Rhea County Tennessee

Census and Marriage Records

1851 through 1900

Compiled by
Bettye J. Broyles

Rhea County Historical and Genealogical Society

Heritage Books
2024

HERITAGE BOOKS

AN IMPRINT OF HERITAGE BOOKS, INC.

Books, CDs, and more—Worldwide

For our listing of thousands of titles see our website
at
www.HeritageBooks.com

A Facsimile Reprint
Published 2024 by
HERITAGE BOOKS, INC.
Publishing Division
5810 Ruatan Street
Berwyn Heights, MD 20740

First printing: 1982

Second printing by Rhea County Historical and Genealogical Society: 1991

Revised and reprinted 1997 by the
Rhea County Historical and Genealogical Society

International Standard Book Number
Paperbound: 978-0-7884-7602-0

INTRODUCTION

This publication is a continuation of ***A Compendium of Rhea and Meigs Counties, 1808 through 1850*** revised and reprinted in 1996 by the Rhea County Historical and Genealogical Society.

The same general format has been followed that was established in the ***Compendium***, with all of the information compiled by family names. The spelling used for the name is as it appeared in the record, sometimes only a vague resemblance to the actual name. Names that could not be deciphered are followed by a question mark. The marriage records for a few years were particularly bad. The first letter of the name usually was clear, but the remainder of the name was a squiggly line almost impossible to read.

MARRIAGES

The marriages were recorded in a number of forms throughout the years. At the end of Volume 1, several pages of original records appeared. In checking these against the recopied portion of the records, several mistakes were noted; i.e., consistant misspelling of some names (McFerson for McPherson in the original records, Willson for Wilson, etc.); last names misspelled so that it changed the name completely (Mynick for Minnix, Casey for Coxey, Edwards for Edmonds, Walker for Waller, Majors for Myers, etc.); leaving out letters (Kelly for Kelley, Mash for Marsh, Lemons or Lemmons, etc.); and changing letters within a name (Purcer for Purser, Evans for Evens, etc.). Unfortunately, all of the original records cannot be checked for errors in later recopying. This is one of the reasons I have consistently used the spelling that appeared in the record even though I knew it to be wrong in many cases.

When the marriage records were recopied, they were not placed in chronological order; i.e., the 1808 through 1838 marriages appear on pages 299 through 458 in Volume 1 rather than at the beginning. The contents of the first four volumes are as follows:

Volume 1– 1808-1881; 1883-1890
Volume 2– 1896-1899
Volume 3– 1899-1902
Volume 4– 1881-1883; 1886-1888; 1890-1902

The marriages in Volume 1 were individually numbered up through page 280 (a total of 1,734 marriages), as were those on the first 14 pages of Volume 4 (142 marriages). In order to make it possible for a researcher to locate the source of the marriage record, the volume and page or marriage number will be found after each entry; i.e., 1-#1322 = Vol. 1, record number 1322; 1-492 = Vol. 1, page 492; 4-2(11) = Vol. 4, page 2, record number 11.

Volumes 2 and 3 consist of a bond and license on each page; therefore, the page number is also the marriage number (425 in Vol. 2 and 432 in Vol. 3). There were roughly 3,700 marriages recorded for the period 1808 through 1900, with another 200 or so that were omitted from the record books but were copied from bonds in the Barnes Papers by Allen in 1832.

The first 14 pages of Volume 4 offer additional information much like the census records, with the following columns: Number, Date of Marriage, Where Married, Names of Parties, Color, Age, Birth Place of Both Parties, Residence of Bridegroom and Bride at Time of Marriage, Occupation of Bridegroom, Name and Official Station of Person by Whom Married, Name and Residence of at least two Witnesses, and Date Recorded. The age and place of birth have been included in the following compilation and follow the name (but only if the place of birth was other than Tennessee).

CENSUS

The following census records were transcribed for this publication: 1860, 1870, 1880, and 1900. Most of the 1890 population schedules for the United States were so badly damaged in a fire in the Commerce Building in 1921 that they were disposed of, including Tennessee. The 1850 Rhea and Meigs County census was included in the ***Compendium*** and will not be repeated in this publication.

The 1850, 1860, and 1870 enumeration included the names of the household members, their age, color, sex, occupation, etc. In 1880, the census was expanded to include additional information, including the place of birth of the household members parents [see 1880 Census in **Appendix A** for a list of the questions and columns to be filled in].

Because of the inclusion in 1880 and 1900 of the relationship of the household members to the head, it was necessary to establish a series of abbreviations as follows (the abbreviation follows the age of the individual):

w = wife	s = son
d = daughter	b = brother
ss = stepson	sd = step daughter
sb = step-brother	ssi = step-sister
m = mother	f = father
si = sister	sil = sister-in-law
sl = son-in-law	bl = brother-in-law
dl = daughter-in-law	ml = mother-in-law
a = aunt	fl = father-in-law
u = uncle	c = cousin
ne = niece	nw = nephew
gm = grandmother	gf = grandfather
gs = grandson	gd = granddaughter

Other abbreviations used include the following:

B = Black or Colored. The letter (B) between the name and age indictes a Black in a White household; a (B) following the census reference indictes an all Black family.
Mu = Mulatto. Indicated the same as above.

f = female and m = male. Where the sex was doubtful based on the name, the letter (f) or (m) was placed between the name and the age so as not to be confused with the father or mother, which always follows the age.

In order to save space, the w, s, and d (wife, son, and daughter) have been omitted where the relationship to the household head is obvious. In a few cases the m (mother) after an age probably should have been ml (mother-in-law), but the relationships are reproduced exactly as they appeared on the census. Several times, the enumerator used son and daughter in the same household where there were two families living (i.e, married son or daughter) instead of grandson or granddaughter. Where this error was obvious, it was corrected in order to avoid confusion.

Since the districts usually were not in numerical order, and the page numbers frequently started over with 1 for each district (1860, 1870, and 1880 census), each entry from a census is referenced by district (a), page (b), and household (c). When the household and family numbers were different, a fourth number was added (d).

	(a) (b) (c)		(a) (b) (c) (d)
Examples:	2 - 10 - 130	or	8 - 286B - 365/367
			(e)

The 1900 census was recorded on consecutively numbered pages, although each page had an A and B part (e). Unless otherwise stated, individuals were born in Tennessee. When different, the State or Country follows the age [1860 and 1870 census only; the 1880 birthplaces were not transcribed].

In the case of the 1900 census where the parent's birthplace also was included, this information follows the individuals birth month and year (f) in the following order: individuals birthplace (g), father's (h) and mother's (i) birthplace. The number of years the individual had been married follows the birth places (j). On the wife's entry, two additional numbers follow the years married (k) and (l). The first number (k) indicates the number of children she has given birth to, followed by the number of children (l) still living in 1900. Three other abbreviations have been used in this portion of the record: Wd = Widowed; D = Divorced; S = Single.

Examples:

(f) (g) (h) (i) (j) (k)(l)		(f)
(Aug 1864-T/Va/NC-M 10-4-3)	or	(Aug 1864-Wd)

Information on foreign-born individuals included the year of emigration (m), number of years in America (n), and whether or not they were naturalized citizens (o). This information appears between the place of birth and the number of years married. "Do" has been used throughout this compilation in place of "Ditto" or "Same as."

(m) (n)(o)
Example: (Dec 1852-Wales/Do/Do-1878/22/Na-M 28)

All of the household heads are listed in **Appendix A** so that a check can be made of adjacent households. This is recommended, especially if you believe a household is incomplete. An excellent example of the enumerators error ocurred on the 1870 census involving my great-grandparents. The listing for adjacent households was as follows:

100	Samuel Craighead	56
	Nancy	56
	Beriah G.	24
	Eleanor	42
101	Nile M. Broyles	51
	Adison M.	17
	Sarah I.	15
	Enoch C.	13
	John W.	6

Eleanor was Nile's wife, but the last name was not shown as Broyles in the Craighead household. This same situation may have occurred in other families. All of the individuals living in a household who had a different last name are cross referenced and appear in parenthesis after the household head in Appendix A.

Bettye J. Broyles

CONTENTS

APPENDIX A– HEADS OF HOUSEHOLD

RHEA COUNTY, TENNESSEE: CENSUS AND MARRIAGE RECORDS

1851 THROUGH 1900

ABBOTT / ABBIT

1880 CENSUS

Martin Abbott 46, Sarah 45, Mary 21, William 18, John 13 12-2-10

1900 CENSUS

Charles Abbit (no dates): non-resident in District 12

Martar Abbit 67 (July 1832-NH/NH/NH-M 44), Sarah 65 (Nov 1834-NH/NH/NH-M 44-4-3) 12-179B-17/19

- - - - - - - - - - - - -

ABEL / ABLE

1860 CENSUS

C.W. Abel 39, Esther W. 31, Catharine 12, Theodore 8, Wright 5, Arrazene (f) 3, Elizabeth FOUST 20 8-20-133

James J. Abel 45 (Merchant), Betsy A. 36, Margaret 21, Misy J. 19, John 5, James T. 3, Mary F. 1 8-22-147

John R. Able 43, Mary M. 37, Margaret J. 8, John R. 5, Mary M. 3, George W. 3/12 8-20-137

Margaret Abel 80 (Pa), Mary R. 45, James K. 14 8-20-135

Robert P. Abel 42, Mary A. 37, Margaret 14, Susan 12, Esther L. 6, Mary J. 3, Alfred L. 5/12 8-20-138

1870 CENSUS

Cain W. Abel 49 (Tanner), Hester E. 44, Darius T. 17, Montreville W. (m) 15, Pherona A. 13, Franklin H. 9, James M. 7, Robert E.L. 4, Cain W. 10/12, Susan FOUST 76 8-10-64

James J. Abel 53 (Retail Merchant), Elizabeth A. 43, Marguerette 31, John A. 15, James F. 13, Mary F. 11, Robert P. 3, William L. 10/12, Mira J. FLEMING 30 8-15-101

John R. Abel 53, Mary M. 47, Margurette Jane 18, John R. Jr. 15, Martha M. 13, George W. 10, Laura I. 2 8-9-57

Mary A. Abel 48, Susan L. 21, Esther L. 16, Mary Jane 14, Alfred L. 10 8-9-56

Mary R. Abel 56 8-11-77

1880 CENSUS

A. S. Abel 21, S. J. 21 8-6-44

C.W. Abel 60, E.L.(?) 53 (w), P.A. 22 (d), I.A.S. 16 (s), C. W. 13 (s), D. L. 7 (d), Jim HINCH (B) 30 6-7-58

F.H. Abel 19: see M. S. Morrison

J.J. Abel 66 (Merchant), Betsy 56, Margaret 31, John 25, J. F. 23 (s), M.F. 21 (d), R.P. 13 (s), W.L. 11 (s) 8-1-2

J.K.P. Abel 35, S. 27 (w), J.E. 8 (s), S.F. 6 (d), J.T. 3 (s), Althia M. 2 (d) 8-5-41

J.R. Abel 62, Jane W. 23 (d), Martha 28 (d), J.R. 25 (s), G.W. 20 (s), S.B. 13 (d) 8-5-42

M.R. Abel 25, J.A. 24, R.R. 6/12 (s): see J.H. Cox

Mary Ann Abel 58, E.L. 25 (d) 8-1-3

Mary R. Abel 66 8-7-59

1900 CENSUS

Edward J. Abel 29 (July 1870-M 10)(Coal Miner), Mary E. 24 (May 1876-T/Ga/Ga-M 10-4-2), Roy T. 7 (July 1892), Gracie H. 3 (Jan 1897) 13-302A-217/225

Franklin H. Abel 39 (Nov 1860-M 16)(Harness Merchant), Mary M. 38 (Nov 1861-M 16-5-4), Mary M. 13 (May 1887), Paul 10 (Ap 1890), Pauline 7 (June 1892), Buford J. 2 (July 1897), Mary A. COULTER 79 (ml) (May 1821-Wd 9-5) 15-273A-95

James C. Abel 82 (May 1818-T/Va/NC-M 6), Eliza F. 69 (Aug 1830-Ky/Va/Ky-M 6-0-0) 10-325A-106/110

James E. Abel 43 (Feb 1857-M 14)(Physician), Harriet M. 38 (Aug 1861-T/T/Va-M 14-4-4), Charles C. 12 (Nov 1887), Florence E. 10 (Sep 1889), Cora L. 6 (Sep 1893), Lila M. 3 (Sep 1896), Amelia ROWAN (B) 7 (July 1882)(Servant) 8-315B-112/116

James J. Abel 85 (Mar 1815-M 46)(Landlord), Elizabeth A. 73 (Oct 1826-M 46-7-5), Margaret 61 (d)(Sep 1838), Mary F. 41 (d)(Ap 1859), Theodore W. JEWELL 44 (Dec 1853-T/NC/NC)(Servant), Fannie THOMAS 28 (Sept 1871-M 1-0-0)(Servant) 8-316A-113/117

James K. Abel 55 (Unk 1845-M 12)(Coal Miner), Mandy 30 (May 1870-T/NC/T-M 12-0-0), Oliver 19 (Sep 1880) (Coal Miner), Ab SMITH 21 (boarder)(Unk 1879-M 0)(Coal Miner), Anna SMITH 16 (boarder)(Unk 1884-M 0-0-0) 8-280A-228/230

John Abel 45 (May 1845-M 9)(Jewelry Merchant), Emma L. 32 (Mar 1868-M 9-4-4), Ida L. 7 (Sep 1892), Ralph K. 4 (July 1895), Tennie E. 3 (Mar 1897), James A. 6/12 (Nov 1899) 8-314B-83/86

John R. Abel 83 (Sep 1816-T/NC/NC-Wd), Martha 43 (d) (Dec 1856), Laura B. 32 (d)(Dec 1867) 15-273B-106

Julia Abel 44, Edith 15, Wright 13: see Calvin Morgan

Lambert Abel 15: see Harriet Corvin

Robert P. Abel 33 (Feb 1867-M 7)(Lawyer), Ada C. 30 (Nov 1869-M 7-2-2), Bruin W. 6 (May 1894), Louisa 5/12 (Jan 1900), Rosie B. COOK 23 (sil)(Mar 1877) 8-312-29/31

William L. Abel 30 (July 1869-M 1)(Physician), Jennie A. 31 (Aug 1868-M 1-1-1), Ollie 3/12 (d)(Mar 1900), Rosa McKINSEY 27 (Dec 1872)(Domestic Servant) 5-233A-107

MARRIAGES

A.L. Able to S.J. Barton, 22 Oct 1879 (same), J.W. Cunnyngham MG 1-#1687

Adaline Abel to Albert N. Spence q.v.

Addaline Abel to Wiley N. Ault q.v.

Altie Abel to Chaley Sharp q.v.

Delia L. Abel to Ben L. Pace q.v.

Esther Abel to J. B. Shipley q.v.

F.H. Abel to M.M. Coulter, 28 Mar 1884 (30 Mar), Thompson Ashburn MG 1-478

H.R. Abel to Julia A. Morgan, 23 Dec 1878 (24 Dec), J. H.(?) Perry MG 1-#1594

Ida I. Abell to B. H. Allen q.v.

J.C. Abel to Eliza F. Coats, 19 Sep 1893, G.W. Brewer MG 4-60

J.R. Abel to Mary Hicks, 20 Oct 1891, W.S. Hale MG 4-30

J.F. Abel to Manassas McDonald, 25 May 1886 (26 May), H.C. Neal --(?) 1-482

J.J. Abel to Elizabeth A. McFarland, 24 Aug 1854 (same), Wm C. Hollins JP 1-#457

J.K.P. Abel to Amanda Ward, 9 Aug 1887 (10 Aug), I.W. Holt JP 1-532

J. P. Abel (35, near Washington) to Harriet Corvin (18, Meigs Co), 4 Jan 1883, I.W. Holt JP, M.R. Abel & Miss Jane Abel W 4-12 (119)

J. R. Abel (28) to Mary E. Hickman (23), 20 Feb 1883, Thompson Ashburn MG, Edward Hickman & Florence Abel W 4-15(142)

J.R.P. Abel to Louisa A. Cowin or Corvin, 11 Jan 1868 (12 Jan), John H. Keith MG 1-#997

John Abel (26) to Lou D. Rogers (22, Sequachie), 4 Oct 1881 (Dayton), John R. Stewart MG, Miss Mary Dodson & F.R. Rogers W 4-2(18)

Lettie E. Abel to James T. Bell q.v.

Margaret Abel to Wiley N. Ault q.v.

Mary J. Abel to F. M. Underwood q.v.

Mary J. Abel to David Williams q.v.

Myra Abel to S.H. Fleming q.v.

P. A. Abel to L. L. Coulter q.v.

R.E. Abel to Myrtle Bodkins, 25 Feb 1888 (26 Feb), John H. Parrott MG 1-542

S. A. Abel to W. H. McFalls q.v.

S. C. Abel to Asahel Johnson q.v.

S. L. Abel to W. J. Ingle q.v.

Sarah F. Abel to Samuel L. Sharp q.v.

Theadore Able to Mary Bohanan, 1 Feb 1872 (4 Feb), Daniel Hodge JP 1-#1226

W. L. Abel to Jennie Darwin, 22 Nov 1898 (23 Nov), J.A. Whitner MG, Robert F. Abel W 2-348

- - - - - - - - - - - - -

ABERCEROMBIE

1880 CENSUS

Jesse C. Abercerombie 28, Ruthey A. 30, Rose A. 6, Sallie E. 3, James W. 9/12 5-7-61

- - - - - - - - - - - - -

ABERNATHY / ABBERNATHY

1860 CENSUS

John C. Abernathy 36, Nancy A. 30, Young L.B. 14, John A. 10, Berry ABERNATHY 74 (NC), Miny 53, Fleming BENNETT 24 (Carriage maker) 2-70-474

1870 CENSUS

Berry Abernathy 85 (NC), Myra 65 (NC), Rebecca 14, Almirah 12, Mary E. 9, Rachel (B) 6 2-13-97

Jas J. Abernathy 34 (Store Clerk): see Jeremiah C. Wasson

John C. Abernathy 47 (Physician), Nancy A. 37, Young L. B. 24 (Physician), John A. 20 (Merchant) 2-13-98

Rachel Abernathy 16 (B): see Berry Abernathy

1880 CENSUS

Eliza Abernathy 54, Jennie 21 (d), Matte BROOKMAN 19 (boarder) 2-22-182

John Abernathy 56 (Physician), Amanda 50, Young 34 (Physician), Emma 35 (dl), Paul 1/12, Luta DAY 21 (boarder), Richard CLEAG (Mu) 20 (Servant-Hastler), Adaline (B) 21 (Cook), John (Mu) 2, Emma (Mu) 1 2-22-181

John Abernathy 30, Permelia 27, Carrie 8, Young 6, John 4, Wallace 2: see Susan Neal

1900 CENSUS

John C. Abernathy 76 (Mar 1824-T/NC/NC-M 55)(Physician), Nancy A. 70 (Aug 1829-M 55-?-0), Berry 19 (gs)(June 1880) 10-327A-148/156

MARRIAGES

Carrie W. Abernathy to R.W. Davidson q.v.

John A. Abernathy to Permela G. Neal, 24 Dec 1870 (25 Dec), Ed F. Lyons MG 1-#1180

Joseph L. Abbernathy to Eliza Cash, 1 July 1868 (same), B. Abbernathy MG 1-#107

Rebecca A. Abernathy to John H. Bryson q.v.

Virginia Abernathy to W. W. Neal q.v.

Y.L. Abbernathy to Emma H. Day, 5 Dec 1878 (same), James Cash MG 1-#1590

- - - - - - - - - - - - -

ACHINSON [ACTKINSON]

1880 CENSUS

John Achinson 33, Bell 30 (w), Cloe LOCKMILLER 48 (si), John 21 (s) [John married Isabella Fike on 24 Dec 1879 in Meigs County]

- - - - - - - - - - - - -

ACRE / ACREY

1860 CENSUS

Albert W. Acre 17 (Blacksmith): see Philip Foust

John W. Acre 61: see Joseph Sykes

MARRIAGES

Mary C. Acre to Joseph Sykes q.v.

Rachel Acre to James H. Cox q.v.

W. Acre to Sarah S. Largent, 7 Sep 1851 (no return) 1-#349

- - - - - - - - - - - - -

ACUFF

1900 CENSUS

James W. Acuff 31 (Jan 1869-M 10)(Furnaceman, Josie 27 (May 1873-M 10-5-5), Lela 8 (July 1891), Carrie 7 (Jan 1893-NY), Clara 7 (Jan 1893-NY), Bertha 4 (July 1895), Ellen 10/12 (Aug 1899), Elizabeth 29 (si)(Mar 1873) 8-312B-25/37

John Acuff 36 (Oct 1863-T/Va/Va-M 10), Mary 35 (Nov 1864-M 10-2-2), Walter 9 (Mar 1891), Nellie 4 (Dec 1895), Emma GARDENHIRE 41 (si) (Nov 1858-T/Va/Va-Wd 0-0), Ed CUNNYNGHAM 22 (bl)(July 1877) 8-286B-367/369

Joseph R. Acuff 45 (Nov 1854-M 6), Mamie(?) S. 25 (Feb 1875-M 6-2-1), Nada J. 3 (May 1897) 11-292A-50

William J. Acuff 38 (June 1861-M 15), Addie I. 34 (Feb 1866-M 15-8-7), Eskell J. 14 (Sep 1885), Bessie A. 11 (Aug 1888), Bird M. 10 (Feb 1890), James H. 7 (July 1892), William L. 5 (Sep 1894), Phares H. 3 (Sep 1896), Lethie L. 4/12 (June 1899) 11-292A-52

MARRIAGES

Emma Acuff to G. W. Gardenhire q.v.

J.D. Acuff to L.E. Grimsley, 23 Jan 1883 (24 Jan), J.W. Burnett MG 1-480

John C. Acuff to Mary E. Cunnyngham, 21 June 1890 (22 June), R.A. Bartlett MG 1-602

Laura A. Acuff to Thomas S. Parham q.v.

Margaret Acuff to W.T. Neal q.v.

W.J. Acuff to Alie I. Card, 8 Aug 1884 (12 Aug), J.W. Burnett MG 1-474

Will Acuf to Josie Cunnyngham, 19 Oct 1890, J.R. Walker MG 4-23

- - - - - - - - - - - - -

ADAMS

1860 CENSUS

Harriet Adams 31, William 11, Rebecca 8, John 6, Narsissa 3, Jackson 3/12, Susan ADAMS 23, William J. 25, John P. 7 2-76-516

Nancy Adams 38 (Va), William L. 13, Ann 9 1-87-592

1870 and 1880– None

1900 CENSUS

Arza Adams 27 (Aug 1872-Oh/Oh/Oh-M 5)(Coal Miner), Ollie 26 (Ap 1874-M 5-2-2), Urius 3 (Mar 1897), Willie 8/12 (Sep 1899) 8-277B-182/183

MARRIAGES

Arthy J. Adams to David H. Hooper q.v.

B.L. Adams to Bertie Morgan, 3 June 1899 (4 June), W.R. Grimsley MG, Robert Pierce W 2-422

J.W. Adams to Blanch Sherrley, 9 Mar 1896 (16 Mar), Wm Turner MG, J.C. Rankin W 2-3

Millie E. Adams to F.A. Bandy q.v.

Synthia Adams to John McMillan q.v.

William S. Adams to Mary A. Newton, 10 Mar 1866 (no return) 1-#893

- - - - - - - - - - - - -

ADCOCK / ADCOX

MARRIAGES

C.W. Adcox to Katie Ray(?), 6 Aug 1888 (16 Sep), W.M. Gordon(?) MG 1-554

Kate Adcock to John Gambell q.v.

- - - - - - - - - - - - -

ADKINS / ATKINS / AIKEN / AIKENS / AKIN / ACKENS / EAKIN / EAKINS

1880 CENSUS

Edmunds Aiken 60, America 50, Allen 16 (s) 3-21-172 (B)

Mary Adkins 29 (Mu): see John Neal

Rosa Aiken 21: see B.F. Roberson

Sarah Aiken 53, Rufus 22, John 13, Marietta 10, Henry 24 (s), Margaret 22 (dl) 2-31-254

1900 CENSUS

Andrew Aiken 70 (Feb 1830-T/Va/T-M 7), Matilda 55 (Unk-M 7-2-2), Melvina HICKS 80 (ml)(Unk-Wd 2-2) 6-244B-93

Ely(?) Adkins 72 (Mar 1828-Ga/Ga/Ga-M 27), Caroline A. 61 (Ap 1833-Ga/Ga/Ga-M 27-4-2)(Washwoman) 2-198B-140/145

Henry Aikens 56: see John Dawson

George A. Eakins 31 (Ap 1869-M 9), Eliza J. 26 (Mar 1874-M 9-6-5), James A. 8 (Oct 1891), John W. 7 (Feb 1893), Elizabeth A. 6 (Ap 1894), Ida P. 4 (Sep 1895), Rosa L. 1 (Nov 1898), Robert G. PELFRY 24 (bl)(Mar 1897-M 4), Matilda F. 21 (sil)(June 1878-M 4-2-2), Foster B. 3 (nw)(Aug 1896), George B. 6/12 (nw)(Sep 1899) 5-230B-46

Joseph Eakens 39 (Ap 1861-M 12), Jennie 28 (Feb 1872-M 12-7-7), William A. 10 (Feb 1890). Mary E. 9 (Feb 1891), Ada J. 6 (July 1893), Harvey L. 5 (July1894), James 3 (Feb 1897), George 2 (Oct 1897), York 1 (Oct 1891) 5-232B-85

Richard Atkins 49 (Unk 1851-Ga/Va/Va-M 24)(Coal Miner), Harriet 39 (May 1861-Ga/Va/Va-M 24-12-8), Jennie 22 (Unk 1878-Ga), Richard 7 (Unk 1883)(Coal Miner), Tabby 14 (Unk 1886), James 12 (Unk 1888), Otto 11 (Unk 1889), Samuel 10 (Unk 1890), George 7 (Unk 1893), Boy 3 (Unk 1897), Patsie SHARP 79 (ml)(Unk 1821) 8-284A-305/307 (B)

MARRIAGES

A.J. Aikens to Matilda Hawkins, 17 Nov 1892, W.S. Hale MG 4-48

Almeda Aiken to Frank L. Lyndon q.v.

George Aikens to Liza J. Pelfrey, 11 Oct 1890, H.B. Burditt MG 4-18

Josephine Aiken to Irvin Yates q.v.

Mahala Aikens to Thomas Phelfrey q.v.

Margaret Eakins to James Nelson q.v.

Martha Eakin to William W. Barton q.v.

Mollie Adkins to Calvin Rankin q.v.

Rhoda Ackens to Charley Phelfrey q.v.

Sallie Eakin to Newton Alton q.v.

- - - - - - - - - - - - -

AIRHEART / AYHEART / AHEART / EARHART / EHEART

1860 CENSUS

George Ahart 48 (NC), Manerva 38, John H. 19, Iverson H. 17, Emily 11, Alvia G. 9, Elorender 2 3-56-382

1870 and 1880 CENSUS– None

1900 CENSUS

Charity Earhart 49 (Ap 1851-Oh/Oh/Oh-Wd 5-5), Willie 21 (Nov 1878-Mo/Oh/Oh)(Coal Miner), George 7 (Feb 1883-Mo)(Coal Miner), Herbert 9 (Aug 1890) 8-289B-429-432

Thomas Earhart 26 (Sep 1873-Mo/Oh/Oh-M 4)(Coal Miner), Nannie 22 (Nov 1877-Oh/Oh/Oh-M 4-2-2), Ed 2 (Jan 1898), Beulah 1 (Feb 1899) 8-289B-428/431

MARRIAGES

Adam J. Aheart to Denira Willson, 15 Sep 1853 (same), W.H. Cunnyngham JP 1-#423

Denirah Aheart to John L. Ramsey q.v.

Thomas Ehert to Nannie P. Love, 13 Mar 1897 (same), A.P. Hayes JP, W.H. Airhart W 2-127

- - - - - - - - - - - - -

ALDERMAN

MARRIAGE

Virginia Alderman to W. F. Leonard q.v.

- - - - - - - - - - - - -

ALEXANDER

1870 CENSUS

Laura Alexander 19: see Stephen Gray

Robert F. Alexander 43, Elizabeth W. 31, George G. 16 (Ind), Addie Z. 13 (Ind), Laura E. 12 (Ind), Sarah E. 2, Catharine A. 5/12, Margarette J. EVERET 11, Martha E. EVERET 7 10-2-13

1880 CENSUS

A.J. Alexander 27, ?.E. 19 (w): see T.J. Kelley

A.S. Alexander 48, S.W. 31 (w), M.L. 8 (d), S.N. 5 (d), D.V. 2 (d), A. 3/12 (d) 8-10-81

J.D. Alexander 30 (Fruit Dealer): see Virginia Leuty

R.F. Alexander 52, Elizabeth 41, George 25, Annie 20, Sarah 12, Catharine 10, Ruth 8, Hiram 6, Cyrus 3 8-3-29

1900 CENSUS

Annie Alexander 10: see Jennie Dickson (B)

George B. Alexander 45 (Jan 1855-Ind/T/Ind-M 17), Sarah A. 35 (July 1864-T/NC/T-M 17-9-7), Cordia 4 (Dec 1885), Robert S. 12 (Dec 1887), Dallas 10 (Sep 1889), Pearl M. 8 (Sep 1891), James G. 6 (Nov 1893), Cyrus B. 4 (Mar 1896), George R. 1 (Dec 1898) 13-296A-119/121

James M. Alexander 58 (Nov 1841-M 40), Margaret D. 58 (Jan 1841-Ga/Ga/Ga-M 40-5-3), Earl 13 (gs)(Mar 1887-T/T/Md) 13-296A-121/123

Thomas Alexander 26 (Jan 1874-M 8)(Carpenter), Ella 26 (Feb 1874-M 8-3-2), Kenneth 4 (May 1896), Jessie 1 (Nov 1898) 8-282A-270/272

William H. Alexander 49 (May 1851-Ala/Ala/Ala-M 25) (Dress Pattern Maker), Rachael 49 (Oct 1850-M 25-4-4), Sarah A. 23 (Aug 1876)(Photographer), John 18 (Nov 1881)(Carpenter), Myrtle 16 (Sep 1883)(Photographer), Ethel 14 (Jan 1886) 8-317A-136/141

MARRIAGES

Addy Alexander to A. T. Marler q.v.

Ella Alexander to Emmit Bowman q.v.

H.J. Alexander to V.E. Green, 27 Ap 1880 (28 Ap), J.F. Perry MG 1-#726

H.M. Alexander to Sallie T. Dandridge, 16 Feb 1899 (same), W.L. Patton MG, W.O. Thomas W 2-382

Harriet Alexander to Sydney Hoslin q.v.

James Alexander to Alice May, 14 Feb 1895, John Ware MG 4-78

James A. Alexander to Mary E. Gibson, 31 May 1899 (4 June), David Davis MG, J.R. McGill W 2-420

Kittie Alexander to J.P. Monyhan q.v.

Louisa C. Alexander to Thomas J. Kelly q.v.

L.F. Alexander to John Smith q.v.

Minny Alexander to J.D. Sullivan q.v.

R. F. Alexander to Elizabeth W. Everett, 23 Dec 1866 (same), W.A. Green JP 1-#925

S. E. Alexander to T. J. Nash q.v.

S. H. Alexander to Mary J. Barger, 7 Aug 1863 (same) 1-#803

Samuel Alexander to Jennie Barnett, 2 Oct 1888 (3 Oct), J. B. Phillips MG 1-555

Thomas A. Alexander to Linnie Ivens [Evens in index], 8 May 1891, R.A. Bartlett, Pastor of 1st Presbyterian Church of Dayton 4-26

Will Alexander to Sarah Killough, 16 June 1892, J.W. Williamson MG 4-38

Wm D. Alexander to Mollie Morgan, 25 Dec 1894, G.R. Baldwin JP 4-74

- - - - - - - - - - - - -

ALLEE

1900 CENSUS

Noah W. Allee 52 (May 1848-Ind/Oh/Oh-M 29)(Clergyman), Rebecca C. 47 (Ap 1853-Ill/Pa/Oh-M 29-3-2), Ellie 18 (Dec 1881-Mo) 3-309A-367/381

- - - - - - - - - - - - -

ALLEN

1860 CENSUS

Samuel Allen 29, Dicey 33, Marthy 11, Mathew 9, Polly T. 7, Sally 5, Jesse 3, James 1 2-71-485

Valentine Allen 57 (Ky), Ann 45, Thomas 22, George 19, Valentine 17, Barbary F. 15, Robert L. 12, Nicholas G. 11 7-4-27

William Allen 23 (Ala)(Merchant), Mary E. 21 6-111-764

1870 CENSUS

Thomas A. Allen 31, Sarah E. 22 6-17-123

Vallentine Allen 61 (Ky), Ann 57, Fanny 25, Robert L. 22, Nicholas 20 7-7-51

William Allen 33 (Retail Merchant), Mary E. 32, John G. 4, Edward N. 2, William P. THOMISON 23 (Retail Merchant) 6-11-69

1880 CENSUS

Margaret F. Allen 30 ("husband left her"), William H. 12, Christea A. 5, Mary E. 5/12 10-30-229/239

N.Q. Allen 29 (Lawyer), Susan C. 27, Kittie M. 3 6-22-1 (Madison Street, Washington)

Robert L. Allen 31 (Merchant), Vesta A. 23, Mary B. 2, James S. THOMISSON 26, Della DARWIN 16 (c) (boarder), Elizabeth SANFORD (B) 29 (Servant, Cook at Hotel), Mary (B) 7 (Nurse) 6-22-5 (Madison St., Washington)

T.A. Allen 43 (Merchant), S.E. 33, C.T. RIDDLE 28 (boarder), W.V. ALLEN 10 (nw), Sallie DAY (Mu) 28 (Servant) 8-1-1

W. G. Allen 42, Mary E. 42, John G. 14, Edward M. 11, Mary 5, Winnie G. 1, M.G. McCROY (f) 15 ("one of the family") 5-9-82

1900 CENSUS

James Allen 32: see Emma Gillespie (B)

James Allen 16: see Jestas Forster

John L. Allen 47 (Feb 1853-NC/NC/NC-M 27), Mary 46 (Jan 1854-NC/NC/T-M 27-9-7), Rachel 21 (Jan 1879), Henry 23 (Feb 1877), Marthy 19 (Mar 1881), John 16 (Oct 1883), Driver 14 (Feb 1886), Margit 11 (Feb 1889), Alinni 8 (Aug 1891), Earnest LOY 5 (gs)(Mar 1895), Wilum 4 (gs)(Mar 1896), Maud 2 (gd)(Jan 1898), Mary BURNETT 82 (ml)(Feb 1818-T/NC/T-Wd 9-7) 12-181B-61/64

Lue Allen 38 (June 1861-Wd 4-4)(Washwoman), Anderson 16 (Feb 1882), Tenny 11 (Mar 1889), Mandy 8 (June 1891), McDonal 5 (Aug 1894) 10-257B-144/148

Matthew Allen 30 (Ap 1870-Ala/T/Ala-M 6), Malicy 25 (Mar 1875-M 6-2-2), Berta 5 (Nov 1895), Anna 3/12 (Feb 1900) 6-246A-116/117

Philip W. Allen 49 (Feb 1851-NY/NY/NY-M 3), Ida 39 (July 1860-Oh/Oh/Oh-M 3-3-1) 9-228A-3

Robert L. Allen 51 (June 1848-T/Ky/T-M 23)(Grocery Clerk), Vesta K. 43 (June 1856-M 23-3-3), Mary B. 22 (Ap 1878), Rosa L. 17 (Mar 1883), Bessie F. 14 (Oct 1883) 15-273-9

Samuel H. Allen 47 (Oct 1852-M 15)(Coke Oven Foreman), Mattie D. 41 (Sep 1880-Miss/SC/SC-M 15-7-7), Maud F. 14 (Aug 1885-Ga), Willie B. 12 (Nov 1887-Ga), Bulah R. 10 (Nov 1889), Lena L. 7 (Ap 1893), Mattie D. 4 (July 1895), Bonnie WALKER 21 (sd)(Aug 1878-Miss/Miss/Miss)(Milinary Store Clerk) 10-328B-181/194

Valentine Allen 57 (Sep 1843-Miss/Miss/Miss-M 34)(Lawyer), Emma 55 (Feb 1845-M 34-5-5), William B. 30 (Jan 1869)(Circuit Court Clerk), Jane K. 28 (Nov 1871), Anna A. 21 (Aug 1879), Maud 17 (Nov 1882) 15-270B-51

William G. Allen 64 (Oct 1835-Ala/T/T/-M 40)(Butcher), Virginia [should have been Mary E.] 62 (July 1837-Va/Va/Va-M 40-8-2), Edward M. 31 (Mar 1869) (Physician), Mary 24 (Dec 1875), Grace 21 (Dec 1878), John G. 34 (s)(Mar 1866-M 0)(Salesman, Gentlemans Furnishings), Versailles 30 (dl)(Aug 1869-M 0) 8-314B-85/88

MARRIAGES

B. F. Allen to I. C. Arrants q.v.

B. H. Allen to Ida I. Abell, 11 Sep 1895, W.A. Howard MG 4-87

Cora Allen to James Gaines q.v.

David Allen to Nancy J. Dotson, 6 Dec 1854 (17 Dec), T.J. Gillespie JP 1-#473

Elizabeth Allen to Solomon Crow q.v.

Emily W. Allen to P.M. Mathis q.v.

Fannie D. Allen to C.D. Broyles q.v.

James Allen to Clemie Day, 6 June 1896 (same), H. Hobart(?) MG, Enoch Suddeth W
2-28 (license) & 2-29 (bond)

James D. Allen to Margarett Jones, 22 Feb 1879 (23 Feb), Wm Morgan JP 1-#1606 & 1-#1692

Jake Allen to Birdie Peak, 7 Ap 1885 (same), Byrd Lucy MG 1-460

John Allen to Elizabeth Singleton, 1 Mar 1856 (2 Mar), Thos Knight JP 1-#538

John G. Allen to Versailles Ault, 24 Feb 1900 (25 Feb), W. L. Patten MG & W 3-126

John G. Allen to Emma Rogers, 30 Sep 1890, M.C. Bruner(?) MG 4-25

John H. Allen to Louissanna Mathews, 4 Jan 1853 (same), W.H. Bell MG 1-#401

Josie Allen to Joseph N. Mitchell q.v.

Lula Allen to William Melton q.v.

Margrett Allen to John H. Hale q.v.

Mima Allen to A. P. Hayes q.v.

Missouri Allen to McHenry Hughes q.v.

Myra J. Allen to Joseph G. Loy q.v.

Nicholas Q. Allen [incorrectly recorded as W.I. Allen] to Susan C. Paine, 2 Sep 1875 (same), S. Phillips MG 1-#1408

P.W. Allen to Ida Greerhart [license] or Gearhart [bond], 12 Mar 1897 (13 Mar), A.H. Low MG, R.J. Murry W 2-126

R.L. Allen to Vesta A. Kelly, 20 June 1877 (same), A.P. Early MG 1-#1504

Thomas Allen to Nancy Thurman, 1 May 1865 (same), Allen Hollan JP 1-#835

Thomas Allen to Elizabeth Norris, 9 June 1885 (same), W.S. Hale MG 1-495

W.G. Allen to Mary E. Thomison, 14 Dec 1859, J.W. Thompson MG 1-#703

W. I. Allen– see Nicholas Q. Allen

William Allen to Susan Moore, 1 Nov 1854 (20 Nov), R.T. Howard MG 1-#463

William O. Allen to Nancy Holland, 20 May 1861 (no return) 1-#754

Winnie G. Allen to Edwin W. Pugh q.v.

- - - - - - - - - - - - -

ALLENDER

1900 CENSUS

Danie Allender 59 (Ap 1841-Wis/NY/NY-M 16), Cora 38 (Sep 1861-Wis/NY/NY-M 16-2-2), Charles 17 (Feb 1883-Wis), Effie 4 (July 1885-Wis) 12-180A-30/32

Eugene Allender 27 (Ap 1873-Wis/NY/NY-M 5)(RR Laborer), Mollie 27 (Ap 1873-M 5-3-2), James 4 (May 1896), Bertha 7/12 (Nov 1899) 14-217B-100/102

MARRIAGE

Myron E. Allender to Mollie Dodson, 6 Mar 1895, G.R. Baldin JP 4-90

- - - - - - - - - - - - -

ALLEY / ALEY

1880 CENSUS

Seth Alley 39, M.H. 37 (w), J.D. 18 (s), D.T. 16 (s), J.H. 15 (s), S.F. 12 (d), S.W. 9 (s), C.H. 5 (s), J.M. 3 (d), J.F. 8/12 (s) 4-32-265

1900 CENSUS

Cua B. Alley 31 (Jan 1869-Va/Va/Va-M 12-5-4)(Seamstress), Raleigh W. 8 (Sept. 1891-T/Ind/Va), John S. 6 (May 1894-Ky/Ind/Va), William F. 5 (Mar 1895), John CRAWLEY 20 (boarder)(Aug 1879-T/NC/T) 13-196B-126/128

George Alley 44 (June 1855-M 13), Nannie 48 (Ap 1852-Ga/Ga/Ga-M 13-4-3), Maud 11 (Feb 1889), Minnie 9 (Nov 1890), Almzo 6 (June 1893) 8-283B-301/303

James M. Alley 33 (Unk 1867-M 7), Adda J. 25 (Oct 1874-M 7-2-2), Walter A. 6 (July 1893), Thomas G. 4 (Sep 1895) 4-224A-202/206 (Spring City-Dayton Road)

Jasper J. Alley 73 (May 1827-M 8), Sarah T. 42 (Mar 1858-Ga/Ga/Ga-M 8-10-8), Flora E.* 16 (sd)(Jan 1884-Ala/Ga/Ga), Margaret E.* 10 (sd)(Ap 1890) 13-303B-257/267 [*probably WYCUFF]

Purcy Alley 34 (Ap 1866-T/Ky/Va-M 5), Mary 19 (Nov 1880-M 5-1-1), Lincoln 2 (June 1898) 1-184B-113/119

Scott W. Alley 27 (June 1872-M 6), Souannah 34 (Mar 1866-M 6-3-2), Carl B. 3 (Sep 1896), Andrew J. 6 (Feb 1894) 4-225A-228/232 (Creed Road)

Seth Alley 59 (Oct 1840-M 40), Mary A. 57 (Mar 1843-T/NY/NC-M 40-3-3), Jefferson D. 38 (Oct 1861), John F. 21 (Oct 1878), William R. 18 (Feb 1882), Earnest 12 (gs)(Aug 1887), Clara E. 3 (gd)(July 1896), Florence 3 (gd)(July 1896) 4-227A-269-273 (Spring City-Washington Road)

William F. Alley 31 (Feb 1869-Ind/Ind/Ind-M 12)(Laborer Saw Mill), Bertha C. 26 (June 1873-M 12-3-1), Marnie 11 (Nov 1888-Ky) 13-305B-296/308

MARRIAGES
Anne Alley to John Trentham q.v.
G.W. Alley to Nancy Ellis, 22 Aug 1885 (same), M.S. Hale MG 1-483
J.D. Alley to Sarah Sharp, 16 Nov 1892, William Morgan JP 4-68
J.J. Aley to S.L. Wycuff, 5 Nov 1891, W.S. Hale MG 4-30
J.M. Alley to Letha Lyle, 21 Oct 1895, F.M. Cook MG 4-92
James H. Alley to Ada Trentham, 3 Sep 1893, R.M. Trentham JP 4-57
Sallie F. Alley to J. A. Campbell q.v.
W.S. Alley to Savanah Wyrick, 27 Mar 1894, R.M. Trentham JP 4-71
William T. Alley to Bertha Clouse, 22 Feb 1888 (same), J.R. Walker ?? 1-547

- - - - - - - - - - - - -

ALLISON
[see also ELLISON]

1900 CENSUS
John H. Allison 52 (Feb 1847-NC/NC/NC-M 31)(House Painter), Margaret L. 48 (Mar 1852-NC/NC/NC-M 31-10-7), Nannie B. 23 (Jan 1877)(School Teacher), Beatrice E. 20 (Dec 1879), Charlotte J. 15 (Oct 1884), Margaret F. 11 (Nov 1888), Nellie G. 6 (Sep 1893) 14-218A-115/117
MARRIAGES
Francis W. Allison to Eliza Riddle, 8 June 1851 (same), E. McKinna JP 1-#342
Mashie Allison to Alex Welch q.v.
Minnie Allison to J.M. Welch q.v.
N. E. Allison to Jessee Tharp q.v.

- - - - - - - - - - - - -

ALSOOP

1900 CENSUS
George Alsoop 35: see Joseph Phillips (B)

- - - - - - - - - - - - -

ALTON

MARRIAGE
Newton Alton to Sallie Eakin, 3 Aug 1880 (4 Aug), S. Breeding JP 1-295

- - - - - - - - - - - - -

AMHURST

MARRIAGE
Robert Amhurst to Mary Arms, 25 Feb 1880 (same), B.F. Holloway JP 1-#1721

- - - - - - - - - - - - -

AMOS / AMES

1880 CENSUS
H.A. Ames 43 (Carpenter), E.C. 57 (w), W.H. 13 (s), J.W. 11 (s), Nancy FILYAN 16 (hired Girl) 4-7-57
MARRIAGES
H.W. Amos to M.M. Cassady, 27 Feb 1886 (28 Feb), J.W. Thompson MG 1-497
Mary A. Amos to Horace S. Lowrey q.v.
Molly Amos to William Travis q.v.

- - - - - - - - - - - - -

ANDERSON

1870 CENSUS
Jennetta Anderson 66 (Ky), Jane 44 (Ky), Caroline 16 (Ky), Jennetta 11 (Ky) 1-23-153
Rens Anderson 20, Rebecca 24, Amanda 6/12: see David Singleton
1880 CENSUS
Andrew Anderson 47 (Physician), Amanda 63 (w), Robert BROWN 28 (ss)(Merchant), Sarah 24 (sd), James GALBRAITH 35 (boarder)(Trader), Jane 34, George MANIS 21 (boarder)(Clerk in Store), Thomas McWHIRTER 28 (boarder)(Proprietor of *Rhea Springs News*), Mary 26, Nancy OBIEN 21 (Servant, Cook), Phena PARIS 14 (Servant, Housekeeper), John WATERHOUSE (B) 26 (Servant) 2-22-183
1900 CENSUS
Andrew Anderson 69 (Nov 1830-T/T/Va-Wd)(Physician) 2-197B-122/127
Jim Anderson 35 (June 1865-Ga/Va/T-M 6)(Machinist), Sallie 22 (July 1877-M 6-1-1), Jammie 1/12 (May 1900), Mancy 67 (m)(Feb 1833), Urean CONLEY 19 (boarder)(Mar 1881-Oh/Oh/Oh), James GRIFFIN (B) 18 (Feb 1882)(Servant) 10-253B-72
John A. Anderson 31 (July 1868-T/T/Iowa-M 11)(Grocery Clerk), Anna D. 25 (Feb 1875-Fla/Ga/Mo-M 1-2-2), Mary I. 4 (Sep 1895-Miss), Adair A. 3 (July 1896-La) 13-299B-176/180
Rebecca Anderson 50 (B): see Matthew Maury
William A. Anderson 61 (Feb 1839-M 0)(Merchant), Catherine K. 38 (May 1862-M 0-5-4), Herbert W. 16 (Mar 1884) 13-304A-263/273
MARRIAGES
Alfred Anderson to Alice Harrold, 28 Oct 1895, S.W. Burnett MG 4-9
Andrew L. Anderson to Amanda M. Brown*, 6 Nov 1875 (9 Nov), G.W. Renfro MG 1-#1419
[*nee Renfrow, widow of Franklin Brown]
James Anderson to Sallie A. Wilson, 6 May 1894, W.A. Howard MG 4-66
Mollie Anderson to Elijah Gannaway q.v.
W.A. Anderson to Mrs. S.C. Snow [nee Bean, widow of F.M. Snow], 15 May 1900 (same), W.R. Grimsley MG, Z.C. Bunn W 3-91 (bond only) & 3-270 (bond & license)
W.L. Anderson to Sarah Dye, 4 July 1888 (same), Calvin Morgan JP 1-570

- - - - - - - - - - - - -

ANDREWS

1880 CENSUS
Elizabeth Andrews 25: see Lucinda Gillespie
Walter Andrews 27: see Charles Jewitt

MARRIAGE
Sarah Andrews to Enoch Suddith (B) q.v.

- - - - - - - - - - - - -

ANGEL

1900 CENSUS
Edmond Angel 26 (Sep 1873-M 6)(Flour Miller), Lenora 26 (Nov 1873-M 6-0-0), Jesse A. 26 (boarder)(Ap 1874) (Flour Miller) 14-216A-61/62
Henry Angel 33 (Unk-M 7)(Furnaceman), Mary 28 (Aug 1871-M 7-2-1)(Washing & Ironing), Mattie 6 (Jan 1894), Charles SPRINGS 31 (boarder)(Mar 1869-Wd) (Sand Cutter Foreman) 10-330A-211/224 (B)
Isaac W. Angel 37 (June 1862-M 9)(Machinist), Selena 26 (Sep 1873-M 9-4-3), Edwin 8 (Feb 1892), Fletcher 5 (Mar 1895), Clementine 2 (Feb 1898), Clementine ANGEL 67 (m)(Dec 1842-T/Va/Va-Wd 2-2) 10-328A-171/181 (B)
James W. Angel 30 (Aug 1869-T/Mo/NC-M 6)(Flour Miller), Artetia B. 26 (May 1874-M 6-3-2), Jacks F. 3 (Jan 1897), Earl P. 1 (Feb 1899), Alice UNDERWOOD 17 (si)(May 1883), Floyd N. GOLLAHAR 13 ("Dead") (Nov 1866-M 12) 14-219A-123/126
John W. Angel 57 (Sep 1844-Mo/NC/NC-M 37)(Flour Miller), Mary J. 57 (Sep 1842-NC/NY/NC-M 37-6-5), Sally C. 22 (Sep 1877), Lizzie M. 19 (Aug 1880), John E. HALEY 18 (gs)(Sep 1881)(Laborer Flour Mill), Eugene 17 (gd)(Feb 1883), Lester W. 10 (gs)(Aug 1889), Mary L. 7 (gd)(Nov 1893), John A. BRADLEY 74 (boarder)(Jan 1826-NC/NC/NC) 14-219B-138/141
William N. Angel 32 (June 1867-T/Mo/NC-M 7), Emma F. 31 (Mar 1869-M 7-3-2), Roy C. 5 (Aug 1894), Ruth M. 3 (Sep 1896) 2-197A-112/117

MARRIAGES
Isaac Angel to Selina Bridgeman, 28 June 1891, W.R. Russell ?? 4-27
J.W. Angel to Mary Thomas, 9 Jan 1892, J.R. Hill MG 4-35
Sallie Angel to Horace A. Blackburn q.v.

- - - - - - - - - - - - -

ANSLEY– see ENSLEY

- - - - - - - - - - - - -

ANTON

1900 CENSUS
Mattie Anton 20: see Willis Taylor (B)

- - - - - - - - - - - - -

ARCHER / ARCHIE / ARCHY

1900 CENSUS
Amy Archer 20: see Charles W. Irwin
Eugene Archy 10: see Milton Ragin (B)

MARRIAGE
Mary Archie to Mitchell Thompson q.v.

- - - - - - - - - - - - -

ARDEN

1900 CENSUS
Walter Arden 50 (Mar 1850-M 12), Phebe 39 (Feb 1861-M 12-4-4), Lena 19 (Aug 1880), Minnie 12 (May 1888), Samuel 8 (Dec 1891) 8-285A-333/335 (B)

- - - - - - - - - - - - -

ARGENT– see LARGENT

- - - - - - - - - - - - -

ARMOR / ARMOUR

1870 CENSUS
Tennessee Armor 25, James M. 7: see Rachel Day

1880 CENSUS– None

1900 CENSUS
James L. Armor 30: see Lucien Hale
Robert Armor 25 (Jan 1875-M 0)(Coal Miner), Minnie 8 (Aug 1881-M 0-0-0) 8-282A-271/273

MARRIAGES
Effie Armour to Zack Martin q.v.
Martha Armour to Lucius Hale q.v.
Isaac A.P. Armor to Tennessee Day, 21 Aug 1861 (no return) 1-#758
R.L. Armor [Armour] to Minnie A. Smith, 28 Feb 1900 (same), W.L. Patton MG, J.W. Selvidge W 3-129
Tennessee Armor to Jack Stinger q.v.

- - - - - - - - - - - - -

ARMS

MARRIAGE
Mary Arms to Robert Amhurst q.v.

- - - - - - - - - - - - -

ARMSTRONG

1900 CENSUS
William A. Armstrong 49 (May 1851-M 22), Sarah I. 42 (Sep 1857-M 22-8-7), Adda B. 19 (Oct 1880), May C. 16 (July 1883), Malissa T. 13 (Dec 1886), Uster M. 10 (Aug 1889), Lady P. 8 (May 1892), Lillie P. 4 (Oct 1895), John P. PARKER 28 (Oct 1871)(Servant) 3-208A-139/151

MARRIAGES
Alfred Armstrong to A.M. Hutchenson, 4 Feb 1870 (9 Feb), J.T. Kimbrough MG 1-#1143
Emaline Armstrong to Robert Countes q.v.

- - - - - - - - - - - - -

ARNDALE

1900 CENSUS
Jack Arndale 37 (Unk 1863-Ga/Ga/Ga-M 0)(Coal Miner), Bettie 25 (Unk 1865-Ga/Ga/Ga-M 0-0-0) 8-283B-299/301

- - - - - - - - - - - - -

ARNOLD / ARNALD

1860 CENSUS

Henry Arnold 37, Mary 40, Samiel B. 18, Sarah A. 17, Elizabeth 14, Mary D. 11, Betha 8, John 6, Jane 4, Lucinda E. 2 3-59-407

1870 and 1880 CENSUS– None

1900 CENSUS

Cora Arnold 14: see James Holland

Lenna Arnold 27, Eugene 8: see Dwight Culver

Sam Arnold 38 (Feb 1862-M 19), Parthenia W. 37 (May 1863-M 19-8-6), John 17 (Aug 1882), James 13 (Dec 1886), Mary 11 (Oct 1888), Pearl 10 (May 1890), Violie 6 (Ap 1894), Floyd S. 3 (Jan 1897) 7-262B-245/250

Samuel B. Arnold 55 (Unk 1845-M 38), Elizabeth 58 (Feb 1842-NC/NC/NC-M 38-12-8), Alfred 22 (Aug 1877), Francis 20 (June 1880), Tennie 17 (ne)(Sep 1883), Ray 5 (gs)(Unk 1895), Lloyd 3 (gs)(Unk 1897), Mary BELL 73 (boarder)(Jan 1827) 15-270A-41

William Arnold 38 (Unk 1862-T/T/NC-M 17), Ellen 31 (Dec 1868-M 17-8-7), Jennie 14 (Oct 1885), Willis 12 (May 1888), Edward 7 (Aug 1892), Lee 6 (Mar 1894), Ernest 4 (Feb 1896), Colonel 2 (Jan 1898), Ada 2/12 (Mar 1900) 15-270A-42 [Wm Arnold married S.E. Johns on 16 Dec 1883 in Meigs County]

MARRIAGES

Benjamin Arnold to Mary Barton, 7 Feb 1861 (no return) [bond shows Pinkney Barton Bm] 1-#744

Frank Arnold to Sarah Ziegler, 12 May 1892, J.Q. Shaver JP 4-41

G.G. Arnold to Lenie K. Culver, 26 July 1891, R.A. Bromlett(?) MG 4-28

Martha Arnold to J.D. Everett q.v.

Sarah Ann Arnold to Bailey Minnich q.v.

\- - - - - - - - - - - - -

ARRANTS

1900 CENSUS

William Arrants 35 (Unk 1865-NC/NC/NC-M 5), Nannie 30 (Unk 1879-M 5-2-2), Frank SEXTON 9 (ss)(Aug 1890) 8-287A-375/377

MARRIAGE

I.C. [Isaac Cross] Arrants to B.F. [Barbara Frances] Allen, 20 Dec 1879 (same), Robert E. Smith MG 1-#2532 [Isaac, son of William and Artamisa Cross Arrants; Barbara, dau of Valentine and Ann Frazier Allen]

\- - - - - - - - - - - - -

ARNWINE / ARWINE

1900 CENSUS

Artney W. Arnwine 41 (Mar 1859-M 20). Maggie 38 (Nov 1861-M 20-11-9), Ernest 19 (Oct 1880), John 18 (May 1882-Calif), Riley 16 (Dec 1883-Calif), Wilbern 15 (Dec 1884), Clarence 12 (Jan1888), Roger 7 (Ap 1893), May I. 5 (Ap 1895), Ruffes R. 3 (Nov 1896), Arthey H. 2 (Jan 1898) 3-204B-78/84 (B)

MARRIAGE

John Arwine to Annie Wilson, 30 Sep 1899 (1 Oct), L.E. Smith JP, Clay Wilson W 3-43

\- - - - - - - - - - - - -

ARTHOR / AURTHOR / ARTHER

1860 CENSUS

Ambros Arther 46, Mary 37, Nancy T. 14, Hartgrove D. 10, William T. 7, John F. 4, James R. 1, Vilet 64 (SC), Magdalin DAVID 86 (Va), Nancy 46, John C. 26 10-30-202

1870 CENSUS

Ambers Arther 58 (Ky), Mary 47, Nancy 24, Hartgrove D. 20, William T. 17, John F. 15, James R. 12, Sarah I. 10, Rosebelle 7, Sidney A. 4, Will ARTHER 75 (SC) 7-8-62

1880 CENSUS

A. Arther 67, Mary 57 (w), S.E. 19 (d), S.A. 13 (d) 7-24-202

H. Arther 30, M.J. 24 (w), A.B. 4 (d), A.J. 3 (d), W.T. 1 (s) 9-32-278

1900 CENSUS

Askinean Arthur 36 (May 1864-M 10)(Coal Miner), Cansas 36 (July 1863-M 10-0-0), Cora HARRIS 14 (May 1886) (Servant) 10-255A-101/102

Hart D. Arthur 48 (Mar 1852-T/Va/Va-M 25), Amanda 42 (Mar 1858-M 25-6-5), Scot 16 (Dec 1883), David 13 (Dec 1886), Mattie 12 (Ap 1888) 8-323B-53/56

MARRIAGES

Body(?) Authur to Kansas Thurman, 17 Sep 1889 (21 Sep), William Morgan JP 1-585

Hart Aurthor to Amanda Haile, 8 Dec 1874 (same), Calvin Morgan JP 1-#1379

Ida Arthur to Thomas Hoffman q.v.

Mary Arthur to Henry Thurman q.v.

Nancy A. Arthur to Frank Fox q.v.

Synda Arthur(?) to T. J. McRoy q.v.

T.W. Auther to G.A. Ballen, 18 July 1886 (same), W.S. Hale MG 1-502

\- - - - - - - - - - - - -

ASLINGER / ASELINGER

MARRIAGES

Cleaver Aslinger to Olivia J. Mills, 3 Dec 1892, T.D. Shelton ?? 4-93

Douglass Aselinger to Nora Morgan, 25 Dec 1900 (same), T.D. Shelton ??, J.F. Wright W 3-262

G.W. Aslinger to Hattie Hutcheson, 11 Sep 1896 (12 Sep), G.W. Curton MG, John Aslinger W 2-66

John Aslinger to Louisa A. Shipley, 9 Oct 1897 (10 Oct), T.F. Shaver MG, C.E. Aslinger W 2-195

Lizzie Aselinger to Andrew Thomas q.v.

\- - - - - - - - - - - - -

ATCHLY / ATCHLEY

1860 CENSUS

John Atchly 55, Mary A. 50 (SC) 10-30-199

Miles Atchley 52, Elizabeth 26, Sarah J. 11, Margaret 9, Abigail 7, Nancy 6, Audley 3 4-46-314

1870 and 1880– None

1900 CENSUS

Elizabeth J.(?) Atchley 56 (Jan 1844-Ala/Unk/SC-M 35-11-7), Francis M. 32 (Oct 1867-Ga), Martha E. 11 (June 1888) 10-326A-129/133

MARRIAGES

G.W. Atchly to Harriet Smith, 24 Sep 1879 (25 Sep), J.W. Robertson ?? 1-#1679

James M. Atchly to Mary Baker, 20 Mar 1862 (same), John Howard MG 1-#778

James M. Atchley to Mary F. Cate, 30 Sep 1897, J.L. McPherson JP 4-98

Jennie Atchley to Robert Jordan q.v.

Miles Atchly to Mary Ann Grisham, 19 Dec 1860 (no return) 1-#737

Nola Atchley to George Dickey q.v.

W.D. Atchley to Bell Blackford, 11 Dec 1892, G.W. Brewer MG 4-48

- - - - - - - - - - - - -

ATKINSON / ATKENSON / ADKINSON

1900 CENSUS

Elijah Atkinson 37 (Sep 1862-T/Va/T-M 9), Ruth 36 (Aug 1863-M 9-4-4), Charles 8 (Mar 1892), Willie 6 (Mar 1894), Jennie 4 (Dec 1895), Anna 7/12 (Nov 1899), Ruth CUNNINGHAM 13 (ne)(June 1886) 8-288A-402/404

John Atkinson 53 (May 1847-T/NC/NC-M 19), Isabel 50 (July 1849-M 19-5-5), James E. 18 (Ap 1881), Martha E. 17 (Feb 1883), Viera E. 12 (Nov 1887), Alace H. 10 (July 1889), Catharine M. 8 (Sep 1891) 5-236A-158 [John Atkinson m. Belle Fike, 24 Dec 1879, Meigs Co]

Thomas Atkerson 54 (Feb 1846-M 29), Virginia 50 (Feb 1850-Ala/Ala/Ala-M 29-7-7), Thomas M. 26 (Jan 1874-Ky), Hugh L. 21 (Aug 1878-Ky), Augusta 19 (Jan 1881), Laura 13 (Oct 1886), Ollie 11 (Feb 1889) 3-205B-97/105

MARRIAGES

Anna Atkinson to W.H. Barley or Bailey q.v.

E.E. Adkinson to Ruth A. Coulter, 30 May 1891, J.R. Walker MG 4-25

Jennie Atkenson to Jonas Smith q.v.

Kate Atkinson to J.D. Cate q.v.

- - - - - - - - - - - - -

ATWOOD

MARRIAGES

Adaline Atwood to James K. Hinds q.v.

Charly Atwood to Nancy Jolly, 2 Dec 1879 (no return) 1-#1700

- - - - - - - - - - - - -

AULT

1860 CENSUS

Charles W. Ault 35, Leah E. 35, Albion 15, Mary J. 13, George W. 11, Thomas J. 5, Olinda 3, William S. 6/12 4-49-330

George W. Ault 29, Rebecca 21, William HARTLY 18, Hugh L.W. JAMES 12 (bound) 3-62-431

Wyly N. Ault 31, Ruth C. 23, William H. 3, James T. 1, Peggy HOWARD 60 2-79-537

1870 CENSUS

Charles W. Ault 46, Manerva T. 26, Albion 24, George W. 21, Thomas J. 16, Orlinda 13, William 11, Charles W. 9 4-1-5

Versa J. Ault 9, George M. 8: see Silvester Wilkey

1880 CENSUS

W.N. Ault 51 (Merchant), J.F. 21 (s)(Store Clerk), M.A. 31 (w), Wiley 16 (s), P.W. 13 (s), S.W. 11 (s), Veruta 9 (d), M.E. 7 (d), S.A. 5 (d), Heildeth(?) 1 (d), T. POPE 38 (boarder)(House Painter) 8-2-20

1900 CENSUS

Charles W. Ault 76 (Jan 1824-T/Pa/T-M 32), Manerva T. 57 (Mar 1843-M 32-0-0), George SMITH 50 (boarder) (Unk 1850-Pa/Pa/Pa)(Carpenter) 8-281B-261/263

Margaret A. Ault 53 (Sep 1846-Wd 8-8), Perry W. 32 (Oct 1867), Emma A. 27 (Mar 1873), Susan A. 24 (Aug 1875), Ida L. 19 (Mar 1881), Lora J. 16 (Sep 1883), George TULLAS (B) 20 (July 1879)(Servant) 8-287B-394/396

Wiley A. Ault 32 (Feb 1868-M 9)(Store Manager), Hester 26 (July 1873-M 9-3-2), Clifford 5 (Jan 1895), Wilfred 5 (Jan 1895) 8-286B-365/367

MARRIAGES

C.W. Ault to Manervia T. Frazier, 20 Feb 1869 (no return) 1-#1046

G.W. Ault to Vesta A. Darwin, 3 May 1876 (same), G.W. Renfro MG 1-#1441

George W. Ault to Rebecca Henry, 29 Dec 1859 (same), John Howard MG 1-#706

Icie D. Ault to Will G. Purser q.v.

Mary Jane Ault to Houston Mansel or Manuel q.v.

Rebecca A. Ault to S.L. Wilkey q.v.

W.N. Ault to Ruth* Howard, 24 July 1855 (same), W.H. Bell MG 1-#510 [*Rutha C. on marriage bond]

Wiley N. Ault to Margaret A. Abel, 10 Oct 1865 (no return) 1-#840

Wiley N. Ault to Margaret Addaline Abel, 10 Oct 1865 (same), A.P. Early MG 1-#865

V.J. Ault to James H. Harrison q.v.

Versailles Ault to John G. Allen q.v.

- - - - - - - - - - - - -

AVERY / AVREY

1900 CENSUS

Charley Avery 22 (June 1877-T/NC/T-M 2)(Coal Puller), Sary J. 19 (Nov 1880-T/NC/T-M 2-1-1), Gustie 1 (July 1898) 10-258A-156/160 (B)

John Avery 57 (Nov 1842-Pa/Conn/Pa-M 33), Margaret 49 (Ap 1850-Wales/Wales/Wales-M 33-1-1) 5-236B-166

MARRIAGES

Charley C. Avery to Sarah Jane Campbell, 6 Sep 1897 (same), W.L. Lillard JP & W 2-175

Ester Avery to James Campbell q.v.

George Joshua Avrey to Julia Ann Reevley, 9 Sep 1893, John Sweeny MG 4-64

Hettie Avery to George Woford q.v.

Mary Avery to Roley Jones q.v.

- - - - - - - - - - - - -

AVY

1900 CENSUS

Willie Avy 19, Frank 15, Lizzie 14, Lillie 11, Mannie 9, Martha 6, Kittie 4, Francis 1: see James Cmpbell (B)

- - - - - - - - - - - - -

AYERS

1900 CENSUS
Alice Ayers 21: see Benjamin F. Mealer
Susie Ayers 23: see George W. Goodrich
William Ayers 31 (Unk 1868-M 6)(Coal Miner), Lottie 26 (Unk 1874-Ga/Ga/Ga-M 6-3-2), Arthur 4 (Sep 1895-Ga), Albert 3 (Mar 1897-Ga) 8-280B-245/247
MARRIAGE
George Ayers to Laura Fleming, 2 Ap 1896 (same), S.W. Burnett MG, Grant Walker W 2-10

- - - - - - - - - - - - -

AYLWORTH

1900 CENSUS
Reuben Aylworth 79, Mary 78: see Fred A. Gregory

- - - - - - - - - - - - -

AXMAKER / AXMACKER

1900 CENSUS
Robert F. Axmacker 50 (Jan 1850-Oh/Germany/Germany-M 15)(Carpenter), Mary E. 32 (May 1868-T/Ala/Va-M 15-7-7), Charles B. 14 (Mar 1886), Walter 12 (Ap 1888), Franklin R. 10 (Mar 1890), Oscar S. 8 (Feb 1892), Lillie L. 5 (Feb 1895), Archie C. 2 (July 1897), Infant 3/12 (Feb 1900) 13-304A-260/270
MARRIAGE
Robert Axmaker to Emma Morgan, 13 May 1885 (same), M.C. Bonner MG 1-496

- - - - - - - - - - - - -

AZZ

1900 CENSUS
George Azz 28 (June 1871-SC/SC/SC-M 4), Laura 22 (Sep 1877-M 4-3-1), Creed 2 (May 1898) 15-273B-99 (B)

- - - - - - - - - - - - -

BACON

1860 CENSUS
Allen Bacon 41 2-72-490
Drury A. Bacon 26, Sarah 27, Mary 2, Amanda 8/12, George M. BIRD 20 3-61-417
1870 and 1880– None
1900 CENSUS
Francis M. Bacon 58 (May 1842-Oh/NY/Conn-M 36) (Merchant), Sally A. 58 (Dec 1841-Oh/NY/NY-M 36-3-2), Lillie E. 9 (adopted dau)(Ap 1891-Ky), Minnie ROGERS 20 (Nov 1879-Ala/Ala/Ala)(Servant), Reuben DANIELS 56 (boarder)(Sep 1843-Oh/Oh/Oh-M 30)(Carpenter) 13-305A-286/296
Samuel Bacon 31 (Feb 1869-T/NC/NC-M 0)(Furnaceman), Florence 32 (Mar 1868-T/NC/NC-M 0-3-3), Lula M. RODDY (sd)(Sep 1889), Lillie 8 (sd)(July 1891), James 7 (ss)(Aug 1892) 10-329B-194/207 (B)
MARRIAGE
D.A. Bacon to Sarah E. Bean, 22 Mar 1853 (24 Mar), A.G. Wright JP 1-#407

- - - - - - - - - - - - -

BADDIRVANS

1900 CENSUS
Margaret Baddirvans 74: see John Hughes

- - - - - - - - - - - - -

BADER

MARRIAGE
George A. Bader to Linda F.M. Taylor, 4 Nov 1887 (24 Nov), Laban Harwood MG 1-537

- - - - - - - - - - - - -

BAGLES
(see also **BOGLE**)

MARRIAGE
Ed Bagles to M.A. Pass, 17 Mar 1885 (18 Mar), W.W. Pyott MG 1-460

- - - - - - - - - - - - -

BAILEY / BAILY

1860 CENSUS
Richard Bailey 50 (Va)(School Teacher), Elmira 26, Geraldein 33, Samuel WILSON 20 (Itenerant) 1-85-580
1870 and 1880– None
1900 CENSUS
Lizzie Baily 55 (Sep 1844-Oh/NY/Pa-M 29-3-2), Percy E. 21 (Feb 1879-Oh/Oh/Oh)(Day Laborer) 10-325A-110/114
William Bailey 39 (May 1861-M 4)(Hardware Salesman), Katie 25 (June 1874-M 4-2-2), Anna L. 2 (Ap 1898), Earnest C. 7/12 (Oct 1899) 10-326B-136/142
MARRIAGES
Annie Bailey to Marion(?) Thompson q.v.
Henry Bailey to Mary Houston, 21 Aug 1881 (Pinhook), W.E. Kangroo JP or MG 4-2 (17) (B)

- - - - - - - - - - - - -

BAIN / BAINE

1900 CENSUS
Charles M. Bain 46 (Feb 1854-T/T/NC-M 25), Rebecca J. 55 (Sep 1844-T/Ga/Ga-M 25-3-3), Milton H. 19 (Sep 1880), Robert T. 17 (Oct 1882), Thomas C. 15 (Mar 1885), William H. HOLLAND 18 (boarder)(May 1882) 9-229A-26
Edward Bain 23: see Wesley Britt
MARRIAGE
Ollie Baine to Samuel W. Smith q.v.

- - - - - - - - - - - - -

BAKER

1870 CENSUS
Samuel Baker 46, Rachel E. 42 (NC), Isaac L. 16, Hariet J. 15, William P. 14, George W. 12, Andrew J. 10, Mary M. 8, James A. 5, Samuel 2 2-7-46

1880 CENSUS

George Baker 22: see Micajah Clack
Lihu Baker 24, Caldenea 24 8-2-14
Samuel Baker 54, Jack 18, Mary 15, James 13, Samuel 11, Martha 10, Thomas 6 12-6-47
Samuel Baker 35, Martha 25, Ida 5, Alice 1 2-35-282

1900 CENSUS

Dallas Baker 29 (Ap 1871-M 7)(RR Laborer), Violet 32 (May 1868-M 7-2-2), Margaret ROBINSON 15 (d) (Sep 1884) 14-215B-57/58 (B)
Ida Baker 22, Mattie 6/12: see George Fields
Lihu Baker 51 (Mar 1849-T/Va/SC-M 23)(Coal Miner), Caldonia 44 (June 1855-M 23-3-3), Lizzie 18 (Ap 1882), Charley 15 (June 1884-Ga)(Coal Miner), Maggie 12 (Dec 1887) 10-321B-34/35
Lizzie Baker 23: see Charles Calloway (B)
Mary J. Baker 31 (Dec 1868-T/T/Ga-Wd 3-3)(Seamstress), Maud E. 12 (Dec 1887), Beulah 10 (June 1889), William R. 8 (Feb 1892) 10-320B-10/10
Rufus Baker 61 (May 1839-Canada/Ver/England-1862/38/N-M 34)(Captalist), Leville 54 (Feb 1845-Oh/Oh/Oh-M 34-2-1) 14-213A-9/9

MARRIAGES

Amanda Baker to Charles MacCay q.v.
Elizabeth Baker to William P. Eaton q.v.
George Baker (23, Meigs Co) to Eliza A. Miller (22), 23 Feb 1882, James Johnson JP, Baxter Clack & Samuel Baker W 4-8(80)
Harriet J. Baker to W.G. Beaver q.v.
I.L. Baker to Manger Watson, 25 Dec 1883 (26 Dec), W.L. West MG 1-473
Jack Baker to Mary Gray, 7 Aug 1889 (8 Aug), W.R. Clack JP 1-588
John Baker to Catharine Mathis, 4 Aug 1891, John Howard MG 4-30
Julia Baker to Ode Zellander q.v.
Julia Louisa Baker to William M. Strong q.v.
Lihugh Baker to Caldonia Morgan, 5 Nov 1876 (7 Nov), William Morgan JP 1-#1467
Margarett Baker to J.B. Dudley q.v.
Mary Baker to James M. Atchly q.v.
William Baker to Nancy Ann Coleston or Coulston, 2 July 1856 (10 July), Thomas Knight JP 1-#556 & 1-#563

- - - - - - - - - - - - -

BALDWIN / BAULDIN

1880 CENSUS

G.R. Baldwin 64 (Carpenter), L.C. 26 (w), J.R. 5 (s), W.H. 1 (s) 4-9-69
H. Baldwin 39, L. 28 (w), Carrie 9, Ida 5, James 4, John 2 3-22-175
John Baldwin 28, Lizzie 27, Joseph 5, Mary 2 2-38-312

1900 CENSUS

Geo R. Baldwin 54 (May 1846-T/Va/Va-M 26)(Justice of the Peace), Levonia 48 (Ap 1852-M 26-5-4), William H. 21 (Dec 1878), Bertie A. 17 (Feb 1883), Mettie M. 14 (June 1886) 14-218A-106/108
Wilum W. Bauldin 63 (July 1836-Va/NC/NC-M 35), Nancy 54 (Dec 1845-M 35-9-8), John [Joseph] 31 (May 1869), Druse 23 (d)(Jan 1877), Bessey 13 (Oct 1886), May 10 (Oct 1889), Claud 4 (gs)(Aug 1895) 12-181B-65/68

MARRIAGES

John R. Baldwin to M.I. Thompson, 18 Sep 1899, J.L. McPherson JP 4-104
Mary E. Baldwin to James F. Walker q.v.

- - - - - - - - - - - - -

BALER– see BOLES

- - - - - - - - - - - - -

BALL

1860 CENSUS

George W. Ball 45 (SC)(Shoemaker), Rachel 47, Margaret 19, John 13, Thomas 10, Liddia 7 6-112-769

1870 CENSUS

William F. Ball 37 (NC), Margarette 25, William 8 1-4-24

MARRIAGES

E.E. Ball to J.A. Marriott q.v.
John L. Ball to Mary J. Caywood, 1 Nov 1875 (4 Nov), S.T. McFerson MG 1-#1418
Lyda A. Ball to Columbus Majors q.v.

- - - - - - - - - - - - -

BALLARD

1900 CENSUS

James M. Ballard 26 (Oct 1873-M 4)(Livestock Dealer), Mintie 25 (Feb 1875-M 4-3-3), James L. 3 (Mar 1897), Bessie 1 (Jan 1899), Flarra 2/12 (Mar 1900) 6-247A-139/140
Joseph Ballard 53 (Feb 1847-M 38), Hetta 52 (Feb 1848-M 38-9-6), Samuel 24 (Nov 1875), Anna 19 (Aug 1880), Clinton 13 (Jan 1887), Lizzie SWAFFORD 16 (gd) (Feb 1884), John WALKER 14 (nw)(Ap 1886) 6-243A-65

MARRIAGES

Catharine Ballard to F.C. Wright q.v.
J.M. Ballard to Mintie Gott, 25 Mar 1896 (27 Mar), A.H. Low MG, R.J. Killough W 2-7
Lewis Ballard to Emeline Hughes, 9 June 1854 (11 June), Wm C. Hollins JP 1-#448
P.N. Ballard to C.P. Day q.v.

- - - - - - - - - - - - -

BALLEN

MARRIAGE

G.A. Ballen to T.W. Auther q.v.

- - - - - - - - - - - - -

BALLEW

MARRIAGES

Etta Ballew to Munroe Ridley q.v.
G.W. Ballew Jr. to Ella Kenedy, 18 Aug 1893, S.S. Franklin JP 4-55
George W. Ballew to Mattie Stringer, 2 June 1893, W.S. Hale MG 4-59

- - - - - - - - - - - - -

BANDY

1860 CENSUS
Francis M. Bandy 25, Nancy J. 26, John R. 4, Sarah J. 2, William M. 1 8-20-131
MARRIAGES
Alice Bandy to G.W. Gibson q.v.
C.F. Bandy to Mary Custer, 18 Dec 1891, R.S. Mason JP 4-34
Elizabeth Bandy to William S. Smith q.v.
F.A. Bandy to Mollie E. Adams, 29 Dec 1891, J.B. Massoner MG 4-37
F.M. Bandy to Nancy J. Bean, 28 Feb 1855, John Crawford JP 1-#486
F.M. Bandy to Melitia Elder, 12 Mar 1895, W.A. Green JP 4-77
J.D. Bandy(?) to Susan T. Fletcher, 11 Nov 1888, Jas Corvin MG 4-44
Mary Ann Bandy to John W. Bean q.v.
Thomas Bandy to Jamia Furgusson, 28 Dec 1878 (29 Dec), B.F. Holloway JP 1-#1595
Wm C. Bandy to Angeline Lemmons, 24 Jan 1854 (31 Jan), Elijah Brewer JP 1-#436

- - - - - - - - - - - - -

BANKS

1880 CENSUS
W.J. Banks 35, N.S. 34 (w), A.T. 12 (s), A.M. 10 (d), J.N. 8 (s), Mary S. 6, H.K. 3 (s), Su A 2/12 (d), Linda LAUTERMILK 65 (ml), M.A. CATES 9, J.B. 5 8-10-86
1900 CENSUS
Henry Banks 23 (May 1877-T/T/Ga), John W. 28 (b)(Jan 1872), Lula 20 (si)(Mar 1880), Rosa 17 (si)(Mar 1883), Ciola 12 (si)(Dec 1887), Lydia 9 (si)(Sep 1890), Mary SMEDLEY 25 (si)(Aug 1874-Wd 3-0), Walter 9 (nw)(Mar 1891) 15-169A-20
Joe Banks 46 (June 1853-Va/Va/Va-M 12), Jennie 28 (Jan 1872-M 12-3-1), Iowa 8 (Sep 1891), Rufe McDONALD 19 (bl)(Coal Miner), Jake BOGGESS 40 (boarder)(Dec 1859)(Servant) 8-313B-56/59 (B)
Thomas Banks 23 (Unk-M 0), Lettie 19 (Ap 1881-M 0-0-0) 8-315B-110/114
MARRIAGES
A.T. Banks to Hugh E. Welch q.v.
Allice Banks to William Smedley q.v.
James Banks to Ella Evans, 28 Aug 1891, John Howard MG 4-30
Joseph Banks to Jennie McDonald, 12 Sep 1887 (same), A. Stone MG 1-528
Mary L. Banks to Charley Sneedley q.v.
Racheal C. Banks to A.H. McReynolds q.v.

- - - - - - - - - - - - -

BANKSTON

1860 CENSUS
Andrew J. Bankston 34 (Va), Nancy C. 36 (NC), Amanda TEAGUE 19 8-12-79
1870 CENSUS
Andrew J. Bankston 50, Nancy C. 47, Elizabeth COWEN 40, Mary E. 8 8-14-99

1880 CENSUS
A.J. Bankston 56, P.A. 33 (w), M.E. 4 (d), A.J. 10/12 (s) 8-19-161
J.H. Bankston 27, M.J. 24 (w), J.E. 4 (d), A.W. 10/12 (s) 8-7-57

1900 CENSUS
Andrew J. Bankston 50 (Oct 1849-T/NC/T-M 25), Darcus A. 53 (June 1847-M 25-6-4), Anna E. 14 (Sep 1885) 3-210B-186/203
George Bankston 17: see Mary E. Hale
Henry Bankston 37 (Nov 1862-M 15)(Blacksmith), Pocahontas 37 (Ap 1863-T/NC/T-M 15-1-1), Onzie 13 (Jan 1887) 8-317B-145/150
Nancy Bankston 35 (Mar 1865-Wd 6-4)(Washwoman), Fanny 20 (Oct 1879)(Washwoman), Martha 12 (July 1887), James H. 9 (June 1890), Creed 1 (May 1899) 6-240B-18
Samuel(?) W. Bankston 21 (Oct 1878-M 1), Lillie A. 18 (Oct 1881-M 1-1-1), Bessie M. 8/12 (Oct 1899) 3-210B-186/204
William O. Bankston 23 (Mar 1877-M 2), Ida M. 21 (Mar 1879-M 2-1-1), Jesse L. 1 (Dec 1898), Mary J. RECTOR 6 (Unk 1894)(Servant) 3-210B-187/205

MARRIAGES
A.J. Bankston to Caroline Teague, 8 Dec 1853 (same), W.C. Hollins JP 1-#431
A.J. Bankston to Anna Phillips, 14 June 1886 (15 June), W.R. Grimsley MG 1-508
Andrew J. Bankston to Polly Ann Malott, 20 Jan 1875 (no return) 1-#1390
Henry Bankston to Lillie Smith, 25 Dec 1898, J.A. Torbett JP 4-95
L. Bankston to R.F.C. Porter q.v.
W.O. Bankston to Ida M. Porter, 31 Jan 1898 (9 Feb), W.K. Fugate JP, W.A. Bankston W 2-246

- - - - - - - - - - - - -

BANNER / BARNER

MARRIAGE
Mary Banner or Barner to Cy Copeland q.v.

- - - - - - - - - - - - -

BARCUS

1900 CENSUS
Benjamin F. Barcus 39 (Mar 1861-Ind/Ind/Del-M 16)(Dry Goods Merchant), Amanda E. 39 (May 1861-Ky/Ky/Ky-M 16-0-0) 10-324B-95/99

- - - - - - - - - - - - -

BARDWELL

MARRIAGE
Frank Bardwell to Minnie Roberts, 29 Feb 1896 (1 Mar), W.L. Lillard JP, G.W. Johnson W 2-2

- - - - - - - - - - - - -

BARGER / BURGER / BARGINS / BARGEN / BERGANS / BURGAN / BURGIN

1860 CENSUS

Carey Bargen 45, Mary 46, Ruthe E. 22, Martha J. 18, Susan 16, Harriet L. 13, Sarah M. 13, Mary E. 10 1-83-570

Robert B. Bargen 49, Ellen 48, Mary J. 17, Abraham F. 14, Robert H. 12 8-16-106

1870 CENSUS– None

1880 CENSUS

Samuel Bergans 25, Ellen 17, Fonster 4 10-29-226/232 (B)

1900 CENSUS

Ellen Barger 87: see Hugh Barger

Hugh Barger 51 (Feb 1849-M 11), Mary H. 36 (Nov 1863-M 11-7-5), Charles B. 19 (Ap 1881), Lodusky E. 17 (Dec 1882), Gertrude 15 (Feb 1885), Nannie 13 (Mar 1887), Uvia 10 (June 1889), Clayton 9 (Mar 1891), Horace 7 (June 1892), Archie 2 (Jan 1898), Linnie 10/12 (July 1899), Ellen BARGER 87 (m)(July 1812-Wd 8-5), William HATFIELD 12 (ss)(Nov 1887) 13-295B-108/110

James R. Barger 24 (Mar 1876-M 2)(Coal Miner), Minerva 19 (Mar 1881-Ga/Ga/Ga-M 2-1-1), Hosea H. 1 (Feb 1899) 13-307A-324/336

John W. Barger 27 (Jan 1873-Ky/T/Ky-M 7), Amanda E. 25 (Mar 1875-M 7-4-4), Fred E. 6 (Oct 1893), Clarence R. 4 (Sep 1895), Grace E. 2 (Jan 1898), Robert F. 1/12 (Ap 1900) 13-295A-98/100

Robert B. Barger 24 (Aug 1875-M 3), Mattie E. 24 (Jan 1876-M 3-2-2), Jesse L. 1 (Sep 1898), Bessie May 5/12 (Dec 1899), James HOWARD 23 (boarder)(Mar 1877) 13-301A-204/212

Samuel Bargin 63 (July 1836-NC/NC/NC-M 17), Ellen 45 (Dec 1854-T/Va/T-M 12-1-1), Louisa McDONAL 64 (Sep 1835-Wd), Horace COPLAN 55 (Oct 1844-NC/NC/NC-Wd) 5-232A-81 (B)

Thomas J. Barger 27 (Aug 1872-M 4), Sarah A. 21 (July 1878-M 4-3-3), Charles T. 2 (Oct 1897), Dulah P. 1 (Nov 1898), unnamed 2/12 (May 1900) 3-202A-41/44

William B. Barger 22, Lushan 19, Jane 16, Anna 15: see Elizabeth A. Fuller

William T. Barger 55 (Jan 1844-T/Va/Va-M 33)(Teamster), Sarah E. 51 (June 1848-T/Va/T-M 33-4-4), Minnie R. 27 (Jan 1873-Ky), Ida E. BEST 20 (Aug 1879-Wd 1-1), Mattie E. 4 (gd)(May 1896), Jasper N. 20 (nw) (Aug 1879)(Coal Miner), Joseph JOHNSON 23 (boarder)(May 1877) 1-302A-219/227

Wyley A.(?) Barger 29 (Aug 1870-M 10), Alice A. 23 (Sep 1876-M 10-3-3), Luella 8 (Oct 1891), Julian T. 5 (Jan 1895), Clara B. 2 (Oct 1897) 4-227A-265/269 (Rhea Springs & Washington Road)

MARRIAGES

E.R. Barger to Ella Darwin, 11 Aug 1899 (13 Aug), W.R. Grimsley MG, R.H. Barger W 3-18

Elizabeth Barger to John W. Everett q.v.

Ida Barger to H.P. Best q.v.

J.M. Burger to Caroline Lindsey, 23 Sep 1887 (25 Sep), B.F. Hollaway JP 1-536

J.N. or J.W. Burger to Nannie Carter, 24 Dec 1900 (25 Dec), W.R. Grimsley MG, N. Burger W 3-261

J.R. Barger to Minerva Harris, 16 Oct 1897 (17 Oct), G.W. Colcord MG, H.N. Best W 2-197

Jennie Barger to J.N. Jordon q.v.

John W. Barger to Amanda E. Wyott, 2 Nov 1892, G.W. Brewer MG 4-48

Julia Barger to Henry Hill q.v.

Martha Barger to George W. Everett q.v.

Martha J. Barger to Newton Casey q.v.

Mary J. Barger to S.H. Alexander q.v.

R.B. Barger to Mattie Painter, 20 Feb 1897 (21 Feb), W.R. Grimsley MG, R.H. Barger W 2-107

Robert H. Barger to Malinda Wyrick, 6 Nov 1867 (same), W.B. Humphrey JP 1-#981

Rutha Burgan to Henry Hughes q.v.

Sam Bargins to Ellen McDonald, 28 Sep 1878 (same), William S. Hale MG 1-290

Susan Barger to Isaac McLandon q.v.

Thomas J. Barger to Sarah A. Smith, 6 Sep 1896, L.E. Smith JP 4-97

Vega Barger to A.E. Grayham q.v.

- - - - - - - - - - - - -

BARKER

MARRIAGES

Elizabeth Barker to Stephen Fuller q.v.

Jennie Barker to George Cunnyngham q.v.

- - - - - - - - - - - - -

BARKSDALE

MARRIAGE

Sarah A.L. Barksdale to H.N. Whittenburg q.v.

- - - - - - - - - - - - -

BARNES / BARNS / BURNS

1900 CENSUS

Alice Barnes 30, Lillie 8, Emma 6: see David W. Reed

Mollie L. Barnes 19: see Nancy Crawford

William L. Barnes 49 (July 1850-M 5)(Tinsmith), Emma E. 30 (Dec 1869-M 5-3-3), Robert L. 4 (Dec 1895), William S. 2 (Feb 1898), Eliza J. 10/12 (July 1899), Mama E. 12 (d)(Sep 1887) 10-321B-37/39

MARRIAGES

Dolly Burns to John Taylor q.v.

Estella M. Burns to Jesse E. Reed q.v.

Jacob Barnes to Callie Reed, 11 July 1891, J.W. Williamson MG 4-28

Jacob Barnes to White Jewell, 21 July 1895, W.L. Lillard JP 4-82

James Barnes to Minnie Buck, 10 Oct 1891, W.C. Daily MG 4-31

John Barnes to Catharine Jocques, 23 Aug 1889 (same), R.S. Mason JP 1-578

Sallie Burns or Burris to John Taylor q.v.

W.F. Barnes to Emma Reid, 2 Oct 1894, J.W. Williamson MG 4-78

W.H. Barnes to Virginia T. Jewell, 8 Jan 1888 (10 Jan), John H. Parrott ?? 1-550

- - - - - - - - - - - - - - -

BARNETT / BURNETT

1860 CENSUS

James Barnet 50, Isaac 22, Elviny 15, Horatio 13, Hanibel L. 11, James K.P. 9, Franklin P. 7, Charlotte 5 5-37-252

Margaret Barnett 56: see R.C. Montgomery

Thomas F. Barnet 65 (Va), Mary 53, Harriet T. 27, Nancy F. 24, Martha J. 17, Eliza A. 17 5-38-257

1870 CENSUS

Isaac Barnett 36, Mary B. 23 (Ala), Elvana C. 5, Mary A. 2 3-7-51

James R. Barnett 59, James P. 21, Franklin 17, Charlotte 14 3-6-39

Sarah A. Burnett 25: see Andrew J. Bryson

1880 CENSUS

Columbus Burnet 20: see William McCarrol

I.W. [Isaac West] Barnett 44, Mary B. 31, Elvana C. 14, Mary A. 11, Sarah J. 9, Harriett A. 7, Florence Y. 6, July 1 5-2-15

James Barnett 71, Julia 41, N. COX 16 (nw) 4-31-257

1900 CENSUS

Isaac W. Barnett 64 (Feb 1836-M 34), Mary 56 (Feb 1844-Ala/T/Ala-M 34-8-8), Revanna 18 (July 1881), Dora 15 (May 1885), Hariet A. CLINE 25 (d)(Nov 1874-M 3-2-2), Anna L. 2 (gd)(Sep 1897), Phillip 6/12 (gs) (Nov 1899) 5-238A-196

James Burnett 24 (Jan 1876), Manerva H. 57 (m)(Mar 1843-Wd 1-1) 7-261B-223/228

Jerry Burnett 34 (Jan 1866-M 6), Margarett 25 (Nov 1874-M 6-3-3), Jonah 5 (Nov 1894), Ulia 4 (Jan 1896), Claytie 2 (May 1898) 7-263A-250/255

Julia Barnett 61 (Ap 1839-Wd 0-0), Malinda WALLER 65 (si)(Sep 1834-Wd 1-1), Doctor M. COX 39 (nw)(Dec 1862) 3-200B-11/11

Lafayette Burnett 44 (Mar 1856-M 19), Delie 39 (Feb 1861-NC/T/NC-M 19-9-9), Milton 19 (Oct 1880), Susan 17 (Dec 1882), Mary 15 (Jan 1885), Parlee 13 (Jan 1887), Maggie 11 (Jan 1889), Lillie 9 (May 1891), Millerd 6 (Mar 1893), Clifford 4 (Feb 1896), Lust 2 (Ap 1898) 12-181A-55/58

Mary Burnett 29: see W.W. Cunnyngham

Mary Burnett 82: see John L. Allen

Mattie Barnett 33: see Frederick Doll

William Barnett 13 (B): see James M. Owens

William L. Burnett 40 (Dec 1859-M 7), Eliza J. 24 (Oct 1875-M 7-2-2), Charles 6 (Feb 1893), Anna J. 1 (Feb 1899) 4-224A-201/205 (Spring City & Dayton Road)

MARRIAGES

A.F. Burnett to A.C. Ponder, 3 Nov 1885 (1 Dec), W.R. Clack JP 1-517

Alice V. Burnett to James A. Jennings q.v.

Cordie D. Burnett to Joseph H. Grenon q.v.

E.L. Burnett to J.W. Purser q.v.

Elvira Barnett to Robert Short q.v.

Elveny Barnett to Henry Young q.v.

George J. Burnett to Adie Couster(?), 4 Mar 1889 (same), W.R. Grimsley MG 1-57

H.E. Burnett to James Purcer q.v.

Harriett Barnett to M.F. Loftis q.v.

J.H. Burnett to Lizzie Ziegler, 4 June 1884 (same), J.H. Weaver MG 1-471

J.S. Burnett to Maggie L. Morgan, 20 Dec 1893, Richard Knight JP 4-62

James E. Burnett to Nettie E. Clouse, 2 Mar 1885 (15 Mar), J.F. Posey MG 1-461

James R. Barnett to July Cox, 18 Sep 1873 (21 Sep), John Howard MG 1-#1302

James R. Burnett to Louisa Morgan, 22 May 1888 (same), M.C. Bruner MG 1-563

James S. Burnett to Myra A. Garrison, 13 Aug 1874 (same), John Howard MG 1-#1349

Jannie Barnett to Samuel Alexander q.v.

Lizzie Burnett to Thomas B. Thompson q.v.

M.E. Barnett to William Eeonis(?) q.v.

Martha Burnett to R.C. Montgomery q.v.

Martha J. Barnett to William Blankenship q.v.

Marthy Barnett to F.M. Loftis q.v.

Mary Burnet to Patrick Wilkey q.v.

Mattie A. Burnett to H.H. Shaver q.v.

Mollie Barnett to Frederick Pall q.v.

Nancy Burnett to Jerry L. Denton q.v.

Nancy F. Burnett to Newton C. Hicks q.v.

Nannie Burnett to W.H. Ledford q.v.

Sallie J. Burnett to J.M. Bolen q.v.

Samuel W. Burnett to Minnie Lockwood, 8 Mar 1897 (11 Mar), Henry W. Webb MG, A.J. Harris W 2-123

Sarah A. Burnett to Thomas H. Robinson q.v.

W.H. Burnett to Selina Hamilton, 14 Ap 1891, John Woolsey MG 4-21

William Barnett to Margarett Bowles, 18 May 1852 (same), A.G. Wright JP 1-#386

- - - - - - - - - - - - -

BARNEY

1900 CENSUS

Ben Barney 16: see Jennie Dickson (B)

- - - - - - - - - - - - -

BARNWELL

MARRIAGE

Isaac Barnwell to Elizabeth James, 28 Nov 1855 (29 Nov), W.R.P. Thompson JP 1-#545

- - - - - - - - - - - - -

BARTLETT

MARRIAGE

Clara L. Bartlett to Elsom C. Sevely q.v.

- - - - - - - - - - - - -

BARTON / BARTIN / BURTON

1860 CENSUS

Alfred Burton 21 (NC), Marthey 34 (NC), James B. 2, Marion 5/12 6-108-739

Azariah Barton 59 (NC), Susan 60, John M. 22, Osker 19, Sarah J. 15, Calvin 36 8-22-146

Elizabeth Barton 42 (NC), Mary E. 22, Sarah C. 17, Martha J. 15, James 13 3-59-404

Elijah Burton 48, Caroline J. 38, Louissa A. 24 1-87-593

Pinkney Burton 23 (NC), Sarah 18 (NC) 6-108-740

Pryor Barton 30, Osker 7, Susan E. 5, Thomas 2, Sarah P. 1 1-86-588
Thomas J. Barton 23, Catharine 21, William W. 2, Misy F. 1 1-87-595

1870 CENSUS

Alfred Burton 28 (NC), Mary 21, James 12, Marion 10, Elizabeth 8, William 3, William [probably HARVESTON] 3 (ss), Sarah A. BURTON 9/12 7-5-35
Caroline J. Barton 49, Rachel KNIGHT 62 1-1-2
Elizabeth Burton 54 (NC), Martha J. 24 (NC), Polly COLLINS 80 (NC), Sarah HUBBERT 27 (NC), Randy HUBBERT 8 7-5-38
Pinkney Burton 35 (NC), Sarah 31 (NC), Caroline 9, Thomas 7, Elizabeth 6, Emaline 2 7-3-25
Thomas J. Barton 36, Catharine Ann 33, William W. 14, Mary Susan A. 11, John C. 10, Thomas A. 8, Robert L. 6, Harriette J. 1 p. 4-3-14

1880 CENSUS

Jane Barton 60, Loretta NORTHRAP 29 (Servant) 1-9-75
Ostear Barton 27, Rilda A. 27 10-28-218/223
Pinkney Barton 46, S.E. 36 (w), J.T. 18 (s), E.J. 14 (d), E.S. 11 (d), Wm I. 9 (s), E.J. 6 (d), Sampson 3 (s) 3-14-110
Pryor Barton 52, Mary 50, S.E. 23 (d), Milo 14, Suther 12. Frank 8 8-4-35
Thomas Barton 46, D.A. 33 (w), M.E. 22 (d), S.H. 17 (s), R.L. 15 (s), O.L. 9 (s), D.L. 5 (d) 11-42-331
W.W. Barton 23, M.G. 22, Elbert 1 4-5-38

1900 CENSUS

Della Barton 26: see Gideon Morgan
Frank Barton 32 (Mar 1878-M 9)(Station Manager), Mollie 31 (Jan 1869-M 9-4-3), Raymon E. 8 (Dec 1891), Ticy 4 (Nov 1895), Cliford 1 (Aug 1898) 10-254B-86
Lafayette L. Barton 45 (Feb 1855-NY/NY/NY-M 21)(Postmaster), Yanjan 45 (Sep 1854-NY/Mass/Mass-M 21-2-2), Ellen 19 (Feb 1881-NY)(Assistant Postmaster), Gleen 16 (Mar 1884-NY) 12-180A-28/30
Milo Barton 34 (Sep 1865-M 6)(RR Yard Master), Alice 31 (Mar 1869-M 6-4-4), Lillie M. 6 (May 1894), Laura E. 4 (Aug 1895), Virgil E. 3 (Feb 1897), Sayburn H. 1 (Feb 1899) 10-325A-109/113
Oscar L. Barton 29 (Jan 1871-M 8), Adda W. 25 (Nov 1874-M 8), Lena A. 6 (Aug 1893) 14-222B-183/187
Souisen Barton 40 (Jan 1860-Wd 0-0), Marsy A. 60 (m) (Mar 1840-Wd 12-5) 10-252A-40
Thomas J. Barton 66 (May 1834-M 20), Delila A. 53 (Ap 1847-M 20-4-4), Katie 19 (Dec 1880), Mattie 16 (Mar 1884), Salla 13 (July 1886) 5-238B-203
Thomas ? Barton 37 (Ap 1863-M 10)(Clothing Merchant), Mary 35 (Aug 1864-Mo/Ireland/Ireland-M 10-5-3), Claude L. 8 (May 1892), John R. 6 (Sep 1893), Ralph C. 1 (Nov 1898) 10-320B-6/6
Witcher Barton 43 (Sep 1857-M 22), Marthy 41 (Sep 1859-T/T/Ga-M 22-6-6), Alburt 21 (Dec 1879), Jessie 15 (Nov 1884), Tom 12 (Mar 1888), Charles 8 (June 1891), Katie 6 (Nov 1893), Molly Rose 5/12 (Oct 1899), Floyad Elbert 21 (s)(boarder)(Dec 1879)(RR Hand) 1-186A-140/147

MARRIAGES

Alfred Burton to Mary D. [nee Arnold] Harviston, 10 Feb 1869 (11 Feb), John Howard JP 1-#1044
C. E. Barton to F. A. Reed q.v.
Della Barton to Edward Culley q.v.
Elizabeth Barton to Thomas K. Green q.v.
Elizabeth Barton to John Prater q.v.
Frank Barton to Mattie or Martha Rogers, 2 Jan 1891, R.A. Bartlett MG 4-24
Jane Burton to John W. May q.v.
Louisa Barton to John M. Lemmons q.v.
M. S. Burton to Samuel Walker q.v.
Mary Burton to Benjamin Arnold q.v.
Oscar Barton to Z.A. Morgan, 10 Sep 1879 (11 Sep), J.F. Perry MG 1-#1674
Oscar L. Barton to Adda W. Ferguson, 1 May 1892, W.G. Mitchell MG 4-41
P.K. Barton to Sarah D. Wright, 24 Aug 1858 (same), G.W. Wallace JP 1-#649
Paralee Burton to Davis Queen q.v.
S. J. Barton to A. L. Able q.v.
Sarah Burton to Houston Hubbard q.v.
Sarah J. Barton to H. M. Rector q.v.
Sudia Barton to Banister C. Smith q.v.
T.A. Barton to Mary A. Cushing, 29 Ap 1890 (29 May), Patrick Jo Farrill MG 1-603
Thos Barton to D.A. Miller, 24 Dec 1879 (same), B.F. Hollaway JP 1-#1699
Thomas J. Barton to Katherine Foust, 10 Mar 1855, John W. Thompson MG 1-#490
W.N. Barton to Mrs. Alice Langly, 18 Sep 1892, R.S. Mason JP 4-50
William W. Barton to Martha F. Akin, 26 Dec 1877 (27 Dec), G.W. Renfro MG 1-#1537

\- - - - - - - - - - - - -

BARTRAM– see BUTTRAM

\- - - - - - - - - - - - -

BASKETT

1900 CENSUS

Frances C. Baskett 58 (Ap 1842-Wd 6-6), Laura F. 31 (Feb 1868), Richard 25 (Mar 1875), Frank 22 (May 1878) (Yard Boss, DC&I Co) 10-329B-201/214

MARRIAGES

Wash Baskett to Mollie Sanders, 10 Feb 1892, R.A. Bartlett MG 4-42
Will Baskett to Esther Thomas, 27 Jan 1896, D.V. Culver MG 4-88

\- - - - - - - - - - - - -

BATES

MARRIAGES

Bessie Bates to W. J. Cowan q.v.
Cordelia Bates(?) to D. W. Merriott q.v.
Oliver Bates to Jane Dooly, 25 Sep 1869 (same), T.N.L. Cunnyngham JP 1-#1112

\- - - - - - - - - - - - -

BATON

1900 CENSUS

William Baton 26: see Eligah Newton (B)

\- - - - - - - - - - - - -

BAUGH

1900 CENSUS
Brice J. Baugh 20: see Charles W. Irwin

- - - - - - - - - - - - -

BEAN

1860 CENSUS
John A. Bean 27, Emily F. 19: see William B. Johnson
John W. Bean 24 (Va), Mary Ann 25, Isaac 1/12 8-20-136
Charles D. Bean 53 (Va), Mary 45, William 23, Jacob 21, Sidney A. 18, Eliza J. 15, Charles 12, Elizabeth 9, Adaline 7 8-14-94
Mary Bean 80 (Md) 1-94-644
Onslow Bean 28: see Joseph Parks
Sarah C. Bean 12: see Elbert S. Cox
1870 CENSUS
Amanda Bean 49 (NC), James T. 22 (NC), Robert 14 (NC), George 11 1-16-103
Franklin L. Bean 24, Ruth 23, Lucy 4 6-12-83
John W. Bean 35 (Va), Mary Ann 35, Isaac Leander 9, Sarah C. 8, William B. 6, Jacob N. 5, Adalade Jane 2, John Walker 1/12 8-7-46
1880 CENSUS
Amanda Bean 59, William 27, Robert 24, George 21 1-15-129
C.T. Bean 27, S.A. 19 (w), I.J. 1/12 (d), W.K. GRAY 40, S.A. 31, J.S. 7 (s) 8-6-50
Lucy Bean 10, Tiney Ruth 11: see John Howard
Mary Bean 58: see S. I. Rogers

1900 CENSUS
Charles D. Bean 29 (June 1870-Mo/T/T-M 7), Lucy G. 29 (Oct 1871-M 7-3-2), Grace G. 4 (June 1895), Sister 2 (Oct 1897) 13-296A-115/117
Charles F. Bean 53 (Mar 1847-T/Va/Va-M 20), Susan A. 39 (Sep 1860-T/Ala/Ala-M 20-7-6), Lizzie E. 17 (Oct 1882), William H. 15 (May 1885), Ruth J. 12 (Nov 1887), Charles R. 9 (Nov 1890), Mary N. 6 (June 1893), Edgar B. 3 (Aug 1896) 13-310B-388/402
Daly C. Bean 24: see Edwin F. Wetmore
Jacob C. Bean 60 (Feb 1840-M 1), Hannah J. 30 (Ap 1870-M 1-1-1), George H. 21 (May 1879)(Coal Miner), Jessie T. 10 (Oct 1889), Dewey M. 2/12 (Mar 1900) 13-306B-315/327
Jacob N. Bean 34 (Feb 1866-M 8), Mary C. 32 (Mar 1868-M 8-4-2), Giles V. 3 (Dec 1896), Oscar D. 1 (Dec 1898) 11-292A-51
John Bean 65 (Unk 1835-S) 13-310B-387/401
John Bean 51 (July 1848-NC/T/T-M 22), Susan 56 (June 1843-T/Oh/T-M 22-14-11), Ruth 18 (Nov 1881), Vinie 16 (Mar 1884), Mary 12 (Dec 1886), Nann 12 (Feb 1888), Lass 11 (Dec 1889), James 9 (Sep 1890), Colman 8 (Jan 1892), Rose 5 (Sep 1894), Ellie 4 (Mar 1896), Larn 2 (Dec 1897), Charles 1 (Jan 1899) 1-183A-84/87
Lucy Bean 33: see John T. Howard
William M. Bean 64 (Unk 1834-T/Va/Va-Wd)(Pensioner), George W. 25 (Mar 1875)(Coal Miner), John A. 24 (May 1876)(Coal Miner), Nannie J. 22 (Feb 1878) 13-307A-328/340

MARRIAGES
Alice Bean to S. J. Rigsby q.v.
Charles D. Bean to Lucy Hoge, 29 Oct 1892, W.A. Green JP 4-47
Eliza J. Bean to H. M. Hensley q.v.
Elizabeth Bean to N. W. Roberts q.v.
Elizabeth Bean to P. L. Eaves q.v.
F.L. [Franklin Locke] Bean to Ruth C. Howard, 10 Jan 1866 (same), R.T. Howard MG 1-#882 [Franklin, son of Edmond and Lucretia Locke Bean; Ruth, dau of Rev. John and Sophia J. Howard]
George Bean or Bear to Mary McCray or McCroy, 21 July 1885 (22 July), James W. Smith JP 1-484
J.T. Bean to Ella Clark, 17 July 1885 (19 July), W.R. Grimsley MG 1-493
John A. Bean to Emily F. Chattin, 24 Aug 1859 (same), A.P. Early MG 1-#695
John W. Bean to Mary Ann Bandy, 21 July 1859 (24 July), D.F. Ward JP 1-#684
Lidea Bean to William C. Lowry q.v.
Lizzie Bean to James C. Winsett q.v.
Mary Bean to William Price q.v.
Mollie Bean to J. F. Gray q.v.
Nancy J. Bean to F. M. Bandy q.v.
S. C. Bean to F. M. Snow q.v.
Sarah E. Bean to D. A. Bacon q.v.
Tinie Bean to W. R. Walker q.v.
W.J. Bean to M.E. Hodge, 10 Dec 1893, W.R. Grimsley MG 4-60
W.T. Bean to Lennie Morgan, 27 Oct 1883 (31 Oct), D. Richardson M 1-474
William Bean to L.B. Moore, 28 Dec 1886 (29 Dec), I.W. Holt JP 1-513
William Bean to Lizzie Brown(?), 3 Feb 1887 (6 Feb), A.W. Frazier JP 1-538
William Beans(?) to Lizzie Rogers, 3 Dec 1887 (4 Dec), W.R. Grimsley MG 1-539

- - - - - - - - - - - -

BEARD

1870 CENSUS
James H. Beard 27, Pocahontas 23, Laura 3, Julia Ann 2, Emily 8/12, William R. BROWN 20 4-16-106
1880 CENSUS
Henry Beard 33, Pocahontas 33, L.J. 14 (d), J.A. 13 (d), Emma 10 (d), R.H. 9 (s), Delilah 7 (d), E.M. 3 (d), Hany REESE 20 (boarder) 4-5-35
1900 CENSUS
James H. Beard 57 (May 1843-M 35), Pocahontas 53 (Ap 1847-M 35-9-8), Florence M. 19 (Sep 1880), White 17 (Sep 1882) 4-224A-206/210
Robert H. Beard 28 (Aug 1871-M 5), Lillie A. 25 (Oct 1874-M 5-3-2), Fred L. 4 (Nov 1895), Henry M. 3 (Oct 1896) 5-237B-191
William Beard 25 (Aug 1874-M 6)(Coal Weighman), Maggie E. 24 (Sep 1875-M 6-2-2), Fred A. 3 (Ap 1897), Mary E. 6/12 (Nov 1899) 13-306A-305/317
MARRIAGES
Delia Beard to Walter Knight q.v.
Ellie Beard to Rylid Gormany q.v. (B)
Emma Beard to S. H. Smith q.v.
Eva Beard(?) to James Vaughn q.v.

Harriet Beard to Thomas J. Bromlett q.v.
James H. Beard to Pocahontas Miller, 8 Aug 1865 (2 Aug) [sic], Daniel Broyles JP 1-#845
Julia Beard to B. S. McClendon q.v.
Laura J. Beard to J. H. Holloway q.v.
Nancy Beard to Robert Johnson q.v.
Robert H. Beard to Lillie A. Bramlett, 21 Jan 1894, W.A. Howard MG 4-63

- - - - - - - - - - - - -

BEASLY / BEASLEY

1870 CENSUS
James E. Beasly 32 (Ga), Elizabeth 23, John W. 3 5-6-41
James M. Beasly 60 (SC), Margarette 56 (NC), Garrett M. 20 (Ga), Thomas 16 (Ga) 5-6-40
John H. Beasley 23 (Ga), Elizabeth 27, Nathan WATSON 22, Rebecca 22 (Ga), James N. 3/12 7-4-30
1880 CENSUS– None
1900 CENSUS
Garrett M. Beasley 18 (June 1878-T/Ga/T-M o), Anna A. 17 (Dec 1882-M 0-0-0) 5-230B-47
John Beasley 55 (Mar 1845-Ga/SC/NC-M 32), Betsey J. 62 (Mar 1838-M 32-1-1), Elijah 16 (Aug 1883) 5-236B-170
John W. Beasley 31 (July 1868-T/G/Ga-M 10), Rebecca A. 38 (Nov 1861-M 10-5-3), Andrew J. 8 (Feb 1892), Alta M. 4 (June 1895), Artie E. 2 (June 1897) 4-227A-267/271 (Spring City & Washington Road)
Thomas W. Beasley 49 (Nov 1850-Ga/NC/NC-M 22), Palina J. 39 (Nov 1861-M 22-9-9), Rosa A. 20 (June 1879), Meda J. 16 (June 1883), James H. 14 (Sep 1885), George W. 12 (Mar 1888), Fred 11 (May 1889), Margarett E. 6 (Oct 1893), Thomas E. 3 (Ap 1897), Hail 8/12 (Oct 1899) 5-230B-48
MARRIAGES
Caroline Beasly to James Pelfry q.v.
E. Beasly to John J. Smith q.v.
G.M. Beasley to Lizza Pelfrey, 25 Aug 1883 (26 Aug), J.M. Bramlett MG 1-472
Garrett Beasly to Mary Eaton, 27 Feb 1872 (same), W.R. Henry JP 1-#1233
James E. Beasly to Elizabeth Minick, 4 Oct 1866 (same), John Howard MG 1-#912
John Beasly to Elizabeth Watson, 18 July 1867 (same), Wm Buttram MG 1-#959
John Beasley or Bundy to Betsy Murry, 14 Sep 1889 (15 Sep), J.M. Bramlett MG 1-594
Lizza Beasley to H. D. Webb q.v.
Madison Beasley to Anney Broyles, 20 June 1899 (21 June)[sic], J.L. Edington MG, G.M. Beasley & G.E. Aikens W 3-5
Rebecca Beasly to Nathan Watson q.v.
Thomas W. Beasly to Palina Josephine Eazell, 17 Ap 1878 (same), J.M. Bramlett JP 1-#1556

- - - - - - - - - - - - -

BEASON

MARRIAGE
Crocket Beason to Anna Shubyrd, 29 Oct 1891, J.W. Cowles JP 4-36

- - - - - - - - - - - - -

BEAVER / BEAVERS / BEEVERS

1880 CENSUS
Elvira Beevers 44, Lora Fine A. 19, William Riley 13, Mary MASON 24 (d), Hester D. MASON 3 (gd) 5-8-70
1900 CENSUS
Alvira Beaver 68 (Ap 1842-SC/SC/SC-Wd 1-1), Mary MASON 38 (d)(Ap 1861-Ga/SC/SC-Wd 2-2), Lilley MASON 14 (gd)(Sep 1885) 5-235A-145
William M. Beaver 29 (Nov 1870-T/Ga/SC-M 8), Nancy C. 24 (Dec 1875-T/Ga/T-M 9-3-1), Laura J. 2 (Feb 1898) 5-325A-141
MARRIAGES
Mary E. Beavers to Richard Masoner q.v.
W.G. Beaver to Harriet J. Baker, 2 Sep 1874 (5 Sep), James Johnson JP 1-#1355
W.R. Beavers to Nannie Howard, 15 Feb 1893, James Carrie(?) MG 4-52
W.R. Beaver to Emma Gravitt, 4 Mar 1890, J.L. Brown JP 4-63

- - - - - - - - - - - - -

BEDDO

1860 CENSUS
Margaret Beddo 36, Ashael 15, Daniel J. 12, Phebe C. 12, Philip T. 7 7-3-17 [widow of Albert W. Beddo]

- - - - - - - - - - - - -

BELL

1860 CENSUS
Granville Bell 25, Mary 32: see John W. Foust
Jack Bell 63, Sophia 58, Lucinda 22, Joseph 16, William H. 5/12, Rufus GOTHARD 14 8-10-60
James P. Bell 14: see Jesse P. Roddy
John Bell 12: see Daniel W. Knox
Leofice Bell 49, Angaline RICHARDS 17, Zipporah RICHARDS 12 6-107-729
Mary A. Bell 17: see Lilborn Boughman
1870 CENSUS
David Bell 23: see James Johnson
James J. Bell 25 (Ala), Phebe J. 33, John W. 8, Mary A. 5 3-14-106
Joseph A. Bell 28, Vina T. 26, John C. 1 5-5-36 (B)
John Bell 35, Nancy 27, Clarett 13, William 11, Margarette 8, Dolly 6/12, Mary J. 12, Joseph 9 3-13-88
Mary Bell 43, Sophia 67 8-21-144 (Mu) & (B)
Peter Bell 55 (Va)(Blacksmith), Ellen 42 (Va), Sallie 18, Mary C. 15, Martha S. 13, Elizabeth 9, Bell M. 6, Heisteller 7, John E. 3, Eliza LODEN 44 1014-90 (B)
Samuel Bell 41, Jane E. 33, Stephen 11, Jane 9 8-21-149 (B)
1880 CENSUS
James Bell 25: see J. H. Rogers
Joseph Bell 38, Viney 36, J.C. 11 (s), S.W. 10 (s), S.J. 7 (d) 8-17-146 (B)
Mary Bell 52, Sophia 77 (m) 8-17-148 (Mu)
Robert Bell 49 (Fisherman), Barbara 27 (sil), Malinda 8 (ne), May 5 (ne), William 1 (nw) 2-31-255

Sam Bell 52, J.S. 42 (w), S.E. 15 (adopted), Lucy YOUNG 84 (m) 8-18-151 (Mu)
Wesley Bell 46, Mary 34, Malinda 10, Elijah 9, Laura 8, Amanda 5, Robert 4, James 1 2-36-295
William Bell 40, Martha 24, Mary 4, Angeline 3, Amanda 1/12 2-42-342

1900 CENSUS
Darysy Bell 22 (Aug 1877-Oh/Oh/Oh-Wd 1-1), Edward 2 (s)(May 1898-Oh/Oh/Oh) 1-189A-200/209 (Spring City)
David Bell 50 (Dec 1849-T/T/Ireland-M 25)(Coal Miner), Liza 44 (June 1855-M 25-7-7), Anna 19 (Dec 1880), Frank 14 (Oct 1885), James 9 (Mar 1891), Mary 7 (Feb 1893) 8-279-209/211
Henry J. Bell 60 (Unk 1840-Ed)(Fisherman), George C. PINION (B) 53 (Jan 1847)(Partner) 2-196A-89/92
James Bell 63 (Feb 1837-M 35), Mary 53 (Mar 1847-M 35-10-9), Frank 29 (Jan 1870), James 21 (Jan 1879), John 18 (Dec 1881), Earnest 15 (Jan 1885), Luther 12 (Feb 1888), Elder 10 (May 1889) 1-186B-149/157
Margiat Bell 52 (Oct 1847-S), Robert 21 (nw)(Oct 1878) 2-192B-28/29
Mary Bell 73: see Samuel B. Arnold
Robert Bell 24 (May 1876-M 2), Susan F. 24 (Sep 1875-NC/NC/NC-M 2-1-1), Conrad C. 8/12 (Sep 1899) 4-226A-242/246 (Rhea Springs & Washington Road)
William Bell 27: see Samuel T. Roberson (B)
William Bell 60 (Dec 1840-M 27), Martha M. 41 (Ap 1859-T/T/Va-M 27-7-5), John H.J. 18 (Mar 1882), William T. 6 (Aug 1893), Addison D. 1 (Mar 1899) 2-192B-27/27
Winnie E. Bell 37 (June 1862-M 21-4-4)(Merchant), Arthur M. 15 (Mar 1885), Edward 7 (Aug 1892), Maud E. 5 (Feb 1895), Lillie E. 2 (Aug 1897) 13-309A-369/383

MARRIAGES
Angy Bell to Perry Jolly q.v.
Grace V. Bell to R.S. or R.T. Hill q.v.
Ida Bell to Ellis Riggs q.v.
Ida Bell to Frank Lynch q.v.
James T. Bell MD (27, Washington) to Lettie E. Abel (27, Dayton), 20 Mar 1882, Thompson Ashburn MG, Richard Rodgers & Miss Flora Grier(?) W 4-8(76)
Jennie Bell to J. F. Moes(?) q.v.
Laura L. Bell to A. E. Davis q.v.
Linda Bell to Howard Patton q.v.
Lucinda Bell to John Johns q.v.
M. E. Bell to Riley Matherly q.v.
Mary Bell to Jack Ensley q.v.
Pleasant Bell to Nancy Dike, 26 Oct 1856 (28 Oct), A.D. Paul JP 1-#558 [duplicated on 1-#565 except year is 1855 and brides name is Dyke]
Priss(?) M. Bell(?) [ink blobs] to John B. Walker q.v.
Robert Bell to Mary Jane Jaquish, 24 Oct 1862 (no return) 1-#789
Robert Bell to Susan F. Rosenbalmer, 3 Jan 1898, A.M. Broyles JP 4-100
Sarah E. Bell to James L. Glanton q.v.
Will Bell to Ida Day, 6 Dec 1900 (same), J.H. Gains MG, B.C. Boyd W 3-253
Winy Bell to Joseph McDonald q.v.
Ziphora Bell to B. Johnson q.v.

\- - - - - - - - - - - - -

BENGERMAN

1900 CENSUS
Edd(?) [numbers written over name] Bengerman 43 (Feb 1857-Wisc/Neb/Oh-M 13), Tenn 43 (Feb 1857-Minn/Minn/Minn-M 13)(School Teacher), Lucinda(?) HART 67 (m)(Sep 1820-Mass/NY/NY-Wd 4-3) 12-179B-20/22

\- - - - - - - - - - - - -

BENNETT / BENNET / BRUNNETT

1860 CENSUS
Fleming Bennett 24 (Carriagemaker): see John C. Abernathy
William Bennet 26, Mary Ann 24, John M. 5, Martha J. 3, Lucinda 1 6-107-727
1870 and 1880– None
1900 CENSUS
Alexander Bennett 27 (Oct 1872-M 3), Ida B. 21 (Oct 1878-M 3-2-1), William S. 1 (July 1898) 10-324A-86/90
John Bennett 25: see David Lane (B)
Miranda Bennett 40 (Unk-Wd 1-1)(Washwoman), Walter 11 (Nov 1878) 8-39A-173/179 (B)
Roscoe Bennett 55 (July 1844-Ga/Ga/T-M 30), Loucinda 60 (Oct 1839-M 30-15-7), Emma 18 (Feb 1882), Will 12 (Jan 1888), Gaither 5 (June 1894), Ida SPRINGS 3/12 (gd)(Mar 1900), Haley GIBSON 49 (boarder)(Ap 1851-T/Ga/T-Wd 3-2)(Washwoman), Maggie THOMAS 14 (boarder)(Feb 1886-T/Ga/T) 8-311A-12/13 (B)
MARRIAGES
Alex Bennett to Ida Claque(?), 28 Oct 1899 (same), J.D. Gathens MG, Pat Rankins W 3-63
Flemming Brunnett to Sarah A. Bryson, 5 Dec 1860 (6 Dec), B. Abernathy MG 1-#735
Jack Bennett to Alie Bollen, 23 Nov 1899 (same), M.B. Hicks JP, Myron Parker W 3-76
Jessey Bennett to Plina Roberts, 17 Sep 1886 (same), J.B. Phillips MG 1-524
John M. Bennett to Cyntha Ann Dagley, 27 Aug 1874 (same), W.W. Lowe JP 1-#1351
Lotty Bennett to William H. Perry q.v.
Sariah Bennet to Turner Smith q.v.
William Bennett to Mary Lemmons, 14 May 1854 (16 May), N.H. Long JP 1-#444

\- - - - - - - - - - - - -

BENSON / BENNISON

1860 CENSUS
Margaret A. Benson 18: see Joshua Riddle
1870 CENSUS
James M. Benson 35 (Store Clerk), Nancy I. 29, Franklin T. 8, William B. 6, John O. 4, Henry C. 2 8-15-104
William B. Benson 24 (Retail Merchant), Julia A. 23, Margarette S. 26 8-19-130
1880 CENSUS
James M. Benson 47, Nancy I. 40, Franklin T. 18, William B. 16, John O. 14, Henry C. 11, Joseph F. 8, Amelia B. 3, Margaret S. 6/30, Rose C. HARRIS 20 ("no kin") 10-27-208/214

William B. Benson 36 (Postmaster, Dayton), Julia A. 34, Molie 9, Hattie 5, T.L. 2 (s) 10-30-233/242

1900 CENSUS

Henry C. Benson 32 (May 1868-M 5)(Grocery Merchant), Alice 27 (July 1872-M 5-2-1), James P. 11/12 (July 1899) 8-314A-66/69

James Benson 68 (Aug 1831-T/NC/NC-M 40), Nancy 60 (Feb 1840-T/SC/Va-M 40-12-9), Arch 23 (Jan 1877), Maggie 20 (May 1880), Bell 16 (June 1883), Edgar 15 (Mar 1885) 8-285B-337/339

James L. Benson 28 (Oct 1871-M 6), Sarah E. 24 (July 1875-M 6-2-2), Nellie E. 5 (Dec 1894), Charles T. 1 (Dec 1898) 2-194B-69/71

Jennie Benson 40 (Jan 1860-Ga/NC/NC-Wd 4-2)(Washwoman), Floyd KEITH 24 (s)(May 1876)(Musician) 10-329B-206/219 (B)

Jung Benson 28 (Oct 1871-M 1), Edna 24 (Nov 1875-Ill/Ky/T-M 1-1-0) 8-285B-336/338

Sarah L. Benson 38 (Oct 1861-T/NC/T-Wd 2-1)(Dressmaker), Gertrude 17 (May 1883) 10-321A-19/19

William B. Benson Jr. 37 (Mar 1863-M 10)(Butcher), Georgia S. 35 (July 1864-Ill/Ky/T-M 10-0-0), Edna F. 9 (adopted d)(June 1890-Kan/England/Ill), Charles C. 8 (adopted s)(Mar 1892-Kan/Eng/Ill), John B. MILLER 59 (fl)(Aug 1840-Ky/Va/Va-M 39)(Butcher), Mary E. MILLER 61 (ml)Oct 1838-M 39-5-4) 8-312-32/34

William B. Benson 55 (June 1844-M 30)(Traveling Salesman, Groceries), Julia A. 53 (Mar 1847-M 30-8-8), Jennie 26 (Ap 1874), Otto 18 (June 1881), Kate 17 (Ap 1883), Edd 15 (Oct 1884), Rose 12 (Mar 1888) 8-313A-43/46

Zack Benson 45 (May 1855-England/Do/Do-1887/13/al-M 9)(Coal Miner), Jennie 25 (May 1875-T/NC/T-M 9-2-1), John L. 6 (Oct 1893-Ky) 10-260A-199/204

MARRIAGES

George Benson to Jane Keith, 26 Oct 1888 (same), Joseph Hoge JP 1-561

Hattie Benson to M.L. Morefield q.v.

Henry C. Benson to Alice Hensley, 27 Dec 1893, James I. Cash MG 4-62

James M. Benson to Nancy I. Gothard, 26 Dec 1860 (27 Dec), R.A. Giddens MG 1-#738

Mary Benson to William G. Rigsby q.v.

Nora Benson to G. F. Spence q.v.

Samuel Benson to Bettie Davis, 5 May 1892, J.W. Cowles JP 4-42

Thomas B.(?) Bennison(?) to Sarah J. Callahan, 14 Nov 1891, W.S. Hale MG 4-35

William B. Benson to Julia A. Collins, 13 Dec 1869 (18 Dec), John H. Keith MG 1-#1131

- - - - - - - - - - - - -

BENTLY

1900 CENSUS

Mary Bently 26, James 2: see Joseph Giles

- - - - - - - - - - - - -

BENTON

MARRIAGE

James Benton to Sarah E. Roberson, 8 July 1866 (12 July), T.N.L. Cunnyngham JP 1-#903

- - - - - - - - - - - - -

BERRY / BARRY

1900 CENSUS

Arch Berry 53 (Sep 1846-M 34), Nancy J. 47 (July 1852-T/Va/Va-M 34-9-7), Samuel 26 (Jan 1874), Sidney S. 19 (May 1881), William E. 15 (Feb 1885) 3-200B-12/12

James Berry 27 (Nov 1872-M 8), Ella 25 (Jan 1875-M 8-3-3), Hattie 6 (Jan 1894), Creed 3 (Ap 1897), Katie 1 (May 1899), Thomas HICKMOT 27 (boarder)(Unk) 6-246A-115/116

John Berry 23 (Sep 1876-M 6), Jessie 23 (Sep 1876-M 6-2-2), Rosie 3 (Sep 1896), Leo 8/12 (Sep 1899) 3-200B-16/17

MARRIAGES

Alice Berry to Foust Weathington q.v.

James Berry to Ella Cagle, 7 Nov 1891, J.W. Knowles JP 4-37

John Barry to Josie Wyrick, 18 Ap 1895, L.E. Smith JP 4-82

- - - - - - - - - - - - -

BESSINGER

MARRIAGE

Frances Bessinger to A. Koppel q.v.

- - - - - - - - - - - - -

BEST / BESS

1900 CENSUS

David Bess 34 (Sep 1865-NC/NC/NC-M 14)(Machinist), Bettie 34 (Jan 1866-Ga/Ga/Ga-M 14-7-5), Earnest 14 (Ap 1886-Ga)(Coal Miner), Odans 12 (Aug 1887), Blanch 10 (Dec 1889), Dennis 7 (Sep 1892), Fred 4 (Jan 1896) 8-277A-177/178

Ida E. Best 20, Mattie 4: see William T. Barger

John Best 24 (Sep 1875-M 0)(Coal Miner), Mollie M. 19 (Aug 1880-M 0-0-0), Burton 21 (b)(May 1879)(Coal Miner), Richard PRYOR 20 (boarder)(Aug 1879)(Coal Miner) 13-320B-235/245

John H. Best 42 (Jan 1858-NC/NC/NC-M 15), Sallie 29 (May 1871-T/Ga/T-M 15), William McK. 3 (Jan 1897), Paralee QUEEN 20 (ne)(Ap 1880-M 0-0-0) 8-317A-137/142

William Bess 50 (Ap 1850-NC/Unk/T-M 23)(Coal Miner), Sarah 43 (Oct 1856-Ga/NC/SC-M 23-10-9), Lithy R. 17 (Oct 1882), Eller 13 (July 1886), Walter 11 (Dec 1888), Hershel 9 (Jan 1891), Mary 6 (Aug 1894), Manda 4 (Oct 1895) 10-258A-153/157

MARRIAGES

H.P. Best to Ida Barger, 11 Aug 1895, G.W. Colcord VDM 4-84

Ida Bess to W. L. Cofer q.v.

John Bess to Mollie Holmes, 12 Ap 1900 (15 Ap), W.A. Bomanyins(?) MG, J. Bess(?) & W.A. Mills W 3-140
Larrind Best to Vester Green q.v.
Vina Bess to William Jones q.v.
Viney Bess to John Godsey q.v.

- - - - - - - - - - - - -

BETTERSON / BRITTERSON

1870 CENSUS

Leroy Britterson 60, Sarah 56, Thomas 22, Rufus 16, Margarette 14, Victori 12, Leroy 10, Tate 8, Arrena (f) 9 6-1-4 (B)

MARRIAGE

Enslow Betterson (22 NC) to Mariah Gillespie (18), 2 June 1881 (Spring City), B.F. Holloway JP 4-3(22) (B)

- - - - - - - - - - - - -

BETTIS / BETTS / BEATIS

1900 CENSUS

Frank Beatis 24 (Dec 1875-M 9)(Furniture Manufacturer), Bettie 22 (Dec 1877-M 9-0-0) 14-219B-133/136
Sallie Bettis 36 (Aug 1863-Wd 1-0)(Washwoman), Minnie SWAFFORD 17 (si)(1883), Colonel SWAFFORD 13 (b)(Aug 1886), Annie NINN 3 (ne)(Ap 1897) 8-315A-90/93 (B)

MARRIAGES

Enzer Bettis to Sallie Thomas, 25 Mar 1885 (same), P.P. Brooks ?? 1-498
James S. Betts to A.M. Johnson, 1 May 1891, R.A. Bramlett MG 4-30

- - - - - - - - - - - - -

BEUGLER

1900 CENSUS

John B. Beugler 41 (Feb 1859-Pa/NJ/NY-M 16)(Photographer), Ella W. 45 (Sep 1854-Oh/NY/NY-M 16-4-4), John C. 15 (Ap 1885-Pa), James W. 13 (Sep 1888-Pa), Clinton P. 11 (Sep 1888), Samuel B. 9 (July 1900), Sarah A. CHASE 67 (ml)(Dec 1832-NY/Mass/NY-Wd 4-2) 8-314B-78/81

- - - - - - - - - - - - -

BEUOIS

1900 CENSUS

Charles Beuois 45 (Mar 1845-NY/Eng/NY-M 7)(Optrician), Verna 31 (Feb 1869-M 7-0-0) 14-216B-79/80

- - - - - - - - - - - - -

BICE / BUICE / BOUCE

1860 CENSUS

Robert W. Bice 33 (Wagonmaker), Elizabeth E. 29, William D. 10, Elementory E. 8, Young C. 6, John R. 4, Sarah J. 2 8-26-175

1870 CENSUS

Margarette S. Buice 28: see William Hickman

MARRIAGES

Elizabeth E. Bice to William M. Payne q.v.
Martha J. Bice to Rufus M. Morgan q.v.
Sarah E. Bouce to F. M. Morgan q.v.
T.J. Bice to Amanda Taylor, 26 July 1860 (same), Wm Morgan JP 1-#721

- - - - - - - - - - - - -

BIDWELL

MARRIAGES

James B. Bidwell to Louiza Parris, 9 June 1876 (10 June), J.J. Ingle JP 1-#1446
Nancy J. Bidwell to Patrick O'Brien q.v.

- - - - - - - - - - - - -

BIGBY

1900 CENSUS

Emily Bigby 14, Willie 12: see Charles Bird (B)

- - - - - - - - - - - - -

BIGERSTAFF

1900 CENSUS

Jennie Bigerstaff 69: see James W. Walker

- - - - - - - - - - - - -

BIGGS

MARRIAGE

Thomas T. Biggs to Deborah C. Cooper, 28 Sep 1857 (same), James Carson ?? 1-#615

- - - - - - - - - - - - -

BILES

1880 CENSUS

Lewis Biles 25: see Jack Suddeth (B)

- - - - - - - - - - - - -

BILLBERRY / BILBERRY / BILBREY/ BILLBURRY

1900 CENSUS

Jerry Bilberry 28 (July 1871-M 7), Eliza 29 (Feb 1871-M 9-0-0) 3-205B-99/107
Joseph O. Bilbrey 26 (June 1873-M 6)(Coal Miner), Nannie A. 28 (Dec 1871-M 6-3-2), Mary L. 3 (Feb 1897), Eva E. 1 (Aug 1898) 13-302B-232/242
William Billburry 35: see Henry Reynolds

MARRIAGE

Jerry Billberry to Eliza Wassen, 25 Nov 1892, J.M. Bramlett MG 4-47

- - - - - - - - - - - - -

BILLINGS

1880 CENSUS

Edward Billings 28 (Miner), Mary 25, Robert 8, William 6, John 2 2-29-232

- - - - - - - - - - - - -

BILLINGSLEY

1900 CENSUS

David Billingsly 49 (Ap 1851-M 17), Anie 47 (Aug 1852-M 17-2-2), Liza 16 (Feb 1884), Reuben 12 (May 1888), Dartin ROBBINSON 61 (boarder)(Mar 1839-La/Miss/T-Wd 3-3) 12-179A-3/3

Eugene Billingsley 16 (B): see Benjamin F. Mealer

MARRIAGES

Annie Billingsley to Harry Simons q.v.

Fannie Billingsley to Ryan Jones q.v.

Sorilda Billingsly to Jack Coulter q.v.

- - - - - - - - - - - - -

BING

MARRIAGE

Adie Bing to John Riggs q.v.

- - - - - - - - - - - - -

BINGHAM

1900 CENSUS

Foss Bingham: see Charley Carr

- - - - - - - - - - - - -

BIRCH

1900 CENSUS

John Birch 35 (Sep 1864-M 11), Raney 30 (Sep 1869-M 11-5-2), Elizabeth 10 (May 1890), Margaret 7 (Mar 1893) 15-272B-87

- - - - - - - - - - - - -

BIRCHFIELD / BURCHFIELD

1860 CENSUS

Willis Burchfield 31 (Blacksmith), Margaret 25, Nancy E. 12, William H. 8, Francis J. 6, Rebecca 4, Margaret 1/12 2-81-553

1870 and 1880 CENSUS– None

1900 CENSUS

Frank W. Birchfield 46 (Dec 1853-T/NC/NC-M 11)(Coal Miner), Caroline 42 (Aug 1857-T/NC/NC-M 11-2-2), Ellen 17 (June 1882-Va), Oscar S. 17 (Feb 1883), James N. 10 (Sep 1889) 11-290A-4

MARRIAGES

Clara Birchfield to Samuel Weller q.v.

Della Birchfield to Frank Martin q.v.

Frank Burchfield to M.C. Flemming, 17 Nov 1888 (same), J.W. Williamson MG 1-555

James Birchfield to Mary E. Conley, 19 Dec 1890, J.W. Williamson MG 4-20

Lillie Birchfield to James Johnson q.v.

Salie Birchfield to W. T. B. Pool q.v.

- - - - - - - - - - - - -

BISHOP

1900 CENSUS

Ann Bishop 19: see William Sawyeur

Frank Bishop 25, Mattie 22: see John Bishop

John Bishop 47 (Unk-M 27), Isabella 50 (Unk-M 27-9-7), Lizzie 20 (July 1879), Mary 18 (Jan 1882), Nannie 16 (June 1884), Glennia A. 13 (Oct 1887), Willie 9 (May 1891), James 4 (Sep 1895), Frank BISHOP 25 (s)(Sep 1874-M 1), Mattie 22 (dl)(July 1877-M 1-0-0) 6-245A-105/105 [John H. Bishop married Isabella Poplin on 8 Aug 1872 in Meigs Co]

Martin Bishop 52 (June 1847-Ala/Germany/Do-M 16), Cliffa 39 (Oct 1861-T/T/Ga-M 16-5-3), Maud 10 (Mar 1890), Zara 4 (May 1896), Edmon 2 (May 1898) 1-188A-178/187

Melvin M. Bishop 20, Cinda 26: see Nancy Bishop

Nancy Bishop 55 (Nov 1835-Wd 3-3), George 35 (s)(Oct 1864-Wd), Martha L. 26 (d)(Dec 1873), Melvin M. 20 (s)(May 1880-M 0)(Coal Miner), Cinda 26 (dl)(Sep 1873-M 0-0-0) 7-261B-222/227

MARRIAGES

Elizabeth J. Bishop to T. N. L. Cunnyngham q.v.

Frank Bishop to Mattie Roddy, 4 July 1898 (no return), Sam Calbough W 2-298

George Bishop to Louisa Wilkey, 4 Ap 1890 (12 Ap), T.F. Shaver JP 1-601

George Bishop to Mary Elder, 27 Nov 1893, R.S. Mason JP 4-60

Hannah Bishop to T. J. Keith q.v.

Martin [Melvin] Bishop to Lucinda Dunning, 23 Sep 1899 (24 Sep), A.B. Hayes JP, R.J. Killough W 3-40

Mary Bishop to Robert Keith q.v.

Mary Bishop to S. R. Keith q.v.

- - - - - - - - - - - - -

BLACK

1900 CENSUS

Edna T. Black 21, Edith B. 17, Joseph W. 15: see Webster Thomas

James A. Black 51 (Dec 1848-Ga/Ga/Ga-M 29)(Coal Miner), Mexico 47 (Ap 1853-M 29-7-7), William M. 27 (Aug 1872-Ga)(Cripple), Fred H. 14 (Nov 1885), James D. 8 (May 1892) 8-289B-425/428

Mathew(?) Black 45 (Mar 1855-NC/NC/NC-M 22)(Coal Miner), Martha 49 (Feb 1851-Ga/NC/NC-M 22-5-4), Silvany 16 (Dec 1882-Ga), Mexico 13 (Mar 1887-Ga), Kewenny 19 [sic] (July 1890 [sic]-Ga), Kilaron 22 (nw)(July 1877-Ga)(Coal Miner) 10-255B-106/109

MARRIAGES

Cordelia Black to J. M. Swafford q.v.

John C. Black to Sallie Mathis, 8 Oct 1897 (9 Oct), F.M. Cook MG, John Holmes W 2-194

Mollie Black to J.M. Colwell q.v.

- - - - - - - - - - - - -

BLACKBURN

1900 CENSUS

Jennie Blackburn 53 (Aug 1846-Oh/Pa/Oh-Wd 4-2), Mary E. 21 (Ap 1879-Oh/Oh/Oh) 8-281B-259/261

Thomas S. Blackburn 29 (May 1871-Oh/Oh/Oh-M 5)(Coal Miner), Margaret 28 (Nov 1871-M 5-1-1), Edgar 1 (Aug 1898) 8-317-135/140

MARRIAGES
Horace A. Blackburn to Sallie Angel, 25 Aug 1900 (26 Aug), R. Walker ?? & W 3-206
Thomas Blackburn to Margaret Hale, 6 Oct 1895, A.P. Hayes JP 4-87

- - - - - - - - - - - - -

BLACKFORD

1900 CENSUS
Edward Blackford 28 (Feb 1872-M 2), Florence 28 (May 1872-M 2-0-0) 8-281A-248/250
MARRIAGES
Bell Blackford to W.D. Atchley q.v.
J.E. Blackford to Florence Bridgemon, 3 Sep 1898 (4 Sep), J.A. Whitner MG, R.J. Killough W 2-319

- - - - - - - - - - - - -

BLACKWELL

1900 CENSUS
William Blackwell 23: see James Stovall
MARRIAGE
Martha Jane Blackwell to Joseph McGille q.v.

- - - - - - - - - - - - -

BLAIR / BLAIN

1900 CENSUS
Bettie Blain 24, Lillie 5, Charles 3: see Margaret Swafford
Lou A. Blair 55 (May 1845-M 32-4-3), William M. 25 (July 1874)(RR Laborer), Hattie M. 23 (Sep 1876)(Dressmaker) 14-216B-80/81
Samuel Blair 20: see Josey McCaleb
William Blair 29 (Jan 1871-M 0), Sarah 18 (Jan 1882-M 0-1-1), Lettie 1 (Mar 1899), Darkes McCALEB 80 (gm) (Unk 1820-T/T/NC-Wd 8-1) 2-194A-52/54 (B)
MARRIAGES
Margaret Blain to T. W. Swafford q.v.
Will Blain to Sarah McCaleb, 20 Nov 1899, M.M. Morris MG 4-104

- - - - - - - - - - - - -

BLAKE

1900 CENSUS
Louis A. Blake 63 (Mar 1837-W.Va/Va/Va-M 36), Rebekah J. 56 (Sep 1843-Oh/Germany/Ind-M 36-1-1)(Boarding House Keeper), Charles A. 20 (s)(Jan 1880-Neb)(Fruit Tree Agent), Charles JULIAN 27 (boarder)(Feb 1873-Kan/Mo/Mo)(Cooper), John PRADY 23 (boarder)(Feb 1877)(Physician), Thomas J. MYERS 25 (boarder) (June 1874-T/T/Oh), William S. MARTIN 22 (boarder)(Jan 1878) 13-299B-175/179

- - - - - - - - - - - - -

BLALOCK

1900 CENSUS
Allie C. Blalock 17: see John C. Reno [Renow]
MARRIAGES
J. Charley Blalock(?): see J. Charley B. Clack
Sallie Blalock to John Renow q.v.

- - - - - - - - - - - - -

BLANCHIT / BLANCET

MARRIAGES
Silas Blanchit to Jane Carter, 10 June 1885 (14 June), J.P. Brown ?? 1-496
Silas Blancet to Alice Williams, 9 Oct 1887 (same), John Howard MG 1-533

- - - - - - - - - - - - -

BLAND

MARRIAGE
Lillie May Bland to William Woolford q.v.

- - - - - - - - - - - - -

BLANK

MARRIAGE
Lucinda Blank to T. B. Cooper q.v.

- - - - - - - - - - - - -

BLANKENSHIP

1900 CENSUS
James D. Blankenship 30 (Nov 1869-T/Va/T-M 5), Louise 23 (May 1877-Ga/SC/SC-M 5-1-1), Hettie L. 4 (Nov 1895) 11-293A-73
MARRIAGES
William Blankenship to Martha J. Barnell, 1 Dec 1853 (no return) 1-#428
William Blankenship to Margarett Crow, 13 Feb 1856 (same), John Howard JP 1-#536

- - - - - - - - - - - - -

BLANKET

MARRIAGE
Sophia Blanket to Thomas Jamison q.v.

- - - - - - - - - - - - -

BLEDSOE

MARRIAGE
William Bledsoe to Josie Mitchell, 19 Oct 1889 (20 Oct), James R. Campbell MG 1-593

- - - - - - - - - - - - -

BLEVINS

1860 CENSUS
Samuel Blevins 27 (Blacksmith), Malinda E. 25, Lucy A. 4, John M. 2: see John B. Murphy
1870 CENSUS
James B. Blevins 29, Julia E. 30, James O. 1, Eillie 1/12, Mary T. 13 5-4-28
Julia Blevins 19: see James A. Darwin
Squire Blevins 52 (NC), Virginia 45 (Va), Sarah E. 26, Susan 22, Martha J. 20, Minnie 18, Joseph T. 16, John W. 13, William J. 11, Squire 7, Joshua F. 3, Mary 6, Minerva E. 3 6-1-1

William P. Blevins 17: see William P. Darwin

1880 CENSUS

J. F. Blevins 25 (Carpenter): see R.C.M. Cunnyngham

James B. Blevins 39, July E. 41, William P. 10, Larrance P. 4, Ida M. 4/12, Samuel D. PIERCE 54 5-3-24

John A. Blevins 50 (Carpenter), Celia 43, Thomas J. 19 6-23-19 (Rural Street, Washington)

S. L. Blevins 29 (Hotel Keeper), M.A. 28 (w), E.E. 7 (d), M.D. 4 (d), E.A. 2 (d); *Boarders*: T.H. HOLLOWAY 22 (Carpenter), E.S. MILLS 24 (Depot Agent), G.H. EIDSON 32 (Engineer), S. ESSEX 30 (Merchant), John MARRITT 20 (Telegraph Operator), W.A. BLEVINS 10 (nw) 4-9-71

Samuel Blevins 74 (Carpenter), Sarah 69, Catharine 42, Tennessee 38, Lucinda 35, Annie 10 or 19 4-8-59

W. A. Blevins 10: see S. L. Blevins

1900 CENSUS

Alfred C. Blevins 69 (May 1831-M 32)(Physician), Virginia C. 48 (Nov 1851-T/Va/Va-M 32-7-5), Charles B. 25 (Jan 1875)(Attorney), Alfred C. 16 (May 1884), Beulah 12 (Jan 1888), Kittie C. 9 (Aug 1890) 10-328B-180/191

Hugh L. Blevins 37 (Oct 1862-M 11)(Coal Miner), Mabel S. 26 (Feb 1874-NH/Ky/T-M 11-4-4), Ethel E. 9 (Oct 1890), Hugh L. 5 (Sep 1894), Garroll V. 3 (Sep 1896), Myrtle 1/12 (Ap 1900) 13-308B-354/367

James B. Blevins 59 (Feb 1841-M 33), Julia E. 61 (Sep 1838-M 33-5-3), Willie P. 30 (May 1870), Lawrence P. 24 (Oct 1875), Ida M. 20 (Jan 1880), Samuel D. PEARCE 74 (bl)(Aug 1825), Margarett STEVENS 66 (sil)(Oct 1833-Wd 0-0) 5-230B-44

John Blevins 21: see Nancy J. Smith

John Blevins 42 (Sep 1857-M 17), Polly A. 34 (May 1866-M 17-7-7), James 15 (Ap 1885), Abrt 12 (Sep 1887), Isac 10 (Nov 1889), Walter R. 8 (Ap 1892), Clay H. 5 (Nov 1894), Idie 3 (Jan 1897), Laura 9/12 (Aug 1899) 10-257A-132/136

Katie Blevins 8: see William Bomires

Mattie Blevins 47 (May 1853-T/T/Va-D), Edna E. 27 (d) (Jan 1873)(Milliner), Margaret D. 24 (Mar 1876), Artie T. 20 (Oct 1879)(Stenographer) 14-214B-35/36

Samuel L. Blevins 68 (Feb 1832-M 45), Malinda 65 (June 1834-T/NC/T-M 45-9-7), Frank R. 31 (May 1869-Wd) (Coal Miner), Thomas R. 22 (May 1878)(Coal Miner) 13-306A-306/318

MARRIAGES

D.M. Blevins to Fanny Hoyle, 22 Dec 1880 (28 Dec), W.W. Lillard MG 1-292

Frank Blevins to Maggie Wyott, 5 Jan 1889 (6 Jan), W.Y. Curton MG 1-562

Hugh Blevins to May Bell Thomas, 6 Ap 1889 (same), W.R. Grimsley MG 1-572

Hugh T.V. Blevins to Melissa Henry, 11 Ap 1855 (same), W.H. Cunnyngham JP 1-#491

J. B. Blevins to J. E. Pearce, 5 Ap 1867 (no return) 1-#950

J. H. Blevins to F. E. Pass, 21 Sep 1880 (29 Sep), D.V. Culver MG 1-296

Joseph T. Blevins to Mary Peterson, 14 May 1876 (17 May), John Howard MG 1-#1443

July [Julia] B. Blevins to R. C. M. Cunnyngham q.v.

Lorina Blevins to William Smith q.v.

Lydia Blevins to Thomas Marsh q.v.

Marthy Jane Blevins to John R. Poe q.v.

Mattie A. Blevins to C. W. Brown q.v.

Nora J. Blevins to F. M. McKenzie q.v.

S. L. Blevins to Malinda Murphy, 7 Sep 1854 (no return) 1-#560

William Blevins to E. A. Hill, 4 Oct 1884 (5 Oct), J.W. Williamson MG 1-#469

- - - - - - - - - - - - -

BLINK

1880 CENSUS

Peter Blink(?) 60, M. 49 (w), M.E. 29 (d), H.T. 26 (s), S.J. 24 (d) 3-28-229

MARRIAGE

Oddie Blink to Lizzie Snyder, 3 Sep 1891, James Carrie(?) MG 4-46

- - - - - - - - - - - - -

BLUFF

MARRIAGE

Dolla Bluff to Henry Syler q.v.

- - - - - - - - - - - - -

BLY / BLYE / BLIE / BLYTHE

1860 CENSUS

Polly Blythe 70, Ellen 24: see Jesse Harwood

1870 CENSUS– None

1880 CENSUS

Ellen Blythe 44: see Mary Harwood

Sarah A. Blye 35 ("husband gone"), Sallie C. 11, Benjamin B. 7, James H. 5, John T. 3 10-26-198/204

1900 CENSUS

Ben B. Blye 27 (Mar 1873-M 0)(Coal Miner), Idia J. 20 (Jan 1880-M 0-0-0) 10-253A-57

Haray Blye 25 (Ap 1875), Sary 57 (m)(Dec 1842-Wd 1-1) 7-262A-228/233

MARRIAGES

B.B. Blye to Syntha Wyrick, 21 Feb 1895, J.W. Romine JP 4-81

B.B. Blythe to Ida Parker, 8 Aug 1899 (same), R.C. Knight JP, E. Fisher W 3-17

James M. Bly to Sarah Byerly, 13 Oct 1866 (same), Wm F. Buttram MG 1-#914

John Blye or Blie to Callie Hensley, 28 Ap 1899 (same), J.W. Romino JP, F.M. Johnson W 2-405

Sarah J. Blythe to H.B. Harvey or Hanney q.v.

- - - - - - - - - - - - -

BODKINS

MARRIAGE

Myrtie Bodkins to R. E. Abel q.v.

- - - - - - - - - - - - -

BOGART / BOGGART / BAGETT

1900 CENSUS

Henry M. Bogart 63 (May 1837-M 41), Frances E. 58 (Feb 1842-T/T/SC-M 41-11-9), Emma L. 22 (Oct 1877), Lizzie E. 16 (Mar 1884), Charles J. 14 (Sep 1885) 3-206A-111/121

James B. Bogart 33 (Dec 1866-M 2), Syntha 22 (Jan 1878-M 2-1-1), Luther F. 1 (Oct 1898) 3-207B-113/146

MARRIAGE

Frances E. Boggart to J.W. McPherson q.v.

Henry Bagett to Cynthia E. Rudder, 21 Aug 1872 (no return) 1-#1248

- - - - - - - - - - - - -

BOGGER

1900 CENSUS

Isaac Bogger 70 (Unk 1830-Wd), Allen 45 (s)(Unk 1855), Mark FOSTER 35 (boarder)(Unk 1865-Va/Va/Va) (Coal Miner) 8-284B-319/321

- - - - - - - - - - - - -

BOGGIS / BOGGESS

1900 CENSUS

Jake Bogess 40: see Joe Banks (B)

Hada Bogges 30, Fred 15, Willie 14: see Jas Campbell (B)

MARRIAGE

Rena Boggis to Frank Marsh q.v.

- - - - - - - - - - - - -

BOGLE / BOGEL

(see also BAGLES)

1900 CENSUS

Hugh Bogel 40: see Bell Kimball (B)

Nancy Bogle 17: see Ashel Templeton

MARRIAGE

Houston Bogle to Bell Kimble, 20 Nov 1900 (same), W.L. Lillard JP & W 3-245

Lula Bogle to Richard Rucker q.v.

- - - - - - - - - - - - -

BOHANNON / BOHANAN

1860 CENSUS

James E. Bohanan 39, Eliza 45, Thomas 17, Robert 16, William 16, George 14, David 12, Mary J. 10, Rufus 8, Joseph 6, Sarah J. 4, James 2 2-71-483

1870 CENSUS

James Bohanan 49, Margaret 46, Mary J. 20, Rufus K. 18, Joseph B. 16, Sarah E. 14, James P. 12, Betsy A. [FINE] 18, Susan M. [FINE] 14, Cordela [FINE] 12, John [DICKEY] 10 2-17-118

Robert B. Bohannon 24, Sarah 22 2-6-37

1880 CENSUS– None

1900 CENSUS

James J. Bohannon 43 (May 1857-M 13), Ellen 34 (Oct 1865-M 13-6-6), Lennea 12 (Oct 1887), Lillie 11 (May 1889), Carl 9 (Feb 1891), Ruth 7 (Sep 1892), Grace 3 (Oct 1896), Rhoda 11/12 (June 1899) 15-174A-111

Philip Bohannon 37 (Feb 1863-M 18), Hanna J. 36 (Ap 1864-M 18-5-4), Susan A. 15 (June 1884), Tinie B. 9 (Aug 1890), Myrtle 4 (Sep 1895) 2-193A-43/44

MARRIAGES

James E. Bohannon to Margarett Fine, 16 Oct 1869 (17 Oct), Allen King MG 1-#1115

Lola Bohannon to G. W. Taylor q.v.

Mary Bohanan to Theodore Able q.v.

R.B. Bohannon to Sarah Brady, 18 Nov 1869 (8 Dec), Z. Rose MG 1-#1125

R.M. Bohannon to Ella Thomas, 13 Dec 1891, J.Q. Shaver MG 4-38

Sarah Bohannon to Leander Clark q.v.

- - - - - - - - - - - - -

BOLEN / BOLLEN / BOLIN / BOWLEN / BOWLIN / BOWLING

1860 CENSUS

James F. Bolen 54 (SC), Elizabeth 39, Sarah TRUSLY 9 7-3-16

Thomas M. Bolen 37, Nancy 37, Asberry 17, William M. 14, Hester E. 12, Benjamin T. 8, Mary C. 6, Sarah E. 4, Thomas J. 2, Nancy A. 1, John P. 39 (SC) 7-4-22

1870 CENSUS

James F. Bowling 63 (SC), Elizabeth 44 7-2-10

Parham Boling 50, Ellen E. 23, John M. 5, Ellen Jane 2 7-3-19

Thomas M. Bowling 47, Nancy 46, Benjamin F. 19, Catharine 18, Sarah 16, Jefferson 14, Angeline 12, Daniel 9, Henry 8, Elizabeth 50 7-2-16

1880 CENSUS

John F. Bolen 73, Elizabeth 50 (w), John D. 62 (b), A.J. (f) 12, J.M. (m) 15 7-22-187 [no relation given for A.J. and J.M.]

T. M. Bolen 58, Nancy 56, Jefferson 22, San 18 (d), Henry 16 8-21-183

1900 CENSUS

Daniel Bolen 35: see Anderson Hendrick

James W. Boling 31: see Daly A. Green

John Bolin 25 (Mar 1875-M 5)(Teamster), Nancy C. 33 (Ap 1867-Ky/T/T-M 5-3-3), Lucinda 8 (May 1892), William H. 4 (Nov 1895), Mindy 1 (Aug 1898), Malinda JORDAN 56 (ml)(Mar 1844-Wd 5-3), James N. JORDAN 26 (bl)(May 1874-Ky), Oscar EVANS 20 (boarder)(July 1879) 13-306A-309/321

John M. Bolin 35 (Mar 1865-M 12), Sallie 39 (Ap 1861-M 12-4-4), Myrtle 11 (Jan 1889), Lawrence 8 (June 1892), Girld 6 (Feb 1894), James R. 2 (Aug 1897) 7-261B-225/230

Nancy Bolin 50 (Unk 1850-Wd 4-4), Georgiana 17 (Dec 1882), Henry 15 (Dec 1884), Louisa J. 12 (gd)(July 1887), John 3 (gs)(Sep 1896) 13-307A-323/335 (B)

Thomas Bollen 50: see David Rhea

MARRIAGES

Alie Bollen to Jack Bennett q.v.

Annie Bolen to W. H. McDade q.v.

Ella Bolen to Thomas Travis q.v.

Elmira J. Bolin to J. Q. A. Shaver q.v.

Catharine Bowling to Freeling Shaver q.v.

Hester E. Bolen to Richard C. Knight q.v.

J.M. Bolen to Sallie J. Burnett, 25 Feb 1888 (26 Feb), J.A. Shaver MG 1-543

John P. Bolin to Mary Cate, 15 Feb 1851 (same), J.A. Mitchell JP 1-#334

John P. Bowlen to Elizabeth Key, 6 Feb 1864 (7 Feb), no MG or JP 1-#817

Margaret Bolin to John Parker q.v.

N.A. Bolen to R.H. Jewell q.v.

Owen M. Bowling to Bertie E. Eaves, 1 Jan 1900 (4 Jan), W.L. Patton MG, M.S. Holloway W 3-103
Sarah Bolen to George Clingon q.v.
Sarah Bowlen to Jacob Lanard q.v.
William Bowlin to Allice F. Story, 3 Ap 1868 (same), William Buttram MG 1-#1007

- - - - - - - - - - - - -

BOLES / BALES / BOWLS / BOWLES / BAILES / BAILS/ BOWLIS / BOLLS / BOLLIS / BOLLES / BOALS

1860 CENSUS
Jacob Boles 50(?) [ink blob], Jane A. 36, Margaret 21, George 18, William 16, John 13, Polly A. 11, Samuel H. 10, Manerva 7, Thomas 5, Robert 2 1-93-636
1870 CENSUS
Daniel Boals 25, Luvena 26, Joseph 5, William 2 2-2-7
George Boals 60 (Va), Pollie 50 (SC), William 21, Emory R. 49, Rufus 16, Sarah E. 15 2-1-6
Jacob Boals 62 (Va), Jennie A. 45, John F. 21, Amanda M. 17, Thomas N. 14, Robert 11 1-17-113
John Boals 31, Mary Jane 21, George R. 2, Malissa J. 8/12 2-1-2
1880 CENSUS
Daniel Boles 36, Lavinia 36, Joseph 14, William 12, George 9, Mary 7, Robert 4, Nettie 1 2-33-270
Jessee Boles 35, Margaret 24, Archibald 3, Noah 1/12, Jane 13, Eliza 8 2-39-319
John Boles 34, Susan 31, Nancy 9, James 6, Andrew 3, Rufus 27 (c) 2-39-321
John Boles 49, Mary 29 (w), Thomas 12, Lucy 10, Elizabeth 8, William 7, John 6, David 3, Cora 1, An 1/12, Rebecca HEMBREE 61 (ml)(occupation listed as "general boss") 2-33-268
William Boles 27, Mary 22, Jane 8, William 6, John 2, Mary FITZGERALD 37 (boarder) 2-33-269
1900 CENSUS
Archey Bowles 33 (Ap 1877-M 1), Mary J. 20 (Aug 1879-M 1-0-0) 6-245B-107/108
Elijah Boles 33 (Feb 1867-M 7), Amanda 23 (May 1877-M 7-2-2), Alta 6 (Jan 1894), Delphia 3 (Nov 1896) 13-299A-171/175
James W. Boles 28 (Feb 1872-M 6), Idie 21 (Oct 1878-M 6-1-1), Albert R. 5 (Jan 1895), Henry J. 19 (b)(Sep 1890), Flora J. McMURTY 17 (c)(June 1882), Charles E. WRIGHT 5 (bl)(Mar 1895) 2-194B-64/66
Jesse L. Baler 56 (Sep 1843-M 23), Margaret A. 44 (Nov 1855-T/T/NC-M 23-4-4), Noah B. 20 (Dec 1879), Richard F. 17 (May 1883), Amy K. 9 (Jan 1892) 2-196B-101/104
Robbert Bails 24 (May 1876-M 1), Sara 19 (Ap 1880-M 1-0-0) 1-185A-118/124
Thomas Bowles 22 (Jan 1868-M 10), Rosnia 27 (June 1872-M 10-5-4), Brigett 8 (Feb 1892), Mary A. 6 (Dec 1893), Johny 4 (Jan 1896), Martha 1 (Jan 1899), Jack KEITH 29 (bl)(May 1871-M 6), Hanah 29 (sil)(Nov 1870-M 6-2-2), Willie 11 (nw)(Oct 1889), Pinctey(?) 0/12 (nw)(May 1900) 7-264A-265/270
William H. Boles 50 (Dec 1849-M 5), Cinda E. 25 (Feb 1875-M 5-0-0), Thomas B. 16 (s)(Jan 1884), Barnet N. 12 (s)(Oct 1887) 2-193B-47/48
William W. Boles 26 (Feb 1874-M 0), Hester P. 16 (Oct 1883-M 0-0-0) 2-193B-47/49
MARRIAGES
Cordelia L. Bales to James A. Sitton q.v.
Daniel Bolls to Melvina Kissiah, 6 Dec 1864 (25 Dec), Asa Newport MG 1-#863
Daniel M. Bailes to Mary Ann Weeks, 11 Aug 1857 (same), R.T. Howard MG 1-#607
Elijah Bowles to Amanda Gill, 23 Sep 1892, W.S. Hale MG 4-51
Fayette Bowles to M. Cox, 19 July 1900, A.M. Broyles JP 4-110
George Bales or Boles to Polly McCuller, 18 Dec 1855 (21 Dec), A.D. Paul JP 1-#559 [Bales] & 1-#566 [Boles]
George T. Bowles to Lorena Bishop, 27 Nov 1889 (same), D.H. Hindman JP 1-586
H.J. Bowles to Floria McMurry, 29 Oct 1900, J.R. Clark MG 2-106
Jacob Bowls to Jane Forney, 11 Dec 1852 (12 Dec), A.D. Paul JP 1-#395
James S. Bowles to Lucy Clark, 19 Jan 1896, W.N. Rose MG 4-88
James W. Bowles to Ida Rice, 7 Jan 1894, W.H. Perkinson JP 4-76
Jessee Bowles to Elizabeth Kirklen, 10 Oct 1865 (15 Oct), S. Phillips MG 1-#852
John Bowles to Mary Jane Emery, 4 Jan 1867 (6 Jan), P.G. Campbell JP 1-#927
Laura J. Bales to W.L. Stephens q.v.
Margarett Bowles to William Barnett q.v.
Martha A. Bowles to Daniel O. Hardbarger q.v.
Martha J. Bowlis(?) to Lee Walker q.v.
Noah Bowles to Mary Dodd, 28 Ap 1899 [bond only], T.N. Johnson W , "License returned not executed, J.T. Howard, C. Clerk" 2-404
Noah Bowles to Z. Cox, 24 Aug 1900, A. M. Broyles JP 4-106
R.C. Bowles to Laura Bell Cox, 23 Oct 1899 (24 Oct), W.N. Rose MG, Noah Bolles W 3-58
S. E. Bowlis to J. H. Chumley q.v.
Samuel A. Bollis to Frances Wilkey, 25 Feb 1899 (26 Feb), W.A. Howard MG, James Houston W 2-388
Shell Bowles to Josie McCulley, 20 May 1894, J.R. Clark MG 4-90
W.W. Bowles to Hester Brown, 11 May 1900, J.H. Keylon JP 4-102
William Boles to Mary Monday, 22 Nov 1870 (same), J.P. Roddy MG 1-#1176
William R. Bowles to Cinda(?) West, 31 Jan 1895, James H. Keelon JP 4-77

- - - - - - - - - - - - -

BOLTON / BOLTIN

1860 CENSUS
Spencer Boltin 79 (SC)(Shoemaker), Mary J. 30 (Va), William H. 14, George W. 12, Louisa M. 10, Mary A. 8, Benjamin C. 4, Franklin 2 6-108-742 (Mu)
1870 and 1880 CENSUS– None
1900 CENSUS
John Bolton 6: see James B. Sims

MARRIAGES

David S. Bolton to Margaret Green, 29 Oct 1898 (30 Oct), W.A. Green JP, J.A. Kelley W 2-341

Florina Bolton to J. A. Ingle q.v.

Nettie Bolton to John Fox q.v.

W.B. Bolton to Mary Stewart, 15 Oct 1898 (16 Oct), W.L. Lillard JP, W.D. Bolton & Peter Bottom W 2-331

- - - - - - - - - - - - -

BOMIRES

1900 CENSUS

William Bomires 27 (July 1872-M 0)(Electrician), Tina 31 (Sep 1868-M 0-1-1), Katie BLEVINS 8 (d)(Sep 1891) 10-323A-69/73

- - - - - - - - - - - - -

BOND

MARRIAGE

Barbary S. M. Bond to John Dyer q.v.

- - - - - - - - - - - - -

BONHAM

MARRIAGE

Orpha Bonham to John A. Foust q.v

- - - - - - - - - - - - -

BOOFER / BOUFER

1870 CENSUS

Lydia Boofer 65: see Abraham Hodge

Jonas Boofer 22, Josephine 28 4-11-72

1880 CENSUS

Jonas Boofer 32, Mary A. 23, Robert M. 9, Thomas J. 7, Mary A. 2, Martha C.(?) 24 (si) 5-4-29

1900 CENSUS

Jonas T. Boofer 53 (Feb 1847-M 21), Mary A. 43 (Sep 1856-M 21-11-6), Nellie 18 (Mar 1882), Lizzie 15 (Jan 1885), Carl 9 (Oct 1890), Martha L. 4 (June 1895), Lida F. 1 (June 1898), Joseph L. 1/12 (Ap 1900) 5-238A-200

Robert M. Boofer 29 (Nov 1870-M 3), Mary D. 26 (Nov 1873-M 3-0-0) 5-238A-198

MARRIAGES

Annie Boofer to John Dagle q.v.

John Boofer to Lyda Jolly, 31 Dec 1864 (1 Jan 1865), J. Howard MG 1-#880

Jonas Boofer to Esther J. Mitchell, 10 June 1869 (no return) 1-#1100

Jonas Boofer to Mary A. Furguson, 4 Nov 1879 (same), John Howard MG 1-#1684

M. E. Boofer to J. C. Mahone q.v.

Robert Boufer to Mary Pierce, 26 Dec 1896 (27 Dec), J.A. Whitner MG, T.H. Buttram W 2-95

- - - - - - - - - - - - -

BOOKER

1860 CENSUS

Adam Booker 51 (Va), Sarah 52, William 25, Mary A. 22, Noah 21, Riley 19, Elizabeth 18, Michael 17, Sarah 14, Jane 11, Adam 10, James 8 4-53-364

1870 and 1880 CENSUS– None

1900 CENSUS

Freddie Booker 6: see Asberry Locke

MARRIAGES

Lydia Booker to Jacob Foust q.v.

P.T. Booker (21, Polk Co) to M.J. Price (20, Gilmore Co, Ga), 5 Jan 1882, M.L. Abbott JP, J.W. Dunahoe & W.N. Raines W (both of Cumberland Co.) 4-9(84)

- - - - - - - - - - - - -

BOONAY

MARRIAGE

Pete Boonay to Rena Buttram, 22 Mar 1877 (same), no MG or JP 1-#1493

- - - - - - - - - - - - -

BOOTH

MARRIAGE

James Booth to Eva Bowman, 1 Jan 1900 (same), W.L. Patton MG, J.H. Trusley W 3-104

- - - - - - - - - - - - -

BORAN / BORING / BOWEN / BOWINS

1900 CENSUS

James Boran 19: see Elen Woody

Jasper N. Bowins 37, Julia 8: see Newt Henry

Lizzie Boring 34, Joshua 8, Nellie 2: see Moses Grier

MARRIAGE

Ellen Bowen to William Woody q.v.

Jasper Bowen to Lillie McHolmes [bond] or McHomes [license], 27 Nov 1900 (same), W.L. Lillard JP, A. Fitzgerald W 3-247

N. L. Bowen(?) to S. A. Stoke q.v.

Rebecca Bowen to A. M. Gadd q.v.

- - - - - - - - - - - - -

BOSLEY

MARRIAGE

Maggie Bosley to James Walker q.v.

- - - - - - - - - - - - -

BOTTOMLEE / BOTTOMLEY

1900 CENSUS

James Bottomlee 39 (Mar 1861-M 10)Coal Miner), Mattie 29 (Oct 1870-Ga/Ga/Ga-M 10-3-3), Satira 9 (Nov 1890), Julia 6 (May 1894), Rosa 2 (Sep 1897) 8-283A-291/293

John Bottomlee 24 (Mar 1874-T/Eng/T-M 6), Martha 23 (Feb 1877-M 6-2-1), Ora E. 1 (Dec 1898) 8-289B-424/427

Moses Bottomlee 38 (July 1861-T/NY/T-M 16)(Fisherman), Lusie 43 (Feb 1857-T/NY/T-M 16-11-7), James 16 (Mar 1884), William 14 (July 1885), Frank Ray 8 (June 1892), Maud 5 (June 1894), Susan G. 4 (Feb 1896), Rosy 11/12 (June 1899) 15-270A-40

Nash Bottomlee 33 (Dec 1866-M 3)(Miner), Sally 22 (May 1878-M 3-0-0), Alexander 10 (Aug 1889), Martha 8 (Oct 1891), Lydia 6 (Jan 1894) 8-289A-421/424

MARRIAGES

James Bottomlee to Elizabeth J. Burwick, no dates [probably 1861], Wm Morgan JP 1-#762

James Bottomlee to Mattie Kiker, 8 Feb 1890 (same), M.C. Bruner MG 1-599

Morris Bottomlee to Lydia Hurt, 17 June 1877 (18 June), Calvin Morgan JP 1-53

Moses Bottomley to L.E. Burchard, 17 Sep 1883 (9 Sep) [sic], F.T. Morgan JP 1-475

BOUCE– see BICE

BOUGHMAN

1860 CENSUS

Lilbourn Boughman 37, Eliza A. 34, Elizabeth I. 4, Mary R. 2, Mary A. BELL 17 2-80-545

BOWEN– see BORAN

BOWER / BOWERS

1870 CENSUS

Francis Bower 43 (Prussia)(Piano Forte Maker), Marguerette 39 (Prussia), Francis M 18 (NY), Angeline B. 15 (NY), Mary L. 13 (NY), Rebecca 11, Sarah S. 6, Henry C. 4 8-16-113

1880 CENSUS

Francis Bower 52, M. 49 (w), M.L. 23 (d), R.J. 21 (d), S.S. 15 (d), H.C. 13 (s), A.S. 8 (s), G.S. 4 (s) 8-7-53

1900 CENSUS

Francis Bower 73 (Feb 1827-Germany/Do/Do-M 47), Margaret 69 (June 1830-Germany/Do/Do-M 47-8-5), Rebecca J. 41 (May 1859), George H. 23 (Oct 1876), William H. 9 (gs)(Jul 1892) 13-301A-205/213

Frank M. Bower 48 (July 1857-NY/Germany/Do-M 25), Nancy V. 49 (Sep 1850-T/Va/T-M 25-6-6), Joseph E. 21 (Nov 1878), Ida E. 19 (Oct 1880), Minnie P. 17 (Ap 1883), Josie Belle 14 (Aug 1885), Mary M. 12 (Jan 1888), Raleigh A. 10 (Dec 1889) 13-300B-196/203

MARRIAGES

Angeline Bowers to James H. Hickman q.v.

Harriet Bowers to J. R. Hoffman q.v.

Henry Bowers to Lin Moss, 29 Nov 1889 (30 Nov), W.R. Grimsley MG 1-583

Linda Bowers to W. P. Johns q.v.

Sarah Bower to Samuel Wilson q.v.

BOWLER

1900 CENSUS

Camilla Bowler 49 (Sep 1850-Oh/Oh/Oh-Wd 1-0) 8-312A-25/26

David Bowler(?) 57 (Oct 1842-M 34), Lurenie 56 (Dec 1844-M 34-12-8), William R. 32 (May 1868), George W. 29 (Jan 1871-Wd), Sarah M. 18 (Jan 1882), Ella F. 15 (Ap 1885), Mattie M. 12 (Jan 1388), Ethel L. 8 (Aug 1891) 2-191B-14/14

MARRIAGE

Darius S. Bowler to Carmilla S. Bucher, 5 Sep 1885 (same), J.H. Locke JP 1-499

BOWMAN / BOMAN / BOMANS / BOYMEN

1870 CENSUS

Elijah Boman 38, Pauline R. 32, John E. 2, Robert D. 2/12, Peter HOLT 8 8-8-52

1880 CENSUS– None

1900 CENSUS

Lemul Bowman 38 (Ap 1862-Ky/Va/Va-M 17), Arabel 32 (Jan 1868-M 17-4-0), Jacob WEST 16 (relation not given)(Mar 1884) 8-287A-379/381

Newton J. Bowman 30 (Feb 1870-M 2)(Coal Miner), Dora 28 (Sep 1871-M 12-8-1), George W. 11 (Nov 1888-Ga) 13-303A-245/255

MARRIAGES

A.J. Bowman to Alice Wright, 12 June 1886 (13 June), I.W. Holt JP 1-508

Emma Boman [or Brown] to L.D. Gorden q.v.

Eva Bowman to James Booth q.v.

Emmit Bowman to Ella Alexander, 6 Aug 1896 (9 Aug), J.J. Krischbaun MG, Thomas Alexander W 2-52

J.N. Bowman to Virginia Olinger, 28 Oct 1888 (27 Oct) [sic], James H. Parrott(?) MG or JP 1-555

L.P. Boymen or Boywer to Dilla Gravitt, 6 Oct 1885 (same), A.J. Pritchett MG 1-500

Louisa Bomans to G. W. Rigsby q.v.

M. E. Bowman to W. T. Green q.v.

Newt Bowman to Dora M. Clanahan, 31 Dec 1887 (same), F.M. Bandy MG 1-547

Phrina Bowman to John Gentry(?) q.v.

BOXLY

MARRIAGE

Catharine M. Boxly to Owen B. Holloway q.v.

BOYD

1880 CENSUS

John W. Boyd 24, Mary 23: see Sam Hensley

1900 CENSUS

Adlanne M. Boyd 24 (July 1875-D 2-2), Bessie L. 7 (Oct 1892), Millie B. 4 (Dec 1895) 3-203A-58/62

John Boyd 44 (Sep 1855-M 14), Mary 42 (Oct 1857-M 14-9-7), William 18 (Dec 1881), Robert 16 (July 1883), Charley 19 (June 1889), Floyed 6 (Dec 1893), Frank 5 (Ap 1895), Bargis 3 (Feb 1897), Lester 1 (Ap 1899) 7-263A-249/254

John A.B. Boyd 35 (Ap 1865-Ill/Oh/Oh-M 12)(Grocery Salesman), Bell 35 (Dec 1864-Ill/Oh/Oh-M 12-2-2), Agnes 8 (July 1891-Ill), Eugene H. 2 (Mar 1878) 10-254A-82

Lillie Boyd 23: see Columbus Gillespie (B)

Rudd Boyd 43 (Ap 1857-M 22), Texas A. 40 (Jan 1860-M 22-9-8), Mary A. 17 (Feb 1883), Laura 14 (Ap 1886), Thomas 10 (Jan 1890), James 8 (Mar 1892), Lizzie 5 (Mar 1895), Henery 2 (Sep 1897), Patilica 2/12 (d) (Mar 1900) 7-263-251/256

Ulusor Boyd 23 (Sep 1876-M 4)(Coal Miner), Maggie 20 (Jan 1880-M 4-2-2), Della 3 (Ap 1897), William 1 (Jan 1899), Carrie PAYNE 14 (sil)(May 1886), John PAYNE 21 (boarder)(Unk 1879)(Coal Miner) 8-279A-212/214

MARRIAGES

Allice Boyd to C. T. Jewell q.v.

E.H. Boyd to Mary C. Foust, 12 Dec 1876 (14 Dec), Samuel Greer TEMEC 1-#1475

John W. Boyd to Mary Housley, 20 Mar 1880 (21 Mar), J.R. Crawford JP 1-#1723

Josie Boyd to William Morrison q.v.

Mary Boyd to John Pogue q.v.

Susie Boyd to Marion Coleman q.v.

Ulyses Boyd to Margaret C. McMillen, 18 Ap 1896 (same), A.P. Hayes JP, J.L. Center W 2-13

\- - - - - - - - - - - - -

BOYER

1900 CENSUS

Samuel Boyer 42 (Aug 1857-Ind/Ind/Ky-M 14), Della 32 (Sep 1867-Ga/Ga/NC-M 14-3-3), Nannie 13 (Aug 1886), Nellie M. 7 (July 1892), Callie D. 6 (Nov 1893) 5-235B-149

\- - - - - - - - - - - - -

BOYLE

MARRIAGE

E. H. Boyle to Syntha E. Moore, 26 July 1870 (no return) 1-#1158

\- - - - - - - - - - - - -

BOYTIN

1900 CENSUS

James Boytin 16: see M. C. Woolfork (B)

\- - - - - - - - - - - - -

BRABSON

1860 CENSUS

John Brabson 3/12: see John Miller

\- - - - - - - - - - - - -

BRACKETT

1900 CENSUS

John H. Brackett 35 (Jan 1865-Ga/NC/NC-M 8)(Coal Miner), Matilda P. 31 (Feb 1869-M 8-6-5), Winona G. 11 (Oct 1888), Rachel E. 7 (Oct 1892), Mary L. 4 (Mar 1896), Hattie J. 2 (May 1898), Alice H. 3/12 (Feb 1900) 13-301A-206/214

MARRIAGES

Etta Brackett to George T. Bryant q.v.

John Brackett to Tillie Wilson, 23 June 1891, William Morgan JP 4-27

\- - - - - - - - - - - - -

BRADFORD

1900 CENSUS

Mary Bradford 39 (Mar 1861-Wd 6-2)(Washwoman), Will HUNT 22 (border)(Mar 1878), Annie MACK 8 (ward) (1892) 8-315A-94/97 (B)

\- - - - - - - - - - - - -

BRADSHAW

1900 CENSUS

Mary Bradshaw 74: see William Y. Denton

MARRIAGES

Dycey Bradshaw to T. P. Sullivan q.v.

James H. Bradshaw to Mary C. Sharp, 25 June 1873 (same), W.R. Henry JP 1-#1284

\- - - - - - - - - - - - -

BRADLEY

1860 CENSUS

William H. Bradley 55, Mary J. 34, Berryman G. 18, John 12, Mary 10, Margaret 5, Robert 1 4-50-340

1870 and 1880 CENSUS– None

1900 CENSUS

John A. Bradley 74: see John W. Angel

\- - - - - - - - - - - - -

BRADY

1860 CENSUS

Angaline Brady 25, James 5, Thomas 3, Mary J. 2: see Thomas Lemons

Charles Brady 22: see Dennis McClendon

Charles Brady 35, Mary L. 39, Farley 11, Micajah 9, Sarah M. 7, Martha J. 5, Anny E. 3, Mary C. 1 2-73-497

Farley Brady 65, Mary 46, Leah 17, Owen R. 14, James P. 11, Amanda 7, Farley S. 3 4-44-301

Hester Brady 45 (SC), John P. 21, Sarah J. 18, James K. 1, Martha E. 7 8-14-93

James Brady 33, Elizabeth 25, Nancy 5, Pleasant 4 9-99-674

Merril Brady 54, Nancy 47, William 20, Samuel H. 15, Sarah A. 12, Hannah E. 10, Greenberry 8, Barnett 5, July McCLENDAN 4/12 9-99-675

Smith Brady 3, Harriet 22, Samuel 3, Newton 1 2-70-475

1870 CENSUS

Angeline Brady 36, James M. 15, Thomas A. 14, Mary J. 12 1-22-147

Charles Brady 32, Zilpha A. 32, Sarah 8, Emily J. 6, William 3, Mary E. 2, Louvenia C. 1 3-20-146

Charles Brady 46, Mary L. 49, Sarah M. 18, Martha J. 17, Anna 14, Caroline 9, Charles 6, Ilas GIPSON (B) 14 2-16-110

Farley Brady 72, Mary Ann 58, James P. 21, Amanda 17, Farley S. 12 4-17-114

James Brady 43, Elizabeth 36 (Va), Nancy J. 14, Pleasant 13 1-21-136

Mariah Brady 30, Nancy J. 13 (B): see Thomas C. Darwin

Merril Brady 63, Nancy 58, Emily 20, Greenberry 18, Barnet 16, Adaline 12 4-15-100

Samuel Brady 22, Emily 21, Sarah 4, Anthony 2 3-19-137

1880 CENSUS

Angeline Brady 48, James 25 12-5-44

Caroline Brady 33, A. B. 9 (d), M. E. 7 (d), J. L. 6 (d) 4-31-249

Charles Brady 42, D.A. 42, S.P. 19 (d), E.J. 17 (d), W.W. 15 (s), M.E. 12 (d), L.E. 10 (d), R.E. 9 (s), H.S. 8 (d), L.L. 4 (s), L.G. 1 (s) 3-13-106

Farley Brady 83, A.M. 68 (w), Amanda 25, F.S. 19 (s), E. MARTIN (f) 18 (Protege) 4-5-37

G.B. Brady 27, B.* 23, P. LINDSEY 26, R.J. 10 (d), L.J. 9 (d), James SMITH 22 8-21-185 [*Barnet, bro of Greenberry B. Brady]

James Brady 31, Phebe 25, Sarah 5, Farley 3, Laura 2, Ella 1/12, Josep THURMAN 18 (Servant) 2-38-315

James Brady 52, Pleasant 24 (s), Anna 17 (d), Martha 1/12 (d) 12-4-29

Smith Brady 51, Harriet 42, Samuel 23, Sarah 19, Martha 14, Addie 12, William 10, Harriet 8, Cleopatra 6, Walter 1, Sarah SELLERS 81 (ml) 2-26-208

W.A. Bradye 39, M.B. 26 (w), J.B. 17 (s), J.H. 16 (s), J.C. 14 (s), E.S. 13 (d), P.H. 12 (d), L.N. 11 (d), Haret 9, Martha 8, N.S. 4 (d), M.M. 2 (d), G.B.S. 2/12 (s) 7-22-190

1900 CENSUS

Andrew Brady 38: see John Swan

Andrew Brady 37 (Oct 1862-M 5)(RR Laborer), Amanda 32 (Sep 1867-M 15-8-5), William H. 15 (Jan 1885), Pearlie A. 13 (Oct 1886)(Domestic Servant), Leroy A.J. 8 (Ap 1892), Maud L. 5 (July 1894), Susan E. 2 (Dec 1897) 2-198A-129/134 (B)

Caroline Brady 53: see Winfield S. McCann

Charles Brady 35 (May 1865-M 12)(Bridge Carpenter), Lizzie 31 (Aug 1868-T/Ky/T-M 12-5-2), Maud 9 (June 1890), Goldie 5 (Jan 1895) 10-323A-59/62

Green B. Brady 47 (June 1852-M 12)(Miller), Laura 29 (Ap 1871-M 12-4-4), Robert T. 11 (June 1888), Ida R. 9 (Aug 1890), Nelie F. 6 (Ap 1894), Bessie L. 2 (Aug 1897), Jane LINDSEY 30 (sil)(Sep 1869) 10-324B-94/98

Henry J. Brady 36 (Ap 1864-M 12), Carra 30 (Feb 1870-M 12-3-3), Houston 11 (Sep 1888), Laner 8 (Sep 1891), Manda 7/12 (Oct 1899) 10-255A-92

James P. Brady 51 (Nov 1848-M 25), Phebe A. 47 (Oct 1853-M 25-12-11), Sarah A. 25 (Ap 1875), Farley W. 23 (June 1876-M 0), Laura J. 22 (Jan 1878), Ella T. 20 (Nov 1879), John J. 18 (July 1881), Amanda A. 17 (Feb 1883), Atta M. 15 (Dec 1884), Florence M. 13 (Sep 1886), Eugene C. 11 (July 1888), Leland E. 6 (July 1893), Roy P. 3 (Nov 1896) 2-196A-96/99

John B. Brady 37 (Aug 1862-M 12), Vinie 28 (Jan 1872-M 12-6-6), Lillie E. 11 (Sep 1888), Gusie or Gertie L. 9 (s)[sic](Nov 1891), Ida C. 8 (Ap 1892), Russel J. 6 (June 1893), Charley H. 3 (May 1897), Willia D. 2 (May 1898), Banister SMITH 47 (fl)(Unk 1853-Wd) 7-262B-244/249

Mary Brady 33 (Feb 1867-Wd 3-3), James 18 (Mar 1882), Jack 16 (Oct 1883), General 14 (July 1885) 12-181A-57/60

Nathaniel B. Brady 44 (Unk-M 16), Sallie C. 39 (May 1861-M 16-6-5), Margie L. 15 (Jan 1885), Freddie W. 11 (May 1889), Ada A. 8 (Dec 1891), Janie V. 6 (Mar 1894), Harry E. 3 (Sep 1896) 10-325A-107/111

Plas Brady 44 (Ap 1856-M 21), Ann 37 (May 1863-M 21-7-6), Marthy 20 (June 1880), Luler 5 (Ap 1884), T. 14 (s)(Ap 1886), Mary 8 (July 1891), Willi 5 (Feb 1895), Walter 1 (Feb 1899) 12-181A-60/63

Samuel S. Brady 43 (Nov 1856-S), Smith 72 (f)(June 1827-M 44), Harriet J. 62 (m)(Ap 1838-M 44-11-6), Harriet E. 27 (si)(June 1872), Cleo P. 26 (si)(Feb 1874), Archable M. GILLESPIE 18 (nw)(Oct 1881), Thomas S. GILLESPIE 16 (nw)(July 1883) 2-195B-86/89

Sellers Brady 42 (July 1857) 14-222B-176/180

MARRIAGES

A. J. Brady to W. D. Hughes q.v.

Amanda B. Brady to W. P. Broyles q.v.

Anny E. Brady to J. F. Johnson q.v.

Barnett Brady to Sallie Whaley, 12 Dec 1883 (13 Dec), J.W. Williamson MG 1-475

Bell Brady to J. F. Broyles q.v.

Charles Brady to Zilpha Ann Gear, 1 Oct 1860 (same), T.H. McFerson JP 1-#729

Charles Brady to Lezzil Wright, 21 Mar 1886 (same), James R. Crawford JP 1-497

E. J. Brady to R. D. Kennedy q.v.

Elizabeth Brady to John J. McCallom q.v.

Ella Brady to John Pearson q.v.

F.M. Brady to A.F. Gross, 1 Ap 1900, William White MG 1-108

Farley Brady to Polly Ann Malony, 8 Feb 1859 (same), A. Johns MG 1-#688

G.B. Brady to Julia A. Linsey, 31 Mar 1888 (same), J.R. Crawford MG 1-548

J. A. Brady to J. C. Dodd q.v.

J.B. Brady to V.C. Smith, 15 Jan 1886 (17 Jan), J.Q. Shaver MG 1-500

J.H. Brady to Cordelia Morgan, 9 Nov 1887 (same), John Howard JP 1-537

J.P. Brady to P.A. Cook, 31 Dec 1873 (1 Jan 1874), E.W. Marsh MG 1-#1323

James Brady to Elizabeth Fugate, 22 Mar 1858 (same), R.T. Howard MG 1-#655

James Brady to Sarah Cantrel, 14 June 1880 (16 Sep)[sic], J.P. Roddy MG 1-#1732

Jane L. Brady to John R. Walker q.v.

L. C. Brady to Isaac Brown q.v.

Laura Brady to D. L. Wright q.v.

Lizzie Brady to Scott McCann q.v.

M. J. Brady to B. T. Hornsby q.v.

Martha L. Brady to James M. Hornesby q.v.

Mary Brady to John P. Moulton q.v.

Mary J. Brady to William H. Daniel q.v.

Mattie Brady to Richard Saffles q.v.

Micajah Brady to A. C. Holland, 11 Aug 1869 (12 Aug), Z. Rose MG 1-#1097
Nancy Brady to Andy Hoskins q.v.
Rebecca J. Brady to Claburn Fugate q.v.
Samuel H. Brady to Emily Willson, no dates or return [probably 1864] 1-#822
Sarah Brady to R. B. Bohannon q.v.
Sereptia Brady to J. D. Franklin q.v.
William A. Brady to Amanda Hughes, 6 June 1861 (no return) 1-#755

- - - - - - - - - - - - -

BRAINE
(see also BAIN / BAINE)

MARRIAGE
Marcus W. Braine to Sallie L. Miller, 1 Jan 1880 (same), J. Howard MG 1-#1709

- - - - - - - - - - - - -

BRAMLETT / BRAMLET

1860 CENSUS
Garlington Bramlet 41, Mary 44, William E. 16, John M. 12, Thomas J. 9, Martha C. 1, George W. EDMONDS 35(?) [ink blob], Mathew EDMONDS 31 3-60-416
1870 CENSUS
Mary Bramlett 50, John 22, Thomas 18, Cyrus 9, George 15 3-7-49
1880 CENSUS
Dicy Bramlett 66: see J. Prater
John M. Bramlett 32, Nancy C. 30, Lila A.T. 5, Dela N. 3, Reta A. 1, Mary BRAMLETT 66 (m) 5-8-75
Thomas J. Bramlett 29, Harriett Ann 29, John C. 5 5-4-27
1900 CENSUS
Cyrus C. Bramlet 41 (July 1858-M 19)(RR Overseer), Hannah E. 36 (Aug 1863-T/NC/NC-M 19-8-5), Charles F. 15 (Feb 1885), Thomas M. 13 (Oct 1887), William W. 7 (Sep 1892), Anna L. 4 (Dec 1895), Bonnie K. 3 (Feb 1897) 5-236A-161
John Bramlet 52 (Feb 1848-T/Ga/T-M 28), Nancy C. 50 (Mar 1850-M 28-15-8), Recta A. 20 (May 1880), Jack R. 17 (Mar 1883), William N. 14 (Sep 1885), Lucretia 13 (Nov 1886), Thomas B. 8 (July 1891), Jessie W. 7 (Jan 1893) 5-237B-182
MARRIAGES
John M. Bramlett to Caroline Minick, 18 Nov 1871 (19 Nov), R.T. Howard MG 1-#1216
Lillie A. Bramlett to Robert H. Beard q.v.
M.C. Bramlett (23) to Hannah E. Denton (18), 3 Nov 1881, A.J. Pritchett MG, J.M. Bramlett & M.E. Denton W 4-5(43)
Ninie Bramlett to T.P. Houston q.v.
Thomas J. Brumlett to Harriet Beard, 10 Aug 1872 (no return) 1-#1244

- - - - - - - - - - - - -

BRAND

1900 CENSUS
William A. Brand 39 (Feb 1861-Ga/Ga/Ga-M 20)(Jeweller), Elizabeth 38 (Unk 1862-Ga/Ga/Ga-M 20-6-1), Joseph A. 19 (Dec 1880-Ga) 8-278A-189/191

- - - - - - - - - - - - -

BRANDON / BRANDIN

1870 CENSUS
James P. Brandin(?) 21: see James K. Hail
1880 CENSUS– None
1900 CENSUS
Bertie Brandon 32 (Ap 1868-T/T/Va-M 16-5-4)(Music Teacher), Minnie I. 11 (Ap 1889), Walter E. 7 (May 1893), Clarence A. 5 (May 1895), Imogene 3 (May 1897) 10-325B-120/124
George Brandon 65 (Aug 1834-M 40)(Grocer), Jane 62 (Feb 1838-M 40-9-8), Mamie ROGERS 21 (d)(Dec 1878-M 0), William ROGERS 25 (sl)(Ap 1875-M 0) (Engineer at Furnace), Harvey VEACH 19 (boarder) (Oct 1880-Ind) 10-324A-90/94
James Brandon 33 (June 1866-M 8)(Saloon Keeper), Mary 24 (May 1876-M 8-3-3), Carl 7 (Feb 1893), Gretchen 3 (Nov 1896), Mande 1 (Ap 1899) 10-321A-16/16
Taylor W. Brandon 18, Margaret A. 18: see Parthenia Thomas

MARRIAGES
Flora Brandon to W.T. Rutherford q.v.
J.W. Brandon to Mary Shannon, 14 Dec 1899 (16 Dec), W.L. Lillard JP & W 3-87
Mamie Brandon to W.A. Rodgers q.v.
Oliva Brandin to John M. Ensor q.v.
S.J. Brandon to Tennie Park, 13 Jan 1900 (14 Jan), W.R. Grimsley MG 3-110
Taylor Brandon to Maggie Breedlove, 21 May 1900 (same), R.C. Knight JP, John White W 3-156
William L. Brandon to Mary W. Cook, 19 May 1893 (23 May), W.T. Drummond MG, W. Lewis Brandon & M.S. Woodall W 2-279

- - - - - - - - - - - - -

BRANNUM / BRANAM / BRANNON

1900 CENSUS
Robert Brannon 47 (Mar 1853-M 20), Mary 33 (May 1867-M 20-3-3), John F. 16 (Aug 1883), Ollie 14 (July 1885), Jennie 11 (June 1888) 13-298B-163/166
William Branam 55 (Dec 1844)(Boarding House Keeper), Josie 39 (Sep 1860-M 22-0-0), Herbert MOORE 2 (ward)(Jan 1898), James H. RUSSELL 27 (boarder) (Mar 1873-M ?) 10-331A-226/241

MARRIAGE
John Brannum to Elizabeth Row, 4 Aug 1869 (no return) 1-#1098

- - - - - - - - - - - - -

BRATCHER / BRACHER / BOUCHER

1870 CENSUS
Elizabeth Bratcher 52, John 35, Benjamin 18, Sarah 16 1-13-87
1880 CENSUS
John Bracher 46, Nancy 47, John 10, General 9, Amanda 5, Cora 4, Charlie 2, George MONDAY 19 (ss), Lorinda 14 (sd) 2-40-327

1900 CENSUS

Benjamin Bracher 55 (Mar 1845-M 3), Lucy 45 (Ap 1855-Ky/Va/T-M 3-0-0), Francis A. GREEN 15 (boarder) (Ap 1885-Ga/Ga/Ga), Lydia E. CHAPLIN 60 (boarder) (Mar 1840-Mass/Mass/Mass-Wd 0-0) 2-199A-144/149

MARRIAGES

Benjamin Bratcher to Catharine Sales, 7 Feb 1872 (10 Feb), John Howard MG 1-#1228

John Boucher to Nancy Monday, 14 May 1873 (same), J.J. Ingle JP 1-#1283

Mary E. Bratcher to Aaron Rhea q.v.

Sarah Bratcher to John Eaton q.v.

- - - - - - - - - - - - -

BREEDEN / BREEDING

1860 CENSUS

Evan Breeden 55 (Va), Abigail B. 55, Nancy P. 23, Asa V. 21, Louisa C. 17, Louisa M. OWENS 24, John G. 19 4-52-354

Stephen Breeden 49, Mary 48, Cynthia A. 22, Thomas J. 20, Mary 18, Lucinda 14, Abigail E. 11 2-75-512

1870 CENSUS

Evan Breeding 65 (Va), Abigail B. 65, Eliza M. 34, John G. OANS 27 (Saddler), John B. BREEDING 37, Nancy J. 34 4-6-36

Stephen Breeding 57, Martha 51, Lucinda 22, Abby E. 19, Mary BROWN 14, James BROWN 12 2-13-93

Thomas Breeding 67 (Va), Margaret 51, Martha REECE 15 2-13-93

1880 CENSUS

H. Breeding 22: see E. Kimbrough

Margaret Breeding 61, Alvira REECE 26 (Servant) 2-41-333

R. Breeding 27: see E. D. Hart

Stephen Breeding 69, Martha 61, Minerva THOMPSON 18 (Servant) 2-38-305

1900 CENSUS

Francis M. Breeden 29 (July 1870-M 6)(Sawmill Laborer), Sarah F. 30 (Sep 1869-M 6-0-0) 14-217B-95/97

John B. Breeding 67 (May 1833-T/Va/T-Wd), Sarah A. 17 (d)(Dec 1882) 2-192B-31/32

MARRIAGES

Abby E. Breeding to Samuel S. Hale q.v.

Cyntha Ann Breeding to Jessee M. Howser q.v.

Hannah J. Breeding to William J. Breeding q.v.

John B. Breeding to Sarah S. Clark, 1 Aug 1870 (2 Aug), Z. Rose MG 1-#1159

Mary A. Breeding to Jerry A. Thompson q.v.

Nancy J. Breeding to William Evans q.v.

S.G. Breeden to Hester Morrell, 23 Nov 1884 (25 Nov), John M. Wolf MG 1-498

Sallie Breeden to Thomas A. Tyler q.v.

Sarah A. Breeding to William M. Owins q.v.

Susan M. Breeding to John D. Owens q.v.

T.J. Breeding to M.M. Ingle, 7 Aug 1869 (8 Aug), Samuel E.(?) Hale MG 1-#1095

William J. Breeding to Hannah J. Breeding, 14 Dec 1852 (16 Dec), A.D. Paul JP 1-#396

- - - - - - - - - - - - -

BREEDLOVE

1900 CENSUS

Charles Breedlove 18: see Jack Moore (B)

Eugene Breedlove 22: see Parthenia Thomas

MARRIAGES

Maggie Breedlove to Taylor Brandon q.v.

Parthena Breedlove to D. L. Thomas q.v.

- - - - - - - - - - - - -

BREIDER

1900 CENSUS

Jeff J. Breider 41: see J. P. Wycuff

- - - - - - - - - - - - -

BRENENAN / BRANEN

MARRIAGES

Florence Branen to Will H. Hayes q.v.

M.G. Brenenan to Sarah E. Rogers, 23 Mar 1886 (same), A.W. Frazier JP 1-486

- - - - - - - - - - - - -

BREWER

1860 CENSUS

Elijah Brewer 66, Mary 68 9-97-656

1870 CENSUS

Elijah Brewer 76, Mary 78, Mary 12 1-22-149

Sarah Brewer 22: see William R. Henry

1880 CENSUS

John Brewer 21, Mary J. 23, Sallie GARRISON (B) 16 (Servant) 5-9-79

John Brewer 48 (RR Laborer), Sarah L. 17, Nancy J. 14, William 10 10-27-209/214

Mary Brewer 88: see James Hayes

1900 CENSUS

Andrew H. Brewer 43 (Nov 1851-T/T/NC-M 23), Sarah F. 52 (Aug 1847-T/T/NC-M 23-0-0) 5-235A-143

George W. Brewer 58 (Mar 1842-T/NC/Ind-M 34)(Minister), Mary J. 53 (June 1846-Ga/Ga/Ga-M 34-3-3), Ruth 25 (Nov 1874)(Dry Goods Saleslady), Rosa L. 21 (Sep 1878), Wilborn 19 (Oct 1880)(Iron Moulder) 10-327A-149/157

Thomas J. Brewer 41 (Feb 1859-Wd)(Saloon Keeper), Walter E. 14 (June 1885-Ala), Maggie 13 (Feb 1887-Ala), Maud 10 (May 1890), John 8 (Jan 1892), John T. 19 (nw)(Jan 1881-Ala/T/Ala-M 1)(Bartender), Mossie 21 (ne)(Sep 1878-M 1-0-0), Mattie 20 (ne)(July 1879-Ala) 10-331B-235/250

MARRIAGES

A. Brewer to Sarah Brewer, 7 Sep 1876 (same), F.J. Paine JP 1-#1459

Ann Brewer to Pleasant Monday q.v.

John Brewer to Mary Zimmaman, 6 Sep 1879 (7 Sep), A.J. Pritchett MG 1-#1673

Nanie(?) Brewer to J. C. Morgan q.v.

Nettie Brewer to E. M. Cooper q.v.

Sarah Brewer to A. Brewer q.v.

Sarah Brewer to L. A. Smith q.v.

- - - - - - - - - - - - -

BREWYE (?)

1880 CENSUS

A. Brewye(?) 37, Lina 35, Mary 10, Geo 13, Catharine 6, L. 6, Ida 2, Catharine KELLY 22 (sil), Ida 2 (ne), Ada 1 (ne) 3-17-16

- - - - - - - - - - - - -

BRIDGEMAN / BRIDGEMON / BRIDGMAN / BRIDGON

1880 CENSUS

John Bridgemon 84, Mary 80, N.H. 52 (d), Mary 50, Rebecca 44, W.C. 27 (nw) 11-39-317

S.D. Bridgeman 58, P.J. 54, Soonia J. 21, S.D. Jr. 19, M.C. 17, Sula 15, Haite 13 8-1-6

1900 CENSUS

Alvia Bridgman 18: see Robert Corn (B)

Celestie Bridgman 26, Leary T. 7, Ray L. 2: see Thomas Jefferson (B)

Dock Bridgman 27 (Unk 1873-M 4) 8-275B-137 (B)

Hoyt C. Bridgman 31 (June 1868-T/Ga/Ga-M 7)(Lumber Dealer), Lilla A. 28 (Oct 1871-T/Mo/Ga-M 7-3-2), Clyde 5 (May 1895), Verria B. 3 (Oct 1896), Baby 0/12 (May 1900) 10-321B-36/38

John L. Bridgmon 52 (Sep 1847-T/T/Ga-M 32)(Lumberman), Mary A. 53 (Ap 1847-M 32-7-6), Frank R. 31 (s)(Unk 1869-Wd)(Lumberman), Herman 15 (gs)(Unk 1884), Effie 13 (gd)(July 1886), Etta 8 (gd)(Dec 1891), Maud 6 (gd)(Ap 1894), Albert C. 24 (s)(May 1876)(Lumberman), Claud 21 (Aug 1878)(Lumberman), Theodore 18 (Dec 1881)(Lumberman) 8-281A-247/249

Matilda Bridgman 43 (Feb 1857-T/Va/NC-Wd 5-5), Sam 24 (Dec 1875-M 0), Jim 21 (Jan 1879), John 14 (Sep 1885) 8-311A-4/4 (B)

Samson Bridgman Jr. 43 (Sep 1856-T/T/Ga-M 19)(Manufacturing Fruit Crates), Lavinia 43 (Dec 1856-M 19-8-5), Jennie 17 (Feb 1883), John L. 14 (Oct 1885), Robbie 13 (Mar 1887), Benn B. 7 (Ap 1893), Juanito 3 (Mar 1897) 8-313B-61/64

Samuel Bridgman 24, Pearl 19: see Isaac Murry (B)

Sarysan D. Bridgman 79 (Oct 1820-T/Va/Va-Wd)(Manufacturing Fruit Crates), Lula 37 (Mar 1863-T/T/Ga), Myrtice LILLARD 14 (gs)(Sep 1885) 8-314B-87/90

Thomas Bridgeman 50 (Unk-Wd), Paul 15 (Unk) 8-314A-76/79 (B)

William Bridgman 28 (July 1871-M 5), Fannie 25 (May 1875-M 5-3-3), Hester 4 (Jan 1896), Dewey 2 (Ap 1898), Arnold 4/12 (Feb 1900) 8-278B-204/206

MARRIAGES

Addie Bridgeman to Ping(?) Talley q.v.

Alva Bridgemon(?) to Robert Cord or Combs q.v.

Bell Bridgeman to Walter Carrington q.v.

Dock Bridgon(?) to Salina Jeffreys, 10 July 1897 (same), S.W. Burnett MG, T.J. Killough W 2-159

Florence Bridgemon to J. E. Blackford q.v.

H.C. Bridgeman to Lillie A. Brooks, 8 Nov 1893, G.W. Brewer MG 4-61

James Bridgeman to Lucinda Garner, 3 July 1890, J.W. Wright MG 4-17

John L. Bridgeman to Mary A. Morgan, 8 Oct 1865 (same), J.W. Williamson MG 1-#843

M. C. Bridgeman to W. W. Lillard q.v.

Samuel Bridgeman to Pearl Murry, 4 July 1899, G.R. Baldwin JP 4-103

Selma Bridgeman to Isaac Angel q.v.

Synthia Bridgeman to Horace Phillips q.v.

W.S. Bridgeman to Fannie White, 21 Ap 1895, A.P. Hayes JP 4-82

- - - - - - - - - - - - -

BRIDGERS

MARRIAGE

Willie Bridgers to Adie Carney or Cassey, 12 June 1883 (same), Thompson Ashburn MG 1-475

- - - - - - - - - - - - -

BRIGHT

1900 CENSUS

Harris Bright 23: see Joseph C. Jones (B)

- - - - - - - - - - - - -

BRIGHTWELL

MARRIAGE

John Brightwell to Sarah F. Thompson, 6 Nov 1854 (12 Nov), Thomas J. Gillespie JP 1-#471

- - - - - - - - - - - - -

BRISON– see BRYSON

- - - - - - - - - - - - -

BRISTOE

1900 CENSUS

Wilum Bristoe 41 (Jan 1857-M 12)(Merchant), Allie 30 (June 1867-M 12-4-3), Claud(?) 8 (Oct 1891), Glenn 5 (Feb 1895), Frank 2 (Mar 1898) 1-184B-110/115

- - - - - - - - - - - - -

BRITT

1900 CENSUS

Wesley Britt 39 (Feb 1861-Ga/Ga/Ga-M 19)(Locamotive Engineer), Rebecca 38 (June 1861-M 19-4-3), Mary 16 (Jan 1884), Ollie 7 (Oct 1892), Gracie 4 (Feb 1896), John FERGUSON 24 (boarder)(Unk 1876) (Coal Miner), Thomas 21 (border)(June 1878)(Coal Miner), Edward BAIN 23 (boarder)(Unk 1877)(Coal Miner) 8-277A-178/179

MARRIAGES

James Britt to Eliza Johnson, 6 Oct 1865 (same), R.T. Howard MG 1-#869

Jane Britt to Reuben Small q.v.

- - - - - - - - - - - - -

BROCK / BROCKE

1900 CENSUS

Sarah Brock 50 (Ap 1850-Wd 8-8)(Farm Boss), Albert 23 (Mar 1877)(Medical Doctor), Saphair 18 (July 1883), Charles 17 (Dec 1882), Joseph 14 (July 1885), Harvy 12 (Feb 1888), Vesta 9 (Oct 1890) 12-181A-54/57

MARRIAGES

Bettie Brock to T.N.L. Cunnyngham q.v.

Callie Brock to Sewell East q.v.

J.F. Brock to M.J. Hughes, 23 Dec 1900 (same), W.L. Lillard JP 3-272

James Brock (23) to Paralee Monehan (22), 11 Dec 1882, C.W. Burch MG, Ben Jenkins & Will Whiatherbee W 4-12(116)

Jennie Brock (or Brick) to Jessie Johnson q.v.

Laurence Brock to Adelia Holms, 6 Oct 1900 (same), W.L. Lillard JP, E. Fisher W 3-231

Mary Brocke to James Hammond q.v.

William Brocke to Caroline Housley, 18 Ap 1885 (same), A.D. Morrison MG 1-493

- - - - - - - - - - - - -

BROGDON / BROGLIN

1900 CENSUS

Amanda Broglin 24: see James M. Watson

Frank Brogdon 69 (Jan 1831-NC/NC/NC-M 44)(Civil War Pensioner), Isbell 60 (Sep 1839-M 44-11-6), Robert E. 8 (gs)(Nov 1891) 4-226A-241/245

MARRIAGES

A.E. Brogdon to Ella Dyer, 14 June 1899 (15 June), R.H. Hutall MG, G.W. Goodrich W 2-426

James Brogdon to Amanda Mitchell, 8 Ap 1896, L.E. Smith JP 4-94

Mary J. Brogdon to Wilburn Clark q.v.

- - - - - - - - - - - - -

BROKE

MARRIAGE

Nancy Broke to Isaac Morris q.v.

- - - - - - - - - - - - -

BRONSON

MARRIAGE

Charles V. Bronson to Laura Morrison, 6 Jan 1892, R.A. Bartlett MG 4-35

- - - - - - - - - - - - -

BROOKMAN

1880 CENSUS

Mattie Brookman 19: see Eliza Abernathy

- - - - - - - - - - - - -

BROOKS

1880 CENSUS

Jeff Brooks 30, Catharine 28, Sampson 2, J.C. 3/12, H.B. 3 (d), Jas GARDENHIRE 30 (boarder) 4-36-294 (B)

P.W. Brooks 24, M.J. 23, C.P. 4 (s), N.J. 1 (d) 4-36-295

1900 CENSUS

Anna(?) Brooks 48 (Sep 1852-T/NC/NC-Wd 12-9), Thomas 20 (July 1879), Charles 18 (Aug 1881), Minna 13 (July 1886), Lula 11 (Aug 1888) 15-268B-8

George Brooks 29 (May 1871-Ga/Ga/Ga-M 8), Mandy 29 (Aug 1870-M 8-5-1), Odellia 2 (Sep 1897) 10-256A-118/122 (B)

James Brooks 82: see Mary J. Ervin

Jefferson Brooks 50 (Mar 1850-T/Ga/Ga-M 22) (Blacksmith), Catharine 52 (May 1848-T/Ga/Ga-M 22-2-2) 14-216A-67/68 (B)

John Brooks 25 (Unk 1875-M 5), Paralee 22 (Jan 1878-M 5-2-2), Rosa 4 (Nov 1895), Roy 2 (Dec 1897) 15-268B-11

Joseph Brooks 34 (July 1865-M 2)(Undertaker), Sophia F. 24 (Jan 1876-M 2-0-0) 10-321A-25/26

Lavinia Brooks 69 (Jan 1831-Ver/Ver/Ver-Wd 0-0), Sarah M. SMITH 64 (si)(June 1835-Oh/Ver/Ver-Wd 0-0) 10-326B-137/144

Maggie Brooks 16: see Louis F. McDonald

Sarah Brooks 65: see W--?--ain Brunnagin(?)

Thomas Brooks 38 (Feb 1862-M 13), Dolly 27 (Jan 1873-M 13-7-6), Anna M. 11 (July 1888), Henry 10 (Nov 1889), Luther 8 (Feb 1892), Bessie 6 (July 1893), Darrell 5 (Ap 1895), Mary 1 (Feb 1899) 13-296B-127/129

William M. Brooks Unk (Unk-M 2), Mary E. 19 (Jan 1881-M 2-2-0) 13-297B-144/147

MARRIAGES

Bell Brooks to Robert Hutson q.v.

F. H. Brooks to Lucy Roberts, 2 Mar 1885 (3 Mar), L.W. Holt JP 1-459

George Brooks to Mandy Hughes, 4 Feb 1892, William Morgan JP 4-34

J.A. Brooks to M.S. Tinsley, 11 June 1889 (same), W.S. Hale MG 1-575

J.A. Brooks to Florence McDonald, 3 July 1897 (4 July), W.L. Lillard JP, A.J. Hawkins W 2-158

J.W. Brooks to Paralee Dobbs, 1 Jan 1895, J.W. Williamson MG 4-81

Lillie A. Brooks to H. C. Bridgeman q.v.

Mattie Brooks to Perry Johnson q.v.

Mattie Brooks to J. W. Lattimore q.v.

N. C. Brooks to Ed Rothgeb q.v.

S. E. Brooks to W. H. Eishhorn q.v.

Sarah E. Brooks to A. Brunagin(?) q.v.

Thomas Brooks to Lottie Shipley, 4 June 1900 (5 June), A. Brunagin MG, Joseph Brooks W 3-164

Thomas C. or E. Brooks to Dollie Laws (or Lomax), 23 Ap 1887 (same), W.S. Hale MG 1-572

W.L. Brooks to Mollie Welch, 27 Jan 1891, J.A. Darr MG 4-23

William Brooks to Mary Walker, 9 Oct 1897 (10 Oct), J.W. Williamson MG, Thomas Brooks W 2-198

- - - - - - - - - - - - -

BROTHERTON

1860 CENSUS

William Brotherton 58 (NC), Ann 40, Thomas 14, Nancy 12, George 11, Liddia 6, Jane 3, Sarah 3, Susan 6/12 3-55-375

1870 CENSUS

Thomas Brotherton 25, Rose Anne J. 23, Mary J. 4, Eliza A. 8/12 3-14-99

MARRIAGE

Thomas Brotherton to Rosannah Kelly, 16 Dec 1865 (17 Dec), William W. Low JP 1-#858 & 1-#1065

- - - - - - - - - - - - -

BROWDER

1870 CENSUS

Jeremiah Browder 52, Sarah 30, Caroline 5 8-21-143 (B)

1880 CENSUS

H. L. Browder 19 (B): see S. H. Cole

MARRIAGE

Stephen Browder to Jane Cox, 23 Jan 1890 (same), James M. Benson JP 1-586

- - - - - - - - - - - - -

BROWNBEAGE

1900 CENSUS

Sidney Brownbeage 54 (Sep 1845-Oh/Pa/Pa-M 13)(School Teacher), Edith A. 37 (Sep 1862-Oregon/Pa/Ill-M 13-2-2), Ethel M. 12 (May 1888-Mich), John F. 8 (Nov 1891), Mary A. 21 (Feb 1879-Mich) 13-305A-290/301

- - - - - - - - - - - - -

BROWN

1860 CENSUS

Creed F. Brown 16: see William B. Killough

Elisha Brown 22, Martha 18, Sarah A. 6/12 4-40-268

Isaac Brown 17: see Lewis C. Ferguson

Jacob Brown 21: see Orville Paine

Jesse S. Brown 51, Ruthe 23, Isaac 18, John 14, Newton 12, Elisha 9, Mary 7, Harriet 5, Richard 3, Amanda 1 4-44-297

Joseph Brown 34, Deatha 35, Newton 12, William 6, John 9, James 5, Henry 1 6-103-701

Newton M. Brown 22, John R. YOUNG 14, Nancy BROWN 54 8-11-69

Obediah H. Brown 48 (Va), Biddy 47 (Va), James 18, Churchwell A. 14, William R. 10 5-39-263

1870 CENSUS

Churchwell A. Brown 24, Nancy Jane 24, Mary Jane 2, William A. 1 5-9-68

Elbert Brown 30, Manda 24, Wm 5, Lafayett 3 2-9-63 (B)

Elisha Brown 35, Martha 27, Sarah A. 10, Jesse C. 2 5-8-56

John Brown 21, Eliza 19 6-1-3

John Brown 25, Mary 30, Zachariah [ROSE] 13, Florence [ROSE] 11, Willie [ROSE] 6, Martin [BROWN] 1 2-12-85

Joseph Brown 25, Adaline 24, George L. 3, Jesse V. 11/12 1-15-98

Joseph Brown 44 (House Carpenter), Dialtha 45, William 18 (House Carpenter), James H. 15, Henry 11, Nathaniel 9, Mary F. 6, Wailey 4 6-1-5

Joseph Brown 23 (NY), Matilda 27, Millie E.J. 9, James T. 7, John F. 2 8-6-38

Mary Brown 14, James 12: see Stephen Breeding

Mary Jane Brown 14: see William G. Willson

Newton Brown 23, Jane 32, Mary E. 8/12, George WOMICK (B) 9 2-12-86

Newton J. Brown 22, Nancy 18, William 10/12 6-5-32

Obediah Brown 59 (Va), Mary M. 48, Harriet A. 18, William C. 16, Mary A. 11 4-13-89

Sabeny Brown 22: see Eliza Haselbarger

Sarah R. Brown 4: see James A. Foster

Thomas J. Brown 31, Alemeda M. 21, William F. 2, Thomas F. 4/12 2-9-64

William Brown 25, Mary J. 23, Florence B. 4/12 2-9-59

William R. Brown 20: see James H. Beard

1880 CENSUS

Andrew Brown 29, Sallie F. 32 (w) 5-9-85

Annie Brown 45: see Andrew Moore (B)

C.A. Brown 34, N.J. 34, M.J. 12 (d), N.A. 10 (s), Obadiah 8, J.T. 6 (s), Tennessee 3, W.L. GARRISON 31 (boarder) 4-12-100

Edna Brown(?) 7: see Moses F. Moore

Gerorge Brown 16, Mary 16, Sarah 11/12, James MILLER 15 (Servant) 1-15-126

Isaac Brown 36, Caroline T. 36, Smith 11, Farley N. 9, Cellers B. 6, Richard 2, Amanda M. 4/12, Mary 25 (si) 6-14-131/133

Isaac Brown 24: see Rebecca Waterhouse (B)

James H. Brown 24 (Carpenter), Rachel R.J. 24, John N. 1 6-18-166/170

John Brown 22 (Waiter) (B): see Jere Wasson

John Brown 36, Mary 42, Zachariah ROSE 23 (ss), Florence 18 (sd), William 15 (ss), Martin BROWN 10 (s), John 6 (s), Arthur 3 (s), Beula 2/12 (d), Caroline BROWN 10 (si) 2-26-203

Joseph Brown Sr. 55 (Carpenter), Daulpha J. 55, Henry C. 22, Nathaniel L. 20, Mary F. 16, Riley S. 13 6-18-165/169

Obediah Brown 70, Polly 58 (w) 12-2-14

Polk Brown 35, Mary 33, Florence 10, Mary 8, Franklin SHULL 36 (c)(Trader) 1-14-114

R. Brown 21: see John McClendon

Robert Brown 28 (Merchant), Sarah 24: see Andrew Anderson

Samuel J. Brown 25 5-7-57

Susan Brown 19 (B): see William Thomas

William Brown 67, Sarah 32 (w) 12-4-33

William B. Brown 26 (Carpenter), Sarah E. 26, Elora E. 5, Laurence N. 2 6-18-167/170

1900 CENSUS

Alice E. Brown 25, Josephine 12, Rachael N. 10, Lucinda E. 7: see Rachael Formens(?) (B)

Ben Brown 29: see Phoebe Rhea (B)

Bessie Brown 8: see Harry D. Martin

Bonnie Brown 21 (1879) 8-275B-140 (B)

Calumma Brown 52 (Unk-M 20), Selina 40 (Unk-M 20-0-0), Chaney O'RANKINS 80 (m)(Unk-Wd 7-2), Harry SWAFFORD 7 (adopted s)(Aug 1892), Nathniel TALLY 6 (adopted s)(Unk), Arnold 4 (adopted s)(Unk) 8-318B-163/169 (B)

Calvin C. Brown 43 (Ap 1857-M 21), Tennessee 38 (Jan 1862-M 21-7-7), Susie S. 17 (Aug 1882), Martin V. 14 (Mar 1886), Mollie B. 11 (Ap 1889), Arthur F. 7 (Nov 1892), Callie V. 3 (Sep 1896), Estella 1 (May 1899) 3-209A-158/172

Charlie Brown 67 (Oct 1832-NY/NY/NY-M 15)(Physician), Birdy 30 (Jan 1870-M 15-0-0)(Dressmaker), Birthy 12 (ne)(Jan 1888) 1-187A-161/169

David Brown 25 (Oct 1874-T/NC/NC), Mary 24 (Mar 1876-M 6-2-2), Edker 4 (Feb 1896), Gracy 2 (Feb 1898) 7-267A-317/322

Edward Brown 14: see Columbia H. Myers

Elbert R. Brown 42 (Jan 1858-M 20), Mary L. 34 (Ap 1866-M 20-7-7), Anna V. 14 (Ap 1886), Walter 11 (Ap 1889), Ida 8 (Jan 1892), Charles 4 (Dec 1895), William 1 (Feb 1899) 2-194B-65/67

Elia Brown 35 (Unk 1865-M 10), Matilda 31 (Mar 1869-M 10-4-4), Judson 10 (May 1890), Anus 8 (May 1892), Henry 6 (Jan 1894), Auston 3 (Aug 1896) 8-285A-325/327 (B)

Eliza Brown 9: see John J.(?) Tucker

Isaac J. Brown 55 (Oct 1844-M 17), Mary F. 36 (July 1863-M 17-3-2), Julia A. 15 (Mar 1885), Cleo 13 (Jan 1887), Ida WOMACK 19 (sil)(May 1881), Lester MARTIN (B) 14 (boarder)(Unk), Evans LAWSON (B) 13 (boarder)(Unk) 6-248A-158/160

James Brown 29 (Aug 1870-M 4), Eva E. 30 (Ap 1870-M 4-1-1), Lura M. 3 (July 1896) 13-304B-279/289

James L. Brown 24 (May 1876-M 0), Malicy 21 (Jan 1879-M 0-0-0), Ada WHITEHOUSE 5 (ne)(Jan 1895-T/NC/T), Cornelia 2 (Ap 1898) 6-243A-70 (B)

Jim H. Brown 45 (Oct 1854-M 22), Rachel J. 44 (May 1856-T/Va/T-M 22-7-5), John N. 21 (May 1879) (School Teacher), Ida A. 16 (Ap 1884), Benjamin F. 11 (Sep 1888), Laura A. 9 (July 1890), Mary J. 6 (Sep 1893) 6-240A-12

John Brown 56 (Ap 1844-M 36), Mary 62 (May 1838-M 36-11-7), John 26 (Mar 1874), Auther 23 (Jan 1877), Beulah 20 (d)(Oct 1879) 10187A-160/168

John C. Brown 44 (Feb 1856-M 13)(Boarding House Keeper), Martha J. 35 (Oct 1864-T/Va/T-M 13-1-1), Loy G. 12 (Aug 1887) 10-331B-244/259

John R. Brown 30 (Ap 1870-M 1)(Manufacturer), Laura N. 17 (Mar 1883-M 1) 13-306A-311/323

Joseph Brown 21: see Louis Sharp

Joseph Brown 31 (Unk-Ala/Va/Ala-M 11)(Furnaceman), Annie 31 (Ap 1869-Ga/Ga/Ga-M 11-4-4)(Washing & Ironing), Virgil R. 9 (July 1890-Ga), Clifford B. 7 (Feb 1893-Ga), Ella M. 5 (May 1895-Ala), Hattie G. 2 (May 1898-Ala) 10-330A-213/226

Joseph Brown 74 (Jan 1826-M 2), Margaret J. 54 (Feb 1846-M 2-1-0), Elmore WRIGHT 34 (boarder)(Sep 1865-M 2), Virginia E. WRIGHT 34 (boarder)(Sep 1865-Ala/Ala/Ala-M 2-2-0) 6-240A-11

Kattie Brown 33: see Fred W. Chattin

Kittie Brown 19: see George W. Foster

Lottie F. Brown 47 (Aug 1852-NY/NY/NY-Wd 11-7), Lucy 20 (Aug 1879-T/NY/NY), Fred L. 17 (Nov 1882), Emory H. 15 (July 1884), Thos K. 10 (Dec 1889), Edeth W. 8 (Jan 1892) 4-225A-227/231 (Clear Creek Road)

Lucion M. Brown 43 (Dec 1856-NC/NC/NC-M 10), Mary 40 (Nov 1859-Ga/Ga/Ga-M 10-4-3), Artie M. 8 (Jan 1892), Charly 6 (July 1893) 10-329B-207/220 (B)

Nathaniel C. Brown 39 (Feb 1861-M 15), Lydia M. 32 (June 1867-Ga/Ga/Ga-M 15-6-5), Hulda L. 14 (Ap 1886), Curtain H. 10 (Aug 1889), Joseph B. 8 (Oct 1891), Hester L. 6 (Mar 1894), Fletcher B. 3 (Nov 1896) 6-240B-13

Richard R. Brown 22 (Sep 1877-M 0), Altha 21 (Dec 1878-M 0-0-0), Edward KIMBRO 19 (boarder)(Dec 1880) 6-246B-132/133

Samuel Brown 45 (Mar 1855-M 19), Laura L. 36 (May 1864-Ga/Ga/SC-M 19-9-9), Robert L. 19 (Jan 1881), William E. 18 (Dec 1882), Luther E. 15 (Mar 1885), Lether E. 13 (May 1887), Rosa L. 10 (June 1889), Walter L. 8 (Dec 1891), Sherman A. 5 (Aug 1894), Mary I. 3 (Feb 1897), McKinley 3/12 (Aug 1899) 5-236A-162

Saphronia Brown 60: see John Morgan

Walter Brown 14: see John Mayott

Will Brown 21 (Aug 1878-M 3)(Coke Puller), Lenny 26 (July 1879-M 3-2-1), Tillie 1 (Sep 1899) 10-258A-158/162 (B)

William Brown 21, Walter 11: see Samuel Vincent

William Brown 46 (May 1854-Ill/Ky/Oh-M 19)(Furniture Merchant), Phebe A. 51 (Jan 1849-Oh/Maine/Oh-M 19-0-0) 8-314B-82/85

William B. Brown 47 (July 1852-M 25)(Carpenter), Sarah F. 46 (Oct 1853-T/Va/T-M 25-8-8), Lawrence E. 22 (Mar 1878), Charles O. 17 (Sep 1882), William W. 13 (Ap 1887), Cornelius F. 10 (Nov 1889), Mabel E. 7 (July 1892), Author 4 (Mar 1896) 6-240A-9

William G. Brown 31 (Ap 1869-M 6), Bertha C. 22 (Oct 1877-M 6-2-2), Alma L. 4 (Ap 1896), Roy E. 11/12 (July 1899) 9-228A-11

William F. P. Brown 55 (Ap 1845-M 33), Mary J. 53 (Jan 1847-M 33-2-2), Mattie ROBINSON 44 (Mar 1856) (House Keeper) 14-218A-113/115

William M. Brown 46 (June 1853-M 19)(Sheriff), Ida* 36 (Jan 1864-M 19-10-9), William M. 18 (Dec 1881) (Jailor), Cleveland 17 (Jan 1883)(Time Keeper, DC&I Co), Robert 15 (Jan 1885)(Telegraph Messenger), Samuel 13 (Ap 1887), Thomas 10 (Aug 1889), Archie 8 (Feb 1892), Hazel 6 (Nov 1893), Ruth 4 (Dec 1895), Joseph 2 (Dec 1897), Sarah GOINS 47 (Unk-M 2-8-5)(House Servant) 10-331B-248/263 [*nee Vyles]

MARRIAGES

Alfred T. Brown to Maud Taylor, 30 Dec 1896, Henry W. Webb MG 4-97

Amanda M. Brown to Andrew L. Anderson q.v.

Anna Brown to Jessie Womack q.v.

Bertie L. Brown to Richard D. Davis q.v.

C. A. Brown to S. E. Miller, 2 Mar 1885 (8 Mar), T. H. McPherson JP 1-479

C.M. Brown to Lillian Martin, 5 May 1891, J.J. Burnett MG 4-26

C.R. Brown to Bertey Marrs, 25 May 1883 (27 May), T.L. Long JP 1-472

C.W. Brown to Mattie A. Blevins, 5 Sep 1889 (7 Sep), J.L. Prater ?? 1-582

Charley Brown to Martha Holston, 31 Jan 1896, J.P. Phillips MG 4-94

Churchwell C. Brown to N.J. McClendon, 18 Feb 1866 (same), Daniel Broyles JP 1-#890

D.R. Brown to Elizabeth B. Loden, 27 June 1873 (3 July), J.P. Roddy MG 1-#1285

Eddie Brown(?) to William Wampler q.v.

Elisha Brown to Sarah Porter, 27 Aug 1874 (13 Sep), E.N. Ganaway JP 1-#1353

F.H. Brown to Mattie E. Crawford, 1 Aug 1893, John F. Price MG 4-59

Florence B. Brown to Charles H. Mills q.v.

G.A. Brown to Sallie F. Gray, 24 Mar 1895, J.F. Hale MG 4-85

G.W. Brown to M.C. Grussham, 2 Aug 1878 (no return) 1-#1572
Gertie Brown to W. M. Trusley q.v.
H.A. Brown (27, Cherokee Co, Ga) to Rachael Grinder (21, Augusta, Ga), 17 Aug 1881, Thompson Ashburn MG CPC 4-3(29) (B)
Herman Brown(?) to Birtie Stephens, 27 Jan 1896, A.N. Jackson MG 4-88
Hester Brown to W. W. Bowles q.v.
Ida Brown to George Foster q.v.
Ida Brown to Abb Mariott q.v.
Isaac Brown to L.C. Brady, 20 Dec 1867 (31 Dec), J.B. McAllen MG 1-#993
Isaac Brown to Rebecca Waterhouse, 30 June 1880 (same), James Johnson JP 1-#1734
J.H. Brown to R.J. Zeigler, 22 Aug 1877 (same), J.H. Locke JP 1-#1507
J.J. Brown to T.A. Earwood, 26 June 1880 (27 June), A.J. Pritchett MG 1-#1733
J.L. Brown to Margaret J. Gay [license] or Gray [bond], 23 July 1897 (24 July), H.B. Burditt MG, Wm Wilkey W 2-164
J.L. Brown to Malisa Cox, 18 Sep 1899 (19 Sep), E.W. Mort MG, Wm Brown W 3-35
James Brown to Jane Miller, 23 July 1867 (same), Daniel Broyles JP 1-#960
James Brown to Emily Cross, 28 Ap 1887 (same), John Howard MG 1-525
James Brown to Eva Card, 2 Feb 1896, W.R. Grimsley MG 4-93
Jessee Brown to Ruth C. Crisp, 26 Oct 1854 (29 Oct), N.H. Long JP 1-#462
Joel A. Brown to Sarah J. Jenkins, 4 Aug 1900 (5 Aug), A.P. Hayes JP, J.S. Brown & L.C. McNabb W 3-195
John Brown to Mary Ann Rose, 1 Aug 1868 (2 Aug), Wm Low JP 1-#1021
John M. Brown to Elizabeth Smith, 25 Nov 1869 (same), W.F. Buttram MG 1-#1127
Joseph Brown to Cornelia Yarnell, 6 May 1891, D.J. Young ?? 4-32
L. A. Brown to James A. Hill q.v.
L. A. Brown to Virginia E. Rodgers, 29 Aug 1891, W. A. Howard MG 4-32
L. C. Brown to A.C. Qualls, 15 Nov 1885 (16 Nov), Taylor Russell JP 1-459
Larkin Brown (32, Cumberland Co) to Catharine Clack (26, Fentress Co), 30 July 1881, James P. Collins JP, Henry Mose & H.H. Stratton W 4-4(32)
Lewis Brown to Marthy Ratlief, 23 Nov 1865 (25 Nov), James Carson MG 1-#873
Lizzie Brown(?) to William Bean q.v.
Maggie Brown to Milton Poge q.v.
Martha J. Brown to John Compton q.v.
Mary Brown to Enoch T. Ritchie q.v.
Mary Brown(?) to J. S. Long q.v.
Mary Brown to Ben Marney(?) q.v.
Mary A. Brown to Jacob Clark q.v.
Mary F. Brown to J. P. Quinn q.v.
Mattie Brown to Spencer Jones q.v. (B)
N.L. Brown to Maggie Gattes, 5 Mar 1885 (same), A.J. Pritchett MG 1-498
Nettie Brown(?) to James R. Sharp q.v.
Owen Brown to Adeline Essex, 24 Sep 1898, R.M. Trentham JP 4-96
Pearly Brown to Clarence McDonald q.v.
R.J.A. Brown to George Henderson q.v.
Richard Brown (26) to Cynthia Crawford (17, Ala), 10 Aug 1882, T.H. McPherson JP, C.C. Jones & G. Marshall W 4-10(93)
Rufus K. Brown to Katie C. Thomas, 12 Mar 1888 (13 Mar), A.D. Stewart MG 1-544
Sallie A. Brown to John Morgan q.v.
Sallie B. Brown to Henry T. Patton q.v.
Sarah Brown(?) to Thomas Whitacer q.v.
Susan Brown to George Henderson q.v.
Susie Brown to Elijah Newton q.v.
Thomas Brown to Mary Noble, 30 Mar 1896, William White MG 4-92
Victoria Brown to George Gillespie q.v.
W.G. Brown to Bertha Broyles, 4 Feb 1894, John T. Price MG 4-63
W.H. Brown to Minnie A. Coal, 29 Nov 1880 (30 Nov), James Johnson JP 1-292
William A. Brown to Eliza J. Winfrey, 13 Oct 1870 (same), John W. Thompson MG 1-#1167
William B. Brown to Sarah Ziegler, 14 Nov 1874 (no return) 1-#1371
William F.P. Brown to Mary J. Roddy, 22 Ap 1867 (25 Ap), S. Phillips MG 1-#949

- - - - - - - - - - - - -

BROWNING

1880 CENSUS
George Browning 26 (Carpenter & Joiner): see Thos Ingle

- - - - - - - - - - - - -

BROYLES / BROILES

1860 CENSUS
Cornelius Broyles 50, Mary H. 27, Onslo G. 26, Robert C. 27 (Reading Medicine) 8-23-157
Daniel Broyles 57, Harriet N. 40, Isaac N. 15, Mary V. 13, Eliza F. 11, Harriet J. 9, William P. 6, James M. 4, Susan A. 25, Mary THOMPSON 70 4-22-353
Joseph Broyles 38 (Blacksmith), Barbary 36, Franklin M. 14, Gillespie 12, William G. 10, Robert N. 8, Darius E. 6, John W. 2 5-33-219
Nile M. Broyles 41, Elenor 32, Mark 19, Addison 7, Isabella 5, Enoch 3 2-75-511
Polly Broyles 70 (Va): see William K. Ganaway
Sanders D. Broyles 37, Delila 34 (Ala), William T. 10, Archald C. 9, Cordelia 7, Alfred 4, Mary E. 2 8-9-52
1870 CENSUS
Daniel Broyles 67, Harriette 50, Isaac N. 24, Mary V. 22, Eliza T. 20, Harriette J. 18, William P. 16, James M. 14, Susan A. 12, John F. 7, Mary THOMPSON 80 4-7-42
Franklin Broyles 23, Paralee 24, Luhanna E. 4, Joseph A. 1 7-7-55
Joseph A. Broyles 48 (Blacksmith), Barbery Ann 46, Robert M. 17, Darius E. 14, John W. 12, Henry C. 9, Andrew A. 7, Sarah A. 4 5-8-62
Nile M. Broyles 51, Eleanor 42, Adison M. 17, Sarah I. 15, Enoch C. 13, John W. 6 2-14-101
Polly Broyles 83 (Va): see William F. Ganaway

Sanders D. Broyles 46, Dillah 52, William T. 21, Archibald C. 19, Cordelia 17, Alfred 14, Mary E. 12, Cornelia 7 8-14-100
William Broyles 19, Catharine 17 3-11-79

1880 CENSUS

Alfred Broiles 33: see Caroline Locke (B)
D. Broyles 77, Harriet 60, Mary 34, E. 32 (d), Jane 29, Wm 26, Jam 24 (s), S.A. 22 (d), J.A. 17 (s) 3-30-245
Darius Broyles 24, Mahala A. 28, Erley B. 3 (d), William P. 2, Adi E. 7/12 5-5-43
F. Mc. Broyles 33, D.P. 33 (w), R.H. 13 (d), J.A. 11 (s), O.M. 10 (s), R.H. 7 (s), W.T. 5 (s), Harit 9/12 7-26-223
I.N. Broyles 35, Mary 29 (w), Scott 5 (s), S.J. 4 (s), Addie I. (d) 3-30-246
James G. Broyles 31, Rhody A. 29, Birtha C. 2, Barba E. 3/12 5-5-38
Joseph Broyles 58 (Blacksmith), Barby A. 55, John W. 20, Henry 18, Andy 17, Barby C. 16 10-31-234/244
Nile Broyles 61, Eleanor 52, Adison 28 (at school), Enoch 23, John W. 16 (Drummer), Belle EASTLAND 25 (d), Henry 23 (sl), Charles 2 (gs), Mark 1 (gs), Albert RAY (Mu) 17 (Servant), Charles SMITH (B) 17 (Servant) 2-26-204
Robert C. Broyles 47 (Doctor), Mary J. 36, Clayton A. 12, Henry Y. 8, Woodville L. 5 5-6-51
S.D. Broyles 56, Delidy 60, A.C. 29 (s), Alfred 24 (s), C.D. 18 (s) 8-2-16
W.T. Broyles 30, Melia 27, S.W. 3, Tom D. 1, Son FLEMMING 14 (ne), Samg 5 (nw) 8-1-4
William Broyles 26, Cathety 26 10-31-235/245

1900 CENSUS

Addison Broyles 47 (Jan 1853-S)(Postmaster, Rhea Springs) 2-199A-146/151
Albert Broyles 36 (Feb 1864-M 10)(Drawing Coke), Sarah 33 (Nov 1866-M 10-7-4), Osca 9 (Sep 1890), Martha J. 8 (Feb 1892), Scenia 6 (Oct 1893), McKinley W. 3 (Oct 1896), Lizzie ROBERDS 21 (Mar 1879)(Servant) 10-253A-64 (B)
Arch C. Broyles 49 (Jan 1851-M 16)(Salesman), Flora 44 (Dec 1855-M 16-4-2), Mabel 12 (Aug 1887), Creed F. 10 (July 1889) 15-270B-49
Charley Broyles 18: see Jim Coaplin (B)
Cornelius D. Broyles 38 (Aug 1861-M 9)(Shipping Clerk), Fannie A. 33 (Ap 1867-M 9-2-2), Willie A. 8 (Oct 1891), Hubert S. 5 (Sep 1894) 15-270B-50
Darius E. Broyles 43 (Jan 1857-M 23), Mahala 49 (May 1851-M 23-9-8), Urecy 23 (Aug 1876)(Dressmaker), Lizzie B. 18 (Nov 1881), Gracey B. 16 (Mar 1884), Sue E. 13 (Jan 1887), Lida P. 10 (Nov 1889), Eunic 8 (Ap 1892) 5-230A-42
Enoch C. Broyles 43 (Ap 185?-M 6), Maggie 31 (June 1868-M 6-1-1), Howard M. 2 (Oct 1897) 2-196B-98/101 [Enoch married Margaret Matlock, dau of Charles L. and Louisa Howard Matlock, on 28 Aug 1895 in McMinn County]
Ida Broyles 3: see Elizabeth Potter
Isaac N. Broyles 55 (Aug 1844-M 27), Mary 49 (Jan 1851-T/Va/T-M 27-8-6), Windfield 25 (Feb 1875), Samuel H. 23 (Dec 1876), Adda 21 (Dec 1878), Thurman C. 19 (Ap 1881), Charles R. 14 (Dec 1885), Ethel 6 (Ap 1894) 14-224A-171/175
James G. Broyles 51 (July 1848-M 30), Rhoda A. 49 (May 1851-M 30-7-4), Barbara E. 20 (Feb 1880), Ula M. 5 (Sep 1894) 5-239A-212
John F. Broyles 37 (Oct 1862-T/Va/T-M 10), Belle 29 (Oct 1870-M 10-4-4), Hattie O. 9 (Jan 1891), Laura A. 7 (Oct 1892), Thomas D. 5 (Nov 1894), Frederick 2 (Sep 1897), Susan A. 42 (si)(May 1858) 14-222A-172/176
Lena Broyles 16: see William T. Gass
Tipton Broyles 50 (Aug 1849-M 26)(Dry Goods Salesman), Permilla 47 (Nov 1852-M 26-7-4), Thomas 21 (Ap 1879), Boston 15 (Sep 1884), Mary 4 (Aug 1895) 8-288A-401/40
William P. Broyles 45 (June 1854-T/NC/NC-M 16), Amanda B. 47 (Dec 1852-T/NC/NC-M 16-2-2), Farley C. 15 (Oct 1884), Homer G. 9 (June 1890) 14-222A-168/172

MARRIAGES

A.C. Broyles to Flora Rogers, 1 Ap 1884 (same), J.H. Weaver MG 1-464
Ada Broyles to Hinegar Buttram q.v.
Adalade Broyles to H.C. Collins q.v.
Albert Broyles to Sarah Gollahu(?), 12 Dec 1889 (same), L.M. Moore ?? 1-594
Anney Broyles to Madison Beasley q.v.
Belle Broyles to Henry Eastland q.v.
Bertha Broyles to W. G. Brown q.v.
C.D. Broyles to Fannie D. Allen, 22 Dec 1890, L.L.H. Carlock MG 4-20
Darius E. Broyles to M.A. Compton, 12 Aug 1875 (same), W.R. Ganaway MG 1-#1404
E. A. Broyles to John W. Whittenburg q.v.
Eliza T. Broyls to B. F. Lee q.v.
Emma Broyles to J. H. Rogers q.v.
F. Mc. Broyles to Darcus Purser, 26 Aug 1865 (27 Aug), John Howard MG 1-#846
J.F. Broyles to Bell Brady, 8 Feb 1890 (9 Feb), John Wolsey MG 1-595
I.N. Broyles to Mary P. Ganaway, 12 Aug 1873 (no return) 1-#1294
James C. Broyles to Roda A. Compton, 5 Ap 1869 (same), Bailey Minick JP 1-#1051
John W. Broyles to A.E. Ganaway, 7 June 1880 (same), John Howard MG 1-#1731
L. B. Broyles to T. D. Broyles q.v.
M. E. Broyles to H. C. Rose q.v.
R.C. (Mrs.) Broyles [nee Jane Mansell] to Joseph Henry Tephtallow q.v.
T.D. Broyles to L.B. Broyles, 29 June 1900 (1 July), J.E. Swicher MG, A.P. Haggard W 3-177
W.P. Broyles to Amanda B. Brady, 24 Dec 1883 (same), J.H. Weaver MG 1-471
W.T. Broyles to P.C. Johnson, 10 Aug 1874 (11 Aug), J.H. Keith MG 1-#1348
William G. Broyles to Catharine Horner, 18 Aug 1869 (same), Bailey Minicks JP 1-#1108

- - - - - - - - - - - - -

BRUCE / BRUSE

1860 CENSUS

Haney Bruse 1: see John N. Ragsdale

MARRIAGE

Sarah E. Bruce to W.J. or M.J. Davenport q.v.

- - - - - - - - - - - - -

BRUMLOW

1900 CENSUS
Beulah Brumlow 10: see James M. Rogers

- - - - - - - - - - - - -

BRUN / BRUNE– see BUNN

- - - - - - - - - - - - -

BRUNAGIN / BRUNNAGIN

1900 CENSUS
W--?--ain Brunnagin 58 (Unk-M 5)(Bricklayer), Sarah 43 (Mar 1857-M 5-0-0), Sarah BROOKS 65 (ml)(July 1834-NC/NC/NC-Wd 3-3) 8-313B-54/57
MARRIAGE
A. Brunagin to Sarah E. Brooks, 25 Dec 1895, G.W. Brewer MG 4-89

- - - - - - - - - - - - -

BRUNER

1900 CENSUS
Henry Bruner 28: see William Eberhart (B)

- - - - - - - - - - - - -

BRUNET / BRUNNET

1860 CENSUS
David S. Brunnet 33, Hannah M. 33, Margaret A. 11, Elijah 8, Betsy J. 6, Sarah C. 4, Mary A. 1, Margaret A. FINE 67 3-68-465
Manerva Brunet 35 (NC), David C. 10, Erastus 7, Daniel 5, Susan A. 1, Leonard WAISNER 25 (NC) 2-74-502

- - - - - - - - - - - - -

BRYANT / BRYAN

1860 CENSUS
John H. Bryant 63, Sarah E. 40, Richard J. 7, Sarah J. 6 8-21-142
1870 CENSUS– None
1880 CENSUS
A.G. Bryant 70, Polly 69, L.E.* 26 (s), M.A. 22 (dl), N.A. 1/12 (gs) 3-17-130 [*Leonidas married Mary A. Johnson on 18 May 1879 in Meigs County]
Joseph Bryant 27, Ann 19, Archibald 1/12, James 21 (b) 2-41-336
M. Bryant 27: see M. M. Thompson (B)
1900 CENSUS
John Bryant 62 (Sep 1837-NY/NY/Conn-M 6)(Grocer), Kate 35 (Dec 1864-Oh/Oh/Oh-M 6-1-1), Jessie 3 (July 1896) 10-325B-114/118
Lesser Bryant 18: see Jack Simpson (B)
Steve Bryant 33: see James Jackson (B)
MARRIAGE
George T. Bryant to Etta Brackett, 10 Dec 1898 (11 Dec), W.R. Grimsley MG, S.W. Bryant W 2-354
J.A. Bryant to Sarah Elsey, 7 June 1890 (same), J.L. Henry JP 1-601
J.A. Bryant to Kate Thomas, 1 Jan 1894, John T. Price MG 4-63
J.T. Bryant to A.V. McFerson, 31 Dec 1877 (1 Jan 1878), M.G. --?--onts MG 1-#1514
Jack Bryant to Matty Williams, 30 Sep 1876 (same), T.D. Kelly JP 1-#1462
Morgan Bryan to Susan J. Cawood, 3 Nov 1879 (4 Nov), James Johnson JP 1-#1683
Sarah T. Bryant to Francis Land q.v.

- - - - - - - - - - - - -

BRYSON / BRISON

1860 CENSUS
Abraham Bryson 66 (Ga), Hanah 33 8-12-80
Andrew J. Bryson 43, Margaret 36, Sarah A. 15, John 14, James 10, Bud 2, Infant 2/12 2-78-527
1870 CENSUS
Abraham Bryson 78 (Ga), Hannah 45, William A. 8 8-9-60
Andrew J. Bryson 54, Margaret J. 45, John H. 24, Thomas S. 12, Robert H.L. 6, Sarah A. BURNETT 25 1-2-10
1880 CENSUS
Andrew Bryson 62 (works in Shoe Shop), Margaret 55 2-22-176
Hanah Bryson 54, W. A. 17 (s) 8-15-125
John Bryson 34 (Saddler), Rebecca 24, Frederick 5, Thomas 2/12 2-22-117
Thomas Bryson 22, Alice 18, Alice 8/12 11-42-339
1900 CENSUS
Margaret J. Bryson 75: see Thomas H. Robinson
Rebecca Bryson 45 (Aug 1854-Wd 27-10-6)(Dressmaker), Marjory I. 20 (Nov 1889), Rebecca A. 16 (Feb 1884), John R. 13 (Dec 1886), Harry W. 10 (Jan 1890) 14-213A-7/7
MARRIAGES
Alice Bryson (Mrs.) to J. H. Secrest(?) q.v.
John H. Bryson to Rebecca A. Abernathy, 27 Sep 1873 (28 Sep), S. Phillips MG 1-#1303
Sallie Brison to S. D. Rudd q.v.
Sarah A. Bryson to Flemming Brunnett q.v.
T.S. Bryson to Alice Carpenter, 16 Nov 1878 (17 Nov), G.W. Wassom JP 1-#1586

- - - - - - - - - - - - -

BUCHANON / BUCKHANON / BUCKANON

1900 CENSUS
Emma Buckhanon 30 (Jan 1870-Wd 4-4)(Washwoman), Flora 16 (Mar 1844), Myrtle 12 (Aug 1897), Maud 8 (Ap 1892), Walter 6 (June 1893), Andrew WHITE 40 (boarder)(Mar 1860-Wd) 10-258A-149/153 (B)
John Buchanon 28 (Unk-M 9), Anna 21 (July 1878-M 9-4-2), Herbert 9 (Mar 1892), Myrtle 3 (Jan 1897) 6-242B-58
Mary Buchanon 56 (Mar 1844-Wd 5-3)(Washwoman), Oscar 13 (July 1886), Delia A. JENKINS 20 (d)(Oct 1879-M 1-0-0)(Washwoman) 6-242B-55
William J. Buchanan 33 (Ap 1867-Va/Va/Va-M 9)(Dentist), Josephine E. 41 (Jan 1859-Ky/Ky/Ky-M 9-7-6), Katherine PIESATT 18 (sd)(June 1881-Va), Ada V. 17 (sd) (June 1882-Va), Martha 15 (sd)(Dec 1884-Va), William 10 (ss)(Mar 1890-Va) 8-317B-149/154

MARRIAGES

D.M. Buchanon to Martha A. Kelly, 19 July 1889 (21 July), R.S. Mason JP 1-576

Daniel Buchannon to Ellen Panky(?), 25 July 1889 (same), Rev. S.W. Wych 1-576

Elizabeth Buchannon to R. T. King q.v.

Elizabeth B..ckhanon to V. L. Hurst q.v.

John Buchanan to Emma McDonald, 3 Sep 1885 (same), S.W. Burnett MG 1-491

John Buchannon to Fannie Wright, 9 May 1891, J.L. Henry JP 4-27

John Buchanan [Buckhannon on license] to Susan J. Webb, 28 Nov 1900 (29 Nov), J.B. Trotter MG, Ben(?) Webb W 3-249

- - - - - - - - - - - - -

BUCHER

MARRIAGE

Carmilla S. Bucher to Darius S. Bowler q.v.

- - - - - - - - - - - - -

BUCK

1900 CENSUS

Molly Buck 32: see Robert Ray

MARRIAGE

Minnie Buck to James Barnes q.v.

- - - - - - - - - - - - -

BUCKNER

1900 CENSUS

Walter Buckner 24: see Mattie Jones (B)

MARRIAGE

Permelia Buckner to James K. Woods q.v.

- - - - - - - - - - - - -

BUETENNER

1900 CENSUS

William Buetenner(?) 37 (June 1862-M 9)(Coal Miner), Martha A. 33 (Sep 1866-M 9-4-4), Unist 7 (June 1892), Orton 5 (Sep 1894), Lucy E. 4 (Jan 1896), Creed D. 2 (Feb 1898) 10-255B-103/105

- - - - - - - - - - - - -

BUFFINGTON

1900 CENSUS

John F. Buffington 19: see William Lindsey

MARRIAGE

W.W. Buffington to M.J. Russ, 19 Jan 1854 (no return) 1-#435

- - - - - - - - - - - - -

BUGUO

1900 CENSUS

Henry H. Buguo 56 (May 1844-Pa/Germany/Do-M 1) (Lawyer), Mary J. 50 (Dec 1849-T/T/NJ-M 31-6-6), Maggie 29 (Oct 1870)(School Teacher), Samuel J. 26 (Nov 1873)(Manufacturer), Helen 22 (Oct 1877), Jennie 17 (May 1883) 12-305A-289/300

- - - - - - - - - - - - -

BUNCH

MARRIAGE

Elizabeth Bunch to G.(?) J. Ridings q.v.

- - - - - - - - - - - - -

BUNN / BUINN / BRUN

1880 CENSUS

Bazelia Buinn 54, Margaret 45, Julius 22, Tennessee 20, Georgian 16, Charlie 17, Horace 14, Luscious 12, Fleacis 10, John 8, Robert 7, Margaret 7, Walter 3 1-9-70

1900 CENSUS

George Bunn 45 (Oct 1854-M 12), Nancy 35 (Aug 1864-T/Ga/NC-M 12-5-3), Edgar 9 (July 1890), Andrew 4 (Aug 1895), Clinton 2 (Mar 1898), Lillie 16 (ne)(Oct 1883) 8-313B-62/65 (B)

Mary H. Bunn 36 (Feb 1864-Wd 6-6)(Washwoman), Elbert 17 (Mar 1883), Pearl 15 (Sep 1885), Henrietta 14 (Dec 1885), Fred 13 (Dec 1884), Ada 8 (Feb 1892), Thomas 5 (July 1894), Henry ESKRIDGE 19 (boarder) 8-315A-91/94 (B)

Reuben Brun 67 (June 1832-T/NC/NC-M 24)(Grocery Merchant), Elizabeth 43 (Mar 1857-T/T/Ky-M 24-3-3), Lula 19 (Sep 1880), Colonel 17 (Mar 1883) 8-313B-60/63

Rhea Bunn 14, Jay 14: see John Pogue

MARRIAGES

S. E. Bunn to G. P. Parker q.v.

Virginia E. Bunn (Mrs.) to Elmore Wright q.v.

- - - - - - - - - - - - -

BUNTIN

1900 CENSUS

Mattie B. Buntin 25: see Olie Hayward

- - - - - - - - - - - - -

BURCHARD

1870 CENSUS

Hamilton Burchard 42 (NY), Jane C. 42, George H. 15, Lucy E. 13, William S. 8, Henry F. 6, Mary G. 4 8-4-27

1880 CENSUS

G.H. Burchard 24, T.I. 24, M.A. 10/12 (d) 8-12-104

H. Burchard 50, J.C. 50, Wm 19, Lucia 23, Henry 16, Gertrude 14, S.C. 10 (d) 8-12-105

1900 CENSUS

George Burchard 44 (Nov 1855-T/NY/T-M 21), Thursday 44 (Mar 1856-M 21-7-7), Walter 17 (Aug 1882), Riley 14 (May 1886), John 12 (Sep 1887), Cora 7 (Jan 1893), Pearl 5 (Sep 1894), James 3 (Feb 1897) 8-288B-411/413

Hamilton Burchard 72 (Jan 1828-NY/Ver/NY-M 47), Jane 72 (Ap 1828-T/SC/NC-M 47-8-6), Gertrude 33 (Ap 1867) 8-289B-422/425

Henry Burchard 36 (Mar 1864-M 18)(Coal Miner), Martha K. 36 (Feb 1864-M 18-7-7), Mary J. 17 (Jan 1883), Horace S. 15 (May 1885), Eva L. 12 (Ap 1888), Winfred D. 8 (June 1891), Grant W. 6 (Nov 1893), Esther B. 4 (Jan 1896), Nellie M. 1 (July 1898) 8-288B-405/407

Henry(?) Burchard 61 (Feb 1839-NY/NY/NY-M 34)(Fruit Grower), Ellen 55 (Aug 1844-Mich/NY/N-M 34-6-4), Ethel 16 (July 1883-Mich) 7-265A-287/292

William Burchard 38 (June 1861-T/NY/T-M 19), Anna 34 (Ap 1866-M 19-10-10), Hattie 17 (Oct 1882), Lillie 15 (Aug 1884), Ansel 13 (Oct 1886), Urchal 11 (Sep 1888), Nora 8 (June 1891), Celia 7 (May 1893), Arnold 5 (Feb 1895), Glennie 3 (July 1896), Edith 3 (July 1896), Gracie 3/12 (Feb 1900) 8-288B-403/405

MARRIAGES

George Burchard to T.E. Stanfield, 1 May 1879 (same), Calvin Morgan JP 1-#1618

H.F. Burchard (18, Cranmore Cove) to Martha McPherson (18), 30 Ap 1882, Calvin Morgan JP, no witnesses 4-14(135)

Hamilton Burchard to Jane C. Gothard, 28 June 1853 (no return) 1-#413

L. E. Burchard to Moses Bottomley q.v.

Minnie Burchard to L. D. Pool q.v.

S. C. Burchard to W. H. Wolf q.v.

William S. Burchard (20) to Annie Die (15), 18 Jan 1882, W. Morgan JP, J.F. Morgan & A.A. Morgan W 8-4-27

\- - - - - - - - - - - - -

BURCHWOOD

1860 CENSUS

Hamilton Burchwod 32 (NY), Janes C. 32, Horace 6, George 4, Lucy 3, Susan 1 8-24-161

\- - - - - - - - - - - - -

BURDETT / BURDIT / BURDITT

1880 CENSUS

E. Burdett 35: see Isaac Jolley

1900 CENSUS

Howard Burdett 50 (Jan 1850-M 23), Mary E. 37 (Jan 1863-M 23-11-8), James 13 (Mar 1887), Clifford C. 8 (Ap 1892), Luella 5 (Feb 1895), Henry C. 3 (July 1897), Rosa L. 1/12 (May 1900) 5-236B-172

John Burditt 25 (Aug 1874-M 4)(Fireman, Saw Mill), Thurza G. 21 (May 1871-Oh/Oh/Oh-M 4-1-1), Cora 3 (Nov 1896) 4-224B-216/220 (Spring City & Dayton Road)

Lillie L. Burdett 16: see Samuel Shelby

Thomas H. Burditt 25 (Sep 1876-M 1), Cyntha 18 (June 1881-M 1-0-0) 3-200B-15/16

William R. Burdett 44 (Sep 1855-Oh/Ver/Oh-M 20), Ida M. 44 (Sep 1855-Oh/Mich/Conn-M 20-5-5), Walter J. 18 (Ap 1882-Oh), Gertrude A. 12 (July 1887-Oh), Mary I. 10 (June 1889-Oh), Lucy L. 6 (June 1893-Oh), George L. 5 (July 1894-Oh), Lantha 79 (m)(Oct 1820-Oh/Conn/Conn-Wd 5-2) 11-290A-6

MARRIAGES

Altie J. Burdett to W. E. Ward q.v.

Elvira Burdett to Jacob Garrison q.v.

F.L. Burdett to J.A. Riggs, 18 Oct 1898, A.M. Broyles JP 4-95

Howard Burdit to Eliza Smith, 15 Aug 1871 (no return) 1-#1204

Howard B. Burdett to Mary L. Smith, 22 Nov 1876 (same), John M. Bramlett MG 1-#1471

J.H. Burditt to Terza Stevens, 5 Aug 1896 (same), P.G. Roddy MG, J.H. Houston W 2-51

Jane Burditt to Joseph Webb q.v.

Martha A. Burdett to Elisha A. Neuby q.v.

Martha J. Burditt to Charles F. Newby q.v.

Mattie Burdett to York Davis q.v.

Rebecca Burdett to Mubcie(?) Pope q.v.

Thomas Burditt to Syntha Phelfrey, 24 Dec 1898 (25 Dec), J.M. Bramlett MG, G.A. Hughes W 2-363

Thomas H. Burdett to M.J. Millican, 11 Oct 1856 (14 Oct), R.T. Howard MG 1-#579

\- - - - - - - - - - - - -

BURDIN

MARRIAGE

J.G. Burdin to Jennie Carter, 15 July 1896 (16 July), H.S. Shaw ??, R.J. Killough W 2-43

\- - - - - - - - - - - - -

BURK

1900 CENSUS

Mandy Burk 45 (Mar 1855-Ga/NC/NC-D 7-6), Allen 17 (Sep 1882-Ga)(Coal Miner), Franklin 13 (Ap 1887-Ga)(Coal Miner), William 9 (Ap 1891-Ga), Glenn 5 (Aug 1894-Ga) 8-284A-311/313

MARRIAGE

Lillie Burk to W. C. Dillard q.v.

\- - - - - - - - - - - - -

BURKETT

MARRIAGE

Leutitia T. Burkett to James L. Miller q.v.

\- - - - - - - - - - - - -

BURKHALTER

1900 CENSUS

Jefferson D. Burkhalter 37 (Dec 1862-Ala/T/Ala-M 7)(Saloon Keeper), Elizabeth 27 (Mar 1873-Ill/Ga/Ga-M 7-1-1), Emma P. 1 (July 1898), Rebecca LOUALEN 22 (Oct 1877)(Household Servant) 10-327B-156/164

Thomas Burkhalter 23: see James D. Smith

MARRIAGE
J. P. Burkhalter to Lizzie Mealer, 9 Oct 1892, G.W. Brewer MG 4-51

- - - - - - - - - - - - -

BURKHART

MARRIAGE
Elizabeth Burkhart to Calvin Stephens q.v.

- - - - - - - - - - - - -

BURKMAN

1900 CENSUS
William P. Burkman 26: see Lemuel M. Cartright

- - - - - - - - - - - - -

BURNELL

1900 CENSUS
Carl Burnell 9: see John Purcer

- - - - - - - - - - - - -

BURNETT– see BARNETT

- - - - - - - - - - - - -

BURREL / BUREL / BURRELL

1900 CENSUS
Holland Burrel 20: see Hiram Moore (B)
Melvin Burrell 45 (Sep 1854-Ga/Ga/Ga-M 21), Louisa 41 (Mar 1839-Ga/Ga/Ga-M 21-4-4), Louis 18 (June 1881-Ga), William 17 (Nov 1882-Ga), Grover C. 16 (Dec 1883-Ga), Martin L. 11 (July 1888-Ga) 8-280B-241/243
Spencer Burrel 35 (Unk 1865-M 16)(Coal Miner), Lola 34 (Unk 1866-M 16-7-3), Nellie 15 (Unk 1885), Ella M. 6 (Unk 1894), Jack 1 (Mar 1899) 8-287B-383/385
MARRIAGE
Mattie Burel to John Cunnyngham q.v.

- - - - - - - - - - - - -

BURSON

1870 CENSUS
Madison Burson(?) 14: see Jacob B. White

- - - - - - - - - - - - -

BURTON– see BARTON

- - - - - - - - - - - - -

BURWICK / BARWICK

1860 CENSUS
Polly Burwick 64 (SC), Mary I. 34, Sarah A. 32, Elizabeth 26, William 24, David H. 20, Liddia C. 2 8-18-123
John Barwick 30, Liddia 32, Mary J. 11, Martha E. 8, Julia 6, William A. 4, Darius W. 2 8-23-155

1870 CENSUS
John M. Burwick 39, Ludia 41, Mary Jane 20, Martha E. 17, Julia A. 15, William A. 13, Darius W. 11, Amanda 9, Arminta 6, David H. 4, Samuel H. 1 8-18-125
Mary Burwick 74 (NC), Sarah 40, William A. 35, Catharine 12 8-5-34
1880 CENSUS
J.M. Burwick 56, Lyddia 56, D.W. 22 (s), E.M. 17 (d), D.H. 15 (s), H.M. 11 (d), S.H. 12 (s), J.T. 9 (s), J.H. 9 (s) 11-41-329
Jas Burwick 30, M.H. 27 (w), T.E. 9 (d), R.H. 5 (s), J.F. 3 (s), C.A. 9/12 (d), L.R. 5 (d) 11-40-322
Mary Burwick 80: see William McPherson
William Burwick 45: see Elbert I. Cox

1900 CENSUS
Bandy Burwick 37: see Julia A. Morgan
David H. Burwick 34 (Mar 1866-M 7), Mary 23 (Aug 1876-M 7-3-2), Orie M. 11 (Jan 1889), Lizzie M. 8 (Jan 1892), Joseph L. 3 (Feb 1897), Minnie E. 1/12 (Ap 1900) 11-293B-85/86
John H. Burwick 24 (July 1875-M 0)(Coal Miner), Sarah E. 19 (May 1887-M 0-0-0) 11-293B-85/85
John M. Burwick 69 (Nov 1830-M 50), Lydia 71 (Nov 1828-M 50-11-9), Ida E. FISHER 13 (gd)(Mar 1887-T/Ind/T), Zella E. 10 (gd)(Feb 1890) 11-293B-84
Samuel Burwick 31 (June 1868-M 10)(Coal Miner), Martha 27 (June 1872-M 10-4-3), William H. 6 (Mar 1894), Martha M. 4 (Dec 1895), Floyd C. 10/12 (July 1899) 11-293B-87/88
MARRIAGES
Amanda Burwick to W. W. McPherson q.v.
Catharine Barwick to W. W. McFerson q.v.
Catharine L. Burwich to Jesse L. Mathews q.v.
D.H. Burwick to Mary Campbell, 28 May 1893, S.S. Franklin JP 4-59
D.W. Burwick to Lisa Walker, 26 Ap 1887 (27 Ap), F.R. Morgan JP 1-535
David Burwick to Ella Pickett, 14 July 1886 (same), Jas P. Walker JP 1-505
Elizbeth J. Burwick to James Bottomlee q.v.
James Burwick to Ada Weller, 19 Ap 1892, R.S. Mason JP 4-40
John Burwick [Byrd marked through] to Lizzie Gothard, 17 Ap 1900 (22 Ap), Heniger Morgan JP, David Burwick W 3-143
Juli Ann Burwick to Jos A. Morgan q.v.
Martha Burwick to John W. Morgan q.v.
Mary Burwick to Hardy Chadwick q.v.
Mintees(?) Burwick to Ed Fisher q.v.
S.H. Burwick to Jannie Walker, 21 Oct 1890, E.F. Givins JP 4-20

- - - - - - - - - - - - -

BUSBY

1880 CENSUS
G.W. Busby or Brisley 29, Thomas H. 6, Susan L. 3 5-1-8
John H. Busby 34, Betsy J. 40 5-2-19
John Busby 13, Margaret Busby 67 (m)("living with son") 5-3-21
Thomas W. Busby 25, Palina J. 19, Rosey A. 11/12 5-3-20

- - - - - - - - - - - - -

BUSUM

1860 CENSUS

Paskill K. Busum 30, Mary A. 28, Nancy E. 1, Henry L. 3 1-86-584

BUTCHELDER

1870 CENSUS

Lynus Butchelder 60 (Conn), Amanda 48 (Ohio), Mark L. 20 (Wisc), Patsey J. 19 (Wisc), Amanda J. 16 (Wisc) 1-3-17

BUTLER / BUTTLAR

1900 CENSUS

James Buttlar 74 (Mar 1826-Va/Va/Va-M 38), Harriet 50 (Ap 1850-M 38-2-2)(Washwoman), Ike 25 (Sep 1874), Wilum 38 (July 1862) 1-184A-104/109 (B)

Joseph Butler 29: see Mattie Stewart (B)

MARRIAGES

Joseph R. Butler to Bessie L. Smith, 22 Aug 1900 (same), G.T. Mussington MG, J---ol Angel(?) W 3-204

Sophia Buttler to James West q.v.

BUTTRAM / BUTRAM / BARTRAM

1860 CENSUS

Elijah Buttram 71 (Va), Nancy [nee Harmon] 64 (Va), John S. 20 6-108-723

Elzy Buttram 37 (Ky), Susan [nee Locke] 31, Tennessee A. 11, Mounterville 9, Robert E. 8, Addison 6, John F. 4 6-106-724

1870 CENSUS

James C. Buttram 41, Syntha P. 37, Malinda T. 16, David O. 5, William F. 7/12 8-14-98

James G. Butram 45, Luvina 25, Lucy A. 22, Mary Jane 20, Sarah A. 15, John M. 13, William A. 7 10-4-25

Samuel Buttram 65 (Ky): see David W. Oldham

Tennessee Buttram 16: see William Fugate

William Buttram 34, Ann C. 32, James S. 13, Elijah 7, Nancy C. 3, John T. 5/12 6-2-10

1880 CENSUS

J.C. Butram 51, S.D. 47 (w), M.F. 26 (d), D.O. 14 (s), W.F. 10 (s), T.H. 8 (s), Wash MORGAN 56 (boarder) 8-17-145

Levena Buttram 34, Lucy A. 32 (si), Mary G. 30 (si), John M. 23 (b), William A. 17 (b), William A. GREEN 26, Sarah M. GREEN 22 or 24 (w), Ethel A. 8/12, Elae E. 8/12 10-26-205/211

1900 CENSUS

Cyntha D. Bartram 67: see Malinda Morgan

John M. Buttram 43 (Sep 1856-M 19)(Coal Miner), Mary J. 38 (June 1861-M 19-7-5), Nora A. 18 (Nov 1881), Maud 14 (Mar 1886), Olsie 9 (Mar 1891), Grace 3 (Feb 1897), Pauline 10/12 (Aug 1899) 8-278A-194/196

MARRIAGES

Amanda Buttram to Newton Lydle q.v.

Catharine Buttram to William C. Edmonds q.v.

Hinegar Buttram to Ada Broyles, 14 Jan 1899 (15 Jan), E.W. Mort MG, C.M. Landreth W 2-374

Mary J. Buttram to P. L. Chambers q.v.

Nancy Buttram to Thomas C. Travis q.v.

Rena Buttram to Peter Boonay q.v.

S. M. Buttram to William A. Green q.v.

W.A. Buttram to M.A. Gannaway, 14 Oct 1890, L. Waldorf MG 4-18

BYERLEY / BYERLY / BYRLEY / BARLY / BARELY / BARLEY / BIRELY

1860 CENSUS

Jasper Barely 34, Malissa D. 25, Sarah J. 2 5-32-211

Jacob Barily 58 (SC), Sarah 57, Mariah 26, Margaret 24, William 22, Lucy 20, James 18, Sarah 16, Nancy 14, Samuel 11 5-31-205

Michael Birely 62, Sarah 53, Martha 16, James 13, Parthena 8 6-105-713

Mike R. Barley 36, Laminia J. 26, Nancy 7, Mary M. 5, Ruth A. 3, Margaret E. 2, Sarah J. 6/12 10-30-200

William M. Birely 29, Sarah 26, Caroline 7, Catharine 6, Michael 4, James 1 6-105-715 [Wm Byerly married Sarah Ann Grammer on 28 Aug 1853 in Roane Co]

1870 CENSUS

Easter* Byrely 53, Rebecca 22: see James Roggers [* listed as Rogrs on 1880 Census]

Jacob Byrely 70 (SC), Sarah 67, Nancy 23, Samuel 21, Mariah CHUMLEY 30, James 6 7-2-18

Joseph Byrely 47, Melissa 40, Sarah Jane 13, Margarette A. 8, Jacob F. 6, Mary A. 5, Melissa T. 1 5-2-13

Margaret Byrely 33: see Franklin Matherly

Michael Byrely 74 (SC), James 23, Martha ROMINES 25, James 2 7-2-17

William D. Byrely 34, Esther A. 26, Alice 9, Elizabeth 6, William N. 4, Emma A. 2, Matilda Jane 1 6-17-121

1880 CENSUS

Jasper Byrly 54, Malissey 47 (w), S.S. 22 (d), Allice 19, J.F. 16 (s), M.A. 15 (d), James M. 9, Tom 11, Martha 7, Emma 5, Hanah 3 7-23-200

Jacob Byerley 83, Margaret 40 (d) 7-25-215

Matilda Byrely 29: see John Morgan

Michel Barly 83: see M. R. Romines

Sam Byrely 33, Sarah 31, W.T. 7 (s), J.H. 4 (d), S.J. 3 (s), C.E. 2/12 (s), John Thomas 4/12 [last name and age marked through] 7-25-214

W.D. Byrly 43, H.A. 36, A.M. 16, W.H. 14, Emma A. 12, M.J. 10, E.A. 8, Hanah 6, Lola 5, T.J. 1, U.G. SUTTELS 1 (gs) 8-18-154

1900 CENSUS

Allen Byerley 19: see William D. Purser

Frank Byreley 27 (Jan 1873-M 2), Sallie 19 (May 1881-M 2-1-1), Wood Ollin 1 (s)(Ap 1899), Jack 22 (b)(July 1878), Addie KNIGHT 14 (sil)(Feb 1886) 7-265B-296/301

Jack Byerly 21 (June 1879-M 1), Kittie 27 (June 1872-T/SC/T-M 1-0-0) 7-266B-310/315

Jacob Beirly 37 (Ap 1863-M 4), Mary E. 22 (May 1878-M 4-1-1), Ada A. 3 (Nov 1896), Mattie 21 (si)(Jan 1879), Thomas 14 (b)(Feb 1886) 5-235B-153

James M. Beyrley 29 (Oct 1870-M 3), Mamie 23 (May 1877-T/T/Ky-M 3-1-1), Dora 2 (Sep 1897)

6-246B-127/128

Margaret Byerley 66: see Lucy Matherley

Sam Byerly 52 (Ap 1848-M 28), Sarah 49 (Dec 1850-M 28-12-9), Dilia 24 (Jan 1876), Charley 20 (Ap 1880), Walter 16 (Oct 1883), Albert 14 (Nov 1885), Adia 12 (Sep 1887), Hattie 10 (Jan 1890), Claud 8 (Mar 1892) 7-266A-303/308

William Byrley 64 (Mar 1836-M 6), July A. 27 (July 1872-T/NC/NC-M 6-3-3), Wiley 15 (July 1884), Dillie 8 (Ap 1892), Mary 4 (Sep 1895), Idia 2 (Jan 1898) 7-267A-121/326

MARRIAGES

A. E. Byerly to S. L. Suttles q.v.

Alice Berly to William Ellison q.v.

Allice Byrley to Alex Clingan q.v.

Amanda J. Byerly to William Morgan q.v.

Anna Mary Byerley to William H. Spring q.v.

Emma Byerley to James Houston q.v.

Emma Byerley to James Webb q.v.

Frank Byerley to Sallie Knight, 8 Jan 1898 (9 Jan), W.R. Knight JP, Will Devault W 2-239

Hannah Byerley to Mort Evens q.v.

J.C. Byerly to Matilda Morgan, 4 Feb 1871 (8 Feb), R.T. Howard MG 1-#1185

J.M. Byerley to Mamie Roddy, 21 Oct 1896, C.G. Gillespie W (bond only) 2-76

Jack Byerley to Kittie Milton, 24 May 1899 (25 May), J.W. Romines JP, D.M. Elder W 2-417

Jacob Byerly to Nicy Thompson, 8 Oct 1872 (same), W.B. McKelvy MG 1-#1258

Jacob Byerley to Ella Webb, 2 Jan 1896, J.W. Romins(?) JP 4-90

Jane Birely to Harvy Roddy q.v.

Jasper Byerly to Malissa Byerly, 20 June 1857 (21 June), J. Howard JP 1-#605

L. E. Byerley to F. K. Knight q.v.

Leuty Byerley to James L. Gothard q.v.

Lucy Byerly to Henry F. Matherly q.v.

Malissa Byerly to Jasper Byerly q.v.

Martha Byerly to Zachariah Romines q.v.

Mary Byerly to W. H. Chumly q.v.

Mary A. Byerley to J. C. Ottinger q.v.

Matude Byerley to Alexander Milton q.v.

Nancy Byerly to James Houseley q.v.

Sarah Byerly to James M. Bly q.v.

Samuel Byerly to Sarah Housler, 31 Jan 1872 (1 Feb), J.W. Williamson MG 1-#1225

Sarah J. Byerley to Manley Yates q.v.

Tennie Byerley to William Roddy q.v.

W.H. Barley or Bailey to Anna Atkinson, 16 Jan 1886 (17 Jan), W.S. Hale MG 1-485

William D. Birely to Hester Ann Chumly, 19 July 1860 (same), John Howard JP 1-#718

William D. Byrley to Julia A. Harris, 24 June 1894, T.F. Shaver JP 4-68

\- - - - - - - - - - - - -

BYRD / BIRD

1860 CENSUS

George M. Bird 20: see Drury A. Bacon

Polly Bird 39, James HENRY 17, Joseph L. 15, Elizabeth A. 11, Harriet A. 8, William C. 6, Mary A. 1 4-42-281

1870 CENSUS

Isaac Byrd 23 (Silversmith), Nancy 20, Elizabeth J. 6/12 3-2-13

1880 CENSUS

David Byrd 56, July A. 39 (w), Sallie 21, Esther 6/12 (d), Tennessee 15, William 14, Martha A. 13, Slator 11, Rufus 9, July V. 6, Susan P. 4, John F. 2 6-13-127/128 (B)

Isaac Bird 33 (Silversmith), Nancy 31, Elizabeth M.A.J. 10, Samantha 8, Elvira A. 4, Pleasant N. 1, Elizabeth CLARK 64 (m) 6-23-20 (Rural Street, Washington)

1900 CENSUS

Andrew C. Bird 37 (July 1862-NJ/NJ/NJ-M 14)(Clergyman), Viola M. 38 (Dec 1861-Wisc/Ver/Ver-M 14-5-3), Maud R. 11 (May 1889-Iowa), Mina R. 7 (Feb 1893-Fla), D. Edson 11/12 (June 1899-Fl) 13-308B-351/364

Charles Bird 38 (Jan 1862-Ga/Ga/Ga-M 7), Kate 27 (Unk 1873-Ga/Ga/Ga-M 7-2-2), Isa 12 (Oct 1887-Ga), Emily BIGBY 14 (sd)(Mar 1886-Ga), Willie 12 (ss) (May 1888-Ga), Melvin HARBIN 19 (nw)(Feb 1881-Ga/Ga/Ga)(Coal Miner) 8-284B-324/326

George Byrd 20, Tennessee 25: see Frank M. Rockholt

Isaac Byrd 53 (Ap 1847-T/Unk/MC-M 31), Nancy 50 (Mar 1850-Ill/T/T-M 31-10-8), Elvira A. 24 (June 1876), Ples H. 21 (June 1878), William 17 (Mar 1883), Kittie M. 15 (May 1885), John R. 12 (Mar 1889) 6-241B-41/41

James F. Byrd 26 (Mar 1874-M 3), Pariserty 22 (July 1871-M 3-2-1), Artie E. 2 (Dec 1897) 2-191A-3/3

James R. Byrd 56 (Ap 1844-T/Va/Va-M 33), Matilda J. 51 (Dec 1848-T/NC/T-M 33-14-13), Joseph L. 18 (Nov 1881), Sarah E. 20 (Aug 1879), Jennie 16 (May 1884), Luella 13 (Jan 1887), John H. 10 (May 1890), Minnie A. 8 (June 1891), Lela B. 5 (Jan 1895), Robert L. 4 (Ap 1896) 6-241A-23/23

Julian Bird 23 (May 1877-M 2), Eliza 19 (Ap 1881-M 2-1-1), Niveiahy(?) 5/12 (Dec 1899) 8-287B-386/388

Sylvester Bird 59 (Aug 1840-NJ/NJ/NJ-M 38)(Bee Keeper), Elizabeth D. 62 (July 1837-NJ/NJ/NJ-M 38-8-7) 13-305A-283/293

William Bird 30 (Oct 1869-M 7), Mary E. 20 (Ap 1880-M 7-2-2), Maggie 4 (May 1896), Mattie 1 (Ap 1899) 8-276B-161/162

MARRIAGES

Bettie Bird to Frank Weathington q.v.

G.D. Byrd to Tennie Rockholt, 19 May 1900 (bond only), P.H. Byrd W 3-154

Isaac Byrd to Nancy Hair, 5 Ap 1869 (6 Ap), W.W. Low JP 1-#1052

James Byrd to Sarah(?) J. Purcer, 21 Mar 1895, J.W. Romines JP 4-79

Nancy S. Byrd to W. M. Norman q.v.

Sydney Bird to W. C. Hope q.v.

William R. Byrd to Mary E. Huskins, 25 Dec 1892, W.A. Howard MG 4-47

\- - - - - - - - - - - - -

CAGLE / CAGEL

1880 CENSUS

M.M. Cagle 44, S. 32 (w), M.S. 15 (d), J.M. 14 (s), M.E. 11 (d), J.R. 8 (d), S.E. 7 (d), A.E. 4 (d), E.E. 11/12 (d) 3-22-181

W. Cagel 24, Sarah 22, D.D. 1 (d), C.D. 4/12 (d) 3-23-182
1900 CENSUS
James M. Cagle 33 (Nov 1866-M 8), Mary M. 27 (June 1870-M 8-3-2), Estel 7 (Oct 1892), Clara 5 (Oct 1894), Feamon HAWKINS 12 (boarder)(Jan 1888-T/Oh/T) 6-249A-171/172
Lot Cagle 60 (Unk-M Unk), Cela A. 52 (Dec 1847-M Unk-10-9), Eva D. 20 (July 1879), Cratie E. 18 (Feb 1882), Luther 13 (Sep 1886), Oscar L. 10 (Feb 1890), Lola D. 3/12 (Feb 1900) 6-241A-30/30
Newton Cagle 43 (Ap 1857-M 22), Sarah J. 41 (Mar 1859-M 22-14-14), Albert W. 18 (Dec 1871), William C. 16 (Sep 1883), Thomas M. 14 (Aug 1885), Samuel 13 (Mar 1887), Berttie E. 10 (Aug 1889), Maud 10 (Mar 1890), Bertha 8 (Aug 1891), Sarah L. 5 (June 1894), Emma E. 5 (July 1894), Hattie M. 4 (July 1895), Calaph Mc 2 (Dec 1897), Mammie 9/12 (Sep 1899), Henry DRAKE 25 (Unk 1875)(Servant) 3-203B-69/74
MARRIAGES
Cordie(?) Cagle to William T. Wright q.v.
Daisy Cagle to Samuel Day q.v.
E.A. Cagle to Florence Wright, 25 Dec 1879 (28 Dec), S.H. McPherson JP 1-#1712
Ella Cagle to James Berry q.v.
James Cagle to Mollie Roberts, 19 Dec 1891, W.A. Howard MG 4-34
M. J. Cagle to Oscar H. Hill q.v.
Missorria Cagle to Clabron Fugate q.v.
Newton Cagle to Sarah Harwood, 14 Mar 1878 (20 Mar), T.H. McPherson JP 1-#1551
Texanna Cagle to Merel Fugate q.v.

- - - - - - - - - - - - -

CAHAN / CAHANA

1870 CENSUS
Selah Cahana 10: see William S. Kelley
1880 CENSUS
Margaret Cahan 26 see H. H. Gambill
MARRIAGES
Cely Cahan to A. J. Mathis q.v.
Dolly Cahan to Franklin Webb q.v.

- - - - - - - - - - - - -

CALDWELL / COLWELL

1860 CENSUS
Audley Caldwell 38, Catharine 36, Ann E. 9, Jonathan M. 6, Mary 3, William 9/12 4-46-313
Jonathan Caldwell 40, Victoria 21 4-46-312
1870 CENSUS
Edly P. Caldwell 48, Catharine 45, Jonathan M. 17, Mary V. 14, William A. 10, Catharine 8 4-18-117
Jonathan Caldwell 51, Victoria 31, Mitta 9, Edley W. 8, Callie 6, Nancy A. 4, James A. 2, Vesta 5/12 4-15-98
Samuel Caldwell 46, Mary F. 31, John 11, Eliza Jane 16, Hugh T. 7, Sarah E. 4, Robert C. 2 4-14-92 (Mu) (B)
1880 CENSUS
J.M. Caldwell 62, Victoria 41 (w), Milla 19, A.W. 17 (s), N.A. 14 (d), James A. 12, V.B. 10 (d), E.W. 9 (d), T.O. 6 (s), J.M. 5 (d), Catharine 1 4-1-4
J.W. Caldwell 27, Catharine 51 (m), Mary 22 (si), Catharine 19 (si), B.F. MARNEY 18 (Servant), J.A. ELLIOTT 33 (boarder)(Mechanic), A.M. CATES 30 (boarder) (Mechanics Assistant) 4-1-1
James Caldwell 48, Permelia A. 30 (w), Thomas A. 2 5-8-69
Manerva Caldwell 55, Jane 21 4-1-5 (B)
Mary Caldwell 50, John 20 (s), Hue 17 (s), E.A. 14 (d), R.K. 13 (s), L.J. 10 (d), J.N. 7 (s), E.G. 4 (s) 4-33-267 (Mu)
Sarah A. Caldwell 36 or 56, Martha A. 54 (si), Rebecca A. 23 (d) 5-7-68
1900 CENSUS
Columbus(?) Colwell 27 (Jan 1873-M 5)(Coal Miner), Callie M. 20 (Nov 1879-M 5-3-3), Cora E. 3 (June 1896), James C. 2 (May 1898), Clem L. 9/12 (Aug 1899) 13-303A-240/250
Curt Caldwell 34 (Ap 1866-M)(RR Laborer), Jennie 40 (si) (June 1860-M 15-0-0) 14-213A-8/8 (B)
John M. Colwell 25 (Sep 1874-M 1)(Coal Miner), Minnie E. 16 (Feb 1884-M 1-1-1), Baby 2/12 (Mar 1900) 3-303A-238/248
Redise Calwell 44: see Nuton Casey
Samuel Caldwell 22 (Nov 1877-M 2)(Coal Miner), Lizzie 18 (Mar 1882-M 2-1-1), Eva 1/12 (Ap 1900) 8-280B-235/237
Victoria Caldwell 61 (Mar 1839-Wd 12-11), James A. 32 (May 1868-Wd)(Grocer & Hardware), Vesta B. 30 (Feb 1870), Eva W. 28 (June 1872), Kittie C. 21 (Feb 1879), Cecil E. 18 (July 1881), Edwin D. 17 (Feb 1883)(Grocery Salesman), Belinda H. DARWIN 72 (si)(Feb 1828) 14-218A-112/114
William J. Caldwell 31 (Sep 1868-T/Ala/Ala-M 10), Sally 38 (Mar 1862-Ga/Ga/Ga-M 10-5-4), Myrtle 6 (Aug 1893), Brown 5 (Mar 1895), Kitty 3 (Dec 1896), May 0/12 (May 1900), Nellie PRYOR 16 (May 1884) (Servant) 8-282B-284/286
MARRIAGES
Ann E. Caldwell to James D. Collins q.v.
Green Caldwell to Victoria Gillespie, 19 May 1898 (22 May), F.P. Nord ??, Zui Fiseherson W. 2-278
J.M. Caldwell to Victoria Darwin, 22 Nov 1859 (no return) 1-#699
J.M. Caldwell to Mollie Black, 1 Dec 1898 (2 Dec), W.S. Hale MG, A.G. ???
John M. Caldwell to Mollie E. Robinson, 22 Aug 1866 (same), B. Frazier MG 1-#908
Jessie May Caldwell to E.P. Johnson q.v.
Lori Caldwell to Willie Davidson q.v.
Mettie Caldwell to T. H. Thomison q.v.
Nancy A. Caldwell to R. J. Patterson q.v.
Robert R. Caldwell to Emma L. Harrison, 1 Dec 1887 (same), L.M. Harris ?? 1-541
S.V. Caldwell to Lizzie Fraley, 8 Oct 1898 (9 Oct), W.S. Hale MG, J.C. Black W 2-329

- - - - - - - - - - - - -

CALHOUN

1900 CENSUS
Jack E. Calhoun 33 (Aug 1866-Ala/Ala/Ala-M 3)(Mechanic), Alice 23 (Feb 1877-M 3-1-0) 13-304B-278/288

MARRIAGE
J.E. Calhoun to Alice Rodgers, 19 Dec 1896 (20 Dec), W.R. Grimsley MG, J.W. Clouse W 2-91

- - - - - - - - - - - - -

CALIFF

1900 CENSUS
Charles Califf 30 (Jan 1870-Ind/Oh/Oh-Wd) 12-179B-26/28

- - - - - - - - - - - - -

CALL

1900 CENSUS
Estill C. Call 26, Dealey 21: see James Prater
MARRIGE
E.C. Call to Delia Prater, 11 Dec 1899 (12 Dec), W.A. Howard MG, W.T. Byerley W 3-85

- - - - - - - - - - - - -

CALLAHAN / CALIHAN

1880 CENSUS
Rufus Calahan 46, Mary J. 46, John T. 21, Mary E. 19, Oranita 18, William H. 16, Sarah J. 14, Lucissa 12, Rufus F. 8, Ro D. 5 5-9-81
1900 CENSUS
Roe Calihan 24 (July 1875-T/SC/T-M 0), Sara 18 (Dec 1881-M 0) 10-259B-186/190
Rufus R. Callahan 63 (Dec 1836-NC/NC/NC-M 47), Mary 63 (Nov 1836-T/NC/T-M 47-10-7) 5-232A-76
MARRIAGES
Bettie Calihan to Isaac Dodd q.v.
G.W. Callahan to S.W. Whaley, 24 Jan 1860 (same), T.W. Crouch MG 1-#1656
Lilla Callahan to James McCallie q.v.
Mintiey Callahan to Norman Yates q.v.
Roe Callahan to Dora Wyatt, 6 Jan 1900 (7 Jan), W.R. Howard MG, J.A. Howard W 3-106
Sarah J. Callahan to Thomas B. Bennison q.v.
W.H. Callahan to Minerva Rogers, 9 May 1886 (same), J.L. Huff(?) JP 1-503

- - - - - - - - - - - - -

CALLOWAY / CALOWAY

1900 CENSUS
Andrew Calloway 40 (Jan 1860-M 11)(RR Laborer), Mattie 28 (Jan 1878-M 11-4-4), John 9 (Aug 1890), Rosa 7 (June 1893), Minnie 6 (Dec 1895), Clayborn 3 (Ap 1897), Sina 23 (si)(Nov 1876)(Washwoman) 14-219B-139/142 (B)
Charles Calloway 26 (Mar 1874-M 3), Lizzie 21 (Aug 1878-Ga/Ga/Ga-M 3-0-0), Lizzie BAKER 23 (boarder)(July 1876-Miss/Miss/Miss) 8-275B-146 (B)
MARRIAGE
Andrew Caloway to Mollie Smith, 20 Feb 1889 (28 Feb), C.J. Peters JP 1-567

- - - - - - - - - - - - -

CALVIN

1880 CENSUS
Lee Calvin 51, Elizabeth 41, Elijah 18, John 16, Emaline 14, Thomas 12, Drucilla 9, Marion 7, Benjamin 4, Margaret 2, Jack GREEN 22 (boarder) 2-30-239
MARRIAGE
Mattie Calvin to G.G. Grant q.v.

- - - - - - - - - - - - -

CAMERON / CAMBON

1870 CENSUS
Lawson Cameron 25, Lydia 22, Lovellar 4, Harriette 1 7-1-8
1880 CENSUS
T.P. Cambon 35, M.J. 23 (w), J.E. 6 (s), L.M. 1 (d), Eliza SPYATT 54 (m), Billy IVES 19 7-28-243

- - - - - - - - - - - - -

CAMMARIS

1900 CENSUS
Moulton Cammaris 45 (Ap 1858?-Ind/Ind/Ind-M 22), Lara 38 (Mar 1862-Ind/Ind/Ind-M 22-2-2), Mary 21 (May 1877?-Ind), Lula(?) 10 (Nov 1886?-Ind) 12-179A-11/12

- - - - - - - - - - - - -

CAMPBELL / CAMBEL

1860 CENSUS
Eli Campbell 42, Easter 63, William 19, Isaac 17, David 15, William C. 14, Marshall B. 11, Martha A. 7, Ester J. 5, Ely H. 3 6-103-705
James Campbell 21, Jane 21, Joseph 1 3-58-397
Malakiah Campbell 28, Margaret 26, Sarah E. 11, John H. 2, Mary 8/12 4-49-335
Preston G. Campbell 56, Martha 48 (SC), Haney(?) C. (f) 23, Margaret I. 18, John R. 16, Rhody E. 13, Ruthe 10 1-83-565
William Campbell 39, Betsy 40, Thomas 16, James F. 13, James [sic] 10, Jane 8, William 4, July 2, Joseph 1/12 6-107-726
1870 CENSUS
Eli Campbell 51 (Ind), Easter 52, Joseph 21, Martha A. 17, Easter J. 16, Eli H. 12 8-3-17
Malaki Campbell 49, Margarette 40, Thomas 4 4-10-67
Nancy E. Campbell 20: see Orson A. Shipley
Preston Campbell 67 (Tanner), Martha 57 (SC), Margaret 27, Roda E. 20, Ruthe E. 18 2-13-92
Thomas Campbell 25, Mary E. 19, Martha E. 2 6-13-94
William Campbell 52, Elizabeth 51, Jane 20, William 14, Joseph 9 6-13-93
1880 CENSUS
Bailey T. Campbell 6: see Bailey Minix
E.L. Campbell 62, Easter 44 (w), Isaac EVERT 35 (sl), Wm 12 (gs), M.T. 10 (gd), J.F. 9 (gs), Jane 5 (gd), Ida 2 (gd) 11-40-323
G.W. Campbell 28, T.E. 21, Eva 4 (d) 11-38-308
James Campbell 37, Manda 39, William R. 10, John T. 6, Margaret E. 5, Calley 5/12 (s) 6-17-162/166

Jeff Campbell 25, Mollie 28, James 8, Annie 3 10-28-213/218 (B) (Mu)
Jinnie Campbell 40, Jasper 21, James W. 17, Alice C. 16 6-14-131/134
Mae Campbell 57, M. 52, S.A. 13 (s) 3-28-226
Martha Campbell 26, C.J. 8 (d) 11-40-324
William Campbell 68 (Farm Laborer), Elizabeth 53, Nancy J. 26, Joseph 16, Sarah E. 10 (gd) 6-23-16 (High Street, Washington)
William H. Campbell 23 (Farm Laborer), Martha E.J.P. 18, Joseph Floyd 11/12 6-23-17 (High Street, Washington)

1900 CENSUS

Alice Campbell 21: see Joseph Gibson
Eliza Campbell 32 (Dec 1867-Wd 5-4), May C. 12 (d)(Dec 1887-Ala/Miss/T), Edgar W. 10 (Dec 1889-Miss), Sarah F. 7 (Jan 1892-Miss), Leroy 4 (Ap 1896-Miss) 5-231A-61
Elizabeth Campbell 70 (Dec 1829-Wd 13-4), Nancy J. MOLES 40 (d)(Dec 1859-M 9)(Washwoman) 6-241B-33
Guss Cambel 55 (Jan 1845-NC/NC/NC-M 22)(Coke Puller), Mollie 51 (Oct 1848-M 22-10-8), Tom 16 (July 1883), Alice 14 (Nov 1885), Maggie 11 (Dec 1888), Cora 8 (Nov 1891), Wade 5 (Dec 1894) 7-265B-293/298 (B)
Hugh Campbell 34: see John F.(?) Humphrey
James Campbell 26 (Unk 1874-M 0), Easter 37 (Unk 1863-M 0-0-0), Willie AVY 18 (ss)(Jan 1882), Frank 15 (ss)(Mar 1885), Lizzie 15 (May 1886), Lillie 11 (Ap 1889), Mannie 9 (Feb 1891), Martha 6 (Aug 1893), Kittie 4 (Mar 1896), Francis 1 (June 1898), Hada BOGGES 30 (sil)(Unk 1870-D 2-2), Fred 15 (nw)(Jan 1885)(Coal Miner), Willie 14 (nw)(Dec 1885) 8-284B-320/322 (B)
James B. Campbel 28 (Oct 1872-M 0), Ella L. 20 (Mar 1880-M 0) 5-232B-93
Jim Campbell 52 (Mar 1848-M 33), Manda 52 (Nov 1847-M 33-10-9), Ida M. 16 (Ap 1884), James R. 12 (Nov 1887), Katie 10 (Mar 1890), Joseph 6 (Oct 1893) 6-242A-51
John M. Campbell 43 (Jan 1857-Pa/Pa/Pa-M 17), Rosa M. (Mar 1854-Oh/Pa/Pa-M 17-7-7), Frank R. 16 (Nov 1883-Pa), Walter M. 15 (Jan 1885-Pa), John M. 13 (Nov 1886), George O. 11 (Nov 1888), Bertha M. 9 (Oct 1890), Mary A. 6 (Feb 1894), Mildred L. 3 (May 1897) 4-227B-271/275 (Road on line between 3rd & 4h Districts)
Joseph Campbell 38 (Unk-T/Va/T-M 5), Martha 33 (June 1866-M 5-7-5), Florance 5 (Dec 1894), John 4 (May 1896), Ada 7/12 (Sep 1899), Henry R. SMITH 16 (ss) (Aug 1883), Alice 14 (sd)(Ap 1886) 6-242A-42
Thomas J. Campbell 36 (Ap 1864-M 14)(Publisher), Harriet 35 (Ap 1865-M 14-7-5), Myrtle A. 11 (July 1888), Constance P. 9 (July 1890), John E. 7 (Nov 1892), Ruth P. 4 (Jan 1896), Martha W. 1 (Feb 1899) 10-322B-53/56
William Campbell 16: see William Lockmiller
William Campbell 20: see William Fifer (B)

MARRIAGES

Alice Campbell to Jack Reed q.v.
Annie Campbell to Jackson Ryan q.v.
Caeli Campbell to Oscar Rodgers q.v.
Charles Campbell to Rachel Mathews, 24 July 1854 (no return) 1-#456
E.H. Campbell to Martha Grigory, 7 Sep 1877 (same), Wm Morgan JP 1-#1509
Elizabeh Campbell to Joseph B. Wood q.v.
Floyd Campbell to Sarah Rising, 27 Aug 1890, R.S. Mason JP 4-15
J.A. Campbell to Sallie F. Alley, 11 Ap 1890 (same), J.R. Campbell ?? 1-600
J.R. Campbell to Eliza J. Whittenburg, 1 Mar 1890 (2 Mar), A.J. Wyrick JP 1-597
James Campbell to Easter Avery, 4 Dec 1899 (same), W.L. Lillard JP, Goss Campbell [signed by X] W 3-79
James F. Campbell to Jane Ellison, 30 May 1857 (same), J. Ingle ?? 1-#600
James H. Campbell to Amanda Holland, 6 May 1869 (same), J. Howard MG 1-#1058
Jane Campbell to Henry Malis q.v.
Jenna Campbell to Joseph Peterson q.v.
Joseph Campbell to Martha Smith, 1 May 1895, H.B. Burdit MG 4-87
Lalia M. Campbell to L. M. Frost or Foust q.v.
Mary Campbell to D.M. Burwick q.v.
Mary Campbell to Samuel Hoge q.v.
Noah A. Campbell to Mary Gattis, 15 Sep 1895, J.M. Bramlett MG 4-86
Sarah E. Campbell to James McCully q.v.
Sarah Jane Campbell to Charley C. Avery q.v.
Susan Campbell to Peter Ellison q.v.
Thomas Campbell to Minnie Coxey, 2 Oct 1897 (3 Oct), J.B. Coulter MG, Burt Reins W 2-192
William W. Campbell to Martha Thompson, 11 Oct 1877 (same), Peter Roddy MG 1-#1517

\- - - - - - - - - - - - -

CANADA

1880 CENSUS

D. Canada 23: see E. Marl

\- - - - - - - - - - - - -

CANELLAR

1900 CENSUS

James Canellar(?) 50 (Ap 1850-M 23), Fanny A. 45 (Dec 1854-M 23-1-1) 2-194A-58/60

\- - - - - - - - - - - - -

CANNALL

MARRIAGE

John F. Cannall or Camell to Bell Green, 11 June 1886 (12 June), W.R. Clack JP 1-501

\- - - - - - - - - - - - -

CANNON

MARRIAGE

Nancy A. Cannon to Hugh Doss q.v.

\- - - - - - - - - - - - -

CANNS

1860 CENSUS
Thomas Canns(?) 17: see Joseph Newell

- - - - - - - - - - - - -

CANSE

1880 CENSUS
J.W. Canse 34, S.J. 31, Joanita 12, O.J. 9 (d), B.C. 6 (d), J.B. 3 (d) 8-6-51

- - - - - - - - - - - - -

CANTRELL / CANTRAL / COTTRELL

1860 CENSUS
Joseph Cantrel 27, Sarah 21, Sarah A. 4 4-52-352
1870 CENSUS
Sarah Cantrell 33, Sarah A. 14, Lorinda Jane 8, Anna LEMMONS 24 1-9-57
1880 CENSUS– None
1900 CENSUS
Charles H. Cantrell 31 (Ap 1869-Ky/T/Ky-M 3)(Coal Miner), Nannie 29 (Sep 1870-M 3-1-1), Claude E. 1 (Aug 1888) 13-308A-347/359
John Cantrell 56: see William R. Myers
MARRIAGES
James N. Cantrell (23, Polk Co) to Rachel A. Hyde (19, Raburn Co, Ga), 26 Oct 1881, M.L. Abbott JP, J.N. Hyde & C. Dunahoo W (both of Clay Co, NC) 4-6(57)
John Cantral to Minerva Yates, 2 Jan 1892, James Carrie(?) MG 4-47
Joseph Cantral to Sarah Lemmons, 12 Jan 1854 (same), Daniel Broyles JP 1-#434
L. J. Cantrell to Thomas C. Gibson q.v.
Martha J. Cantrell to John B. Dudley q.v.
Pete T. Cottrell to Laurie(?) Gaddis, 27 Dec 1894, W.K. Fugate JP 4-75
Robertia Cantrell to Charles Dennis q.v.
Sarah Cantrel to James Brady q.v.
Sarah Cantrell to Marion Watson q.v.

- - - - - - - - - - - - -

CAPP / CAPPS / CAPES / CASE / CASSE

1860 CENSUS
William Capps 30 (Ga), Martha E. 27, Robert 4, Harriet N. 3, Mary J. 3/12 2-76-515
1870 CENSUS
Francis M. Capes 55 (NC), Abigail W. 44, Francis M. Jr. 16, Martha C. 12, Sarah E. 10 8-1-2
1880 CENSUS
F.M. Cass 65, A.R. 55, J.B. 9 (d) 11-39-315
F.M. Capps Jr. 26, C.M. 24, L.J. 3 (d), T.E. 1 (d) 8-9-76
Joseph Capps 23: see Calvin Gillespie (B)
MARRIAGES
F.M. Capps to E.N. Fann, 2 Sep 1876 (3 Sep), J.W. Pence MG 1-#1458
Jane Capps to Moses Williams q.v.
Joseph Capp to Jane Dooley, 3 July 1882 (6 July), G.W. Renfro MG 1-474
Lin or Lou Anna Capps to Perry Elsey q.v.
Mary Ann F. Capps to Seth Hibberd q.v.
Sallie Casse to Joseph Ledford q.v.
Tennie Capps to David Holt q.v.

- - - - - - - - - - - - -

CARAVILE

1900 CENSUS
Andrew B. Caravile 40 (Sep 1859-Ala/Ala/Ala-M 14)(Pattern Maker), Sarah H. 35 (July 1864-Ind/NY/Mich-M 14-3-2), Eloise A. 13 (Jan 1887), Alice G. 11 (Sep 1888), William D. GREGG 62 (c)(Oct 1838-NY/Canada/Do) 13-309B-375/389

- - - - - - - - - - - - -

CARAWAY

1900 CENSUS
William Caraway 54 (Aug 1840-NC/NC/NC-M 23)(RR Section Hand), Rhoda 38 (Oct 1861-M 23-11-10), Lillie 20 (Aug 1879), Lydia M. 17 (May 1883), Thomas H. 15 (Jan 1885), Hattie 13 (Feb 1887), Robert M. 10 (May 1890), Noah I. 7 (Dec 1892), Della 6 (Feb 1894), Hezekiah 4 (Mar 1896), Elizabeth 1 (Oct 1898) 10-327B-164/174

- - - - - - - - - - - - -

CARD

1900 CENSUS
Laurence J. Card 30 (June 1869-M 3), Salina A. 21 (Dec 1878-M 3-2-2), Annie J. 3 (May 1897), Joseph A. 1 (Nov 1898) 13-306B-319/331
Sarah J. Card 61 (Dec 1838-Wd 11-11), Milo M. 21 (Mar 1879), Caswell R. 20 (Mar 1880)(Coal Miner), Mary I. 17 (June 1882) 13-307A-325/337
MARRIAGES
Alie I. Card to W. J. Acuff q.v.
Eva Card to James Brown(?) q.v.
Lawrence Card to Savinia [bond] or Salina [license] McReynolds, 14 Nov 1896 (15 Nov), F.M. Bandy MG, M.L. Holt W 2-82
Letha Card to Hade or Haile Sparks q.v.

- - - - - - - - - - - - -

CARDEN

1900 CENSUS
Laura A. Carden 38, Carl C. 2: see Miles H. McCuiston

- - - - - - - - - - - - -

CARDIFF

MARRIAGE
Nancy C. Cardiff to Thomas Stanford or Swafford q.v.

- - - - - - - - - - - - -

CARGYLE

MARRIAGE
Jordan Cargyle to Nellie Johnson, 5 Oct 1899 (same), R.T. Smith ??, Rufus Suttles W 3-48

- - - - - - - - - - - - -

CARLILE

1900 CENSUS
Andrew Carlile(?) 4: see Birrel G. Hinch (B)

- - - - - - - - - - - - -

CARLOCK

1900 CENSUS
Job W. Carlock 33 (June 1866-M 1)(Merchant), Maud H. 30 Sep 1869-Oh/Oh/Oh-M 1)(Milliner), James E. FURLONG 7 (nw)(Feb 1893-T/Md/Oh) 13-305A-288/299

- - - - - - - - - - - - -

CARMACK

1900 CENSUS
John Carmack 25: see Cate Cuirver (B)
MARRIAGE
Edward Carmack to Maggie Mickey, 15 Dec 1884 (16 Dec), Anderson Love MG 1-492

- - - - - - - - - - - - -

CARMICAL / CARMICLE / CARMICHALL

1870 CENSUS
Julia A. Carmichall 43 (NC), Mary E. 18 (NC) 3-9-62
MARRIAGES
John Carmical to Sinda Pearson, 29 Feb 1868 (1 Mar), T.N.L. Cunnyngham JP 1-#1003
Julie Carmicle to Isah Rice q.v.

- - - - - - - - - - - - -

CARNEY

1880 CENSUS
James Carney 52, Jemima 48 12-2-17
James C. Carney 31, Loutitia 21, Thomas 7, Alfred B. 4, Margaret A. 2, Henry JOHNSON 23 ("wife left him") 6-25-188/192
1900 CENSUS
Alfred Carney 24 (Dec 1875-M 0), Lizzie 24 (Sep 1875-M 0-1-1), Lena 4/12 (Jan 1900) 10-322B-50/53
James Carney 58 (Oct 1841-M 26), Latissa 40 (Dec 1859-M 26-9-7), William 17 (June 1882), Lucy 14 (Feb 1886), Katie 12 (Sep 1887), Avery 9 (Dec 1890), Mynatt 3 (Ap 1897), Thomas CARNEY 26 (s)(Oct 1873-M 5), Manda 25 (dl)(July 1874-T/Va/T-M 5-3-3), Nora 3 (gd)(June 1896), Anna 1 (gd)(Nov 1898), Bertha 4/12 (gd)(Jan 1900) 6-248A-157/158
MARRIAGES
Adie Carney(?) to Willie Bridges q.v.
Alfred Carney to Lizzie Henry, 8 July 1899 (9 July), W.R. Henry JP, George Henry W 3-8
James C. Carney to Loutitia Franklin, 17 Jan 1872 (18 Jan), A.P. Early MG 1-#1222
Thomas Carney to Amanda Roberts, 7 July 1895, W.R. Henry JP 4-82

- - - - - - - - - - - - -

CARPENTER

MARRIAGES
Alice Carpenter to T. S. Bryson q.v.
C.P. Carpenter to Matilda Dupree, 19 May 1886 (20 May), M.C. Bruner MG 1-507
Jane Carpenter to J. W. Fry q.v.
John Carpenter to Martha J. Holt, 2 July 1870 (no return) 1-#1155
Samuel N. Carpenter to Louisa Jane King, 4 Oct 1867 (9 Oct), J.M. Kelly MG 1-#974
Susan Carpenter [nee Franklin] to John Wasson q.v.

- - - - - - - - - - - - -

CARR / KERR / CURR

1900 CENSUS
Charley Carr 49 (Jan 1851-Wd), Dollie 20 (si)(Aug 1880), Flonce 3 (s)(Nov 1896-T/T/Va), Bah 4/12 (s)(Jan 1900), Foss BINGHAM 20 (lodger)(Mar 1880) 7-262A-21/236 (B)
Mary J. Kerr 72: see Joseph H. Watters
William Curr 41 (Nov 1859-T/T/Va-M 17)(Carpenter), Nancy 38 (Ap 1862-Ga/T/T-M 17-6-3), Lillie 13 (Oct 1886-Ga), Lucy 6 (Jan 1894-Ga), Robert 1 (June 1898) 10-250A-11/11

- - - - - - - - - - - - -

CARRINGTON

MARRIAGE
Walter Carrington to Bell Bridgeman, 18 Ap 1900 (same), A.P. Hayes JP, John Sharp W 3-144

- - - - - - - - - - - - -

CARROLL / CARROL

1860 CENSUS
Christopher I. Carroll 10, Wm R. 9: see James Deatherage
James Carrol 13: see Malinda Roberson

1870 CENSUS
Christopher C. Carrol 18 (Ga), Mary J. 18, James C. 1, Henry N. 2/12 4-10-62
Mary Carroll 21: see Banjamin B. Travis
William R. Carroll 18 (Ga), Leara M. 22 5-8-58

MARRIAGES
Andrew Carrol to Manda Winfrey, 26 Mar 1889 or 1884 (27 Mar 1884)[sic, 4 is clear], W.C. Mitchell JP 1-568 [the record prior to this one was dated 1885]
Christopher C. Carroll to Mary Jane Essex, 6 June 1867 (no return) 1-#953
Cleptia Carroll to Jack Suggs q.v.
Emma Carroll to W. N. Hawkins q.v.
Lemay I. Carroll to James A. Landreth q.v.
William R. Carroll to Leury M. Porter, 8 Ap 1869 (same), R.T. Howard M 1-#1054

- - - - - - - - - - - - -

CARSON

1860 CENSUS

James Carson 54, Attaline 39, Samuel J. 21, William C. 12, James B. 10, Susan A. 7, Charlotte E. 5, Lavinia E. 3, William WARD 20, Benjamin VAUGHN 18 3-55-372

1870 CENSUS

James Carson 65 (Dental Surgeon), Adaline 50, James B. 20 (School Teacher), Susan A. 17, Charlotte E. 14, Elizabeth 13, Delia E. 9, Robert H. 6 3-20-143

John C. Carson 43 (Wagonwright), Mary 40, Charles 9, Frances C. 8, Susan 6, Lutitia 2 3-10-72

William C. Carson 22 (Dentist), Dorcas E. 19 2-5-31

1880 CENSUS

William Carson 25 (RR Laborer) 5-11-105 (B)

- - - - - - - - - - - - -

CARTER

1860 CENSUS

Philip L. Carter 53 (Va), Mary 52, Phebe J. 24, Sarah E. 14, James K.P. 13, George H. 12, Pervis T. 9, Philip P. 13 2-71-481

1870 CENSUS

Abner A. Carter 33 (Ga)(Cabnet Workman), Arminda 28, Florence P. 7, William J. 3, Virginia C. 1 8-10-66

1880 CENSUS

Frances Carter 40, S.A. 10 (d), Henry 8, J.E. 4 (s), James 1 4-35-291

Margaret Carter 25 (Cook), William 2, Julia 11/12 1-14-115 (B)

1900 CENSUS

Andy Carter 24 (Mar 1876-M 4)(Coal Miner), Sarah 25 (Ap 1875-M 4-1-1), Anna 10 (Aug 1889), Nancy JOHNSON 70 (ml)(Jan 1830-Wd 10-6) 8-283B-296/298

Bud Carter 32 (Unk 1868-M 16)(Coal Miner), Mattie 26 (Mar 1874-M 16-7-5), Hassie 11 (June 1888), Ina 9 (Ap 1891), Lester 6 (Dec 1893), Grace 3 (Dec 1896), Maud 4/12 (Aug 1899) 8-284B-313/315

George Carter 18 see John Holmes

Omelia Carter 6/12: see Salie(?) Gillespie (B)

Robert T. Carter 51 (Oct 1848-M 21), Cordelia 46 (Oct 1853-M 21-8-7), Catharine 19 (Dec 1880), Nannie S. 16 (Aug 1883), Gus A. 15 (Mar 1885), Samuel H. 12 (Oct 1887), William H. 9 (July 1890), Ruby R. 7 (May 1893), Roy E. 7 (May 1893) 13-308B-358/371

Sanford Carter 22: see Samuel Whitlow (B)

Sanford Carter 21: see Mattie Jones (B)

William Carter 23: see Maggie Roddy

MARRIAGES

A.P. Carter to Mary A. Myres, 3 Mar 1856, "Celebrated by John W Thompson MG" 1-#537

Andy Carter to Pearl Ryan, 8 May 1897 (bond only), James Carter W 2-108 (B)

Andy Carter to Pearl Ryan, 9 May 1897 (license only), J.B. Trotter MG 2-172

Andy Carter(?) to Sarah Lee, 6 Jan 1896, W.S. Hale MG 4-88

Bell Carter or Canter to John Gowins q.v.

Berry Carter to Callie Tipler, 27 Feb 1897 (28 Feb), J.B. Trotter MG, I.K. Brown(?) W 2-121

Birdie Carter to Alfred Hoge q.v.

Callie Carter(?) to Edward Lawson q.v.

F.J. Carter to Lillie Duff, 8 Mar 1891, A.S. Mason JP 4-29

Frances Carter to Byrd Lourey q.v.

George Carter to Clema Morgan, 7 July 1886 (same), Calvin Morgan JP 1-504

Hannibal Carter to Rhoda Northump, 27 Sep 1886 (same), A.H. Frazier JP 1-525

James M. Carter to Vesta Ryan, 5 Feb 1897 (7 Feb), J.B. Trotter MG 2-117

Jane Carter to Silas Blanchit q.v.

Jennie Carter to George Harris q.v.

Jennie Carter to J. C. Burdin q.v.

Margaret Carter to Bailey Smith q.v.

Mary A. Carter to John Kenida q.v.

Nannie Carter to J. N. or J. W. Burger q.v.

Robert Carter to Emma Cleague, 21 Sep 1900 (bond only), Oliver Delaney W 3-223

S. M. Carter to Rebecca Robbs, 6 Oct 1855 (7 Oct), N.H. Long JP 1-#519

Sarah Carter to John Goddard q.v.

Simon Carter to Sarah Pullom, 6 Oct 1889, R.F. Shaver JP 4-63

- - - - - - - - - - - - -

CARTRIGHT / CARTWRIGHT

1900 CENSUS

James Cartright 65 (Unk-T/Va/Va-Wd 1-1) 6-247B-151/152

Lemuel M. Cartwright 50 (Aug 1849-M 27)(Minister), Harriet M. 49 (Jan 1851-M 27), Lena M. 23 (May 1877), William J. 20 (July 1879), Fannie M. 17 (Aug 1882), Robert C. 15 (Oct 1884), Elizabeth R. 13 (Ap 1887), Wm P. BURKMAN 26 (boarder)(Jan 1873-Va/Va/Va)(Minister) 14-213B-18/19

Nathan R. Cartwright 24 (Aug 1875-M 1)(Minister), Grace B. 23 (Mar 1877-Oh/Oh/Oh-M 1-0-0) 14-213A-4/4

MARRIAGES

Mary Cartright to Henry Malis q.v.

N. R. Cartright to Grace B. Watkins, 29 Mar 1899, L. M. Cartright MG 4-105

- - - - - - - - - - - - -

CARY

1900 CENSUS

Thomas Cary 76 (Jan 1824-NY/NY/NY-Wd) 12-179A-2/2

MARRIAGE

William N. Cary to Harriett Fullington, 29 Oct 1865 (same), P.G. Campbell JP 1-#1083

- - - - - - - - - - - - -

CASEY / CASSEY / CASY / CAZY

1860 CENSUS

Wesley Casey 38, Carolin 30 (Ill), John 12, Susan 10, Caisida 7, Elmira 5, Adelia 3, Franklin 1 1-85-582

1870 CENSUS

David Casey 50, Matilda 41, James 25, George W. 16, Nancy A. 15, Sarah E. 13, Rebecca J. 11, Margrette A. CASEY 86 4-16-103

John W. Cazy 53 (NC), Clarisa 43, Susan E. 20, Canzada 18, Elmus N. 16, Cordelia 14, Franklin 10, Mary Jane 6, William E. 2, John C. CAZY 21, Loura Jane 18 1-1-7

1880 CENSUS

J.C. Casey 31, Laura 26, Wm H. 8, J.H. 5 (s), L.E. 3 (d) 4-12-92

Wesley Casey 53, Clarissa 52, Elmer 27, Franklin 20, Mary 16, William 11, Thomas SHELBY 26 (sl), Adella 2 (gd) 1-19-162

1900 CENSUS

John M. Cassey 75 (Ap 1825-T/SC/SC-M 52)(Gardner), Cora 65 (Ap 1835-Ill/Ill/Ill-M 52-4-4), Frank 40 (May 1860) 1-185A-126/132

Nuton Case 50 (Jan 1850-M 16), Harett 48 (Feb 1852-M 16-0-0), William KELLEY 17 (nw)(Ap 1883), Molli 13 (ne)(May 1887), Nettie 9 (ne)(Aug 1890), Redise CALDWELL 44 (boarder)(May 1856-Wd) 1-189A-198/107 (Spring City)

MARRIAGES

Adelia Casey to Thomas Shelby q.v.

E.N. Casey (27) to Harriet Kelly (28), 21 Mar 1883, B.F. Holloway JP 4-13(123)

Elamas Casey to A. Catherine Shelby, 30 May 1874 (31 May), Wm McCully MG 1-#1337

H. C. Casey to C. D. Smith q.v.

John Casey to Mary Jane Swafford, 17 Feb 1866 (same), Allen Howard JP 1-#889

John Casey to Martha Dunkin, 3 Mar 1870 (no return) 1-#1145

John C. Casey to Martha Cox, 19 Sep 1890, J.L. McPherson JP 4-15

Mary J. Casey to I. T. Shelby q.v.

Newton Casey to Martha J. Barger, 19 Mar 1862 (20 Mar), E. Pyott JP 1-#777

Samuel P. Casey to Georgia E. Garrison, 16 Mar 1890 (same), M.C. Bruner MG 1-595

Susan Casey to William Shelby or Shably q.v.

William Casey to Phoeba Housley, 17 Aug 1891, G.J. Liles JP 4-29

William Casey to Bell Moore, 21 May 1892, W.S. Hale MG 4-40

Winnie Casey to Grant McClendon q.v.

Zodec Casey to John W. Duncan q.v.

\- - - - - - - - - - - - -

CASH

1860 CENSUS

Francis A. Cash 33, Elisa 34, Mary A. 9, James W. 5, Thomas J. 2, Catharine J. 4/12 3-54-371

James A. Cash 28 7-6-37

James I. Cash 60, Elizabeth 49, Jane 30, Sarah A. 16, Eliza J. 14, Jesse J. 11 2-80-541

William E. Cash 38 (NC), Lucinda S. 34, Elizabeth J. 14, James J. 12, Jesse W. 9, Sarah A. 1 1-91-624

1870 CENSUS

Francis A. Cash 43, Eliza 45, Mary Ann 18, James W. 15, Jeffrey 12, Catharine 10 1-3-23

James A. Cash 37, Mira A. 21, James A. 3, Florence E. 10 7-6-43

James I. Cash 70, Elizabeth A. 59, Hannah J. 40, Jesse I. 21, Eliza 24, Evangelene 1 2-3-14

Thomas H. Cash 32, Mary M. 28, Henry E. 10, Henrietta B. 8, John C. 3 7-6-42

William Cash 49 (Ala), Lucinda S. 44, James I. 22, Jesse W. 19, Sarah A. 10, Susan REED 21 1-6-39

1880 CENSUS

Albion Cash 14: see Henry DeVault

Asbury Cash 53, Eliza 54, Jeffrey 22, Kate 19 1-18-154

James Cash 79 (Minister), Sarah 54 (w), Jane 1 (d) 2-41-329

Thomas Cash 44, Mary 38, Henrietta 19, Henry 19, John 13, William 9, Flora 6, James 6, Baxter 3 2-40-328

1900 CENSUS

Jeff Cash 40 (Ap 1860-S)(Drugist), Kate 38 (si)(Feb 1862-S) 14-21A-5/5

Jessie Cash (no dates)– non resident in District 12

Jessie Cash 49 (Jan 1851-T/Ala/T-M 28), Hannah 45 (Dec 1854-M 28-7-7), Freeman C. 25 (July 1874), Flora B. 23 (July 1876), Colonen L. 21 (Dec 1878), Hattie E. 18 (Oct 1881), Jessie C. 16 (Oct 1883), Maggie C. 15 (Feb 1885), William G. 6 (July 1893) 14-222B-184/188

Mary Cash 57 (Aug 1842-Wd 10-8), Emma 19 (Sep 1880), Mary 16 (May 1884), M.O.K. 12 (s)(May 1888) 12-180B-45/48

MARRIAGES

Bell Cash to Young Furguson q.v.

Eliza Cash to Joseph L. Abernathy q.v.

H. E. Cash to George C. Eldridge q.v.

Henrietta Cash to L. C. Tallent q.v.

James A. Cash to Myra Ann Spence, 15 Dec 1865 (16 Dec), John Whaley MG 1-#857

Jane E. Cash to Columbus Gibson q.v.

Jesse I. Cash to Mary L. Ladd, 6 Jan 1873 (7 Jan), S. Phillips MG 1-#1270

Jessee W. Cash to Hannah Wasson, 16 Sep 1873 (17 Sep), E.W. Marsh MG 1-#1301

Mary A. Cash to Jessee F. Day q.v.

Mary A. Cash to L. D. Eldridge q.v.

Mirah A. Cash (Mrs.) to H.C. DeVault q.v.

Rebecca Cash to F. M. Thompson q.v.

Sarah Cash(?) to William Fullington q.v.

Sarah Ann Cash to George J. Roddy q.v.

\- - - - - - - - - - - - -

CASIRE

1880 CENSUS

James Casire 46, Sarah 29 (w), Charlie 9, Margaret 4, Thomas 2, Levi 1/12 2-36-296

\- - - - - - - - - - - - -

CASNEY

1860 CENSUS

Thomas J. Casney(?) 44 (NY)(Journeeman Tailor), Martha A. 58, Henry B. 21 1-82-558

\- - - - - - - - - - - - -

CASPER

1900 CENSUS

Josie Casper 23: see Willis Taylor (B)

\- - - - - - - - - - - - -

CASS– see CAPP

- - - - - - - - - - - - -

CASSADY

MARRIAGES
M. M. Cassady to H. W. Amos q.v.
Manerva J. Cassady to William Watson q.v.

- - - - - - - - - - - - -

CASTA

1880 CENSUS
J.W. Casta(?) 29, Hannah 25 (w), T.C. 5 (s), F.B. 4 (d), C.L. 1 (s), W.W. 59 (f), L.S. 54 (m), Jesse REED 18 4-11-84

- - - - - - - - - - - - -

CASTELBERRY

1880 CENSUS
Frank Castelberry 24: see H. R. Rains
Joseph Ca--?--berry 17: see Julia Kelly

- - - - - - - - - - - - -

CASTELL

MARRIAGE
Annie Castell to Patrick Crow q.v.

- - - - - - - - - - - - -

CASTLEMAN

1880 CENSUS
William Castleman 50, Nancy 35 (w), Lula DARWIN 2 (adopted) 1-9-74 (B) (Mu)
1900 CENSUS
William Castleman 65 (Unk-Miss/Miss/Miss-M 35), Nancy 67 (Unk-M 35-0-0) 8-315B-97/101 (B)

- - - - - - - - - - - - -

CASTOR

MARRIAGES
Charles S. Castor to Mary McPherson, 24 Dec 1894, J.F. Hash MG 4-73
James W. Castor(?) to Tennessee Ryan, 16 Dec 1885, Jesse P. Thompson JP 4-73

- - - - - - - - - - - - -

CASTLIN– see COSTELLO

- - - - - - - - - - - - -

CATES / CATE / COATS

1860 CENSUS
John Cates 23, Margaret J. 25, Sarah J. 2 8-13-88
Lucinda Cates 74 (Va), Lousanna 25, Eliza 21 7-5-33
Solomon Coats 34, Loueza 30, William 13, James 11, Sarah J. 9, Mary E. 6, Nancy F. 3 8-12-75
1870 CENSUS
Lucinda Cates 90 (Va), Louisana 30, Joseph 3, John 1, Lucinda J. 13 7-7-50
1880 CENSUS
A.M. Cates 30 (Mechanics Assistant): see J. W. Caldwell
Eliza Cates 50, E. A. 40, Joseph L. 13, Johny 11, J. R. 6: see Jery Whaley
George Cate 22 (Miner): see Timothy Winton (B)
M. A. Cates 9, J. B. 5: see W. J. Banks
Wm Cates 31, S.C. 22, M.F. 4 (d), S.A. 3 (d), W.M. 3/12 (s) 4-8-61
1900 CENSUS
Andrew McC. Cate 43 (Dec 1856-M 19)(Sewing Machine Agent), Fanny A. 40 (June 1859-M 19-6-6), Mentor S. 17 (Sep 1882), Jennie N. 15 (Oct 1884), Lela B. 13 (Jan 1887), Anna L. 10 (Dec 1889), Orville L. 8 (Sep 1891), Ola M. 1 (July 1898) 10-327A-153/161
Horace Cates 28: see Jack Moore (B)
Jim Cates 28: see Phoebe Rhea (B)
John Coats 29 (Jan 1871-M 12), Laura 26 (Unk 1874-M 12-3-3), Amos 10 (Sep 1889), May 6 (June 1893), Mollie 4 (Sep 1895) 15-269A-22
John Cates 41 (Aug 1858-M 3), Pauline 23 (Jan 1877-Ga/T/Ga-M 3-1-1), Annabel 8 (Ap 1891), Lawrence STEVENS 28 (boarder)(Ap 1872-Va/Va/Va) 8-314A-63/66 (B)
John Cates 45 (May 1855-M 18), Laura 42 (Sep 1857-M 18-7-6), George 18 (Mar 1882), Fletcher 16 (Oct 1883), Malcum 13 (Oct 1886), Emmit 9 (July 1890), Florence 8 (May 1892), Burk 6 (June 1894)[last entry marked through], Maud M. 1 (May 1899) 3-206B-113/123
Noah L. Cate 64 (May 1836-M 5)(Sewing Machine Agent), Minnie 45 (Dec 1854-M 5-0-0), Ella L. MILLER 16 (ne)(Feb 1883) 14-217A-86/87
William Cate 50 (Dec 1841-T/T/Ky-M 13)(Shoemaker), Martha 37 (Ap 1863-M 13-7-4), William M. 20 (Mar 1880)(RR Laborer), Della M. 18 (Dec 1881), Hester E. 16 (Oct 1883), Bertha J. 12 (Mar 1888), Albert R. 8 (Oct 1891), Rosa E. 3 (Feb 1897), Infant 0/12 (s)(Mar 1900) 14-214B-26/27
MARRIAGES
Annie Coats(?) to William Smalls q.v.
Eliza F. Coats to J. C. Abel q.v.
Eliza Cate to John W. Hughes q.v.
G. O. Cates to Mary D. Smith, 28 July 1858 (29 July), A. King MG 1-#644
J.D. Cate to Kate Atkinson, 19 Feb 1893, J.M. Hinds MG 4-74
James Cate to Leah Hes, 12 Sep 1870 (no return) 1-#1165
John Cates to Margaret Condley, 17 Mar 1860 (same), A.W. Frazier JP 1-#1660
Joseph Cates to Louisa Largent, 7 June 1851 (9 June), S.R. Hackett JP 1-#340
Lucinda Cates to J. D. Whaley q.v.
Mary Cate to John P. Bolin q.v.
Mary F. Cate to James M. Atchley q.v.
Noah Cate to Lucinda Ray, 18 Ap 1895, L.E. Smith JP 4-82
Sarah Cate to Elias Gothard q.v.
Susanah Cates to William Smith q.v.
W.A. Cate to Mattie Phillips, 25 Dec 1886 (28 Dec), J.T. Nolen MG 1-528

- - - - - - - - - - - - -

CATHBERT

1900 CENSUS

Benjamin Cathbert 41 (Nov 1858-Ga/Ga/Ga-M 1), Willie 23 (Sep 1876-Ga/Ga/Ga-M 1-0-0), Dora 16 (Mar 1884-Ga) 10-327B-163/172 (B)

- - - - - - - - - - - -

CATHEY

1900 CENSUS

Orlena Cathey 58 (Oct 1841-Wd 1-1), Allen 27 (Nov 1872-Ala)(Coal Miner) 10-329B-202/215

- - - - - - - - - - - -

CAUGHT

MARRIAGE

William Caught to Renie Miller, 5 Sep 1896 (6 Sep), F.M. Cook MG, William Eaves [signed by X] W 2-64

- - - - - - - - - - - -

CAULEY

1880 CENSUS

Rufus Cauley 25, F.J. 26, Casey 4 (d), Alvina LAMB 50 (ml), Catharine LAMB 18 (sil), Willie 6 ("child") 8-9-74 (B)

- - - - - - - - - - - -

CAWOOD / CAYWOOD / KEYWOOD

1860 CENSUS

Stephen S. Keywood 37, Louisa A. 37, Andrew N. 6, Mary J. 4, George M. 1, Andrew J. KEYWOOD 34, Susan J. 24 1-89-609 [Stephen Cawood married Louisa A. Nixon on 21 Dec 1852 in Roane Co]

1870 CENSUS

Stephen Cawood 46, Louisa A. 46 (Va), Andrew N. 16, Mary Jane 14, George M. 12, Rebecca CAWOOD 75, Nancy REED 27, Jesse 8, Isabella 3, Polly CRAIG (B) 25, Maggie (B) 5, Willie (B) 4 1-7-43

Susan Cawood 34: see William G. Roddy

1880 CENSUS

Andrew Cawood 24, Parthena 25, Mattie 3, Willie 1, Pettie SCOTT 15 (adopted) 1-11-86

Stephen Cawood 57, Louisa 57, George 21 (s), Rebecca 84 (m), Polly CRAIG (B) 40 (Servant), Willie (B) 10 (Servant), Cora MOORE (B) 10 (Servant), George (B) 16 (Servant), William WARNACK 23 (boarder) 1-12-95

1900 CENSUS

Anderson Cawood 45 (July 1854-M 25), Anie 45 (Sep 1854-M 25-8-8), Wilum 21 (May 1879), Mattie 23 (Oct 1876), Stephen 18 (July 1881), Wash 16 (Dec 1882), Margit 12 (July 1887), Thomas 9 (Ap 1891), James 5 (Mar 1895), Anie 1 (June 1898), Stephen 76 (f)(Feb 1824-Wd)(Cattle Dealer) 1-187A-158/166

Lewis Cawood 41 (Oct 1858-T/Va/Va-M 19), Alice 36 (Feb 1864-M 19-8-8), Eller 17 (Sep 1882), Charles 15 (June 1884), Robbert 12 (June 1887), Mary 11 (Sep 1888), Annie 10 (May 1890), Milli 8 (May 1892), Perl 6 (Aug 1897), Stephen 4/12 (Feb 1900) 1-185A-123/129

Stephen Cawood 76: see Anderson Cawood

MARRIAGES

A.J. Cawood to S.J. Roddy, 14 Feb 1860 (16 Feb), S. Phillips MG 1-#1647

A.N. Cawood to Parthena Foust, 20 Aug 1875 (1 Sep), G.W. Renfro MG 1-#1406

Mary J. Caywood to John L. Bell q.v.

Susan J. Cawood to Morgan Bryan q.v.

- - - - - - - - - - - -

CECIL

MARRIAGE

Nannie B. Cecil to C. M. DeLafayette q.v.

- - - - - - - - - - - -

CENTER / SENTER / CENETER

1900 CENSUS

Nancy Senter 51: see Danie May

William D. Center 67 (Jan 1843-SC/SC/SC-M 25)(Coal Miner), Martha C. 51 (Feb 1849-NC/NC/NC-M 25-6-6), John 24 (July 1875)(Coal Miner), Thomas R. 19 (Oct 1880)(Coal Miner), Eliza J. 17 (Feb 1883), Laura A. 15 (Ap 1885), Rosa I. 12 (Sep 1887) 8-278A-191/193

MARRIAGES

Charley L. Ceneter to Susan A. Russell, 19 Nov 1887 (20 Nov), W.R. Grimsley JP 1-542

Eliza Center to John Wasborne q.v.

Florence Center to W. N. Holden q.v.

- - - - - - - - - - - -

CHADWICK / CHADRICK / CHADDICK

1870 CENSUS

Hardie Chadwick 22, Margurette R. 2: see Richard H. Jordan

William O. Chadwick 61 (Chairmaker), Rachel C. 34 1-23-152

1880 CENSUS

H.H. Chadwick 34, M.J. 30 (w), A.J. 6 (d), S.T. 5 (s) 8-11-96

John Chadwick 39, Becky 35 (w), John 15 (s), Elizabeth 13, Dollie 10, Creed 8, Mollie 6, N.J. 4 (d), J.A. 2 (d) 8-13-109

John Chadrick 52 (Real Estate Agent), Lucretia 43, Martha 15, Amanda TERRY 28 (Servant) 2-22-180

Mary J. Chadrick 69: see W. S. Gillespie

MARRIAGES

Alice Chadwick to Worthy Swift q.v.

Hardy Chadwick to Mary Burwick, 28 Oct 1870 (29 Oct), Wm A. Green JP 1-#1170

Malind Chaddick to James H. Morgan q.v.

- - - - - - - - - - - -

CHAMBERS / CHAMBER / CAMBERS

1860 CENSUS

John W. Chambers 56 (NC)(Silversmith), Frances 33, Susannah H. 23, Richard 17, Charity M. 11 6-110-750

1870 CENSUS
Frances Chambers 49, Susan 31, Charity M. 28, Nancy M. 5 6-11-68
1880 CENSUS
H.D. Chambers 35, M.A. 36, J.A. 11 (d), W.D. 9 (s), J.L. 7 (d), S.E. 1 (d) 11-39-316
Francis Cambers 53, Susanaher H. 41, Nancy M. 15 6-22-8
Tenas Chambers 24 (B): see R. T. Coulter
1900 CENSUS
James A. Chambers 22 (Sep 1878-T/T/NC-M 1)(Comercial), Maggie 22 (Aug 1878-T/England/Do-M 1-1-1), Clyde M. 3/12 (Mar 1900) 3-200A-7/7
John D. Chambers 51 (May 1849-T/Va/T-M 30)(General Merchandise), Vinnie 52 (Aug 1848-NC/NC/NC-M 30-8-6), Homer 18 (July 1882), Lassie 20 (Sep 1879-NC), Lola 16 (June 1884-Ga), Ollie 14 (Sep 1886-Ga), Lister 12 (Aug 1888-Ga) 3-200A-6/6
Malinda(?) H. Chamber 57 (Jan 1843-T/Va/SC-Wd 5-2), Elizabeth 21 (d)(Nov 1878), John F. 13 (s)(Sep 1886) 8-313B-59/62
Susan Chambers 61: see George M. Harrison
MARRIAGES
Maggie Chambers to Felix McCabe q.v.
P.L. Chambers to Mary J. Buttram, 31 Mar 1888 (5 Ap), J.W. Pearce MG 1-545
Susan Chambers to B. B. Travis q.v.

- - - - - - - - - - - - -

CHAMPION

1870 CENSUS
William R. Champion 30 (Ga), Samantha E. 30, Mary Jane 3, William M. 1, Elizabeth SMITH 28 8-17-120
MARRIAGE
Ellen Champion to George Orr q.v.

- - - - - - - - - - - - -

CHANEY

MARRIAGES
C. L. Chaney to Amanda Chaney, 7 Jan 1886 (same), A.W. Frazier JP 1-500

- - - - - - - - - - - - -

CHAPLIN

1900 CENSUS
Lydia E. Chaplin 60: see Benjamin Bracher

- - - - - - - - - - - - -

CHAPMAN

MARRIAGE
John Chapman to Mary Ann Lowry, 1 Nov 1853 (same), R.T. Howard MG 1-#427

- - - - - - - - - - - - -

CHASE

1900 CENSUS
Sarah A. Chase 67: see John B. Beugler

- - - - - - - - - - - - -

CHASTAIN

MARRIAGE
Louisa C. Chastain to Jasper N. McDonald q.v.

- - - - - - - - - - - - -

CHATTIN / CHATTEN

1860 CENSUS
Elizabeth Chatten 105* (NC): see Henry Eaton [*oldest citizen in 1860]
Jesse Chatten 54 (Va): see Robert N. Clack
John Chatten 83 (Va), Catherine 82, Frederick 36 8-24-160
John D. Chattin 52 (Va), Susan 35, John C. 12, William T. 1 3-55-374
1870 CENSUS
Susan Chattin 45, William F. 11, Kate A. 8, Robert P. 7, Mary E. 5, Richard CHATTIN (B) 10 3-19-140
Easter Chattin 16 (B): see Stephen Spence
1880 CENSUS
A.C. Chattin 48, D. 39, Willie 13 (s), Frank 10, Mary 8, James 6, James E. 48 9-32-280 (Mu) (B)
Susan Chattin 55, F.M. 21 (s), R.P. 17 (s), A.M. 15 (d) 3-18-142
1900 CENSUS
Abe Chatin 72 (May 1828-T/Va/Va-Wd) 7-265B-292/297 (B)
Abil Chattin 3/12: see Flora Tellow (B)
Fred W. Chattin 41 (Feb 1859-M 16), Margaret A. 39 (May 1861-M 16-6-6), John D. 14 (Oct 1885), Susan C. 10 (Aug 1890), Kattin A. 8 (Dec 1891), Ernest 6 (May 1894), Annie M. 4 (May 1896), Burch C. 5/12 (Dec 1899), Kattie BROWN 33 (Nov 1866)(Servant) 3-206A-107/117
Isom Chatten 39 (July 1862-T/T/Ga-M 14), Anne 35 (Jan 1864-M 14-7-7)(Washwoman), George 13 (Aug 1886), Marey 11 (Nov 1888), Maud 9 (Oct 1890), Hellen 7 (Nov 1892), Augusta 5 (Ap 1895), Eddie 2 (June 1897), Wallace 8/12 (Sep 1899) 10-252A-47/47 (B)
Lewis Chatten 60 (Jan 1840-M 31), Rose E. 48 (Mar 1852-T/Va/Va-M 31-1-1), Henery R. 10 (Nov 1889) 10-257B-145/149 (B)
Sallie Chaten 32 (B) see James Pursur
Susan Chattin 75 (May 1825-T/Va/SC-Wd 5-4), Mary E. 35 (Mar 1865-T/Va/T) 3-206A-110/120

MARRIAGES
Bell Chattin to Cicero Cook q.v.
Caty Chattin to S. W. Tindell q.v.
Dafney Chattin to Byrd Hinch q.v.
Emily F. Chattin to John A. Bean q.v.
Isam Chattin to Anna Gillespie, 18 Nov 1885 (same), P.P. Brooks ?? 1-484
Mary Chattin to Thomas Houston q.v.
R.C. Chattin to Lucy Shaver, 8 May 1897 (10 May), L.E. Smith JP, I.W. Wilkson W 2-145
W.F. Chattin to Annie Clack, 15 Oct 1884 (same), J.H. Weaver ?? 1-492
W.M. Chattin to Sallie Tullom, 25 Jan 1887 (same), W.S. Hale MG 1-526

- - - - - - - - - - - - -

CHENP(?)

1900 CENSUS
Birt Chenp(?) 26: see Sam McClendon

- - - - - - - - - - - - -

CHILCOAT

1900 CENSUS
John Chilcoat(?) 54 (May 1846-Oh/Oh/Oh-M 30), Elisie 56 (May 1844-Oh/Oh/Oh-M 30-7-6), Francas 18 (Mar 1882-Oh), Franklin 27 (June 1873-Oh)(Pattern Maker) 1-189A-199/208 (Spring City)

- - - - - - - - - - - - -

CHILDS
(see also SCHILL / SCHILDE)

1900 CENSUS
Almy Childs 60(?) (Ap 1840(?)-Mich/Mich/Mich)(School Teacher), Idier 25 (boarder)(Jan 1875) 12-179B-16/18
Taylor M. Childs 53 (Oct 1846-SC/SC/SC-M 23), Nancy C. 44 (June 1855-M 23-1-0), Susan PRAYER 42 (sil)(Ap 1858-M 12-4-2) 2-194A-53/55

- - - - - - - - - - - - -

CHRISTIAN

1870 CENSUS
Hillery Christian 12: see Nicholas Frazier

- - - - - - - - - - - - -

CHUMLEY / CHUMLY

1860 CENSUS
William Chumly 54 (NC), Matilda 47, Hester A. 17, Hugh L. 14 5-31-204
1870 CENSUS
Mariah Chumley 30, James 6: see Jacob Byrely [Barley]
William Chumley 64 (NC), Matilda 57, Jackson S. 33 (Tax Collector) 6-10-64
1880 CENSUS
M. [Mariah] Chumly 46, J.H. 16 (s) 7-25-218
1900 CENSUS
James Chumly 38 (Dec 1863-M 12), Bettie 28 (Feb 1872-M 12-4-4), Dillia V. 11 (Aug 1889), Willie C. 10 (Mar 1890), Dacia T. 8 (Sep 1891), Fredick D. 6 (Feb 1894) 7-267A-325/330
MARRIAGES
Hester Ann Chumly to William D. Birely q.v.
J.H. Chumley to S.E. Bowlin [Boles], 8 Oct 1887 (9 Oct), James A. Crawford JP 1-537
J.S. Chumley to Ann E. Wilson, 24 Nov 1873 (25 Nov), A.P. Early MG [omitted by copier between 1-#1312 & 1-#1313]
J.S. Chumley to Ann E. Wilson, 20 Nov 1873 (22 Nov), A.P. Early MG 1-#1662
W.H. Chumly to Mary Byerly, 24 Nov 1860 (25 Nov), John Lay MG 1-#733

- - - - - - - - - - - - -

CHURCHILL

1880 CENSUS
Wilson Churchill 42 (Ver), Mary 40 (Ver), Eugene 19 (Ver), Lilian 17 (Ver), Delmont 4 (Wisc) 12-1-3

- - - - - - - - - - - - -

CINNAMON

MARRIAGE
Susan Cinnamon to N. W. Rice q.v.

- - - - - - - - - - - - -

CIVILS / SIVILS

MARRIAGE
Jeptha Civils [sic] to Ruth E. Sivils [sic]. 20 Nov 1866 (same), R.T. Howard MG 1-#921

- - - - - - - - - - - - -

CLACK
(see also CLARK)

1860 CENSUS
John T. Clack 29, Harriet J. 22, James T. 9/12, John DONALDSON (B) 40 2-71-484
Micajah Clack 61 (Ky), Margaret 64, Spencer 27 (School Teacher), Micajah 24, William R. 21 (School Teacher), Anny 31 2-73-497
Robert N. Clack 33, Mary J. 23, James L. 1, Eliza A. 35, Rebecca L. 31, Lemesa(?) K. 27, Jesse CHATTIN 54 (Va) 3-65-447
William Clack 43, Galelah G. [Isabella] 41, Martha A. 18, Missouri 16, Leander P. 14, John B. 12, Eliza J. 10, Mary L. 8, George N. 6, William R. 1 3-63-436
1870 CENSUS
John S. Clack 39, Isabella 30, Anna 8, John M. 6, Newton E. 3, William McNEW 11 3-20-144
Marion Clack 47, Mary C. 33 (Switzerland), Susan M. 12, John S. 10 (Student), Vina L. 8, Robert W. 6, George N. 3, Mary A. 1 3-16-114
Micajah Clack 32, Marguerette 26, Mary 8, Bill R. 5, Thomas 2, Louisa HARRIS 19 3-18-134
Micajah Clack 72 (Ky), Margaret 74 2-6-43
Robert N. Clack 41, Mary J. 32, James S. 10, Missouri R. 7, Martha 4, John T. 1, Eliza A. CLACK 48, Vina 38 3-14-103
Spencer Clack 35, Jane 30, Tennessee 7, Ann B. 4, Elizabeth 1 3-18-13
Spencer G. Clack 36, Jane 34, Tennessee 5, Ann B. 4, Aroze(?) A.E. (f) 1 2-6-44
William M. Clack 53, Isabella G. 52, Martha A. 28, Leander P. 24, John B. 22 (School Teacher), Eliza J. 20, Mary L. 18, George N. 16, Wm R. 11, Alexander CLACK (B) 17 (Ga) 3-19-139
William R. Clack 31, Sabra C. 21, Vesta V. 3, Hugh B. 2 2-6-42
1880 CENSUS
John Clack 49, Sarah 37, Annie 19, J.M. 16, Frank 17, N.E. 12 (s), Alice 9, H.E. 7 (d) 3-17-131

Micajah Clack 81, William 41 (s), Caroline 31 (dl), Cesta 12 (gd), Hugh 12 (gs), Margaret 9 (gd), Annie 6 (gd), Micajah 1/12 (gs), George BAKER 22 (Servant) 2-34-281

Spencer Clack 46 (Instructor), Jane 41, Tennessee 16, Anna 14, Kittie 10, Margaret 7, Walter 2 2-35-283

Wm Clack 63, I.G. 61, M.A. 32 (d), Mary 26 (d) 3-18-144

1900 CENSUS

Bernelia Clack 55 (Dec 1844-Ga/Ga/Ga-Wd 3-3), James T. 21 (Sep 1878), John J. 19 (July 1880), Partia 15 (June 1884-Ala) 10-258B-162/166

William M. Clack 83 (May 1817-T/Va/Va-Wd), Martha A. 57 (d)(July 1842), Mary L. 48 (d)(May 1852) 3-207B-135/148

William R. Clack 61 (Feb 1839-M 34), Sabrie C. 51 (Ap 1849-M 34-6-6), Hugh B. 32 (May 1868)(Saw Mill Engineer), Margaret E. 28 (June 1871), Amy L. 26 (Sep 1873)(School Teacher), Sarah C. 24 (Feb 1876) (School Teacher), Raleigh M. 20 (Feb 1880), Anay JOHNSON 71 (si)(Feb 1829-T/Ky/T-Wd 0-0) 2-191B-12/12

MARRIAGES

Alice Clack to S. S. Eaves q.v.

Annabell Clack to E. S. Mills q.v.

Annie Clack to W. F. Charrin q.v.

Anny Clack to James Johnson q.v.

Catharine Clack to Larkin Brown q.v.

Charley B.(?) Clack or Clark [could be Blalock] to Ida Trentham, 1 Ap 1898 (3 Ap), W.S. Hale MG, J.C. Clack W 2-262

E.J. Clack to Thomas Riggins q.v.

J.S. Clack to H.J. Gibson, 23 Jan 1868 (26 Jan), Nathaniel Barnett MG 1-#1653

John S. Clack to Margaret Isabella Wilson, 20 Feb 1867 (21 Feb), A.P. Early MG 1-#938

John S. Clack to Sarah Foust, 20 Feb 1877 (21 Feb), John Howard MG 1-#1486

L. K. Clack to C. P. S. Johns q.v.

M.R. Clack to M.A. Horner, 27 Oct 1860 (1 Nov), James Carson MG 1-#736

R.N. Clack to Mary J. Chattin, 18 Dec 1857 (22 Dec), A. Johns MG 1-#623

Spencer G. Clack to Dealtha Jane Wilson, 9 Ap 1862 (10 Ap), A. Johns MG 1-#779

Susan Clack to James Lemmons q.v.

Susan M. Clack to Houston Hurst q.v.

Taylor Clack to Eliza Williamson, 18 Sep 1889 (same), A.B. Anderson MG 1-582

Vesta V. Clack to Samuel J. Galloway q.v.

William R. Clack to Sabra C. Newport, 11 Sep 1865 (14 Sep), W.W. Low JP 1-#1089

- - - - - - - - - - - - -

CLAFLIN

MARRIAGE

Carrie Claflin to C. D. Foust q.v.

- - - - - - - - - - - - -

CLEAGUE / CLAGUE / CLAGE / CLAIG

1880 CENSUS

J.E. Cleage 30, A.M. 21, Alice 13, Luna(?) 10, Catharine 8, Tim 6, Ida 4, Young 2 3-24-189 (B)

Richard Cleag 20 (Servant), Adaline 21 (Cook), John 2, Emma 1 (B): see John Abernathy

1900 CENSUS

Jefferson Claig 57 (Unk 1847-T/Va/T-M 35), Rachal A. 57 (Unk 1847-T/T/Ga-M 35-15-9), Thomas 20 (Oct 1879), Virgil 15 (June 1884), Loyd 13 (Sep 1886), Susan 12 (Sep 1887), Emma 11 (Mar 1889), Martin 9 (Mar 1891), Louis 8 (Mar 1892) 15-272B-84/84 (B)

MARRIAGES

Annie Clage to B. F. Perry q.v.

Emma Cleague to Robert Carter q.v.

Ida Clague(?) to Alex Bennett q.v.

- - - - - - - - - - - - -

CLANAHAN

MARRIAGE

Dora M. Clanahan to Newt Bowman q.v.

- - - - - - - - - - - - -

CLARDS

1900 CENSUS

James Clards 23 (Ap 1887-M 0)(Fireman, Dayton), Uney 18 (July 1881-Ga/Ga/Ga-M 0), Lee 20 (c)(July 1880-M 0), Sardis 20 (c)(Feb 1880-Ga/T/Unk-M 0) 10-256A-112/116

- - - - - - - - - - - - -

CLARENTS

MARRIAGE

Wm Clarents to Betsy Ann Ives, 16 Oct 1855 (same), J.W. Thompson MG 1-#521

- - - - - - - - - - - - -

CLARK
(see also CLACK)

1860 CENSUS

Sarah A. Clark 19, Amanda F. 14, William L. 12: see Archibald D. Paul

Thomas Clark 39 (NC), Margaret L. 23 (NC), William 4, Mary F. 4 2-73-500

Wiley G. Clark 32, Mary 26 1-85-581

1870 CENSUS

David Clark 25 (NC), Mary C.A. 4, Margaret M. 2 2-13-91

Laura Clark 14 (B): see Wiley G. Clark

Leander W. Clark 22, Sarah A. 29: see Rebecca Paul

Rebecca Clark 65 (NC), Judah 30, John F. 16, James E. 13: see James Lemmons

Sarah Clark 47 (NC), Margaritt M. 23 (NC), Andrew J. 22 (NC), Mary E. 20 (Ga), Henrietta F. 19 (SC), Susan C. 17 (SC), William H. 15 (SC), John A. 14 (Ga), Edward R. 12 (Ga), Eli W. 11 (Ga) 1-14-91

Wilbern Clark 62 (NC), Eveline 19 (NC), Elizabeth 12 2-12-84

Wiley G. Clark 42, Mary E. 37, Laura CLARK (B) 14 1-10-63

1880 CENSUS

Elizabeth Clark 22: see Jacob Roos

Elizabeth Clark 64: see Isaac Bird

Isaac Clark 16: see William Tarwater

Jane Clark 47: see J. W. Thompson

Leander Clark 32, Sarah 25, John 7, Eliza 5, James 3, Rebecca 2/12 2-37-298 [see Wm M. Clack]
Wilburn Clark 68, Mary 34 (w), John 9 (s), Louella 4 (d), Elbert 2 (s) 1-16-137

1900 CENSUS

Harden Clark 18: see Andrew J. Tallent
James A. Clark 45 (Dec 1854-T/T/NC-M 14), Elizabeth 36 (Oct 1863-M 14-3-3), Samuel F. 10 (Dec 1889), Cora L. 7 (Dec 1892), Earnest H. 5 (Jan 1895) 6-247A-140/141
James M. Clark 37 (Mar 1863-Ky/NC/T-M 17), Harriet B. 32 (June 1867-M 17-7-7), William H. 15 (Dec 1884), John T. 13 (June 1886), Jesse S. 12 (Sep 1887), Mary E. 8 (June 1891), Nora A. 6 (July 1894), Alice M. 5 (Ap 1895), Flossie 2 (May 1898), Thomas D. 34 (b) (July 1865-Ky/NC/T) 11-290B-20/20
Jane Clark 67: see Anna Crosby
Mosses D. Clark 29: see James Cunningham
William R. Clark 32 (July 1867-T/T/NC-M 12)(Bed Springs Dealer), Lou 33 (Feb 1867-NC/NC/NC-M 12-6-5), Martha J. 11 (Sep 1888), Elda I. 8 (July 1891), Roseta 6 (Mar 1893), Stella G. 4 (Ap 1896), Dewey 1 (July 1898) 6-242B-57
Wilm Clark 65 (Jan 1835-Oh/Oh/Oh-M 25), Seelby 60 (Feb 1840-Oh/Oh/Oh-M 25-0-0), Liddie DANA 29 (boarder)(Ap 1871)(Housekeeper) 12-179B-15/17

MARRIAGES

A.J. Clark to Grace M. Patterson, 30 Aug 1891, J.R. Walker MG 4-33
Carry C. Clark to George W. Lemmons q.v.
Cenie(?) Clark to Henry Johnson q.v.
Charley B.(?) Clark– see Clack
Elizabeth Clark to Thomas Miller q.v.
Ella Clark to J. T. Bean q.v.
Ellen Clark to Jacob Ross q.v.
Gilbert Clark to Emeline Swafford, 21 Feb 1893 (no return) 4-53
Ida Clark to Bruer(?) Morgan q.v.
J.R. Clark to M.A.M. Powers, 7 June 1900, J.H. Keylon JP 4-105
Jacob Clark to Mary A. Brown, 12 Sep 1882, no MG or JP 4-10(98)
John Clark to Kittie McDonald, 13 Jan 1887 (same), M.C. Bermer MG 1-521 (B)
Jonah Clark to Fannie Vann, 20 Feb 1899, no MG or JP 2-385
L. E. Clark to E. H. Thompson q.v.
Leander Clark to Sarah Bohannon, 18 Feb 1872 (same), Daniel Hodges JP 1-#1231
Lucy Clark to James S. Bowles q.v.
Margaret M. Clark to James P. Sawyer q.v.
Mary Clark to Moses Miller q.v.
Molly Clark to James Sullivan q.v.
Sally Clark to Henry Hoseman q.v.
Sapina or Sophena Clark to James M. McDowell q.v.
Sarah S. Clark to John B. Breeding q.v.
Taylor Clark to Tishie Stephens, 14 June 1885 (same), I.W. Holt JP 1-495
Thomas Clark to Josie Harwood or Howard, 22 July 1890, James Corvin MG 4-45
Wilburn Clark (60, Bale Co, NC) to Mary J. Brogdan or Broglan (49, Blount Co), 30 Oct 1881, S. Breeding JP, Daniel Miller W 4-6(55)

- - - - - - - - - - - - -

CLAWSON

MARRIAGE

A.T. Clawson to Manervia Fletcher, 20 June 1851 (22 June), Daniel Broyles JP 1-#343

- - - - - - - - - - - - -

CLAY

1900 CENSUS

Bird Clay 20 (Feb 1880-Ala/SC/Ga-S)(RR Section Hand), Isaac MURRY 42 (Mar 1858-Ga/Ga/Ga-M 20)(RR Section Hand), Peter HUGHES 25 (May 1875-S)(RR Section Hand) 5-233B-115 (B)

MARRIAGE

Fannie Clay to Robert Mannual q.v.

- - - - - - - - - - - - -

CLAYTON

MARRIAGES

Minnie Clayton to C. F. Marney q.v.
W.A. Clayton to Maggy Powers, 5 Dec 1867 (same), T.N.L. Cunnyngham JP 1-#983

- - - - - - - - - - - - -

CLEMENTS / CLEMENT

1860 CENSUS

Mary L. Clements 23: see Sallie Ryan

MARRIAGES

Thomas Clements to Rosa Hawkins, 19 Mar 1897 (9 Mar) [sic], M.B. Hicks JP, Frank Baskett W 2-128
W.F. Clement to M.T. Fox, 12 Sep 1900 (13 Sep), D.V. Culver MG, Jake or John Brack(?) E 3-214

- - - - - - - - - - - - -

CLEMONS / CLEMMONS

1880 CENSUS

John Clemmons 28: see T. J. Knight

1900 CENSUS

George D. Clemons 34 (Jan 1866-M 0), Isabella 25 (Jan 1875-M 0-1-1), Stella 8 (Nov 1891), Walter L. 6 (Feb 1894), Lillie B. 4 (Oct 1895), Ira K. 3/12 (Feb 1900) 13-300A-181/186

- - - - - - - - - - - - -

CLENDENIN

MARRIAGE

D.C. Clendenin to Harriet S. Waterhouse, 2 Oct 1895, R.A. Owens MG [sic], J.F. Hash or Hook MG [sic] 4-90

- - - - - - - - - - - - -

CLENDON

MARRIAGE

Viola M. Clendon to J. L. Dunlap q.v.

- - - - - - - - - - - - -

CLIFT / CLIFF / CLIFE

1900 CENSUS
Peter J. Clift 53 (Mar 1847) 10-327A-151/159 (B)
Ronie Clife(?) 72: see John Henry(?) Gass
Siah Cliff 24: see Jim Coaplin (B)
MARRIAGE
J.J. Clift to E.L. Reavely, 11 May 1861 (no return) 1-#753

- - - - - - - - - - - - -

CLIFTON

1860 CENSUS
Eldridge Clifton 44 (NC), Allice M. 34, Thomas B. 11, Elizabeth 8, Robert E. 6, Amos B. 5, Eldridge 3, John B. 1, Bailey CLIFTON 84 1-94-645
1870 CENSUS
Alderago Clifton 55 (NC), Alice 45, Thomas B. 21, Elizabeth 18, Robert 16, Amos 14, Alderago 13, John 12, Mary 10, George 8, Alice 6, Rebecca 2, Susan 11/12, Sarah F. MOORE 17 1-16-105
1880 CENSUS
Amos Clifton 25, Nancy 25, Lou Ella 3, William 2/3 [born Sep] 12-6-54
Peter Clifton 60 (NC), Alice 54, Thomas 29, Malinda 32, John 19, Alice 15, Rebecca 12, Susan 9, Aldridge 7, George 17 (s) 12-6-53
Robert W. Clifton 25, Nancy 24 12-6-49
1900 CENSUS
Amos(?) Clifton 49 (Mar 1851-T/NC/T-M 26), Satha 45 (Ap 1854-M 26-6-5), Milburn 20 (Sep 1879), Bell 18 (Mar 1882), Almon 15 (June 1884), Clide 14 (Ap 1886), Auther 8 (July 1891), James 5 (July 1894), Kate 2 (May 1898) 1-183A-85/88
Amos Clifton 31 (June 1868-Ala/Ala/Ala-M 9)(Furnaceman), Sarah 22 (Aug 1877-Ga/Ga/Ga-M 9-1-0), Jeff McCULLIS 35 (boarder)(Unk-Fla)(Furnaceman) 10-328B-177/188 (B)
MARRIAGES
E. B. Clifton to Elijah Smith q.v.
Flora Clifton to Pink Rodgers q.v.
Robert Clifton to Nancy F. Haze, 22 Dec 1875 (23 Dec), James Johnson JP [sic] 1-#1423
Thomas B. Clifton to Mary S. Glass, no bond date (27 Jan 1871), James Johnson MG [sic] 1-#1183

- - - - - - - - - - - - -

CLINE

1900 CENSUS
Hariet A. Cline 25, Anna L. 2, Phillip 6/12: see Isaac W. Barnett
Winnie Cline 68: see Mattie Stewart (B)
MARRIAGE
Susannah Cline to Samuel H. Myres q.v.

- - - - - - - - - - - - -

CLINGON / CLINGAN

1860 CENSUS
William Clingan 33, Caroline M. 36, Mary C. 13, Martha R. 12, William A. 10, Margaret J. 9 8-10-61
1870 and 1880 CENSUS– None
1900 CENSUS
Alexander Clingan 45 (June 1854-M 15)(Station Engineer), Margaret A. 33 (Feb 1867-M 15-5-4), Annie B. 13 (July 1886), Maud B. 11 (May 1889), George W. 6 (Dec 1893-Ala), Maggie N. 2 (June 1897), Robert T. 22 (nw)(Mar 1878)(Coal Miner), Elijah 18 (nw)(Dec 1880)(Coal Miner) 10-329A-186/199
Ellen Clingan 19: see John Swafford
Emma K. Clingan 20: see Isaac N. Shipley
John Clingan 36 (Nov 1863-M 13)(Dry Goods Salesman), Sipie 30 (Sep 1869-M 13-4-4), John G. 12 (Aug 1887), Cora 8 (July 1891), Grover 6 (Sep 1893), Byran 3 (Dec 1896), Linda 18 (ne)(Aug 1881) 8-288A-399/401

MARRIAGES
Alex(?) [ink blob] Clingan to Allice Byrley, 6 Dec 1884 (7 Dec), J.Q. Shaver MG 1-461
Alex Clingan to Margarett Grass, 27 Dec 1879 (28 Dec), R.H. Jordan MG 1-#1711
George Clingon to Sarah Bolen, 3 Nov 1877 (4 Nov), J.R. Crawford JP 1-#1523

- - - - - - - - - - - - -

CLONCE

MARRIAGE
Ollie J. Clonce to Thomas Rouff q.v.

- - - - - - - - - - - - -

CLONIUS

1900 CENSUS
William B. Clonius 27 (May 1873-Va/Va/Va-M 4)(RR Engineer), Millie 21 (Nov 1878-Va/Va/Va-M 4-2-2), Ethel 2 (July 1897-Va), Havas 9/12 (Aug 1899-Va) 10-254A-81

- - - - - - - - - - - - -

CLOUR / CLOYER

MARRIAGES
Nancy N. Clour to Jacob Webb q.v.
Nannie Cloyer to D.J. Doss q.v.

- - - - - - - - - - - - -

CLOUSE

1900 CENSUS
Henry Clouse 74 (Dec 1825-T/T/NC-M 53), Mary E. 75 (Oct 1826-M 53-4-2) 13-304A-269/279
John W. Clouse 58 (Feb 1842-M 19), Martha E. 36 (Oct 1863-T/Ala/T-M 19-7-6), Alvin W. 17 (Sep 1882) (Post Office Clerk), John C. 15 (Feb 1885), Mamie C. 11 (June 1888), Daisy M. 9 (Sep 1890), Margaret M. 5 (Jan 1895), Robert Mc. 1 (Ap 1899) 13-308B-316/328
Lee Clouse 20 (Aug 1879-M 0), Sallie 20 (Feb 1880-Ga/T/T-M 0) 8-283B-303/305

Peter B. Clouse 46 (Mar 1854-M 16)(Coal Miner), Mary A. 32 (Feb 1868-M 16-8-7), William H. 15 (Dec 1884-Mo), James H. 11 (Nov 1888), L. Barton 9 (Feb 1891), Amos B. 7 (Feb 1893), Mary V. 5 (Mar 1895), Saudie B. 3 (Ap 1897), Emma R. 0/12 (May 1900) 13-301B-210/218

MARRIAGES

Annie Clouse to W. M. Pryor q.v.

Bertha Clouse to William T. Alley q.v.

John W. Clouse to Martha E. Everett, 16 Oct 1880 (17 Oct), W.A. Green JP 1-29

Katie C. Clouse to Lafayette Gott q.v.

Nettie E. Clouse to James E. Burnett q.v.

- - - - - - - - - - - - -

COACH

1900 CENSUS

Thomas Coach 20: see Sol Harwood

- - - - - - - - - - - - -

COALLER

1900 CENSUS

Brahat Coaller Jr. 30 (Aug 1869-T/T/Va-M 1)(Undertaker), Sania 25 (Dec 1874-T/Md/T-M 1-1-1), Robert J. 5/12 (Dec 1899), Addie HOLEMAN (B) 19 (Sep 1880) (Servant) 10-254A-80

- - - - - - - - - - - - -

COATNEY

MARRIAGE

Horace Coatney to Callie McDonald, 3 Oct 1879 (4 Oct), W.S. Hale MG 1-#1680

- - - - - - - - - - - - -

COBB / COBBS

1860 CENSUS

George W. Cobb 34 (Ga)(Collecting Officer), Sarah A. 20 6-111-758

1870 CENSUS– None

1880 CENSUS

C.L. Cobb 47, J.H. 45, John 16, Eliza 14, Tom 6, Etta 3 9-31-269

MARRIAGES

Eva Cobb to A. D. Donahoo q.v.

John H. Cobb to Mary Parkinson, 26 May 1891, J.A. Darr MG 4-29

Lizzie Cobb to S. M. Jenkins q.v.

- - - - - - - - - - - - -

COBBAN

1900 CENSUS

Etta M. Cobban 40 (Jan 1860-NY/NY/NY-D 3-3), Harold H. 18 (Feb 1882-Minn), Mary I. 16 (May 1884-Minn), Frankie M. 15 (Mar 1885-Minn) 13-310A-386/400

- - - - - - - - - - - - -

COBURN

MARRIAGE

John Coburn to Martha A. Collier, 1 May 1865 (10 May), John Howard MG 1-#877

- - - - - - - - - - - - -

COCK / COKE

(see also KOCH)

1870 CENSUS

James L. Coke 26, Margaret 15 2-10-69

John R. Cock 26 (Ala)(School Teacher), Sarah J. 24 (Ala), Walter P. 4, Lee M. 2, John C. 8/12 3-15-112

- - - - - - - - - - - - -

COCKRAN / COCHRUM

1900 CENSUS

John Cochran 45 (Jan 1856-Ga/Ga/Ga-M 18), Jane C. 37 (Jan 1863-Ga/NC/NC-M 18-3-3), James B. 17 (Sep 1882), William L. 15 (Oct 1884), Mary C. 10 (June 1889) 7-266A-301/306

John W. Cochrum 29 (Aug 1870-Ga/Ga/Ga-M 10), Nancy E. 28 (Ap 1872-Ga/Ga/Ga-M 10-5-4), Mattie 8 (May 1892-Ga), Lillie 5 (Oct 1894-Ga), Charles 4 (Jan 1896), Lena 1 (Nov 1898) 3-206B-118/129

Lizzie Cochran 45: see Lewis Swafford (B)

- - - - - - - - - - - - -

CODY

MARRIAGES

Frank Cody to Harriet Young, 13 Dec 1896, W.N. Rose MG 4-97

- - - - - - - - - - - - -

COFFER / COFER / COFEN / COFFE

1860 CENSUS

Willis Coffer 39, Nancy 37, Elizabeth 13, Elisa 11, Alexander 8, Willis J. 5, Sarah A. 3, Banister 1 7-6-41

1870 CENSUS

Nancy C. Cofer 47 (Ga), Alexander 18 (Ga), Willis J. 16 (Ga), Banister 7 3-7-44

1880 CENSUS

Alexander Coffer 29, Harriet A. 23, Callie A. 5, Elizabeth C. 3, Amanda 8/12 5-8-78

Banister Coffer 22, Hanah R. 32 (w), Nancy C. COFFER 52 (m) 6-7-60

W.J. Cofer 26, M.T. 21, M.H. 3 (d), R.S. 5/12 (d) 8-14-121

1900 CENSUS

Alexander Cofer 50 (Feb 1850-Wd), Callue A. SEALS 26 (d)(Ap 1874-Wd 3-3), Ina M. 8 (gd)(Dec 1891), Ida M. 8 (gd)(Dec 1891), Virgil McK. 4 (June 1895) 5-232B-86

Elic Coffer 40, Mearin 16, Loyd 7, Lee 4: see Sam Daren(?)

Hannah Coffer 52, Alexander 20: see Frank Dixon

Mary T. Cofer 38 (June 1861-T/Ky/T-Wd 8-3), William R. 6 (Aug 1893), Floyd 3 (Jan 1897), Sarah WARNER 65 (Unk 1835-T/NC/NC-Wd 3-2) 8-316A-114/118

MARRIAGES

Alexander Cofer to Harriet Coley, 22 July 1872 (same), A.J. Pritchett MG 1-#1247

Banister Cofer to Hannah R. Dixon, 3 Ap 1880 (4 Ap), A.J. Pritchett MG 1-#1724

Callie Cofer to Elbert Seals q.v.

Eliza Jane Cofer or Cofen to Martin L. Loftis q.v.

Elizabeth Cofer or Cofin to Carter P. Roland q.v.

John Cofer or Cofen to Tennessee Warren, 10 July 1873 (same), W.R. Henry JP 1-#1286

Lizzie Coffe to James Potter q.v.

Mary Cofer to C. D. Ellison q.v.

M.E.D. Coffer to Maud Smith, 25 Aug 1900 (same), W.L. Lillard JP, Alex Coffer [signed by X] W 3-207

Rosa Cofer to C. F. Gibson q.v.

W.L. Cofer to Ida Bess, 8 Dec 1900 (9 Dec), W.R. Grimsley MG, R.H. Barger W 3-255

- - - - - - - - - - - - -

COGENS / COGGIN

1870 CENSUS

Thomas Cogens 21, Margaret 31 1-17-106

MARRIAGE

Bettie Coggin to John Emory q.v.

- - - - - - - - - - - - -

COKER

MARRIAGE

W.G. Coker to Fanny Foster, 16 May 1877 (18 May), J.M. Bramlett MG 1-#1495

- - - - - - - - - - - - -

COLBUGHAR

1900 CENSUS

Samuel Colbughar 40 (Unk-M 18), Miss 38 (Unk-M 18-6-6), Walter 15 (Aug 1884), Gaston 7 (Sep 1892), Floyd 6 (July 1893), Cleo 3 (June 1896), Lulu 2 (Aug 1897), Oscar 5 (Aug 1894) 6-249B-177/178

- - - - - - - - - - - - -

COLE / COLES / COAL

1870 CENSUS

Erastus Coal 46 (NY)(Millwright), Mary 46 (NY), Samuel 24 (NY), Ada 18 (NY), Emma 16 (NY), Minnie 14 (NY), Scott 12 (NY), Eva 9 (NJ), Ellsworth 6 (NJ), Norman 4 (NJ), Lewis 3 (NJ) 1-21-128

1880 CENSUS

Henry Cole 26, Malinda 22 1-12-100 (B)

John Coles 37 (Cook & Barber)(B): see Jere Wasson

Lossen Cole 36, Lyddie 25, Alice 4 3-20-159 (B)

Mary Coles 56, Minnie 23, Scott 21, Lewis 14, Allen 10/12 (gs), Alpha DYE 16 (boarder) 12-2-18

S.H. Coal 36, E. 39 (w), J.F. 16 (s), S.E. 14 (d), M. 12 (d), Wm 10, Ada 8, Eva 6, Adelia 3, S. 1 (s), H.L. BROWDER (B) 19 (Servant) 3-14-114
[NOTE: last name was spelled Cole at top of p. 15 where household was continued]

MARRIAGES

Ada Coles to Isaac W. Holloway q.v.

Ellen Cole to James Jones q.v.

John Lawson Cole to Lydia Henry, 15 June 1878 (same), J. H. Locke JP 1-290

Maggie Cole to C. W. Wright q.v.

Minnie A. Coal to W. H. Brown q.v.

- - - - - - - - - - - - -

COLEMAN / COALMAN

1860 CENSUS

Wm H. Coleman 23: see Columbus Major

1870 CENSUS

John H. Coalman 38 (Steamboat Pilot), Rachel J. 35, Margurette E. 11, Luella 9, James M. 6, Ada A. 3, Mary Jane 9/12, David EVERET 24 8-21-145

1880 CENSUS– None

1900 CENSUS

James Coleman 28: see Jesse Coleman

Jennie Coleman 42 (Jan 1858-T/Va/Va-Wd 11-5)(Cook, private family), Budd 14 (Feb 1886)(House Servant), Raymond 7 (July 1892), Della 5 (Aug 1894) 10-329B-200/213 (B)

Jesse Coleman 26 (May 1874-M 3), Dellie 21 (July 1878-M 3-2-2), Claud 2 (June 1897), Emitt 7/12 (Oct 1899), James 28 (c)(1872-NC/NC/NC) 7-261B-216/221

Jonas Coleman 60 (Unk 1840-Ala/Ala/Ala-M 15), Lucinda 60 (Unk 1840-M 15-2-2) 8-287A-371/373 (B)

Marion Coleman 23 (Dec 1876-M 8), Louisie 21 (July 1878-M 8-4-2), Docia 2 (Aug 1897), Charley 5/12 (Dec 1899) 7-263A-248/253

Will Coleman 22: see Allie Huskins

William Coleman 56 (May 1844-M 34), Cornelia 53 (Sep 1846-M 34-9-8), Sallie 18 (Ap 1892), Malissie 14 (June 1885), Hattie 11 (Dec 1888), Will O. COLEMAN 22 (c)(June 1877-D) 7-264A-267/272

MARRIAGES

Charles Coleman to Ada Ward or Wood, 3 Mar 1900 (same), W.B. Hicks JP & W 3-187

Emma Coleman to William Rodgers q.v.

J.S. Coleman to D.T. Shaver, 10 July 1896 (12 July), E.B. Waller MG, James Purcer W 2-39

Jones Coleman to Lucinda Jennings, 9 Mar 1885 (11 Mar), Anderson Love ?? 1-459

Marion Coleman to Susie Boyd, 28 Mar 1893, R. Knight JP 4-53

Quinn Coleman to Jane Lawrence, 18 Mar 1890 (22 Mar), J.W. Wright MG 1-600

William Coleman to Emma Denton, 25 Aug 1894, T.B. Trotter MG 4-72

- - - - - - - - - - - - -

COLLETT

MARRIAGE

J.B. Collett to Grace F. Hunter, 21 Aug 1886 (22 Aug), L. Haworth MG 1-502

- - - - - - - - - - - - -

COLLIER / COLYAR

1900 CENSUS

Jeneral F. Collier 29 (July 1870-M 11)(Coal Miner), Maggie 28 (Nov 1871-M 11-5-4), James 8 (Oct 1891), Jake 6 (Mar 1894), Rosa 3 (June 1896), Sylvester 1 (Mar 1899), Mary GREEN 14 (sil)(Nov 1888) 8-283A-293/295

John Collier 36 (July 1863-Ga/Ga/Ga-M 17), Elizabeth 35 (Nov 1864-Ga/Ga/Ga-M 17-6-3), James 14 (July 1885), George 11 (Jan 1889), Hennegar 8 (Nov 1891), Lennie 6 (Oct 1893), Bryant 3 (Oct 1896) 15-271B-66

MARRIAGES

General Collier to Maggie Green, 6 Oct 1889 (same), R.S. Mason JP 1-593

George L. Colyar (24, Franklin Co; RR Conductor from Tracy City) to Theresa L. Neal (?, Giles Co, Va), 15 Dec 1881, H.C. Neal MG, J.R. Neal & Y.L. Abernathy W 4-7(65)

J.A. Collier to Nancy Chumley, 12 Sep 1884 (14 Sep), Calvin Morgan JP 1-462

L.M. Collier to Henrietta Fulking, 4 Dec 1883 (5 Dec), D. Richardson MG 1-465

Martha A. Collier to John Coburn q.v.

COLLINS

1860 CENSUS

Andrew Collins 32, Barbery A. 28, Elizabeth 14 4-46-309

Alfred Collins 34 (NC), Amanda 23, Ira 9, John 1 4-49-332

Henry C. Collins 36, Mary A. 34, James P. 15 (Ala), July A. 13, William P. 11, Alfred W. 9, Catharine 7, John B. 5, Eugene 2 5-33-218

James P. Collins 49, Susan H. 37, James D. 16, Henry C. 14, William G. 11, Elizabeth H. 9, Alfred S. 6, William F. 4, Thomas C. 2 5-35-232

Nancy Collins 60, Buford 22, John T. 14, Bluford TULALDO 9, Margarey 4 4-41-278

Pinkney Collins 41 (NC), Charlotte 38 (NC), Edward L. 11, Robert W. 9, John T. 7, James D. 5, Alfred I. 1 3-60-412

William Collins 28, Ann 25, Cordelia A. 7 4-41-280

William Collins 35 (Dentist): see John Roberson

William Collins 69 (NC), Mary 72 (NC), Eliza MOORE 35 (NC), Thomas S. 18 (NC), Albert D. 16 (NC), Mary E. 5 (NC) 3-60-411

1870 CENSUS

Hugh Collins 45 (Ireland), Nancy J. 30, Mary C. 2 3-18-129

James P. Collins 59, Henry Clay 24, Elizabeth B. 18, Albert S. 16, Millard F. 13, Thomas C. 11 5-4-29

Mariah Collins 13 (Mu): see Micajah Howerton

Mary Collins 40, Dick 7 (B): see Albert P. Early

Mary A. Collins 44, Mary C. 17, Eugenia B. 12, Patrick H. 10, Clarence C. 8, Mary L. 4, Henry L. 4, Edvey E 2 4-12-78

Matilda Collins 17 (B): see Julia Kelley

Nancy Collins 66 (NC): see John Thompson

Pinkney Collins 52 (NC), Charlotte 48 (NC), Edward L. 21, Robert N. 19, John T. 17, James D. 15, Alfred J. 13, Jesse F. 2 3-8-57

Polly Collins 80 (NC) see Elizabeth Burton

William P. Collins 21, Sarah 25, James P. 1 4-1-3

1880 CENSUS

B.M. Collins 42, E.A. 44, Wm E. 11, J.H. 8 (s), Ida S. 6, A. B. 1 (s), J.M. 16 (nw), Amanda DYER 20 (ne) 4-6-45

Edward T. Collins 29, Celia 25 6-12-118

H.C. Collins 34, Adeli 27, S.V. 8 (d), S.T. 6 (s), J.F. 4 (s), O.C. 1 (s) 8-17-147

James P. Collins 69, Elizabeth B. 29 (d), Thomas C. 21 (s) 5-4-33

John T. Collins 27, Lucy V. 24, William D. 1 6-21-187/191

Mary Collins 48 (Cook at Hotel), Peter 5 (B): see William T. Darwin

N.J. Collins 39, John 8 (s), B.A. 5 (d) 3-20-162

P. Collins 62, Charlotte 57, Robert W. 26, James D. 25, Alfred J. 20, Jesse F. 12 5-2-11

1900 CENSUS

Alfred J. Collins 43 (Jan 1857-T/NC/NC)(RR Tie Cutter) 9-228A-1

Beauford M. Collins 62 (Dec 1837-T/NC/NC-M 36), Eliza A. 57 (Nov 1842-M 36-8-3), Andy B. 21 (Feb 1879) 5-233A-99

Edward L. Collins 50 (June 1849-T/NC/NC-M 27), Celia 44 (June 1856-M 27-0-0) 6-243A-66

Elizabeth B. Collins 49: see Thomas C. Collins

George Collins 46 (Ap 1854-T/Ga/T-M 23)(Wood Hauler), Mary A. 44 (July 1855-Ga/Ga/NC-M 23-13-7), Mary E. 16 (May 1884), Lizzie A. 14 (Mar 1886), Beckey J. 11 (May 1888), Lillie M. 7 (Aug 1892), William N. 6 (Oct 1893), Anny B. 2 (Mar 1897) 10-257A-136/140

Henry C. Collins 54 (Jan 1846-M 29)(Bank Cashier), Adelia 47 (Mar 1853-M 29-7-7), James F. 24 (Dec 1875) (Bank Clerk), Oliver C. 21 (May 1879)(Book Keeper), Arch B. 19 (Jan 1881)(Carpenter), William E. 14 (Oct 1885), Lilah M. 12 (May 1888) 14-217A-90/92

James D. Collins 45 (Jan 1855-T/NC/NC-M 19), Maggie 37 (Jan 1863-M 19-6-4), Walter 15 (Feb 1885), Cleo 9 (Jan 1891), John 7 (Ap 1893), Pearl 7 (Ap 1893) 6-247A-145/146

Jesse F. Collins 34 (Jan 1866-T/NC/NC-M 7), Mary 25 (Oct 1874-M 7-4-3), Robert E. 5 (Nov 1894), Maud M. 2 (June 1897), James F. 4/12 (Jan 1900) 6-248A-153/154

John Collins 28 (June 1871-T/Ireland/T-M 6), Addie 25 (Sep 1874-M 6-4-4), Albert 5 (Aug 1894), Luther 4 (Oct 1895), Jessie 2 (Jan 1898), Nancy 2/12 (Oct 1899), Jane COLLINS 62 (m)(Nov 1837-Wd 3-2) 3-209A-159/173

John L. Collins 48 (Jan 1852-T/NC/NC-M 24), Lucy 44 (May 1856-T/Va/Va-M 24-6-6), Della 18 (June 1881), Ida 16 (Mar 1884), Bertha 14 (Mar 1886), Frank 12 (Sep 1888), Hattie 7 (Aug 1892) 5-238B-206

Mary Collins 55 (Unk-Wd 5-5)(Servant), Pate 23 (d)(Unk) 8-319A-174/180 (B)

Robert W. Collins 48 (Dec 1851-T/NC/NC-S) 5-237B-185

Thomas C. Collins 41 (Sep 1858-T/Va/T-M 13), Susan J. 35 (Mar 1863-M 13-7-7), Lena A. 12 (Sep 1887), Clara L. 11 (Jan 1889), Welthy E. 10 (Mar 1890), Denimore S. 8 (Dec 1891), Rosa B. 6 (Dec 1893), James W. 4 (Sep 1895), Susan M. 2 (July 1897), Bettie COMTON 38 (sil)(Nov 1861), Elizabeth B. COLLINS 49 (si)(Sep 1850-T/Va/T) 5-230A-43

Thomas P. Collins 39 (Aug 1860-T/Ireland/Va-M 19)(Carpenter), Eliza 37 (June 1862-M 19-1-1), William 18 (Ap 1882)(Carpenter) 8-317B-148/153

William Collins 64 (May 1835-Ga/Unk/Unk-M 30), Alicy A. 62 (Mar 1837-M 3-5-3) 10-257A-135/139

William Collins 38 (Ap 1862-Ark/T/T-M 3), Belle 25 (Feb 1875-M 3-1-1), Mona L. 2 (Ap 1898), Etta F. WYRICK 28 (sil)(Nov 1871-Wd 2-2)(Cook) 6-242A-45

William E. Collins 31 (Feb 1869-Ind/T/T-M 8), Alace A. 28 (Oct 1871-M 8-4-4), Clara E. 7 (May 1893), Rose E. 5 (Jan 1895), Ova L. 2 (Feb 1898), Amy E. 4/12 (Jan 1900) 5-238A-197

MARRIAGES

A.S. Collins to Nora Rogers, 16 Sep 1893, John T. Price MG 4-54

Alfred Collins to Mandy Henry, 11 Oct 1855 (same), R.T. Howard MG 1-#520

Alfred W. Collins to Mary A. Mitchell, 18 June 1869 (same), A.P. Early MG 1-#1101

Annie Collins to John DeVaney q.v.

B.M. Collins to Eliza Miller, 19 Aug 1863 (no return) 1-#805

Barbara Ann Collins to W. J. Owens q.v.

Belle Collins to W. B. Collins q.v.

Biddie Collins to George Hale q.v.

C.C. Collins to Mollie Fleming, 24 Dec 1888 (25 Dec), D.R. Walker MG 1-558

E.M. Collins to Anna Maley, 8 Nov 1890, W.S. Hale MG 4-18

Edward L. Collins to Celia Wilkey, 5 Nov 1873 (4 Nov), John Howard JP 1-#1307

Elizabeth Collins to Andrew Wyrick q.v.

Elizabeth A. Collins to Albert Morris q.v.

George(?) Collins to Albert Sims q.v.

H.C. Collins to Adalade Broyles, 23 Feb 1871 (same), A.P. Early MG 1-#1187

Ida Collins to Willard Knight q.v.

J.D. Collins (25) to Magie T. Houston (19), 19 Feb 1882, J.M. Bramlett MG, E.L. Collins & G.W. Fisher W 4-9(89)

J.F. Collins to Mary Montgomery, 6 May 1892, J.M. Bramlett MG 4-43

James Collins to Nancy Remeo, 11 May 1886 (13 May), W. S. Hale MG 1-488

James D. Collins to Ann E. Caldwell, 13 Dec 1869 (17 Dec), J.H. Keith MG 1-#1132

John Collins to Bell Wyrick, 25 Dec 1892, A.J. Wyrick JP 4-50

John Collins to Adelia Janoe(?), 19 Aug 1893, W.H. Perkinson JP 4-55

John T. Collins to Lincy Wyrick, 20 Dec 1877 (same), John Howard MG 1-#1533

Julia A. Collins to William B. Benson q.v.

Julia Ann Collins to Samuel L. Pearson q.v.

Lizzie Collins to Philip Suttles q.v.

Malinda Collins to Jackson Thompson q.v.

Mary C. Collins to Z. B. Keith q.v.

Mary J. Collins to John A. Edwards q.v.

Mollie Collins or Colier to John Woody q.v.

Sarah E. Collins to Dock Suttles q.v.

Susan Vida Collins to E.B. Phillips q.v.

Thomas C. Collins to S.J. Compton, 27 Dec 1886 (28 Dec), A.P. Early MG 1-513

W.B. Collins to Belle Collins, 23 Jan 1897 (24 Jan), J.B. Trotter MG, J.K. Brown W 2-115

W.E. Collins to Alice A. Shaver, 1 Nov 1891, J. Howard MG 4-37

William C. Collins to Emeline Partaine, 31 Aug 1865 (same), J.W. Thompson MG 1-#861

William P. Collins to Sarah E. Mitchell, 1 May 1866 (no return) 1-#899

- - - - - - - - - - - - -

COLLOP

1900 CENSUS

Henry Collop(?) 50 (Feb 1850-M) 1-184A-103/107 (B)

- - - - - - - - - - - - -

COLSTON / COLESTON

1860 CENSUS

Sarah Colston 61 (NC): see John M. Houston

1870 and 1880 CENSUS– None

1900 CENSUS

Rachael Colston 50 (Unk 1850-Wd 8-6), Ephraim 24 ((Unk 1875), LaFayette 21 (Unk 1878), Charles 19 (Mar 1881), James 16 (Aug 1883) 13-298B-160/163

MARRIAGES

Ephraim Colston to Ella Tutors, 7 July 1900 (same), W.G. Curton MG, H. Spivey W 3-184

John M. Colston to Sarah Roddy, 30 May 1857 (2 June), A. Johns MG 1-#598

N. Coleston to Caroline Ives, 3 Feb 1851 (same), John Wyatt JP 1-#329

Nancy Ann Coleston to W. M. Baker q.v.

- - - - - - - - - - - - -

COLVILLE / COLVILL

1860 CENSUS

James Colville 40 (Va), Sarah 35, Mary J. 11, Louisa 9, William 8, Thomas 6, Lewis 4, John 1 8-11-72

Warner E. Colville 42 (Merchant), Vesta 37, Richard W. 17, Young 15, Elizabeth 10, Warner 7, Ella 4, Franklin 1 6-113-772

1870 CENSUS

Richard W. Colville 26 (Physician), Mary 24 6-11-74

Warner E. Colville 52, Vesta 47, Elizabeth A. 19, Warner E. 16, Ella Ann 14, Franklin L. 12, Vesta 10, Harriette 7 6-12-81

1880 CENSUS

Richard W. Colville 37 (Doctor), Mary L. 37, Orville E. 8, Frederick E. 5, Young E. 2, Nancy PAINE (B) 27 (Cook) 6-21-191/194

Vesta Colville 19, Harriet 16: see Elvira Paine

1900 CENSUS

Young Colville 54: see Harriet Waterhouse

MARRIAGES

E. A. Colville to Charles R. Roberson q.v.

Elizabeth N. Colville to Alfred Paine q.v.

R.W. Colville to M.L. Paine, 21 Oct 1869 (same), James A. Wallace MG 1-#1117

William Colville to E.M. Waller, 25 Sep 1876 (27 Sep), H.W. Fritts MG 1-#1461

- - - - - - - - - - - - -

COMBOW(?)

1900 CENSUS

Tom Combow(?) 55 (Nov 1845-Va/Va/Va-M 27), Mary J. 45 (July 1854-Va/Va/Va-M 27-4-4), John 26 (Mar 1874-Va), Annie 17 (Ap 1883), Charley 12 (Mar 1888), Geling(?) 11 (s)(Jan 1889), Cary LOYD 34 (c)(Mar 1866-Va/Va/Va-M 6), Sallie 30 (c)(May 1870-M 6-1-1), Pettu V. 3 (c)(Mar 1896) 7-266B-316/321

- - - - - - - - - - - - -

COMMONS

1900 CENSUS

Isaac L. Commons 63 (Oct 1836-Ind/Va/T-M 41), Martha B. 60 (Nov 1839-Ind/Ky/Ky-M 41-5-4), Dora 29 (Aug 1870-Ind), Sheldon HERBECK 41 (boarder)(Jan 1859-Mich/NY/NY) 5-237A-177/177

- - - - - - - - - - - - -

COMPTON / COMTON / CUMPTON

1860 CENSUS

William Cumpton 72, William Jr. 34, Welthey 28, Mahaly 9 5-37-251

1870 CENSUS

William A. Compton 44, Wealthy W. 39, Mahala 19, Sarah E. 8, Susan J. 5 5-10-72

1880 CENSUS

William Compton 53, Wealthy A. 50, Elizabeth S. 16, Susan J. 15 5-5-42

1900 CENSUS

Bettie Comton 38: see Thomas C. Collins

MARRIAGES

John Compton to Martha J. Brown, 1 Jan 1856 (same), A. Johns MG 1-#578

Louissanna Compton to William H. Ward q.v.

M. A. Compton to Darius E. Broyles q.v.

Mahala Compton to Charles W. Good q.v.

Roda A. Compton to James G. Broyles q.v.

S. J. Compton to Thomas C. Collins q.v.

William Compton to Louisanna Mathis, 15 Mar 1862 (16 Mar), John Howard MG 1-#776

- - - - - - - - - - - - -

CONATHY

MARRIAGE

M.W. Conathy to S.J. McGee, 17 Aug 1885 (8 Sep), I.W. Holt JP 1-490

- - - - - - - - - - - - -

CONDIFF

1860 CENSUS

Thomas Condiff 56 (Va), Polly 44, Mary 20, James M. 18, Gabriel J. 16, Parthena 14, Milly C. 12 9-97-654

- - - - - - - - - - - - -

CONDRA / CONDAR / CONDRU / CONDREE

1900 CENSUS

John Condru 22 (Jan 1878-M 0)(Coke Puller), Steler 17 (Mar 1883-M 0-0-0), Walter 15 (b)(Dec 1884) 10-258B-159/163

Mack Condar 22, Maggie 18: see Sarah Cooper (B)

MARRIAGES

A.H. Condra to Octava Long, 19 Nov 1883 (20 Nov), J.H. Weaver MG 1-470

James Condrae to Anna Johnson, 17 Feb 1891, L.M. Moore MG 4-19

John Condra to Estella Lawson, 5 Feb 1900 (same), D.B. Jackson ??, G.W. Brooks W 3-120

- - - - - - - - - - - - -

CONKLIN

1900 CENSUS

Day Conklin 67, Julia 60: see Clara Phillips

- - - - - - - - - - - - -

CONLEY / CONDLEY / CONNELLEY

1900 CENSUS

Elmer Conly 22 (Jan 1878-Tex/Oh/Ky-M 2), Nannie 20 (Sep 1879-M 2-1-1), Luther 1 (Sep 1899) 10-255A-99/100

Frank Conley 47: see John Horten

John C. Connelley 44 (Aug 1855-Minn/Unk-M 12)(Supt Mines), Elizabeth 35 (Dec 1864-NY/Scotland/Do-M 12-5-5), Robert N. 10 (Jan 1890-Minn), Singee 8 (Dec 1891-Minn), Bessie 7 (Mar 1893-Montana), Martha 5 (Nov 1894-Montana), Louisa 4 (Mar 1896-Mon) 13-302A-224/233

John W. Conley 51 (Aug 1848-T/NC/T-M 33), Lucy C. 53 (July 1846-Ga/NC/NC-M 33-4-2), Nancy E. 26 (d) (Mar 1874-S 1-1), Virgil 7 (gs)(Dec 1892) 9-228B-17

Maggie Connelly 20: see George Washington (B)

Mary Conley 46 (Feb 1854-Ky/Ky/Ky-M 25-6-6)(Dress-maker), Evey 9 (d)(Feb 1891-T/Oh/Ky), Charley 5 (s) (Feb 1895), Rachel ROBERTS (B) 58 (July 1841-Ga/Ga/Ga-Wd 0-0)(Servant), Ryle WALTERS 51 (boarder)(Feb 1849-Va/T/T) 7-264B-269/274

Ugean Conley 19: see Jim Anderson

MARRIAGES

Annie Conley to Neiley Shaver q.v.

Cathie Conley to Thomas Jones q.v.

Ellen Conley or Couley to J. N. King q.v.

Elmer Conley to Nannie Janow, 21 Oct 1897 (22 Oct), R.C. Knight JP, B.K.H. Lewis W 2-202

Mackey Conley to Dolly Franklin, 17 Ap 1897 (18 Ap), R.C. Knight JP, Henry Swafford W 2-139

Margarett Condley to John Cates q.v.

Mary E. Conley to James Birchfield q.v.

Minnie Conley to George Shelton q.v.

- - - - - - - - - - - - -

CONNER / CONNERS

1900 CENSUS

Thomas Conner 65 (Jan 1835-T/SC/T-M 41), Violett 67 (Sep 1832-M 41-5-4), Silas C. 29 (Aug 1870-M 5) (Farm Manager), Emma 27 (dl)(Ap 1873-M 5-3-3), Freddie M. 4 (gd)(Jan 1896), William 2 (gs)(Oct 1897), Martha 1 (gd)(Jan 1899), Martha WITT 21 (ne) (Nov 1878), Harriet 17 (ne)(Aug 1882) 5-233A-95

MARRIAGE

James Conners to Alice Smith, 23 Nov 1889 (24 Nov), James F. Murray MG 1-585

- - - - - - - - - - - - -

COOK / COOKE

1860 CENSUS

Brumly Cook 26 (Carpenter), Celia 3: see Alfred Marsh

Joseph W. Cook 35 (Miller), Aletha 28, Sarah J. 14, Thomas J. 9, William W. 6, Phebe A. 5, Eliza D. 4, Nancy T. 1, Margaret WOODARD 36 3-58-401

Osker Cook 26 (Blacksmith), Nancy 34, Martha L. 6, Mary E. 4, John W. 3, Aleatta A. 1, Elijah SNODGRASS 25 (Blacksmith) 1-84-574

1870 CENSUS

Jasper N. Cook 45, Letha 46, Sarah J. 23, Thomas J. 21, William 19, Phebe A. 17, Eliza D. 13, Nancy L. 11, Orinda J. 8, Rufus B. 1/12 4-11-68

Robert F. Cook 65 (SC)(Physician), Callie 59, Sarah M. 33, Robert F. Jr. 17, Arlee C. GAINS 11, George W. 8, John A. 5 3-12-86

1880 CENSUS

C. J. Cook 22: see E. M. Torbett

Celia Cook 22: see Alfred Marsh

Robert F. Cook 27, Ann 25 3-17-132

Sarah M. Cook 40, Altie GAINES 21 (d), George 17 (s), John 15 (s), Charlotte COOKE 60 (m), Mary RAYBURN 20 3-17-132

1900 CENSUS

Charles Cook 21 (June 1878-M 2), Emma 22 (Aug 1877-Tex/Ky/La-M 2-0-0), Onis ENGLAND 26 (boarder) (Oct 1873-SC/SC/SC), Oscar 17 (boarder)(May 1883-SC) 13-296B-123/125

Francis M. Cook 40 (Ap 1860-Tex/T/T/-M 18), Mary E. 35 (Aug 1864-M 18-8-5), Ada M. 11 (Mar 1889), Nola A. 8 (July 1891), James R. 5 (Aug 1894), Maud R. 2 (Aug 1897), Cora T. 7/12 (Oct 1899) 15-269A-27

James Cook 46 (July 1853-T/T/Tex-Wd)(Coke Puller), Sallie 20 (d)(Sep 1879), Carnealy 14 (d)(Mar 1886), Sam H. 11 (May 1889), Mary A. 9 (Ap 1891), Mandy 7 (Nov 1892), Ethel 4 (gd)(Mar 1896), Edd WALKES 9/12 (boarder)(Aug 1890)[sic], Iness WALKES 4 (boarder)(Ap 1896), Anderson WALKES 6 (boarder) (Nov 1893) 10-256A-111/115 (B)

Rosie B. Cook 23: see Robert P. Abel

Sarah M. Cook: see Sarah M. Gaines

Sally Cook 7, George 2: see James Griffin (B)

William G. Cook 49 (Jan 1851-M 17), Sarah 48 (Mar 1852-M 17-5-3), Minnie 16 (Jan 1884), Myrtle 14 (Dec 1885), Mary J. 11 (Feb 1889) 2-196A-91/94 [Wm G. married Sarah Baker on 18 Feb 1883 in Meigs Co]

MARRIAGES

Brumby Cook to Sarah R. Marsh, 19 June 1856 (23 June), J.M. Varnell MG 1-#541

C.C. Cook to Emma E. Johnson, 9 May 1898 (23 May), W.T. Drummond MG, Lewis Brandon W 2-280

C. J. Cook to A. J. Holloway q.v.

Cicero Cook to Bell Chattin, 30 Aug 1895, W.L. Lillard JP 4-86

D. A. Cook to J. P. Brady q.v.

Eliza D. Cook to ?. C. Miller q.v.

James Cook to Margarett Emery, 13 June 1870 (16 June), James Johnson JP 1-#1154

James Cook to Dethaan Marriott, 27 Jan 1883 (23 Jan)[sic] W.S. Hale MG 1-480

Mary W. Cook to William L. Brandon q.v.

Nancy J. Cook to Lewis L. Odel q.v.

Olinda Josephine Cook to John W. Harrison q.v.

Thomas Cook to Anna Womack, 14 Aug 1893, Samuel Washington MG 4-56

William Cook to Jennie Inman, 17 Oct 1891, C.J. Titus JP 4-31

- - - - - - - - - - - - -

COOL

MARRIAGES

Annie Cool(?) to Thomas Evens q.v.

Hanny Cool to William Williams q.v.

- - - - - - - - - - - - -

COOLEY

1900 CENSUS

George S. Cooley 43 (Sep 1856-M 20), Fancy 40 (Mar 1860-M 20-7-7), Lela 17 (May 1883), Ethel M. 15 (May 1885), Reece F. 14 (Mar 1886), Bertha 11 (Feb 1889), James F. 9 (Mar 1891), George S. 6 (Nov 1893), Dewey 1 (June 1898) 6-241B-37

J. Tolbert Cooley 32 (Dec 1867-M 14), Elizabeth 22 (May 1878-M 14-3-3), Mary E. 4 (June 1895), James R. 2 (June 1897), William B. 11/12 (June 1899), Fred 5 (May 1895) 6-241B-36

Jasper N. Cooley 47 (Dec 1852-M 21)(Furnaceman), Louisa 39 (Feb 1861-M 21-10-6), Agnes 16 (July 1883), Harriet D. 14 (June 1885), Nora 11 (Mar 1889), John M. 8 (May 1892), Ethel 5 (June 1894) 10-331A-229/244

MARRIAGES

Bell Cooley to John Killpatrick q.v.

Edward Cooley or Culley to Della Barton, 16 May 1895, W.R. Henry JP 4-76

Eliza Cooley to T. J. Grice(?) q.v.

Harriet Cooley to Alexander Cofer q.v.

Hester Cooley to William Whitfield q.v.

Lou Cooley to Jackson Harris q.v.

- - - - - - - - - - - - -

COOLMILL

1900 CENSUS

Henry Coolmill(?) 55 (Jan 1845-M 35), Blanch 52 (May 1848-M 35-8-5), Hatti 22 (Oct 1877-D 2-1-0) 12-182B-78/81

- - - - - - - - - - - - -

COOPER

1900 CENSUS

Aaron Cooper 70 (June 1829-Pa/NY/NY-M 50)(Merchant), Jane 69 (Ap 1831-NY/Mass/Mass-M 50-8-7) 1-184A-108/113

Elmor Cooper 22 (Jan 1878-Mich/Mich/Mich-M 2), Nettie 20 (Aug 1879-M 2-1-1), Leller 5/12 (d)(Dec 1899) 1-184A-101/105

Laura F. Cooper 20: see George W. Millican

Miller Cooper 50 (Jan 1850-Mich/Mich/Mich-M 4), Bessie 29 (July 1871-M 4-1-0), Hatie 19 (Oct 1880-Wd 2-2)(Cook), Nelli 2 (orphan)(Dec 1897), Della(?) 7/12 (si)(Oct 1899) 1-184A-100/104

Sarah Cooper 24 (June 1875-Wd 4-1), Bertha 9 (Nov 1891-Ky), Mack CONDAR 22 (nw)(Unk 1878)(Coal Miner), Maggie 18 (ne)(Unk 1882) 8-287A-372/374 (B)

MARRIAGES

Alise Cooper to D. H. Girden q.v.

Deborah C. Cooper to Thomas T. Biggs q.v.

E.M. Cooper to Nettie Brewer, 11 Jan 1899, W.T. West MG 4-95

Eliza J. Cooper to James N. Fry q.v.

John Cooper to Sallie Hale, 23 Feb 1893, S.W. Burnett MG 4-52

Milo E. Cooper to Lucy Robinson, 6 June 1890 (11 June), James Johnson JP 1-602

Mollie Cooper to J. A. Garrison q.v.

Robert T. Cooper (36, Bedford Co) to Mary Smith (35, White Co), 25 Nov 1882, W.W. Pyott MG, W.E. Stephens (Evensville) & R.L. Robison (Dayton) W 4-11(106)

Sallie Cooper to Wesley Swafford q.v.

T.B. Cooper to Lucinda Blank, 11 June 1890, James Johnson JP 4-15

- - - - - - - - - - - - -

COPE

MARRIAGE

Margarett Cope to James Hood q.v.

- - - - - - - - - - - - -

COPELAND / COPLAND / COPLIN / COAPLIN / COPELINE

1880 CENSUS

Harris Copeland 24, Caroline 17 10-29-226/233 (B)

1900 CENSUS

Horace Coplan 55: see Samuel Burgin (B)

Irene Copeland 30 (Sep 1869-M 10-3-1)(Washwoman), George 13 (Mar 1887)(Water Carrier at Furnace), Eva HUFF 23 (boarder)(June 1876)(Washing & Ironing) 10-330B-219/233 (B)

Jim Coaplin 32 (Mar 1868-Ga/Ala/Ga-M 8)(Drawing Coke), Fanny 34 (Mar 1866-Ga/Ga/Ga-M 8-5-0), Charley BROYLES 18 (boarder)(Jan 1882)(Drawing Coke), Siah CLIFF 24 (boarder)(Mar 1876)(Carpenter) 10-253A-65 (B)

MARRIAGES

Cy Copeland to Mary Banner or Barner, 2 Ap 1900 (same), J.O. Gaither MG, Riley Gormany W 3-137

Horace Copeland to Rena Day, 18 Mar 1884 (20 Mar), J.H. Locke JP 1-470

M.D. Lafayette Copland to Sary Elizabeth Godsey, 14 Ap 1856 (no return) 1-#530

Van Buren Copeline to Mary Ann Smith, 20 Nov 1876 (same), W.H. Dodd MG 1-#1469

- - - - - - - - - - - - -

COPENHAN

1880 CENSUS

D.M. Copenhan 58, L.A. 45, Rosa EDWARDS 12 (bound) 4-9-70

- - - - - - - - - - - - -

COPINGER / COPPINGER

1900 CENSUS

Charles J. Copinger 39 (Aug 1860-T/Pa/T-M 14), Rhoda A. 29 (Feb 1871-M 14-2-2), Willie 14 (May 1886), Frank 7 (Oct 1892) 6-241B-35

Thomas Coppinger 36 (Feb 1864-M 10), Minnie 28 (Nov 1871-M 10-6-6), Lewis W. 9 (Aug 1890), Harry 7 (July 1892), Thomas B. 6 (Jan 1894), Florence 4 (Oct 1895), Belle 2 (Sep 1897), Mamie 11/12 (June 1899), Margaret COPPINGER 63 (m)(Aug 1836-Wd 5-5) 6-249A-175/176

- - - - - - - - - - - - -

CORBIN

1870 CENSUS

Chesley D. Corbin 38 (SC), Elizabeth G. 38 (Ga), Erby G. 14 (Ga), Sarah M. 13 (Ga), Artatsa M. 11 (Ga), Mary E.F. 9 (Ga), William S. 4 (Ga), Joseph G. 2 (Ga) 1-13-83

- - - - - - - - - - - - -

CORDELL

1900 CENSUS

Hila B. Cordell 12, Pearl 11: see William H. Walker

- - - - - - - - - - - - -

CORDER

MARRIAGE

W.E. Corder to Rosa Lee Davis, 12 Oct 1893, A.D. Hubbard MG 4-57

- - - - - - - - - - - - -

CORDIAL

1880 CENSUS

Izzabel Cordial 58, William R. 19 (s) 5-6-48

- - - - - - - - - - - - -

COREGAN

1880 CENSUS

John Coregan 65, Matilda 49 (w), John 21, Birdie 14 8-7-54

- - - - - - - - - - - - -

CORN

1900 CENSUS

Robert Corn 29 (May 1881), Alvia BRIDGMAN 18 (Mar 1882)(Cook) 10-258B-166/170 (B)

MARRIAGE

Robert Corn to Alva Bridgemon(?), 29 June 1900 (1 July), G. D. Gaither MG, Robert Combs [signed by X] & William Garrison W 3-176

- - - - - - - - - - - - -

CORNETT / CURNUTT

1900 CENSUS

Mary Cornett 39 (July 1860-Ky/Va/Unk-Wd 9-6)(Washwoman), David 13 (Mar 1887), George 10 (Jan 1890), Ollie 8 (Mar 1892), Zoe 6 (Mar 1894), Blanche POWELL 28 (d)(June 1871) 10-328B-176/187

Mary M. Curnutt 75: see Daniel Strader

- - - - - - - - - - - - -

CORVIN / CORVAN / CORWIN / CARVIN / CARWIN / CERWAN

1870 CENSUS

James Carvin 50 (Va), Sarah F. 44, William C. 17, Thomas 16, Louis 14, John 10, Tennessee T. 8, George W. 3, Lorenzo D. 5/12, Moses TURNER 24, Mary J. 20, Samuel 7/12, Sarah FOX 63, Sarah COULTER (B) 18 8-3-20

Pleasant M. Carvin 23, Mary F. 23, Eli James 7, Harriette 5, Samantha A. 2/12 8-14-97

1880 CENSUS

J.T. Corvin 24, S.S. 24 (w), Magie 10, M.S. 9/12 (d) 8-15-128

John Corvin 21, L.A. 20 (w), J.E. 3 (s), S.T.O. 2 (s) 8-20-168 [NOTE: J.A. Gothard 18 was listed at the end of this household, but probably belongs in the next household– see Gothard]

M.D. Corvin 26, S.A. 4: see J. O. Johnson

P.M. Corvin 34, Mary F. 36, Eli 14, Hariet 15, Samantha 10, T.A. 9 (s), S.J. 6 (d), M.E. 4 (d), Levanna 3/12 8-19-164

S.A. Corvin 48, R.S. 15 (d): see Thomas Dobbs

1900 CENSUS

Dollie Corvin 45 (Aug 1854-Wd 5-5), Albert 28 (Unk 1872), Lula 24 (June 1875), William 21 (Dec 1878) (Coal Miner), Virgil 15 (Nov 1884), Cleveland 15 (May 1885), Edward 2 (Mar 1898), Jack WEBB 19 (boarder)(Unk 1881) 15-268B-13

George W. Corvin 33, Ollie 5: see Mary Jane Turner

Hariet Corvin 35 (Feb 1865-Wd 5-4), Lambert ABEL 14 (s) (Dec 1885), Lee CORVIN 10 (s)(Mar 1890), Cora 7 (d)(Ap 1893), Carl 4 (s)(Feb 1896) 15-268B-7

J. Crockett Corvin 41 (Aug 1858-T/Va/T-Wd), Ida A. 17 (Oct 1882), Laura 15 (Oct 1884), Flora 14 (Jan 1886), Richard 7 (June 1892) 13-298A-155/158

James Corvin 83 (Nov 1816-Va/Va/Va-M 25), Delilah 61 (Mar 1839-T/NC/Va-M 25-0-0), Lorenzo D. 30 (Dec 1869), Lucy DENNIS 33 (boarder)(Feb 1867), Mary DENNIS 23 (boarder)(Dec 1876) 15-268B-9/9

John Corvin 41 (Mar 1857-T/Va/T-M 25), Luarah A. 40 (July 1860-M 25-9-2), Samuel O. 22 (Feb 1877), Lawrence H. 19 (May 1887), Walter 16 (June 1884), Hayward 11 (June 1888), Emma 9 (Oct 1891), Maud 5 (Ap 1895), Ova 2 (Ap 1898), Oakley GOTHARD 20 (c)(Mar 1880) 15-268A-6/6

Joseph B. Corvin 39 (Oct 1861-T/Va/T-M 18), Martha L. 40 (Sep 1859-T/Va/NC-M 18-7-7), Ellen T. 17 (Oct 1882), William R. 15 (Sep 1884), Walter E.L. 13 (Nov 1886), Wiley A. 10 (July 1889), Mary E. 7 (Oct 1892), Clara Jane 4 (Sep 1895), Colonel B. 1 (Mar 1899), Polly STEELE 79 (ml)(June 1820-Va/Va/Va-Wd 4-3) 13-297B-143/146

Mary Corvin 17, Sarah 13: see James C. Denson

Ollie Corvin 22 (Mar 1878-M 2)(Coal Miner), Laura 20 (Ap 1880-M 2-0-0) 13-303A-244/254

Pleasant Corvin 55 (Mar 1845-M 31), Mary F. 55 (Aug 1844-T/Va/NC-M 31-10-7), Fred H. 11 (Mar 1889) 15-269A-25/25

Thomas Corvin 46 (May 1854-T/Va/T-M 21), Sarah L. 45 (June 1855-T/NC/T-M 21-9-7), Martha L. 20 (d)(Aug 1879-Wd 1-1), Anna 16 (May 1884), James O. 13 (Jan 1887), Thomas G. 10 (Sep 1889), Mary H. 8 (Jan 1892), John H. 4 (Aug 1895) 13-297B-145/148

Thomas A. Corvin 44 (July 1855-T/Va/T-M 19), Samantha 45 (May 1855-Ga/SC/Ga-M 19-6-6), John W. 18 (Sep 1881), Theodore B. 16 (July 1883), William D. 13 (June 1886), Nancy L. 11 (Mar 1889), Cora Isabelle 7 (June 1892), Earnest Leroy 3 (Oct 1896) 13-298A-156/159

William F. Corvin 49 (May 1851-M 19), Anice 36 (Dec 1863-M 19-7-6), Sally J. 19 (Ap 1881), George W. 16 (Mar 1884), Grover J. 13 (Dec 1888), Dora F. 10 (Jan 1890), Ida 7 (Feb 1893), Bessie M. 3 (Aug 1896) 13-301B-211/219

MARRIAGES

Albert Corvin to Catharine Dobbs, 18 May 1877, W.R. Grimsley MG 1-#1496

Alice Corvin to John Tallent q.v.

E.C. Carwan to Letta E. Foust, 28 July 1884 (29 July), J.H. Weaver MG 1-521

Eli Corvin to Mary F. Steel, 16 May 1862 (no return) 1-#780

Eli Corvin (19) to Vileenia(?) Harrison (16, Meigs Co), 13 Mar 1882, F.M. Bandy MG, J.B. Corvin & W.A. Steel W 4-9(86)

Elizabeth Corvin to Thomas Dobbs q.v.

Ella Corvin to E. R. Barger q.v.

George Corvin to Rilda Corvin, 2 Mar 1894, W.G. Curton MG 4-70

Harriet Corvin(?) to J. P. Abel q.v.

Ida Corvin to James Gothard q.v.

James Corvin to Delila Shipley, 1 Dec 1873 (no return) 1-#1315

John Corwin or Carvin to Lorinda Gass, 29 Dec 1875 (30 Dec), R.H. Jordan MG 1-#1425

Joseph B. Corvin (20, Meigs Co) to Lartha or Laura Steel (22, Meigs Co), 29 Dec 1881, W.R. Grimsley MG, John Steel & W.A. Walker W 4-6(51)

Mary F. Corvin to P. M. Corvin q.v.

Mary Corvin [nee Johnson] to James A. Rogers q.v.

Nancy Carwin to W. C. Teague q.v.

O.P. Corvin to Nettie Pendergrass, 23 Dec 1898 (same), Wm Turner MG 2-362

P.M. Corvin to Mary F. Corvin, 24 May 1869 (29 May), James N. Kelly MG 1-#1060
Phena Corvin to J. L. Turner q.v.
Polly A. Carwin to William Maylott q.v.
R. L. Corvin to Alfred Dobbs q.v.
Rilda Corvin to George Corvin q.v.
Tennessee Corvin to Pleasant Stanley q.v.
Thomas Corvin to Sarah Johnson, 7 Sep 1878 (8 Sep), R.H. Jordan MG 1-#1581
William Corvin to Martha J. Potter, 12 July 1878 (no return) 1-#1567

CORY

1900 CENSUS
John P. Cory 47 (Sep 1852-M 26), Lucindy 47 (July 1852-M 26-11-9), William 19 (Jan 1881), Thomas 17 (Aug 1882), Graves 14 (Sep 1885), Robert 13 (Mar 1887), Gauton 11 (Dec 1888), Mynott 7 (Mar 1893) 6-246B-131/132

COSS

1880 CENSUS
James Coss 34, Adda 30, Willie R.L. 8, Sarah E. 6, Elick F. 3, Malissa M. 1 5-8-76 (B) (Mu)

COSTELLO / CASTOLO / COASTALS / CASTLIN

1880 CENSUS
James Coastals 55, Rachel 57 10-26-202/208
1900 CENSUS
James Castolo 77 (Mar 1823-Ireland/Do/Do-M 33), Rachel 70 (Mar 1830-M 33-2-1) 5-231B-70
MARRIAGE
Annie Costello to Patrick Crow(?) q.v.
Jim Castlin to Rachel Magors, 6 Oct 1879 (no return) 1-#1690

COUCH

1870 CENSUS
Edmond Couch 75 (SC), Rachel 61, Elizabeth 30, Nancy Ann 20, Francis M. 1 8-7-43
John Couch 36, Rachel C. 26, Nancy Jane 8, John 2, Nancy MOYERS 70 8-22-155
Marcel Couch 48, Narcissus 43, William H.H. 15, James F. 13, John Thomas 11, Mary E. 6, Richard 3, Samuel D. 1 8-7-44
1880 CENSUS– None
1900 CENSUS
John Couch 32 (Oct 1867-M 8), Martha 27 (Unk-M 8-4-3), Lillie J. 5 (June 1894), Martha A. 3 (Oct 1896), Annison 7/12 (Oct 1899) 6-248A-162/163
William Couch 23 (Nov 1876-M 3), Reanie 23 (July 1876-M 3-2-1), Annie 2 (July 1897) 6-248B-167/168

MARRIAGES
John Couch to Catharine Moyers, 8 Feb 1859 (9 Feb), William Morgan JP 1-#691
John H. Couch to Martha J. Duckworth, 2 Nov 1877 (11 Nov), W.W. Low JP 1-#1521
Malinda J. Couch to Bird Newman q.v.
Mollie Couch to George Moore q.v.
Nancy Ann Couch to George N. Miller q.v.
Nancy J. Couch to John M. Sexton q.v.
Sarah Couch or Cash to William Fulington q.v.
Tim Couch to Lillie Wigins, 3 Sep 1900, W.K. Fugate JP 4-105
William Couch to Malinda Hughes, 17 Sep 1851 (same), C.A. Holland MG 1-#348

COULTER

1870 CENSUS
Thomas B. Coulter 21, Julia A. 21 (Va), Charles L. 2, Emma A. 1, James FULLER 20, Nancy E. WINSET 27 8-16-112
Thomas J. Coulter 54, Jane P. 45, Kittie Jane 19 (School Teacher), James M. 13, William L. 10, Ruth 6, Robert J.B. 1 8-16-111
Sarah Coulter 18 (B): see James Carvin
1880 CENSUS
R.T. Coulter 22, Mary 22, E.M. 3/12 (d), Mary Ann 58 (m), M.M. 19 (si), Tenas CHAMBERS (B) 24, Curt DYLAND (B) 34 8-10-80
T.B. Coulter 30, J.A. 30 (w), C.L. 12 (s), E.A. 10 (d), J.M. 8 (s), J.B. 4 (s), M.E. 2 (d), James 1/12 (s) 8-9-72
T.J. Coulter 64, J.P. 55 (w), K.J. 29 (d), W.S. 19 (s), R.A. 16 (d), R.J.B. 11 (s) 8-9-73
1900 CENSUS
Addie Coulter 19 (B): see James M. Nelson
Charles L. Coulter 32 (Sep 1867-M 14), Susan A. 33 (Sep 1866-M 14-5-5), Ivan 12 (June 1887), Ralph 9 (June 1890), Walter T. 7 (Ap 1893), Louis O. 3 (Sep 1896), James H. 11/12 (June 1899) 13-296A-118/120
David Coulter 42 (Unk-M 13), Polly 27 (Dec 1870-M 13-3-3), Morris(?) 4 (July 1895), Willard 3 (Aug 1896), Ernest 2 (Sep 1897) 8-318A-158/163 (B)
John B. Coulter 24 (Mar 1876-M 2/12)(Lumber & Grist Milling), Minnie 18 (Nov 1881-M 2/12-0-0), Hugh M. 18 (b)(June 1882)(Lumber & Grist Milling) 3-202B-54/57
Luke L. Coulter 44 (Jan 1856-M 9), Myra 42 (July 1857-T/T/NC-M 9-2-1), Frank A. 17 (Sep 1882), Robert M. 16 (Ap 1884), James B. 14 (May 1886), Stella M. 2 (Dec 1897), Maggie C. PASS 37 (sil)(Sep 1862-T/Va/NC)(School Teacher) 2-107B-113/118
Mary A. Coulter 79: see Franklin H. Abel
Thomas B. Coulter 51 (Dec 1848-M 34)(Sawyer), Julia 51 (Dec 1848-Va/Va/Va-M 34-10-9), Thomas J. 28 (Aug 1871)(Drayman), Mary L. 22 (Ap 1878), James M. 20 (May 1880)(Day Laborer), Hugh M. 17 (June 1882) (Mill Laborer), Julia F. 15 (Ap 1885), Robert J. 10 (Ap 1890) 13-303A-248/258

MARRIAGES
David Coulter to Polly Hale, 10 Oct 1886 (same), J.B. Phillips MG 1-525

Henry Coulter (25, Ga), to Molly McCarty (27), 16 Mar 1883, W.S. Hale MG, W. Powell & J. Chatten W 4-13(130) (B)
J.B. Coulter to Minnie Dungan, 6 Ap 1900 (same), W.R. Grimsley MG, Charles L. Coulter W 3-138
Kittie Coulter to T. N. L. Cunnynham q.v.
L.L. Coulter to P.A. Able, 7 Sep 1880 (8 Sep), W.A. Green JP 1-294
L.L. Coulter to Myra Pass, 27 Jan 1892, J.B. Waggoner MG 4-38
Levena Coulter(?) to James Hubbard q.v.
M. M. Coulter to F. H. Abel q.v.
Ruth A. Coulter to E. E. Adkinson q.v.
Sarah J. Coulter to B. L. Gilmore q.v.

COUNTES

MARRIAGE
Robert Countes to Emaline Armstrong, 4 Sep 1853 (same), John Wyott JP 1-#421

COUSTER

MARRIAGE
Adie Couster(?) to George J. Burnett q.v.

COUTER

MARRIAGE
Jack Couter(?) to Sarilda Billingsly, 4 Aug 1900 (same), T.F. Thatcher MG, George Hickman(?) W 3-194

COVAL / COVALL

1860 CENSUS
William Coval 33 (SC), Charlotte 21, Samuel L. 3, Mary A. RENFROW 18 7-5-32
1870 CENSUS
James Coval 28, Sarah 27, George 6, Susan 3 5-4-25
William Coval 40, Eliza 35, James 12, Peter 9, Caroline 4/12 3-21-148
1880 CENSUS
Samuel L. Coval 22, Mary E. 23, Thomas E. 1 6-13-120
MARRIAGES
James Coval to Sarah Moore, 16 Sep 1860 (same), T.H. McPherson JP 1-#727
Thomas Coval to Mary Porter, 30 Sep 1896 (same), H.B. Burditt MG, R.J. Killough W 2-71
William Covall to Eliza Powers, 17 July 1869 (18 July), John Howard MG 1-#1106

COWAN / COWEN / COWIN

1870 CENSUS
Andrew Cowan 45, Jane 48, Sarah A. 18, Anas 16, William 15, John M. 10, Jane 9, Caldonia 8, Harris 50 8-9-61
Elizabeth Cowen 40, Mary E. 8: see Andrew J. Bankston
1880 CENSUS
Lucinda Cowan 100: see Alfred Etherly (B)
1900 CENSUS
David Cowin 48: see Ben Dyer (B)
William J. Cowan 29 (Sep 1870-Ark/T/Ark-M 9/12)(General Merchandise Salesman), Bessie 21 (Ap 1879-M 9/12) 3-205A-93/101
MARRIAGES
Harrison Cowan to Elizabeth McCarroll, 28 Aug 1865 (same), John H. Keith MG 1-#833
J.S. Cowan to Mrs. Fine Love, 18 Oct 1896 (same), R.C. Knight JP, J.J. Hoge W 2-75
Louisa A. Cowin to J. R. P. Abel q.v.
R.A. Cowan to Alice McDonald, 20 Sep 1879 (22 Sep), J.M. Hall MG 1-#1677
W.J. Cowan to Bessie Bates, 22 Sep 1899 (27 Sep), E.W. Mort MG 3-37
William Cowan to Mary Johnson, 9 Aug 1872 (12 Aug), W. L. Humphrey JP 1-#1243

COWART

MARRIAGE
Thomas Cowart to H.P. Day, 24 Nov 1868 (no return) 1-#1037

COWDEN

MARRIAGE
Rhoda Cowden to Henry Rhea q.v.

COX

1860 CENSUS
Elbert S. Cox 30, Mary A. 30, John B. 8, William H. 7, Charles O. 5, George M. 3, Elbert S. 8/12, Sarah C. BEAN 12 3-61-418
James M. Cox 39, Mary 27, Nancy A. 3, William C. 1 3-58-399
Mat Cox 33, Jane 25, Hardy(?) 5, William 3, Greenberry 5/12 1-88-605
Rebecca Cox 50, Harris 30 (Brick Mason), Julia 21, Nancy A. 16 6-108-737
1870 CENSUS
Elbert S. Cox 43, Mary A. 41, John B. 18, William H. 17, Charles O. 16, George M. 12, Elbert S. 9, Amanda E. 8, Doctor N. 6, Daniel F. 4 6-4-20
John [James?] H. Cox 40 (Wool Carder), Rachel L. 26, Phillip B. 11/12 8-10-65
James M. Cox 37, Mary 36, Nancy A. 12, William C. 11, Robert 9, James M. 6, Mary J. 3, Malinda E. 1 3-5-34
Rebecca Cox 61, Julia 25, Malinda PRITCHET 34, Columbus JONES 16 6-4-24
William Cox 26, Jane 24, John W. 12, Mary E. 6, Sallie Jane 2, William D. 2/12 1-18-115
1880 CENSUS
Elbert S. Cox 52, Mary A. 52, William H. 27, George M. 22, Elbert S. 20, Amanda J. 18, Doctor N. 16, Daniel F. 13, William BURWICK 45 (insane) 6-18-172/275

J.H. Cox 50 (Wool Carder), Racheal S. 37, P.B. 10 (s), R.C. 8 (d), J.H. 5 (s), N.O. 2 (d), M.R. ABEL 25, J.A. 24, R.R. 6/12 8-5-40
John Cox 29, Ann 20, Mary 1, V.T. PERRY 18 (sil) 4-32-260
Let Cox 47 (B): see William T. Darwin
N. Cox 16: see James Barnett
Susan Cox 47: see Julia Kelly
William Cox 32, Blanche 31, Mary 14, Sarah 13, Florence 6, Nettie 4, Hattie 2/12 15-5-43

1900 CENSUS

Barton Cox 31 (Mar 1869-M 11), Magie 38 (Feb 1862-M 11-6-3), James W. 9 (Nov 1890), Clary L. 3 (Dec 1896), Florence E. 1 (Mar 1899) 10-255B-109/112
Doctor M. Cox 39: see Julia Barnett
Ebb S. Cox 39 (Nov 1860-M 15), Amanda T. 33 (Sep 1866-M 14-7-6), Bertha L. 14 (Sep 1885), Virginia M. 13 (Jan 1887), Amanda A. 10 (Aug 1889), Robert T. 9 (Mar 1891), Dixie C. 5 (Dec 1894), Nellie M. 3 (Oct 1896), Cyrus WATERHOUSE 48 (boarder)(Sep 1852) 15-270A-43
Frank Cox 4: see James Crane
George Cox 4: see Albert Stokes (B)
Harriet Cox 65: see John McMahan (B)
James Cox 55 (Feb 1845-M 30)(RR Section Hand), Mary A. 50 (Nov 1849-M 30-10-7), Sarah E. 23 (July 1876), Body 16 (Nov 1883), Hattie 14 (Sep 1885), Thomas 13 (Feb 1887), Lena 9 (Dec 1890) 5-230B-50 (B)
James Cox 25 (Mar 1873-M 5), Lizzie 27 (Feb 1863-M 5-2-2), Hasroy 4 (Mar 1895), Glaspur 2 (July 1897) 10-256A-120/124
James M. Cox 68 (Dec 1831-Wd)(Mail Carrier), Mary J. 33 (d)(Nov 1866), John P. PHIPPS 22 (boarder)(Mar 1878-Ga/Ga/Ga)(RR Laborer) 14-216B-75/76
John Cox 21 (Aug 1878-T/NC/NC-M 2)(Locamotive Fireman), Eva 19 (Oct 1880-M 2-1-1), Earl 4/12 (Jan 1900) 10-324B-98/102
Jossi R. Cox 10: see James Reese
Las Cox 23: see Thomas Sanford (B)
Ollie Cox 21: see Nancy Vaughn
Robert C. Cox 38 (Feb 1861-M 5)(Mowing Machine Salesman), Evaline 32 (June 1868-T/NC/T-M 5-2-2), Hattie M. 3 (May 1897), unnamed 8/12 (d)(Sep 1899) 14-218A-116/118
William M. Cox 28 (Dec 1871-M 1)(RR Section Hand), Belle L. 23 (Sep 1876-M 1-0-0) 5-234A-119/119 (B)

MARRIAGES

Alex Cox to Annis Tipton, 7 Oct 1882 4-11 (B)
Amanda Cox to W. F. Pleasant q.v.
Barton Cox to Martha Wilkey, 19 Jan 1889 (same), T.F. Shaver JP 1-567
Bettie Cox to Anderson Dodd q.v.
Bettie Cox to Merrill McClelland q.v.
E.S. Cox to Mary E. Bean, 23 Ap 1852 (24 Ap), W.H. Cunnyngham JP 1-#363
E.S. Cox Jr. to Tabitha Denton, 31 Dec 1884 (same), J.M. Bramlet MG 1-463
Ellenor Cox to James Short q.v.
Florence Cox to Calvin G. West q.v.
G.M. Cox to Augusta Rice, 5 Mar 1884 (6 Mar), W.S. Hale MG 1-470
Hattie Cox to William Miller q.v.
J.R. Cox to Minnie Shipley, 20 Jan 1895, A.H. Hubbard MG 4-77
James Cox to Lizzie Roddy, 26 Oct 1894, W.A. Howard MG 4-71
James H. Cox to Rachel Acre, 28 Oct 1868 (no return) 1-#1033
James M. Cox to Mary Ann Thurman, 10 June 1854 (11 June), R.T. Howard MG 1-#449
Jane Cox to Stephen Browder q.v.
John Cox to Ann Perry, 18 Feb 1878 (same), F.M. Moore MG 1-#1552
John Cox to Eva Gooden, 28 Ap 1898 (same), W.L. Lillard JP, Charles Gooden W 2-272
July Cox to James R. Barnett q.v.
Katie Cox to William Moore q.v.
Laura Cox to R. C. Bowles q.v.
Laura Cox to Steve Locke q.v.
Lewis Cox to Vesta Ryan, 1 Ap 1894, S.S. Franklin JP 4-65
M. Cox to Fayette Bowles q.v.
Malinda Cox to John W. Pritchett q.v.
Malisa Cox to J. L. Brown q.v.
Martha Cox to John C. Casey q.v.
Mary Cox to Hugh Rhea q.v.
Mary Ann Cox to M. F. Moore q.v.
Myrtle Cox to Thomas Matherly q.v.
Nancy Cox to B. F. Rhea q.v.
Phoebia Cox to Mark Russell q.v.
R.C. Cox to Racheal Welch, 26 Mar 1886 (27 Mar), G.W. Simpson ?? 1-510
Robert Cox to Cislia S. Sullivan, 9 Sep 1858 (same), T.F. Whaley JP 1-#652
Sallie Cox to Thomas B. Thompson q.v.
Tennie Cox to I. B. Young(?) q.v.
W.N. Cox to Betty Garrison (20, Roane Co), 19 May 1881, J.I. Cash MG, A.E. McCobb & Annie(?) Roberts W 4-1(9)
William Cox to Mattie Hayes, 30 May 1896 (same), W.L. Lillard JP, E.L. Rudd W 2-26
William Cox to Bell Waterhouse, 14 Dec 1898 (same), W.L. Lillard JP, James Cox W 2-357
Z. Cox to Noah Bowles q.v.

- - - - - - - - - - - - -

COXEY

1860 CENSUS

John Coxey 8: see John Fellow
John Coxey 24, Nelly JAMES 23, Sarah 2, Mary F. 1/12 3-68-468

1870 CENSUS– None

1880 CENSUS

John Coxey 44, M.J. 33 (w), J.H. 11 (s), Wm 9, Virginia 6, James 3, Mary MARSHALL 44 (si) 9-31-271
John Coxey 27, Lucinda M. 26, Hannah M. 5, Nancy C. 4, Millie 2 6-16-152/155

1900 CENSUS

Hannah Coxey 25: see Harriet Waterhouse
William J. Coxey 63 (Mar 1837-T/Ky/Ky-Wd 7-2), James B. 22 (Ap 1878), Mary MARSHEL 66 (si)(Mar 1834-T/Ky/Ky-S) 3-201A-25/26

MARRIAGES

Jennie Coxey to John Phillips q.v.
John Coxey to Lucinda Hale, 27 Jan 1874 (1 Feb), W.W. Low JP 1-#1327

John Coxey to Kisir Durham, 21 July 1888 (22 July), T.T. Long JP 1-560
Minnie Coxey to Thomas Campbell q.v.

COZART

MARRIAGE
Mary Cozart to Henry Swafford q.v.

COZBY

MARRIAGE
Louisa Cozby to Thomas J. Gist q.v.

CRABLE

MARRIAGE
A.. Crable to Anna Francis, 29 Aug 1887 (31 Aug), no MG or JP 1-527

CRABTREE

1880 CENSUS
William Crabtree 19, Amanda 19, Lentitia 1 2-26-207
MARRIAGE
Letitia Crabtree to Robert Rouse q.v.

CRADLE

1900 CENSUS
Ella Cradle 35 (Aug 1864-NC/NC/NC-Wd 6-2), John 17 (Sep 1882-NC), Calloway 15 (July 1884-NC) 8-284B-315/317 (B)
MARRIAGE
Ella Cradle to John W. Miller q.v.

CRAIG

1870 CENSUS
Bartley C. Craig 30, Jane 27, William 5, John H. 2 7-5-39
Polly Craig 25, Maggie 5, Willie 4 (B): see Stephen Cawood
1880 CENSUS
Bartley Craig 46, Febi J. 30, Willie 14, John H. 12, Justus L. 9, Tiney 6, Robert L. 1 6-25-187/191
Polly Craig 40, Willie 10 (B): see Stephen Cawood
1900 CENSUS
Bart Craig 62 (June 1837-T/NC/T-M 33), Jane 57 (Unk-M 33-6-6), John 31 (Aug 1868), Gus 26 (Aug 1873), Tina 23 (Aug 1876), Callie 17 (June 1882) 6-241B-40

CRAIGHEAD

1870 CENSUS
Samuel Craighead 56, Nancy 56, Beriah G. 24 2-14-100
1880 CENSUS
Samuel Craighead 66, Nancy 66, Beriah 29 2-41-335
1900 CENSUS
Beriah Craighed 53 (Aug 1846-M 17), Annie 42 (July 1857-Ala/Ala/Ala-M 17-6-6), Maggie E. 16 (Sep 1883), Edgar 15 (Feb 1885), Samuel M. 13 (Feb 1887), Cora A. 11 (Ap 1889), Thomas G. 6 (Ap 1894), Nancy 3 (Dec 1896) 2-197A-106/111

CRAIN / CRANE

1870 CENSUS
Sarah Crain 26: see Alfred Hutchison
1880 CENSUS– None
1900 CENSUS
James Crane 26 (Unk-M 7), Martha 25 (Unk-M 7-0-0), Eliza 60 (m)(Mar 1840-Wd 1-1), Frank COX 4 (adopted son)(Unk-Tex) 6-247B-149/150

CRAMER

1900 CENSUS
Andrew Cramer(?) 30 (July 1869-T/Ky/Ky-M 2)(Saw Miller), Carri 23 (June 1876-M 2-1-1), Marget 5/12 (June 1900), Milan CLARKE(?) 24 (June 1875)(Servant) 1-185A-119/125

CRANFIELD

1900 CENSUS
Pleas Cranfield 37 (Nov 1862-M 14), Hattie J. 30 (Nov 1869-M 14-6-4), William W. 11 (Dec 1888), James F. 9 (Dec 1890), Samuel G. 4 (Sep 1895), Mattie L. 2 (Jan 1898) 3-206B-116/126
MARRIAGES
Sisie Cranfield or Stanfield to Lee Price q.v.
William Cranfield to Nancy Jane Wilson, 10 Sep 1866 (13 Sep), T.N.L. Cunnyngham JP 1-#909

CRANMORE

1870 CENSUS
Margarette C. Cranmore 20: see F. Richards
1880 CENSUS– None
1900 CENSUS
James C. (?) Cranmore 55 (Jan 1845-M 34), Lettie 53 (Oct 1846-Ky/Ky/Ky-M 34-12-7), John H. 24 (s)(June 1875-M 3), Jennie 20 (dl)(June 1879-M 3-1-1), Louisa A. 8/12 (gd)(Sep 1899), Josephine 20 (June 1879), James 18 (Mar 1882), Isaac 14 (Nov 1885), Tusky C. 11 (Nov 1889) 15-269A-17

Wayne(?) Cranmore 29 (Nov 1870-M 10), Emily J. 28 (Aug 1871-T/Va/T-M 10-4-4), James M. 9 (Oct 1890), Alice M.E. 7 (Feb 1893), Josie M. 5 (May 1895), Polly A. 10/12 (Aug 1899) 8-311B-20/21

MARRIAGES

Elizabeth Cranmore to Samuel Gill q.v.

Elizabeth Cranmore to J. K. Goad q.v.

John Cranmore to Mariah Smith, 15 Jan 1880 (18 Jan), W.S. Hale MG 1-#1705

Josiah Cranmore to Margarett C. Land, 18 Dec 1867 (19 Dec), J.M. Kelly MG 1-#990

Kittie Cranmore to Robert Duckworth q.v.

Samantha A. Cranmore to William Soward q.v.

- - - - - - - - - - - - -

CRAVIN

1900 CENSUS

Manro Cravin 66 (Mar 1834-Ga/Ga/Ga-M 32), Mary 55 (Feb 1845-Ala/Ala/Ala-M 32-8-2), Frank 17 (May 1893), Sea 11 (June 1888), Manro POWERS 5 (gs) (June 1894), Alic STRINGER 17 (nw)(Oct 1882) 7-265B-295/300 (B)

- - - - - - - - - - - - -

CRAWFORD / CROFFORD

1860 CENSUS

Henry A. Crawford 22 (County Court Clerk): see Robert N. Gillespie

John Crawford 50, Martha 50, James R. 26, Thomas H. 20, Mary Ann 16, John T. 14, Sarah J. 12, Margaret E. 6, Jane GRIFFETT 76 (Va) 7-1-1

1870 CENSUS

Henry A. Crawford 34 (Retail Merchant), Anna M. 28, James T. 9/12 6-9-58

James R. Crawford 36, Mary C. 26, Mary 27, Sarah 22, Margarette E. 16, Jane GRIFFITH 87 (Va), John GRIFFITH (B) 16 (Ala) 7-7-57

1880 CENSUS

Henry A. Crawford 44, Anna N. 38, James T. 10, Mary R.V. 6, Anner E. 4, Henry J. 8/12, Mary A. 37 (si), Margaret E. 26 (si), James WYATT 16 (Farm Laborer), Darthula WYATT (B) 28 (Servant), Monna E. 6 (*), Elsie 4 (*), John GILLESPIE (B) 25 (Servant), Thomas J. GILLESPIE 36 ("living with A.A. Croson, brother") 6-20-183/187 [* daus of Darthula]

J.R. Crawford 46, M.C. 37 (w), Mattie 7 (d), Mary GARRISON 19, Cary DIXON 11, A. GRIFFEN 40 (c) 7-27-233

L. Crawford 50, B.C. 47, Willard 18, S.M. 15 (d), C.T. 12 (s), T.E. 10 (d), R. 8 (d) 3-15-122

Mark Crawford 61, N.A. 31 (w), E.M.J. 7/12: see T.M. Jewell

1900 CENSUS

Henry Crofford 20: see John Swan

Henry A. Crawfrd 64 (Oct 1835-M 31), Anna N. 58 (Mar 1842-M 31-6-6), Mary R. 26 (July 1873), Hannah E. 24 (May 1876), Harry E. 20 (Feb 1880), John R. 17 (June 1882), Martha D. 14 (Ap 1886), Martha A. 57 (si)(Aug 1842), Jennie A. GILLESPIE 18 (ne)(Mar 1882), Mary A. 15 (ne)(Dec 1884), Margaret ROBERTS 52 (Unk)(Servant, Cook) 6-244B-91

James Crawford 66 (May 1834-M 28), Mary C. 56 (Sep 1843-M 28-3-1), Julia KELLY 74 (ml)(Feb 1826-Wd 10-4) 15-273A-92

James H. Crawford 35 (July 1864-Ill/Scotland/England-M 3)(Barber), Mattie E. 26 (Nov 1873-NC/NC/SC-M 3-0-0) 10-329B-203/216

James T. Crawford 30 (Nov 1869)(Book Keeper at Iron Works) 10-331B-237/252

John Crawford 16: see John Purcer

John Crawford 48 (Mar 1852-Fla/Fla/Fla-M 2) 8-284B-318/320 (B)

Lizzie Crawford 38 (Jan 1862-Ga/Unk-M 23-6-3), George H.E. 18 (Mar 1882-Ga/Ga/Ga), Levi E. 9 (June 1890-Ala), James G. 6/12 (Nov 1890) 10-321-24/25

Nancy Crawford 60 (Unk 1840-T/NC/SC-Wd 1-1)(Washwoman), John P. 14 (July 1885-T/England/T), Mollie L. BARNS 19 (d)(Nov 1880-M 0) 10-260A-193/197

Susey Crawford 55: see Philip Henry (B)

MARRIAGES

Cynthia Crawford to Richard Brown q.v.

H.A. Crawford to Anna A. Gillespie, 8 Oct 1868 (same), A. P. Early MG 1-#1031

Henry Crawford to J.D. Murry, 12 Mar 1900, J.L. McPherson JP 4-106 (B)

J.R. Crawford to Mary C. Kelly, 23 Feb 1870 (same), A.P. Early MG 1-#1144

John Crawford to Susie Gillespie, 14 Sep 1898 (same), W.L. Lillard JP, M.L. Eskridge W 2-323

M. E. Crawford to T. J. Gillespie q.v.

Manda Crawford to David Day q.v.

Mary Crawford to John Smith q.v.

Mark W. Crawford to Nancy J. Jewell, 1 Oct 1874 (no return) 1-#1360

Mattie E. Crawford to F. H. Brown q.v.

Sarah J. Crawford to Thomas D. Kelly q.v.

W.E. Crawford to Sarah Ward, 23 Sep 1886 (same), T.H. McPherson JP 1-526

- - - - - - - - - - - - -

CRAWLEY

1900 CENSUS

Aaron Crawley 23 (June 1876-T/NC/T-M 2), Martha 18 (May 1882-M 2-2-1), Loyd 9/12 (Aug 1899), John MARSHALL 37 (boarder)(Feb 1863-Ky) 13-196B-124/126

James A. Crawley 40 (May 1860-T/NC/T-M 17)(Blacksmith), Lizzie A. 36 (Ap 1864-M 17-9-4), Alice 16 (May 1884), Nancy 13 (Jan 1887), Ida 7 (Oct 1892), Dome A. 6 (Sep 1893) 13-299A-170/174

John Crawley 20: see Cua B. Alley

MARRIAGES

Aaron Crawley to Martha Turner, 23 Oct 1897 (24 Oct), W.R. Grimsley MG, E.A. Shelton W 2-203

Caldonia Crawley to Charles E. Giles q.v.

Emma D. Crawley to Thomas D. Ganaway q.v.

James L. Crawley to Annie B. Potter, 3 Nov 1900 (4 Nov), T.D. Shelton ??, E.A. Shelton W 3-238

John Crawley to Mary E. Cusinan or Crisman, 23 Aug 1879 (24 Aug), J.W. Peace MG 1-#1671 & 1-#1695

Orson Crawley to Mary Shipley, 13 Dec 1893, J.W. Clouse JP 4-61

W.A. Crawley to M.E. Mills, 4 Jan 1890 (5 Jan), William Turner MG 1-591

- - - - - - - - - - - - -

CREGE

1900 CENSUS

Edd L. Crege 33 (May 1867-Ga/SC/SC-M 16)(Coal Miner), Rosie 33 (Oct 1866-T/NC/T-M 16-4-4), Andrew 15 (Feb 1885-Ga), Milford 10 (Feb 1890-Ga), Buford 8 (Jan 1892-Ga), Besay 1 (Jan 1899) 10-258A-154/158

William M. Crege 34 (July 1875-M 4)(Carpenter), Samantha 27 (Jan 1873-T/T/Ill-M 4-3-3), Fred 4 (Ap 1896), James R. 2 (Aug 1897), Eddith 1 (Ap 1899), Robert 22 (b)(Nov 1877) 10-254B-84/84

- - - - - - - - - - - - -

CRENS

1900 CENSUS

John Crens(?) 43 (Ap 1857-M 20), Salli 44 (May 1856-M 20-9-7), Ani C. 19 (Feb 1881), Edward 17 (May 1883), Carl 15 (Jan 1885), Author 12 (Sep 1887), Robbert 10 (Ap 1889), John 7 (July 1892), Clide 5 (June 1894), Birthy 4 (May 1896) 12-181A-59/62

- - - - - - - - - - - - -

CRISMAN / CREASMAN / CREASEMAN / CUSINAN

1900 CENSUS

Harvey Creaseman 32 (Ap 1868-M 10), Margaret 23 (Feb 1877-M 10-4-4), William 10 (Sep 1889), Dicie 8 (June 1891), John 4 (Oct 1885), Clay 1 (Sep 1898), Rene WHITE 17 (c)(Unk 1883-T/Ky/T) 13-298B-158/161

Martha Craseman 27, Edith May 11/12: see Miller Goin (B)

MARRIAGES

Burrel Crisman to Martha Goines, 24 Mar 1898 (27 Mar), Sherman Wilson M, John Parker W 2-260

James H. Creasman to Margaret Jordan, 13 May 1891, Wm Turner M 4-27

Mary E. Cusinan or Crisman to John Crawley q.v.

- - - - - - - - - - - - -

CRISP / CRISPE / CRISS

1860 CENSUS

Elias Crisp 47 (Ky), Mary 40, Emly 10, Nancy E. 7 1-83-569

James Crisp 59 (NC), Frances M. 47, Milly A. 18, Sarah M. 12. Marion WATSON 26, Susan E. 28, Manerva 30, William 8, Leander 3, Rebecca J. 1 1-90-615

John R. Crisp 36, Rutha CRISP 80 (NC) 1-87-598

1870 CENSUS– None

1880 CENSUS

Redman Crisp 62, Lucinda 40 (w), John 15, William 14, Ruth 12, Sarah 10, James 11, Robert 7, George 6, Charles 3, Jacob 2 1-9-76

1900 CENSUS

James Crisp 26 (Ap 1874-M 4), Ida 2 (Ap 1877-M 4-2-2), Orral 3 (s)(Mar 1897), Gleen 1 (Feb 1898), Lee 23 (b) (May 1877) 1-186A-137/143

James H. Crisp 59 (Mar 1844-England/Germany/England-1870/30/Na-Wd)(Music Teacher) 10-329A-190/203

John J. Criss(?) 34 (Sep 1865-M 13), Mary 29 (Aug 1870-M 13-6-5), Samuel 12 (Ap 1887), Robburt 11 (May 1889), Clifton 8 (Dec 1892), May 6 (Feb 1894), Anie 4 (Ap 1896), Erinda 1 (Oct 1898) 1-185B-134/141

Thomas W. Crisp 34 (Feb 1866-M 4)(Barber), Ada E. 22 (Aug 1877-M 4-1-1), Carrie B. 2 (Feb 1898) 14-214B-27/28

MARRIAGES

Elias Crisp to Mary Ann Keelon, 4 July 1862 (same), Edward Pyott JP 1-#782

Emeline Crisp to Marion Watson q.v.

J.C. Crisp to Corda Hambrick(?), 25 Nov 1887 (1 Dec), Taylor Russell JP 1-558

J.S. Crisp to M.L. Genoe, 4 Jan 1887 (6 Jan), Taylor Russell MG 1-521

James Crisp to Ellen Shoemaker, 5 Aug 1889 (11 Aug), J.H. Hale JP 1-588

James Crisp to Ida Shelby, 3 July 1896, J.H. Soward MG 4-94

Lee Crisp to Mattie Duncan, 23 Mar 1901 [probably 1900], R.D. Dickson JP 4-107

M. A. Crisp to Luke Edington q.v.

Ruth Crisp to John Gass q.v.

Ruth C. Crisp to Jessee Brown q.v.

Sarah M. Crisp to William Wilby q.v.

Serona Crispe to William Davis q.v.

Thomas Crisp to Ada Shelby, 4 July 1896, J.H. Soward MG 4-94

- - - - - - - - - - - - -

CROCH

MARRIAGE

Richard Croch or Cruch to Betsy Greer, 2 Feb 1867 (no return) 1-#934

- - - - - - - - - - - - -

CROCKETT

1870 CENSUS

Charles Crocket 65, Millie 62, Rhoda 14, Luida 20 6-7-42 (B)

1880 CENSUS– None

1900 CENSUS

Ada Crockett 32 (Unk-S 2-2)(Cook at Hotel), Lee 4 (s)(Aug 1895), William 2 (s)(Feb 1898), Hattie SIMS 38 (si) (Unk-M 3-0-0) 10-323A-64/68

Malinda Crockett 39 (Unk 1861-Va/Va/Va-Wd 7-5)(Washwoman), Charles 20 (Mar 1880)(Coal Miner), Luther 13 (Oct 1886) 8-286B-370/372 (B)

- - - - - - - - - - - - -

CROFTS / CRAFT

1900 CENSUS

Jacob B. Crofts 51 (Sep 1848-M 29), Nancy M 47 (Mar 1853-Ga/Ga/T-M 29-7-5), Larene C. 15 (Oct 1884), Alford B. 13 (Ap 1887) 1-199A-151/156

James Craft (no dates)– non resident in District 12

- - - - - - - - - - - - -

CROMMIN / CRANNION

1880 CENSUS

J.S. Crannion(?) 24, S.M. 18 (w), Robert L. 28 (b), H.A. 52 (m), N.C. 7 (child), May PATTON 18 (c) 8-3-22

James Crommin(?) 27, B.A. 28, N.M. 12 (d), W.W. 10 (s), John H. 8 (s), J. 5 (d), M.C. 2 (d), J.E. 2/12 (s) 8-18-156

CROSBY

1880 CENSUS

Joel Crosby 39 (Plow Agent), Anna 37, George 10, Bertha 9, Earl 8, John 6, Joel 4 2-23-184 [Joel married Anna Stutzman on 10 Sep 1867 in Elkhart, Ind]

1900 CENSUS

Anna Crosby 57 (Jan 1843-Oh/Pa/Germany-Wd 7-7), Bertha A. 27 (Oct 1870-Ind/Ind/Oh), Joel E. 24 (Dec 1875-Ind), James O. 19 (Aug 1880), Anna E. 16 (July 1883), Jane CLARK 67 (boarder) (Aug 1832-T/Va/Fla) 14-226A-245/249 (Rhea Springs-Washington Rd)

George Crosby 30 (Oct 1869-M 4), Louella 27 (Jan 1871-M 4-2-2), Anna E. 3 (Feb 1897), James S. 11/12 (June 1899) 14-221A-150/154 (Spring City-Rhea Springs Road) [George married Louella Ewing]

MARRIAGE

John Crosby to Ida Wright, 2 Feb 1898, W.M. White MG 4-96

CROSS

1900 CENSUS

Jacob H. Cross 44 (July 1855-M 15)(Coal Miner), Sarah 55 (Aug 1844-T/NC/NC-M 15-5-3), John T. 14 (May 1886), Homie(?) HELTON 13 (ne)(Dec 1886-Ala) 13-201B-215/223

MARRIAGES

Annie Cross to Will C. Duff q.v.

Emily Cross to James Brown q.v.

W. F. Cross to Amanda S. Foust, 28 Feb 1887 (1 Mar), G.W. Simpson ?? 1-528 & 1-530

CROW

1870 CENSUS

Louisa J. Crow 40, Eliza Jane 18, John H. 14, William R. 12, Samuel T. 9 4-5-33

1880 CENSUS

Robert N. Crow 64, Elizabeth 75 (w) 5-10-94

1900 CENSUS

John H. Crow 43 (Dec 1856-M 17), Elizabeth 34 (June 1865-T/Va/T-M 17-6-4), Birtha L. 16 (Feb 1884), James W.P. 14 (May 1886), Etta J. 11 (Sep 1888), Ida 3 (Oct 1896) 3-202B-49/52 [John Crow married Elizabeth Eaves on 31 May 1883 in Meigs Co]

Vaughn Crow 45 (Sep 1854-Ga/Ga/Ga-M 4)(Locamotive Engineer), Alice 29 (May 1871-Ala/Ala/Ala-M 4-1-1), James 19 (Sep 1880)(Locamotive Fireman), Oscar 14 (July 1885-Ala), G. 12 (s)(Aug 1887-Ala), Lester 10 (July 1889-Ala), Arthur MULLENIX 12 (ss)(Nov 1887-Ala) 8-312B-40/43

William R. Crow 38 (Oct 1861-M 20), Martha J. 36 (Unk-M 20-3-3), Clement B. 14 (July 1885), Golda L. 13 (Mar 1887), John H. 11 (Sep 1888), Loula 7 (Dec 1892), Thomas 6 (May 1894), Fred 3 (Ap 1897), Ersa HALE 25 (sil)(Unk) 6-245A-103/104

MARRIAGES

A.E. Crow to L.A. Morgan, 9 Mar 1889 (10 Mar), W.G. Curton ?? 1-571

Eliza Crow to George Fisher q.v.

L. J. Crow to A. M. Lowry q.v.

James Crow to Louisa Holland, 19 Feb 1851 (20 Feb), S.R. Hackett JP 1-#335

Louisa Jane Crow to Joshua Garrett q.v.

M. A. Crow to C. H. Smith q.v.

Margrett Crow to William Blankenship q.v.

Patrick Crow to Annie Castell, 26 Oct 1889 (same), James Murrey MG 1-592

Patrick Crow(?) to Annie Costello, 26 Oct 1893 4-58

S.T. Crow (22) to Mary Phillips, 25 Dec 1881, J.M. Bramlett MG, John Coofer & G.W. Fisher W 4-7(63)

Solomon Crow to Elizabeth Allen, 24 July 1860 (same), John Howard MG 1-#720

William Crow (22) to Julia Phillips (22), 12 June 1881, J.M. Bramlett MG, Jas Jones & H.H. Gambell W 4-2(11)

CROWDER

1900 CENSUS

Frank L. Crowder 30 (Ap 1870-NC/NC/NC-M 1)(Mechanic), Ada 19 (Jan 1881-M 1-0-0), Dollie WASHUM 25 (sil)(Dec 1875), Nola 15 (sil)(Sep 1884) 8-276B-157/158

MARRIAGE

John Crowder to Josie Washam, 12 May 1888 (13 May), M.H. Morris ?? 1-551

CRUMLEY

MARRIAGES

Mattie J. Crumley to W. W. Renfro q.v.

Nancy L. Crumley to J. A. Collier q.v.

CRUS

1880 CENSUS

Hugh Crus(?) 25 (RR Foreman), Mary 22 5-11-104

CRUTCHFIELD

MARRIAGE

Mary Crutchfield to C. M. Price(?) q.v.

CULVER

1880 CENSUS

Dwight Culver 45 (Photographer), Eglentine 36, Della 13, Olenna 10, Eugene 7 2-22-185

1900 CENSUS

Dwight Culver 66 (Ap 1834-Mass/Canada/Mass-M 35) (Minister), Eglentine 54 (Sep 1845-Ark/T/Ark-M 35-4-3), Laura ARNOLD 27 (d)(Ap 1873-Wd 2-1), Eugene 8 (gs)(Mar 1892-Ala) 10-323B-75/79

Thomas T. Culver 32: see Calvin J. Turley

MARRIAGES

Clara A. Culver to William Depree q.v.

Lenie K. Culver to G. G. Arnold q.v.

Madeline Culver to S. L. Harvey q.v.

- - - - - - - - - - - - -

CULVERHOUSE

MARRIAGE

Mary Culverhouse to William Dodson q.v.

- - - - - - - - - - - - -

CUMBO / CUNBO

1880 CENSUS

Lentitia Cumbo 27, Robert L. 4/12, David L. 12: see Simon Wyrick

MARRIAGES

John Cunbo to Lydia Doss, 8 June 1900 (same), W.J. McLanis(?) MG, John Pogue W 3-165

- - - - - - - - - - - - -

CUMMINGS

1900 CENSUS

Mon Cummings 26: see John McEntire (B)

- - - - - - - - - - - - -

CUNNINGHAM / CUNNYNGHAM

1860 CENSUS

H.M. Cunningham 41 (Blacksmith), Manet(?) J. 36, Sarah F. 16, Mary L. 14, Cynthia E. 12, July A. 9, John D. 2, Milberry T.E. 5/12 7-2-9

James M. Cunningham 39, Elizabeth E. 39, Thomas D. 15, John W. 13, William V. 10, James H. 8, Margaret F. 3 8-19-126

Thomas N. Cunningham 19, Lorinda J. 18 3-60-410

Wyley H. Cunningham 48, Elvira 43, Charlotte J. 17, Franklin L. 14, Robert C.M. 12, Darius W. 9, James R. 6, Elvira A. 4, Wyly H. 1 3-62-432

1870 CENSUS

Elvira Cunningham 53, Franklin L. 24, Charlotte I. 26, Robert C. 22 (School Teacher), Darius W. 20 (Student), James R. 16, Elvira A. 14, Willie H. 12, Newton LOCKE 57, Mariah KELLY (B) 14 3-21-150

Thomas N.L. Cunningham 30, Lorinda J. 28, William W. 10 (Student), Elvira A. 7, Mary E. 5, John R. 1/12 3-11-32

Jane Cunningham 80 (Va) 3-21-157 (B)

Mary Cunningham 12 (B): see Samuel H. Holloway

William Cunningham 50, Mary 39, Jane M. 21, Grace Ann 19, Sarah E. 16, Nancy M. 14, Wm P. 17 4-2-10 (B)

1880 CENSUS

A.L. Cunnyngham 36 (Minister), S.M. 36, M.E. 14 (d), J.A. 12 (d), A.M. 10 (d), J.M. 8 (s), M.J. 6 (d), L.E. 3 (d) 11-38-310

E. Cunnyngham 62, Isabella 37 (d), D.W. 30 (s), J.R. 27 (s), E.A. 24 (d), W.H. 22 (s), A.B. FILES(?) 23 (boarder), Elvira EAVES* 25 (Teacher), C. GILLESPIE [B} 9, Hoyl DAY (B) 19 4-12-95 [*dau of Pleasant & Elizabeth Bean Eaves]

R.C.M. Cunnyngham 32 (Lawyer), J.B. 29 (w), J.W.C. 2 (s), Mira 7/12, J.F. BLEVINS 25 (bl)(Carpenter) 4-7-58

T.N.L. Cunnyngham 39 (Lawyer), Lorinda J. 37, William W. 19, Elvira A. 16, Mary E. 14, John R. 9, Sarah J. 7, Edgar A. 2 6-22-4 (Madison Street, Washington)

1900 CENSUS

Anna Cunningham 70: see Nancy Rankin (B)

Carrie Cunningham 25: see William McWells

Casper Cunningham 38 (Aug 1861-M 8), Anna 27 (Dec 1872-M 8-5-3), Charley R. 7 (Mar 1893), Sanford H. 5 (Dec 1894), Debby L. 1/12 (May 1900) 6-241A-27

Ed Cunyingham 22: see John Acuff

Elvira A. Cunningham 36: see Myra J. Hodges

George Cunningham 28 (Nov 1871/Ga/Ga/Ga-M 8)(Coal Miner), Jennie 27 (Feb 1873-Ky/Ky/Ky-M 8-3-2), Lenora 7 (Sep 1892), Glennie L. 1 (Sep 1898) 15-272B-83 (B)

James Cunningham 65 (Feb 1835-M 36), Cathern J. 56 (July 1843-M 38-4-3), James 23 (Feb 1877), Ethel 20 (July 1879), Cinda 14 (Oct 1885), James M. JONES 15 (gs)(Mar 1885), Moses D. CLARK 29 (Feb 1871-Ga/Ga/Ga)(Servant) 2-195A-78/81

James Cunningham 38 (Sep 1861-M 12), Lara 28 (Jan 1872-M 12-7-6), Banpler 10 (s)(May 1890), Linis 8 (Sep 1891), Willum 7 (Mar 1893), Frank 5 (Mar 1895), John 2 (July 1897), Lisa 11/12 (June 1899) 1-188A-179/188

John Cunningham 24 (May 1874-M 2), Mary J. 24 (Sep 1875-M 2-1-1), Ninnie F. 1 (Mar 1899) 2-196A-88/91

John Cunningham 32 (June 1867-M 8), Martha E. 26 (Sep 1873-Ga/Ga/Ga-M 8-4-4), Ollie M. 6 (d)(Nov 1893), Anna N. 6 (Mar 1894), Joseph R. 3 (Nov 1896), John K. 1 (Nov 1898) 3-202A-48/51

John R. Cunnyngham 27 (July 1870)(Druggist) 10-320B-5/5

Robert C.M. Cunnyngham 52 (Feb 1848-M 24)(Lawyer), Julia B. 49 (Sep 1850-M 24-7-6), John W.C. 22 (Nov 1877)(Law Student), Nora A. 20 (Sep 1879), Robert L.C. 16 (June 1884), Jean A. 13 (Aug 1886), Thomas P.P. 11 (Sep 1888), Rosa L. 8 (Sep 1891) 14-216B-82/83

Ruth Cunningham 13: see Elijah Atkinson

Thomas N.L. Cunnyngham 59 (Aug 1840-M 4)(Attorney), Bettie N. 46 (Dec 1853-M 4-0-0), Addie B. WALLER 14 (sd)(Sep 1885)(Dry Goods Clerk) 10-325B-116/120

Wiley H. Cunnyngham 41 (July 1858-M 16)(Physician), Ada 39 (May 1861-M 16-5-4), Lela 15 (Ap 1885), Noel 12 (Mar 1888), Golley 9 (Feb 1891), Huston D. 3 (Jan 1897), Roscoe C. MILLER 27 (Nov 1872) (Physician, Partner), Bertha DARWIN 20 (boarder) (Mar 1880) 5-233B-109

William W. Cunnyngham 39 (Aug 1860-M 2)(Druggist), Martha 24 (Ap 1876-Ga/Ga/Ga-M 2-0-0), George 16 (s)(Aug 1883), Ethel 12 (d)(June 1887), Mary BURNETT 29 (Feb 1871)(Servant) 15-271A-56

MARRIAGES

Casper Cunningham to Annie Woody, 15 Oct 1891, W.A. Templeton JP 4-36

Dena(?) Cunnyngham to Thomas Holman q.v.

George Cunningham to Jennie Baker(?), 30 Ap 1892, S.W. Burnett MG 4-40

Henry Cunningham to Jane Foust, 5 Feb 1900 (5 Feb), L.E. Smith JP, John W. Harwood W 3-119

Josie Cunnyngham to Will Acuff q.v.

John Cunningham to Mattie Burel, 25 Jan 1893, J.M. Hill JP 4-54

M. C. Cunningham to Thomas Rhay q.v.

Mary A. Cunningham to William McWells q.v.

Mary E. Cunnyngham to John C. Acuff q.v.

Robert C.M. Cunnyngham to Julia B. Blevins, 31 May 1876 (same), A.P. Early MG 1-#1445

Ruth Ann Cunningham to Benjamin Harris q.v.

T.N.L. [Thomas Newton Locke] Cunnyngham to L.J. [Lorinda Jane] Smith, 28 Sep 1859 (29 Sep), Jas W. Thompson MG 1-#696½ [sic]

T.N.L. Cunnyngham to Kittie J. Coulter, 11 Sep 1883 (same), A.P. Early MG 1-466

T.N.L. Cunnyngham to Elizabeth J. Bishop, 20 Aug 1892

T.N.L. Cunnyngham to ---[erased]--- A. Gibson, 16 Dec 1890, L.L.H. Carlock MG 4-18

T.N.L. Cunnyngham to Bettie Brock, 19 Feb 1896, W.L. Lillard JP 4-95

W.H. [Wylie Houston] Cunnyngham to Ada Darwin, 16 May 1884 (same), A.P. Early MG 1-459

William H. Cunningham to May or Mary E. Holloway, 9 Oct 1858 (24 Sep)[sic], Gilbert Randolph MG 1-#661

William Wylie Cunnyngham (MD) to [Hannah] Minerva Tucker (17, Washington), 30 Aug 1882, J.H. Locke JP, W.L. Locke & C.L. Locke W 4-10(94)

W.W. Cunningham to Julia(?) Fletcher, 21 July 1889, Jas Corvin MG 4-44

- - - - - - - - - - - - -

CURLEY

1870 CENSUS

Nancy Curley 13: see Samuel H. Dickey

- - - - - - - - - - - - -

CURTAIN / CURTON

MARRIAGES

Mattie Curtain to Richard Sneed q.v.

R.J. Curton to Dona Dobbs, 19 or 29 June 1899 (same), G.W. Brewer MG, J.R. Sneed W 3-2

Sarah H. Curtain to Thomas Millsaps q.v.

- - - - - - - - - - - - -

CURTIS

1900 CENSUS

Daniel Curtis 53 (Oct 1846-Md/Md/Md-Wd) 8-287B-385/387 (B)

Will Curtis 40: see Moses Grier

MARRIAGES

Amanda Curtis to T. H. Smith q.v.

John H. Curtis to Mary H. Filpot, 14 Ap 1886 (15 Ap), Jas A. Crawford JP 1-507

Myrtle Grace Curtis to Stanley W. Swaby q.v.

- - - - - - - - - - - - -

CUSHING

MARRIAGES

Margaret Cushing to J. F. Sully q.v.

Mary A. Cushing to T. A. Barton q.v.

- - - - - - - - - - - - -

CUSTER

MARRIAGE

Mary Custer to C. F. Bandy q.v.

- - - - - - - - - - - - -

DAGLEY

1870 CENSUS

Franklin Dagley 26, Susan 18, Charles 2, Henry 9/12 1-8-54

1880 CENSUS

Franklin Dagley 36, Ladie 27, Charlie 11, Henry 10, John 7, Florence 6, Carrie 3 12-1-9

J.I.(?) Dagley 26, Mary 25, Hariet 8, Farley 7, C.D. 5 (d), F.A. 2 (d) 3-28-228

Riley Dagley 34, W.R. 69 (f), A.M. 56 (m), Martha 22 (si), Susan 17 (si), Susan 1 (ne), M.L. 8/12 (nw) 11-42-336

1900 CENSUS

John W. Dagley 28 (Unk 1872-M 6), Mary Ann 22 (Mar 1878-M 6-3-2), Carl F. 4 (Feb 1896), Maud L. 1 (Ap 1899), Charles A. DAGLEY 31 (b)(July 1868)(Salvation Army Work) 3-201B-36/39

William R. Dagley 52 (May 1848-M 16), Sarah A. 38 (Jan 1862-M 16-1-0) 4-225B-235/239 (Ridge Road East of Spring City & Dayton Road)

MARRIAGES

Cyntha Ann Dagley to John M. Bennett q.v.

John Dagley to Annie Boofer, 24 Dec 1893, R.M. Trentham JP 4-62

Martha Dagley to Jack Stephens q.v.

Wm David Dagley to Sarah F. Holloway, 10 Dec 1890, R.A. Dickson JP 4-21

- - - - - - - - - - - - -

DALE

MARRIAGE

Lillie Dale to A. T. Runyan q.v.

- - - - - - - - - - - - -

DALRYMPLE

1860 CENSUS

Allen Dalrymple 56 (SC)(Carpenter): see John N. Ragsdale

- - - - - - - - - - - - -

DALTON

1900 CENSUS

Morgan Dalton 25 (May 1875-M 2)(Coal Miner), Ida 17 (Dec 1882-M 2-1-1), Henry 1 (Dec 1898) 13-302B-236/246

MARRIAGE

Morgan Dalton to Ida Johnson, 1 Oct 1897 (bond only), W. A. Mice W 2-190

- - - - - - - - - - - - -

DANA

1900 CENSUS

Liddie Dana 29: see Wilm Clark

- - - - - - - - - - - - -

DANE

1900 CENSUS

Fanny Dane 18 (B): see Benjamin F. Mealer

MARRIAGE

W.P. Dane to Annie Moore, 16 Dec 1886 (23 Dec), S.H. Price MG 1-521

- - - - - - - - - - - - -

DANIEL / DANIELS / DANNEL / DANNLS / DANALS / DANILL

1870 CENSUS

James O. Daniel 35, Mary Jane 30, William H. 13, John A. 11, Reubin H. 9, Lila A. 2, Lydia A. 4/12, Mary THOMPSON 10 1-19-124

1880 CENSUS

James Daniel 47, Mary 43, John 22, Reubin 20, Delilia 12, Lydia 10, Jamima 2, Riley 1 12-4-36

William Daniel 20 (Mu): see Jere Wasson

William Danill 23, Mary 23, James 3, Jennie 1/12 12-5-41

1900 CENSUS

Elen E. Daniels 72: see John W. Francis

Eline Dannls 19, Sarah 14, Rosi 16, John 11: see Samuel Lemmon

Jenni Daniel 23: see Jestas Forstar

Joseph Daniels 45 (June 1854-M 17)(Civil Engineer), Flora G. 40 (Jan 1860-T/Va/T-M 17-5-4), Walter M.G. 13 (Jan 1887), Jossie 8 (Oct 1891), John B.S. 6 (Ap 1894), Lawrence P. 2 (Oct 1897) 8-312B-38/41

Patrick Daniel 37 (Feb 1863-Ga/Miss/Ga-M 10), Hester A. 32 (Ap 1868-M 10-4-4), Buney S. 9 (Aug 1890-Ga), Gracy E. 6 (Aug 1893), Russell A. 3 (Sep 1896), O'Conner J. 10/12 (July 1899) 7-262B-238/243

Reuben Daniels 56: see Francis W. Bacon

Rilley Danals 26 (Jan 1874), Liddie 22 (si)(May 1878) 12-180B-51/54

MARRIAGES

Annie Daniels to Samuel Lemens q.v.

J.F. Daniel to Ella J. Hughes, 14 Oct 1899 (15 Oct), Bird Henderson MG, G.D. Hughes W 3-53

J.L. Daniels (30, Cedar Springs) to F.A. Greer (24, Pikeville), 24 Ap 1883, T. Ashburn MG, Mary Frazier & Walter Thomison W 4-14(137)

James Oliver Daniel to Mary Jane Lemmons, 3 Oct 1855 (4 Oct), E.R.S. Thompson JP 1-#527

Jennie Daniel to H. B. Ray q.v.

John A. Dannel (24, Meigs Co) to N.A. Lloyd (16), 8 Dec 1881, W.T. West MG, W.C. Watson & W.C. Wolf W 4-6(52)

Lilie Ann Daniel to John Dye q.v.

P. T. Daniel to Hester Shaver, 17 Oct 1889 (22 Oct), R. T. Howard MG 1-593

William H. Daniel to Mary J. Brady, 5 Jan 1875 (8 Jan), Jas Johnson JP 1-#1385

- - - - - - - - - - - - -

DANNY

1860 CENSUS

Sarah Danny(?) 36, John G. 16, Addison A. 9, Joseph C. 6 9-100-686

- - - - - - - - - - - - -

DANSBY

1880 CENSUS

David Dansby 30 (Works in Shoe Shop) 2-24-192

- - - - - - - - - - - - -

DANTY

1900 CENSUS

Aaron Danty 54 (July 1845-NC/NC/NC-M 30), Hattie 57 (May 1843-NC/NC/NC-M 30-6-6), George 26 (June 1874), General 21 (Ap 1879), John 19 (July 1880), Casper 17 (Aug 1883), Mink 12 (Dec 1887), Wilum 9 (Jan 1891) 1-187B-173/182 (B)

- - - - - - - - - - - - -

DARBY

MARRIAGE

H. S. Darby to Cora Morris, 11 May 1886 (same), P. P. Brooks ?? 1-483

- - - - - - - - - - - - -

DARIDGE

MARRIAGE

Sallie T. Daridge to H. M. Alexander q.v.

- - - - - - - - - - - - -

DARR

MARRIAGE

T.P. Darr to Ella Julian, 10 Aug 1874 (21 Aug), P.E. Johnson MG 1-#1352

- - - - - - - - - - - - -

DART

MARRIAGE

C.F. Dart to Mae Morgan, 20 May 1898 (22 May), W.T. Drummond ??, Edward M. Phelps W 2-284

- - - - - - - - - - - - -

DARWIN

1860 CENSUS

James A. Darwin 63 (SC), Bethiah 61 (NC), Belinda 32, Ann 24, Henry C. 17 5-34-231

Thomas Darwin 43, Eliza 38, Orpha J. 17, Mary 15, Rebecca 13, Vesta 11, Tennessee 9, James 7, Henry 5, Alfred 2 4-46-311

William P. Darwin 30 (Merchant), Adelia 21: see Jacob Kelly

1870 CENSUS

Alex Darwin 12 (B): see John N. Miller

Charles Darwin 23 (Va), Lydia 24 (Ga) 5-6-44 (B) (Mu)

Henry C. Darwin 27, Ellen E. 26 (Miss), Eunice M. 1 5-9-63

James A. Darwin 74, Betha 72, Belinda 42, James T. 16 (Ark), Tennessee W. 13 (Ark), Perry Ann 11 (Ark), Mary D. 6 (Ark), Julia BLEVINS 19 5-6-43

Martha J. Darwin 47, Easter A. 19, Mary R. 17, Charles G. 13, Robert 7, William J. 5 5-5-37 (B)

Susan Darwin 30, Mary 7, Andrew 7 (B): see Wm T. Gass

Thomas C. Darwin 53, Eliza Ann 49, Vesta 21, Tennessee 19, James T. 17, Mariah BRADY (B) 30, Nancy J. BRADY (B) 13, Henry C. DARWIN 15, Alfred 12, Addie 9, Ida 9, Ruth GOURD 86 (NC) 4-15-102

William P. Darwin 40, Adelia 30, William P. Jr. 9, James B. 3, Jennie A. 2, Hannah 2/12, William P. BLEVINS 17 5-9-64

1880 CENSUS

Charles Darwin 46, Lydia 31 (w) 5-7-65 (B)

Della Darwin 16: see Robert L. Allen

John Darwin 9 (Servant) (B): see T. C. Darwin

Laidy Darwin 27, Hattie 10, Charity 3, Adia 2, Tom 9/12 8-21-181 (B)

Lula Darwin 2 (Mu): see William Castleman (B)

M.J. Darwin 56, Easter A. 29, Mary R. 27, Charles G. 23, Charles SWAFFORD 4 (nw) 5-8-73 (B)

Mary Darwin 18 (Servant) (Mu): see John Neal

T.C. Darwin 63, Elisa 59, J.C. 25, A.C. 22, Ida 19, Ada 19, Malinda 62 (si), John DARWIN (B) 9 (Servant) 4-7-56

William P. Darwin 50, Adelia 40, William 18, James R. 13, Jennie A. 11, Hannah 9, Thomas A. 7, Eller 6, Nilly 3, Fredick 2, Bathiah 3/12, Perry Ann 20 (ne), Let COX (B) 47 (Farm Laborer), Mary COLLINS (B) 48 (Cook at Hotel), Peter COLLINS (B) 5 5-11-106

1900 CENSUS

Alfred B. Darwin 41 (Feb 1859-M 2), Eliza D. 35 (Ap 1865-M 2-0-0) 5-234A-123

Belinda H. Darwin 72: see Victoria Caldwell

Bertha Darwin 20: see Wyley H. Cunnyngham

Henry C. Darwin 45 (Ap 1855-M 19), Ellen J.S. 41 (Sep 1859-Pa/Pa/Pa-M 19-5-5), Frederick J. 18 (Dec 1881), Thomas B. 14 (Aug 1885), Mary E. 13 (Sep 1886), Orpha E. 10 (Ap 1890), Francis H. 3 (Sep 1896) 14-222A-169/173

James T. Darwin 46 (Mar 1854-Ark/T/T-M 18), Laura L. 36 (Oct 1863-Ky/Ky/T-M 18-8-4), Ollie P. 17 (Nov 1882), Garvie J. 15 (Nov 1884), Sidney L. 6 (s)(Sep 1893), Katie W. 2 (Nov 1897) 5-235A-140

Mary R. Darwin 47 (July 1852-S) 5-231A-55 (B)

William P. Darwin 38 (Jan 1862-M 15), Hariett C. 36 (Sep 1864-M 15-4-4), William C. 13 (June 1886), Adelia C. 9 (July 1890), Elenor 5 (Aug 1894), Darius 1 (Oct 1898), Kate GREY 12 (Dec 1876)(Domestic Servant), Amanda C. PAINE 62 (Aug 1837-T/Va/T-Wd 0-0) 5-234B-131

MARRIAGES

Ada Darwin to W. H. Cunnyngham q.v.

Ann Darwin to Henry C. Rodgers q.v.

Bell Darwin to Andrew Gass q.v.

Della Darwin to J. G. Thomison q.v.

Ella Darwin to W. F. Thomison q.v.

H.C. Darwin to Ellen Shellits, 27 Dec 1880 (5 Jan 1881), D.V. Culver MG 1-294

Hannah G. Darwin to Jesse B. Swafford q.v.

Ida Darwin to J. H. Womack q.v.

Jennie Darwin to W. L. Abel q.v.

Mary B. Darwin to Edward H. Marsh q.v.

Nellie H. or Annie N. Darwin to J. W. Gass

Orpha J. Darwin to R. L. Miller q.v.

Penny A. Darwin to John T. Howard q.v.

Polly Darwin to Will Sawyers q.v.

Rebecca Darwin to John T. Miller q.v.

T. W. Darwin to G. W. Goodrich q.v.

T. W. Darwin to William R. Foster q.v.

Vesta A. Darwin to G. W. Ault q.v.

Victoria Darwin to J. M. Caldwell q.v.

W.P. Darwin to Adelia Gillespie, 23 May 1860 (same), G.W. Renfro MG 1-#713

\- - - - - - - - - - - - -

DAUGHERTY / DAUGHTERY / DOUGHTY / DOUTYS / DOTEY

1860 CENSUS

William Daughtery 30, Mary 31, Mary 4, Eliza J. 1 3-59-402

1870 CENSUS

William Doughty 41, Mary J. 17 3-13-96 (B)

MARRIAGE

Ella F. Dotey to R. N. Magill q.v.

M.B. Daugherty to Naoma Gallahen, 3 Ap 1889 (same), R.S. Mason JP 1-571

William Doutys to Mary C. Johns, 9 Oct 1867 (11 Oct), J.H. Keith MG 1-#976

\- - - - - - - - - - - - -

DAVENPORT

1900 CENSUS

Tabitha Davenport 23: see Edwin R. Gillett

MARRIAGES

M. J. or W. J. Davenport to Sarah E. Bruce, 9 Sep 1883 (same), J.H. Weaver MG 1-476

Sabastian Davenport to Estella M. Germans, 18 Dec 1894, W.W. Dorman(?) MG 4-76

\- - - - - - - - - - - - -

DAVID

1860 CENSUS

Magdalin David 86 (Va), Nancy 46, John C. 26: see Ambros Arthur

1870 CENSUS

John O. David 35 (Boot & Shoemaker), Nancy A. 53 (NC) 10-3-17

1880 CENSUS

John O. David 46 (Boot & Shoemaker) 10-0-230/239

- - - - - - - - - - - - -

DAVIDSON

MARRIAGES

Cora E. Davidson to Will P. McDonald q.v.

R.S. Davidson to Greeley(?) Keith, 19 Mar 1886 (same), G.W. Simpson MG 1-511

R.W. Davidson to Carrie W. Abernathy, 22 Sep 1892, H.C. Neal MG 4-32

Willie Davidson to Lori Caldwell, 13 Sep 1888 (same), W. M. Colston(?) MG 1-554

- - - - - - - - - - - - -

DAVIS

1860 CENSUS

David Davis 53 (NC)(Blacksmith), Sarah 52, John 19, Viney 15, Rufus 17, Martha 12 3-66-456

Henry Davis 35 (Va)(Blacksmith), Ellen 30, Mary 12, Alfred 10, Sarah 8, Clubus(?) 6 (s), Elizabeth 4, Eliza J. 3/12, James KIZIAH 18 4-46-310

Isaac Davis 23, Amanda 18 3-66-457

John Davis 48, Lucinda 36, Elizabeth H. 10, Vesuelia C. 9, Josiah P. 6, Sally 4, Julia A. 2 2-71-482

Lewis J. Davis 35: see Granville H. Wade

1870 CENSUS

David Davis 60 (NC), Sarah 56, Vina 23, Kate DUCKWORTH 34, Martha J. 14, Nancy E. 12, John D. 10, Mary L. 7, Sarah 4 3-16-115

David Davis 35 (Va)(Blacksmith), Rachel 29 (Va), Mariah 11 (Va), Martha C. 9 (Va), Frances 7 (Va), John M. 4 (Va), Henry A. 6/12, George W. 6/12 6-10-62

Henry Davis 45 (Va)(Blacksmith), Ellen P. 40 (Va), Columbia 17 (Va), Julia E. 14 (Va), Eliza Jane 10, John A. 7, William B. 5, Henry W.D. 1 8-19-131

John M. Davis 26: see Snelson Roberts

Rufus Davis 28, Louisa 28, Thomas 1 3-16-119

1880 CENSUS

Ben B. Davis 54, Lucinda 41, Margaret A. 11, Jacob F. 8, Laura B. 7, Lin C. 5, Lucinda M. 2, Dela A. 2/12 6-18-168/171

David Davis 74 (Blacksmith), Sarah 73, S.A. [Vina] 30 (d) 3-22-174

David Davis 48 (Blacksmith), Rachel A. 43, Frances M. 16, John M. 13, Henry A. 10, George W. 10, David I.(?) 9, William A. 7, Anna L. 5, Rachel O. 3 6-13-123/124

Jack Davis 45, M.A. 39, York 20, Reuben 15, Richard 12, Houston 9, Lem 6, Susan 3, L.E. 3/12 (d) 4-9-72

Margaret Davis 18 (B): see Lewis Delonis (Mu)

R.M. Davis 37, L.C. 37, D. 10 (s), J.A. 8 (s), W.E. 4 (s), A.C. 7/12 (d) 3-30-241

1900 CENSUS

Charles M. Davis 35 (Mar 1865-M 10), Sally 25 (Oct 1874-M 10-5-5), Louisa 8 (Feb 1892), Richard 6 (Oct 1893), Bessie 5 (Dec 1894), Florence 3 (Mar 1897), Fanney 1 (Feb 1899), Louisa 70 (m)(Dec 1829-Wd 8-7), Marcella 10 (ne)(Oct 1889) 13-299B-174/178

David Davis 68 (Jan 1832-Va/Va/Va-M 44)(Blacksmith), Rachael 63 (Ap 1837-Va/Va/Va-M 44-13-9), Fanny M. 36 (Nov 1865-Va), Done D. 27 (Nov 1872-Wd) (Coal Miner), William A. 26 (Mar 1874-M 0)(Coal Miner), Della L. 22 (dl)(Nov 1877-Tex/T/T-M 0-0-0), Odie O. 19 (Aug 1880) 13-299B-177/182

Eliza Davis 69: see Creed Shadrick

George W. Davis 30 (Mar 1870-M 9)(Coal Miner), Tressie 23 (July 1876-M 9-0-0) 13-302B-234/244

Henry A. Davis 30 (Mar 1870-Va/Va/Va-M 6)(Blacksmith), Della 23 (July 1876-M 6-3-2), Jesse E. 2 (Nov 1897), Bessie P. 2 (Nov 1897) 13-304A-264/274

John A. Davis 65 (Nov 1836-M 41), Mary A. 58 (Aug 1841-M 41-9-7), Houston H. 28 (Aug 1871), Susan J. 23 (Mar 1877)(School Teacher), Louisa 20 (Ap 1880), Nancy C. 18 (Ap 1883) 5-230A-36/36

James J. Davis 24 (Jan 1876-Ga/Ga/Ga-M 2)(Cooper), Daisey C. 21 (Mar 1879-Ga/Ga/Ga-M 2-1-0) 13-308A-349/362

Jordan Davis 73 (Oct 1821-Ga/Ga/Ga-M 3)(Wood Hauler), Ester 40 (Feb 1860-M 3-0-0), Palee H. HUTCHINS 21 (d)(July 1878-Ga/Ga/Ga-M 2-0-0), Earnest 20 (sl) (Mar 1880-M 2)(Coal Miner), Emmit DAVIS 6 (gs) (Jan 1894-Ga) 10-251B-29 (B)

Joseph A. Davis 33 (May 1867-Ga/Unk-M 5), Mattie D. 23 (Ap 1877-Ga/Ga/Ga-M 5-4-4), Mandy E. 4 (Dec 1895-Ga), Vellia 3 (July 1896-Ga), William O. 2 (Feb 1898), Milbern C. 9/12 (Nov 1899) 3-207A-124/135

Louisa Davis 70: see Charles M. Davis

Mildred Davis 15: see Charles W. Irwin

Miller Davis 10: see Jim Shaver (B)

Richard D. Davis 32 (Ap 1868-M 8)(School Teacher), Bertha T. 23 (Sep 1876-M 8-3-2), Victor D. 4 (July 1895), Earl B. 5 (Nov 1896), Ruth M. 1 (Dec 1898) 4-224B-219/223 (Spring City-Dayton Road)

William Davis 27 (Jan 1873-M 2), Mary E. 23 (Aug 1876-M 2-2-0), Leona 15 (c)(Mar 1885) 15-269A-19/19

York Davis 39 (June 1860-M 2), Martha 26 (May 1874-M 2-0-0) 5-230A-37/37

MARRIAGES

A.E. Davis to Laura L. Bell, 21 Sep 1897 (29 Sep), Wm White MG, W.N. Rose W 2-183

Asbury Davis to Elizabeth Moon, 8 July 1899 (9 July), M.F. Cook MG, T. Morton(?) W 3-9

Augusta C. Davis to Lettie Shirley, 23 Oct 1893, William Turner MG 4-82

Bell Davis to Sam Marler q.v.

Bell Davis to Will Holeman q.v.

Bettie Davis to Samuel Benson q.v.

C. Davis to Samuel Duckworth q.v.

Charley Davis to Sallie Ward, 27 Jan 1890, Jas Corvin MG 4-44

D.D. Davis to M.M. [Mallie M.] Rains, 12 May 1892, R.A. Bartlett MG 4-43

Emaline Davis to Daniel Kennedy q.v.

Fanine(?) Davis to Thomas Gothard q.v.

G.W. Davis to T.L. Melton, 15 Mar 1892, W.S. Hale MG 4-39

H.A. Davis to Dellie Hale, 13 May 1894, R.S. Mason JP 4-66

Isaac Davis to Amanda Frazier, 28 Jan 1860 (29 Jan), A. Johns MG 1-#1654

J.F. Davis to Ellen Sexton, 12 Sep 1896 (same), W.L. Lillard JP 2-67

Jane Davis to Thomas Ellison q.v.
Jordan(?) Davis to Easter Humphrey, 31 Mar 1894, D.H. Hinder(?) JP 4-68
July Ann Davis to Robert Moore q.v.
L. Davis to J. C. Furgerson q.v.
Letha Davis to Wyley Eskridge q.v.
Lewis Jordan Davis to Lucinda C. Jolly, 1 Ap 1861 (4 Ap), D.W. Horner MG 1-#750
Lora Davis to George Nixon q.v.
Mariah E. Davis to Locke Wyrick q.v.
Mary Davis to J. Wasson q.v.
Mary Davis to Wilbert F. Whaley q.v.
Mary E. Davis to W. T. Smith q.v.
Mary R. Davis to Creed Shadwick q.v.
Mattie C. Davis to J. A. Killough q.v.
Mollie Davis to Reese Dean q.v.
Nancy Ann Davis to G. H. Slagle q.v.
Nancy E. Davis to William Dye q.v.
Parthena Davis to Earnest Hutcheson q.v.
Richard D. Davis to Bertie L. Brown, 21 Ap 1892, J. Woolsey MG 4-39
Robert Davis to Mary J. Sherley, 20 Nov 1887, Jas Carrie MG 4-46
Rosa Lee Davis to W. E. Corder q.v.
Samuel B. Davis to Evaline Fine, 21 Aug 1865 (24 Aug), Edward Pyott JP 1-#1073
Sarah E. Davis to Calvin A. Morgan q.v.
Sarah E. Davis to Mason Wright q.v.
Sorena Davis to James Schafer q.v.
T.J. Davis to Mary A. Martin, 10 Dec 1863 (no return) 1-#812
Thomas Davis to Mary Thomas, 14 May 1892, W.S. Hale MG 4-40
Tom Davis to Fannie Whitemer or W. Whitmore, 25 Mar 1866 (26 Mar), I.W. Holt JP 1-511
W.A. Davis to Lillie Nail, 21 Ap 1900 (same), W.S. Hale MG 3-148
Wm Davis to Serena Crispe, 17 Aug 1853 (21 Aug), T.B. Walker MG 1-#418
York Davis to Mattie Burdett, 17 Jan 1898 (20 Jan), H.B. Burdett MG, R.O. Davis W 2-241

- - - - - - - - - - - - -

DAWSON / DOSSON

1860 CENSUS
Josiah Dawson 46, Sarah 37, Elizabeth 23, John 21, Mary 16, Susan 14, Amanda J. 6, Lucinda V. 2, David VARNER 10, Elizabrth WOODEY 20 3-57-388
1870 CENSUS
John F. Dawson 31, Sarah 28, James B. 2, Alice M. 2/12, Evana A. McNEW 12 (Ga) 3-4-24
Josiah Dawson 56, Sarah 40, Amanda J. 16, Victoria 14, William F. 10, Thomas 6 3-4-23
1880 CENSUS
B.F. [Josiah?] Dosson (f) 42 or 52, L.V. 22 (d), Thomas 17 (s) 3-28-219
J.F. Dosson 48, Sarah 38, J.B. 12 (s), A.M. 10 (d), B.F. 8 (s), Charles 5, J.D. 3 (s), Maggie 1 3-27-218
1900 CENSUS
John F. Dawson 61 (Ap 1839-M 33) (Feather Renovator), Sarah 57 (June 1842-M 33-8-7), Douglas B. 28 (Ap 1872)(Coal Miner), Maggie M. 21 (May 1879), Minnie E. 19 (Jan 1881), Robert L. 15 (June 1884), Henry AIKENS 56 (boarder)(July 1843-Germany/Do/Do-1878/21/Na)(Coal Miner) 10-325A-108/112
MARRIAGES
Amanda J. Dawson to Alfred C. Miller q.v.
Elizabeth Dawson to Samuel B. Furgusson q.v.
Josiah Dawson to Sarah F. Thompson, 14 Mar 1853 (15 Mar), James Carson MG 1-#405
Susan Dawson to Robert Smith q.v.

- - - - - - - - - - - - -

DAY

1860 CENSUS
Addison C. Day 39, Hannah P. 39, Anne E. 12, Mary C. 10, Russel B. 9, William K. 7, Nancy J. 5, John 3, Sarah J. LAUDERDALE 16 2-77-518
John Day 67, Rachel 42, Emily [Emma] H. 16, Tennessee N. 15, Hannah P. 11, Richard 9, Virginia 6, Laura 4, Vesta 2, William W. GRIMLY 16 (Mail Rider) 5-32-216
1870 CENSUS
Alfred Day 59, Julia M. 55, Anderson W. 25, Napolean B. 21, Samuel A. 16, James H. 14, Alice RANKINS 14, Sallie McDONALD 24, Martha E. McDONALD 2 5-2-12 (B)
Alfred A. Day 23, Martha A. 22, James S. 3, Napoleon 2, Andrew H. 11/12 5-1-4 (B)
Hannah P. Day 59, Analiza 22, Mary E. 21, Russel B. 19, William J. 17, Nancy J. 15, John A. 13, Sarah J. LAUDERDALE 24 2-5-32
Rachel Day 52, Emma H. 26, Richard 19, Virginia A. 16, Laura A. 14, Vesta L. 12, Tennessee ARMOR 25, James M. 7 5-1-6
1880 CENSUS
George Day 9 (B): see Nettie Roddy
Hoyal Day 19 (B): see E. Cunnyngham
James Day 24, Alice 25, Mary 6, Jennie 3 7-26-228 (B) (Mu)
Lua Day 21: see John Abernathy
Sallie Day 28 (Mu): see T. A. Allen
Samuel Day 27, Mary A. 18 6-12-113 (B) (Mu)
Sarah H. Day 66, Howard 15 (s) 6-13-126/127 (B)
Wyatt A. Day 40, Sallie 30, Martha M. 11, Andrew A. 8, David 6, George T. 5, Harriet O. 3 6-19-175/179 (B)
1900 CENSUS
Alford Day 24, Ollie 16, Lula 2, Willard 1: see Thomas Jefferson (B)
Annie E. Day 73: see William Day
Charles Day 25 (Dec 1874-M 3), Pearl 21 (Ap 1879-M 3-1-1), Cleo 9/12 (Aug 1899), Huell WILKERSON (B) 18 (Jan 1882)(Servant) 3-204-73/78
Henry Day 14: see Ben McDonald (B)
James S. Day 44 (Feb 1856-T/Ga/Va-M 28)(Porter, RR Depot), Alice 45 (Feb 1855-M 28-6-6), Mary 27 (June 1872), Jennie 22 (May 1878), John 19 (Oct 1880), Ida 16 (Aug 1883), Ethel 9 (Oct 1890), Gentry 3 (Aug 1896) 8-312B-36/39 (B)
Samuel F. Day 23 (June 1877-M 11/12), Daisey D. 21 (Jan 1879-M 11/12-0-0) 3-203B-7-/75
William Day 48 (Jan 1852-M 30), Mandy E. 47 (July 1852-M 30-9-8), William G. 20 (June 1880), Thomas A. 17 (Jan 1883), Emmaline A. 14 (Nov 1875), Virginia E.

11 (Feb 1889), John L. 8 (June 1892), Annie L. 4 (Sep 1895), Annie E. DAY 73 (m)(Feb 1827-T/SC/NC-Wd 3-2), Thomas R. GAUT 23 (Ap 1877)(Servant), Robert J. TRUE 22 (Aug 1877)(Servant), Fred RAY 16 (Mar 1884)(Servant) 3-204A-75/81

Wyatt Day 60 (Sep 1839-M 50) 10-257A-134/138 (B)

MARRIAGES

Alfred Day to Nanny Jefferson, 21 Mar 1896 (22 Mar), J.H. Garlington MG, Ben McDaniel W 2-5 (B)

Ann E. Day to James E. Waterhouse q.v.

C.P. Day to P.N. Ballard, 7 May 1897 (8 May), A.H. Low MG, H.M. Swafford W 2-143

Clemie Day to James Allen q.v.

David Day to Manda Crawford, 10 Nov 1895, D.T. Cannary MG 4-92

Emma H. Day to Y. L. Abernathy q.v.

H. P. Day to Thomas Cowart q.v.

Hattie Day to Albert Simons q.v.

Hattie Day to J. C. Montgomery q.v.

Ida Day to Will Bell q.v.

Jane or Janie Day to Ben McDonald q.v.

Jessee F. Day to Mary A. Cash, 4 Oct 1872 (no return) 1-#1256

Lee Day to Sallie Waterhouse, 14 Ap 1881 (same), John Howard JP 1-297 (B)

Lizzie Day to Nick Keith q.v.

Martha Day to Stephen Shields q.v.

Rena Day to Horace Copeland q.v.

Russel B. Day to Sarah A. Foust, 13 Jan 1888, J.P. Thompson JP 4-109

Samuel Day to Daisy Cagle, 11 July 1899, N.K. Fugate ?? 4-111

Samuel A. Day to Nanie Thompson, 26 Dec 1888 (27 Dec), J.D. Billingsley ?? 1-558

Tennessee Day to Isaac A.P. Armor q.v.

Vesta Day to Wyatt Fleming q.v.

DEAKINS

1900 CENSUS

Edward Deakins 22: see Benjamin F. Mealer

DEAN

1870 CENSUS

Caroline Dean 47, Cornelius 19, Margarette 16, James J. 10 8-12-81

1880 CENSUS

William Dean 39, Susan 30, Newton 12, Abijah 6, Josephine 4, Bettie 2 1-11-91

1900 CENSUS

James L. Dean 40 (Sep 1859-T/T/Ala-M 12)(Bank Cashier), Martha 32 (Dec 1867-M 12-3-3), Crawford 10 (Sep 1889), Gladys 8 (June 1891-Kan), Dorothy 2 (Sep 1897) 10-320B-8/8

MARRIAGES

Reese Dean to Mollie Davis, 24 Dec 1891, J.W. Williamson MG 4-35

Thomas J. Dean to Saray T. Kelly, 13 Feb 1866 (15 Feb), J.M. Kelly MG 1-#888

DEARMOND

MARRIAGE

John Dearmond to Ida Harris, 15 Aug 1892, W.A. Howard MG 4-51

DEATHERAGE / DETHERAGE

1860 CENSUS

James Detherage 53, Sarah J. 37, Christopher I. CARROLL 10 (bound), Willum R. CARROLL 9 5-39-264

1870 CENSUS

James Detherage 63, Sarah J. 45, Magie GIDION 82 (Va), Isaac JOLLY 27 5-8-57

1880 CENSUS

James D. Dathrage 72, S.J. 56 (w), M.J. GIDDON 7 (ne) 9-31-262

Nancy Detherage 25, Jane 5, Thomas 1: see Lutitia Smith (B) (Mu)

MARRIAGE

Sarah Deatherage to F. F. Smith q.v.

DEBLIEUX

1900 CENSUS

Julia Deblieux 49 (Feb 1851-La/La/La), Stella 52 (si)(Dec 1847-La/La/La), Amelia 72 (a)(Ap 1828-La/France/La) 10-324B-100/104

DEBORD

1880 CENSUS

G.H. Debord 36, S.M. 31 (w), J.W. 11 (s), R.F. 9 (s), C.S. 7 (d), C.E. 5 (d), R.A. 3 (d), T.H. 10/12 (s), C.B. GATES 6 (ne), James SHANNON 45 (boarder) 8-11-94

DECKER

1900 CENSUS

John C. Decker 49 (Oct 1850-NC/NC/NC-M 27), Mandy A. 51 (Aug 1848-NC/NC/NC-M 27-9-5), Melvina 20 (May 1880-NC), Arthur 16 (June 1883-NC), Garfield 13 (Mar 1887) 15-268B-16

Joseph Decker 23 (July 1876-NC/NC/NC-M 0)(Coal Miner), Mattie 24 (Sep 1875-M 0-0-0) 8-312A-24/25

MARRIAGES

Ella Decker to Walter R. Dukett(?) q.v.

Joseph L. Decker to Mattie E. Elison, 9 Dec 1899 (10 Dec), F.M. Cook MG, L.T. Brady W 3-84

Melvina Decker to W. M. Hartbarger q..v.

DE LAFAYETTE

MARRIAGE

C.M. DeLafayette to Nannie B. Cecil, 1 Mar 1894, R.S. Mason JP 4-69

DELANA

1860 CENSUS
Susan Delana 50 (Va), William 26 1-95-647

- - - - - - - - - - - - -

DELONIS / DELOINE

1880 CENSUS
Lewis Delonis 32, Victory 22, Ida W. 2, Margaret DAVIS 18 6-17-161/165 (Mu) (B)
1900 CENSUS
Ida DeLoine 19, Oliver 14: see Isam Eskridge (B)

- - - - - - - - - - - - -

DELOZIER

MARRIAGES
Cora Delozier to W. C. Ives q.v.
J. E. Delozier to Mary Duff, 9 May 1885 (14 May), Calvin Morgan JP 1-483

- - - - - - - - - - - - -

DELUCE

1900 CENSUS
Frank DeLuce 43 (Ap 1857-Ill/France/Do-M 12)(Stereotypher?), Minnie 36 (Jan 1864-M 12-1-1), Robert E. 11 (June 1888) 2-198B-137/142

- - - - - - - - - - - - -

DEMAY

MARRIAGE
James Demay to Sally Lawson, 23 Jan 1879 (26 Jan), R.H. Jordan MG 1-#1602

- - - - - - - - - - - - -

DENHASN

1880 CENSUS
Rolen Denhasn 56, Catharine WIMPLER 48 (m), Malind 19 (s), William 10 (s), James 10 (s) 10-3-234/243

- - - - - - - - - - - - -

DENIGAN– see DUNCAN

- - - - - - - - - - - - -

DENNING / DUNNING

1900 CENSUS
Alonzo Denning or Dunning 31 (Dec 1868-M 2), Callie 24 (Feb 1876-M 2-1-1), Carrie 1 (Feb 1899) 8-286A-358/360
Charles Denning or Dunning 58 (Unk 1842-M 20), Martha 61 (June 1838-M 20-1-1) 8-286A-357/359
MARRIAGES
Alice Dunning to J. C. Gentry q.v.
Jennie Dunning to Elza Wilkey q.v.
Lucinda Dunning to Martin M. Bishop q.v.
Sarah Dunning to J. L. Riley q.v.
Tom Dunning to Sarah Dye, 15 Dec 1890, R.S. Mason JP 4-24

- - - - - - - - - - - - -

DENNIS / DENIS

1900 CENSUS
John Dennis 57 (Mar 1843-T/NC/SC-M 35)(Carpenter), Mattie M. 59 (Sep 1840-T/Va/Va-M 35-7-6), Taylor S. 32 (July 1867-Wd)(Station Engineer), Charles W. 28 (Feb 1872-D)(Laborer, Shingle Mill) 13-310A-381/395
Lucy Dennis 33, Mary 23: see James Corvin
MARRIAGES
Charles Dennis to Robertia Cantrell, 9 Oct 1897 (same), W.R. Grimsley MG 2-199
Eliza Dennis to Thomas Johnson q.v.
Isham Denis to E.J.K. Hoge, 26 Mar 1871 (same), R.T. Howard MG 1-#1190
S.T. Dennis to Molly Mayberry, 17 Nov 1897 (18 Nov), W.R. Grimsley MG, Robert J. Cirten(?) W 2-207
Syntha Dennis to William Grimsley q.v.

- - - - - - - - - - - - -

DENSKIN– see DUNCAN

- - - - - - - - - - - - -

DENSON

1900 CENSUS
James C. Denson 40 (Oct 1859-Ga/Ga/Ga-M 16), Shrilda L. 36 (June 1863-M 16-4-3), James P. 15 (Nov 1884), William A. 13 (Jan 1887), Eliza L. 10 (Feb 1890), Irene E. 8 (Mar 1892), Leetha A. 2 (Nov 1897), Mary CORVIN 17 (sd)(Feb 1883), Sarah 13 (sd)(Nov 1886) 13-304B-280/290
MARRIAGE
J.C. Denson to M. Manning, 4 Feb 1897 (same), W.R. Grimsley MG, G.W. Dodson W 2-116

- - - - - - - - - - - - -

DENTON

1860 CENSUS
Jeremiah Denton 28 (NC), Jane 27, James J. 10, William H. 12 5-33-220
Nelly J. Denton 17 (NC), Edward 22 (Ind): see Darius Loftiss
1870 CENSUS
Edward Denton 30 (NC), Nancy 26 (NC), William G. 9, Hannah E. 7, Amanda T. 6, Virginia T. 2 5-4-22
James R. Denton 21 (NC), Mary Ann 18 (Ga), Paralee J. 7/12 5-4-24
Jerry Lee Denton 39 (NC), Virginia 38 (NC), William E.M. 9, Guy M. 5 5-4-23
1880 CENSUS
E. Denton 43, Nancy 40, William F. 18, Hannah E. 16, Manda T. 14, Virginia T. 12, Edward H. 9, Nancy C. 7, Susan D. 4, Jerry F. 1 5-1-5
James Denton 30, Mary A. 30, Jerry L. 10, Byron 8, July 6 5-11-107

Jerry Denton 48, Jennie S. 48, William E.M. 19, Guy M. 16, Sarah 9, Mary T. 16 (ne) 5-7-67

1900 CENSUS

Byron S. Denton 27 (Oct 1872-M 9), Anna 26 (Dec 1873-M 9-3-3), Maud 7 (Jan 1893), Charles E. 5 (June 1894), William P. 2 (Dec 1897) 4-224A-203/207

Delia Denton 24, Floyd 22, Grover C. 16: see Joseph Miller

Guy M. Denton 36 (Nov 1863-T/NC/NC-M 12), Martha J. 32 (Mar 1868-M 12-6-4), Thomas R. 11 (Oct 1888), Jennie M. 7 (Aug 1892), Olla L. 5 (Oct 1894), Nellie A. 1 (Dec 1898) 5-234B-135

James Denton 57 (Ap 1849-M 16), Louiza 33 (Dec 1867-M 16-8-8), John H. 15 (Sep 1884), Robert H. 13 (Aug 1886), William 11 (Oct 1888), Benton W. 9 (Dec 1890), James Y. 7 (Oct 1892), Richard J. 5 (Sep 1894), Thomas B. 4 (Sep 1896), Mary A. 2 (Jan 1898) 5-231A-56

James R. Denton 63 (Aug 1836-M 42)(Landlord), Mary A. 58 (Nov 1841-M 42-8-5), George 34 (Dec 1854-D) (Steamboat Engineer), Luther 21 (Sep 1878)(RR Business), Carl 10 (gs)(Jan 1890) 10-259A-171/175

Jerry L. Denton 26 (Unk-M 10), Nancy A. 37 (Oct 1862-M 10-1-1), Walter 8 (Jan 1892) 6-242A-43

John A. Denton 45 (Jan 1855)(Attorney) 10-320B-15/15

Martha Denton 46: see William Rogers

Virginia S. Denton 67: see William E.M. Denton

Will C. Denton 40 (Mar 1860-M 15)(RR Laborer), Sallie A. 29 (Feb 1871-M 15-7-5), Fred E. 13 (July 1886), Blanch G. 9 (Mar 1891), Maud L. 7 (Ap 1893), Charley C. 4 (Aug 1895), Willie R. 1/12 (Ap 1900) 10-259A-172/176

William E.M. Denton 39 (May 1861-M 18), Mary C. 35 (Oct 1864-M 18-4-3), Vina A. 17 (July 1882), Ada S. 13 (July 1886), Clara B. 9 (Sep 1890), Virginia S. DENTON 67 (m)(May 1833-Wd 1-1) 5-230B-45

William Y. Denton 38 (June 1861-M 18)(Warden, County Poor Farm at Washington), Victoria F. (Mar 1861-T/Pa/T-M 18-7-6), Creed 18 (Mar 1882)(Teamster), Mettie 15 (Sep 1884), Cleo 11 (July 1888), Truet 8 (July 1891), Beula 5 (Oct 1894), Gordon 3 (Jan 1897), Willian R. HOWARD 46 (boarder)(Dec 1853-M 16) (Livestock Dealer). *Inmates:* Mary BRADSHAW 74 (Ap 1826-T/Va/T-Wd 0-0), Netta HIGHFIELD 45 (Unk-Ga/Unk-M 16-6-6), Nanny TURK 40 (Unk-S), Rote HOUSLEY 32 (Unk-S), James McCLENDON 22 (Dec 1877-S) 6-243B-77

MARRIAGES

Adelia Denton to George Marshall q.v.

Byron Denton to Annie Fugate, 31 Jan 1892, S.S. Franklin JP 4-34

Caroline Denton to J. D. Rudd q.v.

Edward Denton to Nancy Loftis, 1 Jan 1861 (same), John Day MG 1-#740

Emma Denton to William Coleman q.v.

G.M. Denton to Mattie Harney [Hornsby marked through], 20 Aug 1887 (same), J.M. Bramlett MG 1-538

Hannah E. Denton to M.C. Bramlett q.v.

J.J. Denton to Lori Henderson, 11 Aug 1883 (same), C.T. Houts MG 1-474

James Denton to Sarah Smith, 26 Sep 1867 (same), William Buttram MG 1-#972

Jennie T. Denton to Joseph S. Miller q.v.

Jerry L. Denton to Nancy Burnett, 24 Aug 1890, J.L. Henry JP 4-15

Julia Denton to Rufus McClure q.v.

Lizzie Denton to Walter Lewis q.v.

Nelly Denton to William McCully q.v.

S. A. Denton to Samuel Montgomery q.v.

Tabitha Denton to E. S. Cox Jr. q.v.

W.E.M. [Marion] Denton (20) to Mary C. Houston (17), 6 Oct 1881, John Howard MG, Thomas Smith & N.(?) T. Collins W. 4-2(15)

William Denton to Sallie Vials, 4 Oct 1884 (5 Oct), I.W. Holt JP 1-461

William Y. Denton (20) to Victoria Perry (18, Warren Co), 13 June 1881, R.N. Jordan MG, Byron Blevins & J.M. Bramlett W 4-1(8)

- - - - - - - - - - - - -

DEROSIT

MARRIAGE

Adison Derosit to Virginia Holloway, 20 Feb 1883 (21 Feb), J.P. Roddy MG 1-479

- - - - - - - - - - - - -

DERRICK

1880 CENSUS

Alfred Derrick 20 (Miner): see James Honeycut

MARRIAGE

Alfred Derrick to Rebecca Jolly, 22 Sep 1880 (23 Sep), S. Breeding JP 1-296

- - - - - - - - - - - - -

DE TAR

MARRIAGE

Dorr DeTar to Eva Franklin, 20 Nov 1899 (same), A.P. Hayes JP, Harry(?) Gowing W 3-74

- - - - - - - - - - - - -

DEVANEY / DEVANIE

1870 CENSUS

John H. Devaney 46 (NC)(House Carpenter), Mary Jane 42, Sarah C. 20, John W. 18, William H. 15, Aaron F. 12, Jacob Lee 11, Mary Jane 5, Benjamin J. 3, Cornelia 3 1-4-25

1880 CENSUS– None

1900 CENSUS

John H. DeVaney 77 (June 1822-NC/France/France-M 52), Mary J. 72 (Feb 1828-T/Va/T-M 52-9-8), Sarah C. 50 (Ap 1850), Aaron F. 42 (Feb 1858-Wd), Jacob L. 39 (Nov 1860)(Grocer), Benjamin J. 33 (Mar 1867) 4-224A-207/211

MARRIAGES

Cornela Devaney to C. C. Ferguson q.v.

John W. Devaniie to Margaret A. Thompson, 26 Feb 1876 (27 Feb), G.W. Renfro MG 1-#1438

John W. DeVaney to Annie Collins 24 Sept 1893 John N. Larkin, Priest 4-54

Mary Devaney to Granville T. Furguson q.v.

- - - - - - - - - - - - -

DEVAULT

1880 CENSUS
Henry Devault 33, Ann 30, Mary 12, John 6, William 6, Albion CASH 14 (ss), Florence WRIGHT 20 (Servant, Cook) 2-41-330
1900 CENSUS
Clay Devault 56 (Jan 1844-M 18), Steller 28 (d)(Oct 1871), Will 26 (s)(Oct 1873), Clay 2 (gs)(June 1897), George SMITH 18 (lodger)(May 1882) 7-266A-304/309
Mirah A. DeVault 51 (Mar 1849-M 20-1-1)(Landlady) 7-267A-324/329
MARRIAGES
H.C. DeVault to Mrs. Mirah A. Cash, 18 Feb 1880 (no return) 1-#1717
John Devault to Leah Wyrick, 16 Sep 1896 (17 Sep), J.W. Romines JP, W.F. Purser W 2-68

- - - - - - - - - - - - -

DEW

1900 CENSUS
Eva Dew 7, Ida M. 6, Willard 3: see Thomas Edwards (B)

- - - - - - - - - - - - -

DIALS

MARRIAGE
Minnie Dials to Adison Lemmons q.v.

- - - - - - - - - - - - -

DIARE

1880 CENSUS
Joachin Diare 43 (Dentist) 12-3-22

- - - - - - - - - - - - -

DICK

1900 CENSUS
Andrew Dick 55 (Jan 1845-Ky/Ky/Ky-M 31)(Butcher), Mary E. 45 (July 1854-Ky/Ky/Ky-M 31-4-4), John L. 24 (Aug 1875-Ky)(Civil Engineer), Hayden 9 (Oct 1890-Ky) 10-321B-35/36

- - - - - - - - - - - - -

DICKERSON

1900 CENSUS
David Dickerson 40 (Oct 1859-Mich/Oh/England-M 16), Belle 35 (Dec 1864-Mich/Scotland/Do-M 16-3-3), Lizzie E. 13 (June 1887-Mich), Rena B. 9 (Sep 1890), Arthur C. 4 (Nov 1895) 11-292B-64

- - - - - - - - - - - - -

DICKEY / DEKEY

1860 CENSUS
John W. Dickey 6/12: see Margaret Fine
Samuel H. Dickey 33, Sarah M. 33, Josiah H. 4, James W. 3, John E. REEVELY 24 (Clerk) 2-77-519
1870 CENSUS
Abner Dekey 40, Elizabeth 40, Thomas H. 15, John W. 12, Henry P. 9, Samuel L. 3, Anga M. 10/12 1-3-22 [Abner L. Dickey married Elizabeth E. Waller on 28 Nov 1852 in Roane County]
Samuel H. Dickey 43, Sarah M. 43, Josiah H. 14, James W. 13, John R. 9, Nancy CURLEY 13, Fanny RHEA (B) 13 2-14-102
John Dickey 10: see James Bohanon
1880 CENSUS
Abner Dickey 51, Elizabeth 50, Thomas 25 (Instructor), John 22 (Instructor), Henry 18, Samuel 13, Angie 10, Wilber 6 1-11-87
Jessee Dickey 25 (Merchant), S.A. 23 (w), John 21 (b) (Clerk), W.T. HAYS 50 (boarder)(Carpenter), W.W. RENFRO 24 (boarder), J. PRIGMORE (B) 12 (Servant) 4-8-64
Samuel Dickey 53, Sarah 53, James 22, John 20 (Store Clerk), Robert KELLY (B) 18 (Servant) 2-25-200
1900 CENSUS
George D. Dickey 25 (Dec 1874-M 4), Magnolia 23 (Ap 1877-T/T/Ala-M 4-3-2), Hubert C. 3 (Feb 1897), William 6/12 (Nov 1899) 10-326A-129/134
Sallie E. Dickey 48 (Jan 1852-T/Va/T-Wd 3-3), William M. 30 (Aug 1869)(House Carpenter), Arthur 20 (Aug 1879)(Paper Hanger) 10-320B-12/12
MARRIAGE
George Dickey to Nola Atchley, 29 Feb 1896 (1 Mar), A.W. Jackson MG, L.J. Short W 2-4 & 4-88

- - - - - - - - - - - - -

DICKSON / DIXON

1880 CENSUS
A. Dixon 26, M.C. 21, S.R. 5 (s), D.A. 3 (d), Ida 4/12, John TERRY 15 8-16-139
Cary Dixon 11: see J.R. Crawford
Martha Dixon 63, R.E. 22 (d), J.S. 19 (s) 7-23-197
1900 CENSUS
Alexander Dickson 47 (June 1852-M 15)(Flour Mill Engineer), Samantha 34 (Ap 1866-T/T/Va-M 15-3-3), Walter 15 (Aug 1884), Daisy 12 (Aug 1887), Baby 9/12 (Aug 1899), Lula 20 (d)(Feb 1880) 10-322A-47/49
Frank Dixon 32 (Sep 1867-Pa/Del/Pa-M 1)(Carpenter), Annie L. 25 (Dec 1874-M 1-1-1), Sallie K. 5/12 (Dec 1899), Hannah COFFER 52 (m)(Jan 1848-Pa/Pa/Pa-Wd 2-2), Alexander 20 (b)(Jan 1880), John J. KELLEY 20 (bl)(June 1879) 7-266B-314/319
George Dickson 25 (Sep 1874-Ga), Willie 2/12 (Ap 1900) 8-284B-323/325 (B)
Jennie Dickson 33 (Nov 1866-T/Ga/Va-M 1-2-2)(Washwoman), Ben BARNEY 16 (s)(Dec 1883), Annie ALEXANDER 10 (d)(Sep 1889) 8-318A-160/166 (B)
Robt A. Dickson 75 (Aug 1824-M 19)(Justice of the Peace), Elizabeth 58 (Oct 1841-M 19) 14-217A-93/95
Sam Dickson 25, Emer 17: see James Pursur
Walter Dixon 10: see James A. Hoback
William Dixon 17: see William H. Rogers
MARRIAGES
Cora Dixon to Jasper Webb q.v.
Della Dickson to James Purcer q.v.
Frank H. Dickson to Anne L. Kelly, 4 Jan 1899 (same), E.W. Mort MG, F.H. Dixon & R.J. Killough W 2-369

Hannah R. Dixon to Banister Cofer q.v.
Hugh Dixon to Janie Jones, 22 Jan 1900 (22 Feb)[sic], J.D. Gothen(?) MG, Walter Brickman(?) W 3-114
Ida Dixon to G. N. McQuister q.v.
Nellie Dixon to Tom Paine q.v.
S.R. Dixon to Emma Walker, 6 May 1900 (bond only), A.A. Gilmore W 3-153
Thomas Dickson to M.C. Rowlon, 23 Dec 1886 (same), W.S. Hale MG 1-522
W.D. Dixon to Lotta Doss, 18 July 1891, W.A. Green JP 4-28

DIKE / DYKE

1860 CENSUS
William Dyke 23, Betsy 27, Reediz or Rudiz WITT 13, Reese WITT 11 6-102-691
MARRIAGE
Nancy Dike to Pleasant Bell q.v.

DILL

1900 CENSUS
William Dill 26 (July 1873-Ala/Ala/Ala-M 1), Lela 26 (Feb 1874-Ga/Ga/Va-M 1-1-1), Arthur TAYLOR 8 (ss) (July 1891-Ga/Ga/Ga) 8-314A-67/70 (B)
MARRIAGE
Austin Dill to Emma McClanahan, 18 Feb 1888 (19 Feb), W.B. Grimsley JP 1-543

DILLARD

1900 CENSUS
Green Dillard 32 (May 1868-Ga/Ga/NC-M 8)(Coal Miner), Anna 21 (Feb 1879-Ala/Ala/Ala-M 8-1-1), Charles 6 (Ap 1894) 8-284A-312/314
Horras Dillard 20 (May 1881-NC/Ga/Ga-M 1)(Coal Miner), Sary 19 (Aug 1880-M 1-1-0) 10-257A-137/141
Jasper Dillard 49 (Mar 1850-Ga/Ga/Ga-M 25), Mary 41 (Ap 1859-Ga/Unk-M 25-10-8), Arthur 16 (Sep 1883-Ga), Alice 14 (Dec 1885-Ga), Rainey 10 (July 1889), Green 8 (Feb 1892), Ernest 5 (June 1894), Elisha 2 (June 1897), Pany 7/12 (Oct 1899) 10-257A-138/142
Whit Dillard 30 (Jan 1870-Ga/Ga/NC-M 0)(Coal Miner), Lillie 16 (Mar 1884-Ga/Ga/Ga-M 0-0-0) 8-284A-307/309

MARRIAGES
Charley Dillard to May McIntyre, 25 May 1898 (26 May), W.L. Lillard JP, John Wilson W 2-286
Horace Dillard to Sarah J. Fraley, 29 Oct 1898 (bond only), Jasper Dillard W 2-340
N.G. Dillard to Mary Lemmons, 15 Jan 1891, William Morgan JP 4-23
W.C. Dillard to Lillie Burk, 18 Ap 1900 (Ap 19), Henegar Morgan JP, E. Fisher W 3-145

DILMON / DILEMON / DILLMAN

1870 CENSUS
Hannah Dilemon 25: see Allen Holland
Jacob Dilmon 54 (Va), Margarette 49 (NC), Laura V. 15 6-11-76
1880 CENSUS
Jacob Dillman 58 (Shoemaker), Margaret 55 6-24-23 (Rural Street, Washington)

DIPER

1900 CENSUS
Asker Diper 20: see Laura Sawyer(?)

DISARD

MARRIAGE
Kert Disard to Nannie Foster, 10 Feb 1879 (16 Feb), W.A. Green JP 1-291

DISBANY

MARRIAGE
M. J. Disbany to A. J. Martin q.v.

DOBBS

1880 CENSUS
J.M. Dobbs 31, J.T. 22, J.T 4 (s), P.S. 2 (d) 8-20-167
Thomas Dobbs 29, Esibel 20, M.A. 6/12 (d), R.S. CORVIN 14 (sil), S.A. CORVIN 48 (ml) 8-20-166
1900 CENSUS
Jane T. Dobbs 44 (Dec 1855-Wd 8-8), Ida L. 15 (Nov 1884), Laura 13 (Jan 1887), James A. 10 (Aug 1889), Raleigh 8 (Nov 1891), Arthur 6 (Feb 1894) 13-297B-147/150
MARRIAGES
Alferd Dobbs to R.L. Conlin, 6 Oct 1880 (7 Oct), R.N. Jorden(?) MG 1-294
Altie Dobbs to George Lewis q.v.
Catharine Dobbs to Albert Corvin q.v.
Dona Dobbs to R. J. Curton q.v.
James M. Dobbs to Jane T. Steel, 12 Sep 1874 (13 Sep), Wm A. Green JP 1-#1356
John Dobbs to Lizzie Lewis, 22 Sep 1898 (23 Sep), J.W. Williamson MG, G.L. Lewis [signed by X] W 2-325
Margarett Dobbs to W. T. Walker q.v.
Mary Dobbs to Hays Welsh q.v.
Paralee Dobbs to J. W. Brooks q.v.
Thomas Dobbs to Elizabeth Corvin, 18 May 1879 (20 May), W.R. Grimsley MG 1-#1497

DODD / DOUD

1870 CENSUS
Joseph B. Dodd 31, Margarette 21 7-8-60

William H. Dodd 35, Sarah J. 34, Eliza A. 8, Elizabeth WILSON 76 7-6-41

1880 CENSUS

James W. Dodd 57, Mary 56, Syntha J. 33, Isaac L. 23, Anderson S. 21, Floyd L. 19, Bartley A. 15, George W. 14 6-20-185/189

Joe Dodd 41, Eliza 44, Tom 22, Sallie 20, Aby 4 7-24-204

Joseph B. Dodd 26, Elizabeth J. 22, John C. 4, Edgar J. 1 6-17-156/159

Thomas Doud 33, M.J. 24 (w), G.W. 6 (s), J.N. 3 (s), M.E. 1 (d), E.(?)J. 42 (sil), E. NELSON* 88 (gm) 3-27-214 [* last name is Wilson on 1870 census]

1900 CENSUS

Abbet Dodd 24 (July 1875-M 4), Louisa D. 25 (July 1874-M 4-3-1), Edgar R. 2/12 (Mar 1900) 10-250B-17

Anderson Dodd 45 (Jan 1855-M 1), Sallie 35 (Ap 1865-T/Ky/Ky-M 1-8-6), Myrtle 8 (d)(Mar 1892), Missori HENDERSON 14 (sd)(July 1885), James 12 (ss)(June 1887), Mary A. 11 (sd)(May 1889), William 8 (ss) (July 1891), Emma 3 (sd)(June 1896) 15-272B-89

George N. Dodd 25 (Dec 1874-M 6), Eva 25 (Ap 1875-M 6-2-2), Vesta 4 (Dec 1895), Freeman 2 (Feb 1898) 6-224B-94

Isaac Dodd 44 (Nov 1855-T/SC/T-M 17), Mary E. 36 (Aug 1863-T/NC/T-M 17-3-3), Willie 16 (Sep 1883), Willie [sic] L. 7 (Sep 1892), Greacy M. 2/12 (Mar 1900) 10-258B-169/173

James Dodd 39 (Oct 1860-M 17)(Coal Miner), Sary J. 34 (Nov 1865-M 17-7-4), Linis 16 (Ap 1884), Jannie 12 (May 1888), Willie 5 (July 1894), Uessie 2 (d)(Oct 1897) 10-259A-175/179

James N. Dodd 24 (Mar 1876-M 5), Rhoda E. 25 (Feb 1875-M 5-2-1), Hayman L. 2 (May 1898) 6-244B-95/96

John C. Dodd 47 (Mar 1853-M 19)(Life Insurance Agent), Mary A. 35 (Jan 1865-M 19-6-2), Nannie M. 12 (Jan 1888), Fletcher 9 (Oct 1898) 10-323B-82/86

Joseph B. Dodd 59 (Oct 1840-T/SC/SC-M 3), Ellie 45 (Mar 1855-M 3) 10-252B-51

Sarah J. Dodd 63: see Abner D. Wilkey

Thomas H. Dodd 52 (Oct 1847-T/SC/T-M 27), Mary J. 46 (May 1854-T/T/NC-M 27-10-7), Loyd E. 18 (July 1881), Floyd E. 18 (July 1881), Anna 13 (Mar 1887), Thomas H. 11 (Aug 1888), Wm MINNICK 51 (bl) (Mar 1849) 6-244B-95/95

MARRIAGES

Anderson Dodd to Bettie Cox, 26 Nov 1887 (27 Nov), J.A. Crawford JP 1-537

Anderson Dodd to Sallie Henderson, 22 Nov 1898 (same), W.L. Lillard JP & W 2-347

B.A. Dodd to Mary Hatfield, 25 July 1885 (26 July), J.W. Peace ?? 1-486

E.E. Doud to Irene Mooney, 10 June 1885 (4 July), J.W. Burnett MG 1-493

E.J. Dodd to Susie Vinson or Vinsen, 6 Oct 1900 (7 Oct), John Masoner MG, E. Fisher W 3-232

Eliza Dodd to Abner D. Wilkey q.v.

George Dodd to Caroline Mills, 21 Feb 1890 (23 Feb), William Turner MG 1-595

George Dodd to Eva Mills, 18 Dec 1894, William Turner MG 4-74

Isaac Dodd to Bettie Calihan, 3 Dec 1882, W.S. Hale MG, Bart C. Dodd W 4-12(111)

J.C. Dodd to S.A. Brady, 5 June 1900, L.E. Smith JP 4-105

James Dodd to Sarah J. Wright, 28 Mar 1878 (same), Peter Roddy MG 1-#1553

Joseph Dodd to Elizabeth Whaley, 2 May 1872 (same), W.B. McKelvy MG 1-#1238

Joseph Dodd to Elizabeth Thurman, 5 Dec 1874 (same), N.H. Dodd MG 1-#1378

Joseph B. Dodd to Roseannah Jones, 8 Nov 1866 (same), T.N.L. Cunnyngham JP 1-#920

Joseph B. Dodd to Ella Howard, 5 Nov 1896 (same), G.W. Brewer MG, J.C. Dodd W 2-80

Lafayette Dodd to Hilie R. Real or Reel (bond) or Rud or Reed (license), 18 Aug 1900 (same), W.K. Fugate, H. D. Arthur W 3-199

M. L. Dodd to Jasper N. Howard or Harwood q.v.

Mary Dodd to J. S. Gravitt q.v.

Mary Dodd to Noah Bowles q.v.

Sarah A. Dodd to J. H. Wilson q.v.

Thomas H. Dodd to Mary J. Minicks, 12 Dec 1872 (same), W.H. Dodd MG 1-#1264

W.R. Dodd to Fany or Fannie S.J. Powers, 14 Aug 1898 (same), S.H. Hilton MG, R.J. Killough W 2-309

Walter Dodd to Rhoda Wright, 26 May 1895, B.H. Allen MG 4-81

William A. Dodd to Louvella T. Hoback, 10 Aug 1895, A.H. Low MG 4-84

- - - - - - - - - - - - -

DODGE

MARRIAGE

Laura C. Dodge to C. S. Pardee q.v.

- - - - - - - - - - - - -

DODSON / DOTSON

1860 CENSUS

Abner Dotson 37, Susan 33, James 12, Frances 10, Samuel 8, Abraham 6, Nancy 5, Nathaniel 1 1-90-614

Joel Dotson 41, Elizabeth 39, Martha J. 16, Sarah E. 15, William L. 12, Mary A. 7, Thomas N. 3, George W. 1 2-80-544

Joel Dotson 22, Jane 25, George 4 1-89-611

John Dotson 52, Elizabeth 45, Margaret 23, Thomas 14, Susan 10, James M. 8, Elizabeth 2 9-101-690

Mary Dotson 81, James 40: see Zachariah Key

Jady L. Dotson 26: see Elizabeth Gear

Samuel Dotson 65 (Va), Nelly 30, George W. 18, Amanda C. 14, Zachariah 11, George W. ZIGGLAR 11, Margaret 7, Nancy A. 4, Amanda 10/12 2-74-508

1870 CENSUS

Joel Dodson 55, Elizabeth 45, Mary A. 17, Thomas M. 13, George W. 11, Nancy J. 7, John H. 4 1-11-72

William Dodson 28, Catharine 27, Claton 4, Malinda 2 2-3-13

1880 CENSUS

Ann R. Dodson 56, Mary C. 23 (d)(School Teacher) 5-6-54

Elizabeth Dotson 67, William 17 (s) 2-30-243

Joel Dotson 56, Elizabeth 57, George 20, Nancy 17, John 14, Sarah GILLIAM 80 (ml) 1-17-138

William Dotson 32, Catharine 40, John 13, Malinda 11, Mary 7, Joel 4, Absalom 1 2-37-304

1900 CENSUS

Albert Dodson 28 (Sep 1871-M 5)(Saloon Bartender), Lou 26 (Nov 1873-M 5-2-2), Eugene 3 (Nov 1896-Tex), Arlus 2 (Nov 1897-Tex) 10-320B-9/9

George W. Dodson 40 (July 1859-M 11), Mary A. 39 (Ap 1861-M 11-8-5), Thomas 17 (June 1882), Laura P. 13 (Mar 1887), Sarah A. 9 (Oct 1890), Mary A. 6 (July 1893), Bessie C. 2 (June 1897), William H. 1 (May 1899) 2-194A-59/61

Henry Dodson 53 (Mar 1847-M 30), Martha 45 (May 1853-M 30-6-6), Edward 22 (Ap 1878), Frank 17 (Feb 1883), Minnie 14 (June 1885) 8-316B-131/136

John C. Dodson 33 (Jan 1867-M 8)(Coal Miner), Sarah E. 25 (Oct 1874-M 8-0-0), Minnie RIGGS 11 (boarder) (Ap 1889) 14-217B-101/103

John W. Dodson 34, Maud A. 11, Florence L. 9: see William R. Miller

MARRIAGES

Emaline Dodson to James W. Miller q.v.

G.W. Dodson to Mary Jones, 27 Dec 1889 (Dec 28), W.R. Clack JP 1-589

Henry Dodson to Marthy Hardbarger, 17 Aug 1870 (18 Aug), J.P. Roddy MG 1-#1162

J.C. Dodson to Sarah Dodson, 3 Ap 1893, W.A. Perkinson JP 4-70

J.H. Dodson to N.M. Gilliam, 25 Jan 1887 (29 Jan), Anthony Smith MG 1-518

J.W. Dodson (22) to Delia Ann McCaroll (25), 15 Aug 1881, S. Breeding JP 4-4(31)

Jasper Dodson to Letha Gilliam, 10 Jan 1866 (11 Jan), J.I. Cash MG 1-#886

Joel Dodson to E.J. Smith, 15 Mar 1860 (26 --- 1858)[sic], Thomas Knight JP 1-#2652

Joseph Dotson to Eliza Riley, 7 Ap 1886 (same), A.W. Frazier JP 1-485

Joseph Dodson to Lottie C. Goins, 30 Sep 1896 (same) (license dated 31 Sep), I.M. Barney(?) MG, B.Y. Goin W 2-70

Judia L. Dodson to Hugh Goddard q.v.

Louisa Dotson to Enoch Floyd q.v.

M. C. Dotson to Jessie P. Shipley q.v.

Margarett Dodson to Coleman Smith q.v.

Margarett Dodson to William Roberts q.v.

Mary A. Dodson to William J. Hughes q.v.

Mary Ann Dotson to John B. Robinson q.v.

Mellie Dodson to Myron E. Allender q.v.

Nancy J. Dodson to David Allen q.v.

Samuel Dotson to Nelly Kissiah, 1 Nov 1858 (11 Nov), A.D. Paul JP 1-#665

Sarah Dodson to J. C. Dodson q.v.

Sarah C. Dodson to W. N. Riggs q.v.

Sarah E. Dodson to Vernon M. Dodson q.v.

Thomas Dodson to Manerva Watson, 3 June 1864 (same), W.W. Low JP 1-#1085

Thomas F. Dodson to Lizzie Hughes, 26 Ap 1888 (same), W.R. Clack JP 1-551

Vernon M. Dodson to Sarah E. Dodson, 29 Aug 1867 (no return) 1-#967

William Dodson to Catharine Thompson, 10 Mar 1866 (11 Mar), Daniel Broyles JP 1-#892

William Dodson to Catharine Thompson, 14 Mar 1866 (same), James I. Cash MG 1-#1066

William Dodson (20, Roane Co) to Nancy Teeters (17, Anderson Co), 4 Feb 1883, S. Breeding JP, W. Godby & Albert Morse W 4-13(125)

William Dodson to Mary Culverhouse, 18 June 1897 (20 June), W.R. Grimsley MG, Maynard Stuart W 2-151

- - - - - - - - - - - - -

DOLAN / DOLEN

1900 CENSUS

Bessie(?) Dolen(?) 7, Myrtle 5 see Bill Wilkey

John W. Dolan 49 (Mar 1851-Ark/T/T-M 25), Pheabe L. 40 (Feb 1860-M 25-13-8), Sarah E. 19 (Feb 1881-Ark), Nancy C. 15 (Mar 1885-Ark), Dora D. 10 (Aug 1889-Ark), Maggie L. 6 (Oct 1893), Mishie 4 (Feb 1896), Roscoe 2/12 (Mar 1900) 2-195B-87/90

- - - - - - - - - - - - -

DOLL / DALL

1900 CENSUS

Frederick Doll 41 (May 1859-Germany/Do/Do-1888/12/Na-M 9)(Butcher), Mary 28 (Dec 1871-M 9-4-3), Bena 6 (Dec 1893), Catharine 3 (Dec 1896), Burkett 6/12 (Nov 1899), Mattie BARNETT 33 (sil)(Mar 1867) (Seamstress) 10-329B-204/217

MARRIAGE

Frederick Dall to Mollie Barnett, 24 May 1891, A.W. Frazier JP 4-26

- - - - - - - - - - - - -

DONAHOO / DONAHOE

1900 CENSUS

Andrew Donahoo 52 (Feb 1848-SC/SC/SC-M 2), Marinda E. 28 (July 1871-M 2-3-1), David L. 4 (Nov 1895) 9-228B-14

Clinty Donhoo 41, Floy 10, Ethel 7: see Will Rains

Susan Donaho 38 (Oct 1861-Wd 4-2), Walter 11 (June 1888-T/SC/T), Ethel 4 (Ap 1896) 8-279A-211/213

MARRIAGES

A.D. Donahoo to Eva Cox, 8 Dec 1897 (9 Dec), W.S. Hale MG, R.J. Killough W 2-224

Julia Donahoo to Elijah Pool q.v.

M. S. Donahoe to E. C. Smith q.v.

W.F. Donahoe to Eva Rawlston, 19 Ap 1899 (20 Ap), W.L. Lillard JP, A.J. Hawkins & Walter French Donahoe W 2-403

- - - - - - - - - - - - -

DONALD / DONALS

1860 CENSUS

Harriet Donald 13: see Jason I. Panner

1870 and 1880 CENSUS– None

1900 CENSUS

Wilum Danals 44 (Jan 1856-M 26), Mary 42 (Dec 1857-M 26-12-10), James 22 (July 1877)(Store Clerk), Waltar 18 (Feb 1882), Charley 15 (June 1884), Jessi 13 (July 1886), Shurly 11 (July 1888), Milam(?) 9 (Feb 1891), Luther 6 (May 1894), Tabis 4 (Dec 1895), Wilum 0/12 (June 1900) 12-182A-67/70

- - - - - - - - - - - - -

DONALDSON / DONALSON

1860 CENSUS
John Donaldson 40 (B): see John T. Clack
1870 CENSUS
John Donalson 55, Julia 45, Hiram 20, John A. 18, Calvin 13, Mary 11, Catharine 10, William 9, Sarah 6, Thomas 1 2-10-66
Shepherd Donalson 23, Leonna 20, John L. 6/12 2-12-82 (B)
1880 CENSUS
Hiram Donaldson 26, Amanda 24, Thomas 1 2-34-274 (Mu)
Isabel Donaldson 12, Polk 11, Jack 8: see Calvin Gillespie (B)
John Donaldson 21 (Miner), Delia 15 2-29-233 (Mu)
Shep Donaldson 32, Leonna 30, John 10, Florence 6, George 4, Drucilla 2 2-39-317 (B)
Wash Donaldson 31, Belle 10 (d), Mary GILLESPIE 21 (sd), Robert 5 (ss), William 1 (ss) 2-34-273 (B) (Mu)
1900 CENSUS
George W. Donaldson 48 (Ap 1852-Wd), Talbert 25 (July 1874), William 21 (Feb 1879)(Iron Ore Miner), Samuel 16 (July 1883), Dossie 14 (Feb 1886), Polk K. 11 (Mar 1889), Rackrey 7 (Sep 1892) 2-195A-77/80 (B)
Haram Donaldson 47 (Oct 1852-T/T/Va-M 25), Amanda M. 46 (May 1855-M 25-12-8), Thomas V. 21 (July 1878) (Iron Ore Miner), Louis A. 19 (July 1880), Jesse J. 17 (Oct 1882), Geo E. 15 (Oct 1884), Nathan 12 (Jan 1887), Ethel 9 (Aug 1890), Minnie I. 6 (Jan 1894), Mable L. 3 (Jan 1897) 2-192B-34/35 (B)
Polk Donaldson 30 (Oct 1869-M 10)(Iron Ore Miner), Nancy J. 26 (Aug 1873-M 10-4-4), Bunie V. 9 (July 1891), Silvester 7 (Mar 1893), Bonnie 4 (Dec 1896), Werry 1 (Feb 1899) 2-193B-50/52 (B)
Rebecca Donaldson 49 (Nov 1850-Ga/Ga/Ga-Wd), Lennie E. 27 (sd)(Mar 1873-Jan/T/T) 10-326B-142/150
William Donaldson 74 (Feb 1826-M 41)(Furniture Merchant), Nancy 57 (Oct 1842-Ga/Ga/Ga-M 41-7-4), Sam 23 (Aug 1876)(Physician), Mary E. 19 (May 1881) 8-315B-107/111
MARRIAGES
Amand Donaldson to Robert Pullens q.v. (B)
Bell Donaldson to Tom Gillespie q.v.
Isabel Donaldson to W. M. McCabb q.v.
J.H. Donaldson to Ciller Henry, 11 June 1889 (same), J.W. Barnett MG 1-575
Mary Donaldson to S. H. Reed q.v.
Mary Donaldson to William Henderson q.v.
Pack Donaldson to Jane McCaleb, 19 July 1890, W.R. Clack JP 4-17
Wash Donaldson to Mary Ann Gillespie, 9 Aug 1887 (same), W.R. Clack JP 1-536

\- - - - - - - - - - - - -

DOOLEY / DOOLY

1870 CENSUS
Peter Dooley 46 (Ga), Caroline 42 (Ga), Ellen 22 (Ga), Sarah J. 18 (Ga), Columbus 20 (Ga), Salena 16 (Ga), John 14 (Ga), William B. 12 (Ga), Doctor 9 (Ga), James 5 (Ga), Samuel 3, George 2 3-12-84 (B)
Marion Dooley 24 (Ga), Amanda 22 (Ga), Jane 3 (Ga), William 1 3-12-85 (B)
1880 CENSUS
Marion Dooley 33, Amanda 31, Jane 12, William 10, Beula 7, Belle 5, Thomas 1, Columbus 25 (b), Bedord 21 (b) 2-29-235 (B)
Peter Dooley 54, James 16 (s), George 10 (s), Ida 6 (gd), Anderson GILLESPIE 24 (sl), Salina 23 (d), Samuel DOOLEY 12 (gs), John 22 (s)(at school), Joseph GILLESPIE 5 (gs), Cassie 3 (gs), Lula 2 (gd) 2-28-220 (B)
1900 CENSUS
Marion Dooley 58 (Ap 1842-Ga/Ga/Ga-M 13), Melia 44 (Jan 1856-Va/Va/Va-M 12-8-3), Annie MAGSBY 29 (d)(Nov 1870-M 4-1-1), Earl 3 (gs)(Aug 1896) 10-328B-178/190 (B)
Rachel Dooley 33 (July 1864-M 1-3-1)(Washwoman), Laura 11 (Mar 1889), Ader RUCKER 19 (Aug 1880) 10-252A-43 (B)
MARRIAGE
Jane Dooly to Oliver Bates q.v.
Jane Dooley to Joseph Capp q.v.
Marion Dooley to Melia Rucker, 15 Oct 1887 (16 Oct), J.B. Phillips MG 1-535

\- - - - - - - - - - - - -

DORAN / DOREN

1880 CENSUS
Samuel Doran 33, Martha J. 35, Rufus T. 8, Sarah H. 7, Amos S. 5, John T. 3, Allis M. 1 5-9-87
1900 CENSUS
Rufus L.(?) Doran 29 (Ap 1871-M 8)(Locamotive Fireman), Sarah J. 25 (Ap 1875-M 8-2-0), David MONEYHAN 11 (bl)(Mar 1889) 10-322A-43/45
Sam Doren 53 (Oct 1846-M 30), Martha 51 (Sep 1840-M 30-8-6), Vesty 16 (Mar 1884), Lillie 13 (Sep 1886), Elic COOPER 40 (bl)(Mar 1860-Wd), Mearin 16 (nw) (Jan 1884)(RR Brakeman), Loydd 7 (nw)(Ap 1893), Lee 4 (ne)(Feb 1896) 10-254A-75
MARRIAGES
Cornelia Doran to Levi B. Thurman q.v.
Hattie Doran to G. T. Travis q.v.
Rena Doran to Ollie Smith q.v.
Rufus Doran to Sarah Moonehan, 7 Feb 1892, J.M. Bramlett MG 4-33

\- - - - - - - - - - - - -

DORSETT

1900 CENSUS
Emma Dorsett 50 (Unk-Wd 2-2), Lula 16 (foster dau)(Dec 1883-Ala/Ala/Ala), John W. WEAVER 68 (Aug 1831-NC/NC/NC-Wd)(Dentist) 10-321A-30/31

\- - - - - - - - - - - - -

DORTCH

1900 CENSUS
Ambrose Dortch 17: see Charles E. Irwin

\- - - - - - - - - - - - -

DORTON

1870 CENSUS
James M. Dorton 23, Mary A. 24, Martha A. 4, Eliza R. 1, Mollie 3/12 4-7-45

- - - - - - - - - - - - -

DOSS

1900 CENSUS
Gus Doss 35 (Mar 1865-Ga/Ala/T-M 6), Lettie 24 (Aug 1875-M 6-3-3), Joseph L. 5 (Sep 1894), Fred 2 (May 1898), Arabelle 1/12 (Ap 1900) 13-297A-140/141
Hugh Doss 35 (Dec 1864-T/Ala/T-M 12), Nancy Ann 41 (Oct 1858-T/Ind/Ala-M 12-5-4), Cora Belle 12 (Mar 1888), Cicero A. 9 (Aug 1890), Ida P. 5 (Sep 1894-Ala), Rose Eller 4 (Ap 1896-Ala) 13-297A-139/141
Jasper Doss 50: see William Woody
John Doss 28 (Mar 1872-M 10)(RR Laborer), Ileenie M. 43 (May 1857-M 10-5-4), William L. 9 (Mar 1891), John 7 (Aug 1892), Jesse 5 (Aug 1894), Beulah D. 3 (Sep 1896) 13-302B-226/235
John Doss 80 (Ap 1820-Ala/T/T-Wd)(Fruit Raiser), Nancy 26 (d)(Aug 1873-T/Ala/NC) 13-297A-141/143
John B. Doss 36 (Oct 1863-T/T/NC-M 13), Charlotte 37 (Nov 1862-T/NC/T-M 13-6-6), Ellen 13 (May 1887-Ala), Allen 11 (Sep 1888), Fannie 9 (Aug 1890), Lillie 6 (Feb 1894-Ala), Setlla 4 (Sep 1896), Albert 1 (June 1898) 13-297A-137/139
Matilda Doss 68 (Mar 1832-Wd 6-4), Polly 19 (gd)(Dec 1880)(Washwoman) 10-252A-42 (B)
MARRIAGES
D.J. Doss to Nannie Cloyer, 1 Nov 1888 (same), John Howard MG 1-561
Hugh Doss to Nancy A. Cannon, 4 Nov 1889 (same), W.A. Green JP 1-588
John Doss to Mary Rhodes, 20 Ap 1890, F.M. Capps JP 4-16
Lottie Doss to W.D. Dixon q.v.
Louisy Doss to William H. Doss q.v.
Lynda Doss to John Cumbo q.v.
William H. Doss to Louisy Doss, 24 Jan 1892, W.A. Green JP 4-35

- - - - - - - - - - - - -

DOUD– see DODD

- - - - - - - - - - - - -

DOUGLAS / DOUGLASS / DUGLAS

1900 CENSUS
Eliza Douglas 34 (B): see Benjamin F. Mealer
Luther Douglas 16, Columbus 11: see German See (B)
Michel Duglas 75 (Ap 1825-Ala/Md/Md-M 40), Trucy 80 (Mar 1820-Ga/Ga/Unk-M 40-7-0) 7-265B-289/294 (B)
MARRIAGES
Bell Douglass to Samuel Waterhouse q.v.
Myrtle Douglass to John Howerton q.v.
Sallie Douglass to German See q.v.

- - - - - - - - - - - - -

DOUTYS / DOTEY– see DAUGHERTY

- - - - - - - - - - - - -

DOVERS

1900 CENSUS
James Dovers 43 (Unk-M 21), Lucinda 41 (Aug 1841-M 21-2-2), Linda 24 (Sep 1875) 6-242A-49

- - - - - - - - - - - - -

DOYLE

1900 CENSUS
William Doyle 40 (Nov 1839-Oh/Ireland/Oh-M 13)(RR Bridge Foreman), Mary 31 (June 1868-Ky/Ireland/Do-M 13-6-6), Rose E. 11 (Sep 1888-Ky), Annie B. 10 (Ap 1890-Ky), William W. 8 (Ap 1892-Ky), James 5 (Sep 1894-Ky), Mary 3 (Feb 1896), John M. 2 (Ap 1898) 10-324A-89/93

- - - - - - - - - - - - -

DOZE

MARRIAGE
Elizabeth Doze to R. A. Hill q.v.

- - - - - - - - - - - - -

DRAKE

1870 CENSUS
John Drake 63 (NC), Willis 27, Ann 27 2-5-30
Willis Drake 28, Neoma 27 2-6-41
1880 CENSUS
James Drake 20 (Miner), Elizabeth 22, John 7, James 5, William 4, Nancy 1, Caroline STEVENS 42 (ml) (Seamstress) 2-30-241
Willis Drake 35, O.M. 35, M.E. 6 (d), Thurman 5 3-29-323
1900 CENSUS
Delia Drake 10: see Giles H. Ryan
Henry Drake 25: see Nauron W. Cagle
James A. Drake 64 (May 1836-T/NC/T-Wd), Sherman 21 (s)(Feb 1877) 2-196B-100/103
John Drake 24: see William M. Wiggins
Willis W. Drake 60 (May 1840-T/NC/NC-M 36), May O. 57 (May 1843-M 36-4-2), Sherman D. 23 (s)(May 1847-M 0), Lula M. 17 (dl)(Sep 1882-M 0) 2-193B-45/46
MARRIAGES
Emma Drake to Wyley L. Simpson q.v.
J.W. Drake to Vina Pratt, 8 Jan 1887 (same), W.S. Hale MG 1-522
Mary Drake to John R. Kilgore q.v.
Willis Drake to Naomia Wasson, 25 June 1868 (same), G.W. Renfro MG 1-#1016

- - - - - - - - - - - - -

DREW / DRUE

1900 CENSUS
Jeff Drue 74 (Unk 1828-Ga/Unk/Ga-M 8), Margarett 55 (Unk 1845-Ga/Va/Va-M 8-0-0) 7-265A-285/290 (B)

MARRIAGES
Jeff Drew to Margaret Meadows, 30 Dec 1891, S. Washington MG 4-49
William Drue(?) to Sarah Ruth, 18 Dec 1888 (21 Dec), R.S. Mason JP 1-558

- - - - - - - - - - - - -

DRUMMOND

1900 CENSUS
William T. Drummond 45 (Mar 1855-Mo/Ill/Ill-M 17) (Clergyman), Maggie A. 37 (Oct 1862-Ky/Ky/Ky-M 17-7-4), Daniel W. 15 (Nov 1884-Tex), Maggie J. 11 (Oct 1888-Tex), Elbert J. 9 (Nov 1890-Mich), Earnest L. 5 (May 1895-Ala) 13-309A-361/374

- - - - - - - - - - - - -

DRYMAN / DRYMON/ DRYEMON / DRYMORE

1880 CENSUS
W. Dryemon 25, S.C. 35 (w), M.A. 4 (d), S.E. 2/12 (d), J.R. HUBBARD 17 (ss) 7-24-210
MARRIAGES
Catharine Drymore to Smith Moore q.v.
Rebecca Dryman to James Rennow q.v.
William J. Drymon to S.C. Hubbard, 2 June 1875 (3 June), A.P. Early MG 1-#1398

- - - - - - - - - - - - -

DUANUNG

1880 CENSUS
M.D. Duanung 38, C.M. 38 (w), N.R. 18 (s), J.S. 14 (s), C.A. 12 (s), B.R. 14 (s), S.C. 6 (d) 11-39-318

- - - - - - - - - - - - -

DUCKWORTH

1860 CENSUS
John Duckworth 50, Rebecca 49, John 21, James 19, George W. 17, Doctor B.F. 15, Polly J. 11, Sarah J. 11 4-43-292
Samuel Duckworth 23, Catharin 32, Martha J. 5, Nancy E. 2, John D. 11/12 3-66-255
1870 CENSUS
George W. Duckworth 26, Sarah A. 25, Thomas L. 4, Zachariah R. 3, Sarah R. 10/12 3-1-4
John Duckworth 65 (Shoe & Bootmaker), Rebecca 64, Sarah J. 17, Mary J. 4, Sarah C. 9/12 3-1-5
Kate Duckworth 34, Martha J. 14, Nancy E. 12, John D. 10, Mary L. 7, Sarah 4: see David Davis
1880 CENSUS
Franklin Duckworth 35 (Mill Worker), Emily 37, Susan 8 2-24-194
G.W. Duckworth 36, S.A. 35 (w), T.W. 13 (s), L.R. 11 (s), S.C. 10 (d), H.J. 9 (d), V.A. 8 (d), E.A. 4 (d), A.F. 2 (d) 4-10-78
1900 CENSUS
Robert L. Duckworth 32 (Aug 1867-Md/Md/Md-M 3), Susan K. 19 (Dec 1880-T/T/Ky-M 3-2-1), Samuel W. 1 (Mar 1899) 15-269A-18/18
Sarah Duckworth 33 (Feb 1867-T/T/NC-Wd 6-5), Jeremiah C. 11 (Dec 1888), James A. 9 (May 1891), Isabell 6 (Aug 1893), Cora E. 3 (Aug 1896), William T. 1 (Dec 1898), Berty McANTIRE 15 (ne)(Sep 1884) 5-236B-168/168
MARRIAGES
Betty Duckworth to W. B. McEntire q.v.
Franklin Duckworth to E.L. Franklin, ?? Jan 1871 (22 Jan), Z. Rose MG 1-#1182
J.D. Duckworth to Sarah R. Neal, 22 Dec 1886 (23 Dec), Jesse P. Thompson JP 1-524
Martha J. Duckworth to John H. Couch q.v.
Robert Duckworth to Kittie Cranmore, 19 Jan 1897 (31 Jan), F.M. Cook MG, John Cranmore W 2-114
Samuel Duckworth to C. Davis, 2 Feb 1855 (same), Wm W. Rose MG 1-#501

- - - - - - - - - - - - -

DUDLEY

1860 CENSUS
Calvin G. Dudley 41, Caroline 40, Samuel 18, Benjamin F. 15, Martha J. 13, John 11, James 9, Francis 6, Chessel(?) 3, Moses B. 6/12 1-82-562
1870 CENSUS
Calvin Dudley 51, Caroline 51 (NC), Samuel G. 27, Benjamin 25, John 21, James C. 19, Francis 16, George S. 13, Moses B. 11, General L. 4 2-2-10
MARRIAGES
G. H. Dudley to Bell E. Kincade, 22 Jan 1877 (23 Jan), James I. Cash MG 1-#1488
J.B. Dudley to Margaret Baker, 13 Nov 1857 (no return) 1-#619
John B. Dudley to Marha J. Cantrell, 19 Mar 1854 (same), Daniel Broyles JP 1-#438
Martha J. Dudley to James P. Frank q.v.
Martha M. Dudley to W.R.J. Thompson q.v.

- - - - - - - - - - - - -

DUFF

MARRIAGES
Lillie Duff to F. J. Carter q.v.
Lona Duff to Jack McMillan q.v.
Lorin Duff to John Pickel q.v.
Mary Duff to J. B. Delozier q.v.
Will C. Duff to Annie Cross, 12 Jan 1887 (13 Jan), Calvin Morgan JP 1-531

- - - - - - - - - - - - -

DUISMORE / DUISMOOR

1870 CENSUS
Francis Duismore 67, Lorinda A. 12: see Roland Gass (B)
Joseph Duismoor 14 (B): see Henry H. Miller

- - - - - - - - - - - - -

DUKETT

MARRIAGE
Walter R. Dukett to Ella Decker, 27 Mar 1892, James Corvin MG 4-48

- - - - - - - - - - - - -

DULANEY

MARRIAGE

Vie Dulaney to Isam Eskrick q.v.

- - - - - - - - - - - - -

DULULCH

1900 CENSUS

James Dululch(?) 41 (Feb 1859-M 15), Margt 42 (July 1857-M 15-6-6), George 15 (Feb 1885), Aran 12 (June 1886), Dasker 11 (Jan 1887), Lilli 9 (Feb 1891), Bell 6 (Ap 1894), John 4 (Oct 1895), James EDINGTON 35 (gs)[sic*](Ap 1865) 1-189A-194/203 (Spring City) [*too old to be a grandson; probably son of Luke and Millie Crisp Edington]

- - - - - - - - - - - - -

DUNCAN / DUNKEN / DUNGAN / DRUNKIN / DUGGEN / DENIGAN / DENSKIN

1860 CENSUS

Abgail Duncan 49 (Va), James L. 27, Charles L. 23, Mary 20, Melia A. 19, Sarah R. 17, Semaraus E. 12, Mary A. 9, Henry 9/12 8-14-97

Russel Duncan 48, Mary L. 37, Sandy R. 19, Francis M. 16, Mary S. 15, Charles P. 13, John A. 11, Margaret E. 9, Vesta E. 7, Hiram C. 4, Sarah M. 2 8-17-116

1870 CENSUS

Abigail Dungan 57 (Va), Sarah R. 25, Samiramus E. 22, Mary 19, William GOTHARD 18 8-6-40

Charles L. Dungan 30, Mary Caroline 30, Margarette E.E. 7, Sarah M. 5, Thomas B. 1 8-7-41

James S. Dungan 36, Mary Jane 20, General G. PIERCE 6 8-6-39

Miles A. Dungan 28, Lucinda 25, William A.R. 8, James T.J. 6, John Samuel 4, Charles A. 2, Byrd R. 10/12 8-7-42

Samuel C. Drunkin 47 (NC), Elizabeth 40, John W. 21, Lucinda 19, Mattie 17, Noah M. 15, Cicero 12, James A.M. 6, Joel C.B. 5, Amanda M. 2, Samuel C. 1/12 1-4-26

1880 CENSUS

A.N. Denigan 69, Sarah 37 (d) 8-10-820

C.L. Dungan 40, M.C. 40, Tom 11, Bery 9, Sindy 7, Allice 5, Virginia 6/12 8-10-85

J.S. Dungen 46, M.J. 30 (w), J.A. 9 (s), I.A. 7 (d), V.B. 5 (d), S.V. 3 (s), S.M. 11/12 (d) 8-4-30

J.W. Duncan 34, M.A. 34, J.C. 13 (s), N.E. 11 (d), E.H. 9 (d), E.F. 4 (d), W.M. 1 (d) 4-8-62

John Duncan 38, Cansada 26, Mary 8, Susan 5, William 3, Martha 1 1-11-90

Mary Duncan 75: see J. T. Shelton

Noah Duncan 26, M.F. 24 (w), J.L. 3 (s) 4-5-36

Samuel Duncan 55, Elizabeth 51, Lucinda 29, Cicero 23, James 17, Joel 14, Amanda 12, Samuel 10 1-17-144

1900 CENSUS

James W. Duncan 55 (Mar 1845-M ?)(Carpenter), Mary A. 48 (Ap 1852-M ?-7-6), Magnolia 22 (Aug 1877) (Dressmaker), Frances E. 20 (July 1879), William 18 (Sep 1881), Anna 15 (Sep 1884), Clyde S. RUICBELL 32 (boarder)(June 1867-Ind/Ind/Ind-S)(School Teacher) 13-215A-40/41

John Dunken 51 (Aug 1848-M 35), Cansada 47 (Oct 1852-M 35-9-8), Mattie 21 (Dec 1878), Dara 15 (Feb 1885), Clara 14 (Ap 1889), May 12 (Ap 1888), Freed 8 (Aug 1891) 1-185A-125/131

John C. Duncan 33 (Oct 1866-M ?)(RR Carpenter), Milo P. 29 (June 1870-M ?-3-2), Guy U. 7 (Nov 1892), Maud A. 5 (Dec 1894) 14-223A-192/196

Lucinda E. Dungan 55 (Dec 1844-Wd 10-6), Charles A. 33 (May 1867)(Coal Miner), Simmie R. 27 (d)(Mar 1873) 13-306A-308/320

Samuel Dungan 33 (Aug 1866-M 11)(Coal Miner), Mattie L. 30 (July 1869-M 11-5-4), Mary E. 9 (Feb 1891), Bessie B. 6 (June 1893), Audrey 4 (June 1895), infant 3/12 (d)(Feb 1900) 13-306A-304/316

MARRIAGES

A. Dungan to Elizabeth Horn, no date (no return) [probably 1859] 1-#696

C.L. Dungan (43, Megs Co) to M.E. Montgomery (44, Jefferson Co), 26 Jan 1882, F.M. Bandy MG, Wm Morgan & Wm McPherson W 4-9(85)

Charles L. Dungan to Mary C. Montgomery, 26 Ap 1860 (25 Ap)[sic], D.F. Ward MG 1-#708

Hannah Duggen to W. Thomas q.v.

J.S. Dungan to M.J. Hoge, 23 July 1887 (24 July), W.A. Green JP 1-529

John C. Duncan to Milo Pate Holloway, 23 Dec 1891, R.A. Dickson JP 4-36

John W. Duncan to Zodec Casey, 27 May 1871 (30 May), G.W. Renfro MG 1-#1197

Manerva A. Dungan to W. B. Nichols q.v.

Margaret M. Dunkin or Denskin to E. M. Smith q.v.

Martha Duncan to Alvin G. Ward q.v.

Martha Dunken to John Casey q.v.

Mattie Duncan to Lee Crisp q.v.

Minnie Dungan to J. B. Coulter q.v.

Miles A. Dungan (or Dringan) to Lucinda Newman, 10 July 1860 (12 July), D.F. Ward JP 1-#716

S. M. Dungan to A. L. Morgan q.v.

W.L. Duggen to Fannie E. Rickles, 28 May 1894, John T. Price MG 4-67

- - - - - - - - - - - - -

DUNLAP

1860 CENSUS

Elizabeth Dunlap 50, William 22, James 20, Richard 18, Albert 16 9-100-681

Jacob L. Dunlap 35, Lucinda 30, Betsy S. 3 9-100-683

John Dunlap 33, Polly A. 25, Jacob 4, James F. 1 9-100-682

1870 CENSUS

Elizabeth Dunlap 60, Elizabeth SPAIN 14, John 9, Jacob L. 8 1-20-129

Polly A. Dunlap 38, Jacob L. 14, James 12, John 10 1-19-122

William Dunlap 30, Charlotte 22, Sanders 6, Henry T. 5, James A. 2, Lisa N. 1/12 1-19-128

1880 CENSUS

Elizabeth Dunlap 77, Leonard 18 (s) 12-2-13

Mary Dunlap 40, Jacob 24, James 20, John 17 1-19-157

May Dunlap 8: see James Thompson

Saunders Dunlap 16, Willis 6: see Macey Scarbrough
1900 CENSUS
John Dunlap 37 (Feb 1863-M 17), Martha 32 (Aug 1867-M 17-7-5), Alley 12 (Feb 1888), Rosey 9 (July 1890), Annis 7 (Aug 1892), Ike 4 (July 1895), Mary 2 (Dec 1897) 1-189A-197/206 (Spring City)
John Dunlap 37 (Mar 1863-M 16), Manda 34 (July 1865-M 16-7-7), Charles 14 (Sep 1885), Stanis 12 (Sep 1887), Lannie 10 (Oct 1889), Waltar 8 (Nov 1891), Bess(?) 7 (Feb 1893), John 5 (Mar 1895), Roger(?) 3/12 (Mar 1900) 12-181B-64/67
Polly Dunlap 68 (Feb 1832-Wd 5-3), Jake 31 (s)(Ap 1869), George Jr. 14 (s)(Mar 1886) 1-189A-196/205 (Spring City)
Sanders Dunlap 37 (July 1862-M 13), Mary A. 36 (Aug 1863-M 13-0-0), Joseph WATSON 31 (bl)(Oct 1868), Hannah HAYES 72 (ml)(July 1827-T/NC/T-D 1-1) 14-223A-189/193
MARRIAGES
Elizabeth S. Dunlap to James F. Thompson q.v.
J.L. Dunlap to Viola M. Clendon, 30 May 1883 (31 May), T.L. Long JP 1-472
James F. Dunlap to Maggie Smith, 28 Nov 1883 (29 Nov), T.L. Long JP 1-473
John Dunlap to Polly Ann Edington, 2 Nov 1852 (18 Nov), W. Floyd JP 1-#390
Sanders Dunlap to Mary A. Hase, 19 Feb 1887 (20 Feb), W.T. West MG 1-519
William L. Dunlap to Charlotte McClendon, 1 Aug 1862 (3 Aug), E. Brewer JP 1-#784

- - - - - - - - - - - - -

DUNN

1900 CENSUS
Elin Dunn(?) 61 (May 1839-Wd 9-6), Preston 23(?) (Jan ??), Fillimer 12 (gs)(Ap 1888) 1-186B-148/156
George Dunn 21 (Sep 1878-M 1), Temple 22 (June 1877-T/Va/T-M 1-1-1), Ollie E. 1 (May 1899) 6-246B-126/127
William M. Dunn 57 (Dec 1848-M 23), Nancy J. 42 (July 1857-M 23-2-2), John H. 19 (Mar 1881) 9-228B-19/19
MARRIAGE
Joseph Dunn to Frances J. Tillery, 12 Dec 1887 (14 Dec), M.C. Bruner MG 1-564

- - - - - - - - - - - - -

DUNWOODY

1860 CENSUS
Eliza Dunwoody 7: see Washington Morgan
1870 CENSUS
Albert Dunwoody 22 (B): see Stephen Spence

- - - - - - - - - - - - -

DUPREE

MARRIAGES
David Dupree to R.E. Jones, 26 Jan 1888 (27 Dec), L. Hayworth MG 1-540
Matilda Dupree to C. P. Carpenter q.v.
William Dupree to Clara A. Culver, 2 Jan 1895, G.W. Brewer MG 4-76

- - - - - - - - - - - - -

DURHAM / DENHAM

1880 CENSUS
Columbus Durham 17 (B): see Margaret Pyott
1900 CENSUS
Isaac Dunham 55 (Feb 1845-SC/SC/SC-M 26), Sarah C. 46 (Ap 1854-NC/NC/NC-M 26-7-4), Monroe 14 (June 1885-Ark), Alma 8 (Aug 1891-Ala) 8-279B-224/226
Samuel Durham 35 (Dec 1864-T/T/NC-M 11), Alma 28 (Feb 1872-M 11-4-4), Floyd 10 (Aug 1889), Birtha M. 6 (July 1893), William 4 (Nov 1895), John 2 (Nov 1897) 3-202B-51/54
MARRIAGES
Kisir Durham to John Coxey q.v.
Nancy Durham to G. W. Filyaw q.v.
Preston Durham to Nancy Philyan, 22 Sep 1896, R.M. Trentham JP 4-96
Robert Durham to Frances E. Perkins, 21 June 1884 (same), T.T. Long JP 1-481
Samuel Durham to Alma Thompson, 10 Mar 1888 (same), E.S. Cox JP 1-544

- - - - - - - - - - - - -

DUVALL

MARRIAGE
Mary B. Duvall to Julius Iphofen q.v.

- - - - - - - - - - - - -

DYE / DIE

1880 CENSUS
Alexander Dye 52 (Civil Engineer), Lamina 46, Lulu 21 2-23-188
David Dye 64, Elizabeth 35 (w), Jasper 18, Sarah 10, Adison 6, Amanda 7, William 3, Reubin 2, Callie 1/12 12-3-27
1900 CENSUS
Albert Dye 22 (Oct 1877-M 1), Nancy M. 20 (Sep 1879-M 1-1-1), Ethel 1 (May 1899) 5-237A-180
MARRIAGES
Amand Dye to James E. Edwards q.v.
Annie Die to William S. Burchard q.v.
Eliza Dye to Addison Lemmons q.v.
John Dye (25, Bledsoe Co) to Lilie Ann Daniel (14), 8 Dec 1881, W.T. West MG, W.C. Watson & W.N. Wolf W 4-6(54)
Lula Dye to E. D. Osborn q.v.
Reuben Dye to Missouria C. Shadwick, 14 Ap 1900 (same), A.P. Hayes JP 3-141
Sarah Dye to Tom Dunning q.v.
Sarah Dye to W. L. Anderson q.v.
William Dye to Nancy E. Davis, 25 Sep 1855 (same), A. Campbell JP 1-#518

- - - - - - - - - - - - -

DYER / DYRE

1860 CENSUS
Charles Dyer 32, Nancy J. 30, Mary J. 4 1-85-579
John Dyer 30, Barbary L. 19, Thomas 5/12 1-86-587
William Dyer 57, Rebecca 55, Benjamin A. 27, James Samuel K.P. 14, Mary 12 1-85-578
1870 CENSUS
Abraham Dyer 35 (Ga), Malinda 35, William DYER (B) 13 (Va) 6-15-110
1880 CENSUS
Alfred Dyer 19 5-11-108 (B)
Amanda Dyer 20: see B. M. Collins
Benjamin Dyer 25, Allis 17 10-28-216/221 (Mu)
Elijah Dyer 38, Sarah 36, Ephraim 13, Anna 10, Mary 8, Margaret 6, Flora 3, Harris 1 2-38-310
Isaac Dyer 28, Callie 20, Lora 5, Clement 4, Theopliles 2, Franklin 8/12 10-28-215/220 (Mu)
Jacob Dyer 27 (Printer), Rhoda 30, John 10, Albert 8, Harry 5, Larinia 4, Estella 1, Emma HOUSTON (B) 19 (Cook) 2-21-171
Pryor Dyer 28 (Blacksmith), M.A. 23 (w), Jerry 6 (s), O.T. 4 (s), L.M. 15 (s), M.V. 8 (d) 4-5-41
R.N. Dyre 53, S.A. 22 (w), Malind 5 (d), Tom M. 3 (s), James A. 5/12 (s) 7-22-189
1900 CENSUS
Ben Dyer 47 (Ap 1853-T/T/Va-M 22), Alice 37 (Sep 1862-T/T/Va-M 22-1-1), Aller 11 (d)(Ap 1889), Nelly 13 (boarder)(Oct 1886), David GOWIN 48 (boarder)(Sep 1850), George HENRY 13 (Mar 1887) 10-254B-90 (B)
Cally Dyer 37, Lina M. 5: see Melvin Hight (B)
Ike Dyer 56 (Mar 1844-T/T/Va-M 26), Frank 19 (Sep 1880), Lizzie 16 (Oct 1883), John 13 (Aug 1886) 10-260B-1203/208 (B)
James Dyer 63 (July 1836-T/NC/T-M 24)(Gardner), Eda E. 48 (Ap 1852-M 24-0-0) 4-227B-273/277 (Road on line between 3rd & 4th Districts)
John Dyer 21 (Unk 1879-M 0), Emma 19 (Feb 1881-M 0-0-0) 15-271B-71
Julia Dyer 12: see Nathaniel R. Roberts (B)
Mary Dyer 52 (Ap 1852-S 1-1), Susan 22 (d)(Nov 1877) 5-237A-173
Nancy Dyer 55: see Abraham I. Stever
Rufus Dyer 18 (Unk 1882-M 0)(Miner), Missouri 19 (Unk 1881-M 0) 8-286A-356/358
William Dyre 55 (Jan 1845-M 21), Sarah 62 (Dec 1837-T/Ga/NC-M 21-0-0), James F. PRATER 11 (boarder) (Oct 1888-Mo) 5-238A-194
William Dyer 21 (Unk 1879-M 3), Nancy J. 23 (Unk 1877-M 3-0-0) 8-286A-355/357

MARRIAGES
A.H. Dyre to Malinda Roberson, 19 June 1867 (same), T.N. L. Cunnyngham JP 1-#955
Charles B. Dyer to Nancy J. Vaughn, 2 Nov 1854, "Executed in due time by Thomas V. Atchley JP" 1-#466
Elbert Dyer (29) to Anna W. Mills (18), 4 Oct 1881, W.A. Montgomery MG, Howard(?) Breen or Brun (Cincinnati, Ohio) & J.P. Bauscaum(?) (Grand View) W 4-2(16)
Ella Dyer to A. E. Brogdon q.v.
Emma Dyer to Francis M. Johnson q.v.
John Dyer to Barbery S.M. Bond, 22 Dec 1854 (same), T.V. Atchley JP 1-#479
John Dyer to Emma Jordan, 14 July 1899 (15 July), F.M. Cox MG, R.A.S. Elder W 3-10
Lula Dyer to C. H. Powell q.v.
Rachell Dyer to Isiah Stever or Stover q.v.
William Dyer or Dye to Nancy J. Shadwick, 6 May 1897 (bond only), J.T. Shadwick W 2-142

\- - - - - - - - - - - - -

DYLAND

1880 CENSUS
Curt Dyland 34 (B): see T. Coulter

\- - - - - - - - - - - - -

DYRL

1880 CENSUS
Mary Dyrl 68, Margaret 47 (d), Mary 38 (d), Rachel 20 (d), Susan 7 (gd), M.S. 5 (gd) 9-32-273

\- - - - - - - - - - - - -

DYSEN

1880 CENSUS
Cash Dysen 30, Nany 24, J.C. 9 (d), Jemmie 6 (d), Winie 2 (d), Louis ROBINSON 55 (boarder) 8-8-68 (B)

\- - - - - - - - - - - - -

EALINS

1900 CENSUS
James Ealins 38 (Jan 1862-M 18), Addie 38 (Dec 1861-M 18-8-7), Charles 14 (Sep 1885), John 12 (June 1887), Lillie M. 10 (July 1889), William I. 8 (July 1891), George C. 7 (May 1893), Matilda 5 (Feb 1895), Walter A. 1 (June 1898) 15-272A-75

\- - - - - - - - - - - - -

EARLY / EARLEY

1860 CENSUS
Albert P. Early 42 (Minister), Hannah M. 42, Manerva M. FRAZIER 16, Emily P. 11, Martha EARLY 11, Josephine 9, James A. 7 6-112-771
1870 CENSUS
Albert P. Early 52 (Minister), Hannah M. 52, Mary COLLINS (B) 40, Dick COLLINS (B) 7 6-9-60
James A. Early 18 (Ga): see William I. Irvin
1880 CENSUS
Albert P. Early 62 (Minister), Hannah H. 61 6-22-2 (Madison Street, Washington)
J.A. Early 28, J. ERVIN 30 (si), J.M. 11 (s), Mary 4 (d), Jane ROGERS (B) 40 (Servant) 7-26-226
1900 CENSUS
Hannah M. Early 81: see Benjamin F. Mealer
James Earley 48 (Feb 1852-Ga/T/T-M 19), Mary 39 (Oct 1860-M 19-7-6), Lizzie 17 (July 1882), Emma 15 (June 1884), Critt 12 (July 1887), Albert 8 (Oct 1891), Kattie 4 (Aug 1895), Maybell 1 (Dec 1898) 7-266A-307/312

John Earley 41 (Feb 1859-M 23), Sarah 39 (May 1861-M 23-0-0), Magar 13 (nw)(Ap 1885) 1-189B-207/217
Thomas Early 37 (Dec 1862-M 19)(RR Laborer), Carrie 29 (Oct 1870-M 16-5-5), Maud 13 (Sep 1886), James A. 9 (Ap 1891), John W. 6 (Sep 1893), Idella 5 (Ap 1895), Clas C. 2 (Ap 1898) 14-215A-46/47

MARRIAGES
A.P. Early to Manervia Frazier, 20 Dec 1858 (same), W.H. Bell MG 1-#678
J.A. Early to M.T. Purser, 14 Oct 1880 (same), A.P. Early MG 1-293
Josephine Early to William R. Irwin q.v.
Martha Early to James C. Kelly q.v.

- - - - - - - - - - - - -

EARWOOD

MARRIAGE
T. A. Earwood to S. J. Brown q.v.

- - - - - - - - - - - - -

EAST

MARRIAGES
Ben F. East to Mary E. Lindsey, 18 Dec 1896 (24 Dec), W.T. West MG 2-90
Sewell East to Callie Brock, 28 Oct 1894, J.R. Clark MG 4-79

- - - - - - - - - - - - -

EASTLAND

1880 CENSUS
Henry Eastland 23, Belle 25, Charles 2, Mark 1: see Nile Broyles
MARRIAGES
Henry Eastland to Belle Broyles, 9 Jan 1877 (same), G.W. Wassom JP 1-#1480
[Henry, son of Charles and Sarah Broyles Eastland; Isabella, dau of Nile and Elenor Wilson Broyles]

- - - - - - - - - - - - -

EASTMAN

MARRIAGE
Edwin Eastman to Mrs. Susie C. Hill, 14 Jan 1880 (15 Jan), L.H. McPherson JP 1-#1703

- - - - - - - - - - - - -

EATES [ESTES?]

MARRIAGE
John Eates to Margarett J. McCarroll, 22 Dec 1857 (same), G.W. Nichols JP 1-#624

- - - - - - - - - - - - -

EATON / EATONS

1860 CENSUS
Betsy Eaton 21: see Dorcas F. Fisher
Henry Eaton 66 (Va), Rebecca 61 (NC), Elizabeth CHATTEN 105* (NC) 5-37-249
[*NOTE: On 1850 Census, Elizabeth's last name was Chapman and she was shows as 83 years old]
Joseph Eaton 23: see David Singleton
Joseph Eaton 28, Manerva 27, Mary 10, William H. 8, Baily 6, Samuel 4, Susan 2, George 1 4-50-338
1870 CENSUS
Henry Eaton 67 (Va), Rebecca 65 (NC) 6-3-19
Joseph Eaton 48, Minerva 40, Mary 21, Henry 16, Samuel 13, Alphonsus 12, George 9, Joseph 7, Rebecca 5, John 4, Tennessee 2 6-3-18
1880 CENSUS
W.H. Eaton 28, Melvina 28, Murry M. 6, Lara L. 4, Allis O. 2, Nancy A. 9/12 5-1-9
1900 CENSUS
Adelbert Eaton 45 (May 1855-Ind/England/Ind-M 8), Belle 32 (May 1888-Ill/NY/Pa-M 8-4-4), Ethel I. 15 (May 1885-Iowa), Roy A. 11 (Dec 1888-Iowa), Mary L. 7 (Dec 1892-Iowa), Louis T. 5 (July 1894), Leslie D. 3 (Oct 1897), Florence J. 3/12 (Feb 1900) 11-291A-28
Charley Eaton 8: see James Miligan
James E. Eaton 20 (Feb 1880-Iowa/Ind/Iowa-M 0), Lillie A. 17 (Sep 1882-M 0-0-0) 11-291A-27
John E. Eaton 11, Charles R. 8: see John W. Suttler
Martha Eaton 24, Floyd 8, George 1: see Susan Majors

MARRIAGES
Adaline Eaton to Benjamin Sanders q.v.
Eliza J. Eaton to J.G. Utter q.v.
Henry Eaton to Melvinia Hurst, 20 Aug 1872 (same), A.J. Pritchett MG 1-#1246
J.J. Eatons to M.C. Suttles, 26 Dec 1887 (same), Calvin Morgan JP 1-541
J.J. Eaton to Martha Waller, 18 Sep 1897 (19 Sep), W.S. Hale JP, J.M. Walton(?) W 2-179
Joshua Eaton to Nancy J. Singleton, 23 Nov 1859 (no return) 1-#700
Mary Eaton to Garrett Beasly q.v.
William P. Eaton to Elizabeth Baker, 17 May 1856 (no return) 1-#548

- - - - - - - - - - - - -

EAVES / EVES

1880 CENSUS
Elvira Eaves 25: see E. Cunnyngham
1900 CENSUS
Thomas J. Eaves 48 (Oct 1851-M 21*)(Commercial Traveler, Tobacco), Emely 45 (Aug 1854-M 21-8-8), Charles R. 18 (Mar 1882), Berta E. 20 (Nov 1879) (Music Teacher), William H. 16 (Dec 1883), Alice B. (Aug 1885), Mary E. 12 (Dec 1887), Sarah A. 10 (May 1890), Isaac L. 8 (June 1892), Samuel K. 4 (Feb 1896) 14-216B-78/79 [*married 7 Jan 1879] [Thomas, son of Pleasant L. & Elizabeth H. Bean Eaves; Emily, dau of Isaac & Mary Taylor Cross]

MARRIAGES
Bertie E. Eaves to Owen Bowling q.v.
Ida Eaves to James H. Travis q.v.
S.S. Eaves to Alice Clack, 6 Nov 1895, Wm White MG 4-91

- - - - - - - - - - - - -

EAZELL / EZELL / EZILL / ESEAL

1880 CENSUS
James Eseal 40, N.C. 37 (w), M.J. 20 (d), Josephine 17 (d), J.A. 14 (d), J.M. 10 (s), S.G. 8 (s), J.J. 5 (s), J.H. 2 (s), B.F. 1/12 (s) 4-32-262
1900 CENSUS
George M. Ezell 35 (Mar 1865-M 8), Ellen R. 24 (Jan 1876-Ky/T/T-M 8-4-4), Arthur C. 8 (Ap 1892), Alace J. 4 (July 1895), Ida L. 2 (Sep 1897), Carroll N. 1 (Feb 1899) 5-231B-67
James Ezill 61 (Jan 1838-M 40), Nancy C. 56 (June 1843-Va/NC/NC-M 40-8-6) 5-231B-64
James J. Ezell 22 (Mar 1878-T/T/Va-M 3), Amanda 22 (Jan 1878-M 3-2-2), Rhoda 3 (Dec 1896), Marion 1 (Dec 1898) 5-231B-66
John H. Ezell 20: see Alfred Paine
MARRIAGE
Palina Josephine Eazell to Thomas W. Beasly q.v.

- - - - - - - - - - - - -

EBERHART

1900 CENSUS
William Eberhart 30 (Ap 1870-Ga/Ga/Ga-M 6), Isabella 21 (Unk-Ga/SC/SC-M 6-0-0)(Chambermaid at Hotel), Dolly WILKES 28 (sil)(Hotel Cook), Henry BRUNER 28 (boarder)(Dec 1871-Ga/Ga/Ga)(Handling Iron Ore) 10-327B-161/170 (B)

- - - - - - - - - - - - -

EBERLY / EVERLEY

1900 CENSUS
Peter L. Everly 55 (Feb 1845-Pa/Pa/Del-M 28), Laura L. 47 (Dec 1852-Oh/Oh/Oh-M 28-0-0) 4-224A-209/213 (Spring City and Dayton Road)
MARRIAGE
Clara Eberly to W. H. Palmer q.v.

- - - - - - - - - - - - -

EBLIN

MARRIAGE
W.L. Eblin to Emma C. Morgan, 11 June 1889 (same), F.M. Bandy MG 1-585

- - - - - - - - - - - - -

EDINGTON / EDDINGTON

1860 CENSUS
Luke Edington 30: see Franklin Waterhouse
William R. Edington 27: see Austin J. Evans
1870 CENSUS
Luke T. Edington 39, Millie A. 26, James M. 7, Isaac F. 5, William R. 1, John C. 6/12 1-7-45
William R. Edington 36, Mary M. 27, John E. 7, William S. 5, Jesse 2, Isaac L. 11/12, Prudence McADOO 31 1-18-121
1880 CENSUS
Luke Edington 50, Milla 38 (w), James 16, Isaac 15, William 14, Elvira 3, Malinda 2 1-10-79
Riley Edington 46, Mary 39, John 17, William 14, Jesse 12, Isaac 9, Samuel 7, Clara 5, Moses 2, Mark 1/12 12-1-2
1900 CENSUS
Elvira Eddington 21: see Thomas B. Reid
Frank Edington 35 (Feb 1865-M 11), Maethy 34 (Mar 1866-M 11-5-5), Lee 18 (Jan 1882), Annie 11 (May 1889), Lara 8 (Ap 1892), May 5 (Dec 1894), Paul 1 (Ap 1898), Richard HALAWAY 68 (boarder)(Feb 1833) 1-185A-129/135
James Edington 35: see James Dululch
John L. Eddington 25 (Jan 1875-M 2)(Preacher), Adelia 24 (Nov 1875-M 2-1-1), Catharine 1 (Aug 1898), Nellie HINES 17 (May 1883)(Servant), Andy GRICE 25 (boarder)(July 1875)(School Teacher), Mary J. GRICE 31 (si)(Dec 1868-S)(School Teacher) 5-236A-159
Luke(?) Edington 71 (Mar 1829-M 40), Ann 59 (Mar 1841-M 40-6-6), James 36 (Jan 1864), Wilum 29 (Oct 1871), Ellie 21 (Sep 1879), Bettie 20 (Ap 1880), Samuel 18 (June 1872) 1-185B-131/137
MARRIAGES
F. Edington to Martha Mitchell, 1 Sep 1888 (2 Sep), J.P. Thompson JP 1-552
Luke Edington to M.A. Crisp, 28 Jan 1862 (30 Jan), Edward Pyott JP 1-#773
Polly Ann Edington to John Dunlap q.v.
W.R. Edington to Mary McAdoo, 25 Dec 1861 (same), Jas I. Cash MG 1-#767

- - - - - - - - - - - - -

EDENS / EDEN / ADEN

1860 CENSUS
Leonard Edens 45, Sarah 41. Alexander 11, Betsy A. 7, Elisha 1, William WINSEY 16 8-24-165
MARRIAGE
James Edward Aden or Eden to Lillie A. King, 8 May 1899 (14 May), W.S. Hale MG, James E. Aden & E.S. King [signed by X] W 2-409

- - - - - - - - - - - - -

EDMON

1900 CENSUS
Carson Edmon 25: see Rena Waterhouse

- - - - - - - - - - - - -

EDMONDS / EDMUNDS

1860 CENSUS
Anderson Edmonds 40, Adalaide 39, Malinda 19, Rebecca 17, Dorothy 14, Eliza 12, Ferrel 9, Judy 6, John B. 3, Sarah SHEPHARD 80 (NC) 5-38-259
George W. Edmonds 35, Mathew 32: see Garlington Bramlet

John Edmonds 26, Elizabeth 26, Mary T. 4, Porcha A. 3, Martha J. 1 3-54-370
Newton Edmonds 41, Unity H. 37, Sarepta S. 17, Martha A. 15, Philadelphia E. 12, Newton J. 10, William A. 8, Lorenso W. 6, Caroline H. 4, Tennessee E. 2, John TRUSLY 18 7-3-20
William C. Edmonds 28, Catharine 27, Newton J. 6, Penelope A. 2, Samuel H. 5/12, Penelope EDMONDS 63 6-106-720

1870 CENSUS– None

1880 CENSUS

George W. Edmonds 25, Barshaby M. 25, Fidella F. 5 (d), Mary A.T. 3, Ellie N.(?) 11/12 5-4-28

MARRIAGES

Cassie Edmunds to Charles B. Pickels q.v.
Della Edmonds to Peter Ferguson q.v.
G.W. Edmonds to B.M. Porter, 21 Mar 1874 (22 Mar), M.F. Moore MG 1-#1330
James Edmonds to Elizabeth Minnas, 24 Dec 1850 (same), John Wyott JP
John Edmonds to Elizabeth Rogers, 16 Nov 1854 (18 Nov), J. Howard JP 1-#470
M.A. Edmonds to Nancy Ann Williams, 18 May 1854 (same), R.T. Howard MG 1-#446
Martha Edmonds(?) to Wade McFall q.v.
Sarah E. Edmonds to Elbert E. Harris q.v.
William C. Edmonds to Eliza Crow, 12 Dec 1850 (same), S.R. Hackett JP
Wm C. Edmonds to Catharine Buttram, 27 Oct 1856 (same), R.T. Howard MG 1-#576

\- - - - - - - - - - - - -

EDMONDSON / EDMUNDSON

1880 CENSUS

Thomas Edmundson 35, M.E. 34, N.J. 14 (s), Mary 12 (d), J.R. 10 (s), S.F. 8 (d), M.J. 6 (d), L.E. 3 (s), J.E. 3 (s), D.A. 8/12 (d) 11-39-320

1900 CENSUS

Newton J. Edmundson 33 (Ap 1867-M 4), Viola V. 25 (Sep 1874-Ind/Ind/Ind-M 4-0-0) 11-281B-37

MARRIAGES

James Edmondson to Maggie Rigsby, 4 Mar 1898 (6 Mar), W.J. Kerley (?) MG, L.T. Rigsby W 2-256
N.J. Edmondson to Viola V. Hedlie, 24 Nov 1895, J.H. Morgan JP 4-92
Sarah F. Edmondson to A. S. Sparks q.v.

\- - - - - - - - - - - - -

EDWARDS

1870 CENSUS

John Edwards 41, Mary Jane 27, James D. 11, Sarah A. 7, Ann M. 4, John S. 3 1-2-12
Polly A. Edwards 50, Robert G. 23 (Ala), John B. 21 (Ala), Amanda A. 18 (Ala) 8-22-154
Judge Edwards 14 (Ga): see John Hodges (B)

1880 CENSUS

John Edwards 53, Mary 38, Sarah 18, Ann 14, Sherman 12, Thomas 10, Houston 4, McAllen 5/12 12-2-12
Robert Edwards 33, Jane 36 (w), M.J. 6 (d), W.M. 5 (s), J.B. 3 (s), James B. 2 (s), C.E. 10/12 (d) 8-8-63
Rose Edwards 12: see D.H. Copenhan

1900 CENSUS

Ann Edwards 14: see William McDonald (B)
Dan Edward 45 (Mar 1855-M 24), Maud 49 (Aug 1850-M 24-8-8), Idie 12 (Ap 1887), John 10 (July 1889) 12-180A-34/37
Robert Edwards 53 (Aug 1846-Ala/Ala/Ala-M 30), Ann 59 (Aug 1840-M 30-5-4), James B. 22 (Feb 1879)(Coal Miner), Kate 20 (Aug 1879), Horace HOUSTON 22 (boarder)(May 1878-Ala/Ga/T)(Carpenter) 13-304A-267/277
Shuman(?) Edward 30 (May 1870-M 10), Cora 28 (Nov 1871-M 10-1-1), Harison(?) 8 (Aug 1891) 12-180A-36/39
Susan Edward 50 (May 1850-Wd 8-8), Nettie 16 (Nov 1883), Mary 7 (Ap 1893) 12-180A-35/38
Thomas Edwards 19 (Mar 1880-Ga/Ga/Ga-M 0), Florence 23 (Sep 1876-Ga/Ga/Ga-M 0-3-3), Eva DEW 7 (sd) (Oct 1892), Ida M. 6 (sd)(Mar 1894), Willard 3 (ss) (Aug 1896) 8-317A-140/145 (B)
William N. Edwards 25 (Oct 1874-M 3), Rebecca 29 (July 1870-M 3-1-1), James H. 1 (June 1898), Robert GILL 19 (boarder)(May 1881) 13-300B-198/205
William M. Edwards 23, Vesta 17: see John J.(?) Tudor

MARRIAGES

Fannie Edwards to P. M. Minix q.v.
J.B. Edwards to Mrs. Sallie Shannon (Sherman?), 6 Mar 1900 (same), W.B. Hicks JP, C.L. Meakum(?) W 3-131
James E. Edwards to Amanda Dye, 19 Feb 1900, L.L. Barton JP 4-102
Jennie Edwards to Will McEwen q.v.
John A. Edwards to Mary J. Collins, 15 Ap 1857 (no return) 1-#596
Robert G. Edwards to Ann Gregory, 9 Sep 1871 (same), J. W. Williamson MG 1-#1207
Sarah Edward to Jeff Lytle q.v.
W.M. Edwards to N.V. Tudor, 17 Dec 1899, A.J. Wyrick JP 4-103

\- - - - - - - - - - - - -

EGARTON / EGERTON

1870 CENSUS

Charles F. Egerton 36 (NC), Sarah L. 28 (Ill), Lelia A. 2 (Wisc), Myrta L. 1 (Wisc) 1-3-16

1880 CENSUS

Francis Egerton 47, Sarah 36, Dwight 8, Carrie 6, Frank 5, Jeremiah 2, John A. 2 12-1-5

MARRIAGE

Dwight P. Egarton to Mattie R. Evans, 30 July 1892, L.L. Barton JP 4-74

\- - - - - - - - - - - - -

EICHHORN

MARRIAGES

W.H. Eichhorn to S.L. Elder, 11 Oct 1884 (12 Oct), I.W. Holt JP 1-463
W.H. Eichhorn to S.E. Brooks, 22 or 25 Feb 1889 (28 Feb), W.C. Mise MG 1-566

\- - - - - - - - - - - - -

EIDSON [EDISON?]

1880 CENSUS
G. H. Eidson 32: see S. T. Blevins

- - - - - - - - - - - - -

ELDER / ELDERS

1870 CENSUS
Maggie C. Elder 16: see Nicholas G. Moore
1880 CENSUS– None
1900 CENSUS
Dan Elders 19 (Feb 1881-T/T/NC-M 0)(Day Laborer), Mary 22 (Oct 1877-M 0) 10-250A-8
Delpha Elders 24, Betrice 5, Flossie 2: see Thos Knight
Hezekiah Elder 22 (Mar 1878-T/Unk/Ga-M 4)(Provision Store Clerk), Mattie E. 20 (Sep 1879-Mo/Unk/Ga-M 4-2-1), Ruth 11/12 (June 1899) 10-323B-77/81
Louis F.(?) Elder 46 (June 1853-Ga/SC/SC-M 22), Lucie 45 (Dec 1851-NC/NC/NC-M 22-5-4), William T. 19 (Ap 1881), Mary C. 16 (May 1884), Inez 13 (July 1886), Louis S. 7 (Oct 1896) 15-274B-119
Ras Elder 23 (Jan 1877-T/T/NC-M 2), Rhosie 18 (Jan 1882-M 2-0-0) 10-251B-35
William Elder 30 (June 1869-M 10), Mattie 28 (Mar 1872-T/NC/T-M 10-5-4), Hubert A. 9 (July 1890), Baxter V. 7 (Feb 1893), Bertha M. 5 (Dec 1894), Virgil J. 9/12 (Aug 1899) 11-291B-36
MARRIAGES
Daniel Elder to Mary Monneyhan or Monnyhan, 21 Dec 1899 (same), W.L. Lillard JP, T.F.(?) Knight W 3-92
Hess Elder to Mattie Earps, 24 Dec 1895, M.B. Hicks JP 4-89
J.A. Elder to Mattie Rains, 9 Jan 1889 (10 Jan), D.H. Hickman JP 1-554
James Elder to Mattie Thompson, 6 Sep 1890, H. Cox MG 4-15
Mary Elder to W. R. Trusley q.v.
Mary Elder to George Bishop q.v.
Mary Craton Elder to John D. Morgan q.v.
Melitia Elder to F. M. Bandy q.v.
Ras Elder to Fosie Wilhoit, 7 Jan 1898 (8 Jan), T.F. Shaver MG 2-237
Robert Elder to Delphia Knight, 15 Nov 1893, R.S. Mason JP 4-60
S. L. Elder to W. H. Eichhorn q.v.
Sophia Elder to W. N. Rains q.v.

- - - - - - - - - - - - -

ELDRIDGE / ELDREGE / ELDREDGE

1880 CENSUS
George Eldridge 51, Hariet 40, Lucy 18, Mirtle 13, Synda 10, James 8, Thomas 4, Hariet 2 2-36-292
1900 CENSUS
George Eldrege 11: see James Meadows
Jessie Eldridge 28: see James F. Johnson
William B. Eldredge 23, Mamie L. 23: see Robt M. Kilgore
MARRIAGES
George C. Eldridge to H.E. Cash, no date (no return) [probably 1857] 1-#614
George C. Eldridge (50, Overton Co) to Sarah E. Gone(?) (20, White Co), 20 Dec 1882, D.V. Culver MG, Mrs. Tennie Culver & Miss Della Culver W 4-11(110)
Harriet A. Eldridge to Albion Spence q.v.
L.D. Eldridge to Mary A. Cash, 6 Dec 1852 (no return) 1-#394
W.B. Eldridge to Mamie Kilgore, 21 Aug 1899 (23 Aug), W.G. Drummond MG, H.C. Benson W 3-23

- - - - - - - - - - - - -

ELKINS

MARRIAGES
James F. Elkins to Susan M. Lowe, 17 Sep 1854 (29 Sep), Samuel B. Harwell(?) MG 1-#459
Nathaniel H. Elkins to Jane Lowe, 26 July 1856 (no return) 1-#553

- - - - - - - - - - - - -

ELLIOTT

1880 CENSUS
J.A. Elliott 33: see J.W. Caldwell
1900 CENSUS
George Elliott 53 (Aug 1846-Wd 2-2)(Druggist), Maud 15 (Mar 1885), Robert 13 (July 1886), Martha S. HICKS 69 (m)(July 1830-Wd), May WITT 20 (ne)(Jan 1880), Sophia KENNEDY 32 (Oct 1867)(House Keeper) 14-213A-10/10
Hattie Elliott 12: see Elizabeth Shadrick
MARRIAGES
G.A. Elliott to T.C. Hicks, 19 Mar 1884 (same), S.H. Price MG 1-499
William A. Elliott to Sarah Ann Shadwick, 24 Ap 1886 (same), H.C. Neal ?? 1-486

- - - - - - - - - - - - -

ELLIS

1900 CENSUS
Charles D. Ellis 17, Zerelda M. 15, Habbe 13– see James H. Keylon
Florence Ellis 20: see Eli Gossett
Joseph Ellis 48 (Mar 1852-Ky/Ky/Ky), Sadney L. 42 (b) (Nov 1857-Ky/Ky/Ky), Jane ROGERS (B) 70 (Unk 1830-Wd 0-0)(Servant) 15-273B-94
Richard L. Ellis 35 (Nov 1864-Ky/Ky/Ky) 15-273B-103
Sam Ellis 40 (Sep 1859-M 21), Jane 39 (Feb 1861-M 21-10-10), William A. 20 (Ap 1880)(Watch Repairman), Annie C. 19 (Sep 1881), Maud E. 17 (Jan 1883), Mary V. 15 (July 1884), Miny C. 14 (Feb 1886), Bricy E. 12 (Jan 1887), Tattie L. 11 (May 1889), Winnie C. 8 (Nov 1891), Frank S. 6 (July 1893), Foyster K. 3 (Oct 1896), John STEEL 18 (boarder)(Mar 1882) 10-257B-140/144
Samuel H. Ellis 56 (Feb 1844-T/Mo/T-M 35), Elizabeth 51 (Nov 1848-Ga/Mo/NC-M 35-10-7), Benjamin 16 (July 1883-Ga)(Coal Miner), Samuel H. 15 (Ap 1885-Ga), John S. 11 (May 1889-Ga) 8-311B-23/24

MARRIAGES
Florence Ellis to J. W. Lowrey or Loury q.v.
Laura Ellis to W. T. Wilson q.v.
Laura Ellis to G. H. Harris q.v.
Nancy Ellis to G. W. Alley q.v.
Nannie Ellis to Floyd Jewell q.v.
Sarah Ellis to Michael W. McGentry q.v.
Sidney L. Ellis to Edna E. McDonald, 26 Sep 1900 (same), W.L. Patton MG, J.D. Ellis Jr. W 3-226

- - - - - - - - - - - - -

ELLISON / ELISON / ELLESON
(see also ALLISON)

1880 CENSUS
Wm Elleson 21, Allice 18 (w), Peter 49 (f), Susan 40 (m), Frank 12, Chumly 10, Seney 8, Alfred 4, Buten 2 8-18-152
1900 CENSUS
Cordall Elison 15: see Fill Suttles
Peter Ellison 68 (July 1831-M 45), Susan 60 (Mar 1840-T/Va/Va-M 45-11-5), Cyrus 20 (May 1880-M 1)(Fisherman), Minnie 14 (dl)(Aug 1885-M 1-0-0) 15-271B-65
MARRIAGES
C.D. Ellison to Mary Cofer, 24 May 1891, M.G. Center MG 4-26
Cyrus Ellison to Minnie Wilson, 27 June 1899 (same), J.A. Shelton MG 2-419
Elisha Ellison to Darthula Woodward, 9 June 1852 (10 June), Daniel Broyles JP 1-#376
Frank Ellison to Mattie Moore, 18 Jan 1889 (23 Jan), J. Shaver MG 1-554
Jane Ellison to James F. Campbell q.v.
Mary Ellison to William Rucker q.v.
Mattie Ellison to Sherman Wilson q.v.
Mattie E. Elison to Joseph L. Decker q.v.
Peter Ellison to Susan Campbell, 27 Oct 1856 (same), R.T. Howard MG 1-#575
Susan Ellison to Thomas Martin q.v.
Thomas Ellison to Jane Davis, 19 May 1852 (20 May), D. Broyles JP 1-#276
Wm Ellison to Alice Byerly, 1 May 1880 (2 May), J. Shaver MG 1-#1727
William Ellison to Lillie Morgan, 28 Ap 1896 (same), W.G. Curton MG & W 2-18

- - - - - - - - - - - - -

ELMER

MARRIAGE
Mary E. Elmer to George F. Gordin q.v.

- - - - - - - - - - - - -

ELROD

1900 CENSUS
David A. Elrod 26 (Mar 1874-Ga/Ga/Ga-M 2)(Iron Carrier), Hattie 33 (Oct 1866-Ga/Ga/Ga-M 2-0-0), Harry JONES 17 (ss)(Jan 1883)(Boiler Cleaner) 10-326A-123/127 (B)

MARRIAGE
D.A. Elrod to Hattie Jones, 2 June 1900 (3 June), J.D. Gaither MG & W 3-161

- - - - - - - - - - - - -

ELSEA / ELSEY / ELSIE / ELZY / ELSA / ELSED / ELSOR

1870 CENSUS
M. Elzy 20, Margarette M. 20, Martha L. 1/12 4-4-20

MARRIAGES
Edna Elsor to I. M. Stewart q.v.
John Elsa to Mary A. Shelton, 1 May 1854 (no return) 1-#440
Laura Elsie or Elzie to B.A. or B.H. Grans or Graves q.v.
Mary Elsey to James Fransise or Francisco q.v.
Mattie E. Elsie to W. V. Marler q.v.
Nancy Elzy to Jonathan Tallent q.v.
Nancy Elsey to Thomas Pendergrass q.v.
Perry Elsey to Lin or Lou Anna Capps, 30 Dec 1899 (31 Dec), W.R. Grimsley MG, J.A. Elsea W 3-101
Roby Elsea to Oddie Jones, 20 Nov 1899 (23 Nov), W.R. Grimsley MG, J.A. Elsea W 3-75
Sallie Elsed to L. M. Howell q.v.
Sarah Elsey to J. A. Bryant q.v.
Thomas Elsey or Elsia to Lula Rains, 24 Dec 1900 (25 Dec), W.R. Grimsley MG, Rufus Elsea W 3-260

- - - - - - - - - - - - -

EMERY / EMORY / EMBREE / HEMBREE

1860 CENSUS
Abraham Emory 47, Rhoda 46, James 18 2-71-486
1870 CENSUS– None
1880 CENSUS
Rebecca Hembree 61: see John Boles
1900 CENSUS
Aber Emery 55 (Mar 1845-M 38), Betsy 50 (Jan 1850-M 38-11-6), Frank 15 (Sep 1882), Delia DRILD 15 (ne)(Sep 1884), Robert 3/12 (c)(Feb 1900), Albert EMERY 7 (gs)(Dec 1892), McKinley 2 (gs)(Mar 1898), --?-- MALONE 25 (boarder)(Feb 1875), E.S.C. THOMAS 17 (boarder)(Mar 1883) 10-252B-49 (B)

MARRIAGES
James M. Emory to Martha J. Dotson, 28 Ap 1863 (no return) 1-#797
John Emory to Bettie Coggin, 19 Nov 1886 (21 Nov), C. Morgan JP 1-514
Joseph Emery to Hannah Jane Garrison, 19 May 1860 (same), T.H. McPherson JP 1-#712
Levi Emory to Susan M. Swafford, 3 Oct 1887 (6 Oct), W.A. Green JP 1-552
Margarett Emmory to James Cook q.v.
Mary Jane Emery to John Bowles q.v.
Nettie Emery or Emory to Thos J. Stuters or Stulee q.v.
Thomas Emory to Delila Robards, 4 Jan 1867 (10 Jan), P.G. Campbell JP 1-#928

- - - - - - - - - - - - -

EMMET / EMMIT

1900 CENSUS
Sarah Emmet 35 (Mar 1865-Wd 5-4), Mary 17 (Feb 1882), Andy 10 (Mar 1890), Mannie 6 (Nov 1893) 15-268B-14
MARRIAGE
Mary Emmit to Vance Huston q.v.

- - - - - - - - - - - - -

ENGLAND

1900 CENSUS
Andrew J. England 29 (Jan 1871-Ga/T/Ga-M 9)(Blacksmith), Lillian T. 30 (Dec 1869-Ky/Ga/Ky-M 9-1-1), Andrew C. 8 (Feb 1892) 10-322A-46/48
James England 38 (Feb 1862-M 15)(Grocery Salesman), Lulla 32 (Aug 1867-Ga/Ga/Ga-M 15-5-3), Edward F. 12 (Feb 1888), Carlton J. 9 (July 1890), Perry M. 5 (Oct 1894) 8-286B-366/368
Onis England 26, Oscar 17: see Charles Cook
Perry M. England 66 (Dec 1833-T/NC/T-M 48)(Blacksmith), Elizabeth 64 (Unk-M 48-12-6) 10-321B-39/41
MARRIAGES
A.J. England to Lillian T. Woollen, 12 Ap 1891, S.H. Hilliard MG 4-23
J.A. England to Mary A. Nelson, 19 Jan 1890 (same), R.A. Bartlett MG 1-598
Mary J. England to G. L. Litchfield q.v.
Rosa E. England to C. T. Jewell q.v.

- - - - - - - - - - - - -

ENGLISH

1900 CENSUS
Andrew J. English 56: see John B. Wyatt
MARRIAGE
A.J. English to C.A. Henderson, 14 Aug 1895, A.P. Hayes JP 4-82

- - - - - - - - - - - - -

ENOS / EEONIS / ENUS / ENNIS / ENOUS

1860 CENSUS
William Enus 34, Mary 23, Micheal R. 10, Mariah E. 7, Barbary T. 6, Lucinda 3, James T. 8/12 5-32-215
1870 CENSUS
Mary E. Ennis 46 (Ga), Martha F. 23 (Ala), William W. 22 (Ala), Alexander C. 19 (Ala), Thomas H. 17 (Ala), Austin C. 9 (Ala), Monroe A. 7 (Ala), Laurence M. 10/12 8-2-15
1880 CENSUS
Mary Enous 55, Thomas H. 26, Austin C. 19, Morow A. 16 5-9-80
MARRIAGES
Elizabeth Enos to James J. Thompson q.v.
Michail Enos to Margaritt S.(?) Walker, 30 July 1868 (same), J. Howard JP 1-#1020
Wm Eeonis to M.E. Barnell or Barnett, 4 Nov 1856 (6 Nov), R.T. Howard MG 1-#581

- - - - - - - - - - - - -

ENSLEY / INSLEY / ANSLEY
(see also HENSLEY)

1900 CENSUS
Agnes Insley 30, Lottie 8, Willie 7, Bertha 5: see Edward Jones
Andrew J. Ensley 25 (Nov 1874-T/NC/NC-M 5), Mary J. 25 (Dec 1874-M 5-1-1), John W. 3 (July 1896) 2-199A-153/158
George Ensley 22 (Ap 1878-T/NC/NC-M 5), Nervie E. 19 (Sep 1880-M 3-0-0) 2-197A-110/115
John C. Ensley 53 (Ap 1847-NC/NC/NC-M 31), Mary E. 54 (Mar 1846-NC/Ver/NC-M 31-12-10), John F. 20 (July 1879), Lucie M. 12 (Mar 1888), Robert 10 (Feb 1889), Cora B. 9 (Oct 1890) 2-197A-111/116
MARRIAGES
Jack Ensley to Mary Bell, 21 July 1895, A.M. Broyles JP 4-86
M.J. Ensley to James L. Garrison q.v.
W.J. Ansley(?) to Angess Jones, 31 Jan 1891, L.L.H. Carlock MG 4-24

- - - - - - - - - - - - -

ENSOR

1900 CENSUS
George P. Ensor 33 (Nov 1866-Ky/T/T-M 2), Sarah F. 19 (May 1881-M 2-0-0), Hattie T. 8 (d)(Feb 1892) 4-225B-236/240 (Ridge Road east of Spring City & Dayton Road)
MARRIAGE
John M. Ensor to Oliva Brandin, 9 Aug 1890 (same), A.W. Frazier JP 1-604

- - - - - - - - - - - - -

ERP / EARPS

MARRIAGES
Mattie Earps to Hass Elder q.v.
Viola Erp to George Newman q.v

- - - - - - - - - - - - -

ERWIN / ERWINE / ERVIN
(see also IRVIN)

1860 CENSUS
Dicey Ervin 45 (NC), Andrew J. 21, Eliza J. 24, Rosa 18, Amanda A. 17, Thomas H. 14 2-77-523
1870 CENSUS– None
1880 CENSUS
J.H. Erwin 55, Harry 24 (s), Hattie 20, Grace 14, Sam 12, Justus 10, Alice B. 3-21-171
1900 CENSUS
Andy Ervin 42 (Nov 1857-T/NC/NC-M 21)(Plasterer), Jennie J. 35 (Sep 1864-M 21-4-4), Emma 18 (Aug 1881), Walter 16 (June 1883), David 14 (Nov 1885), Floyd 12 (May 1888) 10-250B-18
Colum--?-- Ervin 27 (Feb 1873-M 8)(Coal Miner), Maggie 25 (Feb 1875-M 8-4-3), Dorsey W. 6 (June 1893), Albat F. 4 (June 1895), Annie M. 1 (May 1899), Walter 18 (b)(Jan 1882)(Coal Miner) 1-302B-233/243

Mary J. Ervin 44 (Unk 1856-T/NC/T-Wd 2-2)(Washwoman), Dock 18 (Ap 1881), James BROOKS 82 (f) (Unk 1818-T/NC/NC-M 57) 8-315B-111/115

MARRIAGES

E. Erwine to B. Harris q.v.

Harry J. Erwin (25, Cartersville, Ga) to Mollie Mills (22, Cleveland), 31 Aug 1881, J.W. Barkman MG, O.E. Mitchell (Atlanta, Ga) W 4-1(5)

Linn(?) Erwin to Maggie Holmes, 17 Oct 1891, W.C. Daily MG 4-31

Tennie Erwin to James Kellin q.v.

Tennie Erwin to L. Whitfield q.v.

William Erwin to Molly Gowins or Goins, 26 Dec 1896 (27 Dec), F.M. Cook MG, William Givens W 2-96

- - - - - - - - - - - - -

ESKRIDGE / ESKRICH

1880 CENSUS

Minnie Eskridge 11 (B)(Servant): see Nettie Roddy

1900 CENSUS

Henry Eskridge 19: see Mary H. Bunn (B)

Isam Eskridge 24 (Mar 1876-T/SC/T-M 1), Victoria 33 (May 1867-M 1-4-2), Ida DE LOINE* 19 (sd)(Jan 1881-T/Ala/T), Oliver 14 (ss)(June 1885-T/Ala/T) 8-311A-5/5 (B) [* probably DULANEY]

Marshal L. Eskridge 43 (Mar 1857-Wd)(Coal Miner), Millie 24 (d)(Unk) 10-327A-152/160 (B)

MARRIAGES

Isam Eskrich to Vie Dulaney, 20 Mar 1899 (same), J.W. Williamson MG, J.J. Hoge W 2-394

Wyley Eskridge to Letha Davis, 25 Dec 1894, L. Diggs MG 4-76

- - - - - - - - - - - - -

ESMINGER / ENSMINGER / ISEMINGER

1900 CENSUS

John T. Ensminger 60 (June 1839-Va/Va/Va-M 28), Sarah A. 56 (Jan 1844-M 28-3-3) 11-292B-68

Joseph Iseminger 82 (Feb 1818-Pa/Germany/Do-Wd)(Retired Merchant), Ellen 48 (d)(Feb 1852-Wisc/Pa/Oh) 13-305A-287/297

MARRIAGE

Martha Esminger* to B. F. Sykes q.v.
[*looks more like Jennings in one place]

- - - - - - - - - - - - -

ESSEX / ESSICK

1860 CENSUS

James Essex 16, Ann 7: see Henry Miller

Louisa Essex 38, Simpson 18, Abbert 16, Lewis P. 12, Louvenea C. 9, Polly A. 6, Elizabeth P. 4, Evaline A. 2 4-41-277

Mary Essex 40 (NC), Prisulla 21, John 18, William A. 13, George W. 12, Mary 10, Cordelia 2 4-43-291

1870 CENSUS

John Essex 26, Sarah J. 19, John N. 1 4-17-115
[John married Sarah Jane Serrett on 31 Jan 1867 in McMinn Co]

Lemoneus Essex 7: see Hugh L.W. Ferguson

Mary Essick 47 (NC), James H. 25, Cordela 12 (Student) 4-11-70

1880 CENSUS

A. or H. Essex 35 (Painter), M.A. 27 (w), Catharine 11/12 4-10-77

John Essex 37, S.J. 30 (w), J.H. 11 (s), S.M. 8 (d), W.A. 5 (s), G.T. 3 (s), R.C. 2/12 (s) 4-4-29

L.P. Essex 28, M.A. 26, T.A. 6, R.M. 5, Ada 3, Miles WHITE 19 (boarder)(Painter) 4--23

S. Essex 30: see S. T. Blevins

1900 CENSUS

Louis P. Essex 55 (Ap 1855[sic]-Wd), Charles A. 15 (June 1884), Mollie 14 (May 1886), Kate 11 (July 1888), Brown 8 (Aug 1891) 4-225A-223/227 (Back Valley Road)

Samuel Essex 18: see Moses Grier

Samuel H. Essex 18, Mollie C. 16: see Elmore Holloway

MARRIAGES

Adelia Essex to Owen Brown q.v.

J.F. Essex to Susannah Waller, 15 July 1874 (16 July), J.P. Roddy MG 1-#1343

Mary Jane Essex to Christopher C. Carroll q.v.

Perscilla Essex to William Pritchett q.v.

- - - - - - - - - - - - -

ETHERLY / ETHERLEY

1870 CENSUS

Alfred Etherley 40, Mary 50, Mollie 10 6-15-108 (B)

1880 CENSUS

Alfred Etherly 58, Mary 56, Mary McCARTY 20 ("husband left"), Cara T. 1, Lucinda COWAN 100 (m) 10-26-200/206 (B) (Mu)

1900 CENSUS

Alford Etherley 63 (Aug 1836-M 6), Lucy 39 (Aug 1860-Ga/Ga/Ga-M 6-1-0), Dollie GRIFFIE 17 (boarder)(Jan 1882) 10-257A-131/135 (B)

MARRIAGE

Alfred Etherly to Lucy Roberts, 15 Nov 1891, S. Washington MG 4-46

- - - - - - - - - - - - -

ETHERTON

MARRIAGE

Nancy J. Etherton to Andrew Webb q.v.

- - - - - - - - - - - - -

EUVERAND / EUVRARD

1900 CENSUS

Joseph E. Euvrard 41 (Sep 1858-Oh/France/Do-M 15), Myrtie E. 36 (Sep 1863-Oh/Oh/Oh-M 15-2-2), Laurence R. 13 (June 1886), Morris W. 11 (Sep 1888) 11-292A-48

Noah H. Euvrand 46 (Oct 1853-Oh/France/Do-M 17), Lizzie N. 43 (May 1858-Ill/Oh/Oh-M 17-0-0) 11-290B-19

MARRIAGE

J.E. Euverand to Myrtie E. Holmes, 5 Jan 1885 (8 Jan), J.H. Snow MG 1-463

- - - - - - - - - - - - -

EVANS / EVENS / EVINS

1860 CENSUS

Austin J. Evans 42, Malinda 48, Moses 18, Emily 20, Esquire 16, James 12, Austin J. 10, William R. EDINGTON 27 9-101-689

John S. Evans 45 (Sadler), Elizabeth 45, Lucy 18, Sarah 16, Ann 14, Quintina 12, Adelia 6, Mary MOORE 68, Christina EVANS 28, Eliza 40 6-112-765

Joseph Evans 40, Sarah J. 38, James G. 13, Clementine 10, John H. 7, Thomas H. 4, Joseph E. 4 5-31-207

1870 CENSUS

Aaron Evans 60, Robert 18 (B): see Joseph S. Evans

Austin Evans 44, Malinda 50, Emily 28, Moses 26, Squire 24, James 22, Austin 20, Lucinda C. 22, Emily A. 1 1-6-37

Joseph S. Evans 50, Sarah J. 48, James G. 23, Clementine 20, John H. 17, Thomas H. 14, Joseph E. 14, Robert F. 5, Mary WREN 74, Aaron EVANS (B) 60, Robert EVANS (B) 18 5-3-19

Lucy Evans 26, Sarah 24, Ann 22, Quintine 20, Delila 15 1-1-6

William Evans 60 (SC), Sarah 50 (SC), Sarah J. 16, William H. 13, James M.J. 13 7-6-45

1880 CENSUS

Aaron Evans 69, June 40, Wm H. 7, Sona A. 6, Gebert E. 4, Neugeni 1 5-8-77 (B)

Austin Evans 63, Malinda 73, Moses 35, Emily 38, Esquire 33, Jackson 20 1-8-64

Charlie Evans 9 (Mu): see Rebecca Hoyal

Joseph S. Evans 60, Sarah J. 58, James G. 33, Clementine 30, John H. 27, Thomas H. 24, Jo E. 24, Robert F. 15, Mary* 84 (m), Christina 56 (d of Mary) 5-6-47 [*last name not shown, but should be MOORE or WREN]

Robert Evans 29, Manda L. 27, Sarah E. 8, Gimima A. 6, Ansker W. 5, Mattie J. 3, Lula W. 7/12 5-6-50 (B)

Sarah Evans 32, Hugh LOCKE 20 (uw), Parthena 19 (ne), Delta 5/12 (ne) 1-11-92

1900 CENSUS

Albert Evans 46 (Ap 1854-M 17), Mary E. 12 (Oct 1867-M 17-6-4), Anna M. 13 (Dec 1886), John E. 11 (Feb 1889), Willie E. 9 (Feb 1891), Samuel A. 7 (May 1893) 8-281A-249/251

Conrad Evans 65 (June 1834-NC/NC/NC-M ?), Martha 59 (May 1841-NC/NC/NC-M ?-0), Caswell WHEELER 54 (May 1846-Wd 1-1)(Servant), Adra 15 (Dec 1884) 14-221B-158/162

James Evans 53 (May 1847-M 24), Lith 43 (Oct 1856-M 24-4-4), Addie 21 (Aug 1878), Charles 19 (Oct 1880), Ader 16 (June 1884), Auther 13 (Nov 1889), James A. THOMPSON 21 (boarder)(Sep 1870)(RR Hand) 1-187B-171/180

John Evans 28: see Sarah J. Snow

John E. Evans 40 (1860-T/Va/Va-Wd)(Cobbler), Samuel 44 (1886), Jesse 8 (1892), Mary MADDISON 20 (d)(Oct 1879-M 2-1-1), James 23 (sl)(Mar 1877-M 2), Grace 6/12 (gd)(Dec 1899) 8-315B-99/103 (B)

Joseph E. Evans 44 (Mar 1856-S), Clemmie 50 (si)(Feb 1850-S) 5-234A-126

Maggie F. Evans 41 (June 1858-Wd 1-1), James F. 13 (s) (Sep 1886), Elizabeth FORD 67 (m)(Oct 1832-Wd 1-1) 5-234A-127

Mary Evans 14: see James G. Thomison

Oscar Evans 20: see John Bolin

Oster J. Evens 50 (Nov 1847-M 15), Mary 30 (Jan 1869-M 16-0-0) 1-188B-187/196

Sarah Evens 35 (Ap 1865-Wd 6-6), Charley 16 (July 1883), Dock 14 (Jan 1886), James 12 (Mar 1888), Elic 5 (Dec 1894), Andy 3/12 (Mar 1899) 12-182A-72/75

Squire Evans 55 (Jan 1845-Wd), Emmie 50 (si)(Ap 1850), Mose 54 (b)(Ap 1846) 1-187B-172/181

Thomas H. Evans 44 (Mar 1856-M 14), Hortense V. 35 (May 1865-M 14-3-1), Ladie H. 9 (Feb 1891) 5-233B-112

MARRIAGES

A.J. Evans to Mary E. Hinds, 1 Dec 1883 (2 Dec), F.L. Long JP 1-473

Annie Evans to J. F. Holloway q.v.

B.A. Evans to Sallie Hayes, 29 Ap 1885 (same), W.S. Hale MG 1-496

Ella Evans to James Banks q.v.

Essquire Evans to Lucind C. Gibson, 29 Dec 1866 (30 Dec), J.B. McCaleb MG 1-#926

Hiram Evins to Sarah L. Row, 27 Aug 1851 (28 Aug), A.D. Paul JP 1-#246

J.G. Evins to Maggee Ford, 21 Oct 1885 (same), A.P. Early MG 1-490

J.L. Evens to Jenni M. Marsh, 9 Sep 1886 (same), John Howard MG 1-506

James Evens to Lila Ann Hinds, 23 Jan 1875 (24 Jn), J.P. Roddy MG 1-#1389

Jemimah Evens to Joseph McDonald q.v.

John Evans to Susie Evens, 9 Nov 1889 (10 Nov), W.S. Hale MG 1-586

Lena R. Evens to J. G. Thomison q.v.

Mart Evens to Hannah Byerley, 26 May 1893, G.W. Brewer MG 4-59

Mary Evens to Addison Locke q.v.

Mattie R. Evans to Dwight P. Egarton q.v.

Moses Evans to Sarah Hays, 8 Nov 1888 (16 Nov), W.G. West MG 1-562

Ocina Evans to Charley Matlock q.v.

Susie Evens to John Evans q.v.

Thomas Evens to Annie Cool(?), 27 Dec 1890 (27 Dec 1889)[sic], L. Harworth MG 1-591

William Evans to Nancy J. Breeding, 17 Oct 1873 (21 Oct), John Howard MG 1-#1305

William Evans to Mary A. Williams, 16 Dec 1889 (same), W.S. Cagle ?? 1-598

\- - - - - - - - - - - - -

EVERETT / EVRETT / EVART / EVERITT / AVERETT

1860 CENSUS

George W. Everet 23, Martha E. 19, Margaret A. 1 8-20-134

John Everet 24, Elizabeth 21, Margaret J. 1 8-17-113

William D. Everett 61 (SC), Elenor 40, John H. 20, James 18 10-28-91

1870 CENSUS

David Everet 24: see John H. Coalman

James J. Everett 25, Sarah A. 19, William J. 2, Mary T. 7/12 6-16-113

Margarette H. Everet 11, Martha E. 7: see Robert F. Alexander
William D. Everett 71 (SC), Elenor 61 (SC), Nancy MORGAN 40, Joseph A. 14, John W. 12, Mary E. 10, William D.S. 7 8-5-33

1880 CENSUS

Isaac Everet 35, William 12, M.T. 10, J.F. 9, Jane 5, Ida 2: see E.L. Campbell
J. B. Evart 31, Cardine 23 (w), F. J. 5 (d), M. E. 3 (d) 11-37-303
J. B. Evert or Erant 32, Caroline 25, S. J. 5 (d), M. E. 1 (d) 11-40-321
W.D. Avrett 81, Nancy MORGAN 40, James 16 8-12-103

1900 CENSUS

George W. Everett 65 (Dec 1834-M 43), Martha E. 59 (June 1840-T/Va/T-M 43-10-8), George W. Jr. 24 (Jan 1876-Ky)(Coal Miner), Lorenzo D. 17 (June 1882-Ky), Nettie L. 15 (July 1884) 13-295A-97/98
James Everitt 28 (Feb 1872-M 7), Mary 25 (Sep 1874-M 7-3-2), James B. 6 (Mar 1894), Walter J. 11/12 (June 1899) 8-287A-374/376
Joseph B. Everett 52 (Feb 1848-Ala/Ala/Ala-M 25), Caroline 44 (Dec 1855-M 25-8-5), Sarah J. 24 (Oct 1875), Martha E. 22 (Mar 1878), Henry J. 16 (Dec 1883), Mollie 13 (May 1887), Ruthie P. 9 (June 1890) 13-308B-357/370
Rufus H. Everett 31 (Nov 1868-Wd), Earl C. 7 (Jan 1893), Samuel R. 4 (Sep 1895), Dewey L. 1 (Oct 1898) 13-295A-97/99

MARRIAGES

Allis Everett to Right Raines q.v.
Delcina Everett to John W. Gilliam q.v.
Elizabeth W. Everett to R. A. Alexander q.v.
G.W. Everett to Crate or Cate Morgan, 7 July 1900 (8 July), W.R. Grimsley MG, J.F. Ivey W 3-185
George W. Everett to Martha Barger, 8 Feb 1858 (10 Feb), W.M. Morgan JP 1-#629
Ina Everett to John Zunistian q.v.
J.D. Everett to Martha Arnold, 8 Aug 1894, J.Q. Shaver MG 4-66
J.I. Everett to Sarah Jane Thurman, 3 Oct 1867 (same), John Howard MG 1-#973
James Everett to Mary J. Grice, 3 Aug 1893, S.S. Franklin JP 4-60
John W. Everett to Elizabeth Barger, 1 Ap 1858 (same), W. M. Morgan JP 1-#636
M. J. Everett to Jacob M. Kelly q.v.
Martha E. Evrett to John W. Clouse q.v.
Sallie J. Evrett or Everett to John Marshall q.v.

- - - - - - - - - - - - -

EVERLEY– see EBERLY

- - - - - - - - - - - - -

EWERS

1900 CENSUS

John E. Ewers 34 (Oct 1842-Oh/Oh/Oh-M 34)(Butcher), Martha M. 57 (Oct 1842-Oh/Oh/Oh-M 34-?), Richard 21 (s)(Feb 1879)(Butcher) 10-320B-4/4
John T. Ewers 24 (May 1876-Oh/Oh/Oh-M 4)(Coal Miner), Nellie G. 24 (Sep 1875-Kan/Ky/Ind-M 4-2-2), Ralph M. 4 (Ap 1896), Bessie M. 2 (Jan 1898) 11-290A-5

MARRIAGES

Ada I. Ewers to J. H. Morgan q.v.
John Ewers to Nellie Toel, 14 July 1895, J.H. Morgan JP 4-91

- - - - - - - - - - - - -

EWING

1870 CENSUS

James G. Ewing 37, Elizabeth 39, Benjamin 15, Jacob 14 Barton 8, Anna A. 7, Ezekiel B. 5 3-13-90

1880 CENSUS

James Ewing 53, C. 50, B.M. 27 (s), J.E. 24 (s), B.M. 17 (s), A.A. 15 (d), E.D. 12 (s), F.J. 9 (d), M.A. 7 (d) 3-22-180

1900 CENSUS

Arthur C. Ewing 63 (Feb 1837-M 42), Sarah F. 58 (July 1841-M 42-4-4) 2-194A-55/57
Bart Ewing 38 (Feb 1862-M 12), Sue 36 (Jan 1864-M 12-6-3), Lela 11 (Jan 1889), Robert 8 (Jan 1892), Jacob 6 (Nov 1893), Beatrice 3 (Unk 1896), Alice 1 (Feb 1898) 3-207B-130/143 [Bart W. Ewing married Susan L. Paul on 28 Feb 1888 in Meigs County]
Elijah B. Ewing 34 (Ap 1866-M 4)(Leather Manufacturer), Julia C. 28 (May 1872-M 4-2-2), Annie B. 2 (Oct 1897), Addie L. 8/12 (July 1899), Georgia THOMAS 19 (Ap 1881)(Servant), --?-- LOVE 33 (boarder)(Dec 1866-NC/NC/Mass)(Tanner & Curier) 14-215A-42/43 [E.B. Ewing married Julia Dickel on 30 Sep 1896 in Meigs County]
Elizabeth Ewing 72 (Ap 1828-Wd 8-6), Jacob 46 (Nov 1853) 3-207A-128/139
Jacob B. Ewing 38 (Dec 1861-M 5), Mary L. 29 (Dec 1870-Tex/T/T-M 5-1-1), Eva Leni 1 (Ap 1899), Elvina FRAZIER 63 (ml)(Feb 1837-Wd 6-1) 2-194A-54/56
John M. Ewing 40 (Aug 1853-M 19), Mattie E. 37 (Nov 1862-M 19-0-0) 2-195B-83/86

MARRIAGES

A. A. Ewing to J. W. Vineyard q.v.
Amanda A. Ewing to H. T. Roddy q.v.
Lennie L. Ewing or Erving to J. W. Moneton q.v.

- - - - - - - - - - - - -

FAIN

1900 CENSUS

Jasper S. Fain 25 (Ap 1875-Indian Territory/Ga/Ga-M 5) (Coal Miner), Sally 20 (Mar 1880-T/Mo/Mo-M 5-3-2), William 4 (Sep 1895), Bessie 2 (July 1897), Gustavas 15 (b)(Ap 1885-Ga/Ga/Ga) 13-303A-237/247

MARRIAGE

Jasper Fain to Sallie Majors, 16 July 1894, R.S. Mason JP 4-66
Sarah E. Fain to Joseph T. Richey q.v.

- - - - - - - - - - - - -

FAIR

1900 CENSUS

James Fair 37 (Mar 1863-NC/Md/NC-M 6)(Coal Miner), Belle 27 (Dec 1872-Ala/Ala/Ala-M 6-0-0) 10-328B-176/186 (B)

- - - - - - - - - - - - -

FAIRBANKS / FURBANKS

1900 CENSUS

Alice Fairbanks 15, Anna P.(?) 11: see Thos J. Mathews

Andrew Fairbanks 53 (Ap 1847-M 26), Mandy 43 (Feb 1857-M 26-11-7), Henry 17 (Sep 1883), Ethel 15 (Sep 1885), Minerva 13 (Oct 1887), Samuel 11 (Mar 1889), Thursday 9 (Sep 1891), Wilburn 2 (Oct 1897) 15-268A-5

Dallie Furbanks 10, Charles 9, Earnest 7, Oscar 3: see Charles Nelson

MARRIAGE

Emma Fairbanks to Charley Nelson q.v.

- - - - - - - - - - - - -

FANN

1870 CENSUS

James M. Fann 38, Jane 42 (NC), Syntha M. 13, Sarah E. 10, George W. 6, Catharine 3, James L. 2 8-8-47

MARRIAGES

Byrd Fann to Maggie Morgan, 14 or 24 Feb 1895, C.E. Money(?) JP 4-78

E. N. Fann to F. M. Capps q.v.

W.H. Fann to Salvina Mills, 22 July 1883 (same), J.H. Pence MG 1-476

- - - - - - - - - - - - -

FARMER

1880 CENSUS

Daniel Farmer 23, Mahala 46 (m), Mary CARROLL 48 (a) (Washwoman), William 8 (c) 2-39-320

1900 CENSUS

Edward J. Farmer 26 (May 1874-M 4)(Coal Miner), Rosella 25 (May 1875-M 4-1-1), Lee W. 1 (Dec 1898) 13-306B-321/333

Lewis Farmer 36 (Oct 1863-M 10), Roda E. 33 (Sep 1866-M 10-2-2), William J. 9 (Feb 1891), Della M. 5 (May 1895) 9-229A-31

- - - - - - - - - - - - -

FARNER

1870 CENSUS

David Farner 14: see Ira M. Whittenburg

George Farner 23, Cathern 25, Sarah J. 6, Nancy L. 5, Mary A. 3, William 1 2-8-55

1880 CENSUS

George Farner 34, Catharine 38, Sarah 15, Nancy 14, Mary 11, William 10, Thomas 7, Benjamin 5, Delia 1 2-34-276

1900 CENSUS

George W. Farner 58 (May 1858-M 38), Cathran 58 (Feb 1842-M 38-4-4), Sarah 35 (Jan 1865), Thomas 21 (May 1879), Bengamon 13 (Dec 1886), Bera 11 (ne) (July 1888) 1-183B-97/101

MARRIAGES

George W. Farner to Catharine Hardbarger, 10 Mar 1864 (no return) 1-#824

Nancy L. Farner to F. M. Godsey q.v.

- - - - - - - - - - - - -

FAULKNER / FALKNER

1860 CENSUS

Martha Falkner 12: see Samuel McAdoo

MARRIAGE

John Faulkner to Amanda Green, 12 May 1884 (15 May), W.R. Clack JP 1-465

- - - - - - - - - - - - -

FAWGER

1860 CENSUS

James P. Fawger(?) 15, Mary J. 12: see Susan Munday

- - - - - - - - - - - - -

FELTY

1900 CENSUS

Della Felty 30: see Ambrose Griffith

- - - - - - - - - - - - -

FENIRAN

1880 CENSUS

John Feniran 36: see John Lee

- - - - - - - - - - - - -

FENNAN / FERMAN

MARRIAGES

George Fennan or Ferman to Flora E. Morgan, 8 Sep 1886 (9 Sept), M.C. Bruner MG 1-506

- - - - - - - - - - - - -

FEREE / FERRIE

1900 CENSUS

John F. Feree 40 (Ap 1860-Oh/Oh/Oh-M 13)(Store Clerk), Carie 52 (My 1868-Oh/Oh/Oh-M 13-0)(Matron) 12-179A-5/6

MARRIAGE

John S. Ferrie to Carrie E. Niles, 21 Nov 1887 (24 Nov), C.B. Riggs ?? 1-543

- - - - - - - - - - - - -

FERGUSON / FURGUSON / FURGUSSON / FURGERSON

1860 CENSUS

Edward Ferguson 44 (Ky), Salina W. 44, Sarilda A. 17, Harrell C. 13, Jemima J. 10, Judy E. 8, Rachel J. 3, Edward H. 1 1-89-610

James C. Fergason 50, Hugh L.W. 23, John T. 21, Addison L. 16 4-41-279

John H. Ferguson 38 (NC), Martha 40 (Ky), Lewis W. 16 (Ky), William H. 14 (Ky), Elisah 12 (Ky), Hugh 10 (Ky), Edward L. 8 (Ky), John A. 6, Jacob V. 3, George W. 1, Elizabeth WRIGHT 61 (NC) 1-84-571

Levi Fergason 58 (NC), Elizabeth 56 (NC), John H. 20, Jane 11 4-42-284

Lewis C. Fergason 37, Martha E. 22, Mary A. 3, Wright S. 2, Isaac BROWN 17 4-44-295

Miller M. Fergason 23, Vesta J. 17, Mary E. 8/12 1-88-601
Robert Ferguson 64 (NC), Mary A. 32, William T. 8, Margaret NEELE 19 4-42-282
Samuel B. Fergason 68 (NC), Enoch D. 16, Cynthia R. 13, James A. 11, Robert N. 4 4-42-283

1870 CENSUS

Hugh L.W. Ferguson 33, Texas A. 21, Patrick 3, Tennessee 1, James C. FERGUSON 60, Lemoneus ESSEX 7 4-13-82
John T. Ferguson 30, Margarette A. 26, Mary Jane 8, Emily L. 4, James J. 2 4-13-81
Levi W. Ferguson 69 (NC), Elizabeth 35, Elvira 10, George 9, Henry 7, Robert 3 4-11-75
Lewis C. Ferguson 46, Martha 32, Mary Ann 13, Wright S. 12, Margarette J. 10, John H. 7, Eliza D. 5, Peter W. 3, Orpha E. 5/12 5-9-65
Milan M. Ferguson 33, Mary E. 11, Lorinda A. 1 1-8-50
Samuel B. Ferguson 77 (NC), Elizabeth 36, Robert M. 15 4-14-90
Vesta Ferguson 30, Samantha 10, William T. 7, Josephine 3 4-13-88
William T. Ferguson 18, Pessy J. 10: see George W. Marshall

1880 CENSUS

H.L.W. Ferguson 43, Texas 25 (w), P.T. 13 (s), T.D. 10 (d), J. 8 (d), A.C. 6 (s), H.C. 3/12 (s), J.C. FERGUSON 72 (f), S.(?)N. 43 (c) 11-42-333
J.T. Ferguson 41, A.P. 31 (w), M.J. 17 (d), E.L. 14 (d), J.J. 11 (s), R. 7 (s), A.P. 3 (d), A.B. 5/12 (d), A.L. FERGUSON 18 (boarder) 4-3-25
L.C. Fergusson 56, Martha E. 42, Margaret J. 20, John H. 17, Eliza D. 15, Peter W. 13, Orpha E. 11, Nancy W. 9, Anney A. 4, Stonwall J. 2 5-3-26
L.W. Ferguson 79, Elizabeth 44 (w), George 18, Henry 16, Robert 14, Harry(?) 10 4-3-18
Lorinda Ferguson 10: see Franklin Waterhouse
S.B. Ferguson 89, Elizabeth 40 (w) 4-3-22

1900 CENSUS

Arthur C. Ferguson 27 (July 1872-M 7), Minnie L. 25 (Sep 1874-Oh/Pa/Oh-M 7-3-3), Arthur R. 6 (Aug 1893), Carroll 4 (Dec 1895), Rosco W. 2 (July 1897) 5-233A-105 [Arthur Craig Ferguson married Minnie Lee Defenderfer on 9 Oct 1892]
Emma F. Ferguson 31, Carrie B. 6: see Andrew J. Wyrick
Hugh L. Ferguson 63 (Oct 1836-M 33), Texas A. 49 (July 1850-M 33-13-12), Farley B. 20 (Mar 1880), Ella B. 17 (Sep 1882), Kate E. 16 (Mar 1884), Lillie M. 12 (July 1887), Charles R. 10 (Feb 1890), Blanch P. 2 (May 1898) 14-222B-182/186
John Ferguson 24, Thomas 21: see Wesley Britt
John T. Ferguson 61 (Aug 1838-M 26), Amanda P. 52 (Ap 1848-M 26-7-5), Adda P. 23 (Mar 1877) 4-224B-220/224 (Back Valley Road)
Patrick T. Furguson 32 (Nov 1867-M 9)(Dry Goods Salesman), Anna A. 29 (May 1872-M 9-1-1), Lillie W. 8 (Dec 1891) 2-199A-150-155
Richard T. Ferguson 27 (Aug 1872-M ?), Flora B. 23 (Ap 1877-M ?), James J. 31 (b)(Nov 1868-M 0)(Teamster), Milo HOLLOWAY 18 (Nov 1881)(Servant, Farm Laborer) 4-224B-221/225 (Back Valley Road)
William P. Ferguson 26 (Mar 1874-M 1), Malinda E. 28 (Mar 1872-M 1-0-0), Thomas SHARP 26 (boarder) (Mar 1874) 5-232B-89
Wilum Furguson 54 (May 1846-Oh/Pa/Pa-M 23), Sarah 51 (Jan 1849-Oh/Oh/Oh-M 23-2-2) 12-180B-52/55

MARRIAGES

Adda W. Ferguson to Oscar L. Barton q.v.
Allice Ferguson to John Sharp q.v.
Bethiah Furgusson to Adam Wyrick q.v.
Bettie Furguson to W. P. Runyan q.v.
C. C. Ferguson to Cornelia Devaney, 24 Oct 1888 (same), J.L. Prater ?? 1-562
Eliza Furgusson to W. H. Miller q.v.
Elizabeth Furgusson to L. W. Furgusson q.v.
Elvira Furguson to James Monday q.v.
Emma Ferguson to Robert W. Thompson q.v.
Granville T. Furguson to Mary Devaney, 20 or 30 Dec 1895, W.L. Patton MG 4-78
H.L.W. Furgusson to Texanna Wassom, 9 Dec 1865 (no return) 1-#855
Hester Ferguson to John Sullivan q.v.
J.C. Furgerson to L. Davis, 29 Sep 1859 (same), L.H. Long JP 1-#1658
J.J. Furguson to Hortense Schoolfield, 7 Dec 1899 (10 Dec), J.E. McKey(?) MG, E.E. Gannaway W 3-81
Jamia Furgusson to Thomas Bandy q.v.
John Furgusson to Permelia Ryburn, 27 Dec 1854 (30 Dec), A.D. Paul JP 1-#476
John T. Furgusson to Ann Foust, 28 Mar 1861 (no return) 1-#749
John T. Furgusson to Amanda P. McChristian, 7 Nov 1871 (no return) 1-#1215
John M. Ferguson to Stacy M. Allison, 22 June 1850 (same), S.F. Foust JP
Josie Ferguson to Wesley Wade q.v.
Julia Ann Ferguson to James McCabe q.v.
L.C. Furgusson to Martha E. Miller, 3 July 1855 (24 July), Levi W. Furguson JP 1-#507
L.L. Ferguson to Ellen M. Riddle, 19 Oct 1890, P.J. O'FARREL ?? 4-24
Lee Ferguson to Silena Hicks, 27 May 1889 (same), W.M. Morgan JP 1-575
Levi W. Furgusson to Elizabeth Furgusson, 27 Sep 1862 (no return) 1-#788
M. Furgusson to James Martin q.v.
Mary A. Furgusson to G. W. Marshall q.v.
Mary A. Furguson to Jonas Boofer q.v.
Mary A. Furgusson to William McCully q.v.
Mary Ann Furgusson to Samuel Travis q.v.
Milow M. Furgusson to Vesta J. Waterhouse. 27 Oct 1858 (no return) 1-#663
P.T. Ferguson to Annie A. Wassom, 25 Nov 1890, J.A. Darr MG 4-28
P.W. Ferguson to Emma Wyrick, 3 Nov 1892, Daniel Broyles JP 4-47
Peter Ferguson to Della Edmonds, 11 Mar 1892, "not solomonized" 4-42
Polk Feruson to Liste(?) Mitchell, 20 Mar 1895, J.F. Hash ?? 4-81
Robert Furgusson to Polly Ann Neal, 31 Aug 1857 (1 Sep), John O. Torbett JP 1-#612
S. R. A. Furgusson to G. H. Hale q.v.
Samantha E. Furgusson to Jacob L. Wasson q.v.
Samuel B. Furgusson to Elizabeth Dawson, 12 Feb 1861 (no return) 1-#745
Sarah Furgusson to William G. Mitchell q.v.
Sarah J. Feruson to G. F. Taylor q.v.

T.H. Ferguson to May Nash, 8 Sep 1900 (9 Sep), Henegar Morgan JP, H.C. Morgan W 3-212
Tennie Ferguson to Floyd Gallahan q.v.
Terza Jane Furguson to Ed Ganaway q.v.
Young Furguson to Bell Cash, 24 Oct 1899 (bond only), J.C. Schoolfield W 3-59

- - - - - - - - - - - - -

FERMAN– see FENNAN

- - - - - - - - - - - - -

FERRETER

MARRIAGE
Mary Ferreter to Cornelius Haley q.v.

- - - - - - - - - - - - -

FIELDING

1880 CENSUS
G.W. Fielding 21, Hettie 16 (w) 3-24-196

- - - - - - - - - - - - -

FIELDS / FRILD / FRIDDS

1900 CENSUS
Delia Frild 15, Robert 3/12: see Aber Emery (B)
George Fields 57 (June 1842-M 13)(Carpenter), Mattie 38 (Oct 1861-M 13-2-2), Albert 18 (Nov 1881)(Coal Miner), Ida BAKER 22 (d)(Aug 1877-M 2-1-1), Mattie 6/12 (gd)(Nov 1899) 8-283A-289/291
MARRIAGE
George Fridds to Mattie Jaquish, 6 June 1896 (same), W.L. Lillard JP, R.J. Killough W 2-27
Mary Fields to Primus(?) Gollaher q.v.

- - - - - - - - - - - - -

FIFER

1900 CENSUS
William Fifer 32 (June 1867-NC/NC/NC-M 1)(RR Section Hand), Irene 29 (July 1870-Va/Va/Va-M 1-0-0), Raymond 7 (ward)(May 1893), Rosie KNOX 4 (ward) (Mar 1896), William CAMPBELL 20 (boarder)(May 1880-Ala/Ala/Ala)(Furnaceman) 10-330B-223/237 (B)

- - - - - - - - - - - - -

FIKE

MARRIAGES
Jane Fike to James White q.v.
John Fike to Margaret Porter, 23 Feb 1861 (no return) 1-#747

- - - - - - - - - - - - -

FILLERS

1900 CENSUS
William D.(?) Fillers 26 (Ap 1874-Ga/Ga/Ga-M 1), Cora A. 21 (June 1878-M 1-1-1), Robert L. 7 (May 1893-Ga), Jesse N. 3 (Dec 1894-Ga), Clara B. 7/12 (Oct 1899) 14-221B-157/161
MARRIAGE
William Fillers to Cora Jones, 10 Dec 1898 (11 Dec), R.A. Dickson JP, W.I. Fillers & R.J. Killough W 2-355

- - - - - - - - - - - - -

FILLS

MARRIAGE
Cassa Fills to B. L. Sherly q.v.

- - - - - - - - - - - - -

FILYAN / FILYOW / FILYAW / FELYAW / FILYOE / FILUMN / PHILYAN

1860 CENSUS
John Fillyow 28 (NC), Rue 27, James A. 6, Matelda 2, Nancy QUILLEN 49, John COXEY 8 4-47-321
1870 CENSUS
John Felyaw 41 (NC), Raicy(?) 40, James A. 16, Matilda 11, William 10, Nancy 5, John 3, George W. 9/12, Nancy QUILLEN 63 (NC), John P. 17 3-1-6
1880 CENSUS
James Filyoe 26, Eliza 27, Susan 6, Joseph 3, Sarah MARTIN 46 (ml) 1-9-68
John Philyan 53, Rose 52, Nancy 16, John 13, G.W. 12 (s), Nancy QUILAN 75 (m) 4-35-288
Nancy Filyan 16: see H. A. Ames
William Filyoe 19, Mary 23, Ada 11/12 1-10-80
1900 CENSUS
George Filumn 30 (May 1870-M 11), Nancy 28 (Jan 1872-M 11-5-4), Edward 6 (Jan 1894), Mable 4 (June 1895), Ruyer(?) 2 (d)(Aug 1897), Hugh 9/12 (Jan 1900), Brits 70 (m)(Jan 1830-Wd), May 26 (si)(Ap 1894) 1-188B-192/201
James Filyow 48 (Jan 1852-M 22), Jane 48 (May 1852-M 22-11-5), John 17 (May 1882), Nannie 15 (Feb 1885), Penny 12 (Jan 1888), Lilly 10 (Dec 1889) 6-246A-120/121
MARRIAGES
Ada Filyaw to W. R. Gilliam q.v.
Ella Filyan to W. H. Shadden q.v.
G.W. Filyaw to Nancy Durham, 1 Sep 1888 (2 Sep), J.P. Roddy MG 1-549
James Filyan to Jane Thompson, 18 Jan 1875 (19 Jan), W.H. Dodd MG 1-#1387

- - - - - - - - - - - - -

FINCH

1900 CENSUS
Hallie Finch 15: see Charles W. Irwin

- - - - - - - - - - - - -

FINE

1860 CENSUS
Isaac Fine 35, Rebecca D. 34, Margaret A. 6, Susan C. 2, Florence M. 2/12 2-74-506
John H. Fine 28, Calesta 29, Cynthia M. 6, Catharine L. 4, Vineth A. 1 2-74-505

Margaret Fine 30, Jacob 22, Mahaly E. 20, Elijah 17, Mary J. 15, Evaline 13, Philip 11, Betsy A. 9, Daniel 7, Susan 5, Adelia 3, John W. DICKEY 6/12 2-77-520
Margaret A. Fine 67: see David S. Brunnet
Nicholas Fine 63 (District of Columbia)(Cooper), Sahinah(?) 53 (NC), James 21, Barbara 18, William 16, Hugh 12, Mary 9, Sidney L. JONES 26, James N. 6, Sidney A. 2, Mary J. 11/12 3-66-453

1870 CENSUS

Calista E. Fine 39, Syntha M. 16, Catharine L. 14, Vinet E. 11, Hannah 8 3-1-3
Betsy A. Fine 18, Susan M. 14, Cordela 12: see James Bohanan

1880 CENSUS

Darthula Fine 16: see Luke Stansbury
Elizabeth Fine 17: see William Wyrick
Isaac Fine 53, Margaret 26 (d), Catharine 21 (d), Florence 20 (d), Sophia 17 (d), Isaac PASS 3 (gs) 2-28-221

1900 CENSUS

John Fine 41 (June 1858-M 23), Catharine 43 (Aug 1856-NC/T/NC-M 23-11-10), Amanda 30 (Oct 1879), Daniel 19 (May 1881), James 17 (May 1883), Grover C. 14 (July 1885), Walter 11 (July 1888), Elijah 9 (Dec 1890), Mollie 7 (June 1892), Cora 6 (Ap 1894), Pole 1 (Aug 1898) 13-198B-162/165

MARRIAGES

C. L. Fine to W. O. Fisher q.v.
Calista E. Fine to William S. Wyrick q.v.
Delia Fine to Richard Jordan q.v.
Evaline Fine to Samuel B. Davis q.v.
Flora or Florence Fine to Reece G. Williams q.v.
John Fine to Catharine Raulston, 26 Dec 1877 (27 Dec), R. H. Jorden MG 1-#1536
John H. Fine to C. E. Paul, 5 Aug 1853 (7 Aug), James I. Cash MG 1-#416
Margarett Fine to James E. Bohannon q.v.
Margaret A. Fine to A. McPheters q.v.
Mary Fine to Levi Tredaway q.v.
Syntha Fine to John S. Knight q.v.

FINLEY

1900 CENSUS

Sterlin Finley 39 (Mar 1861), Nellie 6 (d)(June 1894), Luis 4 (s)(Oct 1895), Sterles 2 (s)(June 1897) 1-188A-174/183 (B)

FINNEY

1900 CENSUS

George E. Finney 59 (Jan 1861-T/Va/T-M 22), Sarah M. 52 (Feb 1848-M 22-7-7), George D. 18 (May 1882), Dollie 16 (Aug 1885), Henry J. 13 (Mar 1887), Hattie M. 10 (June 1889), John H. 4 (May 1896) 4-225A-226/230

FISCUS

1900 CENSUS

Barbara Fiscus 76, Libbie 42, Gladys 6, Alma 2: see George Schatzel

----

FISHER / FEICHER

1860 CENSUS

Dorcas P. Fisher 70 (Md), Betsy EATON 21 5-36-244
George W. Fisher 30, Nancy J. 27, William N. 3, Joseph 2, Mary E. 11/12 5-36-245
Henderson Fisher 37 (NC), Rebecca A. 30, Henry T. 11, George W. 9, William O. 7, Delila S. 5, Mary A. 1, Darcus P. 1 4-48-328
Henry Fisher 42 (NC), Sarah 42, Asberry 16, Emly 14, Elizabeth 12, Ruea H. 8, William G. 6, Ruth GOURD 72 7-5-30
John D. or G. Fisher 38 (Ind), Elizabeth 31, Ruhana I. 11, David E. 6, Noah W. 4, Rebecca M. 2, Tennessee E. 1/12 3-58-395

1870 CENSUS

Asberry F. Fisher 25, Louisa Jane 24, Tennessee 3 7-2-14
David Feicher 35 (Oh), Endera 28 (Pa), Cora M. 10 (Oh), Jedd 5 (Pa), Edith A. 1 1-5-32
Henderson Fisher 44 (NC), Rebecca A. 44, Henry T. 21, George W. 19, William O. 16, Dela S. 14, Darcus P. 10, Mary A. 10, Richard A.R. 8, Louisa A. 4 4-5-32
Henry Fisher 53 (NC), Sarah 54, Emsley 22 (School Teacher), Elizabeth 21, Ruhana 18, William 15 6-9-54
Nancy J. Fisher 37, William N. 13, Joseph E. 12, Mary E. 11, James T. 9 5-9-66

1880 CENSUS

F.A. Fisher 36, L.J. 36, T.E. 13 (d) 8-1-8
W.B. Fisher 26, M.A. 20 (w), H.T. 6/12 (s), Ensly FISHER 37 (b), Eliza FISHER 32 (si) 9-32-279

1900 CENSUS

Adison H. Fisher 38 (Jan 1862-M 15), Mary C. 36 (June 1863-M 15-8-8), Samuel H. 15 (June 1884), Robert T. 14 (Sep 1885), Eliza S. 12 (Jan 1888), Martha J. 8 (June 1891), Thomas J. 10 (July 1889), Mary E. 8 (Jan 1892), Manda H. 6 (Dec 1893), Rebecca A. 2 (Dec 1897) 4-226B-257/261 (Rhea Springs & Washington Road)
Azariah Fisher 56 (Dec 1843-T/NC/T-M 33)(Carpenter), Tomsia 56 (July 1843-M 33-0-0), Mattie KNIGHT 19 (ne)(Nov 1890), Walter A. 17 (nw)(Aug 1882-Tex) 10-250B-19/19
Dorcus P. Fisher 40 (Jan 1859-T/NC/T-Wd 2-1), Joan F. 16 (d)(Aug 1883) 2-226B-258/262
Elizabeth Fisher 52: see William Fisher
Emsley Fisher 53: see Elizabeth Pursur
George W. Fisher 52 (Ap 1848-T/NC/T-M 28), Eliza J. 47 (Nov 1852-M 28-1-1), Solomon S. 26 (adopted s)(Ap 1874), Cora 11 (d)(Oct 1888), Louiza J. LOWERY 70 (m)(Aug 1829-Wd 6-4) 3-201B-35/38
Ida E. Fisher 13, Zella E. 10: see John M. Burwick
John H. Fisher 24 (Feb 1876-M 1), Matilda C. 20 (Nov 1879-T/Ark/T-M 1-1-1), Owen S. 4/12 (Jan 1900) 3-210B-39/42

W. Owen Fisher 46 (Sep 1853-T/NC/T-M 25), Catharine L. 44 (Mar 1856-M 25-8-7), Henry V. 22 (Mar 1878), Syntha E. 14 (Mar 1886), Avazina E. 11 (Oct 1888), Archabald O. 8 (Aug 1891), Charles G. 4 (June 1896) 3-201B-38/41

William Fisher 45 (Oct 1854-M 21), Addie 43 (Feb 1857-M 21-7-6), Summerfield 19 (Jan 1881), Robert 17 (Feb 1883), Lizzie 15 (Feb 1885), Aley 10 (Aug 1887), Garland 7 (June 1892), Willie 3 (Jan 1897), Elizabeth FISHER 52 (si)(Feb 1848) 7-263B-256/261

MARRIAGES

Clistas or Clistis Fisher to J. R. Hurst q.v.

Dealy S. Fisher to Charles T. Smith q.v.

Docia Fisher to Joseph Harwood q.v.

Ed Fisher to Mintee(?) Burwick, 10 Ap 1886 (15 Ap), John P. Walker JP 1-506

Francis A. Fisher to Louiza Jane Knight, 6 Nov 1866 (11 Nov), J. Howard MG 1-#918

George Fisher to Eliza Crow, 30 Dec 1871 (no return) 1-#1220

Hannah Fisher to William B. Fisher q.v.

Hester E. Fisher to Richard Knight q.v.

J.H. Fisher to Matilda Price, 23 Dec 1898, L.E. Smith JP 4-101

Louisa Fisher to David Shelby q.v.

M. M. Fisher to William M. Wheeler q.v.

Noah Fisher to Margarett Rumfelt, 26 Ap 1855 (same), R.T. Howard MG 1-#493

R.A.H. Fisher to M.C. McClendon, 1 Aug 1884 (2 Aug), J. M. Bramlett MG 1-479

Rhuehanna H. Fisher to Thomas J. Knight q.v.

Tennie E. Fisher to J. D. Patton q.v.

W.B. Fisher to Mary A. Whaley, 13 Feb 1879 (same), J.W. Williamson MG 1-#1605 & 1-#1691

W.O. Fisher to C.L. Fine, 16 Sep 1874 (1 Oct), John Howard MG 1-#1358

William B. Fisher to Hannah Fisher, 24 Sep 1858 (26 Sep), J.O. Torbett JP 1-#659

- - - - - - - - - - - - -

FISISCHER [FISCHESSER]

1900 CENSUS

Zeno Fisischer [Fischesser] 55 (July 1844-France/Do/Do-1863/?/?-M 20)(Blacksmith), Mary G. 45 (Aug 1854-Oh/Pa/Oh-M 20-1-1), John R. 18 (Aug 1881-Oh)(Student) 14-218A-110/112

- - - - - - - - - - - - -

FITTS
(see also FRITTS)

MARRIAGES

Thomas Fitts to Kitty Shirley, 21 Nov 1876 (same), W.R. Grimsley MG 1-#1470

William Fitts to Sarah G. Sherley, 7 May 1872 (no return) 1-#1239

- - - - - - - - - - - - -

FITZGERALD / FITZGERLD / FITZGERAL / FITCHGEARL

1870 CENSUS

Paralee Fitzgerald 16: see Henry H. Gamble

1880 CENSUS

Mary Fitzgerald 37: see William Boles

1900 CENSUS

Albert Fitzgerld 47 (Jan 1853-M 19), Barbary A. 43 (June 1856-M 19-9-8), Bell 18 (Ap 1882), Emma M. 14 (May 1886), Archa 11 (May 1889), Addie 7 (Oct 1892), Hattie 6 (Feb 1894), Cordie T. 3 (Sep 1896) 7-263B-260/265

MARRIAGES

Martha Fitchgearl to Robert Wood q.v.

William Fitzgeral to Katie Roberts, 19 Sep 1889 (same), J.P. Roddy MG 1-582

- - - - - - - - - - - - -

FLEMING / FLEMMING / FLEMINGS

1860 CENSUS

William B. Flemings 27, Nancy 19, Samuel H. 24 10-27-180

1870 CENSUS

Mira J. Fleming 30: see James J. Abel

William B. Fleming 37, Nancy J. 29, John H. 10, Sintha L. 4, Cordelia 7/12, Permelia 7/12 10-2-15

Willie Fleming 31, Sarah 29, Mary Jane 6, Wyatt A. 2, Sarah F. 7/12, Amela 56, Sarah E. 16 8-20-140 (B)

1880 CENSUS

Dilla Fleming(?) 8, Jinwey 7: see A. Johnson

Sallie Flemmings 35, Mary J. 14, Wyett 12, Fannie 10, John 8, George 6, Lara 2 8-14-119 (B)

Son Flemming 14, Samg 5: see W. T. Broyles

William Flemings 8, Melia 9: see W. A. Johnson

1900 CENSUS

Annie Fleming 22, LeRoy 4: see Henry Logan (B)

John Fleming 24: see John McEntire (B)

Samuel Fleming 30 (Jan 1870-M 3)(General Merchandise Salesman), Ida 22 (Dec 1877-Ky/T/T-M 3-1-1), Maud B. 2 (Ap 1898) 8-316B-129/133

MARRIAGES

Bell Fleming to J. L. Newman q.v.

C. L. Fleming to D. W. Radcliff q.v.

Fannie Fleming to Charles Thomas q.v.

John Fleming to Annie Logan, 29 Oct 1895, S.W. Burnett MG 4-92

Laura Fleming to George Ayers q.v.

M. C. Flemming to Frank Burchfield q.v.

Mamie Flemming to Ancel M. Gad q.v.

Melis Fleming to C. C. Collins q.v.

Mirah J. Flemming to Daniel Hodges q.v.

S.H. Fleming to Myra Able, 18 Sep 1861 (same), J.W Williamson MG 1-#763

Sallie Fleming to Volentine Rowice q.v.

Samuel H. Flemming to Ida Belle Story, 3 June 1897 (same), G.W. Coleman MG, W.L. Hodges W 2-148

Wm D. Flemming to Nannie Johnson, 19 Aug 1860 (no return) 1-#1649

Wyatt Fleming to Vesta Day, 9 Feb 1896, H. Hubbard MG 4-88

- - - - - - - - - - - - -

FLETCHER

1880 CENSUS
Alice Fletcher 16: see Benjamin Shelow
MARRIAGES
Julia(?) Fletcher to W.W. Cunnyngham q.v.
Lillian Fletcher to Miles Jackson q.v.
Manerva Fletcher to A. T. Clawson q.v.
Susan T. Fletcher to J. D. Bandy(?) q.v.

- - - - - - - - - - - - -

FLEVOPIN

MARRIAGE
Robert Flevopin to Mary Smith, 23 Nov 1882 (same), W.W. Pyott MG 1-472

- - - - - - - - - - - - -

FLINN

MARRIAGE
Carrie E. Flinn to J. A. Swafford q.v.

- - - - - - - - - - - - -

FLORA / FLORE

1900 CENSUS
Henry Flore(?) 28 (Feb 1872-Ga/Unk-M 6)(RR Laborer), Alice 26 (June 1873-M 6-3-2), Willis L. 4 (Dec 1895), Dradie 1 (Aug 1898), Dellie PARKER 9 (Mar 1891) 10-258B-167/171
Theodore Flora 53 (Nov 1846-M 13), Mary Ann 50 (May 1850-M 13-0-0) 13-301B-209/217
MARRIAGE
Theodore Flora to Mary Ann Morgan, 20 June 1885 (21 June), W.R. Grimsley MG 1-493

- - - - - - - - - - - - -

FLOYD

1860 CENSUS
Enoch Floyd 28, Eliza 22, Margaret J. 3, James N. 2 2-72-492
MARRIAGE
Enoch Floyd to Louiza Dotson, 14 Sep 1855 (15 Sep), Archibald Paul JP 1-#517

- - - - - - - - - - - - -

FONDREN / FONDERN

1860 CENSUS
Ananamons Fondren 37 (NC), Sarah 45, George W. 15, Nancy A. 11 7-5-29
1870 CENSUS
Anonymus Fondren 52 (NC)(Shoemaker), Sarah 56, Isaac 23, Nancy A. 21 6-9-61
Samuel Fondern 48, Elizabeth 35, George W. 12, Mary L. 7, Nancy A. 4 6-11-70
MARRIAGE
James Fondren to Sarah Santina Holland, 8 Sep 1853 (same), James H. Locke JP 1-#422

- - - - - - - - - - - - -

FONTENBERRY

MARRIAGE
Nancy Fontenberry to William Sykes q.v.

- - - - - - - - - - - - -

FORD

1870 CENSUS
Mordica Ford 45, Rebecca 32, Sarah E. 16, Mary T. 11, Rosanna C. 9, Charlotte C. 6, Martha E. 2, Margarette E. 4/12 8-13-86
1880 CENSUS– None
1900 CENSUS
Elizabeth Ford 67: see Maggie F. Evans
Thomas Ford 33 (Jan 1867-T/Va/T-M 4)(Day Laborer), Horace MELTON 21 (Unk 1879-T/T/NC)(Partner) 8-275B-147 (B)
MARRIAGES
Carrie Ford to James P. Whitford or Whitfield q.v.
James H. Ford to Rhoda T. Thomison, 20 Nov 1873 (same), A.P. Early MG 1-#1312
Lillie A. Ford to J. C. Hinch q.v.
Maggie Ford to J. G. Evins q.v.
Mordicu or Mordicii Ford to Sarah Crain, 12 Sep 1872 (no return) 1-#1249
Robert Ford to Millie Wyott, 18 May 1891, R.S. Mason JP 4-26

- - - - - - - - - - - - -

FORMENS
(see also FURMAN)

1900 CENSUS
Rachael Formens(?) 62 (Unk 1838-Md/Md/Md-Wd 8-2) (Trashwoman), Alice E. BROWN 25 (d)(Mar 1875-La/Md/Md-Wd 3-3), Josephine 12 (gd)(July 1887-La), Racheal N. 10 (gd)(Mar 1890-La), Lucinda E. 7 (gd) (Mar 1893) 13-303B-255/265 (B)

- - - - - - - - - - - - -

FORNEY

MARRIAGES
Ada Forney to Alex Gormany q.v.
Jane Forney to Jacob Bowles q.v.
West Forney to Queen Sharp, 10 Sep 1887 (18 Sep), L.M. Morris ?? 1-540

- - - - - - - - - - - - -

FORTNER

1880 CENSUS
David Fortner 56, Clarissa 21 (w) 12-7-57
Henry Fortner 54, Nancy 35 (w), Minerva 14, Benjamin 11, Isaac 8, Andrew 6, Martha 4, Mary 1 12-2-15
MARRIAGES
Menny Fortner to J. N. Yarber q.v.
W.H.C. Fortner to Lillie A. C--?--, 24 Dec 1890, W.G. Curton MG 4-22

- - - - - - - - - - - - -

FOSTER / FORSTER

1870 CENSUS

James A. Foster 32, Mary Ann 27, John R. 8, Sarah R. BROWN 5 8-11-71

1880 CENSUS

E.A. Foster 49, Hester 18, Tom 10 11-42-334

Chester Foster 64, Lousa 58, Nellie 14 12-1-8

Leander Foster 23 (NY), Martha 21: see Andrew J. Jolly

Jos Foster 44, M.A. 37 (w), J.R. 18 (s) 8-5-37

1900 CENSUS

Annie L. Foster 31, Harry D. 15, Lois 5: see Chas W. Irwin

George W. Foster 25 (July 1874-Ark/T/T-M 1)(Coal Miner), Ida M. 26 (July 1873-M 1-1-1), Lillie M. 9/12 (Aug 1899), Kittie BROWN 39 (si)(July 1860) 13-306A-312/324

Henry Foster 41 (Jan 1859-Ga/Ga/Ga-M 10), Harriet 48 (June 1851-M 10-8-6), Gertie 16 (Ap 1884), James 13 (Mar 1887), Myrtle 12 (Jan 1888), Henry 8 (May 1892), Alexander 1 (Nov 1898), Andrew WALL 21 (lodger)(Unk 1879-Ala/Ala/Ala), Jacob WALL 22 (lodger)(Unk 1878-Ala/Ala/Ala) 8-275B-139 (B)

Jestas Forstar 84 (Sep 1815-Mass/NY/NY-M 56), Luler 78 (Jan 1822-NY/NY/NY-M 56-11-8), Jenni DANIEL 23 (Jan 1877-NY/NY/NY)(Servant, Cook), James ALLEN 16 (May 1884)(Servant, Farm Hand) 12-180B-41/44

Leander Forster(?) 42 (Jan 1858-M 21), Marthy 40 (Dec 1859-M 21-5-5), Floyad 19 (June 1880), Charly 17 (Feb 1883), Hairl 7 (Dec 1892), Luna 5 (Sep 1894), Edith 3 (Oct 1896) 12-180A-39/42

Mack Foster 35: see Isaac Bogger (B)

Mary A. Foster 57: see Joseph Roberts

MARRIAGES

Allie Foster(?) to Daniel Larson(?) q.v.

Blanche L. Foster to J. K. Franklin q.v.

Fanny Foster to W. G. Coker q.v.

George Foster to Ida Brown, 22 Oct 1898 (24 Oct), R.M. Kilgore MG, Wm Butcher W 2-336

Henry Foster to Harriet Pleston [license] or Preston [index], 26 July 1891, A.P. Early MG 4-27

Leander Foster to Martha Jolley, 2 Sep 1879 (3 Sep), D.V. Culver MG 1-#1672

Linnie Foster to W. L. Givens q.v.

Mack Foster to Hattie Hale, 4 Dec 1892, T.F. Shaver JP 4-46

Maria Foster to Calvin Strickland q.v.

Nannie Foster to Kert Disard q.v.

Nelle M. Foster to Frank A. Miller q.v.

Sally Foster to Jacob W. Moore q.v.

William T. Foster to T.W. Darwin, 9 Nov 1859 (no return) 1-#698

- - - - - - - - - - - - -

FOUST

1860 CENSUS

Elizabeth Foust 49, Mary F. 15, Samuel J. 12 8-23-154

Elizabeth Foust 20: see C. W. Abel

Jacob Foust 54, Ann 53, John 26, Thomas J. 19, Napolean 18, Ann 17, Elizabeth 15, Samuel 13, Rebecca J. 10 4-50-343

James E. Foust 27, Margaret E. 20, Ellen 1 7-3-14 [James married Elizabeth Julia Thompson in 1856 in Pikeville, Bledsoe Co.]

John Foust 70 (Va), Dolly 60 8-21-143

John W. Foust 42 (Carpenter), Mary 42, Martha 20, George W. 16, Sarah A.M. 14, Madison WRIGHT 18 (NC), Granville BELL 25 (Trader), Mary BELL 32 8-9-56

Philip Foust 59, Catharine 54, Albert W. ACRE 17 (Blacksmith) 8-22-152

Philip T. Foust 44, Nancy A. 28, Sarah E. 17, John A. 15, Mary C. 12, William N. 10, Liddy J. 6 Julius M. 3, Phap M. 8/12, William I. FOUST 20 8-21-144

William M. Foust 31, Margaret 24, Parthena A. 5, Barton M. 3, Mary E. 2 2-80-540 [Wm M. Foust married Margaret McPherson on 28 July 1853 in Roane County]

William P. Foust 46, Lentitia 40, Sarah J. 18, Rebecca K. 16, Mary 14, Rufus M. 13, James W. 6, Timothy R. 4, Philip 2 3-65-448

1870 CENSUS

George W. Foust 26, Amaline 23, James E. 3, John Samuel 1 2-5-24

Joab Foust 64 (Blacksmith), Ann 63, Elizbeth C. 24 3-13-91

John Foust 37, Sarah 26, Thomas F. 7 3-13-92

John A. Foust 24, Lydia Jane 19 8-4-26

John W. Foust 52 (House Carpenter), Mary 52, Sarah A. 22 2-5-28

Napolean Foust 30, Susan M. 25 3-13-93

Phillip Foust 69, Catharine 64 8-15-106

Phillip T. Foust 53, Nancy Ann 45, Mary C. 22, William M. 20, Elizabeth J. 15, Julius M. 13, Phillip M. 11, Daily R. 7, George T. 5 8-11-72

Letitia W. Foust 49, Rufus M. 23, Caddie 22, James W. 17, Timothy R. 15, Phillip 12, Letitia E. 10, Amanda S. 6 3-15-109

Samuel O. Foust 22, Mary A. 24, Ann L. 1 3-13-94

Susan Foust 76: see Cain W. Abel

William M. Foust 41, Margaret 34, Parthena A. 15, Barten M. 14, Mary E. 12, John L. 9, James M.C. 7, Latitia Z. 5, Robert F. 2, Elizabeth J. FOUST 30 2-3-15

1880 CENSUS

Frank Foust 22, Elizabeth 18 6-14-132/135

George Foust 36 (House Carpenter), Emma 35, James 12, John 11, Louella 8, George 5, Cora 1/12 2-21-167

Joab Foust 75: see Thomas Foust

John Foust 61 (House Carpenter), Mary 61, Amanda 34 2-21-168

John A. Foust 35 (Blacksmith), S.J. 30, N.A. 9, M.A. 6, W.S. 3, H.C. 2/12 8-4-32

Katharine Foust 75, Philip FOUST 79 [marked through, deceased] 8-13-112

L.M. Foust 60, J.W. 26 (s), P.F. 22 (s), L.E 19 (d), M.S. 14 (d) 3-18-146

M.M. Foust 30, M.S. 20 (w), G.R. 3 (s), F.C. 2 (d), J.N. 5/12 (s), H.M. WALDRUP 30 (boarder) 8-12-100

Margaret Foust 44, John 19, James 17, Lettie 14, Robert 12, Margaret 9, Theodosia 7 2-41-331

N.B. Foust 50, S.M. 35 (w), Annie 7, Jane 5, Florence 2 3-15-121

P.T. Foust 64, N.A. 55, P.M. 20 (s), D.R. 17 (s), G.T. 14 (s) 8-20-175

S.O. Foust 33, M.A. 34, A.L. 11 (d), L.A. 9 (d), S.C. 5 (d), W.N. 1 (s), J. JAMES 29 (boarder), C.C. JAMES 24 (boarder) 3-27-213

Thomas Foust 40, N.A. 34, G.M. 15 (s), J.M. 13 (s), S.M. 12 (d), C. 8 (d), M.A. 3 (d), Joseph 1, Joab FOUST 75 (f) 3-14-109

1900 CENSUS

George Foust 28 (Oct 1871), Nancy A. 75 (m)(Feb 1825-Wd 11-8), Minnie McPHERSON 17 (Aug 1872) (Servant) 8-287A-378/380

George W. Foust 56 (May 1844-M 34), Emma 54 (Dec 1845-M 34-6-4), John S. 31 (Jan 1869), Cora 20 (Ap 1880) 2-197B-116/121

Greely G. Foust 26 (Oct 1872-M 3), Carrie 26 (Nov 1872-Mass/Mass/Mass-M 3-1-1), Maudie M. 4/12 (Oct 1899) 2-198B-136/141

James M. Foust 37 (Ap 1863-M 9), Elizabeth 31 (Nov 1868-Oh/NJ/Ireland-M 9-2-1), Finis M. 8 (Dec 1891), Margaret T. FOUST 64 (m)(Sep 1835-Wd 11-6) 2-192B-26/26

Mary S. Foust 54 (Nov 1845-Wd), Florence 22 (Oct 1877), William 19 (Dec 1880), Sallie 14 (Oct 1885) 3-205A-84/91

Melvin Foust 50 (May 1850-M 24), Maggie 39 (Oct 1860-Ga/Ga/Ga-M 24-10-7), George R. 22 (July 1877), Flora 20 (June 1879), Nola 19 (Dec 1880), Earnest 18 (Mar 1882), Gracie 14 (Feb 1886), Asa 14 (Feb 1886), Roy 10 (Jan 1890), William SMEDLEY 2 (nw)(July 1899), Myrtle GREEN 1 (boarder)(Mar 1899) 8-287-381/383

Philip T. [Theodore] Foust 42 (Jan 1858)(Attorney) 10-327B-158/166

William Foust 24: see Katie Sims (B)

Willie Foust 2/12: see Willis Taylor (B)

MARRIAGES

A. A. Foust to J. A. Hunter q.v.

Amanda Foust to W. F. Cross q.v.

Ann Foust to John T. Furgusson q.v.

David H. Foust to Harriet N. Lewis, 29 Aug 1851 (2 Sep), A.D. Paul JP 1-#347

E. G. Foust to B.E. Gist, 17 July 1858 (no return) 1-#634

E. J. Foust to E. N. Ganaway q.v.

G.G. Foust to Carrie Claflin, 5 Jan 1897 (7 Jan), E.P. Searle MG, B.R.(?) McKay(?) 2-102

George W. Foust to Emma Fraley, 27 Sept 1866 [at Smith's Cross Roads]

James M. Foust to Lizzie Riddle, 28 Feb 1891, J.D. Winchester MG 4-19

Jane Foust to Henry Cunningham q.v.

Jane Foust to A. B. Hodge q.v.

Joab Foust to Lydia Booker, 4 Sep 1880 (5 Sep), T.H. McPherson JP 1-298

John Foust to Sarah B. Jolly, 28 May 1862 (no return) 1-#781

John A. Foust to Orpha Banham, 12 June 1855 (same), A.D. Paul JP 1-#505

John A. Foust to Lydia J. McPherson 3 Sep 1867 (same), Calvin Morgan JP 1-#968

John A. Foust (35, Roane Co) to Deller Hughes (16), 15 May 1881, W.A. Green JP, C.M. Todd & J.N. Jewell W 4-3(26)

Katharine Foust to Thomas J. Barton q.v.

L. J. Foust to H. F. Morgan q.v.

L.M. Foust or Frost to Lalia M. Campbell, 4 June 1892, W.S. Hale MG 4-40

Letta E. Foust to C. C. Cowan q.v.

Louella Foust to B. G. McKenzie q.v.

Mary A. Foust to John T. Smith q.v.

Mary C. Foust to E. H. Boyd q.v.

Mary E. Foust to T. A. Kindrick q.v.

Matty Foust to George M. Spence q.v.

N.B. Foust to S.M. Smith, 28 Jan 1868 (29 Jan), James Carson MG 1-#1001

P.P. Foust to Dartha Smith, 1 Sep 1856 (no return) 1-#569

Parthena Foust to A. N. Cawood q.v.

R. M. Foust to E. B. Moyers, 26 July 1870 (no return) 1-#1157

Samuel O. Foust to Mary Riggins, 3 June 1868 (4 June), T.N.L. Cunnyngham JP 1-#1012

Sarah Foust to John S. Clack q.v.

Sarah Foust to M. S. Riddle q.v.

Sarah A. Foust to Russel B. Day q.v.

Theodosia Foust to D. F. Robinson q.v.

William M. Foust to Margaret L. Laudermilk, 8 July 1875 (9 July), J.W. Pearce MG 1-#1402

- - - - - - - - - - - - -

FOX

1860 CENSUS

David Fox 35 (Tanner), Philip 10, Catharine 7, William 5, Peter 1, Betsy FOX 30 8-10-67

1870 CENSUS

David Fox 41, Elizabeth Jane 35, Phillip 18, Tennessee C. 16, William J. 14, Peter 12, Mary F. 5, James 2 8-14-95

Sarah Fox 63: see James Corvin

1880 CENSUS– None

1900 CENSUS

Henry T. Fox 50 (Feb 1850-T/Mass/Oh-M 25)(Shingle Manufacturer), Alice B. 46 (Aug 1853-T/Va/Va-M 25-4-3), Charles N. 24 (Feb 1876)(School Teacher), William H. 22 (Mar 1878)(Bookkeeper), Franz Eugene 13 (Mar 1887) 13-300A-186/191

James Fox 37 (Mar 1863-M 20), Cordelia 38 (Ap 1862-NC/NC/NC-M 20-6-6), Annie 17 (Dec 1882), Belle 16 (June 1883), Alice L. 14 (Dec 1885), Deck 11 (Mar 1889), Daniel 8 (Mar 1892), Charles 5 (Mar 1895) 13-299A-166/170

Sarah Fox 75: see George McDonald

William Fox 50 (Jan 1850-T/Mass/Oh-M 16)(Bookkeeper), Mary E. 45 (May 1855-M 16-7-5), Trescott E. 14 (Feb 1886), Robert B. 12 (Dec 1887), Louis R. 10 (Dec 1889), Marion M. 8 (Jan 1892), Henry 1 (Jan 1899) 13-300A-187/192

MARRIAGES

Annie Fox to Joseph Martin q.v.

Frank Fox to Dora Hamilton, 8 Dec 1896 (9 Dec), A.H. Low MG, W.D. Fox W 2-87

John Fox to Elizabeth L. Varner, 4 Jan 1855 (7 Jan), A. Campbell JP 1-#481

John Fox to Nettie Bolton, 21 Dec 1898 (27 Dec), W.R. Grimsley MG, A.J. Thomas W 2-359

M. T. Fox to W. F. Clement(?) q.v.

S. Rosa Fox to George McDonald q.v.

William Fox to Molly Seybert, 20 June 1887 (30 June), J.W. Pence ?? 1-529

- - - - - - - - - - - - -

FRALEY / FRALY / FRAILEY / FREILEY / FRAYLEY

1860 CENSUS

John E. Fraley 33, Elvira 31, Mary 9, Catharine 8, Amanda 4, Emy S. 1 5-31-208

1870 CENSUS

John Freiley 73, Mary 70, Elizabeth H. 50, Nancy A. 42, Mary A.J. 39, Rebecca S. 33, John C. 22 8-1-1

1880 CENSUS

James A. Fraley 22, Margaret E. 25, Landa 2 (s), Sarah E. 9/12 6-20-182/186

Samuel H. Fraley 25, Hanaher A. 28, Esquire C. 4, Sarah J. 3, Riley A. 1 6-20-181/185

Sarah Fraley 75: see George Minic

Squire B. Fraley 51, Kisiah 47, John R. 20, Thomas A. 16, Uliss S.J. 14, Nancy J. 10, Squire B. 6 6-20-181/186

1900 CENSUS

Nancy A. Freiley 73 (Mar 1827-S), Rebecah 65 (si)(Dec 1834-S) 11-292A-58

Samuel Fraley 20: see John T. Howard

Samuel H. Frailey 45 (Nov 1854-M 25), Hannah A. 48 (Aug 1851-Ga/Ga/Ga-M 25-9-6), Samuel H. 19 (May 1881), Nellie C. 12 (Dec 1887), Hannah A. 9 (July 1890) 5-232A-78

Tate Friley 24 (Mar 1876-M 2), Martha E. 20 (July 1879-T/Va/T-M 2-1-1), Bertha H. 1 (Oct 1898) 6-240A-6

William C. Fraley 39: see Mary Stanley

MARRIAGES

Amanda M. Fraley to William R. Grimsley q.v.

Della M. Freily to J. F. Wilson q.v.

Eliza Fraley to George Minick q.v.

Emma Fraley to George W. Foust q.v.

G.A. Fraley to Margaret E. Shirley, 30 Aug 1877 (same), Wm A. Green JP 1-#1513

Lizzie Fraley to S.V. Caldwell q.v.

Riley A. Freiley to Andy Hill q.v.

S.B. Fraly to Mary B. Gothard, 28 Feb 1865 (same), John Whaley MG 1-#832

Samuel Fraley to Angeline Gravett, 12 Feb 1875 (17 Feb), J.L. Brown JP 1-#1394

Sarah J. Fraley to Horace Dillard q.v.

Tilda Jane Frailey to Bird Thomas q.v.

Tate Frailey or Fryley to Martha E. Walker, 18 Jan 1898 (19 Jan), W.A. Howard MG, Charley Rudd W 2-242

- - - - - - - - - - - - -

FRANCIS

1900 CENSUS

John W. Francis 60 (May 1840-Oh/Conn/Mass-M 38) (Clerk, Registerars Office), Mary E. 54 (June 1854-Oh/Mass/Ver-M 38-3-3), Elen E. DANIELS 72 (ml) (Aug 1827-Ver/Ver/Ver-Wd 2-1) 10-321A-29/30

MARRIAGES

Anna Francis to A. A. Crable q.v.

John Francis to Almeda Shipley, 11 Feb 1894, W.R. Grimsley MG 4-69

- - - - - - - - - - - - -

FRANCISCO / FRANSISCO

MARRIAGES

George Francisco to Arlene Shipley, 13 Jan 1900 (14 Jan), W.R. Grimsley MG, Andy Green(?) [signed by X] W 3-109

James Fransisco or Fransise to Mary Elsey, 29 Nov 1889 (1 Dec), F.M. Capps JP 1-589

Nettie Francisco to John Thomas q.v.

- - - - - - - - - - - - -

FRANK

MARRIAGES

Isabella Frank to Thomas Miller q.v.

James P. Frank to Martha J. Dudley, 24 Nov 1864 (same), W.W. Low JP 1-#1081

John Frank to Annie Gilliam, 9 Oct 1888 (11 Oct), J.W. Brackman MG 1-556

- - - - - - - - - - - - -

FRANKLIN

1860 CENSUS

Thomas L. Franklin 44 (SC), Rebecca 37, Bennet J. 17, Margaret G. 12, Osker T. 10, James 7, Letiha 4, Joseph 2, John K. FRANKLIN 24 4-47-322

1870 CENSUS

Ben C. Franklin 65 (SC), Lidda 62, Emily L. 27 2-12-87

Bennet J. Franklin 27, Salana E. 19, Thomas L. 6/12 3-9-61

John K. Franklin 33, Nancy I. 28, Bennet L. 3, Lydia J. 1 3-1-1

Thomas L. Franklin 54 (SC), Rebecca A. 47, Susan M. 21 (Ga), Thomas O. 18 (Ga), James D. 15 (Ga), Lottie R. 11, Joseph W. 9, Lucy 4 3-8-60

William Franklin 9: see Peter Shock

1880 CENSUS

B.J. Franklin 32, S.E. 28, T.L. 10 (s), E. 8 (d), E.G. 6 (d), A.J. 4 (d), Baster 2/12 (s) 7-24-205

Bennet Franklin 75, L. A. 72 4-1-6

John Franklin 43 (Carpenter), Blanch 24 (w), B.L. 13 (s), L.J. 11 (d), N.E. 6 (d), L.M. 7/12 (d) 4-1-3

T.L. Franklin 64, R.A. 56, Osker 26, James 23, Joseph 13, Jane HOSKINS 20(?) 7-24-208

Wash Franklin 25: see Timothy Winton (B)

1900 CENSUS

Bennet J. Franklin 62 (June 1837-T/Ga/T-M 31)(House Carpenter), Salena E. 49 (Aug 1850-T/Ky/Ky-M 31-9-6), Annie J. 22 (Nov 1877), Ossue 14 (Mar 1886), William I. 20 (Ap 1880)(Coal Miner), Evan G. DETAR 25 (d)(May 1875-M 0-0-0) 10-322A-48/50

Blanch Franklin 45 (July 1854-Wd 3-3), Mable 27 (d)(Oct 1879), Cora 14 (d)(Mar 1886) 12-180B-40/43

George Franklin 51 (Aug 1849-SC/SC/Va-M 12)(Laborer, Rock Quarry), Winnie 33 (Dec 1866-M 12-6-6), Mabel 11 (May 1889), James 9 (Oct 1890), Estella 7 (Jan 1893), Carrie 5 (Ap 1895), Frederick B. 3 (Mar 1897), Mary J. 9/12 (Sep 1899) 8-317A-138/143 (B)

Harvey Franklin 26 (May 1874-T/Ga/NC-M 10), Hannie 22 (Mar 1878-T/Ga/T-M 0-0), Charles LAMPKIN 23 (boarder)(Unk 1877), Henry LIVELY 60 (Unk 1840-Ga/Ga/Ga-Wd) 8-279B-220/222

James Franklin 46 (Sep 1853-Ga/Ga/T-Wd), William J. 13 (Jan 1887), Robert O. 10 (Sep 1889), Thomas E. 9 (June 1890), Amanda L. 6 (Oct 1893), James H. 3 (Aug 1896) 10-322B-51/54

Joseph W. Franklin 42 (Mar 1858-Ill/Ill/Ill-M 5)(Missionary House), Lee 36 (July 1863-Mo/Ky/Ky-M 5-4-4), Thomas M. 11 (Dec 1888-Col), Mary L. 10 (Aug 1889-Col), Josephine L. 4 (Feb 1896), Joseph W. 2 (Ap 1898) 13-309-365/378

Oscar Franklin 49 (Oct 1850-Ga/Unk-M 19), Mary 49 (Aug 1850-M 19-8-7), Charles H. 18 (Feb 1882), Thomas 15 (Nov 1884), James O. 13 (Sep 1886), Martha A. 11 (Jan 1889), Margaret L. 9 (Jan 1891), Lucy B. 6 (Sep 1893), William E. 4 (Aug 1895) 6-243B-81

Santuelli(?) Franklin 71 (Feb 1829-Miss/SC/Ala-M 47), Artmecy 72 (July 1827-Oh/Md/Pa-M 47-3-2) 6-242A-47

Thomas Franklin 9: see Frank Helton

MARRIAGES

Dollie Franklin to Mackey Conley q.v.

E. L. Franklin to Franklin Duckworth q.v.

Eva Franklin to Dorr DeTar q.v.

Helen Franklin to J. H. Pearson q.v.

J.O. Franklin (31, Ga) to Mary Hicks (27, Bradley Co), 19 Feb 1882, J.L. Shaver MG, T.M. Bolen & T.C. Travis W 4-8(73)

J.O. Franklin to Sereptia Brady, 27 Mar 1886 (28 Mar), J.R. Crawford JP 1-497

J.H. Franklin to Fannie Lively, 24 Aug 1899 (25 Aug), N.D. Reed MG, J.H. Best W 3-25

John K. Franklin to Mary I. McAdoo, 7 Jan 1862 (8 Jan), Jas I. Cash MG 1-#770

John K. Franklin to Blanche L. Foster, 13 Dec 1878 (same), W.F. Rodgers MG 1-#1592

Lentitia Franklin to James C. Carney(?) q.v.

Lizzie Franklin to Henry Gonia(?) q.v.

Lottie Franklin to James Pickett q.v.

- - - - - - - - - - - - -

FRAZIER / FRAZER

1860 CENSUS

Barbary Frazier 71, Mariah L. 35, Abner W. 38 Mary J. 25, Beriah A. 6/12 7-6-39

Manerva M. Frazier 16, Emily P. 11: see Albert P. Early

Passafy T. Frazier 51, Joseph 24, Manerva 17, Nicholas 15, Samuel 12, Sarah J. 9, Onslow G. 3 4-51-347

Ruth L.E. Frazier 53, Samuel I. 20 6-107-732

1870 CENSUS

Abner W. Frazier 49, Mary Jane [nee Craignead] 40, Beriah A. 10, Mary B. 8, Mariah L. 46 7-8-59

Alexander Frazier 60, Eliza 57, Jane 7 6-16-119 (B)

Ana Frazier 44, Nancy 24, James 4 6-12-79 (B)

Nichols Frazier 26, Arena M. 23, Samuel B. 1, Hillery CHASTAIN 12 7-6-44

Pacify T. Frazier 61, Samuel 22, Sarah J. 19, Josephine 20, Lonzo G. 13 4-4-22

Samuel J. Frazier 30 (Lawyer), Ruth L.E. [nee Clawson] 50, Ruth WILSON 25 (Ala), Henry THOMISON (B) (Waiter) 6-7-41

Thomas Frazier 21, Mary 18, William 1 6-12-78 (B)

1880 CENSUS

A. Frazier 59, Mary J. 51, B.H. 20 (s), M.B. 18 (d), M.S. 54 (si) 7-24-203

Amy Frazier 56, Nan 28, Thos D. 25, Ed 15, Wm 11 (B): see Robert N. Gillespie

Birthey Frazier 3: see John Peterson

Eliza Frazier 58, Mary 28, Wm 10, Isaac F. 6 6-24-25 (B)

James Frazier 23 (Lawyer) 6-25-195/199

Samuel J.A. Frazier 41 (Lawyer), Anna A. 3, Alose F. 7 (s), Sallie R. 5 6-25-193/198

Samuel Frazier 30, Josephine 29, James S. 8, Clair B. 3 6-15-135/137

1900 CENSUS

Annie W. Frazier 34, Julia 10, Ida 7: see Geo W. Goodrich

Elvine Frazier 63: see Jacob B. Ewing

Samuel Frazier 52 (Ap 1848-M 30), Josephine 49 (Jan 1851-M 30-7-5), James S. 27 (Sep 1872), Clara 23 (June 1876), Fred B. 19 (Sep 1880), Claudia 17 (Ap 1883), Katie 11 (July 1888) 6-248B-161/162

MARRIAGES

Amanda Frazier to Isaac Davis q.v.

B.A. Frazier to A.B. or A.R. Wiseman, 14 May 1887 (15 May), J.H. Keith MG 1-534

Elmiry Frazier to E. Gregory q.v.

Emily [Emma] P. Frazier to R.N. Gillespie q.v.

L.G. Frazier to V.A. Peterson, 3 Aug 1875 (4 Aug), Wm L. Humphrey MG 1-#1403

Manervia M. Frazier to G. L. Tucker q.v.

Manervia T. Frazier to C. W. Ault q.v.

Manervia Frazier to A. P. Early q.v.

Mary B. Frazier to M. G. McDonald q.v.

Mary E. Frazier to B. K. Mynatt q.v.

Samuel Frazier to Josephine Locke, 27 Jan 1870 (same), A.P. Early MG 1-#1141 [Josephine, dau of James H. and Phoebe Smith Locke]

Samuel Frazier (45) to Sallie Walker, 21 May 1881, S. Breeding JP, C. Gillespie W 4-5(44) (B)

Sarah J. Frazier to William N. Hutchens q.v.

Thomas Frazier to Janis Johnson, 24 Jan 1884 (same), T.N. L. Cunnyngham JP 1-491

- - - - - - - - - - - - -

FREEMAN

1880 CENSUS

Matilda Freeman 14 (B): see W.S. Gillespie

1900 CENSUS

Clint Freeman 21 (May 1879-Ala/Ala/Ala)(Porter, Barber-shop) 10-330B-218/232 (B)

MARRIAGES

Lou Freeman to Richard Lawrence q.v.

Minnie Freeman to Price Gormany q.v.

W.D. Freeman to Sarah E. McCormick, 9 Mar 1886, James Corvin MG 4-45

- - - - - - - - - - - - -

FRENCH

MARRIAGE

Martha French to James G. Rudd q.v.

- - - - - - - - - - - - -

FRESBY

1880 CENSUS

Parthena Fresby 45, Jessee 1: see Jessee May

- - - - - - - - - - - - -

FRITTS
(see also FITTS)

1880 CENSUS

John P. Fritts 43 (Blacksmith), Elizabeth A. 38, Flina(?) C. 5 (d), James C. 2, Mary A. 4/12 5-4-30

MARRIAGE

Benjamin Fritts to Sarah Morgan, 30 Nov 1892, W.M. Turner MG 4-52

- - - - - - - - - - - - -

FROST– see FOUST

- - - - - - - - - - - - -

FRY

1870 CENSUS

Hugh B. Fry 21 (House Carpenter), Minerva 19, Franklin L. 1 3-14-101

Sebra Fry 61 (NC), Jane 17, Ann 28, Mary 20, James N. 16, Ann 13 3-14-105

1880 CENSUS

Joseph M. Fry 39 (Hotel Keeper), Amanda E. 21, Lula B. 7, Jannie C. 4, Nancy E. 3 5-11-102

MARRIAGES

B. A. Fry to Lewis Fugate q.v.

H. B. Fry to Manervia F. White, 21 Nov 1868 (22 Nov), Wm W. Low JP 1-#1036

J.W. Fry to Jane Carpenter, 28 Oct 1869 (same), John Howard MG 1-#1119

James N. Fry to Eliza J. Cooper, 31 July 1863 (no return) 1-#802

- - - - - - - - - - - - -

FUGATE / FUGAT / FUGET / FEWGHET / FEWGET

1860 CENSUS

Martha Fewghet 52 (Va), Lewis 22, Eliza 19, Elbert 17, Catharine SALES 8, Cleborne FEWGET 33 (Va), Rebecca J. 22, Zachariah 1, Sarah SALES 11 3-60-414

William Fewget 25 (Va), Martha 16 (Va) 3-66-452

1870 CENSUS

Calborn Fugat 42 (Va), Rebecca J. 32, Zachariah 10, Meral 8, Martha E. 9, Amanda 7, Lewis 5, Nancy A. 4, Claiborne 3, Elbert S. 2 1-20-135

Martha Fuget 59 (Va), Lewis 30, Elbert 25, Catharine SAILS 16 3-16-113

William Fuget 40 (Va), Martha 29, Victoria 9, Eliza J. 7, John E. 5, Mary 3, Nancy A. 1, Tennessee BUTTREM 16 3-15-111

1880 CENSUS

Clabe Fugate 53, R.J. 43, L.T. 21 (s), M.E. 20 (d), Meril 18, A.J. 16 (d), Louisa 15, N.A. 14 (d), C. 13 (s), E.S. 12 (s), M.R. 10 (d), Thomas 5, S.E. 3 (d), Barnet 1, Va 1/12 (d) 3-25-200

E.S. Fugate 39, M.J. 8 (d), Wm WILSON (B) 25 (Hired Hand) 3-25-201

L.C. Fugate 46, Nancy 35, Wm 5, Lewis 5, Thomas 2 3-22-177

N. A. Fugate 7: see Gilbert Reed

Wm Fugate 51, Martha 39 (w), Eliza 16, John 14, Mary 13, Anna 11, Wm 9, Jas 6, L.T. 6 (s), Sidney 4 (d), Saml G. 2 (s), C.H. 4/12 (s) 3-25-204

1900 CENSUS

Arena Fugate 26: see Andrew J. Garrison

Claburn Fugate Sr. 72 (Nov 1827-Va/Va/Va-M 42), Rebecca J. 64 (Jan 1836-M 42-16-9), Elbert S. 32 (Ap 1868), Mary R. 29 (Dec 1870), Thomas 25 (Feb 1875), Serrah C. 22 (Oct 1877), Barnett 21 (Dec 1878), Victoria A. 19 (Feb 1881), Ediath 10 (gd)(Dec 1889), Oscar 9 (gs)(May 1892) 3-208A-147/160

Claburn Fugate Jr. 33 (Ap 1867-T/Va/T-M 12), Mosurrie 27 (Aug 1872-M 12-7-5), Martin L. 12 (Sep 1887), Gertie I. 11 (Ap 1889), Maud E. 8 (May 1892), Marvin C. 4 (May 1896), Crattie A. 2 (Ap 1898) 3-208A-146/159

Elbert S. Fugate Unk (July Unk-M 17), Ashie A. 42 (May 1858-M 17-1-1), Duglas 16 (Jan 1884) 3-208A-145/158

James Fugate 27 (Jan 1873-T/Va/T-M 1), Jennie 18 (Ap 1882-M 1) 3-210A-180/196

John E. Fugate 36 (Dec 1863-T/Va/T-M 14), Ida A. 35 (Dec 1864-M 14-5-5), Clement W. 13 (Mar 1887), Lavada 11 (Feb 1889), Jewel 8 (Nov 1891), Homer K. 5 (June 1895), Mary A. 2 (Ap 1898), Allin 20 (b)(Feb 1860) 3-210A-180/195

Louis Fugate 23 (Ap 1877-M 2), Myra 19 (Unk 1881-M 2-0-0) 3-210B-184/201

Louis Fugate 65 (Nov 1835-T/Va/Va-M 26), Nancy J. 54 (Sep 1845-M 26-3-3), Thomas L.L. 22 (Mar 1878), James A.G. 19 (Aug 1880), Chester A.A. 18 (Mar 1882) 3-210B-182/199

Merril L. Fugate 38 (Oct 1861-T/Va/T-M 9), Texana 32 (Unk 1868-M 9-3-3), Mara 8 (Nov 1891), Carl 6 (Oct 1893), Otto 4 (July 1895), James GENOW 25 (Unk 1875-Wd)(Servant), Andrew WRIGHT (B) 24 (Unk 1876)(Servant) 3-207B-137/150

William Fugate 24 (Feb 1876-M 5), Rena 25 (Jan 1875-M 5-3-3), Carie 4 (June 1896), Walter 2 (May 1898), Laura A. 3/12 (Mar 1900) 3-210B-185/202

William K. Fugate Sr. 65 (Nov 1834-Va/Va/Va-M 10), Mary E. 45 (Unk 1855-T/NC/Va-M 10-1-1), Samuel C. 21 (Nov 1878), George J.B. 16 (May 1884), Rosa 8 (July 1891) 3-210A-179/194

William M. Fugate 29 (Jan 1871-T/Va/T-M 6), Laura M. 31 (Dec 1868-M 6-3-2), Carl 3 (Ap 1897), Martha J. 11/12 (July 1899) 3-210B-188/206

Zac Fugate 27 (Jan 1873-T/Va/T-Wd), Una 7 (Nov 1892), Dossie 6 (Feb 1894), Bassil N. 2 (Mar 1898) 3-210B-181/198

MARRIAGES

Annie Fugate to Byron Denton q.v.

Bell Fugate to W. W. Smith q.v.

Claburn Fugate to Rebecca J. Brady, 22 Mar 1858, "Returned to office without any indorsement, W.H. Bell, Clerk" 1-#628

Clabron Fugate to Missorria Cagle, 1 Dec 1887 (4 Dec), Taylor Russell JP 1-558

E. J. Fugate to J. D. Patton q.v.

Elizabeth Fugate to James Brady q.v.
E.S. Fugate (41, Rhea Springs) to A. Phillips (23, Rhea Springs), 15 Mar 1882, W.W. Low JP, Geo Julian & John Phillips W 4-8(71)
Elbert Fugate to Amanda Reede, 15 Jan 1873 (16 Jan), John Howard MG 1-#1271
J.M. Fugate to Jennie Hale, 20 Dec 1899, L.E. Smith JP 4-102
Lewis Fugate to B.A. Fry, 12 Feb 1864 (no return) 1-#818
Lewis Fugate to Nancy Jane Smith, 18 Ap 1874 (19 Ap), John Howard JP 1-#1333
Lewis Fugate to Myria Garrison, 7 Feb 1898 (same), L.E. Smith JP, W.A. Smith W 2-248
Martha E. Fugate to H. S. Smith q.v.
Mary Fugate to Francis Johnson q.v.
Merel Fugate to Texanna Cagle, 22 Mar 1891, J. W. Cowls (?) JP 4-22
Nancy A. Fugate to J. H. Jenoe q.v.
Nancy A. Fugate to W. L. Hill q.v.
S. C. Fugate to J. C. Turner q.v.
Victory Fugate to John T. Phillips q.v.
W.K. Fugate to Mary E. Rosė, 24 May 1888 (27 May), Isaac H. Miller MG 1-550
W.K. Fugate Jr. to Laura Hale, 3 Dec 1893, L.F. Smith MG 4-70
Wm K. Fugate Jr. to Rena Garrison, 20 Ap 1894, J.M. Bramlett MG 4-67
Zack Fugate to S. McNutt, 26 Aug 1900, J.W. Pearce MG 4-106

- - - - - - - - - - - - -

FULLER

1870 CENSUS
James Fuller 20: see Thomas B. Coulter
1880 CENSUS– None
1900 CENSUS
Elizabeth A. Fuller 49 (Ap 1851-T/Va/T-D 6-6), William B. BARGER 22 (s)(Feb 1878), Lushan 19 (s)(May 1881), Jane L. 16 (d)(June 1883)(Servant), Anna H. 15 (d)(Feb 1885)(Servant), John H. FULLER 5 (s)(July 1894) 2-198B-135/140
Robert Fuller 22: see Anderson Hendrick
MARRIAGES
Dollie Fuller to Eugene Wilkes q.v.
John Fuller to Mary Moore, 24 Oct 1899 (25 Oct), W.R. Grimsley MG, D.M. Fuller W 3-60
Stephen Fuller to Elizabeth Baker, 16 Feb 1893, H.B. Burdett MG 4-69
Thomas Fuller to Annie Morriss, 11 May 1891, L.M. Moore MG 4-29
Trisday(?) Fuller to A. M. Miller q.v.

- - - - - - - - - - - - -

FULKINS

MARRIAGE
Henrietta Fulkins to L. M. Collier q.v.

- - - - - - - - - - - - -

FULLINGTON

1860 CENSUS
William Fullington 33, Mary 27, Charles P. 11, Harriet 9, Sarah F. 7, Mary 5, George T. 2, Clarissu 11/12 4-45-308
MARRIAGES
Harriet Fullington to William M. Cary q.v.
William Fullington to Sarah Carah or Cash, 14 July 1865 (16 July), W.W. Low JP 1-#1072

- - - - - - - - - - - - -

FULTON

1900 CENSUS
Marie Fulton 15: see Charles W. Irwin

- - - - - - - - - - - - -

FULTS / FEULKS

1880 CENSUS
Henry Feulks 23, L.A. 24, C.H. 5 (d), W.E. 6/12 (s) 3-23-188
MARRIAGE
John Fults to Nellie McDonald, 17 Aug 1889 (same), S.W. Burnett or Bennett ?? 1-577

- - - - - - - - - - - - -

FURLONG

1900 CENSUS
James E. Furlong 7: see Job W. Carlock

- - - - - - - - - - - - -

FURMAN
(see also FORMENS)

1900 CENSUS
George E. Furman 47 (May 1853-NJ/NJ/NJ-M 14)(Mine Boss), Flora E. 36 (July 1863-M 14-5-3), Jennie M. 13 (May 1887), Hazel 10 (Ap 1890), Peyton F. 6 (Feb 1894) 13-304A-262/272

- - - - - - - - - - - - -

FURREY

1900 CENSUS
Joseph W. Furrey 41 (Dec 1859-T/Va/Va-M 16), Izoa A. 33 (July 1876-M 16-7-6), James T. 14 (Aug 1885), Samuel H. 10 (May 1889), Nancy A. 8 (Aug 1891), William M. 4 (July 1895), Harvey 3 (Dec 1897), Bertha E. 8/12 (Sep 1899) 5-231B-63

- - - - - - - - - - - - -

GADD / GAD

1900 CENSUS

John D. Gad 56 (Ap 1844-T/T/SC-M 39), Matilda 55 (Dec 1844-M 39-12-11), Ruth 23 (July 1876), George H. 19 (Sep 1880), Dora E. 17 (Mar 1883), Lorenso D. 13 (Dec 1886), Walter D. 11 (Ap 1889) 13-307B-340/352

James F. Gad 29 (June 1870-M 3), Carrie E. 21 (Feb 1879-Ky/Ky/Ky-M 3-1-1), Etta M. 1 (Nov 1898) 13-295B-109/111

MARRIAGES

A. M. Gadd to Rebecca Bowen, 30 Sep 1885 (7 Oct), J.W. Burnett MG 1-499

Ancil M. Gad to Mamie Flemings, 11 Ap 1900 (same), David Davis ??, J.N. Francis W 3-139

- - - - - - - - - - - - -

GADDIS / GATTIS

1900 CENSUS

Sarah Gaddis 23, James 20, Joseph 11: see John Goins

MARRIAGES

Allie Gaddis to W. A. Lankford q.v.

Florence Gaddis to Arch Gowins q.v.

J.G. Gaddis to Martha E. Kelly, 22 Aug 1897, L.E. Smith JP 4-98

Laurie(?) Gaddis to Pete T. Cottrell q.v.

Mary Gattis to Noah A. Campbell q.v.

Sarah Gaddis to F. C. Smith q.v.

- - - - - - - - - - - - -

GAGE

1900 CENSUS

Frank M. Gage 31: see Jeremiah C. Wasson

- - - - - - - - - - - - -

GAINS / GAINES

1870 CENSUS

Atlee C. Gains 11, George W. 8, John A. 5: see Robert F. Cook

1880 CENSUS– None

1900 CENSUS

Isaac W. Gaines 52 (Feb 1848-M 16)(House Carpenter), Queen 32 (Ap 1868-M 16-6-2), Abraham U. 12 (Dec 1887), Uriah J. 5 (Oct 1894) 10-330A-208/221 (B)

James Gaines 39 (Mar 1861-Ky/Ky/Ky-M 8), Cora 33 (Mar 1867-T/Ga/Ga-M 8-0-0) 8-317A-142/147 (B)

John Gaines 16: see James Rudd

Sarah M. Gaines* 63 (June 1837-T/SC/T-Wd 3-3), Altie C. GAINES 41 (Feb 1859), Mattie SNYDER 22 (Mar 1878)(Servant) 3-206A-112/122 [*listed under Cooke in other years; Sarah M. Cook married Robert J. Gaines on 7 Mar 1855 in Monroe Co; they were divorced in Nov 1869 in Rhea Co]

MARRIAGES

Isaac W. Gains to Queen Gillespie, 29 Jan 1883 (same), John Howard MG 1-481

Isaac W. Gaines (23, Monroe Co) to Queen Gillespie (16), 29 Jan 1883, J. Howard MG, T.D. Kelly & James Cunnyngham W 4-12(118) [Isaac's occupation is shown as School Teacher, but 1900 census lists him as a carpenter)

James Gaines to Cora Allen, 27 Ap 1891, F.J. Paine JP 4-21

Louela Gaines to James Johnson q.v.

- - - - - - - - - - - - -

GAITES / GAITS– see GATES

- - - - - - - - - - - - -

GALBRAITH / GILBRETH / GILBREATH

1870 CENSUS

James H. Gilbreath 26, Jane 24 2-12-89

1880 CENSUS

James Galbraith 35 (Trader), Jane 34: see Andrew Anderson

1900 CENSUS

James H. Galbraith 55 (Aug 1844-M 1)(Landlord), Lelia 29 (Ap 1871-M 1-0-0), James R. 15 (Aug 1884), Georgie C. 13 (July 1886), Nettie C. 10 (Ap 1890), John M. 8 (May 1892), Charles C. 5 (Aug 1894) 2-199A-147/152

John Gilbreath 22: see Nathan D. Reed

MARRIAGES

J.H. Gilbreath or Galbraith to Anney or Amy Reed, 13 Oct 1900 (14 Oct), Robert Walker MG, Charles Viles W 3-234

Minnie Gilbreth to M. D. Smith q.v.

William Gilbreth to Sarah J. Hilton, 14 Oct 1894, W. L. Lillard JP 4-73

- - - - - - - - - - - - -

GALIMO

MARRIAGE

Fred Galimo to Matilda Waller, 2 Dec 1898 (20 Dec), J.B. Phillips MG, R.J. Killough W 2-351

- - - - - - - - - - - - -

GALION

1880 CENSUS

Nancy Galion 32, William 11, James 10, David 8, Joseph 6, Mary 3, Andrew 2/12 1-16-132

- - - - - - - - - - - - -

GALLAHER / GALLAGHER / GALIGER / GALLIAGER / GOLLAHER

1900 CENSUS

Acar Galiger 24 (Nov 1875-M 3)(Drawing Coke), Leucindy 19 (Dec 1880-M 3-1-1), Beuliah 1 (Feb 1899) 10-253A-66 (B)

Catherine B. Galliagher 43 (May 1857-Ireland/Do/Do-1887/12-Wd 10-8), Mary A. 20 (July 1879-Ireland-1887), Susie 18 (June 1881-Ireland-1887), Bridget 16 (Ap 1884-Ireland-1887), Sarah B. 11 (Aug 1888), Cornelius 8 (Sep 1891), Hugh P. 6 (May 1894), Joseph W. 3 (Aug 1896) 10-329A-185/198

David Galiger 30 (Mar 1870-M 7)(Coke Puller), Lennis 24 (Mar 1876-M 7-4-4), Frank 3 (Oct 1896), Robert 6/12 (Nov 1899), Willie 23 (b)(Feb 1877)(Coke Puller) 10-251B-37 (B)

Floyd N. Gollaher 33: see James W. Angel

Joseph Gallagher 31 (May 1869-Ireland/Do/Do-Unk/Unk-Na-M 4)(Coal Miner), Catharine 49 (Unk 1851-Ireland/Do/Do-M 4-16-7), Lena 21 (Ap 1879-NY), John 17 (Sep 1882-NY), Willie 15 (Jan 1885-NY), Josephine 11 (May 1889), Turessa(?) 4 (June 1896) 8-276B-159/160

Richard Gallahar 47 (Unk 1852-M 19), Manerva 45 (Unk 1855-M 19-12-6), Rosa 15 (Aug 1884), Velnea 3 (Nov 1896), Lizzie ROBERTS 19 (sd)(June 1880), Myrtle 17 (sd)(Feb 1883) 8-276A-152/153 (B)

Sam Galiger 52 (Mar 1848-M 11)(Coke Puller), Mealie 28 (Feb 1872-M 11-2-2)(Washwoman), Maybell 9 (May 1891), Uma 7 (Mar 1893), Jimm 22 (boarder)(Aug 1878)(Coke Puller) 10-252A-38 (B)

Susan Gallagher 18: see Patrick Houghey

MARRIAGES

Lucinda Gallagher to George W. Taylor q.v.

Primus Gollaher to Mary Fields, 26 Dec 1890, L.M. Moore MG 4-20 (B)

Sarah Gollaher or Gollahu to Albert Broyles q.v.

- - - - - - - - - - - - -

GALLAHAN / GALLAHEN / GOLLAHON

1900 CENSUS

Floyd Gallahan 33 (Nov 1866-M 12)(Merchant), Tennie 30 (Jan 1870-M 12-2-2), Frederick 11 (Ap 1889), Olive 9 (May 1891) 14-216A-64/65

Naoima Gallahon 64 (Ap 1836-Va/Va/T-D) 14-218A-116/119

MARRIAGES

Floyd Gallahan to Tennie Ferguson, 10 Dec 1887 (11 Dec), J.P. Thompson JP 1-540

Laura C. Gollohan to C. E. Shewman(?) q.v.

Naoma Gallahen to M. B. Daugherty q.v.

- - - - - - - - - - - - -

GALLENDAY

1900 CENSUS

Thomas Gallenday(?) 33 (July 1866-NC/NC/NC-M 10), Margrett 27 (July 1872-M 10-5-2), Mary 6 (Dec 1893), George 4 (Dec 1895) 7-262A-227/232

- - - - - - - - - - - - -

GALLOWAY

1900 CENSUS

Milton Galloway 40 (Feb 1860-M 16), Florida J. 40 (Dec 1859-T/Ga/NC-M 16-7-6), Edmund A. 15 (Feb 1885), Willard C. 13 (Oct 1886), Ralph F. 11 (May 1889), Ermine P. 9 (Ap 1891), Ella A. 3 (Sep 1896), Edna O. 2 (July 1898), Margaret QUINN 65 (ml)(March 1835-NC/NC/NC-Wd 15-12) 14-216A-58/59

MARRIAGES

M.H. Galloway to Jennie Quinn, 25 Dec 1883 (26 Dec), B. Y. Holloway JP 1-505

Samuel J. Galloway to Vesta V. Clack, 17 Sep 1887 (13 Sep), J.B. McCallom MG 1-536

- - - - - - - - - - - - -

GAMBEL / GAMBELL / GAMBILL

1860 CENSUS

Marcus L. Gamble 20, Sarah J. 18 3-63-433

1870 CENSUS

Henry H. Gamble 57 (NC), Martha M. 41, Reuben W. 19 (Ala), Samuel H. NORMAN 5, Paralee FITZGERALD 16 (NC) 5-3-14

1880 CENSUS

H.H. Gambill 66, Martha M. 52, Sam H. NORMAN 15 (gs), Mary REED 50 (Servant), John REED 20 (s), Margaret COHAN 26 (Servant) 5-9-88

M.S. Gambell 40, S.J. 37 (w), M.S. 18 (d), C.M. 16 (s), L.A. 14 (d), M.J. 11 (d), I.M. 7 (d), M.E. 5 (d), R.H. 3 (s), M.L. 10/12 (s), Kate REVESS 24 7-29-245

R.W. Gambell 25, Cansada J. 23, James P. 5, Henry 2, Floyd 10/12 5-7-56

1900 CENSUS

John A. Gamble 31 (Ap 1869-M 4)(Teacher), Kate 27 (Sep 1872-M 4), Josie 10 (Aug 1889) 14-216A-71/72 (B)

John A.(?) Gamble 31 (Ap 1864-M 4)(Teacher), Kate 27 (Sep 1872-4-1-1), Josie D. 10 (Aug 1889) 14-217A-84/85 (B)

Lafayette Gambill 60 (Dec 1839-M 14), Malinda 53 (Aug 1846-M 14-2-2) 8-279A-215/217

Martha Gamble 73 (May 1826-T/T/NC-Wd 4-3), James REUISE 22 (boarder)(Dec 1877), Jack McBRUNE 50 (boarder)(Mar 1850), Mary TAYLOR 33 (Aug 1866-T/T/Ga-Wd 3-1)(Servant), Jessie TAYLOR 4 (boarder) (Jan 1896) 5-231B-69

MARRIAGES

Adeline L. Gamble to I.N. Hutchenson q.v.

John Gambell to Kate Adcock, 31 Oct 1895, G.G. Swann MG 4-90

Joseph Gambell to Marcella Hutchison, 30 June 1888 (same), D.V. Culver JP 1-551

M.L. Gambel to Sarah J. Rodgers, 26 Sep 1858 (same), J.W. Thompson JP 1-#660

Mary Gambill to T. J. Grice q.v.

- - - - - - - - - - - - -

GANN / GAN

1900 CENSUS

Hattie I. Gann 25: see Benjamin F. Mealer

MARRIAGE

Amos Gan to Celista Hill, 22 May 1885 (same), I.W. Holt JP 1-494

- - - - - - - - - - - - -

GANNAWAY / GANAWAY / GANIWAY / GONERWAY

1860 CENSUS

Edward W. Ganaway 27, Tiszat(?) 27, Alonza 3, Aneliza 2, Malissa C. 4/12 5-35-238

Thomas C. Ganaway 28, Mary A. 27, William J. 4, John T. 10/12 5-36-240

William Ganaway 63 (Va), Margaret H.H. 64, Rhody P. 39, Gregory HAMPTON 11, Rhody A. HAMPTON 9 5-35-239
William K. Ganaway 37 (Va), Eliza J. 37, Leonidas J. 11, Mary P. 9, Mary H. 7, William C.B. 5, Orville P. 3, Polly BROYLES 70 (Va) 5-36-241

1870 CENSUS

Edmond Ganaway 37, Louisa Jane 36, Alonza W. 14, Ann Eliza 12, Melissa C. 10, Loretta 8, Martha A. 3, John A. 1 5-10-74
Jane M. Gannaway 20, Martin 30, William J. 2, Mary Ann 8/12, Milly Ann 60 (Va), King HINCH 15, Thomas ROGERS 25 4-2-9 (B)
Thomas Ganaway 38, Mary Ann 38, William Jesse R. 15, John S. 11, Sira M. 3, Sarah E. 9/12 5-8-61
William Ganaway 73 (Va) 5-10-75
William K. Ganaway 48, Eliza Jane 48, Mary P. 19, Martha Ann 17, William C.B. 15, Orville P. 13, Eliza Jane 9, Susan A. 9, Onslow C. 4, Polly BROYLES 83 (Va) 4-3-17

1880 CENSUS

Ed M. Ganaway 39, Elizabeth J. 43 (w), Alonza W. 23, Ann E. 21, Martha A. 13, John A. 11, Walter C. 9, Elmer M. 6, Minney M. 3, Edney 6/12 5-5-41
M.A. Ganaway 48, J.T. 20 (s), C.M. 13 (s), S.E. 19 (d), T.W. 8 (s), O.W. 4 (s), T.C. GANAWAY* 66(?)[probably 48] [*marked through, "dead"] 9-31-266
Rector Ganaway 24, V.J. 20 (w), T.D. 4 (s) 9-31-265

1900 CENSUS

Cyria M. Gannaway 33 (Jan 1867-M 10), Mary A. 33 (Jan 1867-T/NC/T-M 10-3-2), Eldon T. 8 (Oct 1891), Emmett W. 5 (Dec 1894), Mary A. GANNAWAY 68 (m) (July 1831-Wd 8-4)[widow of Thomas C.] 13-308B-355/368
Earnest Ganiway 25 (Sep 1874-M 2)(Harnessmaker), Allice 26 (Mar 1874-M 2-1-1), Graydon 1 (Jan 1899) 10-252B-53
Edward Gannaway 66 (June 1833-M 10), Mary J. 47 (Dec 1852-M 10-0-0), Minnie 23 (d)(May 1877), Edna 20 (d)(Dec 1879) 8-285A-335/337
Onslo G. Gannaway 34 (Mar 1866-T/Va/T-M 13)(Hotel Keeper), Syrana L. 31 (Sep 1868-M 13-0-0), Grace LOVE 25 (Oct 1874-Oh/Oh/Oh)(Servant) 5-234A-117
Thomas Gannaway 23 (Nov 1876-M 0)(Merchant), Emma 23 (June 1876-M 0-0-0), White 27 (u)(Nov 1872) (Clerk), Oliver 24 (u)(Dec 1875)(Photographer) 5-239A-210
Vesta Gannaway 40 (Aug 1859-Wd 8-7), Perry W. 16 (Sep 1883), Darius C. 13 (Sep 1886), Fred R. 9 (Oct 1890), Jesse N. 6 (July 1893), William R. 3 (Oct 1896) 13-295A-100/102
Walter Gannaway 28 (May 1872-M 2)(Tanner), Mandy 26 (Sep 1874-M 2-1-1), Ona G. 1 (Nov 1898) 8-285A-334/336
William Gannaway 45 (July 1854-T/Va/T-M 22), Mary F. 38 (Mar 1862-M 22-10-6), George O. 21 (Mar 1879) (School Teacher), Ova D. 19 (Sep 1880), Lula 18 (Jan 1882), Charles L. 15 (Jan 1885), Hattie R. 12 (Oct 1887), Walter F. 3 (June 1896) 5-238B-208/208

MARRIAGES

A. E. Ganaway to John W. Broyles q.v.
C.M. Ganaway to Mary A. Wright, 3 Mar 1890 (4 Mar), Wm A. Green JP 1-598
E.N. Ganaway to E.J. Foust, 22 June 1876 (same), G.W. Renfro MG 1-#1449
Earnest Ganaway to Alice V. Jordan, 20 Mar 1898, W.R. Grimsley MG 4-99
Edward Ganaway to Teryer Jane Furguson, 18 Aug 1855 (no return) 1-#513
Elijah Gannaway to Mollie Anderson, 11 Sep 1886 (same), J.P. Phillips MG 1-540
J.R. Ganaway to Vesta J. Kennedy, 19 Feb 1876 (20 Feb), J.H. Locke JP 1-#1435
Loretta Ganaway to C. F. Stone q.v.
M. A. Gannaway to W. A. Buttram q.v.
Malissa C. Ganaway to John H. Hamilton q.v.
Mary B. Ganaway to Ira M. Whittenburg q.v.
Mary P. Ganaway to I. N. Broyles q.v.
O.G. Ganaway to S.L. Henderson, 27 Oct 1887 (28 Oct), John H. Parrott MG 1-540
Rhoda R. Ganaway to Samuel Whittenburg q.v.
Thomas C. Ganaway to Mary Ann Rector, 2 Dec 1852 (same), Wm Witcher MG 1-#393
Thomas D. Ganaway to Emma D. Crawley, 25 Nov 1899 (26 Nov), T.D. Shelton MG, E.E. Gannaway W 3-77
William Ganaway to Mary Moore [nee Frazier], 14 Sep 1865 (no return) 1-#847

- - - - - - - - - - - - -

GARDENHIRE

1870 CENSUS

William Gardenhire 22, Mary Jane 25 1-8-47 (B)

1880 CENSUS

James Gardenhire 30: see Jeff Brooks (B)

1900 CENSUS

Emma Gardenhire 41: see John Acuff
Henry Gardenhire 15: see Thomas Nash
William C. Gardenhire 67, Julia 42: see Geo W. Goodrich

MARRIAGES

G.W. Gardenhire to Eliza J. Hale, 17 Jan 1874 (18 Jan), A.J. Mathis MG 1-#1326
G.W. Gardenhire to Emma Acuff, 9 Mar 1889 (20 Mar), W. S. Hale MG 1-569
S. E. Gardenhire to J. B. Walker q.v.

- - - - - - - - - - - - -

GARDNER / GARTNER

1900 CENSUS

Stephen Gartner 40 (Nov 1859-Oh/Oh/Del)(Teacher) 2-198B-139/144

MARRIAGES

Emma Gardner to Henry Porter q.v.
Lula Gardner to John Wilson q.v.

- - - - - - - - - - - - -

GARLAND

MARRIAGE

Ella Garland to James B. Walker q.v.

- - - - - - - - - - - - -

GARNER

MARRIAGES

Elisha Garner to Elsy Gunn or Guin, 23 May 1865 (same), Daniel Broyles JP 1-#838

Lucinda Garner to James Bridgeman q.v.

- - - - - - - - - - - - -

GARRETT / GARRIT / GAERETT

1880 CENSUS

Ellen Gaerett 17: see R. F. Land

1900 CENSUS

Marlar Garret 25 (Mar 1874-M 6), Mary 24 (Ap 1876-M 6-3-3), Nettie 4 (Ap 1896), Lular 3 (Mar 1897), Bertha 1 (Feb 1899) 1-188B-190/199

MARRIAGES

Joshua Garrett to Louisa Jane Crow, 3 Sep 1865 (same), A.P. Early MG 1-#867

Martin Garritt to Mary McCulley, 13 July 1895, H. B. Heiskell JP 4-86

- - - - - - - - - - - - -

GARRISON

1860 CENSUS

Calvin Garrison 38, Eliza M. 36, Melville 14, Myra A. 12, Mary 10, Vesta 8, Clementine 6, James B. 3, Young 1 1-85-583

Jacob Garrison 63 (NC), Emaline 19 1-87-596

John Garrison 71 (NC), Polly 46, James C. 17, Calvin S. 14, Robert W. 12, Elizabeth 8 3-56-387

Joseph Garrison 67 (NC), Mary 58, Hannah 27, Thomas HASE 7 5-37-253

Richard L. Garrison 34 (NC), Mary S. 22, Mam V. 4, Elvira A. 3, Mary E. 1/12 1-83-564

1870 CENSUS

Ann Garrison 11 (B): see James F. Ladd

Eliza A. Garrison 46, Melville 24, Mariah A. 22, Mary 20, Vesta 18, Clementine 16, James B. 13, Young 11, Dreniss(?) 3 7-5-36

Elvira Garrison 10: see James Holloway

Jacob Garrison 75 (NC), Emaline 30, Mary 8, George W. 6, John 5, James L. 2 1-3-15

James Garrison 26, Nancy J. 29, John W. 4, William C. 2 3-4-27

James I. Garrison 30, Catharine 28, Eliza Ann 1 1-19-127

Jane Garrison 34, Amanda 16, Sarah E. 12, Malinda 10, William 9, Charles 7: see Uriah Rawlings (B)

Joseph Garrison 78 (NC), Mary 67, Adam McDONALD 23, Hannah 42, Thomas 15, Mary A. 6, Joseph 1 4-17-112

Richard L. Garrison 45 (NC), Judah H. 25, Mary E. 10, James L. 7, Sarah C. 2, Margarette J. 9/12 1-12-76

1880 CENSUS

Emiline Garrison 38, Mary 19, George 16, John 14, James 12, Elizabeth 9, Jacob 7 2-37-303

James Garrison 39, Jane 39, John 15, Wm 13, T.N. 9 (s), S.M. 6 (d), M.B. 4 (d) 3-27-216

Mary Garrison 19: see J. R. Crawford

Richard Garrison 54 (Dry Goods Merchant), Julia 35 (w), Mary 20, James 17, Sarah 12, Margaret 11, Jeanett 9, John 5, William 2, Lillie 7/12 1-16-135

Sallie Garrison 16 (B): see John Brewer

W.L. Garrison 31: see C.A. Brown(?)

1900 CENSUS

Andrew J. Garrison 50 (Mar 1850-M 27), Eliza 46 (Ap 1864-M 27-8-8), Ton [George Washington] 15 (Dec 1884), Amanda 13 (Jan 1887), John 9 (Oct 1890), Arthur 7 (Mar 1894), Sarah E. 3 (Aug 1896), Arena FUGATE 26 (d)(Feb 1874-Wd 3-3), Betty McCLENDON 23 (d)(Dec 1876-M 0-0-0), Jackson 24 (sl)(Aug 1875-M 0) 14-221B-159/163

Emmaline Garrison 58: see James L. Garrison

Jacob E. Garrison 26 (Ap 1873-T/NC/T-M 2), Amanda M. 25 (July 1874-M 2-1-1), Howell B. 6/12 (Jan 1900), Emet THOMPSON 18 (Sep 1881)(Servant) 2-195B-85/88

James Garrison 37 (Jan 1863-M 16)(Saloon Keeper), Lellian 37 (Nov 1862-M 16-3-3), Frederick 14 (Oct 1885), Gather 9 (Oct 1890), Grover 8 (May 1892) 14-216A-59/60

James C. Garrison 56 (Mar 1844-M 35), Nancy J. 59 (Dec 1840-M 35-5-5), William C. 32 (Dec 1867), Thomas N. 29 (Sep 1870) 3-206A-104/114

James L. Garrison 31 (June 1868-T/NC/T-M 9), Mary J. 28 (June 1871-T/NC/NC-M 9-5-4), Myrtle 8 (Ap 1892), James F. 6 (Jan 1894), Roxy M. 2 (June 1897), Gracie E. 1 (Dec 1898), Emmaline GARRISON 58 (m)(Feb 1842-Wd 6-6) 2-196B-103/107

Jane Garrison 55 (Nov 1844-Wd 8-7), John 24 (Aug 1875), Will 22 (Sep 1877), Lilli 20 (Oct 1879), Laura 15 (Dec 1884) 1-183B-96/100

John H. Garrison 34 (Feb 1866-M 10), Harrie 38 (July 1861-M 10-1-1), Nancy 8 (July 1891) 2-196B-103/108

John W. Garrison 34: see Robert W. Wassom

MARRIAGES

B.L. Garrison to Susie Reed, 4 July 1897, L.L. Barton JP 4-95

Bettie Garrison to J. McClendon q.v.

Betty Garrison to W. N. Cox q.v.

Eliza Garrison to I. E. Morris q.v.

Elizabeth Garrison to C. D. Reed q.v.

Elizabeth Garrison to William McClendon q.v.

Elvira A. Garrison to Moses F. Thompson q.v.

Emiline Garrison to Jacob Garrison q.v.

Gorgia E. Garrison to Samuel P. Casey q.v.

Hannah Jane Garrison to Joseph Emory q.v.

J.A. Garrison to Mollie Looper, 20 Dec 1900, S.A. Waller MG 4-107

J.H. Garrison to Vesta Jane Morriss, 19 Sep 1884 (21 Sep), T.L. Long JP 1-474

Jack Garrison to Janie Kelley, 28 Mar 1885 (same), W.F. Blevins JP 1-491

Jacob Garrison to Elizabeth Erwin, 8 Ap 1850 (9 Ap), Daniel Broyles JP

Jacob Garrison to Emiline Garrison, 22 Feb 1860 (26 Mar), N.H. Long JP 1-#1648

Jacob Garrison to Elvira Burdett, 27 Mar 1875 (same), H.L.W. Furgusson JP 1-#1396

James Garrison to Mary Monday, 27 Nov 1873 (28 Nov), L.M. Moore ?? 1-#1313

James L. Garrison to M.J. Ensley, 2 Aug 1891, J.L. McPherson JP 4-29

John Garrison to Harriett McClendon, 5 Aug 1890, J.P. Thompson JP 4-22

Lethia Garrison to John Reid q.v.
Lillie Garrison to George Ingraham q.v.
Maggie Garrison to W. M. Smith q.v.
Martha Garrison to Elija H. Huff q.v.
Mary Garrison to D. M. Robits q.v.
Myra A. Garrison to James S. Burnett q.v.
Myria Garrison to Lewis Fugate q.v.
Nettie Garrison to J. C. McGee q.v.
R.L. Garrison to Mary L. Holloway, 2 May 1855 (3 May), N.H. Long JP 1-#494
Rena Garrison to William K. Fugate q.v.
Richard L. Garrison to July H. Newport, 3 Ap 1867 (4 Ap), Wm R.S. Thompson JP 1-#946
Sallie Garrison to James Wilkey q.v.
Utah Garrison to May Jewell or Jewett, 18 Jan 1896, G.M. Morris MG 4-93
Vanney Garrison to Thomas H. Ingle q.v.
W.H. Garrison to Louise Peters, 23 Dec 1901 (probably 1900), W.T. West MG 4-107

- - - - - - - - - - - - -

GASS

1860 CENSUS
William T. Gass 38, Ann 57 4-43-290
1870 CENSUS
Leona A. Gass 10, Samuel E. 8: see Orson A. Shipley
Monesa(?) Gass 56, Uria 14, Nelly Ann 12, Andrew 9 4-15-99 (B)
Roland Gass 57, Amanda 36, Andrew J. 13, John C. 11, Allen B. 9, Mary E. 7, Alfred S. 5, Elizabeth F. 2, Amanda A. 11/12, Francis DUISMORE 67 (NC), Lorinda A. DUISMORE 12 5-4-27 (B)
William T. Gass 49, Ann 69, Caroline WEBSTER 31 (NC), Susan DARWIN (B) 30, Mary DARWIN (B) 7, Andrew DARWIN (B) 5 4-11-69
1880 CENSUS
Alfred Gass 21: see Daniel Odem
Sam Gass 17: see J. O. Johnson
W.T. Gass 58, A.K. 56, J.M. 9 (s), S.(?) J.(?) GASS (Mu) 21 (Servant), Justin THOMPSON (Mu) 18 (Servant) 4-36-299
William Gass 25 (Blacksmith), Holland A. 25 (Mu): see Cyrus Henry
1900 CENSUS
Andrew Gass 46 (Jan 1854-M 5), Belle D. 20 (Jan 1876-M 5-3-3), Adelia M. 4 (June 1896), Brown G. 2 (Aug 1897), Maggie G. 1 (Jan 1899) 5-231A-54 (B)
Jacob Gass 29 (Dec 1870-S), Martha PALMER 69 (Sep 1832-Oh/Va/Va-Wd 4-4)(Housekeeper), Wesley H. PALMER 29 (Oct 1870-Mo/NY/Oh-M 1), Clara 21 (dl*)(May 1879-Ind/Pa/Del-M 1), Clarence O. VAN ORSDAL 8 (gs*)(June 1891-T/Mich/Mo), Oden L. VAN ORSDAL 6 (gs*)(Nov 1893-T/Mich/Mo) 4-224A-210/214 [*relationship to Martha Palmer]
John Gass 42 (B): see James L. Pelfrey
John Henry(?) Gass 40 (Mar 1860-M 14), Ruth 35 (Ap 1865-M 14-6-6), Zac(?) 14 (May 1886), Ronia 11 (July 1888), Cinda 10 (May 1890), Betti 7 (July 1892), James(?) 4 (Ap 1896), Clide 1 (July 1898), Ronia CLIFE [CRISP?] 72 (m)(Feb 1828-Wd 3-3) 12-181B-63/66
William T. Gass 78 (Sep 1821-T/T/Va-M 38), Adaline K. 77 (Mar 1823-T/Va/Va-M 38-4-3), Lena BROYLES 16 (Mar 1884)(Servant) 5-234A-120/120
[Wm T. married in 1872 Mrs. Adaline K. Brown Spears, widow of Gen. James G. Spears]
MARRIAGES
Adelia Gass to Brown Spear q.v.
Andrew Gass to Bell Darwin, 26 Aug 1894, W.L. Patton MG 4-64
Delila R. Gass to Owin A. Shipley q.v.
J.W. Gass to Nellie H. or Annie N. Darwin, 27 Nov 1900 (same), J.A. Whitner MG, W.L. Abel W 3-248
John Gass to Ruth Crisp, 23 Dec 1886 (26 Dec), D.B. McNeal JP 1-509
Lorinda Gass to John Corwin or Corvin q.v.
Mary Gass to Charley Phillips q.v.
Samuel Gass to Mary A. Johns, no date (probably 1882), no JP or MG 4-11(109)

- - - - - - - - - - - - -

GASTON

1900 CENSUS
Richard S. Gaston 37 (May 1863-M 7), Sarah E. 24 (May 1876-M 7-3-2), Charlie E. 5 (Jan 1895), George A. 3 (Ap 1896) 6-240B-20/20

- - - - - - - - - - - - -

GATES / GAITES / GAITS

1880 CENSUS
C. B. Gates 6: see G. H. Debord
Mary Gates(?) 13: see W. Morgan
MARRIAGES
John T. Gates to Alice Marler, 6 Nov 1892, W.R. Grimsley MG 4-53
Maggie Gaites to N. L. Brown q.v.
William Gaits to Jane Hair, 20 Sep 1855 (21 Sep), R.T. Howard MG 1-#525

- - - - - - - - - - - - -

GATHER / GAITHER

1900 CENSUS
Jeff D. Gaither 36 (Ap 1864-NC/NC/NC-M 2)(Preacher), Florence 25 (June 1874-M 2-1-1), Eliza G. 1 (Dec 1898), Susan M. KYLE 10 (sil)(Aug 1889) 15-272B-82 (B)
MARRIAGE
Charley Gather to Josie Linch, 5 Jan 1893, S.W. Burnett MG 4-49

- - - - - - - - - - - - -

GAUT / GOUT

1870 CENSUS
Dolly Gout 75 (Va) 8-19-129
1880 CENSUS– None
1900 CENSUS
Thomas R. Gaut 23: see William Day

- - - - - - - - - - - - -

GAY
(see also GRAY)

1880 CENSUS
Sherard Gay 43, Margaret J. 29 (w) 5-7-55
MARRIAGES
J.H. Gay to Lillie M. Wasson, 24 Ap 1889 (same), J.L. Prator ?? 1-572
Margaret J. Gay or Gray to J. L. Brown q.v.

- - - - - - - - - - - - -

GEAR

1860 CENSUS
Elizabeth Gear 50, Caroline 28, Harriet 23, Zilpha A. 21, Jady L. DOTSON 26 3-61-422
MARRIAGES
Emely L. Gear to M. L. Patterson q.v.
Zelpha Ann Gear to Charles Brady q.v.

- - - - - - - - - - - - -

GEARING

MARRIAGE
Elizabeth Gearing to William Hill q.v.

- - - - - - - - - - - - -

GEBTS

1880 CENSUS
Charley Gebts(?) 25 (RR Laborer) 5-11-103

- - - - - - - - - - - - -

GENOE / GENNOE / GENOW / GINNO / GINNOW / JENOE / JANOW / JENNOW

1870 CENSUS
David Genow 25, Emily 27 3-18-128
Hesakiah Genow 22, Sarah 17, James H. 2 3-12-87
James Genow 45, Emaline 43, Edward 18, Mary E. 16, Nancy 12, George W. 10, Jefferson 8, Sarah 6, James 5, Lucinda 1 3-18-126
William R. Genow 24, Sela B. 23, George W. 3, Calvin 20, Charlotte 19 3-18-127
1880 CENSUS
Calvin Janow 30, Charlotte 28, A.J. 7 (d), J.R. 4 (s), Annie 7/12 (d), B.F. TAYLOR 52 (boarder)(Saddler) 4-9-68
David Janow 33, M.L. 10: see A.C. O'Neal
E. Janow 27, W.J. 20, M.B. 1 (d) 3-29-233
H. Janow 32, Sarah 27, H. 11, E. 7, Susan 4, Lina 3, Marion 8/12 3-18-138
Jas Janow 55, E. 50, Martha 27, Nancy 22, Geo 18, J. 16 (s), F.C. 11 (d), Mary 21 (d) 3-19-155
1900 CENSUS
Dack Jenno 27 (Aug 1872-M 2), Annie 24 (Jan 1876-M 2-1-1), Edney 1 (Mar 1899), Franky SINGLETON 41 (ml)(Sep 1858-S) 10-260B-209/214
David Jenow 55 (Feb 1845-M 18), Louisa A. 60 (Mar 1840-T/NC/NC-M 18) 3-209B-172/187
Edward Jannow 48 (Ap 1852-M 22), Nancy J. 42 (Mar 1858-M 22-8-5), Ann P. 13 (May 1887), Robert T. 10 (Oct 1889), Ortha E. 11/12 (June 1899) 4-225B-233/237 (Ridge Road east of Spring City and Dayton Road)
George W. Genow 41 (Feb 1866-M 20), Mahala 41 (Ap 1859-M 20-7-7), Thomas 19 (May 1881), Lener 16 (Aug 1883), Charles 14 (Oct 1885), James O. 11 (June 1888), Magg 9 (May 1891), Truther 7 (Mar 1893), Darius 3 (Sep 1897) 5-234B-134/134
James Genow 25: see Merril L. Fugate
James Genow 31 (July 1868-M 13), Nancy 31 (Feb 1869-M 13-6-6), Sarah E. 12 (May 1888), Robert Y. 10 (Nov 1889), Frank L.M. 8 (Feb 1892), Albert G. 6 (May 1894), Samuel F. 4 (Ap 1896), Laura A. 1 (Feb 1899) 3-210B-183/200
Jeff or Jebb Jeno 33 (Jan 1867), Mary 44 (si)(Nov 1856), Ani 38 (si)(July 1868) 1-190A-212/224 (Spring City)
MARRIAGES
Adelia Janoe(?) to John Collins q.v.
Calvin Ginno to Charlotty Horner, 7 Mar 1868 (11 Mar), W.W. Low JP 1-#1005
David Genow to Mary E. Owens, 30 Oct 1869 (same), Jonathan Chastine MG 1-#1120
Dock Gennoe to Annie Singleton, 23 Feb 1898 (same), W.L. Lillard JP, G.W. Johnson W 2-253
Edward Jennow to Jane Mitchell, 16 Aug 1878 (18 Aug), Wm W. Low JP 1-#1576
Eula Jenoe to Mynatt Phillips q.v.
Flora L. Genoe or Gence to Elvin F. Sharp q.v.
G.W. Jenoe to Mahala Marshal, 12 May 1880 (13 May), T.H. McPherson JP 1-#1729
Hesekiah Ginnow to Sarah L. Wade, 21 Sep 1867 (24 Sep), J.B. McCallom MG 1-#971
Hesekiah Gennoe to Carie Ivester, 31 Jan 1898 (same), W.L. Lillard JP & W 2-245
J.H. Jenoe to Nancy A. Fugate, 28 July 1887 (same), Taylor Russell JP 1-534
James Janow to Jane Henry(?), 3 Dec 1896, J.H. Seward MG 4-96
Lena Jenno or Jones to W. E. Parker q.v.
M. L. Genoe to J. S. Crisp q.v.
Nannie Janow to Elmer Conley q.v.

- - - - - - - - - - - - -

GENTRY

1860 CENSUS
Joshua Gentry 22, Flerney 45, Elizabeth 17, Edwin 16, Martha J. 14, Thomas 13, Samuel 10, Harriet 6, William 4 5-39-262
1870 CENSUS– None
1880 CENSUS
Sirena J. Gentry 57, Sarah N. 23, Josey B. 1 5-2-12
1900 CENSUS
Charlie Gentry (no dates)– non resident in District 12
Robert L.(?) Gentry 25 (Feb 1875-M 3), Birthy 20 (Mar 1880-M 3-2-1), Floyed 8/12 (Oct 1899) 12-180B-50/53
MARRIAGES
Candace Gentry to Maynard Stewart q.v.
Frank Gentry to Minnie Long, 10 Nov 1900 (11 Nov), W.W. Richards MG, Newt(?) Gentry W 3-240
J.C. Gentry to Alice Dunning, 20 Sep 1899 (21 Sep), W.A. Howard MG, Wm Brown W 3-36
John Gentry(?) to Phrina Bowman, 29 Sep 1888 (30 Sep), W.R. Grimsley MG 1-565

Stephen Gentry to Syntha Wilkey, 9 Ap 1893, T.F. Hale MG 4-50

- - - - - - - - - - - - -

GERMANS

MARRIAGE

Estella M. Germans to Sebastian Davenport q.v.

- - - - - - - - - - - - -

GHOLSTON

1900 CENSUS

William Gholston 52 (Mar 1848-M 17), Margaret A. 37 (May 1863-M 17-2-2), William E. 22 (Aug 1877), Carl 10 (Nov 1889) 15-170B-45

- - - - - - - - - - - - -

GIBBS

1870 CENSUS

Sarah A. Gibbs 48 (NC), Asberry 18, Joseph 15 1-20-130

1880 CENSUS– None

1900 CENSUS

Joseph Gibbs 24 (Unk-M 0), Mrs. Joseph Gibbs 23 (Unk-M 0-0) 6-247B-152/153

MARRIAGE

Addison A. Gibbs to Martha J. Newby, 24 June 1872 (26 June), G.W. Renfro MG 1-#1241

- - - - - - - - - - - - -

GIBSON / GIPSON

1860 CENSUS

Jacob Gibson 40 (Ky), Mary M. 43, Columbus 21, Elizabeth A. 18, Andrew J. 15, Lucinda C. 13, Sarah M. 11, Archibald 9, Martha 7 1-91-620

Samuel Gibson 35 (NC)(Blacksmith), Loretta 37, Elias 11, Margaret 9, Matilda 8, Mary J. 7, Charles P. 6, Mary J. [sic] 5, Nancy 3, Thomas F. 6/12 6-36-246

1870 CENSUS

Columbus Gibson 27, Jane E. 24, Thomas E. 4, William 1, Sarah M. 22, Archibald 19, Martha E. 17 105-34

Ilas Gipson 14 (B): see Charles Brady

1880 CENSUS

Andrew Gibson 34 (Merchant), Sarah 28, William 5, James 3, John 1 2-36-289

Columbus Gibson 39, Elizabeth 33, Thomas 13, Willis 11, George 8, James 7, Columbus 5, Charles 3, John 1/12 1-13-108

M.G. Gipson 23, T.S. 32 (w) 8-11-93

Randolph Gibson 30, Sarah 22, William 6, Heterogeneous 2, Mary 1/12 12-5-45

1900 CENSUS

Alvin C.(?) Gibson 41 (Nov 1858-T/Ky/Ky-M 13)(Grocer), Dora L. 35 (July 1864-T/Ga/T-M 13-5-4), Luther H. 12 (Mar 1888-Ga), George M. 9 (Sep 1890), William W. 7 (Oct 1892), Alvin P. 3 (Nov 1896), Lucy D. SELLS 18 (ne)(Jan 1882-Ga) 10-322A-40/42

Carey Gipson 23 (Mar 1877-M 1)(Coke Puller?), Rosie 19 (Jan 1881-M 1-1-0) 10-258A-155/159

Columbus Gibson 25 (May 1875-M 6), Mary 22 (Oct 1877-M 6-3-3), Lara 4 (Sep 1875), Floyad 2 (Mar 1898), Albert 10/12 (July 1899), Lucy 13 (si)(June 1886) 1-186B-153/161

Elisha S. Gibson 68 (Aug 1831-T/SC/T-M 47), Mary A. 64 (Feb 1836-M 47-11-10), Catherine 41 (Jan 1859) 8-315A-92/95

George W. Gipson 44 (Oct 1855-M 7)(Fisherman), Nancy A. 40 (Feb 1860-M 7-4-2), Theodore R. 5 (Dec 1894), Savanna F. 2 (June 1898) 2-196A-93/96

Haley Gibson 49: see Roscoe Bennett (B)

James Gibson 57 (Unk 1843-M 25), Sallie 56 (Mar 1844-T/SC/SC-M 25-1-1), Walter 15 (Mar 1885) 3-205A-87/94

James Gibson 23 (Feb 1873-M 6), Cansada 25 (July 1874-M 6-3-3), Land 5 (s)(Aug 1894), Mattie 2 (Nov 1897), Ruth 11/12 (July 1899) 1-187A-168/176

Joseph Gibson 24 (June 1875-M 0), Ina 26 (Mar 1874-M 0-0), Alice CAMPBELL 21 (sil)(Dec 1878) 8-276B-163/164

Matthew Gibson 51 (Jan 1849-M 24)(Bartender), Sarah F. 57 (Aug 1842-NC/NC/NC-M 24-1-0) 8-314B-86/89

Mathew R. Gibson 27 (Nov 1872-M 8)(Coal Miner), Rula 25 (Oct 1874-M 8-3-3), Henry 6 (Aug 1893), Nora 5 (Feb 1895), May 3 (Jan 1897) 8-288A-398/400

Randolph Gibson 30 (May 1870-Wd), Wheeler 16 (June 1883), Lara 10 (Sep 1889) 12-182B-74/77

William Gibson 32 (Mar 1868-M 5)(Grocer), Tennie 23 (Mar 1887 sic-M 5-1-1), Raymond 3 (Sep 1896) 14-216A-63/64

Wilum R. Gibson 25 (School Teacher): see Wilum Halliet

MARRIAGES

A. [Addie L.] Gibson to T.N.L. Cunnyngham q.v.

A.J. Gipson to Sarah Ingle, 15 Dec 1873 (17 Dec), J.P. Roddy MG 1-#1318

C.F. Gibson to Rosa Cofer, 15 Oct 1898 (16 Oct), W.L. Lillard JP & W 2-334

Columbus Gibson to Jane E. Cash, 13 Dec 1865 (14 Dec), Wm W. Low JP 1-#1068

Columbus A. Gibson to Mary Elizabeth Ingle, 9 Sept 1894, J.M. Hinds MG, Emerson Gibson W

Ella Gibson to William Phillips q.v.

G.W. Gibson to Alice Bandy, 16 Dec 1887 (18 Dec), M.R. Grimsley MG 1-541

G.W. Gibson to Nancy Grisham, 14 Ap 1894, J.W. Cowles JP 4-65

H. J. Gibson to J. S. Clack q.v.

Hettie Gibson to Samuel Ray q.v.

J.E. Gibson to Mary Thomas, 9 Jan 1898, T.D. Shelton ?? 4-93

Lewis Gibson to Malisa T. Keith, 22 Dec 1894, J.Q. Shaver MG 4-75

Louisa Gibson to Thomas Suggs q.v.

Lucind C. Gibson to Essquire Evans q.v.

M. E. Gipson to A. R. Turk q.v.

M.R. Gibson to E.T. Hughes, 27 Dec 1891, W.S. Neighbors MG 4-38

Mahala Gibson to Moses Perkins q.v.

Mary Gibson to J. W. Riley q.v.

Mary E. Gibson to James A. Alexander q.v.

Mollie Gibson to W. J. Jolly q.v.

Nancy C. Gibson to Robert Walker q.v.

Sarah E. Gibson (Mrs.) to W. S. Hallock q.v.

Reuben Gibson to Catharine Zimmerman, 1 Dec 1881 (7 Dec), F.R. Morgan JP 1-477
T.E. Gibson to Hattie Jolley, 13 Jan 1895, J.M. Hinds MG 4-85
Thomas E. Gibson to L.J. Cantrell, 11 Dec 1884 (14 Dec), W.F. West MG 1-461
W.F. Gibson to Teck(?) Lockmiller, 25 Aug 1895, John Ware MG 4-84
W.L. Gibson to Tinnie Marsh, 24 Mar 1895, R.M. Trentham JP 4-77
W.W. Gibson to Emma B. Hicks, 15 Nov 1888 (2 Nov), A.C. Peters MG 1-562

- - - - - - - - - - - - -

GIDEON / GIDDEONS / GIDION

1870 CENSUS
George W. Gideon 50, Rebecca L. RENO 26 (NC), William J. 3, George W. 1 5-8-55
Magie Gidion 82 (Va): see James Detherage
MARRIAGE
G.W. Giddeons to Serena Jolly, 11 Jan 1888 (12 Jan), John Howard MG 1-#998

- - - - - - - - - - - - -

GILBERT

1900 CENSUS
Allen Gilbert 54: see Emma Gillespie (B)
MARRIAGE
Thomas Gilbert to Tempey Johnson, 22 Dec 1883 (25 Dec), F.R. Morgan JP 1-477

- - - - - - - - - - - - -

GILES / JILES

1860 CENSUS
William Giles 35, Elizabeth 33, Penelope A. 10, Elisha K. 8, Henry S. 6, Susan M. 5, Adaline A. 3 2-78-532
1870 CENSUS
William Giles 45, Elizabeth 44, Penelopy 20, Elisha 18, Henry 16, Susan 14, Nodena 12, Rhoda 10, Sarah 8, William 1 3-12-83
1880 CENSUS
Henry Giles 26, Mary 21 Anna 2, Stella 1/12 2-28-222
Wm Giles 55, E.J. 52 (si), P.A. 30 (d), E.N. 28 (s), H.S. 26 (s), M.D. 24 (d), R.E. 18 (d), W.R. 19 (s) 3-26-210
1900 CENSUS
Elisha K. Giles 54 (Ap 1846-Wd), Charles SUTTON 22 (Nov 1877)(Servant 3-202A-47/50
Erwin P. Giles 70 (Feb 1830-Ver/Mass/Mass-M 3)(Merchant), Bettie 44 (Dec 1855-M 3-1-1), Willie 8 (July 1891) 13-309A-367/380
Joseph Giles 24 (Dec 1875-T/T/NC)(Coal Miner), Mary MENTLY 26 (si)(Dec 1873-M 3-4-3), James 2 (nw) (Jan 1897), Bessie JORDAN 12 (ne)(Aug 1887), Della 9 (ne)(Dec 1890) 8-282A-267/269
MARRIAGES
Charles E. Giles to Caldonia Crawley, 13 June 1894, G.W. Colend VDM 4-67
Dena Giles to Columbus Jones q.v.
E.P. Giles to Bettie Harris, 14 Aug 1896 (same), J.A. Whitner M 2-56
H.S. Giles to H.C. Stephenson, 18 Aug 1877 (same), John Howard MG 1-#1512
Henry Giles to Sarah Marshall, 30 Dec 1884 (31 Dec), S.S. Hale MG 1-463
Sallie D. Giles to Harrel Reece q.v.

- - - - - - - - - - - - -

GILL

1900 CENSUS
Jake Gill 35: see Hettie White (B)
John Gill 23 (June 1876-M 8), Hattie 28 (Oct 1871-M 8-3-3), Walter 6 (Sep 1893), Alvin 4 (Ap 1896), Anna M. 1 (Aug 1898) 15-274B-118
John Gill 62 (July 1837-M 32), Martha A. 49 (Unk 1851-M 32-8-6), Waymond 19 (May 1881), Alta 15 (July 1884), Lester 11 (June 1888) 15-271A-62
Robert Gill 19: see William W. Edwards
Samuel Gill 28 (Unk 1872-M 4), Ida 24 (Dec 1875-T/SC/SC-M 4-0), Isabel 8 (Aug 1891), John 7 (Mar 1893), Mary WILSON 69 (ml)(Dec 1830-SC/SC/SC-Wd 5-5) 15-271B-67
MARRIAGES
Alta Gill to Bascomb Nicholson q.v.
Amanda Gill to Elijah Bowles q.v.
John Gill to Hattie McCullough, 4 Sep 1892, J.W. Williamson MG 4-49
Samuel Gill to Elizabeth Cranmore, 16 Sep 1888 (same), W.S. Hale MG 1-553
Samuel Gill to Ida Wilson, 21 Sep 1895, F.M. Cook MG 4-87

- - - - - - - - - - - - -

GILLESPIE

1860 CENSUS
David E. Gillespie 35, Sarah 24, Mary J. 2 2-78-529
James W. Gillespie 38 (Physician), Nancy 30, Ann 1, James WALLACE 25 (Lawyer) 6-113-776
John C. Gillespie 48, Margaret J. 26, Alice 5, Nelly 3, Nancy 2, James W. 4/12 2-78-526 [John C. married Margaret J. McEwen on 31 Jan 1854 in Roane County]
Lucinda Gillespie 37, George T. 3 2-73-496
Robert N. Gillespie 53, Hannah 45, Ann 16, Thomas 14, Robert 12, James 11, William 9, Henry A. CRAWFORD 22 (County Court Clerk) 6-109-744
1870 CENSUS
Allen Gillespie 38, Mariah E. 36, William 15, George W. 13, Mary A. 6, Queen V. 4, Joseph 2, Charles 9/12 6-7-45 (Mu) (B)
Auston Gillespie 60, Brueiller 47, Manda E. 6, Tennessee 15 2-11-78 (B)
Hannah Gillespie 55, Thomas J. 26, James N. Jr. 21, William S. 19, Sarah NICHOLS 21, Julia GILLESPIE (B) 12 6-16-115
Henry Gillespie 22, Harriet 20, James W. 1 7-2-11 (B)
James W. Gillespie 51 (Physician), Nancy 39, Kitty C. 8, William B. 1 6-11-71
Jefferson Gillespie 25, Eliza A. 17 2-11-77 (B)
John Gillespie 46, Susan 27, Eliza 10, Jack 9 6-16-116 (B)(Mu)
Julia Gillespie 12 (B): see Hannah Gillespie

Lucinda Gillespie 46, George G. 14, Mary Robenson GILLESPIE(?) 26, Emma JOLLY (B) 8 2-11-75
Malinda Gillespie 40 (Va), Amos 19, Stephen 17, Jane 15, Ralph 12, Grace 9, Aulston 7, Grace RODDY 65 (Va) 1-13-82 (B)
Mary Gillespie 55, Darthula 18, John 15, Tennessee 7, Anna 4 6-9-59 (B)
Nancy Gillespie 43, Charles L. 15, Samuel J. 13, Mary M. 11, Samuel 10, James E. 5 2-11-76 (B)
Philip Gillespie 21, Elizabeth 20, Manda 2, Sallie 1 2-12-80 (B)
Ralph Gillespie 54, Sallie 46, Eli 17, Siller 14, Jefferson 12, Martha 10, Joseph 8, Thomas 6, Rufus 1 2-11-79 (B)
Robert N. Gillespie 24, Emily P. 21, James 2 6-9-55
Sidney Gillespie 34, Diannah 15, Sallie 7, Willie 4, George W. 6/12 2-12-81 (B)
William S. Gillespie 31 (Store Clerk): see James F. Ladd

1880 CENSUS

Amos Gillespie 27, Mary 25, Sarah 10, Frank 6, Stephen 4, Florence 2, Almeda 1/12 12-7-58 (B)
Anderson Gillespie 24, Salina 23, Joseph 5, Cassie 3, Lula 2: see Peter Dooley (B)
Ann Gillespie 8: see Gracie Roddy (B)
Austin Gillespie 21: see Susan Roddy
C. Gillespie 9 (B): see E. Cunnyngham
Calvin Gillespie 44, Julia 59 (w), Calvin 19 (Miner), Mary HENDERSON 19 (d), William 22 (sl)(Miner), Isabele DONALDSON 12 (sd), Polk 11 (ss), Jack 8 (ss), Joseph CAPPS 23 (boarder)(Miner) 2-28-225 (B) (Mu)
Daniel Gillespie 45, Rose 50 (w) 5-6-49
Eli Gillespie 27, Anna 24, Nellie 6, Mary 2 2-33-266 (B) (Mu)
H.L. Gillespie 55, M.A. 50, Geo 20, Joseph 14, Flivera 8, N.A. 6 4-12-96 (B)
Jack Gillespie 56, Susan A. 37 (w), Eliza A. 21 (d) 6-19-178/182 (Mu)
James W. Gillespie 30, Lennie C. 23, George T. 4, Carry A. 2, E.C. RAWLINGS 51 (a), Jane JOHNSON (B) 28 (Cook)("Left")[probably husband left], Willie J. (B) 4 ("with her"), Mary E. (B) 1 ("with her"), Martha WATERHOUSE (B) 12 (Nurse), James H. MARIOTT (B) 27 (Farm Laborer) 6-21-188/191
Jeff Gillespie 39, Ann 25, Alice 9, John 6, James 5, Anna 3, Franklin 1, Cilla 75 (m) 2-33-271 (B) (Mu)
Jeff Gillespie 21 (Teamster), Emma 17 2-29-230 (B)
John Gillespie 25 (Servant)(B): see Henry A. Crawford
Joseph Gillespie 16 (Servant)(B): see Lucinda Gillespie
Lucinda Gillespie 55, Thomas 23 (s), Elizabeth ANDREWS 25 (Servant), Joseph GILLESPIE (B) 16 (Servant), William DONALDSON (B) 13 (Servant) 2-28-223
Mary Gillespie 21, Robert 5, William 1 (Mu): see Wash Donaldson (Mu)
Mary Gillespie 55, Ann 14 (B): see J. H. Rogers
Mira Gillespie 17, Anna 1 (Mu): see Robert Robinson (B)
Nancy Gillespie 54, Samuel 22 (Miner), Mary HAMPTON 20 (d)(Cook) 2-28-226 (B)
Phillip Gillespie 28, Elizabeth 27, Amanda 12, Columbus 10, John 6, Victoria 3, Rolling 1/12 2-33-272 (B)
Robert N. Gillespie 36, Lilie M. 26, James 11, Charley S. 9, Mary L. 2/12, Amy FRAZIER (B) 56 (Servant, Cook), Nan (B) 28 (Servant, Cook), Thomas D. (B) 25 (Servant), Ed (B) 15, William (B) 11 6-25-193/197 [Robert married Lillie Wilshire on 21 May 1878]
Samuel Gillespie 28, Mary 17 (w), Robert UPTON (B) 20 (Servant), Hugh McCALEB (B) 20 (Servant), James JOLLEY (B) 14 (Servant) 2-28-224
Sarah Gillespie 24, William 13, George 10, Julia 13 (B) (Mu): see Arch McCaleb
Sarah Gillespie 50, Joseph 16, Thomas 14, Rufus 12, Cilla 25, George 5 2-34-275 (B)
Stephen Gillespie 26 (B): see Hugh Heiskell
Thomas J. Gillespie 36: see Henry A. Crawford
W.S. Gillespie 29 (Lawyer), Cara S. 25, Janie S. 2, Mary J. CHADICK 59, Matilda FREEMAN (Mu) 14 (Servant, Cook), Nelson WOMACK (B) 18 (Servant, Laborer) 6-23-12 (Madison Street, Washington)
William Gillespie 25, Martha 29, N.B. 13 4-12-97 (Mu)

1900 CENSUS

Archable M. Gillespie 18, Thomas S. 16: see Saml S. Brady
Andrew Gillespie 46 (Sep 1853-Ind/Oh/Oh)(Coal Miner) 13-304A-266/276
Columbles Gillespie 29 (Nov 1870-M 9), Minerva 25 (Unk-M 9-3-2), Elsie 5 (Oct 1894), Nolan 2 (Oct 1897), Calvin 21 (b)(Dec 1878), Lillie BOYD 23 (Servant) 8-318B-165/171 (B)
Elic Gillespie 45 (Aug 1854-Wd), May K. 22 (Ap 1878), Chaidy 19 (Feb 1881), Anna 16 (Oct 1883), Thomas W. 11 (Dec 1888) 2-193A-37/38 (B)
Emma Gillespie 36 (Aug 1863-Wd)(Boarding House Keeper), James JOLLY 30 (b)(Jan 1870);
Boarders: James WADKINS 22 (Dec 1877) (Furnaceman), William HAMBRICK 23 (Aug 1876)(Furnace Top Filler), James ALLEN 32 (Unk-Va/Va/Va), Allen GILBERT 54 (Feb 1846-Ga/Ga/Ga)(Coal Miner) 10-322A-44/46 (B)
James Gillespie 53 (Feb 1847-T/Va/Va-M 28) 7-264A-262/267
James R. Gillespie 31 (Oct 1868)(Physician) 10-331B-236/251
Jennie A. Gillespie 18, Mary A. 15: see Henry A. Crawford
Joseph Gillespie 33 (Feb 1867-M 8), Mary 33 (Mar 1867-M 8-8-3), Dewey 3 (Aug 1896), Virgie L. 2 (Mar 1898), Emmet 6/12 (Nov 1899), George 40 (b)(Unk 1860-M 1) 15-271-61/62 (B)
Laura A. Gillespie 38 (Jan 1861-D 2-2)(Owns Farm), Jean B. 16 (May 1884), George T. 14 (June 1885) 14-219A-128/131
Philip Gillespie 52 (Mar 1848-M 33), Bettie J. 50 (Jan 1850-M 33-12-8), Mc 16 (July 1883), Belle S. 13 (Aug 1886), Julie 75 (ml)(Unk 1825-Wd 16-10) 2-193A-36/37 (B)
Sallie(?) Gillespie 36 (Unk-Ga/Ga/Ga-Wd)(Washwoman), Florence 18 (d)(Dec 1881-T/Ga/Ga), John S. 6 (s) (June 1893), Omelia CARTER 6/12 (gd)(Dec 1899), James SNELLINGS 61 (boarder)(Unk) 8-318A-157/162 (B)
Sarah Gillespie 70, Persila 38: see James Martin (B)
Thos G. Gillespie 43 (July 1856-T/Va/Va-D)(No Business), Edgar MILLIGAN 16 (Mar 1884)(Saw Mill Fireman), William LOFTIN 73 (Aug 1826-NJ/NJ/NJ-Wd) (Tailor) 14-220A-143/147
Thomas S. Gillespie 56: see Benjamin F. Mealer
Thomas J. Gillespie 55 (Ap 1845-T/T/Va-M 30), Eliza A. 46 (June 1853-T/T/Va-M 30-11-9), John G. 28 (Feb 1872)(School Teacher), Julia 19 (Ap 1881), Charles 16 (Nov 1883), Joseph T. 14 (Dec 1885), Thomas J. 12 (Feb 1888), Mary E. 10 (Feb 1890), Idella 8 (Ap

1892) 2-192B-33/34 (B)
Thomas J. Gillespie 33 (Nov 1866-M 11), Belle S. 30 (July 1869-M 11-5-5), Arthur 11 (Feb 1889), Christiner 9 (June 1892), Bessey 5 (Sep 1894), Gale 3 (Dec 1896), Homer O. 1 (Feb 1899) 2-193A-38/39 (B)
William Gillespie 46 (Jan 1854-Wd)(Blacksmith) 15-271A-60 (B)

MARRIAGES

Addaline Gillespie to Sewell Phillips q.v.
Adelia Gillespie to William P. Darwin q.v.
Alice Gillespie to Cal Moore q.v.
Amanda Gillespie to John Sharp q.v.
Anna Gillespie to Isam Chatten q.v.
Anna A. Gillespie to H. A. Crawford q.v.
Carrie Gillespie to N. M. Hensley q.v.
Columbus Gillespie to Minerva Henderson, 14 May 1892, S.W. Burnett MG 4-40
Eliza Gillespie to Phillip Henry q.v.
Florence Gillespie to Enoch Suddith q.v.
G. H. Gillespie to Joe Rodgers q.v.
George Gillespie to Victoria Brown, 12 Aug 1863
J.W. Gillespie to M.C. Rawlings, 30 Nov 1874 (1 Dec), S. Phillips MG 1-#1375
Jane Gillespie to Robert Kelley q.v.
John Gillespie to Ida Whitfield, 19 Mar 1899, J.H. Keylon JP 4-100
Joseph Gillespie to Mary Wilson, 20 Aug 1891, D.J. Young ?? 4-32
Julia Gillespie to Hugh McCully q.v.
Leander Gillespie to Luther Smith q.v.
Lula Gillespie to George W. Miller q.v.
Mariah Gillespie to Enslow Betterson q.v.
Mariah Gillespie to Frank Peak q.v.
Mary Ann Gillespie to Wash Donaldson q.v.
Mary J. Gillespie to Burton McCaleb q.v.
Minerva Gillespie to Samuel Roddy q.v.
Minnie Gillespie to Arthur Jefferson q.v.
Nellie Gillespie to Henry Jackson q.v.
Queen Gillespie to Isaac W. Gains q.v.
Robert N. Gillespie to Emily P. Frazier, 31 Dec 1867 (same), W.H. Bell MG 1-#994
Sallue Gillespie to Spince Tedder q.v.
Susie Gillespie to John Crawford q.v.
T.G. Gillespie to Laura Peters (21, Harrison, Tenn), 22 Aug 1882, T. Ashburn MG, Miss Sallie Brown & B. Craighead W 4-9(82)
T.J. Gillespie to Lucinda McCaleb, 5 Sep 1855 (5 Jan 1855)[sic], A.D. Paul JP 1-#497
T.J. Gillespie to M.E. Crawford, 30 Dec 1880 (same), A.P. Early MG 1-294
Tom Gillespie to Bell Donaldson, 5 Feb 1889 (no return) 1-577
Tommie Gillespie to W. M. Shelton q.v.
Victoria Gillespie to Green Caldwell q.v.

GILLETT

1900 CENSUS

Edwin R. Gillett 69 (Mar 1831-NY/Conn/NY-M 34)(Pensioner), Matilda S. 63 (Aug 1836-Oh/NY/NY-M 34-0), Tabitha DAVENPORT 23 (boarder)(May 1877-Ky/Ky/Ky)(Music Teacher) 13-309B-377/391

GILLIAM / GILLUM / GUILLIAM / GILLAND / GILLEAND

1860 CENSUS

James Gillam 25, Sophena A. 19, George R. 1 2-81-548
Major C. Gillam 29, Abbey E. 20, Harriet J. 6/12 1-82-554
Nathaniel M. Gillam 70 (Va), Sarah 59 (NC), Sarah R. 20, Lette M. 18, Jesse T. 14 1-82-556

1870 CENSUS

James D. Gilliam 45, Soprona A. 29, George R. 11, William V. 9, James D. 7, Jesse L. 4, Noah M 1 (Va) 2-2-8
Major C. Gilliam 39, Emaline 31, Harriette J. 10, Nancy J. 9, Nathaniel B. 7, John C. 5, Aduline 1 1-12-79
Sally S. Gilliam 70 (NC) 1-12-81

1880 CENSUS

James Gilliam 53, Sophronia 39, George 21, William 19, James 17, Jesse 14, Nora 11, Miranvin 8 (s), Synda 2 (s) 2-40-323
Major Gilliam 49, Emilen 40, Hariet 20, Nancy 18, Nathaniel 17, John 15, Achalin 12, Elizabeth 9, Richard 7, Sarah 5 1-17-145
Sarah Gilliam 80: see Joel Dodson

1900 CENSUS

Dick Gillum 26 (Jan 1874-M 6), Addie 21 (Jan 1879-M 6-2-2), Maggi 3 (Aug 1896), Emma 10/12 (July 1899) 1-186B-152/160
Emma Gillum 64: see Johnson West
Floyd Gilliam 2: see David McCullough
Harriet Gilleand 47 (June 1852-Wd 5-3), William A. 17 (June 1882), Ida L. 14 (Dec 1885) 2-195A-73/76 [see James Henderson 73/75]
James D. Gillum 75: see William V. Gillum
Neton Guillin(?) 28: see Joseph McDonald
Sidney H. Gillum 22 (Oct 1877-Wd)(Cancal--?-- Books) 2-191B-15/15
William V. Gillum 39 (Mar 1861-M 16), Florence A. 36 (Feb 1864-M 6-2-2), Idella 12 (Oct 1887), Paul 9 (Oct 1890), Archibald C. 19 (b)(May 1881), James D. GILLUM 75 (f)(Aug 1824-T/NC/NC-Wd)(Landlord) 2-191B-16/16

MARRIAGES

Alic A. Gilland to James H. Henderson q.v.
Annie Guilliam to John Frank q.v.
G.R. Gilliam (22) to Harriett D. Holloway (21), 1 Sep 1881, Zachariah Rose MG, George Dodson & Pleasant Holloway W 4-5(41)
Harriet Gilliam to Jonathan G. West q.v.
Isabella Gilliam to George W. Parks q.v.
J.D. Gillim to M.M. McFalls, 22 Sep 1885 (24 Sep), L.T. Long JP 1-520 & 1-568
J.P. Gilliam to Linda L. Tallent, 1 Jan 1890 (16 Jan), J.A. Darr MG 1-591
James D. Gilliam to Sophronia A. Paul, no date (no return) [probably 1858] 1-#637
Jesse T. Gilliam to Sephrona F. Johnson, 24 Dec 1866 (no return) 1-#924
John W. Gilliam to Delcina Everett, 27 June 1854 (30 June), N.H. Long JP 1-#465 [1-#503 shows name as Delina Everett and year as 1855]
Letha Gilliam to Jasper Dodson q.v.
Major C. Gilliam to Abegail E. Holloway, 13 Oct 1858, N.H. Long JP 1-#662
N. M. Gilliam to J. H. Dodson q.v.

Nancy Gillum to Jeff Ray q.v.
Nancy Jane Gilliam to James S. Holloway q.v.
S. R. Gilliam to H. B. Harney q.v.
W.R. [Richard Waterhouse] Gilliam to Ada Filyaw, 3 June 1894, J.R. Clark MG 4-74
W.V. Gilliam [misspelled Gillmore on license] to Flovimer A. Hindes, 24 July 1884 (6 Mar), L.T. Long JP 1-545

\- - - - - - - - - - - -

GILMORE / GALMORE

1900 CENSUS
Angeline M. Gilmore 66 (July 1834-Oh/Ver/Mass-Wd 1-1), Albert A. 25 (July 1874-Oh)(Weighmaster at mine) 10-331B-233/248
MARRIAGES
B.L. Gilmore to Sarah J. Colter 3 Dec 1886 (8 Dec), J.D. Drake MG 1-513
Barton L. Gilmore to Essie Haworth, 25 May 1895, John C. Lord MG 4-81
Willy Galmore to Cicero Harris q.v.

\- - - - - - - - - - - -

GINGERY / GENGERY

1860 CENSUS
Margaret Gengery 24: see Thomas McPherson
MARRIAGE
Margarett Gingery to John Wyott q.v.

\- - - - - - - - - - - -

GIRDEN / GERTON

1900 CENSUS
Don Gerton 19, Alisa 21: see William McConnell (B)
MARRIAGE
D.H. Girden to Alise Cooper, 5 Jan 1900 (same), J.C. Dodd JP, Jas Bennet(?) & D.H. Giraton(?) W 3-105

\- - - - - - - - - - - -

GIST

1860 CENSUS
John Gist 29, Nancy A. 22, Amanda M. 3, Sarah E. 5/12 1-88-604
MARRIAGES
B. E. Gist to E. C. Foust q.v.
Thomas J. Gist to Louiza Cozby, no date (no return) [probably 1858]

\- - - - - - - - - - - -

GITGOOD / GETGOOD

1900 CENSUS
James Getgood 47 (July 1852-M 23), Sarah 45 (Ap 1855-M 23-8-8), Mary 22 (Mar 1878), Linter 19 (d)(Oct 1880), Washington 15 (Ap 1885), Charles 12 (Jan 1888), All 8 (s)(July 1891), John 5 (June 1894), Carrie 3 (Oct 1896) 1-189A-201/210 (Spring City)
Parrin Gitgood 24 (Mar 1876-M 1)(RR Section Hand), Artitia 20 (June 1879-M 1-0-0) 10-328B-182/195

MARRIAGE
E.P. Gitgood to Artie Mitchell, 18 Mar 1899 (19 Mar), J.W. Romino JP, J.A. Hand or Hurd W 2-393

\- - - - - - - - - - - -

GITHENS

1900 CENSUS
D. Estaing Githens 45 (Feb 1855-Oh/Oh/Oh-M 16)(Builder & Contractor), Samantha 43 (Dec 1856-Oh/Oh/Oh-M 16-0-0) 14-213A-2/2

\- - - - - - - - - - - -

GITTKENS

1880 CENSUS
E.E. Gittkens 58, B.(?) E. 12 (gd), N.R GITTKENS 62 (w?)[marked through, "Dead") 9-31-268

\- - - - - - - - - - - -

GIVENS

1900 CENSUS
William L. Givens 45 (Jan 1855-T/Ky/T-M 20)(Attorney), Lennie 39 (Aug 1860-M 20-10-5), Claud R. 18 (Sep 1881)(Clerk, Privision Store), Clarice L. 17 (Jan 1883), Edna L. 14 (Nov 1885), Nicholas G. 7 (May 1893), Charles G. 2 (Aug 1897) 10-323B-81/85
MARRIAGE
W.L. Givens to Linnie Foster, 10 Dec 1878 (Dec ??), John W. Thompson JP 1-#1596

\- - - - - - - - - - - -

GLANTON

MARRIAGE
James L. Glanton to Sarah E. Bell, 23 Oct 1880 (28 Oct), W.J. Cunningham MG 1-293

\- - - - - - - - - - - -

GLASS

1880 CENSUS
Harvey Glass 20 (Mu): see Nathan Yearwood (B)
MARRIAGES
M. S. Glass to S. H. Helton q.v.
Mary S. Glass to Thomas R. Clifton q.v.

\- - - - - - - - - - - -

GLENN / GLEN

1900 CENSUS
Henry Glen 38: see Caroline Pullum
MARRIAGE
Henry Glenn to Lucy Renfro, 26 May 1886 (17 June), Anthony Smith MG 1-523

\- - - - - - - - - - - -

GOAD / GOOD / GOURD / GOARD

1860 CENSUS
Robert Goard 76: see Thomas K. Green
Ruth Gourd 72: see Henry Fisher
1870 CENSUS
Ruth Gourd 86 (NC): see Thomas C. Darwin
1880 CENSUS
Tom Good 32, Johny 15 (s), Jane(?)[ink blob] GOOD 75 (m) 9-32-276
1900 CENSUS
John Good 45 (Ap 1855-M 20), Eliza E. 44 (Aug 1855-M 20-6-5), Lena 16 (Sep 1883), Alice 12 (Dec 1887), Lillie 10 (May 1890), Henry 5 (Nov 1894), Bertha M. 2 (May 1898) 15-272B-88
Sally Good 19: see Holliday Spivey
MARRIAGES
Charles W. Goad to Mahala Compton, 22 Dec 1853 (same), T.J. Creede JP 1-#433
J.K. Goad to Elizabeth Cranmore, 29 Ap 1879 (30 Ap), Wm S. Hale MG 1-#1617
John Good to Lennie Miller, 9 June 1888 (10 June), J.Q. Shaver MG 1-550
Mary Good to J. N. Reively q.v.
W.B. Goad to M.M. Snodgrass, 6 Nov 1851 (same), A. Johns MG 1-#354

- - - - - - - - - - - - -

GOADDER

1900 CENSUS
Elbert Goadder 53 (Mar 1847-Mass/Mass/Mass-Wd), Jesty 27 (May 1873-RI/Mass/Canada) 12-179A-11/12

- - - - - - - - - - - - -

GODBY

MARRIAGE
Martha C. Godby to James L. Myrick q.v.

- - - - - - - - - - - - -

GODBYHERE / GODBEHERE / GODBEHIRE / GODSBEHERE

1860 CENSUS
Thomas Godbehere 41, Mary A. 31, William L. 12, Mary S. 9, Martha E. 4 5-51-344
1870 CENSUS
Thomas Godbyhere 52, Mary Ann 42, William L. 21, Mary S. 19, Martha E.J. 14, Addison A.T. 9, Catharine E.A. 3 4-4-24
1880 CENSUS
William L. Godbehere 31, Tenn 33 (w), M.J. 1 (d), Mary WHITTENBURG 40 (sil) 4-31-251
Thomas Godbehere 60, M.S. 28 (d), A.T. 18 (s), C.J. 14 (d) 4-31-252
1900 CENSUS
Allen Godbehere 40 (May 1860-M 11), Eliza 39 (Dec 1860-M 11-6-5), Clemie A. 9 (July 1890), Thos P. 8 (Jan 1892), Mary E. 7 (Jan 1893), Lillie J. 5 (Feb 1895), Ardie M. 3 (Mar 1897) 4-226A-246/250 (Rhea Springs & Washington Road)
Jane Godbehere 21: see Jasper W. McClarin
Wm L. Godbehere 56 (Mar 1844-M 18), Martha E. 45 (Ap 1855-M 18-7-4), Jane 21 (Nov 1878), Samuel T. 19 (July 1880), James H. 16 (Mar 1884), Sarah S. 14 (Ap 1886), Wm J. 8 (Feb 1892), Jesse G. 4 (Ap 1896) 4-225B-231/235 (Ridge Road east of Spring City & Dayton Road)

MARRIAGES
A.T. Godbehire to E.S. Scarbrough, 27 Aug 1889 (29 Aug), A.J. Wyrick JP 1-587
Eliza Ann Godbehere to John McClendon q.v.
Mary S. Godbehere to W. J. McLarrin q.v.
W.L. Godbehere (34) to Elvira Reese (30), 25 Mar 1883, S. Breeding JP, W.P. Morrell & Pheba Wyrick W 4-13(126)
William L. Godbyhere to M.T. Whittenburg, 9 Feb 1878 (10 Feb), John Howard MG 1-#1547

- - - - - - - - - - - - -

GODDARD

1900 CENSUS
James Goddard 41 (Dec 1858-M 16), Doshie 39 (Unk 1861-M 16-5-4), Mollie 15 (May 1885), Della 10 (Feb 1890), Claud 7 (May 1893), Mack 5 (Oct 1895) 15-269A-26

MARRIAGES
Hugh Goddard to Julia L. Dodson, 5 Sep 1860 (6 Sep), T.H. McPherson JP 1-#725
John Goddard to Sarah Carter, 31 Mar 1894, T.F. Shaver JP 4-65

- - - - - - - - - - - - -

GODSEY

1860 CENSUS
John Godsey 35, Elizabeth 30, William 12, Rial 10, John 8, Phebe 6, Charles 4 2-70-479
1870 CENSUS– None
1880 CENSUS
William Godsey 24 (Ship Carpenter), Minirva 24, William 4 2-27-214
1900 CENSUS
George L. Godsey 30 (Oct 1869-Ind/Ind/Oh-M 4), Louella J. 29 (Jan 1871-M 4-2-2), Anna E. 3 (Feb 1897), James S. 11/12 (June 1899) 14-221A-150/154

MARRIAGES
Charley Godsey to Sallie Hollins, 28 June 1898 (same), R.C. Knight JP, Jesse Godsey W 2-296
Clara Godsey to Lee Sherrill q.v.
F.M. Godsey to Nancy L. Farner, 14 June 1891, W.R. Clack JP 4-27
John Godsey to Vinie Bess, 15 June 1898 (same), R. C. Knight JP, R.J. Killough W 2-294
Sarah A. Godsey to William F. Loden(?)
Sary Elizabeth Godsey to M.D. Lafayette Copeland q.v.

- - - - - - - - - - - - -

GOINS / GOINES / GOWINS / GOWING / GONE

1900 CENSUS

Arch Goins 25 (Sep 1874-M 0), Florence 16 (Unk 1884-Ga/Ga/Ga-M 0-0) 15-270B-44

Asbury Goins 23 (Jan 1877-M 3)(Coal Miner), Vesta A. 20 (Nov 1879-M 3-2-1), Clarence E. 9/12 (Aug 1899) 13-302A-216/224 (B) (W) (W)

Benjamin Goin 37 (July 1862-M 11)(Teamster), Saphrony 29 (Oct 1870-M 11-4-3), Rachael C. 7 (Oct 1892), Joanna 4 (June 1895), Frank J. 5/12 (Dec 1899), Elijah 25 (c)(Jan 1875-Wd)(Teamster) 13-306A-310/322 (B)

Bradford Goin 56 (Unk 1844-M 27), Mary 46 (Unk 1854-M 27-8-8), Martha 24 (Nov 1875), Burke 22 (Jan 1878), Jennie 20 (Mar 1880), Culdy 18 (Jan 1882), Emma 14 (Feb 1886), Bettie 12 (Ap 1888), William 9 (Dec 1890), Grover 7 (Feb 1893) 13-296A-122/124 (B)

George Goins 54 (Oct 1845-M 23), Sarah 38 (Oct 1861-M 23-11-8), Dora 16 (Oct 1883), Bertie 15 (Feb 1885), Myrtle 12 (Oct 1887), Minnie 9 (Oct 1890), Stella 6 (May 1894), Raulie 4 (May 1896), Winfield 1 (Aug 1898), Sallie GOINS 85 (si)(Unk 1815), Albert 18 (c)(Sep 1881) 15-271A-63

John Goins 50 (Unk 1850-M 8), Nora B. 25 (Aug 1874-M 8-4-3), Fannie 10 (Sep 1889), Frederic 5 (Nov 1894), Ida J. 4 (Aug 1895), Sarah GADDIS 23 (boarder)(Sep 1876-Ga/Ga/Ga-M 3-0), James 20 (boarder)(Unk 1880-Ga/Ga/Ga), Joseph 11 (boarder)(June 1888-Ga) 15-270B-47

Miller Goin 58 (Unk 1842-M 3), Tilda 50 (Unk 1850-M 3-6-5), Eva N. 19 (Ap 1887), Houston 6 (Jan 1894), Martha CRESEMAN 27 (sil)(Aug 1872-M 1-1-1), Edith May 11/12 (ne)(June 1899) 13-301A-201/208 (B)

Rufus Goin 35 (Unk 1865-M 12), Nancy 27 (Jan 1873-M 12-6-4), William C. 12 (Jan 1888), Hunter 10 (July 1889), Mamie 4 (Dec 1895), Dolly 2 (Mar 1898) 13-295B-111/113 (B)

Sallie Goins 85: see George Goins

Sarah Goins 47: see William M. Brown

MARRIAGES

Albert Goins or Gowins to Bertie or Bettie Gowins, 25 June 1900 (same), Sherman Wilson MG, Roland Kyle W 3-172

Arch Gowins or Gowens to Florence Gaddis, 23 May 1900 (same), Sherman Wilson MG, Lon Stewart W 3-157

Asberry Goins to Vesta Wilson, 2 Jan 1897 (same), F.M. Bandy MG, Hugh Blevins & Asbery Jones W 2-100

Benjamin F. Gowins to Saphrinna Gowins, 17 June 1888 (same), I.W. Holt JP 1-552

Charley Gowings to Nancy Gowings, 2 Mar 1899 (same), ND Reed MG, Charley Givins & Arch Gones(?) W 2-391

Edley Goins or Gowains to Bell Jenkins, 18 Nov 1899 (same), J.P. Houston MG, Rufus Gowains W 3-72

Elijah Gowins to Laura Gowins, 29 Jan 1890 (same), F.M. Capps JP 1-596

Eliza Gowin(?) to George Scott q.v.

John Gowing(?) to Cassie Jordan, 27 Mar 1894, A.D. Hubbard MG 4-73

John Goins to Lizzie Smith, 27 Oct 1900 (same), W.A. Howard MG, A.P. Nichols W 3-235

John Gowins(?) to Bell Cantor or Carter, 14 Nov 1900 (same), Wesley Cranmore MG 3-242

Laura Gowins to Elijah Gowins q.v.

Lottie C. Goins to Joseph Dodson q.v.

Martha Goines to Burrel Crisman q.v.

Matilda Gowins to Miller Goins q.v.

Miller Goins to Matilda Goins, 1 Oct 1896 (same), F.M. Bandy MG, B.F. Goin W 2-72

Molly Gowins to William Erwin q.v.

Nancy Gowings to Charles Gowings q.v.

Roda A. Goins to J. W. Rudd q.v.

Saphrinna Gowins to Benjamin F. Gowins q.v.

Sariah E. Gone(?) to George C. Eldridge q.v. [Sariah, 20 yrs old, born in White County]

W.C. Gowins to Emaline Jordan, 23 Feb 1888 (same), J.W. Pence MG 1-545

William I. Goines to Mary Rudd, 27 Feb 1899 (same), R.C. Knight JP, David Rudd W 2-389

- - - - - - - - - - - - -

GOLESTEN

MARRIAGE

Lucinda Golesten to George Hendenson q.v.

- - - - - - - - - - - - -

GONCE / GOUNCE

1880 CENSUS

John Gounce 71 (Cabnetmaker), Sarah 48 (w), Flora 10 (d), William 8 (s), Lassie 6 (d) 2-21-169

1900 CENSUS

Ellen S. Gonce 64 (Mar 1836-Wd 8-3) 2-198B-141/146

- - - - - - - - - - - - -

GONIA

1900 CENSUS

Henry Gonia 32 (Ap 1868-NY/Mass/NY-M 8)(Coal Miner), Elizabeth 28 (Ap 1872-M 8-3-3), Lassiephine 6 (June 1893), Isaac B. 4 (Jan 1896), Nasie 1 (Jun 1898) 10-322B-55/58

MARRIAGE

Henry Gonia to Lizzie Franklin, 18 Feb 1892, A.W. Frazier JP 4-33

- - - - - - - - - - - - -

GOODALL

1900 CENSUS

Tom Goodall 18: see William Randolph (B)

- - - - - - - - - - - - -

GOODEN / GOODING / GOODIN

1880 CENSUS

Ebinezer Gooding 36, Persif 42 (w), Persis 8 (d), Walter 6 12-3-20

1900 CENSUS

Charley Goodin 20 (July 1879-T/T/Ind-M 1)(RR Brakeman), Mary 21 (Nov 1878-M 1-1-1), Carl 1 (May 1899) 10-259A-179/183

Frank Gooden 25 (Jan 1875-T/T/Ind-M 5)(RR Laborer), Ellen 25 (Ap 1875-T/T/NC-M 5-3-3), Evie 4 (Aug 1895), Eddie 1 (Sep 1898), Grady 4/12 (Jan 1900) 10-259A-176/180

Scott Gooden 45 (May 1855-Wd)(RR Section Boss), Albert 13 (Oct 1886), Fred 2 (Ap 1898), Lizzie SCOTT 40 (ml)(Mar 1860-Ga/Ga/Ga-Wd 4-3), Arty 16 (sil)(Feb 1884), Evy 12 (sil)(Dec 1887), Maud 11 (sil)(May 1889) 10-259A-177/181

MARRIAGES

Eva Gooden to John Cox q.v.

Mary Gooden to Hany(?) Bradford q.v.

- - - - - - - - - - - - -

GOODMAN

MARRIAGE

Nancy Jane Goodman to Francis E. Morefield q.v.

- - - - - - - - - - - - -

GOODRICK

1900 CENSUS

George W. Goodrich 58 (Nov 1831-Ky/Conn/NJ-M 21) (Hotel Keeper), Tennessee W. 42 (June 1857-Ark/T/T-M 21-6-6), Jesse B. 19 (June 1880-Ky), Mary B. 18 (Oct 1881-Ky), Lela A. 16 (Jan 1884-Ky), George G. 12 (Mar 1888), Lula A. 8 (Mar 1892), Adelia D. 6 (Feb 1894): *Boarders at Hotel:* James R. MILLER 21 (Dec 1878-T/T/Va-M 0)(Fire Insurance Agent), Nellie E. MILLER 16 (Nov 1883-T/NC/T-M 0-0), Luther E. MINTON 23 (Feb 1877-M 0)(Telegraph Operator), Flora MINTON 21 (Mar 1879-Mo/T/Ind-M 0-0), Ellen HOOVER 47 (Dec 1852-Ky/Va/Ky-M 26-3-1)(Music Teacher), Kaye 17 (July 1882-Ky), William C. GARDENHIRE 67 (May 1833-M 19)(Landlord), Julia GARDENDIRE 42 (Ap 1858-Tex/SC/Ky-M 19-0), Annie W. FRAZIER 34 (Dec 1865-Tex/SC/Ky-M 13-2-2)(Vocal Culture Instructor), Julia FRAZIER 10 (Sep 1889), Ida FRAZIER 7 (Sep 1892), Ida L. MOODY 36 (Feb 1864-Tex/SC/Ky-M 12-2-2), Herbert MOODY 10 (Jan 1890-Calif/ Ill/Tex), Kenneth MOODY 3 (Dec 1896-Calif), Benjamin SCHOOLFIELD 30 (Oct 1869) (Bookkeeper, Iron Works), James C. MILLER 19 (Sep 1880)(Blacksmith's Helper), Harry HEINEY 31 (Jan 1869-Ind/Ind/Ind) (Mechanical Engineer), Harold MILLER 24 (Feb 1876-RI/RI/Pa)(Chemist), Susie AYERS 23 (Dec 1876-Mo/Mo/Ireland) (Stenographer) 10-320A-2

MARRIAGE

G.W. Goodrich to T.W. Darwin, 21 Ap 1879 (24 Ap), J.M. Hall MG 1-#1615 & 1-#1693

- - - - - - - - - - - - -

GOODSON / GODSON

1870 CENSUS

John Goodson 21: see Alfred Hutchison

MARRIAGE

C.A. Goodson or Godson to L.E. Jones, 22 Dec 1900 (same), W.W. Richards MG, W.H. McDade & S. Goodson W 3-259

- - - - - - - - - - - - -

GOODWIN

1900 CENSUS

Joseph L. Goodwin 23 (Nov 1876)(Physician) 6-242A-44

- - - - - - - - - - - - -

GOOSEBY

1880 CENSUS

James Gooseby 30 (Barber), Sarah 17 (Cook) (B): see Jere Wassom

Sarah Gooseby 15 (Mu): see Robert Robinson (B)

- - - - - - - - - - - - -

GORDON / GORDEN / GORDIN

1900 CENSUS

John Gordon 43 (Unk-M 14), Lizzie 30 (Ap 1870-M 14-5-2), Virgie B. 13 (June 1866), Minnie J. 10 (July 1889) 8-316B-133/138 (B)

Maud Gordon 3: see Charles Harper (B)

MARRIAGES

Charley Gorden to Mary E. Smith, 23 July 1898 (24 July), W.S. Hale MG, Cane Gibson [signed by X] W 2-302

George F. Gordin to Mary E. Elmer, no date, probably Dec 1900, L.L. Barton JP 4-107

L. D. Gorden to Emma Boman or Brown, 5 July 1890 (same), W.G. Gaston ?? 1-603

- - - - - - - - - - - - -

GORMANY / GORMAN / GERMANY

1900 CENSUS

Ada Gormany 23 (Ap 1877-Ala/Ala/Ala-M 9-9-5), Loy 7 (1893), Henry 5 (1895), Maggie 4 (1896), Dan 1 (Sep 1898) 8-315A-94/98 (B)

Louis Gormany 60 (Ap 1840-Ga/Ga/Ga-M 43-2-1), Loy 8 (July 1891) 8-311B-21/22 (B)

MARRIAGES

Alex Gormany(?) to Ada Forney, 13 July 1889 (same), S.W. Burnett MG 1-576

C.C. Gorman to T. M. Watson q.v.

Price Gormany to Minnie Freeman, 4 Jan 1897 (same), S.W. Burnett MG, J.J. Hoge W 2-101

Rylid [Riley in index] Gormany to Ellie Beard, 27 Ap 1899, G.R. Baldwin JP 4-103 (B)

- - - - - - - - - - - - -

GOSSET / GOSSETT / GOSSIT

1880 CENSUS

R. Gossett 19: see Peyton Wite

1900 CENSUS

Eli Gossett 23 (Ap 1877-M 1)(Coal Miner), Nannie M. 27 (Feb 1873-Ga/T/T-M 1-1-1), Floyd J. 4 (d)(Feb 1896), Florence ELLIS 20 (sil)(Jan 1880-Ala), Sam GOSSETT 18 (b)(June 1881)(Coal Miner) 8-311B-22/23

Lon Gossett 26 (Jan 1872-M 1)(Coal Miner), Martha 34 (May 1866-M 1-5-5), Elen LEDFORD 17 (sd)(Jan 1883), Evin 11 (ss)(July 1888), Annes 8 (sd)(June 1891), May 6 (sd)(July 1893), Affie 4 (ss)(May 1896) 10-259B-190/194

Walter C. Gossett 54 (Mar 1846-M 13), Margaret M. 29 (Nov 1870-M 13-6-2), John W. 8 (Mar 1892), Callie 2 (Ap 1898) 8-313B-52/55

MARRIAGES

Eli Gossett to Nannie Jewell, 19 Feb 1899 (21 Feb), W.D. Reed MG, W.R. Gossett W 2-384

Josie Gossit to Albert Wilkey q.v.

L.W. Gossett to Martha Ledford, 15 Feb 1899 (same), R.C. Knight JP, J.J. Hogue W 2-381

Margaret Gossett to James Perry q.v.

Millie Gosset to Wyley Waller q.v.

Riley Gosset to Susan Neal, 5 Aug 1889 (on page with 1896), M.F. Moore MG 4-94

W.C. Gossett to Margaret Webb, 12 Nov 1888 (same), John Howard MG 1-572

\- - - - - - - - - - - - -

GOTHARD

1860 CENSUS

Emalin Gothard 40, Ann 19, Amanda 17, William 15, Rufus 13, Taylor 11, Catharine 9, Doctor 5, Josephine 4, Parthe T. 1, Milo 1 8-12-76

George Gothard 67 (SC), Nancy 56 (NC), Wm B. 26, Susan E. 23 8-17-115

Ira G. Gothard 30 (Blacksmith), Elvida E. 30, Isabella S. 7, Amos L. 5, Alto(?) I. 3, Mary 1/12 8-22-148

John C. Gothard 39 (Shoemaker), Catharine 37, Larkin G. 12, John T. 10, Joseph A. 8, David H. 6, Mary F. 4, Mandy T. 1 8-23-158

Larkin Gothard 43 (SC), Louisa 51, Mary W. 23, Nancy 19, Henry 15, Betsy J. 13 8-22-145

Rufus Gothard 14: see Jack Bell

1870 CENSUS

George Gothard 80, William B. 32, Susan E. 28 8-20-135

Larkin Gothard 60 (SC), Louisa 61, Gustavus H. 25, Elizabeth J. 23, Louisa 18 8-10-68

William Gothard 18: see Abigal Dungan

1880 CENSUS

J.A. Gothard 18, E. Gothard 40 (m), T. 20 (d), Tennessee 18 (d), M.J. 16 (d), William 11, James 9, Thomas 4 8-20-169

L.C. Gothard 43, E.A. 32, J.L. 8 (s), J.W. 20 (s), R.A. 19 (d), A.L. 14 (d), T.C. 12 (s), M.L. 5 (d), D.N. 2 (s) 11-39-319

Larkin Gothard 73 8-2-19

Rosa Gothard 18: see Burton Peirce

Tennessee Gothard 25: see W. Morgan

W.B. Gothard 51, Arrisa 54, S.E. 47 (si) 8-12-99

1900 CENSUS

Aruogia(?) Gothard 73 (Mar 1827-T/NC/NC-Wd 3-2), Sarah NICHOLS 52 (d)(Ap 1848), Henry 25 (gs)(Dec 1874), Della 14 (gd)(Aug 1885) 8-286B-363/365

James D. Gothard 51 (Ap 1849-M 27), Tennessee 44 (July 1855-M 27-11-10), James F. 17 (June 1883), Albert E. 15 (Jan 1885), George A. 11 (Mar 1889), Minnie M. 9 (June 1890), Cora M. 4 (Oct 1895), Roy F. 3 (Ap 1897) 11-293A-80

Kate Gothard 45 (Unk 1855-Wd 6-5), James 27 (Unk 1873) (Coal Miner), Thomas 22 (Unk 1878)(Coal Miner), John 18 (Unk 1882)(Coal Miner) 8-277B-183/185

Minnie Gothard 25: see Calvin Thurman

Oakley Gothard 20: see John Corvin

MARRIAGES

Bettie J. Gothard to F. J. Miller q.v.

David Gothard to Martha Vandergriff, 21 Oct 1899 (22 Oct), John Wane MG, G.F. Vandergriff W 3-57

Elias Gothard to Sarah Cate, 7 Mar 1870 (no return) 1-#1148

James Gothard to Ida Corvin, 8 Jan 1899 (same), Sherman Wilson MG, K.W. Ferguson W 2-371

James L. Gothard to Leuty Byerley, 18 Jan 1881, James Corvin MG 4-45

Jane C. Gothard to Hamilton Burchard q.v.

John Gothard to Mary Thurman, 21 Nov 1891, Wm Morgan JP 4-36

Lizzie Gothard to John Burwick q.v.

Mahala Gothard to Washington Morgan q.v.

Mary Gothard to William Majors q.v.

Mary B. Gothard to S. B. Fraly q.v.

Nancy I. Gothard to James M. Benson q.v.

S. A. Gothard to W. F. Pickett q.v.

Tennie Gothard to Elias Reviley q.v.

Tennie Gothard to James Lyle q.v.

Thomas Gothard to Fanine(?) Davis, 26 Aug 1899 (27 Aug), Sherman Wilson MG, J.S. Gothard W 1-26

William B. Gothard to Arizen Nickels, 23 Nov 1874 (same), Calvin Morgan JP 1-#1373

\- - - - - - - - - - - - -

GOTT

1900 CENSUS

Lafayett Gott 51 (Nov 1848-M 2), Catharine 35 (May 1865-M 2-0-0), Charles K. 26 (Sep 1873), Alford H. 21 (May 1879) 3-206B-114/124

MARRIAGES

Lafayett Gott to Katie C. Clouse, 23 May 1898, W.K. Fugate JP 4-107

Mintie Gott to J. M. Ballard q.v.

\- - - - - - - - - - - - -

GRAHAM / GRAYHAM

1860 CENSUS

Sally Graham 17: see Peter McCully

William Graham 50 (Va), Rebecca 38, Joseph 26, Barbery 14, Rebecca NASH 8 3-59-403

William A. Graham 28, Nancy E. 26, Robert 3, John F. 1, Margaret L. NASH 16 5-36-242

1870 CENSUS

Joseph Graham 38, Emily 18 3-8-53

William Graham 40 Nancy 37, Robert M. 14, Grant 7, General S. 4, Lewis L. 1 3-8-52

1880 CENSUS– None

1900 CENSUS

Asa C. or E. Graham 58 (June 1843-NC/NC/NC-M 33), Evaline E. 45 (Feb 1855-NC/NC/NC-M 33-1-1), Eliza 53 (si)(Ap 1847-NC/NC/NC-S), Addie 11 (d)(June 1888-T/Ky/Ky) 3-211B-201/219

Dock Graham 33 (Unk 1867-M 10), Eliza J. 30 (Dec 1869-M 10-1-1), John L. 9 (Dec 1890) 3-211B-202/220

Leslie Grayham 16: see Major Swafford

Minnie Graham 18, Ida L. 2: see Dock B. Reese

MARRIAGES
A.E. Grayham to Vega Barger, 1 Aug 1900, A.M. Broyles JP 4-106
D.W. Graham to Eliza J. Pearce, 6 June 1894, J.W. Cowles JP 4-85
Eli Graham to Anna Ivinster(?), 13 July 1886 (14 July), Calvin Morgan JP 1-503
James Graham to Mary E. Millican, 3 May 1856 (no return) 1-#544
Joseph Graham to Emily J. Milican, 7 July 1869 (8 July), R.T. Howard MG 1-#2203
Mencores(?) Grayham to Looney Shewbird, 27 Dec 1895, A.M. Broyles JP 4-90
S.L. Grayham to Josie Porter, 22 Dec 1891, W.A. Howard MG 4-34

GRANT

1870 CENSUS
Thomas Grant 36 (NC), Jane 35 (SC), Mahala HENDERSON 45 (SC) 4-9-54
MARRIAGE
G.G. Grant to Mattie Calvin, 10 Aug 1887, James Corvin MG 4-44

GRASECLOSE

MARRIAGE
J.H. Graseclose(*) to Florence Register, 27 Jan 1900, L.W. Cartright MG 4-107
[*last name is Garrison in index]

GRASS

MARRIAGES
Margarett Grass to Alex Clingan q.v.
Sarah Grass(?) to John B. Pugh q.v.

GRASHAM / GRISHAM / GRASSHAM

1860 CENSUS
James W. Grisham 21 (Colier), Elizabeth 19 9-98-663
1870 CENSUS
James M. Grisham 27, Elizabeth 25, Eliza Jane 7, Mary Ann 5, George W. 2, Elizabeth 2/12 4-7-41
1880 CENSUS
Duncan Grassham 70, Lucinda 51 (w) 12-7-55
1900 CENSUS
Isaac A. Grasham 32 (Jan 1868-M 9), Mary L. 26 (Sep 1872-M 9-5-4), George 8 (Jan 1892), Charles D. 7 (Ap 1893-Ark), Laura 4 (Ap 1896), Isaac A. 6/12 (Dec 1899) 2-191A-4/4
MARRIAGES
M. C. Grussham to G. W. Brown q.v.
Mary Grassham to Calvin Lehmer q.v.
Mary Ann Grisham to Miles Atchley q.v.
Nancy Grisham to G. W. Gibson q.v.
Reuben Grassham to Nancy Kirby, 17 May 1892, J.W. Cowles JP 4-42

GRASTY

1900 CENSUS
Mary E. Grasty 71: see James G. Thomison

GRAVES

1900 CENSUS
Alfred W. Graves 58 (July 1841-T/Ireland/Germany-M 11) (Coal Miner), Lucy A. 28 (Aug 1871-T/Ala/T-M 1-5-4), Charles W. 7 (Mar 1892), Jessie A. 5 (July 1894), Robert L. 3 (Mar 1896), Ida L. 11/12 (June 1899), William B. 24 (s)(Nov 1875)((Coal Miner) 9-228A-7
MARRIAGES
Anna Graves to James D. Roddy q.v.
B.A. or B.H. Graves or Grans to Laura Elsie, 13 Nov 1900 (14 Nov), T.D. Shelton MG, J. Wilcox W 3-241
Elizabeth Graves to L. V. Landers q.v.
Nora Graves to John Iles q.v.

GRAVET / GRAVETT / GRAVITT

1860 CENSUS
Cobb Gravet 35 (Ga), Nelly C. 29, Hanah A. 7, William M. 6, Sarah M. 2 5-33-225
1870 CENSUS
Caleb Gravet 40 (Ga), Caroline 40 (NC), Hanna A. 17 (Ga), William 16 (Ga), Sarah M.C. 13, Samuel 10, James 7, Linnah E. 5, Dulcina 3 5-6-42
1880 CENSUS
Caleb Gravett 42, Caroline 40, Samuel 20, James 16, Emmey 14, Dolley 12 6-19-174/178
William M. Gravett 26, Sarah E. 21, Joseph 4, James Samuel 3, William Alfred 8/12 5-11-100
1900 CENSUS
James Gravett 37 (Jan 1863-T/Ga/Ga-M 18), Sallie 36 (Sep 1863-T/T/NC-M 18-7-5), James 15 (Sep 1884), Caleb 13 (May 1887), Olive (Sep 1889), John 7 (Dec 1892), Henry 2 (Aug 1897) 6-243B-73
James S. Gravett 22 (Feb 1878-M 0), Mary E. 21 (Aug 1878-M 0-0) 6-240B-15
Thomas Gravett 23 (Dec 1876-Ga/Ga/Ga), Vina 25 (si)(July 1874-Ga), Nora 21 (b?)(Ap 1879-Ga) 5-232B-90
William Gravett 49 (June 1850-Ga/Ga/Ga-M 30), Sarah E. 41 (Feb 1859-Ga/Ga/Ga-M 30-13-13), Josephus 25 (June 1874), William 19 (Sep 1880), Floyd 18 (May 1882), Charles 16 (Jan 1884), Thomas 14 (Nov 1885), Ira 12 (Oct 1888), Lena 10 (June 1889), Ollie 9 (Feb 1891), Linda 6 (Ap 1894), Kitty 5 (Dec 1894), Nellie 3 (Oct 1896), Cora L. 1 (Jan 1899) 5-235B-148
MARRIAGES
Angeline Gravett to Samuel Fraley q.v.
Dilla Gravitt to L. P. Boymen q.v.
Emma Gravitt to W. R. Beaver q.v.
J.S. Gravitt to Mary Dodd, 17 June 1899 (18 June), Richard Knight JP, N.C. McKelvey W 3-1

James Gravit to Sally Mize, 8 Aug 1883 (9 Aug), J. M. Bramlett MG 1-478
Sally Gravett to William Murphey q.v.
Samuel Gravet (22) to Jane Smith (16), 16 Ap 1883, A.J. Pritchett MG, M.L. Safels(?) & R.J. Jones W 4-14(131)
Samuel Gravitt to Tennie Peterson, June 1889 (2 June), J.L. Brown JP 1-576
William Gravett to Sarah E. Yearwood, 4 Feb 1873 (5 Feb), A.J. Pritchett MG 1-#1276

GRAVIS

MARRIAGE
Rosa Gravis to George Thomas q.v.

GRAY
(se also GAY)

1860 CENSUS
Aaron Gray 23, Rachel 22, Elizabeth 4, Faney GRAY 65, Andrew 13 1-86-589
John Gray 57, Malinda 55, Abraham W. 21, William 19, Benjamin 17, Catharine J. 15, Stephen 12 8-13-89
Nancy Gray 60: see Catharine Martins
Stephen Gray 52, Margaret F. 55 8-19-127
William Gray 26, Charlotte E. 18, Owey or Orvey WATSON 22 4-45-307
1870 CENSUS
Fanny Gray 60: see Martin Hurst
Nancy Gray 72: see Isaac A. Martin
Stephen Gray 62, Margarette F. 66, Laura ALEXANDER 19 8-8-49
William Gray 38, Charlotte E. 35, Calvin A. 6, Joseph E. 3, Mary A. GRAY 40 1-11-69
William K. Gray 30, Stephen B. 22, Benjamin A. 27, Eliza Ann 23, John F. 1 8-3-18
1880 CENSUS
Fanny Gray 68, Andrew 28 2-35-288
John Gray 25, Sarah 30, W.C. 14 (s), M.M. 8 (d), M.E. 6 (d), L.M. 4 (d), S.E. 2 (d), H.P. WEBB 8 3-24-197
W.K. Gray 40, S.A. 31 (w), J.S. 7 (s): see C.T. Bean
William Gray 51, Charlotte 43, Calvin 15, Joseph 12, Mary 9, Thomas 7, Fanny 6, Walter 3 2-30-242
1900 CENSUS
Hattie Gray 27, Herbert 17: see William Swin
George Gray 28 (Aug 1864-Ky/Ky/Ky-M 14)(Coal Miner), Josie 28 (Sep 1863-Ky/Ky/Ky-M 14-2-1), Nancy J. JONES 56 (ml)(Unk-Ky/Unk/Ky-Wd 4-3), William TREADAWAY 30 (boarder)(Aug 1869-Ga/Va/Va) (Furnaceman), Amos READDY 27 (boarder)(Aug 1872)(Coal Miner), Granville SAWYERS 20 (boarder) (May 1880)(Coal Miner), Henry WADE 45 (boarder) (Unk-Va/Va/Va)(Furnaceman) 10-329B-205/218 (B)
George W. Gray 52 (Aug 1847-T/T/Ireland)(RR Carpenter), Rachel A. 53 (Feb 1847-Tex/T/T-M 30-4-3), Uvea 9 (Oct 1880-Ky), Georgia A. 16 (Jan 1884-Ky) 10-326A-126/130
Kate Gray 23: see William P. Darwin
Nathaniel D. Gray 45: see Benjamin F. Mealer
William G. Gray 9: see Charles Reed
William K. Gray 60 (Jan 1840-M 29), Sarah A. 50 (Sep 1849-M 29-2-1), James M. 19 (Oct 1880) 13-300A-185/190
MARRIAGES
Calvin Gray to Attie Minnix, 16 July 1887 (17 July), J.Q. Shaw [probably Shaver] MG 1-583
Catharine J. Gray to Newton A. McGill q.v.
Georgia Gray to Sol Henry q.v.
J.F. Gray to Mollie Bean, 8 Feb 1893, R.W. Wilson MG 4-52
John V. Gray to Ella Stout, 15 Ap 1898 (bond only), W.L. Abel W 2-264
Lorinda Gray to E. P. Wasson q.v.
Lorinda Gray (Mrs.) to T.C. Williams q.v.
M. L. Gray to B. W. Vaughn, 11 June 1857 (no return) 1-#602
Margaret J. Gray [bond] or Gay [license] to J.L. Brown q.v.
Mary Gray to Jack Baker q.v.
Mary A. Gray to Armitt Jones q.v.
Mattie Gray to S. G. Houston q.v.
Sallie F. Gray to G. A. Brown(?) q.v.
W.T. Gray to Lorina E. Thompson, 19 Aug 1889 (20 Aug), Jesse P. Thompson JP 1-578
William Gray to Charlotte Watson, 23 Dec 1858 (same), A. Lowe JP 1-#677

GRAYBEHL

MARRIAGE
J.N. Graybehl (36, Ohio) to Emily A. Graybehl (--, Spring City) 13 Mar 1882, T.N.L. Cunnyngham JP, T.T. McWhorter & G.W. Johnson W 4-7(67)

GREEN / GREENE

1860 CENSUS
Jacob Green 45 (Va), Susan 50, Winna F. 16, Sarah M. 14 1-83-568
Josiah C. Green 27, Hanah C. 25, William A. 2 8-20-132
Mary J. Green 32: see David Morgan
Sarah Green 37: see William Morgan
Sarah H. Green 35, Jane 31: see James Nash
Thomas K. Green 29 (Carpenter), Elizabeth 23, William 6, Susan 4, Calvin 1, Robert GOARD 75 4-45-302
Wm A. Green 35 (Carpenter), Liddia C. 27, John W. 9, Elizabeth A. 7, Sarah J. 5 William T. 3, James J. 3/12 8-16-107
1870 CENSUS
Andrew Green(?) 4: see Thomas Howard
Elijah Green 15: see Rufus B. Sherley
Jacob Green 50, Winna F. 28, Lusa REAS 27 2-8-52
James B. Green 35, Mahala A. 21, Walter J. 1 8-11-73
Julia Green 6 (Ga): see John Hodges (B)
Thomas K. Green 39 (House Carpenter), Elizabeth R. 34, William A. 16, Susan A. 14, Calvin J. 11, Eliza Jane 9, Sarah L. 7, Joseph H. 4, John A. 1 8-19-132
William A. Green 42 (House Carpenter), Lidia C. 37, John W. 19, Elizabeth A. 17, Sarah Jane 15, William T. 13, James J. 10, Vina E. 7, Alexander D. 7, Mariah C. 4, Robert M. 1 8-18-123

1880 CENSUS

Belle Green 10: see John Tinker

J.W. Green 29, N.A. 27, W.H. 5 (s), S.B. 3 (d), S.S. 2 (s), C.W. 8/12 (s) 8-8-64

Jacob Green 64 (Works in Shoe Shop), Lucy 28 (w) 1-18-153

Jessy Green 9, Mattie 7, J.E. 5: see H.D. Riddle

John W. Green 55, Hetta C. 56, Louisa J. 19, Nancy A. 18, Hirem K. 14, Rebecca C. 14 5-5-39

T.K. Green 49 (Carpenter), Elizabeth 45, S.A. 25 (d), Calvin 23, E.J. 21 (d), S.L. 17 (d), J.H. 14 (s), J.A. 12 (s), S. 8 (s), C.R. 4 (s), O.A. 5/12 (s) 8-13-116

Thomas Green 51 (Carpenter & Joiner) 2-27-212

W.A. Green 55, L.C. 46, James J. 20, V.A. 17 (s), M.C. 15 (d), R.M. 12 (s), N.M. 9 (d), A.S.P. 6 (s), A.S. 2 (s) 8-9-75

William A. Green 26, Sarah M. 22 or 24 (w), Ethel A. 8/12, Elae E. 8/12: see Levena Buttram

1900 CENSUS

Albert S. Green 21 (Sep 1879-M 4), Flora 19 (Aug 1880-M 4-2-2), Stella May 2 (Oct 1897), Cora Agnes 1 (Sep 1898) 13-300B-195/202

Calvin Green 42 (Aug 1857-M 12)(Carpenter), Loretta 36 (Sep 1863-M 12-6-5), Nola 10 (Sep 1889), Clarence 8 (Nov 1891), Lella 5 (July 1894), Oza 3 (Oct 1896), Earl 1 (Dec 1898) 8-278B-202/204

Daly A. Green 37 (Feb 1863-T/T/Ga-M 15)(Coal Miner), Mary C. 34 (Aug 1865-T/T/Ga-M 15-3-2), Emmett 13 (Ap 1887), Melvin 10 (Aug 1889), James W. BOLING 31 (boarder)(Nov 1868)(Clergyman) 13-296A-120/122

Francis A. Green 15: see Benjamin Bratcher

Fred Green 35 (Unk 1865-Mich/Mich/Mich-M 11)(Coal Miner), Nannie 28 (Unk 1872-M 11-2-2), Dora 9 (Unk 1891), Albert 6 (Unk 1894) 8-282B-276/278

Hannibal Green 44 (Sep 1855-M 20)(Coal Miner), Nancy 38 (July 1861-M 20-9-9), Lee 19 (Nov 1880)(Coal Miner), Kelly 16 (July 1884)(Coal Miner), Willie 13 (Aug 1886)(Coal Miner), Laura J. 11 (Oct 1888), Caroline D. 10 (Sep 1889), Pearl 8 (Ap 1892), Catharine 6 (Feb 1894), Jean B. 3 (Jan 1897), Nathaniel 1 (Feb 1899) 8-283A-290/292

James J. Green Unk (Unk-M 11)(Merchant), Amanda 32 (May 1868-M 11-3-3), Creed 10 (Aug 1889), Johnie E. 7 (Aug 1892), Bussie A. 4 (Aug 1895) 13-305A-281/291

Jesse Green 29 (Sep 1870-Wd)(Coal Miner), Clay 5 (Jan 1895), May 3 (Mar 1897), Mattie 27 (si)(Aug 1872), Nellie 25 (si)(Dec 1874) 8-287B-384/386

John Green 19 (June 1880-Ga/Ga/Ga-M 1)(Coal Miner), Lou E. 15 (June 1884-T/Ga/T-M 1-0-0) 13-302B-227/237

John R. Green 27 (May 1873-M 7), Elvira 32 (June 1867-M 7-6-5), John F. 12 (Dec 1887), William R. 10 (Aug 1889), Walter 9 (Sep 1890), Emma E. 8 (Dec 1891), Annie B. 5 (Mar 1895), Ethel J. 3 (Sep 1897) 13-308A-343/355

Joseph Green 55 (Feb 1845-Ga/Ga/NC-M 30)(Coal Miner), Maria 55 (Feb 1845-SC/SC/SC-M 30-10-9), Carrie 23 (Ap 1877), Susan 16 (May 1884), Hattie 12 (Nov 1887), Freddie 7 (Oct 1892), Ida 8/12 (Sep 1899) 8-283B-294/296

Liza Green 37: see Alvin P.(?) Morgan

Mary Green 14: see Jeneral F. Collier

Myrtle Green 1: see Melvin Foust

Oscar J. Green 31 (Nov 1868-M 8)(Coal Miner), Minnie M. 30 (Ap 1870-Neb/T/T-M 8-5-3), Wade A. 4 (June 1895), Hugh C. 2 (Feb 1898), Richard E. 1/12 (Ap 1900) 13-308A-348/360

Robert Green 31 (Ap 1869-M 0)(Coal Miner), Lidia 20 (Aug 1879-M 0-0), Alexander 22 (nw)(Unk 1878) (Coal Miner), Charles 20 (nw)(Unk 1880)(Coal Miner) 8-282B-275/277

Sarah Green 45 (July 1854-Wd 4-4), Ethel 20 (Sep 1879), Elfie 20 (Sep 1879), Edwin 18 (Mar 1882)(Coal Miner), Emmet 16 (May 1884) 8-278B-205/207

Thomas J. Green 68 (Feb 1832-T/Va/Va-M 18)(Postmaster), Sarah A. 34 (Mar 1866-M 18-8-6), Eliza D. 16 (Jan 1884), Addie E. 13 (Sep 1886), Anna T. 8 (July 1891), Hattie A. 6 (Nov 1893), Thomas G. 3 (Mar 1897), John W. 8/12 (Sep 1899) 2-199A-154/159

Thomas K. Green 69 (Mar 1831-M 10), Hancock 53 (Sep 1846-SC/SC/SC-M 10-4-3) 8-315B-109/113

Walter Green 33 (Jan 1869-M 2), Josie 20 (Dec 1879-M 2-0) 8-287A-376/378

William A. Green 75 (May 1825-M 50)(Landlord), Lydia C. 64 (Aug 1835-M 50-11-9), Alexander 24 (Sep 1875) (Coal Miner) 13-300B-195/201

William T. Green 42 (Sep 1857-M 4)(Physician), Emma M. 26 (Nov 1873-M 4-3-2), Lena R. 2 (June 1897), Willie I. 1 (May 1899) 13-304A-265/275

MARRIAGES

Allice Green to Henry O. Merrill q.v.

Amanda Green to James McCade q.v.

Amanda Green to John Faulkner q.v.

Andrew Green to Tennessee Jones, 10 Jan 1891, John Q. Shaver MG 4-23

Bell Green to John F. Cannall q.v.

Bell Green to Charles C. Nail q.v.

C.J. Green to Loretta H. Hamilton, 12 Nov 1887 (13 Nov), D. Richardson MG 1-534

Carry Green to John Harvey q.v.

E. A. Green to W.A. or H.A. Yarbough q.v.

Fred Green to Nanney Green or Grice, 25 Ap 1888 (29 Ap), C. Morgan JP 1-570

G.W. or W.G. Green to May Keith, 21 July 1900 (same), Wm A. Green JP, J.A. Green W 3-189

H.C. Green to Annie Hughes, 26 July 1899 (same), R.C. Knght JP, G.G. Howard W 3-14

Henry E. Green– see Greer

I.A. Green to Bertha Tallent, 27 Oct 1900 (28 Oct), W.A. Green JP, Charles Green W 3-237

J.J. Green to Amanda Russell, 29 Sep 1888 (30 Sep), Robert A. Bartlett MG 1-560

Jacob Green to Lucy Reece, 27 Oct 1870 (8 -?-), S. Roberts MG 1-#1172

James B. Green to Mahala A. Riddle, 19 Dec 1867 (same), J.M. Kelly MG 1-#991

Jennie Green to James McConnell q.v.

Jessie Green to Maggie McMillan, 18 Feb 1894, W.A. Green JP 4-70

John Green to Elvira James(?), 22 Feb 1894, W.A. Green JP 4-69

John Green to Evie Suttles, 24 Dec 1898 (25 Dec), W.S. Hale MG, J.L. Fain W 2-365

John R. Green to Nancy Walker, 3 Oct 1888 (same), M.C. Bruner MG 1-563

John W. Green to Nancy A. Kelley, 24 Dec 1874 (29 Dec), J.W. Reece MG 1-#1381
L. A. Green to T. H. Walker q.v.
Maggie Green to General Collin q.v.
Margaret Green to David S. Bolton q.v.
Marion Green to Nancey Walker, 12 Mar 1890 (13 Mar), R.S. Mason JP 1-599
Mary Green to Henry Housley q.v.
Moses Green to Mary A. Newby, 20 May 1898 (same), D. Broyles JP, C.F. Thompson [signed by X] W 2-282
Nancy J. Green to Thyas Jolly q.v.
Nanney Green or Grice to Fred Green q.v.
Oscar J. Green to Minnie M. Johns, 15 May 1892, R.A. Bartlett MG 4-39
R.M. Green to Lyda E. White, 17 Aug 1899 (13 Aug), W.A. Green JP, George Foust W 3-19
Rosie Green to Richard Hughes q.v.
Susan A. Green to George S. Hartman q.v.
Thomas J. Green (50, Washington Co) to Sarah A. Minix (16), 2 Ap 1882, S. Breeding JP, W.H. Eaton & wife W 4-8(79) [see also Thomas J. Greer]
T.K. Green to N.P. Hartbarger, 2 July 1890 (3 July), R.S. Mason JP 1-603
Thomas K. Green to Elizabeth Barton, no dates (between 22 Mar & 13 Ap 1853), Elihu McKinny JP 1-#408
V. E. Green to H. J. Alexander q.v.
Vesta Green to Lennie or Larrind Best, 21 July 1900 (22 July), Henegar Morgan JP, C. Dillard W 3-191
Walter J. Green to Josie Walker, 25 June 1898 (same), A.P. Hays JP 2-295
Winnie F. Green to Samuel Miller q.v.
W.T. Green to M.E. Bowman, 8 Sep 1895, W.A. Green JP 4-86
Wm A. Green to S.M. Buttram, 19 Nov 1878 (21 Nov), J.T. Percy or Perry MG 1-#1588
Wm H. Green to Matilda J. Robinson, 30 Sep 1885 (same), I.W. Holt JP 1-487

- - - - - - - - - - - - -

GREENWOOD

1860 CENSUS
Josiah Greenwood 45 (SC), Elizabeth 44 (SC): see James Thomas
1870 CENSUS
Josiah Greenwood 54 (SC), Elizabeth 50 (SC) 3-18-131
1880 CENSUS– None
1900 CENSUS
Leahbelle Greenwood 10, Thomas H. 15: see Charles W. Irwin

- - - - - - - - - - - - -

GREER / GEER / GRIER

1900 CENSUS
Hattie E. Greer 58 (Sep 1841-NY/NY/NY-Wd 5-3) 8-282B-279/281
Moses Grier 70 (Sep 1829-Va/Va/Ireland-M 48)(Hotel Keeper), Orpha 68 (May 1832-T/Va/T-M 48-1-1), Wetherington S. 32 (s)(Dec 1867-M 2)(Machinist), Jennie 34 (dl)(Aug 1865-Oh/Oh/Oh-M 2-0): *Boarders at Hotel:* Benjamin KENNEDY 56 (Aug 1843-Oh/Oh/Oh-Wd)(Cooper), Will CURTIS 40 (Nov 1859-Ga/NC/Ga-M)(Machinist), Samuel ESSEX 18 (Sep 1881-T/T/Oh)(Matressmaker), Ernest H. HAR-RISON 18 (Oct 1881)(Blacksmith), Will OWENS 27 (Feb 1873-Ill/Ill/Ill)(Day Laborer), Norris KING 21 (Ap 1879) (Day Laborer), William JENKINS 23 (Oct 1876)(Day Laborer), Lizzie BORING 34 (Mar 1866-Wd 6-5) (Servant, Cook), Joshua 8 (cooks son)(Aug 1891), Nelle 2 (cooks dau)(July 1897) 8-312A-28/30
Richard T. Greer 42 (Nov 1857-T/Va/T-M 17), Sue E. 41 (Ap 1859-M 17-5-4), Kittie 14 (July 1885), Millie 7 (Nov 1892), Lucile F. 6 (Ap 1894), Dramond H. 5 (Mar 1895) 10-257B-142/46
MARRIAGES
C. L. Greer (*) to R. L. Thomison q.v.
Callie Greer to Henry E. Greer q.v.
Caroline H. Greer to William Henry q.v.
Eliza A. Geer to Benj Rowden q.v.
F. A. Greer (*) to J. L. Daniels q.v.
Frank A. Greer to Martha J. Thomas, 13 Ap 1887 (14 Ap), M.C. Bruner MG 1-518
Harriet Geer to Vincent Hurst q.v.
Henry E. Greer or Green to Callie Greer, 19 June 1897 (20 June), S.M. Burnett MG, Elbert Husey W 2-154
Jerry Greer to Nettie Jones, 12 Dec 1887 (same), I.W. Holt JP 1-551
Mollie Greer or Green to Len or Lane Hardin q.v.
Patsy Greer to Richard Croch q.v.
R.T. Greer (26, Pikeville*) to S.E. Johnson (24, Dayton), 8 May 1883, T. Ashburn MG, Walter Thomison & W.A. Templeton W 4-14(139) [* NOTE: C.L. and F.A. Greer also born in Pikeville]
Thomas J. Greer to Elizabeth Mathis, 5 Dec 1872 (same), W.H. Dodd MG 1-#1263

- - - - - - - - - - - - -

GREERHART

MARRIAGE
Ida Greerhart [bond] or Gearhart [index] to P.W. Allen q.v.

- - - - - - - - - - - - -

GREGG

1880 CENSUS
Edward L. Gregg 45 (Carpenter), Catharine 39, Mattie W. 18, Abraham 11, Jinette 9, Charles E. 5, Fannie 2 5-7-64
1900 CENSUS
William D. Gregg 62: see Andrew B. Caravile
MARRIAGES
Jenett Gregg to Foster A. Kyle q.v.
Matty Gregg to Robert T. Howard q.v.

- - - - - - - - - - - - -

GREGORY / GRIGORY

1860 CENSUS
Richard Gregory 62 (SC), Anna 62, Sarah 32, Catharine 28, George 23, Lucinda 20, Brittania 16 8-26-177

1870 CENSUS

Richard Grigory 80 (SC), Sarah Jane 42, Catharine 38, Lucinda 30, Brit Ann 22 8-20-138

1880 CENSUS

Sarah Gregory 55, Suider 37: see M. Mayers

1900 CENSUS

Fred A. Gregory 28 (Feb 1872-Iowa/Ill/NY-S), Clara A. 53 (m)(June 1846-NY/N/NY-Wd 1-1), Reuben AYLWORTH 79 (gf)(Nov 1820-NY/NY/NY-M 55), Mary 78 (gm)(July 1821-NY/NY/NY-M 55-1-1) 14-223A-188/192

James Gregory 26 (Ap 1874-T/NC/T-D), Cornelius 24 (b) (Ap 1876), Nancy PRESTWOOD 52 (m)(May 1848-T/England/SC-Wd 4-4) 2-197A-105/110

Lucinda Gregory 64: see William McEwen

William R. Gregory 50 (Nov 1849-M 27), Mary T. 41 (Dec 1858-M 27-10-10), Charles A. 16 (July 1883), Edna O. 15 (Feb 1885), Mary L. 13 (Feb 1887), Rosa L. 10 (Sep 1887), Louis 7 (Jan 1893), Lucy 7 (Jan 1893), Thomas R. 3 (Aug 1896), Hugh L. 1 (Feb 1899) 14-222B-179/183

MARRIAGES

Ann Grigory to Robert G. Edwards q.v.

E. Gregory to Elmiry Frazier, 25 Feb 1860 (26 Feb), A. Johns MG 1-#1650

James Gregory to Ann E. Thompson, 6 Nov 1871 (7 Nov), J.W. Peace MG 1-#1214

James Gregory to Annie Monsey, 6 Mar 1896, Wm White MG 4-92

Martha Grigory to E. H. Campbell q.v.

- - - - - - - - - - - - -

GRENON

MARRIAGE

Joseph H. Grenon to Cordie D. Burnett, 30 Nov 1889 (1 Dec), M.C. Bruner MG 1-592

- - - - - - - - - - - - -

GREUNITZ

1900 CENSUS

Otto Greunitz 31 (Ap 1869-Germany/Do/Do-1880/19/Na) (Music Teacher) 10-321A-18/18

- - - - - - - - - - - - -

GREW

1880 CENSUS

W.A. Grew 55, S.C. 46, James J. 20, D.A. 17 (s), M.C. 15 (d), R.M. 12 (s), N.M. 9 (d), A.S.P. 6 (s), A.S. 2 (s) 8-9-75

- - - - - - - - - - - - -

GRICE / GRISE

1870 CENSUS

James N. Grice 55 (NC), Nancy 44 (Va), Thomas J. 24, Elijah T. 22, Susan R. 16, John C. 12, James F. 8, Mary E. 4 7-3-22

1880 CENSUS

Nancy Grice 57, T.J. 30 (s), M.E. 14 (d), A.H. 8 (gs), N.S. 5 (gd), L.T. 32 (s) [marked through, "Dead"] 7-29-250

1900 CENSUS

Andy Grice 25: see John L. Eddington

Frank J. Grice 44 (Feb 1854-T/NC/Ind-M 10)(Coal Miner), Maggie 37 (Oct 1862-M 10-2-1), Mary L. JOHNSON 16 (sd)(Nov 1883) 11-293A-76

Mary J. Grice 31: see John L. Eddington

MARRIAGES

E.T. Grice to Nancy Mathis, 8 Feb 1872 (same), R.T. Howard MG 1-#1229

Isie(?) Grice to John S. Spencer q.v.

J.F. Grice to Maggie Johnson, 8 Sep 1888 (9 Sep), E.F. Gwinn JP 1-560

Mary E. Grice to John J. Smith q.v.

Mary J. Grice to James Everett q.v.

Nanny Grice or Green to Fred Green q.v.

Susan A. Grise to William R. Smith q.v.

T.J. Grice to Mary Gambill, 1 July 1853 (same), James R. Crawford JP 1-497

T.J. Grice to Eliza Cowley, 14 Ap 1888 (15 Ap), J.R. Crawford JP 1-549

- - - - - - - - - - - - -

GRIEVER
(see also GUIRVER)

MARRIAGE

Mary Griever to Charley Ross q.v.

- - - - - - - - - - - - -

GRIFFIE

1900 CENSUS

Dollie Griffie 17: see Alford Etherly (B)

- - - - - - - - - - - - -

GRIFFIS

MARRIAGE

George Griffis to Lillie Hooper, 19 Feb 1895, W.R. Grimsley MG 4-79

- - - - - - - - - - - - -

GRIFFIN / GRIFFEN

1880 CENSUS

A. Griffen 40: see J. R. Crawford

1900 CENSUS

Eliza J. Griffin 33: see Joseph Rose

George Griffen 35 (Sep 1864-Ga/Ga/Ga-M 14)(Coal Miner), Elizabeth 23 (Mar 1877-Ga/Ga/Ga-M 14-5-2), Joseph 14 (May 1886-Ga), Benjamin 13 (June 1887-Ga) 10-254B-89 (B)

James Griffin 23 (Unk 1877-M 1), Anna 23 (Unk 1877-M 1-2-2), Sally COOK 7 (sd)(Unk 1893), George 2 (ss) (July 1898), Myrtle GRIFFIN 14 (si)(Unk 1886) 8-287B-389/391 (B)

James M. Griffin 67 (Jan 1833-NC/NC/NC-M ?), Sarah 66 (May 1834-NC/NC/NC-M ?) 14-215B-48/49

James Griffin 18 (B): see Jim Anderson

MARRIAGES

James Griffin to Beckey Wilson, 9 July 1895, J.B. Phillips MG 4-82

West or Wist Griffin to Ella Love, 1 Mar 1898 (same), J.B. Phillips MG, Westley Griffin & Roscoe Bennett W 2-255 (B)

- - - - - - - - - - - - -

GRIFFITH / GRIFFETT

1860 CENSUS

Jane Griffett 76 (Va): see John Crawford

1870 CENSUS

Jane Griffith 87 (Va): see James R. Crawford

John Griffith 16 (B): see James R. Crawford

1880 CENSUS

A. Griffith 37, Jane 33, C.H. 7 (d), Victor 10, Luther 2, Emmett RHEA 25 (boarder) 4-8-60

1900 CENSUS

Ambrose Griffith 57 (Mar 1841-M 32)(Hide Dealer), Jennie G. 54 (Mar 1846-Va/Va/Va-M 32-4-3), Cora A. 27 (Dec 1872)(Teacher), Luther C. 22 (Mar 1878), Della FELTY 30 (ne)(Aug 1869) 14-216A-60/61

Viola Griffith 28 (Sep 1871-Ala/Ireland/Ala-Wd 2-2), John A. 3 (Sep 1894), Grace 5 (Ap 1895) 14-221A-147/151

William Griffith 61 (Ap 1839-M 8)(Wood Chopper), Franzinia 39 (Feb 1861-M 8-4-4), Florence 13 (Sep 1886), Dolly A. 7 (Nov 1892), Allie 4 (Sep 1895), Charles W. 2 (June 1897), Robert 7/12 (Oct 1899) 13-305B-298/310

MARRIAGES

Andrew F. Griffith to Viola Johnson, 23 Ap 1894, W.H. Perkinson JP 4-66

Rebecca E. Griffith to James E.M. Newport q.v.

- - - - - - - - - - - - -

GRIGSBY

MARRIAGE

J.F. Grigsby (30, McMinn Co) to Nancy J. Johnson (20), 27 June 1881, no MG or JP, W.D. Holloway W 4-2(13)

- - - - - - - - - - - - -

GRIMSLEY / GRIMSLY

1860 CENSUS

William W. Grimsly 16: see John Day

1870 and 1880 CENSUS– None

1900 CENSUS

James M. Grimsley 58 (Sep 1841-M 27)(Blacksmith), Sarah R. 49 (Nov 1850-M 27-2-1), Lester M. 22 (Dec 1877)(Blacksmith) 13-305B-300/312

William Grimsley 29 (July 1870-M 10)(Repairer), Cynthia 28 (Sep 1871-M 10-2-2), John F. 9 (Aug 1890), James W. 4 (Oct 1895), Roy HOUSTON 28 (boarder)(Ap 1872-Ala/T/Ga) 13-299B-179/184

William R. Grimsley 50 (Mar 1850-M 25), Amanda M. 56 (Jan 1844-M 25-2-2), James E. 22 (Dec 1877), Pearl C. 14 (Nov 1885) 13-310A-382/396

MARRIAGES

L.E. Grimsley to J.D. Acuff q.v.

William Riley Grimsley to Amanda M. Fraley, 30 Dec 1874 (31 Dec), R.H. Jordan MG 1-#1383

Willie Grimsley to Syntha Dennis, 19 Oct 1889 (20 Oct), W.A. Green JP 1-588

- - - - - - - - - - - - -

GRINDER

MARRIAGE

Rachael Grinder (21, Augusta, Ga) to H.A. Brown q.v. (B)

- - - - - - - - - - - - -

GROSS

1880 CENSUS

J.H. Gross 74 (Merchant), Mary 73, Phebe 16 4-9-73

Manda Gross 48, Bob 1: see J.F. Tallent

1900 CENSUS

Alfred Gross 47 (June 1853-M 24)(Carpenter), Laura 37 (Jan 1863-M 24-2-2), Maud O. 15 (Ap 1885) 14-216B-77/78 [A.F. Gross married Laura A. Odom on 13 Sep 1876 in Meigs County]

Thomas A. Gross 25 (Ap 1875)(Publisher) 10-331B-247/262

MARRIAGE

A. F. Gross to F. W. Bandy q.v.

- - - - - - - - - - - - -

GRUESWELL

1860 CENSUS

Elijah Grueswell 27 (Tailor), Sarah 23 8-22-150

- - - - - - - - - - - - -

GRUSON

MARRIAGE

John Gruson to Margaret Mathis, 3 Aug 1878 (3 Sep), Calvin Morgan JP 1-#1579 [last name spelled Grason in index]

- - - - - - - - - - - - -

GUESS

1900 CENSUS

Manda Guess 64 (Nov 1833-Wd 11-7), John 35 (Nov 1864), Addie 30 (Aug 1869), Sallie 20 (Jan 1880) 3-203A-63/67 (B)

- - - - - - - - - - - - -

GUINN / GUIN / GUNN / GINN / GWIN

1860 CENSUS

William Guin 65 (Carpenter), Margaret 60, John 19 6-110-752

William F. Guin 31, Susan 31, Eliza 5 2-79-533

1870 CENSUS

William Guinn 77 (House Carpenter), Margurett 76 6-11-72

William F. Guinn 36, Susan 34 (SC), Eliza 14 (SC) 4-3-16

1880 CENSUS
Margaret Ginn 86 (Pensionr) 6-16-143/145
MARRIAGES
Eliza Gunn to Dock(?) Reese q.v.
Elzy Gunn or Guin to Elisha Garner q.v.
Nannie Gwin to Allie Jones q.v.

- - - - - - - - - - - - -

GUIRVER

1900 CENSUS
Cate Guirver(?) 55 (Dec 1844-M 27), Annie 54 (Unk-M 27-3-2), Nannie 24 (Oct 1874-D 2-1), William 28 (unk), Melvin JONES 8 (gs)(Oct 1891); *boarders:* James WILKERSON 31 (Ap 1869-Ga/Ga/Ga), John CARMACK 25 (Unk), George HILL 20 (Unk), Frank HILL 8 (Unk) 8-318A-155/160 (B)

- - - - - - - - - - - - -

GUNTER

1900 CENSUS
William C. Gunter 29 (Ap 1871-M 9), Lottie 27 (Ap 1873-M 9-5-4), Annie 8 (Oct 1891), Maggie 6 (Oct 1893), Mandie 4 (Sep 1895), Carney 1/12 (May 1900) 8-316B-126/130

- - - - - - - - - - - - -

GWILLIM

1900 CENSUS
David Gwillim 41 (May 1859-Wales/Wales/Wales-1868/32/Na-M 19)(Coal Miner), Mary 37 (Dec 1862-Oh/Wales/Wales-M 19-6-6), William 17 (Jan 1883) (Grocery Clerk), Thomas 15 (Aug 1884)(Coal Miner), Reese 13 (June 1886), Ann 11 (Aug 1888), Gertrude 9 (July 1890), Elwer(?) 7 (Aug 1892) 8-277B-187/189
Rees Gwillim 67 (Mar 1833-Wales/Wales/Wales-1869/30/Na-M 2), Florence 40 (Feb 1860-M 2-1-1), Isaac R. 3/12 (Jan 1900), Robert WALKER 34 (boarder)(May 1866-Wd)(Preacher) 8-278A-188/190
Tal Gwillim 24: see Benjamin F. Mealer
MARRIAGE
Carrie J. Gwillian to S. B. Hillock q.v.

- - - - - - - - - - - - -

HAAS

1900 CENSUS
Joseph Haas 33 (Sep 1866-Germany/Do/Do-1885/15/Na-M 6), Anna 22 (Feb 1878-Ind/Ind/Ind-M 6-3-3), Emma 5 (Sep 1894), Lena 3 (Sep 1896), Norman J. 1 (Sep 1898) 6-24A-1
MARRIAGES
Joseph Haas to F.A. Harris, 9 July 1893, W.A. Howard MG 4-58
Lillie Haas to C. E. Hayes q.v.

- - - - - - - - - - - - -

HACKETT

1860 CENSUS
Samuel R. Hackett 62, John 24, Harriet H. 58 6-113-778
1870 and 1880 CENSUS– None
1900 CENSUS
Humphrey Hackett 55 (Unk 1845-M 34), Ann 53 (Unk 1847-M 34-0), Arthur LOTHARAGE 16 (May 1884) 15-272B-86 (B)
MARRIAGE
Margaret Hackett to L. C. Ragsdale q.v.

- - - - - - - - - - - - -

HACKLER / HACKER

1860 CENSUS
Richard Hacker 17: see James T. Nanny
1870 and 1880 CENSUS– None
1900 CENSUS
Morgan Hackler 51 (Mar 1849-M 6), Margarett A. 34 (Feb 1866-T/Ireland/T-M 6-2-2), Lillie A. 15 (June 1884), Flora A.M. 5/12 (Dec 1899) 3-206A-105/115
MARRIAGE
Martha Hackler to John Lincoln q.v.

- - - - - - - - - - - - -

HACKMAN

MARRIAGE
John Hackman to Martha E. Martin, 24 Aug 1853 (25 Aug), Benjamin Wallace MG 1-#420

- - - - - - - - - - - - -

HACKNEY

1880 CENSUS
Jacob Hackney 28, Thomas 22: see Cyrus Henry

- - - - - - - - - - - - -

HAGGARD

1900 CENSUS
Andrew P. Haggard 37 (Aug 1862-Ga/T/T-M 14)(Attorney), Arrena 31 (May 1869-Ga/Ga/Ala-M 14-4-3), Clark 13 (Jan 1887-Ga), Effie 10 (Feb 1890), William C. 4/12 (Jan 1900) 10-320B-14/14 [A.P. married Arrena Desdemona Clark in Georgia]

- - - - - - - - - - - - -

HAIR / HARE

1870 CENSUS
Jane Hair 45, Susan A. 23, Pleasant 21, Henry 18, Mary M. 7 3-2-12
1880 CENSUS– None
1900 CENSUS
Henry Hare 51 (Feb 1849-S), Jane 100* (m)(June 1800-Wd 1-1) 5-234B-133 [*oldest citizen in county in 1900]
MARRIAGES
Jane Hair to William Gaits q.v.
Mary Hair to W. C. McKelvey q.v.
Nancy Hair to Isaac Byrd q.v.

- - - - - - - - - - - - -

HAIRCE

1870 CENSUS
Mary Hairce 44, Barbara 22, Melvina 18, Hannibal 17, Canedy 15, Gilbert 12, Virnon 10 6-4-21

- - - - - - - - - - - - -

HALBERT

MARRIAGE
Ellvira Halbert to Henry Houston q.v.

- - - - - - - - - - - - -

HALE / HAIL / HAILE

1860 CENSUS
George Hale 60, Susan 31, George H. 18, Margaret E. 16, James 14, Lucinda 12, Manerva 8, Linda 4, Susan 1 3-65-450
Scott Hale 42, Martha 39, Andrew 21, Elissa 18, John H. 16, James P. 13, Andrew J. 11, William S. 10, Allen 1, Elizabeth McFARLAND 81 (SC) 5-34-230
1870 CENSUS
George Hail 70, Susan 42, Lucinda 17, Minerva 15, Mary 13, Rebecca 9 3-19-135
George H. Hail 28, Syntha R. 23 3-14-100
James Hail 22, Jane 27, Laura 1, William 4 3-19-136
James K. Hail 23, Mary J. 20, William 3, Martha A. 1, James P. BRANDIM(?) 21 6-14-99
Scott Hail 54, Martha J. 46, Manda J. 19, Eliza A. 25, William 18, Allen 12, Bartin 6 6-14-96
1880 CENSUS
James Hale 31, Jane 33, L.O. 12, M.A. 10, Geo 4, John 1 3-30-242
Martha J. Hail 57 (m), Allen 20 (s), Joseph B 15 (s) 10-30-227/236
Susan Hale 53, Rebecca 17 (d) 3-19-149
William Hail 54, H.E. 50, Hanah E. 19, Wilford 17, L.J. 8 8-19-159
William S. Hail 23 (Minister), Sarah E. 19, Dollie L. 3, Martha A. 10/12 10-30-227/235
1900 CENSUS
Allen Hale 41 (Ap 1859-M 5), Frankie 35 (Mar 1865-M 5-0) 8-314A-74/77
Aquilla M. Hale 50 (Jan 1850-M 30)(Cobbler), Mary J. 46 (Nov 1853-M 30-3-2), Emmie 13 (May 1887) 8-312B-39/42
Berkelder Hail 12: see Arabela J. Reel
Ersa Hale 25: see William R. Crow
George I. Hale 24 (May 1876-M 6), Biddie 25 (July 1874-T/Ireland/T-M 6-3-3), James T. 5 (Sep 1894), Lillie J. 4 (Nov 1896), John H. 9/12 (Sep 1899) 3-209A-162/176
Isac Hale 54 (Dec 1845-T/Ga/NC-M 10)(Coke Puller), Jossie 32 (Nov 1867-Ga/Ga/Ga-M 10-7-6), Mary 11 (Sep 1888), Eller 9 (Dec 1890), Mattie 7 (Feb 1893), Jinnie 4 (June 1895), Andrew 1 (Oct 1898) 10-256A-116/120 (B)
Joseph B. Hale 35 (Ap 1865-T/T/NC-M 1), Lina 37 (Mar 1863-M 1-0), Martha HALE 77 (m)(Oct 1822-NC/Ireland/NC-Wd 9-6) 8-311B-14/15
Lucien Hale 28 (Aug 1871-M 2)(Coal Miner), Martha 22 (July 1877-M 2-1-0), James L. ARMOR 30 (bl)(Jan 1870-M 2)(Coal Miner) 8-277B-186/188
Mary E. Hale 24 (Oct 1875-Wd 2-2), Ethel 5 (Aug 1894), Claud 3 (Ap 1897), George BANKSTON 17 (b)(Unk 1883) 15-271A-57
Mary J. Hale 57 (June 1842-T/NC/NC-Wd), John C. 21 (s) (Jan 1879) 3-209A-166/180
Pafee(?) Hale 27 (Feb 1873-T/Va/T-M 6)(Painter), Mannie 23 (Ap 1872-M 6-2-2), Lum 4 (Feb 1896), Henry 1 (Oct 1899), Radin D. HALE 67 (m)(Feb 1833-Wd) 10-260A-194/199
Susan Hale 77 (Nov 1822-Wd 9-4)(Seamstress), Becky 36 (Mar 1864)(Dressmaker) 6-224A-88
Thomas Hale 33 (Mar 1867-M 6), Mary 24 (Aug 1875-T/NC/NC-M 6-2-1), Samuel 5 (Mar 1895), Josa LOCKE 38 (si)(Unk-M 1-0)(Washwoman) 6-245B-111/112
Thomas Hale 22 (Jan 1888-M 3)(Coal Miner), Lena 22 (Nov 1877-M 3-1-1), Lucile 1 (Nov 1898) 8-278A-196-198
Will Hale 18 (Oct 1881-M 0)(Coal Miner), Loveler 14 (Dec 1885-M 0-0) 10-256A-114/118 (B)
William S. Hale 43 (May 1857-T/T/NC-M 25)(Coal Miner), Ellen S. 39 (Dec 1860-M 25-10-7), May M. 12 (Ap 1888), Charles V. 9 (Sep 1890), James N. 7 (Nov 1892), Walter H. 2 (Sep 1897) 13-302A-220/228
Wolford Hayle 37 (May 1863-M 16), Mary J. 52 (Nov 1847-M 16-1-1), Samuel 14 (Jan 1886) 15-269A-21
MARRIAGES
Allen Hale to Vird Wright, nee Travis (36), 1 Ap 1883, T.N. L. Cunnyngham JP, T.J. Gillespie (of Washington) W 4-13(124)
Allen Hale to Frankee Henry, 1 Nov 1896 (same), R.C. Knight JP, A.H. Williamson W 2-79
Amanda Haile to Hart Author q.v.
Annie E. Hail to J. M. Spisor q.v.
Bart Hale to Liney Tucker, 11 Mar 1899 (same), R.C. Knight MG, R.J. Killough W 2-392
Delia Hale to C. H. Jones q.v.
Dellie Hale to H. A. Davis q.v.
Eliza J. Hale to G. W. Gardenhire q.v.
Fannie Hale to Enoch Suddeth q.v. (B)
G.H. Hale to S.R.A. Furgusson, 8 Ap 1869 (no return) 1-#1053
George Hale to Biddie Collins, 10 Sep 1893, W.H. Perkinson JP 4-55 [NOTE: a second entry, 4-59, spells last name Hall]
Hattie Hale to Mack Foster q.v.
Ida B. Hale to Eugene Phillips q.v. (B)
Isaac Hale to Josephine Pullam, 16 Nov 1889 (17 Nov), S.W. Wych ?? 1-584
James Hale to Mary Jane Maryott, 16 Jan 1866 (19 Jan), J.H. Keith MG 1-#884
James Hale to Jane Loy, 11 Dec 1867 (12 Dec), G.W. Renfro MG 1-#987
Jennie Hale to J. M. Fugate q.v.
Jennie Hale to Peter Rue q.v.
Jssse Hale to Callie Wheeler, 12 Sep 1899 (same), J.S. Phillips MG, Joseph Phillps W 3-31
John H. Hale to Margaret Allen, 11 July 1867 (same), R.T. Howard MG 1-#958
John P. Hale to Emma P. McKeehen, 4 Oct 1889 (same), W. S. Hale MG 1-586
Julia C. Hail to Lewis Jackson q.v.
Laura Hale to W. K. Fugate q.v.
Laura Hale to Jack Keith q.v.

Lemuel I. Hale to Maggie Houston, 12 June 1886 (13 June), J.Q. Shaver MG 1-507
Lisa(?) Hale to John Winfry(?) q.v.
Lucinda Hale to John Coxey or Casey q.v.
Lucius Hale to Martha Armour, 27 Nov 1897 (bond only), A.P. Hayes W 2-215
Lucy Hailes to George Williams q.v.
Malinda Hale to Solomon Harwood q.v.
Margaret Hale to Thomas Blackburn q.v.
Mary Hale to Charles H. Sanford q.v.
Mattie Hale to James Majors q.v.
Mattie Hale to P. G. Travis q.v.
Milley Hale to Alex Ran q.v.
Minerva Hale to H. J. Morehall q.v.
Polly Hale to David Coulter q.v.
S.H. Hail to Jervin Swafford, 15 Oct 1887 (16 Oct), J.M. Bramlett MG 1-538
Sallie Hale to John Cooper q.v.
Samuel S. Hale to Abby E. Breeding, 29 Jan 1873 (4 Feb), J.P. Roddy MG 1-#1273
Thomas Hale to Mary Harris, 30 Sep 1893, W.G. Curtain MG 4-56
Viola Hale to John Richey q.v.
W.O. Hale to Mary E. Swafford, 15 Dec 1890, W.G. Mitchell JP 4-33
Walter Hale to May Weatherly, 27 Ap 1896 (same), W.S. Hale MG, G. Pryor W 2-17
William Hale or Hail to Ellen Travis, 16 Oct 1875 (17 Oct), A.J. Mathis MG 1-#1415 & 1-291
William M. Hale to Louella Thomas, 27 Jan 1900 (28 Jan), G.H. Musington MG, Isaac Hale [signed by X] W 3-116

- - - - - - - - - - - - -

HALEY

1900 CENSUS
John E. Haley 18, Eugene 17, Lester W. 10, Mary L. 7: see John W. Angel
MARRIAGES
Cornelius Haley to Mary Ferreter, 22 Jan 1877 (23 Jan), B. J.M. Sutey(?) MG 1-#1481
Ward Haley to Mary L. Roddy, 13 Jan 1857 (15 Jan), A. Johns MG 1-#588

- - - - - - - - - - - - -

HALL

1880 CENSUS
J.M. Hall 52 (Minister), M.A. 36 (w), A.C. 13 (d), Geo 11, T.E. 9 (d), M.C. 6 (d), R.R. 3 (s), A.J. 10/12 (d) 11-37-306
1900 CENSUS
Eli Hall 19: see Thomas Travis
Emma Hall 40 (Dec 1859-Wd 5-5)(Washwoman), Ethel 16 (June 1893), Lora 15 (Mar 1884), Hallie 12 (Jan 1887), Beverly 12 (Mar 1888), Linar 8 (Dec 1891) 7-26aB-224/229
Farrel Hall 63 (Jan 1837-M 40), Martha 60 (June 1840-M 40-8-8), Rudolphus 23 (June 1876-M 0), Elbert 21 (Jan 1879), Lester 16 (May 1884) 15-272A-78
George Hall 39, William 16: see Monroe R. Miller
John Hall 39 (Jan 1861-M 20), Sallie 35 (July 1864-M 20-8-6), Willie 12 (May 1888), Mary E. 9 (June 1890), Anna M. 8 (Feb 1892), Sydney R. 5 (Dec 1894), Roy C. 4 (Feb 1896), Emma 2 (Mar 1898) 15-273-98
John M. Hall 40 (June 1859-M 18), Nancy J. 38 (Aug 1861-T/Va/T-M 18-4-4), Obie B. 17 (Sep 1882)(Coal Weighmaster), Victor C. 16 (Jan 1884)(Driver at Mines), John A. 15 (Feb 1885)(Driver at Mines), Lena 13 (Dec 1886), Abbie M. 21 (Sep 1878)(Music Teacher), Gaither HENEGAR 24 (boarder)(Aug 1875-Ala/Ala/Ala)(Barber) 13-309A-362/375
Maud Hall 20: see William B. Smith
Susan Hall 50 (Nov 1849-Wd 3-2)(Seamstress), William C. 26 (Dec 1873), Samuel S. 13 (Jan 1887) 6-242B-59
Thomas J. Hall 35 (Sep 1864-M 12), Sarah L. 32 (Sep 1867-M 12-5-5), Louis L. 10 (Feb 1890), Ida A. 5 (Mar 1895), John T. 4 (Mar 1896), Reece D. 1 (July 1898), Roscoe N. 1/12 (May 1900) 4-224B-212/216 (Spring City & Dayton Road)
MARRIAGES
Abbie Hall to T. M. Taylor q.v.
Dalt Hall to Maudie Smith, 29 July 1899 (30 July), W.L. Lillard JP, R.C. Knight W 3-15
George Hall to Biddix Collins– see George Hale
J.F. Hall to Ollie Wright, 22 June 1889 (31 June), Daniel Broyles JP 1-481
James Hall to Alice Hickson, 13 May 1885 (same), P.P. Brooks ?? 1-494
Letha E. Hall to Charles L. Kilgore q.v.
Lori Hall to J. C. Thurman q.v.
Mary Hall to Henry Parks q.v.
Nettie Hall to T. E. Travis q.v.

- - - - - - - - - - - - -

HALLIBURTON / HALLYBURTON

1900 CENSUS
Homer Halliburton 30 (Ap 1870-M 3), Lavinia 26 (Mar 1874-M 3-0-0), Corra McDONALD 24 (sil)(Dec 1875), Mina WYBEL 2 (ne)(Jan 1898-Oh/Oh/T), Mollie A. SUGGS 57 (m)(Nov 1843-Wd), Mamia 20 (si) (Dec 1879) 10-255A-98/99
MARRIAGE
Homer H. Hallyburton to Lovenia McDonald, 20 Ap 1897 (same), J.A. Whitner MG, W.M. Dickey W 2-140

- - - - - - - - - - - - -

HALLOCK / HALLIET

1900 CENSUS
Wilum Halliet 66 (Dec 1833-T/NY/NY-M 12), Sarah 46 (Mar 1854-M 12-7-7), Jane 14 (June 1885), Chalton 12 (Ap 1888), Wilum R. GIBSON 25 (boarder)(Feb 1875)(School Teacher) 1-187B-167/175
MARRIAGE
W.S. Hallock to Mrs. Sarah E. Gibson, 19 Mar 1898 (20 Mar), Spencer Tonnell(?) MG, R.J. Killough W 2-259

- - - - - - - - - - - - -

HAMBRICK

1900 CENSUS
William Hambrick 23: see Emma Gillespie (B)

MARRIAGE

Corda Hambrick to J. C. Crisp q.v.

- - - - - - - - - - - - -

HAMBY / HAMBIE / HANBY / HANSBY

1900 CENSUS

Hinery Hansby 24 (Ap 1876-T/T/Va-M 4)(Coal Miner), Mary 21 (Feb 1879-Ga/T/T-M 4-2-1), Grachy 2 (Feb 1898) 10-255B-105/108

James L. Hamby 14, Lillie M. 12, Nancy A. 7, William P. 5, Harvey 2, Samuel P. 10: see William H. Hensley

Ralie Hansby 55 (Jan 1845-M 25)(Coal Miner), Mary S. 38 (Ap 1862-Va/Va/Va-M 25-6-4), George 14 (July 1885), Josey 9 (Aug 1890) 10-255B-110/113

Reuben L.(?) Hanby 55 (Aug 1844-M 26), Kinsey J. 47 (Jan 1853-M 26-10-7), Lizzie M. 18 (Nov 1881), John E. 13 (Feb 1887), Samuel T. 11 (Mar 1889), Hughston R. 6 (Mar 1894), Martha M. 3 (Sep 1896) 5-231B-71/71

MARRIAGES

Flora Hamby to Loyd Rector q.v.

Reuben Hambie or Hamby to Eliza J. Minick, 5 Feb 1872 (no return) 1-#1227

Reuben Hamby to Sansada J. Magors, 28 Jan 1875 (29 Jan), John W. Williamson MG 1-#1391

- - - - - - - - - - - - -

HAMELL

MARRIAGE

Ruban Hamell to Sarah McGee, 23 Sep 1858 (24 Sep), N.H. Long JP 1-#658

- - - - - - - - - - - - -

HAMILTON

1860 CENSUS

Jacob Hamilton 30 (Blacksmith), Martha J. 23, John H. 3, William S. 1/12, Sarah RECTOR 57 5-35-235

1870 CENSUS

Jacob M. Hamilton 40, Martha J. 33, John H. 13, William S. 11, Parthena 9, Loretta E. 7, Salina 5, Isa 1, Louisa E. RECTOR 28, Salina E. RECTOR 22 5-10-76

1880 CENSUS

Jacob M. Hamilton 50, Martha J. 45, Lorretta A. 15, Felina E. 13, Idona A. 9, Eliza M. 7, Dora 2, Oza W. 11 (s) 5-4-36

John H. Hamilton 22 (Cabnetmaker), Melissa C. 20, Lawrence C. 3, Herbert W. 1 5-5-37

1900 CENSUS

Corda Hamilton 13: see Kirk Loydd

Elbert Hamilton 50 (Feb 1850-M 21)(Blacksmith), Martha 43 (Oct 1856-M 21-10-10), Bill 17 (Dec 1882), Mally 15 (Feb 1885), Flecher 13 (Nov 1886), Minie 11 (Mar 1889), Annie 8 (Nov 1891), Tom 6 (Feb 1894), Floyed 3 (Ap 1897), Crocket JOHNSON 29 (Mar 1881) 10-253B-74

Elizabeth Hamilton 37, Mary 20: see Wm J. Pendergrass

Jacob M. Hamilton 70 (Mar 1830-M 44)(Blacksmith), Martha J. 63 (Oct 1836-M 44-1-1), George W. 18 (Aug 1881) 5-234A-129

John H. Hamilton 42 (June 1857-M 24)(Physician), Malissa 40 (Feb 1860-M 24-9-7), Lawrence 23 (May 1877) (School Teacher), Herbert W. 21 (Mar 1879), Albert D. 15 (Jan 1885), Etha J. 12 (Sep 1887), Martha A. 5 (May 1895), Anna M. 2 (Sep 1897) 5-236A-156

Lizabeth Hamilton 57: see Tilman Mace

Minnie Hamilton 18: see John Morgan

Rhoda Hamilton 39 (Aug 1860-Ky/Ky/Ky-M 23-11-10), Lavinia 20 (Oct 1879-Oh/NC/Ky), Lillie 15 (Oct 1884-Oh), Liner 10 (Feb 1890), Othello 7 (Sep 1892), Lola 7 (Sep 1892), Laucaste 4 (June 1895), Burnice 3 (May 1897), Summite 2/12 (Mar 1900), Nancy PICKLE 18 (d)(Feb 1882-Oh-M 3-2-2), Ethel 3 (gd)(Sep 1896), Lavinia 6/12 (d)(Nov 1899) 10-323-61/64 (B)

MARRIAGES

Dora Hamilton to Frank Fox q.v.

Jacob M. Hamilton to Martha J. Rector, 11 June 1855 (4 July), Sewell Phillips MG 1-#504

John H. Hamilton to Malissa C. Ganaway, 16 June 1876 (18 June), A.C. Peters MG 1-#1448

Lizzie Hamilton to S. T. McSwen q.v.

Loretta A. Hamilton to C. J. Green q.v.

Nancy Hamilton to Robert Pickle q.v.

Parthenia Hamilton to Hugh A. Locke q.v.

Selina Hamilton to W. H. Burnett q.v.

T.J. Hamilton to Bettie Harwood, 3 Jan 1888 (25 Jan), A.D. Stewart MG 1-544

Valia Hamilton to William McDonald q.v.

W.S. Hamilton to Ada Smith, 13 Nov 1886 (same), John Howrd MG 1-532

- - - - - - - - - - - - -

HAMLIN

MARRIAGE

Dottie A. Hamlin to John Skyles q.v.

- - - - - - - - - - - - -

HAMMOND

MARRIAGE

James Hammond to Mary Brocke, 30 Mar 1871 (same), W.R. Henry JP 1-#1191

- - - - - - - - - - - - -

HAMPTON / HAMTON

1860 CENSUS

George Hampton 11, Rhody A. 9: see William Ganaway

Henry Hampton 57 (Va)(Carpenter), Mary 44 (Ky), Sarah E. 15, Robert 2, Ann T. 7 10-30-201

1870 CENSUS– None

1880 CENSUS

Mary Hampton 20: see Nancy Gillespie (B)

1900 CENSUS

James W. Hamton 39 (Aug 1860-M 20), Rebecca 36 (Ap 1864-M 20-13-10), Milh [sic] 18 (Aug 1881)(RR Hand), Bessy 17 (Feb 1882), Luther 14 (May 1886), Araker 12 (May 1888), Arthur 10 (Dec 1889), Cary 9 (Feb 1891), Berthy 8 (Ap 1892), Ray 6 (Ap 1894), Robbert 3 (June 1896), Lillie 3/12 (Feb 1900), Charles HAMTON 39 (b)(Feb 1861) 1-184B-116/122

MARRIAGES
Margaret Ann Hampton to Geo W. Hoslin or Hoplin q.v.
Mattie Hampton to Frank Smith q.v.

- - - - - - - - - - - - -

HANES / HAINES / HAYNES– see HINDS

- - - - - - - - - - - - -

HANEY / HAYNEY / HANNEY

MARRIAGES
Ella Hanney to D. B. Thompson q.v.
L. J. Hayney to James Trusley q.v.
Rachael Jane Haney to N. T. Posey q.v.

- - - - - - - - - - - - -

HANKINS
(see also HAWKINS)

1860 CENSUS
James H. Hankins 41, Caroline 32, James 14, Matilda 12, Jane 10 3-66-454
1870 and 1880 CENSUS– None
1900 CENSUS
Hattie Hankins 13: see Jack Lee (B)

- - - - - - - - - - - - -

HANKS

1860 CENSUS
David Hanks 40, Elizabeth 35 9-97-657
1870 and 1880 CENSUS– None
1900 CENSUS
Charley Hanks 19: see Dan Smith (B)

- - - - - - - - - - - - -

HANSFORD

MARRIAGE
Joseph Hansford to Minerva Holloway, 19 July 1884 (20 July), Jesse P. Thompson JP 1-465

- - - - - - - - - - - - -

HANSON
(see also HENSON)

1860 CENSUS
James L. Hanson 62 (Va), Mary A. 40, Rhody L. 2 3-57-392
MARRIAGE
Eva Hanson to Percival Johnson q.v.

- - - - - - - - - - - - -

HARBIN

1900 CENSUS
Melvin Harbin 19: see Charles Bird (B)

- - - - - - - - - - - - -

HARDBARGER / HARTBARGER / HASHBARGER / HARCHBARGER / HASELBARGER

1870 CENSUS
Elizabeth Haselbarger 37, William A. 18, Martin J. 14, John S. 5, Sarah R. 1, Sebeny BROWN 22 2-15-107
Phillip Hardbarger 20, Barbara 17, Daniel 18: see Livi Tredway
Rufus Hardbarger 23, Mary E. 19, Samuel H. 4, Winney J. 2, Martha J. 18 1-5-33
1880 CENSUS
Betsy Harshbarger 48, Samuel 16, Belle 12 2-38-313
Helen Hardbarger 45: see William Wilson
William Hashbarger 29, Mary 26, Callie 1 2-38-311
1900 CENSUS
Edward Hardbarger 18, Charles 7, Cordelia 2: see Elijah Norris
Sam Hartbarger 39 (Ap 1861-M 11), Mary 26 (Mar 1874-M 11-5-5), Meni 9 (Oct 1890), Alice 7 (Sep 1892), Helen 5 (July 1894), Jessi 3 (June 1896), John 1 (Ap 1899) 1-185B-132/138
William A. Hashbarger 48 (June 1852-M 25), Mary J. 47 (Jan 1853-M 25-5-5), Eliza 16 (Ap 1884), John M. 14 (July 1885), Jackson 7 (Aug 1892), Joseph RUCKER 29 (Feb 1871)(Servant) 3-207B-136/149
MARRIAGES
Catharne Hardbarger to George W. Farmer q.v.
Carrie Hartbarger to Mrs. Annie Hensly, 4 Sep 1892, D.H. Hindman JP 4-51
Daniel O. Hardbarger to Martha A. Bowles, 19 May 1858 (same), Asa Newport MG 1-#638
Daniel O. Hartbarger to Mary Jane Touzer, 14 Ap 1868 (16 Ap), J.P. Roddy MG 1-#1008
Emma A. Hartbarger to P. A. Norris q.v.
Lillie Hartbarger to Thomas Morgan q.v.
Marthy Hartbarger to Henry Dodson q.v.
N. P. Hardbarger to T. K. Green q.v.
R.N. Hartbarger to Mary E. Smith, 3 Nov 1864 (5 Nov), W.W. Low JP 1-#1078
Rufus Hartbarger to Lydia Wilson, 9 Aug 1890 (10 Aug), Richard Knight JP 1-603
Samuel Hashbarger to Mary McClelland, 3 July 1889 (5 July), C.J. Titus JP 1-580
W.M. Hashbarger to Melvina Decker, 17 Nov 1900 (18 Nov), F.M. Cook MG & W 3-244

- - - - - - - - - - - - -

HARDIN / HARDEN / HARDAN

1870 CENSUS
Mary A. Harden 45: see John Wyatt
1880 CENSUS
Mary A. Harden 58, Lottie 30, Sarah A. 1: see Jas W. Rice
1900 CENSUS
John S. Hardin 36 (Ap 1864-M ?)(Livery Stable Keeper), Minnie L. 28 (May 1872-M ?-2-2), Raymond F. 2 (Nov 1897), infant 1 (Dec 1898), Phoebe NEAL 18 (Nov 1881)(Servant) 14-219B-132/135
Joseph D. Hardin 32 (July 1867-M 0)(Livery Stable), Maud D. 21 (Jan 1879-M 0-0) 14-219B-131/134
Solomon Harden 45 (Ap 1855-M 12), Isadore 42 (Ap 1858-M 12-6-3), Solomon 22 (May 1878), George 20 (Ap

1880), Ellen T. 18 (Nov 1881), Jennie 17 (Mar 1883), Martha 15 (May 1885), Annie 13 (Feb 1887), Lena 10 (Dec 1889) 13-298A-153/156

MARRIAGES

J.D. Hardin to Mollie Spence, 2 Ap 1889 (3 Ap 1884)[sic], J.H. Parrott ?? 1-568

J.D. Hardin to Maud Holt, 14 Feb 1900, J.A. Whitner MG 4-105

John S. Hardin to Minnie B. Johnson, 3 Feb 1897, A.N. Jackson MG 4-97

Len or Lane Hardin to Mollie Greer or Green, 17 Ap 1899 (same), W.L. Lillard JP, S.T. Stuart W 2-401

Lucinda E. Hardin to James W. Rice q.v.

Massie Harden to Jones Sykles q.v.

Nancy Harden to Henry Sykles q.v.

Roxie Harden to McDuffey Stone q.v.

- - - - - - - - - - - - -

HARELSTON

MARRIAGE

Margaret Harelston to G. W. Standifer q.v.

- - - - - - - - - - - - -

HARMON

1900 CENSUS

Leonard Harmon 58 (Jan 1841-M 33)(Cabnet Worker), Sarah J. 55 (July 1844-M 33-0), Ann N. PATTISON 51 (si)(Oct 1848) 14-215B-50/51

Phebe Harmon 29: see Mary Morris (B)

MARRIAGE

Jacob Harmon to Kissiah Low, 19 Dec 1851 (no return) 1-#357

- - - - - - - - - - - - -

HARMONY

1900 CENSUS

David Harmony 30: see Henry Swafford (B)

- - - - - - - - - - - - -

HARNEY– see HORNEY

- - - - - - - - - - - - -

HARP

MARRIAGE

Elizabeth Harp or Haress to R. H. Perry q.v.

- - - - - - - - - - - - -

HARPER

1900 CENSUS

Charles Harper 36 (May 1864-Ga/Ga/Ga-M 8), Molly 25 (Sep 1874-T/Va/Va-M 8-2-0), Maud GORDON 3 (ne) (Dec 1896) 8-318B-162/168 (B)

- - - - - - - - - - - - -

HARREL

MARRIAGE

M. M. Harrel to W. R. Stanly q.v.

- - - - - - - - - - - - -

HARRIS / HARRISS

1860 CENSUS

Dawson Harris 58 (NC), James 12 2-81-552

Edward Harris 35 (Ga), Agatha 37 (SC), George W. 15 (Ill), James P. 13, Thomas N. 11, John C. 9, William 4 4-44-298

Margaret C. Harris 19: see Martin McCully

Nancy A. Harris 10/12: see Nancy Martin

Smith Harris 23, Leah E. 23, George W. 10/12 2-77-522

1870 CENSUS

Dawson Harris 62 (NC): see Martin McCullough

James Harris 61, Stephen 21, Tennessee 17, Nancy 14, Mary 13, Eliza 30, Stephen HARRIS 63 6-14-101

Louisa Harris 19: see Micajah Clack

Sarah Harris 12: see Thomas K. Thompson

Samuel Harris 21, Tennessee 17: see George L. Tucker

William C. Harris 37 (NC), Margarette E. 23 (NC), Roey B. 7 (NC), Texas A. 4, William E. 2, Joseph B. 5/12 5-8-59

William H. Harris 24, Nancy A. 27, Sarah M. 5, Robert E. Lee 3, George W. 8/12, Elizabeth MATHEWS 66, Luhanna MATHEWS 43 1-2-0

1880 CENSUS

Rose C. Harris 20: see James M. Benson

F.A. Harris 22, D.A. 19, B.S. 1 (s), W.F. 2/12 (s), J.M. MARTIN 27 8-16-138

William Harris 44, Margaret E. 33, Rowley B. 17, Texas A.M. 14, William E. 12, Joseph B. 15, July A. 7, Cornelia M. 4 6-19-177/182

1900 CENSUS

Benjamin Harris 30 (Jan 1870-M 2), Mary 23 (Sep 1876-M 2-2-2), Barnett 1 (Jan 1899), Lillie 3/12 (Feb 1900) 6-245B-108/109

Cora Harris 14: see Sakinean Arthur

George V.(?) Harris 38 (July 1861-M 5)(Coal Miner), Laura 32 (July 1867-M 5-3-3), Roy T. 4 (Dec 1895), Rosa N. 2 (Sep 1897), Babe 0/12 (May 1900) 10-328A-170/180

James Harris 21 (Oct 1878-M 1), Jane 17 (Oct 1882-M 1-0) 10-324A-87/91

Joseph Harris 40 (Sep 1859-M 12)(Carpenter), Adeline 32 (Ap 1868-M 12-?-?), Louise 16 (Mar 1884), Martha 13 (Ap 1887), Walter 10 (July 1889), Eva LANE 22 (d)(Sep 1877-Wd 2-1), Etta 3 (gd)(Feb 1897) 8-279B-221/223

Phill Harris 50 (Jan 1850-M 16), Rachel 29 (Feb 1871-M 16-5-5), Nelson 11 (Sep 1888), Elishue 9 (May 1891), Linnie 7 (May 1893), Alford 4 (Nov 1895), Kittie 1 (Jan 1899) 7-264A-264/269

Roy Harris 38 (Unk-T/NC/NC-M 6), Nancy J. 39 (Jan 1861-M 6-2-2), Ida B.V. 4 (Dec 1895), John F. 1 (Dec 1898) 6-248A-160/161

Sam Harris 32 (Ap 1868-M 5)(Coal Miner), Winny 28 (Feb 1870-M 5-0) 10-255B-102/104

Samuel Harris 56 (Aug 1843-M 30)(Grocer), Tennessee F. 47 (Ap 1853-M 30-9-8), Robert B. 23 (June 1876) (Grocery Salesman), Richard G. 14 (Mar 1886), Carrie S. 11 (Feb 1889), Mandie 8 (Ap 1892) 10-327B-159/168

Vesty Harris(?) 25: see Ben McDonald (B)

William Harris 32 (Feb 1868-T/NC/NC-M 11), Octavia 29 (Aug 1870-T/T/NC-M 11-4-4), Maud 9 (July 1890), John 7 (Mar 1893), Lester 5 (Sep 1894), Ethel 1 (Nov 1898) 6-216A-122/123

William C. Harris 64 (June 1836-NC/NC/NC-M 38), Margaret 63 (Jan 1837-NC/Germany/NC-M 38-6-5), Berry A. 13 (Dec 1886) 6-245B-112/113

MARRIAGES

B. Harris to E. Erwine, 15 May 1856 (20 May), E.E. Wasson JP 1-#561

Benjamin Harris to Harriett Knox, 17 Aug 1863 (18 Aug), D.W. Knox JP 1-#804

Benjamin Harris to Ruth Ann Cunningham, 15 Dec 1864 (16 Dec), Wm Low JP 1-#1087

Bettie Harris to E. P. Giles q.v.

Bettie Harris to Wesley Hawkins q.v.

Charley Harris or Haries to Sarah Marriott, 20 Ap 1900 (same), J.W. Williamson MG, Clem Wilson W 3-146

Cicero Harris to Gilly Galmore, May 1889 (same), A.W. Frazier JP 1-573

E.B. Harris to Amanda Randolph, 21 June 1890, M.C. Bruner MG 4-17

E.G. Harris to N.P. Thurman, 18 Aug 1885 (23 Aug), B.F. Holloway JP 1-482

Elbert Harris to Sarah E. Edmonds, 26 May 1877 (27 May), B.F. Holloway JP 1-#1502

Eva Harris to W. H. Lane q.v.

F. A. Harris(?) to Joseph Haas q.v.

G.W. Harris to Laura Ellis, 20 Mar 1895, J.C. Dodd JP 4-91

George W. Harris to Mary Turk, 16 Sep 1868 (17 Sep), A.L. King MG 1-#1029

George Harris to Jennie Carter, 8 Oct 1887 (9 Oct), W.J. Kirley ?? 1-533

Ida Harris to John Dearmond q.v.

Julia A. Harris to William D. Byrley q.v.

J. B. Harris to Mary Marler, 30 Oct 1897 (same), W. A. Howard MG 2-206

Jackson Harris to Lou Cooley, 14 June 1887 (same), M.C. Bruner MG 1-565

M. E. Harriss to J. A. Selcer q.v.

Maggie Harris to S. F. Thompson q.v.

Mary Harris to Thomas Hale q.v.

Mary A. Harris to John Thompson q.v.

Miles Harris (24, Warren Co) to Nancy Woodey (21), 6 Oct 1881, W.S. Hale MG, Clinton Turnbill(?) & Bill Mires W 4-2(20)

Minerva Harris to J. R. Barger or Booger q.v.

Nancy E. Harris to James Kisjah q.v.

P. C. Harris to W. W. Ruthgab or Ruthgate q.v.

S.S. Harris to M.L. Smith, 24 July 1894, R.S. Mason JP 4-67

Sallie Harris to John Hensley q.v.

Sallie M. Harris to William Miller q.v.

Samuel Harris to Tennessee Howard, 6 Nov 1869 (7 Nov), A.P. Early MG 1-#1122

Texas Harris to S. S. Knight q.v.

Vina Harris to M. McCullam q.v.

W.A. Harris to Octavia Milton, 20 June 1889 (23 June), J.L. Henry JP 1-580

W.O. Harris to Myra Hayes (or Hogue), 3 May 1890, James Johnson JP 4-77

- - - - - - - - - - - - -

HARRISON

1860 CENSUS

William Harrison 25, Mary 19 8-12-78

1870 CENSUS– None

1880 CENSUS

Elizabeth Harrison 58, George M. 22 (s), James Henry 21 (s) 6-13-121

Nath Harrison 36, S.S. 34, Sarah NEAL 12 (protégé) 4-5-39

Thomas Harrison 50, Alice 31, Emma 18, Lula 5, Susan 2/12 (B)(Mu): see Jere Wasson

William Harrison(?) 26, N.E. 25, I.F. 6 (s), R.N. 4 (d), Ida 2 4-2-17

1900 CENSUS

Allen F. Harrison 41 (May 1859-Ind/NC/NC-M 18)(Missionary), Alice C. 39 (Jan 1861-Ind/Oh/Ind-M 18-4-2), William N. 13 (July 1886-Kan), Harlin C. 9 (Dec 1890-Kan), Anna ROSE 12 (adopted d)(July 1887-La/Germany/La) 13-309B-374/388

Charles Harrison 23 (Dec 1876-M 1), Mary A. 19 (Oct 1880-M -1-1) 9-229A-23

Ernest H. Harrison 18: see Moses Grier

George M. Harrison 42 (June 1857-M 19), Nancy F. 35 (Feb 1865-M 19-9-8), John W. 18 (Dec 1881), Susan E. 15 (May 1885), Verissy 12 (Oct 1887), Ada L. 11 (May 1889), James H. 9 (Feb 1891), Ida M. 5 (Jan 1895), George W. 1 (June 1898), Charles W. 5/12 (Dec 1898), Susan CHAMBERS 61 (ml)(Dec 1838-T/NC/T-D 1-1) 6-249A-176/177

James Harrison 41 (Mar 1859-M 19), Verised J. 39 (Nov 1860-M 19-6-5), George W. 17 (Dec 1882), Floyd 15 (Nov 1884), Thurgon or Spurgon 6 (Sep 1893), Rebecca 4 (June 1895), Mattie 1 (July 1898) 5-237A-178/178

James H. Harrison 41 (Jan 1859-M 22), Alice S. 38 (Oct 1861-NC/NC/NC-M 22-10-10), Hampton J. 19 (May 1881), Lafayette F. 17 (Mar 1883), Callie B. 15 (Feb 1885), Crockett P. 12 (July 1887), Bessie L. 10 (Aug 1889), David O. 6 (Jan 1894), Florence E. 3 (June 1897), Winnie M. 2/12 (Mar 1900), Willie May 9 (Jan 1891) 4-227-268/272 (Spring City & Washington Road)

Mar--?-- O. Harrison 35 (Unk-M 2), Sitha J. 42 (Sep 1858-M 2-3-3), Bertha A. TALLENT 21 (sd)(May 1879), Alma 17 (sd)(Aug 1882), Edward F. 14 (ss)(Mar 1886) 8-315B-108/112

Minnie Harrison 13: see Perry McWillis (B)

MARRIAGES

Amanda J. Harrison to A. L. Wilkey q.v.

Ann Harrison to Rolston Morgan q.v.

Emma L. Harrison to Robert R. Caldwell q.v.

Georg M. Harrison to Maney M. Travis, 14 Nov 1880 (same), John Howard MG 1-293

James H. Harrison (22) to V.J. Ault (21), 21 Mar 1882, T.H. McPherson JP, G.W. Ault & Eliza Dodd W 4-8(74)

John W. Harrison to Orlinda Josephine Cook, 5 July 1878 (7 July), Peter Roddy MG 1-#1566

Mattie Harrison to Rolla Jones q.v.
Nathan M. Harrison to Sarah Reavely, 21 Mar 1870 (no return) 1-#1149
Robert Harrison to Ethel Lile [license[or Lyle [index], 4 July 1899 (same), L.E. Smith JP, J. Lyle W 3-7
Vileenia(?) Harrison (16, Meigs Co) to Eli Corvin q.v.
William Harrison to Elizabeth Vaughn, 14 Sep 1872 (no return) 1-#1251

- - - - - - - - - - - - -

HARROD / HORRID

MARRIAGES
James Harrod (19, McMinn Co) to Maggie Meyers (16, Bledsoe Co), 26 Feb 1882, J.W. Peace MG, J.B. Corvin & E.A. Peace W 4-8(78)
Jourden Horrid to Elizabeth Ollfred, 23 Jan 1862 (no return) 1-#772

- - - - - - - - - - - - -

HARROLD

MARRIAGE
Alice Harrold to Alfred Anderson q.v.

- - - - - - - - - - - - -

HARSHAW

1880 CENSUS
S. C. Harshaw 25 (B): see H. R. Porter

- - - - - - - - - - - - -

HARSH

1900 CENSUS
Philip H. Harsh 43 (June 1856-Oh/Oh/Oh-M 21), Ida N. 43 (June 1856-Oh.NY/NY-M 21-7-7), Blanche 20 (Mar 1880-Oh), Ray C. 18 (Oct 1881-Minn), Harry H. 16 (Aug 1883-Iowa), Vera H. 14 (June 1885-Minn), Clinton 12 (Oct 1881-Minn), Frances E.W. 9 (June 1890-Minn), Gaddis G. 7 (Ap 1892-Minn) 6-255A-90

- - - - - - - - - - - - -

HART

1880 CENSUS
E.D. Hart 35, J. 29, C.S. 14 (s), John 7, S.E. 4 (d), M.A. 2 (d), R. BREEDING 27 (Hired Hand) 3-23-187
1900 CENSUS
Alice Hart 24 (Unk 1876-M 5-0) 8-275A-129 (B)
Henry Hart 64 (Mar 1836-Conn/Conn/Conn-M 30)(Real Estate Agent), Eller 54 (Ap 1846-Pa/Pa/Pa-M 30-4-3), Hettie 25 (Feb 1875), Grace 17 (Ap 1883) 1-186A-139/146
Lucinda Hart 67: see ---?--- Benjamin

- - - - - - - - - - - - -

HARTLEY

1860 CENSUS
William Hartley 18: see George W. Ault
1870 and 1880 CENSUS-- None
1900 CENSUS
John M. Hartley 18 (Mar 1882-Tex/T/T-M 0), Eliza 21 (June 1878-M 0-0) 6-248A-155/156
Samuel Hartley 20: see Elzie Wilkey
MARRIAGE
John Martin Hartley to Lizie Tilly or Tilley, 13 Oct 1899 (15 Oct), N.D. Reed MG, H.M. Hartley W 3-52

- - - - - - - - - - - - -

HARTMAN

MARRIAGE
George S. Hartman to Susan A. Green, 11 Sep 1897 (12 Sep), L.C. Carter MG, C.J. Green W 2-177

- - - - - - - - - - - - -

HARVESTER

MARRIAGE
Mary S. Harvester to William Myers q.v.

- - - - - - - - - - - - -

HARVEY / HARVY

1870 CENSUS
Thomas J. Harvey 58 (NY), Martha A. 58, Franklin HULL 11 1-13-84
1880 CENSUS
John Harvy 67 (B): see Jacob Krichbaum
MARRIAGES
John Harvey to Carry Green, 4 July 1900 (same), W.D. Reed MG, R.L. Armor W 3-180
S.L. Harvey to Madeline Culver, 7 Jan 1897 (same), A.N. Jackson MG, R.J. Killough W 2-112
Susan Harvey or Hanney to Warren Rhea q.v.

- - - - - - - - - - - - -

HARVISTON / HARFESTON / HARVERSON

1900 CENSUS
Mandy Harvison 70 (Unk 1830) 15-268B-10
Margaret Harverson 65 (Unk 1835-Wd 1-1) 8-286A-348/350
MARRIAGES
Mary O. Harviston to Alfred Burton q.v.
Kittie Harfeston to John Woody q.v.

- - - - - - - - - - - - -

HARWOOD / HAWOOD / HAYWARD

1860 CENSUS
Jesse Harwood 56 (SC), Mary 40, Benjamin D. SMITH 16, Francis E. HARWOOD 6, Mary A. 4, Joseph A. 1, Polly BLYTHE 70, Ellen BLYTHE 24 3-65-449
John Harwood 36 (Blacksmith), Sophia 35, Ruthe C. 14, Margaret J. 9, Sophia 4, John T. 6/12, Hiram PRESLEY 10 (bound) 6-110-756
Rufus M. Harwood 32, Julia A. 29 (Va), William 15, John 13, Claiborn 11, Solomon 8, Joseph 5, Martha J. 3, Elizabeth 1/12 3-63-439
[Rufus drowned in Tennessee River in 1865]

1870 CENSUS
Jesse Harwood 65 (SC), Mary 40, Francis A. 14, Mary Ann 13, Samantha J. 9 3-4-25
Julia A. Harwood 45 (Va), Claiborne 20, Solomon 18, Joseph 14, Martha 13, Elizabeth 10, Mary 2 3-15-110
1880 CENSUS
J.A. Harwood 52, C. 28 (s), Joseph 24, Martha 24, E. 18 (d), Mary 13 3-25-203
Mary Harwood 58, Francis 26 (s), S. J. 18 (d), Ellen BLYTHE 44 (si) 3-29-238
Ruth Harwood 51, W.C. 24 (d), M.E. 22 (d), J.W. 17 (s) 3-27-217
1900 CENSUS
Claborn Harwood 49 see William J. Pendergrass
Frank Harwood 46 (Dec 1853-T/SC/T-M 12), Tressie 32 (Mar 1868-M 12-6-3), Fredy K. 10 (Oct 1889), Ben H. 7 (Ap 1893), Tennessee 2 (Feb 1898) 7-265A-288/293
John W. Harwood 37 (Jan 1863-M 6), Sallie 24 (May 1876-Ky/Ky/Ky-M 6-3-3), Ida B. 5 (Nov 1894), Alice B. 3 (Ap 1897), Charles D. 1 (Nov 1898) 3-203B-67/72
Gile Hayward 26 (Dec 1873-NY/NY/NY-M 0)(Physician), Mima M. 28 (Mar 1872-Mich/Mich/NY-M 0-0), Mattie B. BUNTIN 25 (boarder)(Nov 1874) 13-309B-372/386
Ruthy Harwood 70 (Nov 1829-T/T/NC-Wd 0) 3-212A-209/217
Susie Harwood 20, Clifford 6/12: see Meridith M. Paul
Sol Harwood Unk (Unk-M 23), Mary M. 53 (Nov 1846-M 23-5-5), Joseph 22 (July 1877), Idel 20 (Sep 1879), R. Morgan 17 (Jan 1883), Laura P. 5 (Nov 1894), Gracie A. 11/12 (June 1899), Thomas COACH 20 (Aug 1879)(Servant) 3-207A-123/134
William Harwood 54 (Sep 1845-M 28), Martha 43 (Dec 1856-M 28-12-11), John M. 27 (June 1872), William C. 20 (Feb 1880), James T. 17 (Sep 1882), Julia A. 16 (Mar 1884), Lula 12 (July 1887), Gertie 10 (Aug 1889), Jesse W. 8 (Feb 1892), Hugh C. 4 (Jan 1896) 6-248B-170/171
William Harwood 37 (Mar 1863-M 7), Marrire 22 (Mar 1878-M 7-1-1), Talma F. 10/12 (July 1899) 3-200B-13/14
MARRIAGES
Alice Harwood or Howard to Will Rockholt q.v.
Bettie Harwood to T. J. Hamilton q.v.
F.A. Harwood to Trussie Wilkey, 10 May 1887 (same), Taylor Russell JP 1-533
H.B. Haywood to Ruth Wilson, 18 Jan 1875 (same), James A. Wallace MG 1-#1386
Jennie Harwood to Therlow Reid q.v.
John Harwood to Jane Wilson, 24 Aug 1874 (25 Aug), W.W. Low JP 1-#1354
John Harwood to Susie Paul, 13 May 1899 (bond only), Therlow Reed W 2-411
John W. Harwood to Sallie Reynolds, 2 Jan 1894, J.W. Cowles JP 4-65
Joseph Harwood to Dorcia Fisher, 22 June 1887 (same), Taylor Russell JP 1-533
Josie Harwood to Thomas Clark q.v.
Laura Harwood to R. T. King q.v.
M. J. Harwood to C. A. Sparks q.v.
Martha Harwood to William Pendergrass q.v.
Mary Harwood to James G. Ray q.v.
Mary A. Harwood to John A. Riggs q.v.
Mary A. Harwood to A. C. Roberts q.v.
Mollie Harwood to William Pendergrass q.v.
Rachel Clementine Harwood [license] or Howard [index] to Thomas Shook q.v.
Rossey Hawood or Howard to Byrd McDonald q.v.
S.H. Harwood to Laura Moore, 5 Sep 1900 (same), W.L. Lillard JP, W.C. Bailey W 3-209
Samantha Harwood or Howard to John Tanksley q.v.
Sarah Harwood to Newton Cagle q.v.
Sarah Harwood to Joseph Watson q.v.
Solomon Harwood to Malinda Hale, 4 Aug 1876 (6 Aug), John Howard MG 1-#1454
W.C. Harwood to Mariah McMillan, 21 Dec 1892, J.W. Cowles JP 4-47
William Harwood to Catharine Reeds, 23 Dec 1865 (24 Dec), W.W. Low JP 1-#1090
William Harwood to Martha Parker, 16 Sep 1871 (19 Sep), W.N. Clack JP 1-#1208

- - - - - - - - - - - - -

HASEMER– see HOSEMAN

- - - - - - - - - - - - -

HASSEY / HASEY

MARRIAGES
Eliza Hassey to Young Loy q.v.
J.W. Hasey to Martha McClaren, 16 Sep 1884 (18 Sep), W.L. West MG 1-461

- - - - - - - - - - - - -

HASSLER / HAUSLER / HOSTLER / HARSLER / HOSLIN / HOSSLIN

1860 CENSUS
George W. Hostler 21, Margaret 16 5-32-210
1870 CENSUS
George W. Harsler 31, Sarah F. 25, John A. 1 4-7-44
MARRIAGES
Columbus Hassler to Cora Price, 24 Dec 1892, R.A. Dickson JP 4-44 1-#710
George W. Hosler to Margaret Ann Hampton, 4 May 1860 (11 May), R.F. McDonald JP 1-#710
George W. Hoslin to Sary F. Holloway, 12 Feb 1868 (13 Feb), G.W. Renfro MG 1-#1002
Sarah Hausler to Samuel Byerly q.v.
Sydney Hoslin to Harriett Alexander, 9 Nov 1854 (23 Nov), Orville Paine JP 1-#467

- - - - - - - - - - - - -

HATFIELD

1880 CENSUS
Hans Hatfield 46: see Scruggs Yearwood
1900 CENSUS
William Hatfield 12: see Hugh Barger
MARRIAGE
Mary Hatfield to B. A. Dodd q.v.

- - - - - - - - - - - - -

HAWK

1900 CENSUS

Charles Hawk 40 (Feb 1860-Ind/Oh/Oh-M 17), Lutichie 40 (Ap 1860-Unk/Oh/Oh-M 17-6-3), Warn 15 (Nov 1884-Ind), Lerni 7 (Dec 1892), Danal 4 (Dec 1895), Margaret QUICK 73 (boarder)(May 1827-Wd 1-2-0) 12-179A-10/11

- - - - - - - - - - - - -

HAWKINS
(see also HANKINS)

1870 CENSUS

Ambus L. Hawkins 28: see Joseph A. Zigler

1880 CENSUS– None

1900 CENSUS

Andy J. Hawkins 38 (June 1866-M 13)(Coal Miner), Mandy 28 (Ap 1872-M 13-6-4), Daisy M. 12 (Nov 1887), Herbert C. 9 (Mar 1891), Della Lee 5 (Ap 1895), Andrew M. 10/12 (July 1899) 13-301B-214/222

Belle Hawkins 39 (Ap 1861)(Seamstress), William 8 (s) (Sep 1891), Richard 16 (nw)(Jan 1884), Fannie 41 (si)(Mar 1859-S 1-1)(Seamstress) 10-31A-224/239

Darkey C. Hawkins 58: see Jerry Hawkins

Feamon Hawkins 12: see James M. Cagle

Henry Hawkins 27 (Aug 1872-M 9)(RR Switchman), Girdie 23 (Aug 1877-M 9-4-0) 10-259B-182/186

Henry C.(?) Hawkins 49 (Sep 1850-Ga/Ga/Ga-M 27), Amanda 48 (Oct 1851-Ga/Unk/Ga-M 27-6-4), Joseph 20 (Mar 1880-Ga)(Butcher) 10-328A-169/179

Jerry Hawkins 25 (Mar 1875-T/Unk/NC-M 0), Mary 25 (May 1875-M 0-0), Darkey C. HAWKINS 58 (m)(Jan 1842-NC/Ireland/Unk-Wd 8-8) 10-324B-99/103

Louis Hawkins 38 (Unk 1862-M 13)(Coal Miner), Tennie 30 (Unk 1870-M 13-7-6), Maynard 12 (Jan 1888), Ethel 10 (May 1890), John 9 (Jan 1893), Willie 5 (Mar 1895), Alice 2 (Nov 1897), Carrie 3/12 (Ap 1900) 8-279B-223/225

Oscar Hawkins 25 (May 1875-M 3)(RR Foreman), Florence 22 (July 1877-M 3-2-0) 10-259B-188/192

West Hawkins 35 (Mar 1865-M 14)(Coal Miner), Bettie 29 (Ap 1881-M 14-3-3), Mary A. 9 (Feb 1891), Allice 7 (July 1892), Robert 3 (Aug 1896) 10-255A-102/103

William B. Hawkins 32 (July 1867-Oh/Oh/Oh-M 14), Delila 36 (June 1863-M 14-8-6), Tunin 13 (s)(Jan 1887), Elisa A. 11 (Ap 1889), Gilbert E. 9 (Aug 1890), Charles S. 8 (Mar 1892), William C. 4 (Mar 1896), George H. 2 (Mar 1898), Isiac A. PERRY 20 (Feb 1880)(Miner) 3-212A-210/228

MARRIAGES

A.J. Hawkins to Mandy McDonald, 28 Aug 1886, Calvin Morgan JP 1-532

Bell Hawkins to W. A. Jorden q.v.

Elmer M. Hawkins to S.A. Reed, 9 Feb 1896, G.W. Morris MG 4-88

H.B. Hawkins to Gertie(?) Phillips, 31 July 1890 (5 Aug), W.S. Hale MG 1-604

J.L. Hawkins to Lennie Smith, 8 Jan 1887 (9 Jan), Calvin Morgan JP 1-531

Jerry Hawkins to Mary Millard, 14 Ap 1900 (same), W.L. Lillard JP & W 3-142

Lillie M. Hawkins to Earnest N. Keith q.v.

Matilda Hawkins to A.J. Aikens q.v.

Nancy J. Hawkins to E. P. Tipton q.v.

Oscar Hawkins to Florence Henderson, 10 Aug 1897 (bond only), R.J. Killough W 2-172 (bond marked through) & 2-174 (bond only)

Phebe Hawkins to Charley R. Middleton q.v.

Rosa Hawkins to Tom Clements q.v.

W.M. Hawkins to Emma Carroll, 20 Sep 1897 (same), J.S. Best MG, J.M. Pogue W 2-181

Wesley Hawkins to Bettie Harris, 20 Aug 1887 (21 Aug), Calvin Morgan JP 1-534

- - - - - - - - - - - - -

HAWORTH

MARRIAGE

Essie Haworth) to Barton L. Gilmore q.v.

- - - - - - - - - - - - -

HAWS

1870 CENSUS

Jane Haws 73: see Samuel H. Holloway

1880 CENSUS

Jane Haws 83: see Samuel Holloway

MARRIAGE

Leapatra Haws to Samuel H. Holloway q.v.

- - - - - - - - - - - - -

HAYDEN

MARRIAGE

Martha A. Hayden to J. W. Martin q.v.

- - - - - - - - - - - - -

HAYS / HAYES / HAYSE / HASE / HAZE

1860 CENSUS

James Hase 30, Sarah 39, John 12, James C. 10, William R. 8, Thomas S. 5, Sarah E. 3, Samuel 2 9-98-671

James H. Hase 44, Liddia 39, Pleasant 14, Rebecca 13, Joanah 11, Elijah 7, Nancy 5, James 3, Sarah 1/12 9-97-658

John Hase 21, Nancy 20, Elizabeth 4, Liddia 2 9-97-659

Thomas Hase 7: see Joseph Garrison

1870 CENSUS

James Hayse 55, Lydia 49, Pleasant G. 25, Jeannie(?) 21, Elijah 17, Nancy 15, James 12, Sarah 10, Lydia 8, Micah 4 1-23-151

John Hayes 32, Nancy 32, Mary E. 12, Lidia 10, Joseph 8, Rebecca 6, Mira 4, Sallie 11/12 1-16-101

1880 CENSUS

H. F. Hays 26: see R. W. Holloway

James Hayes 64, Lydia 59, James 22, Sarah 19, Lydia 17, Lucy 1/12, Mary BREWER 88 (m), James VEDETOE 20 (boarder), Rebecca HAYS 16 (boarder) 12-6-51

W. T. Hays 50: see Jessee Dickey

1900 CENSUS

Alvin Hayes 46 (Nov 1853-Oh/Oh/Oh-M 7)(Bookkeeper), Jennie 37 (Sep 1862-M 7-5-5), William 17 (Nov 1882-Oh)(Coal Miner), May 16 (May 1884-Oh), Phebe 13 (June 1886-Oh), Florence 12 (Feb 1888-Oh), Kate L. 6 (Feb 1894), Henry SWAIN 23 (boarder)(May 1877-Oh/Oh/Oh)(Magazine Clerk), Sherman 19 (boarder)(Unk 1881/Oh/Oh/Oh)(Coal Miner) 8-277B-179/180

Charles C. Hayes 74 (July 1825-Oh/Md/NJ-M 49)(Farm Bureau?), Ruth W. 70 (Jan 1830-Oh/Oh/Mass-M 49-6-5) 9-229B-35

Charles L. Hayes 27, Dora 23, John H. 1 see John M. Howard

Hannah Hayes 72: see Sanders Dunlap

James Hays 24 (Nov 1875-M 1), Maggie 21 (Oct 1878-M 1-1-1), Lemner 0/12 (May 1900) 12-182B-81/84

Jesse Hayes 15: see John A. Patterson

Jessie Hayes 18, George R. 2: see Edward Townsend

John M. Hayes 30 (July 1869-T/NC/T)(Livery Stable Keeper) 10-331B-239/254

Thomas C. Hays 37 (Oct 1862-Oh/Oh/Oh-M 7), Florence 25 (May 1875-M 7-3-3), Jessee 15 (Oct 1884-Oh), George 6 (Oct 1893), Hermann 4 (Sep 1895), Minie 2 (Nov 1897), Elic 63 (Nov 1836-Oh/Pa/Pa-Wd) 10-259B-192/196

MARRIAGES

A.P. Hayes to Mima Allen, 19 Oct 1892, J.D. Winchester MG 4-5

C.E. Hayes to Lillie Haas, 19 Sep 1891, W.A. Templeton JP 4-37

Charley L. Hayes to Dora Howard, 1 Sep 1897 (same), G.W. Brewer MG, C.R. Hayes & J.M. Hayes W 2-170

Elizabeth Haze to Joseph Vetito q.v.

Emily Hays to J. R. Morrell q.v.

George Hayes to Jessie Townsell, 19 June 1897 (20 June), R.G. Knight JP, John Hosey W 2-153

J.M. Haze to Prescilla Smith, 24 Nov 1854 (28 Nov), W.C. Danly MG 1-#572

Joannah Hayse to Robert Miller q.v.

John M. Haze to Eliza Jane Reese, 4 Nov 1862 (6 Nov), J.P. Thompson JP 1-#790

Laura Hayes to William Stultz q.v.

Mary Hase to Sanders Dunlap q.v.

Mattie Hayes to William Cox q.v.

Myra Hayes or Hogue to W. O. Harris q.v.

Nancy F. Haze to Robert Clifton q.v.

Nellie Hayes to Enoch White q.v.

Sallie Hayes to B. A. Evan q.v.

Sallie E. Hayes to J. W. Walker q.v.

Sarah Hays to Moses Evans q.v.

Thomas E. Hayes to Florence Sharp, 11 Feb 1894, D.E. Broyles JP 4-65

Will H. Hayes to Florence Brenen, 3 July 1896 (5 July), W.S. Hale MG, J. Brooks W 2-37

- - - - - - - - - - - - -

HEAD

1900 CENSUS

James Head 34 (Mar 1866-Ga/Ga/Ga-M 8)(Mine Contractor), Della 27 (June 1872-M 8-4-3), Walter 7 (Feb 1893), Jessie 4 (July 1895), Willie 2 (Feb 1898) 8-278B-206/208

William F. Head 29 (July 1870-M 10)(Coal Miner), Sarah 25 (Jan 1875-M 10-3-3), Sula 7 (Oct 1892), Gertrude 4 (Dec 1895), Herbert 1 (July 1898) 8-277A-170/171

- - - - - - - - - - - - -

HEADLEE / HEADLEY / HEDLIE

1900 CENSUS

John B. Headlee 51 (Dec 1848-Ind/Pa/Pa-M 26), Louisa 48 (May 1852-Ind/T/Oh-M 26-5-4), Blanche E. 15 (Dec 1884-Ind), Bertha F. 4 (Mar 1896) 11-291B-38

Walter B. Headlee 22 (Oct 1877-Ind/Ind/Ind-M 4), Eva A. 20 (Oct 1879-M 4-1-1), Birdie E. 3 (Jan 1897) 11-291B-41

MARRIAGES

Viola V. Hedlie to N. J. Edmondson q.v.

Walter Headley to Eva Pickett, 22 Feb 1896 (23 Feb), C.E. Mowry JP, F.M. Rigsby W 2-1

- - - - - - - - - - - - -

HEATON

MARRIAGE

Henry Heaton to Annie Tramelt, 4 Mar 1888 (same), J. Howard MG 1-560

- - - - - - - - - - - - -

HECK

1880 CENSUS

--?--utin Heck(?) 34, M. 27, A.M. 6, A.J. 3 3-24-194

- - - - - - - - - - - - -

HEDGECOTH

1900 CENSUS

Allice Hedgecoth 31, Carl A. 10, Carmon J. 6: see Bailes W. H. Lewis

MARRIAGE

Nathan Hedgecoth to Allie Lewis, 25 Sep 1888 (2 Oct), M.C. Bruner MG 1-564

- - - - - - - - - - - - -

HEINEY

1900 CENSUS

Harry Heiney 31: see George W. Goodrich

- - - - - - - - - - - - -

HEISKELL / HASKEL / HASKELL

1870 CENSUS

Hugh B. Heiskell 38, Rhoda Jane 30 (Va), Florence 13, Wade 11, Frank 10, Ada E. 9, John 6, Hugh B. 5, Sallie C. 3, Frederic 1, Mary MARNEY (B) 17, Sarah MARNEY (B) 5/12 1-10-64

Luther M. Heiskell 41, Ellen 39, Martha 15 (Mo), Daniel 14 (Mo), Pole 12 (Mo), Emma A. 6 (Mo), Minnie 1 1-4-28

1880 CENSUS

Hugh Heiskell 48, Rhoda 38, Florence 22, Wade 21, Franklin 20, Addie 18, John 16, Hugh 14, Kate 13, Frederic 9, Willie 8, Richmond 6, Stephen GILLESPIE (B) 26 (Servant) 1-18-151

Isaac Heiskell 40, Sarah 35, Susan 9 (sd), infant 1/12 ("died 1 June 1880") 1-12-94 (B)

Luke Heiskell 50, Ellen 48, Daniel 24, Emma 16, Minnie 1 1-8-67

1900 CENSUS

Daniel Haskel 44 (Ap 1856-Miss/T/T-M 16), Bell 38 (Oct 1861-M 16-4-3), Morton 11 (Sep 1888), James 8 (Sep 1891), Paul 3 (Mar 1897), Vinna Fry HUNT 50 (Unk 1851) 1-186B-150/158

Edward Haskell 5: see Henry Logan (B)

Humpry Haskel 68 (Nov 1831-T/Va/T-M 6), Susan 42 (June 1857-M 6-0), Addi 35 (d)(July 1864), Katine 33 (d)(Feb 1867) 1-188B-189/198

Luther Haskel 71 (Jan 1821-T/Va/T-M 3), Nelli 48 (Ap 1852-M 3-0) 1-186A-145/153

MARRIAGES

Annie Heiskell to Henry Robinson q.v. (B)

Daniel Heiskell to Bell Roses(?), 13 June 1884 (15 June), S.H. Price MG 1-545

Emma Heiskell to J. L. Hoyal q.v.

Florence Heiskell to R. M. Robinson q.v.

H.B. Heiskell to Carrie Wallis, 7 Mar 1900, J.A. Whitner MG 4-105

John Heiskell to Anna Love, 28 Oct 1887 (27 Oct)[sic], J.B. Phillips MG 1-535

L.M. Heiskell to Nellie James, 27 Ap 1897, Wm White MG 4-96

M. E. Heiskell to T. J. Robinson q.v.

Minnie E. Heiskell to Samuel E. Paul q.v.

- - - - - - - - - - - - -

HELTON / HILTON

1900 CENSUS

Frank Helton 39 (Feb 1861-M 5), Sally 38 (Unk 1862-M 5-4-3), Cleveland RAINS 13 (ss)(Unk 1887), Thomas FRANKLIN 9 (ss)(Unk 1891) 15-269B-31

Homie(?) Helton 13: see Jacob H. Cross

Marion Helton 38 (Feb 1862-M 1)(Coal Miner), Katie 25 (Jan 1875-Ga/Ga/Ga-M 1-3-1), Augustus 13 (May 1887), Samuel R. 10 (Ap 1890), infant 0 (d)(May 1900) 13-305B-294/306

Sarah J. Helton 52: see Louis F. McDonald

Thomas I. Helton 42 (Ap 1858-M 15)(Coal Miner), Lannie 30 (Jan 1870-M 15-6-5), Charles E. 13 (July 1886) (Coal Miner), Wilburn R. 9 (July 1890)(Coal Miner), Herbert 6 (Aug 1893), Earnest 5 (Ap 1895), Fred F. 1 (Ap 1899) 13-303B-251/261

Willie Helton 34 (Mar 1866-Oh/Ireland/Ky-Wd 0)(Laundering) 10-327B-163/173

MARRIAGES

Ellen N.J. Helton to James E. McBride q.v.

Frank Hilton to Sally Roberts, 11 Mar 1894, W.L. Lillard JP 4-73

S.H. Helton to M.S. Glass, 25 Dec 1884 (same), I.W. Holt JP 1-462

S.H. Helton to Susan Letner, 15 Jan 1887 (same), A. W. Frazier JP 1-522

S.H. Helton to Willie Jones, 22 July 1890 (23 July), D.V. Culver MG 1-597

Sarah J. Hilton to William Gilbreath q.v.

Thomas Helton to Sainne McJunkins, 16 May 1885 (17 May), J.R. Crawford JP 1-494

- - - - - - - - - - - - -

HENDERSON

1860 CENSUS

John R. Henderson 20, Anna 28, William 5/12 5-39-261

1870 CENSUS

Mahala Henderson 45 (SC): see Thomas Grant

William Henderson 55, Florina 56, Samuel L. 21, Harriett 16, William 13 5-7-53

1880 CENSUS

C.F. Henderson 42, M.J. 34, J.F. 14 (s), T.J. 13 (s), C.C. 10 (s), W.H. 8 (s), L.C. 7 (d), Flora 1 (d) 9-30-256

I.(?) J. Henderson 48, Sarah 33 (w), J.T. 14 (s), S.L. 12 (d), J. ?. 6 (s), W.M. 9/12 (s) 4-36-298

John Henderson 22: see Nathan Yearwood (B)

S.L. Henderson 30, S.E. 26, F.M. 2 (d) 9-30-253

William Henderson 44, Margaret 37, Allen 9 (d?), John 5 (s) 8-18-157

William Henderson 66, Fanny 66, H.P. 26 (d), William 24, Sam 22 9-30-257

William Henderson 22, Mary 19: see Calvin Gillespie (B)

1900 CENSUS

Alvin Henderson 37 (June 1862-M 17)(Saw Mill Sawyer), Eliza J. 26 (Oct 1863-M 17-5-5), Robert F. 16 (Feb 1884), Sarah L. 14 (Feb 1886), Charles L. 7 (Ap 1893), William H.B. 5 (Aug 1896), Rebecca 9/12 (Aug 1899) 9-228B-18

Anna Henderson 62 (Ap 1838-Wd 8-7), Minnie 20 (June 1879-D 0) 6-240A-2

George Henderson 35 (May 1865-M 3)(Station Engineer), Lucinda 37 (Nov 1862-M 3-0) 10-321A-26/27

Hariet Henderson 43 (Aug 1856-Wd 5-5), Robert 11 (Aug 1888), John R.J. 10 (Dec 1889), Flora J. PEARCE 22 (d)(June 1877) 9-228B-16

Hattie Henderson 38 (Oct 1861-Ga/Ga/Ga-M 7-3-3)(Washwoman), Archie 6 (Dec 1893), Annie M. 3 (Oct 1896), Garland 5/12 (Jan 1900), George JOHNSON 24* (boarder), Warren JACKSON 25* (boarder) 8-318A-160/165 (B) [*no month or year included]

James Henderson 24 (Feb 1876-M 0), Alice A. 19 (Oct 1880-T/Ga/T-M 0-0) 2-195A-73/75

James F. Henderson 63 (May 1837-M 29)(Gardner), Sarah N. 67 (Feb 1833-M 29-1-1) 4-224B-222/226 (Back Valley Road)

John Henderson 34 (Jan 1866-M 11), Edner 29 (Oct 1870-Ga/Ga/Ga-M 11-4-4), Frank 10 (Dec 1889), Cattie 7 (Mar 1893), Ray 3 (Sep 1896), Ralph 10/12 (July 1899) 10-258B-161/165

John Henderson 27 (May 1873-M 2), Rachel 20 (Ap 1880-T/NC/T-M 2-1-1), Gracy 1 (Jan 1899) 10-156B-121/125

John F. Henderson 34 (June 1865-M 12)(Coal Miner), Rilla 28 (Jan 1872-T/Oh/T-M 12-7-6), Claude A. 10 (Aug 1889), Gertrude 9 (Ap 1891), Clyde L. 6 (July 1893), Gordon G. 4 (Nov 1895), Glenn J. 2 (Nov 1897), Minnie M. 6/12 (Nov 1899) 13-308A-345/357

Jonah Henderson 15, Horace 13: see William Smith

Lucy C. Henderson 25, Orville R. 2: see Calobis(?) Russell

Richard Henderson 56 (May 1844-M 30), Mary 41 (May 1859-Ga/Ky/Ga-M 30-13-8), Thomas E. 22 (June 1877), Monro 14 (June 1885), Alice 13 (Sep 1886), Thad 12 (Oct 1887), Columbus 9 (Unk 1891), Francis 5 (Dec 1896) 8-289A-414/417

Sams J. Henderson 27 (Ap 1873-M 6), Lida L. 27 (Ap 1873-M 6-4-3), George W. 5 (July 1894), Samuel W. 10/12 (July 1899), Martha E. WRIGHT 26 (Mar 1894) (Servant) 9-228B-13

Samuel Henderson 45 (Sep 1854-M 13)(Station Engineer), Mary 32 (Sep 1867-M 13-3-3), Fred 11 (Jan 1889), Jessie 5 (Nov 1894), Ethel 3 (Sep 1896) 8-277A-175/176

Sue Henderson 34: see John W. Hudson

Thomas Henderson 38 (Jan 1862-M 10)(Bookkeeper), Alice 28 (Jan 1872-M 10-5-4), Nellie 9 (Jan 1891), Eneasi(?) 7 (Ap 1893), Tessa 3 (Sep 1896), Edwin 2 (Jan 1898) 10-250A-4

Thomas J. Henderson 68 (Feb 1832-M 28)(Gardner), Sarah 54 (June 1845-M 28-4-3), James M. 26 (Feb 1874) (Hotel Waiter), George W. 21 (Sep 1878), Callie N. 19 (Jan 1881), Benjamin 16 (Aug 1883) 14-223A-186/190

William Henderson 25 (Oct 1874-T/T/Ga-M 0), Martha 17 (Unk 1883-Ala/Ala/Ala-M 0-0) 8-289A-420/423

MARRIAGES

A. Henderson to Daniel Mitchell q.v.

Bell Henderson to Oliver Stricklan q.v.

C. A. Henderson to A. J. English q.v.

Caldonia Henderson to F. H. Sneed q.v.

Carin(?) Henderson to Jack Houston q.v.

Elizabeth A. Henderson to H. R. Mathis q.v.

Florence Henderson to Oscar Hawkins q.v.

Franklin Henderson to Sarah Neal, 19 Sep 1872 (same), D. Broyles JP 1-#1253

George Henderson to Susan Brown, 17 Mar 1881 (same), James Johnson JP 1-297 (B)

George Henderson to R.J.A. Brown, 16 June 1884 (17 June), I.W. Holt JP 1-520

George Henderson to Lucinda Golesten, 11 Jan 1896, J.W. Williamson MG 4-88

H.C. Henderson to Harriet Henderson, 20 Oct 1886 (same), H.B. Burdett MG 1-526

Harriet Henderson to A. M. Pearce q.v.

Harriet Henderson to H. C. Henderson q.v.

Hettie Henderson to Ben White q.v.

Jacob Henderson to Ida Smith, 24 Dec 1897 (25 Dec), Jas Bramlett MG, Elmer Wright & Jake Henderson W 2-232

James Henderson to Hettie Lowry, 11 Ap 1893, J.D. Gaither MG 4-50

James M. Henderson to Alice A. Gilland, 7 Sep 1899, J.H. Keylon JP 4-101

James T. Henderson to Jane Thurman, 11 Jan 1859 (same), William Morgan JP 1-#690

John Henderson to Roda Small, 21 June 1887 (same), Calvin Morgan JP 1-531

John Henderson to Salley Kelly, 19 Oct 1887 (same), B.F. Holloway JP 1-542

Lori Henderson to J.J. Denton q.v.

M. J. Henderson to C. T. Houts q.v.

Mary Henderson to Melvin Hight q.v.

Mary E. Henderson to Bryan Pelfrey q.v.

Minerva Henderson to Columbus Gillespie q.v.

Miranda Henderson to J. F. Travis q.v.

S. L. Henderson to O. G. Ganaway q.v.

Sallie Henderson to Anderson Dodd q.v.

Sally Henderson to George Shaw q.v.

Samuel Henderson to Eliza C. Smith, 8 Mar 1877 (same), G.H. Ryan JP 1-#1490

Samuel A. Henderson to A. Mitchell, 15 Aug 1879 (19 Aug), J.M. Bramlett MG 1-#1669 & 1-#1694

Sarah Henderson to A. C. Morgan q.v.

William Henderson to Mary Donalson, 14 Jan 1880 (15 Jan), James Johnson JP 1-#1710

HENDRICK / HENDRICKS

1900 CENSUS

Anderson Hendrick 30 (Feb 1870-T/NC/T-M 2)(School Teacher), Dora 28 (Feb 1872-Ga/Ga/Ga-M 2-0), Robert FULLER 22 (boarder)(Dec 1877)(Hardware Salesman), Daniel BOLEN 35 (boarder)(June 1864) (Coal Miner) 10-250B-13

MARRIAGE

A.F. Hendricks to Dora Pence, 21 Sep 1897 (22 Sep), J.A. Whitner MG, Wolford Hagie(?) W 2-184

HENEGAR

1880 CENSUS

Kate Henegar 16, Lulu 9: see Thomas Robinson

1900 CENSUS

Gaither Henegar 24: see John Hall

HENNINGER

1900 CENSUS

James F.(?) Henninger 46 (July 1853-M 12)(Dry Goods Merchant), Kate 33 (Dec 1866-M 12-6-6), Elba 11 (Ap 1889), Sophronia 8 (June 1891), Alice E. 7 (Dec 1892), Martha A. (Mar 1895), James S. 2 (Dec 1897), baby 0/12 (d)(May 1900), Josephine KIKER 17 (Sep 1882)(House Servant) 10-323B-79/83

HENRY / HENERY

1860 CENSUS

Andrew J. Henry 18: see R. C. Montgomery

Calvin Henry 33, Isabella 40 3-55-378

Cyrus Henry 21 3-62-430

George Henry 65 3-62-429

Hiram Henry 52, Delila 48, Snelson 20, Addison 19, James K. 17, Martha 14, Georgea 12, Joseph 6 3-58-396

Solomon Henry 50, Mary 44, Joel 15, Elizabeth 12, Addison L. 10, Newton 7, Solomon 6, Franklin L. 4, Mary 1 3-62-427

William Henry 22, Rachel F. 19: see Newton Locke

1870 CENSUS

Calvin Henry 52, Isabella 53 3-8-58

Cyrus Henry 30, Cassa 22, Mary C. 2, Melton LOCKE (B) 15, Rufus LOCKE (B) 18, Joseph LOCKE (B) 17 6-15-103

George W. Henry 27, Elizabeth 23, William 2, Solomon 7/12 6-15-104

James Henry 24, Mary 21, America P. 4, Tennessee 2, Malinda 9/12, Hiram HENRY 60 3-9-64

John Henry 52, Mary 27 (Ga), John 2 (Ind), Elizabeth RUSSELL 16 1-16-102

Oliver O. Henry 37 (Md), Kate 34, Willshier 12, Trendel 19 4-6-37

Solomon Henry 59, Mary 46 (NC), Newton 16, Solomon 14, Franklin 13, Mary 11, James 9 3-8-59

Uria Henry (f) 54, Ruey (f) 45 3-21-149

William R. Henry 37, Rachel F. 29, Thomas N. 8, Cyrus F. 6, Oliver 3, Florence 3/12, Sarah BREWER 22, Asbery LOCKE (B) 17, Phillip (B) 11, Priscilla 13 (B), Lydia A. (B) 15 6-10-65

1880 CENSUS

Bryant Henry 23 (B): see John L. Ramsey

Calvin Henry 55, Isabella 59 (w), Rhoda 30 (si) 3-13-102

Cyrus Henry 41, Cassi 34, Mary C. 11, Rebecca J. 10, William W. 7, Malissa A. 6, Susan T. 4, Mary WASSOM 50 (m), Mariah SMITH 21 (ne), Frank S. HENRY 26 (b), James HENRY 19 (b), William GASS (Mu) 25 (Blacksmith), Holland A. (Mu) 25 (Servant), Thomas HACKNEY 22, Jacob HACKNEY 28 6-15-138/140

Frank S. Henry 26, James 19: see Cyrus Henry

Joel L. Henry 35, Mary J. 29, Eliza M. 4, Franklin F. 4/12 6-16-150/153

Mary C. Henry 33, America P. 14, Malinda 11, John H. 9, Elizabeth 3: see Orlena Nanney

Newton L. Henry 26, July L.S. 17 6-17-154/157

William R. Henry 47 (County Court Clerk), Rachel F. 40, Thomas N. 18, Cyrus F. 16, Florence 11, William P. 7, Lular 4 6-3-121

1900 CENSUS

Casey Henry 52 (Oct 1847-Wd 5-5), Rebecca 29 (Nov 1870), William 27 (Mar 1873), Susan 22 (Oct 1877) 6-246A-121/122 [Casey, widow of Cyrus]

Frank Henery 43 (Feb 1857-T/NC/T-M ?), Malila 39 (Feb 1861-M ?-6-3), Charles V. 11 (June 1888), Cyrno W. 5 (Feb 1895), Floyd F. 2 (Nov 1897) 10-252B-50 [F.L. Henry married Mality Wright on 1 Feb 1883 in Meigs County]

George Henry 13: see Ben Dyer

George R. Henry 36 (May 1864-M 4), Callie 21 (Oct 1878-M 4-3-2), Drusila J. 3 (Oct 1896), Willie G. 1 (June 1898), William HEMBRY 13 (Mar 1887)(House Servant) 2-193A-42/43

Joel L. Henry 55 (Dec 1844-M 27), Mary J. 49 (Feb 1851-T/T/Va-M 27-7-5), Fred F. 20 (Jan 1880)(Grocery Salesman), Gracie 17 (Aug 1882), Samuel E. 14 (Dec 1885), James M. 12 (Mar 1888) 6-242B-54

Milton Henry 48 (Feb 1853-Va/Va/Va-M 6), Maggie 37 (Unk 1863-M 6-1-1), Charles 14 (Sep 1885), Maggie 13 (Ap 1887), Pearl L. 10 (Sep 1889), Zella 3 (May 1897) 8-281B-254/256 (B)

Newt Henry 54 (Mar 1846-M 25), Emmaline 45 (Nov 1854-M 25-9-9), Mort 16 (Nov 1885), Miny 14 (July 1884), Evey 12 (Nov 1887), Norris 8 (June 1891) Laura 7 (Ap 1893), Nevie A. 3 (Ap 1877), Jasper B. BOWINS 37 (lodger)(Aug 1862-T/SC/SC-D)(Stonemason), Julia 8 (lodger)(Dec 1891-Ala) 7-266A-305/310

Newton Henry 46 (July 1853-M 21), July 39 (Aug 1860-T/T/Va-M 21-7-6), Addia 19 (June 1880), Sallie 18 (Nov 1881), Saib 15 (Aug 1884), Walter 13 (Aug 1886), Pearl 11 (Mar 1889), Robert 8 (July 1891) 10-250B-14

Perry Henry 9, Melissa 6: see Jack Ryan (B)

Philip Henry 50 (Jan 1850-T/Va/Va-M 16), Lizzie 35 (Ap 1865-Ala/Unk/T-M 16-8-6), George 13 (Aug 1886) Susan T. 16 (Mar 1884), Will 12 (May 1888), Leviler B. 10 (Feb 1890), Leonor M. 8 (May 1892), Luther 4 (Dec 1896), Susey CRAWFORD 55 (ml)(Aug 1854 sic-M 1-1-1), Charley REED 25 (boarder)(Feb 1875-Va/Va/Va), Robert STOVALL 22 (boarder)(Mar 1888-Ga/Unk-M 1), Dan JOHNSON 19 (boarder)(Mar 1881)(Coal Miner) 10-253-67 (B)

Ruie Henry 80: see John M. McPherson

Solomon Henry 45 (Jan 1855-M 18)(Carpenter), Elizabeth 40 (Ap 1860-M 18-9-5), John 16 (Feb 1884), William H. 9 (Oct 1890), Edgar 7 (Feb 1893), Lucy 6 (Mar 1894), Arch D. 2 (June 1897) 15-274A-113

Susan Henry 10: see David Ryne (B)

William R. Henry 68 (Ap 1832-Wd) 9-229A-25

MARRIAGES

A.J. Henry to Tennessee Murphy, 26 Ap 1866 (same), John Howard MG 1-#898

Calvin Henry to Isabella Kenedy, 4 Nov 1850 (same), W.H. Cunnyngham JP

Ciller Henry to J. H. Donaldson q.v.

Elizabeth Henry to George Henry q.v.

Cyrus W. Henry to Cassa Wassum, 10 Oct 1867 (same), T.N.L. Cunnyngham JP 1-#977

Frankee Henry to Allen Hale q.v.

George Henry to Elizabeth Henry, 12 Feb 1864 (same), John Wyott JP 1-#819

James Henry to Mary Nanny, 13 July 1865 (same), J. Howard MG 1-#844 & 1-#875

James Henry to Malissa Walker, 25 July 1891 (probably 1896), P.G. Roddy MG 4-89

Jane Henry to James Janow q.v.

Joel L. Henry to Mary J. Rudd 29 Nov 1873 (30 Nov), Timothy P. --?-- [Dunn?] MG 1-#1314

John Henry to Annie Ryan, 18 Nov 1886 (same), J.R. Crawford JP 1-510

Lizzie Henry to Alfred Carney q.v.

Lydia Henry to John Larson Cole q.v.

Maggy Henry to Elijah Huff q.v.

Mandy Henry to Alfred Collins q.v.

Mary Henry to Peter G. Roddy q.v.

Melissa Henry to Hugh T.V. Blevins q.v.

N.L. Henry to Julia Rudd, 17 Aug 1879 (same), John Howard MG 1-#1670

Phillip Henry to Eliza Gillespie (22, Jackson Co, Ala), 7 July 1881, P.G. Roddy MG, Anderson Parker & Jack Gillespie W 4-1(2) (B)

Rebecca Henry to George W. Ault q.v.

Sol Henry to Georgia Gray, 3 June 1900 (same), J. E. Senekes(?) ??, Wash Brewer W 3-163

Solomon Henry to Mary Wassam, 26 Mar 1866 (same), R.T. Howard MG 1-#894

Solomon Henry (27, occupation, Dry Goods Clerk) to Bettie Smith (23), 19 Jan 1882, H.P. Waught MG, Cyrus Waterhouse W 4-9(87)

William Henry to Caroline H. Geer, 31 Mar 1864 (same) R.T. Howard MG 1-#826

William R. Henry to Rachel F. Locke, 31 May 1858 (same), W.H. Bell MG 1-#632

- - - - - - - - - - - - -

HENSLEY / HENSELY
(see also **ENSLEY** and **HOUSLEY**)

1870 CENSUS
Henry M. Hoosely [sic] 34, Eliza Jane 23, Emma L. 6, Napoleon 3, Alice Jane 11/12 8-12-126
1880 CENSUS
H.M. Hensley 49, E.J. 33 (w), W.L. 15 (d), N.M. 13 (s), A.J. 11 (d) 8-20-173
1900 CENSUS
Ellen Hensley 20: see William H. Jones
Emanuel Hensley 49 (Oct 1850-Va/Va/T-M 31), Susan J. 50 (May 1850-M 31-13-11), Victoria 15 (May 1885), Henry J. 7 (Sep 1892) 13-304A-261/271
Henry M. Hensley 61 (Unk 1839-Ga/Ga/Ga-M 1), Nannie 31 (Mar 1869-M 1-3-2), Minervah 1/12 (Feb 1900), Lillie ROTHJEB 7 (sd)(Feb 1893) 8-287B-393/395
Napoleon M. Hensley 31 (Dec 1868-M 0)(Attorney), Carrie 22 (Dec 1877-M 0-0) 10-325A-105/109
Tom Hensley 53 (Mar 1847-M 28), Mary 49 (Jan 1851-M 28-5-5), Frank 21 (Mar 1879), Miny 18 (Dec 1881), Ethel 16 (Feb 1884), Bob 12 (Sep 1887), Hattie 10 (Mar 1890) 10-257B-143/147
William H. Hensley 22 (Ap 1878-M 1), Mary A. 30 (Ap 1870-T/Va/T-M 1-8-5), James L. HAMBY 14 (ss)(Ap 1886), Lillie M. 12 (sd)(Jan 1888), Nancy A. 7 (sd) (Jan 1893), William P. 5 (ss)(May 1895), Harvey W. 2 (ss)(Aug 1897), Samuel P. 10 (nw)(Sep 1887-NC) 13-303B-258/268
MARRIAGES
Alice Hensley to Henry C. Benson q.v.
Bernetha M. Hensley to W. M. Russell q.v.
Callie Hensley to John Blye q.v.
Eliza J. Hensley to T. J. Sneed q.v.
H.M. Hensley to Eliza J. Bean, 22 June 1863 (no return) 1-#798
H.M. Hensley to Nancy Rotgeb, 19 May 1899 (same), N.D. Reed MG, W.L. Lillard W 2-415
James Hensley or Hosey to May or Mary Ellen Jones, 3 Feb 1900 (same), W.L. Lillard JP, Arlin(?) Jones(?) W 3-117
John Hensley to Sallie Harris, 1 Oct 1893, J.L. Brown(?) JP 4-59
John Hensley to Maryline Milis, 18 Mar 1896 (22 Mar), W.R. Grimsley MG 2-6
Laura Hensley to W. King Lloyd q.v.
Mrs. Annie Hensley to Carrie Hartbarger q.v.
N.M. Hensley to Carrie Gillespie, 27 June 1899 (same), W.L. Patton MG, G. Gillespie W 3-4

\- - - - - - - - - - - - -

HENSON
(see also **HANSON**)

1900 CENSUS
Elbert Henson 43 (Unk-Wd)(Shoemaker) 10-327B-162/171 (B)
Lucia Henson 13: see Charles W. Irwin
Maria Henson 43 (Ap 1857-T/T/Ala-M 23-15-9)(Washwoman), Isaac 22 (Sep 1877), Hillard 20 (Jan 1880), Willie 16 (Ap 1884), Eliza 14 (Oct 1885), Herbert 12 (Dec 1887), Elizabeth 9 (Jan 1891), Lillie M. 7 (Mar 1893), Robert 5 (Oct 1894), Henry TULLESS 51 (boarder)(Oct 1848-D), Sadie 17 (boarder)(Jan 1883) 8-313A-51/54 (B)
MARRIAGES
Hagus Henson to Ellen Lively, 8 Dec 1899 (9 Dec), N.D. Reed MG, J.N. Franklin W 3-82
Louisa Henson to J. B. Russell q.v.

\- - - - - - - - - - - - -

HERBECK

1900 CENSUS
Sheldon Herbeck 41: see Isaac L. Commons

\- - - - - - - - - - - - -

HERBERT

MARRIAGE
P. Herbert to E.J. Loy, 1 Mar 1886 (4 Mar), D.B. McNeal JP 1-508

\- - - - - - - - - - - - -

HERRICH

1900 CENSUS
John Herrich 48 (Mar 1852-M 25), Renidy(?) 46 (Mar 1854-M 25-3-3), Magar 21 (Jan 1879), Revis 22 (d) (Dec 1882) 1-189B-211/223 (Spring City)

\- - - - - - - - - - - - -

HERRING

1900 CENSUS
Jessie J. Herring 66: see William Lindsey
Thomas Herring 22 (July 1877-NC/NC/NC-M 2), Tilda 16 (Nov 1883-M 2-1-1), William 1 (Feb 1899) 8-284B-322/324

\- - - - - - - - - - - - -

HES

MARRIAGE
Leah Hes to James Cate q.v.

\- - - - - - - - - - - - -

HIBBS

1900 CENSUS
Mollie Hibbs 37 (Nov 1862-Ga/Ga/T-M 23-8-6), Gussie 16 (Oct 1883-T/Ga/Ga), Minnie 14 (Oct 1886), George 11 (Aug 1888), Retta 9 (Mar 1891), Blanche 5 (July 1894), Kate MARLER 21 (d)(Nov 1878-Wd 1-1), Media 2 (gd)(Feb 1898) 8-280A-227/229
MARRIAGE
Katie Hibbs to John Marler q.v.

\- - - - - - - - - - - - -

HICKEY

1900 CENSUS
Andrew Hickey 26 (Mar 1874-M 4), Laura 26 (June 1874-M 4-2-2), Tennessee 1 (Dec 1898), Leona 11/12 (July

1899), Bryant 35 (Unk 1865)(Servant) 3-209A-163/177 (B)

Daniel F. Hickey 39 (Feb 1861-M 7/12), Lucy 22 (Unk 1878-M 7/12), Hattie 13 (Unk 1887), Horace 10 (Unk 1890), Odessa 6 (Nov 1893), Margerie J. 3 (gd) (Unk 1896), Creasy PHILLIPS 7 (d)(Unk 1893) 3-209A-164/178 (B)

Jake Hickey 43 (Ap 1857-M 26), Harriet 40 (Aug 1859-M 26-13-6), Henry 18 (Feb 1882), Florence 16 (Ap 1884), Girllie 10 (Feb 1890), James 6 (Feb 1894), Emmer 3 (Nov 1896), Lizzia WILLIAMS 20 (d)(Aug 1879-M 6-3-3), Edward 6 (gs)(July 1893), Carl 2 (gs) (Nov 1897), Paul 6/12 (Nov 1899) 2-198B-143/148 (B)

Mary J. Hickey 41 (May 1859-Wd 7-3), Rufes 13 (Feb 1887), Charles H. 11 (Oct 1889), Harvey H. 6 (May 1894) 5-231B-68

Richard Hickey 18 (Oct 1881-M 1/12), Annie 17 (Unk 1883-M 1/12), Frank WILKARSON 25 (Dec 1874) (Logman) 3-208B-157/170 (B)

William Hickey 5: see Hulda Wasson (B)

MARRIAGES

Charlotte Hickey to Richard Rhea q.v.

D.F. Hickey to Martha Wasson, 7 Aug 1897, J.G. Isabell MG 4-97

D.F. Hickey to Lucy Phillips, 17 Dec 1899, M.M. Morris MG 4-102

Florence Hickey to Frank Rhea q.v.

Lizzie Hickey to James Williams q.v.

Richard Hickey to Ann Baker, 25 May 1900, M.M. Morris MG 4-106 (B)

\- - - - - - - - - - - - -

HICKMAN / HICKAMON

1860 CENSUS

John R. Hickamon 29, Catharine 29, Margaret L. 2 8-13-84

Elias Hickamon 69 (Va), Margaret 65 8-13-85

Henry Hickamon 35, Lamera E. 31 8-13-86

William Hickman 26, Elizabeth 25, Alexander 2, Samuel H. 1, David HICKEMON 23 8-10-62

1870 CENSUS

Alexander Hickman 48, Ann Eliza 39, Margarette K. 17, James H. 15, Elias E. 12, Mary A.E. 10, John A. 7, Harriette G. 3, Emily A. 3/12 8-17-115

Henry Hickman 46, Samira E. 41 8-8-51

William Hickman 36, Elizabeth A. 35, Alexander 13, Heneger 11, David 9, Robert 2, Margarette HICKMAN 70, Margarette S. BUICE 28 8-11-121

1880 CENSUS

A. Hickman 57 (Minister), A.E. 49 (w), I.S. 22 (s), M.I. 20 (d), J.A. 17 (s), H.J. 12 (d), M.A. 10 (d), U.S. 7 (d) 8-8-71

J.H. Hickman 25, A.B. 25 (w), Etta 1 (d), E.E. 22 (b) 8-8-62

John Hickman 55, Vilaet 41 (w), Robert 22, Martin 14, S.V. 10 (d), Nettie 8, George 5, Bill 11 (ss) 8-8-69 (B)

W.H. Hickman 46, E.A. 45 (w), S.H. 22 (s), D.O. 18 (s), R.B. 12 (s), W.E. 7 (d) 8-20-171

1900 CENSUS

Anna L. Hickman 67: see James H. Hickman

Charles Hickman 30 (Sep 1869-Oh/Oh/Oh-M 5), Anna 28 (Mar 1872-England/Do/Do-M 5-0-0) 8-288B-407/409

James H. Hickman 45 (June 1854-M 22), Angeline B. 45 (Aug 1854-NY/Europe/Do-M 22-3-3), Etta B. 21 (Feb 1879), Raleigh 15 (June 1884), Margaret A. 13 (Aug 1886), Anna L. 67 (m)(Mar 1833-T/Va/Va-Wd) 13-301A-202/209

Samuel H.(?) Hickman 40 (Jan 1860-M 10)(Locamotive Engineer), Emma 28 (Ap 1872-Va/Va/Va-M 10-3-3), Cora G. 9 (June 1890), Bessie O. 6 (Jan 1894), Lela E. 4 (May 1896-Tex), Oscar SABIN 40 (boarder)(Unk 1860-Pa/Pa/Pa)(Carpenter) 8-276A-153/154

MARRIAGES

Charley Hickman to Annie Moon, 30 Sep 1895, J.H. Seward MG 4-86 [spelled Hickmott in index]

H. J. Hickman to John T. Price q.v.

Harriett Hickman to George Prater q.v.

J.O. Hickman to Sallie A. Ritchey, 26 Oct 1896 (29 Oct), W.A. Howard MG, W.S. Walker W 2-78

James H. Hickman to Angeline Bowers, 19 Feb 1878 (21 Feb), W.A. Green JP 1-#1546

M. K. Hickman to R. A. Holeman q.v.

Margaret Hickman to Jerry Rawlings q.v.

Mary E. Hickman to J. R. Abel q.v.

Mattie Hickman to Jeff Suggs q.v.

Monroe Hickman to Ida Worthington, 6 July 1900 (same), no MG or JP, Wm Kelley W 3-182

Rosa A. Hickman to Donaldson Howard q.v.

S.H. Hickman to Emma Shelton, 25 Feb 1889 (26 Feb), J.R. Walker MG 1-572

Virginia L. Hickman to Joseph P. Martin q.v.

\- - - - - - - - - - - - -

HICKMONT / HICKMOT

1900 CENSUS

James Hickmont 89 (May 1811-England/Do/Do-M 45), Charlotte 86 (June 1818-England/Do/Do-M 45-7-5) 8-289A-412/414

Thomas Hickmot 27: see James Berry

\- - - - - - - - - - - - -

HICKS / HIX

1860 CENSUS

Joseph Hicks 61 (Va), Jane 46, Newton C. 19, John T. 14, Mary J. 12, Eliza A. 10, Sarah C. 7, Susan J. 1 5-34-228

1870 CENSUS

Jane Hicks 55, John T. 23, Mary Jane 22, Eliza Ann 18, Susan J. 11 4-11-71

Newton C. Hicks 27, Nancy F. 33, Robert N. 7, Mary Jane 5, Martha A. 2, Josephine 1/12 4-11-73

1880 CENSUS

Jane Hicks 68, E.A. 30 (d), Robert 18 (gs) 4-6-42

Newton Hicks 40, N.F. 42, R.N. 18 (s), M.J. 16 (d), M.A. 13 (d), M.F. 10 (d), L.J. 8 (s) 4-6-46

1900 CENSUS

Charles Hicks 18 (Oct 1881-M 1), Ida 22 (July 1876-M 1-0) 2-194B-68/70

Eliza Hix 63: see W. Mathew Hix (B)
James Hicks 20: see James Walker
John Hicks 56 (Dec 1843-T/Va/NC-M 29)(House Carpenter), Margaret 46 (Oct 1853-M 29-9-7), Addy 21 (Sep 1878-Wd 1-1), Robert 18 (Mar 1882), Nola 15 (July 1884), Maud 13 (Oct 1886), George W. 9 (June 1890), Lillie 6 (Mar 1894), Donie 6 (gd)(Ap 1894) 10-331A-227/242
John S. Hicks 46 (Nov 1853-M 26), Mary E. 46 (Oct 1853-Ga/NC/NC-M 26-5-5), Charly T. 21 (Sep 1878), Ira A. 19 (May 1881), Effie J. 15 (May 1885), Bartley I. 12 (Sep 1887) 7-265B-300/305
Joseph Hicks 32 (Aug 1867-M 3)(Minister), Nannie 26 (Feb 1874-Ky/Ky/Ky-M 3-1-1), Joseph 10/12 (July 1899) 10-321A-20/21
Martha S. Hicks 69: see George Elliott
Melvina Hicks 80: see Andrew Allen
Milton B. Hicks 35, Nannie 34: see Benjamin F. Mealer
W. Mathew Hix 25 (May 1875-M 1), Lara J. 21 (May 1879-M 1-0), Eliza HIX 63 (m)(Dec 1836-Wd 10-6), Polk 43 (b)(Sep 1856), Allie 19 (si)(Dec 1882), Reace SPRINGS 13 (nw)(June 1886), Mandie 11 (ne)(Dec 1888) 3-200A-5/5 (B)
William Hicks 58 (Jan 1842-NC/NC/NC-M 38)(Coal Miner), Nancy 55 (Sep 1844-M 38-9-7), James 21 (Nov 1878), Ollie 18 (June 1881), George 14 (Ap 1886) 8-282B-280/282
William T. Hicks 49 (Oct 1850-Wd), Addie 21 (June 1878), Winton 10 (June 1889), Berton 7 (Dec 1892), John 4 (Aug 1895), Thomas A. KIRBY 20 (Sep 1879)(Servant) 2-195B-81/84

MARRIAGES

A.J. Hicks to Bettie J. Vincent, 24 Oct 1890, W.R. Clack JP 4-28
Addie Hicks to Henry Ludwig q.v.
Alfie Hicks to Jackson A. Smith q.v.
Annie Hicks to A. J. Sneed q.v.
Charles Hicks to Ida Jolly, 25 Mar 1900, Jas H. Keylon JP 4-102
Emma B. Hicks to W. W. Gibson. 15 Nov 1888 (20 Nov), A.C. Peters MG 1-562
J.G. Hicks to Margaret E. Phillips, 7 Sep 1870 (8 Sep), Wm Ganaway MG 1-#1164
Lou Hicks to T. M. Whaley q.v.
M. M. Hicks to J. T. Wright q.v.
Martha Hicks to R. A. Porter q.v.
Mary Hicks to J. O. Franklin q.v.
Mary Hicks to J. E. Abel q.v.
Mary J. Hicks to S. S. Knight q.v.
Milton B. Hicks to Nannie A. Mealer, 28 June 1892, G.W. Brewer MG 4-39
Newton C. Hicks to Nancy F. Burnett, no date (5 Sep 1861), J. Howard MG 1-#760
S. C. Hicks to S. S. Knight q.v.
Sarah Hicks to James Walker q.v.
Silena Hicks to Lee Ferguson q.v.
T. C. Hicks to G. A. Elliott q.v.
Viola Hicks to Luther H. Marler q.v.
Wm Hicks to Lora Locke, 20 May 1899 (21 May), L.E. Smith JP, Charles Hicks W 2-416

- - - - - - - - - - - - -

HICKSON / HIXON

1900 CENSUS

Benjamin Hixon 12, Jean H. 8, Emma 3: see Mariel K. Rhea (B)
Will Hickson 39 (Feb 1862-M 11)(Grocery Salesman), Amy 30 (Sep 1869-M 11-4-4)(Seamstress), Edy G. 9 (Aug 1890), James P. 7 (Nov 1892), Wyley 4 (Ap 1896), Willie 5/12 (Dec 1899) 10-251A-28/28

MARRIAGES

Alice Hickson to James Hall q.v.
John Hixon to Sopprina Rhea, 22 Dec 1887 (same), B.F. Holloway JP 1-539
W.C. Hixon to Sarah A. Purcer, 21 Sep 1889 (22 Sep), John J. Parriott ?? 1-588

- - - - - - - - - - - - -

HIDER [HYDER]

1900 CENSUS

Niles C. Hider 37 (Ap 1863-M 13), Lizzie 39 (Dec 1860-M 13-8-4), Wilum 12 (Sep 1887), Jussi 6 (July 1893), Jan 3 (Aug 1896), Francas 2 (May 1898), Barder MIZE 18 (boarder)(Ap 1882)(RR Hand) 1-188A-181/190

- - - - - - - - - - - - -

HIGBY

1900 CENSUS

Nelson Higby 79 (Oct 1825-NY/NY/NY-M 31), Julia(?) 62 (June 1837-Pa/Pa/Pa-M 31-1-1) 12-179A-7/8
Nelson Higby Jr. 30 (Mar 1870-Mich/NY/Pa-M 6)(Tooth Dentist), Jessi 33 (Feb 1867-NJ/NY/NY-M 6-2-2), Ralph 4 (Aug 1895), Huller 4/12 (Feb 1900) 12-179A-8/9

MARRIAGE

Nelson C. Higby to Jossie G. Huntington, 4 Jan 1894, W.L. Patton MG 4-69

- - - - - - - - - - - - -

HIGHBARK

1860 CENSUS

Clara Highbark 55: see Calvin Tharp

- - - - - - - - - - - - -

HIGHFIELD

1900 CENSUS

Betta Highfield 45: see William Y. Denton

- - - - - - - - - - - - -

HIGHT / HITE

1880 CENSUS

C.C. Hite 31 (Carpenter), Ellen 22 (w), M. 3 (d), E.D. 1 (s) 4-10-82

1900 CENSUS

Melvin Hight 19 (Dec 1880-T/Ga/Ga-M 0), Mary 21 (Oct 1878-M 0-0), Cally DYER 37 (a)(Mar 1863-T/T/Ala-M 20-10-9), Lina M. 4 (c)(Dec 1895) 8-313-50/53 (B)

MARRIAGE

Melvin Hight to Mary Henderson, 13 Sep 1899 (same), B.J. Jones MG, Jackson Garmany W 3-33

- - - - - - - - - - - - -

HILEARY

1900 CENSUS

Henry Hileary 52 (Feb 1842-Oh/Oh/Oh-Wd), Perry 12 (Mar 1888), Aron 10 (May 1890), Wilm 8 (Ap 1892), Maud 4 (Jan 1896) 12-180B-48/51

- - - - - - - - - - - - -

HILEY

MARRIAGE

Cal G. Hiley to Cora B. Shelton, 28 Sep 1887 (29 Sep), W.A. Green JP 1-528

- - - - - - - - - - - - -

HILL

1860 CENSUS

William P. Hill 10: see George W. Wallace

William Hill 34 (Day Laborer), Elizabeth 23, John C.L. 4, Louisa 3, Francis M. 1 1-92-626

1870 CENSUS

Francis M. Hill 27, Susan E. 28, Luretta E. 6, James R. 5, Sarah E. 2 4-14-94

1880 CENSUS

Isaac Hill 34: see William Tarwater

James W. Hill 46, Ellen 36, John W. 15, Betsy A. 13, Reuben A. 11, William G. 9, Sarah L. 8, Mary E. 6, Parattie(?) 3, James A. 1 6-18-171/174

Susan Hill 40, Louisa 16, E. 12 (d), James 14, Jack 8, D.A. 3 (d) 3-24-192

1900 CENSUS

Elic Hill 56 (Ap 1844-NC/Ga/SC-Wd), Albert 18 (Dec 1871), Walter 16 (Feb 1884), Cushie 12 (Mar 1888), Magie 10 (May 1890), William A. 8 (Ap 1892) 7-264B-275/280

George Hill 20, Frank 18: see Cate Guirver(?) (B)

James A. Hill 29 (June 1871-M 7/12), Laura A. 23 (Unk 1877-Ga/Ga/Ga-M 7/12) 3-207A-130/142

James A. Hill 23 (Aug 1876-T/NC/T-M 1), Rubey An 22 (May 1877-M -0) 5-232A-77

John M. Hill 69 (May 1832-Oh/Mass/Conn-M 15)(Machinist), Sopha 44 (Mar 1856-Oh/Switzerland/Do-M 15-0-0) 10-331A-231/246

John W. Hill 36 (Dec 1863-Ind/Ind/Ind-M 14), Rebeca E.(?) 32 (May 1868-M 14-6-5), Eliza E. 13 (Ap 1887), William A. 11 (June 1888), James C.A. 8 (Dec 1891), John W. 6 (Jan 1894), Mellinda M. 1 (June 1899), W. Baily RECTAR 9 (nw)(Feb 1891) 3-202A-46/49

Judson B. Hill 49 (Aug 1850-NY/Conn/Pa-M 23), Harriet M. 53 (Jan 1847-Wisc/Ver/NY-M 23-3-2), Sybil H. 18 (Nov 1881-Wisc), William J. 15 (Aug 1884-Wisc) 11-292A-47

Luther Hill 18: see Sam McClendon

Mattie E. Hill 21 (July 1878-Wd 3-3), C. Luther 4 (Ap 1896), Mandy B. 2 (Dec 1897), Nancy C. 1 (Feb 1899) 3-210A-177/192 (see Timothy McNutt)

Oscar H. Hill 27 (Feb 1873-M 5), Mary J. 27 (Nov 1872-M 5-2-1), Theondo 5 (Sep 1894), Henry JOHNSON 26 (boarder)(Unk) 6-248B-169/170

Rheuben A. Hill 31 (Unk-M 13), Lizzie 25 (Sep 1874-M 13-4-4), George 10 (Ap 1890), Willia 6 (Jan 1894), Pearl 4 (Feb 1896), Charles 7/12 (Oct 1899) 6-241A-25

Roda Hill 60 (May 1840-Wd 4-4), Frank P. 24 (May 1876) 3-207A-130/141

William L. Hill 30 (Oct 1869-M 4), Nancy A. 34 (Mar 1866-T/Va/T-M 3-3), James E. 3 (Nov 1896), Claburn P. 2 (Jan 1898), Thomas F. 1 (Jan 1899) 3-208B-148/161

MARRIAGES

Alexander Hill to Catharine Maynard, 8 June 1854 (9 June), E. Brewer JP 1-#447

Andy Hill to Riley A. Freiley, 15 May 1899 (same), J.B. Trotter MG, Joe Payne W 2-413

Celista Hill to Amos Gan q.v.

E. A. Hill to William Blevins q.v.

Ed Hill to Alice Worthington, 3 Mar 1894, R.A. Dickson JP 4-66

Edward Hill to Nancey Stephens, 17 Feb 1886 (18 Feb), B.F. Holloway JP 1-515

Henrietta Hill to John Smith q.v.

Henry Hill to Julia Barger, 24 Feb 1900, G.R. Baldwin JP 4-102

J.W. Hill to R.E. Porter, 19 June 1886 (20 June), T.H. McPherson JP 1-519

James A. Hill to L.A. Brown, 12 Nov 1899, M.F. McCuiston JP or MG 4-104

John Hill to Ellen Peak, 30 Ap 1898 (same), J.B. Phillips MG, Joseph Rose(?) W 2-273

Katie Hill or Hibbs to John Marler q.v.

Oscar H. Hill to M.J. Cagle, 19 Nov 1893, S.S. Franklin JP 4-64

R.A. Hill to Elizabeth Doze, 25 Sep 1886 (28 Sep), J.R. Crawford JP 1-541

R.S. Hill to Dora Moore, 22 Sep 1891, J.J. Burnett MG 4-30

R.S. or R.T. Hill to Grace V. Bell, 2 July 1893, G.W. Brewer MG 4-58

Susie C. Hill (Mrs.) to Edwine Eastman q.v.

Thomas Hill to Malinda D. Parker, 18 Aug 1868 (19 Aug), J.P. Roddy MG 1-#1026

W.L. Hill to Nancy A. Fugate, 23 Nov 1895, W.K. Fugate JP 4-89

W.P. Hill to Nancy Riggens, 20 Nov 1869 (21 Nov), T.N.L. Cunnyngham JP 1-#1126

Will Hill to Elizabeth Gearing, 22 June 1854 (23 June), E. Brewer JP 1-#450

William G. Hill to Mary Powell, 4 Aug 1896 (same), W.L. Lillard JP, John W. Hill W 2-50

- - - - - - - - - - - - -

HILLIARD / HILLYARD

1900 CENSUS

Humbusby(?) Hilliard 46 (Ap 1854-Ga/Ga/Ga-M 18)(Coal Miner), Lizabeth 43 (Sep 1856-Ga/Ga/Ga-M 18-8-6), Martha V. 18 (July 1881-Ga), Mary L. 6 (Oct 1883-Ga), Gillie 10 (Mar 1890), Harrett 8 (May 1882), Floyd 3 (Ap 1897), Morgan 3/12 (Feb 1900) 10-255B-107/110

Nancy J. Hillyard 34 (Nov 1865-Wd 2-2), Tressa 7 (Nov 1892), Alexander 2 (Mar 1898) 10-322B-49/52

MARRIAGE

John Hilliard to Nancy J. Meeton, 20 Ap 1889 (21 Ap), Joseph Hoge JP 1-573

- - - - - - - - - - - - -

HILLOCK

MARRIAGE

S.B. Hillock to Carie J. Gwillian, 8 Sep 1892, J.S. Petty MG 4-42

- - - - - - - - - - - - -

HILTON– see HELTON

- - - - - - - - - - - - -

HINCH / HURCH / HURCE

1870 CENSUS

King Hinch 15: see Jane M. Gannaway (B)

Thompson Hurce 34, Pamelia M. 34, Lucy A. 16, Virginia A. 7, Susan M. 3, Barbara 1 6-4-23

1880 CENSUS

Fanny Hinch 25, Lulu 1/12 (B): see Jere Wasson

James B. Hinch 30: see Lutitia Smith (B)

Jim Hinch 30 (B): see C. W. Abel

1900 CENSUS

Birrel G. Hinch 52 (Mar 1848-T/Ala/T-M 12)(Coal Miner), Dafney 50 (May 1850-Ga/Ga/Ga-M 12-4-2), Andrew CARLILE(?) 4 (nw)(Oct 1895) 10-251A-27 (B)

John Hinch 66 (Ap 1834-M 12), Lillie A. 40 (Mar 1860-M 12-4-3)(Dressmaker), Welcker 19 (Mar 1881), Archie D. 10 (Aug 1889), Harry F. 8 (May 1892), Robert L. 4 (Aug 1895) 14-217A-85/86

MARRIAGES

Byrd Hinch to Dafney Chattin, 26 Sep 1889 (same), A.B. Anderson MG 1-587

Elizabeth Hinch to Martin V. Reed Jr. q.v.

Fanny Hurch to Mark Reynolds q.v.

J.C. Hinch to Lillie A. Ford, 31 Dec 1887 (1 Jan 1888), S.H. Price(?) MG 1-543

John Hinch to Lorinda Holloway, 10 Nov 1895, R.A. Dickson JP 4-91

- - - - - - - - - - - - -

HINDMAN / HINDEMAN

1900 CENSUS

Eliza J. Hindman 47: see Hany Schaefer

MARRIAGE

Kati Hindeman to Harry Schafer q.v.

- - - - - - - - - - - - -

HINDS / HINES / HYNES / HANES / HAMES / HAINES / HAYNES

1860 CENSUS

Belle Haynes to William Rose q.v.

Robert D. Hines 33, Sarah L. 32, Phebe E. 6, Della A. 3, Lucinda 1 1-90-617

Thomas Hanes 83 (Pa), James 67, Cleopatra 20 5-33-217

1870 CENSUS

Alexander Hanes or Haimes 21, Hettie 23, Thomas G. 5, Charles 2 1-13-86 (B)

Robert D. Hanes 43, Sarah 43, Phebe E. 16, Delilah A. 12, Lorinda J. 11, Mary E. 9, Florence A. 6, James M. 2, Major D. 2/12 1-6-38

1880 CENSUS

J. Hames 27, C.C. 24: see S. O. Foust

L.J. Haines or Hainira 39 (Wheelwright), S.J. 34 4-8-63

Robert Hinds 53, Sarah 53, Mary 19, Florence 17, James 12, David 10 1-13-103

1900 CENSUS

James Hynes 32 (Aug 1867-M 12)(Preacher), Lucy 31 (Ap 1861-M 12-4-4), Inbur 11 (d)(Oct 1888), Rosi 9 (d) (Mar 1891), Allie 7 (d)(Sep 1892), Rosco 4 (Oct 1895) 1-187B-166/174

Major D. Hinds 30 (May 1870-M 9), Martha 26 (Mar 1864-M 9-5-5), Lillie 8 (Ap 1892), Hester 6 (Aug 1893), Caroline 5 (May 1895), Euene 4 (s)(Aug 1896), Alonso 1 (Ap 1899), Caroline INGLE 49 (sil)(Oct 1850) 1-188A-183/192 [David Hinds married Martha Ingle on 10 May 1891]

Nellie Hines 17: see John L. Eddington

Norman A. Haynes 51 (Mar 1849-Ind/Oh/NJ-M 27), Martha 49 (Feb 1851-Ind/Md/Md-M 27-5-5), Celistia 18 (June 1881-Ind), John S. 12 (July 1887), Oliver 8 (Aug 1891) 5-232B-87

MARRIAGES

Flovimer A. Hinds to W. V. Gilliam q.v.

James Hinds to L.G. Ingle, 6 Oct 1887 (same), James Johnson JP 1-536

James C. Hinds to Phebe C. Holloway, 18 Dec 1854 (30 Dec), Asa Newport MG 1-#475

James K. Hinds to Adaline Atwood, 17 Sep 1868 (29 Sep), A. Newport MG 1-#1030

James P. Hinds to S.A. Paul, 24 Dec 1854 (same), Asa Newport MG 1-#480

Lila Ann Hinds to James Evens q.v.

Lorinda Hinds to G. M. Ingle q.v.

Mary E. Hinds to A. J. Evans q.v.

Robert D. Hinds to Sarah Lu Hollaway, 17 Feb 1853 (24 Feb), A. Newport MG 1-#403

- - - - - - - - - - - - -

HINKEL

1900 CENSUS

Walter Hinkle 26: see William Ryan

MARRIAGE

Sallie Hinkel to T. J. Pope q.v.

- - - - - - - - - - - - -

HIPS

1900 CENSUS

John Hips 35 (Jan 1865-NC/NC/NC-M 13), Martha 28 (Dec 1871-M 13-6-4), Charles 6 (May 1894), Britler(?) 4 (d)(Dec 1896), Robert 3 (May 1897), Almon 2 (Ap 1898), Henry 12 (b)(May 1888) 1-183A-89/92

MARRIAGE

Nancy Hips to M. P. Reed q.v.

- - - - - - - - - - - - -

HOBACK

1900 CENSUS

James A. Hoback 53 (Jan 1847-M 31)(Sawyer), Sarah A. 52 (Jan 1848-M 31-5-5), Artie B. 30 (Aug 1869), Sterling L. 19 (July 1880), Leonard 16 (June 1883)(Broom-maker), Walter DIXON 10 (adopted s)(Mar 1870) 13-304B-277/287

Levi Hoback 23 (Ap 1877-M 0)(Teamster), Minnie B. 16 (July 1883-M 0-0-0) 13-305B-299/311

MARRIAGES

Levi Hoback to Minnie McJunkins, 7 Feb 1900 (same), A.P. Hayes JP, A.B. Dodd W 3-121

Louella T. Hoback to William A. Dodd q.v.

W.C. Hoback to Bell Marcum, 16 Nov 1889 (17 Nov), W.S. Hale MG 1-585

- - - - - - - - - - - - -

HODGE / HODGES

1860 CENSUS

Daniel Hodges 35, Nancy 56, Mary 21, James 19 10-27-182

William C. Hodge 19, Nancy A. 20, Mary E. 1 4-51-345

1870 CENSUS

Abraham Hodge 33, Jane 21, Anna 7/12, Lydia BOOFFER 65 3-6-37

Daniel Hodges 45 (Saddler), Nancy 64 10-2-14

John Hodges 22, Harriet 20 (Ga), Judge EDWARDS 14 (Ga), Julia GREEN 6 (Ga) 8-4-29 (B)

William C. Hodge 30 (Blacksmith), Nancy A. 30, Mary E. 12, William 8, John W. 4, Margarette A. 1 3-5-29

1880 CENSUS

A. Hodge 42, Lidia 25 (w), B.J. 1 (d), A.L. 10 (d), L.B. 8 (d), Lyda [BOOFER, see 1870 census] 75 (m), William WRIGHT 24 (Hired Hand) 3-14-108

Danil Hodge 58, M.J. 38 (w), H.L. 5 (s), Kettie 8 (adopted d) 8-2-17

David Hodge or Wadye 45, Permelia P. 33, Martha 21, Nancy E. 19, Mary 15, William 12, John 9, Malinda J. 3 5-10-96

Houston A. Hodge 33, Sarah B. 36, Annie V. 6, John Wesley 3, Vesty O. 2 5-10-97

Mark Hodge 24: see Scruggs Yearwood

William Hodges 40 (Blacksmith), W.A. 40, W.E. 2 (d), J.M. 13 (s), M.A. 11 (d), M.B. 7 (d), N.L. 5 (d), E.D. 1 (d), R.N. MILLIGAN 25 3-15-120

1900 CENSUS

James H. Hodge 47 (Jan 1853-M 9)(Carpenter), Adda H. 31 (May 1869-M 9), Grace B. 7 (Mar 1893), Mary E. 5 (Ap 1895), Daniel ODOM 65 (July 1834-T/NC/T-Wd)(Carpenter) 14-218A-117/120

Melinda Hodge 40 (Unk-Ga/Ga/T-Wd 6-6), Bertha 21 (May 1879), Susie 16 (Sep 1883), Hester 13 (Aug 1886), Hattie N. 12 (Oct 1887), Robert L. 9 (Mar 1891) 10-322A-49/51

Myra J. Hodges 59 (June 1840-Wd 2-1), William L. 25 (Nov 1874) (Jewelery Merchant), Elvira A. CUNNINGHAM 36 (June 1863)(Servant) 8-312-30/2

Rice Hodge 20 (Unk 1880-Ala/Ala/Ala-M 4), Cora 20 (Unk 1880-T/Ala/Ala-M 4-0), Jink KNOTT 30 (boarder) (Oct 1869-D) 8-275A-134 (B)

MARRIAGES

A.B. Hodge to B.W. Kelly, 24 Ap 1859 (same), John Wyott JP 1-#692

A.B. Hodge to Jane Foust, 28 Dec 1869 (27 Dec)[sic], T.N.L. Cunnyngham JP 1-#1039

A.B. Hodge to Malinda Parker, 11 Dec 1877 (16 Dec), John Howard MG 1-#1530

Annie L. Hodge to E. T. Hunter q.v.

Birtha Hodge to Peter Schill or Shilde q.v.

Callie Hodges to Lee Marcum q.v.

Daniel Hodges to Nancy Fleming, 12 Jan 1850 (13 Jan), Benjamin Wallace MG 1-#291

Daniel Hodges to Mirah J. Flemming, 12 Sep 1872 (18 Sep), J.W. Williamson MG 1-#1250

J.F. Hodge to Addie Odom, 8 June 1891, J.A. Darr MG 4-26

John Hodge to Mrs. Mary Johnson, 22 June 1889 (24 June), J.L. Prater ?? 1-581

Jonas Hodges to Martha C. Jones, 12 Ap 1898 (same), W.R. Grimsley MG, F.M. Hodge W 2-268

Katie L. Hodges to George D. McAndrus q.v.

Louisa J. Hodge to John McDonald q.v.

Molly Hodge to Riley N. Millican q.v.

Rice Hodges to Cora Mitchell, 11 Oct 1897 (same), J.W. Wassum MG, E.B.A. Bonner W 2-196

Wm Hodge to Nancy Woodby, 18 Sep 1857 (same), J. Howard JP 1-#613

- - - - - - - - - - - - -

HOFFMAN / HUFFMAN

MARRIAGES

Elbert Huffman to Mary J. Wyrick, 29 Sep 1863 (no return) 1-#808

J.R. Hoffman to Harriet Bowers, 30 Ap 1891, J. Waldorff MG 4-21

Thomas Hoffman to Ida Arthur, 31 Oct 1899 (same), W.L. Lillard JP, J.M. Hayes W 3-64

- - - - - - - - - - - - -

HOGUE / HOGES / HOGE

1860 CENSUS

Samuel Hogue 22, Mary E. 18, Joseph P. 4/12 8-15-99

1870 CENSUS

Joel W. Hoge 32, Margarette I. 26, Samuel B. 2, Mattie L. 11/12 8-3-21

Joseph J. Hoge 63 (County Court Clerk), Nancy 60, Mary 26, Elizabeth K. 22, Joseph 21, Martha E. 19, William B. 17, Flavius J. 11 6-9-57

1880 CENSUS

Joseph Hoge 30, Mary T. 24, Robert R. 5, Crawford L. 3, William P. 1 5-8-79

Mary Hoge 5: see R. T. Martin

N. L. Hoge 8: see J. O. Johnson

1900 CENSUS

Joseph Hogue 50 (Sep 1849-M 27), Mary 44 (Mar 1856-M 27-9-8), Bradford 23 (Jan 1877)(Coal Miner), Floyd 21 (Jan 1879)(Coal Miner), James 19 (May 1881), Dexter 12 (June 1887), Eddie 7 (Feb 1893), Herbert 2 (June 1897), Ida 16 (d)(Sep 1883) 8-278B-207/209

Robert Hogue 25 (Dec 1874-M 2)(Coal Miner), Flora 23 (May 1879-M 2-1-1), James C. 1 (Dec 1898) 8-280B-244/246

Samuel B. Hoge 32 (June 1867-M 7)(Coal Miner), Laura 26 (Jan 1874-M 7-3-3), William R. 5 (Oct 1894), Esther H. 4 (Oct 1895), Mary I. 2 (Jan 1898) 13-303B-250/260

MARRIAGES

Alfred Hoge to Birdie Carter, 29 Aug 1896 (same), J.B. Phillips MG, G.W. McMillen W 2-61

B.L. Hogu or Hogue to Ellen Jones, 18 Aug 1900 (19 Aug), A.P. Hays JP, G.W. McMillin W 3-200

E. J. K. Hoge to Isham Denis(?) q.v.

J.W. Hoge to Elizabeth Nichols, 17 Dec 1857 (same), Wm Morgan JP 1-#622

Joel W. Hoge to Margarett J. Montgomery, 24 Feb 1866 (4 Mar), Wm A. Green JP 1-#891

Joseph Hoge to Mary Killough, 28 Dec 1873 (same), W.R. Henry JP 1-#1321

Lucy Hoge to Charley D. Bean q.v.

M. E. Hoge to W. J. Bean q.v.

M. L. Hoge to J. S. Dingan q.v.

Mary A. Hoge to John C. Rogers q.v.

Margaret I. Hoge to Robert Tate Martin q.v.

Nathaniel Hoges to Angeline Myres, 2 Sep 1869 (3 Sep), W.L. Humphrey JP 1-#1109

R.J. Hoge to Flora Wyatt, 17 Nov 1897 (same), A.P. Hays JP, Ed Misger(?) W 2-2-8

S.B. Hoge to Laura F. Owins, 24 Sep 1893, John Seving(?) MG 4-56

Samuel Hoge to Mary Campbell, 28 July 1858 (same), D.F. Ward JP 1-#643

- - - - - - - - - - - - -

HOLBROOK

MARRIAGE

Edith Holbrook to S. T. Walker q.v.

- - - - - - - - - - - - -

HOLCOMB

MARRIAGE

Sarah Holcomb to N. G. Moates q.v.

- - - - - - - - - - - - -

HOLDER / HOLDEN

1900 CENSUS

Andy Holden 37 (May 1863-Ga/Ga/SC-M 14)(Coal Miner), Ella 33 (Ap 1867-M 14-4-2), Della 9 (Aug 1890), Willie 2 (Jan 1898), Sarah HOLDEN 67 (m)(July 1822-SC/SC/SC-Wd 10-2) 8-282A-269/271

Ed Holden 9: see John Hughes

Sarah Holden 67: see Andy Holden

William Holden 25 (May 1875-M 2)(Coal Miner), Mattie F. 22 (Dec 1877-M 2-1-1), Fred E. 1 (Jan 1899), Mary 16 (si)(June 1883) 8-277A-173/174

MARRIAGES

Hettie Holder to John Hughes q.v.

Hettie Holder to Levi Thurman q.v.

W.N. Holder to Florence Center, 24 Dec 1897 (same), A.O. Hayes JP, J.J. Hoge W 2-231

- - - - - - - - - - - - -

HOLES

1860 CENSUS

Thomas P. Holes 18: see John W. Hulse

- - - - - - - - - - - - -

HOLLAND / HAWLAND

1860 CENSUS

Allen Holland 57, Polly 61, Nancy E. 22, Permelia C. 20, James K.P. 15, John M. HOLLAND 30, James T. 12, Amanda A. 10, Robert N.M. 9, Allen L. 7 6-106-721

Thomas R. Holland 54 (Ga), Sibila 39, Martha A. 12, Anagamia C. 9, Hannah P. 7, Emily S. 5, Elizabeth 4, Nancy L. 3, John E. 2 4-51-348

1870 CENSUS

Allen Holland 68 (Ga), Mary 72, James P. 22, Robert 19, Allen L. 15, Hannah DILEMON 25 6-15-111

Thomas R. Holland 63 (Ga), Sarah S. 48, Hannah J. 20, Emily Isabelle 19, Nancy L. 13, Ruth E. 16, John Evans 11, Mary A. 9, Elijah H. 6, Henry J. McNEW 17 4-6-39

1880 CENSUS

S.S. Holland 58, Hannah 31 (d), John 22 (s), M.A. 19 (d), E.H. 17 (s) 4-31-248

1900 CENSUS

Elijah H. Holland 37 (May 1863), Hannah J. 50 (si)(Sep 1849) 14-222A-167/171

James Holland 29 (Oct 1870-T/Va/T-M 4)(Blacksmith), Tennessee 28 (Aug 1871-M 4-3-2), Oscar A. 3 (Aug 1896), Ida S. 2 (Feb 1898), Cora ARNOLD 4 (Jan 1886)(Servant) 8-311B-19/20

John F.(?) Holland 42 (Ap 1858-M 4), Mary J. 37 (Nov 1862-M 4-0) 14-222A-166/170

John I. Hawland 46 (Jan 1854-Oh/Oh/Oh-M 17), Mary E. 39 (Dec 1858-Oh/Oh/Oh-M 17-9-6), Ima J. 15 (Feb 1885-Oh), Harry K. 12 (July 1887), Mable S. 11 (Feb 1889), Pavin B. 9 (Oct 1890), Ernest W. 7 (May 1893), Marion J. 4 (June 1895) 2-107B-115/120

William H. Holland 18: see Charles M. Bain

MARRIAGES

A. C. Holland to Micajah Brady q.v.

Allen Holland to Jennie Rogers, 1 July 1888 (same), John Howard MG 1-548

Amanda Holland to James H. Campbell q.v.

E. S. Holland to J. D. Wheeler q.v.

J.K. Holland to Jane Parker, 20 Feb 1874 (23 Feb), W.H. Dodd MG 1-#1328

James F. Holland to Tennie V. Prater, 9 Oct 1895, W.A. Howard MG 4-91

Louisa Holland to James Crow q.v.

Mary A. Holland to James A. Torbett q.v.

Nancy Holland to William O. Allen q.v.

Nancy L. Holland to Charles Hollaway q.v.

Permelia C. Holland to S. A. J. Walker q.v.

Ruthy J. Holland to T. B. Holloway q.v.

Sarah Santina Holland to James Fondren q.v.

- - - - - - - - - - - - -

HOLLINS

MARRIAGE

Sallie Hollins to Charley Godsey q.v.

- - - - - - - - - - - - -

HOLLOMAN / HOLLAMAN / HOLMAN / HOLEMAN

1900 CENSUS

Addie Holeman 19 (B): see Brahat Coaller Jr.

Guy Holman 63 (Feb 1837-T/Va/NC-M 49)(Grocer), Hester A. 59 (Mar 1841-M 48-17-11), James A. 35 (May 1865)(Hotel Porter), William A. 31 (Jan 1869-Wd) (Restaurant Clerk), Guy F. 28 (June 1871-Wd)(Hotel Waiter), Moses 25 (Sep 1874)(Day Laborer), Mary A. 23 (Nov 1876), Amanda B. 21 (July 1878), Ida M.S. 19 (Sep 1880), Birdie P. 17 (July 1882), Stanton 14 (Jan 1886), Adelia 10 (June 1889), Cordelia 10 (June 1889), Emanuel 6 (gs)(May 1884), Alonzo 5 (gs)(Aug 1884), Gracie E. 3 (d)(Aug 1896), Maud Mc 3 (gd) (Aug 1896), Annie F. 2 (gd)(Feb 1898) 10-330A-215/228 (B)

Ike Holloman 40: see Marquis Morrison

James L. Hollaman 15: see John Rickel

MARRIAGES

G.F. Holeman to Emma Randolph, 11 Feb 1894, B.F. Tipton MG 4-68

Mary Holman to S. W. Clift q.v.

R.A. Holeman to M.K. Hickman, 26 Dec 1870 (same), F. Campbell MG 1-#1181

Thomas Holman to Dena(?) Cunningham, 19 Feb 1890 (same), L.M. Moore ?? 1-594

Will Holeman to Bell Davis, 29 Ap 1893, J.D. Gaither MG 4-50

HOLLOWAY / HOLLAWAY/ HOLAWAY / HOLDAWAY

1860 CENSUS

Isaac Hollaway 29, Mary 27, Thomas 2, Virginia C. 1, Sarah 4/12 1-86-590

James Hollaway 58 (NC), Elvira 50, John M. 28, Richard 26, Samuel H. 22, Ann 21, James 18, William 16, Harriet 10 1-87-594

James P. Hollaway 26, Nancy J. 23, Sarah E. 1 1-82-555

Joseph P. Hollaway 49 (NC)(Blacksmith), Elizabeth C. 46, Nancey 24, Berry T. 21, Eliza A. 17, Lavinia 13, Lorinda 11, Leander 10 1-88-600

Major Holloway 56 (NC), Major B. 19, Thomas H. 17, Robert G. 14, Francis MAJORS 24, Delila 23 1-90-618

Milo Hollaway 13: see Rufus N.B. Sherly

Pleasant Hollaway 38, Harriet 39, Sarah 15, Mary 12, Eliza 10, John 8, Nancy 3, Harriet 1 1-87-591

Richard H. Holoway 35, Louisa 19, Phebe A. 2, Misy E. 1 1-91-619

Sterling Holloway 42, Emly 29, Landon N. 9, Thomas B. 8, Charles R. 7, John H. 5, Mary L. 2, Darius W. 8/12 8-15-104

William T. Holoway 28, Lucinda 26, Sarah A. 4, William H. 3, John N. 1 1-90-616 [Wm T. married Lucinda C. Hines on 6 Jan 1855 in Roane Co]

1870 CENSUS

Isaac W. Holloway 38, Thomas G. 12, Virginia C. 11, Sarah E. 9, Columbus G. 8, Joseph F. 5 1-6-36

James Holloway 68 (NC), Elvira 60, John M. 39, Richard G. 37, Ann 24, William D. 22, Elvira GARRISON 10 1-1-1

James S. Holloway 36, Nancy J. 33, Sarah E. 11, Phebe T. 8 1-12-80

Joseph Holloway 59 (NC), Benjamin F. 30 (Blacksmith), Eliza A. 27, Louvenia 23, Elmore 16 4-18-118

Major Holloway 65 (NC), William T. 38, Lucinda C. 36, Sarah A. 14, William H. 12, John N. 11, Mary E. 10, Elizabeth Jane 8 1-6-35

Milo S. Holoway 23 (Merchant), Ada 20 2-5-34

Pleasant M. Holloway 47, Harriette 50 (Va), Eliza Ann 20, John S. 17, Nancy E. 14, Harriette 12, Minerva J. 8, Elmina 8 1-18-119

Richard Holloway 44, Louisa 28, Phebe A. 12, Mira A. 10, Luella R. 6, Mary L. 5, Sarah F. 1, Patriarch 2/12 1-12-78

Samuel H. Holloway 32, Lopatry 29, Elvira Jane 3/12, Jane HAWS 73, Mary CUNNINGHAM (B) 12 1-2-11

Sterling H. Holloway 53, Emily 39, Landon N. 19, Thomas B. 18, Charles R. 17, John H. 14, Mary E. 12, Darius W. 10, Andrew J. 9 4-9-55

1880 CENSUS

B.F. Holloway 41, Emma 33, Ida Lee 5, Floyd 5, J.E. 1 (s) 4-36-293

C. Holloway 24, W.L. 24, O.S. 2 (s) 4-31-247

Elvira Holloway 70, Miller 49, Richard 47, Ann 40, Francis HOLLOWAY 81 (sil) 1-10-77

Isaac Holloway 50, Addie 27 (w), Virginia 21 (d), Columbus 18 (s), Joseph 6 (s) 1-13-104

J.P. Holloway 69, L.L. 33 (d), L.E. 26 (s) 4-36-296

Major Holloway 76, Malinda 37 (w), General 6 (s), George 4 (s), John (s) 1-13-105 [Major married Malinda Hughes Treadway on 25 Sept 1872 in Roane Co]

Milo Holloway 33 (Merchant), Adda 30, Eva 9, Anna 7, William 4, Schipka 1 (d) 2-24-344

Mira Holloway 19: see Wade McFalls

Pleasant Holloway 56, Harriet 60, Eliza 30, Nancy 24, Hariet 21, Minerva 17, Almira 178 1-12-101

R.W. Holloway 53, E.J. 39 (w), P.E. 21 (d), M.A. 20 (d), L.R. 16 (d), M.L. 14 (d), S.F. 11 (d), W.P. 10 (d), N.L. 5 (d), H.F. HAYS 26 4-1-8

S. Holloway 64, E. 48 (w), John 24 (s), D.W. 20 (s), A.J. 19 (s), Mary 18 (d) 4-33-266

Samuel Holloway 43, Leopatra 40, Elvira 10, Jack 8, James 6, Walter 4, Kelley 2, Jane HAWS 83 (ml) 1-10-82

T.H. Holloway 22: see S. T. Blevins

Tom Holloway 28, R.E. 27 4-33-274

W.D. Holloway 35: see John Thompson

1900 CENSUS

Andrew J. Holloway 39 (Jan 1861-M 16), Celia J. 42 (July 1857-Tex/T/T-M 16-7-5), Sterling C. 15 (Dec 1884), Anne E. 12 (Aug 1887), Thomas H. 10 (Nov 1889), Lena E. 5 (June 1894), Jarman A. 10/12 (July 1899), Emily HOLLOWAY 69 (m)(Feb 1831-Wd 1-1) 4-226A-252/256 (Rhea Springs-Washington Road)

Emily Holloway 46 (Dec 1853-Wd 6-6), James F. 21 (July 1878)(Dealer in Furs), Ethel 18 (Sep 1881)(Dressmaker), Albert 16 (Nov 1883), Kelso 14 (Mar 1866) 14-215A-47/48

Elmore Holloway 46 (Mar 1854-M 20)(Town Marshall), Louisa R. 61 (June 1859-Oh/Germany/Do-M 20-5-5), Samuel H. ESSEX 18 (s)(Sep 1881), Mollie C. ESSEX 16 (d)(July 1883) 14-217A-88/90

Floyd Holloway 23: see Benjamin F. Mealer
Frank Holoway 34 (Nov 1865-M 12), Anie 32 (Oct 1867-M 12-2-2), James 9 (Aug 1890), Alice 7 (July 1892) 1-187A-164/172
Harriet Holloway 80, Nancy E. 44: see George W. Smith
John Holloway 44 (Feb 1856-M 10), Leora J. 33 (Sep 1866-M 10-4-3), Alta B. 16 (Oct 1883), Cratie M. 16 (Aug 1891), Logan M. 4 (June 1895), Darius M. 3 (Oct 1896), William THOMPSON (B) 18 (June 1881) (Servant) 3-202B-57/60
Luty [Leopatra] Holloway 60 (Jan 1840-Wd 10-8), Eller 30 (d)(Ap 1870), Lillie 27 (May 1873), James 23 (Ap 1877), Walter 21 (Jan 1879), Calli 20 (Jan 1880), Line 17 (d)(Sep 1882), Viny 16 (May 1884), Mathy 13 (Sep 1886) 1-165B-130/136
Milo Holloway 8: see Richard T. Ferguson
Milo S. Holloway 53 (Mar 1847-M 29)(Insurance Agent), Adda 50 (May 1850-M 29-8-7), Anna A. 27 (Sep 1872) (Deaf & Dumb), Reese W. 19 (Jan 1881) (Drayman), Laura 16 (May 1884), Maggie M. 13 (June 1887) 13-216B-76/77
Richard Halaway 68: see Frank Edington
Richard Holloway 75 (Aug 1824-T/T/NC-M 45), Eliza J. 52 (May 1838-T/NC/T-M 45-8-6), Thomas G. 42 (nw) (June 1857)(RR Carpenter), Allen H. McFALLS 83 (f)(Dec 1817-NC/NC/NC-Wd) 14-223A-191/195
Thomas B. Holloway 48 (Sep 1851-M 25)(Postmaster), Ruth E. 47 (Feb 1853-M 25-0) 14-216A-66/67

MARRIAGES

A.J. Holloway to C.J. Cook, 19 Jan 1884 (20 Jan), J.M. Bramlett MG 1-462
Abegail E. Holloway to Major C. Gilliam q.v.
B.F. Holloway to Emma Pass, 27 Oct 1874 (same), G.W. Renfro MG 1-#1365
Charles Hollaway to Nancy L. Holland, 22 Dec 1875 (23 Dec), W.W. Lowe JP 1-#1424
Charley Holloway to Mary Moneyhan, 27 Feb 1897, S.J. Brumlow [signed by X] W, "This license was returned not used, J.T. Howard, Clerk" 2-120
Delila J. Holloway to William F. Majors q.v.
Elie Holloway to Carl Stookey q.v.
Eliza Ann Holloway to James Price q.v.
Elvina Hollaway to Gus Smith q.v.
H.C. Holloway to Mary L. Thompson, 8 Oct 1886 (10 Oct), J.D. Drake ?? 1-507
Harriet D. Holloway to G. R. Gilliam q.v.
Isaac W. Hollaway to Mary J. Hollaway, 8 Sep 1856 (13 Sep), E.E. Wasson JP 1-#570
Isaac W. Hollaway to Ada S. Coles, 10 Ap 1875 (11 Ap), J.P. Roddy MG 1-#1397
J.F. Holloway to Annie Evans, 19 Jan 1889 (20 Jan), W.R. Clack JP 1-571
J.H. Holloway to Laura J. Beard, 5 Nov 1888 (9 Nov), J.M. Bramlett MG 1-562
J.H. Hollaway to Mary C. Kincannon, 25 Jan 1880 (6 Jan) [sic], J.N. Bramlett JP 1-292
James S. Holloway to Nancy Jane Gilliam, 17 Aug 1858 (19 Aug), J.I. Cash MG 1-#648
Jeane Holloway to James A. Thompson q.v.
Lizzann Holloway to James Prints q.v.
Lorinda Holloway to John Hinch q.v.
Lucinda Hollaway to J. Newton Willis q.v.
Lucinda J. Holloway to James M. Majors q.v.
Luretta Hollaway to H. C. Sherrill q.v.
M.B. Hollaway to Mary Hughes, 24 Sep 1866 (27 Sep), Asa Newport MG 1-#1063
Maggie Holloway to D. M. Rhea q.v.
Mary Hollaway to A. J. Trentham q.v.
Mary E. Hollaway to J. M. Reede q.v.
Mary E. Holloway to H. T. Rogers q.v.
May or Mary E. Holloway to William H. Cunnyngham q.v.
Mary J. Holloway to Isaac W. Hollaway q.v.
Mary L. Holloway to R. L. Garrison q.v.
Milo Pate Holloway to J. C. Duncan q.v.
Milo S. Holloway to Adda A. Peters, 5 May 1870 (same), T.K. Munsey MG 1-#1151
Minerva Holloway to Joseph Hansford q.v.
Nora L. Holloway to Thomas H. Wyler q.v.
Owen B. Holloway to Catharine M. Boxley, 14 Ap 1853 (17 Ap), A.D. Paul JP 1-#410
Pheba R. Hollaway to N. C. McFall q.v.
Phebe C. Holloway to James C. Hinds q.v.
R.W. Holloway to Eliza Jane McFalls, 15 Ap 1855 (18 Ap), J.I. Cash MG 1-#492
Samuel H. Hollaway to Leopatra Haws, 12 Oct 1867 (17 Oct), G.W. Renfro MG 1-#978
Sarah Hollaway to William Treadway q.v.
Sarah F. Holloway to William D. Dagley q.v.
Sarah Lu Hollaway to Robert D. Hinds q.v.
Sary F. Hollaway to George W. Hoslin q.v.
T.B. Hollaway to Ruthy J. Holland, 15 Dec 1874 (16 Dec), W.W. Low JP 1-#1380
Virginia Holloway to Adison Derosit q.v.
William Holloway to Sarah Treadaway, 8 Jan 1879 (9 Jan), J.P. Roddy MG 1-#1600

\- - - - - - - - - - - -

HOLLOWFIELD

MARRIAGE

Samuel Hollowfield to Linda Moore, 12 May 1885 (same), Calvin Morgan JP 1-483

\- - - - - - - - - - - -

HOLMES / HOLMS / HOMES

1900 CENSUS

George W. Holmes 33 (July 1866-M 13)(Coal Miner), Jennie A. 30 (May 1870-M 13-5-5), Bertha A. 13 (June 1886), William M. 11 (Aug 1888), Mary L. 10 (Jan 1890), James H. 6 (Ap 1894), Thomas H. 1 (Aug 1898) 13-301A-203/211
Green Holmes 68 (Unk 1838-Ga/Ga/Ga-M 42), Ann 62 (Unk 1838-Va/Va/Va-M 42-5-0) 7-265B-291/296 (B)
John Holmes 28 (Dec 1871-M 2)(Coal Miner), Caroline 22 (Aug 1877-M 2-0), George CARTER 18 (boarder) (Unk 1882)(Coal Miner) 8-279-214/216
Mary Holmes 34 (Jan 1866-M 5-1-1), Price JONES 15 (boarder)(July 1884-T/England/Wales) 10-323A-62/66
Thomas H. Holmes 67 (Sep 1842-M 34), Mary E. 53 (Nov 1846-M 34-9-7), Thomas G. 17 (Aug 1882)(Coal Miner), Walter H. 10 (July 1889) 13-301A-203/210

MARRIAGES

Adelia Holmes to Laurence Brock q.v.
Anna Homes to W. A. Mills q.v.

John Holmes to Caroline Mooneyhan, 24 Dec 1898 (same), W.S. Hale MG, J.L. Fain W 2-364
Lou or Lori Holmes to Wiley Scott q.v.
Maggie Holmes to Linn(?) Erwin q.v.
Mollie Holmes to John Bess q.v.
Myrtle E. Holmes to J. E. Euverard q.v.
Polly A. Holmes to Pat McMahan q.v.
Samuel Holmes to Nancy Neal, 31 May 1891, R.S. Mason JP 4-26

- - - - - - - - - - - - -

HOLSTON

1900 CENSUS
George Holston 17: see Katie Sims (B)
MARRIAGE
Martha Holston to Charley Brown q.v.

- - - - - - - - - - - - -

HOLT

1870 CENSUS
Eliza A. Holt 51, Martha J. 22, David L. 16, William R. 13 8-17-118
Peter Holt 8: see Elijah Boman
1880 CENSUS– None
1900 CENSUS
David A. Holt 48 (Jan 1854-M 2), Tennessee 20 (June 1879-M 2-1-0) 13-303B-256/266
MARRIAGES
David Holt to Tennie Capps, 20 Dec 1897 (21 Dec), W.R. Grimsley MG, W.T. Bowman W 2-226
Emma(?) Holt to Thomas Kanly q.v.
Martha J. Holt to John Carpenter q.v.
Maud Holt to J.O. Hardin q.v.
William R. Holt to Sallie Wathern, 5 Feb 1900 (8 Feb), W.R. Grimsley MG, W.F Sullivan W 3-118

- - - - - - - - - - - - -

HONEYCUT

1880 CENSUS
James Honeycut 46 (Miner), Nancy 45, Pleasant 20 (Miner), Mary 15, Louisa 13, Emily 10, Rosa 7, May 5, Alfred DERRICK 20 (boarder)(Miner) 2-30-245

- - - - - - - - - - - - -

HOOD

1860 CENSUS
Rozannat(?) Hood 47 (NC), Rufus 21, Joseph 14, James 7, Robert L. 2 1-93-635
1870 CENSUS
Joseph Hood 22, Elizabeth 28, John F. 8, James A. 3, David M. 1, Helen HOOD 32, James R. 4, Eliza E. 2 1-18-118
Rufus Hood 32, Susan 23, Margaret 6, Sarah 3, Charles 1, James D. 15 2-1-1
1880 CENSUS
James Hood 30, Margaret 28, Mary 9, Rebecca 1 2-34-277
Joseph Hood 35, Elizabeth 38, James 13, David 12, Nancy 8, Milo 5 2-34-279
Robert Hood 20, Martha 20, Mary 1, Rosa HOOD 65 (m) 2-34-280
Rufus Hood 47, Susan 33, Margaret 15, Sarah 13, Charles 11, Samuel 9, Rolla 6, Jane 3, Thomas 1 2-34-278
1900 CENSUS
Charley Hood 31 (Jan 1869-M 9), Idia L. 42 (July 1857-T/NC/T-M 9-9-8), Hallie 17 (July 1882), Roy 8 (Dec 1891), Jargin 6 (Sep 1893), Clara S. 1 (Dec 1898) 7-263B-253/258
Chris Hood 27 (Unk 1873-M 5)(Coal Miner), Mattie 38 (Feb 1862-Ga/Ga/Ga-M 5-7-4), Willie HUGHES 10 (ss)(Nov 1889-Ga/Ga/Ga), Rena SOWERS 16 (sd) (May 1884-Ga-M 0-0), John SOWERS 27 (ssl)(Unk 1873-M 0)(Coal Miner) 8-287B-387/389
James H. Hood 46 (Nov 1853-T/Ga/T-M 20)(Telegraph Superintendent), Alice 40 (Sep 1859-M 20-5-5), Lillie E. 18 (Mar 1882)(Telegraph Operator), Willie E. 12 (Sep 1887), Carl H. 9 (June 1890), Annie M. 8 (May 1892), Jessie 5 (Oct 1894) 10-321A-27/28
Robert Hood 45 (July 1854-T/NC/NC-Wd), Adl M. 16 (d) (Jan 1884), Lucy 13 (d)(Oct 1886), William10 (s) (Mar 1890), Eller 9 (d)(Nov 1892), May 8/12 (gd)(Sep 1899) 7-267A-320/325
Ruffus Hood 65 (July 1834-T/T/NC-M 30), Sousie 54 (Jan 1846-M 30-13-13), Thomas B. 21 (Aug 1878), Edd 19 (Sep 1880), John 17 (Feb 1883), Robert 15 (May 1885), Ruffus 13 (Jan 1887), Luie(?) 11 (s)(May 1889), George 7 (June 1892) 7-263B-258/263
Sam Hood 28 (Oct 1871-M 2), Florence 35 (May 1865-M 2-0), Sousie McCULLOUGH 12 (ne)(May 1888) 7-273B-259/264
MARRIAGES
Annie Hood to Ben McCullough q.v.
Charley Hood(?) to Ida Reeder, 23 Dec 1890, W.R. Clack JP 4-28
J.R. Hood to Jane Morgan, 26 Dec 1896 (27 Dec), R. Knight JP, W.F. Byerley W 2-97
James Hood to Margaret Cope, 11 Jan 1876 (12 Jan), Asa Newport MG 1-#1431
Jane Hood to A. S. McCuistine q.v.
Sallie Hood to Adison L. McCuller q.v.
Samuel Hood to Florence Wright, 5 July 1898 (4 July), David Davis MG, W.F. Purser & R.J. Killough W 2-236

- - - - - - - - - - - - -

HOOK

1900 CENSUS
William Hook 55 (Aug 1844-Ky/Scotland/Ky-M 5)(Pensioner), Tabicaa 37 (Oct 1862-Ky/Ky/Ky-M 5-0-0) 14-213A-1/1

- - - - - - - - - - - - -

HOOPER / HOPPER

MARRIAGES
David H. Hooper to Arthy J. Adams, 22 Dec 1870 (same), J.W. Pearce MG 1-#1179
J.R. Hopper to M.M. Wampler, 10 July 1884 (11 July), W.S. Hale MG 1-491
Lillie Hooper to George Griffis q.v.

- - - - - - - - - - - - -

HOOVER

1900 CENSUS
Ellen Hoover 47, Kate 17: see George W. Goodrich
James R. Hoover 58 (Oct 1843-Ky/Ky/Ky-M 26)(School Teacher) 10-331B-242/257

- - - - - - - - - - - - -

HOPE

1880 CENSUS
J.N. Hope 36 (or 46), Prudence 26, Allice 5, Hugh 3, Gather 2 8-2-12
1900 CENSUS
Hardin Hope 53 (Feb 1847-T/Ala/T-M 3)(Pensioner), Sidney 51 (Mar 1849-M 3-0) 14-221A-154/158
MARRIAGE
H.C. Hope to Sydney Bird, 20 Oct 1897, J.H. Keylon JP 4-99

- - - - - - - - - - - - -

HORN

1870 CENSUS
Marion Horn 27 (Engineer), Ruth 26 3-5-32
MARRIAGE
Elizabeth Horn to A. Dungar q.v.

- - - - - - - - - - - - -

HORNER / HARNER

1860 CENSUS
Doctor W. Horner 43 (NC)(Blacksmith), Louisa 34 (NC), Margaret O. 16, Nancy A. 13, Louisa [Lucretia] M. 11, Louisa J. 9, Catharine D. 6, William F.J. 1 3-54-367
1870 CENSUS
William F. Harner 12: see William J. McLerrin
MARRIAGES
Catharine Horner to William G. Broyles q.v.
Charlotty Horner to Calvin Ginno q.v.
Louisa Horner to William Walters q.v.
Louisa V. Horner (widow) to James White q.v.
M. A. Horner to M. R. Clack q.v.
N. A. Horner to J. N. Ward q.v.

- - - - - - - - - - - - -

HORNEY / HARNEY

1870 CENSUS
Henry Horney 30, Sarah R. 30, John Y. 4, Martha J. 3, Sarah E. 1/12 2-3-17
1880 CENSUS– None
1900 CENSUS
Rebecca Horney 49, Thomas 26, Lee 22: see Mary J. Rogers
MARRIAGES
H.B. Harney to S.R. Gilliam, 30 Nov 1863 (no return) 1-#810
H.B. Harney to Sarah J. Blythe, 12 Aug 1883 (no return) 1-477
Mattie Harney [Hornsby marked through] to G.M. Denton q.v.

- - - - - - - - - - - - -

HORNSBY

1900 CENSUS
Albert Hornsby 60 (Feb 1840-M 33), Darker 55 (Oct 1844-M 33-10-9), John 30 (Jan 1870), Henry 21 (Ap 1879), Thomas 18 (July 1881), Harur 17 (Feb 1883), John 11 (gs)(Sep 1888), Van 9 (gs)(Mar 1891), Elizabeth JOHNSON 36 (d)(Feb 1864-Wd 6-6), Lillie 16 (gd) (Jan 1884), Florence 10 (gd)(Mar 1890), Della 8 (gd) (July 1891), Fred 7 (gd?)(Ap 1893), Jesse 5 (gd)(Ap 1895), Bulah 3 (gd)(Jan 1897) 2-93B-49/51 (B)
MARRIAGES
B. T. Hornsby to M. J. Brady, 1 Mar 1852 (no return) 1-#366
James M. Hornsby to Martha L. Brady, 24 Mar 1855 (same), Nathaniel Barrett MG 1-#488

- - - - - - - - - - - - -

HORRID– see HARROD

- - - - - - - - - - - - -

HORTOEN

1900 CENSUS
John ? Hortoen 65 (Feb 1835-Ind/Va/Ky-M 36), Margarett 60 (June 1839-M 36-2-1), Frank CONLEY 47 (boarder)(Mar 1863-Oh/Oh/Oh-M 25) 7-264B-270/275

- - - - - - - - - - - - -

HOSEMAN

MARRIAGE
Henry Hoseman [bond] or Hasemer [license] or Housemier [index] to Sally Clark, 9 Dec 1888 (11 Dec), R.S. Mason JP 1-557

- - - - - - - - - - - - -

HOSKINS / HASKEN / HUSKINS

1880 CENSUS
Jane Hoskins 20(?): see T. S. Franklin
1900 CENSUS
Allie Huskins 25 (Sep 1874-T/NC/T-S)(Dressmaker), Boss 12 (b)(Oct 1887-T/NC/T), Maudie 4 (d)(Jan 1896), Will COLEMAN 22 (boarder)(June 1877-T/NC/T) (Coal Miner) 10-259B-187/191
MARRIAGES
Andy Huskins to Nancy Brady, 7 Feb 1893, T.F. Shaver JP 4-51
J.W. Hasken to Sarah C. Rector, 6 Feb 1862 (no return) 1-#774
Mary F. Huskins to William R. Byrd q.v.

- - - - - - - - - - - - -

HOUGHEY

1900 CENSUS
Patrick Houghey 48 (Mar 1852-Ireland/Do/Do-1873/27/Na-M 5)(Retail Liquor Dealer), Mary 30 (Feb 1870-Ireland/Do/Do-M 6-2-1), Robert E. 4 (Sep 1895), Susan GALLAGHER 18 (June 1881-Ireland/Do/Do)(Servant) 8-316-122/126

- - - - - - - - - - - - -

HOUPT

MARRIAGE

Franklin Houpt to Sarah Wyrick, 5 Jan 1851 (same), J.O. Torbett JP 1-#328

- - - - - - - - - - - - -

HOUSE

1860 CENSUS

John House 33 or 53 (Va)(Carpenter), Lavinia 35, Martha J. 11, Amanda 7, John 1 2-81-549

John House 40 (Miller) 2-76-517

MARRIAGE

John House or Hewse to Amanda Paul, 13 Oct 1866 (15 Oct), W. R.S. Thompson JP 1-#919

- - - - - - - - - - - - -

HOUSER / HOWSER

1900 CENSUS

John Houser 29: see Arva Morgan

Milton Howser 30 (Jan 1870-M 13), Tennie 30 (Oct 1869-M 13-8-7), Henry 12 (Jan 1888), David 8 (Unk 1892), Marion 7 (Oct 1893), Joseph 6 (Jan 1894), Jefferson 5 (May 1895), Rena 2 (Jan 1898), Floyd 3/12 (Feb 1900) 8-285B-341/343

MARRIAGES

Jesse M. Houser to Cynthia Ann Breeding, 24 Oct 1865 (no return) 1-#851

Matilda Howser to Thomas Trusley q.v.

Thomas B. Houser [license, bond, & index] or Housley [bond] to Mrs. Mary Keith, 17 Dec 1899 (18 Dec), W.L. Patton MG, T.G. Henry(?) W 3-89

- - - - - - - - - - - - -

HOUSLEY / HOUSELEY / HOUSLY / HAUSLY / HASLY / HOWSERLEY
(see also HENSLEY and ENSLEY)

1870 CENSUS

Samuel D. Housely 47, Rebecca A. 46, Samuel R. 22, Sarah C. 20, John 19, James A. 17, Henry 14, Mary E. 12, Frances A. 10, William T. 17, Rowlen C. 3 7-4-31

1880 CENSUS

J.E. Hausly 26, Nancy 30 (w), L.T. 4 (d), Julia 7/12 (d) 7-25-217

John Hausly 28, M.F. 28, B.A. 4 (d), H.C. 8/12 (d) 7-24-209

S.R. Hasly 32, Mary 22, Henry 5, Sam 3, Florence 8/12, Sarah 25 (si), Allice 4 (ne), Branon 1 (nw) 7-25-216

Sam Hously 57, R.A. 56, Henry 22, Billy 15, Raten 12, Mary BOYD 22 (d), John W. BOYD 24 (sl) 7-25-219

1900 CENSUS

John Housley 49 (Oct 1850-Wd)(Coal Miner), George 16 (Nov 1885)(Coal Miner), Johnny 13 (Dec 1887), Roly B. 3 (Mar 1897) 10-252A-39

Nancy Hously 50 (Dec 1849-M 27-5-4), Addie 19 (s?)(June 1882), Walter 13 (s)(Sep 1886) 7-265B-297/302

Rote Hoysley 32: see William Y. Denton

Samuel Housely 20 (Oct 1880-T/T/Va-M 2)(Coal Miner), Alice 17 (Dec 1882-M 2-1-1), Gladis 1 (Nov 1898) 10-256A-110/14

William G. Housley 36 (Sep 1863-M 19), Conly B. 34 (Nov 1865-M 19-10-8), Flora A. (May 1882), Floyd 16 (May 1884), Dora I. 13 (Nov 1886), J. Houston 11 (Aug 1888), Cyrus R. 9 (Oct 1890), Ernest 5 (Aug 1894), Carol L. 3 (May 1897), unnamed 1/12 (Ap 1900) 3-201A-22/23

MARRIAGES

Caroline Housley to William Brooke q.v.

Emma L. Housley to George S. Powell q.v.

Henry Howserley (24, Marion Co) to Ann Prater (21, DeKalb Co, Ala), 1 Sep 1881, John Q. Shaver MG, John Boyd & Sam Byerley W 4-1(7)

Henry Housley to Mary Green, 11 Nov 1895, J.W. Williamson MG 4-94

James Houseley to Nancy Byerly, 7 Nov 1874 (no return) 1-#1368

John Housley to Margaret Minnix, 2 Aug 1873 (3 Aug), R.H. Jordan MG 1-#1291

John Hously to Mabel Claire Vaughn, 25 Aug 1900 (26 Aug), W.L. Lillard JP 3-205

Mary Housley to John W. Boyd q.v.

Nancy Housley to Ben Johnson q.v.

Nancy Housley(?) to Jim Sneed q.v.

Phoeba Housley to William Casey q.v.

Samuel Hensley [sic] to Alice Johnson, 11 Sep 1897 (same), W.S. Hale MG, W.C. Dillard W 2-176

W. Housley to C.B. Morgan, 23 Ap 1881, J.A. Crawford JP 4-6(60)

- - - - - - - - - - - - -

HOUSTON / HUSTON

1860 CENSUS

John M. Huston 27 (NC)(Carpenter), Eliza J. 24, Edgar A. 2, John H. 2/12, Margaret HUSTON 63 (NC), Sarah COLSTON 61 (NC) 6-111-759

Thomas Houston 25, Sarah A. 22, Robert P. 1/12, Samuel HOUSTON 19 3-63-434

1870 CENSUS

John M. Houston 37 (NC)(House Carpenter), Eliza J. 35, Edgar A. 12, John H. 9, Margarette T. 7, --?-- Lydia 4, Mary L.A. 1, Margarette 74 (Scotland) 6-7-44

Thomas A. Houston 35, Sarah A. 37, Mary C. 5, Thomas P. 1 6-4-26

1880 CENSUS

Emma Houston 19 (B): see Jacob Dyer

J.M. Houston 47 (Carpenter), Eliza J. 44, Edgar A. 21 (Carpenter), John H. 18, Margaret Linn 16, Elida 14, Mary L.A. 10, Ida L.E. 8, William R. 1, Margaret HOUSTON 84 (m) 5-2-10

Thomas A. Houston 45, Sarah A. 52, Mary C. 15, Thomas D. 10, Laura LAWSON 3 ("taken to raise") 6-12-110

1900 CENSUS

Alfred C. Houston 61 (Oct 1838-NC/NC/NC)(Butcher) 13-302A-223/231

James A. Houston 33 (Feb 1867-M 8), Jennie 34 (Nov 1863-T/NC/SC-M 8-3-3), Rosa C. 6 (June 1893), Adda M. 4 (Sep 1895), Maud M. 2 (Mar 1898), Thomas ROBINSON 52 (border)(Jan 1848), Walter KIMBRO 18 (boarder)(Unk) 6-246B-129/130

John Houston 39 (Mar 1861-T/Pa/Oh-M 7), Lorinda J. 35 (Sep 1864-M 7-3-3), James W. 7 (Feb 1893), Cora 5 (Oct 1894), Katie Lee 2 (Jan 1898), Tilman McMILLEN 18 (Ap 1882)(Servant) 4-227B-272/276 (Road on line between 3rd & 4th Districts)

John M. Houston 66 (Oct 1833-NC/NC/Scotland-M 43), Eliza J. 65 (Nov 1834-M 43-8-6), Mary L.A. 31 (Feb 1869), William R. 21 (May 1878), Edgar NEWMAN 18 (boarder)(Feb 1882-T/T/G) 5-237B-183/183

Horace Houston 22: see Robert Edwards

Mary Houston 29 (Mar 1871-T/T/Ga-D 4-4)(Washwoman), Alice 10 (Sep 1889), Viety 7 (Aug 1892), Lillie M. 5 (July 1894-Va) 10-329A-193/206 (B)

Roy Houston 28: see William Grimsley

Thomas Houston 30 (Aug 1869-M 4)(Merchant), Ninie C. 23 (Oct 1876-M 4-2-2), Lela P. 2 (July 1897), Ada I. 11/12 (June 1899) 5-237B-188/188

MARRIAGES

Elida(?) Houston to P. W. Pierce q.v.

Henry Houston to Ellvira Halbert, 24 Aug 1898 (same), J. McPherson MG, L. Whitaker W 2-312

Ida Houston to R. F. Runyan q.v.

J.H. Houston to Riner(?) Runnions, 17 Ap 1892, John Woolsey MG 4-41

Jack Houston to Carin(?) Henderson, 12 Feb 1887 (13 Feb), Byrd Terry ?? 1-521

Jack Houston to Emma Matherly, 3 Oct 1887 (same), J.Q. Shaver MG 1-534

James Houston to Emma Byerley, 30 Aug 1888 (20 Sep), T.F. Shaver JP 1-560

James A. Houston to Jennie McCullough, 13 Mar 1892, Richard Knight JP 4-42

John M. Houston to Eliza J. Rhea, 24 Dec 1856, "Returned without any Indorsement, W.H. Bell, Clerk" 1-#586

Kitty Houston to Melton Johnson q.v.

Maggie Houston to Lemuel I. Hale q.v.

Maggie T. Houston to J. D. Collins q.v.

Mary Houston to Henry Bailey q.v.

Mary C. Houston to W. E. M. Denton q.v.

S.D. Houston to Eliza C. Travis, 10 Ap 1865 (same), John Howard MG 1-#876

S.G. Houston to Mattie Gray, 15 Jan 1890 (same), J.A. Darr(?) MG 1-591

Samuel Houston to Malinda Kennedy, 3 Mar 1861 (6 Mar), John Wyott JP 1-#748

Sarah Houston to John Rhea q.v.

T.P. Houston to Ninie(?) Bramlett, 7 Jan 1897 (same), W.A. Howard MG, John Vaughn W 2-103

Thomas Houston to Mary Chattin, 18 July 1887 (19 July), Byrd Long MG 1-530

Thomas A. Houston to Sarah A. Minicks, 24 Sep 1855 (27 Sep), J. Howard JP 1-#526

Vance Houston to Mary Emmit, 28 May 1898, G.R. Baldwin JP 4-95

- - - - - - - - - - - - -

HOUTS

MARRIAGE

C.T. Houts to M.J. Henderson, 19 Feb 1864 (same), John Wyatt JP 1-#820

- - - - - - - - - - - - -

HOWARD
(see also **HARWOOD**)

1860 CENSUS

Peggy Howard 60: see Wyly A. Ault

Robert T. Howard 35 (Baptist Preacher), Penelope J. 35, Thomas J. 15, William A. 11, John M. 9, Tennessee T. 7, James 5, Robert T. 3, Richard H. 6/12 6-104-707

Ruth Howard 23, William C. 4, Mary E. 2, Sarah J. 2/12 3-60-413

1870 CENSUS

Charles P. Howard 22 (Ga), Millie Jane 20 8-14-94

John Howard 46 (Blacksmith), Sophia 45, Sophia J. 13, John L. 10 2-3-95

Robert T. Howard 42 (Minister), Penelope 43, Thomas J. 25 (House Carpenter), William 21, John M. 15, Robert T. Jr. 13, Richard H. 10 6-11-75

Ruth Howard 40, William 14, Mary 12, Sarah J. 10, John W. 7 3-6-35

Thomas Howard 56 (SC), Harriette 54 (NC), Mary 29 (Ga), Julia A. 19 (Ga), Jesse 15 (Ga), Palestine 13 (Ga), Robert P. 11, Matilda C. 8, Andrew GREEN or Green Andrew Howard 4 8-12-80

William Howard 21: see Sarah J. Parks

1880 CENSUS

James A. Howard 26 (Mail Con--?--), Carlene L. 25, Jane McDONALD (B) 8 (Servant) 6-24-22 (Rural Street, Washington)

John Howard 56 (Minister), John T. 20 (Store Clerk), Lucy BEAN 1 (gd), Tiney Ruth BEAN 11 (gd), Solome MASON 45 6-22-9 (Madison Street, Washington)

John M. Howard 29 (Retail Merchant), Rhuehanna 29, Darah 4 6-25-189/193

Wm Hawrd [sic] 35, M.A. 24, J.M. 8 (s), A. 6 (d), Belle 4, Jam 3, C. 4/12 (s) 3-19-151

1900 CENSUS

Callie Howard 46 (July 1853-T/T/NC-Wd 7-6), Charles F. 18 (Feb 1882), Richard A. 16 (Ap 1884), Lela M. 13 (May 1887), Troy J. 10 (May 1890), Mary 7 (Oct 1892), Nellie 5 (Feb 1895), Olivia JAMES 50 (si)(Dec 1849-T/T/NC) 10-323B-80/84

Charles Howard 52 (Jan 1848-Ga/SC/SC-M 31), Millie 50 (May 1850-T/Ga/T-M 31-8-7), Alfred 20 (Mar 1880), Tennessee 16 (July 1883), Mary 13 (Aug 1886), Richard T. 10 (Sep 1889), Oliver 7 (June 1892) 13-297A-138/140

James Howard 24 (Dec 1875-S)(Grocer) 10-320B-11/11

James Howard 23: see Robert B. Barger

James G. Howard 56 (May 1844-M 22)(Ferryman), Mary E. 55 (Nov 1844-T/T/Va-M 22-4-4), William J. 21 (May 1879)(Fisherman), John S. 18 (May 1882)(Fisherman), Mary M. 15 (Jan 1885), James C. 12 (Dec 1887) (Fisherman) 3-204B-79/85

Jasper Howard 45 (Aug 1854-M 11), Lou 31 (July 1869-M 11-6-6), Willie D. 15 (Oct 1884), Cyntha D. 9 (Sep 1890), James M. 8 (May 1892), Taylor 5 (June 1894), Jerusha C. 4 (May 1896), Robert L. 2 (Mar 1898), Martha D. 9/12 (May 1900) 6-248A-154/155

John L. Howard 29 (Jan 1871-M 9)(RR Section Hand), Myrtle 25 (Feb 1875-M 9-4-4), Mary E. 7 (Aug 1892), James J. 6 (Mar 1894), Willie A. 3 (Aug 1897), George C. 2 (Ap 1898) 5-230A-51 (B)

John M. Howard 49 (Mar 1851-M 29), Hamie 48 (Jan 1852-M 29-1-1), Dora HAYES 23 (d)(Mar 1877-M 2-1-1), Charles L. HAYES 27 (sl)(Jan 1873-M 2)(Livery Stable Keeper), John H. 1 (gs)(June 1898) 10-321A-22/23

John T. Howard 40 (Nov 1859-M 15)(County Court Clerk), Pennie A. 40 (Jan 1860-Ark/T/Ark-M 15-7-6), Marguerit 14 (Sep 1885), George W. 13 (May 1887), Sophia 11 (Ap 1889), Lillie B. 7 (Sep 1891), Lylton 4 (Nov 1895), Ruth 2 (Jan 1898), Stoma HOWARD 52 (sm)(Mar 1862-Wd 0), Lucy BEAN 33 (ne)(Feb 1867-S)(Dry Goods Saleswoman), Samuel FRALEY 20 (lodger)(Feb 1880) 10-260A-200/205

Robert Howard 42 (Nov 1857-M 16)(Landlord), Mattie 37 (Jan 1863-M 16-1-1), Gladis 5 (Aug 1894), Penelope 73 (m)(Feb 1826-Wd 1-1) 10-255A-95/95

Titus Howard 26: see Creasia Hudson (B)

William Howard 52 (Mar 1848-M 29), Mary E. 50 (Oct 1849-T/T/Ky-M 29-7-4), Alace T. 28 (Aug 1871), Bertha 20 (Sep 1879), Corda B. 14 (July 1885) 5-232B-88

William R. Howard 48: see William Y. Denton

MARRIAGES

Alice Howard or Harwood to Will Rockholt q.v.

Donaldson Howard to Rosa A. Hickman, 27 Oct 1899 (28 Oct), J.G. Isabell MG, Wm Kelery W 3-61

Dora Howard to Charley L. Hayes q.v.

Eliza Howard to J. A. Sullivan q.v.

Ella or Ellen Howard to Joseph B. Dodd q.v.

Harriet Howard to Lewis Turner q.v.

James A. Howard to C.L. James, 18 Oct 1877 (same), Robert E. Smith MG 1-#1518

Jasper N. Howard to M.L. Dodd, 1 Nov 1890, no MG or JP 4-25

John Howard to Delmie Mason, 21 Aug 1887 (same), W.A. Howard MG 1-526

John M. Howard to Ruhana Nanny, 23 Feb 1871 (same), J. Howard MG 1-#1188

John T. Howard to Penny A. Darwin, 21 Sep 1884 (same), Thompson Pulburn(?) MG 1-524

Louisa Jane Howard to James P. Shipley q.v.

Margaret Howard to John W. Willis q.v.

Nannie Howard to W. R. Beavers q.v.

Palestine Howard to William Turner q.v.

Polly Howard to John Stofer q.v.

Robert T. Howard (26, occupation, Merchant in Chattanooga) to Matty Gregg (20, Bradley Co), 27 Dec 1881, J. Howard MG, J.N. Evans (of Evensville) & W.A. Humphries W 4-5(50)

Rossey Howard or Harwood to Byrd McDonald q.v.

Ruth Howard to W. N. Ault q.v.

Ruth C. Howard to Franklin L. Bean q.v.

Samantha Howard or Harwood to John Tanksley q.v.

Tennessee Howard to Samuel Harris q.v.

Tinie Howard to James Jones q.v.

Vicey E. Howard to John A. Thomas q.v.

William A. Howard to Mary E. Ingle, 13 Nov 1870 (same), Allen S. King MG 1-#1174

- - - - - - - - - - - - -

HOWE

1880 CENSUS

James Howe 56 (Miller), Hester 46, Thomas 19, Anna 17, James 12, Emelin WASSON (B) 23 (Servant, Cook) 2-23-189 [James married Hester A. Hand on 20 March 1853 in Roane County]

MARRIAGE

Annie Howe to John B. Wasson q.v.

- - - - - - - - - - - - -

HOWELL / HOWEL

1860 CENSUS

John Howell 59, Elizabeth H. 55, James H. 23, Rachel J. 18, John V. 17, Jackson J. 13, Samuel HOWELL 30, Ruth J. 28, William H. 1 7-1-5
[Samuel married Ruth J. Blevins on 10 Nov 1857]

Joseph A. Howell 28 (Merchant), Viney 21 8-22-151 [Joseph married Vinie McCorkle on 1 Ap 1860 in Meigs County]

1870 CENSUS

Elizabeth Howel 66, Rachel J. 29, John V. 28, Jackson P. 23 7-3-20

1880 CENSUS– None

1900 CENSUS

Moses Howell 13: see Katie Sims (B)

Moses Howell 56 (June 1843-NC/Va/NC-Wd), Joanna 20 (June 1879), John F. 1 (gs)(Dec 1398), Moses 15 (nw) (Jan 1885-T/NC/NC) 10-329B-198/208 (B)

MARRIAGES

L.M. Howell to Sallie Elsed, 14 Nov 1883 (15 Nov), F.M. Bandy MG 1-488

Rachel J. Howell to Thomas F.(?) Whaley q.v.

Sam Howell to Tinie Scroggins, 2 Feb 1889 (3 Feb), John Howard MG 1-566

W.E. Howell to Lena E. Kilgore, 4 Sep 1893, R.M. Kilgore MG 4-57

- - - - - - - - - - - - -

HOWERTON / HOWARDON

1860 CENSUS

Micajah Howerton 64 (Va), Jane 54 5-33-221

Sarah Howerton 47 (Ga), George 24, Mary 21, Alfred WHITE 9 5-6-39 (B)

1870 CENSUS

Micajah Howerton 77 (Va), Jane 67, Mariah COLLINS (Mu) 13 5-6-38

1880 CENSUS

George Howerton 34, John E. 9, James A. 7, Saear E.J. 4, Sarah 60 (m) 5-8-71/72 (B)

Peter Howerton 59, Emaline 48, Sarah E.S. 10, Napoleon 9 10-26-199/205 (B)

1900 CENSUS

George Howardon 56 (Jan 1844-T/Ga/Ga-Wd) 5-231A-52 (B)

James Howardon 26 (Aug 1873-S) 5-231A-53 (B)

MARRIAGES

John Howerton to Myrtle Douglass, 2 Aug 1891, D.E. Broyles JP 4-28

Stacia Howerton to Elmore Randolph q.v.

- - - - - - - - - - - - -

HOYAL / HOYLE / HOYL / HOWAL

1860 CENSUS
John Hoyal 60 (Va)(Physician), Rebecca A. 40, Virginia A. 18, Catharine B. 14, John 1 6-112-770
1870 CENSUS
John Hoyal 69 (Va)(Physician), Rebecca 50, John 12, James 8, Mary JOHNSON (B) 31 6-12-80
1880 CENSUS
Rebecca Hoyal 59, John 21, James 17, Charlie EVANS (Mu) 9 (Servant), Delia WHITTENBURG 22 (Servant), James THOMPSON 27 (Servant) 1-18-152
1900 CENSUS
Charles Hoyal 26: see Harley Wasman
Hairny(?) Hoyl(?) 47 (June 1852-NY/NY/NY-M 16)(Minister), Rose 41 (Feb 1859-NY/NY/NY-M 16-4-4) (School Teacher), Farmer 15 (Mar 1885-NY), Anis 11 (Sep 1888-Calif), Alas 9 (Oct 1890-NY), Howard 6 (July 1890-NY) 12-179B-18/20
James Hoyal 37 (June 1862-T/Va/T-M 17), Hattie 27 (Nov 1873-M 17-2-2), Ellen 3 (Nov 1886), Barbra 8 (Feb 1892) 1-186A-139/145
Marjorie Hoyal 38, Marjorie 16: see Wm C. Payne
MARRIAGES
Charley Howal to Mary Johnson, 20 Sep 1898 (bond only), Andrew Colong(?) W 2-324
Fannie Hoyle to D. M. Blevins q.v.
J.L. Hoyal to Emma Heiskell, 23 Oct 1883 (24 Oct), A.P. Early MG 1-466
James L. Hoyal to Hettie W. Hart, 25 Mar 1896, J.A. Whitner MG 4-93
L. J. Hoyle or Hale to John Wimpey q.v.

- - - - - - - - - - - - -

HUBBARD / HUBBERT / HIBBARD

1860 CENSUS
Elizabeth Hubbard 61 (SC), Huston 24, Sarah E. 40 3-59-408
1870 CENSUS
Sarah Hubbert 27 (NC), Randy 8: see Elizabeth Burton
1880 CENSUS
J. R. Hubbard 17: see W. Dryemon
1900 CENSUS
Bidgan(?) Hubbard 78 (Ap 1822-NY/NY/NY-M 11), Jenni 65 (June 1834-Ind/Ind/NC-M 11-0-0)(Miliner) 12-179A-4/4
MARRIAGES
Houston Hubbard to Sarah Burton, 10 Jan 1861 (same), John Howard MG 1-#741
James Hubbard to Levena Coulter, 24 June 1886 (27 June), W.G. Curton MG 1-501
S. C. Hubbard to William J. Dryman q.v.
Sarah E. Hubbard to Dotson Moore q.v.
Seth Hibbard to Mary Ann F. Capps, 20 Sep 1862 (21 Sep), W.W. Low JP 1-#787

- - - - - - - - - - - - -

HUDLESTON / HUDDLESTON

1860 CENSUS
Margaret Huddleston 12: see Larkin Majors
MARRIAGES
John Hudleston to Polly Vetito, 9 Oct 1855 (11 Oct), Elijah Brewer JP 1-#535
W.W. Hudleston to M.J. Majors, 11 Dec 1853 (15 Dec), Asa Newport MG 1-#432

- - - - - - - - - - - - -

HUDSON / HUTSON

MARRIAGES
J.B.S. Hutson to Mrs. E.I. Trier, 12 Oct 1898 (same), G.W. Brewer MG & W 2-230
John Hudson to Lizzie Keith, 16 Nov 1894, L. Diggs MG 4-71
Robert Hutson to Bell Brooks, 23 Sep 1899, G.R. Baldwin JP 4-101 (B)

- - - - - - - - - - - - -

HUFF

1900 CENSUS
Elizah Huff 24 (Sep 1875-T/NC/T-M 3), Maggie 20 (Nov 1878-M 3-1-1), George 2 (Mar 1898) 7-266A-306/311
Eva Huff 23: see Irene Copeland
MARRIAGES
Elijah H. Huff to Martha Garrison, 7 Sep 1893, J.W. Peace ?? 4-61
Elijah Huff to Maggie Henry, 3 Dec 1896, J.H. Seward MG 4-96

- - - - - - - - - - - - -

HUGHES / HUGHS

1860 CENSUS
Allen Hughes 53 (NC), Narcissa 50 (NC), Mary J. 22, Henry C. 20, Andrew J. 20, Amanda 17, John 12, James M. 10 1-91-622
John W. Hughes 49 (NC), Margaret 20, Elizabeth 20, Malissa 13, William 7, Elender 8/12 7-2-6
William Hughes 24 (Day Laborer), Mary 21, Rhody 2, Samuel 14, Martha 8 1-89-612
1870 CENSUS
Calvin Hughes 36, Fanny E. 32 (NC), William 8, Nancy C. 5, Mary M. 2, Martha J. 3/12 7-8-62
John W. Hughes 59 (NC), Eliza 30, William G. 16, Sarah E. 10, Asberry G. 8, George W. or M. 6, John N. 4 7-1-4
McHenry Hughes 39, Missouri 31 (NC), Sarah T. 11, James M. 9, Fidelity 4, Mima E. 2 7-4-28
Thomas B. Hughes 26, Rachel 21 (Ky) 8-1-7
1880 CENSUS
Charlie Hughes 27, Orlena 24, Thomas 6, Charlie 2, Mary 1/12 2-32-264 (B)
F.B. Hughes 37, R. 31 (w), Ida 11 11-39-313
M.H. Hughes 49, M. 44 (w), S.T. 20 (d), J.M. 17 (s), Dellia 12, Mintie E. 10, Jennie 8, Claerind 6, Johney 4 (s), Wm E. 2, J.J. 8/12 (s) 8-5-39
Moses Hughes 64, Indiann 61, Jery 22, Margaret 14 5-2-18 (B)
Munroe Hughes 29, Eliza 25, M.J. 9 (d), M.A. 5 (d) 8-17-141 (B)
Walker Hughes 70, S.E. 21 (d), J.C. McCAREY(?) 10 (gs) 11-41-330

1900 CENSUS

Charles Hughes 51 (Feb 1849-T/Va/T-M 27), Arlinia 43 (Mar 1857-T/Africa/T-M 27-13-11), Mary 20 (Jan 1880), Parelee 19 (Nov 1881), Nancy 6 (Aug 1883), Sam 3 (Mar 1887), Maggie 11 (May 1889), John M. 9 (Nov 1890), Hays 7 (Feb 1893), Van D. 4 (Dec 1895), Vesta B. 2 (July 1897), Henry SCOTT 47 (Aug 1852-Va/Va/Va)(Teamster) 2-95A-79/82 (B)

Charley Hughes 21, Isom 34, Wright 39, Alford 26: see Lou Weathington (B)

George Hughes 64 (Ap 1836-T/T/Pa-M 31), Ann E. 47 (Jan 1853-M 31-6-5), Jim G. 21 (Jan 1879), Arthur 19 (Jan 1881)(Coal Miner), Ben J. 11 (Aug 1888), Bertha C. 9 (Dec 1891) 10-260A-197/202

George A. Hughes 31 (June 1868-M 7)(RR Tie Cutter), Beckean S. 26 (Feb 1874-M 7-4-3), Media J. 7 (May 1893), George T. 5 (Jan 1895), Samuel D. 2 (June 1897) 9-229B-34

Jake Hughes 23: see Fannie Johns (B)

James A. Hughes 22: see Tate Martin

John Hughes 28 (Oct 1871-M 3), Hettie 20 (Jan 1880-M 3-1-1), Eddie 1 (Jan 1899), Margaret BRADDIRVANS 74 (gm)(Feb 1826-NC/NC/NC-Wd 4-0), Ed HOLDEN 9 (bl)(Feb 1891) 8-283B-298/300

John Hughes 22 (Jan 1878-M 2)(Coal Miner), Rebecca 19 (Nov 1880-Ga/T/T-M 2-0), Edd 19 (b)(Mar 1881-T/Va/T)(Mine Laborer), Dellie LOWERY 10 (sil)(Oct 1889) 10-259B-189/193

John Hughes 21 (Unk 1879-M 2)(Coal Miner), Mary J. 20 (Oct 1879-M 2-2-1), Jannie G. 8/12 (Sep 1899), Willie MATHEWS 6 (bl)(Oct 1883), Pollie SHAW 86 (gml) (Jan 1824-Wd 1-0) 10-259A-173/177

Peter Hughes 25: see Bird Clay (B)

Rufus Hughes 19 (Unk 1881-Ga/Ga/Ga-M 2), Rileda(?) 18 (Aug 1881-Ga/Ga/Ga-M 2-0) 8-287B-390/392

Tennie Hughes 24: see Norris P. Lawrence

Thomas Hughes 26 (Jan 1874-M 2)(Iron Ore Miner), Charlat 18 (Feb 1882-M 2-1-1), Devirda 7/12 (Oct 1899) 2-195B-80/83 (B)

Willie Hughes 10: see Chris Hood

MARRIAGES

A.J. Hughes to Kittie Rodgers, 30 Nov 1900 (1 Dec), W.R. Grimsley MG, W.J. Bean W 3-250

Amanda Hughes to William A. Brady q.v.

Annie Hughes to H. C. Green q.v.

Annie Hughes to Samuel Standifer q.v.

Callie Hughes to James Moore q.v.

Carrie Hughes to J. A. Iveston q.v.

Deller Hughes to John A. Foust q.v.

E. T. Hughes to M. R. Gibson q.v.

Elizabeth C. Hughes to Thomas J. Hughes q.v.

Ella J. Hughes to J. F. Daniel q.v.

Emaline Hughes to Lewis Ballard q.v.

Emeline Hughes to Richard Rue or Rice q.v.

Emma Hughes to Frank Tullass q.v.

Henry Hughes to Tutha Burgan, 7 July 1862 (10 July), Ed Pyott JP 1-#783

Ivery Hughes to Monroe Spiller q.v.

J.H. Hughes to Calvin(?) Sharp, 16 Jan 1888 (same), W.S. Hale MG 1-546

J.T. Hughes to Caroline Neal, 12 Jan 1884 (13 Jan), J.W. Barnett MG 1-520

James Hughes to Sarah Jane Mitchell, 24 Ap 1854 (same), Thomas V. Atchley JP 1-#441

Joab Hughes to Polly Ann Minick, 6 Feb 1877 (same), P.G. Roddy MG 1-#1485

John Hughes to Hattie Holder, 20 Feb 1897 (21 Feb), R.P. Hogue JP, T.S. Blackburn W 2-118

John D. Hughes to Rebecca Lourey, 11 June 1898, no MG or JP, G.W. Hughes W 2-293

John H. Hughes to Mary J. Mathis, 25 Sep 1897 (26 Sep), F.M. Cook MG, W.H. Smith W 2-187

John W. Hughes to Margaret Mathis, 31 May 1858 (3 June), Orville Paine JP 1-#631

John W. Hughes to Eliza Cate, 7 Dec 1869 (29 Dec), Wm L. Humphrey JP 1-#1130

John W. Hughes to Louisa Wright, 15 June 1878 (same), J. Howard MG 1-#1562

Lizza Hughes to Thomas F. Dodson q.v.

M. J. Hughes to J. F. Brock q.v.

Malinda Hughs to John R. Treadaway q.v.

Malinda Hughes to William Couch q.v.

Mandy Hughes to George Brooks q.v.

Margaret Hughes to George Johnson q.v.

Martha J. Hughes to T. B. Walker q.v.

Mary Hughes to M. P. Hollaway q.v.

Mary Hughes to Louis Swafford q.v.

Matilda E. Hughes to Enoch White q.v.

McHenry Hughes to Missouri Allen, 23 Aug 1855 (same), A. Johns MG 1-#515

Milly Hughes to Joseph Mitchell q.v.

Mollie Hughes to F. S. Sharp q.v.

R.C. Hughes to Frances Moore, 12 May 1855 (same), R.T. Howard MG 1-#495

Renor Hughes to John Soward q.v.

Richard Hughes to Rosie Green, 6 July 1896 (same), M.B. Hicks JP, J.M. Washburn W 2-38

Richard Hughes to Mary Swafford, 18 June 1897 (same), S.G. Sanders MG, I.K. Dyer W 2-152

Sarah Hughes to Thomas Martain q.v.

Sarah Ann Hughes to P. M. Varner q.v.

Tennie Hughes to Arthur L. Manans(?) q.v.

Thomas J. Hughes to Elizabeth C. Hughes, 18 Sep 1867 (no return) 1-#969

W.D. Hughes to A.J. Brady, 24 July 1892, W.S. Neighbors MG 4-42

W.G. Hughes to Mary Vincan, 26 Dec 1887 (same), L. Hayworth MG 1-539

W.L. Hughes to Katie Wilkey, 31 July 1890 (same), A.W. Frazier JP 1-604

William J. Hughes to Mary A. Dodson, 23 Dec 1857 (24 Dec), N.H. Long JP 1-#625

- - - - - - - - - - - - -

HULL

1870 CENSUS

Franklin Hull 11: see Thomas J. Harvey

- - - - - - - - - - - - -

HULSE

1860 CENSUS

John W. Hulse 30 (Dentist), Elvira 34, Polly L. 8, Hanah J. 6, Sarah C. 4, James B. 2, Thomas P. HOLES 18 8-19-130

- - - - - - - - - - - - -

HUMPHREY / HUMPHREYS

1860 CENSUS
Mary Humphrey 15: see Newton Locke
William L. Humphreys 36 (Va), Susan E. 26, Jesse F. 5, Thomas P. 3, Sarah E. 8/12 8-26-174
1870 CENSUS
William L. Humphrey 48 (Va), Susan E. 37, Jesse F. 15, Sarah E. 11, Margarette J. 8, Adaline D. 5, William L. 3, James L. 1 8-20-136
1880 CENSUS– None
1900 CENSUS
John F.(?) Humphrey 39 (Ap 1861-M 16)(Lumberman), Rosa A. 37 (July 1863-T/T/Va-M 16-5-2), Annie M. 12 (May 1888), Hazel G. 6 (Nov 1893), Hugh CAMPBELL 34 (boarder)(Mar 1866-Wd), Milton O'BEE 39 (boarder)(Nov 1860-M 12) 10-327B-157/165
Morris Humphrey 66 (Ap 1834-Oh/Oh/Oh-M 42), Sarah C. 63 (July 1836-Oh/Oh/Oh-M 42-3-1), Odessa S. 22 (June 1877-Oh) 11-290A-1
MARRIAGES
C.H. Humphreys to Lona L. Smith, 23 June 1892, Z.M. McGee MG 4-38
Easter Humphrey to Jordan(?) Davis q.v.
Hinny(?) Humphreys to Easter Jones, 27 Ap 1884 (same), W.S. Hale MG 1-470
William Humphrey to S.E. Rector, 13 Feb 1851 (same), Wm Ganaway MG 1-#333

- - - - - - - - - - - - -

HUNT

1880 CENSUS
John Hunt 45, Rachel 46, Mary 17 1-8-148
1900 CENSUS
Virna Fry Hunt 50 see Danniel Haskel
Will Hunt 22: see Mary Bradford (B)
Willis Hunt 37 (July 1862-M 19), Rosie 29 (Jan 1870-Ga/Ga/Ga-M 19-4-0) 10-257B-146/150 (B)

- - - - - - - - - - - - -

HUNTER

1900 CENSUS
Lark Hunter 33 (Ap 1867-Ga/Ga/Ga-M 9)(Coal Miner), Vira 39 (Oct 1860-Ga/Ga/Ga-M 9-8-5), Daisy 9 (Mar 1891-Ala), Willie E. 7 (July 1892), Robert 5 (Feb 1895), Mary 16 (gd)(Oct 1883-Ga), Nancy 18 (gd)(Ap 1881-Ga), Margaret RAIDEN or RIDUE 25 (sil)(Oct 1874-G/Ga/Ga-D 3-1), Laura 3 (ne)(July 1896) 8-283B-295/297
Pleasant E. Hunter 56 (Nov 1843-T/Va/SC-M 31), Harriett B. 54 (Nov 1845-NC/NC/NC-M 31-8-5), John W. 26 (Sep 1873), Ivina I. 19 (Dec 1880), Etha E. 16 (Oct 1883), Samuel 14 (July 1885), Pilar C. 13 (Mar 1887) 5-233B-111 [Pleasant married Harriett B. Whitesides on 12 Mar 1869]
Thomas Hunter 27 (May 1873-Ga/Ga/Ga)(Day Laborer) 10-331A-223/238 (B)
MARRIAGES
A.J. Hunter to Kissiah Wilkey, 2 Aug 1866 (same), T.N.L. Cunnyngham JP 1-#906
E.T. Hunter to Annie L. Hodge, 11 Sep 1889 (12 Sep), John Howard MG 1-593
Elva Hunter to Joseph Tucker q.v.
Grace F. Hunter to J.B. Collett q.v.
J.A. Hunter to A.A. Foust, 18 Ap 1899 (23 Ap), L.E. Smith JP, J.M. Stoker W 2-402

- - - - - - - - - - - - -

HUNTINGTON

1880 CENSUS
Hiram Huntington 55, Anna 49, Fred 19, Ella E. 18, Henry L. 15, Jessie E. 13, Alice 10, Gertrude 7 2-3-21
1900 CENSUS
Anna Huntington 67 (Sep 1832-NY/NY/NY-Wd 7-5), Eller 37 (d)(Jan 1862-NY-S)(Dr Med), Girty 27 (d)(July 1872-NY-S)(School Teacher) 12-179-12/14
MARRIAGES
Alice Huntington to John B. Merritt q.v.
Jossie G. Huntington to Nelson G. Hughby q.v.

- - - - - - - - - - - - -

HUPANS

1900 CENSUS
Robbert D. Hupans(?) 74 (Feb 1826-M 47), Sarah 73 (Feb 1827-M 47-7-6), Lara 41 (d)(Mar 1859), Maud 19 (gd)(Nov 1881), Albert 16 (gs)(Nov 1883), Hattie 15 (gd)(Mar 1885) 1-187A-163/171

- - - - - - - - - - - - -

HURD

1900 CENSUS
Jeff Hurd 23: see Katie Sims (B)

- - - - - - - - - - - - -

HURLEY

1900 CENSUS
Higey T. Hurley 12: see Charles Wycuff
MARRIAGE
Eliza H. Hurley to Charley Wycuff q.v.

- - - - - - - - - - - - -

HURST

1870 CENSUS
Huston Hurst 19, Granvil 32, Mornville 30, Armilda 27, Nancy E. 21 2-7-45
Martin Hurst 42, Fanny GRAY 60, Mary E. KING 65 (Va), Thomas A. 21 2-8-53
1880 CENSUS
Granville Hurst 40, Mary 33, John 6, Earnest 3, William 2, Addie 5/12, William LONG 20 (boarder) 2-35-287
John Hurst 24, Martha 21, Joseph 3, Mary 1, unnamed 1/12 (s) 2-38-308
Mary Hurst 54, Canada 24, Gilbert 22, Vincent 20 5-1-7

1900 CENSUS

Canada Hurst 44 (Nov 1855-M 0), Mary 12 (Ap 1888-Ga/T/Ga-M 0-0) 5-237B-187

Hanable Hurst 46 (Sep 1853-M 22), Eliza A. 44 (Ap 1856-M 22-5-5), James R. 21 (Feb 1879), William C. 19 (Jan 1881), Rosa A. 5 (Nov 1884), Bettie J. 13 (Sep 1886), John C. 5 (Mar 1895) 5-237B-190

John Hurst 52 (Dec 1847-M 24), Martha E. 41 (Mar 1859-M 24-10-8), Charley W. 20 (May 1880), Martha J. 14 (July 1885), Gaither 9 (Aug 1890), Esther E. 7 (Mar 1893), Arch 4 (Nov 1895), Luther 1 (June 1898) 3-201B-34/37

Joseph Hurst 22 (Nov 1877-M 0), Calista 17 (Ap 1883-M 0-0) 4-226B-259/263

Vincent Hurst 40 (May 1860-M 11), Matilda J. 38 (June 1865-M 1-7-3), Walter L. 9 (Mar 1891), Lillie M. 6 (June 1893), Goldie B. 4 (June 1895) 6-247B-148/149

MARRIAGES

Barbara Ann Hurst to Thomas J. Pelfrey q.v.

Canada Hurst to Mary H. Smith, 24 Ap 1900 (same), A.B. Burdett ??, Wm McCulley W 3-150

Granvill Hurst to Mary E. King, 2 Sep 1873 (4 Sep), J.P. Roddy MG 1-#1298

Hanibal Hurst to Ann Smith, 10 Ap 1878 (11 Ap), A.J. Pritchett MG 1-#1554

Houston Hurst to Susan M. Clack, 18 Nov 1874 (19 Nov), J.P. Roddy MG 1-#1372

J.R. Hurst to Cistas Fisher, 11 Nov 1899 (12 Nov), J.M. Bramlett MG, R.H. Williams W 3-69

John E. Hurst to Marthy E. Smith, 13 Aug 1875 (15 Aug), J.M. Bramlett MG 1-#1405

Lucy Hurst to Thomas Smith q.v.

M. A. Hurst to W. R. Smith q.v.

Martin Hurst to Mary Ann Miller, 31 Dec 1873 (same), A.L. King MG 1-#1322

Mary Hurst to Doctor Martin q.v.

Melvinia Hurst to Henry Eaton q.v.

Nancy E. Hurst to W. H. Johnson q.v.

Rosa Hurst to Charley Keylon q.v.

V.L. Hurst to Elizabeth Buckhannon, 17 Sep 1885 (same), John Howard MG 1-491

V.L. Hurst to Jane Smith, 2 Jan 1889 (same), J.L. Brown JP 1-559

Vincent Hurst to Harriet Geer, 12 Ap 1864 (same), John Howard MG 1-#827

- - - - - - - - - - - - -

HURT

MARRIAGE

Lydia Hurt to Norris Bottomlee q.v.

- - - - - - - - - - - - -

HUTCHENS / HUTCHINS

1900 CENSUS

Earnest Hutchins 20, Paree H. 21: see Jordan Davis (B)

Edward P. Hutchins 45 (Dec 1854-Oh/Ver/Ver-M 12), Mary J. 39 (June 1860-Oh/Scotland/Do-M 12-4-4), Frances W. 10 (May 1890), Robert P. 8 (Oct 1891), Ralph C. 6 (July 1893), Clarence T. 4 (Jan 1896) 11-292A-59

Sarah M. Hutchins 72 (Jan 1828-Ver/Conn/Ver-Wd 1-1) 11-292B-60/60

MARRIAGE

William N. Hutchens to Sarah J. Frazier, 12 Nov 1872 (same), John Howard MG 1-#1261

- - - - - - - - - - - - -

HUTCHINSON / HUTCHESON / HUTCHERSON / HUCHISON

1860 CENSUS

Alfred Hutcheson 52, Matilda 49, Darius C. 2, Charles C. 17, Tennessee 15, George W. 13, Samantha 11, Ada 8, Leander 6, David WARD 21, William 18 8-11-71

Isaac Huchison 33, Rutha 30, Charles A. 10, Margaret 8, Catharine A. 6, Emily 3, James W. 1 8-13-87

1870 CENSUS

Alfred Hutchison 63, Matilda 59, John GOODSON 21, Sarah CRAIN 26 8-13-88

Charles M. Hutcheson 34, Harriette W. 31, Charles P. 9, James M. 6, Benjamin L. 3 8-22-150

Darius C. Hutcheson 36, Mary Jane 24, Mary Ann L. 6, Samantha T. 4, Adda A. 3, Charles R. 1, Tobe HUTCHESON (B) 19 8-12-83

Jefferson Hutcheson 28, Crassey 30, Albert 14 8-22-151 (B)

Samuel W. Hutcheson 35, Susan E. 37, John L. 13, Mary C. 11, Charles W. 8 8-13-89

Vilena(?) [erased and written over] Hutchison(?), Matilda A. 5, William A. 4, Oliver L. NORMAN 17 8-13-87

1880 CENSUS– None

1900 CENSUS

Jefferson Hutchison 30 (Mar 1870-M 5), Mary 26 (Unk 1874-M 5-3-3), Fred 4 (Oct 1895), Lola 2 (July 1897), Fletcher 10/12 (Aug 1899) 8-285A-326/328 (B)

Mary A. Hutchinson 64: see William H. Rogers

Nanna Hutcheson 45 (Nov 1855-Wd 1-1), James B. 17 (Dec 1872), Elizabeth C. RENFRO 72 (m)(Feb 1828-Wd 7-6) 14-221A-148/152

MARRIAGES

A. F. Hutcheson to M. A. Woods q.v.

A. M. Hutchenson to Alfred Armstrong q.v.

Albert Hutcheson to Sallie Wright, 14 July 1895, J.W. Francis MG 4-83

Ben Hutcheson to Agnes Shelton, 12 June 1886 (13 June), E.G.H. Ryan ?? 1-503

C.N. Hutcheson to Martha E. Marler, 25 Feb 1889 (27 Feb), J.R. Walker MG 1-571

Earnest Hutcheson to Parthena Davis, 6 Dec 1897 (7 Dec), D.B. Jackson MG 2-222

Hattie Hutcheson to G. W. Aslinger q.v.

I.N. Hutchenson to Adelia L. Gamble, 9 Mar 1877 (14 Mar), H.A. Green JP 1-#1491

J.B. Hutcheson (24, Bledsoe Co) to N.E. Renfro (26, McMinn Co), no date but recorded 1 Dec 1882, W.W. Pyott MG, D.T. Hill (of Spring City) & E.A. Lowry (of Pikeville) W 4-11(105)

Josie Hutcheson to Judge Turner q.v.

L.V. Hutchinson to H.W. Standfield q.v.

Louvena Hutchinson to Samuel G. Thompson q.v.

Lumie Hutcheson to Anna Logan, 26 Sep 1900 (same), J.D. Gather MG, Munsel(?) Smith W 3-227

Marcella Hutchison to Joseph Campbell q.v.
Mary Hutcheson to Andy Jones q.v.
R. T. Hutcherson to C.H. Mathewson q.v.
Randia(?) Hutcheson to Thomas Swafford q.v.
S.W. Hutcherson to Mary A. Rodgers, 3 Ap 1876 (5 Ap), W.W. Lillard MG 1-#1440
Samantha M. Hutchenson to Marion M. Owenby q.v.
Vilena Hutchesson to L. D. Powers q.v.

- - - - - - - - - - - - -

HUTSELL

1880 CENSUS
D. M. Hutsell (m) 23 3-21-166
1900 CENSUS
Addie Hutsell 38 (July 1861-Wd 6-5), Joseph R. 16 (Dec 1883), Walter S. 14 (Mar 1886), Charley 9 (Mar 1891), John H. 6 (Sep 1893), Nina L. 3 (Aug 1896) 10-322-42/44

- - - - - - - - - - - - -

HYDE

1900 CENSUS
Ellen Hyde 33 (June 1866-T/NC/SC-S 1-1)(Dressmaker), John 15 (Mar 1885-Ala/Ga/T)(Grocery Salesman) 8-311A-10/11
MARRIAGE
Rachel A. Hyde (19, Raborn Co, Ga) to Jas N. Cantrell q.v.

- - - - - - - - - - - - -

IGOU

MARRIAGE
A.C.P. Igou to Tennessee C. Whaley, 23 Oct 1855 (same), J. Ballison JP 1-#532

- - - - - - - - - - - - -

ILES

MARRIAGES
Hannah E. Iles to J. A. Patton or Bolton q.v.
Jesse Iles or Ples to Alice Thomas, 30 May 1896 (bond only), J.A. Potter W 2-25
John Iles to Nora Graves, 11 June 1898 (12 June), T.D. Shelton MG, Wm Burton W 2-292
M.V. Iles or Ides to Sallie Wright, 22 June 1888 (24 June), W.A. Green JP 1-552

- - - - - - - - - - - - -

INER (?)

1900 CENSUS
Clay Iner(?) [ink blob] 27, Annie 21: see Louisa Wright

- - - - - - - - - - - - -

INGLE / INGLES

1870 CENSUS
Jesse Ingle 47, Mary A. 44, Caroline 19, Sarah E. 17, Mary 15, Lousa 13, Elisha N. 11, Amanda 9, Martha 7, James 5, Lucinda 1, Alfred 19 2-2-11
John Ingle 24: see William P. Thomison
Samuel Ingle 43, Julia 43, Emily 20, William J. 17, Elizabeth A. 15, John T. 9, Eliza E. 6, James O. 3, Julia A. 35 6-6-36
Thomas H. Ingle 21, Van 4 2-3-12
1880 CENSUS
J.E. Ingle 24 (Merchant), N.E. 20 (w), A.S. 2 (s), Ray 1/12 (s), J.T. 18 (b) 8-3-24
Jessee Ingle 56, Mary 54, Caroline 27, Amanda 19, Martha 16, Thomas 14, Lucinda 11 2-40-325
Martin Ingle 21, Lorinda 20 1-17-141
Thomas Ingle 31, Van 25, Elvira 7, William 5, Mary 2, Florence 1/12, George BROWNING 26 (c)(Carpenter & Joiner) 2-40-326
1900 CENSUS
Thomas H. Ingle 52 (Nov 1848-M 30), Van 43 (Oct 1855-T/NC/T-M 30-10-8), Florence A. 20 (May 1880), James F. 17 (Jan 1883), Minnie B. 14 (Oct 1886), Ray A. 8 (Aug 1891), Nettie A. 6 (Jan 1894), Walter B. 3 (Jan 1897) 2-192A-23/23
Caroline Ingle 49: see Majar O. Hynes [Hinds]
MARRIAGES
Amanda Ingle to Asa Stincipher q.v.
Barbary Ellen Ingle to William J. Wasson q.v.
E. J. Ingle to G. W. McCarter q.v.
E.M. Ingle to Lorinda Hinds, 8 Oct 1879 (9 Oct), J.P. Roddy MG 1-#1681
J.A. Ingle to Florina Bolton, 31 Dec 1883, J.W. Pearce MG 1-519
Jefferson Ingle to Mary Majors, 21 Feb 1853 (23 Feb), J.I. Cash MG 1-#404
L. G. Ingle to James Hinds q.v.
M.M. Ingle to T.J. Breeding, 7 Aug 1869 (8 Aug), Samuel E.(?) Hale MG 1-#1095
Mary A. Ingle to Z. F. Long q.v.
Mary E. Ingle to William A. Howard q.v.
Sarah Ingle to A. J. Gipson q.v.
Thomas H. Ingle to Vanney Garrison, 21 May 1870 (22 May), James I. Cash MG 1-#1152
W.J. Ingle to S.L. Able, 26 Dec 1873 (31 Dec), R.T. Howard MG 1-#1319
William Ingles to July Kenedy, 8 Jan 1888 (same), T.H. McPherson JP 1-543

- - - - - - - - - - - - -

INGLESOE

MARRIAGE
Jinna Inglesoe to R. P. Jones q.v.

- - - - - - - - - - - - -

INGRAHAM

MARRIAGE
George Ingraham to Lillie Garrison, 24 June 1887 (3 July), Calvin Morgan JP 1-530

- - - - - - - - - - - - -

INMAN

MARRIAGE
Jennie Inman to William Cook q.v.

- - - - - - - - - - - - -

IPHOFEN

MARRIAGE

Julius Iphofen to Mary B. Duvall, 18 Oct 1888 (19 Oct), J. M. Bramlett MG 1-561

- - - - - - - - - - - - -

IRVIN / IRWIN
(see also ERWIN)

1870 CENSUS

William I. Irvin 28, Josephine 19 (Ga), James 1, James A. EARLY 18 (Ga) 7-5-37

1880 CENSUS

J. Ervin 30, J.M. 11, Mary 4: see J.A. Early

1900 CENSUS

Charles W. Irwin 31 (Nov 1868-Oh/Oh/Oh-M 4)(School Teacher), Minnie V. 32 (Feb 1868-Neb/Germany/Do-M 4-0)(Boarding House): *Boarders and students:* Annie L. FOSTER 31 (Dec 1868-SC/SC/SC-M 3-2-2), Harty D. 15 (May 1885-Wash/SC/SC), Lois 5 (June 1894-Fla), Hallie FINCH 15 (Dec 1884), Marie FULTON 15 (Ap 1885), Gertrude MOREY 17 (May 1883-Iowa), Mildred DAVIS 15 (Feb 1885-Neb), John E. MARTIN 16 (May 1884-NC/Wisc/Wisc), Trudie ROGERS 17 (May 1883-Ala/Miss/Miss), Ambrose DORTCH 17 (Jan 1883), Katie RIKARD 18 (Feb 1882-La/La/La), Lucia HENSON 15 (Mar 1885-Fla/England/Fla), Mary PAVEY 17 (Jan 1883-Iowa/Canada/Ill), Leahbelle GREENWOOD 10 (May 1890-Ala), Thomas H. GREENWOOD 15 (Dec 1884-Ala), Nancy H. SMITH 41 (May 1859-NC/NC/NC-Wd 0), Harry A. STONER 17 (Ap 1883-Oh/Oh/Oh), Frank PAUL 23 (Ap 1877-Maine/Ver/NH), Brice J. BAUGH 20 (Mar 1880-Ark/Va/Miss), J. Harold MITCHELL 16 (May 1884-Oh/Oh/Oh), Amy ARCHER 20 (Jan 1880-Oh/Oh/Oh) 13-310A-385/399

MARRIAGES

James M. Irvin to Hester Odom, 13 May 1899 (21 May), G. W. Brewer MG, A. Purser W 2-412

William I. Irwin to Josephine Early, 23 July 1867 (same), J.H. Keith MG 1-#961

- - - - - - - - - - - - -

ISERNINGER
(see also ESMINGER)

1900 CENSUS

Joseph Iserninger 82 (Feb 1818-Pa/Germany/Do-Wd)(Retired Merchant), Ellen 48 (d)(Feb 1852-Wisc/Pa/Oh) 13-305A-287/297

- - - - - - - - - - - - -

IVENS / IVINS / IVINGS

1880 CENSUS

James Ivins 28, D. 28, Roby 1 11-42-337

M.S.R. Ivings 30: see John McClendon

MARRIAGE

Linnie Ivens or Evens to Thomas A. Alexander q.v.

- - - - - - - - - - - - -

IVES / IVIS

1860 CENSUS

William Ivis 85 (Va), Betsy 67 6-103-7-3

1870 CENSUS– None

1880 CENSUS

Billy Ives 19: see T. P. Cambron

MARRIAGES

Betsy Ann Ives to William Clarents q.v.

Caroline Ives to N. Coleston q.v.

George Ives to Polly Ann Stanly, 2 Feb 1851 (same), J. Wyott JP 1-#330

Martin Ives to Elizabeth Stanley, 22 Jan 1852 (no return) 1-#360

W.C. Ives to Cora Delozier, 18 Dec 1892, G.W. Brewer MG 4-49

- - - - - - - - - - - - -

IVESTER / IVINSTER / IVUSTER / IVERSTER / IVESTON

1900 CENSUS

Bulah Ivester 17: see John Neal

Jesse W. Iverster 26 (Oct 1873-M 4)(Coal Miner), Sarah 32 (Ap 1868-Ga/Ga/Ga-M 4-2-2), Henry W. 3 (Nov 1896), Mira SMALL 15 (gd)(Nov 1884) 13-302B-228/238

Park Ivester 17: see Robert J. Kilouge [Killough]

MARRIAGES

Anna Ivinster to Eli Graham q.v.

Carie Ivester to Hezekiah Gennoe q.v.

J.A. Iveston to Carrie Hughes, 25 June 1892, R.S. Mason JP 4-39

Jennie Ivuster to L. P. Turner q.v.

Jesse Ivester to Sallie Thurman, 1 Jan 1896, A.P. Hayes JP 4-89

- - - - - - - - - - - - -

IVEY / IVY

1900 CENSUS

Edward H. Ivey 24 (Sep 1875-M 2), Emma 19 (Mar 1881-M 2-2-2), William 3 (Ap 1897), Bridget 8/12 (Nov 1899) 8-316B-123/127

John F. Ivy 44 (Sep 1855-M 26), Linda 48 (Unk 1857-M 26-10-9), Gertie 17 (Oct 1882), James 13 (Sep 1886), Elijah 10 (Feb 1890), Lillie M. 8 (May 1896), Bertha E. 5 (July 1894) 15-274B-120

MARRIAGES

E.H. Ivey to Emma Ridley, 2 Dec 1898 (3 Dec), W.L. Lillard JP, Pat Smith W 2-353

Eliza M. Ivey to J. W. Simpson q.v.

- - - - - - - - - - - - -

IVIL

MARRIAGE

James A. Ivil (31, Campbell Co) to Frances E. Smith (22), 4 Jan 1883, James Johnson JP, W.M. Wilson & James Brock W 4-12(113)

- - - - - - - - - - - - -

J -----?------ [ink blob]

1900 CENSUS

Wairick R. J---?--- 39 (Jan 1861-Ky/Ky/Ky) 8-284B-316/318 (B)

- - - - - - - - - - - - -

JACKSON

1860 CENSUS

George W. Jackson 21, Ruth 22, Nancy F. 4 8-12-81

1870 CENSUS– None

1880 CENSUS

James Jackson 25, Rebecca 25, Julus 5, Sarah A. 3, Jery A. 1, James F. 4/12 5-3-18 (B)

1900 CENSUS

Henry Jackson 65 (Unk 1835-Ga/Ga/Ga-M 14), Charity 63 (Unk 1837-Ga/Ga/Ga-M 14-0), Ella 11 (gd)(Unk 1888-Ala/Ala/Ala), Elussion 8 (gs)(Unk 1892-Ga), Mary WINNIS 45 (si)(Mar 1865-NC/NC/NC-Wd 0) 15-273B-107 (B)

James Jackson 38 (Feb 1862-T/SC/SC-M 13)(Coal Miner), Sam McDERMIT 22 (boarder)(May 1878), Steve BRYANT 33 (boarder)(Oct 1866-Ala/Ala/Ala) 8-318B-169/175 (B)

James Jackson 33 (Mar 1867-T/Va/T-M 7)(Coal Miner), Hester 18 (Oct 1881-M 7-2-2), Susie 15 (Dec 1884), Buford 5 (Sep 1894), Hubbard S. 10 (ward)(Dec 1889), Henry MAYS 23 (May 1877-Ga/Ga/Ga-M 1) (Coke Puller) 10-256A-115/119 (B)

James H. Jackson 60 (Dec 1839-NC/NC/NC-M 18), Texas C. 39 (Mar 1861-T/NC/T-M 18-9-8), Thomas W. 16 (Aug 1883), Hebron 15 (Mar 1885), Carie 13 (May 1887), Naomie 12 (May 1888), Andrew 11 (May 1889), Marlow 8 (Oct 1891), Etter 6 (Nov 1893), Innur 2 (June 1897), Noah SHOEMAKER 60 (fl)(Mar 1840-NC/NC/NC-M 43) 2-197A-108/113

Joseph Jackson 50 (June 1849-M 19), Mary E. 35 (Mar 1865-T/Miss/T-M 19-8-5), Aney 15 (Oct 1884), David 13 (Mar 1887), Meedy 11 (Aug 1888), Edy 9 (Oct 1890) 10-254A-79 (B)

Reuben Jackson 37: see John Swan

Waldo Jackson 19 (Aug 1880-M 7), Nora 22 (Mar 1878-T/Ga/Va-M 7-2-2), Clarence 5 (Dec 1894), Walter A. 5/12 (Jan 1900) 8-311A-9/10 (B)

Warren Jackson 25: see Hattie Henderson (B)

MARRIAGES

Annie Jackson to Haas Swafford q.v.

D.B. Jackson to Lulu Stegall, 22 Sep 1900 ("license returned not executed"), G.W. Goodrich W 3-225

Elizabeth Jackson to Linsey Jackson q.v.

Florena Jackson to James Robinson q.v.

H.H. Jackson to Mary Travis, 22 Dec 1885 (24 Dec), J.R. Crawford JP 1-487

Henry Jackson to Nellie Gillespie, 11 Sep 1890, W.R. Clack JP 4-17

Ida Jackson to James McGee q.v.

James Jackson to Elizabeth Milican, 28 June 1851 (29 June), A.G. Wright JP 1-#344

Lewis Jackson to Julia C. Hail, 15 May 1889 (16 May), S. W. Wyat MG 1-574

Linsey Jackson to Elizabeth Jackson, 3 July 1889 (4 July), D.H. Hindman JP, 1-581

Martha Jackson to Rafe Williams q.v.

Miles Jackson to Lillian Fletcher, 29 Dec 1892, E. Provine MG 4-52

- - - - - - - - - - - - -

JAKES

1900 CENSUS

Robert Jakes 24 (May 1876-M 4), Mary 36 (Oct 1863-M 4-6-5), Ella B. 2 (June 1897), John N. MANESS 15 (ss) (Oct 1884)(Coal Miner), Charles 11 (ss)(Oct 1888) (Coal Miner), Willie 9 (ss)(July 1890), Walter 6 (ss) (Oct 1893) 8-279B-222/224

- - - - - - - - - - - - -

JAMES

1860 CENSUS

Columbus James 8: see John W. Pritchett

Henry James 16: see John Wyatt

Hugh L.W. James 12: see George W. Ault

John James 47 (Tiner), Penelope 16, Charles 14, Oliva 11, Elizbeth 9, Caroline 7, Tennessee 5 6-111-762

Nelly James 23, Sarah 2, Mary F. 1/12: see John Coxey

William G. James 10: see Thomas McPherson

1870 CENSUS

John James 59, Penelope 24, Olivia 20, Caroline 16, Tennessee 13 6-9-56

1880 CENSUS

Horris [Horace] James 50, William C. 14, Charles W. 12, Mary A. 9 5-7-63

John James 70 (Tanner), Penelope 36 (d), Orlina 31 (d), Elizabeth 29 (d), Tennessee 25 (d), Rachel E. 9 (gd) 6-22-3

Margaret James* 60 (m), Mary A. GOTHARD 39 ("living with mother"), John F. 18, Susan I. 15, Isaac N. 2 10-30-228/237 & 238 [* see also JONES]

1900 CENSUS

Charles James 34 (Oct 1865-M 10), Darthula 36 (Feb 1864-M 10-4-4), Ethel 10 (Nov 1889), Mathew 8 (July 1891), Thopis 3 (July 1896), Marchie 2 (June 1897) 8-285B-323/345

James T. James 36 (Aug 1863-M 13), Eliza 35 (Mar 1865-M 13-7-3), Caswell 12 (Mar 1888), Joseph W. 11 (Ap 1889), Arthur M. 5 (July 1894) 13-299A-172/176

Margaret James 86 (Unk 1814-Wd 4-3), Peter 23 (s)(Unk 1877) 8-286B-369/371 [see also JONES]

Olivia James 50: see Callie Howard

Samuel James 36 (Nov 1863-M 1), Sarah 35 (Unk 1865-M 1-6-3), Florence 15 (Sep 1884), Sally 13 (Sep 1886), Nancy 10 (Ap 1890), Mary 7 (Sep 1892), Willie 5 (July 1894) 8-287A-382/384

Sarah James 36 (May 1864-M ?-6-3)(Washwoman), Lizzie SMITH 17 (d)(Feb 1883), Maggie 12 (d)(July 1887), Ida 10 (d)(Feb 1890) 8-312A-27/29

MARRIAGES

C. L. James to James A. Howard q.v.

Charley James to D.A. Morgan, 26 Oct 1889 (27 Oct), S.H. Hilliard MG 1-581

Elizabeth James to Isaac Bomwell q.v.

Elvira James to John Green q.v.

H.W. James to L.C. Wilson, 3 Oct 1887 (same), F.J. Paine JP 1-529

Nellie James to L. M. Heiskell q.v.
Rosa James to Wallace Waller q.v.
Tennie D. James to E. F. Waterhouse q.v.
Tommie James to Lula McPherson, 12 Mar 1897 (14 Mar), W.A. Green JP, Pete Jones W 2-125

- - - - - - - - - - - - -

JAMISON / JEMESON

1880 CENSUS
Benjamin Jemeson 22, Catharine 20 2-32-258
MARRIAGE
Thomas Jamison to Sophia Blanket, 12 July 1887 (13 July), H.R. Glenn ?? 1-583

- - - - - - - - - - - - -

JANOW– see GENOE

- - - - - - - - - - - - -

JANSON

1900 CENSUS
Jem Janson (no dates): Non-resident in District 12

- - - - - - - - - - - - -

JAQUISH / JACQUISH / JAQUESS / JOCQUES

MARRIAGES
Catharine Jocques to John Barnes q.v.
Emely Jacquish to Thomas H. Woods q.v.
John H. Jaques to Elizabeth Witt, 30 Jan 1886 (31 Jan), C. Morgan JP 1-520
Katie Jacques to James Miller q.v.
Mary Ann Jaquish to Robert Bell q.v.
Mattie Jaquish to George Fridds q.v.
Nannie Jacquish to Robert Walker q.v.
Roby Jacquish to Mary Manis, 8 Aug 1896 (9 Aug), B.S. Hale MG, B. Suttles [signed by X] W 2-54

- - - - - - - - - - - - -

JARVIS

1880 CENSUS
John Jarvis 45, Emma 39, G.E. 14 (d), N. 13 (d), A.E. 11 (s), Young 9, Ada 6 3-22-176

- - - - - - - - - - - - -

JEFFERS

1900 CENSUS
John F. Jeffers 51 (Jan 1849-NC/NC/NC-M 12)(Coal Miner), Mahala 45 (Oct 1854-T/NC/NC-M 12-3-3), Charles W. 16 (Oct 1883)(Coal Miner), Edmond M. 13 (June 1886)(Coal Miner), Nora M. 11 (Ap 1889), Decatur J. 9 (Aug 1890), Della B. 7 (Aug 1892) 13-309B-378/392
MARRIAGE
Eliza Jane Jeffers to Zachariah Lewis q.v.

- - - - - - - - - - - - -

JEFFERSON

1900 CENSUS
Thomas Jefferson 57 (Mar 1831-Md/Unk-M 40)(Carpenter), Harrit 60 (Jan 1830-SC/Va/Va-M 40-11-7), Tiblin N. 15 (Sep 1884), Celstie BRIDGMAN 26 (d)(June 1873-M 2-3-2), Leary T. 7 (gd)(Ap 1893), Ray L. 2 (gd)(Dec 1897), Alford DAY 24 (sl)(Jan 1876-M 2), Ollie 16 (d)(Mar 1884-T/Md/SC-M 2-2-2), Lula 2 (gd) (July 1897), Willard 1 (gs)(Feb 1899) 7-264B-271/276 (B)
MARRIAGES
Arthur Jefferson to Minnie Gillespie, 25 Aug 1888 (26 Aug), S. Carter MG 1-572
Frank Jefferson to Mahala Waldon, 11 Mar 1888 (same), Calvin Morgan JP 1-548
Maggie Jefferson to Turner Pullin(?) q.v.
Nanny Jefferson to Alfred Day q.v.
Reuben Jefferson to Lena Watkins, 2 May 1896 (21 May), J.B. Phillips MG, R.J. Killough W, Rufus Jefferson Bm 2-20
Will Jefferson to Ida Merriott, 2 May 1896 (same), J.B. Phillips MG, Rube Jefferson W 2-49

- - - - - - - - - - - - -

JEFFREYS

MARRIAGES
Minnie Jeffreys to Elijah Thurman q.v.
Salina Jeffreys to Dock Bridgon(?) q.v.

- - - - - - - - - - - - -

JENKINS

1860 CENSUS
Edmond Jenkins 60 (Va), Anna 35, Frances 14, Benjamin 13, Catharine 9, Love A. 7, Elizabeth 5, James 4, Edmond 3, Louisa 1 1-92-629
1870 and 1880 CENSUS– None
1900 CENSUS
Edward L. Jenkins 48 (Jan 1852-M 21)(Stonemason), Josie 33 (Jan 1867-Ala/Ga/Ga-M 21-10-5), John E. 15 (July 1874), Lillie M. 11 (Jan 1889), Florence L. 5 (May 1895), Walter F. 2 (Jan 1898), Pink 6 (nw)(Aug 1883) 13-303B-253/263
Wm Jenknis 23: see Moses Grier
Wm Jenkins 19: see Louis Sharp
MARRIAGES
Bell Jenkins to Edley Gains or Gowains q.v.
L. V. Jenkins to Andy Smith q.v.
M. C. Jenkins to J. W. Ruth q.v.
S.M. Jenkins to Lizzie Cobbs, 14 Feb 1889 (same), J.P. Thompson JP 1-567
Sarah J. Jenkins to Joel Brown q.v.

- - - - - - - - - - - - -

JENNINGS

MARRIAGFS
J.C. Jennings to Emma Mealer, 7 Sep 1886 (8 Sep), M.C. Bruner MG 1-506

James A. Jennings to Alice V. Burnett, 9 Mar 1886 (same), M.C. Bruner MG 1-485
Lucinda Jennings to Jones Coleman q.v.

- - - - - - - - - - - - -

JESTER

1900 CENSUS
John B. Jester 51 (May 1849-SC/SC/SC-Wd), Luella J. 12 (May 1889), December 8 (Dec 1891), John F. 6 (Feb 1894) 14-218A-107/109 (B)

- - - - - - - - - - - - -

JEWELL / JEWEL

1860 CENSUS
John Jewel 50 (Ga), Martha J. 46 (Ky), Mary C. 20, James M. 18, John H. 15, Emly A. 13, Nancy E. 11, George H. 9, Thomas M. 7, Theodore W. 5, Rufus H. 3, Charles T. 1 10-28-187
1870 CENSUS
Edley A. Jewel 22, Mary A. 19, Caloy E. 4/12 10-2-10
James Jewell 28, Mary Ann 23, Charles T. 1, John H. 25, Louisa McDONALD 21 (Ala) 10-3-22
John Jewel 58, Martha Jane 56 (Ky), Nancy Jane 19, George W. 17, Thomas M. 15, Theodore W. 13, Rufus H. 11, Charles T. 9, Lonanzie LEA 16 8-16-110
1880 CENSUS
J.H. Jewell 36, L.F. 32, S.E. 8 (s), J.F. 5 (s) 8-3-27
J.M. Jewell 38 (Gristmiller), M.A. 34, C.T. 10 (s), Magneta 8 (d), U.?. 6 (d), R.E. 3 (s) 8-21-182
John Jewell 68, M.J. 65, T.W. 23 (s) 8-14-118
R.H. Jewell 23, N.A. 21, C.R. 1 (s), Betsy BALEW 70 (ml) 8-21-184
T.M. Jewell 27, C.T. 20 (b), N.J. CRAWFORD 31 (si), Mark CRAWFORD 61 (bl), E.M.J. 7/12 7-27-229
1900 CENSUS
Charley Jewell 36 (Mar 1864-T/NC/SC-M 16), Allice 39 (Aug 1860-M 16-6-6), Cleavlin G. 15 (Nov 1884), George W. 14 (Mar 1886), Vesty M. 12 (May 1888), Ethel M. 9 (Sep 1890), Creed T. 6 (Sep 1893), Albert E. 3 (Oct 1896) 7-265B-299/304
James Jewell 58 (Feb 1842-T/NC/SC-M 23)(Coal Miner), Mary 53 (Mar 1846-Ala/Ala/Ala-M 32-8-5), Maud 15 (Nov 1886) 10-261A-215/220
John H. Jewell 56 (May 1844-T/SC/NC-M 15)(Carpenter), Mary T. 35 (Ap 1865-M 15-5-5), Ryle W. 11 (June 1882), Emmy J. 9 (Jan 1891), Myrtle M. 6 (Jan 1893), Edney E. 3 (July 1896), Lea 8/12 (Sep 1899) 7-262A-229/234
Sody E. Jewell 28 (Nov 1871-M 8), Victory 30 (Mar 1870-Ky/T/T-M 9-2-2), William J. 7 (June 1892), Frances L. 2 (May 1898) 10-252B-56/56
Theodore W. Jewell 44: see James J. Abel
MARRIAGES
C.T. Jewell to Allice Boyd, 18 Dec 1883 (20 Dec), J.R. Crawford JP 1-473
C.T. Jewell Jr. to Rosa E. England, 12 Nov 1889 (same), S.H. Hilliard MG 1-588
E.A. Jewell to N.A. McDonald, 11 Jan 1870 (same), John H. Keith MG 1-#1137
Elizabeth Jewell to P. M. Purcer q.v.
Flora Jewell to Samuel M. Scott q.v.
Floyd Jewell to Nannie Ellis, 4 July 1894, R.S. Mason JP 4-68
J.H. Jewell to L.F. McDonald, 15 Feb 1871 (same), J.W. Williamson MG 1-#1186
J.H. Jewell to Mary T. McCallie, 9 Feb 1885 (same), John Howard MG 1-459
J.M. Jewell to Mary Ann McDonald, 14 Aug 1868 (same), C.T. McDonald JP 1-#1024
Mary Jewell to William B. Purcer q.v.
May Jewell or Jewett to Utaw Garrison q.v.
Nancy J. Jewell to Mark W. Crawford q.v.
Nannie Jewell to Eli Gosset q.v.
Nola Jewell to J. M. Killough q.v.
R.H. Jewell to N.A. Bolen, 4 Jan 1878 (6 Jan), J.R. Crawford JP 1-#1540
Virginia T. Jewell to W. H. Barnes q.v.
White Jewell to Jacob Barnes q.v.

- - - - - - - - - - - - -

JEWITT

1880 CENSUS
Charles Jewitt 49, Mary 40, Alice 20, John 18, Mary 13, Mariah POWEL 22 (Servant), Charles 1, Walter ANDREWS 27 (Laborer) 12-2-19
1900 CENSUS
Mary N. Jewett 61 (Sep 1837-Mass/Mass/Conn-Wd 3-2), Alas 40 (d)(Sep 1859-Minn/Mass/RI-S), Mary 32 (d) (May 1867-Minn) 12-179A-9/10

- - - - - - - - - - - - -

JINK

1900 CENSUS
Wm Jink 25: see Lee A. Kelly (B)

- - - - - - - - - - - - -

JOHENIGAN

MARRIAGE
J. P. Johenigan to Flora Johnson, 25 May 1894, J. W. C---?--- JP 4-67

- - - - - - - - - - - - -

JOHNS

1860 CENSUS
Andrew Johns 50 (Baptist Preacher), Catharin 50 (Va), Charles P. 17, Martha E. 11, McCampbell 9, Jane W. 8, George T. WITSON [WILSON?] 21, Nancy H. 19, Albert T. 7/12 3-64-441
1870 CENSUS
Mary C. Johns 28: see John A. Walker
William R. Johns 27, Elizabeth 33 8-17-117
1880 CENSUS
W.R. Johns 46, Betsey A. 55 (si) 8-8-70
1900 CENSUS
Matilda Johns 65 (Unk 1835-Ga/T/T-Wd 10-8), Allen 29 (s) (Unk 1871-D)(Coal Miner), Frank 24 (Unk 1876), George 10 (Unk 1890) 8-275A-133/133 (B)

Milton N. Johns 35 (Mar 1865-Miss/NC/NC-M 9), Cordelia 25 (Jan 1875-Ga/Ga/Ga-M 9-4-0), Thomas MITCHELL 12 (bl)(Nov 1887-T/Ga/Ga), Pearl 8 (sil)(May 1892) 8-275A-121/121 (B)

Nannie Johns 45: see James L. McCuiston

William P. Johns or Jones 24 (Ap 1876-Neb/T/T-M 2)(Coal Miner), Lula 23 (Oct 1876-M 2-1-1), James A. 8/12 (Sep 1899) 13-308A-348/361

MARRIAGES

Bertha Johns to James L. McCuiston q.v.

C.P.S. Johns to L.K. Clack, 16 Ap 1866 (17 Ap), J.B. McAllen MG 1-#896

Caroline Johns to John A. Walker q.v.

John Johns to Lucinda Bell, 1 Dec 1869 (2 Dec), Wm L. Humphrey JP 1-#1128

Mary A. Johns to Samuel Gass q.v.

Mary C. Johns to William Doutys q.v.

Minnie M. Johns to Oscar J. Green q.v.

Nancy Johns to G. W. Wilson q.v.

W.P. Johns to Linda Bowers, 28 Sep 1898 (bond only), W. M. Johns W 2-327

JOHNSON

1860 CENSUS

Edmund Johnson 42 (NC), Anna M. 32, Eliza A. 13, Phebe L. 12, John W. 10, Mary J. 8, Lewis M. 5, Sarah T. 2 1-94-639

James Johnson 42 (Clerk), Antinely(?) 14, William 7, Calvin 5, Barnet 3, Antinely P. JOHNSON 41, Sellers 21, John O. 19 1-91-621

James W. Johnson 21, Mary J. 24, Nancy 22, Samuel L. 1 8-13-91

John Johnson 61, Polly 57, Mahaly I. 21, Richard J. 19, Humphrey V. 17, Nicholson 14, Neoma E. 11 2-75-509

Mary Johnson 35, Meary J. 12, Benjamin F. 10 8-25-173

Mary A. Johnson 44, John T. 21, Asabel 17, Isabella W. 14, William 9, Permelia 7, Charles W. MOSS 40 (NY) (Trader) 8-22-149

Sidney Johnson 27, Henegar 5, Delvora 1: see Ander Trim

William B. Johnson 37, Martha G. 38, Catharine 11, George W. 9, James F. 5, Nancy E. 2, Susan E. 1, John A. BEAN 27, Emly F. 19, Elizabeth McFARLAND 82 (SC) 10-28-186

William J. Johnson 46, Sarah 47 (SC), Richard 17, Cyrus I. 11, Sarah L. 8, Rebecca M. 5 8-13-90

1870 CENSUS

Asabel Johnson 27, Susan C. 21 8-15-105

Edmond Johnson 55 (NC), Ann M. 39 (NC), John 18 (Ky), Lewis 13, Sarah 10, George 9, James 7, Martha 4, Jesse 2 1-15-100

James Johnson 51, Anna 41, Nettia 23, William 18, Calvin 16, Burnet 13, Sally SHORT 25, Mary 8, Margarette 6, David BELL 23 1-15-99

John O. Johnson 62 (NC), Rebecca 58, James L. 24, George W. 21, Mary D. 17, Sarah L. 14, Delilah ROGERS 83 (Va) 8-6-37

Lott Johnson 36, Rose Ann 8, Clay 38, John E. 5, William B. 3, Riley S. 1, Milley 75, Aggie 17, Rolen McDONALD 30 (Va) 4-7-46 (B)

Margarette Johnson 30, Jarret F. 2: see James Pierce

Martha Johnson 58, Craven S. 27, Benjamin 21, Martha C. 18 3-11-80

Martha C. Johnson 47 (Va), George W. 19, James F. 15, Nancy E. 12, Susan E. 10, Annette P. 8, Martha I. 6 10-4-24

Mary Johnson 31 (B): see John Hoyal

Mary A. Johnson 55, Permelia C. 17 8-15-108

Pleasant Johnson 23, Adaline 18 1-18-117 (B)

Richard Johnson 53 (Tanner), Nancy J. 39, Atsa Jane 15, Elizabeth 14, Jesse 12, Mary 10, Jarves 9, Lempy 7, Richard L. 5, Martha 3, Henry 1, Sarah 4/12 2-14-103

1880 CENSUS

A. Johnson 37 (Merchant), Catharine 31, Mintie 9 (d), Everet(?) 6, Etta 4, Delta 2, Dilia FLEMING(?) 8 (ne), Jinwey 7 (nw) 8-2-18

George Johnson 26, Lena 25 8-1-5 (B)

George W. Johnson 29, Mary 21, S.A. 5/12, Dany(?) LEUTY 23 (bl), M.P. JOHNSON 40 (c) 3-24-193

Harvey Johnson 52, Mary 53, James 24, Josephine 26, Pasala(?) 22 (d), E. 20 (d), Margarita 18, Wm 15, T. 12 (s) 4-11-85 [Harvey married Mary Ann Parsley on 31 Dec 1852 in Roane Co]

J.O. Johnson 72, Rebica 68 (w), M.D. CORVIN 26 ("living in family"), S.A. 4 (d), Sam GASS 17 (gs), N.L. HOGE 8 (boarder) 8-15-127

Jack Johnson 16, Leah DAY (B) 20 6-14-133/135

James Johnson 62, Annie 50 (w), Barnet 28 (s) 1-15-123

Jane Johnson 28, Willie J. 4, Mary E. 1 (B): see James W. Gillespie

L. M. Johnson 28 3-24-190

M. P. Johnson 40: see George W. Johnson

Martha G. Johnson 58, James F. 25 (s), Susan E. 20 (d), Aminta P. 18, Martha J. 15, Willie U. WHEELER 10 (gs) 10-27-206/212

Robert Johnson 16 (B): see William Roddy

S.A. Johnson 52, Sarah 35 (w), N.J. 12 (d), J.T. 10 (s), W.R. 8 (s), S.A. 5 (d), J.H. 3 (s), E.C. 1 (d) 3-16-127

W.A. Johnson 30, H.S. 24 (w), Virginia 2, N.B. 1 (s), William FLEMINGS 6 (nw), Melia FLEMINGS 9 (ne) 8-4-31

1900 CENSUS

Alexander Johnson 33 (Aug 1866-T/Va/T-M 11)(Brickmason), Mary E. 29 (Ap 1871-Ala/Ala/Ala-M 11-6-3), Isaac 8 (Ap 1892), Robert 2 (May 1898), John 3/12 (Feb 1900) 10-325B-121/125 (B)

Anay Johnson 71: see William R. Clack

Arne Johnson 36 (May 1864-Ga/Ky/Ga-M 11), Laura 32 (Mar 1868-Ga/Ga/Ga-M 11-7-6), Mary 10 (Oct 1889-Ga), Walter 9 (Nov 1891-Ga), Frank 8 (May 1892-Ga), Eliza A. 6 (Aug 1893), Eli 5 (May 1895), Len 5 (May 1895) 8-317A-139/144 (B)

Asahel Johnson 57 (Ap 1843-M 30)(Hardware Merchant), Susan C. 51 (Aug 1848-M 30-5-4), Della 22 (Oct 1877) 8-317B-151/156

Charles Johnson 32, Alice 22: see Sarah Trusly

Charles E. Johnson 44 (Jan 1856-Mich/Pa/NY), Sarah C. 67 (m)(Dec 1832-NY/NY/NY-Wd 3-1) 13-299B-176/181

Crocket Johnson 29: see Elbert Hamilton

Dan Johnson 19: see Philip Henry (B)

Elizabeth Johnson 36, Lillie 16, Florence 10, Della 8, Fred 7, Jesse 5, Bulah 3: see Albert Hornsby (B)

Emmett P. Johnson 26 (Aug 1873-M 7)(Hardware Merchant), Jessie 25 (May 1875-M 7-2-2), Imogene E. 5 (Sep 1894), Harry C. 1 (Mar 1899), Mary JOHNSON 60 (c)(June 1839) 8-313A-44/47

George Johnson 24: see Hattie Henderson (B)

George Johnson 49 (Dec 1850-T/T/Va-M 22), Marry E. 47 (Mar 1852-M 22-6-5), Stanten I.(?) 20 (Dec 1879), Frank 16 (Feb 1884), Ona 13 (Sep 1886), Mary 10 (Aug 1889), Paulean 5 (Feb 1895) 10-253A-62

George W. Johnson 40 (Unk 1860-M 18), Cornelia 33 (Unk 1867-M 18-7-4), Edward 17 (Jan 1883), Jennie 9 (Oct 1890), Cyrus 5 (Oct 1894), Lena 3 (Mar 1897) 15-270B-46/46

Henry Johnson 26: see Oscar H. Hill

Hurman Johnson 39 (Dec 1860-Ky/Ky/Germany-M 15) (Coal Miner), Maggie 40 (Mar 1860-T/Ga/T-M 15-8-5), Stella 12 (Feb 1888), Marion 7 (June 1892), Jennie 5 (Jan 1895), Terressa 3 (Jan 1897), Henry 11/12 (June 1899) 8-280B-237/239

James Johnson 60, Elmira 40: see Bertie Wasson (B)

James A. Johnson 49 (Oct 1850-T/T/Va-M 14), Sarah V. 50 (Unk 1850-M 14-1-1), Auther 14 (s)(Jan 1886), Lillie E. 11 (d)(Ap 1887) 3-211A-196/214

James F. Johnson 44 (Jan 1856-M 14), Montie 34 (Jan 1866-M 14-6-5), Lillie 12 (Jan 1888), Irene 10 (June 1889), Henry G. 9 (Oct 1890), James C. 7 (Feb 1893), Gladys R. 5 (Nov 1894), Jessie ELDRIDGE 28 (sil) (Ap 1872) 10-325B-117/121

James H. Johnson 35 (May 1865-M 8)(House Carpenter), Lillie 23 (Jan 1877-M 8-4-3), Minnie 7 (Mar 1892), Olie 4 (Sep 1895), Isie 2 (May 1898) 10-326B-139/146

John Johnson 40 (Unk 1860-Ga/Ga/Ga-Wd), Arthur 13 (s) (Ap 1889), Sallie LOVE 53 (ml)(Unk 1847-Ga/Ga/Ga-Wd 2-0) 8-282B-281/283 (B)

Joseph Johnson 23: see William T. Barger

Margaret Johnson 56: see William A. Jordan

Marshall Johnson 27 (Mar 1873-Ky/Ky/Ky)(Barber) 8-315B-101/105 (B)

Mary L. Johnson 16: see Frank J. Grice

Mose Johnson 20: see Lon Weathington (B)

Nancy Johnson 70: see Andy Carter

Newton Johnson 38 (Aug 1861-M 18), Emity 39 (Nov 1860-M 18-7-7), Lida 17 (Dec 1882), Frank 15 (Nov 1884)(Coal Miner), Walter 12 (July 1887)(Coal Miner), James 9 (Mar 1891), Mattie 7 (Dec 1892), Cordelia 4 (Aug 1895), Arthur 1 (Aug 1898) 8-278A-193/195

Perry Johnson 34 (May 1866-Va/WVa/WVa-M 8), Mattie 23 (Mar 1877-T/Ky/T-M 8-2-2), Burnice A. 7 (Feb 1893), Jesse 4 (Mar 1896) 8-311A-7/7

Robert Johnson 27 (May 1873-M 6)(RR Laborer), Nannie 24 (Dec 1875-M 6-5-5), Nettie E. 7 (Aug 1892), Robbie J. 6 (July 1893), Oliver 5 (Mar 1875), Louie 3 (Dec 1896), Viola 1 (Feb 1899) 14-219A-127/10 (B)

Vessa Johnson 25, Pearl 5: see Lutitia McDowel

William Johnson 28 (Oct 1871-Ga/Ga/Ga-M 13)(Coke Puller), Sallie 30 (Oct 1869-Ga/Ga/Ga-M 13-3-3), George 11 (July 1888-Ga), James RUSSELL 27 (boarder) (May 1873-Ga/Ga/Ga)(Coke Puller) 10-256B-123/127 (B)

William A. Johnson 49 (Jan 1851-M 24), Hattie 47 (June 1852-T/Va/Va-M 24-3-3), Jennie 32 (d)(Oct 1867), Nannie 31 (d)(Feb 1869), May 16 (d)(May 1884) 8-316-118/122

MARRIAGES

A. M. Johnson to James S. Betts q.v.

Abbie Johnson to Joseph Johnson q.v.

Adaline Johnson to William Marsh q.v.

Alexander Johnson to Ellen Powers, 26 July 1888 (same), L.M. Morris MG 1-551

Alice Johnson to Samuel Hensley q.v.

Alsia Jane Johnson to William Walker q.v.

Amber Johnson to Serephenae Moore, 9 Nov 1870 (10 Nov), Asa Newport MG 1-#1173

Anna Johnson to James Condrae q.v.

Asahel Johnson to S.C. Abel, 4 Jan 1870 (5 Jan), J.H. Keith MG 1-#1135

B. Johnson to Ziphora Bell, 24 Dec 1863 (same), A.P. Early MG 1-#815

Ben Johnson to Nancy Housley, 19 Ap 1896 (same), C.H. Pettis PC, L. Blom W 2-15

C. C. Johnson to S. J. Wheeler q.v.

C.H. Johnson to Alice Trusley, 23 Dec 1896 (same), G.W. Coleman MG 2-93

Crawford Johnson to Nettie Murphy, 14 June 1890 (same), S.W. Mych MG 1-601

D. Johnson– see James A. Rogers

Ed Johnson to Minerva Pope, 9 Mar 1894, A.P. Hayes JP 4-74

Edna Johnson to Thomas J. Smith q.v.

Edward Johnson to Matilda Osby, 30 June 1887 (same), Byrd Terry ?? 1-583

Eliza Johnson to James Britt q.v.

Ellen Johnson to John S. Monsey q.v.

Emma Johnson to Jefferson Wright q.v.

Emma E. Johnson to C. C. Cook q.v.

Emmet P. Johnson to Jossie May Caldwell, 6 Dec 1893, R.A. Owen MG 4-61

Flora Johnson to J. P. Johenigan q.v.

Francis Johnson to Mary Fugate, 25 Nov 1885 (24 Nov) [sic], T.H. McPherson JP 1-516

Francis M. Johnson (20, Polk Co) to Emma Dyer (21, Walker Co, Ga), 22 Dec 1881, J.W. Cunnyngham MG, W.E. Craword & J.F. Cole W 4-5(49)

G.W. Johnson to Mary E. Leuty, 22 May 1878 (same), R.E. Smith MG 1-#1569

George Johnson to Margaret Hughes, 5 Mar 1887 (same), W.S. Hale MG 1-522

Henry Johnson to Cenie(?) Clack, 10 Nov 1899 (same), J.W. Williamson MG 3-68

Ida Johnson to John A. Stephens q.v.

Ida Johnson to Morgan Dalton q.v.

Issabella M. Johnson to William P. McGilla q.v.

J.F. Johnson to Anny E. Brady, 2 Aug 1873 (3 Aug), James Johnson JP 1-#1290

James Johnson to Amy Clack, 2 Sep 1864 (15 Sep), Asa Newport MG 1-#862

James Johnson to Lillie Birchfield, 25 June 1891, M.C. Bruner MG 4-27

James Johnson to Louela Gaines, 29 Aug 1891, R.S. Mason JP 4-33

Jane Johnson to Hugh McCaleb q.v.

Janey or Josey Johnson to James McDonald q.v.

Janis Johnson to Thomas Frazier q.v.
Jessie Johnson to Jennie Brock or Brick, 13 July 1887 (same), C. Morgan JP 1-529
John Johnson to Sydney Trim, 21 Dec 1858 (same), John B. Murphy JP 1-#676
John Johnson to Annie Love, 12 Nov 1887 (same), G.D. Collins ?? 1-535
John Johnson to Lizza Yarnell, 27 Feb 1893, J.B. Phillips MG 4-54
John W. Johnson to Margaret J. Louder, 26 May 1871 (same), James Johnson JP 1-#1198
Joseph Johnson to Abbie Johnson, 9 Nov 1899 (11 Nov), L.L. Barton JP, H.L. Hawkins W 3-67
Joseph C. Johnson to Loduskia Barger, 23 June 1900 (same), W.R. Grimsley MG, J.R. Barger W 3-169
Katie Johnson to R. H. Parks q.v.
Kittie Johnson to S. L. Paul q.v.
Lottie M. Johnson to Henry Uster q.v.
Louisa Johnson to William Thompson q.v.
Lucy Johnson to William Wills q.v.
M. H. Johnson to W. H. Manis q.v.
Maggie Johnson to J. F. Grice q.v.
Malia Johnson to A. W. Walker q.v.
Margaret Johnson to W. L. Wade q.v.
Martha Johnson to Jimmie(?) Small q.v.
Mary Johnson (Mrs.) to John Hodge q.v.
Mary Johnson to Charley Hoyal q.v.
Mary Johnson to William Cowan q.v.
Mary Jane Johnson to John W. Stout q.v.
Melton Johnson to Kitty Houston, 18 Sep 1886 (19 Sep), W.S. Hale MG 1-509
Milton Johnson to Delia Mitchell, 16 Aug 1890 (17 Aug), J.W. Wright MG 1-604
Minnie B. Johnson to John S. Hardin q.v.
Moody Johnson to J. M. Killough q.v.
N.B. Johnson to Lucy McPherson, 10 Jan 1887 (11 Jan), S.S. Hale MG 1-516
Nancy Johnson to W. J. Stovall q.v.
Nancy J. Johnson to J. F. Grigsby q.v.
Nannie Johnson to John Russell q.v.
Nannie Johnson to William D. Flemming q.v.
Nellie Johnson to Jordan Cargyle q.v.
Nelly Johnson to James Roddy q.v.
P. C. Johnson to W. T. Broyles q.v.
Percival Johnson to Eva Hanson, 31 Aug 1885 (4 Sep), M.C. Bruner MG 1-517
Perry Johnson to Mattie Brooks, 19 Dec 1889 (same), W.S. Cagle ?? 1-595
Richard T. Johnson to Susan T. Jones, 12 Sep 1865 (same), "Solemnized" (no name) 1-#850
Robert Johnson to Nancy Beard, 1 Sep 1894, W.H. Perkinson JP 4-72
S. E. Johnson to R. T. Greer q.v.
Sam Johnson to Maggie Walker, 23 Oct 1880 (24 Oct), W.M. Morgan JP 1-294
Samuel Johnson to Jane Qualls, 5 Nov 1886 (same), A.J. Pritchett MG 1-573
Sarah Johnson to Thomas Carvin q.v.
Sarah E. Johnson to Joseph McAndrews q.v.
Sephrona F. Johnson to Jesse T. Gilliam q.v.
Steve Johnson to Mary Logan, 24 Sep 1883 (same), J.W. Williamson MG 1-465
Susannah Johnson to John R. Mynott q.v.
Tempy Johnson to Thomas Gilbert q.v.
Thomas Johnson to Eliza Dennis, 21 Jan 1888 (22 Jan), W. R. Grimsley MG 1-544
Viola Johnson to Andrew F. Griffith q.v.
W.H. Johnson to Nancy E. Hurst, 3 Feb 1873 (5 Feb), J.P. Roddy M 1-#1275
William Johnson to Hallie Thomison, 21 Dec 1876 (same), A.P. Early M 1-#1478
Zippora Johnson to John Milton q.v.

- - - - - - - - - - - - -

JOLLY / JOLLEY

1860 CENSUS

Alexander Jolly 28 (Miller), Nancy A. 29, Henry R. 7, Theias(?) 6, Susan E. 4, James W. 1 1-94-637 [Alexander married Nancy A. Fuller on 15 Jan 1852 in Roane County]
Andrew J. Jolly 30, Nancy 23, Sarah 6, Martha 1, Andrew J. JOLLY 23 3-67-461 [Andrew married Nancy Clark on 8 Mar 1853 in Roane County]
James W. Jolly 34, Martha 34, Lucinda 15, Granville 12, Isaac 10, Samuel 7, James 5, William 2 3-66-451
John Jolly 50, Liddia 54, William F. 21, Nancy J. 10, Sarah 18, Caroline 15 3-54-366
William Jolly 57, Nancy 57, Sarena 21, William 16, Savannah 1 4-52-356

1870 CENSUS

Andrew J. Jolly 40 (Miller), Nancy 33, Sarah F. 16, Martha R. 11, Polly A. 8, Harriette 4, William J. 2 4-15-97
Emma Jolly 8 (B): see Lucinda Gillespie
Isaac Jolly 27: see James Detherage
Nancy A. Jolly 38 (Ill), Matthias 16, Henry 17, Susan 14, James 11, Rebecca 9, John 6 2-9-58
William Jolly 68, Elizabeth 68 (SC), Savannah 11 4-6-34

1880 CENSUS

Andrew J. Jolly 50, Nancy 43, Harriet 15, William 11, Samuel 8, John 3, Leander FOSTER 23 (sl)(NY), Martha 21 (d) 12-1-1
Angeline Jolly 46, James 21, Rebecca 19 (Cook), Rhoda 13 2-30-244
Henry Jolly 26, Margaret 24, Lee 5, Ida 3, Delia 2 2-36-294
Isaac Jolley 40, S.T. 22 (w), I.B. 3 (d), W.P. 1 (s), E. BURDETT 35 9-30-260
James Jolly 14 (B): see Samuel Gillespie
Rebecca Jolley 20: see William Tarwater

1900 CENSUS

Andrew J. Jolly 70 (Feb 1830-M 49), Nancy 64 (Ap 1836-M 29-7-7), Molley 35 (Mar 1865), John 23 (June 1876) 12-180A-38/41
Henry T. Jolley 47 (Mar 1853-M 25), Peggie A. 50 (Feb 1850-M 25-8-8), Delia 22 (Sep 1877), James W. 16 (Oct 1883), Grover C. 15 (Feb 1885), Thomas A.H. 12 (Feb 1888), Lucie 10 (Jan 1890), Benton M. 7 (Sep 1892) 2-194B-70/72
James Jolly 30: see Emma Gillespie (B)
Jane Jolly 26, Kate 11/12: see Ellen Peak (B)
Robert L. Jolley 24 (Nov 1876-M 6), Minnie B. 19 (Ap 1881-M 6-2-1), Charles 5 (May 1895) 2-194B-71/73
Sam Jolly 25 (July 1874-M 2), Hattie 18 (July 1881-M 2-1-0) 12-180A-37/40
William P. Jolley 21 (May 1878-M 0), Angie C. 23 (Aug 1877-M 0-0) 2-192B-27/28

Wilum J. Jolley 31 (July 1868-M 1), Molley 20 (Mar 1880-M 1-0) 12-181B-66/69

MARRIAGES

Hattie Jolley to T. E. Gibson q.v.

Henry Jolly to Peggy Ann Miller, 15 Jan 1874 (same), J.J. Ingle JP 1-#1325

Ida Jolly to Charles Hicks q.v.

Isaac Jolly to Susan Sharp, 3 Mar 1872 (same), W.R. Henry JP 1-#1234

J. J. Jolley to S. E. Shuman or Sherman, 8 June 1889 (9 June), W.R. Clack JP 1-579

James Jolly to Jane Peak, 30 May 1896 (same), G.W. Brewer MG, Oliver Strickland [signed by X] W 2-23

Lee Jolly to Minnie Keylon, 5 May 1894, J.M. Hinds MG 4-90

Lucinda C. Jolly to Lewis J. Davis q.v.

Lyda Jolly to John Boofer q.v.

Martha Jolly to Leander Foster q.v.

Nancy Jolly to Charly Atwood q.v.

Perry Jolly to Angy Bell, 13 Aug 1899, A.M. Broyles JP 4-101

Rebecca Jolly to Alferd Derrick q.v.

Rebecca Jolly to Samuel Travis q.v.

Rosanna Jolly to C. C. Wilkey q.v.

S. A. Jolly to A. L. McClendon q.v.

Sam Jolly to Lottie Reed, 15 Jan 1899, no MG or JP 4-95

Sarah B. Jolly to John Foust q.v.

Sarah F. Jolly to Peter D. Mitchell q.v.

Serena Jolly to G. W. Giddeons q.v.

Susan Jolly to G. W. Prater q.v.

Thyas Jolly to Nancy J. Green, 1 Jan 1873 (same), Allen L. King MG 1-#1268

W.J. Jolly to Rena Loy, 29 Dec 1892, W.T. West MG 4-49

W.J. Jolly to Mollie Gibson, 1 Jan 1899, W.T. West MG 4-105

William Jolly to Elizabeth Knox, 20 Sep 1864 (22 Sep), Jas Carson MG 1-#1080

- - - - - - - - - - - - -

JONES

1860 CENSUS

Margaret Jones* 36 (Va), Mary A. 23, Margaret 18 7-2-10 [*see also Margaret James, 1880 and 1900 census]

Sidney L. Jones 26, James N. 6, Sidney A. 2, Mary J. 11/12: see Nicholas Fine

1870 CENSUS

Columbus Jones 16: see Rebecca Cox

John Jones 68 (Ga), Ann 69 (NC), Mary Ann 15 1-1-3

Margarette Jones 52, Mary A. 33 (Va), Margarette F. 26 (Va), John F. 8, Susan I. 6, William H. 3, Samuel B. 6/12, Juliann 6/12 10-3-16 [see note above]

Thomas Jones 37 (Wheelwright), Malinda Jane 34, Mary Ann 15, Elizabeth C. 13, George W. 9, Charles T. 7, Angeline 4, Robert G. 3, Eliza Jane 3/12 1-1-4

William L. Jones 18: see Thomas H. McPherson

1880 CENSUS

Eliza Jones 42, Lulu 16, George 12: see Jere Wasson

James Jones 27, Elma 28, Elena 9 5-4-32

John Jones 77, Annie 80 4-7-51

John Jones 35 (Miner), Lucy 25, Robert 5, Jane 2, Henry 1/12 2-31-249

Joseph Jones 40 (Preacher), Rosa 20 (w), Elizabeth 6, Eliza 5, Martha 4 2-29-234 (B)

Mat Jones 23, M.H. 19 (w), Jacob 20 (b) 3-30-239 (Mu)

Susan Jones 28: see Jack Suddeth (B)

Taylor Jones 32, Lucy 22, William A. 1, Clemey K. 10/12 5-6-52

1900 CENSUS

Armitt P.(?) Jones 33 (Feb 1867-Wales/Do/Do-1868/32/Na-M 10)(Coal Miner), Mary A. 28 (Dec 1871-Ky/T/Tex-M 10-5-4), Eddie 9 (Ap 1891), Maggie M. 7 (Jan 1893), Cora H. 5 (Feb 1895), Marion 3 (May 1897), David S. 1 (Mar 1899) 10-327A-150/158

Charles Jones 25 (July 1874-T/T/Va-M 0)(Station Engineer), Cordelia 17 (Dec 1882-M 0-0), Amelia 62 (m) (Mar 1838-Va/Va/Va-Wd 7-6) 13-302B-230/240

Christopher Jones 65 (Feb 1835-Wales/Do/Do-1863/36/Na-M 39)(Saloon Keeper), Eliza 54 (Sep 1835-England/Do/Do-1863/36-M 39-4-3), Mary RIDER 39 (d)(Ap 1861-England-Wd 1-1), Ellen 16 (gd)(Sep 1883-Ohio/Va/Eng) 10-330B-221/234

Columbus C. Jones 54 (Unk 1836-M 10), Madina A. 43 (Nov 1846-M 10-6-5), William E. 11 (Nov 1888), James R. 9 (Sep 1890), Laura E. 6 (Sep 1893), Nicie M. 4 (Feb 1896), Spencer T. 2 (Feb 1898) 3-202A-44/47

Edward Jones 55 (Aug 1844-England/Do/Do-1868/32/Na-M 33)(Brickmason), Jane 55 (Ap 1845-Wales/Do/Do-M 33-8-6), Elizabeth 23 (July 1876-Pa), Jackson 20 (Aug 1879-Eng)(Brickmason), Alice 18 (Feb 1882-Eng), Agnes INSLEY 30 (d)(Mar 1870-Pa-M 9-3-3), Lottie 8 (gd)(Jan 1892-Ala), Willie 7 (gs)(Jan 1893-Ala), Bertha 5 (gd)(Dec 1894-Ala) 8-281A-250/252

Eli H. Jones 59 (June 1840-England/Do/Do-1865/35/Na-M 37)(Brickmason), Elizabeth 59 (June 1840-Eng/Do/Do-M 37-10-6), Richard H. 24 (Feb 1876-Pa) (Brickmason), Emily 19 (Jan 1881-Eng), Sarah E. 16 (Nov 1883-Eng) 8-281A-251/253

Eli H. Jones 32 (Nov 1867-England/Do/Wales-1868/31/Na-M 10)(Bricklayer), Alice 34 (July 1865-Scotland/Do/Do-M 10-4-4), Maggie M. 9 (Dec 1890), James M. 5 (Nov 1894), Millie J. 2 (Nov 1897), Lillie M. 6/12 (Dec 1899), Malinda 28 (si)(Ap 1872) 8-276A-154/155

Fannie Jones 49 (Ap 1851-SC/SC/SC-Wd 10-5), Floyd 19 (1881)(Day Laborer), Eugene 21 (1879)(Day Laborer), Jake HUGHES 23 (boarder)(Unk)(Day Laborer) 8-315A-89/92 (B)

George W. Jones 52 (May 1848-M 24), Manerva 42 (Feb 1858-T/Va/Va-M 24-8-8), Robert H. 23 (Nov 1876) (Mail Carrier), Cora H. 21 (Jan 1878), Mary A. 19 (Dec 1880), Sarah M. 15 (Oct 1884), William T. 14 (Feb 1886), Samuel M. 11 (Ap 1889), Edna B. 6 (Sep 1893), Luella G. 7/12 (Nov 1899) 14-215B-56/57

Harry Jones 17: see David A. Elrod (B)

James Jones 41 (Sep 1858-Eng/Do/Do-1882/17/Na-Wd) (Bricklayer), Charles H. 20 (Jan 1880-Eng/Do/Wales-1882/17)(Day Laborer), Edwin 18 (Dec 1881-Eng-1882/17), Elizabeth 12 (Jan 1888-Ala) 10-323A-66/70

James Jones 49 (July 1850-T/SC/T-M 25), Elvira 49 (Dec 1850-T/SC/T-M 25-3-0) 5-237B-184/184

James N. Jones 15: see James Cunningham

John Jones 25 (Jan 1875-Ga/Ga/Ga-M 1)(Sawmill Laborer), Nellie 18 (Ap 1882-M 1-0) 13-310B-390/404

John R. Jones 30: see Marquis Morrison

Joseph C. Jones 68 (Dec 1831-Ga/Ga/Ga-M ?), Rose 49 (Oct 1850-Ga/Ga/Ga-M ?-3-3), George R. 19 (Aug 1880)(Driver in Coal Mines), Ellen 14 (Oct 1885), William 13 (June 1886), Harris BRIGHT 23 (boarder) (July 1876)(Coal Miner), Pellum MONTGOMERY 26 (boarder)(Day Laborer) 10-331B-234/249 (B)

Matthew Jones 45 (June 1854-M 20), Melinda 34 (Unk-M 20-8-6), Arthur 18 (Oct 1881), Mattie 16 (July 1883), Annie 13 (Oct 1886), William 11 (Mar 1889), Clyde 9 (Oct 1890), Morgy 7 (Feb 1893) 10-328A-172/182 (B)

Mattie Jones 35 (Oct 1865-Ala/Ga/Ala-Wd 5-3)(Washwoman), Willis P. POWELL 15 (s)(Aug 1884-T/Va/Ala), Daniel POWELL 10 (Jan 1890), James JONES 6 (s) (Jan 1894); *Boarders:* Sanford CARTER 21 (Jan 1879), Walter BUCKNER 24 (1876), John STOVALL 20 (Unk), William M. WILKS 34 (Aug 1865-Ga/Ga/Ga), Birdie PEASSALL 17 (Unk) 8-316A-117/121 (B)

Melvin Jones 8: see Cate Guirver (B)

Nancy J. Jones 56: see George Gray (B)

Price Jones 15: see Mary Holmes

Roley Jones 40 (Feb 1869-M 15), Mary 31 (Mar 1879-Pa/Pa/Wales-M 15-5-5), James 9 (Ap 1881), Luther 17 (May 1883), John 13 (Oct 1886), Maggie A. 11 (May 1889), Flora 7 (Aug 1892), Cecial 4 (July 1895), Arlie 1 (July 1898) 5-236B-165

Speich Jones 20: see Louis P. Thatcher

William Jones 50 (Unk 1850-Ga/Ga/Ga-M 4), Mattie B. 22 (June 1877-M 4-1-0), Calvin 13 (Dec 1886) 8-287A-373/375 (B)

William H. Jones 33 (Jan 1867), Cora 17 (si)(May 1883), Ellen HENSLEY 20 (si)(Dec 1879-M 0-0) 1-260B-207/212

William L. Jones 35 (July 1864-T/T/Va-M 14)(Station Engineer), Addie 36 (July 1863-M 14-4-2), Mattie C. 14 (Dec1885), Kate 12 (July 1887) 13-302A-221/229

MARRIAGES

Agness Jones to W. J. Ansley(?) q.v.

Alice M. Jones to W. H. Spanier(?) q.v.

Allie Jones to Nannie Gwin, 2 Jan 1890 (same), J.W. Wright MG 1-582

Andy Jones to Mary Hutcheson, 14 Ap 1890 (same), C.M. Moore ?? 1-603

Andy Jones to Martha Powell, 18 May 1892, J.R. Hill MG 4-39

Armitt Jones to Mary A. Gray, 20 Mar 1890 (26 Mar), R.A. Bartlett MG 1-596

C.C. Jones to Mary E. Nelson, 7 July 1883 (8 July), T.H. McPherson JP 1-478

C.H. Jones to Delia Hale, 29 Nov 1899 (30 Nov), John P. Houston MG, W.L. Jones W 3-78

Columbus Jones to Dena Giles, 10 Oct 1886 (same), T.H. McPherson JP 1-517

Cora Jones to William Fillers q.v.

Crit Jones to William Reed q.v.

D.W. Jones to Alice Morgan, 16 Aug 1887 (same), M.C. Bruner MG 1-564

Dora Jones to John R. Shaddin q.v.

Easter Jones to Hinny(?) Humphreys q.v.

Elizabeth Jones to W. M. Varner q.v.

Ellen Jones to B. L. Hogue q.v.

Eriphomy Jones to G. W. Lowry q.v.

Evan Jones to Flora Lillins or Tellins, 30 Sep 1886 (same), A.W. Frazier JP 1-525

Hattie Jones to D. A. Elrod q.v.

Hattie Jones to Munroe Smith q.v.

Hesekiah Jones [or James] to Margaret T. Peace, 28 Jan 1871 (same), J.P. Peace MG 1-#1184

J.F. Jones to Adda McCroy, 23 Dec 1884 (24 Dec), W.S. Hale MG 1-490

Jack Jones to Laura Wyatt, 18 Sep 1900 (19 Sep), W.L. Lillard JP, G. Kiker W 3-220

James Jones to Ellen Cole, 4 Oct 1876 (5 Oct), A.J. Pritchett MG 1-#1466

James Jones to Tinie Howard, 9 Nov 1887 (10 Nov), J.W. Peace MG 1-586

Janie Jones to Hugh Dixon q.v.

L. E. Jones to C. A. Goodson q.v.

Laura Jones to William White q.v.

Lena Jones or Jenno to W. E. Parker q.v.

Leuthy Jones to L. H. Patten q.v.

Margaret Jones to James D. Allen q.v.

Margaret Jones to Luke Mosely q.v.

Martha C. Jones to Jones Hodges q.v.

Mary Jones to G. W. Dodson q.v.

Mary Jones to Peter Pharris q.v.

Mary A. Jones to R. W. Walker q.v.

Mary A. Jones to W. L. Rider q.v.

Mary A. Jones to William Reece q.v.

Mary or May Ellen Jones to James Hensley q.v.

Mat Jones to Malinda Ray, 7 Nov 1879 (no return) 1-291 (B)

Mattie Jones to Thomas Monday q.v.

Nancy Jones to Hugh McLarmore q.v.

Nancy Jones to Carril(?) Rankin q.v.

Nettie Jones to Jerry Greer q.v.

Oddie Jones to Robert Elsea q.v.

R. E. Jones to David Dupre q.v.

R. P. Jones to Jinna Inglesoe, 30 Dec 1861 (31 Dec), S. Phillips MG 1-#768

Roley Jones to Mary Avery, 13 Sep 1885 (13 Sep), J.M. Bramlett MG 1-510

Rolla Jones to Mattie Harrison, 20 Sep 1879 (21 Sep), John Howard MG 1-#1678

Roseanna Jones to Joseph Dodd q.v.

Ryan Jones to Fannie Billingsley, 18 Dec 1893, J.W. Williamson MG 4-64

Sam Jones or James or Janus to Sarah Smith, 3 Ap 1899 (4 Ap), M.D. Reed MG, Sam Smith [signed by X] & R.J. Killough W 2-399

Sarah E. Jones to John H. McGuire q.v.

Spencer Jones (21, Richmond, Va) to Mattie Brown (21, Loudon Co), 25 Nov 1881, M.L. Abbott JP, Mary K. Abbott W 4-6(53) (B)

Susan Jones to James Melton q.v.

Susan T. Jones to Richard T. Johnson q.v.

Tandy J. Jones to Martha J. Pierce, 15 Ap 1867 (16 Ap), J.M. Kelly MG 1-#948

Taylor Jones to Lucy Standifer, 30 Dec 1876 (same), A.J. Pritchett MG 1-#148

Tennessee Jones to Andrew Green q.v.

Thomas Jones to Jane Lemmons, 27 July 1853 (31 July), Elijah Brewer JP 1-#414

Thomas Jones to Cathie Conley, 15 Ap 1896 (same), A. Hickman MG, G.W. Hickman W 2-12

W. Jones to Vina Purcell, 23 Mar 1887 (same), S.W. Burnett ?? 1-518
W.F. Jones to Mary Nipper, 15 Oct 1898 (same), W.L. Lillard JP, P. Bottom W 2-332
William Jones to Mattie Bell Smith, 11 June 1896 (same), G.H. Pettis PC, J.W. Hudson W 2-30
William Jones to Vina Bess, 13 Dec 1896 (same), G.W. Brewer MG, Doc Geno W 2-89
Willie Jones to S. H. Helton q.v.

- - - - - - - - - - - - -

JORDAN / JORDEN / JORDON / JOURDAIN

1860 CENSUS
Cyrus Jorden 23 (Ga), Susan 29, Elmira 7, Caroline 5, Susannah 3, Theola 6/12 8-25-170
1870 CENSUS
Richard H. Jordan 47 (Ga)(Minister), Robert O. 23, Jesse B. 16, Minnie G. 11, Nancy C. 8, Tennessee 5, Hardie CHADWICK 22, Margurette R. 2 8-13-92
William A. Jordan 24, Sarah Jane 35, Nancy 46, Rawston BUICE 9 8-14-93
1880 CENSUS
A. Jordan 37, M.J. 16 (d), Robt 13, Frank 12, Bell 10, Alfred 7, Sitta 3, John 3/12 9-30-259
R.O. Jordon 33, M.A. 27 (w), Trudie 6, M.C. 3 (d), R.H. 1 (s), Chas S. 1 (s) 8-7-56
1900 CENSUS
Bessie Jordan 12, Bella 9: see Joseph Giles
Frank R. Jourdain 32 (Ap 1868-M 9), Anna M. 42 (Jan 1858-M 9-3-3), Lula 8 (July 1891), Anabella 6 (Aug 1893), Bertha 3 (Sep 1896) 5-238A-195
James Jordan 38 (Jan 1862-M 8), Jennie 29 (Oct 1870-Ky/T/T-M 8-4-1), Minnie 3 (Aug 1896) 13-308B-356/369
Jessie B. Jordan 47 (June 1852-T/Ga/T-M 23), Catharine 45 (Nov 1854-M 23-10-7), Azza 13 (Sep 1886), Gollahighan 12 (Feb 1888), Manuel 8 (Aug 1891), Mary M. 6 (Mar 1894), Mack 2 (June 1897) 15-271B-70 [Jesse married Catherine Elizabeth Minnis on 5 Dec 1875 in Bradley County]
Malinda Jordan 56, James N. 26: see John Bolin
Ozias Jordan 76 (Jan 1824-Ga/SC/SC-Wd), William B. 35 (Aug 1864), Henegar 27 (Ap 1873)(Coal Miner) 13-306A-313/325
Richard Jordan 21 (Sep 1878-M 2), Delia 21 (June 1878-M 2-2-2), Nola 2 (Jan 1898), Pearl 4/12 (Jan 1900) 15-268B-12
Robert O. Jordan 53 (Dec 1846-M 27), Mary A. 48 (Mar 1852-M 27-6-5), Richard H. 21 (Oct 1878), William A. 16 (Aug 1883), Lillie E. 12 (Dec 1887) 13-308A-346/358
William A. Jordan 55 (Ap 1845-Wd)(Merchant), Margaret JOHNSON 56 (sil)(Feb 1844-Wd 1-0)(Housekeeper) 13-305B-297/309

MARRIAGES
Alice V. Jordon to Earnest Ganaway q.v.
Cassie Jordan to John Gowing(?) q.v.
Charlotte Jordan to Thomas Lyons q.v.
Emaline Jordan to W. C. Gowins q.v.
Emma Jorden to John Dyer q.v.
Henegar Jordan to Lillie Nail, 26 Aug 1899, no MG or JP, J.C. Bridgeman W 3-27
J.N. Jordon to Jennie Barger, 20 Dec 1891, W.R. Grimsley MG 4-34
John Jordan to Malinda White, 1 Aug 1861 (same), W.A. Green JP 1-#757
John W. Jordan to Ginnie Price, 20 Aug 1893, R.S. Mason JP 4-55
Mahala Jordan to Adam Watson q.v.
Margaret Jordan to James H. Creasman q.v.
Mollie Jordan to John McMillan q.v.
Osiras Jordon to Susan Morgan, 8 June 1852 (no return) 1-#378
Richard Jordan to Delia Fine, 14 Jan 1898 (16 Jan), W.G. Curton MG, Roland Kyle W 2-240
Robert Jordan to Jennie Atchley, 17 Oct 1887 (10 Oct)[sic], F.J. Paine JP 1-528
W.A. Jorden to Bell Hawkins, 31 Dec 1900 (same), W.S. Hale MG, O. Sabin W 3-267
W.G.Z. Jordan to G. W. Willhoit q.v.

- - - - - - - - - - - - -

JULIAN

1900 CENSUS
Charles Julian 27: see Louis A. Blake
MARRIAGE
Ella Julian to T. P. Darr q.v.

- - - - - - - - - - - - -

JUSTICE

1880 CENSUS
John Justice 20, Tennessee 22, Mary 2 1-14-121 (B)

- - - - - - - - - - - - -

KANLY

MARRIAGE
Thomas Kanly to Emma(?) Holt, 22 Feb 1889 (same), D. Richardson MG 1-565

- - - - - - - - - - - - -

KAYLOR

MARRIAGES
A. Kaylor to Mary Rodgers, 3 July 1900 (same), H. Morgan JP 3-178
Asbery Kaylor to Elizabeth Parson, 7 July 1897 (1 July) [sic], R.C. Knight JP 2-157
W.P. Kaylor to Mattie Parson, 12 May 1896, R.J. Kainy(?) W "Duplicate of license which was stole from said Kayler" 2-22

- - - - - - - - - - - - -

KEATHLEY

MARRIAGE
Samuel M. Keathley to Della A. White, 19 Mar 1896, G.W. Brewer MG 4-92

- - - - - - - - - - - - -

KEBLER

MARRIAGE
Aggie Kebler to G. V. Robinson q.v.

KEEDY / KEELY

1900 CENSUS
Howard Keely 50 (Ap 1850-Pa/Pa/Pa-D) 11-293B-86/87
Zachariah T. Keedy 51 (Nov 1848-M 14), Mary 45 (Dec 1854-Va/Va/Va-M 14-2-2), Hester 14 (Nov 1885), Robert TREADWAY 19 (boarder)(Jan 1887) 13-295B-110/112
MARRIAGES
Hester Keedy to Robert Treadway q.v.
Salina Keedy to Burty Sells q.v.

KEELING / KEELEN / KEELIN / KELLON / KEYLON

1870 CENSUS
George W. Keelon 8: see Aaron C. Owens
Sarah Kellon 7: see Franklin Locke
1880 CENSUS– None
1900 CENSUS
Charles Keylon 23 (Mar 1877)(Ore Shoveler) 10-321A-17
Elexander Keylon 47 (Sep 1852-M 12), Parthenia 48 (Ap 1852-M 12-6-4), Lillie M. 17 (Oct 1882), Luther C. 22 (nw)(Ap 1878), Susan 74 (m)(Sep 1825-T/Va/Va-Wd 9-6) 2-193B-46/47
James H. Keylon 55 (Jan 1845-M 11), Mary 44 (Jan 1856-M 11-11-10), Charles M. Unk (Unk), John B. 17 (Feb 1883), James L. 14 (Sep 1885), Virgil P. 10 (Nov 1889), Claude A. 6 (Feb 1894), Charles D. ELLIS 17 (ss)(Nov 1882), Zerelda M. 15 (sd)(Oct 1884), Habbe 13 (ss)(Oct 1886) 2-194B-72/74
MARRIAGES
Charley Keylon to Rosa Hurst, 15 Sep 1900 (16 Sep), W.S. Hale MG, W.P. Pelfrey W 3-219
James Kellin* to Tennie Erwin, 29 July 1896 (30 July), W. S. Hale MG, J. Brooks W 2-47 [*last name spelled Keylon in index]
John Keeling to Elizabeth Loy, 1 Sep 1860 (2 Sep), J.I. Cash MG 1-#724
Mary Ann Keelen to Elias Crisp q.v.
Minnie Keylon to Lee Jolly q.v.
William E. Keelon to Priscilla Loy, 3 Ap 1861 (4 Mar), E. Pyott JP 1-#751

KEENER

1900 CENSUS
Fanny Keener 33: see Thomas Prater
MARRIAGE
Margaret Keener to David Wilcoxson q.v.

KEENEY

1900 CENSUS
Henry Keeney 35 (Aug 1864-Ky/Pa/Ky-M 15), Sally C. 35 (Jan 1865-Ky/Ky/Ky-M 15-5-4), Basil E. 14 (Sep 1885-Ky), Ethel J. 12 (Mar 1888-Ky), Gladys P. 10 (Dec 1889-Ky), Jessie M. 7 (Ap 1893) 11-290B-14

KEETY

MARRIAGE
Tennessee Keety to Rev. J.J. Krischbaunn q.v.

KEEVER

MARRIAGE
Walter E. Keever to Jennie Riddle, 26 Aug 1896 (same), G.W. Coleman MG, Joe F. Benson W 2-60

KEITH

1860 CENSUS
John H. Keith 21, Ann E. 24, John H. 10/12, Elizabeth LOWERY 11 (bound) 10-27-184
Nicholas Keith 50, Eliza J. 45, Jane 19, Mary 15, Margaret 13, Neely 12, Thomas 10, Brownlow 9, Ann 7, Tennessee 5, Robert 4, Sarah MITCHELL 13 (adopted) 10-27-185
1870 CENSUS
Jackson Keith 57, Nancy 37, Jesse 22, Charles R. 19, Syntha A. 17, William J. 15, Louvena 13, James H. 11, Abraham L. 9, Jackson Jr. 5, Nancy A. 3, George F. 8/12, Catharine 70 (SC) 8-2-16 (B)
John H. Keith 31 (Physician), Ann E.C. 34, John H. 10, Martha U. 8, Mary Ida 5, Sallie M. 3 8-15-103
Neeley Keith 21 (Miller), Sally 22 7-1-7
Nicholas Keith 61 (Wool Carder), Eliza Jane 55, Margarette M. 23, William T. 20 (Miller), Zachariah B. 19 (Miller), Nancy A. 17, Tennessee E. 15, Robert 14 8-20-141
1880 CENSUS
Charles Keith 31, Jane 21, G.F. 9 (s), Frank McDONALD (B) 8 8-16-137
Isam Keith 36, Mary 29 6-16-147/150 (B)
Jock Keith 57, Jane 50, Jess 33, J.H. 21 (s), A.L. 19 (s), Jack 15, Viney 23 (d), Nany 13 (d), G.F. 11 (s), Willie 12, Nichols 7, Eba 5 (d), Edda 2 (s), Dora 2, A.G. 1 (s), Alice 1/12 (gd) 8-19-160 (B)
1900 CENSUS
Charles Keith 49 (B): see Neely M. Keith
Earnest D.(?) Keith 26 (Jan 1874-Ga/T/T-M 6)(Miller), Lillie 22 (June 1877-Ga/Ga/Ga-M 6-2-2), Claude 5 (Ap 1895), Wallace 3 (May 1897) 10-252B-52
Floyd Keith 24: see Jennie Benson (B)
Hugh Keith 26: see Samuel Whitlow (B)
Jack Keith 29, Hanah 29, Willie 11, Pinctney 0/12: see Thomas Bowles

Jessie Keith 53 (Oct 1846-Wd 0), Joe 11 (s)(Jan 1889), Floyd 7 (Sep 1892), Nineva 3 (Aug 1896), Ruff SUTTLES 28 (bl)(Nov 1871-M 0)(Keeper at Furnace), Lizzie 24 (si)(Mar 1876-M 0-0), Corra SUTTLES 7 (ne)(Nov 1892) 10-252A-44 (B)

Nancy Keith 71 (Mar 1829-Wd 19-14), Jack 33 (Dec 1867-Wd), Floyd 30 (Nov 1869), Glover 19 (Aug 1880), Orvil 12 (Feb 1888) 10-252A-45 (B)

Neely M. Keith 52 (Mar 1848-M 6), Hannah E. 35 (Nov 1864-M 6-2-2), Mary L. 16 (May 1884), Estelle 11 (May 1889), Baxter V. 4 (Dec 1895), Anna R. 2 (Jan 1898), Charles KEITH (B) 49 (Oct 1850)(Servant) 13-196A-117/119

Nich Keith 28, Lizzie 19: see Ben McDonald (B)

Robert Keith 21 (Oct 1878-M 1)(Grocer), Mabel 18 (July 1881-M 1-0) 10-328A-168/178

MARRIAGES

Ann Keith to W. T. Perser q.v.

Charley Keith to Lucinda Officer, 19 Feb 1889 (10 Feb) [sic], A. Stone MG 1-566

Earnest N. Keith to Lillie N. Hawkins, 31 Jan 1894, Jas I. Cash MG 4-70

Greeley(?) Keith to R. S. Davidson q.v.

J.C. Keith to James O. Whaley q.v.

Jack Keith to Laura Hale, 22 Dec 1897 (23 Dec), R.T. Smith MG, James Day W 2-229

Jane Keith to George Benson q.v.

John H. Keith to Ann E.C. Moyers, 21 July 1858 (no return) 1-#640

Lizzie Keith to John Hudson q.v.

Lizzie Keith to Rufus Suttles q.v.

Mary Keith to James O. Whaley q.v.

Mary Keith (Mrs.) to Thomas B. Houser or Housley q.v.

Mary Keith to G. W. or W. G. Green q.v.

Melissa T. Keith to Lewis Gibson q.v.

Mollie Keith to J. W. McFalls q.v.

N.J. Keith to Jessie L. Lockmiller, 16 Nov 1893, R.S. Mason JP 4-60

N.M. Keith to H.E. Shipley, 20 Mar 1894, James I. Cash MG 4-76

Nick Keith to Lizzie Day, 22 Dec 1899 (24 Dec), L. Burks MG, A. Day W 3-97

Robert Keith to Mary Bishop, 30 Jan 1895, J.W. Smith MG

Robert Keith to Mabel Walker, 1 Nov 1898 (same), J.A. Whitner MG, C. Givens W 2-342

S.R. Keith to Mary Bishop, 10 Aug 1897 (bond only), J.P. Keith W 1-109

Samuel Keith to Mary J. Swafford, 31 Mar 1886 (same), F.M. Bandy MG 1-488

T.J. Keith to Hannah Bishop, 15 Sep 1894, D.V. Culver MG 4-71

Z.B. Keith to Mary C. Collins, 9 Sep 1873 (same), John H. Keith MG 1-#1300

\- - - - - - - - - - - - -

KELLY / KELLEY / KILLEY

1860 CENSUS

Jacob Kelly 49, Julia F. 37, Mary C. 16, Thomas D. 11, Vesta A. 6, Roy B. 4/12, William P. DARWIN 30 (Merchant), Adelia DARWIN 21 6-109-748

James Kelly 43 (Va), Betsy 43 (Va), Mary J. 21, John W. 19, Malissa 17, James A. 15, Sarah T. 13, William S. 12, Virginia J. 10, Thomas J. 8, Nancy A. 6, Margaret E. 5, Jacob M. 3 8-21-140

John Kelly 41 (Tailor), Rachel E. 26, Mary W. 1, David R. 1/12 1-95-648

William Kelley 56, William A. 22 7-3-12

1870 CENSUS

Delilah Kelly 54, Louisa 25, Martha 17, John 13, Catharine 11 4-14-93

George W. Kelley 32, Isabella J. 25 3-14-98

James J. Kelley 51 (Va), Elizabeth 53 (Va), James A. 26, Virginia 20, Thomas J. 19, Nancy Ann 17, Margarette E. 16, Jacob M. 13, Ellen B. 9, Emma A. 6 8-8-54

Julia Killey 46, Thomas D. 21, Vesta A. 14, William B. 10, Jacob 8, Matilda COLLINS (B) 17 6-4-25

Mariah Kelly 14 (B): see Elvira Cunnyngham

Samuel Kelly 55: see Thomas J. Marsh

William Kelley 65, William A. 31 (Miller) 7-1-3

William S. Kelley 22, Mary F. 22, Ellen E. 6/12, Selah CAHANA 10 8-18-122

1880 CENSUS

Andy Kelley 22, Catharine 22, John A. 1, Andrus JOHNSON 9 ("living with me") 6-12-114 & 6-12-115 (B)

Ballen Kelley 20 (B): see Julia Kelley

Catharine Kelly 22, Ida 2, Ada : see A. Brewye(?)

Floyd O. Kelley 5, Ida E 2: see Sarah A. Mariott (B)

J.A. Kelly 36, Texas 27 (w), J.H. 5 (s) 8-7-55

J.J. Kelley 63, Marget 26 (d), E.B. 9 (d), M.D. 6 (d), Franklin 1 (gs) 8-7-61

J.M. Kelley 23, M.J. 22 (w), J.A. 2 8-6-46

James Kelly 34, M.A. 28, Martha 9 (d), A.H. 8 (d), N.A. 3 (d), M.A. 3/12 (d) 3-24-191

Julia Kelley 56, William 20, Jacob 18, Susan COX 47 (boarder), Joseph CASTELBERRY(?) 17 (Hired Laborer), Ballen KELLEY (B) 20 (Hired Laborer), Isaac TUCKER (B) 16 4-12-94

Robert Kelly 18 (B): see Samuel Dickey

T.J. Kelley 29, L.E. 22, Edgar 3, A.J. ALEXANDER 27 (boarder), ?.E. 19 (w) 8-6-49

W.A. Kelley 41, E.A. 36, M.M. 8 (d), I.R. 6 (s), B.E. 4 (d), W.D. 10/12 (s), William KELLEY 76 (f), David SINGLETON 76 (fl), Frankey 25 (sil), R.A. 4 (ne), James 7 ("living in family") 7-29-246

William Kelley 76: see W. A. Kelley

1900 CENSUS

Andy Kelly 47 (Mar 1853-M 13), Maggie 40 (Aug 1869-T/NC/NC-M 13-6-6)(Washwoman), Richard 17 (Aug 1892), King 11 (Sep 1888), Robert 7 (Nov 1892), Barn 5 (Dec 1894), Marry 3 (Mar 1897), Lee R. (Jan 1899) 10-250B-15 (B)

Eugene Kelly 20, Tennie 21, Arthur F. 5/12: see Jos Kelly

James Kelly 52 (Ap 1848-M 30), Margurett A. 49 (Aug 1850-M 30-8-7), Mary T. 22 (Nov 1877), Louisa 18 (May 1882), Georgian 14 (Oct 1885), Mamie J. 12 (Ap 1888) 3-207A-120/131

James A. Kelly 56 (Nov 1843-T/Va/Va-M 6), Mollie E. 27 (Oct 1872-M 6-3-3), Thomas E. 5 (Dec 1894), Winnie D. 2 (Dec 1897), Earnest E. 11/12 (July 1899) 5-273B-108

John J. Kelley 20: see Frank Dixon

John T. Kelly 44 (Nov 1855-M 20), Victoria 35 (Feb 1865-Ky/Ky/Ky-M 20-3-3), Mary E. 13 (Jan 1887-Ky), Jim E. 11 (Jan 1889-Ky), Ethel 8 (Nov 1891) 3-207A-122/133
Joseph Kelly 50 (Mar 1850-Wd)(Merchant), Arthur S. 21 (Mar 1878), Minnie 13 (Dec 1886), Myrtle 11 (Jan 1889), Susan 9 (June 1890), Luther K. 23 (s)(Nov 1876-M 3), Lena 18 (dl)(Oct 1881-M 3-1-0), Eugene 20 (s)(Oct 1879-M 1). Tennie 21 (dl)(Dec 1878-M 1-1-1), Arthur F. 5/12 (gs)(Jan 1900) 15-274A-115
Julia Kelly 74: see James Crawford
Lafayette Kelly 18, Minnie 15: see Robert T. Simpson
Lee A. Kelly 52 (Jan 1848-T/Va/SC-Wd 4-3), Lula MEDLOCK 28 (d)(Ap 1872-M 4-4-1), Brownlow 30 (sl) (Unk 1870-M 4), William KELLY 24 (s)(July 1875), Sarah 19 (Jan 1882), Georga WHITE 5 (gd)(Mar 1894), John WLLIAMS 48 (boarder)(Unk 1848-Ind/Ind/Ind-Wd), Richard SHARP 19 (boarder)(Unk 1881), William JINK 25 (boarder)(Unk 1875-D) 8-275B-141 (B)
Luther K. Kelly 23, Lena 18: see Joseph Kelly
Richard Kelley 36 (Feb 1864-T/Ga/T-M 12)(Coke Oven Boss), Carry 31 (June 1868-M 12-6-5), Clarence 10 (Aug 1889), Purser 7 (Oct 1892), Tamora A. 5 (Dec 1894), Nally 2 (Dec 1897), Miny B. 4/12 (Jan 1900), Minie KELLY 21 (si) (Aug1879-T/Ga/T) (School Teacher) 10-253B-69 (B)
Steve Kelly 48 (June 1851-M 12), Alonza KELLY 40 (b)(June 1860-M 15), Mark KELLY 35 (b)(Aug 1864-M 12) 8-284B-314/316 (B)
Thomas D. Kelley 50 (June 1849-M 26)(RR Hand), Sarah 51 (Oct 1850-T/NC/T-M 26-5-5), John J. 22 (Jan 1877), James W. 17 (Mar 1883), Thomas C. 15 (Oct 1884), Ned 7 (Mar 1893) 5-235A-142
Wilum Kelly 17, Molli 13, Nettie 9: see Nuton Casey
William Kelly 23: see Bup Matlock (B)
William Kelly 26: see Bertie Wasson (B)
William Kelley 61 (Mar 1839-M 29)(Mail Carrier), Lizzie A. 56 (Jan 1844-T/SC/NC-M 29-6-6), Bud 26 (Nov 1873), David 20 (Aug 1879), Alford B. 17 (Nov 1882), Sammy 14 (Feb 1886) 7-265A-284/289
William Kelly 31 (Mar 1869-Ky/Ky/Ky-M 8), Lussie 25 (July 1874-M 8-3-3), Rudolph 7 (Sep 1892), Floria 5 (Jan 1895), Eugene 1 (Aug 1898), Clenia SHARPE 4 (ne)(Dec 1895) 2-197A-107/112
William B. Kelley 40 (Feb 1860-M 16), Ada 40 (May 1860-Ky/Md/Ky-M 16-3-2), Lee 13 (May 1887), Jesse J. 11 (Mar 1889) 6-244A-87

MARRIAGES
Adie Kelly (Mrs.) to T. J. Robinson q.v.
Ann E. Kelly to Jesse F. McDowell q.v.
Anne L. Kelly to Frank H. Dickson q.v.
B. W. Kelly to A. B. Hodge q.v.
Catharine Kelly to William H. Shelton q.v.
Clara Kelly to Francis Porter q.v.
Dellie Kelly to James White q.v.
elizabeth Kelley to W. H. Rice q.v.
Ellen B. Kelley to W. R. Sullivan q.v.
Harriet Kelly to E. N. Casey q.v.
Jacob Killey [Kelly] to Adie Locke, 15 Jan 1885 (same), A.P. Early MG 1-459
Jacob M. Kelly to M.J. Everett, 5 Oct 1876 (same), W.A. Green JP 1-#1463
James Kelly to Margaret Taylor, 21 Ap 1871 (same), Daniel Broyles JP -#1193
James C. Kelly to Martha Early, 19 Feb 1867 (same), Beriah Frazier MG 1-#936
James H. Kelly to Bell V. Rucker, 5 June 1894, R.M. Kilgore MG 4-68
Janie Kelley to Jack Garrison q.v.
John W. Kelly to Rachel E. Rector, 6 June 1857 (7 June), E. E. Wasson JP 1-#601
Louiza Kelly to Sam Porter q.v.
Maggie Kelley to James Lowrey q.v.
Malissa A. Kelly to W. N. Smith q.v.
Martha A. Kelly to D. M. Buchanon q.v.
Martha E. Kelly to J. G. Gaddis q.v.
Mary C. Kelly to J. R. Crawford q.v.
Nancy A. Kelley to John W. Green q.v.
Robert Kelley to Jane Gillespie, 24 Ap 1884 (same), James Johnson JP 1-469
Rosannah Kelly to Thomas Brotherton q.v.
Salley Kelly to John Henderson q.v.
Sary T. Kelly to Thomas J. Dean q.v.
Thomas D. Kelly to Sarah J. Crawford, 13 Nov 1873 (same), A.P. Early MG 1-#1308
Thomas J. Kelly to Louisa C. Alexander, 9 Feb 1876 (10 Feb), H.C. Peters MG 1-#1434
Thursday Kelly to William Roberts q.v.
V. T. Kelley to Wesley Raines q.v.
Vesta A. Kelly to R. L. Allen q.v.
Will Kelly to Minnie Muncey, 24 Jan 1900 [probably 1901], A.M. Broyles JP 4-110
William A. Kelly to Eliza Ann Singleton, 27 Oct 1870 (same), D. Hodge JP 1-#1169
William S. Kelly to Molly F. Strebick, 17 Nov 1868 (same), no MG or JP 1-#1035

- - - - - - - - - - - - -

KEMMER

1900 CENSUS
David C. Kemmer 35 (Feb 1865-M 11), Tressa F. 38 (Sep 1861-M 11-4-3), Thomas R. 9 (Jan 1891), Walter R. 7 (Mar 1893), William J.B. 3 (Sep 1896) 2-197B-117/122
MARRIAGE
D.C. Kemmer to Florence Rose, 26 Oct 1888 (28 Oct), S.H. Price MG 1-570

- - - - - - - - - - - - -

KENNEDY / KENEDY / KENIDA

1860 CENSUS
Daniel Kennedy 40, Mary E. 32, Sarah E. 12, Darius E. 3, Vesta E. 11/12 3-62-424
John Kennedy 26, Mary 26, Isabella 1, Samuel 6/12, Elizabeth E. McMURRY 25 3-61-423
1870 CENSUS
Daniel Kennedy 51, Emaline 42, Darius E. 12, Vesta I. 10, Daniel 8, James A. 6, Calvin N. 3 3-9-65
James Kennedy 25, Mary 24, Julia 5, Tennessee 2 3-10-71
1880 CENSUS
D. Kennedy 56, M.E. 50 (w), D.E. 22 (s), R.D. 18 (s), J.A. 15 (s), C.N. 12 (s) 9-31-263

James C. Kenedy 41, Mary F. 34, July A. 12, Malinda T. 10, Celia J. 5, Rachel E. 4, Vesta M. 7/12 6-12-112

1900 CENSUS

Benjamin Kennedy 56: see Moses Grier

Daniel Kennedy 79 (Nov 1821-T/Pa/T-M 45)(Retired, Old Age), Mary E. 71 (Jan 1829-M 45-8-6) 9-228A-6

James Kennedy 35 (Ap 1865-M 13), Mattie 29 (Aug 1870-M 13-4-4), Edward 11 (Jan 1889), Stella 8 (Oct 1891), Della 5 (June 1894), Daisey E. 2 (May 1898), Betsy McMURRY 60 (boarder)(Unk) 6-247B-144/145

John W. Kennedy 31 (Dec 1868-M 6), Amy M. 23 (May 1877-Oh/Oh/Pa-M 6-3-3), Robert L. 5 (Ap 1895), Myrtle 2 (Ap 1898), John 3/12 (May 1900) 9-228A-5

Julius A. Kennedy 49 (Mar 1851-T/Ind/NC-M 24), Julia J. 48 (May 1852-T/Va/T-M 24-13-10), Finley 19 (July 1880), Hattie M. 16 (May 1884), Joseph H. 14 (Aug 1885), Alice B. 13 (Sep 1886), Samuel H. 10 (May 1890), Cora E. 6 (Feb 1894) 6-249B-178/179 [J.A. married Julia Bishop on 23 Ap 1876 in Meigs Co]

Sophia Kennedy 32: see George Elliott

MARRIAGES

Daniel Kenedy to Ann Long, 3 Feb 1851 (6 Feb), Daniel Broyles JP 1-#331

Daniel Kenedy to Emaline Davis, 19 May 1856, Robert T. Howard MG 1-#550

Ella Kenedy to G. W. Ballew Jr. q.v.

J.N. Kennedy to Mabel Lee, 17 Ap 1894, R.A. Bartlett JP 4-69

James Kennedy to Mary Wright, 10 Mar 1863 (12 Mar), John Wyott JP 1-#794

John Kenida to Mary A. Carter, 10 Aug 1888 (same), Calvin Morgan JP 1-570

July Kenedy to William Ingles q.v.

Malinda Kenedy to James Robertson q.v.

Malinda Kennedy to Samuel Houston q.v.

Mamie Kenedy to O. L. Tichner q.v.

R.D. Kennedy (20) to E.J. Brady (17), 26 Nov 1881, T.H. McPherson JP, James C. Garrison & James Cunnyngham W 4-4(37)

Vesta J. Kennedy to J. R. Ganaway q.v.

William G. Kennedy to Rachel C. Winfrey, 1 Aug 1876 (same), E.N. Ganaway JP 1-#1452

- - - - - - - - - - - - -

KENT

1900 CENSUS

Robert Kent 20: see Marquis Morrison

- - - - - - - - - - - - -

KERLEY

1900 CENSUS

Daniel L. Kerley 45 (Feb 1855-M 22), Milla C. 44 (Oct 1855-M 22-5-4), Martin 21 (Feb 1879), Ida 16 (May 1884), Lizzie 11 (Ap 1889), Jesse 3 (Oct 1896) 6-246A-123/124

George W. Kerley 66 (Jan 1834-T/NC/T-M 47), Elizabeth C. [nee Acree] 66 (Jan 1834-T/NC/NC-M 47-6-4), Clarence E. 38 (Jan 1862-Ky-M 15), Nancy J. 38 (Ap 1862-Wd 0-0 sic], Elizabeth 14 (gd)(Oct 1885-T/Ky/T), George F. 13 (gs)(Sep 1886), William F. 12 (gs) (Nov 1887) 6-246A-114/115

Jesse Kerley 34 (Aug 1865-M 3), Mary 30 (Oct 1869-M 3-0) 6-246A-117/118 [Jesse married Mary Wasson on 15 Ap 1897 in Meigs Co]

MARRIAGE

J.A. Kerley to Nancy J. Richey, 23 Dec 1885 (24 Dec), P.G. Roddy MG 1-517

- - - - - - - - - - - - -

KERR– see CARR

- - - - - - - - - - - - -

KERRICK

1860 CENSUS

John W. Kerrick 28 (Va), Sarah 22, Catharine 4, Bushsor(?) T. 2 1-94-643

- - - - - - - - - - - - -

KERSEY

1860 CENSUS

John Kersey 31 (SC)(Carpenter), Elizabeth 32, James B. 1 6-109-746

John Kersey 64 (SC), Roxan 65 (NC), Rachel 35, Sarah 29, Mary A. 9, Manerva 6, Sarah A. 3, George M. 2 1-95-646

Wiley Kersey 35 (SC), Mary E. 19 1-82-557

- - - - - - - - - - - - -

KERTAIN
(see also CURTAIN / CURTON)

1900 CENSUS

Will Kertain 20: see Robert J. Kilonge

- - - - - - - - - - - - -

KESLER / KISLER / KESSLER

1880 CENSUS

G.M. Kisler 30, E.L. 25, G.S. 6 (s) 3-28-225

H. Kisler 53, R.H. 54, D.P. 21 (d), J.F. 21 (d), R.A. 19 (s), L.A. 16 (d) 3-28-224

1900 CENSUS

Iseael Kesler 43 (Oct 1856-Pa/Pa/Pa-M 22)(Lumber Dealer), Elizabeth 37 (Dec 1862-Pa/Pa/Pa-M 22-7-4), Nancy 18 (May 1882-Pa)(Lumber Mill Bookkeeper), Hellen 11 (Nov 1888), Edward 9 (Mar 1891) 10-325A-111/115

MARRIAGE

Pauline Kessler to John Koch q.v.

- - - - - - - - - - - - -

KEY / KEYS

1860 CENSUS

Elener E. Key 14: see Cornelius Shaver

Green B. Keys 27: see Rufus B. Sherly

William Key 31, Kate 30, Nancy 9, Elizabeth 7, Margaret 5, William 3, Sarah 2, John WEEKS 26 7-6-43

Zachariah Key 36, Martha 28, William 7, Lotty 3, Andrew I. 12, Mary DODSON 81, James DODSON 40 2-80-547

MARRIAGES

Elizabeth Key to John P. Bowlen q.v.

Z. Key to Martha Dodson, 19 Jan 1850 (same), Asa Newport MG

- - - - - - - - - - - - -

KIBBLE

1880 CENSUS

Elder Kibble 21 ("parted from here") 6-14-130/132

- - - - - - - - - - - - -

KIKER

1880 CENSUS

T.J. Kiker 36, H.A. 32, H.A. 10 (s), Henry 7, M.E. 6 (d), F.A. 5 (d), J.E. 1 (s) 9-32-277

1900 CENSUS

George Kiker 23 (June 1876-Ga/Ga/Ga)(Merchant), Luther 13 (b)(Feb 1886-T/Ga/Ga), Oscar 11 (b)(Dec 1885) 8-281B-262/264

Josephine Kiker 17: see James F.(?) Henninger

Laura Kiker 15: see Samuel H. Hixon

MARRIAGE

Mattie Kiker to James Bottomlee q.v.

- - - - - - - - - - - - -

KILGORE

1900 CENSUS

Jane Kilgore 47 (Mar 1853-Ga/Ala/NC-Wd 9-5), Parker 20 (d)(Mar 1880-Ga), William H. 13 (Sep 1886-Ga), Gussie 7 (Feb 1893) 13-297A-141/144

John Kilgore 27, Archer 22, George 4/12: see George M. Neuman

Robert M. Kilgore 61 (Mar 1839-Oh/Oh/Oh-M 33)(Clergyman), Asenath M. 60 (Mar 1840-Mich/Ver/NY-M 33-3-2), Louis A. 15 (adopted s)(Ap 1885-SC/Unk/Maine), Mamie L ELDREDGE 23 (d)(July 1876-Iowa/Oh/Mich-M 0-0), William B. 23 (sl)(Dec 1876-Iowa/Do/Do-M 0)(Painter) 13-309A-370/384

MARRIAGES

Charles L. Kilgore to Letha E. Hall, 4 Sep 1893, R.M. Kilgore MG 4-57

John R. Kilgore to Mary Drake, 25 Jan 1899 (same), G.W. Brewer MG, G.C. Newman W 2-377

Lena E. Kilgore to W. E. Howell q.v.

Mamie Kilgore to W. B. Eldridge q.v.

- - - - - - - - - - - - -

KILLOUGH / KILOUGE

1860 CENSUS

Pulaski Killough 34 (Collecting Officer), Sarah 28, Robert 5, Mary 4, Thomas 2, Mary KILLOUGH 70 (SC) 6-110-755

Robert Kellough 40 (Keeping Confectionary), Casander 26, Joseph A. 2, James H. 3/12 6-111-760

William B. Killough 31 (Merchant), Mary D. 19, Theodore 8, James 6, Catharine 2, Creed F. BROWN 16 (Clerk) 6-111-763

1870 CENSUS

Pulaski Killough 43 (Retail Merchant), Sarah 23, Robert 15, Mary 14, Sarah 9, Elley 4 6-8-49

Robert Killough 52, Casander 38, Joseph 12, James 10 6-8-50

1880 CENSUS

C.S. Killough (f) 47, Laura 23 6-24-27 (Rural Street, Washington)

Joseph A. Killough 22, Martha C. 19 6-13-123/123

Pulaski Killough 56 (Keeping Drug Store), Sarah 31, Eller 14, Sarah 19 6-23-15 (Jefferson Street, Washington)

Robert J. Killough 25 (Druggist), Ellen A. 25 days (d) 6-24-24 (Rural Street, Washington)

1900 CENSUS

Joseph Kllough 41 (Aug 1859-M 20)(Carpenter), Martha C. 39 (May 1861-Va/Va/Va-M 20-7-6), Lillian J. 19 (Dec 1880), Maud 17 (Jan 1883), Alma 15 (Ap 1885), Roy 13 (Feb 1887)(Water Boy), Gertrude 10 (Mar 1890), Earl 4 (Mar 1896) 10-250B-21

Mack Killough 40 (Feb 1860-M 14)(Carpenter), Nellie 29 (May 1871-M 14-2-2), Jack 12 (July 1887), Beatress 4 (Oct 1895) 10-260A-196/201

Robert J. Kilouge 46 (Nov 1854-M 26)(Bookkeeper), Laura 38 (Oct 1861-M 26-3-3), Eler M. 18 (May 1882), Albert 15 (Jan 1884), Jimmie G. 9 (May 1891), Will KERTAIN 20 (boarder)(May 1880-Va)(Coal Miner), Park IVESTER 17 (boarder)(June 1882) 10-252B-55

MARRIAGES

Ella Killough to G. B. Morgan q.v.

J.A. Killough to Mattie C. Davis, 14 Jan 1880 (same), J. Howard MG 1-#1704

J.M. Killough to Moody Johnson, 4 Feb 1880 (no return) 1-#1713

J.M. Killough to Nola Jewell, 17 Oct 1886 (same), John Howard MG 1-532

Laura Killough to R. J. Killough q.v.

Mary Killough to Joseph Hoge q.v.

R.J. Killough to Laura Killough, 16 Jan 1873 (same), W.R. Henry JP 1-#1272

Robert Killough to Casandra Trim, no date (no return) [probably 1856] 1-#577

Sarah Killough to Will Alexander q.v.

- - - - - - - - - - - - -

KILLPATRICK

1900 CENSUS

John Killpatrick 31 (Feb 1869-T/NC/T-M 8), Bell 25 (Nov 1874-Ind/Ind/Ind-M 8-6-4), Arthur L. 8 (Ap 1892), Clisa A. 6 (Nov 1894), Estle W. 1 (d)(June 1898), Ira W. 7/12 (Oct 1899), Margarett E. 55 (m)(Sep 1844-Wd), Samuel SWAFFORD 18 (boarder)(Feb 1882) 5-238A-193

MARRIAGE

John Killpatrick to Bell Cooley, 15 July 1891, J.M. Bramlett MG 4-29

- - - - - - - - - - - - -

KIMBALL / KIMBLE

1900 CENSUS
Bell Kimball 33 (Oct 1867-Wd 3-3)(Washwoman), Minnie 14 (June 1885), Roy 7 (Dec 1892), Clyde 4 (Jan 1896), Hugh BOGEL 40 (boarder)(Dec 1859)(Coal Miner) 8-313B-57/60 (B)
MARRIAGE
Bell Kimble to Houston Bogle q.v.

KIMBROUGH / KIMBRO

1880 CENSUS
E. Kimbrough 59, L.J. 47 (w), M.E. 22 (d), Sarah 19 (d), M.C. 16 (s), Newton 13, L.J. 9 (d), Robert 7, H. BREEDING 22 (boarder) 3-21-167
1900 CENSUS
Edward Kimbro 19: see Richard R. Brown
Elisha M. Kimbrough 35 (Dec 1864) 11-290B-23
Robert or David B. Kimbrough 27 (Jan 1873-S) 3-208B-154/167
Walter Kimbro 18: see James A. Houston
MARRIAGE
M. E. Kimbrough to J. B. Stephens q.v.

KINCADE

MARRIAGE
E. Kincade to G. H. Dudley q.v.

KINCANNON

1860 CENSUS
James Kincannon 37 (Wagonmaker), Adeline 30, Jane E. 11, William 9, Thomas 7, Franklin 5, Cordelia 3, Mary 1, Samuel LAUDERDALE 15 2-79-534
1870 CENSUS
James Kincannon 46 (Wagonwright), Adeline 42, Jane 20, William 18, James F. 14, Cordelia 13, Mary 11, Sarah P. 9, Tennessee 7 3-1-7
1880 CENSUS
J. Kincannon 52 (Wheelwright), Adaline 43 (w), James 30, William 27, A.M. 22 (d), Tennie 16, Sarah 18, Sarah LAUDERDALE 35 (sil)
1900 CENSUS
Thomas W. Kincannon 20 (Jan 1880-M 2), Martha J. 19 (Jan 1881-M 2-1-1), Rina M. 1 (May 1899) 3-211B-205/223
James F. Kincannon 44 (Jan 1856-M 21)(Carpenter), Sarah J. 41 (Aug 1858-T/T/NC-M 21-9-9), A. Ethel 18 (Dec 1881), Artie C. 17 (d)(June 1883), Charles J. 14 (Oct 1885), Rosa M. 12 (Sep 1887), Roscoe F. 10 (Oct 1889), S. Pearl 8 (July 1891), Maggie M. 7 (Ap 1893), H. Irvin 4 (May 1896), Hattie J.B. 1 (Nov 1898) 3-211A-194/212
James M. Kincannon 77 (Feb 1823-Wd), Jennie E. 50 (d) (June 1849), William A. 49 (s)(Jan 1851), Delia 37 (d) (Oct 1862), Sarah P. 37 (Jan 1863) 3-211B-198/216
MARRIAGES
Franklin Kincannon to Sarah Parks, 10 Ap 1879 (same), D.V. Culver MG 1-#1611
Mary C. Kincannon to J. H. Hollaway q.v.
T. L. Kincannon to Oliver M. Spence q.v.
Thomas W. Kincannon to Mattie Phillips, 5 Jan 1898, J.A. Torbett JP 4-99

KINDRICK

MARRIAGE
T.A. Kindrick to Mary E. Foust, 25 Dec 1877 (same), J.P. Roddy MG 1-#1535

KING

1870 CENSUS
Allen L. King 46, Martha E. 26, Mary E. 24, Emstus E. 17, Julia H. 16, John D. 11, Lodera K. 10, Amanda C. 6 2-8-54
John H. King 32, Nancy A. 31, Joseph N. 9, William R. 7, Robert F. 6, Margarette T. 4, Mary E. 6/12 5-7-52
Mary E. King 65 (Va), Thomas A. 21: see Martin Hurst
Sebastion S. King 27 (SC)(Retail Merchant), Annie E. 20 2-16-13
1880 CENSUS-- None
1900 CENSUS
David C. King 46 (Ap 1854-M 18), Lucinda 33 (Unk 1867-Ala/T/T-M 18-9-7), Lafayette 12 (Feb 1888), Maud E. 10 (Mar 1890), David 8 (Jan 1892), George E. 6 (Mar 1894), McKinley 4 (Mar 1896), DeWitt 2 (Ap 1898), Elijah A. 2/12 (Mar 1900) 8-281B-256/258
James T. King 35 (July 1864-M 18)(Station Engineer), Mary E. 35 (Aug 1864-T/Va/Ind-M 18-6-4), Livy M. 15 (Sep 1884), Samuel L. 14 (May 1886), William R. 7 (May 1893), Eula M. 3 (Aug 1896) 6-241A-32
Joseph N. King 38 (July 1861-S)(crippled)(Hog Raiser) 9-229A-32
John King 38 (May 1862-T/SC/T-M 17)(Boiler Maker), Lillie M. 34 (Jan 1866-M 17-5-4), Mabel 15 (Oct 1884), Guy V. 9 (Oct 1890-Ga), Egbert R. 8 (Jan 1892), Lorinda M. 1 (July 1898), Lorinda G. WUMBLE(?) 68 (May 1832-Wd 12-10) 8-312A-33/35
John H. King 61 (June 1838-T/NC/Va-M 39), Nancy A.C. 61 (Ap 1839-T/Va/Va-M 39-9-7), John 18 (Aug 1881), Mary E. RUSSELL 29 (d)(July 1870-D 1-1), Caroline 4 (gd)(Aug 1895) 9-228B-15
Luke M. King 72 (Unk-T/Va/NC-M 42), Ruth 61 (Jan 1839-M 42-7-6), Robert T. 27 (Mar 1873-M 0), Laura 26 (dl)(Mar 1874-M 0-0), Jasper 29 (sl)(May 1871-M 10) 6-248A-157 [Luke married Ruth Emmaline Ford on 23 Dec 1857]
Norris King 21: see Moses Grier
Robert T. King 27, Laura 26: see Luke M. King
MARRIAGES
Anna King to John Wilkey q.v.
Charley King to Alica Smith, 26 Sep 1893, W.S. Hale MG 4-57
Hannah King to Moses Phillips q.v.
Hatte King to William Stone q.v.

J.N. King to Ellen Couley or Conley, 13 Dec 1900 (same), T.F. Shaver MG, G.H. West W 3-256
Julia H. King to F. A. Simpson q.v.
Kate King to Jasper Price q.v.
Lillie A. King to James Edward Aden q.v.
Louisa Jane King to Samuel N. Carpenter q.v.
M. E. King to E. S. Martin q.v.
Mary E. King to Granville Hurst q.v.
Minnie M. King to James McKinley q.v.
Phebe King to G. W. Prisley q.v.
R.T. King to Elizabeth Buchannon, 12 Jan 1892, S.S. Franklin JP 4-34
R.T. King to Laura Harwood, 7 Sep 1899 (bond only), Threnda(?) Reed W 3-30
S. R. King to B. N. Turk(?) q.v.

- - - - - - - - - - - - -

KINSER

1880 CENSUS
J.L. Kinser 43, Elizbeth 36 (w), R.F. 14 (s), Mary 11, William 9, Tom 7, Samuel 4, Emma 11/12 8-19-165

- - - - - - - - - - - - -

KIRBY / KERBY

1870 CENSUS
Jeston Kirby 43, Malinda J. 15, Nancy A. 14, William H. 11, John B. 9, Samuel 7 3-2-11
1880 CENSUS
Justin Kerby 52, Jane 24 (d), Nancy 22 (d), William WASHING 2 (gs), Charlie 1/12 (gs), Cordelia 5 (gd) 2-41-334
Martha Kirby 29: see George Pinion (Mu)
1900 CENSUS
John B. Kirby 47 (Feb 1853-M 22), Martha A. 51 (Sep 1849-M 22-6-3), Van B. 13 (Sep 1886), Frank L. 11 (Ap 1889), Amanda WARES 6 (ne)(Aug 1893), Dewitt 3 (nw)(Mar 1897), Jeston KIRBY 71 (m)(Dec 1828-Wd 5-5) 2-195B-82/85
William Kirby 48 (Aug 1851-M 20), Mary J. 43 (Dec 1856-M 20-6-6), William J. 18 (Aug 1881), Henry B. 16 (Ap 1884), Samuel E. 13 (June 1886), Milo 10 (Dec 1889), Jener R. 7 (June 1892), Laura E. 3 (Aug 1897) 2-196A-94/97

MARRIAGES
Ella Kirby to J. R. Sisson q.v.
J.B. Kirby to Marthy Pinion, 17 Nov 1878 (18 Nov), James Johnson JP 1-#1587
Jane Kirby to John Walton q.v.
Nancy Kirby to Ruben Grassham q.v.
Nancy Kerby to John Withshan(?) q.v.
Samuel Kirby to Sarah Swafford, 29 May 1886 (30 May), W.S. Hale MG 1-487
Thomas J. Kirby to Malinda McFalls, 10 May 1853 (12 May), D. Broyles JP 1-#411
William H. Kirby (23) to Mary McDaniel (23), 11 Aug 1881, S. Breeding JP, Marcus Duckworth W 4-3(27)

- - - - - - - - - - - - -

KIRKLEN / KIRKLIN / KIRKLAN / KIRKLAND

1860 CENSUS
George W. Kirklan 40, Martha P. 36 (NC), Mary A. 18, Cynthia 16, Elizabeth 14, Adam 11, Nancy 7, Catharine 5, George 1 2-72-494
1870 CENSUS
Adam Kirkland 57, Mary 56 (Va), Crawford 21, Catharine 18, Margarette 16, Minerva 13 1-17-107
1880 CENSUS
Adam Kirklin 60, Mary 66, Catharine 24, Mary 22, Minerva 20, Rufus SELVAGE 17 (Servant) 1-16-133
1900 CENSUS
Add Kirklen 82 (Feb 1818-T/Scotland/Holland-M 55)(Molder?), Mary 87 (May 1813-Va/NJ/NJ-M 55-0-0) 1-183B-95/98
MARRIAGES
C. L. Kirkland to N. J. McDaniel q.v.
Elizabeth Kirklen to Jesse Bowles q.v.
Nancy M. Kirklen to H. P. Parker q.v.

- - - - - - - - - - - - -

KIRKLER

1900 CENSUS
Julli(?) Kirkler 45 (Feb 1855-NC/NC/NC-Wd 3-2), Chippi 22 (Ap 1878-NC)(Machines), Willie 20 (Nov 1879-NC) 12-179B-25/27

- - - - - - - - - - - - -

KIZIAH / KEZIAH / KISSIAH / KISJAH

1860 CENSUS
David Keziah 30, Metelda 30, George W. 6, Nancy A. 4, Sarah E. 2 4-44-299 [David married Matilda McCarroll on 9 Oct 1851 in Roane County]
James Kiziah 18: see Henry Davis
Thomas Keziah 30, Emaline 35, Margaret 75, James 21, Lorena 18(?) [ink blob] 2-73-501 [Thomas married Emaline Garrett on 22 Jan 1851 in Roane Co]
MARRIAGES
James Kisjah to Nancy E. Harris, 23 May 1864 (25 May), W.W. Low JP 1-#1084
Mary Ann Kiziah to A. J. Reeder q.v.
Melvina Kissiah to Daniel Bolls q.v.
Nelly Kissiah to Samuel Dotson q.v.

- - - - - - - - - - - - -

KNIGHT

1860 CENSUS
Richard Knight 23, Mary 24, John P. 4, James T. 7/12, Anthony SMITH 17 7-5-36
Thomas Knight 54 (NC), Philadelphia G. 44, Tennessee 19, Louisa J. 16, John S. 16, Thomas 15, Richard 13, Stephen 11, Philadelphia 4 7-7-44
1870 CENSUS
Delpha Knight 52, Thomas J. 24 (Retail Merchant), Stephen 21, Catharine 18 7-1-6
Rachel Knight 62: see Caroline J. Barton

Richard Knight 23, Hettie 22, Stephen F. 3, John L. 1 7-2-13

Richard C. Knight 33, Mary Ann 33, John S. 14, James L. 11, Mary RAWLINGS 21 7-3-24

1880 CENSUS

Philadelphia Knight 64: see R. Knight

R. Knight 33, H.E. 32, S.F. 12 (s), J.T. 11 (s), M.A. 9 (d), T.W. 6 (s), M.E. 3 (d), T.V. 4/12 (d), Philadelphia KNIGHT 64 (m) 7-27-234

T.J. Knight 35, R. 26 (w), Thomas 7 (s), P. 4 (d), Wilburn 2 (s), John CLEMMENS 28, Wright MAJORS 22 7-25-213

1900 CENSUS

Addie Knight 14: see Frank Byrely

Charley Knight 25 (Mar 1875-M 4), July 20 (Jan 1880-M 4-4-1), Lester 1 (Mar 1899) 7-266B-308/313

Cornelius R. Knight 56 (Nov 1843-Oh/Maine/Oh-M 34), Elizabeth A. 54 (Jan 1847-Oh/Pa/Oh-M 34-6-5), Solomin 18 (Nov 1881-Ind) 4-227B-274/278 (Road on line between 3rd & 4th Districts)

Frank S. Knight 32 (Oct 1867-M 9), Pollie A. 29 (Feb 1871-M 9-3-3), Arnold 7 (Mar 1893), Artie 5 (Mar 1895), Freed 3 (Ap 1897) 7-261B-217/222

Henery Knight 29 (Unk 1881-T/NC/Ga-M 0), Victory 26 (Feb 1872-M 0-1-1), Ollie 1/12 (Ap 1900) 10-258A-157/161 (B)

James Knight 61 (May 1839-T/NC/NC-M 33)(Pensioner), Martha A. 62 (Jan 1838-T/NC/NC-M 33-3-3) 14-218A-108/110

James Knight 27 (Oct 1872-M 5)(Coal Miner), Mollie 25 (Jan 1874-T/Ga/Ga-M 5-2-2), Freedia 3 (Nov 1896), Harry 2 (Ap 1898) 10-252A-46

Mattie Knight 19, Walter A. 17: see Asriah Fisher

Richard Knight 53 (May 1847-Wd), Tyler 31 (s)(Mar 1869) (School Teacher), Mary A. 28 (July 1871), Thomas W. 25 (Oct 1874), Martha E. 22 (June 1877), Tennessee V. 20 (Feb 1880), Floyd 17 (Nov 1882), Richard B. 14 (Sep 1885), Albert L. 11 (Mar 1889) 7-267A-319/324

Richard C. Knight 62 (Aug 1837-M 46)((Justice of the Peace), Mary A. 62 (Sep 1837-T/NC/NC-M 46-2-0), Kate 24 (gd)(Feb 1878)(School Teacher), Robert E.L. 20 (gs)(May 1880)(Provision Store Clerk), Mattie 17 (gd)(Mar 1883), Sarah 15 (Feb 1885) 10-323B-78/82

Thomas Knight 54 (Nov 1845-T/NC/T-M 27), Louhannie 49 (Nov 1850-M 27-7-7), Delpha ELDERS 24 (d) (Aug 1875-Wd 2-2), Tennessee J. 15 (d)(Oct 1884), Lucy 11 (d)(Ap 1889), Betrice ELDERS 5 (gd)(Nov 1894), Flossie 2 (gd)(Feb 1898) 7-263B-257/262

Thomas K. Knight 28 (Feb 1872-M 7)(Station Engineer), Lola E. 26 (Mar 1874-M 7-3-3), James N. 6 (Aug 1893), Beulah 4 (Ap 1896), Agnes 1 (Feb 1899) 10-331A-230/245

Villers(?) E. Knight 31 (Jan 1869-Ind/Oh/Oh-M 11), Alice E. 26 (Mar 1874-M 11-5-4), Merrill H. 10 (Dec 1889), Mary A. 9 (Ap 1891), Hattie C. 7 (Jan 1893), Agnes E. 5/12 (Jan 1900) 4-227B-275/279 (Road on line between 3rd & 4th Districts)

Walter B. Knight 26 (Mar 1874-M 5), Adelia G. 26 (Aug 1873-M 5-3-2), Bryan 2 (Jan 1898) 4-227B-276/280 (Road on line between 3rd & 4 Districts)

Wilard(?) S. Knight 28 (Nov 1871-Ind/Ind/Ind-M 6), Ida 24 (June 1875-Ind/T/T-M 6-3-3), Eva M. 5 (May 1895), Allice P. 2 (Feb 1898), Clarence F. 5/12 (Dec 1899) 3-201B-32/34

MARRIAGES

Delphia Knight to Robert Elder q.v.

F.K. Knight to L.E. Byerley, 15 Oct 1893, T.F. Shaver JP 4-56

H.B. Knight to Victoria Newby, 14 June 1889 (same), M.B. Hicks JP 2-425

John S. Knight to Syntha Fine, 3 Nov 1874 (same), John Howard MG 1-#1367

Jos Knight to Mollie Lewis, 10 Feb 1895, J.Q. Shaver MG 4-78

Lena(?) Knight to C. L. Neal q.v.

Louisa Jane Knight to Francis A. Fisher q.v.

Mollie Knight to George Washburn q.v.

Richard Knight to Mary Ann Spence, 19 July 1855 (same), J. Crawford JP 1-#512

Richard Knight to Hester E. Fisher*, 11 Jan 1867 (15 Jan), P.G. Campbell JP 1-#931 [*the record is clearly Fisher, but other sources list her last name as Bolen]

S.S. Knight to S.C. Hicks, 29 Jan 1870 (30 Jan), Bailey Minicks JP 1-#1142

S.S. Knight to Mary J. Hicks, 7 Feb 1880 (9 Feb), J.M. Bramlett MG 1-#1715

S.S. Knight to Texas Harris, 27 Mar 1884 (30 Mar), P.G. Roddy MG 1-474

Sallie Knight to Frank Byerley q.v.

Tennessee Knight to James Prator q.v.

Thomas J. Knight to Rhuahanna H. Fisher, 5 Ap 1872 (same), J.W. Williamson MG 1-#1235

Walter Knight to Delia Beard, 20 Aug 1895, R.M. Trentham JP 4-84

Willard Knight to Ida Collins, 3 Dec 1893, A.J. Wyrick JP 4-69

- - - - - - - - - - - - -

KNOX

1860 CENSUS

Benjamin Knox 34, Jesse 14, Jeremiah 12, Susan O. 10, Betsy C. 7, Sarah E. 1 3-56-385

Daniel W. Knox 52, Sarah A. 49, Nancy A. 16, Solomon A. 13, Elijah 12, Sarah E. 6, John BELL 12 (bound), James LEA 3 9-98-670

Elizabeth Knox 58(?) (SC), Liddia 14 3-56-383

James Knox 17, Denira 20 3-56-384

1870 CENSUS– None

1880 CENSUS

Samuel Knox 39, Susan 33, John 13, Adria 12, Bryant 8, Louella 4, Catharine 6, Deldoraun (f) 9 1-19-155

1900 CENSUS

Rosia Knox 4: see William Fifer (B)

MARRIAGES

Benjamin Knox to Mary Jane Robinson, 9 July 1860 (same), T. McPherson JP 1-#717

David C. Knox to Rachel Mathis, 28 Feb 1864 (same), E. Pyott JP 1-#821

Daniel C. Knox to Rachel Mathis, 28 Feb 1864 (same), E. Pyott JP 1-#828

Elizabeth Knox to William Jolly q.v.

Harriet Knox to Benjamin Harris q.v.

Henry Knox to Bell Thompson, 27 May 1890 (same), J.W. Zillender MG 1-601

James Knox to Jenisa Jane McClaring, 18 Jan 1860 (19 Jan), D.W. Horner ?? 1-#1659
Lyda Knox to James H. Ward q.v.

KOCH
(see also **COCK**)

MARRIAGE
John Koch to Pauline Kessler, 25 Sep 1899 (27 Sep), R.C. Knight JP, Rhea Moench(?) W 3-41

KOPPEL

MARRIAGE
A. Koppel to Frances Bessinger, 27 May 1886 (3 June), Julius Oches, Hebrew Minister 1-507

KRICHBAUM / KIRCHBAUM / KRISCHBAUM / CRISBURN

1880 CENSUS
Jacob Krichbaum 53, Elizabeth 53, Franklin 26, Adda 16, Jacob 13, Phillip 10, Robert 8, Gracie 6, John HARVY (B) 67 (Servant) 1-15-131
John Kirchbaum 27: see Benjamin Shelow
1900 CENSUS
Tenn Crisburn(?) 43 (Nov 1857-T/T/England-Wd), Charles 13 (s)(May 1887) 1-183B-91/94
MARRIAGES
J.J. Krischbaum (Rev.) to Tennessee Keety, 5 Feb 1891, W. C. Daily MG 4-23
Tennie A. Krischban to H. T. Smith q.v.

KYLE / KILE

1870 CENSUS
David Kyle 39 (Va), Caroline 37, Nancy H. 8, William 3, Edwin 1 5-2-11
Robert Kyle 46 (Va), Louvenia 42, Harriett H. 8, Sarah C. 6, James 2, Ellen 1/12 8-22-152
1880 CENSUS
David Kyle 49, Ellen 42, Nancy H. 18, William D. 14, George M. 9, Foster A. 7, Caroline M. 4, Robert C. 1 5-10-95
R. Kyle 59, L. 52 (w), S.C. 16 (d), James 12, Ellen 10, R.G. 6 (s) 8-18-158
1900 CENSUS
David Kile 23 (Mar 1877-M 6), Amanda 23 (Sep 1876-T/NC/T-M 6-3-3), Arther A. 5 (July 1894), Mollie 4 (Nov 1895), Florence 10/12 (Aug 1899) 3-206B-117/127
Ellen Kyle 63 (Aug 1836-T/Va/Va-Wd 6-6), Foster A. 27 (Mar 1873-M 3), Jennie 26 (dl)(July 1873-M 3-1-0), Caroline 24 (d)(Ap 1876), Robert C. 21 (s)(Feb 1879) 5-232A-74
George R. Kyle 26 (Unk 1876-T/Va/T-M 2), Bird 21 (Oct 1878-M 2-2-1), Clarence 0/12 (May 1900) 15-271B-72
Robert Kyle 79 (Ap 1821-Va/Va/Va-Wd), Sally 32 (d)(Sep 1867-T/Va/Va), James 29 (s)(June 1870), Ellen 27 (d) (May 1873) 15-272A-73
Susan M. Kyle 10: see Jeff D. Gaither (B)
William Kyle 41 (Sep 1838-Va/Va/Va-M 2), Narcissa(?) W. 38 (Mar 1862-Va/Va/T-M 2-0-0), LeVera 11 (May 1889-Va) 15-273B-104
William D. Kyle 32, George M. 29: see Caroline McDonald
MARRIAGES
David Kyle to Ellen McDonald, 25 Oct 1860, John W. Thompson MG 1-#693
David Kyle to Amanda A. Wilson, 30 Sep 1894, John Hill JP 4-71
Foster A. Kyle to Jennett Gregg, 14 Sep 1897 (15 Sep), J.A. Whitmore MG, J.A. Howard W 2-178
Nannie H. Kyle to W. P. Kyle q.v.
W.P. Kyle to C.S. Witt or Wilt, 24 Nov 1886 (25 Nov), L. Harworth(?) MG 1-524
W.P. Kyle to Nannie H. Kyle, 26 July 1890 (28 July), W.L. Lillard JP, R.J. Killough W 2-304

LACEWELL

1900 CENSUS
William L. Lacewell 53 (Sep 1846-T/T/NC-M 34)(Grocer), Mary E. 52 (Jan 1848-T/NC/Va-M 34-7-5), Lucy C. 22 (June 1877-Ga), Rose Ann 21 (Dec 1878-Ga) 13-300A-184/189

LADD

1860 CENSUS
James F. Ladd 43 (Ky), Sidney A. 42, Thomas F. 11, Mary L. 8, Sarah E. 6, Hanah 4, Ludiske 1, Franklin ROGERS 21 5-31-206
1870 CENSUS
James F. Ladd 53 (Ky)(Retail Merchant), Sidney A. 52, Thomas F. 21 (Clerk in Store), Mary L. 18, Adelia A. 15, Loduska 11, William S. GILLESPIE 31 (Clerk in Store), Ann GARRISON (B) 11 4-8-47
MARRIAGES
Hannah E. Ladd to Joel L. McPherson q.v.
Mary J. Ladd to Jesse I. Cash q.v.

LAMB

1880 CENSUS
Alvira Lamb 50 (m), Catharine 18, Willie 8: see Rufus Cauley (B)

LAMATER

MARRIAGE
Mearl D. Lamater to Allen W. Schmit q.v.

LAMBERT

1900 CENSUS
Phena Lambert 29 (Sep 1870-Ky/Ky/Ky-D 16-6-1)(Boarding House), Jesse R. 5 (Dec 1894) 14-215A-37/38

\- - - - - - - - - - - - -

LAMPKIN

1900 CENSUS
Charles Lampkin 23: see Harvey Franklin

\- - - - - - - - - - - - -

LAND

1860 CENSUS
Benjamin F. Land 22, Caroline J. 16 7-6-38
Sarah Land 70, Richard F. 30, Sarah T. 19, Margaret T. 11, Martha C. 1 8-21-141
1870 CENSUS-- None
1880 CENSUS
R.F. Land 52, M.C. 20, Ellen GARRETT 17 8-6-45
1900 CENSUS
Rhoda Land 73: see Elijah Morris
MARRIAGES
Francis Land to Sarah T. Bryant, 14 Aug 1857 (same), G.W. Nichols JP 1-#608
M. C. Land to J. H. Montgomery q.v.
Margaret C. Land to C. A. Morgan q.v.
Margaret C. Land to Josiah Cranmore q.v.
N. R. B. Land to John Wright q.v.
Sarah Land to William T. Walker q.v.

\- - - - - - - - - - - - -

LANDERS / LANDER

1900 CENSUS
Frank Lander 49 (Aug 1850-Maine/Do/Do-M 24), Melissa H. 51 (Oct 1848-Maine/Do/Do-M 24) 13-296B-129/131
MARRIAGE
L.V. Landers to Elizabeth Graves, 17 Ap 1886 (18 Ap), W.S. Hale MG 1-485

\- - - - - - - - - - - - -

LANDFORD

1900 CENSUS
Frank Landford 19: see Charles F. Roberson

\- - - - - - - - - - - - -

LANDIS

1900 CENSUS
Henry B. Landis 47 (Aug 1852-Ind/Pa/Oh-M 18)(Nurse), Mary E. 41 (Dec 1858-Ind/Va/Oh-M 18-6-6), Charles C. 18 (Mar 1892-Ind), Asta E. 16 (Feb 1884-Kan), Mattie P. 14 (Jan 1886-Kan), Wilma L. 11 (Aug 1888-Kan), Loyd B. 9 (Dec 1890-Kan), Freddy A. 6 (Mar 1894-Mich) 13-309B-379/393

\- - - - - - - - - - - - -

LANDRETH

1860 CENSUS
David M. Landreth 30 (NC), Permelia 26 (NC), Rozanna 8 (NC), Nelly C. 7 (NC), Edward F. 5 , James H. 3, Rachel J. 6/12 5-34-229
1870 CENSUS-- None
1880 CENSUS
James W. Landreth 38 (Carpenter), Mary E. 29, Lea N. 17, John W. 13, James E. 10, Charles M. 2 5-4-35
1900 CENSUS
James Landreth 58 (Aug 1841-NC/NC/NC-M 26), Mary E. 48 (Dec 1851-T/NC/T-M 26-12-7), Charles 21 (Feb 1874), Daniel M. 19 (July 1880), William A. 18 (Ap 1882), Cyntha 16 (May 1884), Sarah L. 12 (July 1887), Cora 10 (Jan 1890), Emma B. 8 (June 1892) 5-239A-211/211
Lee Landreth 38 (Ap 1862-NC/NC/NC-M 14), Elizabeth 28 (July 1871-M 14-5-5), James A. 12 (Ap 1888), Albert W. 9 (Feb 1891), David W. 5 (Mar 1895), Mary S. 3 (Sep 1896), Henry A. 1 (Dec 1898) 5-237A-181/181
MARRIAGE
James A. Landreth to Lemey(?) I. Carroll, 3 Dec 1892, D.E. Broyles JP 4-47

\- - - - - - - - - - - - -

LANE

1870 CENSUS
Albert Lane 24, Orlena 22, John W.F. 1 5-7-54
1880 CENSUS-- None
1900 CENSUS
Alonzo Lane 50 (Unk-M 14), Annie 30 (Unk-M 14-3-3), Stella 13 (Unk), Enlis 11 (Unk), Clifton 8 (Unk), Louis TIGNER 41 (boarder)(May 1859) 8-318B-166/172 (B)
Caroline Lane 40 (Oct 1839-Wd 7-2), Hiram 17 (Oct 1882) (Coal Miner), Rachel 12 (July 1887) 8-280B-242/244
David Lane 46 (Unk 1854-Wd), John BENNETT 25 (Unk 1875)(Partner) 8-275B-144 (B)
Eva Lane 22, Etta 3: see Joseph Harris
Joseph Lane 3: see Sam Walters (B)
MARRIAGES
Bessie Lane to William Mice q.v.
L. Lane to Tama or Tanna Staples, 25 Aug 1886 (same), P.P. Brooks ?? 1-504
W.H. Lane to Eva Harris, 24 Dec 1894, A.P. Hays JP 4-75

\- - - - - - - - - - - - -

LANGLY

MARRIAGE
Alice Langly (Mrs.) to W. N. Barton q.v.

\- - - - - - - - - - - - -

LANKFORD

1880 CENSUS
J.T. Lankford 21, N.E. 24, N.E. 4 (d), D.F. 3 (s), J.M. 11/12 (s), F.R. 17 (b), S.E. 23 (boarder) 3-18-139
J.W. Lankford 29, S.M. 19 3-18-140

MARRIAGES
S. M. Lankford to H. F. Smith q.v.
W.A. Lankford to Alia Gaddis, 10 Oct 1893, J.W. Cowles JP 4-64

- - - - - - - - - - - - -

LARGENT / ARGENT

MARRIAGES
John Argent to Sharlett Thomas, 31 Mar 1888 (16 Ap), M.C. Bruner MG 1-563
Louisa Largent to Joseph Cates q.v.
Sarah S. Largent to W. Acrey q.v.

- - - - - - - - - - - - -

LARSON– see LAWSON

- - - - - - - - - - - - -

LATHAM

MARRIAGE
James Latham to Fannie Latham, 21 Nov 1878 (same), John Howard MG 1-290 (B)

- - - - - - - - - - - - -

LATIMORE / LATTIMORE

MARRIAGES
J.W. Lattimore to Mattie Brooks, 19 May 1886 (same), Byrd Perry ?? 1-505
S.C. Latimore (43, Monroe Co) to K.E. Robinson (38), 23 Jan 1883 (at Lorrain, Tenn), S. Phillips MG, Polk Brown & But Robinson W 4-13(121)

- - - - - - - - - - - - -

LATMIR

1870 CENSUS
Samuel Latmir 40, Elizabeth 24, Julia F. 4, Robert 4/12, Emily 4/12 8-12-82 (B)

- - - - - - - - - - - - -

LAUDERDALE / LODERDALE

1860 CENSUS
Nancy Lauderdale 9: see Charles Reivley
Samuel Lauderdale 15: see James Kincannon
Sarah J. Lauderdale 16: see Addison C. Day
1870 CENSUS
Sarah J. Loderdale 24: see Hannah P. Day
1880 CENSUS
Sarah Lauderdale 35: see J. Kincannon

- - - - - - - - - - - - -

LAUDERMILK / LAUTERMILK

1880 CENSUS
Linda Lautermilk 65: see W. J. Banks
MARRIAGE
Margaret L. Laudermilk to William M. Foust q.v.

- - - - - - - - - - - - -

LAVENDER / LAVEINDER

1900 CENSUS
Balam Lavender 44 (Sep 1855-M 7), Eliza P. 32 (Mar 1868-M 7-3-3), Sarah E. 13 (Nov 1887), Ollie W. 10 (Feb 1890), James R. 5 (Jan 1895), Elsa M. 3 (Nov 1896), Lucy W. 8/12 (Feb 1900) 2-196B-99/102
Calvin D. Lavender 28 (Nov 1867-M 6), Laura E. 19 (Dec 1880-Ky/T/T-M 6-1-1), Clemma L. 2 (June 1897) 14-217A-92/94
George Laveinder 34 (Dec 1865-M 4), Jane 35 (June 1865-M 4-1-1), Lucy 2 (Nov 1897) 1-185A-124/130
Sarah J. Lavender 61 (Feb 1839-Wd 10-9), Jefferson D. 19 (Ap 1881) 14-217B-98/100
William S. Lavender 24 (Aug 1875-M 2), Lula S. 17 (Mar 1883-Ky/Ky/Ky-M 2-1-1), Claud H. 1 (Mar 1899) 14-217B-99/101
MARRIAGES
Amanda Lavender to Walter Powell q.v.
J.B. Lavender to Eliza P. Turner, 3 Dec 1893, R.A. Dickson JP 4-62
Mary A. Lavender to B. F. Perkins q.v.
Sarah Lavender to William Talley q.v.
Will Lavender to Lula Worley, 10 Mar 1898, F.F. Treadgill MG 4-100

- - - - - - - - - - - - -

LAWHORN

1900 CENSUS
Joel A. Lawhorn or Lanham 55 (Jan 1845-M 22), Florence C. 45 (Dec 1854-M 22-8-2), Irma 10 (d)(Aug 1889), Mary S. 7 (d)(Sep 1892), William T. 29 (s)(Feb 1871-M 14), Mary C. 34 (dl)(Nov 1865-M 14-2-1), Thomas C. 12 (gs)(Nov 1888) 13-301A-200/207
MARRIAGES
Nancy S. Lawhorn to William C. Smith q.v.
M. C. Lawhorn to W. T. Lawhorn q.v.
W.T. Lawhorn to M.C. Lawhorn, 10 Feb 1896, W.A. Green JP 4-94

- - - - - - - - - - - - -

LAWRENCE / LAWRANCE

1900 CENSUS
James J. Lawrence 26 (June 1873-Ky/Ky/Ky-M 0)(Telegraph Operator), Lena 26 (Oct 1873-Ky/Ky/Ky-M 0-0) 10-331B-243/258
Norris P. Lawrence 33 (Mar 1867-Mich/NY/NY-M 7) (School Teacher), Leila 28 (Dec 1871-Tex/T/NC-M 7-3-3), Meda 6 (Jan 1894-Mich), Linley E. 2 (Jan 1898), Leta 9/12 (Aug 1899), Tennie HUGHES 24 (boarder) (Mar 1876-T/Wales/Oh)(Student) 13-310A-383/397
Stuvor Lawrance 63 (Mar 1837-Miss/Unk/Unk-M 9)(Coke Puller), Annie 70 (Aug 1829-M 9-5-1), Acker 14 (Aug 1885), George SANDERS 57 (ss)(May 1843-Wd) (Preacher), Robert 8 (sgs)(Dec 1890) 7-265B-290/295 (B)
Wilford Lawrence 35 (Mar 1865-Mich/Mich/Mich-M 14) (School Teacher), Addie 35 (June 1864-Mich/NY/NY-M 14-1-1), Ivan D. 7 (June 1892-Mich) 13-310A-384/398

MARRIAGES

Jane Lawrence to Quinn Coleman q.v.

R.S. Lawrence to Charlotte Price, 8 June 1885 (same), J. Waldarf MG 1-492

Richard Lawrence to Lou Freeman, 23 Mar 1887 (same), Byrd Terry ?? 1-523

- - - - - - - - - - - - -

LAWSON / LAUSON / LASSON / LARSON

1880 CENSUS

Jasper Lauson 12 (B): see H. M. Perser

John Lasson 28 (Miner), Mary 22, William 4, Alfred 1 2-31-246

Laura Lawson 3: see Thomas A. Houston

1900 CENSUS

Edd Lawson 52, Callie 19: see Bird Lowery (B)

Evans Lawson 13 (B): see Isaac K. Brown

Telly Larson 25, Isabel 10, Ellie 9, Edwin 3: see John Rue

William M. Lawson 60 (July 1840-M 17), Martha J. 48 (Mar 1852-Tex/T/Ky-M 17-4-4), James H. 16 (Sep 1883)(Teamster), Annabel 14 (Aug 1885), William H. 11 (June 1888), John B. 9 (Aug 1890) 13-300A-190/195

MARRIAGES

Alfred Lawson to Allis Romines, 28 July 1856 (no return) 1-#554

Alfred Lawson or Larson to Tellola Ridly, 8 Dec 1888 (same), W.S. Hale MG 1-569

Daniel Lawson or Larson to Allie Foster(?), 25 Jan 1888 (same), J.W. Williamson MG 1-546

Edward Lawson to Callie Carter(?), 10 June 1893, S.S. Franklin JP 4-58

Estella Lawson to John Condra q.v.

Richard Lawson to Visa or Vina McDowel, 16 Aug 1893, A. D. Hubbard MG 4-57

Sally Lawson to James Demay q.v.

W.M. Lawson (42, McMinn Co) to Mattie J. Moore (28, Texas), 7 Dec 1883 [should be 1882 since it was recorded on 9 Ap 1883], J.W. Burnett M, C.H. Morgan & A.T. Nichols W 4-13(127)

- - - - - - - - - - - - -

LAWYER

1870 CENSUS

James P. Lawyer 25, Sarah A.S. MUNDAY 43 (Va), Hamilton L. 14, Martha A. 12 1-14-89

- - - - - - - - - - - - -

LEDBETTER

MARRIAGE

Ann Ledbetter to James Watson q.v.

- - - - - - - - - - - - -

LEDFORD / LEADFORD

1900 CENSUS

Elen Ledford 17, Evin 11, Annes 8, May 6, Affie 4: see Lon Gossett

Joseph Leadford 34 (Sep 1865-T/NC/NC-M 12)(Coal Miner), Sallie 31 (Jan 1869-M 12-5-5), Lillie B. 11 (July 1888), Elbert J. 9 (Aug 1890), Arthur 6 (June 1893), Jimie 4 (Feb 1896), Vance 1 (Oct 1898) 7-264B-277/282

William H. Leadford 31 (Jan 1869-T/NC/T-M 10)(Brickmason), Nannie 26 (Ap 1874-M 10-3-3), Iverson 7 (Jan 1892), Glen 3 (Aug 1896), Irenia 1/12 (Ap 1900) 10-258B-168/172

MARRIAGES

Joseph Ledford to Sallie Cape, 14 July 1887 (same), Calvin Morgan JP 1-534

Martha Ledford to L. W. Gossett q.v.

W.H. Ledford to Nannie Burnett, 19 Sep 1890, R.A. Bartlett ?? 4-15

- - - - - - - - - - - - -

LEE / LEA

1860 CENSUS

James Lea 3: see Daniel W. Knox

Thomas Lea 30, Acady 20, Sarah E. 1/12, Sarah 74 (SC), Andrew I. 27 (Day Laborer) 9-100-680

William Lea 32, Sarah M. 19, Archy 2, Sarah E. 2/12 9-100-679

1870 CENSUS

Arcada Lee 29, Sarah E. 8, Thomas 5, James 12 2-10-72

Lonanzie Lee 16: see Theodore W. Jewell

1880 CENSUS

John Lee 54 (Shoemaker), Ann 50, James 24 (RR Laborer), Joseph 22 (RR Operator), Frank 20 (RR Operator), M.J. 16 (d), Charlie 14, John FENIRAN 36 (boarder) (RR Laborer), L.C. TILLERY 40 (boarder) 4-10-76

1900 CENSUS

Albert E. Lee 29 (Feb 1871-Oh/Oh/Pa-M 2), Eva M. 20 (June 1879-Oh/Wisc/Oh-M 2-0-0), Anna L. 6 (Oct 1893), Clarence S. 4 (Sep 1895) 11-292B-69

Duarie Lee 22 (Jan 1878-Oh/Oh-Pa-M 4), Lenore W. 21 (Ap 1879-Ind/Oh/Ind-M 4-1-1), Arthur H. 3 (May 1897) 11-292B-63

Jack Lee 35 (Jan 1866-M 10), Delia C. 30 (Mar 1870-T/Va/Ky-M 10-2-1), Roy 13 (Mar 1887), Harriet A. STAPLEY 70 (ml)(Unk 1830-Ky/Ky/Ky-Wd 14-3), Hattie HANKINS 13 (ne)(Ap 1887) 8-285A-329/331 (B)

Josephine Lee 49 (Mar 1851-Pa/Pa/Oh-Wd 5-5)(Landlady), Willis W. 13 (Nov 1886-Oh/Oh/Pa) 11-292A-55

Reuben B. Lee 26 (Nov 1873-Oh/Oh/Pa-M 5), Alice 21 (June 1878-Pa/Pa/Pa-M 5-2-2), Roderick B. 3 (May 1897), Hazel B. 1 (Ap 1899-Pa) 11-292A-54

MARRIAGES

A.E. Lee to Eva Mae Russels, 25 Aug 1898 (31 Aug), E.W. Mort MG 2-314

A.T. Lea to Arcada Miller, no dates 1-#580

B.F. Lee to Eliza T. Broyles, 18 Nov 1897 (24 Nov), L.M. Cartwright MG, W.A. Ault W 2-210

D.H. Lee to Leonora Wilson, 1 May 1896 (4 May), W.A. Howard MG, R.B. Lee & Duane Lee W 2-19

Mabel Lee to J. N. Kennedy q.v.

Nellie E. Lee to W. S. B. Poe q.v.

Sarah Lee to Andy Carter(?) q.v.

T.P. Lee to Aminda Miller, 4 July 1857 (5 July), T.J. Gillespie JP 1-#557; also 1-#562 & 1-#564

William Lea to Sarah Wrydenhour, 24 Dec 1856 (25 Dec), W.H. Cunnyngham JP 1-#587

- - - - - - - - - - - - -

LEECH

1900 CENSUS

Arvell Leech 14 (Aug 1885)(Student), Hallie 24 (si)(June 1875) 13-305B-292/303

LEETH

MARRIAGE

Lillie Leeth to P. A. Minton q.v.

LEFFEW

1870 CENSUS

Keziah Leffew 39, William H. 11, Elizabeth 9, Pleasant H. 5, Jane McDUFFEY 35 3-6-38

MARRIAGE

Lydia Leffew to Will Smith q.v.

LEIGH

1900 CENSUS

Viola Leigh 39 (Unk-Wd 2-1)(Washing & Ironing), Dean STAPLES 19 (boarder)(Furnaceman) 10-329B-198/211 (B)

LEMONS / LEMMONS / LEMANS

1860 CENSUS

John Lemons 65, Sarah 45, Lucinda 17, Louisa 16, John 13, Amy 12, George 10, James 8, Blanch L. 6 1-86-585

Lorinda J. Lemons 20: see John Monroe

Ruben Lemons 24, Rebecca 31, Amy or Anny 3, Mary 2 2-80-542

Thomas Lemons 96 (Va), Elizabeth 68 (Va), Angaline BRADY 25 (Va), James 5 (Va), Thomas 3 (Va), Mary J. 2 (Va) 9-98-665

William Lemmons 61 (Va)(Blacksmith), Anny 45, Elizabeth 18, William 16, Richard 14, Samuel 12, Addison 11, Elvira 9, James 4 9-101-687

1870 CENSUS

Anna Lemmons 24: see Sarah Cantrell

George W. Lemmons 20, Mary 26, Lorinda J. 2/12 3-3-20

James Lemmons 21, Susan Jane 25, Rebecca CLARK 65 (NC), Judah 30, John F. 16, James E. 13 1-12-75

John M. Lemons 26, Louisa 33, John M. 1 1-7-44

William Lemmon 72, Sarah 58, James F. 16 1-3-21

William Lemmons 27, Samuel 24, Elizabeth 16, Addison L. 20 1-22-142

1880 CENSUS

Adison Lemons 27, Eliza 19, Alice 3, Jasper 2, Marion 1/2 12-3-26

James Lemons 26, Susan 28, Rebecca 9, William 7, James 5, Hattie 3, unnamed 1/12 (d) 12-4-37

John Lemons 39, Eliza 43, John 11, Amanda 9, William 7, James 5, Perry 2 12-4-32

Richard Lemons 36, Paralee 44, Lorinda 8, Franklin 6, Martha 3, Lou Ella 1 12-4-31

Sarah Lemons 68 1-19-156

Samuel Lemons 29, Betsy 26, James 9, Jessee 7, Samuel 4, Almeda 2 12-4-38

1900 CENSUS

Adison Lemans 60 (Feb 1840-M 6), Betti 34 (Mar 1866-M 6-1-1), Jasper 20 (s)(Ap 1880), Nomi 15 (d)(May 1885), Henry 13 (Jan 1887), Alas 10 (d)(Dec 1889), Charley 9 (Mar 1891) 12-182B-80/83 [Addison married Elizabeth Holms on 18 Dec 1895 in Meigs Co]

Amos A. Lemons 50 (Aug 1849-Ga/Ga/NC-M 7)(Furniture Worker), Vinie E. 36 (Jan 1864-M 7-6-4), James C. 16 (Jan 1884)(Saw Mill Laborer), Adaline C. 13 (Oct 1886), Thomas H. 5 (June 1894), Jennie E. 2 (Jan 1898) 14-219B-134/137

Frank Lemons 26 (Feb 1874-M 2), Maggie 25 (Nov 1875-M 2-2-2), William R. 1 (Jan 1899) 9-228A-4

George Lemons 50 (Mar 1850-M 16)(Coal Miner), Mary 29 (May 1871-M 16-1-1), Maggie 13 (Mar 1887) 8-280B-238/240

Samuel Lemmon 55 (Oct 1844-M 1), Ann 34 (Sep 1865-M 1-4-4), Sam 24 (d)(Feb 1876), Elisie 14 (d)(Aug 1885), Sarah 10 (d)(June 1889), Maggie 8 (May 1892), Samuel 4/12 (Jan 1900), Eline DANNELS 19 (sd)(Mar 1884), Sarah 14 (sd)(Dec 1885), John 11 (ss)(Oct 1888), Rosi 14 (sd)(July 1885) 2-182B-79/82

Vista Lemons 17: see James W. Pelfry

MARRIAGES

Addison Lemmons to Eliza Dye, 8 Dec 1875 (9 Dec), H.B. Heiskell JP 1-#1422

Adison Lemmons to Minnie Dials, 30 Aug 1882 (31 Aug), no MG or JP 1-481

Allie Lemons to James Ray q.v.

Angeline Lemmons to William C. Bandy q.v.

Anney Lemmons to William M. Watson q.v.

Archer Lemon to Vinie Wade, 22 Feb 1894, A.L. Parker MG 4-85

B. L. Lemmons to William Reese q.v.

Frank Lemons to Maggie Lewis, 17 Ap 1898, J.W. Crayne MG 4-99

George W. Lemmons to Carry C. Clark, 2 Oct 1869 (3 Oct), A.J. Mathis MG 1-#1113

James Lemmons to Susan Clarke, 8 Jan 1869 (no return) 1-#1041

Jane Lemmons to Thomas Jones q.v.

John M. Lemmons to Louisa Barton, 7 Feb 1865 (9 Feb), W.W. Low JP 1-#1082

Joseph Lemmons to Salissa Meeks, 10 Ap 1852 (11 Ap), W.S. Wright JP 1-#387

Mary Lemmons to William Bennett q.v.

Mary Lemmons to N. G. Dillard q.v.

Mary E. Lemons to Thomas Walker q.v.

Mary Jane Lemmons to James A. Daniel q.v.

Richard Lemmons to Elizabeth McClendon, 9 Mar 1867 (same), H.B. Heiskell JP 1-#942

Richard Lemmons to Pairlee Roberts, 19 Jan 1870 (no return) 1-#1138

Sam Lemons to Martha Loy, 8 Jan 1889 (10 Jan), D.L. Ferris(?) MG 1-567

Samuel Lemmons to Elizabeth Roberts, 6 June 1870 (9 June), H.B. Heiskell JP 1-#1153

Samuel Lemons to Nancy Rhea, 5 Nov 1885 (6 Nov), W.T. West MG 1-519

Samuel Lemens to Annie Daniels, 2 Ap 1899, W.T. West MG 4-100
Sarah Lemmons to Joseph Cantral q.v.
Sarah Lemmons to William Thompson q.v.

LENOIR

MARRIAGE

Calvin Lenoir to Laeond Smith, 15 Dec 1885 (same), P.P. Brooks ?? 1-483

LEONARD / LANARD

MARRIAGES

Jacob Lanard to Sarah Bowlen, 5 June 1868 (same), Edward Pyott JO 1-#1013
W. F. Leonard to Virginia Alderman, 28 July 1887 (same), --?-- Drake MG 1-527

LETNER / LITNER

1870 CENSUS

Caswell Litner 25, Eliza C. 26, Lydia 3, Martha J. 6/12 6-13-87

1880 CENSUS– None

1900 CENSUS

James Letner 23 (July 1876-M 1), Lean 22 (May 1878-M 1-1-1), William 6 (May 1894), Roscoe C. 2/12 (Ap 1900), Calvin LETNER 72 (f)(May 1828-Wd), Sheridan 4 (b)(Jan 1896) 13-310B-389/403

MARRIAGES

Calvin Letner to Mary Grassham, 19 Feb 1887 (20 Feb), Anthony Smith MG 1-517
Susan Letner to S. H. Helton q.v.
Will Letner to Emma Riggs, 19 Feb 1887 (20 Feb), A. Smith MG 1-518

LETSON

1900 CENSUS

Rinnie T. Letson 34 (July 1865-Ga/Ga/Ga-Wd 2-2), Earl H. 16 (Nov 1883-Ga)(Coal Miner), Olonzo T. 15 (Mar 1885-Ga) 13-309A-364/377

LEUTY

1860 CENSUS

Burton Leuty 32 (Merchant), Virginia 24 (Va), Mary LEUTY 61 4-47-318
Stanton W. Leuty 39, Harriet O. 30, Mary E. 6, James F. 4, Virginia T. 10/12 3-65-446

1870 CENSUS

Burton Leuty 43 (Retail Merchant), Virginia 36 (Va), Mary E. 8, John S. 5, Catharine 3, Brutella 9/12, Mary LEUTY 74, Vina LEUTY 65 (Ga) 4-8-50

1880 CENSUS

Dany(?) Leuty 23: see George W. Johnson
H.O. Leuty 50, Virginia T. 19, G.A. McDONALD 33 1-29-225/230
Virginia Leuty 48, M. L. 18 (d), J. S. 14 (s), Virginia 13, B. A. 10 (d), J. B. 8 (s), Thomas 6, J. D. 4 (s), Hannah THOMPSON (B) 22 (Servant), Joseph REYNOLDS 18 (boarder)(Printer), J.A. ALEXANDER 30 (boarder) (Fruit Dealer) 4-10-83

1900 CENSUS

Harriet Leuty 72, Tenie 27: see Eli McDonald
James Leuty 29 (May 1871-T/?/Va-M 6), Nellie 24 (Mar 1876-Calif/T/Oh-M 6-2-2), Loy C. 4 (Aug 1895), Annie M. 7/12 (Nov 1899) 3-203A-64/68
James T. Leuty 43 (July 1856-M 8), Evaline 35 (Nov 1864-M 8-0) 3-207A-126/137
Virginia Leuty 68, Caty 32, Birdy 30: see Herbert Payne

MARRIAGES

Burton Leuty to Virginia McPherson, 11 Ap 1860 (12 Ap), S. Phillips MG 1-#1661
Mary E. Leuty to G. W. Johnson q.v.
Mary L. Leuty to H. B. Payne
T.B. Leuty to Julia A. McPherson, 30 July 1866 (no return) 1-#905

LEWIS / LOUIS

1870 CENSUS

Barbara Lewis 20: see William Marshall

1880 CENSUS

B.H.M. Louis 39 (School Teacher), S.A. 38 (w), W.A. 12 (s), Allien S. 10 (d), Ida R. 8, Mollie R. 6, O.G. 4 (s) 8-3-26

1900 CENSUS

Arch N. Lewis 53 (Mar 1847-T/Va/Va-M 22), Margaret A. 49 (Jan 1851-M 22-10-5), Cynthia 19 (Jan 1881-Ga), Lindsay E. 14 (Feb 1886), Sarah C. 9 (Aug 1890), James W. 2 (Aug 1897) 13-296A-113/115
Ascar [Oscar] Lewis 24 (Ap 1876-T/Ga/Ga-M 1)(Painter), Elen 22 (Ap 1878-M 1-1-1), Lewdward 11/12 (June 1899) 10-251B-31
Bailes M.H. Lewis 59 (Dec 1840-Ga/SC/SC-M 39)(Painter), Sarah 58 (Feb 1842-Ga/SC/SC-M 39-8-5), Allice HEDGECOTH 31 (d)(Sep 1868-M 11-3-1), Carl A. 10 (gs)(July 1889), Carmon J. 6 (gd)(Aug 1893) 10-253A-58
Harrson Lewis 56 (Mar 1844-T/NC/NC-M 0), Margaret L. 22 (Dec 1877-M 0-0) 5-233A-102
Harrison Lewis 7: see Davis Weaver
John Lewis 50 (May 1850-M 26), Margaret 39 (July 1860-M 26-11-10), Manuel 14 (Nov 1885), Abbie 12 (Nov 1887), Charlie 10 (Jan 1890), Mary A. 7 (June 1892), Lee 1 (May 1899) 6-247B-150/151

MARRIAGES

Allie Lewis to Nathan Hedgecoth q.v.
George Lewis to Altie Dobbs, 11 Dec 1896 (bond only), J.W. Banks W 2-88
Harriet N. Lewis to David H. Foust q.v.
Harrison E. Lewis to Maggie L. Neal, 29 Sep 1899 (1 Oct), L.E. Smith JP 3-42
Lizie Lewis to Jack Smithers q.v.
Lizzie Lewis to John Dobbs q.v.
Maggie Lewis to Frank Lemons q.v.

Mollie Lewis to Joseph Knight q.v.
Oscar G. Lewis to Ella Sneed, 23 Sep 1898 (25 Sep), W.L. Lillard JP, B.M.H. Lewis & Oscar Lewis W 2-326
S. A. Lewis to Julia Lowe, 17 Aug 1889 (18 Aug), John Howard MG 1-579
Walter Lewis to Lizzie Denton, 25 Dec 1890, J.J. Burnett MG 4-20
William Lewis to Rebecca Monday, 16 Feb 1869 (18 Feb), Asa Newport MG 1-#1045
Zachariah Lewis to Eliza Jane Jeffers, 3 Nov 1866 (4 Nov), T.N.L. Cunnyngham JP 1-#917

- - - - - - - - - - - - -

LIGHTFOOT

1900 CENSUS
Mary Lightfoot 24 (Ap 1876-T/Va/T-S)(Washwoman), Earnest LIGHTFOOT 5 (s)(June 1894), Edd ROBERTSON 4 (s)(Oct 1895), Walter PHILLIPS 2 (s)(Mar 1898), Mary LIGHTFOOT 55 (m)(Ap 1845-M 38-10-3) 10-258A-151/155 (B)

- - - - - - - - - - - - -

LILLARD

1880 CENSUS
Robert W. Lillard 54, Sarah A. 52, Sarah J. 27, William W. 26 (Studying Medicine), John M. 21, Eidfall A. 19, James M. 6, Adavie 12 6-16-142/144
1900 CENSUS
Myrtice Lillard 4: see Sarysan D. Bridgman
Wigfall Lillard 39 (Ap 1861-M 8)(Dry Goods Salesman), Ida A. 29 (Oct 1870-M 8-1-1), Ida P. 6 (June 1893) 11-290B-16
William L. Lillard 52 (July 1847-M 30)(Justice of the Peace), Mary A. 47 (Mar 1853-M 30-7-2), George R. 23 (May 1877)(Day Laborer), Walter C. 9 (Aug 1890) 10-326A-131/136 [W.L. Lillard married M.A. Neil on 1 June 1871 in Meigs Co]
MARRIAGES
A. C. Lillard to H. M. Purser q.v.
Ella Lillard to T. D. Thomas q.v.
Sarah J. Lillard to P. M. Purcer q.v.
W.D. Lillard to Ida Walker, 25 July 1891, J.R. Walker MG 4-28
W.W. Lillard to M.C. Bridgeman, 4 Sep 1884 (same), J. Waldord MG 1-470

- - - - - - - - - - - - -

LIMERLY

MARRIAGE
Henry Limerly to Matilda K. Pressly, 19 Oct 1852 (same), C.A. Wallard MG 1-#385

- - - - - - - - - - - - -

LINCOLN

1900 CENSUS
Martha Lincoln 26 (Ap 1874-D 5-3)(Washwoman), Frank 8/12 (Oct 1899) 8-318A-159/164 (B)
MARRIAGES
John Lincoln to Martha Hackler, 14 Aug 1887 (15 Aug), G.D. Collins MG 1-584
John M. Lincoln to Sary Wright, 27 Aug 1866 (28 Aug), Asa Newport MG 1-#1062

- - - - - - - - - - - - -

LINDSEY / LINSEY / LINSY

1880 CENSUS
P. Lindsey 26, R.J. 10, L.J. 9: see G.B. Brady
1900 CENSUS
Jane Lindsey 30: see Green B. Brady
Robert B. Linsy 52 (Sep 1847-Ireland/Do/Do-1844/46/Na-M 17)(Sawmill Operator), Math 37 (Sep 1862-M 17-1-1), Maggi 15 (Aug 1884), Charles 7 (orphan)(Nov 1872) 1-183B-90/93
William Lindsey 39 (Ap 1861-Ga/SC/Ga-M 13), Jennie 41 (Nov 1858-T/SC/SC-M 13-8-5), Newton 11 (July 1888), Chaney 8 (May 1892), Mabel 4 (Oct 1895), John F. BUFFINGTON 19 (July 1880-Ga/Ga/T)(Coal Miner), Jessie J. HERRING 66 (Aug 1833-SC/SC/SC-Wd) 8-276A-149/150
MARRIAGES
Caroline Lindsey to J. M. Burger q.v.
Julia A. Linsey to G. B. Brady q.v.
Mary E. Lindsey to Ben F. East q.v.
Robert B. Lindsey (36) to Marrie Richey (15, Meigs Co), 15 Mar 1883, J. Howard MG, Sam Frazier & Enoch Richey W 4-13(129)

- - - - - - - - - - - - -

LINE / LINER

1900 CENSUS
William C. Line 41 (Feb 1859-M 10), Sarah A. 25 (June 1874-T/T/NC-M 10-4-4), Flora 9 (Nov 1890), Ernest W. 6 (July 1893), Blanche 4 (Oct 1895), Courtney 2 (Dec 1897), Amanda RAULSTON 70 (ml)(Unk 1830-NC/NC/NC-Wd 6-6) 13-295A-102/104
MARRIAGE
James Liner to Tina Scott, 19 Oct 1890, F.M. Capps JP 4-19
W.C. Line to S.A. Ragleston, 10 Nov 1889, James Carrie MG 4-46

- - - - - - - - - - - - -

LITCHFIELD

1900 CENSUS
Samuel W. Litchfield 54 (Jan 1846-Ind/England/Do-Wd)(Carpenter), Marion A. 25 (Ap 1875-Ind)(Carpenter), Jennie 20 (July 1879-Ind), Ethel 18 (Nov 1887-Fla), Charles F. 15 (Nov 1884-Fla), Richard J. 13 (Ap 1887-Fla), Walter F. 9 (July 1890-Fla), Theodore 6 (June 1893-Fla): *Boarders:* Arthur MANOUS 26 (Mar 1874-SC/SC/SC-S)(Carpenter), Blennie WOODALL 19 (Feb 1881-NC/NC/NC-S)(Carpenter), Ollie PINE 23 (Ap 1877-Ind/Pa/Oh) 13-307A-329/341
MARRIAGE
G.L. Litchfield to Mary J. England, 12 Aug 1898 (14 Aug), W.J. Drummond MG, J.A. Anderson W 2-308

- - - - - - - - - - - - -

LITEL

1880 CENSUS
Sam Litel 28, Catharne 36 (w), A.J. 4 (d), Delila 6/12 (d) 4-33-271

- - - - - - - - - - - - -

LIVELY

1900 CENSUS
Henry Lively 60: see Garvey Franklin
MARRIAGES
Annie Lively to A. B. Smith q.v.
Ellen Lively to Hague Henson q.v.
Fannie Lively to J. H. Franklin q.v.
Joseph Lively to Mattie Nash, 20 Aug 1900 (same), W.L. Lillard JP, W.G. Curen(?) W 3-202

- - - - - - - - - - - - -

LOAD

1880 CENSUS
James E. Load 4: see John Peterson

- - - - - - - - - - - - -

LOCKE

1860 CENSUS
Addison Locke 39 (Physician), Mary 20, Susan E. 15, James L. 13, John B. 11, Mary 9, Cordelia 7, Hugh 1, Isaac KNIGHT 21 1-95-651
Franklin Locke 46, Isabella 37 6-107-731
James H. Locke 44, Adaline 36, Ollinda J. 17, Mary E. 15, Leah Ann 12, Josephine 9, William L. 5, Charles L. 2 6-106-725
Newton Locke 47, William HENRY 22, Rachel F. 19, Mary HUMPHREY 15 6-107-730
1870 CENSUS
Addison Locke 57 (Physician), James L. 24 (Overseer), Delia 16, Hugh A. 11, Nancy E. 7, John WHEELER 27 (Physician) 1-1-5
Alfred Locke 21, Elizabeth 18, Barton 10 6-12-85 (B)(Mu)
Anderson Locke 64, Vina [KELLY] 22, Joseph 21, John 18, Andrew 15, Jane 13, Barton 9, Mollie 2, John 5 6-13-89 (B)
Asbery Locke 17, Phillip 11, Priscilla 13, Lydia A. 15 (B): see William R. Henry
Caroline Locke 48, Jeremiah 23, Alfred 21 1-2-13 (B)
Franklin Locke 58 (Retired Lawyer), Isabella T. 55, Sarah KELLON 7 6-12-84
James H. Locke 54, Adaline 48, Malinda J. 25, Mary 23, Lea A. 20, William L. 15, Lusians(?) 13, James H. 6, Adaline 8 6-13-90
Jane Locke 33, William B. 10, Samuel V. 10, George A. 7 5-3-20
Melton Locke 14, Rufus 18, Joseph 17 (B): see Cyrus Henry
1880 CENSUS
Alfred Locke 35, Malinda 35, Lunna 8, Fanny 5, Babe 1 6-25-190/194 (B)
Asbury Locke 27, Tilda 25, Charley 4, Mary Frances 1 6-17-155/158 (B)(Mu)
Caroline Lock 80, Alfred BROILES 33 (s), Horace PETERS 23 (sl), Mary 21 (d), Charlie LOCKE 7 (gs), Anna 1 (gd) 1-19-163 (B)
Hugh Locke 20, Parthena 19, Delta 5/12: see Sarah Evans
J. C. Locke 28: see J. H. Rogers
James H. Locke 64, Orlinda J. 31, Mary E. 28, Leah A. 23, William L. 22, Charles L. 21 (Law Student), Adea 18, James H. 16 6-14-128/129
Mary J. Locke 44, William BARTON 19, Samuel V. 19, George A. 15, Anna A. 4, Mary E. 4, Darthula WADE 22 ("living about"), Floyd 5/12 6-17-160/164 (Mu)
1900 CENSUS
Alfred Locke 54 (May 1847-M 25), Lizzie 52 (Unk-M 25-5-4), Anna 11 (Unk), Malco 6 (Mar 1894) 6-243A-72 (B)
Asberry Locke 49 (Unk-M 25)(Laborer, Rock Quarry), Matilda 48 (Aug 1851-M 25-7-7), Charles 22 (June 1878), John R. 19 (June 1881), Richard 17 (May 1883), Ardler 13 (Dec 1886), Samuel H. 10 (Aug 1889), Lula R. 6 (June 1893), Freddie BOOKER 6 (Unk) 6-245B-109/110 (B)
Charles Locke(?) 24: see Bertie Wasson (B)
Hugh A. Locke 41 (July 1859-M 20)(Grist Miller), Parthena E. 39 (May 1861-M 20-3-3), Adison L. 18 (Ap 1882), Hester A. 14 (Oct 1885) 5-231A-68
James H. Locke 47 (Mar 1853-Wd), Eva L. 13 (Oct 1886), Osborn 11 (Aug 1888), Iva L. 7 (Oct 1892) 5-236A-157 [James H. married Susan W. Taylor on 5 Oct 1884 in Meigs County]
Jane Locke 57 (Aug 1842-S), Leah 52 (si)(Oct 1847-S), Charles L. 42 (b)(Dec 1857-S)(Grocery Dealer) 6-243B-78
Josa Locke 38: see Thomas Hale
John C. Locke 48 (Aug 1851-Wd)(Lawyer), Charles L. 17 (Aug 1882), David R. 11 (Dec 1888) 14-216A-65/66 [John married Flora Rhea on 17 May 1881, Meigs Co]
Maggie Locke 46: see George W. Morgan
Robert Lock 3, James C. 2: see Hulda Wasson (B)
William L. Locke 44 (July 1855-M 5), Pink M. 34 (Nov 1865-Ky/Md/Oh-M 5-3-3), Neil G.L. 3 (June 1896), William R. 2 (Dec 1898), Arnold M. 3/12 (Feb 1900), Mary 55 (si)(Jan 1845), James 36 (b)(Oct 1863) 6-246B-125/126

MARRIAGES
Adie Locke to Jacob Kelly q.v.
Addison Locke to Mary Evans, 11 Aug 1855 (12 Aug), S. Phillips MG 1-#646
G.R. Locke to Maggie Snow, 5 Feb 1895, J.H. Snow MG 4-78
Hugh A. Locke to Parthenia E. Hamilton, 11 Sep 1878 (same), D.H. Carr MG 1-#1582
James Locke to Alice Wasson, 3 July 1897, J.G. Isabell MG 4-97
Jane Locke to Henry Rhea q.v. (B)
Josephine Locke to Samuel Frazier q.v.
Lora Locke to William Hicks q.v. (B)
Louisa C. Locke to James M. Sweeton q.v.
Malinda Locke to Moses Porter q.v. (B)
Mollie Locke to Horace Peters q.v. (B)
Mollie Locke to Luther Smith q.v. (B)
Rachel F. Locke to William R. Henry q.v.
Steve Locke to Laura Cox, 15 Aug 1892, W.H. Dunbar MG 4-41

W.L. Locke to Pink Morrison, 31 July 1895, J.A. Whitener MG 4-90

- - - - - - - - - - - - -

LOCKENBEE / LOCKERBY

1880 CENSUS
Samuel Lockerby 45, Aurelia 36, Charlie 15, Allis 13 12-1-7
MARRIAGE
C.L. Lockenbee to Mary Miller, 23 Ap 1890, A.J. Christian ?? 4-178

- - - - - - - - - - - - -

LOCKEY

1900 CENSUS
Alvis Lockey 28, Ida 24: see Marquis Morrison

- - - - - - - - - - - - -

LOCKMILLER

1900 CENSUS
Marlone(?) Lockmiller 21 (Jan 1879), Manda 43 (a)(Oct 1856) 6-249A-174/175
Scruggs Lockmiller 26 (July 1873-M 3), Nannie 20 (July 1879-M 3-0) 10-321B-33/34
William Lockmiller 27 (Aug 1872-M 3), Mary M. 24 (Aug 1875-M 3-1-1), Della M. 1 (June 1898), Willie CAMPBELL 16 (bl)(Feb 1884) 6-248B-166/167
William Lockmiller 57 (Mar 1843-M 37), Mary 59 (Mar 1841-M 37-11-7), Buck 18 (Mar 1882), Lydia 11 (Unk 1889), Lemuel 6 (Unk 1894) 15-274A-116
MARRIAGES
Jessie L. Lockmiller to N. H. Keith q.v.
Scruggs Lockmiller to Nannie Parker, 14 Aug 1896 (16 Aug), W.L. Lillard JP, J. Brooks W 2-45
Teck(?) Lockmiller to W. F. Gibson q.v.

- - - - - - - - - - - - -

LOCKWOOD

1900 CENSUS
Blanchy Lockwood (no dates): non-resident in District 12
MARRIAGE
Minnie Lockwood to Samuel W. Burnett q.v.

- - - - - - - - - - - - -

LODEN / LODAN

1870 CENSUS
Eliza Loden 44: see Peter Bell (B)
1880 CENSUS– None
1900 CENSUS
James Loden 63 (Ap 1837-M 42), Hariet 63 (July 1836-M 42-8-4), Tomas 34 (Mar 1866-Wd)(RR Hand), Alrage 27 (July 1872)(RR Hand), Ellie PRICE 8 (gd)(Ap 1892), Susan 60 (si)(May 1840) 12-182A-71/74
Vigia(?) Lodan(?) 30 (June 1869-M 8), Nasty(?) 25 (May 1875-M 8-3-2), Claud 6 (June 1893), Lillie 4 (Oct 1895) 12-182A-70/73
MARRIAGES
E.J. Loden to Vesta Miller, 8 Jan 1892, James M. Ledford ?? 4-43
Elizabeth Loden to James M. Majors q.v.
Elizabeth B. Loden to D. R. Brown q.v.
William F. Loden to Sarah A. Godsey, 22 Aug 1898, George Morris ?? 4-99

- - - - - - - - - - - - -

LOFTISS / LOFTIS / LOFTES / LOFTIN

1860 CENSUS
Coleman Loftiss 25 (School Teacher): see James Pierce
Darius Loftiss 33 (NC), Anna 30 (NC), Mary 6 (Va), Creed 4, Nelly J. DENTON 17 (NC), Edward DENTON 22 (Ind) 5-35-233
George Loftiss 25, Amanda 20, Susan J. 4, Samuel T. 2, Nancy E. 1 5-32-214
Martin Loftiss 55 (Va), Tabitha 56, Francis M. 23, William D. 21, Susan 3, Nancy 16, Eliza 14, Martin L. 12 5-32-213
1870 CENSUS
Francis M. Loftis 34 (NC), Harriett S. 32, Mary T. 6, Thomas M.C. 4 5-7-47
Martin Loftis 65 (Va), Tabitha 66 (Va) 5-5-34
Martin L. Loftis 21 (NC), Eliza Jane 21 (Ga) 5-5-35
1880 CENSUS
Martin L. Loftis 32, Margaret A. 23, William M. 8, Sarah T. 2, Mary E. 8/12, Tabitha LOFTIS 77 (m), Thomas M. 14 (nw), John T. 11 (nw) 5-7-62
1900 CENSUS
Martin L. Loftes 52 (Oct 1847-Va/Va/Va-M 24), Margaret A. 44 (Jan 1856-M 24-10-8), Sarah T. 22 (Dec 1877), Mary E. 20 (July 1879), Cyntha A. 17 (Dec 1882), Walter M. 15 (Ap 1885), James T. 11 (Sep 1888), Samuel A. 9 (Oct 1890), Cleveland 4 (May 1896), Artie May 2/12 (Mar 1900) 13-300B-194/200
William Loftin 73: see Thomas G. Gillespie
MARRIAGES
F.M. Loftis to Marthy Barnett, 4 Ap 1861 (no return) 1-#752
M.F. Loftis to Harriett Barnett, 7 Jan 1868 (no return) 1-#995
M.L. Loftis to Margaret A. Smith, 8 Sep 1877 (same), A.J. Pritchett MG 1-#1510
Martin Loftis to Mariah Porter, 12 June 1896 (13 June), H. B. Burditt MG, M.L. Loftis Jr. [signed by X] & M.L. Loftix Sr. [signed by X] W 2-31
Martin L. Loftis to Eliza Jane Cofer, 20 Oct 1868 (31 Oct), B. Minix JP 1-#1034
Nancy Loftist(?) to Edward Denton q.v.

- - - - - - - - - - - - -

LOGAN

1870 CENSUS
Henry Logan 32 (Ga), Leu 24 (NC), Florance 4, Pinkney 3, Lueller 1 10-1-5 (B)
1880 CENSUS
Wily Logan 51, L.I. 41 (w), Florence 14, Pinkney 11, Lewella 10, G.A. 9 (d), A.B. 6 (d), S.A.P. 5 (d), Bess 3, Len A. 1 (d) 7-27-237 (B)

1900 CENSUS

Henry Logan 75 (Unk-NC/NC/NC-Wd), Ella 33 (Unk-T/NC/NC), Andrew 26 (Unk), Laura 25 (Oct 1874), Annie FLEMING 22 (d)(Feb 1878-M 4-2-1), LeRoy 4 (gs)(Unk), Edward HASKELL 5 (gs)(Unk) 8-311A-2/2 (B)

MARRIAGES

Anna Logan to Lumie Hutcheson q.v.

Annie Logan to John Fleming q.v.

Anthony Logan to Catharine Warren, 10 Feb 1852 (12 Feb), A.D. Paul JP 1-#362

George Logan to Anna Morris, 20 Nov 1897 (21 Nov), D.B. Jackson MG, R.J. Killough W 2-211

Ginger Logan to Will Williams q.v.

Mary Logan to Steve Johnson q.v.

- - - - - - - - - - - - -

LOMAS / LOMAX

1870 CENSUS

William E. Lomas 35 (Va)(Miller), Rebecca A. 23, Malaki 3, Pleasant G. 7/12, Susan LOMAS 50 (Va) 1-17-112

MARRIAGE

Dollie Lomax to Thomas C. or E. Brooks q.v.

- - - - - - - - - - - - -

LONG

1860 CENSUS

Leonard Long 32, Myra 33, Serena E. 7, William J. 7/12 2-74-503 [Leonard married Myra Waterhouse Paul on 18 May 1852]

Nicholas H. Long 42, Margaret P. 37, Mary P. 14, Zachary D. 12, Amanda C. 10, Elizabeth 8, Archibald D.P. 6, Stephen N.H. 4, Cyrena 3/12, Elizabeth LONG 84 1-84-572

1870 CENSUS

Lenard Long 42, Margaret E. 16, Serena E. 17, William J. 10, Elizabeth A. 8, Mary 11/12 2-16-115

Nicholas H. Long 52, Margarett J. 46, Zachari T. 22, Amanda C. 20, Elizabeth K. 19, Archibald D.P. 16, Stephen N. 13, Addison L. 7 1-10-66

1880 CENSUS

Elizabeth Long 18: see Franklin McCabe

Leonard Long 34, Margaret 27, Lydia 9, Jane 7, John 4, James 1 2-35-285

Margaret Long 56, Archibald 26, Stephen 22, Adison 16 1-18-149

S.E. Long 27: see J.L. McPherson

W.H. Long(?) 24, C. 25, A.F. 3 (d), H.F. 1 (s) 4-32-259

W.H. Long 37, M.H. 36 (w), M.E. 7 (d), J.H. 2 (s) 3-21-168

William Long 30: see Granville Hurst

Zachariah Long 33, Mary 56, Nellie 3, Mary 2, Idenna 11/12 1-18-150

1900 CENSUS

Addison Long 37 (Nov 1862-M 12)(Cattle Dealer), Isabella 32 (Feb 1868-M 12-0-0) 14-215A-45/46

Frank W. Long 48 (Sep 1851-T/NC/NC-M 15), Callie 35 (Jan 1865-M 15-6-5), George H. 14 (June 1886), William H. 12 (Dec 1887), Benjamin H. 9 (Jan 1891), Sallie 9 (Jan 1891), James F. 8 (June 1892) 3-209B-170/185

James N. Long 24 (July 1875-M 6), Mamie E. 21 (Sep 1878-M 6-1-1), Sallie F. 3 (Ap 1897) 2-194B-66/68 [James married Mamie Curton on 15 July 1894 in Meigs County]

John S. Long 27 (Feb 1873-T/NC/T-M 4), Mary 20 (Sep 1879-M 4-1-1), Carl 2 (Aug 1897) 3-205B-101/110

John W. Long 43 (June 1856-NC/NC/NC-M 25), Josy 43 (June 1856-M 25-10-8), Wilbur 23 (Ap 1877), John 15 (June 1885), William 13 (Mar 1887), Essey 10 (Nov 1889), Jewell 8 (July 1891), Arkey 6 (Dec 1893), Bart 2 (Sep 1897), Lee 1 (Ap 1899) 2-195A-74/77

William H. Long 57 (Feb 1843-T/NC/NC-M 24), Mary 56 (May 1844-T/Va/T-M 24-2-2), John H. 21 (May 1878), Berttie 15 (Jan 1885) 3-203A-65/69

Zac Long 52 (Aug 1847-M 24), Mary 44 (June 1855-M 24-12-8), Farmer 13 (Sep 1886), Burtha 12 (Feb 1888), Vira 10 (d)(July 1889), Anzi 9 (d)(Nov 1890), Sarah 6 (Mar 1894) 1-188B-188/197

MARRIAGES

A.L. Long to Bell Wassom, 11 Feb 1888 (12 Feb), B.F. Holloway JP 1-544

Amanda C. Long to James M. Phillips q.v.

Ann Long to Daniel Kenedy q.v.

Elizabeth Long to William Pass q.v.

J.S. Long to Mary Brown, 4 Feb 1896, L.E. Smith JP 4-93

Leonard J. Long to Margaret E. Owens, 20 July 1870 (no return) 1-#1156

Mary J. Long to F. A. McCabe q.v.

Minnie Long to Frank Gentry q.v.

Mollie Long to William B. McEntyre q.v.

Nellie Long to Charley Smith q.v.

Octava Long to A. H. Condra q.v.

Suda Long to A. J. Moore q.v.

Thomas Long to Frances Standifer, 30 Dec 1899 (6 Jan 1900), David Davis MG, Jack SUGGS W 3-102

Z.T. Long to Mary A. Ingle, 8 Aug 1876 (10 Aug), J.P. Roddy MG 1-#1455

- - - - - - - - - - - - -

LOTHARAGE

1900 CENSUS

Arthur Lotharage 16: see Hemphrey Hackett (B)

- - - - - - - - - - - - -

LOUALEN

1900 CENSUS

Rebecca Loualen 22: see Jefferson D. Burkhalter

- - - - - - - - - - - - -

LOUDER

MARRIAGE

Margarit J. Louder to John W. Johnson q.v.

- - - - - - - - - - - - -

LOUVEL

1860 CENSUS

Nancy Louvel(?) 10: see Mary White

- - - - - - - - - - - - -

LOVE

1860 CENSUS
James A. Love 21: see Joseph Parks
1870 and 1880 CENSUS– None
1900 CENSUS
Ella Love 30 (Unk 1870-D 0), Wiley McDUFFY 35 (boarder)(Unk 1865-Ga/Ga/Ga-M 4) 8-275B-135 (B)
Francis E. Love 51 (Sep 1848-Oh/Oh/Oh-M 28)(RR Section Hand), Amy 44 (Jan 1856-Oh/Oh/Oh-M 28-7-5), Maggie B. 13 (Oct 1886-Oh), Jessie 11 (Dec 1889-Oh), William S. 8 (Feb 1892-Oh) 5-234A-121
Grace Love 25: see Onslo G. Gannaway
James Love 34 (Feb 1866-M 10), Vesta 25 (Ap 1875-M 10-5-5), Bertha 9 (Ap 1891), Walter 5 (Ap 1895), James 3 (Dec 1896), Vesta 1 (Mar 1899) 10-330A-214/227 (B)
Sallie Love 53: see John Johnson (B)
MARRIAGES
Anna Love to John Heiskell q.v.
Annie Love to John Johnson q.v.
Ella Love to West Griffin q.v. (B)
James Love to Vesta McDonald, 28 Dec 1889 (same), F.J. Paine JP 1-590
Maddison Love to M. Lucinda Winfrey, 9 Mar 1878 (21 Mar), B.F. Holloway JP 1-#1550
Nannie P. Love to Thomas Eheart or Airhart q.v.
Sarah E. Love to Joseph E. Parks q.v.

- - - - - - - - - - - - -

LOVELACE

1900 CENSUS
Jessie A. Lovelace 28 (July 1871-M 10)(Coal Miner), Mary E. 29 (July 1870-Ala/T/T-M 10-5-3), William H. 9 (Dec 1890-Ala), Jennie V. 1 (June 1898) 15-272A-81
MARRIAGE
Eliza Lovelace to J. A. Loyd q.v.

- - - - - - - - - - - - -

LOVING

MARRIAGE
Myra E.A. Loving(?) to William A. Thompson q.v.

- - - - - - - - - - - - -

LOW / LOWE

1860 CENSUS
Andrew Lowe 67, William 32, Amanda 28, Jane E. 3, George A. 10/12, Nancy McADOO 18, James A. LOWE 22 (School Teacher) 3-69-472
1870 CENSUS
John Low 22, Sela 22 (Ga), Samuel 1 3-11-75
N. Low 69 (England)(Music Teacher), Francis 24 (Eng): see Jamiah C. Wasson
William W. Lowe 42, Amanda M. 39, Jane E. 3, George A. 10, Letitia 8, Jesse G. 6, James W. 3, John H. 5/12 3-1-2
1880 CENSUS
William Lowe 52, Jane 23 (d), G.H. 21 (s), L.M. 18 (d), J.G. 15 (s), J.W. 12 (d), C.C. 5 (s) 3-20-161
1900 CENSUS
--?-- Lowe 33: see Elijah B. Ewing
Charles C. Lowe 25 (Ap 1875-M 1), Violet N. 31 (Sep 1868-M 1-1-1), Whitten M. 6/12 (Dec 1899), Mary LOWE 56 (m)(Aug 1843-T/NC/T-Wd) 3-209B-174/189
MARRIAGES
Kissiah Low to Jacob Harmon q.v.
Jane Lowe to Nathaniel H. Elkins q.v.
Julia Lowe to S. A. Lewis q.v.
Susan M. Lowe to James F. Elkins q.v.
William W. Lowe to M.M. Thompson, 15 Mar 1855, J.W. Thompson MG 1-#498

- - - - - - - - - - - - -

LOWRY / LOWREY / LOUREY / LAURAY

1860 CENSUS
Elizabeth Lowery 11: see John H. Keith
George W. Lowery 26, Euphemy 25, Andrew J. 4, Cetha C. 2 3-64-442
1870 CENSUS– None
1880 CENSUS
Louisa J. Lauray 69, John H. CROW 21 (s), Susan ROGERS 40 ("husband left her"), Thomas 5 6-25-186/190
1900 CENSUS
Andy Lowry 35 (Sep 1864-M 7)(Teamster), Jenny 45 (May 1855-M 7-0-0) 8-316B-127/131 (B)
Bird Lowery 34 (Oct 1865-M 3), Fanny E. 46 (Dec 1853-Ga/Ga/Ga-M 3-13-10) Asberry CARTER 21 (ss)(Jan 1879-T/Va/Ga), Alen 8 (ss)(Oct 1881), Viney 15 (sd) (Aug 1884), Alford 11 (ss)(Nov 1888), Emmer 11 (sd) (Jan 1889), Callie LAWSON 19 (sd)(May 1881-T/Va/Ga-M 7-2-1), Edd 52 (ssl)(Aug 1847-T/Miss/Miss-M 7), Pelem MONTGOMERY 30 (boarder)(Feb 1870-Ga/Ga/G) 10-251A-23 (B)
Dellie Lowery 10: see John Hughes
James Lowry 39 (Aug 1861-T/SC/T-M 9), Maggie 28 (Nov 1871-M 9-3-3), Navadia 7 (June 1892), William 5 (Mar 1895), Mary E. 1 (July 1898) 7-265A-281/286
John Lowery 44 (Mar 1856-Wd)(Coal Miner), George 11 (Aug 1898) 10-259B-191/195
Louisa J. Lowery 70: see George W. Fisher
Posey C. Loury 60, Ruhannie 57: see John Rue
William B. Lowry 30 (July 1869-T/Va/T-M 1)(Insurance Agent), Cora B. 27 (Mar 1873-Ga/Ga/Ga-M 1-1-1), Robert A. 5/12 (Dec 1899) 11-293A-77
William J. Lowry 36 (Feb 1864-M 6)(City Marshall), Mattie 24 (June 1875-M 6-4-4), Clara J. 5 (Aug 1894), William J. 4 (Jan 1896), Marion L. 1 (Sep 1898) 10-328B-179/192 [W.J. married Mattie Hodges on 7 Oct 1893]
MARRIAGES
A.M. Lowry to L.J. Crow, 28 Jan 1875 (same), John M. Bramlett MG 1-#1392
Byrd Lourey to Frances Carter, 2 Dec 1896 (6 Dec), J.B. Trotter MG 2-83
E.A. Lowry to Willie(?) Mynott, 24 Dec 1893, W.A. Howard MG 4-61
G.W. Lowry to Eriphomy Jones, 28 Feb 1855 (29 Feb), R.T. Howard MG 1-#485

Hannah J. Lowery to David Malony q.v.
Hattie Lowry to James Henderson q.v.
Horrace S. Lowery to Mary A. Amos, 31 Oct 1893, L.L. Barton JP 4-57
J.W. Lowrey or Loury to Florence Ellis, 4 July 1900 (same), W.L. Lillard JP 3-179
James Lowrey to Maggie Kelly, 4 Oct 1891, T.F. Shaver JP 4-31
Louisa Lowry to Dunkin McClarin q.v.
Mary Ann Lowry to John Chapman q.v.
Rebecca Lourey to John D. Hughes q.v.
Rosa Lourey to Samuel Wilkey q.v.
William C. Lowry to Lidea Bean, 26 Nov 1856 (no return) 1-#584

- - - - - - - - - - - - -

LOY / LAY

1860 CENSUS
Yancy Loy 45, Mary 40, Elizabeth 25, Jane 22, George 20, Priscilla 18, Malinda 16 1-96-652
1870 CENSUS
Malinda Loy 32, Hubbert W. 12, Jane A. 10 1-2-14
Yancy Loy 52, Eliza 25, John W. 7, Nancy A. 4, Martha J. 2, Sarah S. 4/12 1-22-143
1880 CENSUS
Eliza Loy 30, John 15, Nancy 13, Martha 11, Sarah 8, Joel 6, James 2 12-5-40
1900 CENSUS
Earnest Loy 5, Wilum 4, Maud 2: see John L. Allen

MARRIAGES
Arlie Loy to John W. Short q.v.
E. J. Loy to P. Herbert q.v.
Elizabeth Loy to Lay to John Keeling q.v.
Florence Lay to John Simms q.v.
Jane Loy to James Hale q.v.
Joseph G. Loy to Myra J. Allen, 28 Oct 1894, James Jordan JP 4-77
Martha Loy to Sam Lemons q.v.
Priscilla Loy to William E. Keelen q.v.
Rena Loy to W. J. Jolly q.v.
Yancy Loy to Eliza Hassey, 14 Mar 1865 (17 Mar), W.W. Low JP 1-#1088

- - - - - - - - - - - - -

LOYD / LLOYD / LOYED

1860 CENSUS
Harrison Loyed 14: see Sarah Wilson
1870 and 1880 CENSUS– None
1900 CENSUS
Cary Loyd 34, Sallie 30, Petty V. 3: see Tom Combow(?)
Kirk Loyd 32 (Aug 1867-Va/Va/Va-M 2), Laura 25 (May 1875-M 2-1-1), Roy 1 (Sep 1899), Corda HAMILTON 13 (ne)(Unk 1887-T/T/Va) 7-264A-266/271
MARRIAGES
J.A. Loyd to Eliza Lovelace, 6 Oct 1886 (same), James R. Stewart MG 1-511
N. A. Lloyd to John A. Dannel q.v.
Nelia Loyd to John Morgan q.v.
W. King Loyd to Laura Hensley, 27 Dec 1897 (28 Dec), E.W. Mort(?) MG, W.K. Loyd & John Cembo(?) W 2-234

- - - - - - - - - - - - -

LUCAS

MARRIAGE
Will Lucas to Harriet Mitchell, 21 Aug 1896 (17 Sep), R.W. Rawlings MG 2-59 (Note on bond: "Returned and not used")

- - - - - - - - - - - - -

LUDWIG

MARRIAGE
Henry Ludwig to Addie Hicks, 28 June 1893, R.S. Mason JP 4-58

- - - - - - - - - - - - -

LUSTERS / LUSTOR

MARRIAGES
Mahala Lustor(?) to Luke Marriott q.v.
Mahala Lusters to Horace Peters q.v.

- - - - - - - - - - - - -

LUTTEN

MARRIAGE
Isaac Lutten to Louisa Roberts, 25 Dec 1886 (same), J.Q. Shaver MG 1-512

- - - - - - - - - - - - -

LYLES / LYLE / LILES

1900 CENSUS
Thomas B. Lyle 14: see John W. Wassom
MARRIAGES
Anny Liles to James Pearson q.v.
Ethel Lile to Robert Harrison q.v.
James Lyle to Tennie Gothard, 20 Jan 1895, F.M. Cook MG 4-82
Jesse Lyles to Rachel Majors, 25 Nov 1872 (same), Thomas Coward JP 1-#1262
Letha Lyle to H. M. Alley q.v.
Walter Lyles to Mary F. Smith, 4 Aug 1900 (5 Aug), --?-- Atchley MG, F.M. Smith & Frank(?) Allison [signed by X] W 3-193

- - - - - - - - - - - - -

LYNCH / LINCH / LUNCH

1900 CENSUS
Frank Lunch 39 (Unk 1861-T/Ireland/Do-M 7)(Coal Miner), Ida 25 (May 1875-M 7-3-3), James E. 6 (Aug 1893), Clarence 5 (Oct 1894), Elmer D. 2 (July 1897) 8-279A-210/212

MARRIAGES

Frank Lynch to Ida Bell, 19 Oct 1892, J.D. Winchester MG 4-53

Josie Linch to Charley Gather q.v.

- - - - - - - - - - - - -

LYNDON

MARRIAGE

Frank L. Lyndon to Almeda Aiken, 15 July 1897 (19 July), G.W. Colend(?) VDM, Frank E. Lyndon W 2-160

- - - - - - - - - - - - -

LYON / LYONS / LION

1870 CENSUS

Oliver Lyon 63 (NJ)(Wagonwright), Harriet A. 55 (Brazil) 2-13-96

1880 CENSUS

Oliver Lyons 72 (Wheelwright), H. 64 (w), M.C. MAPLES 59 (sil), Anna May LYONS 6 (adopted d) 4-10-79

R.C. Lyons 51 (Stonemason), E.A. 39 (w), R.T. 4 (s), John P. 2 (s) 4-2-11

Thomas Lyons 18: see W.O. Shipley

1900 CENSUS

John Lyons 22 (Oct 1877-T/Ireland/Ga-M 3), Callie E. 20 (Mar 1880-M 3-0-0) 14-217B-103/105

Martin Lyons 64 (July 1835-Pa/Ireland/Do-M 33)(Farm Manager), Elizabeth 58 (Oct 1841-M 33-7-6), Ephraim 22 (Jan 1878)(Bartender), Mary 20 (Mar 1880), Robert 17 (Mar 1883)(Grocery Clerk) 8-276B-158/159

Richard C. Lyons 70 (Jan 1830-Ireland/Do/Do-1848/52/Na-M 34)(Stonemason), Elizabeth 60 (May 1840-Ga/Ga/Ga-M 34-4-2), Richard T. 23 (Feb 1877-Ga) 14-217B-104/106

Robert L. Lyons 19 (Mar 1881-T/Pa/T)(Confectioner) 8-311A-1/1

William Lyons 25 (Jan 1875-M 4), Ella 21 (Oct 1878-Ga/Ga/Ga-M 4-2-2), Jessie 2 (Oct 1897), Alice May 11/12 (June 1899) 13-298A-157/160

MARRIAGES

Gid Lion to Martha Pendergrass, 2 July 1878 (3 July), C.W. Peace MG 1-#1564

Thomas Lyons to Charlotte Jordan, 21 Sep 1886 (31 Sep), W.R. Grimsley MG 1-508

- - - - - - - - - - - - -

LYPOLD

MARRIAGE

A.M. Lypold to Katie McGarn, 22 Dec 1888 (23 Dec), W.T. West MG 1-557

- - - - - - - - - - - - -

LYTLE / LYDLE

MARRIAGES

Jeff Lytle to Sarah Edward, 15 Sep 1888 (16 Sep), C.B. Riggs MG 1-553

Newton Lydle to Amanda Buttram, 22 Ap 1879 (no return) 1-#1616

- - - - - - - - - - - - -

McADOO

1860 CENSUS

Mary McAdoo 18: see Jesse P. Thompson

Nancy McAdoo 18: see Andrew Lowe

Samuel McAdoo 74 (SC), John A. 11, Martha FALKNER 12 6-105-716

1870 CENSUS

Prudence McAdoo 31: see William R. Edington

MARRIAGES

Mary McAdoo to W. R. Edington q.v.

Mary J. McAdoo to John K. Franklin q.v.

- - - - - - - - - - - - -

McAFEE

1900 CENSUS

Charles McAfee 39 (Mar 1861-Pa/Unk-M 10), Mary V. 42 (Feb 1858-M 10-4-3), Edith 15 (May 1885) 13-297A-136/138

MARRIAGES

Charles McAfee to Mary Pendergrass, 20 Oct 1889 (23 Oct), F.M. Capps JP 1-590

Luther McAfee to Sullivan Moore, 10 Sep 1892 [possbly 1891], J.R. Hill MG 4-41

- - - - - - - - - - - - -

McALLEN

1880 CENSUS

Eliza McAllen 20 (School Teacher): see J. O. Shaver

- - - - - - - - - - - - -

McALLEY
(see also McCULLY)

1900 CENSUS

Paul McAlley 32 (Dec 1867-M 12), Martha 31 (Feb 1869-M 12-?), Maud 10 (Sep 1889), Flaura 8 (June 1891), John 7 (Oct 1891), Lucy 4 (Ap 1896), Creed 2 (Ap 1898), Charles 3/12 (Mar 1900) 1-186B-154/162

- - - - - - - - - - - - -

McALPIN / McCARPEN / McCOLPIN

1860 CENSUS

John McAlpin 65, Temperance M. 39, Robert 10, Polly A. 8, William 7, Susan 6, Rachel 3, Catharine M. 3 3-68-467

1870 CENSUS

Temperance McCarpen 51, Robert F. 19, Susan 16, Frances 13, Martha C. 12, James A. 9, Daniel H. 7 3-2-9

MARRIAGES

Catharine McAlpin to H. M. McNew q.v.

John NcColpin to Rachel Nash, 14 Oct 1852 (same), W.H. Bell MG 1-#383

Sarah McColpin to William Majors q.v.

Susan McAlpin to William A. Smith q.v.

- - - - - - - - - - - - -

McANDREWS

MARRIAGE
Joseph McAndrews to Sarah E. Johnson, 6 May 1891, James Johnson JP 4-63

- - - - - - - - - - - - -

McANDRUS / McANDRENS

1900 CENSUS
Geo(?) B. McAndrens 38 (Aug 1861-T/Ind/T-M 8), Kate V. 29 (Feb 1871-Oh/Oh/Oh-M 8-3-3), Joseph C. 7 (Feb 1893-Kan), George E. 4 (Aug 1895), John R. 2 (Mar 1898) 8-317B-147/152
MARRIAGE
George D. McAndrus to Katie L. Hodges, 24 May 1892, W.S. Neighbors MG 4-40

- - - - - - - - - - - - -

McBEE

1900 CENSUS
Milton O. McBee 39: see John F. Humphrey

- - - - - - - - - - - - -

McBIVINS

1880 CENSUS
John McBivins(?) 40, Lyda 33, E. 11 (d), Robert 7, John 3: see Sam Walker

- - - - - - - - - - - - -

McBRIDE

MARRIAGE
James E. McBride to Ellen N. J. Helton, 11 Sep 1886 (11 Aug)[sic], I.W. Holt JP 1-511

- - - - - - - - - - - - -

McBROOM

1900 CENSUS
Robert McBroom 26 (Aug 1874-M 7), Mary 28 (May 1871-M 7-4-4), William 5 (Dec 1894), Harry 3 (June 1896), Robert 1 (Oct 1897), Paul 6/12 (Nov 1899) 5-234B-132
MARRIAGE
Robert McBroom to Mary Wright, 19 Mar 1894, James I. Cash MG 4-76

- - - - - - - - - - - - -

McBRUNE

1900 CENSUS
Jack McBrune 50: see Martha Gamble

- - - - - - - - - - - - -

McCABE

1870 CENSUS
Francis McCabe 27 (Scotland), Mary J. 25, James A. 3, Nicholas A. 1, Zachary 6/12 2-17-119
James B. McCabe 35 (Scotland), Manda 23, Francis A. 3, Jacob M. 2, Mary L. 10/12 2-8-51
Franklin McCabe 35, Amanda 22, James 13, Nicholas 11, Zachariah 9, Amanda 8, Florence 6, Lillie 1, Elizabeth LONG 18 (Servant) 2-40-324
1880 CENSUS– None
1900 CENSUS
Francis A. McCabe 57 (Mar 1843-Ireland/Do/Do-M 22), Amanda E. 42 (July 1857-M 22-9-6), Gilbert G. 19 (July 1880), Clyde R. 16 (Ap 1884), Lella B. 4 (Dec 1895), Condon R. 6/12 (Nov 1899) 2-198A-130/135
Hayle W. McCabe 5, Thomas P. 2: see William H. Rector
James McCabe 33 (May 1867-T/Scotland/T-M 12)(RR Section Foreman), Julia A. 29 (Jan 1871-M 12-5-4), Barry 10 (Jan 1890), Cleo 8 (Aug 1891), Bertha C. 4 (May 1896), Bruce 6/12 (Nov 1899) 14-214A-23/24
John McCabe 38 (Jan 1862-Scotland/Ireland/Do-M 16), Bettie 33 (June 1866-T/Va/Va-M 16-7-5), George W. 13 (June 1887), William B. 10 (Sep 1889), Frank A. 9 (May 1891), Laura N. 6 (Jan 1894), Lieutenant G. 1 (Nov 1898) 2-198B-142/147
Nicholas McCabe 31: see Marquis Morrison
MARRIAGES
Felix McCabe to Maggie Chambers, 28 Mar 1885 (same), W.A. Green JP 1-505
Frank McCabe to Manda Reede, 30 July 1877 (5 Aug), Wm W. Low JP 1-#1506
F.A. McCabe to Mary J. Long, 14 Aug 1866 (15 Aug), W.W. Low JP 1-#1092
J.M. McCabe to Lezzie Smith, 8 Nov 1884 (9 Nov), J.N. Thompson MG 1-498
James McCabe to Amanda Green, 12 Nov 1864 (14 Nov), W.W. Low JP 1-#1076
James McCabe to Julia Ann Ferguson, 19 Feb 1888
Lillie McCabe to R. T. Minnick q.v.
Nick A. McCabe to Lizza Vandergriff, 10 Oct 1896 (11 Oct), W.R. Grimsley MG 2-73
W.M. McCabe to Isabel Donaldson, 24 Aug 1893, W.R. Clack JP 4-54
Z.T. McCabe to Jennie M. Rector, 8 Aug 1896, A.J. Wyrick JP 4-97
Zack T. McCabe to Martha Rector, 20 Oct 1893, R.M. Trentham JP 4-62

- - - - - - - - - - - - -

McCAIN

1900 CENSUS
Wlliam H. McCain 40 (Ap 1860-M 6), Laurie C. 29 (Mar 1871-M 6-3-3), James W.M. 16 (Dec 1884), Susan B. 14 (Dec 1886), Myrtle E. 12 (Sep 1888), Lilley 8 (June 1891), Bettie E. 4 (Oct 1895), Giler A. 3 (Sep 1897), Martha R. 2 (Dec 1898) 2-192A-21/21
MARRIAGE
Amanda J. McCain to C. L. Sturgis q.v.

- - - - - - - - - - - - -

McCALEB / McCABB

1860 CENSUS

Archibald McCaleb 41, Nancy P. 33, Andrew 71, Eliza P. 44 or 64 (Va) 2-72-493

1870 CENSUS

Albert McCaleb 66, Darcus 45, Luke 15, Samuel 13, Hugh 10 2-10-70 (B)

Arch McCaleb 51, Mary J. 45, Martha McCALEB (B) 16, Elizabeth McCALEB (B) 13 2-10-67

Martha McCaleb 16, Elizabeth 13 (B): see Arch McCaleb

Peter McCaleb 40 (Fla), Ester 36, Henry 20, Martha 18, Albert 16, Ann 14, Hariet 12, Thomas 9, Fanny 3, Arcina 1 2-10-68 (B)

1880 CENSUS

Albert McCaleb 75, Darkus 48 (w), Samuel 21, Hugh 18, Martha 18 (dl) 2-33-267 (B)(Mu)

Arch McCaleb 61, Jane 54, Sarah GILLESPIE (B) 24, William (Mu) 13 (Servant), George (Mu) 10 (Servant), Julia (B) 13 (Cook) 2-32-263

Hugh McCaleb 20 (B): see Samuel Gillespie

Jacob McCaleb 9 (B): see George Roddy

1900 CENSUS

Darkes McCaleb 80: see William Blair

James A. McCaleb 21: see James Reed (B)

Josey McCaleb 37 (Dec 1863-Wd 0-0), Samuel BLAIR 20 (nw)(May 1880) 2-193B-51/53 (B)

Samuel McCaleb 45 (Sep 1854-M 20), Martha C. 35 (July 1864-M 20-8-7), Nancy D. 15 (Feb 1885), Bettie A. 13 (May 1887), Albert 10 (Aug 1889), Hugh 8 (Mar 1892), Lennis 5 (Dec 1894), Belle 3 (Ap 1897), Viney L. 1 (Dec 1898), Berton 24 (Feb 1876-M 2)(Servant) 2-194A-57/69 (B)

MARRIAGES

Burton McCaleb to Mary J. Gillespie, 15 Feb 1898, Z.T. Morris MG 4-100

Elizabeth McCaleb to Thomas H. McPherson q.v.

Ester McCaleb to Daniel Moore q.v.

Henry McCaleb to Amanda Young, 2 Aug 1900, W.T. West MG 4-105

Hugh McCaleb to Jane Johnson, 16 Sep 1884 (17 Sep), W. R. Clack JP 1-469

Jane McCaleb to Peck Donaldson q.v.

Lucinda McCaleb to T. J. Gillespie q.v.

Sallie McCaleb to James Martain q.v.

Sarah McCaleb to Will Blain q.v.

- - - - - - - - - - - - -

McCALL

MARRIAGE

Doris McCall to R. J. Wilson q.v.

- - - - - - - - - - - - -

McCALLIE

MARRIAGES

James McCallie to Lilla Callahan, 24 Dec 1889 (same), W.S. Hale MG 1-589

Mary T. McCallie to J. H. Jewell q.v.

- - - - - - - - - - - - -

McCAMEY / McCAMIREE

1870 CENSUS

Andrew McCamey 29, Drisiller 27, Manervy J. 9, Nancy A. 8, Mary I. 4, James B. YOKELY 13 2-15-108

MARRIAGE

Hugh McCamiree to Nancy Jones, 25 June 1856 (26 June), W.H. Cunnyngham JP 1-#551

- - - - - - - - - - - - -

McCARPEN– see McALPIN

- - - - - - - - - - - - -

McCARROLL / McCARROLE

1860 CENSUS

Elizabeth McCarrol 41, Mary 15, Eliza A. 6: see Aggy McCulla

1870 CENSUS– None

1880 CENSUS

John McCarrol 70, Permelia 65, John 28, Delilia 23, Louisa 22 2-41-332

William McCarrol 29, Sarah 31, Nancy 8, Hattie 3, Columbus BURNET 20 (bl) 2-29-228

MARRIAGES

Delia Ann McCarroll to J. W. Dodson q.v.

Elizabeth McCarroll to Harrison Cowan q.v.

Harvy McCarrole to Elizabeth Teige, 23 Nov 1852 (same), W.C. Hollins JP 1-#392

Margaret J. McCarroll to John Estes q.v.

Sarah McCarroll to Jeremiah Rose q.v.

- - - - - - - - - - - - -

McCARTER

MARRIAGES

G.M. McCarter to E.J. Ingle, 19 Ap 1856 (26 Ap), no MG or JP 1-#543

Maggie McCarter to Mark Roddy q.v. (B)

- - - - - - - - - - - - -

McCARTY

1880 CENSUS

Mary McCarty 20, Cata T. 1: see Alfred Etherly (B)

MARRIAGE

Molly McCarty to Henry Coulter q.v. (B)

- - - - - - - - - - - - -

McCEAVER

1900 CENSUS

Charlie McCeaver 10: see Bertie Wasson (B)

- - - - - - - - - - - - -

McCHOLISTER

1900 CENSUS

Hugh McCholister 36: see William D. Wright

- - - - - - - - - - - - -

McCLANAHAN / McCLENAHAN

MARRIAGES

Dora McClenahan(?) to Newt Bowman q.v.
Emma McClanahan to Austin Dill q.v.
Mattie McClenahan to Clarence L. Miller q.v.

- - - - - - - - - - - - -

McCLARIN / McCLARING / McLARIN / McLARRIN / McLERRIN

1860 CENSUS

Hugh McClaren 67 (Scotland): see Catharine Rush

1870 CENSUS

William J. McLerrin 27, Lucretia M. [nee Horner] 21, Martha C. 3, William D. 7/12, William F. HARNER 12 3-3-18

1880 CENSUS

Jasper McClarin 35, Mary 30, Marma 13, Wiley 11, Hariet 7, John 4, Anna 2, James 1 1-8-62

1900 CENSUS

James McClerin 26 (Ap 1874-T/Ga/T-M 6)(Furnaceman), Millie 27 (Jan 1873-M 6-0), Newton McDERMIT 27 (boarder)(RR Section Hand) 10-328B-179/191 (B)

Jasper W. McClarin 58 (Ap 1842-M 7), Mary J. 49 (July 1850-M 7-0), Jane GODBEHERE 21 (ne)(Nov 1876) 4-226A-247/252 (Rhea Springs & Washington Road)

MARRIAGES

Dunkin McClarin to Louisa Long, 30 May 1857 (1 June), D.W. Horner MG 1-#599

Jenisa Jane McClaring to James Knox q.v.

Martha McClaren to J. W. Hasey q.v.

S. A. McLarrin to W. H. Tallent q.v.

W.J. McClarrin to Mary C. Marrs, 21 Oct 1874 (22 Oct), G.W. Renfro MG 1-#1364

W.J. McLarrin to Mary J. Godbehere, 19 Nov 1893, A.L. Parker MG 4-85

- - - - - - - - - - - - -

McCLELLAND / McCLELLAN

1900 CENSUS

Albert O. McClelland 46 (Ap 1854-Oh/Pa/Pa-M 17), Sarah 36 (July 1863-Oh/Oh/Oh-M 17-4-4), Anna 13 (May 1887), Ada 10 (Ap 1890), Emma 7 (Oct 1892), Alda NEWTON 15 (d)(Oct 1884-M 0-0), Eugene NEWTON 20 (sl)(July 1879-M 0) 6-241B-34

Mary McClennand 89: see David Woodey

Tom McClelland 45 (Dec 1854-M 20), Victory 41 (May 1859-M 20-11-7), Jal 17 (Aug 1882), Wright W. 15 (Aug 1884), Mary 11 (Nov 1887), Addison 9 (Feb 1891), Clarence 5 (Mar 1895-Indian Territory), Ben 4 (Sep 1896-Ind Ter), Robert 6/12 (Nov 1899) 10-253B-73

MARRIAGES

Altie McClellan to Euene Newton q.v.

J.C. McClelland to Alice Smith, 22 Dec 1890, Bird Henderson MG 4-20

Mary McClelland to Samuel Hardbarger q.v.

Merril McClelland to Mettie Cox, 30 Sep 1874 (1 Oct), J.K. Crawford ?? 1-#1359

Thomas J. McClellan to Dora V. Miller, 5 Feb 1880 (15 Feb), F.H. McPherson JP 1-#1716

Vera McClelland to J. W. Wright q.v.

- - - - - - - - - - - - -

McCLENDON / McCLENDAL

1860 CENSUS

Dennis McClendon 35, Mary 31, Nancy J. 14, Rebecca A. 11, Merril 10, Elizabeth 8, Thomas J. 6, Addison 2, Adaline 2, Charles BRADY 22 9-99-676

July McClendon 4/12: see Merril Brady

Sanders McClendon 22, Polly A. 20 9-99-673

Willis McClendon 31 (NC), Elizabeth 26, John 5, Amanda 2, Mary C. 2/12 9-99-672

1870 CENSUS

John McClendal 71 (NC), Nancy 70 (NC), Malinda 31 1-20-131

Mary McClendal 41, Rebecca A. 21, Merrell B. 19, Sarah E. 18, Thomas 16, Addison 12, Adeline 12, Mary C. 7, Melvina 2 5-10-70

Sanders McClendon 33, Farley Ann 30 (NC), Julia Ann 10, Simon(?) 8, John L. 5, Vesta R. 3, Young L. 7/12 1-9-59

Willis McClendal 41 (NC), Elizabeth 33, John 15, Amanda 12, Mary 10, Harriette 9, Benjamin S. 6, Elizabeth J. 3 1-21-137

1880 CENSUS

A. McClendon 21, Sarah 21, S.H. 8/12 (s) 3-13-101

Adaline McClendon 22: see John Pyott

Elaigon(?) McClendon 65, Mada J. 65, James A. 10 (Ga) 10-26-203/209

John McClendon 25, Annie 24, A.J. 5 (s), M.E. 4 (d), J.T. 4/12 (s), R. BROWN (*) 30, M.C.R. IVINS (*) 30 4-35-286 [*males, relation not recorded]

M. McClendon 26, Bettie 25, D.R. 4 (s), M.S. 3 (d), N.A. 1 (d) 8-19-163

Malinda McClendon 35, Ancil 10 (s) 1-19-161

W. McClendon 52, E.L. 45, C.N. 22 (d), Mary 20, Harriet 19, Sherman 17, E.J. 13 (d), S.B. 4 (d) 4-35-285

1900 CENSUS

Ansel G. McClendon 31 (Aug 1868-M 10), Ellen 31 (Nov 1868-M 10-6-2), Hoyal L. 6 (June 1893), Lawrence A. 3 (Nov 1896), Malinda MADGETT 62 (m)(Ap 1836-T/NC/at sea-Wd 1-1) 4-226B-255/259 (Rhea Springs and Washington Road)

Benjamin McClendon 35 (Dec 1864-T/NC/SC-M 8), Julia A. 32 (Mar 1868-M 8-2-1), Kate 6 (Oct 1893) 14-221B-162/166

Jackson McClendon 24, Betty 23: see Andrew J. Garrison

James McClendon 19: see Hiram Moore (B)

James McClendon 22 see William Y. Denton

Jessie McClendon 6: see Mary Scarbrough

Sam McClendon 65 (Sep 1834-T/NC/NC-M 40), Annie 59 (Feb 1841-NC/NC/NC-M 40-8-7), Young 30 (Sep 1869), Birt CHENP(?) 26 (gs)(Ap 1874), Luther HILL 18 (boarder)(Mar 1882) 1-185B-133/139

Willis McClendon 72 (May 1828-NC/NC/NC-Wd), Mary 40 (Dec 1859), Flora A. 11 (July 1888), Nancy J. 8 (July 1891) 14-221B-161/165

MARRIAGES

A.L. McClendon to S.A. Jolly, 26 Aug 1878 (27 Aug), W.W. Low JP 1-#1578
Alice McClendon to Jeff Smith q.v.
Alice McClendon to J. M. Mosier q.v.
Amanda McClendon to George Marshall q.v.
B.S. McClendon to Julia Beard, 17 Jan 1892, J.W. Cowles JP 4-43
Bettie McClendon to D. M. Mitchell q.v.
Charity McClendon to James E. Thompson q.v.
Charlotte McClendon to William L. Dunlap q.v.
Elizabeth McClendon to Richard Lemmons q.v.
Grant McClendon to Winnie Casey, 31 Jan 1893, James Johnson JP 4-52
Harriet McClendon to John Garrison q.v.
J. McClendon to Bettie Garrison, 11 Feb 1900, J.A. Torbett JP 4-102
John McClendon to Ann Munday, 5 June 1874 (8 June), James Johnson JP 1-#1332
John McClendon to Eliza Ann Godbehere, 1 Oct 1893, W.J. McLarrin MG 4-61
M. C. McClendon to R. A. H. Fisher q.v.
N. J. McClendon to Churchwell C. Brown q.v.
Viney McClendon to Frank Walker q.v.
Willis McClendon to Elizabeth Garrison, 17 Dec 1852 (20 Dec), W. Lloyd JP 1-#397

\- - - - - - - - - - - -

McCLURE

1900 CENSUS

Jehu N. McClure 30 (Mar 1870-Ga/Ga/Ga-M 10), Jane 30 (Mar 1870-Ga/Ga/Ga-M 10-6-5), Bertha 9 (May 1891-Ga), Fanny 7 (June 1892-Ga), Lizzie 5 (Aug 1894-Ga), Johnnie 4 (Mar 1896-Ga), Joseph 2 (June 1898), James 9/12 (Aug 1899) 15-268A-2/2
John M. McClure 54 (Aug 1845-Ga/Mo/Mo-M 34), Mary A. 54 (Feb 1846-Ga/Ga/Ga-M 34-10-8), Nervy A. 24 (Ap 1876-Ga), Ida 22 (May 1878-Ga), Minnie 14 (Sep 1885-Ga), Ada 12 (May 1887-Ga), George 11 (Feb 1889-Ga) 3-206B-115/125

MARRIAGE

Rufus McClure to Julia Denton, 13 Dec 1889 (14 Dec), J.M. Bramlett MG 1-594

\- - - - - - - - - - - -

McCOLLEND

MARRIAGE

Jesse McCollend to Penelopy White, 25 Oct 1875 (same), John Howard MG 1-#1416

\- - - - - - - - - - - -

McCONNELL

1900 CENSUS

William McConnell 25 (July 1874-M 6), Lou 25 (July 1874-T/Mo/T-M 6-0), Don GERTON 19 (boarder)(June 1880-NC/NC/NC-M 0), Alie 21 (boarder)(May 1879-T/Mo/T-M 0-0) 8-315A-93/96 (B)

MARRIAGE

James M.C. McConnell to Jennie Green, 24 Dec 1898 (28 Dec), R.C. Knight JP, J.J. Jolly W 2-366

\- - - - - - - - - - - -

McCORMICK

MARRIAGE

Sarah E. McCormick to W. D. Freeman q.v.

\- - - - - - - - - - - -

McCOSLEN

1880 CENSUS

John McCoslen 19: see N. J. Vinyard

\- - - - - - - - - - - -

McCOY / MACOY

1880 CENSUS

Calvin McCoy 54, Susan 18 (d), E.L. 8/12 (? female) 4-31-256
Martha McCoy 44, Thomas 17, Mary J. 15, N.A. 13 (d), J.C. 12 (s), Adaline 9 (d), John 7 (s) 7-23-195

1900 CENSUS

Rena A. McCoy 20: see John F. McCulloch

MARRIAGES

Calvin McCoy to Sarah J. McCully, 25 Sep 1878 (26 Sep), A.J. Pritchett MG 1-#1583
Charles MacCoy to Amanda Baker, 3 May 1886 (same), P.P. Brooks ?? 1-482

\- - - - - - - - - - - -

McCRAVEN

MARRIAGE

Mattie McCraven to Robert Powers q.v.

\- - - - - - - - - - - -

McCROY / McCAREY
(see also McROY)

1880 CENSUS

J. C. McCarey(?) 10: see Walker Hughes
M. G. McCroy 15: see W. G. Allen

MARRIAGES

Adda McCroy to J. F. Jones q.v.
Mary McCroy to George Bean q.v.

\- - - - - - - - - - - -

McCUISTON / McCUSTINE / McQUISTON / McCHRISTIAN

1870 CENSUS

David McCuiston 53, Seythia 54 (Ky), Andrew 16, Mary L. 5, Melissa 2 2-7-48
Miles H. McCuiston 32, Elizabeth J. 31, Seitha J. 11, George N. 10, Laura A. 8, James L. 7, Ellen 5, Samuel D. 4, Calop L. 2/12 2-7-50 [M.H. married Elizabeth C. Turk on 25 Dec 1857]

1880 CENSUS

Miles McChristian 43, Betsy 42, George 20, Laura 18, James 16, Hariet 15, Samuel 13, Caleb 12, Miles 7, Andrew 5, Arthur 3, Ida 1 2-35-296

Thomas McCuiston 25, ?.V. 18 (w), Mary 50 (m) 4-12-99

1900 CENSUS

George McCuiston 40 (Dec 1860-M 17)(Teamster), Ida T. 38 (Ap 1862-M 17-7-3), John C. 12 (Ap 1888), Miler E. 10 (Feb 1890), Clarence L. 8 (Mar 1892) 2-191B-18/18

Miles H. McCuiston 64 (Dec 1836-M 47), Elizabeth J. 62 (Jan 1838-M 47-13-12), Caleb J. 29 (June 1870) (Blacksmith), Miles F. 27 (June 1872)(Clergyman), Andrew W. 25 (June 1874)(Blacksmith), Arthur P. 23 (July 1876), Anna B. 21 (Aug 1878), Fred A. 19 (Sep 1880), Laura A. CARDEN 38 (d)(Nov 1861-M 3-1-1), Carl C. CARDEN 2 (gs)Mar 1897) 2-191A-5/5

Samuel D. McCuiston 33 (Oct 1866-M 6), Sarah E. 26 (Jan 1874-M 6-4-3), Stella G. 4 (June 1895), Virgil E. 3 (Dec 1896), Benjamin C. 3/12 (Feb 1900), James M. PRICE 28 (May 1872) 2-191A-6/6
[Samuel married Sarah E. Price]

MARRIAGES

A.S. McCustine to Jane Hood, 12 Jan 1891, W.R. Clack JP 4-24

Amanda P. McChristian to J.T. Ferguson q.v.

G.N. McQuiston (22) to Ida Dixon (19), 16 Feb 1882, James Johnson JP, John Edmond & George Stonecipher W 4-9(81)

H. E. McChristian to William Williams q.v.

James L. McCuiston to Bertha Johns, 14 Aug 1898, J.A. Torbett JP 4-103

Mary J. McChristian to William A. Stegall q.v.

S. J. McChristian to E. F. Talent q.v.

McCULLAM / McCALLOM / McCALLEN

MARRIAGES

John J. McCallom to Elizabeth Brady, 17 Oct 1857 (22 Oct), Nathaniel Bennett MG 1-#617

M. McCullam to Vina Harris, 2 Jan 1855 (15 Jan), N.H. Long JP 1-#499

Mary McCallen to W. A. Wooden q.v.

McCULLOUGH / McCULLOCH / McCULLOUCH / McCULLEN / McCULLY / McCULLEY / McCULLA
(see also McALLEY)

1860 CENSUS

Aggy McCulla 64 (NC), Elizabeth McCARROL 41, Mary 15, Eliza A. 6, William McCULLA 23 4-49-329

David McCulla 29 (SC), Mary E. 26, Wallas 6, Margaret J. 4, Sarah A. 2, John T. 1 2-75-510

Elizabeth McCulla 16: see Franklin Milligan

Martin McCully 38 (SC), Viney 28, Margaret A. 5, Addison L. 2, John T. 6/12, Margaret C. HARRIS 19 2-81-551

Peter McCully 25, Lucinda 32, Sally GRAHAM 17 4-43-288

Ruth McCulla 27, Pamelia 6: see John W. Thompson

1870 CENSUS

Adam McCullouch 41, Ann J. 43, Robert M. 13, Sarah C. 10, Letitia 8, Malinda E. 6, John L. 3 6-3-14

Elizabeth McCullough 73, Nancy 24, Elizabeth 1 3-8-55

James McCullough 19, Sarah E. 21 6-3-15

James McCullough 18, Sarah 22 3-7-47

Martin McCullough 50 (SC), Louvina 36 (NC), Margaret 14, Adison 12, John F. 11, Benjamin 8, Manda J. 5, Mary E. 3, Dawson HARIS 62 (NC) 2-1-5

Peter McCullough 48 (Miller), Eglentine A. 43, William 10, Sarah E. 7, John F. 3 3-7-43

William McCully 30, Nelly J. 25 (NC), John H. 4, Napoleon B. 2, Mary T. 8/12, Nellie OANS 32 4-1-4

William H.H. McCulley 29, Rachel E. 29, George W. 3, Margarette E. 10/12 1-17-110

1880 CENSUS

Martin McCullough 60, Lavinia 48, Adison 21, John 17, Benjamin 16, Jane 14, Mary 11, Charles 9, Thomas 7 2-39-318

P. McCullough 55, Tiney [Eglentine] 53, Frank 14 4-31-254

William McCullough 20, Mary 18 4-31-255

William McCullough 54, Nellie 36 (w), J.H. 14 (s), N.B. 12 (s), M.J. or M.T. 9 (s), Amanda 5, Margaret 1 4-3-26

1900 CENSUS

Addison McCullough 47 (July 1862-T/NC/NC-M 14), Sarah E. 33 (Nov 1866-M 14-7-3), William W. 12 (June 1887), Charley B. 9 (Dec 1890), Mary D. 2 (July 1897), Emma E. 4/12 (Jan 1900) 2-192A-24/24

Ben McCullough 44 (Nov 1835-T/SC/NC-M 17), Margret A. 35 (Oct 1864-M 17-7-5), Manda 15 (Sep 1884), Bertha 13 (Dec 1886), Sousin 11 (Mar 1889), Delia 7 (Dec 1892), Myra 3 (June 1896) 7-264A-261/266

David McCullough 67 (Feb 1833-SC/SC/SC-M 28), Sarah 64 (Sep 1836-T/T/Ky-M 28-7-3), Pollie A. 20 (May 1880), Floyd GILLIAM 2 (gs)(Aug 1898) 2-191B-13

John F. McCulloch 33 (Unk 1867-Wd), William E. 7 (Aug 1892), John F. 6 (Feb 1894), Tina A. 2 (Sep 1897), Reny A. McCOY 20 (ne)(Oct 1879) 4-225A-225/229 (Back Valley Road)

Nellie McCulley 57 (July 1842-Wd 7-7), Jenni 23 (Ap 1877), Maggi 21 (June 1879) 1-189A-195/204 (Spring City)

Susie McCullough 12: see Sam Hood

Tina [Eglentine] McCullough 70: see Burt Revis

William P. McCullough 38 (Aug 1861-M 20), Mary A. 35 (Jan 1865-T/T/NC-M 20-9-5), Mary E. 13 (June 1886), Tinie J. 10 (Feb 1889), James L. 7 (Dec 1892), Emet F. 4 (Sep 1895), Anna B. 1 (Sep 1898) 5-236B-167

Wilum McCully 25 (Mar 1875-M 5), Sara 20 (Nov 1879-M 5-3-2), May 2 (Sep 1897), Right 5/12 (Jan 1900) 1-187A-155/163

MARRIAGES

Adison L. McCuller to Sallie Hood, 22 July 1886 (same), J.P. Roddy MG 1-508

Amanda McCulley to Clark Vittito q.v.

Ben McCullough (20) to Annie Hood (18), 12 Nov 1882, J.J. Krichbaum(?) MG, Joseph Bolls & Jesse Bolls W 4-11(108)

Eliza McCully to Franklin Milican q.v.

Elizabeth McCully to Eli Partain q.v.

Ella M. McCully to L. A. Shanan q.v.

H. A. McCully to Thomas A. Weeks q.v.

Hattie McCullough to John Gill q.v.
Hugh McCully to Julia Gillespie, 23 Feb 1881 (24 Feb), James Johnson JP 1-297 (B)
J.F. McCullough to Emma Neal, 2 July 1893, W.F. Moore MG 4-56
James McCully to Sarah E. Campbell, 13 Nov 1869 (14 Nov), Bailey Minicks JP 1-#1124
Jennie McCullough to James A. Houston q.v.
Josie McCulley to Shell Bowles q.v.
Mary McCullough to Burkett Revis q.v.
Mary McCulley to Martin Garrett q.v.
Nancy McCully to Houston White q.v.
Nelly McCully to Rubin Owens q.v.
Permelia McCully to Joseph Martin q.v.
Peter McCully to Augusta Whittenburg, 24 Sep 1865 (same), A. Hollan JP 1-#849
Polly McCuller to George Boles q.v.
Sarah E. McCully to James C. Milican q.v.
Sarah J. McCully to Calvin McCoy q.v.
W.E. McCulley to Sarah Thompson, 4 Sep 1895, H.B. Heiskell JP 4-86
William McCully to Nelly Denton, no date [probably 1864], R.T. Howard MG 1-#829
William McCully to Mary A. Furgusson, 12 Jan 1880 (same), A.J. Pritchett MG 1-#1707
William H. McCulley to Sarah Simpson, 8 Jan 1878 (no return) 1-#1542

McCULLUS

1900 CENSUS
Jeff McCullus 35: see Amos Clifton (B)

McDADE

MARRIAGE
W.H. McDade to Annie Bolen, 22 Dec 1900 (same), Wm A. Green MG, S. Goodson W 3-258

McDANIEL / McDANIELS / McDANIL

1860 CENSUS
Greenberry McDaniel 46 (SC), Elbey 31, John 17, Elizabeth 13, Thomas H. 12, Aron J. 7, Columbus 3 5-39-260
1870 CENSUS
Thomas H. McDanel 21, Adaline 18 (Ill) 5-7-49
MARRIAGES
Elizabeth A. McDaniels to William O. Shadrick q.v.
Jasper N. McDaniel to Louisa C. Chastain, 11 Oct 1865 (12 Oct), J.B. McCullen MG 1-#841 & 1#870
Mary McDaniel to William H. Kirby q.v.
N.J. McDaniel to C.L. Kirkland, 15 Jan 1896, W.T. West MG 4-88
Rhoda McDaniel to Henry Rumfeld(?) q.v.
Sebsan(?) McDanil to Victoria Bradford, 4 Nov 1883 (5 Nov), Byrd Lucy MG 1-460

McDERMIT

1870 CENSUS
A. McDermet 30, Margaret P. 28, Jane 3: see J.C. Wasson
1880 CENSUS– None
1900 CENSUS
Newton McDermit 27: see James McClearin (B)
Sam McDermit 22: see James Jackson (B)

McDONALD / McDONAL

1860 CENSUS
Bryant R. McDonald 63 (Va), Elizabeth 52 (Va), Mary E. 25, Floied J. 21, Georgia A. 15, Sidney C. 12, Charles T. 27, Caroline 25, Caroline E. 3/12 10-29-192
James McDonald 37 (Carpenter), Catharine 37, John F. 11, Letty A. 7, Henry S. 5, Virginia L. 3 8-18-121
John McDonald 27 (Va)(Miller), Louisa J. 27, Mary E. 5 10-27-181
Lewis McDonald 33 (Tanner), Nancy 23 (Va), Stanton W. 2 8-10-65
Nancy McDonald 53 (Va), Louissea 30, Caroline 28, Milton 21 10-28-190
Roland F. McDonald 35, Virginia E. 26, Alice 5, Nancy 1, C.C. RICHARDS 19 1-27-183
1870 CENSUS
Adam McDonald 23, Hannah 42, Thomas 15, Mary A. 6, Joseph 1: see Joseph Garrison
Aubern McDonald 35, Mahala 17, Delilah A. ?, Martha J. ? 10-3-19 (B)(Mu)
Bryan R. McDonald 73 (Va), Elizabeth 64 (Va), George A. 22, Sidney C. 21, Martin SPRADLING 19, Mary E. SWAFFORD 17 10-2-9
George McDonald 50 (Va) 8-22-156 (B)
Green McDonald 56 (SC), Elba 51, Elizabeth 22, Isaiah 16, Columbus 12 5-7-48
Green A. McDonald 39, Laura A. 22 (NC), Sidney C. 2, William 4, John P.W. 10/12 10-3-18 (B)
John McDonald 36 (Tanner), Louisa Jane 36 8-11-69
Lewis McDonald 40 (Va), Louesa 35, Mary Ann 19, Ellen 9, Caroline 7, William 4, Edy F. 3/12 8-4-25 (B)
Lewis F. McDonald 43, Nancy 33 (Va), Stanton W. 12, Harriette 8, Joseph F. 4, Edna E. 3 8-13-91
Nancy McDonald 65 (Va), Caroline 35, Milton G. 28 10-2-11
Rolen McDonald 30 (Va)(B): see Lott Johnson
Rowlen F. McDonald 45, Orpha Jane 36, Alice 15, Nancy 11, William P. 1 10-4-28
Sallie McDonald 24, Martha E. 2: see Alfred Day (B)
Samuel McDonald 45, Letha Isabella 28, Catharine 12, Charles 10, Emma C. 6, James A.L. 4, Mary V. 2, Scrap (f) 2/12 8-5-31 (B)
1880 CENSUS
Frank McDonald 8 (B): see Charles Keith
G. A. McDonald 33: see H. O. Leuty
G. B. McDonald 68: see T. H. McDonald
George McDonald 65 (B): see S. F. McDonald
Green McDonald 67 (Servant) 2-27-210
Henry McDonald 30, M.J. 24, Angeline 8, Darius 5, W.C. 3 (s) 4-2-10
Jane McDonald 8 (B): see James A. Howard

L.F. McDonald 54, Nancy 44, S.N. 21 (s), H.M. 17 (d), J.F. 14 (s), E.C. 11 (d), George McDONALD (B) 65 (Servant) 8-17-142
Lewis McDonald 52, Liewiza 41, William 13, Benjamin 6, Joseph 6 10-29-226/231 (B)
Nancy McDonald 73, Caroline 49, Milton G. 38, Wm SAWYERS 20 (no relation) 10-28-214/219
R. McDonald 41, Mary 21 (w) 5-9-83 (B)(Mu)
R.F. McDonald 55, O.J. 46, Nancy 21, William P. 11, Mary E. 9, Annie B. 7, Luvenia 6, Cora C. 4 10-29-222/227
Rolly McDonald 37, Ann 24, Stanton 7, Stanley 4, Adie 1/12 (marked through, probably deceased) 7-28-244 (Mu)
Sam McDonald 50, Leathy 39 (w), Emma 16, Juncy 12, Virginia 11, Jennie 9, Alice 8, Sarah 7, Clawice 5, Rufus 2, Hait 7/12, Catharin 22 (d), Vesty B. 3, Mollie A. 3/12 8-11-89 (B)(Mu)
Sam McDonald 47, Letha B. 30 (w), Catharine 21, Ema 16, James 13, Virginia 11, Sarah 7, Allis 6, Clarence 3, Rufus 4, Wyatt 10/12 10-28-212/217 (B)(Mu)
T.H. McDonald 31, S.D. 28 (w), J.G. 9 (s), M.L. 3 (d), W.L. 1 (d), G.B. McDONALD 69 9-30-254
William McDonald 23: see Adam Watson

1900 CENSUS
Amos McDonald 43 (Dec 1857-Ind/Ind/T-M 15)(Station Engineer), Cordia 36 (Oct 1863-M 15-5-3), Maud 13 (Aug 1887), Herbert 11 (Dec 1889), Bessie 6 (May 1894) 10-251B-36/36
Ben McDonald 28 (Ap 1872-T/Va/Va-M 3), Jane 41 (Dec 1858-T/NC/T-M 3-6-4), Vesty HARRIS(?) 25 (sd)(Jan 1877-Wd 0)(Servant), Lizzie KEITH 19 (sd)(Feb 1881-M 0-0), Nick 28 (ssl)(May 1872-M 0), Henry DAY 14 (ss)(June 1885) 10-253B-68 (B)
Caroline McDonald 69 (July 1830-T/Va/Va-S), William D. KYLE 32 (nw)(Oct 1867-T/Va/T), George M. KYLE 29 (nw)(Dec 1870) 15-272A-74/74
Corra McDonald 24: see Homer Halliburton
David McDonald 49 (Unk-Va/Va/Va-M 6), Sallie 28 (Unk-M 6-3-2), William 8 (Mar 1892), Mizie 5 (Mar 1895) 10-328B-177/189 (B)
Eli McDonal 53 (Dec 1846-T/Va/Va-S), Harriet LEUTY 72 (Ap 1828-T/Va/Va-Wd 3-3), Tenie 27 (ne)(Aug 1872) 10-260B-208/213
Frank McDonald 30 (May 1870-M 0)(Merchant), Nannie K. 27 (Nov 1872-M 0-0) 13-305B-291/302
George McDonald 37 (Ap 1863-M 10)(Sawyer), Rosa S. 46 (Nov 1853-T/Mass/Oh-M 10-0), Sarah FOX 75 (m)(May 1825-Oh/Eng/Eng-Wd) 13-300A-188/193
Henry McDonald 51 (Ap 1849-M 28), Margaret 45 (Mar 1855-M 28-4-4), Darius 27 (Mar 1873), Sarah J. 20 (Feb 1880), Sylvester 17 (May 1883), Grant 14 (Aug 1885) 14-222B-175/179
James McDonald 33 (Jan 1867-M 4), Mattie 34 (Dec 1865-Ga/T/Va-M 4-1-0) 8-315A-95/99 (B)
James McDonald 40 (Unk-Ala-M 16)(House Carpenter), Annie 30 (Ap 1870-Ala-M 16-9-7), Katie 15 (Oct 1884-Ala), Deward 12 (Dec 1887-Ala), Carl 8 (Jan 1892), Mamie 7 (Jan 1893), Alice 4 (May 1896), Willie 2 (July 1897), Otis 4/12 (Aug 1899) 10-330A-212/225 (B)
James F. McDonald 38 (Feb 1862-M 17), Mary E. 35 (Jan 1863-M 17-9-8), Martha J. 17 (Ap 1883), John T. 14 (Dec 1886), Margaret R. 10 (Oct 1889), Dellas E. 6 (Jan 1894), Mary L. 3 (July 1896), James 6/12 (May 1900), Anna 6/12 (May 1900) 9-229A-22
Joseph McDonald 58 (May 1842-M 4), Catharin 48 (Sep 1851-M 4-0), Neton GUILLIN(?) 28 (nw)(Nov 1871) 1-183B-95/99
Lewis F. McDonald 73 (Sep 1826-T/Va/Va-M 43), Nancy 63 (Aug 1836-T/Va/Va-M 43-5-4), Joseph F. 37 (June 1862), Edna 32 (Dec 1867), Maggie BROOKS 16 (Jan 1884)(Servant), Sarah J. HELTON 52 (July 1847-Wd 5-4)(Servant) 15-268A-1
Louisa McDonal 64: see Samuel Burgin (B)
Milton G. McDonald 60 (Aug 1839-T/Va/Va-Wd), Carl 13 (Aug 1886), John WHITE 60 (Unk 1839-Wd) 3-206B-119/130
Robert McDonald 62 (Mar 1838-T/Va/Va-M 13)(Coke Oven Laborer), Agnes 56 (Ap 1844-M 13-6-1), Janie 23 (Oct 1876), Maggie SCOTT 16 (gd)(Mar 1884), Mary 14 (gd)(Mar 1886), Willie 10 (gs)(Feb 1890) 13-305B-295/307 (B)
Robert McDonald 56 (Aug 1843-Va/Va/Va-M 26), Ann 47 (Mar 1853-M 26-3-1), Stanly 22 (June 1873) 10-257A-133/137 (B)
Rufe McDonald 19: see Joe Banks (B)
Samuel McDonald 60 (Unk 1840-Wd), Hoyt 20 (Unk 1880), Walter 17 (Unk 1883) 8-281A-252/258 (B)
Stanton McDonald 42 (Ap 1858-M 7), Eulalia 31 (Dec 1869-Ala/Ala/Ala-M 7-3-3), Ethel 6 (Mar 1894), Edith L. 2 (June 1897), Louis C. 1 (Oct 1898), Sarah F. BENNETT 68 (ml)(June 1832-Ga/Ga/Ga-Wd 5-4), Albert G. 32 (bl)(July 1868-Ala/Al/Ga)(Grocery Salesman) 15-268A-3
Tom McDonald 50 (July 1849-SC/SC/SC-M 23)(Coal Miner), Mary F. 42 (Aug 1858-T/T/Va-M 23-9-7), Ida S. 22 (Ap 1878), Lora B. 19 (Sep 1880), Eller M. 18 (Feb 1882), Hester 15 (Dec 1885), Nolla 11 (Mar 1889), James 10 (Feb 1890), Tominy W. 6 (June 1893) 10-251A-26 (B)
W. Edward McDonald 28 (May 1872-T/T/Ga) (Broommaker) 13-300A-182/187
William McDonald 47 (May 1853-T/Va/T-M 18), Ada 35 (Mar 1865-M 18-7-7), John T. 17 (Jan 1883), James S. 14 (May 1886), Martha S. 13 (Ap 1887), George W. 8 (July 1891), Della 7 (Feb 1893), Joseph A. 4 (May 1896), Rosa A. 1 (Jan 1899) 6-242B-60
William McDonald 31 (Sep 1868-M 9)(Physician), Cora E. 28 (Dec 1871-M 9-3-1), Raymond 5 (Sep 1894) 14-217A-86/88
William McDonald 30 (Aug 1869-T/Va/T-M 4)(School Teacher), Jovelia 22 (Oct 1877-Ky/NC/Ky-M 4-1-1), Cleocle 3 (Oct 1896) 10-252A-41 (B)
William McDonald 36 (Unk-M 0), Emma 26 (Unk-M 0-0), Ann EDWARDS 14 (boarder)(Unk) 8-314A-75/78 (B)

MARRIAGES
Ada McDonald to E. L. Sanders q.v.
Alice McDonald to Charley Hart q.v.
Alice McDonald to R. A. Cowan q.v.
Annie McDonald to William Shields q.v.
Ben McDonald to Jane or Jennie Day, 30 May 1897, H. Hobbart MG 2-171
Byrd or Myred McDonald to Rossey Harwood or Howard, 22 Sep 1900 (23 Sep), W.R. Grimsley MG, Wm M. Kelley W 3-224
Callie McDonald to Horace Coatney q.v.

Charles McDonald to Sallie Swafford, 24 Dec 1885 (no return) 1-485
Charley McDonald to Nelie Stewart, 4 June 1887 (6 June), S.W. Burnett ?? 1-583
Charley McDonald to Mariah Weatherns(?), 8 Mar 1890 (same), F.J. Paine JP 1-586
Clarence McDonald to Pearly Brown, 26 Dec 1899 (same), I.H. Gaines MG, Clem McDonald & Helen Jones W 3-99
David McDonald [only name on bond] 2-219
David McDonald to Sallie Wilson, 25 Dec 1897 (same), J.B. Phillips ?? 2-233
Delilia McDonald to James N. Sharp q.v.
Edna E. McDonald to Sidney L. Ellis q.v.
Ellen McDonald to David Kyle q.v.
Ellen McDonald to Sam Bargins q.v.
Emma McDonald to John Buchanan q.v.
Florence McDonald to J.A. Brooks q.v.
George McDonald to S. Rosa Fox, 30 Mar 1891, J.R. Walker MG 4-19
Henry S. McDonald to Mary J. McFalls, 22 May 1872 (25 May), Daniel Broyles JP 1-#1240
J. McDonald to A. Scudder, 13 Aug 1887 (same), L. Haworth MG 1-527 & 1-533
James McDonald to Janey or Josey Johnson, 22 Dec 1888 (23 Dec), M.C. Bruner MG 1-563
Jennie McDonald to Joseph Banks q.v.
John McDonald to Louisa J. Hodge, no date, but between 19 May and 22 June 1852 1-#375
Joseph McDonald to Winy Bell, 20 July 1855 (22 July), T. J. Jack JP 1-#509
Joseph McDonald to Jemimah Evans, 14 Feb 1895, J.W. Gillespie JP 4-78
Kittie McDonald to John Clark q.v.
L. F. McDonald to J. H. Jewell q.v.
Lena McDonald to John Purcer q.v.
Lizzie McDonald to John Martin q.v.
Lovenia McDonld to H. H. Hallyburton q.v.
M.G. McDonald to Mary B. Frazier, 7 Oct 1884 (9 Oct), T. Ashburn MG 1-466
Manassas McDonald to J. F. Abel q.v.
Mandy McDonald to A. J. Hawkins q.v.
Mary Ann McDonald to J. M. Jewell q.v.
Mary E. McDonald to J. E. Sawyers q.v.
Mary J. McDonald to William R. Mathewse q.v.
Mollie McDonald to Herbert Stokes q.v.
N. A. McDonald to E. A. Jewell q.v.
Nellie McDonald to John Fults q.v.
R.F. McDonald to Orpha J. Paine, 16 Oct 1866 (same), W. H. Bell MG 1-#915
S. E. McDonald to J. H. Jewell q.v.
Sarah McDonald to Malvin Mills q.v.
Sydnia C. McDonald to Thomas H. Roddy q.v.
Vesta McDonald to James Love q.v.
W.M. McDonald to Valia Hamilton, 18 Aug 1895, Leroy(?) Biggs MG 4-86
William Payne McDonald to Cora E. Davidson, 19 May 1891, J.R. Walker MG 4-25

- - - - - - - - - - - - -

McDOWELL / McDOWEL

1860 CENSUS
Thomas C. McDowell 30, Lutitia 33 (NC), Nancy C. 8, Martha J. 6, Joseph C. 4, William R. 2, James M. 6/12 7-8-50
1870 and 1880 CENSUS– None
1900 CENSUS
Joseph C. McDowell 44 (Sep 1855-M 24), Elizabeth 42 (Jan 1858-M 24-11-9), Thomas W. 23 (Mar 1877), Martha J. 19 (Ap 1881), Nora 16 (Sep 1883), Lula 14 (Sep 1885), Joseph J. 12 (Oct 1887), Eliza 8 (June 1891), Myrtle 6 (Oct 1893), James 6/12 (Nov 1899) 5-238B-202
Lula M. McDowell Unk: see William D. Wilkey
Lutitia McDowel 73 (Feb 1827-NC/NC/NC-Wd 2-2), William R. 42 (Oct 1857), James M. 40 (Nov 1859), Vessa JOHNSON 25 (Dec 1874-T/Ga/T)(House Servant), Pearl JOHNSON 5 (Mar 1895) 5-238A-199
Major McDowell 33 (Oct 1866-SC/Va/SC-M 1)(RR Section Hand), Mary 22 (Feb 1878-Ga/a/T-M 1-0-0) 10-324B-97/101 (B)
Thomas W. McDowell 23: see Samuel A. Wilkey
MARRIAGES
James M. McDowell to Sapina or Sophena Clark, 17 Nov 1900 (same), F.M. Cook MG 3-243
Jesse F. McDowell to Ann E. Kelly, 23 Feb 1869 (no return) 1-#1047
Vader McDowell to William Wilkey q.v.
Visa or Vira McDowel(?) to Richard Lawson q.v.

- - - - - - - - - - - - -

McDUFFY / McDUFFEY

1870 CENSUS
Jane McDuffey 35: see Keziah Leffew
1880 CENSUS– None
1900 CENSUS
Wiley McDuffy 35: see Ella Love (B)

- - - - - - - - - - - - -

McELWEE

1870 CENSUS
Thomas B. McElwee 54, Martha [nee Matlock] 50, Charles 20, Julia A. 17, Hugh 14, Henry 11 2-15-104
1880 CENSUS– None
1900 CENSUS
Charles L. McElwee 50 (Oct 1849-M 20), Mary A. 42 (Ap 1858-T/Ky/T-M 20-5-3), Martha J. 17 (Jan 1883), John R. 14 (May 1886), Lillie M. 9 (May 1891) 2-196A-90/91
MARRIAGE
Ned McElwee (23, McMinn Co; occuption, Railroad) to Annie Rucker (?, McMinn Co), 23 Feb 1882, S. Breeding JP, John Roberson & wife W 4-7(70) (B)

- - - - - - - - - - - - -

McERVIN

1870 CENSUS
Mary McErvin 8: see James Rice

McEWEN / McUEN

1860 CENSUS
Merrel McUen 25, Malinda A. 20, Ruthe J. 2/12 5-40-266
1870 and 1880 CENSUS– None
1900 CENSUS
William McEwen 24 (Oct 1875-M 3)(Coal Miner), Jennie 25 (Aug 1874-T/Ala/T-M 3-2-2), Lizzie 2 (Nov 1897), Estelle 1 (May 1900), Lucinda GREGORY 64 (a)(June 1835-S) 13-304A-268/278
MARRIAGE
Will McEwen to Jennie Edwards, 23 Oct 1896 (25 Oct), W.R. Grimsley MG, Zack Martin W 2-77

McFALL / McFALLS

1860 CENSUS
Daniel McFalls 67 (NC), Mary 63 9-100-684
Francis McFalls 30, Caroline 30, Amanda 14, Daniel L. 6, Joseph E. 5, Rebecca A. 2, Hulda 1/12 9-100-685
Hamp McFalls 40 (NC)(Carpenter), Mary 37, Samantha 17, Ward V.(?) 9, Wright S. 1, Jacob L. WASSON 19, Mary A. 19, Victoria 4/12 4-43-294
Robert McFalls 33 (NC), Barbary A. 34, Mary 11, Darius 9, Joseph 7, Caroline 4 4-44-300
1870 CENSUS
Allen H. McFalls 50 (NC), Mira 48, Wright L. 12, Martha 20, Joseph H. 1, Mary A. 1/12 1-12-77
Robert McFalls 46 (NC), Barbara Ann 46, Darius 18, Joshua R. 16, Mary Jane 14, Sarah A.C. 8, Martha 10, General G. 3 4-14-95
1880 CENSUS
Wade McFalls 60, Mira 58, Wright 21 (s), Phebe 18 (dl), James 7 (s), Mira HOLLOWAY 19 (gd), Lorinda REECE 1/12 1-17-142
1900 CENSUS
Allen H. McFalls 83: see Richard Holloway
Joseph R. McFalls 50 (Nov 1849-M 30), Aloy A. 59 (Jan 1841-M 30-3-3), William D. 21 (Feb 1879), James R. 17 (Dec 1882), Rufus J. 12 (Jan 1888)
4-224A-208/212 (Spring City & Dayton Road)
MARRIAGES
Eliza Jane McFalls to R. W. Holloway q.v.
J.W. McFalls to Mollie Keith, 9 July 1892, James Corvin MG 4-45
M. A. McFalls to J. D. Gilliam q.v.
Malinda McFalls to Thomas J. Kirby q.v.
Martha McFalls to Samuel Roberts q.v.
Mary Ann McFalls to Jacob L. Wassum q.v.
Martha J. McFalls to Henry S. McDonald q.v.
N.L. McFall to Pheba R. Holloway, 9 Ap 1880 (15 Ap), J.P. Roddy MG 1-#1725
Samantha McFalls to Zachariah T. Wassum q.v.
W.H. McFalls to S.A. Able, 16 Sep 1875 (20 Sep), J.J. Ingle JP 1-#1411
Wade McFall to Martha Edmonds(?), 20 Mar 1899, G.W. Morris MG 4-104

McFANILES

1900 CENSUS
Wash McFaniles 21 (May 1879-M 2), Martha 19 (Ap 1881-M 2-0) 12-180A-33/36

McFARLAND

1860 CENSUS
Elizabeth McFarland 81 (SC): see Scott Hale
Elizabeth McFarland 82 (SC): see William B. Johnson
MARRIAGES
Elizabeth McFarland to J. J. Abel q.v.
Lizza McFarland to Jeff Miller q.v.

McGANN

1900 CENSUS
Winfield S. McGann 47 (June 1855-Va/Va/Va-M 12), Bettie E. 38 (July 1872-M 12-4-4), Kattie J. 9 (Sep 1890), Dora E. 7 (July 1892), Otha W. 4 (Oct 1895), Mollie B. 3 (May 1897), Caroline BRADY 53 (ml)(Unk 1847-Wd) 3-211A-192/210
MARRIAGE
Scott McGann to Lizzie Brady, 17 July 1889 (21 July), W.F. West MG 1-577

McGARN

MARRIAGE
Katie McCarn to A. M. Lypold q.v.

McGEE

1900 CENSUS
Jesse C. McGee 41 (Nov 1858-M 8)(Sheriff's Deputy), Mattie 28 (Oct 1871-T/Va/T-M 8-3-2), Lula L. 7 (Jan 1893), William B. 4 (Jan 1896) 14-216B-81/82
Thomas McGee 52 (Ap 1847-M 22), Sarah 40 (Ap 1860-M 23-3-3), Martha 21 (Nov 1879), Rosi 1 (July 1898) 1-186B-146/154
MARRIAGES
J. McGee (24, Polk Co) to Lulah Marshall (17, Meigs Co), 1 Mar 1883, T.H. McPherson JP, J.M. Johnson & H.M. Marshall W 4-14(140)
J.C. McGee to Nettie Garrison, 1 Jan 1892, J.B. Wagoner MG 4-36
James McGee to Ida Jackson, 10 Sep 1885 (13 Sep), H.B. Burdett MG 1-513
S.J. McGee to M.W. Conathy q.v.
Sarah McGee to Ruban Hamell q.v.

McGENTRY

MARRIAGE
Michael W. McGentry to Sarah Ellis, 11 July 1887 (same), F.J. Paine JP 1-584

- - - - - - - - - - - - -

McGILL / McGILLE / MAGILL

1870 CENSUS
William McGill 52, Ellen 46, Mary 22, Sarah 20, William 12, John 8, Margarette 6, Amanda 3 4-6-35
William P. McGill 35, Isabella M. 25, Thomas D. 7, Alice E. 5, Mary M. 1 8-15-107
1880 CENSUS– None
1900 CENSUS
Robert McGill 53 (Mar 1847-M 25)(Coal Miner), Mary P. 45 (Dec 1854-T/NC/T-M 25-2-1), Thomas H. 21 (July 1878-M 1)(Coal Miner), Addie I. 19 (dl)(Sep 1880-NC/NC/NC-M 1-1-1), Edith M. 4/12 (gd)(Jan 1900) 13-305B-293/305
MARRIAGES
Joseph McGille to Martha Jane Blackwell, 3 June 1867 (30 June), W.W. Low JP 1-#956
Mary McGill to Robert McGill q.v.
Newton A. McGille to Catharine J. Gray, 3 Oct 1866 (4 Oct), J.M. Kelly MG 1-#911
R.N. Magill to Ella F. Dotey, 25 Dec 1886 (27 Dec), J. Waldrof MG 1-516
Robert McGill to Mary McGill, 24 Dec 1886 (25 Dec), A. W. Frazier JP 1-513
T. H. McGill to Ada Queen, 5 Nov 1898 (same), W. R. Grimsley MG, Robert McGill W 2-343
William P. McGille to Issbella M. Johnson, 16 Nov 1861 (no return) 1-#765

- - - - - - - - - - - - -

McGOUGHY

MARRIAGE
Issabella McGouhy to Washington Morgan q.v.

- - - - - - - - - - - - -

McGOWEN

1880 CENSUS
Robert McGowen 33 (Miner), Mary 23, Susan 6, Charlie 4, Willis 1 2-31-248

- - - - - - - - - - - - -

McGUIRE / McGUYER

1860 CENSUS
James W. McGuyer 33, Nancy 38 (Ga), John H. 12, Mary 10, Robert J. 8, William M. 5, James M. 2 8-21-139
1870 CENSUS– None
1880 CENSUS
Elija McGuire 56, Eliza 57, Becky 44, M.A. 28 (d), M.S. 26 (d), B.F. 23 (s), J.B. 20 (s), W.G. 5 (gs), Nola 5/12 (gd) 8-16-134
MARRIAGES
John H. McGuire to Sarah E. Jones, 9 Sep 1868 (11 Sep), R.H. Jordan MG 1-#1027
Sarah McGuire to John L. May q.v.

- - - - - - - - - - - - -

McHALEY

1860 CENSUS
Henry McHaley 21 (School Teacher), Sarah A. 1 8-12-74

- - - - - - - - - - - - -

McHOLMES / McHOMES

MARRIAGE
Lillie McHolmes or McHomes to Jasper Bowen q.v.

- - - - - - - - - - - - -

McHONE

1900 CENSUS
John J. McHone 52 (May 1848-Wd), Eliza J. 20 (Aug 1879), Martha L. 18 (Dec 1881-Ga), Ulysses 13 (July 1887-Ga) 5-236A-155/155

- - - - - - - - - - - - -

McINTYRE / McENTIRE / McENTYRE / McANTIRE

1900 CENSUS
Berty McAntire 14: see Sarah Duckworth
James McIntyre 21: see John C. Willson
John McEntire 36 (Mar 1864-Ga/Ga/Ga)(Furnaceman), Mon CUMMINGS 26 (Jan 1874)(Furnaceman), John FLEMING 24 (Mar 1876)(Furnaceman) 10-323A-61/65 (B)
Tara(?) McIntyre 27 (Jan 1873-D 1-1), Etta 6 (Oct 1893) 3-203A-65/70
MARRIAGES
Jennie McEntir(?) to Henry Payne q.v.
May McIntyre to Charley Dillard q.v.
W.N. McEntire to Betty Duckworth, 21 Dec 1877 (23 Dec), Wm W. Low JP 1-#1534
William B. McEntyre to Mollie Long, 11 Jan 1894, J.W. Cowles JP 4-65

- - - - - - - - - - - - -

McJUNKINS / McJUNKIN / McJENKINS

1900 CENSUS
Balu(?) McJenkins 32 (Feb 1868-M 11)(RR Brakeman), Winnie 27 (Mar 1873-M 11-3-2), Haggie 10 (d)(Dec 1889), James 8 (Dec 1891) 10-259A-180/184
James McJunkin 40 (July 1859-M 18)(Coal Miner), Florence 37 (May 1863-M 18-6-4), Eva L. 12 (Nov 1887), Freddie 7 (Feb 1893), Sudsa M. 5 (May 1895) 8-278A-192/194
Samuel McJunkin 34 (Feb 1866-Ga/Ga/Ga-M 9)(Machinist), Eva 29 (Oct 1870-M 9-2-2), Clarence 4 (Aug 1895), Earl 3/12 (Mar 1900) 8-276A-151/152

MARRIAGES
David McJunkins to Minnie Wilkey, 13 Oct 1888 (14 Oct), J.W. Williamson MG 1-555
M. McJunkins to Florida Rector, 10 Ap 1886 (11 Ap), Calvin Morgan JP 1-514
Minnie McJunkins to Levi Hoback q.v.
Sainne McJunkins to Thomas Helton q.v.
Samuel McJunkin to Eva Pickel, 17 Dec 1890, R.S. Mason JP 4-24

- - - - - - - - - - - - -

McKEEHEN / McKEHAN

1860 CENSUS
James McKehan 45, Martha 27, Margaret 5, Sarah J. 1, Elvira F. 1/12 5-37-248
1870 and 1880 CENSUS– None
1900 CENSUS
James McKeehen 34 (Nov 1865-M 13)(Blacksmith), Emma 32 (Mar 1868-M 13-6-5), Callie 11 (Oct 1888), Ernest 9 (May 1891), Annie 6 (July 1893), Lakie 4 (Oct 1895), Dollie M. 1 (May 1899) 14-213B-15/15
MARRIAGE
Emma P. McKeehen to John P. Hale q.v.

- - - - - - - - - - - - -

McKELVEY

MARRIAGE
N.C. McKelvey to Mary Hair, 21 Aug 1894, W.G. Curton MG 4-71

- - - - - - - - - - - - -

McKEMP

1900 CENSUS
James McKemp 12: see Grant Walker (B)

- - - - - - - - - - - - -

McKENZIE

1900 CENSUS
Benjamin G. McKenzie 34 (Feb 1866-M 7)(Attorney), Louella 29 (Oct 1870-M 7-3-3), James G. 6 (Sep 1893), Cora G. 3 (Jan 1897), George J.W. 3/12 (Feb 1900), Maggie 11 (d)(Nov 1888) 10-324A-88/92
George C. McKenzie 39 (Jan 1861-T/Va/T-M 17)(Cashier), Nancy N. 40 (June 1859-T/T/Ga-M 17-8-7), Charlotte 16 (Dec 1885), George A. 14 (May 1886), Irby E. 12 (Mar 1888), Bedford T. 9 (July 1890), Emmett H. 7 (Sep 1892), Robert J. 4 (Sep 1895), Fred J. 1 (Oct 1898) 8-313A-48/51 [George marred N.N. Hardin on 6 Feb 1883 in Meigs County]
James L. McKenzie 26 (May 1874-M 1)(Physician), Anna M. 20 (June 1879-M 1-1-1), Heremigh 7/12 (Oct 1899) 13-309A-360/373
MARRIAGES
B.G. McKenzie to Louella Foust, 21 Dec 1891, John T. Price MG 4-49
F.M. McKenzie to Nora J. Blevins, 7 Aug 1885 (same), T.H. McPherson JP 1-516

- - - - - - - - - - - - -

McKINLEY

1900 CENSUS
John McKinley 63 (Mar 1837-Scotland/Do/Do-1881/19/Na-Wd)(Butcher), Mary NEWMAN 35 (d)(Sep 1864-Scotland/Do/Do-M 15-6-4), Herbert J. 39 (sl)(Mar 1861-England/Do/Do-1881/19/M 15)(Clerk), Tom 12 (gs)(May 1888-Mich), John 9 (gs)(Dec 1890), Annie 5 (gd)(Oct 1894-Mich), Marnie A. 6/12 (gd)(Nov 1899) 8-313A-47/50
MARRIAGES
James McKinley to Minnie M. King, 9 Nov 1889 (same), W.R. Beard(?) ?? 1-584
Marim(?) McKinley to Edward Morgan q.v.

- - - - - - - - - - - - -

McKINNEY

1880 CENSUS
Joe McKinney 26, Gracie 20, Isabel 1/12, Amanda YOUNG 18 (Servant), Easter 4, Mira 2/12 1-8-61 (B)
1900 CENSUS
Jane McKinney 66: see George Moats
John McKinney 35 (Feb 1865-S) 13-299A-167/171
MARRIAGE
Siller McKinney to William Randolph q.v.

- - - - - - - - - - - - -

McKINSEY

1900 CENSUS
Rosa McKinsey 27: see William L. Able

- - - - - - - - - - - - -

McLANDON

MARRIAGE
Isaac McLandon to Susan Barger, 10 Dec 1865 (same), W. W. Low JP 1-#1075

- - - - - - - - - - - - -

McLANE

1900 CENSUS
Mack McLane 50 (Mar 1850-Ala/Unk./T-M 24), Margrett 50 (Mar 1850-M 24-11-10), Mary E. 22 (May 1878), Emmarn N. 20 (Feb 1880), Noah N. 13 (Aug 1886), Hannie 12 (Mar 1888), Maroe 9 (Sep 1890), Fred 8 (Mar 1892), Vestie 6 (Aug 1893), Millie 5 (Oct 1896), Carra E. 24 (sd)(Sep 1875) 10-252B-54 (B)

- - - - - - - - - - - - -

McLEER

1870 CENSUS
Joseph McLeer 27 (Merchant), Susan 20: see Jeremiah C. Wasson

- - - - - - - - - - - - -

McLEMORE

1860 CENSUS

Thomas McLemore 34, Mary 28, William 11, Ellen 8, James 6, Isaac 4, Elizabeth 2 2-32-256

- - - - - - - - - - - - -

McMAHAN

1900 CENSUS

John McMahan 26 (Unk-M 2), Miranda 40 (Unk-T/T/Ga-M 2-2-2), Jesse 3/12 (Feb 1900), Harriet COX 65 (ml) (Unk-Ga-Wd 9-6) 6-248B-165/166 (B) [John married Miranda Cox on 19 Nov 1898 in Meigs Co]

MARRIAGES

Ellen McMahan to William A. Minton q.v.

Maggie McMahan to J. C. Tramble q.v.

Pat McMahan to Polly A. Holmes or Homes, 20 Ap 1900 (same), W.D. Reed MG, E. Fisher W 3-147

- - - - - - - - - - - - -

McMARTY / McMURTY

MARRIAGE

James McMarty or McMurty to Hattie Waller, 27 July 1880 (1 Aug), James Johnson JP 1-292

- - - - - - - - - - - - -

McMILLEN / McMILLIN / McMILLIAN / McMULLEN

1880 CENSUS

A. E. McMillin 19: see Gid Sharp

1900 CENSUS

Calvin H. McMillan 51 (Nov 1848-M 30), Susan M. 44 (July 1855-M 30-7-5), Mary B. 22 (Ap 1878), Harrison D. 18 (Jan 1882), Walter 12 (Dec 1887) 13-307B-341/353

Columbus McMillan 26 (Unk 1874-M 5)(Miner), Sarah 25 (June 1874-M 5-1-1), Ray (Unk 1895), Thomas WILSON 30 (bl)(Unk 1870) 8-281B-258/260

Edward McMillan 20 (Nov 1879-M 4), Nannie F. 21 (Mar 1879-M 4-2-2), Rosa M. 2 (Jan 1898), Nancy E. 1 (Jan 1900) 4-224B-218/222 (Spring City & Dayton Road)

Franklin McMillan 56 (Jan 1844-M 36), Sarah 55 (Sep 1844-M 36-9-5), Sallie TEASELY 16 (d)(July 1883-M 0-0), Fred 22 (sl)(Nov 1877-M 0)(Coal Miner), Perry WATSON 25 (boarder)(Unk 1875-Ky/Ky Ky) (Coal Miner), George PRITCHET 38 (boarder) (July 1861-M 15)(Coal Miner) 8-277A-169/170

George McMillan 46 (Unk 1854-M 21)(Carpenter), Alice 42 (Ap 1858-M 21-6-2), James 9 (June 1890), Gertrude 5 (Oct 1894) 8-276B-165/166

James M. McMillan 42 (Sep 1857-M 22), Elizabeth 59 (May 1841-M 22-10-6) 8-286B-368/370

Joe(?) McMillan 54 (Oct 1845-T/NC/T-M 48), Bethenia 68 (Oct 1851-T/NC/NC-M 48-9-7) 3-200B-13/13

John McMillan 27 (Dec 1862-M 11)(Coal Miner), Cynthia 26 (June 1863-M 11-3-3), Mary 7 (Feb 1893), Clay 5 (June 1894), Roy 2 (Feb 1898) 8-289B-423/426

Louisa McMillan 37 (Unk-Wd 1-1) 10-331B-246/261

Tilman McMillen 18: see John Houston

MARRIAGES

C.W. McMillan to Sallie Wilson, 24 Dec 1894, A.P. Hayes JP 4-75

Ed McMillen to Nancy Neal, 25 Mar 1897 (26 Mar), L.E. Smith JP, C.K. Knight W 2-131

Florence McMillan to James L. Roberts q.v.

Jack McMillan to Lona Duff, 31 May 1891, R.S. Mason JP 4-26

John McMillan to Synthia Adams, 31 July 1889 (same), M.C. Bruner MG 1-578

John McMillan to Bell Walker, 10 Aug 1894, R.S. Mason JP 4-71

John McMillan to Mollie Jordan, 28 Jan 1899 (29 Jan), W. A. Green JP, J.S. Allen W 2-378

Maggie McMillin to Newt Welsh q.v.

Maggie McMillan to Jessie Green q.v.

Margaret C. McMillen to Ulyses Boyd q.v.

Mariah McMillan to W. C. Harwood q.v.

Mariah McMillen to George Smith q.v.

Martha McMillin to George Pritchett q.v.

Mary L. McMillen to W. G. M. Thomas q.v.

Samuel McMillan to Lulla Wilkey, 15 Ap 1894, John S. Wicey(?) MG 4-69

Sarah McMillen to John Townsend q.v.

Sudie McMillen to Fred Tinsley q.v.

Susan McMullen to George W. Smith q.v.

Texas McMillan to James L. Pritchett q.v.

Tom McMillen to Jennie Wooday, 8 June 1898 (same), A.P. Hayes JP, W.A. Snedley W 2-290

- - - - - - - - - - - - -

McMURRY / McMURRAY / McMAURY

1860 CENSUS

Elizabeth E. McMurry 25: see John Kennedy

Sarah McMurry 52 (NC), Rhoda E. 18, John H. 18 3-62-426

William McMurry 23, Eliza A. 32 3-54-369

1870 CENSUS

Elizabeth McMurry 22: see Peter Minnick

Rhoda McMurry 28: see Robert Montgomery

William McMurry 45, Eliza A. 42, William 9, John H. 3 3-13-89

1880 CENSUS

Elija McMurry 53, E.A. 51 (w), J.H. 13 (s) 3-15-119

J.E. McMury 40, ?.N. WYOTT 37, M.J. 38 (w), P.J. 13 (s), N.A. 11 (d), T.N. 6 (s), R.H. 4 (d), M.J. 1 (d) 9-31-264

R.E. McMurray 33: see C. Smith

1900 CENSUS

Betsy McMurry 60: see J. Kennedy

Eliza A. McMaury 71 (Oct 1828-Wd), William A. 8 (gs) (May 1892-Ala/T/Ala), William S. 8 (gs)(May 1892) 3-204A-76/82

Eveline McMurry 50: see Martin Wilkey

Flora J. McMurry 17: see James W. Boles

MARRIAGES

E. McMurry to Eliza Moore, no date (4 Feb 1860), John Howard MG 1-#685

Floria McMurry to H. J. Bowles q.v.

M. McMurry to J. C. Moore q.v.

Mary McMurry to J. Smith q.v.

William McMurry to Ann Wright, 13 Dec 1879 (no return) 1-#1698

- - - - - - - - - - - - -

McNABB / McNAB

1870 CENSUS

Thomas L. McNabb 17, Julius M. 15, Zachariah L. 13, William B. 11, Jacob A. 9, James A. 7: see Zachariah Rose

1880 CENSUS– None

1900 CENSUS

Lattimore B. McNabb 80 (Mar 1820-Oh/Scotland/Ireland-M 23)(Carpenter), Olive E.H. 65 (Aug 1834-Oh/Oh/Oh-M 23)(Dressmaker) 14-213A-6/6

Love McNabb 24 (Dec 1875)(Livery Stable Keeper) 10-329B-199/212 (B)

Smith McNabb 47 (Jan 1853-Ky/Unk-M 6)(Mine Laborer), Dora 22 (Dec 1877-M 6-3-2), Veatric 4 (Oct 1895-Ala), Phonso 3/12 (Feb 1900) 10-258A-148/152 (B)

MARRIAGE

N.P. McNabb to Mary Sneedley, 6 Dec 1900 (same), J.A. Shelton MG 3-251

- - - - - - - - - - - - -

McNEAL

1880 CENSUS

James McNeal 59 (Minister), Ellen 55, James 18, Nancy 20, Lorena 14, Mabelina 11, Maud 1/12 12-4-35

MARRIAGE

Adaline McNeal or McKeal to John J. Tidwell q.v.

- - - - - - - - - - - - -

McNELIS

MARRIAGE

William McNelis to Mary A. Cunningham, 10 Jan 1891, Patrick J. O'Farrell MG 4-20

- - - - - - - - - - - - -

McNETIS / McNELIS

1900 CENSUS

Mike McNetis 45 (Nov 1854-Ireland/Do/Do-M 20)(Teamster), Mary A. 39 (July 1861-Ind/Oh/NY-M 20-8-8), Annie 19 (Nov 1880-Oh), Mary 17 (Mar 1883), Gracie 15 (Dec 1885), Agnes 12 (May 1888), Ellen 9 (Feb 1891-Ky), Maggie 6 (Ap 1894-Ky), James F. 3 (Ap 1897), Lizzie 0/12 (May 1900), James McNETIS 47 (b)(Nov 1852-Ireland/Do/Do-S) 2-192A-20/20

- - - - - - - - - - - - -

McNEW

1870 CENSUS

Evana A. McNew 12: see John F. Dawson

Henry J. McNew 17: see Thomas R. Holland

MARRIAGE

H.M. McNew (*) to Catharine McAlpin, 8 Feb 1873 (9 Feb), W.W. Low JP 1-#1277 [*McKew in index]

- - - - - - - - - - - - -

McNUTT

1900 CENSUS

Timothy McNutt 22 (June 1855-M 22), Rebecca 43 (Nov 1856-M 22-10-8), Mattie E* 21 (July 1878), Serepthia 17 (Mar 1889), Narsus 12 (May 1888), Joseph R. 9 (Sep 1890), Elizabeth 7 (Sep 1892), Mike C. 5 (Feb 1895), Ulo 2 (June 1897) 3-210A-175/190 [*marked through– see Mattie E. Hill]

MARRIAGE

S. McNutt to Zack Fugate q.v.

- - - - - - - - - - - - -

McPHAIL

1900 CENSUS

Mary McPhail 58 (Aug 1841-Ga/T/T-Wd 11-8), Emma 28 (Sep 1871-T/T/Ga), Sarah 26 (May 1874), John D. 24 (Feb 1876), Martha E. 22 (Dec 1877), Nancy M. 20 (June 1879), Loucresia 18 (Aug 1881), Eva 16 (July 1883), Dora 14 (July 1885) 3-210B-181/197

- - - - - - - - - - - - -

McPHERSON / McFERSON

1860 CENSUS

James A. McPherson 32, Mary A. 32, John F. 13, Liddia J. 11, Cynthia E. 9, James H. 7, William W. 5, Mary E. 3, Nancy C. 2/12 8-16-108

James D. McPherson 50 (Va), July A. 48 (Va), Amanda J. 25 (Va)(School Teacher), John M. 24, Mary L. 17 (School Teacher), Emly P. 15, Stephen I.M. 13, Julia F. 11, William P. 4 4-47-323

Thomas McPherson 29, Elizabeth 30, Adelia 4, Andrew B. 2, William G. JAMES 10 (bound), Margaret GENGERY 24, John REDENER(?) 10 3-57-390

1870 CENSUS

Jacob McPherson 14 (B): see Thomas H. McPherson

James A. McPherson 48, Mary Ann 44, John F. 21, Syntha E. 17, James H. 15, William W. 13, Mary E. 11, Nancy C. 9, Thomas A. 7, Martha K. 5, Sarah D. 3 8-6-35

James D. McPherson 60 (Va), Julia A. 59 (Va), John M. 35 (Va), William P. 14 4-9-56

Joel L. McPherson 28 (Va)(Merchant), Hannah E. 18 4-8-48

Thomas H. McPherson 39, Amanda J. 36, Adaline 14, Andrew B. 12, Ann V. 9, Lucinda I. 4, Jacob McPHERSON (B) 14, William J. JONES 18 3-4-26

1880 CENSUS

J.L. McPherson 39, H.E. 26 (w), J.T. 11 (s), S.A. 8 (d), M.M. 6 (d), J.S. 5 (s), F.L. 3 (s), W.B. 2 (s), S.E. LONG 27 (Housekeeper), James TALLEY 28 (Farm Hand) 4-35-290

J.M. McPherson 46, C. 26 (w), Mary THOMPSON 15 (c) 11-42-340

James D. McPherson 70, J.A. 68 (w), William 28 (s) 4-35-292

Thomas McPherson 49, A.J. 47 (w), A.D. 24 (d), F.J. 14 (d), J.W. 8 (s), Lilly 6 (d), E.J. 3 (d), J.A. WRIGHT 14 (Hired Hand) 3-27-215

William McPherson 25, L.C. 22 (w), Mary BURWICK 50(?) [ink blob] (ml) 11-40-328

1900 CENSUS

Amanda McPherson 66 (Mar 1834-Va/Va/Va-Wd 3-3), Lela 26 (d)(Mar 1874-T/T/Va) 3-205B-100/108

James W. McPherson 28 (Ap 1872-T/T/Va-M 4/12), Frances E. 19 (June 1880-M 4/12-0-0) 3-205B-00/109

John M. McPherson 63 (Oct 1836-Va/Va/Va-M 21), Catharine J. 48 (Feb 1852-M 21-4-4), Harriet A. 19 (Oct 1880), James T. 17 (Aug 1882), Samuel W. 15 (Nov 1884), Mary N. 3 (May 1887), Ruie HENRY 80 (boarder)(Aug 1819) 4-226A-244/248 (Rhea Springs and Washington Road)

Joel L. McPherson 59 (Oct 1840-Va/Va/Va-M 31)(Lawyer), Hannah E. 47 (Dec 1852-T/T/Ky-M 31-13-11), Frank C. 23 (Dec 1876)(Hotel Clerk), Cinna G. 17 (Sep 1882)(Teacher), Elizabeth H. 15 (Oct 1884), Lewis N. 13 (Aug 1886), Louisa C. 11 (Sep 1888), Joel M. 8 (Feb 1892), Mary McPHERSON 26 (d)(Aug 1873-D 1-1), Jack D. (gs)(Oct 1895) 14-213B-17/17

Mary McPherson 26, Jack D. 4: see Joel L. McPherson

Susan McPherson 49 (Jan 1851-M 25-11-9)(Washwoman), George P. 21 (Nov 1878)(Fireman, Station Engine), Minnie 17 (July 1882)(Dressmaker), Dora 5 (June 1884), Luria F. 14 (June 1885), Dilsia 12 (Ap 1888), Zoe 10 (Aug 1889), Onie M. 7 (May 1893) 10-325B-122/126

MARRIAGES

A. V. McFerson to J. T. Bryant q.v.

Adelia McPherson to W.Y. or W.G. Vinyard q.v.

Amanda J. McFerson to Thomas McFerson q.v.

Emma McPherson to Thomas Roddy q.v.

H.W. McFerson to Lyda Catharine Barwick, 14 July 1877 (17 July), C. Morgan JP 1-#1505

J.W. McPherson to Frances E. Boggart, 16 Feb 1900 (20 Feb), Wm White MG, H.T. Roddy W 3-123

Joel L. McFerson to Hanah E. Ladd, 4 Oct 1869 (5 Oct), Z. Rose MG 1-#1114

John McPherson to Catharine J. Thompson, 15 Mar 1879 (18 Mar), E.L. Burnett MG 1-#1093

John F. McFerson to Mary E. Morgan, 1 Feb 1877 (6 Feb), C. Morgan JP 1-#1484

Julia A. McPherson to T. B. Leuty q.v.

Lucy McPherson to N. B. Johnson q.v.

Lula McPherson to Tommie James q.v.

Lyda J. McFerson to John A. Foust q.v.

Martha McPherson to H. F. Burchart or Burchard q.v.

Mary McPherson to Charles S. Castor q.v.

Snyde McPherson to Smythe B. Moulton q.v.

Syntha McPherson to Noah Myers q.v.

Thomas McFerson to Amanda J. McFerson, 19 July 1869 (20 July), J.W. Thompson MG 1-#1093

Thomas H. McFerson to Elizabeth McCaleb, 27 Dec 1852 (30 Dec), J. Stancel MG 1-#399

Virginia McPherson to Burton Leuty q.v.

W.W. McPherson to Amanda Burwick, 5 Ap 1888 (6 Ap), F.R. Morgan JP 1-580

W.W. McPherson to Missouri Shadwick, 8 Sep 1898 (bond only) 2-320

\- - - - - - - - - - - - -

McPHETERS / McPHEATERS

1900 CENSUS

Alfred McPheaters 75 (Dec 1824-M 14), Margaret 48 (Dec 1853-M 14), Azariah 12 (Ap 1888), Jesse L. 9 (Sep 1890) 4-225A-230/234 (Creek Road)

MARRIAGE

A. McPheters to Margaret A. Fine, 21 Ap 1887 (same), S.H. Price MG 1-530

\- - - - - - - - - - - - -

McREYNOLDS

MARRIAGES

A.H. McReynolds to Racheal C. Banks, 11 Ap 1899 (same), W.L. Patton MG, J.F. Henninger W 2-400

Ella McReynolds to James Rodgers q.v.

Savinia [bond] or Selina [license] McReynolds to Lawrence Card q.v.

\- - - - - - - - - - - - -

McROY / McEROY

(see also **McCROY**)

MARRIAGES

Amos McEroy(*) to Rebecca Simpson, 14 Mar 1881 (15 Mar), James Johnson JP 1-297
[*index lists Amos as McCroy]

T.J. McRoy to Synda Auther, 17 Jan 1885 (same), T.F. Shaver JP 1-464

\- - - - - - - - - - - - -

McSWAIN / McSWEN

MARRIAGE

S.R. McSwain or McSwen to Lizzie Hamilton, 12 Dec 1894, J.F. Hash MG 4-76

\- - - - - - - - - - - - -

McWHIRTER

1880 CENSUS

Thomas McWhirter 28 (Proprietor, *Rhea Springs News*), Mary 24: see Andrew Anderson

\- - - - - - - - - - - - -

McWILLIS / McWELIS

1900 CENSUS

Perry McWillis 67 (Dec 1832-Ala/Ala/Md-M 18)(Stonemason), Susan 50 (Nov 1849-T/T/Md-M 18-4-1), Minnie HARRISON 13 (ne)(June 1886) 1-198A-125/130 (B)

William McWelis 30 (Mar 1870-Ireland/Do/Do-Unk/Unk/Na-M 10)(Coal Miner), Mary 29 (Dec 1870-Ireland/Do/Do-M 10-5-4), Annie 8 (Jan 1892), James P. 4 (Nov 1895), Louisa 2 (Oct 1897), Paul F. 6/12 (Nov 1899), Carrie CUNNINGHAM 25 (sil)(Ap 1875-NY) 8-276B-60/161

\- - - - - - - - - - - - -

MACAHAN

1870 CENSUS
Martha Macahan 40, Margarette M. 15, Sarah I. 12, Sela O. 10, Elvira 8 10-1-7

- - - - - - - - - - - - -

MACE

1900 CENSUS
Tilman Mace 32 (Jan 1868-NC/NC/NC-M 11), Catharine 32 (Feb 1868-M 11-5-5), Johney 9 (Oct 1890), Mary E. 8 (Jan 1892), William L. 6 (July 1893), James Mc 2 (Ap 1898), Emma O. 10/12 (July 1899), Lizabeth HAMILTON 57 (ml)(Oct 1842-NC/T/T-Wd) 10-260B-211/216

- - - - - - - - - - - - -

MACK

1900 CENSUS
Annie Mack 8: see Mary Bradford (B)
MARRIAGE
Lou Ella Mack to Emmit Robertson q.v.

- - - - - - - - - - - - -

MACKADOW
(see also McADOO)

1880 CENSUS
Elys Mackadow 38, C.I. 37 (w), M.A. 13 (d), J.C. 9 (s), R.B. 6 (d) 7-28-238

- - - - - - - - - - - - -

MADDISON

1900 CENSUS
James Maddison 23, Mary 20, Grace 6/12: see John E. Evans (B)
MARRIAGE
Manervia Maddison to Thomas Walter q.v.

- - - - - - - - - - - - -

MADGETT

1900 CENSUS
Melinda Madgett 62: see Ansel G. McClendon

- - - - - - - - - - - - -

MAGSBY

1900 CENSUS
Annie Magsby 29, Earl V. 3: see Marion Dooley (B)
MARRIAGE
John Magsby to Annie Rucker, 18 Mar 1900 (same), G.T. Mussington MG, Floyd Maryott(?) W 3-133

- - - - - - - - - - - - -

MAHAFFY

1860 CENSUS
Hiram Mahaffy 34, Jane 40, Jesse L. 9, Russel H. 7, Mary I. 4, Sarah H. 1 1-82-563

- - - - - - - - - - - - -

MAHAN

1900 CENSUS
Bridget Mahan 17: see William Small
Polly Mahan 60 (Nov 1840-M 25-8-4), Mary 19 (Sep 1880), Ellen 13 (Dec 1886), Daniel 11 (Nov 1888) 8-283A-287/289

- - - - - - - - - - - - -

MAHONEY / MAHONE

1900 CENSUS
John L. Mahoney 49 (Mar 1851-Ind/Ireland/Do-M 18)(RR Section Hand), Rose E. 37 (Oct 1862-Ky/Ireland/Do-M 18-9-5), Mary A. 17 (Jan 1883), Rosa G. 15 (Oct 1884), John D. 8 (May 1892), Jennie P. 4 (Aug 1895), James L. 1 (Oct 1898) 5-234A-116
MARRIAGE
J.C. Mahone to M.E. Boofer, 12 Sep 1882 4-10(99)

- - - - - - - - - - - - -

MAJORS / MAGORS

1860 CENSUS
Columbus Majors 24, Mary A. 24, Martha J. 5, John T. 2, William H. COLEMAN 25 3-61-421
David Majors 30, Jane 31, Larkin 11, David 5 1-96-653
Elias Majors 28, Martha 23, John 7, Betsy 8/12 1-92-630
Francis Majors 24, Delila 23: see Major Holloway
James M. Majors 33, Lucinda J. 34, Sarah C. 4, William W. 2 1-82-560
Larkin Majors 54, Betsy 56, James 18, George 14, Margarey HUDDLESTON 21 1-92-627
1870 CENSUS
David Majors 44, Martha J. 48, David 14, Bernetta 9 1-16-104
William F. Majors 30, Margarette 32, Mary E. 12 (Mo), James 6, Sarah J. 3, Robert L. 7/12 1-17-111
1880 CENSUS
Francis Majors 46, Margaret 41, James 14, Sarah 12, Robert 10, Eliza 8, Laura 6, Luther 2, Mary UNDERWOOD 20 (sd) 1-15-128
James Majors 44, Susan 40, Mary 20, N.J. 19 (s), Milton 17, William 10, Martha 8 James 6, Andrew 3, Sarah 2 3-16-128
John Majors 50, Mary 30 (w), Jane 10, Robert 8, Walter 6, William 3, Charlie 1 1-15-127
Wright Majors 22: see T. J. Knight
1900 CENSUS
Andy Majors 24 (Jan 1876-M 4)(Coal Miner), Annie 24 (July 1875-M 4-4-3), Virgil 2 (Aug 1897), Verdie 2 (Aug 1897), Florida PLUNING 15 (ne)(Mar 1885) 13-302B-229/239

Francis M. Majors 64 (Dec 1835-M 30)(RR Hand), Margett 61 (Dec 1838-M 30-10-7), Robbirt 30 (Feb 1870), Luther 22 (May 1878), Henry 17 (Feb 1883), Bell J. 15 (Dec 1884) 1-184A-107/112

James Majors 24 (Nov 1875-M 5)(Coal Miner), Mattie 19 (July 1880-M 5-2-0) 8-278A-195/197

Susan Majors 60 (Sep 1839-T/SC/SC-Wd 10-7), Samuel 17 (Feb 1883)(Coal Miner), Martha EATON 24 (d)(Feb 1876-Wd 2-2), Floyd 8 (gs)(Oct 1891), Georgia 1 (gd) (June 1898), Asberry TAYLOR 21 (boarder)(Unk 1879)(Coal Miner) 8-279B-225/227

William Majors 26 (Aug 1873-M 4)(Coal Miner), Mollie 21 (Aug 1878-M 4-2-2), Myrtle 4 (Aug 1895), Bertha 1 (July 1898) 8-277A-176/177

MARRIAGES

Andy Majors to Nannie Thurman, 24 June 1896 (same), W. S. Hale MG, J. Holmes W 2-33

Cansada J. Magors to Rheuben Hamby q.v.

Columbus Majors to Lyda H. Ball, 28 Feb 1868 (same), R.T. Howard MG 1-#1048

Francis M. Majors to Margarett Underwood, 5 Dec 1863 (no return) 1-#811

Henry Majors to Hattie Tharp, 25 Dec 1900, S.A. Walker MG 4-107

James Majors to Mattie Hale, 2 Jan 1895, A.J. Wyrick JP 4-83

James M. Majors to Lucinda J. Holloway, 16 Sep 1854 (19 Sep), N.H. Long JP 1-#464

James M. Majors to Elizabeth Loden, 26 Dec 1862 (no return) 1-#791

Jane Majors to Marcus Wright q.v.

M. J. Majors to W. W. Hudleston q.v.

Mariah Majors to John Orr q.v.

Martha Majors to J. F. Waller or Wallis q.v.

Mary Majors to Jefferson Ingle q.v.

Mary Majors to Wiley Kirsey q.v.

Nicy Majors to Russell Thompson q.v.

Noah Majors– see Noah Myers

Rachel Majors to Jim Casttin(?)

Rachel Majors to Jessee Lyles q.v.

Sallie Majors to Jasper Fain q.v.

William Majors to Sarah McColpin, 5 Oct 1852 (same), W. H. Bell MG 1-#381

William Majors to Mary Gothard, 12 Dec 1895, W.L. Lillard JP 4-91

William F. Majors to Delila J. Holloway, 19 Nov 1858 (20 Nov), A. Newport MG 1-#671

- - - - - - - - - - - - -

MALEW

1880 CENSUS

Betsy Malew 70: see R. H. Jewell

- - - - - - - - - - - - -

MALEY

1900 CENSUS

Kate Maley 21: see Alex Ridley

Patrick Maley 60 (Unk 1840-Ireland/Do/Do-1859/41/?-M 40), Kate 55 (Unk 1845-Ireland/Do/Do-M 40-11-9), John 36 (Nov 1863-Va)(Brickmason), Charles 30 (Unk 1870), William 22 (May 1878), Kate 20 (Unk 1880), Sarah 18 (Unk 1882), Thomas 16 (Unk 1884), Mary 15 (Nov 1884) 15-273B-101

MARRIAGES

Anna Maley to E. M. Collins q.v.

Delia Maley to Alex Ridley q.v.

Katie Maley to J. R. Ramsey q.v.

- - - - - - - - - - - - -

MALIS / MELIS
(see also MOLES)

1860 CENSUS

Samuel Melis 51, Jane 53, Emaline 24, Elizabeth 23, Samuel 22, George W. 19, Usabyen(?) 15, James 13 6-102-695 (Mu)

MARRIAGES

Henry Malis to Jane Campbell, 4 Dec 1887 (same), John Howard MG 1-537

Henry Malis to Mary Cartright, 8 Mar 1897 (9 Mar), J.B. Trotter MG, J. Campbell W 2-124

- - - - - - - - - - - - -

MALONE / MALONY

1900 CENSUS

---?--- Malone 25: see Aber Emery (B)

John C. Malone 46 (Jan 1854-M 18)(Machinist), Martha 45 (Aug 1855-M 18-5-4), Edgar 20 (Dec 1879)(Machinist), Lawrence L. 16 (Sep 1883), Charles B. 14 (June 1885), Annie 12 (Aug 1887), Willie 3 (Oct 1896), John WEST 21 (nw)(Dec 1878) 15-272B-90

MARRIAGES

David Malony to Hannah J. Lowery, 4 Oct 1854 (5 Oct), W.W. Rose MG 1-#460

Polly Ann Malony to Farley Brady q.v.

- - - - - - - - - - - - -

MALOTT / MAYLOTT

MARRIAGES

Polly Ann Malott to Andrew J. Bankston q.v.

William Maylott to Polly A. Carwin, 17 July 1868 (18 July), J.M. Kelly MG 1-#1019

- - - - - - - - - - - - -

MANIS / MANNIS / MANOUS / MANANS / MANUS / MANESS

1880 CENSUS

George Manis 21: see Andrew Anderson

1900 CENSUS

Arthur Manous 26: see S. W. Litchfield

Ephraim H. Manus 45 (Feb 1855-M 20), Elizabeth 38 (Dec 1861-M 20-9-9), Annie G. 20 (May 1880), Charles M. 17 (Nov 1882), Vina J. 14 (Oct 1885), Edd H. 12 (Ap 1888), William A. 10 (Sep 1889), Pearl 8 (Aug 1891), Luke 6 (Nov 1893), John H. 4 (Oct 1895), Laura 2 (Jan 1898) 3-210A-176/191

John N. Maness 15, Charles 11, Willie 9, Walter 6: see Robert Jakes

Thomas J. Manis 23 (Sep 1876-M 1), Sarah E. 17 (Aug 1882-M 1-0) 2-194A-60/62

MARRIAGES
Arthur L. Manans to Tennie Hughes, 14 June 1900 (20 June), W. Woodford MG, G.P. Woodall W 3-167
Mary Manis to Robert Jacquish q.v.
Thomas J. Mannis to S. E. Pickel, 6 Ap 1899, Z.T. Morris MG 4-101
W.H. Manis to M.H. Johnson, 21 Jan 1884 (24 Jan), F.R. Morgan JP 1-475

- - - - - - - - - - - - -

MANNING

MARRIAGES
Ida Manning to W. J. Young q.v.
M. Manning to J. C. Denson q.v.

- - - - - - - - - - - - -

MANNUAL

MARRIAGE
Robert Mannual to Fannie Clay, 31 Dec 1898 (same), R.C. Knight JP, Robert Pullmer(?) W 2-368

- - - - - - - - - - - - -

MANSEL / MANSELL

1870 CENSUS
Houston Mansel 21, Jane 21, Charles D. 10/12 6-13-91
MARRIAGES
Houston Mansel to Mary Jane Ault, 28 Jan 1869 (no return) 1-#1043
Jane Mansell (Mrs. R.C. Broyles) to Joseph Henry Tephtallow q.v.

- - - - - - - - - - - - -

MAPLES

1880 CENSUS
M. C. Maples 59: see Oliver Lyons

- - - - - - - - - - - - -

MARCUM

MARRIAGES
Bell Marcum to W. C. Huback q.v.
Lee Marcum to Callie Hodges, 19 Ap 1889 (20 Ap), R.S. Mason JP 1-575
Lee Marcum to Annie Wycoff, 5 Oct 1890, R.S. Mason JP 4-17

- - - - - - - - - - - - -

MARIOTT / MARRIOTT / MERRIOTT / MERRIT / MARYOTT / MAYATT / MAYROTT / MEARIET

1860 CENSUS
Wm N. Merriott 53, Nancy A. 39, William N. 16, John 14, James 13, Mary 11, Margaret 9, Scott 7, Thomas 5, Ness 2 6-113-775
1870 CENSUS
Leandia Mariott 35, Mary Jane 15, Sarah A. 7, Eli 9, Tennessee 5 1-9-58 (B)
Nancy Mariott 49, James 23, Henry S. 17, Thompson N. 15, Nancy P. 11, Alfred 9 6-14-97
William N. Marriott 27, Mary J. 28, Peter J. 3, Nancy A. 1: see Peter Minnick
1880 CENSUS
James H. Mariott 27 (B): see James W. Gillespie
John Marriott 20 (Telegraph Operator): see S. T. Blevins
Sarah A. Mariott 56, William A. 25, John Henry 21, Deltha A. 23, David William 18, Floyd O'KELLEY 5 (orphan), Ida E. 2 (orphan, "no kin") 10-30-232/241 (B)
1900 CENSUS
Ali Mayatt 58 (Dec 1841-M 8), Idia 38 (Ap 1862-M 8-12-3), Walter 15 (Aug 1884), Mantie 2 (July 1897), James H. 10/12 (Aug 1899) 10-256B-126/130 (B)
David Mayatt 38 (July 1861-T/Va/NC-M 12)(Coal Miner), Cordelia 27 (Ap 1873-M 12-4-3), Henry O. 8 (Oct 1891), John J. 6 (Sep 1893), Elizabeth 4 (Jan 1896) 10-260B-210/215 (B)
Floyd Mayrott 24 (Jan 1876-M 2)(Coal Miner), Maggie 29 (May 1871-M 2-3-1), Maybell 2 (Sep 1898) 10-250A-9 (B)
John Mayott 50 (Dec 1849-T/T/NC-M 12), Angline 43 (Oct 1856-M 12-1-1), Walter BROWN 14 (nw)(Aug 1885) 7-266B-313/318 (B)
Thomas Meariet 62 (Sep 1837-NY/NJ/NY-M 40)(Fruit Grower), Almer 60 (Feb 1840-NY/NY/NY-M 40-3-2) 12-179A-13/15

MARRIAGES
Abb Mariott to Ida Brown, 3 Oct 1891, S. Washington MG 4-46
D.W. Merriott to Cordelia Bates(?), 15 Ap 1888 (21 Ap), J. B. Phillips MG 1-547
Deathaan Marriott to James Cook q.v.
Floyd Mariott to Maggie Moore, 23 June 1897 [bond], 22 June [license & return], George S. Sanders MG, J.T. Randolph W 2-155 (B)
Ida Merriott to Will Jefferson q.v.
J.A. Marriott to E.E. Ball, 12 Ap 1869 (13 Ap), R.T. Howard MG 1-#1055
James C. Mariott to Mary C. Smith, 24 Jan 1872 (same), W.G. Allen JP 1-#1223
John B. Merritt to Alice Huntington, 6 May 1893, Charles H. Abbott MG 4-58
Luke Marriott to Mahala Lustor, 17 Ap 1892, William Morgan JP 4-39
M. M. Mariott to A. R. Poe q.v.
Margaret Maryott to John A. Mathis q.v.
Mary Jane Maryott to James Hale q.v.
Sarah Marriott to Charles Harris or Haries q.v.
W.N. Mariott to Mary Jane Minick, 26 Dec 1865 (same), R.T. Howard MG 1-#860

- - - - - - - - - - - - -

MARL

1880 CENSUS
E. Marl 52, S.A. 47, Hester 23, Joseph 20, J.H. 17 (s), D. CANADA 23 (hired Man) 3-13-105

- - - - - - - - - - - - -

MARLER / MEALER / MALER / MARLOW

1860 CENSUS

Nicholas Marler 35, Elizabeth J. 27, Francis M. 10, Christina 8, George W. 6, Alfred T. 5, Margaret T. 1 8-15-101

1870 CENSUS

Nichodemus Marler 46, Elizabeth Jane 37, Francis M. 20, Christena 19, George W. 16, Alfred T. 15, Margarette T. 11, Martha E. 9, Mary M. 4, Simona A. 3 8-4-23

1880 CENSUS

N. Marler 57, E.J. 49 (w), M.T. 19 (d), Martha 17, M.M. 15 (d), Alice 13, Florence 11, J.F. 7 (d), Frank 12 8-6-48

1900 CENSUS

Alfred T. Marler 45 (Dec 1854-M 21), Addie V. 43 (Jan 1857-Ind/T/Ind-M 21-12-11), Lela J. 17 (Jan 1883), Robert H. 15 (Mar 1885), Nicholas 13 (Jan 1887), Mattie L. 11 (Feb 1889), Laura A. 8 (Dec 1891), Lillie T. 6 (Jan 1894), Bessee M. 4 (Feb 1896), Fletcher 2 (Feb 1898), infant 0/12 (May 1900) 13-307B-334/346

Benjamin F. Mealer 63 (Feb 1837-Ga/NC/NC-M 42)(Hotel Keeper), Martha 58 (Aug 1840-Ga/Va/SC-M 42-1-1), Nannie HICKS 34 (d)(July 1865-Ga-M 7-0), Milton B. 35 (sl)(Jan 1865-Canada/Do/Do-1866/33/Na-M 7) (Attorney), Eliza DOUGLAS (B) 34 (June 1865-Ga/Ga/Ga-M 15-4-4)(Cook at Hotel), Fanny DANE (B) 18 (June 1871-T/Ga/Ga)(Cook at Hotel), Eugene BILLINGSLEY (B) 19 (Unk)(Hotel Porter); *Boarders at Hotel:* Thomas J. GILLESPE 56 (Ap 1844-Wd) (Clerk & Master, Chancery Court), Tal GWILLIM 24 (Feb 1876-T/Wales/Do)(Grocer), Edward DEAKINS 22 (Nov 1877)(Clothing Salesman), Hattie L. GANN 25 (July 1874-Ky/Ky/Ky) (Dry Goods Saleslady), Alice AYERS 21 (Feb 1879-Mo/Mo/Ireland)(Stenographer), Floyd HOLLOWAY 23 (May 1877-T/T/NC) (Bartender), Nathaniel D. GRAY 45 (Mar 1855-Miss/NC/NC-M 18)(Saloon Keeper), Hannah M. EARLY 81 (Aug 1818-T/Va/T-Wd 50), Albert W. SAILLIE 21 (Ap 1879-T/T/French Canada)(Commercial Traveler, Notions), Belle S?AGRANGE(?) 37 (Feb 1863 WVa/Oh/Oh)(Milliner) 10-320A-1/1

Charles Maler 32 (Ap 1868-Ga/Ga/Ga-M 10), Lucy C. 25 (Dec 1874-Oh/Oh/Oh-M 10-2-1), William 8 (June 1891) 10-259A-174/178

F. Marion Marler 56 (Mar 1844-T/T/Va-M 28), Susan 55 (Mar 1845-T/T/Ky-M 28-2-2), Lizzie 23 (Ap 1877) 3-205A-91/99

Francis M. Marler 31 (May 1869-M 5), Blanche M. 24 (Dec 1875-T/T/Va-M 5-2-2), Arville 3 (Oct 1896), Versa V. 1 (Oct 1898) 13-308B-336/348

George W. Marlow 46 (Dec 1853-M 25), Margaret J. 46 (Jan 1854-T/NC/NC-M 25-11-11), James M. 22 (Dec 1877), Maggie 20 (Oct 1879), Thomas 18 (Ap 1882), Annie 16 (Feb 1884), Mona 14 (Mar 1886), Mattie 10 (Aug 1889), Lester 8 (Mar 1892), Ollie 6 (Ap 1894), Allen 4 (Ap 1896) 6-244B-97/98

Kate Marler 21, Media 2: see Mollie Hibbs

Luther Marlow 24 (June 1875-M 0), Viola 18 (July 1881-M 0-0) 6-244B-96/97

Nichodemus Marler 76 (Nov 1823-T/T/NC-M 56)(Landlord), Elizabeth J. 68 (Feb 1832-T/Va/T-M 56-15-4), Florence D. 29 (June 1870) 13-307B-335/347

MARRIAGES

A. D. Marler to Cyrus Walker q.v.

A.T. Marler to Addy Alexander, 24 July 1878 (no return) 1-#1571

Alice Marler to John T. Gates q.v.

Charles L. Mealer to Lucy Yaunt, 25 Ap 1890 (27 Ap), W.S. Cagle ?? 1-600

Clare A. Marler to Richard L. Robertson q.v.

Emma Mealer to J. C. Jennings q.v.

Francis M. Marler to Blanche Rudd, 28 Ap 1895, W.R. Grimsley MG 4-83

John Marler to Katie Hibbs [bond] or Hill [license], 25 July 1896 (26 July), W.R. Grimsley MG, F.M. Marler W 2-48

Lizzie Mealer to J. D. Burkhalter q.v.

Luther H. Marler to Viola Hicks, 26 Jan 1900 (27 Jan), W.A. Howard MG, T.J. Gillespie W 3-115

Martha E. Marler to C. N. Hutcheson q.v.

Mary Marler to J. B. Harris q.v.

Nanny or Naomia A. Marler to Milton B. Hicks q.v.

Sam Marler to Bell Davis, 14 Ap 1888 (15 Ap), J.R. Crawford JP 1-549

Tennie Marler to Ben Rutledge q.v.

W.V. Marler to Mattie E. Elsie, 10 June 1899 (11 June), M.G. Curton MG, J.O. Crawley W 2-424

- - - - - - - - - - - - -

MARNEY / MANNEY

1860 CENSUS

Andrew Marney 32, Eva A. 25, Mary A. 4, George W. 1 2-72-488 [Andrew married Iva M. Martin on 18 Ap 1855 in Meigs County]

1870 CENSUS

Andrew Manney 38, Mary 14, George 12, Eligah 10, William 6, Archibald 2 2-9-61

Mary Marney 17, Sarah 5/12 (B): see Hugh B. Heiskell

Sarah Manney 40, Elizabeth 13, Benjamin 10, David 3 2-9-60 (B)

1880 CENSUS

B. F. Marney 18: see J. W. Caldwell

David Marney 11 (B): see Jessee Roddy

MARRIAGES

Ben Marney(?) to Mary Brown, 8 Mar 1890 (9 Mar), C.J. Titus JP 1-599

C.F. Marney to Minnie Clayton, 30 Sep 1887 (31 Sep), E.S. Cox JP 1-532

- - - - - - - - - - - - -

MARS / MARRS / MARE

1880 CENSUS

Aaron Marrs 56, Alvira 52, William 23, Lucinda 25, James 21, Nancy 18, Amanda 16, Oscar 14, Birtie 11 1-12-102

1900 CENSUS

George Mars 65 (July 1824-M 40), Nancy 58 (Nov 1841-M 40-7-6) 12-180A-31/33

George Mars Jr. 22 (Mar 1878-M 1), Anglean 17 (Oct 1882-M 1-1-0) 12-180A-31/34

Isaac Mars 30 (Oct 1869-M 12), Lizzie 31 (Oct 1868-M 12-3-3), Wilson 10 (Jan 1890), Katie 7 (Mar 1893), James 3 (Feb 1897), Elizabeth PARMER 85 (boarder)(Jan 1815-NY/NY/NY-Wd 4-2) 12-180A-32/35

Tom Mare 38 (July 1861-M 8), Liddie 25 (Oct 1874-M 8-2-1), Mary 4 (Sep 1895) 1-189B-208/218 (Spring City)

MARRIAGES

Bertey Marrs to C. R. Brown q.v.

Mary C. Marrs to W. J. McClarrin q.v.

- - - - - - - - - - - - -

MARSH / MARCH

1860 CENSUS

Alfred March 60 (NC), Celia 61, Nancy J. 24, Brumly COOK 26 (Carpenter), Celia COOK 3 4-51-349

John L. Marsh 36, Anna 33, Grover L. 14, Edward W. 12, Alfred T. 10, John T. 8, Simon A. 6, Addison B. 4 1-83-567

Onslow Marsh 35, Mary 24, William 6, James A. 4, Susan 3, Edweny 1 1-85-575

Thomas Marsh 31, Elizabeth 27, Oliver N. 3, Martisha 1 4-51-351

1870 CENSUS

Onslo G. Marsh 44, Mary C. 35, William H. 16, James A. 14, Lottie S. 12, Edwine Jane 10, Thomas 8, Sila E. 5, Virginia M. 3 1-9-56

Orinda Marsh 50, Alfred T. 20, John F. 17, Simon A. 15, Adison B. 13 4-11-74

Selah Marsh 72 (NC): see Mary E. Torbett

Thomas J. Marsh 40, Elizabeth L. 38 (NC), Oliver N. 13, Thomas A. 8, Nancy O. 6, Agnes E. 3, John C. 5/12, Samuel KELLY 55 4-9-57

1880 CENSUS

Alfred Marsh 30, Angie 26, Ira 4, Waverly 2, Thomas 1/12, Celia COOK 22 (sil) 1-9-73

Martha Marsh 48 (Washwoman), Franklin 24, William 19 2-24-197 (B)

Mary Marsh 46, James 23, Thomas 18, Celia 16, Jennie 14, Pearce 8, Tennie 6 1-9-72

1900 CENSUS

Angie Marsh 45 (Ap 1854-Wd), Linard 24 (Feb 1876), Waverly 22 (Ap 1878), Thomas 20 (Feb 1880), Mary 18 (Feb 1882), Bessie 16 (Jan 1884), Della 14 (Nov 1886) 1-185A-135/161

Bertha Marsh 13: see Thomas J. Smith (B)

Frank Marsh 53 (Unk 1847-SC/SC/SC-M 3)(Blacksmith), Mattie 15 (ne)(Dec 1884)(Private Cook), William 8 (nw)(Aug 1891), Martha 72 (m)(Unk 1828-SC/SC/SC-Wd 4-2) 2-198A-124/129 (B)

MARRIAGES

A.T. Marsh to Martha J. Roberts, no date [between 8 Oct & 6 Nov 1851] 1-#353

Alfred T. Marsh to Austillie J. Whittenburg, 1 Sep 1873 (no return) 1-#1299

C. E. Marsh to J. E. Thompson q.v.

Edward W. Marsh to Mary B. Darwin, 7 Jan 1867 (no return) 1-#929

Frank Marsh to Rena Boggis, 16 Aug 1884 (17 Aug), J.P. Thompson JP 1-470

Jenni M. Marsh to J. L. Evens q.v.

Mary E. Marsh to Thomas F. Torbett q.v.

O.G. Marsh to Virginia Torbett, 16 Sep 1856 (no return) 1-#573

Onslow G. Marsh to Mary C. Stockton, 7 Aug 1852 (12 Aug), S. Roberts MG 1-#382

Sarah R. Marsh to Brumby Cook q.v.

Thomas Marsh to Lydia Blevins, 25 Dec 1892, R.A. Dickson JP 4-44

Tinnie Marsh to W. L. Gibson q.v.

William Marsh to Adaline Johnson, 16 June 1883 (17 June), B.F. Holloway JP 1-475

- - - - - - - - - - - - -

MARSHALL / MARSHEL

1860 CENSUS

Sally Marshel 68, Polly 22 3-68-469

1870 CENSUS

George W. Marshall 39 (Blacksmith), Mary 42, William T. FERGUSON 18, Pessy J. FERGUSON 10 4-13-85

John Marshall 23, Elizabeth 27 3-11-76

John P. Marshall 44, Margarette 38, Henry J. 16, George M. 14, Mahala 11, Sarah J. 9, Martha 6, Texas 4, John 5/12 3-5-30

William Marshall 47 (Ky), Mary 53, Benjamin F. 21, Arrena J. 19, Mary 17, Amanda T. 16, Coffel 13, Thomas 7, Barbara LEWIS 30 3-11-77

1880 CENSUS

G.W. Marshall 54, M.A. 52, M.E. 9 (d), James O. 5 4-11-87

Jeff Marshall 26, M.E. 24, B.L. 5 (s), Theodore 1 3-19-150

Mary Marshall 44: see John Coxey

Posey Marshall 54, Margaret 50, George 24, S.J. 19 (d), ?.B. 15 (d), L.V. 13 (d), John 10, Lorinda 7, A.F. 3 (s) 3-13-103

1900 CENSUS

Bert L. Marshall 25 (Feb 1875-M 4), Eva L. (Sep 1877-Ky/Ky/T-M 4-1-1), Hattie A. 1 (June 1898) 6-240A-10

George M. Marshal 44 (Mar 1856-M 8), Amanda 42 (Dec 1857-T/NC/T-M 8-2-2), Euclid S. 7 (June 1892), Elizabeth J. 5 (Sep 1894) 3-211A-193/211

Jefferson N. Marshall 46 (Oct 1853-M 26), Minerva E. 45 (Nov 1854-M 26-6-5), George P. 19 (Mar 1881), Walter F. 13 (Nov 1886), Carrie M. 7 (Aug 1892) 5-235B-150

John Marshall 37: see Aaron Crawley

Mary Marshall 66: see Willie J. Coxey

Theodore J. Marshall 21 (Jan 1879-M 1), Della L. 18 (Feb 1882-M 1-0) 5 -233A-98

MARRIAGES

Amanda E. Marshall to Harris Smith q.v.

Burket Marshall to Lena Simons, 25 Dec 1895, J.B. Trotter MG 4-88

Frank Marshall to Texas Marshall, 24 Sep 1891, J.W. Williamson MG 4-32

G.W. Marshall to Mary A. Furgusson, 17 Mar 1870 (same), B. Minicks JP 1-#1147

George Marshall to Amanda McClendon, 24 July 1891, J.M. Bramlett MG 4-30

George Marshall to Adelia Denton, 6 Dec 1900 (7 Dec), H. B. Burditt MG, Bert Marshall W 3-252

H.J. Marshall [or Morehall] to Minerva Hale, 4 Dec 1873 (5 Dec), John Howard MG 1-#1317

J.T. Marshall to Della West, 30 Nov 1898 (1 Dec), J.M. Bramlett MG, G.W. Johnson W 2-350
John Marshall to Sallie J. Everett, 7 Aug 1900 (same), W.R. Grimsley MG, James Knight W 3-196
Lulah Marshall to J. McGee q.v.
Mahala Marshall to G.W. Jenoe q.v.
Robert Marshall (25) to Susan Smith (18), 2 June 1881, B.F. Holloway JP, no witness 4-3(21) (B)
Sarah Marshall to Henry Giles q,v,
Texas Marshall to Frank Marshall q.v.

MARTIN / MARTAIN

1860 CENSUS

Catharine Martin 61, William A. 30, Mary E. 27, Isaac A. 27, Nancy GRAY 60 8-19-128
Manerva Martin 29, Napoleon T. 6, Samuel S. 4, Sampson 2 4-41-276
Nancy Martin 60, Elbert 13, Nancy A. HARRIS 10/12 4-40-272

1870 CENSUS

Elbert S. Martin 23 (House Carpenter), Nancy 27, Armilda J. 6, Moana 3, Thomas A. 1, Ancil 1 1-20-132
Isaac A. Martin 37, Ruth 27, Joseph P. 3, Nancy Jane 1, Catharine MARTIN 74, William A. 45, Mary E. 42, Nancy GRAY 72 8-8-50

1880 CENSUS

E. Martin 18: see Farley Brady
I.A. Martin 40, Ruth 37, J.P. 13 (s), N.J. 11 (d), W.A. 56 (b) 8-6-47
J. M. Martin 27: see F. A. Harris
James M. Martin 20, Mary A. 25 6-16-148/150
R.T. Martin 20, Margaret 35 (w), M.A. 1 (d), Maggie HOGE 5 (adopted d) 8-10-84
Sarah Martin 46: see James Filyoe
W. A. Martin 56: see I. A. Martin
William Martin 21, Martha 19, James 1 2-42-341 (Mu)

1900 CENSUS

Belle J. Martin 39 (Oct 1860-T/T/NC-M 1-6-4)(Washwoman), Leonard C. 10/12 (s)(July 1899), Charles(?) E. WOODY 17 (d)(Mar 1883)(Washwoman), Darius C. 11 (s)(Oct 1888), Lillie B. 7 (d)(Nov 1892) 6-242B-56
Birdie Martin 38: see James F. Walker
Franklin Martin 41 (Ap 1858-M 21), Sarah E. 41 (Nov 1858-M 21-9-9), Mary L. 19 (Feb 1881), Vesty A. 17 (Ap 1883), Cordley A. 14 (May 1886), Ellen V. 11 (Dec 1887), George W. 10 (Mar 1890), Addie J. 8 (May 1892), Dock 6 (Ap 1894), Laura E. 3 (Sep 1896), Mattie J. 11/12 (June 1899) 2-192B-30/31
Franklin Martin 22 (Mar 1878-M 2)(Blacksmith Helper), Belle 22 (June 1877-M 2-1-1), Harry 1 (Sep 1898) 10-323A-68/72
Gilbert Martin 32 (June 1867-M 9), Sally R. 48 (Dec 1851-Ga/NC/Ga-M 9-7-4), Rose Lee 7 (Aug 1892) 13-297A-136/136
Harry D. Martin 51 (Nov 1848-M 29)(Blacksmith), Amavia 45 (July 1854-M 29-4-4), Lillian 28 (d)(Mar 1872-D 1-1), Maud 17 (Mar 1883)(Dressmaker), Bessie BROWN 8 (gd)(Feb 1892) 10-323B-72/76
James Martin 22 (Jan 1878-M 1), Sallie 20 (Ap 1880-M 1-1-1), Henry P. 11/12 (June 1899), Sarah GILLESPIE 70 (gm)(Unk 1830-Wd 10-5), Persila GILLESPIE 38 (a)(Dec 1862) 2-193A-39/40 (B)
James H. Martin 31 (Nov 1868-T/T/Va-M 4), Manda 23 (Mar 1877-T/T/Va-M 4-2-2), James G. 2 (Sep 1897), Thomas M. 9/12 (Sep 1899) 3-205B-98/106
John Martin 33 (Sep 1866-M 0), Lizzie 45 (Unk-M 0-0), Lillie TULLON 11 (adopted d)(May 1889) 8-318B-170/176 (B)
John E. Martin 16: see Charles W. Irwin
Joseph Martin 43 (May 1857-M 18), Amanda J. 48 (May 1852-M 18-2-2), Joseph 17 (Nov 1882), Samuel L. 14 (July 1885) 13-195A-101/103
Joseph Martin 22 (Nov 1877-M 4), Mary J. 19 (June 1880-M 4-1-1), Emma L. 1 (Ap 1899), Sarah N. MARTIN 68 (m)(Oct 1831-T/T/NC-Wd 11-6) 10-326B-135/141
Joseph P. Martin 33 (Feb 1867-M 11), Virginia 32 (Mar 1868-M 11-2-2), Ray 8 (Oct 1891), Annie R. 6 (Oct 1893) 13-307B-339/351
Lester Martin 14 (B): see Isaac K. Brown
Lewis Martin 63 (Aug 1836-Md/Unk/Md-Wd) 10-257A-130/134 (B)
Nancy Martin 62 (Unk 1838-Wd 9-5), Robert F. 18 (gs)(Feb 1882) 15-269B-33/33
Ruth Martin 57 (Jan 1843-Wd 2-2)(Landlady), Nancy J. 31 (d)(Feb 1869) 13-307B-338/350
Tate Martin 49 (Nov 1850-M 23)(Coal Miner), Margaret 54 (May 1846-M 23-5-5), Mary 20 (June 1879), James A. HUGHES 22 (boarder)(Jan 1878) 13-306A-307/319
William S. Martin 22: see Louis A. Blake

MARRIAGES

A.J. Martin to M.J. Disbany, no dates probably 1854, "Celebrated by John W. Thompson MG" 1-#455
Alice Martin to William W. Parks q.v.
Caroline Martin to W. M. Minick q.v.
Doctor Martin to Mary Hurst, 16 Jan 1891 [probably 1892], W.G. Taylor JP 4-43
E. J. Martin to John Thompson q.v.
E.S. Martin to M.E. King, 14 Oct 1871 (no return) 1-#1210
Frank Martin to Della Birchfield, 18 July 1897 (same), A.N. Jackson MG, James Morgan W 2-162
J.W. Martin to Martha A. Hayden, 25 Dec 1885 (same), Saban Haworth MG 1-490
James Martin to M. Furgusson, 24 May 1851 (25 May), John O. Torbett JP 1-#339
James Martin to Mary A. Trusley, 8 Nov 1879 (20 Nov), W. S. Hale MG 1-#1685
James Martin to Sallie McCaleb, 20 Sep 1898, J.H. Keylon JP 4-96
John Martin to Lizzie McDonald, 13 Dec 1891, W.S. Hale MG 4-35
John Martin to Lizzie Rucker, 10 Oct 1899 (same), R.T. Smith JP, S.D. Shillus W 3-50 (B)
John Martin to Bell Woody, 13 Dec 1898 (same), J.B. Trotter MG 2-356
Joseph Martin to Permelia McCully, 12 Oct 1874 (18 Oct), William McCully MG 1-#1361
Joseph Martin to Amanda Wilkey, 18 Nov 1884 (same), F. M. Bandy MG 1-461
Joseph Martin to Minnie Suttler, 6 Sep 1881, James Corvin MG 4-44

Joseph Martin to Mary Moon, 14 July 1895, J.R. Clack MG 4-85
Joseph Martin to Annie Fox, 29 Dec 1900, L.C. Line W, "Returned Not Executed" 3-266
Joseph P. Martin to Virginia L. Hickman, 18 Sep 1890 (20 Sep), J.R. Walker MG 1-587
Lillian Martin to C. M. Brown q.v.
Lizzie Martin to J. D. Roddy q.v.
Lula Martin to John Travis q.v.
Martha E. Martin to John Hackman q.v.
M.C. Martin to Amanda Roscoe, 26 Feb 1891, J. Waldorf MG 4-23
Mary Martin to Robert Peterson q.v.
Mary A. Martin to T. J. Davis q.v.
Mary Elizabeth Martin to Solomon Wyrick q.v.
Mary Lou E. Martin to Samuel Shadwick q.v.
N.T. Martin to Sary N. Thompson, 3 Mar 1871 (7 Mar), D. Broyles JP 1-#1189
Nannie Martin to Perry J. Reid q.v.
R.M. Martin to Catharine Templeton, 12 Oct 1874 (13 Oct), W.H. Bell MG 1-#1362
Robert Tate Martin to Margarett J. Hoge, 3 Nov 1877 (4 Nov), C. Morgan JP 1-#1522
Thomas Martin to Peggy A. Thompson, 5 Nov 1856 (6 Nov), J.O. Torbett JP 1-#582
Thomas Martin to Sarah Hughes, 13 Feb 1873 (14 Feb), W.L. Humphrey JP 1-#1278
Thomas Martin to Susan Ellison, 24 Dec 1887 (25 Dec), W.G. Curton ?? 1-544
Zack Martin to Effie Armour, 14 Jan 1899 (15 Jan), R.C. Knight JP, R.J. Killough W 2-375

- - - - - - - - - - - - -

MARYMAN

1900 CENSUS
Robert W. Maryman 62: see John G. Wallingford
William Maryman 24 (June 1875-Ind/Unk/Ind-M 2)(Clerk, Iron Works), Allice 22 (Aug 1877-Oh/Oh/Oh-M 2-0-0) 10-320B-13/13

- - - - - - - - - - - - -

MASON / MASONER

1860 CENSUS
Ruthe Mason 47, Solama 25, Berreman G. 7 5-40-267
1870 CENSUS
Ruth Mason 55 (NC), Saloma 35, Richard 18 5-6-45
1880 CENSUS
Solome Mason 45: see John Howard
1900 CENSUS
Bob Mason 60 (Mar 1840-Wd)(Coal Miner), Allice 16 (d) (Nov 1883) 10-260A-195/200
James Mason 25: see Rosa Wade
Mary Mason 38, Lilley 14: see Alvira Beaver

MARRIAGES
Delmia Mason to John Howard q.v.
Richard Masoner to Mary E. Beavers, 20 Dec 1872 (same), A.J. Pritchett MG 1-#1265

- - - - - - - - - - - - -

MASSEY

MARRIAGES
James Massey to N.J. Smith, 9 Nov 1858 (10 Nov), L.(?) Knight JP 1-#667
Jennie Massey to William Meeks q.v.

- - - - - - - - - - - - -

MASSINGALE

MARRIAGE
Sallie Massingale to James C. Morgan q.v.

- - - - - - - - - - - - -

MASTON

1900 CENSUS
Bob Maston 11, Joey A. 8: see Fill Suttles

- - - - - - - - - - - - -

MATHERS

MARRIAGE
Sallie Mathers or Wathens to William R. Holt q.v.

- - - - - - - - - - - - -

MATHERLY / MATHERLEY

1870 CENSUS
Franklin Matherly 26, Lucy 30, William H. 4, Sarah E. 7/12, Margaret BYRELY 33 7-3-26
1880 CENSUS
H.F. Matherly 33, Lucy 42, W.H. 12 (s), S.E. 11 (d), J.T. 8 (s), J.R. 4 (s), J.E. 1 (s) 7-24-206
1900 CENSUS
Henry Matherley 29 (Feb 1871-M 6), Maude 26 (June 1873-M 6-1-1), Maybell 1 (May 1899) 10-253A-59/59
Lucy Matherley 62 (Ap 1838-Wd 2-1), Johny 18 (Jan 1882), Ernest 2 (gs)(July 1897), Margaret BYERLEY 66 (si)(Oct 1833), Ryley MATHERLY 25 (s)(Ap 1875-Wd) 7-264A-263/268
Ryley Matherly 25, Ernest 2: see Lucy Matherley
Thomas Matherley 26 (Dec 1873-M 2), Marrey L. 26 (Dec 1873-M 2-1-1), Carl 1 (Feb 1899) 10-253A-60/60
MARRIAGES
Emma Matherly to Jack Houston q.v.
Henry Matherly to Bell Wyrick, 16 June 1888 (24 June), T.F. Shaver JP 1-550
Henry F. Matherly to Lucy Byerly, 25 Ap 1866 (same), J.W. Williamson MG 1-#897
Riley Matherly to M.E. Bell, 1 Aug 1896 (2 Aug), J.W. Romines JP, J.H. Chumley W 2-40
Thomas Matherly to Myrtle Cox, 19 Aug 1897 (20 Aug), J.W. Romines JP, --?-- Matherly & R.J. Killough W 2-167 [NOTE: the groom was shown as Thomas Cox on the license]

- - - - - - - - - - - - -

MATHEWS /MATHIS / MATHUS / MATHEW / MATHES / MATTHEWS / MATHEWSE

1860 CENSUS

Berreman G. Mathews 57 (NC), Catharine W. 61, Berryman G. 4, Thomas J. 2 5-38-258

James Mathews 98 (Va), Lusetta 23, Luisana 21 5-33-224

1870 CENSUS

Andrew J. Matthews 48 (NC), Mary 44, Nancy A. 17, Mary M. 14, Theodocia E. 12, Pamelia E. 9, Andrew J. 6 3-7-50

Berry G.Matthews 67 (NC), Catharine 71 (NC), Catharine M. 30, Berryman G. 14, Thomas J. 12, John Walker 5, Catharine E. 1 5-7-51

Elizabeth Mathews 66, Luhanna 43: see William H. Harris

Emily Matthews 41 (NC), Sarah F. 16, William R. 14, Mary A. 10, George W. 8, Cresser Ann 6, James B. 4, Joseph M.H. 1, Pleasant MATTHEWS 41 4-16-104

John A. Matthews 24, Margarette E. 19, James A. 2 6-14-98

Nancy Mathes 17: see John J. Smith

1880 CENSUS

T. J. Mathis 22, M. C. 22, M. J. R. 10/12 (d), Catharine MATHIS 80 (gm), S. E. L. 10 (c) 9-30-255

1900 CENSUS

John T. Mathews 44 (Ap 1856-NC/NC/NC-M 12), Mary E. 32 (Aug 1868-NC/NC/NC-M 12-3-2), Jessie 10 (Jan 1890-NC), Kemilia 7 (Aug 1892) 10-260A-201/206

Ruth Mathews 19: see James D. Smith

Thomas J. Mathews 50 (Feb 1849-M 25), Sarah N. 43 (July 1856-M 25-9-7), Jessie F. 21 (June 1878), Mollie J. 19 (Jan 1881), Thomas J. 16 (Nov 1883), William Y. 12 (Feb 1888), Sarah L. 9 (Jan 1891), Gertie B. 6 (Oct 1893), Joseph A. 3 (Jan 1897), Alice FAIRBANKS 15 (boarder)(May 1885), Anna P.(?) FAIRBANKS 11 (boarder)(Feb 1889) 15-268A-4/4

Wesley Mathis 31 (Dec 1866-Ala/Ala/Ala-M 6), Sally 23 (Mar 1877-Ga/Ga/Ga-M 6-1-1), Pearl 6 (Ap 1894-Ga), Birdie 21 (ne)(Oct 1878-Ala) 8-275A-122 (B)

Willie Mathews 16: see John Hughes

MARRIAGES

A.J. Mathis to Cely Cahan, 3 Jan 1876 (4 Jan), W.H. Dodd MG 1-#1430

Berryman Mathis to Mary Standifer, 17 Ap 1878 (14 Ap) [sic], A.J. Mathis MG 1-#1555

Catharine Mathis to John Baker q.v.

Celia Mathis to W. J. Smith q.v.

Edward A. Mathus to Rutha J. Mathus, 21 Aug 1857 (same), A.D. Paul JP 1-#1032 [NOTE: this record was on page with records from 1868]

Elizabeth Mathis to Thomas J. Greer q.v.

Eva Mathis to Mern(?) Waller q.v.

Eveline Mathis to William Smith q.v.

H.R. Mathis to Elzabeth A. Henderson, 30 Dec 1861 (2 Jan 1862), J.W. Williamson MG 1-#769

James J. Mathis to Lizzy Snow, 23 Sep 1875 (same), Thomas F. Hale MG 1-#1413

Jesse L. Mathews to Catharine L. Burwick, 23 Oct 1889 (same), J.J. Kirchbaum PE 1-584

John Mathis to Nancy Rose, 26 Sep 1880 (27 Sep), John Howard JP 1-296

John A. Mathis to Margarett Maryott, 3 May 1867 (5 May), R.T. Howard MG 1-#952

Louissana Mathew(?) to John H. Allen q.v.

Louisanna Mathis to William Compton q.v.

Margaret Mathis to John W. Hughes q.v.

Margaret Mathis to John Gruson q.v.

Mary J. Mathis to John H. Hughes q.v.

Mary M. Mathis to S. L. Shaver q.v.

Missouri Mathis to J. H. Travis q.v.

Nancy Mathis to E. T. Grice q.v.

Nancy Mathis to A. J. Pritchett q.v.

Nancy A. Mathis to William Sweatman q.v.

P.M. Mathis to Emely W. Allen, 19 Mar 1853 (20 Mar), R. T. Howard MG 1-#406

Rachel Mathis to David or Daniel C. Knox q.v.

Rachel Mathews to J. H. Willson q.v.

Rachel Mathewse to Charles Campbell q.v.

Rutha J. Mathus to Ed A. Mathus q.v.

Sallie Mathis to John C. Black q.v.

Sallie Mathis to Rudy H. Smith q.v.

Sarah Jane Mathis to John J. Smith q.v.

Thomas J. Mathis to Missouri K. Shaw, 7 Sep 1878 (8 Sep), A.J. Mathes MG 1-#1580

William R. Mathewse to Mary J. McDonald, 5 July 1854 (6 July), Orville Paine JP 1-#452

- - - - - - - - - - - - -

MATHEWSON

MARRIAGE

C.H. Mathewson to R.T. Hutchenson, 3 Ap 1867 (no return) 1-#947

- - - - - - - - - - - - -

MATLOCK / MEDLOCK

1900 CENSUS

Brownlow Medlock 30, Lula 28: see Lee A. Kelly (B)

Bup Matlock 37 (Ap 1863-M 3), Lula 26 (Unk 1874-M 3-4-1), Georgia 4 (July 1895), William KELLY 23 (bl) (Unk 1877) 8-275A-125/125 (B)

MARRIAGE

Charley Matlock to Ocina Evans, 20 Dec 1888 (same), F.J. Paine JP 1-557

- - - - - - - - - - - - -

MAXWELL

1880 CENSUS

Houston Maxwell 28, Tennessee 32, Matilda TROUT 14 (sd), William 10 (ss), John 7 (ss), Jasime 5 (sd), Parthena MAXWELL 1 (d) 1-10-85

- - - - - - - - - - - - -

MAY / MAYS

1880 CENSUS

Jesse May 69 (Lumberman), Parthena FRESBY 45 (Housekeeper), Jesse 1 (s) 12-4-20

1900 CENSUS

Danie May 35 (Feb 1865-M 6)(Butcher), Lou M. 27 (May 1873-M 6-2-2), Floyd A. 4 (Oct 1895), John R. 2 (Feb 1898), Nancy SENTER 51 (boarder)(Ap 1849) 8-312B-41/44

Henry Mays 23: see James Jackson (B)

Thomas E. May 25 (Oct 1874-Ga/Ga/Ga-M 7)(Coal Miner), Lizzie T. 22 (Sep 1877-Ga/NC/Ga-M 7-4-3), Ora 4 (Jan 1896), Mattie 2 (Mar 1898), James C. 0/12 (May 1900) 13-301B-208/216

MARRIAGES

Alice May to James Alexander q.v.

Alice May to W. F. Shipley q.v.

Bronnie or Brownie May to William Salts or Sults q.v.

Byrney E. May to J. T. Smith q.v.

John L. May to Sarah McGuire, 23 Dec 1876 (24 Dec), Wm R. Grimsley MG 1-#1479

John W. May to Jane Burton, 27 Sep 1886 (same), A.W. Frazier JP 1-504

Lizzie May to Joel Rogers q.v.

- - - - - - - - - - - - -

MAYBERRY

MARRIAGE

Molly Mayberry to S.T. Dennis q.v.

- - - - - - - - - - - - -

MAYFIELD

1900 CENSUS

Charles Mayfield 27: see Florence Ray (B)

Robert Mayfield 27: see Nancy Mitchell (B)

- - - - - - - - - - - - -

MAYNARD / MANARD

1880 CENSUS

May Manard 20: see H. M. Perser

MARRIAGE

Catharine Maynard to Elexander Hill q.v.

- - - - - - - - - - - - -

MEADOWS / MEDOWS

1900 CENSUS

Eph Meadows 37 (Oct 1862-M 16)(RR Laborer), Eliza A. 34 (Ap 1866-T/T/NC-M 16-0-0) 14-214B-30/31

Jack Meadows 43 (Unk 1857-Ky/Ky/Ky-M 6) 8-275B-138 (B)

James Meadows 28 (Oct 1861-M 4)(RR Laborer), Novella 23 (Nov 1867-T/T/NC-M 4-2-2), Laura 1 (Aug 1898), Joseph W. 5/12 (Jan 1900), George ELDREGE 11 (nw)(Jan 1889) 14-214B-31/32

MARRIAGES

Alfred Medows to Margaret A. Wilson, 11 July 1885 (12 July), S. Washington MG 1-492

Jack Meadows(?) to Bettie Swafford, 5 Mar 1888 (same), L.M. Morris ?? 1-548

James Meadows to Novia Oakes, 24 Feb 1898, R.A. Dickson JP 4-99

- - - - - - - - - - - - -

MEALER– see MARLER

- - - - - - - - - - - - -

MEANALLERY

1880 CENSUS

B. N. Meanallery 7: see A. J. Pritchett

- - - - - - - - - - - - -

MEDAIN

1880 CENSUS

Muck Medain 20, Margaret 21, Mary E. 1, James F. 7, Cora L. 3 6-13-124/125 (B)

- - - - - - - - - - - - -

MEDARIS

1900 CENSUS

Charles Medaris 63 (Sep 1837-Ind/Va/Va-M 19), Caroline L. 58 (Mar 1842-Germany/Do/Do-M 19-0), Silas F. PERKINS 34 (boarder)(July 1865-T/England/Germany-Wd), Marrie A. 13 (boarder)(July 1886) 6-240A-8/8

- - - - - - - - - - - - -

MEDLEY

1900 CENSUS

Clinton Medley 26 (June 1873-T/T/NC-M 0), Lucy 20 (Feb 1880-Ga/NC/NC-M 0-0-0) 11-292B-67

Joseph A. Medley 22, Earnest 19: see Sarah J. Snow

- - - - - - - - - - - - -

MEDOD

1900 CENSUS

Shaw P. Medod(?) 67 (Ap 1850-M 4), Emma 49 (Ap 1851-M 4-3-2), Harmon 16 (Mar 1884) 1-186A-143/151

- - - - - - - - - - - - -

MEE

1880 CENSUS

George Mee 17: see John Thompson

J.F. Mee 51, L.A. 40 (w), C.A. 9 (s), P.M. 7 (s), S. 4 (d) 3-15-115

M.L. Mee* 25, L.C. 24 (w), J.E. 3 (s), Della 1, James 73 (f) 4-2-13

William T. Mee* 28, S.E. 28, Ida 10(?), M.D. 5 (d), Floyd 3, Ada 1 4-2-15

[*NOTE: the last name was the same on both these entries, but both were impossible to decipher with certainty]

- - - - - - - - - - - - -

MEEKS

MARRIAGES

Salissa Meeks to Joseph Lemmons q.v.

William Meeks to Jennie Massey, 8 Feb 1887 (same), I.W. Holt JP 1-521

- - - - - - - - - - - - -

MEETON

MARRIAGE

Nancy J. Meeton to John Hilliard q.v.

- - - - - - - - - - - - -

MELBIA

1880 CENSUS

E.L. Melbia(?) 57, E.S. 39 (w), F. 3 (d), S.H. 1 (s), A.F. 15 (s), C.D. 12 (s) 3-29-231

- - - - - - - - - - - - -

MELENDY

1900 CENSUS

Bryant H. Melendy 64 (Feb 1836-NH/NH/NH-M 22), S. Jeanette 49 (Sep 1850-NY/Ver/NY-M 22-4-4), Willie A. 17 (Mar 1883-Mich), LaRue 14 (July 1885-Mich), Leslie L. 12 (June 1887-Mich) 11-292B-61/61

MARRIAGE

E.B. Melendy to Nettie Morrison, 6 Oct 1900 (9 Oct), Smith Sharp MG, E. Fisher W 3-230

- - - - - - - - - - - - -

MELTON– see MILTON

- - - - - - - - - - - - -

MERRILL / MERILL

1870 CENSUS

Joel Merrill 37 (Mich)(Bootmaker), Sarah H. 42 3-15-108

1880 CENSUS

J.J. Merrill 49 (Shoemaker), S. 50 (w), Allice MERILL 25 (sil), Nettie 4 (d*), J.D. 2 (s*) 8-10-87 [*relationship to Allice]

1900 CENSUS

Sarah Merrel 76: see Frank Rigsby

MARRIAGE

Henry O. Merrill to Allice Green, 11 May 1876 (same), C. Morgan JP 1-#1442

- - - - - - - - - - - - -

MERTIN

1900 CENSUS

John K. Mertin 57 (Ap 1843-Germany/Do/Do-1871/29/Na-Wd?)(Butcher) 10-323A-71/75

- - - - - - - - - - - - -

MESSER

1900 CENSUS

Printos S. Messer 31 (Mar 1869-Mich/Oh/Ind-M 8)(Stone-mason), Cora E. 28 (Feb 1872-Mich/Germany/Mich-M 8-4-4), Olive E. 7 (July 1892-Mich), Vesta B. 6 (Ap 1894-Mich), Roswell 4 (Nov 1895-Mich), Orlena N. 1 (Dec 1898) 13-308A-350/363

- - - - - - - - - - - - -

METZGAR

1900 CENSUS

George W. Metzgar 41 (Sep 1858-Oh/Pa/Pa-M 16), Nancy L. 42 (Aug 1857-Oh/Oh/Del-M 16-6-6), Hazel E. 15 (Feb 1885), Charles H. 13 (Mar 1887), Myrtle M. 11 (Feb 1889), William S.C. 8 (Sep 1891), Dwight L. 6 (Ap 1894), Paul S. 2 (Nov 1897) 5-234B-136

- - - - - - - - - - - - -

MICKEY

MARRIAGE

Maggie Mickey to Edward Carmack q.v.

- - - - - - - - - - - - -

MIDDLETON

1900 CENSUS

Charles Middleton 48 (Nov 1851-M 7)(Blacksmith), Phoebe 34 (Feb 1866-M 7-0-0) 10-323A-58/61

MARRIAGES

Charley R. Middleton to Phebe Hawkins, 26 Oct 1893, R.S. Mason JP 4060

Sallie Middleton to A. E. Weaver q.v.

- - - - - - - - - - - - -

MIKELS / MICKELS

1900 CENSUS

John Mikels 63 (June 1837-T/Va/T-M 25), Sarah E. 50 (Jan 1850-M 25-7-6), Mary E. 19 (Nov 1880), Angie E. 18 (May 1882), Samuel R. 17 (May 1883), William N. 15 (June 1884), Daniel F. 11 (Mar 1889), Hannah C. 9 (Mar 1891) 5-232A-84

MARRIAGE

Elizabeth J. Mickels to Joseph Roads q.v.

- - - - - - - - - - - - -

MILEN

MARRIAGE

Mary Ann Milen (18, White Co) to Thomas Ship-ley q.v.

- - - - - - - - - - - - -

MILES

1900 CENSUS

Andy Miles 45 (Mar 1855-M 13)(Coal Miner), Annie 31 (Mar 1869-M 13-4-4), William J. 12 (Dec 1887)(Coal Miner), Pearl V. 8 (Sep 1891), Jesse L. 6 (May 1894), Albert A. 3 (May 1897) 13-303A-241/251

- - - - - - - - - - - - -

MILICAN / MILLICAN / MILIGAN

1860 CENSUS

Franklin Milligan 32, Eliza 30, Elizabeth McCULLA 16 5-36-243

George Milligan 28, Jane 28, Mary J. 1, Liddea 2/12 8-11-68

1870 CENSUS

Calvin Millican 40, Sarah 49, Peter P. 12, Martha 11, Eliza J. 6, Victoria 2 3-8-54

Franklin Milican 36, Eliza 40, William R. 1, Lovina MILICAN 36 3-8-56

1880 CENSUS

Frank Milican 52, Viney 12, J.E. 9 3-26-209

R. N. Milligan 25: see William Hodges

1900 CENSUS

Edgar Millican 16: see Thomas G. Gillespie

Franklin Millican 71 (July 1828-T/Unk-M 48), W. Riley 31 (s)(Ap 1869) 3-200A-2/2

George W. Millican 33 (Jan 1867-M 10)(Journalist), Emma 32 (July 1867-Va/Va/Va-M 10-3-3), Edith 8 (Jan 1892), Earl E. 4 (June 1895), George E. 2 (Aug 1897), Laura F. COOPER 20 (ne)(Aug 1879-Va/Va/Va) 10-325A-112/116

James Miligan 19 (Nov 1880-M 0), Tilda 22 (Jan 1878-M 0-1-1), Claud 0/12 (May 1899), Charles EATON 8 (nw)(July 1891) 10-258B-164/168

Perry Miligan 43 (Nov 1856-M 23), Manda 46 (May 1854-M 23-8-7), John 14 (Dec 1885), Sallie 12 (Nov 1887), George E. 8 (Feb 1892), Willie 4 (Sep 1895) 10-258B-163/167

MARRIAGES

Elizabeth Milican to James Jackson q.v.

Emily J. Milican to Joseph Graham q.v.

Franklin Milican to Eliza McCully, 19 Feb 1852, "Without any official return being made, W.H. Bell, Clerk" 1-#356

G.W. Milican to Jane Shubert, 14 Ap 1856 (16 Ap), Thomas Knight JP 1-#531

George W. Milican to Nancy Singleton, 1 Jan 1851 (no return) 1-#327

James Millican to Tilda Suttles, 19 July 1899 (same), W.L. Lillard JP, James Phillips W 3-12

James C. Milcan to Sarah E. McCully, 18 Nov 1851 (same), W.M. Ganaway MG 1-#355

M. J. Millican to Thomas H. Burdett q.v.

Maggie Millican to George W. Tumlin q.v.

Mary E. Millican to James Graham q.v.

Riley N. Millican to Molly Hodge, 14 Aug 1878 (same), John Howard MG 1-#1575

W.R. Milican to Molley Perry, 9 May 1900, L.E. Smith JP 4-110

MILLARD

1900 CENSUS

Wesley D. Millard 42 (Ap 1858-M 25), Martha E. 42 (Jan 1858-M 25-11-10), Calvin W. 20 (Sep 1879), Josephine 17 (Sep 1882), John J. 14 (Mar 1886), Freddie L. 12 (Sep 1887), Lavannie E. 10 (May 1889), Rhoda A. 8 (Aug 1891), Samuel P. 8 (Aug 1891), William J. 6 (Dec 1893), Zacharia S. 4 (Dec 1895), James A. 1 (May 1899) 5-237A-174

MARRIAGES

James Millard to Maggie Wright, 2 Ap 1890 (same), R.S. Mason JP 1-597

Mary Millard to Jerry Hawkins q.v.

MILLER

1860 CENSUS

Henry Miller 48, Eliza 44, Eliza J. 16, Joseph 14, Pocahontus 12, Jane 10, James ESSEX 16, Ann ESSEX 7 4-41-274

John Miller 65 (SC), Cynthia 55 (SC), Sarah E. 19 (Ga), John F. 12, Andrew 10, Mary J. 6, John BRABSON 3/12 4-42-285

Peter W. Miller 45, Rebecca 43, John H. 17, Wright S. 16, James L. 14, Delila A. 12, Zachary L. 11, Peerce(?) C. 9, Alfred C. 8, Peter W. 6, Benjamin F. 4, Sarah L. 3, Elbert S. 1 4-43-287

Thomas Miller 55 (Ga), Emaline 50, Jane 21, Moses 18, Hannah 16, Peggy A. 15, Amanda 13, Thomas 11, Samuel 9, John 6, Eliza 2 2-72-490

William Miller 38, Mary 25, John L. 13, Thomas 12, Robert 10, Peggy A. 8, David 6, Mary 4, Clinton 1 2-72-491

1870 CENSUS

Ann Miller 15 (B): see Henry H. Miller

Henry H. Miller 59, Eliza Jane 55, Margarette A.T. 15, Ann MILLER (B) 15, Joseph DUISMOOR (B) 14, Samuel D. PIERCE 41 4-10-61

John H. Miller 27, Susan 25, Josiah 4, Mary 1, Alex DARWIN (B) 12 4-17-111

John T. Miller 32, Rebecca E. 24 4-16-107

Moses Miller 25 (Tanner), Pollie 29, Elizabeth A. 3 2-11-74

Rebecca Miller 53, Alfred C. 18, Peter W. 16, Sarah L. 13, Elbert S. 11, Rebecca J. 9 4-17-109

Thomas Miller 54, Emaline 50, Jane 31, Hannah 26, Thomas 24, Margaret A. 22, Manda 20, Samuel 18, John 14, Eliza A. 10 2-11-73

William R. Miller 54, Mary 45, Thomas 21, Robert 18, Margaret A. 17, David 15, Mary 13, Clinton 10, William 8, John L. 1 2-9-65

Wright S. Miller 26, Orpha J. 26, Bertha E. 4, Martha W. 9/12 4-16-108

1880 CENSUS

A.H. Miller 26, E. 27 (w), M.J. 8 (d), Eliza 6 (d), J.H. 4 (s), Flora 18 (sil) 3-19-152

F.J. Miller 52 (Shoe & Bootmaker), B.J. 36 (w), Virginia 19, M.S.J. 17 (d), M.R. 13 (d), S.F. 12 (d), J.D. 5 (s), G.C. 4 (s), J.L. 2 (s), B.D. 2/12 (s) 8-4-34

H. H. Miller 69, E. J. 65 (w) 4-4-30

H.M. Miller 37, E. 24 (w), James 4, Hester 2, P. or R. 9/12 (d), S.D. 68 (m) 4-33-270

J.T. Miller 43, Rebecca 33, W.W. 9 (s), R.C. 7 (s), E.B. 24 (ne) 4-4-31

James Miller 15: see George Brown

Moses Miller 29, Polly 39 (w), Betty 12, John 10, Moses 6, Wilburn 5, Jackson 4, Eva 1 1-16-136

Robert Miller 28, Joanne 30, Sylvesta 5, Columbus 3, Florence 3/12 12-6-48

Russell Miller 60, Mary 50, David 22, Clinton 19, Mary 17, William 15, Louis 10 (gs) 2-37-299

S. D. Miller 68: see H. M. Miller

S.H. Miller 38, R.A. 28 (w), Viney 11, Lettie 5, J.D. 4 (s), Tenn 2 (d), Martin 9/12 4-33-269

Sam Miller 24, Clanenelee(?) 21, L.M. 2 (d) 3-28-223

Samuel Miller 26, Winnie 35, William 9, Charles 8, Sarah 3 2-27-217

Thomas Miller 31, Belle 26, Elizabeth 6, Wiley 5, Russel 2 2-37-302

Thomas Miller 32, John 22 (b), Jane 36 (si), Eliza 21 (si), William LONG 22 (boarder) 2-32-262

W.H. Miller or Millet 29, E.A. 35 (w), R.S. 10 (d), S.J. 8 (d) 9-31-270

1900 CENSUS

Betsy J. Miller 53 (Dec 1846-T/SC/Va-Wd 7-6), John 26 (Ap 1874-T/Va/T)(Carpenter), Bede 20 (Ap 1880), Milton 18 (May 1882), Charlie 15 (Nov 1884), Frank J. 10 (June 1889) 8-315B-98/102

Charles G. Miller 60 (May 1840-Oh/Mass/Mass-M 21)(Pensioner), Frances A. 58 (May 1842-Canada/Ver/Scotland-M 21-2-1), Daisy 15 (May 1883-Oh) 14-213B-14/14

Clinton Miller 37 (May 1863), Polley 74 (m)(Unk 1826-Wd 10-5), Mary 40 (si)(Oct 1858) 2-193B-44/45

Ella L. Miller 6: see Noah L. Cate

Fannie Miller 20 (1880)(Cook) 8-315B-100/104 (B)

George Miller 32 (Oct 1867-M 3), Lula 25 (Unk-T/T/Ga-M 3-2-2) Burkett 2 (d)(Ap 1898), son 5/12 (Jan 1900), John 23 (boarder)(Unk), Len PERKINS 22 (boarder) (Unk) 8-318B-164/170 (B)

Harold Miller 24: see George W. Goodrich

Hiram Miller 60 (Feb 1840-M 14), Draltha 59 (Ap 1841-M 14-0) 1-185A-128/134

Jacob S. Miller 36 (May 1864-M 16), Harriet C. 34 (Ap 1866-M 16-4-2), Monsey M. 8 (June 1891), Dulcey D. 1 (July 1898) 5-237A-179/179

James Miller 39 (Oct 1861-M 18), Marget 43 (Feb 1857-M 18-0) 1-185A-121/127

James Miller 27 (Nov 1872-Ill/Ky/T-M 1)(Public School Teacher), Minnie A. 27 (Oct 1872-Mo/T/Mo-M 1-1-1), Charles L. 7/12 (Oct 1899) 13-300B-197/204

James C. Miller 19: see George W. Goodrich

James R. Miller 21, Nellie E. 16: see George W. Goodrich

Jasper Miller 57 (Ap 1843-Ga/NC/NC-M 8), Harriet 36 (Dec 1860-Ga/Ga/Ga-M 8-2-2), Thomas L. 16 (June 1883-Ga), Lillie 7 (Dec 1892-Ga), Lizzie 5 (June 1894-Ga) 8-280B-240/242

John B. Miller 59, Mary E. 61: see William B. Benson Jr.

John F. Miller 61 (Aug 1838-M 30), Rebecca 53 (Jan 1847-M 30-2-2), Walter W. 29 (Sep 1870), Roscoe C. 27 (Nov 1872), Lawrence SMITH 18 (May 1878)(Servant) 4-224A-204/208 (Spring City & Dayton Road)

John L. Miller 31 (Mar 1869-M 6), Ida B. 22 (Oct 1877-M 6-2-2), William A. 5 (Feb 1895), Cordia S. 3 (Mar 1897) 2-193A-41/42

Joseph Miller 32 (Oct 1867-M 8)(Stage Driver), Virginia T. 31 (Sep 1868-T/NC/NC-M 8-4-4), Elsie 7 (Oct 1892), Evelina 5 (Sep 1894), Elenore 3 (June 1896), John H. 2 (Ap 1898), Delia DENTON 24 (sil)(Aug 1875-T/NC/NC), Floyd 22 (bl)(Dec 1877), Grover C. 16 (bl) (Nov 1883) 5-234B-130/130

Moses Miller 58 (Dec 1841-M 40), Polley 60 (June 1840-M 40-7-5), John 40 (May 1860-M 11), Anie 37 (Ap 1863), Wilber 34 (July 1865), Wilum 30 (Sep 1869), Elise 27 (Oct 1872-M 5-1-1) 1-183A-82/85

Malauchton Miller 54 (Sep 1845-Oh/Oh/Oh-M 27), Nettie 47 (Sep 1852-Oh/NY/Oh-M 27-3-1) 11-292A-57/57

Monroe R. Miller 44 (June 1855-Wd), Malissa 18 (Feb 1882), Cora G. 15 (Aug 1884), James R. 10 (Feb 1890), Martha S. 8 (Feb 1892), Arche G. 5 (Sep 1894), Lillie M. 3 (Ap 1897), George HALL 19 (boarder)(May 1861-M 10), William 16 (boarder)(Aug 1883) 3-306B-322/334

Roscoe C. Miller 27: see Wiley H. Cunnyngham

Samuel H. Miller 58 (May 1842-M 25), Rebecca A. 51 (Feb 1849-M 25-8-7), Jerry D. 24 (May 1876), Tennessee 22 (Mar 1878), Martin L. 20 (Aug 1879), Sophia A. 17 (Oct 1882), Marie S. 16 (Oct 1883), Mandy J. 15 (Jan 1885), Jevrona E. 12 (d)(Feb 1888) 3-211A-197/215

White B.(?) Miller 33 (1866-M 10)(Attorney), Mamie L. 32 (Dec 1867-Ga/Ky/T-M 10-3-3), Burkett M. 9 (June 1890), Vaughn 8 (Ap 1892), Austin G. 5 (July 1894) 10-321A-23/24

William R. Miller 34 (May 1866-M 11), Sarah M. 34 (July 1865-M 11-0), Alice M. 12 (ne)(June 1887), John H. DODSON 34 (Mar 1866-Wd)(Partner), Maud A. 11 (boarder)(Oct 1888), Florence L. 9 (boarder)(Oct 1890) 2-194A-62/64

MARRIAGES

A.C. Miller to Margarett J. Thompson, 15 Sep 1874 (16 Sep), H.L.W. Furguson JP 1-#1357

A.M. Miller to Thusday(?) Fuller, 12 Oct 1890, J.W. Wright MG 4-18

Alfred C. Miller to Amanda J. Dawson, 17 Aug 1870 (18 Aug), J.W. Thompson MG 1-#1161

Amanda Miller to James Yancy q.v.

Arcada Miller to A. J. Lea q.v.

Arminda Miller to T. P. Lee q.v.

Arthur L. Miller to Rebecca Wasson, 3 Ap 1892, W.G. Mitchell JP 4-73

Clarence L. Miller to Mattie McClenahan, 2 Aug 1898 (same), W.R. Grimsley MG, W.W. Lister W 2-305

D. A. Miller to Thomas Barton q.v.

D. V. or A. V. Miller to Thomas J. McClellan q.v.

Eliza Miller to B. M. Collins q.v.

Eliza A. Miller to George Baker q.v.

Elizabeth D. Miller to James C. Pearce q.v.

F.J. Miller to Bettie J. Gothard, 20 July 1874 (22 July), T.P. Dunn MG 1-#1345

Frank A. Miller to Nelie M. Foster, 10 Oct 1899, R.A. Hutsell MG 4-103

George W. Miller to Lula Gillespie, 24 Ap 1897 (25 Ap), A.W. Randolph MG, James Richardson W 2-141

Hannah Miller to L. S. H. Smith q.v.

Henry H. Miller to Eliza J. Pearce, 6 Jan 1853 (12 Jan), J. Stencel MG 1-#402

J.R. Miller to Nellie E. Todd, 19 Oct 1899 (same), G.W. Brewer MG, T. Gwillim W 3-56

James Miller to Katie Jacques, 18 July 1888 (22 July), W.L. Thurman ?? 1-547

James L. Miller to Leutitia T. Burkett, 25 Sep 1885 (26 Sep), A.P. Early MG 1-#866

James W. Miller to Emaline Dodson, 12 July 1854 (no return) 1-#454

Jane Miller to James Brown q.v.

Jeff Miller to Lizza McFarland, 16 Nov 1886 (same), T.F. Shaver JP 1-515

John Miller to Malinda Roberson, 17 Oct 1861, "Returned not executed" 1-#764

John H. Miller to Susan Smith, 9 Dec 1865 (no return) 1-#856

John T. Miller to Rebecca Darwin, 21 Oct 1869 (no return) 1-#1116

John W. Miller to Ella Cradle, 30 Sep 1890 (same), W.L. Lillard JP 3-228 (B)

Joseph S. Miller to Jennie F. Denton, 20 Nov 1891, J.M. Bramlett MG 4-37
L. J. Miller to W. H. White q.v.
Lennie Miller to John Good q.v.
Leonard Miller: see Leonard WELLER
Maggie V. Miller to George L. Morgan q.v.
Martha A. Miller to Elbert Pearce q.v.
Martha E. Miller to L. C. Furgusson q.v.
Mary Miller to C. L. Lockenbee q.v.
Mary Ann Miller to Martin Hurst q.v.
Mattie Miller to Elias Roberts q.v.
Moses Miller to Mary Clark, 14 Jan 1867 (15 Jan), P.G. Campbell JP 1-#930
Peggy Ann Miller to Henry Jolly q.v.
Pocahontas Miller to James H. Beard q.v.
Renie Miller to William Caught q.v.
Robert Miller to Joannah Hayse, 24 Oct 1872 (27 Oct), James Johnson MG [sic] 1-#1259
S. E. Miller to C. A. Brown q.v.
S.K. Miller to B.T. Walker, 13 Dec 1894, James Johnson JP [sic] 4-78
Sallie L. Miller to Marcus W. Braine q.v.
Samantha Miller to J. P. Russell q.v.
Samuel Miller to Winna(?) Green, 27 Oct 1870 (same), J.P. Roddy MG 1-#1168
Samuel Miller to Clarenda Ward, 24 Nov 1877 (25 Nov), B.F. Hollaway JP 1-#1528
Thomas Miller to Elizabeth Clark, 14 May 1868 (17 May), P.G. Campbell JP 1-#1010
Thomas Miller to Issabella Frank, 23 Dec 1872 (26 Dec), A.L. King MG 1-#1267
Vesta Miller to E. J. Loden q.v.
W.F. Miller to Sitha Tallent, 20 Nov 1890, R.A. Bartlett MG 4-23
W.S. Miller to Orpha J. Darwin, 27 Ap 1865 (28 Ap), W.W. Low JP 1-#1070
William Miller to Sallie M. Harris, 15 June 1887 (16 June), James Johnson JP 1-589
William Miller to Hattie Cox, 20 May 1897, W.T. West MG 4-97
?. C. Miller to Eliza D. Cook, 18 Oct 1876 (same), B.F. Hollaway JP 1-#1465

- - - - - - - - - - - - -

MILLS

1880 CENSUS
Charles Mills 53 (Retired Merchant), Sarah 41, George 22, Mary 21, Anna 16, Charles 13, Walter 4 2-22-178
E.S. Mills 24 (Depot Agent): see S. T. Blevins
1900 CENSUS
Hettie Mills 64 (Mar 1836-Wd 6-4)(Fruit Picker), Kittie SHIRLEY 22 (d)(May 1878-Wd 2-1), Ethel 2 (gd)(Oct 1897) 13-296B-132/134
Walter Mills 22: see Jack Simpson (B)
MARRIAGES
Anna W. Mills to Elbert Dyer q.v.
Caroline Mills to George Dodd q.v.
Charles H. Mills to Florence B. Brown, 4 May 1893, C.G. Jones MG 4-50
E.S. Mills to Annabell Clack, 31 Aug 1885 (1 Sep), S. Phillips MG 1-520
Eva Mills to George Dodd q.v.
Harriet Mills to Gilbert Shipley q.v.
Kittie Mills to Calvin Shipley q.v.
M. E. Mills to W. A. Crawley q.v.
Malvin Mills to Sarah McDonald, 28 June 1884 (28 July) [sic], J.W. Burnett MG 1-466
Maryline Mills to John Hensley q.v.
Mollie Mills to Harry J. Erwin q.v.
Ollivia J. Mills to Cleaver Aslinger q.v.
Salvina Mills to W.H. Fann q.v.
W.A. Mills to Anna Homes, 16 July 1886 (17 July), M.C. Bruner MG 1-506

- - - - - - - - - - - - -

MILLSAPS

MARRIAGE
Thomas Millsaps to Susan H. Curtain, 7 Jan 1879 (8 Jan), H.B. Heiskell JP 1-#1585

- - - - - - - - - - - - -

MILTON / MELTON

1870 CENSUS
DeCalb C. Melton 23 (Retail Merchant), Amanda A. 21, Mary A. 4, David O. 2, Missouri 19 8-22-158
1880 CENSUS– None
1900 CENSUS
Carley Melton 50 (June 1849-England/Do/Do-M 14)(Coal Miner), Sarfina 33 (Nov 1866-T/Ind/T-M 14-6-5), Henry 12 (Ap 1888), Lenia 10 (May 1890), Frank 8 (Ap 1892), Nora 4 (July 1895), Elley (Aug 1898) 10-254B-83
Heiskel Melton 19, James 7: see Hiram Moore (B)
Horton Melton 21: see Thomas Ford (B)
James Melton 36 (Aug 1863-M 14), Susin 35 (July 1864-T/Va/Va-M 14-4-4), Brathia 13 (Nov 1886), Icie 10 (Mar 1880), Walter 8 (Ap 1892), Mary 1 (July 1898) 7-262A-233/238
James L. Milton 26: see Andy H. Vincent
Robert W. Melton 37 (Oct 1862-Wd), James A. 4 (July 1895), Susie C. 1 (Mar 1899), Martha J. 30 (si)(Unk 1870), Barnie A. 23 (b)(Unk 1877) 3-209B-171/186
William Milton 50 (Oct 1849-T/Va/Va-M 5), Luty 23 (Mar 1878-M 5-3-3), Maggie 18 (June 1881), Alford 6 (July 1894), Pearl 4 (Mar 1896), Lunce 4/12 (Jan 1900) 7-266B-311/316
MARRIAGES
Alexander Milton to Natuda Byerley, 3 Mar 1888 (same), A.P. Early MG 1-543
James Melton to Susan Jones, 24 Oct 1885 (25 Oct), James R. Crawford JP 1-490
John Milton to Zippora Johnson, 11 Jan 1866 (same), A.P. Early MG 1-#881
Kittie Milton to Jack Byerley q.v.
Lula Melton to Allend Rawlings q.v.
Maggie Melton to Clyde Wyrick q.v.
Octavia Milton to W. A. Harris q.v.
T. L. Milton to G. M. Davis q.v.
William Melton to Lula Allen, 11 July 1893, W.A. Howard MG 4-58

- - - - - - - - - - - - -

MINICK / MINNIX / MINIX / MINNICK / MINICKS / MINICH

1860 CENSUS

Baily Minick 34, Sarah E. 13, Polly A. 11, William H. 9, Nancy C. 7, Eliza J. 5, Tennessee 3, Rebecca M. 1 5-37-250

George Minick 33, Sarah 40, William 10, Margaret 8, Mary Jane 6, Alfred VAUGHN 16 3-55-373

Peter Minick 44, Rachel 48, Mary J. 17, Eliza A. 16 3-63-435

1870 CENSUS

Baily Minnix 54 (NC), Sarah A. 27, Mary A. 20, William H. 18, Nancy C. 16, Louisa Jane 14, Tennessee 12, Rebecca M. 11 5-4-26

George Minnick 46, Eliza Jane 44, William 21, Margarette 19, Mary J. 16, Sarah A. 4, Alta E. 1 3-4-22

Peter Minnick 54, Rachel 58, Elizabeth McMURRY 27, Mary J. 28, Peter J. 3, Nancy A. 1 3-7-46

1880 CENSUS

Bailey Minix 64, Sarah A. 36 (w), Bailey T. GAMBELL 6 (gs) 5-2-16

George Minic 56, Eliza 54, Sarah 14, Hariet 11, William 31 (s), Sarah FRALEY 75 (ml) 2-27-219

Peter Minnick 64, Fanny 35 (w), Anne 12 (d), James 7 (s) 9-31-267

1900 CENSUS

Baily Minick 83 (Nov 1816-NC/NC/NC-M 19), Sarah A. 40 (Mar 1860-M 19-0), Baily T. 25 (gs)(Aug 1874-M 0), Lily 21 (gdl)(Nov 1878-T/Ireland/T-M 0-0) 5-238A-201

William Minnick 51: see Thomas H. Dodd

MARRIAGES

Altie Minnix to Calvin Gray q.v.

Bailey Minnich to Sarah Ann Arnold, 27 Sep 1860 (same), J. Howard MG 1-#726

Caroline Minick to J. M. Bramlett q.v.

Eliza A. Minick to C. H. Reynolds q.v.

Eliza J. Minick to Reuben Hamby q.v.

Elizabeth Minick to James E. Beasly q.v.

George Minick to Eliza Fraley, 2 Oct 1864 (same), John Howard MG 1-#878

Lottie J. Minick to W. A. Smith q.v.

Margaret Minnix to John Housley q.v.

Mary J. Minicks to Thomas H. Dodd q.v.

Mary Jane Minick to W. N. Mariott q.v.

P.M. Minix to Fannie Edwards, 9 Aug 1879 (same), J.M. Bramlett MG 1-#1666

Polly Ann Minick to Joab Hughes q.v.

R.T. Minnick to Lillie McCabe, 19 Aug 1899 (20 Aug), W.A. Howard MG & W 3-20

Rebecca N. Minicks to Charles Perry q.v.

Sarah A. Minicks to Thomas A. Houston q.v.

Sariah A. Minix to Thomas J. Green q.v.

Tennessee Minicks to H. F. Porter q.v.

W.H. Minix to Lisa Ann Runnels, 12 Aug 1879 (13 Aug), J.M. Bramlett MG 1-#1667

W.M. Minich to Caroline Martin, 29 Mar 1851 (30 Mar), W.H. Cunningham JP 1-#337

William Minick to Abba J. Wilkey, 29 Dec 1871 (same), John Howard MG 1-#1219

- - - - - - - - - - - - -

MINNIS

MARRIAGE

William Minnis to Mary Stoops, 19 Nov 1864 (same), John Howard MG 1-#879

- - - - - - - - - - - - -

MINTON

1900 CENSUS

James F. Minton 54 (Nov 1845-Ga/NC/NC-M 30), Nancy E. 45 (May 1855-NC/NC/NC-M 30-11-8), Robert L. 18 (Feb 1882-NC), John R. 15 (Sep 1884-Ga), Nancy A. 13 (Unk 1887-Ga), Maggie L. 8 (Mar 1892-Ga), Martha A. 4 (May 1895-Ga) 8-286A-349/351

Luther E. Minton 23, Flora 21: see George W. Goodrich

Mary B. Minton 63 (Jan 1837-NC/NC/NC-Wd 9-7), Julius 22 (s)(Oct 1877-Ga/NC/NC-M 4), Lizzie 22 (dl)(Feb 1878-T/Calif/T-M 4-2-2), Charlie 3 (gs)(May 1897-Ala), Eveline 1 (gd)(Mar 1899), Pinkney 19 (s)(Ap 1881-Ga-M 0), Lillie 15 (dl)(Dec 1884-Ala/Ala/Ala-M 0-0) 8-314B-79/82

Riley Minton 23 (Unk 1877-Ga/Ga/Ga-M 3)(Miner), Cleo 21 (Ap 1879-M 3-1-1), Mabel 1 (Dec 1898) 8-286A-359/361

MARRIAGES

J.J.R. Minton to Cleopatra Nichols, 3 Oct 1897 (5 Oct), F.M. Cook MG, Sam Shadwick(?) W 2-193

P.A. Minton to Lillie Leeth, 23 Dec 1899 (same), J.W. Williamson MG, T.H. Patton W 3-96

William A. Minton to Ellen McMahan, 26 Dec 1900 (26 Jan 1901), W.F. Ward MG, James Mintee W 3-264

- - - - - - - - - - - - -

MITCHELL / MICHEL

1860 CENSUS

John Mitchell 30 (Colier), Nancy A. 27, Abigail 3, Jane 1 9-97-662

Margaret Mitchell 58, Elizabeth 25, Betsy J. 23, Mary V. 5, Elvira J. 1, Samantha J. 1/12 4-41-275

Robert Michel 59 (Va), Susan A. 18, Josephine 16, Sarah E. 14, Buenvesta 12, Mary A. 9, Nancy WOODWARD 50, Betsy WOODWARD 65 5-38-255

Sarah Mitchell 13: see Nicholas Keith

William Mitchell 26, Sarah A. 25, Welthey A. 1 5-33-222

1870 CENSUS

David Mitchell 40, Catharine 42, Martha 20, David 15, Daniel 12, Tennessee 2, Martha SMITH 71 4-14-96

James Mitchell 25, Sophia 28, David M. 4, Josephine 1 4-5-29

John Mitchell 44, Nancy A. 34, Aha 13, Nancy J. 11, Loucenia 10, Martha E. 8, Joseph N. 4 4-6-40

Susan A. Mitchell 32, Booney V. 23: see Jacob B. White

William G. Mitchell 36, Sarah A. 35, Martha A. 11, Ella J. 8, John H. 4, Eliza 2 4-12-76

1880 CENSUS

David Mitchell 65, Catharine 48 (w), Tennessee 12 4-7-54

David Mitchell 21, A.N. 24 4-7-55

James Mitchell 34, Sophia 38, David 13, Josephine 10, James 8, Charles 6, Amanda 3 2-26-206

Nancy Mitchell 47, Viney P. 17 (d), Martha 15, J.N. 2 (s) 3-19-54

P.G. Mitchell 23, S.F. 26, Flora 4, F.B. 1 (d) 4-7-53
William Mitchell 45, S.A. 43, Wealthy 21, Emma 17, John 14, Eliza 10, Charles 8, Floyd 4 4-3-21

1900 CENSUS

Charles Mitchell 26 (Sep 1873-M 2), Allie M.B. 22 (Aug 1877-T/NC/T-M 2-1-1), Robert O. 2 (Nov 1898) 3-211A-190/208
Daniel Mitchell 40 (Oct 1859-M 20)(Coal Miner), Erie E. 40 (Feb 1860-M 20-7-6), Charles T. 15 (Feb 1885), Tennie E. 10 (June 1889), Joseph M. 7 (Jan 1893), Reuben J. 3 (Feb 1897) 13-304B-274/284
David M. Mitchell 34 (May 1866-M 11), Bettie J. 33 (May 1867-T/NC/T-M 11-3-2), Manda J. 10 (Oct 1889), James W. 6/12 (Nov 1899) 3-211A-189/207
James Mitchell 54 (May 1846-M 15), Martha 48 (Dec 1851-M 16-4-3), John 15 (Feb 1885), Arch 13 (Nov 1886), Thomas 11 (July 1888) 3-207B-131/144
J. Harold Mitchell 16: see Charles W. Irwin
Joe Mitchell 65 (Unk 1835-Ga/Ga/Ga-M 35), Nellie 55 (Unk 1845-Ga/Ga/Ga-M 35-10-6) Raulie 16 (1884), May 11 (1889), Bertha 9 (1891) 8-275A-123 (B)
John Mitchell 53 (Ap 1847-M 28), Catharine L. 45 (June 1854-M 28-8-6), Marmartician 12 (d)(Jan 1888), John R. 9 (Nov 1892), Green P. 5 (Ap 1895) 10-261A-213/218
Joseph Mitchell 31 (Nov 1868-M 10), Josephine 23 (June 1876-M 10-4-4), John B. 8 (Jan 1892), Bertha M. 7 (Mar 1893), Nellie K. 4 (Aug 1895), Earnest K. 8/12 (Sep 1899) 4-224A-205/209 (Spring City & Dayton Road)
Nancy(?) Mitchell 25 (Unk 1875-D 3-2), Mitles 9 (Aug 1890), Gracie 1 (Aug 1898), Harvey 21 (b)(1879), Robert MAYFIELD 27 (boarder)(1873) 8-275A-132 (B)
Thomas Mitchell 12, Pearl 8: see Milton N. Johns (B)
William J. Mitchell 30 (May 1870-M 6), Susan 29 (Ap 1871-M 6*), Roscoe M. 5 (May 1895), David E. 3 (Feb 1897), Laura B. 1 (Aug 1898), Katie J. 4/12 (Jan 1900), Nancy TRENTHAM 60 (si)(May 1840-S) 4-225B-238/242 [*number of children not indicated]

MARRIAGES

A. Mitchell to Samuel A. Henderson q.v.
Amanda Mitchell to James Brogdon q.v.
Artie Mitchell to E. P. Gitgood q.v.
Cora Mitchell to Rice Hodges q.v.
D.M. Mitchell to Bettie McClendon, 16 Jan 1889 (20 Mar), W.T. West MG 1-559
Daniel Mitchell to A. Henderson, 8 Oct 1879 (same), D.V. Culver MG 1-#1688
Delia Mitchell to Milton Johnson q.v.
Esther J. Mitchell to Jonas Boofer q.v.
Hattie Mitchell to Will Lucas q.v.
James Mitchell to Martha A. Watson, 8 July 1883 (same), John Howard MG 1-481
James A. Mitchell to Minnie A. Ragsdale, 18 Oct 1888 (same), J.P. McPherson MG 1-555
James W. Mitchell to Susannah Wiggins, 4 Oct 1894, L.E. Smith JP 4-85
Jane Mitchell to Edward Jennow q.v.
Joseph Mitchell to Milly Hughes, 12 May 1854 (14 May), A.D. Paul JP 1-#443
Joseph N. Mitchell to Josie Allen, 5 Feb 1891, A.L. Darr MG 4-28
Josie Mitchell to William Bledsoe q.v.
Kate Mitchell to John Ward q.v.
Lillie Mitchell to James Watson q.v.
Liste(?) Mitchell to Polk Ferguson q.v.
M. J. Mitchell to James Rector q.v.
M. J. Mitchell to Lewis White q.v.
Martha Mitchell to F. Edington q.v.
Mary A. Mitchell to Alfred W. Collins q.v.
Mary Ann Mitchell to Jacob Womack q.v.
Nancy Mitchell to James Pullam q.v.
Peter D. Mitchell to Sarah F. Jolly, 24 Nov 1875 (same), W.W. Low JP 1-#1420
Sarah E. Mitchell to William P. Collins q.v.
Sarah E. Mitchell to Jacob Myres q.v.
Sarah J. Mitchell to W. T. G. Wright q.v.
Sarah Jane Mitchell to James Hughes q.v.
Tennie Mitchell to Harvey Peters q.v.
Viney Mitchell to L. E. Smith q.v.
William G. Mitchell to Sarah Furguson, 13 Aug 1858 (no return) 1-#647

- - - - - - - - - - - - -

MITTS

MARRIAGE

Louisa J. Mitts to Obediah Triming(?) q.v.

- - - - - - - - - - - - -

MIZE / MISE / MICE / MAISE

1880 CENSUS

John Mise 45, Edna E. 31, Mary E. 18, Sallie 13, John 12, Manila J. 8, July A. 7, Martha E. 6 6-17-164/168

1900 CENSUS

Aron Maise 72 (Jan 1828-Wd) 1-187A-162/170
Barder Mize 18: see Niles C. Hides
John Mize 63 (Feb 1837-M 36), Edna E. 59 (May 1841-NC/NC/NC-M 36-6-6) 6-240B-16
John Mize Jr. 34 (July 1865-M 14), Kittie 31 (Ap 1869-M 14-6-5), Mattie 3 (Ap 1887), Ashley 8 (Sep 1891), Jesse 6 (Mar 1894), Henry C. 4 (Nov 1893), Alic 3 (Aug 1896) 6-240B-17

MARRIAGES

Arthur Mize to Mary Watson, 9 Nov 1900 (same), W.G. Curton MG, John Mize W 3-239
Ellen Mize to John R. Wyatt q.v.
Henry Mice to Litha C. Reese, 9 Oct 1885 (same), A.I. Long JP 1-523
John Mize to Mila W. or A. Webb, 2 Jan 1886 (3 Jan), A.J. Pritchett MG 1-515
Julia Mize to William Ogle q.v.
Nely J. Mize to W. B. Webb q.v.
Sally Mize to James Gravit q.v.
William Mize or Maze to Bessie Lane, 24 Oct 1898 (same), Benjamin J. Jones MG, William Majers & Frank Benton W 2-338 (B)

- - - - - - - - - - - - -

MOATES / MOATS / MOTES

1900 CENSUS

George Moats 45 (Mar 1855-NC/Ga/Ga-M 22), Lula 36 (Sep 1863-Ga/Ga/Ga-M 22-8-8), James R. 19 (Feb 1881-Ga), John H. 16 (Jan 1884-Ga), William W. 15

(Ap 1885), Mattie 11 (Aug 1888), Robert 9 (Feb 1891), Cyrus E. 6 (Oct 1893), Della 4 (July 1895), Jane McKINNEY 66 (ml)(Mar 1834-NC/NC/NC-Wd 5-2) 3-299A-168/172

MARRIAGES

N.G. Moates to Sarah Holcomb, 13 Sep 1899 (17 Sep), F.M. Cook MG, J.B. Swafford W 3-34

Vina Motes to Lin Stuart q.v.

- - - - - - - - - - - - -

MOLES
(see also MALIS / MELIS)

1900 CENSUS

Robert Moles 27 (July 1872-T/Ky/Unk-M 7), Mattie 30 (Unk-M 7-5-4), Richard 16 (Ap 1885), Dake C. 12 (Unk), John 5 (July 1894), Nellie 2 (July 1897) 6-243A-71

MARRIAGES

Henry Moles (52, Washington) to Rebecca Ryan (37, Washington), 14 Nov 1881, John Howard MG, Harris O. & Nancy Ryan W 4-5(45)

Robert Moles to Mattie Price, 29 Sep 1892, S.S. Franklin JP 4-51

- - - - - - - - - - - - -

MONEHAN / MOONAHAN / MOONEHAN / MOONEYHAN / MONEYHAN / MONNYHAN / MONYHAN

1900 CENSUS

David Mooneyhan 11: see Rufus L.(?) Doran

Jesse Moonyhan 13: see Charles Sharp

MARRIAGES

Caroline Mooneyhan to John Holmes or Homes q.v.

J.P. Monyhan to Kittie Alexander, 26 June 1890 (same), M.C. Bruner MG 1-603

Mary Moneyhan to Charles Holloway q.v.

Mary Monnyhan to Daniel Elder q.v.

Paralee Moonahan to Matthew Louis Poe q.v.

Paralee Monehan to James Brock q.v.

Sarah Moonehan to Rufus Doran q.v.

Synda Moneyhan to Charles Sharp q.v.

- - - - - - - - - - - - -

MONDA

1870 CENSUS

Shelby Monda 56, Matilda 56 (Ga), Rebecca 27, Elizabeth 23, Susan 21, Mary 18, Malissa 10 2-1-4

- - - - - - - - - - - - -

MONDAY / MUNDAY / MONDY / MANDY

1860 CENSUS

Nancy Monday 26, Sarah E. 7, Mary L. 6, James H. 2, Eliza J. REESE 16, James 3 Lucinda C. 3 1-90-613

Pleasant Monday 31 (Blacksmith), Webby A. 33, Margaret 9, Ann 7, Mary M. 2, Calvin 1 9-97-660

Steve(?) Monday 28, Liddia 25 1-82-559

Susan Monday 33 (Va), James P.* TAUZER 15, Mary J.* 12, Anna E. MONDAY 8, Hamilton L. 4, Martha N. 2 2-81-550 [*bro & sis of Susan]

1870 CENSUS

Nancy Monday 35, James 11, George 7, Lorinda 3, John 1 1-11-70

Pleasant Munday 41, Webby A. 43 (NC), Ann 17, Calvin 11, George W. 9, Elijah 7, Charles 4 1-22-150

James(?) H. Monday 33 (House Carpenter), Adaline F. 25, Thomas J. 3, Amanda E. 2 2-5-27

1880 CENSUS

James Monday 22, Elvira 21, Matilda 1, Margaret 11 (si) 4-3-19

James Monday 48 (Carpenter & Joiner), Adaline 40, Thomas 13, Amanda 11, Laura 9, John 6, Anna 4, Maud 1 2-22-174

Pleasant Monday 52 (General Carpenter), Catharine 49 (w), Calvin 21, George 19, Elijah 17, Charles 14 12-6-50

1900 CENSUS

Charles Mandy 35 (Jan 1865-M 9), Nanni 30 (Feb 1870-M 9-5-5), Coleman 9 (Mar 1891), Grover 7 (Ap 1893), Nelli 5 (Mar 1895), Blain 3 (Dec 1896), Noah 1 (Oct 1898) 12-182A-68/71

James H. Monday 64 (Aug 1836-M 41)(Landlord), Adiline F. 57 (Nov 1842-M 41-11-7), Amanda E. 28 (May 1872), Laura F. 25 (Dec 1874), John A. 24 (May 1876)(Soldier, Private), Annie 22 (Aug 1877), Margie M. 8 (Dec 1881), Jesse C. 16 (Ap 1884) 2-196A-95/98

Ples Monday 63 (Mar 1837-M 42), Catharine 64 (Feb 1836-M 42), Call 40 (s)(May 1860), Freed 25 (Dec 1874), Lize 32 (Jan 1868), Gather 30 (Mar 1870), Virgil(?) 22 (May 1878), Abe 15 (June 1884), Dora 10 (May 1890), Bird 5 (June 1894), Byant 2 (July 1897) 12-182A-73/76

Thomas J. Monday 33 (Aug 1866-Wd)(Carpenter), Bessie L. 13 (d)(Aug 1886-T/T/Ky), Nellie G. 9 (Feb 1881) 2-199A-145/150

MARRIAGES

Ann Monday to John McClendon q.v.

James Monday to Elvira Furguson, 2 Aug 1876 (5 Aug), D. Broyles JP 1-#1453

James R. Mondy to Nancy Ryan, no date, but between 19 Feb & 29 Mar 1851 1-#336

Jessie Monday to Charlie Simpson q.v.

Margarett Monday to William T. West q.v.

Mary Monday to James Garrison q.v.

Mary Monday to William Boles q.v.

Myrtle Monday to J. C. Simpson q.v.

Nancy Monday to John Boucher q.v.

Pleasant Monday to Ann Brewer, 9 June 1858 (same), N.H. Long JP 1-#633

Rebecca Mondy to William Louis q.v.

Sarah E. Mondy to Zachariah T. Morris q.v.

Thomas Monday to Mattie Jones, 14 Oct 1886 (same), J.S. Phillips MG 1-525

- - - - - - - - - - - - -

MONETON

MARRIAGE

J. W. Moneton to Lennie L. Ewing or Erving, 18 Dec 1894, J.B. McCallon MG 4-75

- - - - - - - - - - - - -

MONROE / MUNROE

1860 CENSUS

John Monroe 59 (Va), Ethaenda P. 56 (Va), George O. 25 (Va), James T. 21, Lorinda J. LEMMONS 20 2-78-531

1870 CENSUS

James T. Monroe 30 (Va), Lorinda J. 27, Saritha 4, Ana A. 2, John M. 15, Sarah G. 9 1-22-148

1880 CENSUS

James Monroe 50, Jane 37 (w), Sarah 14, J.D. 10 (s), Mary 7, George 3, S.A. 2 (d), J.N. 3/12 (s) 4-1-7

1900 CENSUS

James T. Monroe 68 (Aug 1831-Va/Va/Va-Wd)(Gardner), Jesse C.(?) RICE 70 (boarder)(Oct 1827-T/England/Do-Wd)(Gardner) 14-223A-190/194

MARRIAGE

Iza Munroe to Charley Roberson q.v.

- - - - - - - - - - - - -

MONSEY / MUNSEY / MONNSEY / MONZY / MANZY / MINSEY / MINCEY / MENCY

1860 CENSUS

R.T. Monzy 48 (Va)(School Teacher), Eliza 47 (Va) 6-112-768

1870 CENSUS

Richard T. Manzy 59 (Va)(School Teacher), Eliza A. 60 (Va) 7-7-56

Thomas K. Monsey 54 (Va)(School Teacher), Mary 43, Virginia P. 23, Emma L. 22, Orlena A. 19, John S. 6, Zach E. 12, Thomas K. 10 2-4-21

1880 CENSUS– None

1900 CENSUS

Andrew Mency 24 (Mar 1876-M 3), Illier(?) 18 (May 1882-M 3-1-1), Jennie 1 (Ap 1899) 1-189B-205/214

David J. Mency 53 (Sep 1846-M 30), Ullersy(?) 45 (Oct 1854-M 30-10-10), Mathy 26 (Ap 1874-Wd 1-1), Jerry 9 (gs)(Jan 1890), Wilum 24 (Oct 1876), Minie 21 (Aug 1878), Mary 18 (Sep 1882), John 14 (May 1886), Thomas 12 (Ap 1888), Manda 10 (Jan 1890), Sallie 8 (Feb 1892), Uleus 4 (d)(Ap 1896) 1-189A-202/211 (Spring City)

William Mincy 26 (Oct 1874-T/T/Va-M 3), Carie 25 (Dec 1874-M 3-1-1), Ollie 1 (Oct 1898) 3-209B-173/188

MARRIAGES

A.J. Mincey to Ida Genow or Janoe, 24 Feb 1898 (same), A.M. Broyles JP, Floyd Gallahan W 2-254

Annie Minsey to James Gregory q.v.

John S. Monsey to Ellen Johnson, 26 July 1876 (same), J.W. Williamson MG 1-#1451

Maggie Monnsey to C. H. Wilson q.v.

Minnie Munsey to Will Kelly q.v.

- - - - - - - - - - - - -

MONTGOMERY

1860 CENSUS

Christina Montgomery 49, Martha A. 21, James H. 18, Margaret E. 16 8-14-92

Howard T. Montgomery 25, Susan 26, Manerva [STANFIELD] 8, Thursey [STANFIELD] 6, John H. MONTGOMERY 1 8-18-122

R.C. Montgomery 43, Margaret BARNETT 56, Andrew J. HENRY 19 6-108-735

1870 CENSUS

Christina Montgomery 60, Martha 38, Lonzo 1 8-4-22

Robert Montgomery 54, Rhoda A. 26, Elizabeth 6, Samuel C. 3, James H. 1, Rhoda McMURRY 28 6-5-28

Thomas H. Montgomery 37 (Va), Susan 39, Minerva STANFIELD 18, Thursday E. 14, John MONTGOMERY 11, Malinda A. 9, Gentha J. 7, Jacob 4, Saimme(?) E. 2 8-5-32

1880 CENSUS

C.T. Montgomery 75, M.C. 42 (d), R.S. 11 (gd) 8-13-107

Elizabeth Montgomery 15, Samuel 13, Robert C. 10, Mary A. 6: see Leander Pierce

T.H. Montgomery 50, S.B. 49, M.A. 18 (d), J.J. 16 (d), J.C. 14 (s), S.E. 1 (d), R.F. 9 (s) 8-12-106

1900 CENSUS

Howard Montgomery 66 (Dec 1833-Va/Va/Va-M 43), Susan 68 (June 1831-T/Va/Va-M 43-10-8) 8-289A-417/420

Jacob Montgomery 33 (July 1866-T/Va/T-M 10), Hattie 24 (Sep 1875-T/Va/Va-M 10-4-3), Effie 7 (July 1892), Lola 4 (Nov 1895), Maynard (Feb 1899) 8-289A-415/418

Pellum Montgomery 26: see Joseph C. Jones (B)

Pelem Montgomery 30: see Bird Lowrey (B)

Raulston Montgomery 28 (Sep 1871-T/Va/T-M 8), Mattie 25 (Ap 1875-Ark/Oh/Iowa-M 8-3-3), Ada 7 (Ap 1893), Roy 4 (July 1895), Willis 2 (May 1898) 8-289A-416/419

Samuel Montgomery 33 (May 1867-M 9), Sarah A.D. 29 (Aug 1870-T/NC/NC-M 9-4-4), Minnie C. 8 (Ap 1892), Jeramiah C. 7 (Ap 1893), William F. 5 (Dec 1894), Carie B. 2 (Oct 1897) 5-231A-60

William Montgomery 62 (May 1838-Ga/Ga/Ga-M 3), Frankie 30 (Unk 1870-M 3-1-1), Nellie 6 (May 1894) 8-289A-412/415

MARRIAGES

Andy Montgomery to Frances Swain, 26 Aug 1889, S. Washington MG 4-45

Charles Montgomery to Annie Phillips, 24 Feb 1898, F.F. Treulgill MG 4-100

J.C. Montgomery to Hattie Day, 3 Dec 1890, W.A. Green JP 4-21

J.H. Montgomery to M.C. Land, 4 Jan 1879 (5 Jan), Calvin Morgan JP 1-#1599

Jennetta Josephine Montgomery to M. A. Morgan q.v.

Joseph E. Montgomery to Sarah Jane Whittenburg, 13 Dec 1867 (19 Dec), S. Phillips MG 1-#988

Linda Montgomery to Thomas Nichols q.v.

M. E. Montgomery to C. L. Dungan q.v.

Margarett J. Montgomery to Joel W. Hoge q.v.

Mary Montgomery to Benjamin Murphy q.v.

Mary Montgomery to J. F. Collins q.v.

Mary C. Montgomery to Charles L. Dungan q.v.

R.C. Montgomery to Rhoda Ann Wilkey, 6 Sep 1862 (no return) 1-#786

R.C. Montgomery to Martha Burnett, 13 Oct 1889, H.B. Burditt MG 4-84

R.F. Montgomery to Mattie Ossler, 20 Mar 1892, G.W. Colcord VDM 4-40

T.L. Montgomery to Tennessee C. Trotter, 15 Ap 1898 (17 Ap), T.F. Shaver MG, A.L. Morgan W 2-270
Roda A. Montgomery to Leander Pearce q.v.
S. R. Montgomery to J. W. Romines q.v.
Samuel Montgomery to S.A. Denton, 21 Mar 1891, J.M. Bramlett MG 4-29
T.H. Montgomery to Susan Stanfield, 21 Nov 1857 (22 Nov), G.W. Nichols JP 1-#620

- - - - - - - - - - - - -

MOODY

1900 CENSUS

Ida L. Moody 36, Herbert 10, Kenneth 3: see George W. Goodrich

- - - - - - - - - - - - -

MOON

MARRIAGES

Annie Moon(?) to Charley Hickmon(?) q.v.
Elizabeth Moon to Asbury Davis q.v.
Julia Moon to W. N. Myers q.v.
Mary Moon(?) to Joseph Martin q.v.

- - - - - - - - - - - - -

MOONEY

MARRIAGE

Irene Mooney to E. E. Doud q.v.

- - - - - - - - - - - - -

MOORE

1860 CENSUS

David Moore 18, Nancy A. 32, Emaline 26, Sally 21, William 16, Emaline 14, Henry 12 8-10-63
Elisha Moore 33, Milsbery 34, Francis M. 9, Mary E. 7, James M. 5, Thomas 3, Mary 1, William 17 7-8-51
Jordan Moore 25, Martha 22, Tate 1 6-108-741
Kezziah Moore 50, Sarah M. 17 6-108-738
Mary Moore 68: see John S. Evens
Robert Moore 23, Julia A. 18 8-10-64
William Moore 19: see Henry Wasson

1870 CENSUS

Albert D. Moore 24 (NC), Sarah 30, Thomas L. 2, Eliza A. 5/12, Eliza MOORE 44 (NC) 7-7-52
David Moore 25, Mary E. 31 7-4-29
Jeremiah Moore 30, Sarah 28, Robert 9 6-2-9
Moses F. Moore 35 (NC)(Wool Carder), Mary A. 33, Arabella Jane 11, Elbert S. 7 6-4-22
Nicholas G. Moore 25 (Retail Merchant), Amanda J. 22, Beriah F. 1, Maggie C. ELDER 16, William M. SNIDER 18 (Clerk in Store) 8-15-103
Rebecca Moore 60, William B. 26, Abner W. 21, Emma 19, Rebecca 17, Juliana Emma 11 10-3-20
Sarah F. Moore 17: see Alderago Clifton
Smith Moore 24 (SC), Nancy C. 23 (SC), William H. 4 6-16-118

1880 CENSUS

Andrew Moore 24 (Miner), Jaolene 21, Eugene 1/12, Annie BROWN 45 (ml) 2-31-251
David Moore 38, Emeline 40 (w) 7-26-224
George Moore 16, Cora 10 (B): see Stephen Cawood
George D. Moore 34, Amanda 34, Finley 20, George 18, July 15, Robert 13, Elizabeth 10, William 9, Rufus 2 10-27-207/213
James Moore 64, N.J. 36 (w), Malinda 12 (d), J. 10 (d), M.E. 8 (d), John T. 3 8-13-113
Lewis Moore 69: see John W. Opal
Moses F. Moore 45, Mary A. 43, Elbert S. 17, Edna BROWN(?) 7 5-2-13
Rebecca Moore 72, William D. 37, Mary J. 30, Adda E. 27: see W.A. Templeton
Smith Moore 35, N.C. 31, W.H. 14 (d), Valentine 8, John 6, Sarah 5, David 4, Steave 6/12 7-22-194
N.G. Moore 35, A.J. 32, R.F. 11 (s), E.W. 8 (s), D.R. 6 (d), M.L. 3 (d), Emma 6/12 7-28-241

1900 CENSUS

Beriah F. Moore 31 (Ap 1869-M 3)(Electrician), Annie 26 (Mar 1874-M 3-0) 10-322B-52/55
Evan Moore 47 (Aug 1852-Ky/Ky/Ky-M 7)(Blacksmith), Ada L. 28 (Mar 1872-T/NY/NY-M 7-1-1), John C. 4 (May 1896), Mary L. 5/12 (Dec 1899) 2-198B-133/138
Herbert Moore 2: see William Branam
Hiram Moore 35 (July 1864-T/T/NC-M 3), Mary 36 (Oct 1863-T/Ky/T-M 3-5-4), Will H. 18 (Ap 1882), Thomas H. 13 (Ap 1887), Eugene 10 (Mar 1890), Carrie 8 (Mar 1892), Albert COTEN 19 (foster s)(Unk-T/Ga/T); *Boarders:* Jefferson WILSON 38 (Dec 1861), Heiskel MELTON 19 (Unk), James MILTON 17 (Unk)(Coal Miner), William WILSON 19 (Ap 1881-Ga)(RR Section Hand), James McCLENDON 19 (Mar 1881)(RR Section Hand), Holland BURREL 20 (Mar 1880) 10-328A-173/183 (B)
Jack Moore 77 (Unk 1823-M 37), Emma 49 (Dec 1850-NC/NC/NC-M 37-16-8), John 28 (Oct 1871)(Coal Miner), Lillie 3 (Ap 1887), Rena WILSON 19 (Dec 1880-T/T/Ala)(Servant); *Boarders:* Noah TRIPLETT 30 (Unk 1870), Jacob WHITE 32 (Unk 1868), Horace CATES 28 (Unk 1871), Charles BREEDLOVE 18 (Unk 1882)(Coal Miner) 15-272A-79/79 (B)
James C. Moore 51 (Feb 1849-M 25)(Iron Ore Miner), Mary C. 37 (July 1862-M 25-6-5), Martha J. 16 (July 1883), Alace A. 14 (Sep 1885), Isaac V. 10 (July 1889), Samma 10/12 (Aug 1899), Benjamin PHILLIPS 19 (boarder)(Oct 1880) 5-231B-72
John N. Moore 35 (June 1864-Ky/T/T-M 14), Sarah A. 33 (Feb 1867-M 14-6-5), Elijah L. 13 (Aug 1886), Chloe O. 10 (Aug 1889), Amy I. 8 (Dec 1891), Elmer L.(?) 4 (Jan 1896-Ark), Ruel M. 1 (Aug 1898) 2-196A-92/95
Kelley Moore 35 (Dec 1864-M 11)(Iron Ore Miner), Alice 29 (Oct 1870-M 11-5-4), Guene 9 (May 1891), Rasey 6 (Sep 1893), James W. 4 (Mar 1896), Allie 1 (June 1898) 2-195A-76/79 (B)
Nathan B. Moore Unk (Unk-M 3)(Watch Repairer), Elizabeth 32 (Feb 1868-M 3-1-1), Esley 3 (Aug 1897) 8-327B-146/151
Nicholas G. Moore 55 (Dec 1844-M 32), Amanda J. 52 (Aug 1847-M 32-8-5), Earnest W. 28 (July 1871)(Coal Miner), Emma M. 20 (Dec 1879), Robert L. 16 (Sep 1883) 10-322A-45/47

MARRIAGES

A.D. Moore to Rebecca Stephens, 26 Mar 1874 (same), W.H. Dodd MG 1-#1331

A.J. Moore to Suda Long, 24 Dec 1851 (same), A.D. Paul JP 1-#358

A.J. Moore to Susan Porter, 8 Mar 1886 (same), Taylor Russell JP 1-512

Annie Moore to W. P. Dane q.v.

B.F. Moore to Annie Sneed, 29 May 1897 (30 May), A.H. Low MG, T.M. Whaley W 2-147

Bell Moore to William Casey q.v.

Cal Moore to Alice Gillespie, 25 Aug 1888 (26 Aug), W.R. Clack JP 1-559

Daniel Moore to Ester McCaleb, 2 Dec 1889 (5 Dec), J.H. Hale JP 1-590

Dora Moore to R. S. Hill q.v.

Dotson Moore to Sarah E. Hubbard, 24 Jan 1867 (25 Jan), Charles Lamb JP 1-#933

Easter Moore to James Reed q.v.

Eliza Moore to E. McMurry q.v.

Evan Moore to Lucy A. Stibbins, 18 Jan 1899 (same), W.L. Lillard JP 2-376

F.C. Moore to Nancy Reavely, 20 Jan 1855 (21 Jan), Benjamin Wallace MG 1-#482

F.C. Moore to Sarah Powers, 14 Ap 1870 (same), William Buttram MG 1-#1150

Frances Moore to R. C. Hughes q.v.

George Moore to Mollie Couch, 31 Dec 1892, J.R. Clark MG 4-52

Girdie Moore to W. Z. Rothwell q.v.

J.C. Moore to M. McMurry, 8 May 1857 (9 May), R.T. Howard MG 1-#650

Jacob W. Moore to Sally Foster, 13 Mar 1877 (14 Mar), B.F. Holloway JP 1-#1492

James Moore to Callie Hughes, 9 Aug 1891, R.S. Mason JP 4-28

L. B. Moore to William Bean q.v,

Laura Moore to S. H. Harwood q.v.

Linda Moore to Samuel Hollowfield q.v.

M.F. Moore to Mary Ann Cox, 7 Mar 1855 (8 Mar), R.T. Howard MG 1-#524

Maggie Moore to Noah Tallant q.v.

Maggie Moore to Floyd Mariott q.v. (B)

Mariah Moore to John P. Smith q.v.

Mary Moore to William Ganaway q.v.

Mary Moore to John Fuller q.v.

Mattie Moore to Frank Ellison q.v.

Mattie J. Moore to W. M. Lawson q.v.

R. J. Moore to W. A. Templeton q.v.

Robert Moore to July Ann Davis, 23 Feb 1858 (same), W.M. Morgan JP 1-#653

Sammie Moore to Louis B. White q.v.

Sarah Moore to James Coval q.v.

Serephenae Moore to Amber Johnson q.v.

Sillvan Moore to Luther McAfee q.v.

Smith Moore to Catharine Drymore, 5 June 1866 (6 June), Charles Lamb JP 1-#901

Susan Moore to William Allen q.v.

Syntha E. Moore to E. H. Boyle q.v.

W.M. Moore to Katie Cox, 23 Sep 1899 (24 Sep), S.G. Frazier MG, M.M. Hodges W 3-38

- - - - - - - - - - - - -

MOREFIELD

MARRIAGES

Francis E. Morefield to Nancy Jane Goodman, 28 June 1876 (same), John Howard MG 1-#1450

M.L. Morefield to Hattie Benson, 3 Sep 1890, J.R. Walker MG 4-18

- - - - - - - - - - - - -

MORELAND / MOORELAND

MARRIAGES

Alex Mooreland to Isabella Parks, 2 July 1888 (22 July), W.R. Clack JP 1-560

Wesley Moreland to Rachel Scott, 4 July 1885 (5 July), C. Morgan JP 1-493

- - - - - - - - - - - - -

MORGAN

1860 CENSUS

Calvin Morgan 38 (Wagonmaker), Sarah L. 27, Virginia C. 7, Tennessee E. 5, Julia A. 4, Peter C. 3/12 10-27-179

Charles Morgan 43 (Carpenter), Emeretta 36, Henry S. 18, Franklin R. 16, William B. 14, Thomas C. 12, Rufus W. 10, Mary E. 7, Josephine 4, Parlen 1 8-25-168

David Morgan 34, Nancy 34, Joseph A. 5, John W. 3, Mary E. 4/12, Mary J. GREEN 32 10-30-198

Elias Morgan 41 (Wagonmaker), Tensey J. 30, William B. 15, John D. 13, James C. 11, Jerome 9, Lavenia 6, Lofty MORGAN 65 (SC), John 30 (Wagonmaker) 10-29-196

Francis M. Morgan 24, Sarah 26, Missouri H. 1 10-27-178

Lewis Morgan 40 (Blacksmith), Elizabeth 30, Parthena 12, Caroline 4, Joseph C. 1 8-23-159

Lewis Morgan 66 (SC)(Wagonmaker), Elizabeth 53 (SC), Henry L. 21, Doskey TAYLOR 50 10-28-188

Martin Morgan 40 (SC), Mary 28, Elizabeth 10, Cornelius 8, Adolphus L. 6, Cordelia 4, Therisa 9/12, Thomas M. MORGAN 42 8-18-119

Rufus Morgan 28, Martha J. 29, Jarrelda 7, Albion P. 5, Edmond T. 2, James F. 1/12, Margaret L. BICE 22 10-29-197

Sarah Morgan 42, William H. 17, Elizabeth A. 14, James W. 13, Mary A. 10, Asberry H. 7, Louissa C. 5 8-18-124

Washington Morgan 57 (SC)(Blacksmith), Susannah 64, George 23, Mary Ann 33, William 22 8-25-171

Washington Morgan 35 (Carpenter), Margaret J. 28, Sidney A. 8, John 8, Abigail J. 6, Eliza DUNWOODY 7 8-9-54

William Morgan 40, Judy M. 38, Mary A. 18, Caroline A. 15, Albert A. 13, Newton F. 9, Theodore 6, Henry F. 3, Gideon B. 8/12, Sarah GREEN 37 8-26-176

1870 CENSUS

Calvin Morgan 48 (Wagonwright), Sarah L. 41, Virginia C. 17, Tennessee E. 15, Julia A. 13, Peyton C. 10, Flora E. 7, Alice 3, Henry C. 1 10-2-12

Calvin A. Morgan 24, Sarah E. 19 (Va), Mary E. 2 8-19-133

Charles Morgan 52 (Millwright), Emmeritta 47, William B. 24, Rufus W 20, Mary E. 16, Josephus 14, Paralee 11, George W. 8, Charles H. 5 8-2-10

Elias H. Morgan 50 (Wagonwright), Tomesa J. 42, William B. 26 (Tooth Dentist), John D. 23 (Tooth Dentist), James C. 20, Jerome R. 17, Lavena 14, Tennessee K. 9, Mattie C. 8 10-1-6
Franklin R. Morgan 26, Laura 17, Sampson 9/12 8-2-11
Gideon T. Morgan 35, Catharine M. 28, Mary H. 8, Hettie A. 5, Rufus H.L. 3, Elizabeth I. 2, Catharine J. 4/12, Elizabeth MORGAN 74 (SC) 10-1-1
James H. Morgan 25 (Ala), Sarah M. 22 8-2-14
Lewis Morgan 50 (Blacksmith), Elizabeth 40, Parthena E. 19, Caldonia H. 13, Joseph C. 11, George L. 6, Robert E. 4, James L. 1 8-16-109
Martin Morgan 50 (SC), Mary 40, Elizabeth L. 20, Cornelius H. 18, Adolphas 16, Cordelia E. 14, Theresa A. 10, Darthula A. 6, Sarenia C. 4, Samantha 1 8-5-30
Nancy Morgan 40, Joseph A. 14, John W. 12, Mary E. 10, Wm D.S. 7: see William D. Averett
Sarah A. Morgan 38, Margarette 20, Irena 12, Julia A. 6, George W. 3 8-8-53
Sarah J. Morgan 53, William H. 27, James W. 23, Mary A. 20, Asberry H. 17, Louisa C. 15 8-7-45
Washington Morgan 68 (SC)(Millwright), Susan 74 (NC), John H. 13, George D. 11 8-2-12
William Morgan 22, Manda 19 7-2-15
William Morgan 50, Judah 48, Albert A. 22, Newton F. 19, Theodore W. 17, Henry F. 14, Gideon B. 11 8-20-137
William F. Morgan 32 (House Carpenter), Sarah C. 28, Cory W. 3, Bruce C. 1 8-10-67

1880 CENSUS

A.A. Morgan 46, Flora 47, A.B. 18 (d), K.M. 14 (d), A.A. 12 (s), Carry 10, Jamey 7, M.C. 6 7-26-222
A.C. Morgan 35, M.C. 27 (w) 8-20-174
A.S. Morgan 26, Sallie 15 (w) 8-13-111
C.A. Morgan 35, S.E. 29 (w), M.E. 12 (d), J.E. 9 (d), H.N. 7 (s), C.P. 4 (s), Minta 1 (d) 8-11-88
Calvin Morgan 57 (Carpenter), Sarah L. 52, Tennessee E. 25, Paton Coy 20, Flora C. 16, Allis 13, Henry C. 11, Delia E. 8 10-28-217/222
Charles Morgan 61, E.R. 57 (w), N.B. 35 (s), R.W. 30 (s), M.E 27 (d), Joe 24, Paralee 21, L.W. 18 (s) 11-38-307
Elias H. Morgan 61 (Wagonmaker), Tennessey J. 52, Jerome R. 26, Louvinia C. 24, Kentucky T. 19, Mattie C. 17 10-28-220/225
F.R. Morgan 37 (Carpenter), Lisa 27 (w), M.S. 10 (s), N.E. 8 (d), M.M. 5 (d), B.M. 4 (s), L.B. 2 (d) 11-37-305
Houston Morgan 37, S.M. 35 (w), Tom 14, Jane 8, Wm 6, Mary 2 11-40-327
H.F. Morgan 23, S.J. 25 8-11-92
J.A. Morgan 23, J.A. 24 8-13-108
J.W. Morgan 22, M.S. 23, L.A. 1 (d) 8-13-110
John Morgan 26, Matilda BYERLY 29 (si), J.W. WATTS 20 7-24-207
John D. Morgan 33 (Doctor-Dentist), Mary C. 29, Idela M. 5, Lenah 4, Earl 2 10-28-219/224
Louis Morgan 60 (Blacksmith), Eliza 50, J.C. 21 (Blacksmith), G.S.M.C. 17 (s), R.U. 12 (s), J.L. 9 (s), Clay 3 8-4-33
M.J. Morgan 49 (m), A.P. 24 (s), E.T. 21 (s), J.F. 18 (s) 8-11-91
Mary Morgan 50, Elizabeth 30, C.H. 28 (s), D.A. 18 (d), S.C. 15 (d), S.J. 13 (d), S.M. 8 (d) 8-12-101
Nancy Morgan 40, James 16: see W.D. Avrett
W. Morgan 81, M. 45 (w), G.D. 19 (gs), J.H. 21 (gs), Tennessee GOTHARD 25 (Hired), Mary GATES(?) 13 (Servant) 11-37-302
W.F. Morgan 41, S.C. 41 (w), G.W. 13 (d), I.P. 7 (d), E. 5 (s) 11-40-326
W.H. Morgan 37, J.I. 24 (w), W.E. 4/12 (s), J.W. 31 (b), M.A. 27 (si), A.H. 26 (b), L.C. 23 (si) 8-9-79
Wash Morgan 56: see J. C. Butram
White Morgan 31, Reece 24 (w) 5-9-84
William Morgan 60, J.M. 58, A.A. 32 (s), N.F. 29 (s), T.N. 26 (s), G.B. 20 (s) 8-2-13
William N. Morgan 33, Manda P. 25, John P. 9, William H. 7, James C. 4, Daniel P. 3, George W. 6/12 10-30-227/234

1900 CENSUS

Adolphus Morgan 46 (Ap 1854-M 20), Sarah 37 (Jan 1863-M 20-11-9), Lawrence 19 (Nov 1880), Hilton 16 (Nov 1883), Gideon 13 (July 1886), Maud 11 (Nov 1888), Viola 9 (Sep 1890), Earl 8 (May 1892), Zo 6 (Feb 1894), Bulah 4 (Oct 1845), Earnest 2 (Feb 1898) 8-286A-345/347
Alvin P.(?) Morgan 46 (May 1854-M 16), Ella 36 (July 1863-M 16-8-5), Roscoe 3 (Sep 1886), Ralph 12 (Ap 1888), Clide 9 (July 1890), Ray 8 (Feb 1892), Roy 3 (Jan 1897), Liza GREEN 37 (sil)(Jan 1861) 8-278B-200/202
Andrew A. Morgan 32 (July 1867-M 1), Ellen 16 (May 1884-M 1-1-1), William D. 2/12 (Mar 1900) 10-255A-94
Arva Morgan 48 (Feb 1852-T/NC/T-Wd 0)(Merchant), Bertha GREEN 15 (ne)(Ap 1885), James A. 7 (nw) (Sep 1892), John HOUSER 29 (boarder)(Nov 1870) (Coal Miner) 8-277B-182/184
Brownlow Morgan 23 (May 1877-M 3), Ida 27 (Mar 1873-M 3-3-2), Bertie M. 2 (Dec 1897), James F. 9/12 (Aug 1899) 11-291A-25
Calvin Morgan 77 (Mar 1823-M 50), Sarah 71 (Oct 1828-M 50-12-7), Julia ABEL 44 (d)(Ap 1856-Wd 4-2), Edith 15 (gd)(Nov 1884), Wright 13 (gs)(Jan 1887) 8-277B-181/182
Calvin Morgan 56 (Ap 1844-M 32), Sarah E. 49 (Ap 1851-Va/Va/Va-M 32-6-4), Ina F. 13 (June 1886) 8-282B-278/280
Calvin Morgan 30 (Ap 1870-M 14), Nannie 27 (Jan 1873-M 14-6-2), Nettie 13 (Feb 1887), Edward 4 (May 1896) 15-269A-24
Charles Morgan 82 (Mar 1818-T/SC/SC-Wd)(Landlord), William B. 54 (June 1845), Parie 40 (Nov 1859) 11-291A-22
Douglas Morgan 30 (Mar 1870-NC/T/NC-M 3), Vesta 21 (Ap 1879-T/T/Va-M 3-1-1), Mattie A. 2 (Aug 1899) 6-240A-4
Ed T. Morgan 43 (Oct 1856-M 10)(Merchant), Marion 30 (June 1869-Scotland/Do/Do-M 10-3-3), Archie 7 (July 1892), Roy 4 (May 1896), Loyd 10/12 (July 1899), Flossie ROMINES 20 (Jan 1880-Ind/Ind/T)(Servant) 8-277B-184/186
Elizabeth Morgan 70 (Ap 1830-T/T/Va-Wd 13-7), Robert E. 35 (May 1865)(Brickmason) 8-311B-16/17
Frank R.(?) Morgan 56 (Oct 1843-M 31), Laura 46 (Ap 1854-M 31-13-11), Julia A. 18 (Mar 1882), Blaine 15 (Aug 1884), Flora A. 13 (Nov 1886), Charles G. 10 (Dec 1889), Lena E. 7 (Aug 1892) 11-291A-20

Fred Morgan 34 (July 1865-M 12), Mandy D. 35 (June 1864-M 12-4-3), John H. 9 (Jan 1891), Bessie M. 5 (July 1894), Charles M. 3 (Jan 1897) 6-254A-101/102

George L. Morgan 36 (Nov 1863-M 12)(Locamotive Engineer), Maggie 39 (June 1860-Va/Va/Va-M 12-6-4), Harry L. 11 (Feb 1889), Vinnie D. 8 (Ap 1892), Mabel 6 (May 1894), Gladys 1 (Aug 1898) 8-311B-15/16

George W. Morgan 38 (Jan 1862-M 9)(Carpenter), Mary A. 34 (Nov 1865-T/T/NC-M 9-3-3), James H. 7 (Aug 1892), Charles C. 5 (Dec 1894), Hudson G. 2 (Dec 1897), Maggie LOCKE [nee Snow] 46 (sil)(Dec 1853-T/T/NC-Wd 0-0) 11-290B-18

Gideon B. Morgan 38 (Oct 1861-M 16)(Carpenter), Ella 34 (Ap 1866-M 16-6-3), Charles R. 18 (July 1881), Myrtice 8 (June 1891), Eva 4 (Sep 1895), infant 0/12 (d)(May 1900), Della BARTON 26 (Unk 1874)(Servant) 8-282B-274/276

Henry Morgan 27 (Jan 1873-T/Va/T-M 2), Lula 23 (July 1876-M 2-2-2), Pearl 1 (Sep 1898), Wheeler 1 (Sep 1899) 6-245B-105/106

Henry Morgan 41 (Oct 1858-M 12)(Grocery Clerk), Edith 33 (Sep 1866-Oh/Oh/Oh-M 12-3-2), Merle 7 (June 1892), Bernice 6 (Nov 1893) 8-279A-213/215

Henry C. Morgan 32 (Jan 1868-M 8)(Coal Miner), Nancy 34 (Aug 1865-WVa/Oh/Oh-M 8-1-0) 8-278A-190/192

Henry F. Morgan 43 (June 1856-M 20)(Carpenter), Lydia J. 45 (Feb 1855-M 20-5-4), Edgar 19 (May 1881)(Grocery Salesman), Veda 15 (Mar 1885), Anna 11 (July 1888), Luther 4 (Feb 1896) 8-282B-285/287

Houston Morgan 60 (Unk 1840-M 35), Sarah 60 (Unk 1840-M 35-?-?), Allie 13 (d)(Unk 1887), Martha 9 (d) (Unk 1891) 8-288B-410/412

James Morgan 25 (May 1875-M 5), Sallie 21 (Feb 1879-M 5-2-0) 7-262A-236/240

James Morgan 40 (May 1860)(Merchant), Mattie J. 26 (Dec 1873-M 7-0), Ida A. 10 (Oct 1889) 8-277A-168/169

John Morgan 29 (Jan 1871-M 6), Cornelia 30 (Mar 1870-Va/Va/Va-M 6-3-3), Carey B. 5 (Feb 1895), William C. 3 (Jan 1897), Dania P. 1 (Dec 1898), Minnie HAMILTON 18 (ne)(Mar 1882-T/Va/Va) 7-262A-234/239

John Morgan 44 (Oct 1855-M 17)(Postmaster), Sallie A. 36 (Feb 1864-Ga/Ga/Ga-M 17-9-8), Pearl F. 16 (Sep 1883)(Assist Postmaster), Willie N. 15 (Dec 1884) (Assist Postmaster), Walter E. 12 (Jan 1888), Luther B. 10 (Sep 1889), Clyde J. 8 (Oct 1891), Edgar B. 6 (Mar 1894), Pauline H. 2 (Nov 1897), Whitney 5/12 (Jan 1900), Saphronia BROWN 60 (ml)(June 1839-Ga/SC/SC-Wd) 10-251B-34

John D. Morgan 52 (June 1847-M 27), Mary C. 48 (Sep 1851-M 27-10-8), Della 25 (Oct 1874), Lena 24 (May 1876), Olliver 19 (Jan 1881), Logan 16 (Jan 1884), Carrol 13 (Aug 1886), Clide 11 (Ap 1889), May K. 7 (Feb 1893) 8-282A-273/275

John H. Morgan 29 (June 1870-M 11), Maggie 28 (May 1872-M 11-4-4), Ambros 10 (Feb 1890), Clebert 7 (Sep 1892), Mary 5 (Dec 1894), Martha 1 (Sep 1898) 6-247A-133/134

John W. Morgan 46 (Mar 1854-M 22)(Coal Miner), Martha E. 46 (Dec 1853-M 22-8-8), William B. 16 (July 1883)(Coal Miner), Darius F. 15 (Mar 1885), Nancy J. 12 (Sep 1887), Anice 10 (May 1890), John D. 8 (Ap 1892), Albert L. 4 (June 1895) 11-293B-92/93

Joseph Morgan 41 (Jan 1859-M 8)(Blacksmith), Nannie 36 (Nov 1863-T/Va/T-M 18-7-7), Charles 17 (Dec 1882), Frederick 14 (June 1885), Essie 12 (Sep 1887), Pansy 10 (Dec 1889), Virgil 7 (Aug 1892), Edith 3 (Feb 1897), Mildred 4/12 (Feb 1900) 8-318A-153/158

Josephus Morgan 44 (Feb 1856-M 8), Maggie E. 38 (Jan 1862-Canada/Ireland/Scotland-M 9-0-0) 11-291A-24

Julia A. Morgan 44 (Nov 1835-Wd 6-2), Searge W. 17 (July 1882), David B. 15 (May 1885), Bandy BURWICK 37 (Ap 1863-D 0-0) 8-286B-364/366

Lewis Morgan 65 (Nov 1834-M 34), Francis A. 64 (Dec 1836-NC/Unk-M 34-4-2) 6-240B-14

Luther R. Morgan 19 (Aug 1880-M 1), Jane A. 22 (May 1878-M 1-1-1), Eva V. 4/12 (Jan 1900) 11-291A-31

Malinda Morgan 46 (Nov 1853-Wd 3-2), Eva P. 14 (May 1886), Calla R. 12 (Mar 1888), Cyntha D. BARTRAM 67 (m)(Aug 1832-Wd 1-1) 5-230A-41

Martha J. Morgan 68 (June 1831-Wd 2-0) 8-277B-185/187

Monroe Morgan 36 (June 1863-T/Ala/Ala-M 19), Jenettie 36 (June 1863-M 19-8-8), Eddie 17 (Dec 1882) (Miner), Sinnie 14 (Aug 1885), Jacob 13 (Jan 1887), Ira 11 (Jan 1889), Bruce 9 (July 1890), Clayton 7 (July 1892), Dossie 6 (Mar 1894), Buena V. 3 (Oct 1896) 8-286B-362/364

Roy Morgan 8, Maggie W. 6: see Jim P. Wycuff

Rufus W. Morgan 50 (Ap 1850-M 15), Bettie 40 (Dec 1859-T/NC/T-M 15-6-4), Addie 12 (Mar 1888), Mattie 7 (Jan 1893), Mary P. 5 (Mar 1895), Ella 1 (Sep 1898) 11-290B-21

Serena Morgan 33 (July 1866-T/SC/T), Samantha 30 (si) (Dec 1869), Leona 26 (si)(Dec 1873) 8-285B-342/344

Theodore Morgan 46 (July 1853-M 18)(Carpenter), Nora F. 40 (July 1859-M 18-6-6), Gertrude 17 (Jan 1883), Grace B. 14 (Dec 1885), Iuay T. 11 (July 1888), Maria 7 (Sep 1892), Madge 5 (June 1894), Ruth 11/12 (June 1899) 8-282A-272/274

White Morgan 50 (Unk 1850-M ?), Reece 45 (Unk 1855-M ?-0) 8-289A-413/416

William Morgan 23 (Jan 1877-M 0)(Miner), Ivy 18 (Nov 1881-M 0-0) 8-288B-409/411

William Morgan 56 (Oct 1843-M 30), Anna 55 (Unk-M 30-12-11), Daniel P. 24 (June 1875), George W. 20 (Nov 1879), Thomas M. 18 (Ap 1882), Susan D. 15 (Ap 1884), Bertha E. 13 (Jan 1887), Delia A. 11 (Dec 1888), Cora T. 9 (May 1891), Charles G. 4 (Dec 1895) 6-245A-100/101

William F. Morgan 62 (Aug 1837-T/SC/NC-M 34), Sarah S. 60 (Jan 1840-T/NY/T-M 34-5-2), Ida P. 27 (Oct 1872), Earnest N. 25 (Oct 1874), Byron 6 (gs)(Nov 1893) 11-290A-7

William H. Morgan 57 (Ap 1843-M 20), Jane E. 44 (July 1855-Ky/T/Ky-M 20-7-7), Walter 20 (Jan 1880), Sarah C. 18 (Oct 1881), Elsie J. 16 (Sep 1883), Bruce B. 14 (Jan 1886), Lawson E. 11 (July 1888), Esra H. 9 (Feb 1891), Etta A. 7 (May 1893), James W. MORGAN 47 (b)(May 1847-S) 13-300B-193/199

MARRIAGES

A.C. Morgan to Sarah Henderson, 14 Aug 1883 (same), W. S. Hale MG 1-475

A.L. Morgan to S.M. Dungan, 7 Feb 1880 (8 Feb), Calvin Morgan JP 1-#1714

Albert H. Morgan to Addie L. Stephens, 3 Feb 1890 (same), A.W. Frazier JP 1-587
Alice Morgan to D. W. Jones q.v.
Alice M. Morgan to Pollard R. Wade q.v.
Allison Morgan to Tabitha J. Nichols, 4 Aug 1856 (5 Aug), A. Campbell JP 1-#568
Bertie Morgan to B. L. Adams q.v.
Brown Morgan to Ida Clark, 20 Mar 1897 (21 Mar), C.E. Moway JP, S.B. Fann W 2-130
C.A. Morgan to Margaret C. Land, 28 Oct 1877 (same), Calvin Morgan JP 1-#1519
C.B. Morgan to W. Housley q.v.
Caldonia Morgan to Lihugh Baker q.v.
Calvin A. Morgan to Sarah E. Davis, 29 Mar 1867 (same), Wm L. Hurmprey JP 1-#944
Clema Morgan to George Carter q.v.
Cordelia Morgan to J. H. Brady q.v.
Crate or Cate Morgan to G. W. Everett q.v.
D. A. Morgan to Charley James q.v.
Daniel Morgan to Clem Smith, 12 Ap 1884 (13 Ap), C. Morgan JP 1-480
David Morgan to Nancy Wiseman, 6 Feb 1855 (8 Feb), J. Whaley MG 1-#483
E. L. Morgan to James Winters q.v.
Edward Morgan to Marim(?) McKinley, 20 Aug 1890, M.C. Bruner MG 4-19
Emma Morgan to Robert Axmaker q.v.
Emma C. Morgan to W. L. Eblin q.v.
F.M. Morgan to Sarah E. Bouce, 24 Mar 1858 (1 Ap), Wm Morgan JP 1-#635
F.R. Morgan to Laura Pickett, 17 Aug 1868 (same), C. Morgan JP 1-#1025
Flora E. Morgan to George Ferman q.v.
G.B. Morgan to Ella Killough, 2 Aug 1884 (3 Aug), D. Richardson MG 1-466
G.T. Morgan to C.M. Pearson, 3 Feb 1861 (4 Feb), Wm A. Green JP 1-#743
George L. Morgan to Maggie V. Miller, 21 Ap 1888 (22 Ap), J.H. Parrott MG 1-547
George W. Morgan to Mary Snow, 3 Sep 1890, C.E. Mowrey JP 4-17
H.F. Morgan to L.J. Foust, 1 Jan 1880 (same), J.H. Perry MG 1-#1708
I. A. Morgan to W. W. Morgan q.v.
J.C. Morgan (22, Dayton) to Nanie(?) Brewer (18, McMinn Co), ? Sep 1882, J.A. Nicholson MG, E.(?)M. Hewell(?) & N.F. Morgan(?) W 4-2(14)
J.D. Morgan Jr. to Vesta Woodey, 10 Oct 1896 (11 Oct), W.S. Hale MG, J.B. Harre W 2-74
J.F. Morgan to Mattie Underwood, 19 Oct 1892, J.D. Winchester MG 4-53
J.H. Morgan to Ada I. Ewers, 12 Oct 1887 (13 Oct), Calvin Morgan JP 1-39
James Morgan to Ella Taylor, 9 Oct 1892, John F. Price MG 4-47
James C. Morgan to Sallie Massingale, 22 Dec 1895, W.A. Howard MG 4-87
James H. Morgan to Malind Chaddick, 12 Jan 1869 (same), Wm L. Humphrey JP 1-#1042
Jane Morgan to J. R. Hood q.v.
Jennie Morgan to James Oldham q.v.
John Morgan to Nelia Loyd, 3 May 1894, R. Knight JP 4-66
John Morgan to Sallie A. Brown, 13 Jan 1883 (14 Jan), J.F. Shaver MG 1-472
John D. Morgan to Mary Craton Elder, 11 Mar 1873 (same), A.P. Early MG 1-#1279
John W. Morgan to Martha Burwick, 23 Aug 1877 (same), Calvin Morgan JP 1-#1508
Joseph Morgan to Maggie E. Murry, 7 May 1893, Henry Morgan JP 4-57
Joseph A. Morgan to Julia Ann Burwick, 30 May 1878 (same), C. Morgan JP 1-#1560
Julie Morgan to Ace Neuman q.v.
Julia E. Morgan to Roby L. Rodgers q.v.
Julia A. Morgan to H. R. Abel q.v.
Kittie J. Morgan to Wilber B. Peak q.v.
L. A. Morgan to A. E. Crow q.v.
Laura J. Morgan to J. M. Nelson q.v.
Lennie Morgan to W. T. Bean q.v.
Lillie Morgan to W. J. Truex q.v.
Lillie Morgan to William Ellison q.v.
Louisa Morgan to James R. Burnett q.v.
Luther Morgan to Jane Swafford, 21 Nov 1898 (29 Nov), C.E. Munsey JP 2-345
Lydia Morgan to Watt Reid q.v.
M.A. Morgan (18, Ala) to Jennette Josephine Montgomery (18), 18 Sep 1881, W.S. Hale MG, Cornelius Morgan & Cliff Morgan W 4-2(19)
Mae Morgan to C. F. Dart q.v.
Maggie Morgan to Byrd Fann q.v.
Maggie L. Morgan to J. S. Burnett q.v.
Mary A. Morgan to John L. Bridgeman q.v.
Mary Ann Morgan to Theodore Flora(?) q.v.
Mary E. Morgan to John F. McPherson q.v.
Mary Elizabeth Morgan to T. M. Solomon q.v.
Mattie Morgan to J. D. Stansberry q.v.
Matilda Morgan to J. C. Byerly q.v.
Mintin Morgan to Thomas Shirley q.v.
Mollie Morgan to William D. Alexander q.v.
Nora Morgan to Douglass Aselinger q.v.
Nora Morgan to J. M. Price q.v.
Rolston Morgan to Ann Harrison, 13 Mar 1886, James Corvin MG 4-44
Rufus M. Morgan to Martha J. Bice, 16 June 1851 (7 July), E. McKenna JP 1-#341
Ruphus W. Morgan to Bettie Thompson, 28 Dec 1885 (31 Dec), C. Morgan JP 1-483
Sarah Morgan to Benjamin Fritts q.v.
Susan Morgan to Osiras Jordon q.v.
T.W. Morgan (28) to Nora Pass (22), 27 Dec 1881, W.W. Lowe JP, N.F. Morgan & J.G. Love W 4-5(46)
Tennie E. Morgan to W. E. Pass q.v.
Thomas Morgan to Lillie Hartbarger, 1 Feb 1894, F.M. Cook MG 4-63
Thomas C. Morgan to Manervia Swafford, 17 Aug 1867 (same), W.L. Humphrey JP 1-#965
Virginia C. Morgan to W. H. Varnell q.v.
W.H. Morgan to Lula Vinson, 21 Dec 1897 (22 Dec), W.A. Howard MG, J.H. Harrington W 2-227
W.W. Morgan to I.A. Morgan, 14 Dec 1876 (same), S. Green or Greer MG 1-#1477
Washington Morgan to Issabella McGoughy, 26 Feb 1859 (27 Feb), W.H. Bell MG 1-#687
Washington Morgan to Mahala Gothard, 5 Dec 1873 (same), W.L. Humphrey JP 1-#1316
William Morgan to Amanda J. Byerly, 1 Aug 1869 (no return) 1-#1107

William Morgan to Ibie Nichols, 23 Ap 1900 (same), no MG or JP, W.A. Morgan W 3-149
Z. A. Morgan to Oscar Barton q.v.

- - - - - - - - - - - - -

MORRELL / MERRELL

1870 CENSUS
Eldridge Merrell 42, Susan 37, Hester 13, Joseph 10, James 8 3-10-70
MARRIAGES
Hester Morrell to S. G. Breeden q.v.
J.R. Morrell (20) to Emily Hays (21, Greene Co), 26 Nov 1881, T.N. McPherson JP, J.C. Garrison & James Cunnyngham W 4-4(36)

- - - - - - - - - - - - -

MORRIS / MORRISS

1860 CENSUS
Isaac Morris 47, Ann E. 51, Manerva 20, Ephraim 17, Albert 15, Zachariah 13, Dicey A. 10, James 6 6-99-678
1870 CENSUS
Aaron Morris 45, Delila A. 43, Mary 19, Lucinda 17, John 16, William 14, James 12, Nancy 10, Amanda E. 8, Os--?--* (s) 5, Burt--?--* 2 (d) 1-20-134 [*ink blob over names]
Albert Morris 24, Elizabeth A. 23, Vesta Jane 1 1-3-20
Ann Morris 61 (NC), Luvisa 38, James 17 1-20-133
Lucinda Morris 60 (NC), Peter 23 (NC), Angeline 16 (NC), Jane 15 (Ga) 10-4-27
1880 CENSUS
Albert Morris 36, Elizabeth 33, Vesta 12, Amanda 3, Andrew 7/12 2-27-301
Isaac Morris 68, Eliza 72, James 26 12-2-16
1900 CENSUS
Catharine Morris 56 (Nov 1843-D 5-3)(Seamstress), Deliah 19 (Jan 1881), Samuel H. 18 (Mar 1882) 6-243B-76
Elias R. Morris 21: see James D. Rigsby
Mary Morris 45 (Unk-M 17-3-2), Jesse WOMAC 28 (boarder)(Dec 1871-D 0), Pheba HARMON 29 (boarder) (Ap 1871-T/Ga/T-M 14-1-0)(Cook, Private Home) 10-329B-197/210 (B)
Mathew M. Morris 45: see Jeff Thompson (B)
Peter T. Morris 63 (Feb 1837-NC/Unk/Va-M 28)(Furnaceman), Adaline 47 (Sep 1852-M 28-12-9), Annie 26 (July 1873-Wd 5-3), William I. 25 (Ap 1875)(Furnaceman), Charley F. 21 (Ap 1879)(Furnaceman), Jesse G. 19 (Nov 1880)(Furnaceman), James M. 17 (July 1882)(Furnaceman), Mozina 15 (June 1884), Henry W. 13 (July 1886), Julia 12 (Ap 1888), George A. 9 (gs)(June 1890-NC), Gracie F. 8 (gd)(Jan 1892-NC), Fred L. 2 (gs)(Ap 1898-NC) 10-330A-209/222 (B)
MARRIAGES
Anna Morris to George Logan q.v.
Annie Morris to Thomas Fuller q.v.
Albert Morris to Elizabeth A. Collins, 6 May 1866 (same), W.W. Low JP 1-#1069
Cora Morris to H. S. Darby q.v.
George Morris to S.A. Thompson, 17 Sep 1899, G.W. Reed MG 4-101
I.E. Morris to Eliza Garrison, 1 Mar 1889 (5 Mar), C.R. Riggs MG 1-569
Isaac Morris to Nancy Broke, 8 Jan 1891, L.L. Barton JP 4-22
Vesta Jane Morriss to J. H. Garrison q.v.
Zachariah T. Morris to Sarah E. Monday, 11 Sep 1868 (same), Edward Pyott JP 1-#1064

- - - - - - - - - - - - -

MORRISON

1880 CENSUS
F.M. Morrison 40 (Editor), W.C. 30, L.E. 12 (d), F.E. 6 (d), Gertrude 6/12 8-4-36
M.S. Morrison 36 (Editor), Catharine 28, Charles 3, Albert 10/12, F.H. ABEL 19 (boarder)(Clerk in Dry Goods Store) 8-1-10
1900 CENSUS
Francis M. Morrison 60 (Jan 1840-M 33)(Newspaper Editor), Winniva C. 58 (Jan 1842-M 33-6-3), Gertrude 20 (Nov 1879-Kan)(Dry Goods Saleslady) 8-315B-106/110
John Morrison 38 (Mar 1862-Ga/NC/NC-M 7), Nellie C. 27 (June 1872-T/SC/T-M 7-4-4), Thomas F. 6 (Aug 1893), Lee B. 5 (Feb 1895), Mandy M. 3 (Mar 1897), Samuel W. 1 (Aug 1898) 13-296B-125/127
Marquis Morrison 56 (Jan 1844-M 23)(Boarding House Keeper), Katharine 40 (Sep 1859-M 23-9-9), Alberta 20 (Aug 1879), Walter 18 (Nov 1881), Ethel 16 (Jan 1884), Lula 14 (Jan 1886), Marcus 12 (Jan 1888), Emmet 10 (May 1890), Thomas 5 (Nov 1894), Garrett 2 (Dec 1897); _Boarders:_ John R. JONES 30 (Feb 1870-Oh/Wales/Do)(Saloon Keeper), Ike HOLLOMAN 40 (Mar 1860-Wd)(Saloon Bartender), Nicholas McCABE 31 (Dec 1868-T/Ireland/T-Wd)(RR Section Foreman), Marshal WALLER 19 (May 1881), Robert KENT 20 (Mar 1880-WVa/WVa/WVa), Alvis LOCKEY 28 (Jan 1872-M 0)(Carpenter), Ida LOCKEY 24 (Jan 1876-T/T/Germany-M 0-0) 10-320B-3
Mary C. Morrison 51 (May 1849-Iowa/T/T-D 6-3), Nettie 19 (Feb 1881-Kan/Oh/Iowa)(School Teacher), Mary SHARP 85 (m)(Nov 1814-T/SC/SC-Wd 3-2) 13-309A-363/376
MARRIAGES
Alexander Morrison to Sary E. Robertson, 8 Nov 1863 (no return) 1-#809
Florence E. Morrison to Will Robeson q.v.
James Morrison to T.M.A. Thompson, 6 Jan 1873 (same), L. Moon MG 1-#1269
Laura Morrison to Charles V. Bronson q.v.
Nettie Morrison to E. B. Melendy q.v.
Pink Morrison to W. L. Locke q.v.
William Morrison to Josie Boyd, 18 Jan 1890 (19 Jan), R.S. Mason JP 1-598

- - - - - - - - - - - - -

MORTON

1900 CENSUS
James B. Morton 36 (Ap 1864-M 9)(Carpenter), Minnie E. 26 (Nov 1873-T/Ind/T-M 9-5-1), Ruth A. 1 (Oct 1898), John F. 40 (b)(Oct 1859-M 0)(Carpenter), Sarah E. 20 (sil)(Dec 1879-T/Ky/Ky-M 0-0) 13-309A-366/379

MARRIAGE

J.F. Morton to S.C. Thomas, 4 May 1900 (same), W.R. Grimsley MG, J.W. Morton W 3-152

- - - - - - - - - - - - -

MOSELEY

MARRIAGE

Luke Moseley to Margaret Jones, 15 Aug 1888 (25 Aug), J.B. Phillips MG 1-553

- - - - - - - - - - - - -

MOSES

1900 CENSUS

Hanna(?) Moses 70 (Jan 1820-Wd), Marthy 30 (gd)(Ap 1870), Willie 7 (gs)(Mar 1890) 1-185A-122/128

Jess Moses 32 (May 1868-M 16), Liliea 31 (Mar 1869-T/Ga/Ga-M 16-8-8), Harris 4 (Sep 1885), Bob 13 (Mar 1887), Anderson 11 (Jan 1889), Barbie 8 (June 1891), Violia 7 (Ap 1893), Miny 5 (May 1895), Mary L. 3 (Ap 1897), Texas (Ap 1899) 7-266A-302/307

- - - - - - - - - - - - -

MOSIER

MARRIAGE

J.M. Mosier to Alice McClendon, 4 Dec 1897 (5 Dec), R.J. Garbet or Goslit MG, J.F. Parham(?) & R.J. Killough W 2-220

- - - - - - - - - - - - -

MOSS

1860 CENSUS

Charles W. Moss 40: see Mary A. Johnson

1870 CENSUS

James M. Moss 25, Eliza Jane 25, Margarett E. 2 1-8-49

1880 CENSUS– None

1900 CENSUS

Thomas G. Moss 52 (Oct 1847-T/SC/T-M 27), Josie M. 46 (Sep 1853-M 27-11-9), Rebecca A. 22 (Feb 1878), Pearl E. 20 (Feb 1880), Oscar C. 17 (Ap 1883), Edgar E. 14 (Dec 1885), Charles G. 10 (Aug 1889), Bronci J. 7 (Aug 1892), Nellie J. 4 (Sep 1895), John WALKER (B) 14 (Unk 1886)(Servant) 3-209A-157/171

MARRIAGES

J.P. Moss to Jennie Bell, 21 Dec 1888 (25 Dec), W.R. Clack JP 1-565

Linn Moss to Henry Bowers q.v.

- - - - - - - - - - - - -

MOULTON / MOLTON

1860 CENSUS

John P. Moulton 25, Mary 24, Farly N. 1/12 2-70-478

1870 and 1880 CENSUS– None

1900 CENSUS

Elic Molton 31 (May 1869-T/Va/T-M 13), Matilda 31 (Feb 1869-M 13-6-4), Lealer 8 (Jan 1892), Elic F. 5 (June 1894), Cary 2 (Aug 1897), Cleo J. 8/12 (Oct 1899), Griffin SUTTLES 21 (boarder)(Jan 1879) 7-265B-298/303

Newton F. Moulton 40 (May 1860-Wd 4-4), Stella M. 15 (Jan 1885), Maggie M. 13 (Dec 1886), Eula L. 10 (Aug 1889), Bessie M. 8 (Feb 1892) 14-214A-24/25

Smith Moulton 27 (Aug 1872-M 1), Sydnah A. 28 (Jan 1872-M 1-1-1), Helen 9/12 (Aug 1899) 14-213B-17/18

MARRIAGES

John P. Moulton to Mary Brady, 21 Aug 1857 (27 Aug), Math Barnett MG 1-#610

Smythe B. Moulton to Snyda McPherson, 22 Aug 1899, R.A. Dickson JP 4-101

- - - - - - - - - - - - -

MOWREY / MOWRY / MAURY / MOREY

1900 CENSUS

Charles E. Mowrey 65 (Oct 1834-NY/Mass/Ver-M 43), Nancy E. 59 (Nov 1840-NY/NY/NY-M 43-7-5) 11-291B-44

Gertrude Morey 17: see Charles W. Irwin

Henry Mowry or Moury 26 (Dec 1873-Mich/Mich/NY-M 4)(Coal Miner), Ethel 22 (May 1878-M 4-1-1), Gladdis 3 (Mar 1897), James WINSETT 20 (bl)(Aug 1879) (Coal Miner) 8-282A-268/270

Matthew Maury 39 (June 1860-Ky/Ky/Ky-M 7)(General Manager, --?--)[ink blob], Anna L. 34 (June 1865-Va/Va/Va-M 7-0), Rebecca ANDERSON (B) 50 (Unk 1850-Va/Va/Va)(Servant) 8-287B-391/393

- - - - - - - - - - - - -

MOYERS– see MYERS

- - - - - - - - - - - - -

MUENCH

1900 CENSUS

Theodore Muench 44 (Feb 1856-Ind/Germany/Do-M 16) (Deputy County Trustee), Libbie 36 (Ap 1864-Ind/Ind/Ind-M 16-1-1), Salla 10 (May 1890) 10-327B-160/169

- - - - - - - - - - - - -

MULOY

1900 CENSUS

Kattie Muloy(?) 45 (Feb 1855-Wd 4-4), Frank 17 (May 1883), Mandy 16 (Mar 1884), Walter 12 (Aug 1887), Henry 9 (Ap 1891) 7-266B-315/320

- - - - - - - - - - - - -

MULKEY / MULKY

1880 CENSUS

Jonathan Mulky 39, Elizabeth J. 30, James R. 16 10-26-197/202

MARRIAGE

Jonathan Mulkey (32, Gilmore Co, Va) to H. Revis (26), 1 Oct 1882, J.A. Crawford JP, Get(?) Gaise(?) & Abe Powell(?) W 4-10(100)

- - - - - - - - - - - - -

MULLENIX

1900 CENSUS
Arthur Mullenix 12: see Vaughn Crow

- - - - - - - - - - - - -

MULLENS

1880 CENSUS
Archibald Mullens 33, Martha 16, Sissie 8, Joseph 6, Elizabeth 3 1-12-98

- - - - - - - - - - - - -

MURAT

1880 CENSUS
Luke Murat 45, L.J. 33, A.M. 10, C. 6, S.S. 5, S.A. 1, Sidney HOUSTON 20 3-18-141 (B)(Mu)

- - - - - - - - - - - - -

MURPHY / MURPHEY

1860 CENSUS
John B. Murphy 65 (NC)(Blacksmith), Lucy R. 6, Permelia J. PETERSON 31, Samuel BLEVINS 27 (Blacksmith), Malinda E. 25, Lucy A. 4, John M. 2 6-112-766
Samuel M. Murphey 37 (Blacksmith), Jane 19, Gustavas 16, John 14, Tennessee 12, Margaret 11, Mountaville 7 6-102-693
1870 CENSUS
Gustavus Murphy 25, Sarah 22 6-5-29
1880 CENSUS
Gus Murphey 35, S.E. 30, L.M. 10 (d), G.W. 6 (s), C.A. 4 (d), J.T. 2 (s) 3-14-111
William Murphy 30 (RR Laborer), Malinda C. 22 6-19-173/177
1900 CENSUS
Jane Murphy 65 (Feb 1835-NC/NC/NC-Wd 5-2)(Washwoman), Mamis 30 (s)(Ap 1870-T/NC/NC)(RR Hand), Martha 25 (d)(Mar 1875), Blain 20 (gs)(May 1880), Harison 7 (gs)(Jan 1893) 1-187A-159/167 (B)
William Murphy 60 (Unk 1840-Ireland/Do/Do-1873/26/Na-M 21), Sary 43 (Sep 1857-Ga/Ga/Ga-M 21-8-7), William R. 19 (Nov 1880), Dellie 16 (Jan 1884), Brigett 14 (Jan 1886), Ellen 12 (Sep 1887), Mary 9 (May 1891), Gertrude 6 (July 1893), Landun 4 (May 1896), George TROTTER 17 (lodger)(Unk) 10-260B-204/209
MARRIAGES
Benjamin Murphey to Mary Montgomery, 2 Oct 1851 (same), W.H. Cunnyngham JP 1-#351
G.G. Murphy to Sarah Smith, 8 May 1869 (9 May), T.N.L. Cunnyngham JP 1-#1059
Malinda Murphy to S.L. Blevins q.v.
Nancy Murphey to Samuel Travis q.v.
Nettie Murphey to Crawford Johnson q.v.
Tennessee Murphy to A. J. Henry q.v.
W.A. Murphy to Sarah J. Wisemer, 24 Nov 1877 (25 Nov), Rich Holland MG 1-#1527
William Murphey to Sally Gravett, 29 Dec 1879 (same), B. F. Ziegler JP 1-#1701

- - - - - - - - - - - - -

MURRY / MURRAY

1900 CENSUS
Isaac Murry 42: see Bird Clay (B)
Isaac Murrey 43 (July 1856-Ga/Ga/Ga-M 20)(RR Laborer), Kate 40 (Jan 1860-Ga/Ga/Ga-M 20-7-6), Willie 14 (Oct 1885), Isaac M. 10 (July 1889), Lonnie 8 (Dec 1891), Grover C. 6 (Oct 1893), Pearl BRIDGMAN 19 (d)(Feb 1881-Ga-M 0-0-0), Samuel 24 (sl)(Dec 1875-M 0)(Coal Miner) 14-215B-49/50 (B)
MARRIAGES
Beckey Murry to John Beasley q.v.
J. D. Murry to Henry Crawford q.v.
Maggie E. Murry to Joseph Morgan q.v.
Pearl Murry to Samuel Bridgeman q.v.

- - - - - - - - - - - - -

MUSSINGTON

1900 CENSUS
George Mussington 38 (Nov 1861-Jamaca, West Indies/Do/Do-1870/29/Na-M 4)(Minister), Annie 23 (Jan 1877-Va/Va/Va-M 4-2-2), Selina 3 (Aug 1896-Va), George T. 1 (May 1899-Va) 10-326A-125/129 (B)

- - - - - - - - - - - - -

MYERS / MYRES / MEYERS / MAYERS / MOYER / MOYERS

1860 CENSUS
Calvin Myers 27, Rachel 21, William 4, John T. 3 6-103-704
Lesly Myers 52, Mary 30, Rachel C. 16, Christopher 14, Angaline 12, Noah 8, Joseph 1 8-18-120 [Lesley Myres married Mary Gregory on 24 Nov 1857 in Meigs Co]
Wiley Myers 50, Sarah 41, Joseph 22 (Clerk), Mathus A. 20, Mary J. 17, Sarah P. 15, Casander 12, Nancy K. 9, Rufus L. 9, Robert R. 7, Elizabeth N. 5, John T. 3, Addison B. 1 8-19-129
William Myers 42 (Pa), Nancy 33 (Va), George 18, Mary 14, Abigail 12, Catharine 9, William 8, Susan 6, Alexander 2, Samuel 4/12 8-17-119
1870 CENSUS
Lesley Myers 58, Mary 40, Joseph C. 12, Richard L. 10, Zarilda L. 6, Catharine T. 3 8-20-139
Nancy Moyers 70: see John Couch
Rachel Myers 35, William 16, John 14 6-12-82
William M. Meyers 59, Sarah 50, Mary J. 28, Sarah P. 24, Nancy K. 19, Rufus S. 19, Robert R. 17, Elizabeth E. 16, John T. 12, Albion B. 11 3-15-07
1880 CENSUS
C.C. Myers 32, M. 38 (w), J.R. 12 (s), W.T. 7 (s), S.J. 4 (d), D.E. 3/12 (d) 8-7-60
David Meyer 38, S.M. 33 (w), C.C. 10 (d), A.J. 6 (d), E. 4 (s) 4-11-88
M. Mayers 50, Sarah 17, S.A. 18 (d), Tennie 13 (d), George 7, Sarah GREGORY 55 (si), Suider 37 (si) 8-15-126
Wm R. Moyer 45, E.C. 37 (w), Sam 21, J.S. 18 (s), W.H. 17 (s), M.M. 14 (d), J.R. 11 (s), C.H. 10 (s) 8-15-130

1900 CENSUS

Columbia H. Myers 36 (Oct 1863-M 14), Mattie J. 36 (Dec 1863-T/NC/NC-M 14-3-3), Samuel 13 (Aug 1886), Vesta 10 (Oct 1889), Charles 7 (July 1892), Edward BROWN 16 (boarder)(Aug 1883) 13-300B-199/206

David Moyer 58 (Jan 1842-Pa/Pa/Pa-M 34), Sarah M. 54 (May 1846-Oh/Pa/Pa-M 34-3-3), Adelia N. 25 (Sep 1874), Iva N. 18 (Feb 1882), Harry M. 17 (Mar 1883) 14-222B-177/181

Homer L. Meyers 22 (Aug 1877-Ky/Ky/Ky-M 0)(Dentist), Nina 17 (Aug 1882-Oh/Ind/Ind-M 0-0-0) 10-331B-238/253

James Myers 39 (Mar 1861-T/T/NC-M 19), Belle 38 (Aug 1861-M 19-7-7), Anna E. 16 (Nov 1883), Martha 14 (Mar 1886), Darthulah 10 (Dec 1889), Arvie Caroline 8 (Jan 1892), Polly L. 5 (Feb 1895), Alice Udiana 10/12 (July 1899), Aster POWERS 17 (boarder)(Mar 1883) 13-297B-148/151

Noah Myers 51 (Mar 1849-M 25), Cynthia E. 46 (Dec 1853-M 25), Julia A. 16 (June 1883), Minnie E. 11 (June 1888), Flossie M. 8 (Sep 1891) 11-293A-74

Patrick D. Myers 68 (Oct 1831-M 48)(Jeweler), Martha J. 65 (Nov 1834-M 48-11-10), Cora B. 27 (Oct 1872) (School Teacher), Stella May 20 (Dec 1879)(School Teacher) 13-308B-359/372

Ray V. Meyers 31 (Mar 1869-Oh/Pa/Oh)(Mining Engineer) 10-331B-241/256

Thomas J. Myers 25: see Louis A. Blake

William C. Myers 23 (Feb 1877-M 4)(Coal Miner), Cordelia 20 (July 1879-M 4-2-1), Oscar H. 3 (Sep 1896), John F. 25 (b)(May 1875)(Coal Miner), G. Earnest 21 (b) (Mar 1879)(Coal Miner) 13-300A-183/188

William M. Myers 44 (Oct 1855-T/T/NC-M 12), Mary S. 24 (Dec 1875-M 12-0) 5-232A-79

William R. Myers 63 (Aug 1836-M 43), Elizabeth C. 57 (July 1842-NC/NC/NC-M 43-8-6), John CANTRELL 56 (bl)(Mar 1844-NC/NC/SC-Wd) 13-297B-149/152

MARRIAGES

Abigal Myres to William Tolsten q.v.

Angeline Myres to Nathaniel Hoges q.v.

Ann E. Moyers to John H. Keith q.v.

Catharine Moyers to John Couch q.v.

Catharine T. Myres to Luther Parker q.v.

E. B. Moyers to R. M. Foust q.v.

Ester Myers to Leonard Weller q.v.

Fannie Myers to John D. Olinger q.v.

J.R. Myres to Anney Thompson, 3 Dec 1891, W.G. Curton MG 4-34

Jacob Myres to Sarah E. Mitchell, 13 Mar 1867 (same), L.M. Renfro MG 1-#943

M.A. Moyers to J.C. Keith, 18 Sep 1867 (same), Heil Buttram MG 1-#970

Maggie Meyers to James Harrod q.v.

Martha Myers to Darth Webb q.v.

Mary A. Myers to A. P. Carter q.v.

Noah Myers to Syntha McPherson, 4 Mar 1875 (same), Calvin Morgan JP 1-#1395

R.L. Myers or Majors to Mary Rose, 2 June 1892, W.R. Grimsley MG 4-38

Samuel H. Myres to Susannah Cline, 18 July 1866 (same), J.W. Williamson MG 1-#904

William M. Myers to Mary S. Harvester, 20 Feb 1887, Jas Corvin MG 4-46

W.N. Myers to Julia Moon, 2 Mar 1881 (6 Mar), W.S. Hale MG 1-297

William C. Myres to M.A.R. Woody, 1 Oct 1853 (same), S.R. Hackett JP 1-#425

- - - - - - - - - - - - -

MYERSON

MARRIAGE

J.A. Myerson to Susan E. Swafford, 17 May 1876 (18 May), Calvin Morgan JP 1-#1444

- - - - - - - - - - - - -

MYNATT / MYNOTT

1860 CENSUS

John R. Mynatt 25, Susannah 27, James B. 2, Preston 21: see William Snelson

Lenville Mynott 24 (Day Laborer), Jemima A. 27, Martha C. 7/12 1-89-608

1870 and 1880 CENSUS– None

1900 CENSUS

Barton K. Mynatt 75 (Mar 1825-M 43)(Physician), Mary E. 71 (Jan 1829-M 43-3-1), Samuel C. 42 (Aug 1857) 6-244A-84

MARRIAGES

B.K. Mynatt to Mary E. Frazier, 14 Ap 1857 (15 Ap), W.H. Bell MG 1-#595

John R. Mynott to Susanah Johnson, 7 July 1855 (8 July), A.D. Paul JP 1-#508

Willie(?) Mynott to E. A. Lowry q.v.

- - - - - - - - - - - - -

NAIL

1900 CENSUS

Charles C. Nail 25 (Oct 1874-M 4)(Coal Miner), Lizzie B. 23 (Jan 1877-M 4-3-2), Charles C. Jr. 2 (Oct 1897), infant 1 (s)(Mar 1899) 13-305A-284/294

Robinson Nail 52 (Oct 1847-M 26)(Carpenter), Belle M. 44 (Aug 1855-T/NC/T-M 26-12-7), John G. 23 (Jan 1877), Eva B. 17 (Aug 1882-Tex), Gertrude J. 14 (May 1886), Abraham L. 11 (Ap 1889), Raleigh D. 9 (Jan 1891) 13-305A-282/292

MARRIAGES

Charles C. Nail to Bell Green, 19 Jan 1896, W.R. Grimsley MG 4-93

Lillie Nail to Henegar Jordan q.v.

Lillis Nail to W. A. Davis q.v.

- - - - - - - - - - - - -

NANCE

MARRIAGE

Annie Nance to G. M. Scott q.v.

- - - - - - - - - - - - -

NANNY / NANNEY

1860 CENSUS

James T. Nanny 43 (NC)(Blacksmith), Orlena 43, Mary C. 14, Ruehany 11, William 6, Pulaski 4, Richard HACKER 17 6-110-754

1870 CENSUS

James T. Nanny 54 (NC), Orlena 53, Ruhanna J. 23, William T. 16, Pulaski 12, Nicholas NANNY 80 (NC) 6-8-51

1880 CENSUS

Orlena Nanney 61, Pullaski 23, Mary C. HENRY 33, America P. 14, Malinda 11, John H. 9, Elizbeth 3 6-23-18 (High Street, Washington)

MARRIAGES

Mary Nanny to James Henry q.v.

Ruhana Nanny to John N. Howard q.v.

- - - - - - - - - - - - -

NASE

1880 CENSUS

Godfre Nase 31, M.N. 24 (w) 8-21-178

Isaac Nase 47, N.C. 49, Suda 24, John 20, Nela 13, Willie 9 9-21-179

- - - - - - - - - - - - -

NASH

1860 CENSUS

James Nash 35, Nancy C. 39, John W. 7, William J. 6, Thomas P. 4, James H. 1, William 10, Sarah H. GREEN 35, Jane GREEN 31 8-16-109

Margaret L. Nash 16: see William A. Graham

Rebecca Nash 8: see William Graham

1870 CENSUS– None

1880 CENSUS

John Nash 14, Samuel 12: see William Wyrick

1900 CENSUS

John W. Nash 45 (Unk 1853-M 22), Effie 40 (Jan 1860-Iowa/Pa/Ind-M 22-8-7), Nettie 17 (Mar 1883-Mo), James L. 14 (Aug 1885-Mo), William 11 (June 1888-Mo), John T. 8 (June 1891-Mo), Efie 3 (Aug 1896), George E. 11/12 (June 1899) 8-279A-218/220

Thomas Nash 43 (May 1857-M 3), Sally 39 (Mar 1861-Ky/T/T-M 3-2-2), Robert 12 (Jan 1888), Henry GARDENHIRE 15 (July 1884)(Coal Miner), May NASH 19 (ne)(June 1880) 8-280A-232/234

MARRIAGES

James M. Nash to Nancy Green, 16 Dec 1851 (same), E. McKinery JP 1-#356

May Nash to T. H. Ferguson q.v.

Nettie Nash to Joseph Lively q.v.

Rachel Nash to John McColpin q.v.

T.J. Nash to S.E. Alexander, 2 July 1883 (5 July), D. Richardson MG 1-477

T.J. Nash to Sarah E. Walker, 30 Sep 1897 (bond only), W.R. Walker W 2-191

W.J. Nash to L.L. Rush, 20 Oct 1891, W.A. Green JP 4-30

- - - - - - - - - - - - -

NATHAN

1880 CENSUS

H. M. Nathan 35: see J. H. Rogers

- - - - - - - - - - - - -

NEAL / NEIL / NEELE

1860 CENSUS

Calvin Neil 20 (NC), Manerva 17 4-43-289

Eliza J. Neil 29, Eglentine 11, Mary Ann 8, Sterling 10: see George W. Wallace

Margaret Neele 17: see Robert Ferguson

1870 CENSUS

Calvin Neal 32, Minerva 23, John R. 7, Sarah M. 4, Susan A. 3, James H. 2 3-6-40

James Neal 64, Elizabeth 56 (NC), Sarah 34, Madison 15 4-13-84

Leander Neal 40 (NC)(Blacksmith), Susan 43 (NC), James 21 (Ga), Ellender 18 (Ga), Eli Thomas 16 (Ga), George W. 10 (Ga), Nancy A. 8 (Ga), William 2 6-16-114

Mitchel Neal 24, Rebecca A. 21, Susan E. 3, Mary Ann 7/12 4-13-83

William W. Neal 45 (Preacher), Susan L. 38, William W. 13, Permelia G. 17, John S.P. 10, Francis H. 7, Thena L.L. 4 2-6-36

1880 CENSUS

Calvin Neal 42, M.A. 40, J.R. 17 (s), S.M. 16 (d), S.A. 17 (d), J.H. 14 (s), C.L. 9 (s), W.C. 8 (s), C.F. 7 (d), M.L. 5 (d), W.F. 5/12 (d) 4-31-253

John Neal 41 (Lawyer), Mary 38, Amanda 9, Permelia 7, John 5, Nora 3, George 1, Mary ADKINS (Mu) 29 (Servant, Milk Maid), Mary DARWIN (Mu) 18 (Servant, Cook) 2-24-193

Sarah Neal 12: see Nath Harrison

Susan Neal 49, John 21 (Lawyer), Franklin 19 (Printer), Theona 15, Mary COX (Mu) 21 (Servant, Cook), Minnie (Mu) 5, Lula (Mu) 1, John ABERNATHY 30 (sl) (Merchant), Permelia 27 (d), Carrie 8, Young 6, John 4, Wallace 2 2-21-172

1900 CENSUS

Addie R. Neal 21 (Ap 1879-S)(Housekeeper), Jean B. WILSON 10 (Oct 1889), Hazen S. 6 (Dec 1893), Hattie M. 4 (June 1895) 14-219B-135/138

Christopher Neal 30 (Nov 1871-M 5), Lena T. 20 (June 1879-T/Oh/Oh-M 5-2-2), Alta A. 2 (Oct 1897), Cora A. 7/12 (Oct 1899), Samuel WIBEL 42 (boarder, visitor)(Dec 1857-Ind/Pa/Pa) 4-227B-277/281)(Road on line between 3rd & 4th Districts)

G. Calvin Neal 61 (Jan 1839-NC/NC/NC-M 44), Manervia F. 60 (Jan 1840-M 44-12-10), Manary E. 17 (d)(June 1882), Laura A. 11 (gd)(June 1888) 3-200A-3/3

John Neal 28 (June 1871-Ga/SC/SC-M 8)(Station Fireman), Sally 26 (July 1873-Ga/Ga/SC-M 8-2-1), Oscar W. 4 (Oct 1895-Ga), Bulah IVESTER 17 (Sep 1882)(Servant) 8-282A-265/267

John Neal 19: see Rosa Wade (B)

John R. Neal 39 (Dec 1860-T/NC/T-M 15), Martha L. 28 (May 1872-T/Va/?-M 15-8-6), Rinda 12 (Nov 1887), Franklin 10 (Nov 1889), Charles F. 9 (Feb 1891), Ella

May 7 (June 1893)[marked through, probably dead], James I. 5 (Aug 1894), Ernest F. 3 (Aug 1896), Albert M. 2 (May 1898) 3-200A-1/1

Low M. Neal 50 (Feb 1850-T/NC/NC-M 22), Lucinda 43 (Feb 1857-T/T/Va-M 22-9-8), Samuel E. 23 (May 1877-M 0), Rosa E. 17 (dl)(Aug 1882-M 0-0), Granville C. 18 (Jan 1882), Frederick 15 (Mar 1885), William 12 (Nov 1887), Phoeba J. 9 (Oct 1890), Robert 7 (Ap 1893), Lida M. (July 1897) 4-225A-224/228 (Back Valley Road)

Meredith A. Neal 29 (Aug 1870-T/NC/Ga-M 11)(Coal Miner), Mary J. 27 (June 1872-Ga/Ga/Ga-M 11-5-3), William A. 9 (June 1890-Ga), Lillie A. 8 (Feb 1892), Earnest W. 1 (Mar 1899) 13-301A-207/215

Phoeba Neal 18: see John S. Hardin

Sarah Neal 23 (Dec 1876-D 4-2), Lula 6 (June 1893-T/Ga/T), Stella 2 (Feb 1898) 3-205A-87/95

Tullock Neal 50 (Mar 1850-T/NC/NC-M 23), Margaret 49 (Aug 1850-M 23-2-2), Floyd M. 21 (Jan 1879), Reese M. 11 (Dec 1888) 14-223A-187/191

W. Calvin Neal 27 (Dec 1872-T/NC/T-M 2), Eliza E. 18 (Mar 1882-T/T/Va-M 2-1-1), Tennie M. 1 (Ap 1899) 3-200A-4/4

MARRIAGES

Amanda B. Neal to W. E. Wheelock q.v.

C.L. Neal to Lena(?) Knight, 23 Jan 1895, E.A. Lowrey ?? 4-83

Caroline Neal to J. T. Hughes q.v.

Emma Neal to J. F. McCullough q.v.

Fanny J. Neal to Samuel Wyrick q.v.

Ida Neal to J. H. Wilson q.v.

John T. Neal to Mattie Perry, 1 Sep 1886 (same), M. F. Moore ?? 1-509

Maggie L. Neal to Harrison E. Lewis q.v.

Malica Neal to William Tefferteller q.v.

Nancy Neal to Ed Millen q.v.

Nancy Neal to Samuel Holmes q.v.

Permelia Neal to John A. Abbernathy q.v.

Polly Ann Neal to Robert Furgusson q.v.

Rachel L. Neal to Elisha A. Thurman q.v.

S. B. Neal to J. W. Pelfrey q.v.

Samuel Neal to Rosie Stinner, 25 Dec 1899, R.M. Trentham JP 4-105

Sarah Neal to Franklin Henderson q.v.

Sarah R. Neal to J. D. Duckworth q.v.

Susan Neal to Riley Gosset q.v.

Tennie Neal to Van Thurman q.v.

Theona L. Neal to George L. Colyar q.v.

W.T. Neal to Margaret Acuff, 12 Dec 1890, W.G. Mitchell JP 4-33

W.W. Neal to Virginia Abernathy, 29 Nov 1880 (30 Nov), J.R. Hixon MG 1-293

\- - - - - - - - - - - - -

NECLING

1880 CENSUS

Martin Necling 35 (Miner), Mary 29, John 12, Henry 10, Lucy 8, Perlina 6, Jane 1/12 2-31-252

\- - - - - - - - - - - - -

NEELY

MARRIAGE

William Neely to Eliza Smith, 17 Jan 1890 (19 Jan), W.R. Clack JP 1-597

\- - - - - - - - - - - - -

NELSON

1860 CENSUS

Andrew J. Nelson 31 (NC), Elizabeth 31, Samuel R. 8, Mary K. 1 8-14-96

1870 CENSUS– None

1880 CENSUS

E. Nelson 88: see Thomas Doud

1900 CENSUS

Charles Nelson 25 (Feb 1875-M 1), Emma 25 (Ap 1875-M 1-6-4), Dallie FURBANKS 10 (sd) (May 1890), Charles 9 (ss)(Unk 1891), Earnest 7 (ss)(Mar 1893), Oscar 3 (ss)(Sep 1896) 15-271B-68

Charles Nelson 56 (Feb 1844-SC/Va/SC-M 19), Bettie 49 (Ap 1851-SC/SC/Va-M 19-0-0) 8-321B-34/36 (B)

James M. Nelson 51 (Sep 1848-Oh/Oh/Oh-M 5), Laura J. 44 (Ap 1856-Ga/T/Ga-M 5-0)(Hotel Keeper), John R. 10 (Mar 1890), Mabel 7 (Oct 1892), Addie COULTER (B) 19 (Ap 1887)(Servant), James WILLIAMS 26 (boarder)(Ap 1874)(Bookkeeper) 13-299B-178/183

John C. Nelson 64 (June 1835-M 41)(Mining Engineer), Louisa 62 (Feb 1838-M 41-6-4), Samuel 34 (Jan 1866), Louisa 2[illegible] (Mar 1871), Ralph A. 9 (gs)(Dec 1891) 10-326A-127/131

William Nelson 54 (Nov 1845-Ga/Ga/Ga-M 37), Amanda 45 (Unk 1855-Ga/NC/NC-M 37-7-5), Margaret 21 (Feb 1879-Ga), Drew F. 20 (Feb 1880-Ga)(Miner), Thomas 18 (Aug 1881)(Miner), Julia 10 (June 1889) 8-281B-257/259

MARRIAGES

Albert Nelson to Polly Phillips, 4 Jan 1890 (5 Jan), J.M. Bramlett MG 1-594

Charley Nelson to Emma Fairbanks, 6 May 1899 (7 May), F.M. Cook MG, C. Goins W 2-408

J.M. Nelson to Laura J. Morgan, 19 Sep 1895, J.A. Whitner MG 4-85

James Nelson (23, Meigs Co) to Margaret Eakins (23, Meigs Co), 4 Aug 1881, M.L. Abbott JP, B.F. Johnson, C.G. Riddle [*], D.S. Allison[*], & S.B. Robertson W 4-1(4) & 4-7(64) [* both signed by X]

Mary Nelson to S. D. Rudd q.v.

Mary A. Nelson to J. A. England q.v.

Mary E. Nelson to C. C. Jones q.v.

Mary S. A. Nelson to Thomas Stewart q.v.

\- - - - - - - - - - - - -

NESTOR

1900 CENSUS

Hillary Nestor 44 (Mar 1856-WVa/WVa/WVa-M 14)(Piano Dealer), Mary A. 38 (Aug 1867-M 14-3-3), French 21 (Oct 1878-WVa)(Piano Dealer), Maysell 13 (Dec 1886), Fred H. 11 (Aug 1888) 14-215A-44/45

\- - - - - - - - - - - - -

NEUBY / NEWBY / NUSBY

1900 CENSUS

Elisha A. Neuby 48 (Mar 1852-M 8), Martha A. 44 (May 1856-M 8-4-3), Emily R. 22 (Nov 1877), Abie E. 6 (Nov 1893), Netie A. 5 (Sep 1894), George W. 2 (July 1897) 14-223A-196/200

Fayet C. Neuby 33 (May 1867-M 11), Martha J. 28 (Ap 1878-M 11-4-4), Alta J. 9 (July 1880), Hattie L. 6 (Sep 1893), Rebecca A. 5 (Feb 1895), Clyde M. 2 (Jan 1898) 14-223A-197/201

James F. Neuby 49 (Feb 1851-M 23), Rosa J. 41 (Dec 1858-M 23-13-8), Mary R. 21 (Nov 1878), John A. 17 (Feb 1882), Cora E. 15 (Aug 1884), George W. 13 (Oct 1886), Eliza E. 9 (Oct 1890), Lloyd J. 7 (Jan 1893), Perry E. 5 (Aug 1894), Thomas E. 3 (Feb 1897) 14-223B-200/204

Reiley N. Neuby 46 (Ap 1854-Wd), George F. 14 (June 1886), John R. 11 (Aug 1888) 14-223A-199/203

Robinson Neuby 50 (Nov 1849-M 25), Frances C. 49 (Ap 1851-T/SC/SC-M 25-10-7), Frank W. 24 (Ap 1876), James M. 21 (Nov 1878), Elisha T. 19 (May 1881), Mary J. 14 (Ap 1886), Louella S. 12 (Ap 1888), Eliza E. 7 (June 1892), Charles F. 4 (Mar 1896) 14-223A-198/202

MARRIAGES

Charles F. Newby to Martha J. Burditt, 12 Sep 1889, R.A. Dickson JP 4-63

Elisha A. Nusby to Martha A. Burdett, 14 Aug 1892, R.A. Dickson JP 4-51

Martha J. Newby to Addison A. Gibbs q.v.

Mary A. Newby to Moses Green q.v.

Victoria Newby to H. B. Knight q.v.

\- - - - - - - - - - - - -

NEWELL

1860 CENSUS

Joseph Newell 46, Mary 34, Nancy A. 13, Leralda I. 11, Martha C. 9, Mary C. 6, Joseph C. 12, Thomas CANNS(?) 17 8-11-70

1870 and 1880 CENSUS– None

1900 CENSUS

James Newell 21 (July 1878-M 1), Martha M. 19 (Ap 1881-M 1-1-0) 5-232B-94

James M. Newell 40 (Oct 1859-M 19)(Carpenter), Ella 39 (Oct 1860-M 19-7-5), Elizabeth 15 (Mar 1885), Jessie 10 (Jan 1890), Webb 8 (May 1892), Edward 5 (June 1894), Hubert 3 (June 1896) 8-317B-150/155

\- - - - - - - - - - - - -

NEWMAN / NEUMAN

1860 CENSUS

Jacob Newman 42, Elizabeth 28, Bird 18, Lucinda 16, Samuel 13, George W. 8, Andrew J. 5, Solmound W. 3 8-14-95

John Newman 34, Sidney A. 22, Rachel 1 5-31-203

1870 and 1880 CENSUS– None

1900 CENSUS

Edgar Newman 18: see John M. Houston

George M. Neuman 29 (Mar 1871-M 4), Viola 38 (Nov 1861-Ga/Ga/Ga-M 4-2-2), Edward 16 (Ap 1884-NC), John KILGORE 27 (sl)(May 1873-M 1), Archer 22 (sd)(Feb 1878-Ala/Ala/Ga-M 1-1-1), Georgy 4/12 (gd) (Jan 1900) 8-276A-150/151

Herbert J. Newman 39, Mary 35, Torn 12, John 9, Annie 5, Marnie A. 6/12: see John McKinley

MARRIAGES

Ace Neuman to Julia Morgan, 28 Oct 1890 (no return) 4-25

Bird Newman to Malinda J. Couch, 12 Aug 1868 (16 Aug), R.H. Jordan MG 1-#1023

Conrad Newman to Saphira Teague, 8 Nov 1860 (11 Nov), Wm A. Green JP 1-#731

George Newman to Viola Sharp, 11 July 1896 (same), W.L. Lillard JP 2-42

J.L. Newman to Bell Fleming, 19 Aug 1896 (21 Aug), W.A. Green JP, I.C. Newman W 2-58

Lucinda Newman to Miles A. Dungan q.v.

R.C. Newman to M.C. Travis, 29 May 1900 (same), W.A. Brumagin ??, S.W. Pearcy W 3-158

\- - - - - - - - - - - - -

NEWPORT

1860 CENSUS

Asa Newport 57 (Blacksmith), Elizabeth 57, James F.M. 24, Julia H. 15, Sabeny C. 12 1-94-640

1870 CENSUS

Asa Newport 67, Elizabeth 67, Clementine UNDERWOOD 10 (Mo) 1-17-109

James F. Newport 34, Rebecca E. 27, Mary E. 3, William C. 2 1-17-108

MARRIAGES

Elizabeth Newport to Jesse Stonecipher q.v.

James F.M. Newport to Rebecca E. Griffith, 1 June 1866 (3 June), J.C. McAllen MG 1-#902

July H. Newport to Richard L. Garrison q.v.

Sabra C. Newport to William R. Clack 1.v.

\- - - - - - - - - - - - -

NEWTON

1900 CENSUS

Eligah Newton 26 (June 1873-Ga/Ga/Ga-M 1), Souisey 19 (June 1880-M 1-0), William BATON 26 (boarder) (June 1873-Wd) 10-253B-71 (B)

Eugene Newton 20, Alda 15: see Albert O. McClelland

MARRIAGES

Elijah Newton to Susie Brown, 28 Ap 1899 (26 Mar), D.B. Jackson MG 2-406

Eugene Newton to Alitie McClellan, 25 Dec 1899 [bond only], W.H. McCully W 3-98

Mary A. Newton to William S. Adams q.v.

\- - - - - - - - - - - - -

NICHOLS / NICKELS / NICHOLAS / NICHOLDS

1860 CENSUS

Andrew J. Nichols 35, Sarah 26, Nathaniel 11, James 3 8-15-100

A. Nicholas 32, Sarah E. 12, Wm B. 4, Andrew T. 2 8-15-102

1870 CENSUS

Arvazine Nichols 43, William B. 14, Andrew T. 12 8-4-24

Nat Nichols 22, Eliza A. 18 10-1-3

Sarah Nichols 21: see Hannah Gillespie

1880 CENSUS

A.T. Nicholds 22, S.E. 32 (si), H.C. 5 (s) 8-12-102

J.L. Nichols 22, Emma 17 (w), C.O.P. 1/12 (d) 8-21-177

W.B. Nichols 24, M.A. 27, J.T. 5 (s), A.P. 2 (s), A.B. 8/12 (d) 8-10-81

1900 CENSUS

James Nichols 42 (June 1857-M 22), Emma 36 (Jan 1864-M 22-12-5), Floyd 14 (Feb 1886), Edna 11 (Feb 1889), Henry C. 8 (June 1891) 9-288B-406/408

Thomas Nichols 42 (Mar 1858-M 17), Malinda 40 (Oct 1859-M 17-8-6), Vesty 12 (Nov 1887), Elsa 9 (July 1890), Willie 8 (May 1892), Lizzie 5 (Ap 1895), Hobart 3 (Mar 1897), John 11/12 (June 1899) 8-289A-418/421

MARRIAGES

Arizen Nichels to William B. Gothard q.v.

Cleopatra Nichols to J. J. R. Minton q.v.

Elizabeth Nichols to J. W. Hoge q.v.

Ibie Nichols to William Morgan q.v.

Tabetha J. Nichols to Allison Morgan q.v.

Thomas Nichols to Linda Montgomery, 13 Dec 1883 (same), C. Morgan JP 1-471

W.B. Nichols to Manerva A. Dungan, 20 Dec 1875 (same), C. Morgan JP 1-#1426

- - - - - - - - - - - - -

NICHOLSON

MARRIAGE

Bascomb or Bascant Nicholson to Alta Gill, 21 July 1900 (same), Sherman Wilson MG, Cyrus Ellison [signed by X] W 3-190

- - - - - - - - - - - - -

NILES

MARRIAGE

Carrie E. Niles to John S. Ferrie q.v.

- - - - - - - - - - - - -

NINN

1900 CENSUS

Annie Ninn 3: see Sallie Bettis (B)

- - - - - - - - - - - - -

NIPPER / NIPPUR

1900 CENSUS

William Nippur 29 (Oct 1870-M 7)(Stonecutter), Mary 26 (June 1873-Ga/T/T-M 7-4-4), Nora 6 (Dec 1893), Cattie 4 (Aug 1895), Lucy 2 (July 1897), Lee 11/12 (June 1899) 10-250A-10

MARRIAGE

Mary Nipper to W. F. Jones q.v.

- - - - - - - - - - - - -

NITITO

1900 CENSUS

Stephen Nitito(?) 30 (Mar 1870-M 12), Manda 28 (Ap 1872-M 12-3-3), Parthynia 12 (Jan 1888), Allie 3 (Sep 1896), Charles 1 (Ap 1899) 1-188B-191/200

- - - - - - - - - - - - -

NIXON

1900 CENSUS

George Nixon 23 (May 1877-T/T/Ga-M 0)(Bricklayer), Lora 23 (Unk 1877-T/T/Ga-M 0-0) 8-278B-198/200

Samuel H. Nixon 51 (July 1848-T/Ga/Va-M 31)(Bricklayer), Julia A. 51 (July 1848-Ga/Ga/Ga-M 31-10-4), Charles A. 14 (May 1886-Ga), Fred 12 (May 1888), Walter 10 (Mar 1890), Laura KIKER 15 (Jun 1884-Ga) 8-278A-197/199

MARRIAGE

George Nixon to Lora Davis, 24 Feb 1900 (25 Feb), A.P. Hayes JP, Fred Greer W 3-127

- - - - - - - - - - - - -

NOBLE

MARRIAGE

Mary Noble to Thomas Brown q.v.

- - - - - - - - - - - - -

NOBLETT

MARRIAGE

Savannah Noblett to John H. Rector q.v.

- - - - - - - - - - - - -

NORMAN

1870 CENSUS

Oliver L. Norman 17: see Vilena Hutchison

Samuel H. Norman 5: see Henry H. Gamble

1880 CENSUS

Samuel H. Norman 15: see H. H. Gambill

1900 CENSUS

Clinton Norman 35 (Sep 1864-M 15), Minerva E. 27 (Aug 1862-M 15-7-7), Martha J. 14 (Mar 1886), Samuel H.C. 12 (Sep 1887), Louellen 10 (Oct 1889), John S. 8 (Aug 1891), Edward L. 6 (Nov 1893), Nancy C. 3 (June 1896), Sarah M. 1 (Feb 1899) 5-232A-73

William J. Norman 25 (Nov 1874-Ga/Ga/Ga-M 0), Nancy S. 22 (Sep 1877-M 0-0) 8-276B-162/163

MARRIAGE

W. M. Norman to Nancy S. Byrd, 22 Dec 1899 (23 Dec), N.D. Reed MG, W.R. Woody W 3-95

- - - - - - - - - - - - -

NORRIS / NORRISS

1900 CENSUS

Elijah Norris 50 (July 1849-Ga/Ga/Ga-M 1), Malinda 30 (Jan 1870-M 1-4-3), John 17 (s)(Oct 1882)(Coal Miner), Grover 11 (Sep 1888), Alice WILSON 11 (sd)

(Mar 1889), Edward HARTBARGER 18 (ss)(Nov 1881), Charles 7 (ss)(Dec 1892), Cordelia 2 (sd)(Jan 1898), Rhoda LAND 73 (ml)(Unk 1827-NC/NC/NC-Wd 4-3) 15-269B-29

Grover C. Norris 11: see William H. Walker

MARRIAGES

Elizabeth Norriss to Thomas Allen q.v.

E.A. [Elijah] Norris to Emma(?) A. Hartbarger, 9 June 1899 (10 June), J.M. Cook MG, John Colyar W 2-423

John Norris to Della Sexton, 7 Sep 1900 (same), F.M. Cook MG, W.R. Walker W 3-211

Mahala Norriss to Nathan Watson q.v.

Mamie Norris to W. W. Walker q.v.

William Norris to Mahala Webb, 8 Jan 1870 (11 Jan), W.F. Buttram MG 1-#1136

- - - - - - - - - - - - -

NORTHRUP / NORTHOP / NORTHRAP

1880 CENSUS

Loretta Northrap 29: see Jane Barton

1900 CENSUS

Earnest Northop 10: see Albert Stokes (B)

Mary Northrup 53 (Unk 1847-Germany/Do/Do-Wd 7-6), Waldrin 28 (s)(Mar 1872-T/NY/Germany), Charles 15 (s)(Ap 1885) 3-201B-40/43

MARRIAGE

Roda Northump to Hannibal Carter q.v.

- - - - - - - - - - - - -

NORTON

1900 CENSUS

Harvey H. Norton 2: see Nancy Rankin (B)

- - - - - - - - - - - - -

NYE

1900 CENSUS

A.F. Nye 49 (Nov 1850-Oh/Pa/Oh-M 28)(Barber), Anna 43 (Sep 1856-Oh/Oh/T-M 28-4-3), Sylvia 17 (Sep 1882-Oh) 8-315B-102/106

Earl G. Nye 25 (June 1874-Oh/Oh/Oh-M 5)(Barber), Lena R. 24 (Oct 1875-T/NC/T-M 5-2-2), Fred A. 3 (Nov 1896), Dick 9/12 (Aug 1899) 10-324A-84/88

- - - - - - - - - - - - -

OAKES

1900 CENSUS

George W. Oakes 58 (May 1842-T/Va/T-M 37), Mary J. 57 (Oct 1842-NC/NC/NC-M 37-8-7) 14-214B-29/30

MARRIAGE

Novia(?) Oakes to James Meadows q.v.

- - - - - - - - - - - - -

OASIS

1870 CENSUS

William J. Oasis 45, Nancy E. 35, James B. 12, Lucinda 2 2-16-116

- - - - - - - - - - - - -

O'BRIEN / OBIEN

1880 CENSUS

Nancy Obien 21: see Andrew Anderson

MARRIAGE

Patrick O'Brien to Nancy J. Bidwell, no date (8 Nov 1874), W.W. Low JP 1-#1369

- - - - - - - - - - - - -

ODEL

MARRIAGE

Lewis L. Odel to Nancy J. Cook, 13 Ap 1872 (14 Ap), H.B. Haskiel JP 1-#1236

- - - - - - - - - - - - -

ODOM / ODEM

1880 CENSUS

Daniel Odem 47 (Carpenter), M.J. 43 (w), A.L. 18 (d), Hester 17 (d), M.M. 15 (d), H.E. 12 (d), S.G. 9 (s), Alfred 8, Alfred GASS 21 (Carpenter) 4-8-65

1900 CENSUS

Daniel Odom 65: see James H. Hodge

MARRIAGES

Addie Odom to J. F. Hodge q.v.

E. A. J. Odom to Braxton Walker q.v.

Hester Odom or Odaw to James M. Irvin q.v.

- - - - - - - - - - - - -

ODY

1880 CENSUS

Edward Ody 24 5-7-66 (Mu)

- - - - - - - - - - - - -

OFFICER

MARRIAGE

Lucinda Officer to Charley Keith q.v.

- - - - - - - - - - - - -

OGLE / OGILL

1870 CENSUS

Henry Ogill 20, Nancy A. 18: see William Webb

1880 CENSUS– None

1900 CENSUS

Sarah L. Ogle 36 (Mar 1861-Wd 6-6), Dellie M. 16 (Oct 1883), Fletcher L. 12 (May 1888), Heneretta J. 9 (June 1890), Robert 7 (Dec 1892), Anna L. 4 (May 1896) 5-235A-138 [John H. Ogle married M.S.L. Caggle on 27 Nov 1881 in Meigs County; John H. was taxed in Rhea County in 1875]

William D. Ogle 29 (Mar 1871-M 9)(RR Laborer), Julia 28 (Aug 1871-T/T/NC-M 9-3-3), Nancey 5 (Dec 1894), John H. 3 (Mar 1897), James L.M. 1 (May 1899) 6-240B-19

MARRIAGES
Della Ogle to Yank Webb q.v.
Henry Ogle to Nancy Webb, 20 Jan 1870 (same), W.F. Buttram MG 1-#1139
William Ogle to Julia Mize, 26 Mar 1892, H.B. Burdett MG 4-41

- - - - - - - - - - - - -

O'KELLY / O'KELLEY

1860 CENSUS
Benjamin O'Kelly 24 (NC) 7-4-21
Benjamin O'Kelley 46 (NC)(Carpenter), Cassey [Cassander] 46, Nancy E. 25, Martha J. 23, Mary J. 19, Keziah E. 16, Francis M. 13, Clarrissa A. 11, James 11, Thomas E. 7, Irena A. 3 7-1-4

- - - - - - - - - - - - -

OLDHAM

1870 CENSUS
David W. Oldham 28, Pamela E. 37, Mary J. 6, Sarah E. 4, Samuel H. 3, Todd 1, Samuel BUTTREM 65 (Ky) 8-22-157
1880 CENSUS
David Oldham 38, P.E. 48 (w), M.J. 15 (d), S.E. 14 (d), S.H. 13 (s), T.T. 12 (d), J.T. 10 (s), F.J. 7 (d) 11-37-301
Y.P. Oldham 36, N.M. 35, Dana 18 (nw) 8-13-114
1900 CENSUS
David Oldham 38 (Mar 1862-M 9)(Coal Miner), Addie A. 23 (Oct 1876-M 9-3-3), Sarah E. 5 (May 1895), Bertha A. 2 (Nov 1897), unnamed 5/12 (Dec 1899) 11-293B-90/91
Emily Oldham 67 (Ap 1833-M 35-7-6), Fannie 26 (Jan 1874) 8-286A-347/349
James Oldham 29 (Oct 1870-M 7), Jennie 26 (Mar 1874-M 7-2-2), Fred 5 (Mar 1895), Maud 2 (Ap 1898) 8-286A-350/352
MARRIAGES
D.R. Oldham to Jenny Rogers, 6 July 1889 (7 July), W.S. Hale MG 1-577
David Oldham to Parmela E. Sullivan, 28 Mar 1863 (no return) 1-#795
James Oldham to Jennie Morgan, 16 Oct 1893, F.M. Cook MG 4-62
Mary J. Oldham to James R. Wilson q.v.
S.H. Oldham to Genette Shadrick, 20 Sep 1897 (21 Sep), Henegar Morgan JP, R.J. Killough W 2-182

- - - - - - - - - - - - -

OLINGER

1900 CENSUS
John Olinger 60 (Mar 1840-M 32), Arabelle 59 (Oct 1840-M 32-5-4), James W. 21 (Sep 1878)(Coal Miner), Henry B. 19 (June 1880) 11-291B-43
John D. Olinger 27 (Jan 1873-M 6), Fannie B. 18 (Nov 1881-M 6-3-3), Grace 5 (Oct 1894), Albert 4 (Feb 1896), Lucy 1 (May 1899) 11-293A-75
MARRIAGES
Elizabeth Olinger to W. M. Walker q.v.
John D. Olinger to Fannie Myers, 26 Mar 1893, C.E. Munsey JP 4-50
Virginia Olinger to J.N. or J.V. Bowman q.v.

- - - - - - - - - - - - -

OLIVER

MARRIAGES
Fannie Oliver to J. T. Oliver q.v.
H. O. Oliver to P. J. Snow or Senow, 26 Dec 1891, R.A. Bartlett MG 4-36
J. T. Oliver to Fannie Oliver, 14 Dec 1889 (same), Wm Morgan JP 1-599

- - - - - - - - - - - - -

OLLFRED

MARRIAGE
Elizabeth Ollfred to Jourden Horrid q.v.

- - - - - - - - - - - - -

O'NEAL / O'NEIL

1870 CENSUS
Abraham O'Neal 72 (Va), Millia 47, Louisa Jane 20, Francis M. 16, Houston H. 12 8-19-134
1880 CENSUS
A.C. O'Neal 59, L. ?1 [ink blob] (w), David JANOW 33 (sl), M.L. 10 (gd) 3-29-237
1900 CENSUS
Amos O'Neal 19: see Wiley Simpson
MARRIAGES
James O'Neal to Laurie O'Neal, 5 Sep 1887 (same), John H. Parrott ?? 1-527
Joseph O'Neal to Alice Pyane, 28 Ap 1888 (29 Ap), J.B. Phillips MG 1-548
Samuel O'Neil to Malinda J. Williams, 25 Mar 1887 (same), Calvin Morgan JP 1-531

- - - - - - - - - - - - -

OOTEN

1900 CENSUS
Albert Ooten 19: see Hiram Moore (B)

- - - - - - - - - - - - -

OPAL

1880 CENSUS
John W. Opal 32 (Jailor), Nancy A. 22 (w), Mary M. 12 (d), William D. 9 (s), James T. 6/12 (s), James L. WEBB 1 (nw), Lewis MOORE 69 (prisoner) 6-24-no household number, Jailhouse

- - - - - - - - - - - - -

O'RANKINS

1900 CENSUS
Chaney O'Rankins 80: see Calumma Brown (B)

- - - - - - - - - - - - -

ORLANDER

1870 CENSUS
Murphey Orlander 37 (Oh), Mary Ann 21, Margarette C. 4, Marion F. 1 8-12-84

- - - - - - - - - - - - -

ORR

MARRIAGES
George Orr to Ellen Champion, 20 Ap 1889 (same), W.R. Brice ?? 1-573
John Orr to Mariah Majors, 30 Aug 1852 (same), Wm Floyd JP 1-#379

- - - - - - - - - - - - -

OSBORN / OSBURN

1880 CENSUS
Rachael Osburn 13 (B): see Rebecca Paul
1900 CENSUS
Edwin B. Osborn 50 (Feb 1850-Oh/Conn/Conn-M 20) (Store Supt), Florence C. 48 (Aug 1851-Mich/NY/NY-M 20-1-1), Jessie C. 18 (Mar 1882-Mich) 13-302B-231/241
Edwin D. Osborn 41 (Jan 1859-Oh/Oh/Oh-M 16) (Surveyor), Lulu K. 41 (May 1859-Ind/NY/NY-M 16-5-3), Edwin D. 13 (Aug 1886), Lewis C. 7 (June 1892), Roy P. 10 (July 1899) 14-213B-10/20
Lucinda Osborn 78: see Joseph Phillips (B)
MARRIAGES
E.D. Osborn to Lula Dye, 29 Mar 1884 (same), S.H. Price MG 1-482
Lucy Osborn to Riley Wood q.v.

- - - - - - - - - - - - -

OSSLER

MARRIAGE
Mattie Ossler to R. F. Montgomery q.v.

- - - - - - - - - - - - -

O'SULLIVAN

1900 CENSUS
Patrick O'Sullivan 61 (Feb 1839-Ireland/Do/Do-1853/45/Na-M 25), Dicy A. 62 (Oct 1837-Va/Va/Va-M 25-5-4) 4-225B-239/243 (Rhea Springs & Washington Road)

- - - - - - - - - - - - -

OTTINGER

1900 CENSUS
James(?) Ottinger 49 (Jan 1851-T/Pa/Pa-M 16)(Coal Miner), Mary A. 35 (May 1865-M 16-5-4), Henry 10 (Ap 1890), Willie 7 (Jan 1893), Anna 5 (Jan 1895), James 2 (Mar 1898) 8-280A-230/232
MARRIAGES
Florence Ottinger to Effie Shipley q.v.
J.C. Ottinger to Mary A. Byrley, 14 Oct 1884 (16 Oct), I.W. Holt JP 1-463
Raymon Ottinger to Amanda Wright, 27 Nov 1897 (28 Nov), R. Knight JP, J.W. Wright W 2-213

- - - - - - - - - - - - -

OUTEN

MARRIAGE
Salina Outen to John Wasson q.v.

- - - - - - - - - - - - -

OVERBY

1870 CENSUS
Edward Overby 21 (B): see J. Wasson

- - - - - - - - - - - - -

OWENS / OWINS / OANS / OWINGS

1860 CENSUS
Louisa M. Owens 24, John G. 19: see Evan Breeden
Ruben Owens 30, Nelly 30, James 1 6-107-728
William M. Owens 28, Sarah A. 24, Margaret J. 3, William S. 1 4-52-355
1870 CENSUS
Aaron C. Owens 51 (NC), Lucinda 51 (SC), Lovey Ann 29, George W. KEELON 8 3-2-14
John G. Oans 27: see Evan Breeding
Nellie Oans 32: see William McCully
William M. Oans 38 (Miller), Sarah A. 34, William 10, Louiza A. 9, Thomas J. 5, Zorilda E. 2, Franklin 11/12 2-17-123
1880 CENSUS
James Owens 21, Elizabeth 17, Mary 2, Martha 1/12 2-38-306
Millie Owens 54, James 20 (s) 11-42-335
William Owens 54, Barbara 51, Lucinda 12 2-37-300
1900 CENSUS
George W. Owens 66 (Aug 1833-T/T/SC-M 42), Mary A. 69 (June 1830-NC/NC/NC-M 42-7-5), William W. 41 (Jan 1859)(Coal Miner) 13-300B-192/198
[George W. Owen married Mary Alexander on 24 Aug 1854 in Roane County]
James M. Owens 35 (Feb 1865-T/Ill/T-M 18), Rachael A. 34 (Unk 1866-M 18-5-5), Martha 17 (June 1883) [name and date marked through], Samuel 14 (June 1885), Mollie 13 (Oct 1887), Margaret A. 12 (Feb 1888), James M. 8 (Sep 1892), William BARNETT (B) 13 (Unk 1887)(Servant) 3-207B-138/151
Will Owens 27: see Moses Greer
MARRIAGES
Esther Owens to Alonzo Raper q.v.
Hattie Owens to Everett Sparks q.v.
James Owings to E.J. Myrick, 5 Jan 1876 (same), W.W. Low JP 1-#1427
James Owens (21) to Rachael Watson (21, Meigs Co), 21 Jan 1882, A. J. Pritchett MG, E. D. Pierce & G. W. Fisher W 4-10(96)
John D. Owens to Susan M. Breeding, 15 Aug 1866 (same), J.M. McCullum MG 1-#907
Laura F. Owins to S. B. Hoge q.v.
M. C. Owens to J. F. Smith q.v.
Margaret E. Owens to Leonard J. Long q.v.
Martha Owens to Burch Shell(?) q.v.
Mary E. Owens to David Genow q.v.
Rubin Owens to Nelly McCully, 17 May 1854 (same), John Howard JP 1-#445

W.J. Owens to Barbara Ann Collins, 9 Jan 1874 (same), Allen L. King MG 1-#1324
William J. Owens to Elizabeth Paul, 21 Nov 1864 (24 Nov), Asa Newport MG 1-#864
William M. Owins to Sarah A. Breeding, 12 Sep 1854 (same), A.D. Paul JP 1-#458

- - - - - - - - - - - - -

OWNBY / OSBY

MARRIAGES
Marion M. Ownby to Samantha M. Hutchenson, 2 Mar 1867 (no return) 1-#941
Matilda Osby to Edward Johnson q.v.

- - - - - - - - - - - - -

PACE

MARRIAGE
Ben L. Pace to Delia L. Abel, 9 Dec 1897 (same), J.F. Hash MG 2-225

- - - - - - - - - - - - -

PADUCE

1870 CENSUS
Tempy Paduce 23 (B): see James Prater

- - - - - - - - - - - - -

PAINE / PAYNE

1860 CENSUS
F. J. Paine 28 (Merchant): see Joseph Parks
Orville Paine 60, Elvira [nee Locke] 50, Orpha J. 25,
Hannibal 21, Mary L. 17, Ann 15, Alfred 12, Susan 7, Bird PAINE 50 (Physician), Jacob BROWN 21 5-38-256
1870 CENSUS
Caroline Paine 20, William 2 (B): see Darius Waterhouse
Elvira Paine 62, Ann 23, Alfred 22, Susan 16, Nancy PAINE (B) 19, William PAINE (B) 14 5-6-46
Flavius J. Paine 37, Amanda C. 32 5-3-15 [F.J. married Amanda Caroline Latham on 22 Jan 1837 in McMinn County]
Nancy Paine 19, William 14 (B): see Elvira Paine
1880 CENSUS
Elvira Paine 74, Alfred 32, Elizabeth N. 28, William C. 8, Flavius J. 7, Charles M. 5, Lila M. 3, Goldie L. 1, Vesty COLVILLE 19, Harriet 16 5-10-91
F.J. Paine 48, Caroline A. 23 (w), Frankey WALKER 18 (Hired girl) 5-10-93
Nancy Paine 27 (B): see Richard W. Colville
William Payne 48 (Lawyer), Mary 50, Lula 22, Herbert 20, Margie 18, Alice 11 2-23-187
1900 CENSUS
Abraham Payne 70 (Jan 1830-England/Do/Do-Wd) 11-293A-79
Alfred Paine 51 (June 1848-M 29), Elizabeth 48 (Aug 1851-M 29-10-10), Flavius J. 27 (July 1873), Charles M. 25 (Feb 1875), Lillie M. 23 (Mar 1877), Goldie L. 22 (Oct 1878), Orville 19 (Oct 1880), Mable P. 17 (Nov 1882), Colville 14 (June 1885), Vesta A. 13 (Feb 1887), Susan A. 11 (Jan 1889), John H. EZELL 20 (boarder) (Jan 1880) 5-231A-59
Amanda C. Paine 62: see William P. Darwin
Carrie Payne 14, John 21: see Ulusor Boyd
Herbert Payne 40 (Feb 1860-M 13), Mary 37 (July 1862-M 13-0), Virginia LUTY 68 (ml)(June 1832-Wd 8-7), Caty 32 (sil)(Oct 1867), Birdy 30 (sil)(Oct 1869) 1-189A-193/202 (Spring City)
Will Payne 27 (Aug 1872-M 2), Sallie 27 (May 1873-Ala/Ala/Ala-M 2-1-1), Fawn STEVENS 6 (ss)(Jan 1894-Ala/Ala/Ala) 8-316B-124/128 (B)
William C. Payne 68 (Aug 1831-M 40)(Lawyer), Mary L. 70 (Feb 1830-Oh/Va/Va-M 40-7-4), Alice G. 31 (d) (Oct 1868), Marjorie HOYAL 38 (d)(Oct 1861-Wd 1-1), Marjorie 16 (gd)(Nov 1883) 14-221B-156/160
William C. Paine 28 (June 1871-M 6), Mary 27 (June 1872-M 6-4-3), Ira L. 5 (Aug 1894), Elsie R. 3 (Sep 1896), Perry P. 1 (Feb 1899) 5-235A-139
MARRIAGES
Abraham Payne to Mrs. Louisa Wright, 7 Dec 1900 (13 Dec), G.W. Brewer MG, Charley Viles W 3-254
Alfred Paine to Elizabeth N. Colville, 27 Sep 1870 (same), J.A. Wallace MG 1-#1166
Alice Pyane(?) to Joseph O'Neil q.v.
Algeline Paine to Charles M. Todd q.v.
Evaline Paine to J. W. Williamson q.v.
H.B. Payne to Mary L. Leuty, 25 Jan 1887 (same), Geo W. Simpson ?? 1-527 [Herbert, son of Wm C. Payne; Mary, dau of Burton & Virginia Leuty]
Henry Payne to Jennie McEntire, 22 May 1893, James Johnson JP 4-54
M. L. Paine to R. W. Colville q.v.
Orpha J. Paine to R. F. McDonald q.v.
Susan C. Paine to W. I. [Nicholas Q.] Allen q.v.
Tom Paine (19) to Nellie Dixon, 3 Aug 1882, J.F. Peters MG, N. Whittenburg & John Edmonds W 4-7(68)
W.C. Paine to Mary Wilkey, 14 Sep 1893, F.J. Paine JP 4-56
William M. Payne to Elizabeth E. Bice, 21 Ap 1869 (same), Calvin Morgan JP 1-#1056

- - - - - - - - - - - - -

PAINTER / POINTER

1900 CENSUS
Robert Pointer 24 (July 1875-T/T/Ga-M 3), Malinda 22 (Dec 1877-M 3-0) 3-205A-88/96
Thomas Painter 67 (Oct 1832-M 30), Paralee A. 49 (Dec 1850-M 30-4-2), Thomas ROWDEN 86 (u)(Unk 1813-Wd) 15-273B-109
MARRIAGE
Mattie Painter to N. B. Barger q.v.

- - - - - - - - - - - - -

PALMER / PALMOUR / PARMER

1870 CENSUS
Semeour Palmour 33 (Ga), Francis 34 (Ga), Benjamin U. 11 (Ga), Sinthe M. 9 (Ga), Sarah M. 8 (Ga), Marcus M. 5 (Ga), John B. 3 (Ga), Susan E. 1 (Ga), Wilson BREWER 67 (NC), Elizabeth 64 (NC) 2-1-3
1880 CENSUS-- None

1900 CENSUS

Elizabeth Parmer 85: see Isaac Mars

Martha Palmer 67, Wesley H. 29 (s), Clara 21 (dl): see Jacob Gass

MARRIAGE

W.H. Palmer to Clara Eberly, 22 Dec 1899 (24 Dec), A.J. Wyrick JP, Charles Hayes W 3-93

- - - - - - - - - - - - -

PANKEY / PANKY

MARRIAGES

Ellen Panky(?) to Daniel Buchannon q.v.

Mary Pankey(?) to Jonas Rucker q.v.

- - - - - - - - - - - - -

PANNER

1860 CENSUS

Jason I. Panner 37 (NY), Elizabeth A. 37, Alfred B. 19, Clarissa C. 11, Franklin 9, Sorena C. 4, Harriet DONALD 13, Ellen WILEY 13 9-99-677

- - - - - - - - - - - - -

PARDEE

MARRIAGE

C.S. Pardee to Laura C. Dodge, 16 June 1891, J.A. Darr MG 4-26

- - - - - - - - - - - - -

PARHAM

MARRIAGE

Thomas S. Parham to Laura A. Acuff, 31 July 1892, L.L. Barton JP 4-84

- - - - - - - - - - - - -

PARKER

1860 CENSUS

Prudence Parker 52, Margaret J. 39, Ellen 21, Elizabeth 18, Malinda 14, Prudence 12, Charlotte 9 2-73-499

1870 CENSUS

George Parker 67, Docia 50, Samuel 16, Martha A. 14, Anna 10, Allie 9 1-9-62

John Parker 23, Angeline 20, James 1 6-15-107

John Parker 21, Mary T. 18, James 4, Thomas 1 1-9-61

Robert Parker 53, Sarah 51, Nancy 23, Anderson 20, Malinda 15, Joseph 18, Jane 14, Laka 12, Arbana 10, Martha 8 6-15-106

1880 CENSUS

Anderson Parker 30, Adda 25 (w) 6-16-151/154

George P. Parker 34, Sarah M. 34 (w), Rufus D. 11, Margaret J. 8, Thomas L. 4, Rittie M. 1, George W. PARKER 73 (f) 6-19-176/181

Samuel Parker 26, Ann H. 28, July 3, William E. 1, Ida J. 5/12 7-17-153/156

1900 CENSUS

Anderson Parker 50 (Oct 1849-M 23)(Blacksmith), Adda 46 (May 1854-M 23) 10-324A-92/96

Ann Parker 48 (July 1851-Wd 2-2), Fred 17 (Oct 1882), Alma 10 (June 1889) 7-267B-327/332

Davis ?. Parker 43 (Dec 1856-Ky/Ky/Va-Wd)(Sawmill Sawyer), Burton T. 15 (Oct 1884-T/Ky/T)(Sawmill Laborer), William K. 11 (May 1879)(Sawmill Laborer) 4-224B-213/217 (Spring City & Dayton Road)

Dellie Parker 9: see Henry Flore(?)

Edd W. Parker 21 (Aug 1878-M 2), Linnie J. 23 (May 1877-M 2-0) 10-250B-16

John P. Parker 28: see William A. Armstrong

Louiza Parker 53, Elvin 8: see John Pogue

Margarett E. Parker 29 (July 1870-NC/NC/NC-Wd), Mattie 11 (May 1889-NC), Belle G. 4 (Aug 1895-NC) 3-209A-167/181

Myrum Parker 18: see John A. Whitner

MARRIAGES

Anderson Parker to Ada Rudd, 3 July 1875 (4 July), J.R. Crawford JP 1-#1401

David Parker to Manervia C. Riburn, 15 Aug 1853 (23 Aug), A.D. Paul JP 1-#417

Elizabeth Parker to George W. Small q.v.

Ellen Parker to E. F. M. Treadaway q.v.

G.P. Parker to S.E. Bunn, 8 Mar 1889 (same), J.W. Williamson MG 1-569

H.P. Parker to Nancy M. Kirklen, 31 Jan 1888 (same), I.W. Holt JP 1-552

Ida Parker to B. B. Blythe q.v.

Jane Parker to J. K. Holland q.v.

John Parker to Margaret Bolin, 4 June 1889 (same), F.M. Capps JP 1-580

John J. Parker to Mary E. Shipley, 9 Oct 1888 (14 Oct), Rev. W.G. Curtin 1-561

Kittie Parker to John W. Pogue q.v.

Lake Parker to Alexander Rice q.v.

Luther Parker to Catharine T. Myres, 4 Aug 1885 (6 Aug), W.R. Grimsley MG 1-48

Malinda Parker to A. B. Hodge q.v.

Malinda D. Parker to Thomas Hill q.v.

Margaret H. Parker to R. D. Sneed q.v.

Martha Parker to William Harwood q.v.

Mattie Parker to E. L. Rudd Jr. q.v.

Nannie Parker to Scruggs Lockmiller q.v.

Nancy Parker to H. H. Rawlings q.v.

Orbanna Parker to David Rice q.v.

Permelia Parker to David Woody q.v.

Samuel Parker to Ann Roddy, 16 Jan 1876 (same), J.R. Crawford JP 1-#1429

W.C. Parker to Tinie Scott, 20 Oct 1888 (same), John H. Parriott ?? 1-559

W.C. Parker to Mary Roe, 26 Feb 1890 (same), F.M. Capps JP 1-596

W.E. Parker to Lena Jones or Jenno, 30 Aug 1897 [bond only], B.M. or W.H. Lewis W 1-169

- - - - - - - - - - - - -

PARKINSON

MARRIAGE

Mary Parkinson to John H. Cobb q.v.

- - - - - - - - - - - - -

PARKS / PARK

1860 CENSUS

Joseph Parks 40 (Merchant), Sarah J. 42, James A. LOVE 21 (Merchant), Margaret SYKES 23 (School Teacher), F.J. PAINE 28 (Merchant), Onslow BEAN 28 (Merchant) 6-109-745

1870 CENSUS

Lucy Parks 36 (NC), Mary E. 16, Thomas A. 15, Sarah J. 12, Reubin H. 10, Henry W. 5, Margarett C. 5 1-4-27

Sarah J. Parks 52, William HOWARD 21 6-10-67

1880 CENSUS

L.M. Parks 48, Thomas 23, Reuben 18, Henry 5, M. 12 (d) 3-26-227

Sarah J. Parks 65 6-22-10 (Madison Street, Washington)

1900 CENSUS

Henry H. Parks 35 (Nov 1864-T/T/NC-M 10), Mary E. 28 (May 1872-M 10-4-4), Laura K. 8 (Mar 1892), Wilmoth 6 (Dec 1893), Lucy P. 4 (Oct 1895), Maud M. 3/12 (Mar 1900), Lucy PARKS 60 (m)(Nov 1839-NC/NC/NC-Wd 7-5), Fred A. 16 (nw)(Nov 1880) 3-212A-208/226

Thomas A. Parks 44 (Mar 1856-T/T/NC-M 5), Emma A. 36 (Feb 1864-T/Conn/T-M 15-3-3), Joseph 13 (Aug 1886), Lucy 11 (July 1888), Birtha 6 (May 1894) 3-212A-207/225

MARRIAGES

George W. Parks to Isabella Gilliam, 1 Jan 1896, J.H. Keylon JP 4-91

Henry Parks to Mary Hall, 18 Oct 1890, J.M. Bramlett MG 4-24

Isabella Parks to Alex Mooreland q.v.

Joseph E. Parks to Sarah E. Love, 22 June 1852 (same), W.H. Bell MG 1-#374

R.H. Parks to Katie Johnson, 14 Sep 1889 (13 Sep), J.P. Thompson JP 1-592

Sarah Parks to Franklin Kincannon q.v.

T.A. Parks to Emma Thompson, 26 May 1885 (same), S.H. Price MG 1-493

Tennie Park to S. J. Brandon q.v.

William M. Parks to Alice Martin, 26 Mar 1897 (no return) 4-97

- - - - - - - - - - - - -

PARMALEE / PARMERLEE

1880 CENSUS

Nelson Parmalee 48 (Carpenter & Joiner), Sylva 47, Myrtie 18, John 9 12-3-23

1900 CENSUS

Cilia Parmerlee 66 (Sep 1833-Ver/Ver/Ver-Wd 2-2)(Dressmaker), Nelson PHILLIPS 15 (gs)(Dec 884) 12-180B-44/47

MARRIAGE

M. A. Parmalee to E. T. Phillips q.v.

- - - - - - - - - - - - -

PARSON

MARRIAGES

Elizabeth Parson to Asbery Kaylor q.v.

Mattie Parson to W. P. Kaylor q.v.

- - - - - - - - - - - - -

PARTAIN / PARTAINE / PARTIN / PARTEN

1870 CENSUS

Elizabeth Parten 47 (NC), Sarah 11, James P. 8, Abraham L. 6 1-11-73

William W. Partn(?), Amanda 43, Leruah 22, Nancy E. 19, Barshaby M. 17, William F. 16, Mary 7, Eugene 5, Reubin 4, Jacob 3, Tennessee 6/12, Sarah 18 5-10-71

MARRIAGES

Eli Partain to Elizabeth McCully, 7 Nov 1867 (no return) 1-#980

Emeline Partaine to William C. Collins q.v.

- - - - - - - - - - - - -

PASS

1860 CENSUS

James H. Pass 37 (Va)(Millwright), Ellenor 36 (Va), William E. 15, Emily P. 13, Martha A. 11, Eliza J. 8, Mary 4, Nora F. 1 3-59-406

1870 CENSUS

James H. Pass 47 (Va), Eleanor 47 (NC), William E. 24 (NC), Emma P. 22 (NC), Martha A. 20 (NC), Jane 18, Miral 14, Nora 11, Margaret 9, Elizabeth 7, James A. 4, John 2 2-4-19

1880 CENSUS

Isaac Pass 3: see Isaac Fine

James Pass 57, Elleanor 56, William 35, Martha 32 (Seamstress), Mira 25, Nora 20, Margaret 18, Florence 15, James 14, John 11 2-41-338

1900 CENSUS

Maggie C. Pass 37: see Luke L. Coulter

William A. Pass 55 (Mar 1845-Va/Va/NC-Wd), James C. 16 (Dec 1883), Payton A. 12 (Nov 1887), Ola M. 8 (Aug 1891) 8-282B-277/279

Willie Pass 24: see Mattie Rector (B)

MARRIAGES

Emma Pass to George B.F. Hollaway q.v.

F. E. Pass to J. H. Blevins q.v.

M. A. Pass to E. H. Bagles q.v.

Myra Pass to L. L. Coulter q.v.

Nora Pass to T. W. Morgan q.v.

W.E. Pass (37, NC) to Tennie E. Morgan (27), 28 Dec 1882, D. Richardson MG, N.F. Nelson & A.P. Morgan W 4-12(117)

William Pass to Elizabeth Long, 3 Mar 1879 (no return) 1-#1608

- - - - - - - - - - - - -

PATRICK

MARRIAGE

Henry Patrick to Jane Robisson, 4 Ap 1896 (5 Ap), W.A. Green JP, J.P. Martin W 2-11

- - - - - - - - - - - - -

PATTERSON

1860 CENSUS

Robert Patterson 26 (Day Laborer), Sarah E. 20, Greenberry 2 1-89-607

1870 and 1880 CENSUS– None
1900 CENSUS
Ann N. Patterson 51: see Leonard Harman
Elbert M. Patterson 33 (Mar 1867-T/T/Calif-M 13), Dicie L. 31 (Sep 1868-T/T/NC-M 13-7-4), Alice M. 12 (June 1887), Franklin A. 11 (Sep 1888), Oscar M. 8 (Dec 1891), Maggie L. 1 (Sep 1898) 2-194A-61/63
John A. Patterson 25 (Oct 1874-Miss/Miss/Miss-M 7), Alta 23 (Aug 1876-Mo/Oh/Oh-M 7-3-3), William 5 (Aug 1894-Tex), Otto 2 (Aug 1897-Tex), Rufus 6/12 (Dec 1899), Jesse HAYES 15 (boarder)(Oct 1884-Oh/Oh/T) 8-289B-430/433
MARRIAGES
Grace M. Patterson to A. J. Clark q.v.
Robert J. Patterson to Nancy A. Caldwell, 9 June 1891, J.R. Walker MG 2-27
M.S. Patterson to Emily L. Gear, 23 Ap 1859 (24 Ap), A.P. Early MG 1-#689

\- - - - - - - - - - - - -

PATTON / PATTEN

1860 CENSUS
Alexander Patten 26 (NC), Margaret C. 22, Elizabeth 7 10-29-193
1870 CENSUS
John Patten 55 (Ga), Sarah 50 2-9-62 (B)
1880 CENSUS
Hay Patton 18: see J. S. Crannion(?)
S.M. Patton 25, M.O. 4 (d), J.M. 3 (s), M.L. 11/12 (d) 3-20-163
1900 CENSUS
Benjamin F. Patton 51 (Ap 1849-M 14)(Minister), Mattie K. 30 (Aug 1869-Ky/Ky/Ky-M 14-5-4), Claude R. 11 (Aug 1888-Ky), Bertha L. 8 (Oct 1891-WVa), Mary L. 4 (June 1895-Ky), Benjamin F. 10/12 (July 1899), Annie E. 42 (sil)(Feb 1858)(School Teacher) 10-327A-147/155
Hiram Patten 33 (Ap 1867-M 11), Malinda 27 (Feb 1873-M 11-3-3), Willie 7 (Nov 1892), Bessie 5 (Dec 1894), Berthy 2 (Dec 1897) 7-263B-254/259
Jeffe Patton 39 (Ap 1862-M 10), Tennie 32 (Feb 1868-M 10-4-4), Coral 9 (Mar 1891), Charley 7 (Dec 1892), Carrie 5 (Mar 1895), Cattin(?) 5/12 (Dec 1899) 7-262A-236/241
John Patton 69 (Jan 1831-Ireland/Do/Do-1834/66/Na-M 45) (Furnace Manager), Esther 63 (Dec 1836-Ireland/Do/Do-M 45-2-2), Mamie 44 (Ap 1856-NY/NY/NY), Cora 30 (Mar 1870-Oh/NY/NY) 14-217A-87/88
Martan Patten 52 (Feb 1848-Wd)(Preacher), Nancy 19 (Aug 1880), Forest 16 (June 1884), Nellie 10 (May 1890) 12-179B-19/21
Will L. Patten 29 (Aug 1870-M 4)(Minister), Clara L. 25 (Sep 1874-T/Eng/NY-M 4-2-2), Lucile F. 3 (Jan 1897), Winnifrew S. 1 (Jan 1899), Anna ROSE 10 (Ap 1890)(Servant) 8-314B-81/84
MARRIAGES
Fanny Patton to William Sexton q.v.
Henry T. Patton to Sallie B. Brown, 6 Dec 1886 (14 Dec), George W. Sampson ?? 1-528
Howard Patton to Linda Bell, 23 July 1889 (24 July), W.R. Clack JP 1-587
J.A. Patton [or possibly Bolton] to Hannah E. Iles, 20 Dec 1893, J.W. Clouse JP 4-60
J.D. Patton to E.J. Fugate, 19 or 22 Oct 1884 (22 Oct), Taylor Russell JP 1-460 & 1-492 [dates differ on license]
J.D. Patton to Tommie E. Fisher, 16 Ap 1890 (17 Ap), M.C. Bruner MG 1-596
John J. Patton to Candace Sharp, 25 Aug 1884 (same), Jas A. Wallace MG 1-466
L.H. Patton to Leuthy Jones, 24 July 1856 (27 July), W.H. Cunningham JP 1-#567

\- - - - - - - - - - - - -

PAUL / PALL / POLL

1860 CENSUS
Archibald D. Paul 61, Rebecca 45, Nancy E. 24, Sarah A. CLARK 19, Amanda F. 14, William L. 12, Archibald D. PAUL 9, Samuel E. 2 2-74-507 [Archibald married Rebecca Clark on 29 Oct 1854 in Roane Co]
1870 CENSUS
Rebecca Poll 51, Leander W. CLARK 22, Archibald D. PAUL 14, Samuel 12, Sarah A. CLARK 29 2-17-117
1880 CENSUS
Rebecca Paul 64, Archibald 24 (s), Samuel 20 (s), Rachael OSBURN (B) 13 (Servant, Cook), William RUKER (B) 9 (Servant) 2-37-297
1900 CENSUS
Arch D. Paul 44: see Samuel E. Paul
Frank Paul 23: see Charles W. Irwin
Meridith M. Paul 68 (Jan 1832-NC/NC/NC-M 15), Tennessee 48 (Feb 1852-T/NC/T-M 15-8-7), Charles 24 (ss)(Dec 1875), Edward 23 (ss)(July 1877), Thomas 12 (s)(Nov 1887), Artie 11 (d)(May 1889), Alice 9 (d) (July 1890), Mandy 9 (d)(July 1892), Susie HARWOOD 20 (sd)(July 1879-M 1-1-1), Clifford 6/12 (gs)(Nov 1899) 6-248B-163/164
Pharis Paul 45: see Samuel J. Wheeler
Samuel E. Paul 42 (Dec 1857-M 3)(Teacher), Minnie E. 31 (Oct 1868-M 3-1-1), Ellen H. 1 (Jan 1899), Arch D. 44 (b)(Sep 1855)(Supt RR Work) 14-219A-122/125

MARRIAGES
Amanda Paul to John House(?) q.v.
C. E. Paul to John H. Fine q.v.
Elizabeth Paul to William J. Owens q.v.
Frances Paul to Edward M. Phelps q.v.
Fredrick Pall to Mollie Barnett, 24 May 1891, A.W. Frazier JP
Narcissa C. Paul to Cornelius Wissener q.v.
S. A. Paul to James P. Hinds q.v.
S.L. Paul to Kittie Johnson, 22 Nov 1890, W.S. Hale MG 4-18
Samuel E. Paul to Minnie E. Heiskell, 30 Nov 1897 (1 Dec), J.A. Whitmer MG 2-216
Sherman Paul (22, McMinn Co) to Mary Emaline Porter (21), 10 Aug 1881, J.M. Bramlett MG, Bailey Minnik & T.J. Bramlett W 4-4(39)
Sophronia A. Paul to James D. Gilliam q.v.
Susie Paul to John Harwood q.v.

\- - - - - - - - - - - - -

PAVEY

1900 CENSUS
Mary Pavey 17: see Charles W. Irwin

PEAK

1880 CENSUS
Albert Peak 34, Charity 28, Matilda 13 2-32-265 (B)
Amos Peak 29, Ellen 26, Harris 9, Ada 4, Standifer 5 3-18-137 (B)
1900 CENSUS
Ellen Peak 52 (Unk-T/T/NC-Wd 10-7), Jane JOLLY 26 (d) (Feb 1874-M 4-1-1), Kate 11/12 (gd)(June 1899), Clent PEAK Unk, Lennie Unk, Blucer Unk, Eddie 10 8-317A-141/146 (B)
Horace Peak 24: see Olliver Strikland (B)
Jackson Peak 61 (Ap 1839-M 25), Amanda 49 (May 1851-M 25-12-10), Essie 21 (Oct 1878), William 15 (Dec 1884), John A. 11 (July 1888), Thomas 10 (May 1890), Nellie M. 5 (Oct 1894), Arthur 4 (Dec 1895), Ana M. 8/12 (Aug 1899) 14-217B-105/107 (B)
MARRIAGES
Birdie Peak to Jake Allen q.v.
E. M. Peak to Walter Pearson q.v.
Ellen Peak to John Hill q.v.
Frank Peak to Mariah Gillespie, 25 Jan 1882, James Johnson JP, C.K. Gillespie & Nancy Gillespie W 4-7(66) (B)
Jane Peak to James Jolly q.v.
Wilber B. Peak to Kittie J. Morgan, 27 Aug 1899 (same), T.G. Davis ??, J.M. Head W 3-28

PEARCE / PIERCE / PEIRCE / PEACE

1860 CENSUS
Elbert Pierce 24, Martha 22, Perry W. 2 5-34-227
James Pierce 72, Rachel 66, Samuel 26, Margaret L. 22, Julia E. 20, Coleman LOFTISS 25 (School Teacher) 5-34-226
Margaret Peirce 59, James 38, Sarah 21, Sallie S. 26, Susan 24, Thomas 22, Margaret 18, Margaret J. 8, Irena 1 8-12-82
Robert Peirce 19, Catharine 22, Adellia 1, --- [ink blob, possibly Miron] SHIPLEY 21 8-13-83
1870 CENSUS
Elbert D. Pierce 39, Martha A. 35, Perry White 11 5-5-31
General G. Pierce 6: see James L. Dungan
James Peirce 49, Leann 33, Zarilda J. 8, Robert R. 6, Margarette JOHNSON 30, Jarret F. 2 8-12-79
Jesse Pierce 38, Jane 25, Harriette A. 9, Hannah 6, Mary F. 1 8-11-70 (B)
John Pierce 46, William J. 15, John F. 14, Nancy A. SWAFFORD 20, Aron 11/12, Margarette 12 8-19-127
Samuel D. Peirce 41: see Henry H. Miller
1880 CENSUS
Burton Peirce 36, L.M. 40, M.R. 19, Evander 8, N.(?)C. 7, L.M. 5, A.C. 4, T.C. 2, W.G. 22 (b), S.A. 20 (sil), Rosa GOTHARD 18 (c) 11-38-309
David Pierce 33, Teressa 23, Elbert 1, Sarah PHILLIPS 12 (ne) 1-18-147
Elbert D. Pierce 49, Martha A. 44, Perry W. 21, Mary D. 6 (d), Hester A. THOMPSON 17 (ne) 5-3-22
Leander Pierce 50, Rhoda A. 36 (w), Elizabeth MONTGOMERY 16, Samuel 13, Robert C. 10, Mary A. 6 6-12-111
W.G. Pierce 22, S.A. 20: see Burton Peirce
1900 CENSUS
Ambrose A. Pierce 43 (Oct 1856-M 11)(Pharmacist), Mary A. 35 (Jan 1865-M 11-3-3), Leola S. 10 (Jan 1890) 10-321A-21/22
Elbert D. Pierce 69: see Perry Pierce
Flora J. Pearce 22: see Hariet Henderson
Perry Pierce 41 (Jan 1859-M 10), Elida 40 (Ap 1860-M 10-5-3), Maud A. 9 (July 1891), John D. 2 (July 1897), William E. 6/12 (Nov 1899), Elbert D. PIERCE 69 (f) 4-224B-217/221 (Spring City & Dayton Road)
Rhoda A. Pearce 56 (Mar 1844-Wd 9-6), Celia C. 18 (Sep 1881), Willie E. 16 (July 1883) 5-238B-209
Samuel D. Pearse 74: see James B. Blevins
MARRIAGES
A.M. Pearce to Harriett Henderson, 4 Aug 1871 (same), W.R. Henry JP 1-#1203
Elbert Pearce to Martha A. Miller, 28 Feb 1856 (15 Feb) [sic], no MG or JP 1-#539
Eliza J. Pearce to Henry H. Miller q.v.
Eliza J. Peace to D.W. Graham q.v.
J. E. Pearce to J. B. Blevins q.v.
Jennie Pearce to J. B. Zeigler q.v.
James C. Pearce to Elizabeth D. Miller, 12 Ap 1857, John W. Thompson MG 1-#594
L.D. Peace to Ada B. Scales, ? Dec 1889 (26 Dec), J.W. Peace MG 1-591
Leander Pearce to Rhoda A. Montgomery, 31 July 1879 (same), J.M. Bramlett MG 1-#1665
Lucinda Pierce to R. A. Phillips q.v.
Margaret T. Peace to Hezekiah James q.v.
Margarett L. Pierce to Isaac G. Stevens q.v.
Martha L. Pierce to Tandy J. Jones q.v.
Mary Pierce to Robert Boufer q.v.
P.W. Pierce to Elida Houston, 24 Jan 1891, F.J. Paine JP 4-24
Robert Pierce to Minnie Reynolds, 12 Dec 1895, W.M. Turner MG 4-91

PEARCY

1900 CENSUS
Samuel H. Pearcy 36 (July 1863-Wd)(Undertaker), Carl O. 7 (s)(July 1892) 10-327B-158/167
MARRIAGE
S.H. Pearcy to Effie Powell, 14 Aug 1900, W.L. Patton MG 4-106

PEARMAN / PEARMON

1880 CENSUS
Henry A. Pearman 22, Edna 25 6-12-116
1900 CENSUS
Henry Pearmon 48 (Jan 1852-T/Va/NC-M 24)(Blacksmith), Sidney 48 (June 1851-M 24-0), Horace C. 18 (c)(Dec 1881), Ida SMITH 10 (Jan 1890)(House Servant)

10-326A-130/135 [Henry L. married Sidney Rudd on 28 June 1875 in Meigs Co]

- - - - - - - - - - - - -

PEARSLEY

1900 CENSUS
Thomas Pearsley 57: see Joseph E. Rains

- - - - - - - - - - - - -

PEARSON / PERSON

1860 CENSUS
Samuel Pearson 28, July A. 31, Mary E. 7, Sarah STEPHENS 62 (NC) 3-57-391
Silas Pearson 39 (Va), Jane 33, Mary E. 8, Charles H. 6, Martha J. 3, Margaret E. 5/12 1-92-628
Thomas Pearson 70 (NC), Nancy 28, James 20, William H. 5, Nancy 3, Margaret 1 3-56-386
1870 CENSUS
James H. Pearson 28 (Retail Merchant), Hellen A. [Augusta] 22 2-5-25 [Jas, son of Thomas & Frances Pearson; Helen, dau of Bennett & Lydia Tunnell Franklin]
1880 CENSUS
James Pearson 38 (Blacksmith), H.A. 32 (w), J.T. 9 (s), J.C. 8 (s), W.A. 6 (s), L.O. 3/12 (d) 4-8-67
1900 CENSUS
Henry Pearson 28: see Maggie Roddy
James H. Pearson 60 (May 1840-M 31), Hellen A. 52 (Mar 1848-T/SC/Ky-M 31-7-6*), James T. 29 (Nov 1870) (Sawmill Engineer), John C. 28 (Mar 1872), Lydia O. 20 (Mar 1880), Harvey B. 17 (Aug 1883), Anna M. 14 (Mar 1886) 2-192B-29/30
[*deceased child was Lorena Alice, 1877-1878]
John Pearson 16 (Dec 1883-Ga/Ga/Ga) 8-275A-127 (B)
MARRIAGES
C. M. Pearson to G. T. Morgan q.v.
J.H. Pearson to Helen Franklin, 13 Dec 1869 (10 Dec), Z. Rose MG 1-#1133
James Pearson to Anny Liles, 18 Oct 1852 (24 Oct), Daniel Broyles JP 1-#384
John Pearson to Ella Brady, 30 Dec 1901 (probably 1900), M.E. McCuiston MG 4-107
Samuel L. Pearson to Julia Ann Collins, 21 June 1860 (24 June), J. Carson MG 1-#715
Sinda Pearson to John Carmical q.v.
Walter Pearson to E.M. Peak, 16 Aug 1899, G.R. Baldwin JP 4-104

- - - - - - - - - - - - -

PEASSALL

1900 CENSUS
Birdie Peassall 17: see Nattie Jones (B)

- - - - - - - - - - - - -

PEELER / PEALER

1880 CENSUS
W.D. Pealer 38, Elizabeth 42 (w), E.W. 17 (d), C.A. 13 (d), H.H. 8 (s), Hattie 6 (d), B.J. 3 (d) 8-5-36
MARRIAGE
W.D. Peeler to Elizabeth Shoemaker, 12 Jan 1880 (13 Jan), J.H. Perry MG 1-#1702

- - - - - - - - - - - - -

PELFREY / PHELFREY

1870 CENSUS
James Phelfrey 30, Caroline 27 (Ga), James T. 1 6-3-16
Thomas J. Phelfrey 34, Nancy 68, Pricey E. 26, James R. SMITH 11, Eliza A. 10, Mary E. 8 6-2-11
1880 CENSUS
T.J. Pelfrey 44, Barbary 35, Washington 7, Perry 5, Bynum 3, Tate 1 5-1-6
1900 CENSUS
Byron Pelfrey 23 (Ap 1877-M 3), Mary E. 25 (Aug 1874-M 3-2-2), Lewis F. 2 (July 1897), Mandy M. 11/12 (June 1899) 5-237B-189
Charles M. Pelfrey 27 (Jan 1873-M 6), Rhoda P. 21 (May 1879-M 6-3-3), Rosa C. 5 (Dec 1894), Mary E. 3 (Ap 1897), Ida L. 1 (Nov 1898) 6-241A-26
James L.(?) Pelfrey 30 (Oct 1869-M 11), Mahalay 31 (Dec 1868-M 11-5-5), Mary L. 9 (Aug 1890), Cora M. 8 (Jan 1892), James W. 6 (Mar 1894), Bessie L. 2 (Aug 1897), Andrew J. 8/12 (Sep 1899), John GASS (B) 42 (boarder)(Ap 1858) 4-224A-211/215 (Spring City & Dayton Road)
James N. Pelfrey 60 (Jan 1840-T/T/Va-M 0), Lizzie F. 21 (Nov 1878-M 0-0), Bascom 20 (s)(Feb 1880-T/T/Ga), Elija 14 (s)(Oct 1885), Lizzie WEBB 55 (si)(Sep 1844-T/T/Va-M 2-0-0) 6-247B-147/148
James W. Pelfrey 27 (Sep 1872-T/T/Ga-M 6)(RR Tiecutter), Sarah B. 23 (July 1876-M 6-3-3), Ida P. 5 (Jan 1894), Thomas A. 3 (Dec 1896), Rettie E.L. 1 (Feb 1899), Vesta LEMONS 17 (Ap 1882)(Servant) 9-228A-2
Perry Pelfrey 24 (June 1875-M 2), Eliza 19 (Dec 1880-M 2-1-0) 10-323B-74/78
Robert G. Pelfrey 24, Matilda F. 21, Foster B. 3, George B. 6/12: see G.A. Eakins
Thomas Pelfrey 63 (July 1836-T/T/NC-M 28), Barbara 53 (Jan 1847-M 28-7-7), Tate 21 (Mar 1879), Julia 16 (May 1884), Lura 13 (Jan 1887), Lorena RUDD 5 (boarder)(Unk) 10-323B-73/77
William E. Pelfrey 29 (Feb 1871-M 8), Hester 25 (July 1874-T/NC/T-M 8-2-2), Clement 5 (July 1894), Samuel J. 1 (Nov 1898) 6-247B-147/148
MARRIAGES
Bryan or Byron Pelfrey to Mary E. Henderson, 12 June 1896 (19 June), H.B. Burditt MG, R.J. Killough W 2-32
Charley Phelfrey to Rhoda Ackens, 18 June 1893, J.M. Bramlett MG 4-54
J.W. Pelfrey to S.B. Neal, 2 Sep 1893, J.M. Bramlett MG 4-67
J.W. Pelfrey to Florence E. or D. Reel, 13 Nov 1899 (15 Nov), J.M. Bramlett MG, J.R. Smith W 3-70
James Pelfrey to Caroline Beasly, 20 Mar 1868 (22 Mar), Wm Buttram MG 1-#1006
Liza J. Pelfrey to George Aikens q.v.
Lizza Pelfrey to G. M. Beasley q.v.
Robert Pelfrey to Frances Rul or Reel, 3 Sep 1896 (4 Sep), H.B. Burdett MG 2-41
Syntha Phelfrey to Thomas H. Burditt q.v.

Thomas J. Phelfrey to Barbara Ann Hurst, 4 Oct 1871 (no return) 1-#1211
Thomas J. Phelfrey to Mahala Aikens, 18 May 1889 (19 May), H.B. Burdett MG 1-574
W.E. Phelfrey to Hester Suttles, 1 Nov 1891, John Howard MG 4-37
W.P. Phelfrey to Lizzie Phillips, 15 Ap 1898 (17 Ap), J.M. Bramlett MG 2-269

- - - - - - - - - - - - -

PENCE

MARRIAGE
Dora Pence to A. F. Hendricks q.v.

- - - - - - - - - - - - -

PENDERGRASS

1900 CENSUS
Wm J. Pendergrass 37 (Nov 1862-NC/NC/NC-M 9), Martha J. 41 (Oct 1858-T/T/Va-M 9-2-1), Oscar W. 8 (Aug 1891), Claborn HARWOOD 49 (bl)(May 1849), Elizabeth HAMILTON 37 (sil)(May 1863-Wd), Mary 20 (ne)(Aug 1879-Pa/Va/Va) 3-209A-168/183
MARRIAGES
Martha Pendergrass to Gid Lion q.v.
Mary Pendergrass to Charles McAfee q.v.
Nettie Pendergrass to O. P. Corvin q.v.
Thomas Pendergrass to Nancy Elsey, 10 Oct 1889 (13 Oct), W.R. Grimsley MG 1-592
William Pendergrass to Mollie Harwood, 6 Ap 1886 (7 Ap), Taylor Russell JP 1-512
William Pendergrass to Martha Harwood, 29 Sep 1890, J.W. Williamson MG 4-17

- - - - - - - - - - - - -

PENS

1860 CENSUS
Betsy Pens 38: see Dempsey Sykes

- - - - - - - - - - - - -

PEOPLES

MARRIAGE
Elizabeth A. Peoples to George L.M. Wheeler q.v.

- - - - - - - - - - - - -

PERKEVILLE

MARRIAGE
James Perkeville [Pirkle?] to Annie Peters, 1 Ap 1900, R.A. Dickson JP 4-102

- - - - - - - - - - - - -

PERKINS / PARKINS

1880 CENSUS
Nelson Perkins 26 (B): see John Robinson
Robert Perkins 45, Malinda 40, A.D. 17 (d), J.C. 13 (s), E.D. 11 (d) 3-26-205
1900 CENSUS
Brainard Perkins 59 (Oct 1840-Ver/Ver/Ver-M 15)(Fruit Grower), Mary A. 39 (Ap 1861-M 15-2-2), Merrill 13 (June 1886), Brainard 9 (Aug 1890) 14-220A-140/144
Len Perkins 22: see George Miller (B)
Silas F. Perkins 34, Maggie A. 13: see Charles Medaris
William H. Perkins 50 (June 1849-NC/NC/NC-M 22), Nancy J. 54 (Oct 1845-M 22-5-1), Rachel M. 22 (May 1878) 2-198B-138/143
MARRIAGES
Adaline Parkins to K. M. Thompson q.v.
B.F. Perkins to Mary A. Lavender, 18 May 1885 (13 June), S.H. Price MG 1-496
F.L. Perkins to Sarah Sharp, 11 June 1898 (same), W.L. Lillard JP, R.J. Hairress W 2-291
Frances E. Perkins to Robert Durham q.v.
J.J. Perkins (25, Jefferson Co) to Anna Quinn (18, McMinn Co), 31 Jan 1882, Thompson Ashburn MG, John Birnett & Lizza Zeigler W 4-10(97)
Moses Perkins to Mahala Gibson, 16 May 1878 (18 May), H.B. Heiskel JP 1-#1559
Robert Perkins to Margaret M. Wyrick, 28 May 1884 (29 May), B.F. Holloway JP 1-464
Write Perkins to Mary Thomas or Thurman, 31 Dec 1887 (same), W.S. Hale MG 1-546

- - - - - - - - - - - - -

PERRY

1880 CENSUS
J.F. Perry 30 (Minister), M.V. 30 (w), W.E. 6 (s), S.J. 4 (d), O.W. 2 (s) 8-13-115
James Perry 26, M. 25 (w, Martha 8, Anna 6, Mary 4, Alvin 2, Isaac 3/12 3-25-202
V. T. Perry 18: see John Cox
1900 CENSUS
Andrew J. Perry 52 (July 1847-M 16), Malissa 33 (Unk 1866-M 16-6-5), Nora Vesta 15 (May 1885), Flora M. 7 (Oct 1892), Samuel T. 4 (Feb 1896), Alice D. 2 (Ap 1898), Jack D. 7/12 (Nov 1899), William H. SMITH 25 (Ap 1875)(Servant) 3-204B-82/89
Isaac A. Perry 20: see William B. Hawkins
John Perry 58 (Dec 1841-Italy/Do/Do-1871/28/Na-M 14), Josephine 36 (May 1864-Ky/Ky/Ky-M 14-0) 10-327B-154/162
MARRIAGES
A.J. Perry to Malissa E. Smith, 28 Oct 1882 (29 Oct), J.W. Thompson MG 1-473 & 4-11(103)
Ann Perry to John Cox q.v.
Annie Perry to Henry Young q.v.
B. F. Perry to Annie Clage, 14 May 1885 (same), P. P. Brooks ?? 1-494
Charles Perry to Rebecca N. Minicks, 6 Jan 1876 (same), W.R. Henry JP 1-#1428
Della Perry to W. D. Wilkey q.v.
James Perry to Margarett Gossett, 24 Aug 1871 (same), W.R. Henry JP 1-#1205
Mattie Perry to John R. Neal q.v.
Molly Perry to Lindsey Pritchett q.v.
Molley Perry to W. R. Millican q.v.
R.H. Perry to Ann Elizabeth Harp, 19 May 1877 (20 May), A. Hickman MG 1-#1498
Victoria Perry to William Y. Denton q.v.

William Perry to M.F. Walker, 16 July 1880 (same), A.J. Pritchett MG 1-296
William H. Perry to Lotty Beannett, 30 Nov 1875, W.R. Henry JP 1-#1421

- - - - - - - - - - - - -

PETERS

1860 CENSUS
Agnes Peters 65 (Va), Nancy 42, Betsy 38, Cynthia 32 2-78-528
1870 CENSUS
Agnes Peters 75 (Va), Nancy 46, Elizabeth 43, Sintha 37 2-6-38
Horace Peters 15, Calvin 10 (B): see Joseph B. Peters
Joseph B. Peters 52 (Merchant), Susana M. 47, Margaret C.A. 16, Joseph L. 11, Laura A. 9, Horace PETERS (B) 15, Calvin (B) 10 2-4-33
1880 CENSUS
Horace Peters 23, Mary 21: see Caroline Locke (B)
Joseph Peters 62 (Retired Merchant), Susanna 57, Joseph 21, Laura 18 2-22-179
Nancy Peters 63, Elizabeth 60 (si)(Seamstress) 2-22-175
1900 CENSUS
Samuel Peters 30 (Ap 1870-M 5), Nanie 23 (July 1879-M 5-2-1), Mary 3 (June 1896), Washington 1 (July 1898) 1-184B-111/117
MARRIAGES
Adda A. Peters to Milo S. Holloway q.v.
Annie Peters to James Perkeville [Pirkle?] q.v.
Cornelia Peters to William P. Thomison q.v.
Harvey Peters to Tannie Mitchell, 7 May 1887 (8 May), Anthony Smith MG 1-535
Horace Peters to Mollie Locke, 22 Nov 1879 (24 Nov), B.F. Holloway JP 1-#1718
Horace Peters to Mahala Lustors, 11 Sep 1894, W.H. Baine MG 4-70
J.F. Peters (32, W Va) to Martha Ann Peters (25, Blount Co), 25 Aug 1881, A. Selcer MG, J. Peters & J. Selcer W 4-3(30) (B)
Laura Peters to T. G. Gillespie q.v.
Louie Peters to W. H. Harrison q.v.
Martha Ann Peters to J. F. Peters q.v. (B)
Samuel Peters to Nannie Rhea, 7 Aug 1895, W.N. Rose MG 4-104

- - - - - - - - - - - - -

PETERSON

1860 CENSUS
John Peterson 25, Lucinda C. 24, Vesta A. 4, Joseph A. 2 6-105-712
Joseph Peterson 70 (Miller), Jane 50 3-58-398
Permelia J. Peterson 21: see John B. Murphy
Robert Peterson 39 (Blacksmith), Mary J. 25, William C. 7, Lucy 4 6-102-697
Thomas Peterson 36, Sarah A. 31, Nancy M. 11, Mary J. 6, Margaret E. 4, Robert 1 6-106-719
1870 CENSUS
Elizabeth Peterson 45: see Harvey Roddy
John Peterson 36, Lucinda C. 35, Vesta A. 16, Joseph 13, John R. 10, Sidney C. 9, Catharine 6, Delia E. 2 6-8-53
Robert Peterson 40 (Ala)(Blacksmith), Mary 36, William 17, Lucy 14, Emma 1 6-8-52
Thomas Peterson 46 (Ala), Sarah A. 40, Nancy M. 20, Mary J. 17, Robert 10, Sarah C. 8, Amanda T. 5, Virginia 1 6-11-77
1880 CENSUS
John Peterson 46 (Blacksmith), Eliza M. 34, Louisa E. 14, Dellie E. 12, Sallie R. 10, Cora L. 6, James E. LOAD 4 (ss), Birthey FRAZIER 3 (gd) 6-22-11
Thomas Peterson 53, Sarah A. 48, Robert 20, Sarah C. 17, Manda T. 14, Virginia A. 10, Emily G. 7, Joseph T. 4, Margaret J. WYATT 7 (gd) 8-19-175/180
MARRIAGES
Emma Peterson to John Pogue q.v.
James Peterson to Elizabeth Wright, 5 Mar 1864 (same), A.P. Early MG 1-#823
John Peterson to Catharine Trim, 31 May 1853 (same), J. Wyott JP 1-#412
Joseph Peterson to Jenna Campbell, 26 Dec 1852 (27 Dec), John Wyott JP 1-#398
Mary Peterson to Joseph T. Blevins q.v.
Nancy M. Peterson to John Wyott q.v.
Robert Peterson to Mary Martin, 7 Feb 1851 (same), John Wyott JP 1-#332
Robert Peterson to Tilda Saffles, 25 Dec 1886 (26 Dec), P.G. Roddy MG 1-515
Sarah Peterson to J. D. Roddy q.v.
Tennie Peterson to Samuel Gravitt q.v.
V. A. Peterson to L. G. Frazier q.v.
Virginia Peterson to James Whittle q.v.

- - - - - - - - - - - - -

PETTYGREW

MARRIAGE
William Pettygrew to Jennie Peyton, 17 Sep 1889 (same), J.W. Burnett MG 1-585

- - - - - - - - - - - - -

PEYTON

MARRIAGE
Jennie Peyton to William Pettygrew q.v.

- - - - - - - - - - - - -

PHARRIS / PARRIS

1880 CENSUS
Rhena Paris 14: see Andrew Anderson
MARRIAGES
Louiza Parris to James B. Bidwell q.v.
Peter Pharris to Mary Jones, 24 May 1855 (same), Wm C. Hollins JP 1-#502

- - - - - - - - - - - - -

PHELPS

MARRIAGE
Edward M. Phelps to Frances Paul, 20 May 1898 (25 May), N.W. Allen MG, C.F. Dart W 2-283

- - - - - - - - - - - - -

PHILEMON / PHILYMON

MARRIAGES

J.W. Philymon to Martha Reed, 17 Jan 1885 (19 Jan), W.H. Walis(?) MG 1-495

Nancy Philyan to Preston Durham q.v.

- - - - - - - - - - - - -

PHILLIPS

1860 CENSUS

James C. Phillips 30 (NC), Martha 24 (Ga), Carter F. 9 (Ga), Malinda R. 2 5-35-234

1870 CENSUS

James Phillips 40 (NC), Martha 36 (Ga), Rena E. 15, Julia 10, Mary E. 6, Martha 5 5-5-30

Robert A. Phillips 51, Jane 44, James M. 26, Amanda P. 22, Robert M. 18, Margarette E. 16, Asha 11, Martha 6 4-1-6 [R.A. married Jane Reed on 17 Oct 1844 in Roane County]

1880 CENSUS

Harris R. Phillips 34, Elizabeth 34, William J. 12, Martha C. 9, Girtie L. 7, James C. 5, Allis 2 5-11-101

J.C. Phillips 54, Mary 21 (w), July E. 20, Mary E. 16, John 9, Sarah C. 3 5-1-4

Lucy Phillips 6: see Robert Robinson (B)

Robert Phillips 62, Jane 56, A.J. 21, Martha 17 3-25-199

Sarah Phillips 12: see David Pierce

Tom Phillips 30, E.R. 28 (w), Nora 10, C. 7 8-8-67

1900 CENSUS

Benjamin Phillips 19: see James C. Moore

Carter Phillips 54 (May 1846-M 28), Elizabeth 53 (Mar 1847-M 28-8-6), Marthy 25 (Sep 1874), Jim 23 (Aug 1876), Allice 21 (Jan 1879), Rosey 18 (Sep 1881), John PRYOR 18 (boarder)(Dec 1881) 10-256B-124/128

Clara ?. Phillips 40 (Jan 1860-Mich/Do/Do-Wd 3-0)(Corres. Sec., Sou. Ad.), Albert K. 15 (ss)(Ap 1885), Bessie I. 9 (sd)(Oct 1890), Arthur J. 8 (ss)(May 1892), Day CONKLIN 67 (f)(Jan 1833-Mich/Do/NY-M 25) (School Teacher), Julia 60 (m)(Aug 1839-NY/NY/NY-M 25-0-0 sic), Mary A. PHILLIPOT 18 (boarder) (Aug 1881-Wisc/T/Wisc)(Student) 13-308B-352/365

Creasy Phillps 7: see Daniel F. Hickey (B)

John Phillps 31 (Unk 1869-T/NC/NC-M 2), Virginia 26 (Mar 1874-M 2-1-1), Birtha J. 6/12 (Nov 1899) 3-201A-26/27

John T. Phillips 50 (Nov 1849-T/Va/T-M 0), Vesta J. 32 (July 1867-M 0-0-0), Cora E. 13 (d)(May 1887), Luther 10 (s)(Feb 1890), Minett 21 (s)(Jan 1879-M 0), Bula 16 (dl)(Ap 1884-M 0-0) 4-227A-266/270 (Rhea Springs & Washington Road)

Joseph Phillips 51 (Dec 1848-M 29)(Furnace Hand), Mary 49 (Aug 1850-SC/SC/SC-M 29-5-0), Lucinda OSBORN 78 (ml)(Unk-SC/SC/SC-Wd 3-2), George ALSOOP 35 (boarder)(May 1865-T/Va/Va)(Furnace Hand) 10-328A-166/167 (B)

Joseph E. Phillips 53 (June 1846-Ga/NC/NC-M 23)(Mail Carrier), Delia A. 55 (July 1844-NC/NC/NC-M 23-3-1) 14-216A-72/73

Minett Phillps 21, Bula 16: see John T. Phillips

Nelson Phillips 15: see Cilis Parmerlee

Robert A. Phillips 81, Cinda A. 61: see Robert M. Phillips

Robert M. Phillips 48 (Nov 1851-M 23), Cordelia 40 (Ap 1860-8-6), Robert T. 22 (Oct 1877), Luther 15 (Oct 1884), Benjamin P. 10 (May 1890), Fredie M. 7 (Nov 1892), Gertrude 5 (Ap 1895), Robert A. 81 (f)(Feb 1819-M 10), Cinda A. 61 (m)(Ap 1840-M 10-3-2) 2-196B-97/100

Walter Phillips 2: see Mary Lightfoot (B)

Well Phillips 59 (B): see Jeremiah C. Wasson

William Phillips 28 (May 1872-M 9)(Charge of Coke Oven), Ellie 26 (Jan 1874-M 9-4-4), Arvil C. 8 (July 1891), Virgil L. 7 (Sep 1892), Cyrus R. 4 (Ap 1896), Clara E. 2 (Mar 1898) 10-256B-125/129

MARRIAGES

A. Phillips to E. S. Fugate q.v.

Anna Phillips to A. J. Bankston q.v.

Annie Phillips to Charles Montgomery q.v.

Carrie Phillips to Jack Turner q.v.

Charley Phillips to Sallie Randolph, 20 July 1897 (same), H. Hilbert MG 2-163

E.T. Phillips (34, Baltimore, Md) to M.A. Parmalee (20, Chittenden, Vt), 16 Jan 1882, D.V. Culver MG, Thomas Johnson & John Robinson W 4-9(90)

Edward B. Phillips to Susan Vida Collins, 6 June 1893, John L. Price MG 4-55

Ethel Phillips to Q. A. Tallent q.v.

Eugene Phillips to Ida B. Hale, 28 Ap 1900 (same), J.D. Gaither MG 3-151

Gertie(?) Phillips to H. B. Hawkins q.v.

Horace Phillips to Synthia Bridgeman, 3 Oct 1899 (same), R.T. Smith ?? 3-46

J.C. Phillips to Mary E. Smith, 24 Feb 1880 (same), W.A. Hale MG 1-#1720

James Phillips to Onis Smith, 26 Dec 1900 (same), W.L. Lillard JP 3-265

James M. Phillips to Amanda C. Long, 1 Dec 1870 (8 Dec), John Howard MG 1-#1177

John Phillips to Jennie Coxey, 4 June 1898 (5 June), J.M. Bramlett MG, G.W. Frazier W 2-288

John Phillips to Vesta J. Thompson, 29 Mar 1900, L.M. Cartright MG 4-104

John M. Phillips (20, Putnam Co) to Rittie M. Scott (14, White Co), 9 June 1881, D.V. Cluver MG, Charles A. Quiner & Frank Ditty W 4-1(10)

John T. Phillips to Victory Fugate, 11 Feb 1878 (13 Feb), W.W. Low JP 1-#1544

Julia Phillips to William Crow q.v.

Lizzie Phillips to W. P. Phelfrey q.v.

Lucy Phillips to D. F. Hickey q.v.

Margaret E. Phillips to J. G. Hicks q.v.

Mary Phillips to S. T. Crow q.v.

Mary Phillips to Henry Romines q.v.

Mattie Phillips to Thomas W. Kincannon q.v.

Mattie Phillips to W. A. Cate q.v.

Melvin Phillips (30, Rhea Springs) to Emaline Wasson (24, Rhea Springs), 9 Dec 1881, Thompson Ashburn MG, Mrs. Anna Crosby (Rhea Springs) & Miss Anna Williams (Moleston, Ala) W 4-5(42) (B)

Moses Phillips to Hannah King, 13 June 1885 (14 June), W.S. Hale MG 1-495

Mynott Phillips to Bula Jenoe, 30 Aug 1899 (3 Sep), A.M. Broyles JP, W.K. Fugate W 3-29

Polly Phillips to Albert Nelson q.v.

R.A. Phillips to Lucinda Pierce, 10 Jan 1891, J.W. Cowles JP 4-21

R.M. Phillips to Cordelia Russell, 20 Nov 1876 (21 Nov), W.W. Low JP 1-#1468
Sewell Phillips to Addaline Gillespie, 31 July 1856 (1 Aug), T.K. Munsey MG 1-#555
William Phillips to Ella Gibson, 13 Sep 1890, R.A. Bartlett MG 4-15

- - - - - - - - - - - - -

PHILPOT / FILPOT / PHILLIPOT

1880 CENSUS
I.L. Philpot 33, S.E. 31, Mary 13, A.E. 3 (d), Joseph 3/12 (s) 4-12-93
1900 CENSUS
Mary A. Phillips 18: see Clara ? Phillips
MARRIAGE
Mary H. Filpot to John H. Curtis q.v.

- - - - - - - - - - - - -

PHIPPS

1900 CENSUS
John P. Phipps 22: see James M. Cox

- - - - - - - - - - - - -

PICKARD

1900 CENSUS
Frank Pickard 47 (July 1852-NC/NC/NC-M 21), Ella L. 41 (July 1858-Ind/NC/Ind-M 21-4-2), Lena M. 20 (July 1820-Ind), Charles J. 9 (Feb 1891) 11-293A-81
Matilda L. Pickard 70 (Sep 1829-NC/NC/NC-Wd 6-3) 11-293A-82

- - - - - - - - - - - - -

PICKETT / PICKET

1860 CENSUS
Cassan Picket 78, Joseph S. 42 8-17-117
P.M. Picket 42 (NC), Eliza 35, Mary C. 16, Lewis R. 15, John W. 13, James F. 9, Laura 8, William T. 1 8-23-156
1870 CENSUS
Eliza Picket 46, James 20, William 13 10-1-4
1880 CENSUS– None
1900 CENSUS
James F. Pickett 49 (Aug 1850-T/NC/NC-M 29), Maggie S. 46 (July 1853-T/Va/Va-M 29-12-10), John S. 18 (May 1882), Mattie B. 14 (June 1885), William H. 11 (June 1888), Jessie C. 7 (Jan 1893) 11-290A-11
James T. Pickett 23 (Jan 1877-M 3)(Coal Miner), Charlotte A. 21 (Nov 1878-T/T/Ga-M 3-1-1), John S. 1 (Sep 1898) 11-290B-12
MARRIAGES
Duskie(?) Pickett to Marion Rigsby q.v.
Ella Pickett to David Burwick q.v.
Eva Pickett to Walker Headley q.v.
James Pickett to Lottie Franklin, 21 Dec 1896 (24 Dec), J.H. Morgan JP, F.M. Rigsby W 2-92
James F. Pickett to Mary Swafford, 12 June 1868 (14 June), Wm L. Humphrey JP 1-#1014
James F. Pickett to Margaret D.E. Walker, 14 Nov 1870 (15 Nov), J.W. Williamson MG 1-#1175
Laura Pickett to F. R. Morgan q.v.
Rosie Pickett to Dennis Rowan q.v.
W.F. Pickett to S.A. Gothard, 7 July 1879 (no return) 1-#1620

- - - - - - - - - - - - -

PICKLE / PICKEL

1900 CENSUS
Alberta Pickle 8/12: see Sam Walters (B)
James Pickle 39 (Nov 1860-M 19), Texas 38 (Dec 1861-Ga/Ga/Ga-M 19-8-5), James P. 15 (Ap 1886), Nellie 11 (Mar 1889), Napoleon 8 (Ap 1892), Rosa E. 5 (Ap 1895), Pealie 1 (Sep 1898) 8-288B-408/410
Nancy Pickle 18, Ethel 3, Lavinia 6/12: see Rhoda Hamilton (B)
Nimrod Pickle 61 (Unk-M 29)(Blacksmith), Lucy 42 (May 1858-M 29-2-2) 8-313B-55/58 (B)
MARRIAGES
Charles B. Pickel to Causie Edmunds, 13 Jan 1892, S.W. Burnett MG 4-33
Eva Pickel to Samuel McJunkin q.v.
John Pickel to Lorin Duff, 7 Aug 1889 (same), R.S. Mason JP 1-577
Robert Pickle to Nancey Hamilton, 2 July 1896 (same), J.B. Phillips MG, Moses Porter [signed by X] W 2-36
S. E. Pickel to Thomas J. Mannis q.v.

- - - - - - - - - - - - -

PIESATT

1900 CENSUS
Katharine Piesatt 18, Ada V. 17, Martha 15, William 10: see Wm J. Buckhanon
MARRIAGE
Margaret Piesatt to J. M. Ross q.v.

- - - - - - - - - - - - -

PINE

1900 CENSUS
Ollie Pine 23: see Samuel W. Litchfield

- - - - - - - - - - - - -

PINION

1880 CENSUS
George Pinion 28, Lucinda 52 (m), Martha KIRBY 29 (si) 2-26-209 (Mu)
1900 CENSUS
George C. Pinion 53 (B): see Henry J. Bell
MARRIAGE
Marthy Pinion to J. B. Kirby q.v.

- - - - - - - - - - - - -

PIRKLE– see PERKEVILLE

- - - - - - - - - - - - -

PLEASANT

1900 CENSUS

Benjamin F. Pleasant 75 (Mar 1825-Ky/Va/T-Wd)(Physician) 10-331B-240/255

MARRIAGE

W.F. Pleasant to Amanda Cox, 9 July 1883 (10 July), I.W. Holt JP 1-479

- - - - - - - - - - - - -

PLISTON

MARRIAGE

Harriet Pliston or Preston to Henry Foster q.v.

- - - - - - - - - - - - -

PLUNING

1900 CENSUS

Florida Pluning 15: see Andy Majors

- - - - - - - - - - - - -

POE

MARRIAGES

A.R. Poe to M.M. Mariott, 1 Aug 1855 (same), J. Crawford JP 1-#511

Frank Poe to Nancy A. Arthur, 15 Ap 1879 (same), J.A. Shaver MG 1-#1614

John R. Poe to Martha Jane Ble.ins, 31 July 1867 (no return) 1-#962

Matthew Louis Poe (28, Ga) to Paralee Moonahan (20, White Co), 24 July 1881, J.W. Hughes JP, Lewis Rogers, Hennegar Morgan & Wm Snow W 4-1(3) & 4-7(61)

W.S.B. Poe to Nellie E. Lee, 1 June 1898 (5 June), A. Hickman MG, W.S. Bert Poe & Arthur S. Kelley W 2-287

- - - - - - - - - - - - -

POESTON

MARRIAGE

Nancy E. Poeston to James L. Wyrick q.v.

[recopied records show last name as Ponder and a Nancy E. was the dau of William R. Ponder; the original marriage record is definitely spelled Poeston]

- - - - - - - - - - - - -

POGUE / POGE

1900 CENSUS

John Pogue 27 (Dec 1872-Ind/Oh/NC-D), James W. 25 (b)(Oct 1874-T/Oh/NC), Louiza PARKER 53 (m)(Jan 1847-NC/T/Ga-M 10-9-7), Elvin PARKER 8 (sb)(Dec 1891-T/T/NC), Rhea BUNN 14 (sb)(May 1886-T/Ind/NC), Jay BUNN 14 (sb)(May 1886) 6-249A-173/174

MARRIAGES

John Pogue to Emma Peterson, 6 Jan 1889 (same), W.Y. Curton MG 1-562

John Pogue to Mary Boyd, 16 Oct 1898, T.A. Coppinger W "License Returned" 2-335

John W. Pogue to Kittie Parker, 19 July 1892, J.W. Peace MG 4-63

John W. Pogue to Lillie Tilly, 2 June 1900 (same), W.J. McLarin(?) MG, Theo Moence W 3-162

Joseph Pogue to Flora Wycuff, 25 June 1900 (same), W.S. Hale MG, J.J. Alley(?) W 3-171

Louella Pogue to John A. Porter q.v.

Milton Poge to Maggie Brown, 31 Dec 1897 (1 Jan 1899) [sic], R.T. Smith ??, John Sharp W 2-367

- - - - - - - - - - - - -

PONDER

1870 CENSUS

William R. Ponder 49, Margaret 45, Nancy E. 19, Sarah F. 17, Atey(?) C. 15, Jonathan V. 13, Margaret C. 11, William P. 5 1-12-90

1880 CENSUS

Hamilton Ponder 32, Elizabeth 34, Ellen 6, William 4, Almeda 1 2-39-316

MARRIAGES

A. C. Ponder to A. F. Burnett q.v.

H. W. Ponder to Margarett E. Wyrick, 18 Ap 1872 (no return) 1-#1237

Margaret C. Ponder to G. W. Wyrick q.v.

Nancy E. Ponder(?) – see Poeston

- - - - - - - - - - - - -

POOL / POOLE

1900 CENSUS

Elijah Pool 33 (Jan 1867-T/SC/T-M 12), Julia 1871-T/SC/SC-M 12-7-5), John 10 (Jan 1890), Linas 8 (May 1892), William 4 (May 1896), Hubert 1 (Aug 1898), George 4/12 (Jan 1900) 8-286B-361/363

Lorenzo Poole 72 (Unk 1828-SC/SC/SC-M 29)(Coal Miner), Martha 64 (Aug 1836-T/Ala/T-M 29-6-4), William M. 25 (July 1874)(Locamotive Fireman), Lorenzo Jr. 29 (Jan 1871-M 7), Minnie 20 (dl)(July 1879-M 7-1-1), James F. 5 (gs)(July 1894) 8-279B-226/228

William T. B. Poole 37 (Aug 1862-Ga/Ala/Unk-M 8) (Furnace Engineer), Sarah E. 27 (Feb 1873-M 8-4-2), Maud 4 (Aug 1895), Edith 1 (June 1898) 10-326B-139/147

MARRIAGES

Elijah Pool to Julia Donahoo, 22 Feb 1888 (same), Calvin Morgan JP 1-548

L.D. Pool to Minnie Burchard, 11 Oct 1892, William Turner MG 4-48

Minnie Pool to J. F. Wright q.v.

W.T.B. Pool to Salie Birchfield, 20 Mar 1891, R.S. Mason JP 4-22

- - - - - - - - - - - - -

POPE

1880 CENSUS

Burrell Pope 37, Harriet 37, Caroline 10, William 7, Minerva 4, Susan 1/12 1-9-69

J. Pope 38 (House Painter): see W. N. Ault

1900 CENSUS

James F. Pope 58 (Jan 1842-Wd)(House Painter), Henry P. 17 (Feb 1883), Ernest N. 12 (Feb 1888), Josephine 7 (Sep 1882) 14-223A-193/197

Monroe Pope 54 (Sep 1845-M 11)(House Painter), Rebecca 46 (July 1853-M 11-0-0) 14-223A-195/199

Thomas Pope 40 (Sep 1859-M 21), Sallie 39 (Mar 1861-M 21-8-5), Ninni 15 (Mar 1884), Adda 14 (Mar 1886), Gilbert 8 (June 1891), Martha 6 (Jan 1894), Chaim(?) 4 (Dec 1896) 12-179B-21/23

MARRIAGES

Minerva Pope to Ed Johnson q.v.

Monroe Pope to Rebecca Burdett, 20 Jan 1891, D. Broyles JP 4-20

T.J. Pope to Sallie Hinkel, 11 June 1887 (12 June), W.S. Hale MG 1-526

PORTER

1860 CENSUS

John A. Porter 25, Eliza 21 3-65-445

Rebecca M. Porter(?) 15: see John White

Reuben W. Porter 34, Elizabeth 25, Sarah 8 3-55-377

Samuel Porter 75 (SC), Rebecca 70 (NC) 3-55-379

William Porter 36, Amanda 33, Lucy 12, Nancy 10, Bersheba 8, Francis 6 4-50-341

1870 CENSUS

John A. Porter 35, Eliza Jane 30, James S. 9, John A. 7, Rebecca E. 2, Blanch L. 15 3-3-21

John W. Porter 20, Malissa 20, Mariah 5/12 7-5-33

Rebecca Porter 83: see Reuben Porter

Reuben Porter 46, Elizabeth 44, Susan 8, William R. 2, Leatha 20, Henry 9, Samuel 2, Rebecca 83 (NC) 4-1-1

1880 CENSUS

H.B. Porter 33, A.E. 24 (w), Jane 2, S.J. 1 (s), William PORTER 35 (b), S.C. HARSHAW (B) 25 (Servant), Henry PORTER (B) 19 (Servant) 3-14-113

Henry Porter 19 (B): see H. R. Porter

J.W. Porter 26, Tilda M. 34, Mariah S. 9, William H. 7, Jenette 5, Mary E. 1 5-10-92

John A. Porter 46, Eliza J. 39, James S. 19, John A. 17, Rebecca E. 11, Mary A. 10, William J. 6, Robert H. 5, Ida M. 1, Rebecca M. PORTER 96 (m), William PORTER 18 (c) 6-12-119

Rebecca M. Porter 96: see John A. Porter

William Porter 35: see H. R. Porter

William Porter 18: see John A. Porter

1900 CENSUS

Henry Porter 27 (June 1872-M 6), Emma 24 (Aug 1875-M 6-3-3), John 4 (June 1895), Joseph 1 (Aug 1898), Carie 1 (May 1899) 5-233A-96

James Porter 28 (Dec 1870-M 5)(RR Engineer), Lizzie 23 (Ap 1877-T/T/Ala-M 5-1-1), Maud L. 3 (Ap 1897) 10-259A-178/182

James S. Porter 28 (Sep 1871) [marked through] 3-206A-108/119

James S. Porter 39 (Aug 1860-M 2), Clarinda M. 24 (Oct 1875-T/NC/T-M 2-2-2), James R. 1 (July 1898), Bessie M. 2/12 (Feb 1900), John H. WARD 59 (f)(Mar 1841-NC/Unk-Wd) 3-208A-140/153

John Porter 51 (June 1848-Oh/Oh/Oh-M 28), Mary J. 51 (Jan 1849-Ind/Oh/Oh-M 28-5-5), Frederick E. 24 (Aug 1875-Oh), Irene 23 (Ap 1877-Oh), Harvey D. 21 (May 1879-Oh), Albert 19 (Feb 1881-Oh)(Telegraph Operator), Mary E. 16 (Sep 1883-Oh) 6-240B-22

John Porter 55 (Aug 1844-M 33), Malissa 47 (Feb 1853-M 33-9-7), Serepta 18 (Sep 1881), Rosa 11 (June 1888), Laura 10 (Feb 1890) 5-233A-97

John A. Porter Sr. 66 (June 1833-T/Va/Va-Wd), Humphrus 17 (Ap 1833) 3-202A-45/48

John A. Porter Jr. 37 (Jan 1863-M 11), Luella 27 (Jan 1873-M 11-5-5), Otha C. 9 (Nov 1890), Azli 7 (s)(Sep 1892), Sarah L. 6 (Mar 1894), Ora A. (d)(Ap 1895), Lucella M. 2 (Oct 1897) 4-226B-261/265 (Rhea Springs & Washington Road)

Letha M. Porter 59, James S. 33: see Rheuban F. Porter

Moses Porter 27 (June 1872-T/T/NC-M 7)(Stonecutter), Malinda 27 (Feb 1873-M 7-4-1), Charles S. 9 (Nov 1890), Nettie THOMAS 18 (boarder)(July 1881) 10-329B-186/209 (B)

Rheuban F. Porter 19 (Nov 1880-M 3), Margaret C. 19 (Jan 1881-T/Unk/Ga-M 3-3-1), Olanzo 2 (Oct 1897), Letha M. PORTER 59 (m)(Unk 1841-Wd 6-3), James PORTER 33 (b)(Mar 1867) 3-208A-142/155

Robert F. Porter 27 (Mar 1873-M 0), Lena 18 (July 1881-M 0), Hattie E. 2 (d)(Dec 1898) 4-226B-260/264 (Rhea Springs & Washington Road)

William H. Porter 38 (July 1861-M 17), Susan A. 39 (Mar 1861-M 17-4-3), Tilda 13 (Jan 1887), James S. 10 (May 1889), Mary J. 9 (Aug 1890) 4-227B-278/282

William J. Porter 27 (Jan 1873-M 4), Emma 26 (June 1873-M 4-3-3), Birtha A. 3 (June 1898), John A. 1 (July 1899), William J. Jr. 1/12 (May 1900) 3-211A-191/209

MARRIAGES

A. P. Porter to J. L. Rector q.v.

B. M. Porter to G. W. Edmonds q.v.

Francis Porter to Clara Kelly, 17 Dec 1896, J.H. Howard MG 4-97

H.F. Porter to Tennessee Minicks, 27 Feb 1878 (same), J.M. Bramlett MG 1-#1548

Henry Porter to Emma Gardner, 23 Mar 1895, H.B. Burdit MG 4-87

Ida M. Porter to W. O. Bankston q.v.

John A. Porter to Eliza J. White, 6 Dec 1859 (no return) 1-#702

John A. Porter to Louella Pogue, 2 Feb 1889 (3 Feb), W.G. Curtain ?? 1-566

John W. Porter to Malissa Smith, 2 Sep 1869 (same), R.T. Howard MG 1-#1110

Josie Porter to S. L. Grayham q.v.

Leathy Porter to Rheubeun Porter q.v.

Leury M. Porter to William R. Carroll q.v.

Margaret Porter to John Fike q.v.

Mariah Porter to Martin Loftis q.v.

Mary Porter to Thomas Coval q.v.

Mary Emaline Porter to Sherman Paul q.v.

Moses Porter to Malinda Locke, 4 Mar 1890 (same), J.W. Wright MG 1-595

Nancy Porter to James M. Smith q.v.

R.A. Porter to Martha Hicks, 17 Aug 1887 (18 Aug), J.M. Bramlett MG 1-539

R. E. Porter to J. W. Hill q.v.

R.F.C. Porter to L. Bankston, 17 Jan 1900, L.E. Smith JP 4-102

Rheubeun Porter to Leathy Porter, 19 Feb 1876 (same), A.J. Pritchett MG 1-#1437
Sam Porter to Louiza Kelly, 24 Dec 1901 [probably 1900], J.F. Leuty JP 4-109
Sarah Porter to Elisha Brown q.v.
Susan Porter to or A. J. Moore q.v.
W.H. Porter to S.A. Woods, 14 Sep 1883 (15 Sep), M.F. Moore MG 1-478

- - - - - - - - - - - - -

POSEY / POSSY

1900 CENSUS
John Possy 62: see John Potter
MARRIAGES
B. C. Posey to B. F. Rose q.v.
Martha Posey to John Potter q.v.
N.T. Posey to Rachael Jane Haney, 22 Mar 1881 (same), A.P. Early MG 1-298
W.D. Posey to Beckey Roe, 21 Sep 1897 (same), R.C. Knight JP, J.C. Nipper W 2-173
Wylie or Wiley D. Posey to Josephine Wathern, 10 June 1898 (same), C.E. Mowry JP, J.D. Olinger W 2-297

- - - - - - - - - - - - -

POTTER

1870 CENSUS
Thomas C. Potter 47, Margarette 46, William 17, Abijah 15, Sarah 13, Martha 11, Laura 4, Rhoda 1 6-14-100
1880 CENSUS
Arter M. Potter 39 ("A lone woman living about"), Cluisa E.M. 2 (s) 6-19-172/176
1900 CENSUS
Elizabeth Potter 62 (Oct 1837-T/NC/Ga-Wd 10-7), Wm 40 (July 1859), Isaac 27 (Sep 1872), Jack 25 (Mar 1875) (Brakeman), Lillie 23 (July 1879), Ida BROYLES 3 (gd)(Feb 1897) 8-311A-8/8
John Potter 37 (Jan 1862-M 8)(RR Engineer), Martha 24 (Mar 1876-T/Ga/Ga-M 8-3-3), Wolford 7 (Ap 1893), Lelia 3 (Sep 1896), Lennia 6/12 (Nov 1899), John POSEY 62 (fl)(Oct 1847-Ga/Ga/Ga-Wd) 10-259B-184/188
Silas Potter 34 (Mar 1866-M 11)(RR Locamotive), Martha A. 34 (Feb 1866-M 11-1-1), Jackie E. 9 (Aug 1890) 10-259B-183/187
MARRIAGES
Anna B. Potter to James L. Crawley q.v.
James Potter to Lizzie Coffe, 25 July 1894, W.S. Hale MG 4-67
John Potter to Martha Posey, 16 Jan 1892, J.W. Williamson MG 4-36
Martha J. Potter to William Corvin q.v.

- - - - - - - - - - - - -

POWELL / POWEL

1880 CENSUS
A.W. Powell 26, M.H. 24, V.E. 5 (d), M.M. 4/12 (d), Sarah W. 1 [last name & age marked through] 7-28-242
Daniel N. Powell 62, Mary A. 60, Daniel Squire Powell 21 (s) 10-26-196/201
Mariah Powel 22, Charles 1: see Charles Jewitt
1900 CENSUS
Blanche Powell 28: see Mary Cornett
Carrie M. Powell 24: see Jackson Suddath (B)
Charles H. Powell 34 (Feb 1866-M 6)(School Teacher), Lula 25 (Mar 1875-M 6-3-3), Ulysis 5 (Nov 1894), Lucy A. 3 (Nov 1896), Estella D. 1 (Sep 1898) 10-326A-132/138 (B)
Lewis J. Powell 43 (Jan 1856-Ga/Ga/Ga-M 24)(Blacksmith), Haritt M. 44 (Ap 1856-NC/Ala/Unk-M 24-7-6), Lewis N. 17 (Jan 1883-Ga), Erasca A. 14 (Ap 1886-Ga), John B. 13 (Jan 1887-Ga), Joe H. 11 (July 1888-Ga), William A. 8 (May 1892-Ga), Carl B. 6 (Sep 1894-Ga) 10-253A-63
Willis P. Powell 15, Daniel 10: see Mattie Jones (B)
MARRIAGES
C.H. Powell to Lula Dyer, 4 Jan 1894, Lenny Deggs MG 4-64
Effie Powell to S. H. Pearcy q.v.
George S. Powell to Emma L. Housley, 8 Ap 1897 (same), J.A. Whitner MG 2-137
Martha Powell to Andy Jones q.v.
Mary Powell to William G. Hill q.v.
Walter Powell to Amanda Lavender, 15 Jan 1895, R.A. Owen MG 4-79

- - - - - - - - - - - - -

POWERS

1860 CENSUS
James Powers 35, Eliza J. 25, John A. 14, Nancy C. 12, Lorasadow 10 (s), Sarah E. 7, James R. 1 3-67-462
1870 CENSUS
John T. Powers 25, Mary M. 28, Virgil 5, Floyd 3, Robert L. 1 4-9-59
1880 CENSUS– None
1900 CENSUS
Aster Powers 17: see James Myers
John Powers 34 (Dec 1865-Ala/Ala/Ala-M 3)(Coke Puller), Mary 26 (Ap 1874-Ala/Va/Va-M 3-0) 7-264B-274/279 (B)
Manro Powers 5: see Manro Cravin
MARRIAGES
Eliza Powers to William Covall q.v.
Ellen Powers to Alexander Johnson q.v.
Fany or Fannie S.J. Powers to W. R. Dodd q.v.
John Powers to Carrie Sellers, 24 Dec 1891, J.R. Hill MG 4-37
John Powers to Mary Williams, 15 July 1898 (same), W.L. Lillard JP, P.J. Johnson W 2-300
L.D. Powers to Vilena Hutchesson, 22 June 1870 (no return) 1-#1199
M. A. M. Powers to J. R. Clark q.v.
Maggy Powers to W. A. Clayton q.v.
Nancy Jane Powers to T. G. Robertson q.v.
Robert Powers to Mattie McCraven, 9 Oct 1892, S.W. Burnett MG 4-51
Sarah Powers to F. C. Moore q.v.

- - - - - - - - - - - - -

PRADY

1900 CENSUS
John Prady 23: see Louis A. Blake

- - - - - - - - - - - - -

PRATER / PRATOR

1870 CENSUS

James Prater 32, Tennessee V. 27, John T. 8, Mary Jane 5, James W. 3, Henry H. 1, Tempy PADUSE (B) 23 7-2-12

1880 CENSUS

J. Prater 52, M.A. 45, Ann 19, J.A. 16 (s), M.E. 12 (d), R.N. 6 (s), W.C. 3 (s), Dicy BRAMLET 66 (m) 7-25-212

James Prator 42, T.V. 38 (w), J.T. 18 (s), M.J. 15 (d), J.W. 13 (s), N.H. 11 (s), T.V. 8 (d), Delia A. 1 7-28-240

1900 CENSUS

James Prater 62 (Ap 1838-T/Va/T-M 39), Tennessee 57 (Nov 1842-M 39-8-7), Oscar 19 (Feb 1881), Dealey CALL 21 (d)(Feb 1879-M 0-0), Estill C. CALL 26 (sl)(Aug 1873-Mich/NY/Mich-M 0)(Well Driller) 7-266B-312/317

James F. Prater 11: see William Dyre

Mary Prater 63: see Thomas Prater

Susan Prater 42: see Taylor M. Childs

Thomas Prater 25 (June 1874-Ark/SC/Ga-Wd), Mary 4 (Nov 1895), Willie 3 (Jan 1897), Mary PRATER 63 (m)(Feb 1837-Ga/Ga/Ga-S), Fanny KEENER 33 (boarder)(May 1867-D 7-5) 8-288A-397/399

MARRIAGES

Ann Prater to Henry Howserley q.v.

Delia Prater to E. C. Call q.v.

G.W. Prator to Susan Jolly, 18 Feb 1888 (19 Feb), Calvin Morgan JP 1-549

Georg Prater to Harriett Hickman, 17 May 1879 (18 May), W.A. Green JP 1-291

James Prator to Tennessee Knight, 6 Oct 1860 (7 Oct), B.H. Jordan MG 1-#730

John Prater to Elizabeth Burton, 3 Sep 1880 (4 Sep), J.R. Crawford JP 1-295

John T. Prater (20) to Mariah Smith (21, Meigs Co), C.G. Roddy MG, John Morgan & Thomas Whaley W 4-1(6)

M. J. Prator to A. Purcer q.v.

Tennie V. Prator to James F. Holland q.v.

Thomas W. Prater to Cassy Ward or Wood, 10 Sep 1893, A.D. Hubbard MG 4-57

- - - - - - - - - - - - -

PRATT

MARRIAGE

Vina Pratt to J. W. Drake q.v.

- - - - - - - - - - - - -

PRESLEY / PRESTLEY / PRISLEY / PRESSLY

1860 CENSUS

Hiram Presley 10: see John Harwood

1870 and 1880 CENSUS– None

1900 CENSUS

George W. Presly 53 (Nov 1846-T/NC/T-M 11)(Coal Miner), Rhoda 30 (Oct 1869-M 11-5-4), Paul A. 10 (Jan 1890), Simon A. 8 (Ap 1892), George W. 4 (May 1896), Jasper T. 10/12 (July 1899) 8-283A-288/290

Nathan Presley 37, Nettie 23: see John Rush

MARRIAGES

G.W. Prisley to Pheba King, 26 Nov 1888 (27 Nov), Eli Hays JP 1-559

James W. Prestly to Olly Zimerle, 22 Jan 1852 (same), E. McKinna JP 1-#361

Matilda K. Pressly to Henry Limerly(?) q.v.

- - - - - - - - - - - - -

PRESNELL / PRESSNEAL

1900 CENSUS

John Pressneal 39 (Sep 1860-M 17)(Coal Miner), Mary 36 (Oct 1863-M 17-1-1), Clay H. 16 (May 1884) 10-255B-103/106

William Presnell 37 (May 1863-M 16)(Coal Miner), Lizzabeth 36 (May 1864-M 16-6-5), Burthy 15 (June 1884), Nora 14 (Aug 1883), May 8 (Mar 1892), Edca 6 (s) (Feb 1894), Lawrance 4 (Ap 1896) 10-255B-104/107

- - - - - - - - - - - - -

PRESTON

1860 CENSUS

Rector Preston 58: see William G. Roddy

1870 CENSUS

Rector Preston 67: see William G. Roddy

Thomas Preston 41, Nancy 30, Minty 12, Silah 10, Isaac 8, Benjamin 6, Eliza 4, Louisa 6/12 1-14-93 (B)

1880 CENSUS– None

1900 CENSUS

James Preston 25 (Ap 1875-M 6), Kisir 24 (May 1876-M 6-1-1), Maggi 2 (Jan 1898) 1-187A-157/165

MARRIAGES

Birtie Preston to Andrew Walls q.v.

Jennie Preston to Walter Strickland q.v.

- - - - - - - - - - - - -

PRESTWOOD / PRESSWOOD

1880 CENSUS

Miles Prestwood 54 (Ship Carpenter), Jane 26 (w), Andrew 19 (Ship Carpenter), Alice 16, Bernie 6, Girtie 4, Nora 1 2-27-213

1900 CENSUS

Barry Prestwood 26 (May 1874-T/T/Ga-M 2)(Carpenter), Jennie 23 (Mar 1877-M 2-1-1), Romeo 1 (July 1898), Miles V. PRESTWOOD 73 (f)(July 1826-T/NC/T-Wd) (Carpenter) 3-209A-160/174

Nancy Prestwood 52: see James Gregory

MARRIAGE

Cora Presswood to Elijah Wiggins q.v.

- - - - - - - - - - - - -

PREWET / PREWIT

1860 CENSUS

Martha Prewet 18: see Jeffrey West

Polly Prewit 45, Martha 19, Caroline 15, Sarah 13, Dorehewly(?) 11 6-104-709

- - - - - - - - - - - - -

PRICE

1880 CENSUS

John Price 39, Catharine E. 45 (w), Louisa E. 17, Martha A. 14, Jasper L. 10, William R.H. 7 6-23-21 (Rural Street, Washington)

1900 CENSUS

Alonzo S. Price 43 (Unk 1857-England/Do/Do-?/?/Na-M 7)(Granite Cutter), Margaret J. 27 (Mar 1873-M 7-1-1) 13-300A-191/197

Gillan S. Price 51 (Jan 1849-Ark/T/T-M 31), Mary J. 51 (Nov 1849-M 31-9-8), John A. 30 (Feb 1870), William A. 22 (Sep 1877), Lavada E. 14 (June 1885), Katie E. 11 (Dec 1888) 3-203A-58/61

Henry T. Price 35 (Oct 1864-T/T/Va-M 12)(Dry Goods Salesman), Eva L. 35 (Sep 1864-SC/SC/SC-M 12-0) 14-220A-141/145

James M. Price 28: see Samuel D. McCuiston

Jasper Price 29, Catharine 26: see Luke M. King

Jeff Price 53 (Aug 1846-Ga/Ga/Ga-M 24)(Coke Roller), Hattie 42 (Jan 1858-Ala/Ala/Ala-M 24-11-10), Mary A. 24 (Ap 1876), Challott 22 (Mar 1878), Flareance 20 (Aug 1879), John 14 (Mar 1886), Ellen 11 (Dec 1888), Columbus 9 (Dec 1890), Love 6 (May 1894), Parycity 5 (May 1895), Ulis 1 (Nov 1898) 7-264B-272/277 (B)

John Price 55 (May 1845-Wd) 6-242A-46

Joseph Price 36 (Sep 1863-M 2)(Teamster), Nora 27 (Oct 1872-M 2-1-1), Jack 5 (May 1895), Charlie 11 (July 1888), Ella 10 (May 1890), Fred 7 (Oct 1892) 8-314A-64/67

Nancy C. Price 55, Julia A. 17: see Joseph Thorp

Susan Price 60, Ellie 8: see James Loden

MARRIAGES

Charlotte Price to R. S. Lawrence q.v.

Cora Price to Columbus Hassler q.v.

Georg Price to Lutitia Thurman, 5 Jan 1895, Eli Hayes JP 4-81

Ginnie Price to John W. Jordan q.v.

Henry J. Price to Cora A. Snowden, 1 Ap 1900 (same), W.L. Lillard JP 3-136

J.M. Price to Sallie Thompson, 12 Feb 1889 (15 Feb), J. Johnson JP 1-567

J.M. Price to Nora Morgan, 28 Feb 1899 (1 Mar), C.E. Mowrey JP, Josephus Morgan W 2-390

Jasper Price to Katy King, 30 Aug 1890, J.L. Henry JP 4-15

Jasper Price to Kate King, 4 Dec 1897 [bond only], Robert Milo W 2-221

John T. Price to H.J. Hickman, 13 May 1894, W.A. Templeton JP 4-67

Lee Price to Susie Standfield or Cranfield [both names on record], 25 Aug 1893, S.S. Franklin JP 4-56

Lee Price to Mary Rudd, 24 Nov 1897 (same), W.R. Henry JP, R.J. Killough W 2-212

M. J. Price to P. T. Booker q.v.

Matilda Price to J. H. Fisher q.v.

Mattie Price to Robert Moles q.v.

William Price to Mary Bean, 10 Feb 1893, S.S. Franklin JP 4-50

\- - - - - - - - - - - - -

PRIGMORE

1880 CENSUS

J. Prigmore 12 (B): see Jessee Dickey

MARRIAGE

W. Houston Prigmore to Mary Thompson, 26 Oct 1878 (28 Oct), J.W. Thompson MG 1-290

\- - - - - - - - - - - - -

PRINCE / PRINTS

MARRIAGES

C.M. Prince(*) to Mary Crutchfield, 16 Aug 1886 (same), P.P. Brooks ?? 1-503 [* last name also looks like Privt]

James Prince (34) to Eliza Ann Holloway (30), 10 June 1881, M.L. Abbott JP, Pleasant Holloway & W.H. Todd W 4-1(1)

James Prints to Lizzann Holloway (34), 30 June 1881, M.L. Abbott JP, Pleasant Holloway & W.J. Todd W 4-7(62)

\- - - - - - - - - - - - -

PRITCHETT / PRITCHET

1860 CENSUS

Andrew J. Pritchet 34, Nancy 34 5-33-223

John W. Pritchett 27, Melinda 27, Columbus JAMES 8 (bound) 6-105-711

1870 CENSUS

Andrew J. Pritchett 44, Cassanna 44, James A. 14, Rowlan J. 12, Jefferson D. 9, Sarah L. 3 5-5-32

Malinda Pritchet 34: see Rebecca Cox

William Pritchett 36, Priscilla 26, George W. 8, Linzie 3 4-3-13

1880 CENSUS

A.J. Pritchett 54, Cassander 54, J.D. 18 (s), B.N. MEANALLEY 7 (gs), M. WEBB 45 (Servant), M.M. 3 (d) 5-1-1 [Andrew J. married Cassy Jones on 28 Ap 1867 in Meigs County]

1900 CENSUS

George Pritchet 38: see Franklin McMilan

George W. Pritchet 36 (July 1863-T/NC/T-M 16), Martha B. 32 (Mar 1868-M 16-6-6), Andrew J. 16 (Mar 1885), Wealthy A. 13 (Oct 1886), James 8 (Aug 1889), Joe 7 (Oct 1892), Oscar 6 (Feb 1894), Minta 2 (June 1897), Roy 2/12 (Mar 1900) 3-200B-14/15

James L. Pritchet 35 (July 1864-T/SC/T-M 5), Tex 26 (May 1874-M 5-4-3), Inda B. 4 (Sep 1895), Samuel A. 2 (July 1897), Charles B. 1 (Jan 1899) 3-201A-30/32

Jeffe Pritchett 38 (Dec 1861-M 5), Mandy 28 (Feb 1871-T/NC/T-M 5-2-2), Jim F. 5 (May 1895), Classia 1 (June 1898) 10-256A-119/123

William Pritchet 65 (July 1834-SC/Va/NC-M 37), Percilla 59 (Sep 1840-T/NC/NC-M 37-4-3), William J. 22 (Aug 1877-M ?) 3-201A-31/33

MARRIAGES

A.J. Pritchett to Nancy Mathis, 10 June 1850 or 1854, "No official return made, returned to office 1856, W.H. Bell, Clerk" 1-#453

George Pritchett to Martha McMillin, 15 July 1884 (28 Feb 1885)[sic], J.W. Thompson JP 1-496

J.D. Pritchett to Amanda Sneed, 7 Aug 1894, H.B. Burditt MG 4-64
James L. Pritchett to Texas McMillan, 7 Jan 1894, A.J. Wyrick JP 4-65
John W. Pritchett to Malinda Cox, 10 Dec 1854 (same), J.O. Torbett JP 1-#478
Lindsey Pritchett to Molly Perry, 3 July 1889 (5 July), M.F. Moore MG 1-578
Malinda Pritchett to W. Waller q.v.
Nancy J. Pritchett to Wesly Watson q.v.
William Pritchett to Perscilla Essex, 1 Ap 1863 (no return) 1-#796

- - - - - - - - - - - - -

PROCTOR

1900 CENSUS
George Proctor 38 (Mar 1862-SC/SC/SC-M 13)(RR Laborer), Mattie 30 (Jan 1870-Ala/Ala/Ala-M 13-10-6), Ellen 61 (m)(Mar 1839-SC/SC/Ala), Otho 12 (Ap 1888-Ala)(Hotel Servant), Georgia 7 (May 1893), Pat 4 (Oct 1895), Jepo 4 (Oct 1895), Leona 5/12 (Nov 1899) 14-214B-34/35 (B)

- - - - - - - - - - - - -

PROFFITT

MARRIAGE
Mary E. Proffitt to James M. Wade q.v.

- - - - - - - - - - - - -

PRYOR / PRYER

1900 CENSUS
Abraham Pryor 28 (Unk-M 0)(Coal Miner), Callie 22 (Unk-M 0-0) 10-324A-91/95 (B)
Green H. Pryor 32 (Oct 1867-M 8)(Coal Miner), Samantha 21 (Aug 1878-M 8-0) 9-229A-28
James Pryor(?) 57 (Jan 1841-M 35), Martha 57 (Aug 1843-T/NC/NC-M 35), Rebeir 16 (Dec 1884) 1-183A-88/91
Jessi Pryor 44 (Nov 1855-M 24), Marthy 40 (June 1859-M 24-5-5), Anie 23 (Jan 1877), Plinnis(?) 18 (d)(Nov 1881), Dellie 16 (Dec 1883), Clay 14 (Mar 1886), Lee 11 (Aug 1888) 1-187B-170/179
John Pryor 18: see Carter Phillips
Mary Pryer 51 (Mar 1849-NC/Scotland/NC-Wd), Nathan A. 20 (s)(Ap 1880), Richard A. 18 (Oct 1881)(Coal Miner), May A. 16 (May 1884), Mary A. 13 (Dec 1886), Georgia A. WEST 24 (d)(Jan 1876-M 8-5-2), William 5 (gs)(Aug 1894), Richard A. 0/12 (gs)(May 1900) 10-255B-108/111
Nellie Pryor 16: see William J. Caldwell
Richard Pryor 20: see John Best
Will Pryor 23 (Nov 1876-T/T/NC-M 5), Amin 20 (Feb 1880-M 5-2-1), Icie 2 (Sep 1897) 10-256A-113/117

MARRIAGES
A.B. Pryor to Alice Sharp, 11 Dec 1899 (same), J.W. Romines JP, Moses Hamile(?) [signed by X] W 3-86
Georgie Ann Pryor to John West q.v.
Green Pryor to Samantha West, 13 Dec 1891, Will Morgan JP 4-36
W.M. Pryor to Annie Clouse, 27 Aug 1894, W.S. Hale MG 4-72

- - - - - - - - - - - - -

PUGH

1860 CENSUS
Stewart H. Pugh 52, Sarah 44, William R. 5 9-98-664
1870 and 1880 CENSUS– None
1900 CENSUS
Benjamin Pugh 51 (July 1848-Ga/Ga/Ga-M 10), Emma J. 24 (July 1875-SC/SC/SC-M 10-3-3), Beulah 7 (Dec 1892-Ga), Nettie M. 6 (Ap 1894-SC), Ruskin V. 2 (Aug 1897-SC) 15-270A-39
John H. Pugh 51 (May 1849-T/Va/Va-M 27), Rebecca 49 (Dec 1850-T/Va/Va-M 27-7-5), Warren 24 (July 1875), Walter 20 (Jan 1880), Ernest 16 (Oct 1883), Alta 20 (Feb 1880), Ada 13 (Oct 1886) 3-204B-80/86

MARRIAGES
Edwin W. Pugh to Winnie G. Allen, 9 July 1900 (same), W.L. Patton MG, John G. Allen W 3-186
John B. Pugh to Sarah Grass(?), 17 July 1883 (same), D. Richardson M 1-469

- - - - - - - - - - - - -

PULLENS / PULLIN / PULLOM / PULLAM / PULLUM / POLLAN / PULLMAN

1900 CENSUS
Caroline Pullum 58 (Mar 1842-Ga/Ga/Ga-Wd 7-3), Ella 20 (June 1879-Ga)(Washwoman), Ida VAUGHN 12 (gd)(Ap 1888), John T. WORTHINGTON 6 (gs)(May 1894), Annie D. PULLUM 4 (gd)(Jan 1896), Henry GLEN 38 (boarder)(Sep 1861-Ga/SC/Ga)(House Carpenter) 10-342A-83/87 (B)
Robert Pollan 38 (Ga/Ga/T-M 6), Anne 36 (Oct 1863-M 6-1-1) 8-316A-116/120 (B)

MARRIAGES
James Pullam to Nancy Mitchell, 21 Nov 1888 (same), C.D. Collins MG 1-558
Josephine Pullam to Isaac L. Hale q.v.
Mary Pullman to Louis Worthington q.v.
Robert Pullens to Amand Donaldson, 25 Mar 1891, James M. Beeson JP 4-19 (B)
Sarah Pullom to Simon Carter q.v.
Turner Pullin to Maggie Jefferson, 14 Sep 1890, Simon Carter MG 4-16

- - - - - - - - - - - - -

PURCELL

MARRIAGES
Darthula Purcell to James Thomas q.v.
Vina Purcell to W. Jones q.v.

- - - - - - - - - - - - -

PURCER / PURSER / PERCER / PERSER

1860 CENSUS

James Purser 67 (SC), Elizabeth 68 (SC), Rebecca 26, Polly 22 7-5-28

Pleasant M. Purser 40, Elizabeth 25, Darcus P. 15, William T. 12, Henry M. 9, Robert O. 7, James RENFROW 17 7-4-26

William Purser 28, Sarah 19 7-4-24

1870 CENSUS

Pleasant M. Purser 50, Elizabeth 34, William T. 21, Henry M. 19, Robert O. 17, Mary T. 9, Albert 7, Emily J. 5, John 3, Sarah A. 10/12 7-7-53

William Purser 47, Mary C. 32, Miller 8, William F. 6, Scrap(?) 10/12 (d) 7-9-54

1880 CENSUS

H.M. Purser 29, A.C. 23, W.N. 3 (s), Jinnie 9/12, May MANARD 20, Jasper LAUSON (B) 12 7-22-188

P.M. Purser 60, Elizabeth 52, M.T. 19 (d), A. 16 (s), Ema 14 (d), John 12, Anne 10, James 8, N. 6 (s), Beaky PURSER 48 (si) 7-27-236

R.O. Purser 27, E.M. 23, W.G. 3 (s), E.M. 1 (s) 7-27-235

W.B. Purser 50, M.C. 44, William 17, S.C. 9 (d), P.A. 8 (d), James 6, J.W. 5 (d) 7-28-239

W.T. Purser 31, N.A. 27 (w) 9-32-272

1900 CENSUS

Albert Pursur 37 (Mar 1863-M 14), Mary J. 35 (Ap 1865-M 14-5-5), Henry W. 13 (Sep 1886), Lester 10 (Aug 1889), Ector 7 (Nov 1892), Charles O. 3 (Aug 1896), James L. 2 (Ap 1898) 10-250A-1

Elizabeth Pursur 63 (Nov 1837-Wd 7-7)(Landlady), Nich 26 (Mar 1874), Emesly FISHER 53 (boarder)(Nov 1846) 10-250A-2

James Pursur 27 (Dec 1882-M 2), Estell 21 (Aug 1879-M 2-2-1) 7-261B-219/224

James Pursur 29 (Feb 1872-M 1)(Teamster), Dellia 22 (July 1878-M 1-1-1), baby 1/12 (May 1900), Sam DICKSON 25 (boarder)(Nov 1875-M 0)(Mine Engineer), Emer 17 (boarder)(July 1882-Ga/Ga/Ga-M 0), Sallie CHATEN (B) 32 (Ap 1868-Wd 3-0)(Servant) 10-250A-5

John Pursur 33 (Feb 1867-M 12)(Coal Weigher), Lumid 30 (Ap 1870-Ga/SC/Ga-M 12-5-4), Floey 10 (Aug 1889), Frank 8 (Dec 1891), Lillie 5 (Aug 1894), Jewell 1 (Feb 1899) 10-251A-25

John Purcur 25 (Nov 1874-M 3), Ellen 29 (May 1871-M 3-3-2), Vance 1 (June 1898), Carl BURNETT 9 (ss)(Jan 1891), John CRAWFORD 16 (c)(Mar 1884) 7-267A-326/331

Mameray J. Pursur 20 (Sep 1879), Emma V. 18 (si)(Feb 1882), Robert L. 16 (b)(Jan 1884)(Office Boy), Freed 11 (b)(Nov 1889), Bettie C. 7 (si)(July 1892) 10-251A-22

Miller Pursur 39 (Jan 1861-M 16), Sary J. 48 (Mar 1852-M 16-5-5), Myrtle A. 15 (Nov 1884), Gertie C. 14 (Dec 1885), William R. 12 (July 1888), Sary E. 11 (Feb 1889), Tennie A. 9 (Mar 1891) 7-261B-220/225

Ray Pursur 36 (Oct 1863-M 1), Emma J. 25 (Ap 1875-M 1-0), Lawice(?) KNIGHT 27 (lodger)(Nov 1872) 7-261B-226/231

Robert Pursur 47 (Nov 1852-M 25)(Blacksmith), Mosalipie 43 (May 1857-T/T/Ga-M 25-10-7), Elija 21 (Jan 1879)(Blacksmith), Edgar 19 (Jan 1881), Henery 16 (July 1883), Elic 14 (Mar 1886), Maud 10 (June 1889), Beulah 7 (Dec 1892) 10-250B-12

William B. Pursur 70 (May 1830-T/NC/NC-M 30), Mary C. 59 (Dec 1840-M 30-5-3), Allen BYERLEY 19 (lodger)(May 1881) 7-261B-218/223

William G. Purser 23 (Feb 1877-M 2)(Grocery Salesman), Icie 20 (June 1879-M 2-1-1), Maurine 6/12 (Nov 1899) 8-314A-69/72

MARRIAGES

A. Purcer to M.J. Prator, 1 Oct 1885 (1 Nov), J.O. Shasne or Shanon JP 1-500

Ann Purser (Mrs.) to T. M. Whaley q.v.

Darcus Purser to F. Mc. Broyles q.v.

Emma J. Purser to W. F. Purser q.v.

H.M. Purser to A.C. Lillard, 31 Dec 1874 (same), J.R. Crawford JP 1-#1384

J.W. Purser to E.L. Burnett, 6 Feb 1897 (7 Feb), A.H. Low MG, S.T. Knight W 2-06

James Purcer to H.E. Burnett, 25 Sep 1897 (26 Sep), J.W. Romine JP, J.H. Jewell W 2-188

James Purcer to Della Dickson, 26 Nov 1898 (27 Nov), W.L. Patton MG, R.J. Killough W 2-349

John Percer to Lena McDonald, 8 Dec 1887 (11 Dec), John H. Parrott MG 1-538

M. T. Purser to J. A. Early q.v.

P.M. Purcer to Elizabeth Jewell, 28 Dec 1859 (29 Dec), J. Whaley MG 1-#705

P.M. Purcer to Sarah J. Lillard, 4 Mar 1884 (5 Mar), J.R. Crawford JP 1-471

Robert O. Purser to E.M. Rudd, 28 Nov 1874 (29 Nov), J.R. Crawford JP 1-#1376

Sarah A. Purcer to W. C. Hixon q.v.

Sarah J. Purcer to James Byrd q.v.

W.F. Purser to Emma J. Purser, 12 Jan 1899 (same), E.W. Mort MG, E. Fisher W 2-373

W.T. Perser to Ann Keith, 23 Dec 1872 (25 Dec), W.B. McKelvy MG 1-#1266

William B. Purcer to Mary Jewell, 11 Dec 1867 (same), R.T. Howard MG 1-#985

William G. Purcer to Sarah Spence, 1 Mar 1860 (same), John B. Murphy JP 1-#1651

Will G. Purser to Icie D. Ault, 15 Dec 1898 (same), W.L. Patton MG, Brack B. Blevins W 2-358

- - - - - - - - - - - - -

PYOTT

1860 CENSUS

Edward Pyott 46 (Va), Margaret 44 (Va), John E. 21 (Va) (School Teacher), Joel J. 18, Henry C. 15, William W. 13, Samuel A. 12, Towsen F. 10, Stephen C. 6 2-79-535

James H. Pyott 37 (Va), Martha J. 27, Louiza 8, Mary H. 3, Eliza V. 1 1-82-561 [James H. married Martha J. Derrick on 19 June 1851 in Roane County]

1870 CENSUS

Edward Pyott 58 (Va), Margaret 54 (Va), Joel J. 28, William W. 26 (Minister), Samuel A. 22 (School Teacher), Lowison F. 19, Stephen C. 16 2-4-20

John E. Pyott 31 (School Teacher), Barbra C. 24, James H. 1 2-4-22

1880 CENSUS

John Pyott 42 (Lawyer), Barbara 34, James 11, John 9, Charles 6, Anna 3, Cora 1, Adaline McCLENDON 22 (Servant) 2-25-199

Margaret Pyott 64, Henry 35 (s), Samuel 31 (s)(Instructor), Columbus DURHAM (B) 17 (Servant) 2-42-343

MARRIAGE

John E. Pyott to Barbara Catharine Hoyal, 10 June 1866

- - - - - - - - - - - - -

QUALLS

MARRIAGES

A. C. Qualls to L. C. Brown q.v.

Jane Qualls to Samuel Johnson q.v.

- - - - - - - - - - - - -

QUEEN

1880 CENSUS

Adam Queen 25, Malinda 21, Mary 2 1-12-97

1900 CENSUS

John Queen 20, Lizzie 13: see William Weatherbee

Nancy Queen 44 (May 1856-Ga/Unk/Ga-Wd 9-6)(Washwoman), Lizzie 15 (Feb 1885-NC), Mary 12 (Aug 1887-Ga) 13-295B-112/114

Paralee Queen 20: see John H. Best

MARRIAGES

Ada Queen to T. H. McGill q.v.

Davis Queen to Paralee Burton, 19 Aug 1899 (20 Aug), N. D. Reed MG, J.H. Franklin W 3-22

- - - - - - - - - - - - -

QUEENER

MARRIAGE

Callie Queener to James W. Rose q.v.

- - - - - - - - - - - - -

QUICK

1900 CENSUS

Margaret Quick 75: see Charles Hawk

- - - - - - - - - - - - -

QUILLEN / QUILAN

1860 CENSUS

Nancy Quillen 49: see John Fellyow

1870 CENSUS

Nancy Quillen 63 (NC), John P. 17: see John Felyow

1880 CENSUS

Nancy Quilan 75: see John Philyan

- - - - - - - - - - - - -

QUINN

1900 CENSUS

Margaret Quinn 65: see M. Galloway

MARRIAGES

Anna Quinn to J. J. Perkins q.v.

Jennie Quinn to M. H. Galloway q.v.

J.P. Quinn to Mary F. Brown, 14 Feb 1883 (same), T.N.L. Cunnyngham JP 1-479

- - - - - - - - - - - - -

RADCLIFFE / RATLIEF

MARRIAGES

D.W. Radcliffe to C.L. Fleming, 13 Oct 1891, R.A. Bartlett MG 4-31

Marthy Ratlief to Louis Brown q.v.

- - - - - - - - - - - - -

RADCRISP

1870 CENSUS

John Radcrisp 35, Lucinda 30, John S. 5, William 4, Ruth J. 3, Sarah F. 1 1-3-19

- - - - - - - - - - - - -

RADGER

1900 CENSUS

J.A. Radger 18 (Jan 1882-M 1), Anie 19 (Mar 1881-M 1-1-1), Luther 1 (d)(Mar 1899) 1-189B-209/220 (B)

James Radger 50 (Ap 1850-M 21), Ellen 45 (Ap 1855-M 21-1-1) 1-189B-209/219 (Spring City) (B)

- - - - - - - - - - - - -

RAGIN

1900 CENSUS

Milton Ragin 29 (Mar 1871), Henry SILAS 35 (Unk 1865-Wd)(Partner), Eugene ARCHY 10 (lodger)(Oct 1889) 8-275B-145 (B)

- - - - - - - - - - - - -

RAGLESTON– see RAULSTON

- - - - - - - - - - - - -

RAGSDALE

1860 CENSUS

DeWitt Ragsdale 24, Margaret A. 20 6-113-777

John N. Ragsdale 34 (Physician), Caroline E. 27, Robert B. 3, Haney Bruce 1, Allen DALRYMPLE 56 (SC)(Carpenter) 10-29-194

MARRIAGES

D.C. Ragsdale to Margarett Hackett, 22 July 1858 (same), Sewell Phillips MG 1-#642

Minnie A. Ragsdale to James A. Mitchell q.v.

- - - - - - - - - - - - -

RAIDEN

1900 CENSUS

Margaret Raiden or Ridue 25, Laura 3: see Lark Hunter

- - - - - - - - - - - - -

RAINES / RAINS

1880 CENSUS

H.R. Rains 40, N.D. 33, James 8, Westly 1, Frank CASTLEBERY 24 (boarder) 9-32-274

Wesly Rains 32, V.J. 30, S.B. 4 (d), H.W. 5/12 (s), J. RAINS 79 (f) 8-9-78

1900 CENSUS

Cleveland Rains 13: see Frank Helton

Joseph E. Rains 34 (July 1865-M 16)(Coal Miner), Jennie 32 (Aug 1867-M 16-4-4), Lucius E. 15 (July 1884) (Teamster), Fred H. 13 (Sep 1886), Addie M. 11 (Aug 1888), James T. 8 (Aug 1891), Thomas PEARSLEY 57 (boarder)(Unk 1843-M ?)(Teamster), William WORLEY 33 (boarder)(Mar 1867)(Sawmill Laborer) 13-306B-318/330

Will Rains 32 (Mar 1868-Wd)(RR Brakeman), Clinty DONHOO 41 (si)(Oct 1858-NC/T/T-Wd 6-3), Floy 10 (nw) (Feb 1890), Ethel 7 (ne)(Sep 1892-Indian Territory/ Ga/NC) 10-251B-32

Wright Rains 31, Elizabeth 29, Burnette 5, John W. 2: see James A. Walker

MARRIAGES

Lula Rains to Thomas Elsey or Elsie q.v.

M. M. Rains to D. D. Davis q.v.

Mattie Raines to J. A. Elder q.v.

Right Raines to Allis Everett, 15 Ap 1888 (same), W. R. Grimsley MG 1-547

W.A. Raines to L.E. Rice, 8 Nov 1893, T.F. Shaver JP 4-70

W.N. Rains to Sophia Elder, 24 Dec 1888 (25 Dec), J.W. Williamson MG 1-579

Wesley Raines to V.J. Kelley, 4 Feb 1875 (same), A. Hickman MG 1-#1393

Wright Raines to Craty Walker, 4 July 1894, W.A. Green JP 4-64

RAMSEY

1860 CENSUS

John L. Ramsey 44, Diana 30, William B. 12, Samuel L. 10, Louisa J. 7, Stephen SPENCE 28 7-5-35

1870 CENSUS

Samuel Ramsey 21: see Albert P. Early

1880 CENSUS

John L. Ramsey 65, V.A. 50 (w), J.A. 18 (s), S.B. 12 (d), Bryant HENRY (B) 23 (Servant) 3-20-158

S. S. Ramsey 30 3-20-160

Scott Ramsey 27: see Jere Wasson

MARRIAGES

J.R. Ramsey to Katie Maley, 25 Aug 1898 (same), W.S. Hale MG, J.H. White W 2-213

John L. Ramsey to Deniah Aheart, 24 Nov 1859 (same), W.H. Bell MG 1-#701

RAN

MARRIAGE

Alex Ran to Milley Hale, 16 Dec 1884 (same), P.P. Brooks ?? 1-464

RANDOLPH

1880 CENSUS

Kelley Randolph 25, Moriah 7, Ulsey 5: see Louisa Ryon (B)

1900 CENSUS

Elmer Randolph 40 (May 1860-T/Unk/NC-M 14)(Coal Miner), Stacia 25 (Aug 1874-T/T/Va-M 14-6-4) (Seamstress), Blie 15 (Feb 1885)(Mine Laborer), Lilie 14 (Feb 1886), Henery 11 (Ap 1890), Nolia 9 (May 1891) 10-251A-24 (B)

James Randolph 57 (Mar 1843-T/T/NC-M 12), Rachel 30 (Dec 1869-M 12-7-4), Eddie 15 (Mar 1885), William 10 (Aug 1889), Sary 7 (Dec 1892), Ryley 5 (Aug 1894) 10-256B-127/131 (B)

Jeptha Randolph 56 (June 1843-M 28)(House Carpenter), Mary E. 45 (Mar 1855-T/Va/T-M 28-14-10), Robert 17 (Oct 1882), James 15 (Nov 1881), Emma 13 (Nov 1886), John 11 (Mar 1889), Minerva 9 (Jan 1891), Frank 7 (Mar 1893), Jeptha 5 (July 1894), Winnie A. 2 (Ap 1898) 13-298B-165/169

Mona Randolph 22: see Will Thurmon (B)

William Randolph 45 (Dec 1854-T/ ? /NC-M 19)(Scale Boss), Celler 46 (Feb 1858-T/Miss/Miss-M 19-10-9), James 18 (Mar 1882), Deller 14 (Aug 1885), Corra 12 (Aug 1887), Bessy 11 (Jan 1889), Lou 9 (Sep 1890), Emmur 7 (Nov 1892), Luther 4 (Dec 1895), Toliver J. 35 (b)(Sep 1864-Wd), Peter ROBINSON 25 (boarder) (July 1874), Tom GOODALL 18 (boarder)(Mar 1882) (Coal Miner) 10-251B-33 (B)

MARRIAGES

Amanda Randolph to E. B. Harris q.v.

Elmore Randolph to Stacia Howerton, 31 Mar 1885 (same), W.F. Blevins JP 1-580

Emma Randolph to G. F. Holeman q.v.

Frances Randolph to Daniel Sullivan q.v.

I.T. Randolph to S.L. Robeson, 27 July 1890, S. Carter MG 4-16

Mary Randolph to William Thurman q.v.

Sallie Randolph to Charley Phillips q.v.

William Randolph to Siller McKinney, 27 Dec 1883 (same), W.S. Hale MG 1-480

RANKIN / RANKINS

1870 CENSUS

Alice Rankins 14: see Alfred Day (B)

1880 CENSUS

Jane Rankin 51, Corill 26 (s), C.C. 23 (s) 8-14-120 (Mu)(B)

1900 CENSUS

Edward O. Rankin 37 (July 1862-Ind/Ireland/NY-M 14) (Bricklayer), Emma S. 41 (Feb 1859-Ky/Ky/Ind-M 14-2-2), Edward M. 13 (May 1887-Ind), Bessie O. 6 (Feb 1894-Ky) 10-321B-35/37

Floyd Rankins 21 (Unk 1879-M 2), Addie 20 (Nov 1880-M 2-2-0), Elsie WALTERS 22 (sil)(May 1878) 15-271A-59 (B)

Josie Rankns 9: see William Young (B)

Nancy Rankin 38 (Unk 1862-Ga/Ga/Ga-Wd 6-3), Dora 25 (Ap 1875-Ga/Ga/Ga-Wd 2-2), Anna CUNNINGHAM 70 (ml)(Unk 1830-Ga/Ga/Ga-Wd 3-1), Harvey H.

HORTON 2 (gs)(July 1897) 15-272A-80 (B)

MARRIAGES

Calvin Rankin to Mollie Adkins, no date, probably 1882 4-11(107)

Carril(?) Rankins to Nancy Jones, 30 June 1891, D.J. Young ?? 4-32

Floyd Rankins to Addie Walters, 22 Aug 1897 (same), S.W. Burnett MG [license only] 2-185

Maggie Rankins to William Young q.v.

- - - - - - - - - - - - -

RANSOM

MARRIAGES

Clara Ransom to Willis Stewart q.v.

Synda Ransom to Grant Walker q.v.

- - - - - - - - - - - - -

RAULSTON / RAUSTON / RAWLSTON / ROLSTON / RAGLESTON / RAYSTON

1870 CENSUS

Daniel Raulston 35, Rebecca M. 35 (NC), Catharine E. 12 (NC), Martha C. 10, Poindexter 7, William 5, James 3, Sarah A. 1/12 8-17-116 [Daniel married Amanda Rebecca Lowe about 1856 in North Carolina]

1880 CENSUS

Dan Rayston 50, Manda 48, Pendleton 20, William 18, Jinney 15, S.A. 9 (d) 8-15-132

1900 CENSUS

Amanda Raulston 70: see William C. Line

Deck Raulston 38 (Nov 1861-M 11), Nancy E. 37 (Nov 1862-M 11-4-3), Sarah L. 9 (Aug 1890), John 7 (Ap 1893), Ben M. 5 (Jan 1895) 13-297A-142/145

James Rolston 33 (May 1867-M 13), Annie 34 (July 1865-Ark/T/T-M 13-5-5), James R. 12 (Feb 1888), Darrel 9 (Sep 1890), William J. 8 (Ap 1892), Rosa E. 4 (Aug 1895), Mollie C. 2 (May 1898) 13-307B-337/349

MARRIAGES

Catharine Rauston to John Fine q.v.

Eva Rawlston to W. F. Donahoe q.v.

Deck Raulston to Nancy Shirley, 11 Feb 1890, James Corvin MG 4-45

James Raulston to Annie Stone, 29 Ap 1888, James Corvin MG 4-45

S. A. Ragleston to W. C. Line q.v.

- - - - - - - - - - - - -

RAVIN

MARRIAGE

Mary Ravin to Samuel Washington q.v.

- - - - - - - - - - - - -

RAWLINGS /ROLLINS / ROLLINGS

1860 CENSUS

Adam Rawlings 75 (Va), Viny 70 (Va) 6-113-773 (B)

P.T. Rawlings 34, Elizabeth C. 32, Malinda C. 4, Fred G. THOMAS 30 6-109-747

1870 CENSUS

David Rawlings 46, Margarette 44, Syntha 17, Sirena 15, Catharine 13, Sela 10, Ellen 8, Emma 3 6-8-48

Mary Rawlings 21: see Richard C. Knight

Phillip T. Rawlings 44, Elizabeth C. 42, Malinda 13, William M. WILSON 38 (Physician) 6-8-47

Uria [Viney?] Rawlings 86 (Va), Jane GARRISON 34, Amanda 16, Sarah E. 12, Malinda 10, William 9, Charles 7 6-7-43 (B)

1880 CENSUS

A. Rawlings 25, Nancy 26, Albert 6, Ronna 6/12, Serena 6/12 7-24-211

E.C. Rawlings 51: see James W. Gillespie

Sidney D. Rawlins 23: see John Trusley

1900 CENSUS

Albert Rollings 25 (Dec 1874-T/Ga/T-M 7)(Blacksmith), Lulu 25 (Ap 1875-M 7-2-1), Ethel 1 (Sep 1898) 10-329A-183/196

Alford Rowlins 22: see Lon Weathington (B)

Archie Rollings 47 (Oct 1852-Ga/T/Ga-M 27)(Blacksmith), Nancy 52 (Aug 1847-M 27-8-3), Cordelia 19 (Nov 1882), Charley 17 (May 1884) 10-328B-175/185

MARRIAGES

Allend Rawlings to Lula Melton, 21 Jan 1893, W.A. Howard MG 4-47

Daisey B. Rollins to J. B. Tanksley q.v.

H.H. Rawlings to Nancy Parker, 18 Sep 1872 (19 Sep), W.G. Allen JP 1-#1252

Jerry Rawlings to Margaret Hickman, 26 Dec 1900 (25 Dec) [sic], J.A. Bowman MG, Jack Coulter W 3-263

M. C. Rawlings to J. W. Gillespie q.v.

- - - - - - - - - - - - -

RAYBURN / RAYBIN / RYBURN / RIBURN

1880 CENSUS

Mary Rayburn 20: see S. M. Cook

1900 CENSUS

Charly Raybin 38 (Aug 1861-Ala/SC/SC-M 10), Azia 41 (July 1858-M 10-1-1) 7-265B-294/299 (B)

MARRIAGES

Manervia C. Riburn to David Parker q.v.

Pamelia Ryburn to John Furgusson q.v.

- - - - - - - - - - - - -

REAL / REEL

1880 CENSUS

James Real 52, Hannah 54, W.M. WASSON 54 (boarder) 4-10-80 (B)

1900 CENSUS

Arabela J. Reel 40 (July 1859-T/NC/T-Wd 6-4), Alexander SWAFFORD 20 (s)(Mar 1880), Berkelder HAIL 12 (s)(Ap 1888) 5-238B-205

MARRIAGE

Halie R. Real or Reel to Lafayette Dodd q.v.

- - - - - - - - - - - - -

RECTOR

1860 CENSUS

James Rector 24, Margaret 22 5-35-237

Jesse Rector 65, Sarah C. 21, Jesse L. 19, Louisa E. 17, Washington T. 15, Silvira E. 12 5-35-236
[NOTE: it is possible that Sarah Rector 57 on last line

of previous household of Jacob Hamilton belongs with Jesse]
John Rector 34, Elvira 30, Thomas H. 9, Landon L. 7, James K. 6, Azariah B. 4, Mary J. 3, Sarah L. 1, William T. 2/12 3-69-471
Landon Rector 62, Polly 57, Houston M. 25, Landon 16 2-70-473
Sarah Rector 57: see Jacob Hamilton
William Rector 21, Manerva 22 2-77-524

1870 CENSUS

Louisa E. Rector 28, Salina E. 22: see Jacob N. Hamilton
William H. Rector 31, Minerva 31 (Va), James L. 4, Ellen 6/12 4-9-53

1880 CENSUS

William Rector 41, L.C. 32 (w), J.L. 14 (s), M.E. 11 (d), J.H. 5 (s), M.E. 2 (d), M. 5/12 (d) 4-34-279

1900 CENSUS

Mary J. Rector 6: see William O. Bankston
Mattie Rector 45 (1855-Wd 1-1), Willie PASS 24 (s)(1876) 8-282B-282/284 (B)
John Rector 26 (June 1873-T/T/Mo-M 2)(RR Laborer), Savannah 22 (Mar 1878-Ala/Ala/Ala-M 2-1-1), John C. 1 (Feb 1899) 14-220A-139/143
W. Baily Rectar 9: see John W. Hill
William H. Rector 61 (Feb 1839-M 27), Serrild A. 52 (Jan 1848-M 27-8-4), Sallie 17 (July 1882), William T. 14 (June 1885), Elizabeth 11 (Oct 1888), Hayle W. McCABE 5 (gs)(Oct 1894), Thomas P. 2 (gs)(Jan 1897) 3-203A-60/64

MARRIAGES

Florida Rector to M. McJunkins q.v.
H.M. Rector to Sarah J. Bartin, 13 Aug 1862 (15 Aug), W. W. Low JP 1-#785
J.L. Rector to Lilley Yount, 2 Feb 1885 (same), A.P. Early MG 1-459
J.L. Rector to A.P. Porter, 15 Nov 1889 (17 Nov), J.M. Bramlett MG 1-594
James Rector to M.J. Mitchell, 2 Oct 1856 (same), J.R. Burchfield MG 1-#574
Jennie M. Rector to Z. T. McCabe q.v.
John H. Rector to Savanah Noblett, 30 Ap 1898 (1 Mar) [sic], J.A. Torbett JP, B.T. McCabe W 2-275
L. E. Rector to William Humphrey q.v.
Loyd Rector to Flora Hanby, 12 Nov 1887 (same), I.W. Holt JP 1-537
Martha Rector to Zack T. McCabe q.v.
Martha J. Rector to James M. Hamilton q.v.
Mary Ann Rector to Thomas C. Ganaway q.v.
Rachel E. Rector to John W. Kelly q.v.
Sarah Rector to Cornelious Shaver q.v.
Sarah C. Rector to J. W. Hasken q.v.
Wlliam Rector to Manerva Watson, 13 Nov 1858 (14 Nov), S.H. Dickey JP 1-#668
William H. Rector to Louisa C. Smith, 31 Jan 1873 (2 Feb), R.T. Howard MG 1-#1274

\- - - - - - - - - - - - -

REECE / REESE / REACE / REES / REAS

1860 CENSUS

Benjamin Reese 40, Mary A. 40 (NC), Elizabeth 21, Mary A. 19, Lucy 17, Delitha 14, Thomas B. 12, Benjamin T. 10, George H. 6, Josephine 4 1-84-573
Eliza J. Reese 16, James 13, Lucinda C. 3: see Nancy Munday
Elvira Reese 8: see Thomas Breeden

1870 CENSUS

Benjamin Reese 56, Elizabeth 36, Lucy 25, Dilla 23, Thomas 21, Benjamin F. 20, George W. 18, Josephine 14, Mary 4/12 1-10-65
Elizabeth Reese 28: see Snelson Roberts
Lusa Reas 27: see Jacob Green
Martha Reece 15: see Thomas Breeding

1880 CENSUS

Alvira Reece 26: see Margaret Breeding
Benjamin Reece 50, Eliza 25 (d), Thomas 23, George 21, Josie 10 (gd), Mary 10 (d) 1-18-146
Henry Reese 20: see Henry Beard
Lorinda Reece 1/12: see Wade McFalls
Lucy Reece 24: see William Thompson

1900 CENSUS

Alexander Reece 10, Nancy E. 5: see Alexander Ridley
James Reese 57 (May 1843-M 8), Mary F. 33 (Oct 1866-M 8-0-0), Jossi R. COX 10 (ne)(Aug 1889) 2-196B-102/105
Dock B. Reese 55 (Feb 1845-Wd), Addie V. 14 (Mar 1886), Minnie GRAHAM 18 (d)(Ap 1882-M 3-1-1), Ida L. 2 (gd)(May 1898) 2-196B-103/106

MARRIAGES

Dock Reese to Eliza Gunn, 9 May 1874 (12 May), John Howard MG 1-#1336
Eliza Jane Reese to John M. Hase q.v.
Elvira Reese to W. L. Godbehere q.v.
Harrie or Harrel Reece (30, NY) to Sallie D. Giles (20), 14 Dec 1882, T.H. McPherson JP, J.F. Dawson & J.B. Dawson W 2-12(114)
Litha C. Reese to Henry Mice q.v.
Lucy Reece to Jacob Green q.v.
William Reece to Mary A. Jones, 29 Ap 1871 (30 May), G.W. Renfro MG 1-#1195
William Reese to B.L. Lemmons, 27 Dec 1873, "Not Executed, J.B. Chumly, Clerk" 1-#1320

\- - - - - - - - - - - - -

REED / REID / REEDE

1860 CENSUS

Gilbert Reed 38, Mary A. 37, Catharine 16, Charles 15, John M. 14, Nathan 13, Hanna M. 8, Thomas F. 7, Amanda 3, Adaline 8/12 3-68-464

1870 CENSUS

Gilbert Reed 55, Mary Ann 48, Catharine L. 26, Charles H. 25, John N. 24, Nathan D. 21, Amanda 13, Samuel H. 9, Delilah L. 7, Gilbert B. 5 4-1-7
James Reed 44 (Ga), Hannah 45 (Ga) 4-8-52 (B)
Nancy Reed 27, Jesse 8, Isabella 3: see Stephen Cawood
Susan Reed 21: see William Cash

1880 CENSUS

Charles Reed 35, S.E. 36, J.A. 13 (s), P.E. 9 (s), N.M. THOMPSON 23 (boarder) 4-11-89
David Reed 35, Jane 36, William 18, Emily E. 10, Martha A. 7, Albert 6, Watson 5, Robert L. 3, Benjamin 3, Nathan 1 5-3-23
Gilbert Reed 57, M.A. 57, D.L. 17 (d), G.B. 14 (s), N.A. FUGATE 7 (gd), Joseph SHARP 17 (Hired Hand) 4-7-49

Jesse Reed 18: see J. W. Casta
John Reid 33, M.E. 22, A.E. 6 (d), N.L. 3 (s), Alonzo 1 4-7-50
Mary Reed 50 (Servant), John 20 (s): see H.H. Gambill
N.D. Reed 31 (Merchant), M.T. 22 (w), Frank A. 2 (s), W.S. 3/12 (s), S.H. 19 (b) 8-3-23 [N.D. married Margaret T. Stanfil in 1874]

1900 CENSUS

Aaron A. Reed 55 (Feb 1845-Oh/Pa/Pa-M 9), Ida W. 37 (Oct 1862-Oh/Oh/Oh-M 9-2-2), Grace 8 (May 1892), Thomas D. 6 (May 1894), Alexander R. REED 85 (f)(Aug 1814-Pa/Pa/Ireland-Wd), Julia A. WILSON 59 (d)(Oct 1840-Oh/Pa/Pa-Wd 8-5) 11-292B-66
Barlow Reed 30 (Mar 1870-M 9), Madan(?) 25 (Mar 1875-M 9-5-5), Benjamin 8 (Mar 1892), Alas 7 (Ap 1893), Floyed 4 (Oct 1896), Mamie 2 (July 1897), Ethal 8/12 (Sep 1899) 12-181A-58/61
Charles Reed 55 (May 1845-M 22), Samantha E. 56 (May 1844-T/T/NC-M 22-3-2), Lorinda WASSOM 30 (d) (May 1870-M 6-1-1), James C. 2 (gs)(Ap 1898), William G. GRAY 9 (s)(July 1890) 14-222B-181/185
Charley Reed 25: see Philip Henry (B)
Crave D. Reed 31 (July 1868-M 9), Emma E. 29 (Nov 1870-T/NC/T-M 9-3-3), Ethel 6 (July 1893), Emma 5 (Ap 1895), Bula 1 (Aug 1898) 2-191A-9/9
David W. Reed 57 (May 1843-M 31), Jane 50 (Jan 1850-M 31-11-8), Benjamin 22 (July 1877), Nathan 21 (Feb 1879), John 15 (Mar 1885), Alice BARNES 22 (d) (May 1870-D), Lillie 8 (gd)(May 1892), Emma 6 (gd) (Jan 1894) 11-294A-94/95
Frank Reed 22 (Dec 1877-M 2)(General Merchant), Ethel 19 (Mar 1881-M 2-1-1), Alvin (Feb 1899) 8-316A-121/125
James Reed 72 (June 1827-Ga/Ga/Ga-M 40), Esther 66 (Ap 1834-M 40-12-6), James A. McCALEB 21 (Sep 1878) 14-215B-55/56 (B)
Jessie C. Reed 27 (Nov 1872-M 3), Steller 19 (Oct 1880-Oh/Oh/Ind-M 3-1-1), Grace 1 (Aug 1878) 1-185A-141/149
John A. Reed 32 (Jan 1868-Ala/Ala/Ala-M 2)(Coal Miner), Maggie 16 (Feb 1884-Ill/Ill/Ill-M 2-1-1), Viola D. 1 (Mar 1899) 13-306B-320/332
John M. Reed 53 (Jan 1847-M 27), Mary E. 42 (June 1857-M 27-13-9), Elonzo 21 (Mar 1879), Eddie A. 15 (Sep 1884), James G. 13 (Aug 1886), Thomas T. 2 (Sep 1888), Isey P. 6 (Aug 1893), Landon S. 5 (May 1895), Gilbert B. 3 (Jan 1897) 6-243B-79
Loretta Reed 67: see Smith B. Richards
M. Therlow Reed 23 (Nov 1876-M 1), Jennie 21 (Oct 1878-M 1-0) 3-201A-28/30
Mart Reid 28 (Dec 1871-M 7)(Dry Goods Salesman), Elizabeth 26 (Ap 1874-M 7-3-3), Offie M. 5 (Mar 1875), Helen E. 3 (Oct 1896), Nessie 4/12 (Jan 1900) 14-219A-119/122
Mart V. Reid 58 (July 1841-T/NC/T-M 33)(Commercial Trader), Susan* 49 (Jan 1851-M 33-7-5), Susan A. 25 (Ap 1875), Joseph 17 (Aug 1882), Offie 16 (Nov 1883) 14-214A-22/23 [*nee Boyd]
Nathan D. Reed 51 (Ap 1849-M 26)(General Merchant), Margaret T. 41 (July 1858-M 26-5-3), Sammy 19 (Feb 1881)(General Merchant), Anny 17 (Jan 1883), John GILBREATH 22 (boarder)(Nov 1877-Oh/Oh/Oh) (Grocery Salesman) 8-316A-120/124
Robert Reed 49 (Aug 1850-NC/Ireland/Do-M 26), Tuler(?) 49 (Jan 1851-T/NC/NC-M 26-4-4), James 16 (Aug 1883-NC), Robbert 14 (July 1885-NC), Jasper 12 (Jan 1888-NC), Tuler 10 (Ap 1890-NC) 12-179A-1/1
Robert L. Reed 23 (Sep 1876-M 0)(Coal Miner), Alice 19 (Ap 1881-M 0-0) 11-294A-93/94
Thomas B. Reid 22 (Mar 1878-M 1)(Dry Goods Salesman), Mabel N. 20 (Nov 1879-M 1-0), Elvira EDDINGTON 21 (May 1879)(Servant) 14-219A-120/123
Watson Reed 24 (Oct 1875-M 2)(Coal Miner), Lydia 21 (Sep 1878-M 2-1-1), William 1 (Jan 1899) 11-294A-96/97
William R. Reed 25 (Ap 1875-M 6)(Coal Tipper), Crit 23 (Mar 1877-T/T/Va-M 6-2-2), Charles L. 3 (Oct 1896), Willie J. 1 (Mar 1899) 11-294A-95/96

MARRIAGES

Ada Reed to Cain Wilkey q.v.
Amanda Reede to Elbert Fugate q.v.
Anney or Amy Reed to J. F. Gilbreath q.v.
C.D. Reed to Elizabeth Garrison, 27 June 1891, J.P. Thompson JP 4-27
Callie Reed to Jacob Barnes q.v.
Catharine Reede to William Harwood q.v.
Charles Reede to C.E. Wassom, 13 June 1878 (same), John Howard MG 1-#1561
David Reede to Jane Roberts, 20 Dec 1867 (same), W.W. Low JP 1-#992
Elizabeth Reed to J. W. Scott q.v.
Emma Reid to W. F. Barnes q.v.
F.A. Reed to C.E. Barton, 17 Mar 1898 (27 Mar), J.W. Crane MG, W.J. Tallent W 2-258
J.M. Reede to Mary E. Holloway, 2 Ap 1873 (6 Ap), John Howard MG 1-#1282
Jack Reed to Alice Campbell, 13 Oct 1899, no MG or JP, Dan Burwick [signed by X] W 3-54
James Reed to Easter Moore, Aug 1895, Wm Walton MG 4-87
Jesse E. Reed to Estella M. Burns, 28 Aug 1897, G.W. Morris ?? 4-98
John Reid to Lethia Garrison, 27 July 1896, L.L. Barton JP 4-98
Joseph Reed to Martha Sherrill, 27 Nov 1897, R.A. Dickson JP 4-98
Lottie Reed to Sam Jolly q.v.
M.L. Reed to L.C. Rice, 2 Jan 1890 (same), J.W. Williamson MG 1-589
M.P. Reed to Nancey Hips, 17 Jan 1885 (18 Jan), I.W. Holt JP 1-462
Manda Reede to Frank McCabe q.v.
Martin V. Reed Jr. to Elizabeth Hinch, 6 Dec 1893, R.A. Owen MG 4-62
Nannie Reed to W. D. Vandenter q.v.
Patsey Reed to Andy Waldo q.v.
Perry J. Reid to Nannie Martin, 8 Feb 1894, J.W. Clews(?) JP 4-67
Robert Reid to Mary Sherrill, 16 May 1897, G.W. Morris MG 4-98
S. A. Reed to Elmer M. Hawkins q.v.
S.H. Reed to Mary Donaldson, 29 June 1900 (same), G.W. Brewer MG, J.F. Gilbreath(?) W 3-174
Susie Reed to B. L. Garrison q.v.
Therlow Reid to Jennie Harwood, 4 May 1899 (bond only), R.J. Killough W 2-407

Watt Reid to Lydia Morgan, 2 Ap 1898 (3 Ap), H. Morgan JP, D.H. Burwick W 2-263
William Reed to Crit Jones, 20 May 1895, J.Q. Shaver MG 4-86

REEDER

MARRIAGES
A.J. Reeder to Mary Ann Kiziah, 20 Ap 1854 (same), A.D. Paul JP 1-#439
Ida Reeder to Charley Hood (?) q.v.

REEDY / READDY

1900 CENSUS
Amos Readdy 27: see George Gray (B)
John B. Reedy 30 (Mar 1870-Oh/Ireland/Do-M 3)(Weighmaster DC & I Co), Blanche 23 (Nov 1876-Oh/Oh/Oh-M 3-2-2), Rowena 2 (July 1897-Oh), Sherman 10/12 (July 1899) 10-326B-143/151

REGISTER / REGESTER

1900 CENSUS
Burt---s Regester 53 (Feb 1847-Oh/Oh/Oh-M 20), Kate 41 (Aug 1858-Ind/Ind/Ind-M 20-2-2), Neth(?) 9 (d)(Dec 1870-Oh) 1-186A-141/148
James Regester 72 (Ap 1828-Pa/Pa/Pa-Wd)(Hotel Keeper), Clara B. 34 (Nov 1865-Pa/Pa/Pa), Sarah J. 31 (Oct 1868-Pa), Kate F. 27 (Dec 1870-Pa) 14-219B-136/139
Jesse B. Regester 28 (June 1872-Pa/Pa/Pa-M 3)(Physician), Blanch L. 23 (Sep 1876-T/Pa/Pa-M 3-1-1), James G. 1 (Sep 1898) 14-219A-121/124
MARRIAGE
Florence Register to J. H. Graseclose(?) q.v.

RENDEN

1880 CENSUS
W.R.(?) Renden(?) 58, M.J. 54, S.E. 24, J.S. 21, W.P. 13, C.M. 18, B.A. 8 4-31-250

RENFRO / RENFROW

1860 CENSUS
George W. Renfro 35 (Methodist Preacher), Elizabeth C. 28, Marthy A. 7, William W. 6, Nancy E. 4, Josiah A. 2, Mary D. 3/12 2-78-525
James Renfrow 17: see Pleasant M. Purser
Martha Renfrow 48, Lavinia A. 10 7-5-31
Mary A. Renfrow 18: see William Coval
1870 CENSUS
George W. Renfro 46, Elizabeth C. 41, Martha A. 17, William W. 16, Nancy E. 14, Josiah A. 12, Mary D. 10, Sally D. 7, James R. 4 1-2-8
1880 CENSUS
W. W. Renfro 24: see Jessee Dickey
1900 CENSUS
Elizabeth C. Renfro 72: see Nanna Hutcheson
Ollie Renfro 22, Daniel 25: see Rosa Wade (B)
MARRIAGES
C. R. Renfro to C. H. Richards q.v.
Lucy Renfro to Henry Glenn(?) q.v.
N. E. Renfro to J. B. Hutcheson q.v.
W.W. Renfro to Mattie J. Chumley, 16 Jan 1883 (17 Jan), D.V. Culver MG 1-478

RENOW / RENNOW / RENO / RENYEW / RENON

1870 CENSUS
Rebecca L. Reno 26 (NC), William J. 3, George W. 1: see George W. Gideon
1880 CENSUS
W.G. Renon 24, M.C. 26, N.K. 9 (d), John 8 (s), Martha E. 3 (d), Robert 8/12 (s) 8-5-43
1900 CENSUS
John C. Reno 31 (July 1869-M 4), Sarah E. 33 (May 1867-M 4-2-1), Carrie B. 8 (Oct 1891-Ga), Allie C. BLALOCK 17 (sd)(Feb 1883) 11-290A-8
MARRIAGES
E.A. Renow to Rebecca Singleton, 28 Ap 1869 (same), J.W. Hewse JP 1-#1057
James Rennow to Rebecca Dryman, 1 Mar 1869 (no return) 1-#1049
John Renow to Sallie Blalock, 14 Nov 1895, A.P. Hayes JP 4-89
M. L. Renow to Will Weatherly q.v.

REVELY / REAVELY / REVILEY / REAVLEY / REEBELY

1860 CENSUS
Charles Reivley 54, Cyanthia 48, Elizabeth L. 23, William J. 15, Hugh P. 13, Robert H. 10, Martha J. 6, Nancy LAUDERDALE 9 8-9-53
John E. Reevely 24 (Clerk): see Samuel H. Dickey
MARRIAGES
E. L. Reavely to J. J. Clift q.v.
Elias Reviley to Tennie Gothard, 25 June 1900 (same), Geo J. Avrey MG, F.G. Revely W 3-170
J.N. Reively to Mary Goad, 18 June 1900 (same), J.D. Shelton MG, B.J. Graves W 3-168
Julia Ann Reavley to George Joshua Avrey q.v.
Nancy Revely to F. C. Moore q.v.
Sarah Reavely to N. M. Harrison q.v.

REVIS / REVESS / RIVAS / RIVIS

1880 CENSUS
Cela J. Rivis 26, William R. 9, Burkett 5, James T. 1 5-10-89
Kate Revess 24: see M. S. Gambell
William Revis 32, Hariet 23, Susan 4, Cora 3 12-4-34

1900 CENSUS

Burt Revis 24 (Unk-M 6), Mary 29 (Nov 1870-T/T/NC-M 6-3-3), Thomas 5 (Dec 1894), Addison R. 4 (Dec 1895), Harry 1 (Jan 1899), Vina [Egletine] McCULLOUGH 70 (ml)(Mar 1830-NC/NC/NC-Wd 10-5) 6-246B-130/131

William B. Revis 32, Lincy 18: see Lee A. Smith

MARRIAGES

Burkett Revis to Mary McCollough, 26 Aug 1893, John Howard MG 4-59

H. Revis to Jonathan Mulkey q.v.

Mary M. Rivas to Enos Turner q.v.

Richard Revis to Lyna A. Smith, 20 Jan 1900 (21 Jan), W.L. Lillard JP, L.A. Smith W 3-113

REYNOLDS / RUNNELS / RANNAL

1870 CENSUS

Calvin Reynolds 30 (Pa), Eliza A. 26, Rachel S. 1 3-7-45

Joseph Reynolds 24, Ellen 32, Ned 11, Pollie 7, Nancy 62 2-15-105 (B)

1880 CENSUS

Joseph Reynolds 18 (Printer): see Virginia Leuty

1900 CENSUS

Henry Reynolds 47 (Nov 1853-Ind/NC/NC-M 27), Rosia 47 (July 1852-NC/NC/NC-M 27-2-2), Roy R. 23 (July 1876-Ind)(Sawyer), Albert M. 12 (Mar 1888), William BILLBURRY 35 (lodger)(Mar 1865) 7-267B-329/334

John W. Reynolds 50 (1850-T/T/Va-M 14), Maggie 29 (1871-M 14-11-6), Flora 10 (July 1889), Artie 9 (May 1891), Louise 6 (June 1893), Wm 5 (Jan 1895), Ada 4 (Mar 1896), Enzar 1 (Mar 1899), William SWAFFORD 28 (boarder)(Sept 1871) 15-272B-85 (B)

MARRIAGES

Calvin H. Reynolds to Eliza A. Minick, 8 July 1865 (10 July), John Howard MG 1-#874

John W. Rannal to Maggie Swafford, 16 Oct 1885 (same), W.S. Hale MG 1-485

Lisa Ann Runnels to W. H. Minix q.v.

Mannie Reynolds to Roby Price q.v.

Mark Reynolds to Fanny Hurch, 1 May 1886 (3 May), J.B. Phillips ?? 1-519

Neytie(?) Reynolds to Enoch West q.v.

Sallie Reynolds to John W. Harwood q.v.

RHEA / RAY / RHAY

1860 CENSUS

Aaron Rhea 61 (SC), Blanche 59, Aaron 14 9-98-666

Henry Rhea 26, Rhoda A. 26, William 4, Doctor I. 2 9-97-655

Hugh Rhea 18, Mary C. 20 1-85-577

James Rhea 35, Louisa Jane 32, Wright S. 12, James 10, Alexander 8, Bryant 5, Priscilla 4, Florence 6/12, James SMITTY 18 3-67-459

John Rhea 26, Sarah 26, James 6, Warren 1 9-98-669

Pleasant Rhea 42, Mariah 45, William 17, Tennessee 14, Robert 12, Lucinda 9, Joseph 7, James 4, Mary A. 19 3-60-414

Warren Rhea 20, Susan 27, Anna L. 7, Mary J. 1 9-98-668

1870 CENSUS

Aaron Ray 68 (SC), Blanchey 67 (Va), Jefferson 9 1-22-144

Aaron Ray Jr. 24, Elizabeth 22, William 3, Hughey 6/12 1-22-145

Benjamin F. Rhea 28 (Ga), Nancy A. 20, John N. 1 3-6-42

Fanny Rhea 13 (B): see Samuel H. Dickey

Henry Ray 34, Rhoda 30, Nancy 6, Samuel 4 1-22-146

Henry Ray 37, Martha 36, Julia 16, Nancy 11, Sally 9, Henry 6, Vina 4, Napolion 2, Jeremiah 1/12 3-17-124 (B)

Hughey Ray 25, Mary C. 24, Edweeney 9, Amanda C. 5, John C. 2, Elizabeth 6/12 1-17-114

James Ray 50, Louisa J. 45, Wright S. 22, James 20, Alexander 18, Bryant W. 16, Priscilla A. 14, Florence D. 11, David R. 7, Robert E.L. 5 3-16-116

Lawson Ray 35, Elizabeth 27, Malinda 8, Charles 7, Lewis 5, Richard 3, Phebe 2 3-17-122

Mariah Ray 33, Robert 22, Lucinda 18, Joseph 16, James 14 3-10-69

Richard Ray 4, John 2 (B): see Samuel Ray

Samuel Ray 37, Lucy J. 32, James C. 8, Samuel W. 6, Thomas 4, Mary L. 2, Ann E. 7/12, Martha 25, Susan 6, Richard RAY (B) 4, John (B) 2 3-17-121

Susanna Ray 36, Mary Jane 11, Jefferson 9, John H. 6, Isabella 2 1-10-67

1880 CENSUS

Aaron Ray 35, Elizabeth 26, William 12, Brown 8, Dock 7, James WEST 26 (Servant) 1-14-116

Albert Ray 17 (Mu)(Servant): see Nile Broyles

Emmett Rhea 25: see A. Griffith

Henry Ray 46, Rhoda 35, Nancy 13, Samuel 11, James 9, Aaron 7 12-5-42

Henry Rhea 56, Martha 50, Sarah 17, Henry 16, Viney 15, M.B. 9, Frank 6, S.P. 3, Jerry 8 3-21-169 (B)

Hugh Ray 35, Mary 36, Edweny 19, Amanda 15, John 12, Hugh 8, Mary 5, George 3, Jefferson RAY 19 (nw) 1-17-139

Lawson Rhea 50, E. 40, Charlie 16, L.C. 14, Emaline 14, Phebe 9, G. 8, Lawson 6, Solerance 3, Parallee 5 3-21-170 (B)

Lewis Rhea 49, E. 40, Clarisa 18, L.B. 16, E.M. 14, N.A. 11, G.B. 9, Loso(?) 6, P.C. 4, F. 2 3-30-240 (B)

M.E. Rhea 61 (m), Rhea 33 (s), Lucinda 26, Jane 21, Willim SMITH 16 (gs), P.M. 18 (gs) 3-15-123

Thos Rhea 16, Lauson 14, S.F. 9, C. 7, John 2 3-29-236 (B)

1900 CENSUS

David Rhea 32 (Mar 1868-M 1)(Lawyer), Marget 32 (Ap 1868-M 1-0), Thomas BOLLEN 50 (May 1850-Wd) (Servant) 1-186A-138/144

Florence Ray 20 (1880)(Servant), Charles MAYFIELD 27 (boarder)(1873) 8-275A-128 (B)

Frank Rhea 25 (Jan 1875-Wd) (RR Laborer) 14-216A-69/70 (B)

Fred Ray 16: see William Day

Henry Ray 35 (Dec 1864-M 14)(RR Laborer), Mary J. 31 (May 1869-M 14-6-3), Thomas E. 13 (Nov 1886), Cara L. 8 (Feb 1892), Annie M. 1 (May 1899) 2-198A-132/137 (B)

Henry Ray 65 (Mar 1835-M 45), Rhoda 64 (Ap 1836-M 45-9-2) 12-182B-77/80

Hugh Ray 45 (Mar 1845-M 35), Mary 50 (Ap 1850-M 35-9-6), Hugh 25 (May 1873), George 20 (Ap 1880), Mary 17 (Aug 1882) 1-184B-111/116

James Ray 29 (Sep 1870-M 2), Almelia 32 (Feb 1878-M 2-1-1), Samuel 3/12 (Feb 1900) 12-182B-76/79

James G. Ray 46 (Dec 1850-M 15), Mary E. 40 (Unk 1860-M 15-10-9), John 17 (Nov 1882), Pleasant R. 15 (Jan 1885), Valina 12 (Feb 1888), Robert C. 10 (Feb 1890), Tennessee A. 8 (Dec 1891), Laura P. 5 (July 1894), Joseph 3 (Jan 1897), Listia O. 11/12 (Oct 1899) 3-205A-86/93

Mariel K. Rhea 61 (Mar 1839), Frank 25 (boarder)(May 1875)(Teamster), Tobi 21 (Mar 1877)(RR Laborer), Benjamin HIXON 12 (gs)(Aug 1887), Jean H. 8 (gd) (May 1892), Gladis H. 5 (gd)(Ap 1895), Emma 3 (gd) (Feb 1897) 14-214B-33/34

Phoebe Rhea 26 (Sep 1873-Wd 2-1)(Boarding House Keeper), John 8 (May 1892), Ben BROWN 29 (boarder) (Dec 1870-NC/NC/NC), Jim CATES 28 (boarder) (Unk) 8-311B-13/14

Richard Ray 30 (Mar 1870-M 8), Slattie 23 (1877-M 8-5-3), Richard 7 (Feb 1893), Mattie 4 (Dec 1896), John B. 6/12 (Jan 1900) 3-208B-153/166 (B)

Robert Ray 52 (Feb 1848-S), John A. 22 (nw)(Mar 1878), Molly BUCK 22 (Dec 1867)(Servant), James SMITH 14 (Unk 1886)(Servant) 3-205A-89/97

Samuel Ray 30 (Ap 1870-M 7), Hettera 22 (Dec 1877-M 7-3-3), Henry 4 (Aug 1895), James 2 (Ap 1897), Wilum 9/12 (Ap 1899) 12-182B-75/78

Thomas Rhea 33 (June 1866-M 4)(Day Laborer), Clara 25 (Ap 1875-M 4-3-2) 14-216A-70/71 (B)

MARRIAGES

Aaron Rhea to Mary E. Bratchen, 28 Dec 1865 (29 Dec), Ed Pyott JP 1-#1067

Alice Rhea to Jeff Thompson q.v.

B.F. Rhea to Nancy Cox, 6 May 1866 (same), John Howard MG 1-#900

Blancha J. Rhea to Francis M. Short q.v.

D.M. Rhea to Maggie Holloway, 24 Jan or June 1899, J.L. McPherson JP 4-104

Ediwie or Elmire Ray to Joseph Teague q.v.

Eliza J. Rhea to John M. Houston q.v.

Frank Rhea to Florence Hicky, 17 Dec 1893, J.W. Cowles JP 4-68

H.B. Ray to Jennie Daniel, 13 Aug 1898, J.M. Hercules MG 4-95

Henry Rhea to Jane Locke, 19 Nov 1885 (no return) 1-484

Henry Rhea to Rhoda Cowden, 3 Aug 1856 (same), N.H. Long JP 1-#590

Hugh Rhea to Mary Cox, 28 Ap 1858 (same), N.H. Long JP 1-#682

Hugh Ray to Bertie Tharp, 22 July 1900, W.T. West MG 4-105

James Ray to Allie Lemons, 7 Ap 1899, W.T. West MG 4-101

James G. Ray to Mary Howard, 20 Jan 1887 (same), T.H. McPherson JP 1-521

Jeff Ray to Nancy Gillum, 25 Nov 1880 (25 Nov), J.P. Roddy MG 1-294

Jennie Ray to Benjamin Riddle q.v.

Katie Ray(?) to C. W. Adcox q.v.

John Rhea to Sarah Houston, 25 Mar 1855 (same), N.H. Long JP 1-#489

Lucinda Ray to Noah Cate q.v.

Malinda Ray to Mat Jones q.v. (B)

Mary Ann Rhea to George Smith q.v.

Nannie Rhea to Samuel Peters q.v.

Nancy Rhea to Samuel Lemons q.v.

O. T. Ray to James Smith q.v.

Phebe Ray to Henry Turk q.v.

Richard Rhea to Charlotte Hickey, 2 June 1892, J.W. Cowles JP 4-42

Samuel Ray to Hattie Gibson, 3 Jan 1894, W.T. West MG 4-63

Sopprina Rhea to John Hixon q.v.

Thomas Rhay to M.C. Cunnyngham, 29 Jan 1889 (31 Jan), James H. Hale JP 1-569

Thomas Rhea to Clearisa Stephens, 6 Mar 1896, R.A. Dickson JP 4-93

W.S. Rhea to Jennie Rice, 23 July 1879 (same), John Howard MG 1-291

Warren Rhea to Susan Harvey or Hanney, 9 May 1854 (same), N.H. Long JP 1-#442

- - - - - - - - - - - - -

RHODES / ROADS

MARRIAGES

Joseph Roads to Elizabeth J. Mickells, 17 Sep 1855 (same), John Crawford JP 1-#516

Mary Rhodes to John Doss q.v.

- - - - - - - - - - - - -

RICE

1860 CENSUS

Jossiah Rice 50 (SC), Ruthe 50 (NC), William L. 19, James 16, Nathan 15, Sarah F. 12, Charlotte E. 10, Nancy E. 8, Martha C. 6 5-39-265

1870 CENSUS

Amedia Rice 39, Emily 40, Alexander 18, Francis 16, David 14, Samuel 12, John 10, Margarette 8, Mary A. 7, Bred(?) 2 3-11-74

Isaiah Rice 58 (Ga), Ruth 60 (NC), Charlotte 21, Nancy 19, Martha 16, John 12, Sarah 8, Fanny 61, John 16, Mary 4/12 6-3-13

James Rice 25, Elizabeth 23, Mary McERVIN 8 6-5-33

1880 CENSUS

James W. Rice 37, Elizabeth L. 34, William H. 10, James F. 6, Charley W. 4, Leyton M. 4, Mary E. 2, Mary A. HARDEN 58 (ml), Lottie RICE 30 (si), Sarah A. 1 (d) 6-20-180/184

1900 CENSUS

Henry Rice 29 (Sep 1870-T/NC/T-M 6), Lizzie 24 (Ap 1876-M 6-3-3), Myrtle L. 5 (July 1894), Birttie A. 4 (Mar 1896), Henry W. 1 (Sep 1898-Tex) 7-265A-282/287

Jesse C.(?) Rice 70: see James T. Monroe

Sharlott E. Rice 51 (Jan 1849-T/T/NC-Wd 6-3), Nancy J. 13 (Dec 1886), George W. 12 (Ap 1888) 5-232A-75

MARRIAGES

Alexander Rice to Lake Parker, 21 Ap 1877 (22 Ap), W.H. Dodd MG 1-#1494

Augusta Rice to G. M. Cox q.v.

David Rice to Orbanna Parker, 23 Nov 1877 (25 Nov), T.H. McPherson JP 1-#1526

Florence Rice to J. T. Tallant q.v.

Frances Rice to James Shaufner(?) q.v.

Ida Rice to James W. Bowles q.v.

Isiah Rice to Julia Carmicle, 24 July 1871 (same), J. L. Brown JP 1-#1201
L. C. Rice to M. L. Reed q.v.
L. E. Rice to W. A. Raines q.v.
James W. Rice to Lucinda E. Harden, 9 Sep 1868 (same), John Howard MG 1-#1028
Jennie Rice to W. S. Rhea q.v.
Martha Rice to A. L. Smith q.v.
N.W. Rice to Susan Cinnamon, 11 Dec 1867 (same), W.M. Buttram MG 1-#986
Rachel E. Rice to T. A. Young q.v.
W.H. Rice to Elizabeth Kelly, 3 Sep 1893, T.F. Shaver JP 4-61

- - - - - - - - - - - - -

RICHARDS

1860 CENSUS
Angaline Richards 17, Zipporah 12: see Lodice Bell
C.C. Richards 19: see Roland F. McDonald
1870 CENSUS
F. Richards 47, Sarah C. 78 (SC), Martha 18, Margarette C. CRANMORE 20 8-18-124
1880 CENSUS– None
1900 CENSUS
Olivia J. Richards 43 (Mar 1857-Ky/Ky/Ky-Wd 4-4), Florence 22 (Aug 1877-Ky), Ida 21 (Dec 1878), Charles H. 16 (Aug 1883)(Livery Stable Laborer), Bert B. 15 (Nov 1884)(Livery Stable Laborer) 14-219A-129/132
Smith B. Richards 43 (June 1857-T/Mo/?-M 22)(Carpenter), Julia M. 40 (Sep 1857-Wisc/Eng/NH-M 22-6-6), Victor E. 19 (July 1880)(Carpenter), Reece H. 16 (Oct 1883)(RR Laborer), Alberta M. 11 (May 1889), Nellie A. 9 (Feb 1891), Lilla B. 7 (Feb 1893), John W.M. 4 (Oct 1895), Loretta REED 67 (boarder)(Sep 1832-NY/NY/NY-Wd 4-0) 14-219A-126/129
MARRIAGES
C.H. Richards to C.E. Renfro, 16 Oct 1883 (same), W.S. Hale MG 1-472
Lew(?) Richards to James Young q.v.

- - - - - - - - - - - - -

RICHARDSON

1900 CENSUS
Noris Richardson 27 (June 1872-M 2), Mary 21 (Sep 1878-Tex/Ala/Mo-M 2-1-0) 5-235A-147

- - - - - - - - - - - - -

RICHEY / RITCHIE

1870 CENSUS
Mary Richey 37, Mary 14, Enoch 10, Martha 7 6-15-105
1880 CENSUS
Mary Richie 48, Enoch 20, Sarah M. 19 6-15-137/139
1900 CENSUS
David Ritchie 50 (Jan 1850-Ala/T/Ala-M 29), Serepta J. 52 (Feb 1848-M 29-2-1) 11-292A-56/56
Enoch Ritchie 40 (Sep 1859-M 7), Mary 41 (May 1859-M 7-8-8), John 18 (Aug 1881), Louie [marked through, Hanie written above; no age or date], Eddie L. 14 (May 1886), Ethel 10 (Aug 1889), Vinnie 8 (Ap 1892), Robert 6 (Dec 1893), Mammie 5 (June 1895), Louie SWAFFORD [TUTORS marked through below Swafford] 18 (d) (June 1881-Wd) 3-203B-71/76
Robert T. Ritchie 46 (May 1854-M 18), Lennie B. 36 (May 1864-M 18-5-4), Dora I. 15 (Aug 1884), James A. 11 (Dec 1888), Ella J. 7 (Oct 1892), Jesse R. 5/12 (Dec 1899) 11-292A-53
MARRIAGES
Enoch T. Ritchie to Mary Brown, 22 Sep 1880 (no return) 1-292
John Richey to Viola Hale, 25 July 1898 (same), J.W. Williamson MG 2-303
Joseph T. Richey to Sarah E. Fain, 11 Oct 1877 (same), J.W. Pace(?) MG 1-#1516
Mattie Richey to Robert B. Lindsey q.v.
Nancy J. Richey to J. A. Kerley q.v.
Sallie A. Ritchey to J. O. Hickman q.v.
Vesta Richey to Harry Wolfe q.v.

- - - - - - - - - - - - -

RICKETTS

MARRIAGE
Major Ricketts to Minnie Tucker, 16 Jan 1895, W.L. Lillard JP 4-83

- - - - - - - - - - - - -

RICKLES / RICKEL

1900 CENSUS
John Rickel 45 (Mar 1855-M 22), Susanah 38 (Nov 1861-M 22-5-3), Anna H. 19 (July 1880), Jara P. 15 (Jan 1885), James L. HOLLAMAN 15 (nw)(Feb 1885) 2-194B-63/65
MARRIAGE
Fannie E. Rickles to W. L. Duggen q.v.

- - - - - - - - - - - - -

RIDDLE / RIDLE

1860 CENSUS
Joshua Riddle 45, Martha 43, Milo S. 20, Mary 18, Mahala 12, Florence E. 7, Hirame D. 4, Margaret A. BENSON 18 8-23-153
1870 CENSUS
Josh I. Riddle 55, Martha 53, Mary O. 24, Hiram D. 12 8-11-75
Milo S. Riddle 30, Sarah E. 27, William O. 1 8-11-74
1880 CENSUS
C. T. Riddle 28: see T. A. Allen
H.D. Riddle 23, Martha 63 (m), M.O. 37 (si), W.J. 11 (gs), Jessey GREEN 9 (gs), Mattie 7 (gd), J.E. 5 (gd) 8-20-176
M.S. Riddle 44, S.E. 37 (w), W.O. 11 (s), R.I.S. 8 (s), S.J. 7 (d), H.C. 1/12 (d) 8-5-38
1900 CENSUS
Hiram Riddle 43 (June 1856-M 14), Drusilla 40 (Jan 1860-M 14-4-4), John 13 (Feb 1887), Roy I. 11 (May 1889), Maggie A. 9 (Nov 1891), Jesse D. 4 (May 1896) 8-287A-377/379
Thomas Riddle 28 (Sep 1871-M 5), Anna 24 (June 1875-M 5-2-2), Milo C. 3 (Nov 1896), Lucille 11/12 (June 1899), Charles 15 (b)(Unk 1885), Gus SMITH 26

(boarder)(Nov 1873-M 0)(Coal Miner), Laura 24 (boarder)(Oct 1875-M 0-0) 8-285B-339/341

MARRIAGES

Benjamin Riddle (22) to Jennie Ray (26), 23 May 1881, W.A. Howard MG, Jas Bohannon & Jack Ray (both of Hamilton Co) W 4-3(23)

Eliza Ridle to Francis W. Allison q.v.

Ellen M. Riddle to L. L. Ferguson q.v.

Jennie Riddle to Walter E. Keever q.v.

Lizzie Riddle to James M. Foust q.v.

M. S. Riddle to Sarah Foust, no date (11 Sep 1861), W. A. Green JP 1-#761

Mahala A. Riddle to J. B. Green q.v.

Thompson [Thomas] I. Riddle to Annie Smith, 5 May 1895, F. Alexander MG 4-79

- - - - - - - - - - - - -

RIDER

1900 CENSUS

James F. Rider 30 (Dec 1869-T/Ga/Ga-M 11) (Painter), Maggie 30 (Oct 1869-T/T/Ark-M 11-6-5), Adellie 8 (Aug 1891), Rufus 7 (Nov 1892), Frederick 6 (Ap 1893), Hattie 4 (Aug 1895), Pearlie L. 1 (Ap 1899) 14-213A-3/3

Mary Rider 39, Ellen 16: see Christopher Jones

Mattie Rider 42 (Jan 1858-Ga/Ga/Ga-Wd), Sam 18 (Ap 1882), Annie 16 (Ap 1884) 3-208B-150/163

MARRIAGE

W.L. Rider to Mary A. Jones, 19 Jan 1892, R.A. Bartlett MG 4-43

- - - - - - - - - - - - -

RIDINGS

MARRIAGE

G.(?) J. Ridings to Elizabeth Bunch, 24 Dec 1878 (same), B.T. Ziegler JP 1-#1589

- - - - - - - - - - - - -

RIDLEY / RIDLY / RIDGLEY

1900 CENSUS

Alex Ridley 21 (Oct 1878-Ga/Ga/Ga-M 0), Delia 25 (Unk-T/Ireland/Do-M 0-0), Kate MALEY 21 (sil) (Nov 1878-T/Ireland/Do) 8-318B-161/167

Alexander Ridley 73 (Unk 1826-Wd)(Old Age Pensioner), Fannie 30 (d)(June 1869-D 3-3)(Housekeeper), Alexander REECE 10 (gs)(Aug 1889), Nancy E. 5 (gd) (July 1894), Rose A. RIDLEY 10/12 (gd)(July 1899), Nancy A. SMITH 28 (d)(May 1872-M 11-3-3), John F. 30 (sl)(Jan 1870-M 11)(Coal Miner), John A. 9 (gs) (Ap 1890), Samuel A. 6 (May 1894), William R. 2 (Feb 1898) 9-228A-10

Roe Ridley 31 (Sep 1868-Ga/Ga/Ga-M 11)(Furnace Stoveman), Etta 28 (Aug 1871-Tex/Mo/T-M 11-5-4), Ernest 11 (Jan 1889), Lettie E. 8 (June 1891), Bertie 7 (Ap 1893), William T. 4 (July 1895) 8-316B-132/137

William H. Ridgley 72: see Jesse D. Thomas

MARRIAGES

Alex Ridley to Delia Maley, 9 Nov 1899 (same), J.A. Whitner MG 3-66

Eliza Ridley to J. Y. Rue q.v.

Emma Ridley to E. H. Ivey q.v.

Munroe Ridley to Etta Ballew, 9 Oct 1886 (10 Oct), J. Shaver MG 1-510

Nancy Ridley to John F. Smith q.v.

Tellola Ridley to Alfred Lawson q.v.

- - - - - - - - - - - - -

RIDNER / REDENER

1860 CENSUS

John Redener(?) 10: see Thomas McPherson

William R. Ridner 22, Elizabeth 47 (Ky), Thomas 10 3-55-376

- - - - - - - - - - - - -

RIGGINS / RIGGENS

1870 CENSUS

Richard Riggins 64 (NC), Cristener 64 (Va), John H. 38, Thomas 36, Silas 30, Sarah 32, Charles 27 3-13-87 (B)

MARRIAGES

Mary Riggins to Samuel O. Foust q.v.

Nancy Riggens to W. P. Hill q.v.

Thomas Riggins to E.J. Clack, no date (14 Aug 1878), no MG or JP 1-#1574

- - - - - - - - - - - - -

RIGGLE

1880 CENSUS

Elijah A. Riggle 20, Florence 14 (w) 6-17-157/161

John Riggle 92, Faribee 67 (w): see Z.T. Sneed

- - - - - - - - - - - - -

RIGGS

1900 CENSUS

Ellis Riggs 27 (June 1871-M 9)(Coal Miner), Ida A. 25 (Feb 1875-M 9-3-1), Altie 2 (Feb 1898) 14-217B-102/104

John A. Riggs 51 (May 1849-M 1), Fanny E. 52 (May 1848-M 1-0), Robert 16 (s)(Aug 1883-T/T/Ga) [probably deceased, name marked through], Richard 15 (Feb 1885), William 7 (July 1892), Chapman 5 (Aug 1894), Arthur 5 (Aug 1894) 3-211A-199/217

Minnie Riggs 11: see John C.(?) Dodson

MARRIAGES

Ellis Riggs to Ida Bell, 25 Dec 1892, W.H. Parkinson JP 4-54

Emma Riggs to Will Lehmer q.v.

J.A. Riggs to F.L. Burdett, 18 Oct 1898, A.M. Broyles JP 4-95

J.M. Riggs to Arminda Smith, 2 Jan 1885 (6 Jan), T.H. McPherson JP 1-463

John Riggs to Adie Bing, 23 Feb 1889 (24 Feb), M.F. Moore MG 1-574

John A. Riggs to Mary A. Harwood, 17 Ap 1889 (21 Ap), J.H. Hale JP 1-579

W.N. Riggs to Sarah C. Dodson, 4 Dec 1888 (same), J.P. Thompson JP 1-554

- - - - - - - - - - - - -

RIGSBY

1880 CENSUS
B.F. Rigsby 27, Mary J. 40 (w), S.A. 9 (d) 8-11-90
1900 CENSUS
Frank Rigsby 56 (June 1843-M 30), Jane 71 (Oct 1829-M 30-1-1), Sally 28 (d)(Oct 1871), Sarah MERREL 76 (sil)(Mar 1824-Wd 0-0) 8-279A-208/210
James D. Rigsby 39 (May 1861-M 15)(Blacksmith), Carrie 38 (Feb 1862-Ga/Ga/Ga-M 15-5-5), Sarah A. 14 (Mar 1886), James A. 11 (July 1888), Charles M. 9 (June 1890), Minnie E. 7 (Ap 1893), Elias R. MORRIS 21 (Mar 1879-Ga/Ga/Ga)(Coke Oven Laborer) 13-302A-218/226
Mar--?-- F. Rigsby 29 (Jan 1871-M 10), Eliza R. 25 (May 1875-M 10-3-3), Charles H. 8 (Feb 1892), Russie E. 5 (June 1894), Walter H. 2 (Sep 1897) 11-290B-13
Nelson Rigsby 11, Effie M. 9, Ina 5, Iva 5: see Wm Wilson
Robert J. Rigsby 34 (May 1866-M 13), Eliza J. 30 (Feb 1870-Ga/Ga/Ga-M 13-2-2), John W. 9 (June 1890), Esther A. 6 (July 1893-Ga) 11-291A-32
Samuel J. Rigsby 28 (July 1871-M 6), Alice M. 27 (Mar 1873-M 6-1-1), Effie D. 4 (Mar 1896) 11-291A-33
William D. Rigsby 41 (Mar 1859-M 18), Sarah C. 41 (Mar 1859-M 18-4-4), Edith I. 17 (Sep 1882), Wed W. 16 (Oct 1883), Vernie E. 14 (July 1885), William H. 12 (Oct 1887) 11-290B-15
MARRIAGES
G.W. Rigsby to Louisa Bomans, 15 Sep 1887 (same), J.M. Hall MG 1-528
M. L. Rigsby to W. L. Wilson q.v.
Maggie Rigsby to James Edmondson q.v.
Marion Rigsby to Duskie(?) Pickett, 24 Mar 1891, E.F. Gurice(?) JP 4-21
S.J. Rigsby to Alice Bean, 6 or 16 Dec 1894, C.E. Muncy JP 4-75
Wm D. Rigsby (22) to Sarah C. Walker (22), 24 Nov 1881, W.R. Grimsly MG, F.M. Snow & Wm Morgan W 4-4(38)
Wm G. Rigsby to Mary Benson, 5 Jan 1857 (8 Jan), W.M. Morgan JP 1-#589

- - - - - - - - - - - - -

RIKARD

1900 CENSUS
Katie Rikard 18: see Charles W. Irwin

- - - - - - - - - - - - -

RILEY / REILLEY

1900 CENSUS
James Riley 32 (Mar 1868-M 10), Mary 32 (Jan 1868-M 10-5-3), Moxie 5 (Feb 1895), Jesse 2 (Aug 1897), Della M. 7/12 (Nov 1899) 8-318B-168/174
Sarah Riley 56 (Oct 1843-T/Va/Va-Wd 0) 8-286A-351/353
MARRIAGES
Eliza Riley to Joseph Dodson q.v.
J.L. Riley to Sarah Dunning, 21 Oct 1886 (same), W.S. Hale MG 1-510
J.W. Riley to Mary Gibson, 12 Sep 1890, R.A. Bartlett MG 4-16

- - - - - - - - - - - - -

RISING

MARRIAGE
Sarah Rising to Floyd Campbell q.v.

- - - - - - - - - - - - -

RIVERS

1880 CENSUS
William Rivers 14 (B): see John Robinson

- - - - - - - - - - - - -

ROACH

1900 CENSUS
John B. Roach 26 (Jan 1874-M 1)(Coal Miner), Crocia 21 (Jan 1879-M 1-1-1), Tillman 5/12 (Dec 1899), William ROSE 19 (boarder)(Dec 1880)(Coal Miner) 13-305B-302/214

- - - - - - - - - - - - -

ROBARDS / ROBERDS

1880 CENSUS
Margaret Roberds 28: see Simon Cumbo
1900 CENSUS
Lizzie Roberds 21: see Albert Brayls (B)
MARRIAGE
Delila Robards to Thomas Emory q.v.

- - - - - - - - - - - - -

ROBBINS

1900 CENSUS
John Robbins 30 (Oct 1869-Ga/Ga/Ga-M 0)(RR Laborer), Bell 21 (Aug 1878-M 0), Dessa 6 (Dec 1893) 14-216A-68/69 (B)
Newton Robbins 67 (Aug 1842-NC/NC/NC-M 27), Mary A. 60 (Ap 1840-NC/NC/NC-M 22-8-7), George 26 (Nov 1873-NC), Cora A. 21 (Oct 1878-NC), Adaline 19 (Oct 1880-NC), Galiman O. 13 (Mar 1887-NC) 3-209A-167/181

- - - - - - - - - - - - -

ROBBS

MARRIAGE
Rebecca Robbs to S. M. Carter q.v.

- - - - - - - - - - - - -

ROBERTS / ROBITS

1860 CENSUS
Hughe Roberts 35, Jane 30, James 12, John 6, William 4, Harriet 1 2-70-476
1870 CENSUS
Snelson Roberts 60 (NC)(School Teaher), Willie 2, Emma 7/12, John M. SWEETEN 21, John M. DAVIS 26, Elizabeth REESE 28 1-8-55
Joseph Roberts 42, Dicy E. 37, Iseral S. 14, Sarah A. 8, George W. 7 2-20-71

Valentine Roberts 56 (Blacksmith), Mary 40, Margurette 26, Nancy 20, Lucinda 12, Mary A. 3, James S. 2 1-21-140

Watson Roberts 21, Ana M. 18, Mary L. 1 5-9-67

1880 CENSUS

James Roberts 35 (Miner), Susan 24, Armilda 12, Joel 8, Alexander 6, Alice 4, Martha 3/12 2-31-247

John Roberts 21, America 19, E.J. 8/12 (d) 4-4-28

John Roberts 43 (House Carpenter), Terressa 44, McDonald 17 (House Carpenter), John 8 2-27-216

1900 CENSUS

Joseph Roberts 43 (July 1856-Ireland/Do/Do-1864/35/Na-M 15), Alice 45 (May 1855-T/NY/T-M 15-3-3), Ira W. 14 (Ap 1886), Elsie 11 (Jan 1889), Thane O. 8 (July 1891), Mary A. FOSTER 57 (sil)(Ap 1843-T/NC/T-Wd 1-1) 8-317B-152/157

Lizzie Roberts 19, Myrtle 17: see Richard Gallahar (B)

Lorenza Roberts 40 (Unk-M 14), Sallie 35 (Mar 1865-M 14-9-7), Nellie 13 (Feb 1887), Charlie 10 (Jan 1890), Rettie 8 (Oct 1892), Harris 7 (Mar 1893), Ella 5 (Ap 1895), Lizzie 2 (Feb 1898), Taylor 5/12 (Dec 1899) 6-244B-98/99

Margaret Roberts 52: see Henry A. Crawford

Nannie Roberts 29 (Mar 1871), Lillie 16 (si)(Nov 1883) 12-180B-47/50

Nathaniel R. Roberts 29 (Oct 1870-M 9)(Barber), Dillard 24 (Oct 1875-Miss/NC/NC-M 9-1-0), Julia DYER 12 (ward)(Dec 1887) 10-326A-132/137 (B)

Rachel Roberts 58 (B): see Mary Conley

William Roberts 52 (Feb 1848-M 22), Tennie 43 (Ap 1857-T/NC/T-M 22-5-5), Florance 21 (Oct 1878), John 19 (Feb 1881), Jessie 16 (July 1883), Nannie 13 (July 1886), Willie 9 (Ap 1891) 10-259B-185/189

MARRIAGES

A.C. Roberts to Mary A. Harwood, 30 Sep 1877 (same), Wm W. Lowe JP 1-#1511

Amanda Roberts to Thomas Carney q.v.

D.M. Robits to Mary Garrison, 6 July 1880 (8 July), Stephen Breeding JP 1-295

Elias Roberts to Mattie Miller, 19 June 1887 (same), F.J. Paine JP 1-583

Elizabeth Roberts to Samuel Lemmons q.v.

James L. Roberts to Florence McMillan, 7 Feb 1889 (same), W.G. Mitchell JP 1-568

Jane Roberts to David Reede q.v.

John Roberts to Amerrica Winefrey, 1 Jan 1879 (same), B.F. Hollaway JP 1-#1597

Katie Roberts to William Fitzgeral q.v.

Lizzie Roberts to J. M. Wright q.v.

Louisa Roberts to Isaac Lutten q.v.

Lucy Roberts to Alfred Etherly q.v.

Lucy A. Roberts to F. H. Brooks q.v.

Martha J. Roberts to A. T. Marsh q.v.

Minnie Roberts to Frank Bardwell q.v.

Mollie Roberts to James Cagle q.v.

N.W. Roberts to Elizabeth Bean, 9 May 1891, J.W. Williamson MG 4-29

Pairlee Roberts to Richard Lemmons q.v.

Plina Roberts to Jessey Bennett q.v.

Sally Roberts to Frank Hilton q.v.

Samuel Roberts to Martha McFalls, 14 Nov 1874 (17 Nov), J. Waller MG 1-#1370

William Roberts to Margarett Dotson, 25 June 1863 (no return) 1-#799

William Roberts to Thursday Kelley, 11 Oct 1899 (same), W.L. Lillard JP & W 3-51

\- - - - - - - - - - - - -

ROBINSON / ROBERTSON / ROBERSON / ROBESON / ROBISON / ROBESON

1860 CENSUS

Daniel Roberson 35, Susan M. 36, Sarah E. 10, John 7, Eliza T. 4, Mary A. 1 1-94-642

Francis Robertson 61 (Va), Turner G. 15 (NC) 3-68-466

Harvey Roberson 50 (Va)(Miller), Mahaly 49, Thomas H. 16, Nancy A. 13 4-47-320

James Roberson 55, Elizabeth 50, Felix A. 27, Mary J. 23, James O. 19, Catharine E. 16, Thomas J. 12, David T. 9, Harvey M. 7 1-89-606

John Roberson 61, Hannah 51, Benjamin F. 27, Elbert P. 24, Brunetta A. 22, Eliza R. 20, Samuel 18, John M. 16, Rufus 10, William COLLINS 35 (Dentist) 1-88-603

Malinda Roberson 27, Tennessee E. 18, Malinda E. 16, James CARROLL 13 3-62-425

Samuel Robinson 49, Mary 45, Mary E. 16, John W. 14, Thomas F. 12, Charles R. 9, James L. 3 1-85-576

Sarah A. Roberson 37 (NC), William A. 30, Margaret 22 2-78-530

1870 CENSUS

Henry Robinson 55 (Va), Mahala 56, Thomas H. 27 2-5-26

Hiram Robeson 41 (NC), Sarah 37 (Ky), Daniel R. 17 2-12-88

James Robinson 65, Elizabeth 60, Catharine 24, Thomas J. 23, David F. 21, Henry M. 19, Charles VAUGHN 13, James 11, Ernest 7, Mabel 4 (Ga) 1-5-30

John Robinson 71, Hannah 61, Eliza R. 30, Samuel P.C. 28, Rufus M.C. 19 1-5-29

Mary Robinson 56, Thomas F. 22, Charles H. 18, James L. 12 6-13-92

Noah Robinson 20, Margaret 25, John F. 2, James 7/12 2-15-106

Robert Robinson 33, Louisa 32, Amanda 7 1-18-116 (B)

Susan Robinson 37, John 18, Eliza 13, Mary 11, James 8, Jesse 6 3-13-95

1880 CENSUS

B.F. Roberson 48, E.G. 43 (w), J.C. 7 (s), Maggie 5, J.H. 2 (s), Rosa AIKEN 21 (Hired Girl) 4-1-2

C.R. Robinson 29 (Merchant), Eler A. 23, Eula M. 2 5-6-53

Dilsie Robinson 35, Henry 19, Lee 17, Walter 6, Frederic 3, Lewis 1/12 1-8-66 (B)

James Robinson 75, Elizabeth 70, Catharine 38, David 29, Earnest VAUGHN 17 (gs), Mabel 13 (gd), Idella 10 (gd) 1-8-65

John Robinson 82, Samuel 39 (s), Brunette 39 (s), Rufus 29 (s), Addie 26 (dl), Earnest 1/12 (gs), Nelson PERKINS (B) 26 (Servant), William RIVER (B) 14 (Servant) 1-11-93

John Robertson 28, Susan 46 (m), Mary 21 (si), James 18 (b), Jesse 15 (b) 7-22-186

Louis Robinson 55: see Casy Dysen

Mary Robinson 66, Thomas F. 32, James S. 22 6-14-129/130

Robert Robinson 48 (Barber), Louisa 47, Mira GILESPIE 17 (boarder), Sarah GOOSEBY 15 (boarder), Amanda WASSON 16 (adopted), Stephen WASSON 26 (boarder), Lucy PHILLIPS 6 (ne), Anna GILESPIE 1 2-21-173 (B)(Mu)

Thomas Robinson 38, Sarah 36, Harvey 65 (f), Mahala 67 (m), Kate HENEGAR 16 (boarder), Lulu 9 (boarder) 2-24-196

1900 CENSUS

Bre---(?) Robbinson 63 (Aug 1836-D)(Farm Boss) 1-186B-147/155

Charles Robertson 48 (Sep 1851-M 24), Ella A. 43 (Sep 1856-M 24-7-6), Earl 18 (June 1881), Grover 15 (Sep 1884), Callie 12 (Ap 1888), Hester 8 (July 1891), Thomas 6 (Sep 1893), Samuel 4 (Ap 1896) 15-273A-93

Charles F. Roberson 29 (Oct 1870-M 7), Elizabeth 30 (Jan 1870-M 7-3-3), William F. 5 (Nov 1894), Giles W. 4 (Nov 1895), Mary F. 1 (July 1898), Mary L. 50 (a) (Mar 1850-S), Frank LANDFORD 19 (Nov 1880-T/Germany/T-S)(Servant) 2-193B-48/50

Danil Robinson 44 (Jan 1856-Wd), Celler 8 (Feb 1892), James 6 (Jan 1894), Mable VAUGHN 31 (ne) (Oct 1868) 1-187A-156/164

Dartin Robbinson 61: see David Billingsly

Edd Robertson 4: see Mary Lightfoot (B)

Elizabeth G. Robinson 62 (June 1837-Wd 4-4), John C.(?) 27 (Nov 1872), Maggie 25 (Dec 1874), Horace J. 23 (Ap 1877), Samuel P. 19 (Dec 1880) 14-222B-174/178

James Robertson 48 (Jan 1852-M 15), Mary E. 38 (May 1862-M 15-7-6), Callie 13 (Sep 1886), Urittie 11 (d) (Sep 1888), Lillie 9 (Sep 1890), Charley 7 (Ap 1893), Maggie 5 (July 1894), Pealer(?) H. 7/12 (Oct 1899) 7-263A-252/257

James M. Roberson 33 (Feb 1867-M 4)(Dry Goods Salesman), Annie 26 (Ap 1874-M 4-1-1), Lorea 3 (Ap 1897) 8-314A-71/74

Jerry Robertson 64 (Ap 1836-M 36)(Coke Puller), Mary 64 (May 1836-T/T/Va-M 36-11-7), Lawrence 20 (Feb 1880), Aalic 17 (Sep 1882), Cordelia 15 (Oct 1884) 10-256B-129/133 (B)

Mahala Robinson 88: see T. H. Robinson

Margaret Robinson 15: see Dallas Baker (B)

Mattie Robinson 44: see W. F. Brown

Peter Robinson 25: see William Randolph (B)

Peter Robertson 50 (Oct 1849-T/Unk/Va-M 19)(RR Laborer), Jennie 37 (Feb 1863-M 19-0-0) 10-260A-202/207 (B)

Robert Robinson 61 (Aug 1838-T/Va/T-M 40)(Barber), Lusizie 65 (Feb 1835-M 40-0) 2-198A-126/131 (B)

Rufus M. Robinson 49 (Mar 1851-M 19), Florence 42 (July 1857-Va/T/Va-M 9-4-4), Loy H. 17 (Sep 1882), Hannah 16 (Ap 1884), Hoyal 8 (Jan 1892), Ruth 2 (Aug 1897) 14-216B-83/84

Samuel P.C. Robinson 59 (Mar 1841-M 22), Addie R. 44 (July 1855-T/NC/T-M 22-8-8), Earnest O. 20 (Ap 1880), Eva M. 18 (May 1882), Annie P. 15 (Oct 1884), Gladdis 13 (Sep 1886), Mary E. 10 (Oct 1889), Sammie 8 (Mar 1892), Paul 5 (Aug 1894), Lester O. 3 (Nov 1896) 14-213B-16/16

Samuel T. Roberson 39 (Feb 1861-M 16)(School Teacher), Sarah 37 (Mar 1863-T/NC/T-M 16-3-3), Ira 16 (Mar 1884), James B. 14 (July 1885), Pearly E. 8 (July 1891), William BELL 27 (boarder)(Dec 1872-NC/Australia/NC)(Baker) 10-326B-133/139

Thomas Robinson 52: see James A. Houston

Thomas H. Robinson 58 (May 1842-T/Va/T-M 30), Sarah A. 55 (Aug 1844-M 30-0-0), Mahalah 88 (m)(May 1812-T/Va/Va-Wd 3-2), Margaret J. BRYSON 75 (ml)(Sep 1824-Wd 12-3) 4-225B-234/238 (Ridge Road east of Spring City & Dayton Road)

William Robeson 33 (Feb 1867-M 7)(Dry Goods Salesman), Florence E. 25 (Nov 1874-Kan/T/T-M 7-0-0) 10-321A-19/20

MARRIAGES

Amanda Robinson to Stephen Wasson q.v.

B.F. Robinson to E.G. Roddy, 20 Nov 1871 (21 Nov), Zachariah Rose MG 1-#1217

Brunette Roberson to William M. Stubbs q.v.

Charley Roberson to Iza Munroe [marked through], 14 Sep 1890, S. Washington MG 4-49

Charles Robinson to Lizzie Ryan, 24 Dec 1893, J.M. Hinds MG 4-79

Charles R. Roberson to E.A. Colville, 24 Feb 1876 (same), A.P. Early MG 1-#1436

D.F. Robinson to Thodosia Foust, 24 Sep 1889 (25 Sep), J.L. Prater ?? 1-580

Emmit Robertson to Lou Ella Mack, 20 Jan 1900 (same), R.C. Knight JP, Wm Kelly W 3-112

G.V. Robinson to Aggie Kebler, 30 Sep 1890, A.W. Frazier JP 4-17

Henry Robinson to Annie Heiskell, 14 Jan 1892, A.W. Frazier JP 4-35 (B)

James Robertson to Malinda Kenedy, 26 Mar 1852 (29 Mar), D. Broyles JP 1-#369

James Robison to Florena Jackson, 30 Oct 1888 (same), Joseph Hoge JP 1-561

Jane Robisson to Henry Patrick q.v.

John B. Robinson to Mary Ann Dotson, 22 Oct 1873 (23 Oct), H.B. Haskiel JP 1-#1306

K. E. Robinson to S. C. Latimore q.v.

Lucy Robison to Milo E. Cooper q.v.

M. A. Robinson to A. J. Vaughn q.v.

Malinda Roberson to John Miller q.v.

Malinda Roberson to A. H. Dyre q.v.

Mary Jane Robinson to Benjamin Knox q.v.

Mary M. Robinson to Joseph Young q.v.

Matilda J. Robinson to William H. Green q.v.

Molly E. Robinson to John M. Caldwell q.v.

R.M. Robinson (30) to Florence Heiskell (24, Sweetwater, Tenn), 16 Nov 1881, Thompson Ashburn MG, T.T. McWhorter & Will Montgomery (of Rockwood) W 4-4(33)

Richard L. Robertson to Clara A. Marler, 11 Dec 1898 (15 Dec), W.R. Grimsley MG, R.J. Kellough W 2-386

S. L. Robeson to I. T. Randolph q.v.

Sarah E. Roberson to James Benton q.v.

Sary E. Robertson to Alexander Morrison q.v.

T.G. Robertson to Nancy Jane Powers, 9 Dec 1867 (same), J.B. McAllen MG 1-#984

T.J. Robenson to M.E. Heiskell, 23 Oct 1871 (same), G.W. Renfro MG 1-#1212

Thomas J. Roberson to Mrs. Addie Kelly [nee Locke], 26 Dec 1888

Thomas H. Robinson to Sarah A. Burnett, 15 Aug 1870 (16 Aug), G.W. Renfro MG 1-#1160

Will Robeson to Florence E. Morrison, 1 June 1893, G.W. Brewer MG 4-58

- - - - - - - - - - - - -

ROCKHOLT

1900 CENSUS

Frank M. Rockholt 59 (Jan 1841-M 32), Susan A. 62 (Ap 1838-M 32-6-6), Alice 21 (Oct 1879), James 20 (Feb 1880), Tennessee BYRD 25 (d)(Dec 1874-M 0-0), George BYRD 20 (sl)(Nov 1879-M 0) 6-244A-86

William Rockholt 28 (Mar 1872-M 3), Alice 24 (Feb 1876-M 3-2-2), Malvin 2 (Dec 1897), Mettie 7/12 (Oct 1899) 6-243B-75

MARRIAGES

Tennie Rockholt to G. D. Byrd q.v.

Will Rockholt to Alice Howard or Harwood, 13 Jan 1897 (14 Jan), W.R. Henry JP, R.T. King W 2-104

- - - - - - - - - - - - -

RODDY / RODDYE / RIDDY

1860 CENSUS

David M. Roddy 50, Betsy 37, Wright 15, Mary J. 13, David M. 11, Cathrin C. 9, Bryant 5, Mark L. 3, Ann R. 1/12 1-95-650

Harvey Roddy 43, Richard C. 20, John T. 18, Rachel J. 16, Edmond 14, Peter G. 12, Harriet A. 10, James R. 7, Ellen M. 5, Betsy RODDY 40 7-7-46

Jesse P. Roddy 36, Emily 34, James M. 17, William P. 6, Robert C. 4, James P. BELL 14 1-92-631

Susan Roddy 41, James 22, Liddia A. 19, Thomas 17, John 15, Jane 13, Margaret 10, Jesse RODDY 85 1-93-634

William G. Roddy 35, Amanda 23, John 6, Nancy 3, Margaret RODDY 56, Elizabeth 23, George 21, Rector PRESTON 58 1-93-633

1870 CENSUS

David M. Roddy 60, Elizabeth B. 48, Wright S. 25, David M. Jr. 21, Catharine C. 19, Briant M. 15, Mark 13, Ann 10, Bell 7 1-13-88

Elizabeth Roddy 50 (Va), Samuel 15, Mahala 14, Mark 8 1-15-94 (B)

Grace Roddy 65 (Va): see Malinda Gillespie (B)

Harvey Roddy 52, Jane 44, Richard C. 27, John T. 25, Peter G. 21, Harriette A. 19, James R. 17, Ellen 14, Sarah E. 3, Elizabeth PETERSON 45 6-6-38

Henry Roddy 31, Carilla 25 (Va), Thomas 1 1-15-95 (B)

James L. Roddy 33, Margarette E. 26, Frank 3, Mary 1 1-15-96

Susan Roddy 48, Thomas 27, John 23, Jane 22, Emma 20, Margaritte 10, Anna 8/12 1-15-97

William G. Roddy 45, Amanda 33, John F. 16, Nancy A. 13, Sarah E. 10, Jesse 6, Susan 1, Margarette RODDY 65, Elizabeth 28, George P. 30, Rector PRESTON 67, Susan CAWOOD 34 1-14-92

1880 CENSUS

David Roddy 70, Betsy 57, Catharine 27, Mark 22, Belle 17 1-13-110

George Roddy 40, Sarah 35, Charles 5, James 3, Carrie 2/12, Mary SHORT 18 (sd), Margaret 16 (sd), Jacob(?) McCALEB (B) 9 (Servant) 1-15-122

Gracie Roddy 70, Ann GILLESPIE 8 (gd), Mark RODDY 18 (Servant) 1-14-119 (B)

Harvey Roddy 63, Jane 50, Richard C. 40, Sarah E. 13 6-16-145/147

Henry Roddy 40, Corilla 27 (w), Thomas 13, Mary 9, Isham 6, Henry 2, William 1/12 12-7-56 (B)

James D. Roddye 26, Samuel D. 4, Martha E. 2 6-17-159/163

Jessee Roddy 56, Emily 54, William 26, Robert 24, Margaret 19, Amanda 17, Charlotte 15, Walter 12, David MARNEY (B) 11 (Servant), William WOODS (Mu) 15 (Servant) 1-13-112

John L. Roddye 37 (Shoemaker), Martha E. 27, William C. 5, Mary K. 3, Robert S. 8/12, C.L. COLVILLE 20 6-21-185/189

Mary Roddy 18 (Mu): see Gracie Roddy (B)

Nettie Roddy 31, Jesse 4, Mary 2, Burton 5/12, George DAY (Mu) 9 (Servant), Minnie ESKRIDGE (B) 11 (Servant) 1-15-124

Peter G. Roddy 31 (Minister), Mary Frances 20 6-17-158/162

Samuel Roddy 25 (B): see William Roddy

Susan Roddy 62, John 26 (s), Austin GILLESPIE (B) 21 1-14-118

William Roddy 55, John 26, Sarah 19, Jessee 16, Susan 11, William 8, Samuel RODDY (B) 25 (Servant), Robert JOHNSON (B) 16 (Servant) 1-14-113

1900 CENSUS

Bryant B. Roddy 45 (Mar 1855), Cathran 49 (si)(May 1851), Marke 42 (b)(June 1857), Elizabeth RODDY 77 (m)(June 1822-Wd 9-6) 1-184B-115/121

Elizabeth Roddy 38 (Ap 1852-Wd 6-6), Bert 22 (ss)(July 1877), Nora 16 (d)(Ap 1884), Richard 13 (s)(Aug 1886), Ida 10 (Ap 1890), Nellie 8 (Jan 1892), James 5 (June 1894), Mary 1 (June 1898) 6-248B-168/169

Henry T. Roddy 28 (July 1871-M 3), Amanda 27 (June 1873-M 3-2-2), Url T. 1 (July 1898), Emma E. 2/12 (Mar 1900) 3-207A-129/140

James Roddy 62 (Aug 1837-M 30)(RR Hand), Margett 59 (Nov 1840-M 30-6-4), Frank 21 (Nov 1867), Salli 28 (May 1872), Wilum 23 (July 1876), Claud 13 (May 1886) 1-184A-105/110

John Roddy 55 (Feb 1845-M 2), Sarah 45 (Jan 1855-M 2-0), May 12 (ne)(Feb 1881) 1-184A-102/106

John T. Roddy 57 (Sep 1842-M 27), Martha 47 (Feb 1853-M 27-10-8), Robert 20 (Oct 1879), James F. 18 (Oct 1881), Anna J. 17 (Jan 1883), Cary E. 13 (Oct 1886), Sallie 11 (July 1888), Mattie 3 (Aug 1896) 6-245B-110/111

Lula M. Roddy 10, Lillie 8, James 7: see Saml Bacon (B)

Maggie Roddy 40 (June 1859-Wd 5-3)(Boarding House Keeper), Julia 19 (June 1890), Jefferson 17 (Sep 1882)(Furnace Laborer), Frederick 9 (Dec 1890); _Boarders:_ Clem WILSON 32 (Dec 1867-Ga/Ga/Ga-M ?)(Day Laborer), Foster STENSON 24 (Ap 1876-Ga/Ga/Ga)(Furnaceman), William CARTER 23 (Sep 1876-D)(Furnaceman), Henry PEARSON 28 (Unk-Ga/Ga/Ga)(Day Laborer), Emily WILSON 14 (Sep 1885-Ga/Ga/Ga)(Hotel Cook) 10-322B-56/59

Peter Roddy 52 (Nov 1847-M 21), Mary F. 40 (June 1859-M 21-8-8), Frank 20 (Jan 1880), Elizabeth 17 (Dec 1882), Harvey 15 (Dec 1884), Albert 12 (June 1887), Rosa 10 (May 1890), Solomon 6 (Oct 1893), Lonnie 4 (Feb 1896), John 2 (Oct 1897) 6-249A-172/173

Thomas Roddy 25 (May 1875), Jaspher 22 (b)(Mar 1878), Maud 20 (si)(Ap 1880), Lizzie 18 (si)(Jan 1882), Emma RODDY 55 (m)(Jan 1845-Wd 5-5) 1-188A-182/191

Wilum Roddy 75 (Feb 1825-M 18), Manda 40 (Sep 1859-M 18-3-3), Rectar 15 (s)(Mar 1884), James 12 (s)(Feb 1882), Anie 7 (d)(Oct 1890), Wilum 28 (nw)(Aug 1871) 1-184A-99/103

MARRIAGES

Ann Roddy to Samuel Parker q.v.

Annie P. Roddy to J. H. Thomas q.v.

C. J. Roddy to S. L. Rose q.v.

E. G. Roddy to D. F. Robinson q.v.

E. J. Roddy to John H. Travis q.v.

Edward Roddy to Jane Spence, 8 Oct 1851 (same), John Wyott JP 1-#352

Elizabeth Roddy to Calvin Wright q.v.

Ellen M. Roddy to Samuel Travis q.v.

Georg J. Roddy to Sarah Ann Cash, 2 May 1867 (same), G.W. Renfro MG 1-#951

George P. Roddy to Sarah J. Short, 4 Oct 1873 (5 Oct), A.L. King MG 1-#1304

H.T. Roddy to Amanda A. Ewing, 20 Sep 1897 (22 Sep), William White MG 2-180

Harvy Roddy to Jane Birely, 14 June 1860 (same), John Howard MG 1-#714

J.D. Roddy to Sarah Peterson, 17 July 1880 (18 July), J.R. Crawford JP 1-295

J.D. Roddy to Lizzie Martin, 7 Feb 1883 (8 Feb), John Howard MG 1-479

James Roddy to Nelly Johnson, 18 Nov 1873 (19 Nov), A.L. King MG 1-#1310

James D. Roddy to Anna Graves, 19 Sep 1875 (20 Sep), John Howard MG 1-#1412

James L. Roddy to M.E. Whittenburg, 21 Aug 1865 (23 Aug), R.T. Howard MG 1-#868

John P. Roddy to Sallie L. White, 22 Mar 1889 (24 Mar), W.R. Clack JP 1-571

Lizzie Roddy to James Cox q.v.

Lydda Ann Roddy to J. W. Thompson q.v.

Mamie Roddy to J. M. Byerley q.v.

Mark Roddy to Maggie McCarter, 23 Dec 1880 (same), Jas Johnson JP 1-292 (B)

Mary J. Roddy to William F. P. Brown q.v.

Mary L. Roddy to Ward Haley q.v.

Mattie Roddy to Frank Bishop q.v.

Peter G. Roddy to Mary Henry, 1 Jan 1879 (same), John Howard MG 1-#1598

R.S. Roddy to Susie Roddy, 9 July 1890, J. Johnson JP 4-17

S. J. Roddy to A. J. Cawood q.v.

Samuel Roddy (28) to Minerva Gillespie (16), 22 Mar 1883, J.P. Roddy MG, Isaac Brown & Eliza Lee W 4-13(128) (B)

Sarah Roddy to John M. Colston q.v.

Susie Roddy to R. C. Roddy q.v.

Thomas Riddy [i is clear] to Emma McFerson, 3 Feb 1869 (4 Feb), M.L. Clendenin MG 1-#100

Thomas H. Roddy to Sydnia C.(?) McDonald, 13 Dec 1876 (same), J.H. Keith MG 1-#1476

W.G. Roddy to Amanda Whittenburg, 27 Nov 1883 (same), James Johnson JP 1-465

William Roddy to Tennie Byerley, 19 Aug 1899 (20 Aug), E.H. Lowrey ??, S.B. Roddy W 3-21

- - - - - - - - - - - - -

ROGERS / RODGERS

1860 CENSUS

Franklin Rogers 21: see James F. Ladd

Henry T. Rogers 25 (Va), Mary E. 25, James A. 8/12 2-80-546

John C. Rodgers 23, Alex 23, Leminamas L.(?) 3, Stephen 1 8-17-114

1870 CENSUS

Delilah Rogers 83 (Va): see John O. Johnson

Henry C. Rogers 35, Ann 34, Lillie 1 4-15-101

Henry L. Rogers 35, Mary E. 35, James A. 10, Letha E. 9, William H. 7, Nathaniel M. 5, Sarah E. 3, Martha J. 1 2-2-9

James Rogers 57 (Ga), Mary 31, Fanny 9, James 6, Caroline 4, Easter BYRELY* 58, Rebecca 22 10-4-29
[* ROGERS on 1880 census]

Susan Rogers 42, Patience E. 23, David A. 19, James W. 16, John P. 14, Rebecca G. 11, Margarette E. 2 8-9-59

Thomas Rogers 25 (B): see Jane M. Gannaway

1880 CENSUS

Easter Rogers 68, Rebecca 32: see James Rogers

H.C. Rogers 46 (Physician), Ann S. 46, L.J. 11 (d), J.C. 9 (s), J.H. 7 (s), W.A. 5 (s), Nora 3 (d) 8-14-117

J.H. Rogers 55 (Dry Goods Merchant), M.W. 51 (w), Flora 28, F.R. 21 (s), Sara 19, Emma 9, Ella 6, J.C. LOCK 28, James BELL 25, H.M.(?) NATHAN(?) 35 (Telegraph Operator), Ronnie VALENTINE (B) 35, Mary GILLESPIE (B) 55 (Servant), Ann GILLESPIE (B) 14 8-14-123

James Rogers 68, Mary J. 41 (w), Fanny 20, James M. 16, Caroline 13, William 8, Thomas 5, Mary R. 1, Easter ROGERS 68 (m), Rebecca 22 (si) 10-26-198/203

Jane Rogers 40 (Servant)(B): see J. A. Early

Joel Rogers 44 (Carpenter), S.S. 20 (w), J.C. 1 (s) 8-4-29

L.C. Rogers 28, M. 31, J. 7 (d), A.A. 4 (d), J.O. 3 (s), P.L. 1 (s) 11-40-325

S.I. Rogers 30 (m), W.R. 6 (s), K.E. 3 (d), Mary BEAN 58 (m) 8-9-77

S.R. Rogers 50 (m), M.S. 30 (d), J.W. 25 (s), R.B. 22 (d), Magie 11 (?), R.W. WALKER 28 (Printer) 8-6-52

1900 CENSUS

Emily Rogers 53 (Aug 1846)(Seamstress), Rebecca 41 (si) (Jan 1857)(Seamstress) 13-303A-247/257

Frederick R. Rogers 42 (Sep 1857-M 13)(Bank Cashier), Mary 39 (Aug 1860-M 13-4-3), Lyd 10 (Aug 1889), Margaret 8 (Sep 1891), Frederick R. 5 (May 1893) 8-316A-119/123

James H. Rogers 29 (Dec 1878-M 3)(RR Agent), Emma B. 30 (May 1870-T/T/Va-M 3-2-2), Lucile 1 (Nov 1898), Wendell 6/12 (Dec 1899) 14-218A-111/113

James M. [A. in marriage record] Rogers 46 (Sep 1853-M 15)(Carpenter), Mary D. 47 (Mar 1853-T/NC/T-M 16-2-1), Beulah BRUNLOW 10 (adopted d)(Nov 1889-Ala/Unk) 13-303A-246/256

James O.(?) Rogers Unk (Unk-M 5)(Coal Miner), Callie 20 (Jan 1880-M 5) 11-293B-88/89

John P. Rogers 44 (Mar 1856-M 24), Mary J. 43 (May 1857-M 24-10-9), James M. 21 (Jan 1879), George W. 19 (Nov 1880), Suder 17 (Mar 1883), Myrtie 15 (Ap 1885), Walter H. 11 (Mar 1889), Edward 8 (Mar 1892), Fred 8 (Mar 1892), William 4 (June 1895) 13-303A-249/259

Lewis G. Rogers 48 (June 1851-M 29)(Coal Miner), Margaret G. 53 (Oct 1846-M 29-7-6), Mary E. 18 (Sep 1881), Henry L. 16 (May 1884)(Coal Miner), Maggie L. 10 (July 1889) 11-293A-83

Mary J. Rogers 61 (Ap 1839-Wd 8-5), James 37 (Nov 1862) (Coal Miner), William 26 (June 1873)(Coal Miner), Thomas 24 (May 1876)(Coal Miner), Mary 20 (Oct 1879), Elizabeth 17 (Oct 1882), Rebecca HORNEY 49 (si)(Dec 1850-Wd 4-0), Thomas 26 (nw)(Unk 1874) (Coal Miner), Lee 22 (Unk 1878)(Coal Miner) 8-283A-292/294

Minnie Rogers 20: see Francis W. Bacon

Robert Rogers 21 (Feb 1879-M 1)(Coal Miner), Julia E. 19 (Sep 1880-M 1-1-1), Ethel E. 4/12 (Jan 1900) 11-293B-91/92

Thomas L. Rodgers 57 (Jan 1843-M 34)(Drayman), Jolly S. 49 (Nov 1850-M 34-8-6), Hoxie A. 26 (May 1874), Minie L. 23 (July 1876), Fred O. 17 (July 1882), Anny M. 16 (Mar 1884) 10-254B-85

Trudie Rogers 17: see Charles W. Irwin

William Rogers 25, Mamie 21: see George Brandon

William Rogers 28 (June 1871-M 4)(Coal Miner), Emma 22 (July 1877-M 4-0), Martha DENTON 46 (ml)(Unk 1856-Wd 1-1) 8-283B-302/304

William A. Rogers 42 (June 1857-NY/England/Do-M 20) (Farm Manager), Margaret E. 43 (Feb 1857-Pa/Pa/Pa-M 20-7-4), Amand 17 (Aug 1883-Va), William H. 14 (Nov 1885-Va), Mark W. 12 (Jan 1888-Oh), Edith 9 (Sep 1890) 8-276B-155/156

William E. Rodgers 31 (Oct 1868-WVa/Va/Va-M 2)(School Teacher), Cora 24 (Oct 1875-Oh/Oh/Oh-M 2-2-1), William F. 1 (June 1898) 5-234A-124

William H. Rogers 40 (Feb 1860-M 12)(General Merchant), May 30 (Unk-M 12-2-2), Leland W. 10 (Ap 1890), Madge 5 (Oct 1894), Mary A. HUTCHINSON 64 (m) (Unk T/NC/NC-Wd 1-1), William DIXON 17 (boarder)(Nov 1882)(Night Watchman) 8-318B-167/173 [Wm H. married May Neil, 26 Feb 1889, Meigs Co]

William R. Rogers 26 (Oct 1873), Kittie E. 23 (si)(Dec 1876) 13-307A-327/339

MARRIAGES

Alice Rodgers to J. E. Calhoun q.v.

Elizabeth Rogers to John Edmonds q.v.

Flora Rogers to A. C. Broyles q.v.

Gad Rogers to Allis Wampler, 4 Oct 1877 (no return) 1-#1514

H.E. Rogers to Malissa Smith, 24 Sep 1872 (25 Sep), D. Broyles JP 1-#1255

H.T. Rogers to Mary E. Holloway, 19 Nov 1859 (23 Nov), A.D. Paul JP 1-#672

Henry C. Rodgers to Ann Darwin, 27 Oct 1867 (same), A.P. Early MG 1-#979

J.H. Rogers to Emma Broyles, 17 Nov 1897 (18 Nov), J.A. Whitner MG & W 2-223

James Rodgers to Ellen Wester, 24 July 1878 (25 July), J. Johnson JP 1-290

James Rodgers to Ella McReynolds, 8 Ap 1890 (same), F.M. Bundy MG 1-597

James A. Rogers (28, Marion Co) to Mary Corvin, nee D. Johnson (28, Bledsoe Co), 22 Dec 1881, W.A. Green JP, T.T. Corvin & J.O. Johnson W 4-5(48)

Jennie Rogers to Allen Holland q.v.

Jennie Rogers to D. R. Oldham q.v.

Joe Rodgers to G.H. Gillespie, 12 Jan 1900, R.A. Dickson JP 4-102

Joel Rogers to Lizzie May, 17 July 1886 (same), Calvin Morgan JP 1-501

John C. Rogers to Mary A. Hoge, 15 Aug 1874 (16 Aug), R. T. Howard MG 1-#1350

Kittie Rogers to A. J. Hughes q.v.

Lizzie Rogers to William Beans(?) q.v.

Lou D. Rogers to John Abel q.v.

Martha or Mattie Rogers to Frank Barton q.v.

Mary Rodgers to A. Kaylor q.v.

Mary A. Rodgers to S. W. Hutcherson q.v.

Minerva Rogers to W. H. Callahan q.v.

Nora Rogers to A. S. Collins q.v.

O. A. Rodgers to Edmond Sandys q.v.

Oscar Rodgers to Celia Campbell, 28 Mar 1896 (29 Mar), H. Morgan JP, D.R. Oldham W 2-9

Pink Rodgers to Flora Clifton, 19 Oct 1895, W.T. West MG 4-84

Robert L. Rodgers to Julia E. Morgan, 9 Jan 1899 (17 Jan), H. Morgan JP 2-372

Sarah Rodgers to Joseph Clark q.v.

Sarah E. Rodgers to M. G. Brenenan q.v.

Sarah J. Rodgers to M. L. Gambel q.v.

Susan Rogers to Gee Waller q.v.

Virginia E. Rodgers to L. A. Brown q.v.

W.A. Rodgers to Mamie Brandon, 21 Dec 1899 (21 Dec), J.A. Whitner MG 3-90

William Rodgers to Emma Coleman, 10 Sep 1896 (same), W.L. Lillard JP, W.M. Rogers W 2-65

ROLAND / ROLAN / ROWLON

1870 CENSUS

Carter Rolan 21 (Ga), Elizabeth 23, Willis J. 1, Mary J. 1 3-6-41

MARRIAGES

Carter P. Roland to Elizabeth Cofer, 17 June 1868 (same), W.M. Buttram MG 1-#1015

M. C. Rowlon to Thomas Dickson q.v.

ROMEO

MARRIAGE

Nancy Romeo or Remeo to James Collins q.v.

ROMINES / ROMANS

1870 CENSUS

Martha Romines 25, James 5: see Michael Byrely

1880 CENSUS

M.R. Romines 30, J.Z. 15 (s), Michel BARLY [BYRELY] 83 (f) 7-22-19

1900 CENSUS

Flossie Romines 20: see Ed R. Morgan

George W. Romines 39 (Mar 1861-M 18), Mary 34 (Nov 1865-M 18-9-6), Dora 16 (June 1884), Lafayette 14 (Aug 1885), Ruth 8 (Mar 1892), Martha 6 (Jan 1894), Ella M. 4 (May 1896), Sudie 10/12 (July 1899) 15-269B-37

James W. Romines 35 (Sep 1864-M 11), Susie R. 31 (Feb 1869-T/Va/T-M 11-5-3), Zach A. 10 (July 1889), Lester H. 8 (Aug 1891), McKinley E. 3 (Aug 1896) 7-267A-318/323

MARRIAGES

Allis Romines to Alfred Lawson q.v.

Christopher Romines to Lucinda Stoops, 24 May 1865 (same), Joseph L. Brown JP 1-#837

Henry Romines to Mary Phillips, 22 Jan 1887, James Corvin MG 4-45

J.W. Romines to S.R. Montgomery, 1 June 1888 (3 June), T.F. Shaver JP 1-550

Katie Romans to C. G. Thomas q.v.

Martha Romines to William Simmamons q.v.

Zachariah Romines to Martha Byerly, 22 Dec 1863 (same), John Howard MG 1-#813

ROPER / RAPER

1870 CENSUS

Sarah Roper 35 (NC), Nathaniel 17 (NC), Charles 14 (NC), Calzina 7 (NC), Alonzo 5 (NC), William RUSSELL 23 (Ga), Andrew RUSSELL 55 (NC) 1-5-32

MARRIAGES

Alonzo Raper (18, NC) to Esther Owens (15, Washington Co, Tenn), 7 Mar 1882, N. Whittenburg MG, Mary Owens & Amanda Whittenburg W 4-12(112)

Lucinda Roper or Rosser to J. A. Tieague q.v.

Nathaniel Raper to Adaline Russell, 24 May 1871 (no return) 1-#1196

ROSCOE

MARRIAGE

Amanda Roscoe to M. C. Martin q.v.

ROSE / ROSES

1860 CENSUS

Margaret Rose 52, Columbus T.A. 18, John W. 16, James M. 13, Mary E. 10, Sarah J. 4 4-53-360

1870 CENSUS

Adaline Rose 20, Alic 15 (B): see Zachariah Rose

Margarette Rose 55, John W. 23, James M. 22, Mary E. 19, Sarah J. 13 4-5-31

Zachariah Rose 13, Florence 11, Willie 6: see John Brown

Zachariah Rose 61 (NC), Sarah* 68, Adaline ROSE (B) 20, Alic (B) 15, Thomas L. McNABB 17, Julius M. 15, Zachariah L. 13, William B. 11, Jacob A. 9, James A. 7, Virgil ROSE 6 4-8-51 [* nee Cate Bunch]

1880 CENSUS

David C. Rose 24, Mary M. 20, Edmond L. 1 6-14-134/136

H.C. Rose 30 (Physician), M.E. 22, Charles 2 8-2-11

Joseph Rose 27, N.J. 22 (w), J.F. 7 (s), M.M. 4 (d), J.W. 1 (s) 8-20-172

M. Rose 70, John 31 (s), James 29, Mary 26, S. J. 21 (d) 4-34-277

Nathan W. Rose 35, Susan 29, Richard O.R. 9, Edna J. 8, James L. 7, Martha F. 4, James W. 2 5-10-90

W.F. Rose 44, N.J. 43, Belle 19, S.A. 16 (d), S.J. 14 (d), ?.A. 12 (s), A.F. 8 (d), C.H. 2 (s) 4-11-91

Zachariah Rose 23, Florence 18, Wm 15: see John Brown

1900 CENSUS

Anna Rose 10: see Will L. Patton

Anna Rose 12: see Allen F. Harrison

Arthur Rose 20: see Samuel Umbarger

Henry C. Rose 50 (May 1850-M 23)(Physician), Elizabeth 42 (May 1858-M 23-2-1), Christiana 16 (Dec 1883) 8-312B-42/45

James W. Rose 20 (Nov 1879-M 0)(Coal Miner), Callie 18 (Ap 1882-M 0-1-1), Nora 0 (May 1900) 13-305B-301/313

John A. Rose 45 (Aug 1854-M 15)(Coal Miner), Mary R. 45 (June 1854-M 15-1-1), Ella M. 13 (Aug 1886) 8-283A-286/288

John M.(?) Rose 51 (July 1848-T/T/NC-S), Susan J. 39 (si) (May 1861-S) 4-226B-253/257 (Rhea Springs & Washington Road)

Joseph Rose 62 (Unk 1838-M 27), Nancy J. 48 (Feb 1852-M 27-12-6), Joshua F. 26 (Nov 1873)(RR Brakeman), Herbert F. 11 (Jan 1889), Albert C. 9 (Dec 1890), Jennie V. 3 (Nov 1896), Eliza J. GRIFFIN 33 (Aug 1866-T/T/Ala-Wd 0)(Servant) 13-304B-276/286

Maggie A. Rose 42 (Sep 1857-Wd 8-8), William M. 23 (Ap 1877-Ga)(Station Engineer), Leonard R. 20 (June 1879-Ga), Bessie C. 19 (Mar 1881-Ga), Jessie C. 16 (Aug 1883-Ga), Lula B. 14 (Sep 1885-Ga), Joseph A. 11 (July 1888-Ga), Charles F. 9 (Nov 1890), Glenn A. 7 (Ap 1893) 10-321B-38/40

Nancy Rose 38 (Oct 1851-Wd 7-4), Martha 15 (Jan 1885-Ark), Thomas S. 10 (Mar 1888), Mary 6 (Ap 1884) 3-201A-21/22

Samuel Rose 44 (June 1856-M 17), Jane 35 (Feb 1865-M 17-6-6), Jessie 19 (Ap 1884)(RR Hand), Anie 14 (Ap 1886)(Quiltmaker), Samuel 10 (Oct 1899), Jefferson 7 (Sep 1892), James 4 (Nov 1895), Burda 2 (d)(Feb 1898) 1-184B-112/118

Solomon Rose or Rise 29 (Oct 1870-Ga/Va/Va-M 8), Fannie 26 (July 1873-Ala/Ala/Ala-M 3-1-1), Claudie 5 (Oct 1894) 8-318B-171/177 (B)

William Rose 53 (Unk 1847-T/SC/SC-M 33)(Coal Miner), Liza 43 (Dec 1856-T/T/SC-M 33-7-5), Emma 23 (July 1876), Lura 15 (Aug 1884), Walter 14 (Mar 1886), Dora 7 (Mar 1893), Etta 2 (Mar 1898) 8-278B-199/201

William Rose 19: see John B. Roach

MARRIAGES

B.F. Rose to B.C. Posey, 6 Oct 1897 (same), W.R. Grimsley MG, R.J. Killough W 2-200

Beatris L. Rose to Samuel Umbarger q.v.

Bell Roses(?) to Daniel Heiskell q.v.

Florence Rose to D. C. Kemmer q.v.

Foster Rose to Dinah Woods, 13 Dec 1890, Wm R. Russell MG 4-20 (B)

H.C. Rose to M.E. Broyles, 22 Nov 1876 (23 Nov), John W. Williamson MG 1-#1472

James W. Rose to Callie Queener, 14 July 1899 (16 July), J.P. Houston MG, Joseph Rose [signed by X] W 3-11

Jeremiah Rose to Sarah McCarroll, 30 Mar 1867 (no return) 1-#945

Justin Rose to Maggie Vaughn, 5 May 1887 (same), John Howard MG 1-523

Mary Rose to R. L. Myers or Majors q.v.

Mary Ann Rose to John Brown q.v.
Mary E. Rose to W. K. Fugate q.v.
Nancy Rose to John Mathis q.v.
S.L. Rose (26, Polk Co; Merchant) to C.J. Roddy (18), 20 May 1883, Z. Rose MG, J.T. Roddy & Virgil Rose (both of Roddy, T) W 4-14(134)
William Rose to Belle Haynes, 25 Mar 1898 (same), Wm A. Green JP, Charlie Dunnag(?) W 2-261

\- - - - - - - - - - - - -

ROSENBALMER / ROSENBAULM

1900 CENSUS
John Rosenbaulm 45 (Ap 1855-Va/Va/Va-M 27), Martha L. 43 (Feb 1857-Va/Va/Va-M 27-2-2), Sarah J. 26 (May 1874-Va-M ?) 4-226A-243/247
MARRIAGE
Susan F. Rosenbalmer to Robert Bell q.v.

\- - - - - - - - - - - - -

ROSS / ROOS / ROUSE / ROUS / REUISE

1870 CENSUS
William F. Rous 34 (Retail Merchant), Nancy J. 32, Isabela 8, Serena E. 6, Sarah E. 4, John A. 2, Amanda 4/12 2-6-35
1880 CENSUS
Jacob Roos 39 (Blacksmith), Evaline 30, Charlie 4, Robert 2, James 1, Elizabeth CLARK 22 (sil) 1-14-117
1900 CENSUS
Charles Ross 26 (Ap 1874-M 3), Mary 28 (Feb 1872-M 3-1-1), Loyd 1 (Oct 1898) 1-185A-120/126
James Reuise 22: se Martha Gamble
Joab Ross 59 (Jan 1841-Germany/Do/Do-1870/23/Na-M 25)(Blacksmith), Evaline 50 (Jan 1850-NC/NC/NC-M 25-6-6), Mathis 19 (May 1881), Lizzi 13 (Ap 1887), Hatty 1 (May 1889), Ellie [Elmeady] 9 (Oct 1891) 1-183B-98/102
MARRIAGES
Charley Ross to Mary Griever, 8 Dec 1897, W.T. West MG 4-99
J.M. Ross to Margaret Pieratt(?), 27 Feb 1895, F. Alexander MG 4-77
Jacob Ross to Ella [Evaline] Clark, 28 Oct 1875 (29 Oct), J. P. Roddy MG 1-#1417
Robert Rouse [Ross] to Letitia Crabtree, 20 Nov 1898, W.T. West MG 4-96

\- - - - - - - - - - - - -

ROTHGAB / ROTHGEB / ROTHJEB

1900 CENSUS
Lillie Rothjeb 7: see Henry M. Hensley
MARRIAGES
Ed Rothgob to N.C. Brooks, 4 Jan 1890 (5 Jan), W.S. Hale MG 1-590
Nancy Rothgeb to H. M. Hensley q.v.
W.W. Rothgab to P.C. Harris, 21 May 1890 (same), S.G. Hilliard MG 1-600

\- - - - - - - - - - - - -

ROTHWELL

MARRIAGE
W.Z. Rothwell to Girdie Moore, 27 May 1892, E.F. Garrison(?) JP 4-41

\- - - - - - - - - - - - -

ROUFF / ROFF

1900 CENSUS
Alexander Roff 22: see William C. Webb
MARRIAGE
Thomas Rouff to Ollie J. Clonce, 19 May 1891, J.R. Walker MG 4-29

\- - - - - - - - - - - - -

ROW / ROWE

1900 CENSUS
William L. Rowe 47 (June 1852-T/NC/Ala) 9-229A-24
MARRIAGES
Elizabeth Row to John Brannum q.v.
Sara L. Row to Hiram Evins q.v.

\- - - - - - - - - - - - -

ROWAN / ROWEN / ROWICE

1900 CENSUS
Amelia Rowan 17 (B): see James E. Abel
Valentine Rowen 67 (Unk 1833-M 20), Sallie 65 (Unk 1835-Ala/Ala/Ala-M 20-8-6); Fannie* 28 (Sep 1871-D 1), John 26 (Aug 1873), Melina 17 (July 1882), Delia 16 (Mar 1884), Carrie THOMAS 8 (gd)(Nov 1891), Frank VINEYARD 45 (boarder)(Unk 1855-Oh/Oh/Oh)(Coal Miner), Henry WRIGHT 21 (boarder)(Unk 1889-NC/NC/NC)(Coal Miner) 5-273B-100 (B) [* nee Fleming Thomas]
MARRIAGES
Dennis Rowan to Rosie Pickett, 26 Nov 1888 (27 Nov), E.F. Garvin(?) JP 1-556
Volentine Rowice (39, McMinnville, T) to Sallie Fleming (37, Jackson, Ala), ? Oct 1882 (recorded 5 Oct), R.H. Jewell JP, Mary J. & W.F. Fleming (of Dayton) W 4-11(102) (B)

\- - - - - - - - - - - - -

ROWDEN

1900 CENSUS
Thomas Rowden 86: see Thomas Painter
MARRIAGE
Benjamin Rowden to Eliza A. Geer, 26 Nov 1857 (same), W.H. Cunnyngham JP 1-#621

\- - - - - - - - - - - - -

RUCKER / RICKER

1880 CENSUS
James Rucker 11 (Mu): see Nathan Yearwood (B)
William Rucker 9 (B): see Rebecca Paul

1900 CENSUS

Ada Rucker 19: see Rachel Dooley (B)

James Ricker 37 (May 1863-M 1)(RR Hand), Sarah 25 (Ap 1875-M 1-0) 1-189B-210/222 (Spring City) (B)

Joseph Rucker 29: see William A. Hashbarger

MARRIAGES

Annie Rucker to Ned McElwee q.v.

Annie Rucker to John Magsby q.v.

Bell V. Rucker to James H. Kelly q.v.

Jonas Rucker to Mary Pankey, 14 Oct 1895, S.W. Burnett MG 4-92

Lizzie Rucker to Henry Tulliss(?) q.v.

Melia Rucker to Marion Dooley q.v.

Richard Rucker to Lula Bogle, 18 Feb 1886 (same), P. P. Brooks ?? 1-499

William Rucker to Mary Ellison, 14 July 1900 (bond only), J.B. Phillips W 3-188

- - - - - - - - - - - - -

RUDD / RUDE

1860 CENSUS

Elijah Rudd 38 (Tailor), Eliza 30, Alexander 18, Sarah 15, James 12, Mary 9, Adelaide 6, Mareteh(?) 3 6-110-753

1870 CENSUS

Elijah L. Rudd 50, Eliza G. 40 (Va), Sarah E. 24, James G. 21, Mary J. 18, Adda F. 16, Eliza M. 11, Julia T. 9, Elijah L. 6 6-16-114

1880 CENSUS

Burl Rudd 46: see Thomas Sneed

Elijah L. Rudd 60, Eliza G. 54, Sarah E. 35, Eligeh L. 17 6-21-189/192

Levi Rudd 53, C.M. 33 (w), M.C. 20 (d), C. 18 (d), John 16, James 14, Sam 12 3-18-145

Mary Rudd 49, Solomon H. 24, Charles T. 14: see Henry A. Pearman

T.(?) Rudd 25, E. 27, J.C. 3 (s), M.M. 2 (d), J.H. 2/12 (s) 4-12-98

W.M. Rudd 45, M.T. 30 (w), S.A. 13 (d), M.J. 11 (d), J.R. 9 (s), J.H. 7 (s), Marks 2 (s) 8-7-53

1900 CENSUS

Charles Rudd 34 (Jan 1866-M 12), Mary F. 30 (May 1870-T/Va/T-M 12-0-0) 6-241A-24

Elijah L. Rudd 79 (Nov 1820-M 59), Eliza G. 74 (July 1825-Va/Va/Mass-M 59-8-7), Sarah 55 (d)(Feb 1845) 5-233B-110

James Rudd 49 (July 1850-M 16), Rhoda A. 32 (June 1867-M 16-5-1), Ether L. 1 (Aug 1898), John GOINS 16 (bl)(Mar 1884), Charlie RUDD 19 (s)(Jan 1881) 8-312A-27/28

James G. Rudd 42 (Unk 1858-M 25), Mattie 49 (July 1850-Va/Va/Va-M 25-5-3), Ella 21 (May 1879), Freddie 15 (Dec 1884) 8-285B-344/346

Lorena Rudd 5: see Thomas Pelfrey

MARRIAGES

Ada Rudd to Anderson Parker q.v.

Blanche Rudd to Francis M. Marler q.v.

Charley B. Rudd to Maggie Smith, 1 Oct 1900 (same), W.L. Lillard JP, C.T. Rudd W 3-229

Charles T. Rudd to Mary Walker, 4 Feb 1888 (no return) 1-546

E.L. Rudd Jr. to Mattie Parker, 26 Feb 1891, John Howard MG 4-26

E. M. Rudd to Robert C. Purser q.v.

J.D. Rudd to Caroline Denton, 14 Aug 1895, T.M. Baily or Bandy MG 4-87

J.W. Rudd to Roda A. Goins, 28 July 1885 (same), John Howard MG 1-490

James G. Rudd to Martha French, 27 Feb 1872 (28 Feb), W.B. McKelvey MG 1-#1232

Julia Rudd to N. L. Henry q.v.

Mary Rudd to William I. Goines q.v.

Mary Rudd to Lee Price q.v.

Mary J. Rudd to Joel L. Henry q.v.

Rebecca M. Rudd to Thomas Sneed q.v.

S.D. Rudd (24; occupation, Tramp) to E.J. Sneed (35), 12 May 1881, J.H. Locke JP 4-3(24)

S.D. Rudd to Mary Nelson, 5 Sep 1890, H. Cox MG 4-15

S.D. Rudd to Sallie Brison, 1 Sep 1896 (same), A.P. Hayes JP, Daniel Rudd Jr. W 2-63

- - - - - - - - - - - - -

RUDDER

MARRIAGE

Cynthia E. Rudder to Henry Bagott q.v.

- - - - - - - - - - - - -

RUE / ROE

1900 CENSUS

John Rue 37 (May 1863-M 10), Elizabeth 62 (Oct 1837-Ga/T/T-M 10-9-6), James 16 (s)(Ap 1884), Charles 11 (s)(June 1888), Telly LARSON* 25 (sd)(Jan 1875-Ga/T/Ga-M 13-5-3), Isabel 10 (sgd)(Nov 1889-T/Sweden/Ga), Ellie 9 (sgd)(Ap 1891-T/Sweden/Ga), Edwin 3 (sgs)(Aug 1896-T/Sweden/Ga), Posey C. LOURY 40(?) (boarder)(Unk-NC/NC/NC-M 40), Ruhannie 57 (boarder)(Sep 1842-T/SC/T-M 40-13-2) 8-316B-134/139 [nee Ridley]

MARRIAGES

Beckey Roe to W. D. Posey q.v.

Caroline Roe to Jim Shipley q.v.

J.Y. Rue to Eliza Ridley, 5 May 1890 (same), W.R. Brisco MG 1-600

Mary Roe to W. C. Parker q.v.

Peter Rue to Jennie Hale, 4 May 1896 (6 May), H.B. Burdett MG, J.N. Vaughn W 2-21

Richard Rue to Emeline Hughes, 25 Jan 1854 (no return) 1-#437

- - - - - - - - - - - - -

RUL / RULS

MARRIAGES

Florence E. or D. Ruls or Reels to J. W. Pelfrey q.v.

Frances Rul to Robert Pelfrey q.v.

- - - - - - - - - - - - -

RUMFELT / RUMPHELT

MARRIAGES

Henry Rumphelt to Rhoda McDaniel, 1 Mar 1852 (same), M.C. Atchley MG 1-#367

Margarett Rumfelt to Noah Fisher q.v.

- - - - - - - - - - - - -

RUNYAN / RUNYON / RUNNIONS

1880 CENSUS

Isaac Runyon 45, R.M. 40, S.E. 18 (d), L.J. 16 (d), W.P. 14 (s), J.B. 12 (s), E.L. 10 (s), R.F. 8 (s), O.C. 3 (s), F.T. 2/12 (d) 4-6-44 [Isaac married Rivannah M. Blevins on 25 July 1860 in Meigs Co]

1900 CENSUS

Byron Runyan Unk (Unk)(Grocery Salesman) 14-218B-118/121

Charlotte Runyons 70: see Tom Thompson (B)

Isaac Runyon 65 (Dec 1834-M 38), Revanna 60 (Nov 1839-M 38-14-8), Elias T. 30 (Feb 1870-Wd)(School Teacher), Anna T. 20 (Mar 1880) 5-233A-100

Robert F. Runyan 31 (Nov 1868-Wd), Hellan R. 1 (d)(Oct 1898), Sarah E. 37 (si)(June 1862) 5-233A-103

William P. Runyan 33 (Aug 1866-M 10), Bettie 30 (Jan 1870-M 10-4-4), Willie W. 8 (Dec 1891), Cora M. 7 (May 1392), Robert W. 4 (Dec 1895), Benjamin F. 2 (Ap 1898) 4-227B-279/283 (Clear Creek Road)

MARRIAGES

A.T. Runyan to Lillie Dale, 19 Feb 1891 (at 5:30 PM), D.E. Broyles JP 4-18

Oscar Runyan to Lillie Travis, 28 Oct 1899 (29 Oct), D.E. Broyles JP, R.T. Runyan W 3-62

R.F. Runyan to Ida Houston, 5 Mar 1897 (7 Mar), W.A. Howard MG, J.B. Runyan W 2-122

Riner(?) Runnions to J. H. Houston q.v.

W.P. Runyan to Bettie Furguson, 5 Mar 1891, F.J. Paine JP 4-19

- - - - - - - - - - - - -

RUSH

1860 CENSUS

Catharine Rush 47, Rebecca 22, Joseph 20, Hugh 17, William 13, Hugh McCLAREN 67 (Scotland) 3-63-437

1870 CENSUS

Catharine Rush 59 (NC), Rebecca A. 33 3-14-104

1880 CENSUS– None

1900 CENSUS

John Rush 54 (Mar 1846-M 15), Alice 56 (June 1844-M 15-6-6), Virgil 13 (Oct 1886), George A. 8 (Jan 1892), Harry 7 (May 1893), Maud M. 2 (Oct 1897-Ala), Nettie PRESLEY 23 (d)(Jan 1877-M 3-1-0), Nathan 37 (sl)(Mar 1863-M 3) 15-274B-117

Rebecca A. Rush 54 (June 1845) 2-199A-152/157

MARRIAGE

L. L. Rush to W. J. Nash q.v.

- - - - - - - - - - - - -

RUSS

MARRIAGE

M. J. Russ to W. W. Buffington q.v.

- - - - - - - - - - - - -

RUSSEL / RUSSELL / RUSSELLS

1870 CENSUS

Andrew Russell 55 (NC), William 23 (Ga): see Sarah Roper

Elizabeth Russell 16: see John Henry

1880 CENSUS

F. Russell 60 (Millright), Sarah 52, J.F. 19 (s) 3-26-206

1900 CENSUS

Calonis(?) Russell 47 (Oct 1852-NC/NC/NC-M 25)(Sawmill), Laura A. 45 (Jan 1855-NC/NC/NC-M 25-6-5), George L. 20 (Jan 1880)(Sawmill Fireman), Melvin J. 17 (Feb 1883)(Sawmill Laborer), Luther A. 13 (Dec 1886)(Sawmill Laborer), Elbert F. 11 (Dec 1888), Lucy C. HENDERSON 25 (d)(Jan 1875-NC-Wd 4-1-1), Orville R. 2 (gs)(Aug 1897-Ga/Ga/NC) 14-217A-89/91

James Russell 27: see William Johnson (B)

James H. Russell 27: see William Branam

James W. Russell 52 (Dec 1847-Wd)(Miller), Nancy E. 15 (Oct 1884), Lenna 13 (Nov 1886), Thomas 10 (Dec 1889), Martain J. 8 (Ap 1892), Taylor 6 (Aug 1893), Samuel 4 (Sep 1895) 2-108B-134/139

Marcus Russell 21 (June 1878-M 2), Phebe 21 (Nov 1878-M 2-2-0) 13-296A-116/118

Mary E. Russell 29, Caroline 4: see John H. King

Nancy E. Russell 15, Thomas 11: see Granville H. Wade

Pery Rusel 55 (Ap 1845-Pa/NC/Ga-M 19), Sarah 39 (May 1861-M 19-6-4), James 16 (Ap 1884), Robbut 10 (Nov 1889), Ader 6 (Feb 1894), McKenly 4 (Ap 1896) 1-186A-144/152

William H. Russell 59 (Jan 1841-Ga/NC/Ga-M 24)(Lineman), Nancy E. 40 (Ap 1860-M 24-12-9), Cora M. 20 (Oct 1879), Julia A. 17 (June 1883), Robert 14 (July 1885), Mary E. 11 (Nov 1888), Alice E. 9 (Feb 1891), Hattie E. 7 (Mar 1893), William B. 3 (Sep 1896), Grace 11/12 (June 1899) 14-215A-36/37

William M. Russell 64 (May 1836-M 0)(Pensioner), Burnette M. 6 (June 1883-M 0-0) 13-296A-114/116

William M. Russell 41 (Unk 1859-Ga/T/T-M 16), Arrenia 35 (Unk 1865-Ga/Ga/NC-M 16-6-4), Maggie 12 (June 1888-Ga), Lola 7 (Mar 1892), Andy 5 (July 1895), Walter 4 (Oct 1896) 3-200A-8/8

MARRIAGES

Adaline Russel to Nathaniel Raper q.v.

Amanda Russell to J. J. Greene(?) q.v.

Cordelia Russell to R. M. Phillips q.v.

Eva Mae Russell to A. E. Lee q.v.

Holliday Russell to Lucy Snyder or Sydneys, 1 Dec 1897 (same), L.R. Nichols MG, H.P. Best W 2-217

J.B. Russell to Louisa Henson, 20 Jan 1888 (25 Jan), Calvin Morgan JP 1-549

J.P. Russell to Samantha Miller, 29 Oct 1884 (30 Oct), J.M. Bramlett MG 1-478

James W. Russell (34, Monroe Co) to Tennessee Wade (17), 21 Oct 1881, W.W. Lowe JP, J.E. Evans & S.V. Davis W 4-6(58)

John Russell to Nannie Johnson, 8 Sep 1891, L.L.H. Carlock MG 4-33
Mark Russell to Phoebia Cox, 22 Sep 1897 (23 Sep), W.A. Green JP, J.J. Green W 2-185 [bond only] & 2-186 [bond & license]
Mary J. Russell to John Shaker q.v.
Susan A. Russell to Charley L. Ceneter q.v.
Thomas L. Russell to L.C. Wade, 28 Dec 1877 (30 Dec), W.W. Low JP 1-#1539
W.M. Russell to Bernetha M. Hensley, 24 Feb 1900 (25 Feb), David Davis MG, W.A. Andrew W 3-125

- - - - - - - - - - - - -

RUTH

MARRIAGES
Frankie Ruth to B. F. Suttler or Suttles q.v.
J.W. Ruth (54, Franklin Co) to M.C. Jenkins (25, Dupline? Co, NC), 10 Jan 1883, I.W. Holt JP, Andy Smith & M.G. Gibson W 4-12(120)
Sarah Ruth to William Drue(?) q.v.

- - - - - - - - - - - - -

RUTHLEDGE

MARRIAGE
Ben Ruthledge to Tennie Marler, 7 Ap 1886 (same), F. M. Bandy MG 1-488

- - - - - - - - - - - - -

RUTHERFORD

MARRIAGES
J.F. Rutherford to Lula Thomas, 10 Aug 1889 (1 Aug), M.C. Brunner MG 1-578
W.T. Rutherford to Flora Brandon, 8 Jan 1893, G.W. Brewer MG 4-49

- - - - - - - - - - - - -

RYAN / RYON / RYNE

1860 CENSUS
Harris Ryan 52 (Ky), Lucinda 24, Giles 22 (Tanner), Mary E. 19, Rebecca 15, Darius 12 7-3-12
Sallie Ryan 50 (NC), Mary L. CLEMENTS 23 6-102-694
1870 CENSUS
David Ryan 48 (NC), Julia 32, Sallie 11, Tennessee 8, William 4, Martha 3, Slater 1 6-5-31 (B)
Giles H. Ryan 30, Elizabeth 24, Elizabeth M. 6/12 5-7-50
Harris Ryan 62 (Va), Nancy A. 45, Lucinda 30, Rebecca 25, Martha 4 6-17-122
James Ryan 23, Luanna 16 6-16-117 (B)(Mu)
Louisa Ryan 35, James 17, Henry 14, William 12, Elmore 9, Tolbert 6 6-17-126 (B)
Sarah Ryan 50 (NC), Abner 19, Dartha A. 18, John 16, David 13 6-17-125 (B)
1880 CENSUS
G.H. Ryon 42, Eliza C. 34, E.N. 10 (d), N.R. 8 (s), L.C. 6 (d), J.C. 4 (s), L.E. 2 (d) 7-29-251
Henry H. Ryon 72, Nancy A. 52 (w), Larinda 36, Rebecca 35, Martha A. 13, George W. 14, John 9 6-12-109
Louisa Ryon 44, Henry Giles 23, William T. 21, J. Elmore 19, Torbet 13, Kelley RANDOLPH 25 (Hotel Laborer)("Parted with wife"), Ulsey 5, Moriah E. 7 10-20-231/240 (B)
1900 CENSUS
David Ryne 82 (Aug 1817-NC/NC/NC-M 43), Julia 67 (Unk-M 43-10-5), Franklin 18 (Ap 1882), Susan HENRY 10 (gd)(Unk) 6-248A-158/159 (B)
Giles H. Ryan 64 (Nov 1835-M 35), Elizabeth 54 (Oct 1845-M 35-9-6), John 24 (Nov 1875), Rosa A. 16 (June 1883), Delia DRAKE 10 (adopted d)(Unk) 6-242B-62
Jack Ryan 29 (Nov 1870-M 5), Annie 23 (Ap 1876-T/NC/Va-M 5-1-1), Julia 4 (Sep 1895), Perry HENRY 9 (nw)(Unk), Melissa 6 (ne)(July 1893) 6-249B-179/180 (B)
William Ryan 29 (Mar 1871-M 7), Ida M. 27 (Oct 1872-M 7-4-3), John H. 7 (Ap 1893), William U. 3 (Feb 1897), Charlie C. 9/12 (Aug 1899), Walter HINKLE 26 (u) (Aug 1874) 6-243A-63
MARRIAGES
Annie Ryan to John Henry q.v.
Giles H. Ryan to Elizabeth Smith, 28 Jan 1866 (same), R.T. Howard MG 1-#885
Harris Ryan to Nancy A. Singleton, 27 Dec 1862 (no return) 1-#792
Jackson Ryan to Annie Campbell, 16 Feb 1898 (same), W.L. Lillard JP 2-252
L. M. Ryan to J. F. Walker q.v.
Lizzue Ryan to Charles Robinson q.v.
Martha Ryan to M. C. Smith q.v.
Nancy Ryan to James R. Mondy q.v.
Pearl Ryan to Andy Carter q.v. (B)
Rebecca Ryan to Henry Moles q.v.
Sallie Ryan to Charley Smuthers q.v.
Tennessee Ryan to James W. Castor(?) q.v.
Vesta Ryan to Lewis Cox q.v.
Vesta Ryan to James M. Carter q.v.
W.H. Ryan to Ida Sanfransisco, 2 July 1892, W.S. Hale MG 4-38

- - - - - - - - - - - - -

SABIN

1900 CENSUS
Oscar Sabin 40: see Samuel H.(?) Hickman

- - - - - - - - - - - - -

SAFFLES / SAPHELS

1880 CENSUS
James Saphels 28, S.B. 24 (w), J.D. 7 (d), S.B. 1 (d) 3-25-198
S. Saphels 40, Berby 36 (w), Albert 21 (s), M.D. 17 (d), Norma 15, J.W. 13 (s), J.F. 11 (d), Andy 8, M.E. 6 (d), Sela 4, J.H. 2 (s), M.S. 2 (d) 3-33-183
MARRIAGES
Richard Saffles to Mattie Brady, 12 Jan 1892, T.F. Shaver JP 4-34
Tilda Saffles to Robert Peterson q.v.

- - - - - - - - - - - - -

SAILLIE

1900 CENSUS
Albert W. Saillie 21: see Banjamin F. Mealer

- - - - - - - - - - - - -

SALES / SAILS

1860 CENSUS
Catharine Sales 8, Sarah 11: see Martha Fewghet
Hampton Sales 50, Mary 40, Harrison 20, Caroline 18, Louiza 16, Kesiah 14, Catharine 12, Sarah 10, Daniel 8, Liza 4, Judy(?) 2, Eliza STONE 18, Sarah 16, James W. 9, James M. 1 3-67-460
1870 CENSUS
Catharine Sails 16: see Martha Fugate
MARRIAGES
Catharine Sales to Benjamin Bratcher q.v.
G.H. Sales to Mary Stone, 6 Nov 1859 (no return) 1-#697
Sarah Sales to Vanburen Thompson q.v.

- - - - - - - - - - - - -

SALTS

MARRIAGE
William Salts or Sults or Swets to Bronnie or Brownie May, 10 or 17 Feb 1895 [0 written over 7 or vice versa], A.D. Hubbard MG 4-76

- - - - - - - - - - - - -

SAMPLER

1880 CENSUS
L. L. Sampler 25: see Jere Wasson

- - - - - - - - - - - - -

SANDERS / SAUNDER

1900 CENSUS
George Sanders 57, Robert 9: see Stuvor Lawrance (B)
MARRIAGES
Benjamin Sanders to Adaline Eaton, 26 June 1855 (no return) 1-#496
E.L. Sanders to Ada McDonald, 9 Mar 1892, A.C.. Peters MG 4-43
Mollie Sanders to Wash Baskett q.v.

- - - - - - - - - - - - -

SANDRANS

1900 CENSUS
Larance Sandrans 48 (Nov 1851-Oh/Eng/Eng-M 27)(Plasterer), Emarlia 49 (Nov 1852-Oh/Oh/Oh-M 27-6-6), Ara 20 (d)(June 1879-Oh), Ray 18 (Dec 1881-Oh)(RR Hand), Martin 8 (July 1891) 12-180B-46/49

- - - - - - - - - - - - -

SANDYS

MARRIAGE
Edmond Sandys to O.A. Rodgers, 3 Feb 1885 (same), I.W. Holt JP 1-460

- - - - - - - - - - - - -

SANFORD / STANFORD

1880 CENSUS
Elizabeth Sanford 29 (Cook at Hotel), Mary 7 (B): see Robert L. Allen
1900 CENSUS
Thomas Sanford 30 (Mar 1870-Ga/Ga/Ga-M 4)(Coal Miner), Nancy 32 (Dec 1868-NC/SC/SC-M 4-0-0), Las COX 23 (boarder)(Unk 1877) 8-287B-388/390 (B)
MARRIAGES
Charles H. Sanford to Mary Hale, 30 May 1877 (24 June), G.W. Wassom JP 1-#1501
Thomas Stanford to Nancy C. Cardiff, 6 June 1896, J.A. Brown W 2-28 (B) [NOTE: the following page, 2-29, shows Thomas Swafford to Nancy C. Cardiff, on the same date]

- - - - - - - - - - - - -

SANFRANSISCO

MARRIAGE
Ida Sanfransisco to W. H. Ryan q.v.

- - - - - - - - - - - - -

SANKS

MARRIAGE
Ed E. Sanks to W. J. Slupe or Sleepe q.v.

- - - - - - - - - - - - -

SAWYERS / SAWYEUR

1880 CENSUS
William Sawyers 20: see Nancy McDonald
1900 CENSUS
Eli T. Sawyers 69 (Aug 1830-T/Va/SC-M 34)(Landlord), Isabella J. 61 (Ap 1839-M 34-2-1) 2-197B-118/123
Frank Sawyers 63 (Nov 1836-Pa/Pa/Pa-M 29), Sarah 50 (July 1849-Ind/Pa/Pa-M 29-4-4), Perl 17 (June 1882-Ind), Nellie 13 (Dec 1886-Ind), Grover 10 (Dec 1889-Ind), Ruth 5 (Jan 1895-Ind) 12-180A-29/31
Granville Sawyers 20: see George Gray (B)
Laran Sawyer(?) 67 (Jan 1853-NY/NY/NY-M 24), Jane 50 (Aug 1847-NY/NY/NY-M 24-4-4), Lee 22 (Mar 1878-NY), Carl 17 (Sep 1880-NY), Adns(?) 13 (Mar 1887-Wis), Asker DIPER 20 (Ap 1880)(Servant) 12-179B-22/24
William Sawyeur 40 (Aug 1859-M 13), Mary C. 40 (Ap 1860-M 13-1-1), Robert C. 12 (Aug 1887-Ga), Ann BISHOP 19 (lodger)(Ap 1881-Ala/Ala/Ala) 10-260A-198/203
MARRIAGES
J.E. Sawyers to Mary E. McDonald, 28 Dec 1868 (same), J.W. Thompson MG 1-#1040
James P. Sawyer to Margaret M. Clark, 26 Dec 1871 (28 Dec), H.B. Heiskell JP 1-#1218
Will Sawyers to Polly Darwin, 5 Mar 1886 (6 Mar), B.F. Holloway JP 1-516

- - - - - - - - - - - - -

SCALES

MARRIAGE
Ada B. Scales to L. D. Peace q.v.

- - - - - - - - - - - - -

SCARBROUGH / SCARBERRY

1870 CENSUS
Mary Scarberry 36, Priscilla 10, Eliza S. 8 1-19-126
1880 CENSUS
Mary Scarbrough 48, Priscilla 20, Eliza 19, Saunders DUNLAP 16 (nw), Willis 6 (nw) 1-10-84

1900 CENSUS
Mary Scarbrough 69 (Mar 1831-T/NC/Spain-Wd 2-2), Priscilla 40 (d)(Sep 1859-T/SC/T), Josie McCLENDON 6 (ne)(Ap 1894) 4-226A-248/252 (Rhea Springs & Washington Road)
William Scarbrough 51 (May 1849-M 22)(Carpenter), Saprona C. 49 (May 1851-M 22-5-5), Sarah F. 20 (Feb 1880), Bertie E. 18 (Oct 1881), Willie R. 15 (July 1884), Charley E. 13 (May 1887), Elsie H. 11 (Jan 1889) 10-258A-152/156

MARRIAGE
E. S. Scarbrough to A. T. Godbehire q.v.

- - - - - - - - - - - - -

SCHAFER / SCHAEFER
(see also SHAUFNER)

1900 CENSUS
Haney Schaefer 41 (July 1858-Pa/Pa/At sea-M 10)(Plasterer), Kate M. 36 (July 1836-Oh/Pa/Oh-M 10-5-5), Claude H. 9 (Aug 1890), Dawn I. 7 (Jan 1892), Blanche M. 5 (Dec 1894), McKinley H. 3 (Jan 1897), Howard C. 1 (May 1899), Eliza J. HINDMAN 47 (sil) (July 1852-Oh/Pa/Oh) 10-326B-144/152

MARRIAGES
Harry Schafer to Kati Hindeman, 13 July 1889 (same), R.A. Bartlett MG 1-579
James Schafer to Sorena Davis, 14 Feb 1895, Leroy Diggs MG 4-78

- - - - - - - - - - - - -

SCHATZEL

1900 CENSUS
George L. Schatzel 49 (June 1850-Pa/Germany/Do-M 23) (Repairer), Juliet 48 (Mar 1852-Oh/Germany/Do-M 23-0), John P. 44 (b)(Mar 1856-Tex/Germany/Do-S)(Woodworker, Wagon), Barbara FISCUS 76 (ml) (Oct 1823-Germany/Do/Do-Wd 9-6), Libbie 42 (sil) (Mar 1858-Oh/Germany/Do-Wd 2-2) (Seamstress), Gladys 6 (ne)(Ap 1894), Alma 2 (ne)(Oct 1897) 13-299B-180/185

- - - - - - - - - - - - -

SCHILL / SCHILDE
(see also CHILDS)

1900 CENSUS
August Schill 58 (Mar 1842-Germany/Do/Do-1861/39/Na-M 32), Mary 53 (Feb 1847-T/Va/Va-M 32-3-3), Peter 23 (Aug 1876-NC) 10-323A-60/63
MARRIAGES
Lou Schill to Andrew Snyder q.v.
Peter Schill or Schilde to Bertha Hodge, 15 Sept 1900 (same), W.L. Lillard JP, P. Schill & John White W 3-218

- - - - - - - - - - - - -

SCHMIT

MARRIAGE
Allen W. Schmit to Mearl A. Lamater, 21 Dec 1887 (same), R.A. Bartlett MG 1-539

- - - - - - - - - - - - -

SCHOOLFIELD

1880 CENSUS
W.B. Schoolfield 56, M.A. 41, Elizabeth 22, M.C. 17 (s), G. R. 14 (s), Harriet 12, J.C. 8 (s) 4-7-52
1900 CENSUS
Benjamin Schoolfield 30: see George W. Goodrich
William B. Schoolfield 76 (Ap 1824-Wd), Elizabeth J. 43 (d)(May 1858), Mary C. 40 (d)(Ap 1860), John C. 26 (s)(Aug 1873) 4-227A-270/274 (Spring City & Washington Road)
MARRIAGE
Hortense Schoolfield to J. J. Furguson q.v.

- - - - - - - - - - - - -

SCHRIMPSHIRE / SHARPSHIRE / SHRAPHIER

1860 CENSUS
Mary I. or J. Sharpshire 28: see Rufus B. Sherly
1870 CENSUS
Mollie Shraphier 36: see Rufus B. Sherly
MARRIAGES
James Schrimpshire to Franey Smith, 26 Sep 1891, R.A. Bartlett MG 4-32
Tressa Scrimpshire to John B. Webb q.v.

- - - - - - - - - - - - -

SCOTT

1870 CENSUS
John A. Scott 33 (Ind), Narcissus 23, Isaac C. 3, Doctor Y. 8/12 3-14-102
1880 CENSUS
James H. Scott 50, Paisity 28 (w) 5-11-98
Rettie Scott 15: see Andrew Cawood
1900 CENSUS
Annie Scott 24 (Dec 1875-M 0-1-1)(Washing & Ironing), May WHITFIELD 7 (d)(June 1892-T/Ga/T) 10-323A-63/67
Arthur Scott 18: see H. Toliver (B)

Henry Scott 47: see Charles Hughes
James Scott 65 (Feb 1835-T/T/NC-M 32)(Pensioner), Paricity 48 (June 1851-NC/T/T-M 32-0-0) 7-264B-273/278
Jonah Scott 26 (May 1874-M 5)(Coal Miner), Adah 21 (July 1878-M 5-3-0), Jane 67 (ml)(Unk 1833-Wd 8-7) 15-269B-28
Lizzie Scott 40, Arty 16, Evy 12, Maud 11: see Scott Gorden or Gooden
Maggie Scott 16, Mary 14, Willie 10: see Robert McDonald (B)
Sam T. Scott 18 (Mar 1882-M 0), Floria 16 (Dec 1883-M 0-1-1), Raymon 2/12 (Mar 1900) 10-260A-193/198

MARRIAGES

G.M. Scott to Annie Nance, 16 Oct 1899 (same), W.L. Lillard JP, E.T.M. Hale or E.T. McHale W 3-55
George Scott to Eliza Gowin(?), 17 Oct 1890, F.M. Capps JP 4-22
J.W. Scott to Elizabeth Reed, 5 May 1898, L.L. Barton JP 4-100
Loucy Ann Scott to John N. Steel q.v.
Rachel Scott to Wesley Moreland q.v.
Rittie M. Scott to John M. Phillips q.v.
Samuel M. Scott to Flora Jewell, 2 Aug 1899 (same), W.L. Lillard JP, J.R. Denton W 3-16
Tina Scott to James Liner q.v.
Tinie Scott to W. C. Parker q.v.
Wiley Scott to Lou or Lori Holmes, 15 Sep 1900 (16 Sep), David Davis MG, Wyley Scott & Miller Gaines(?) [signed by X] W 3-217

- - - - - - - - - - - - -

SCOVILLE

1900 CENSUS

James W.V. Scoville 61 (Sep 1838-Ind/NY/NY-M 27)(Dry Goods Merchant), Frank K. 56 (May 1854-NY/Ind/Ind-M 27-2-2), Maude R. 21 (May 1879-Ind), Claud THOMPSON 20 (boarder)(Ap 1880)(Partner) 14-215A-41/42

- - - - - - - - - - - - -

SCROGGINS / SCROGINS

1870 CENSUS

Thomas B. Scrogins 18, Barbra E. 19, Sarah J. 1/12 7-6-46

1880 CENSUS

J.A. Scroggins 46, M.A. 38 (w), E.E. 17 (d), E.C. 14 (s), M.A. 12 (d), J.C. 10 (s), R.M. 7 (s), S.A. 4 (d), M.E. 2 (d) 3-22-178

1900 CENSUS

Call Scroggins 29 (Sep 1870-M 4), Emma 22 (Aug 1877-M 4-2-1), Girtie 11/12 (June 1899-Ala) 7-265A-283/288

MARRIAGES

David Scroggins to Orris Wyrick, 27 Oct 1900 (same), T.A. Shelton MG, Y.W. Yatter(?) W 3-236
Emaline Scroggins to Nehemiah Shipley q.v.
Liza Scroggins to Mart Wilkey q.v.
M. E. Scroggins to J. M. Shaver q.v.
Mary A. Scroggins to Turner P. Smith q.v.
Tinia Scroggins to Sam Howell q.v.

- - - - - - - - - - - - -

SCRUGGS

1880 CENSUS

James Scruggs 22: see Scruggs Yearwood

- - - - - - - - - - - - -

SCUDDER

MARRIAGE

A. Scudder to J. McDonald q.v.

- - - - - - - - - - - - -

SEALS

1900 CENSUS

Callie A. Seals 26, Ina M. 8, Ida M. 8, Virgil McK. 4: see Alexander Cofer

MARRIAGE

Elbert Seals to Callie Cofer, 25 Feb 1891, J.W. Williamson MG 4-25

- - - - - - - - - - - - -

SECREST / SEACREST

1900 CENSUS

John H. Seacrest 40, Alice L. 38: see John W. Wassom

MARRIAGE

J.H. Secrest to Mrs. Alice Bryson, 24 Sep 1893, W.P. Perkinson JP 4-55

- - - - - - - - - - - - -

SEDMAN

1900 CENSUS

William Sedman 46 (Mar 1854-England/Do/Do-1880/20/Na-M 20), Eliza* 43 (Oct 1856-England/Do/Do-1880/20/Na-M 20-7-7), George 19 (Mar 1881-Pa), Frank 16 (July 1883-Oh), Edith 14 (Nov 1885-Oh), William 8 (Nov 1891-Oh), Archie 6 (Dec 1893-Oh), Ray 4 (Dec 1895-Oh), Clyde 3 (Jan 1897-Oh) 3-209A-165/179 [* nee Gibson]

- - - - - - - - - - - - -

SEE / SEA

1900 CENSUS

German See 67 (Oct 1832-M 0), Sarah 39 (May 1861-M 0-0), Luther DOUGLAS 16 (s)(Dec 1883-Ga), Columbus 11 (s)(Ap 1889-Ga) 10-326A-124/128
Sally Sea 20: see Samuel Whitlow (B)

MARRIAGE

German See to Sallie Douglass, 4 Nov 1899 (5 Nov), G.T. Mussington MG, R.S. Mason W 3-65

- - - - - - - - - - - - -

SELCER

MARRIAGE

J.A. Selcer to M.E. Harris, 4 July 1883 (8 July), J.M. Bramlett MG 1-476

- - - - - - - - - - - - -

SELLERS

1860 CENSUS
Joseph W. Sellers 38, Nancy 35, Sarah E. 12, Catharine E. 11, William L. 9, Margaret 7, Martha 5, James H. 3 3-56-381
1870 CENSUS
Joseph W. Sellers 50, Nancy 49, Sarah E. 21, Catharine C. 20, Wlliam L. 18, Margarette 16, Martha J. 15, James H. 12 3-9-66
1880 CENSUS
Sarah Sellers 81: see Smith Brady
MARRIAGE
Carrie Sellers to John Powers

- - - - - - - - - - - - -

SELLS

1900 CENSUS
Lucy D. Sells 18: see Alvin C.(?) Gibson
MARRIAGE
Burty Sells to Salina Keedy, 3 Dec 1896 (same), M.G. Hicks JP, R.J. Killough W 2-84

- - - - - - - - - - - - -

SELVIDGE / SELVAGE

1880 CENSUS
Rufus Selvage 17: see Adam Kirklin
MARRIAGE
J.W. Selvidge to Louella Smith, 28 Feb 1900 (same), W.L. Patton MG, R.L. Armor W 3-130

- - - - - - - - - - - - -

SEVELY

MARRIAGE
Elsom C. Sevely to Clara L. Bartlett, 5 Ap 1894, R.A. Bartlett MG 4-69

- - - - - - - - - - - - -

SEXTON

1860 CENSUS
Elizabeth Sexton 41, William 14, John M. 6 8-9-58
Halley Sexton 48, Mary A. 19, James P. 2 8-9-59
James Sexton 19 (Fisherman) 8-9-55
Tollover Sexton 70 (SC)(Carpenter), Rebecca 65, Sarah M. 14, Martha E. 8 8-9-57
1870 CENSUS
Holly Sexton 63, Mary Ann 28, James P. 13, Tennessee J. 9, Nancy 6 8-21-147
Elizabeth Sexton 50, William 24, Milo 18 8-21-148
1880 CENSUS
Elizabeth Sexton 60, W.M. 33 8-18-155
J.P. Sexton 23, N.J. 22 (w) 8-18-153
M.A. Sexton 37, Tenie 20 (d), N.A. 16 (d), Ida A. 4 (gd) 8-18-150
Milo Sexton 26, N.J. 20 (w), Eliza 3 (d), W.J. 1/12 (s) 8-19-162
1900 CENSUS
Frank Sexton 9: see William Arrants
James P. Sexton 43 (June 1857-M 4), Ellen 36 (Dec 1863-T/Va/T-M 4-2-2), America D. 18 (Mar 1882), Henry C. 16 (Aug 1883), Robert 12 (July 1888), Edna 11 (Jan 1889), Oscar L. 3 (Nov 1896), Patrick 1 (July 1898) 15-270B-48
[James P. married Ellen Walker on 1 Jan 1896]
William M. Sexton 55 (Ap 1845-M 16)(Sawmill Fireman), Fanny 32 (Dec 1867-Ala/Ala/Ala-M 16-6-0) 13-309B-371/385
MARRIAGES
Alice Sexton to J. B. Ward q.v.
Della Sexton to John Norris q.v.
Edna Sexton to John Stanley q.v.
Ellen Sexton to J. F. Davis q.v.
J.P. Sexton to N.J. [Nancy Jane] Swafford, 31 Oct 1879 (no return), R.L. Allen ?? 1-#1682 & 1-#1689 [marked through]
J.P. Sexton to Martha E. Swafford, 13 May 1886 (16 May), W.G. Curton ?? 1-501
John M. Sexton to Nancy J. Couch, 28 Jan 1876 (same), Wm M. Grimsley MG 1-#1432
Nannie Sexton to William Arrants q.v.
William Sexton to Fanny Patton, 28 May 1883 (1 June), W.S. Hale MG 1-476

- - - - - - - - - - - - -

SEYBERT

MARRIAGE
Molly Seybert to William Fox q.v.

- - - - - - - - - - - - -

SHADDIN / SHADDEN

1900 CENSUS
Martha Shadden 63 (July 1836-Wd 6-5), William W. 14 (Feb 1886) 5-230A-38
William Shaddin 23 (Jan 1887-M 5), Ella 18 (Mar 1882-M 5-2-2), Pearl 3 (Feb 1897), Lawrence 11/12 (June 1899) 6-264A-119/120
MARRIAGES
John R. Shaddin to Dora Jones, 4 July 1891 (no return) 4-27
W.H. Shadden to Ella Filyan, 9 Feb 1896, R.M. Trentham JP 4-93

- - - - - - - - - - - - -

SHADWICK / SHADRICK / SHADICK

1860 CENSUS
Wm Shadrick 50 (Chairmaker), Aggy 51 (NC), John 21, Jane 18, Harden 14, Malinda 14 8-17-118
1870 CENSUS
Adaline Shadwick 36, Mary J. 12, William G. 9, Henry 4, Sarah A. 3 3-2-10
1880 CENSUS– None
1900 CENSUS
Creed Shadick 28 (Dec 1871-M 7)(Coal Miner), Bettie 23 (Mar 1877-M 7-1-1), William 2 (Oct 1897), Eliza DAVIS 69 (ml)(May 1831-Wd 9-5) 8-286A-352/354
Elizabeth Shadrick 60 (Unk 1840-Wd 4-4), Hatty ELLIOTT 12 (gd)(Unk 1888) 8-281B-255/257

Hard Shadrick 54 (Jan 1846-M 28), Mary J. 49 (July 1850-M 28-5-4), Dora 18 (Oct 1881), Lydia M. 8 (Mar 1892) 8-286B-360/362

John Shadrick 34 (Unk 1866-M 9), Mary J. 26 (Oct 1873-T/Ga/T-M 9-0) 15-272A-77

Prudence Shadrick 51 (Unk 1849-Ky/Ky/Ky-Wd 12-10), Arvazene 12 (Unk 1888-Ky), Sally 10 (Unk 1890) 8-286A-353/355

Samuel T. Shadrick 25 (May 1875-M 4), Mary L. 24 (Feb 1876-Ga/Ga/NC-M 4-2-2), Mary J. 4 (Mar 1896), Ella A. 1 (June 1898) 8-286A-354/356

William Shadrick 27 (July 1873-M 13), Tilda A. 29 (Aug 1870-Ga/Ga/Ga-M 13-1-0), Rachael SHADRICK 68 (m)(Dec 1831-Wd 8-3) 8-285A-332/334

MARRIAGES

Creed Shadwick to Mary R. Davis, 14 Oct 1892, William Morgan JP 4-64

Elizabeth Shadwick to William J. Soward(?) q.v.

Genette Shadwick to S. H. Oldham q.v.

J.T. Shadwick to Joe A. Yoder, 26 Dec 1891, R.S. Mason JP 4-34

Missouri Shadwick to W. W. McPherson q.v.

Missouri C. Shadwick to Reuben Dye q.v.

Nancy J. Shadwick to William Dye or Dyer q.v.

Samuel Shadwick to Mary Lou E. Martin, 18 Ap 1896 (19 Ap), J.H. Morgan JP, Worthy Swift W 2-14

Sarah Ann Shadwick to William A. Elliott q.v.

William O. Shadrick to Elizabeth A. McDaniels, 12 Nov 1864 (13 Nov), John W. Williamson MG 1-#842

- - - - - - - - - - - - -

SHAHAN– see SHANNON

- - - - - - - - - - - - -

SHAKER

MARRIAGE

John Shaker to Mary J. Russell, 1 Dec 1888 (same), John H. Parrott ?? 1-556

- - - - - - - - - - - - -

SHALLIDAY

1900 CENSUS

Martin or Mation Shalliday 55 (Sep 1844-Scotland/Do/Do-1881/19/Na-M 26)(Mining Contractor), Margaret 50 (Mar 1850-Scotland/Do/Do-1881/19-M 26-10-7), Jas 23 (June 1876-Scotland-1881/Na), Annie 21 (Dec 1878-Scotland-1881/Na)(Milliner), Margaret 17 (Oct 1882-Mass), Agnes 15 (Jan 1885), Virginia 8 (Ap 1892) 10-327B-155/163

- - - - - - - - - - - - -

SHANKLE

1900 CENSUS

Rachel(?) Shankle 59 (Feb 1841-Ga/T/T-Wd 7-6), Lou 25 (Ap 1875-Ga/Ala/Ga), Ida 23 (Feb 1877-Ga), Julia 21 (Ap 1879-Ga), Birtha 16 (Sep 1883-Ga) 15-273B-105

- - - - - - - - - - - - -

SHANNON / SHAHAN

1880 CENSUS

Jas Shannon 45: see G. H. Debord

Joe A. Shannon 46 (Railroad Hand), Willi M. 48, Lucinda 27, Mary J. 7 (d), Joseph R. 2/12 (s) 10-28-211/216

MARRIAGES

J.A. Shahan to Ella M. McCully, 24 Feb 1883 (25 Feb), J.W. Burnett MG 1-464

Lucinda Shannon to James H. Stallings q.v.

Mary Shannon to J. W. Brandon q.v.

Mrs. Sally Shannon or Sherman to J. B. Edwards q.v.

- - - - - - - - - - - - -

SHARP

1880 CENSUS

Calvin Sharp 52, John 54 (b) 9-30-258

Gid Sharp 45, Eliza 36, J.E. 16 (s), J.F. 13 (s), S.M. 11 (d), C.A. 7 (s), S.L. 5 (s), D.E. 2 (d), A.E. McMILLIN 19 (ne) 9-30-261

Joseph Sharp 17: see Gilbert Reed

Rufus M. Sharp 25, Livice F. 25, Calvin L. 5, Hiram M. 2 5-5-40

1900 CENSUS

Charles Sharp 25 (Unk 1875-M 3)(Coal Miner), Cinda 20 (Ap 1880-M 3-1-0), Jesse MOONYHAN 13 (bl)(Unk 1887) 8-279A-216/218

Clenia Sharp 4: see William Kelly

Frank M. Sharp 50 (Mar 1850-M 20), Jane 45 (Ap 1855-M 20-7-5), Hattie 18 (Ap 1882), Birthy 15 (d) (Feb 1885), John 13 (Mar 1887), Jessie 8 (Nov 1891), Nelli 4 (Jan 1896) 1-184A-109/114

James R. Sharp 28 (July 1871-M 2)(Coal Miner), Nettie T. 19 (Nov 1880-M 2-1-1), Leon 1 (d)(Nov 1898) 5-234A-128

John Sharp 30 (Sep 1869-M 3)(Shoe Repairer), Allie 22 (July 1877-M 8-5-3), Cornelius 5 (d)(Sep 1894), Arthur 2 (May 1898), George 2 (Dec 1897) 8-276B-164/165

John Sharp 27 (Aug 1872-M 8), Callie 26 (Sep 1873-M 8-0) 10-258A-150/154 (B)

John Sharp 36 (Ap 1864-M 11)(Iron Ore Miner), Amanda 30 (Mar 1870-M 11-6-4), Richard 8 (Feb 1892), Lilard A. 6 (May 1894), Claud U. 3 (Aug 1896), Victoria F. 1 (Sep 1898) 2-193A-35/36 (B)

Jud Sharp 66 (Unk-Wd), Vina 17 (Jan 1883)(Washwoman), John 14 (Oct 1885), Carrie 13 (July 1886), Annie 1 (May 1899) 6-247A-135/136 (B)

Lavadia A. Sharp 32 (Dec 1867-S 3-3), Rosa E. 13 (d)(Jan 1897), Perry E. 11 (s)(Jan 1889) 9-228A-8

Louis Sharp 24 (Unk 1876-M 7)(Coal Miner), Sallie 26 (Aug 1873-M 7-0), Joseph BROWN 21 (boarder)(Unk 1879)(Coal Miner), William JENKINS 19 (boarder) (Unk 1881)(Coal Miner) 8-280A-229/231

Mary Sharp 85: see Mary C. Morrison

Patsie Sharp 79: see Richard Atkins (B)

Richard Sharp 19: see Lee A. Kelly (B)

Thomas Sharp 26: see William P. Ferguson

William Sharp 52 (Oct 1847-Ky/Ky/Ky-M 31), Mary A. 48 (Ap 1852-Oh/Oh/Oh-M 31-6-5), Nellie M. 11 (Feb 1889) 13-307B-332/344

MARRIAGES

Alice Sharp to A. B. Pryor q.v.

Andy Sharp to Addie Smith, 17 July 1896 (17 Aug), J.B. Phillips MG, Riley Garmany & Add Smith W 2-44

Calvin(?) Sharp to J. H. Hughes q.v.

Candace Sharp to John L. Patton q.v.

Charley Sharp to Altie Abel, 22 July 1894, R.S. Mason JP 4-67

Charles Sharp to Synda Moneyhan, 12 June 1897 (13 June), W.S. Hale MG, Frank Ellison W 2-149

Elvin F. Sharp to Flora L. Gonce, 20 Dec 1893, W.L. Patton MG 4-84

F.S. Sharp to Mollie Hughes, 29 July 1894, J.W. Williamson MG 4-66

Florence Sharp to Thomas E. Hayes q.v.

James N. Sharp to Delilia McDonald, 28 Dec 1889 (no return) 1-582

James R. Sharp to Nettie Brown(?), 11 Nov 1897 (12 Nov), J.M. Bramlett MG, W.W. Smith W 2-205

John Sharp to Amanda Gillespie, 14 Aug 1889 (15 Aug), J.W. Bowman MG 1-577

John Sharp to Tinnie Stewart, 5 Sep 1890, A.W. Frazier JP 4-16

John Sharp to Allice Ferguson, 19 Sep 1891, R.S. Mason JP 4-31

Josie Sharp to William Swan q.v.

Mary C. Sharp to James A. Bradshaw q.v.

Queen Sharp to West Forney q.v.

Samuel L. Sharp to Sarah F. Abel, 9 Dec 1894, A.P. Hayes JP 4-74

Sarah Sharp to J. D. Alley q.v.

Sarah Sharp to F. L. Perkins q.v.

Susan Sharp to Isaac Jolly q.v.

- - - - - - - - - - - - -

SHARPSHIRE– see SHRIMPSHIRE

- - - - - - - - - - - - -

SHAUFNER
(see also SCHAFER)

MARRIAGES

Emma Shaufner(?) to John Tucker q.v.

James Shaufner(?) to Frances Rice, 17 May 1889 (same), A.W. Frazier JP 1-575

- - - - - - - - - - - - -

SHAVER / SHAVIN

1860 CENSUS

Cornelius Shaver 56, Jane 47 (SC), James M. 24, Jesse A. 22, Andrew H. 18, Theodore F. 15, Samuel L. 14, Elenor E. KEY 14, Nancy J. TRUSLEY 31, William TRUSLEY 2 7-2-7 [Cornelius married Jane Moore on 16 Oct 1832 in Blount County]

John Shaver 85: see Samuel Wilkey

John Q. Shaver 26, Elmira J. 18 7-2-8

1870 CENSUS

Cornelius Shaver 63, Jane 57 (SC), Samuel L. 23 7-8-63

Jesse A. Shaver 31, Harriet 21, Eunice 2, Louisa J. 3/12 7-1-1

John Q. Shaver 38, Elmira J. 28, Nancy J. 9, Jesse A. 7, Henry H. 4, Hester Ann 2, Freeling H. 26 7-1-9

1880 CENSUS

J.Q. Shaver 46, E.J. 38, Jesse 18, Hose 14, Hester 12, Allice 8, Delia 2, Eliza McALLEN 20 (boarder)(School Teacher) 7-23-201

S.J. Shaver 35, J.A. 15 (s), M.E. 13 (d), L.E. 11 (d), D.E. 7 (d), E.H. 1 (s) 7-23-198

S.L. Shaver 33, M.C. 31, C.A. 8 (s), T.F. 6 (s), J.T. 3 (s) 7-29-249

T.F. Shaver 36, M.C. 27 (w), J.M. 7 (s) 7-23-199

1900 CENSUS

Freeling T. Shaver 55 (Oct 1844-T/T/SC-M 20), Catharine 47 (Jan 1853-T/SC/T-M 20-2-2), Cordia 17 (Dec 1882), Offie 14 (Oct 1885) 7-264A-268/273

Huston Shaver 45 (Ap 1876-M 7), Martha A. 25 (Nov 1874-M 7-3-3), Hudson J. 6 (Feb 1894), Wallace A. 4 (Oct 1895), Dewey M. 2 (Ap 1898), Joe THOMPSON (B) 51 (lodger)(Jan 1842-NC/Unk/NC-Wd) 7-263A-246/251

Jessee Shaver 38 (May 1862-M 13), Mollie 32 (Dec 1867-M 13-6-6), Birtie 12 (May 1888), Ivy 10 (Sep 1887), Creed 9 (May 1891), Ethel 6 (June 1894), Roby 4 (Jan 1896), Noah 1 (Dec 1898) 7-262B-240/245 [Jesse A. married Maud Molly Brown on 17 July 1887 in Meigs County]

Jim Shaver 55 (Jan 1845-M 5), Sarah 40 (July 1859-Ga/Unk-M 5-1-1)(Washwoman), Miller DAVIS 10 (ss) (Mar 1890) 7-267B-328/333 (B)

John Shavin 66 (Nov 1833-M 40), Emma J. 57 (Dec 1842-T/SC/Ga-M 40-7-5), Ida B. 18 (Ap 1882), Ollie 14 (Dec 1885) 7-262B-239/244

John M. Shaver 27 (Nov 1872-M 7), Martha 21 (Aug 1878-M 7-2-2), Theodora W. 5 (July 1894), James E. 1 (Nov 1898) 7-263A-247/252

Lafayette Shaver 53 (Oct 1846-M 20), Mary C. 51 (Sep 1848-T/NC/T-M 20-5-5), John T. 23 (Mar 1877), Florence 19 (Jan 1881), Henry 17 (Mar 1883), Walter U. 14 (Sep 1885), William G. 12 (Jan 1888), Fred R. 10 (Jan 1890) 7-262B-242/247

Nealy Shaver 27 (Aug 1872-M 3), Annie 23 (July 1877-Ky/Oh/Ky-M 3-1-1), Hattie 5 (d)(Dec 1894), Ellen 2 (d) (Feb 1898) 7-262B-243/248

Thomas F. Shaver 25 (June 1874-M 6)(Coal Miner), Mary M. 22 (July 1877-M 6-2-2), Ida P. 3 (Sep 1896), Scott H. 2 (May 1898), John SOWARD 27 (boarder)(Dec 1892) 10-250A-3/3

MARRIAGES

Alice A. Shaver to W. E. Collins q.v.

Cornelius Shaver to Sarah Rector [nee Barton], 11 Mar 1874 (same), P.E. Johnson MG 1-#1329

Cornelius Shaver to Vina Wilkey, 30 Ap 1893, J.B. Trotter MG 4-50

D. T. Shaver to J. S. Coleman q.v.

Freeling Shaver to Catharine Bowling, 17 Jan 1880 (18 Jan), J.R. Crawford JP 1-#1697

H.H. Shaver to Mattie A. Burnett, 20 Aug 1893, W.A. Howard MG 4-56

Hester Shaver to P. T. Daniel q.v.

Lucy Shaver to R. C. Chattin q.v.

J.M. Shaver to M.E. Scroggins, 27 Aug 1893, J.B. Trotter(?) MG 4-55

John Q. Shaver to Elmira J. Bolin, 23 Dec 1859 (25 Dec), T. Knight JP 1-#704

Neiley Shaver to Annie Conley, 7 Dec 1896 (same), T.F. Shaver MG 2-85

S.L. Shaver to Mary M. Mathis, 2 Sep 1871 (3 Sep), R.T. Howard MG 1-#1206
S.L. Shaver to Catharine J. Singleton, 29 July 1879 (no return), W.R. Henry, Clerk 1-#1664

- - - - - - - - - - - - -

SHAW

1880 CENSUS
George Shaw 24, Sarah 23, Joe 1, Samuel 1/12 1-10-81
1900 CENSUS
Pollie Shaw 86: see John Hughes
MARRIAGES
George Shaw to Sally Henderson, 2 Dec 1877 (7 Jan 1878), A.J. Mathis MG 1-#1543
George Shaw to Sallie Henderson, 26 Jan 1878 (27 Jan), A.J. Mathis MG 1-290
Missouri K. Shaw to Thomas J. Mathis q.v.

- - - - - - - - - - - - -

SHEARER

1900 CENSUS
Titus Shearer 67 (Mar 1833-Oh/NC/NC-M 20), Margaret E. 54 (Feb 1846-Oh/SC/Oh-M 20-3-2), Frank A.S. 16 (Nov 1883-Oh), Nannie E. 13 (Nov 1886-Oh) 14-222B-180/184

- - - - - - - - - - - - -

SHEEP

1880 CENSUS
Lillie Sheep 18, Annie 2/12: see Benjamin Shelow

- - - - - - - - - - - - -

SHELBY / SHELVY

1860 CENSUS
Samuel Shelvy 41 (Carpenter), Sarah 41, John 16, Catharine 13, Isaac T. 12, William 6, James 3, David 11/12 5-37-247
1870 CENSUS
Samuel Shelby 53 (House Carpenter), Sarah 53, Aggie C. 23, Isaac T. 21, William 16, James 15, David 10, George W. 7 4-10-63
1880 CENSUS
Alfred Shelby 31 (Carpenter), Harriet 19 (w), L.E. 3 (d), Charlie 2 4-10-81
Thomas Shelby 26, Adella 2: see Wesley Casey
William Shelby 25, Susan 28, Addie 4, Ada 2 1-10-83
1900 CENSUS
David Shelby 46 (June 1853-M 16), Louisa A. 34 (Nov 1865-M 16-8-6), William O. 15 (May 1885), Sarah A. 13 (Jan 1887), James H. 10 (Oct 1889), Jacob A. 7 (Aug 1892), Cleo B. 3 (d)(Aug 1896), David S.H. 1 (Sep 1898) 4-226B-256/260
George W. Shelby 35 (June 1864-M 11)(Sawmill Laborer), Kansas 27 (May 1873-Ala/Ala/Ala-M 11-4-3), William L. 7 (Sep 1892-Ala), Henry C. 6 (Feb 1894), Savannah 1 (July 1898) 4-224B-214/218 (Spring City & Dayton Road)
Samuel Shelby 76 (Mar 1824-T/Va/Va-M 16)(Gardner), Mary T. 48 (Mar 1852-M 16-0), Lillie L. BURDETT 16 (ne)(Feb 1884) 14-217B-97/99
Thomas F. Shelby 53 (Oct 1846-M 19)(Teamster), Mary J. 34 (Oct 1865-T/T/Ill-M 19-9-7), John M. 18 (Oct 1881)(Deaf & Dumb), Floyd 16 (July 1883)(Day Laborer), Elbert 14 (Aug 1885)(Day Laborer), Clara 11 (Aug 1888), Cordia B. 10 (May 1890), Leonard 7 (May 1893), Willie H. 3 (Jan 1896) 14-217B-96/98
William Shelby 46 (Sep 1853-M 26), Susan 49 (Sep 1850-T/T/Ill-M 26-6-5), Nelie 19 (Aug 1880), Walter F. 13 (Ap 1887), Earnest 7 (Nov 1892) 4-226A-251/255 (Rhea Springs & Washington Road)
Wilum N. Shelby 48 (May 1852-M 15), Amen 39 (Ap 1861-M 15-0) 1-185A-127/133

MARRIAGES
Ada Shelby to Thomas Crisp q.v.
Addie Shelby to Henry L. Smith q.v.
Catharine Shelby to Elamas Casey q.v.
David Shelby to Louisa Fisher, 3 Aug 1884 (8 Aug), T.H. McPherson JP 1-476
I.T. [T.F.?] Shelby to Mary J. Casey, 28 Dec 1880 (29 Dec), B.F. Holloway JP 1-296
Ida Shelby to James Crisp q.v.
James Shelby to Lucy Turner, 21 Feb 1885 (22 Feb), J.M. Bramlet MG 1-464
Thomas Shelby to Adelia Casey, 29 July 1874 (2 Aug), Wm McCully MG 1-#1347
Tilda Shelvy to E. West q.v.
William Shelby* to Susan Casey, 30 May 1874 (31 May), Wm McCully MG 1-#1338 [*original record shows last name as Shably instead of Shelby]

- - - - - - - - - - - - -

SHELL / SHULL

1880 CENSUS
Franklin Shull 36: see Polk Brown
1900 CENSUS
James Shell 24 (Jan 1876-M 1), Martha 17 (Sep 1882-M 1-1-1), James A. 11/12 (June 1899) 3-208A-141/154
MARRIAGE
Burch Shell to Martha Owens, 14 Aug 1898, J.A. Torbett JP 4-103

- - - - - - - - - - - - -

SHELLY

1880 CENSUS
Jacob F. Shelley 25 (Minister) 5-7-58

- - - - - - - - - - - - -

SHELOW

1880 CENSUS
Benjamin Shelow 42, Annie 41, Willie 16, Lillie SHEEP 18 (d), Annie 2/12, Alice FLETCHER 16 (ne), John KIRCHBAUM 27 (boarder) 1-11-89

- - - - - - - - - - - - -

SHELTON

1870 CENSUS

James M. Shelton 50, Mary Jane [nee Rice] 34, William H. 14, James M. 13, Mary J. 11, Sarah E. 9, Andrew J. 7, John W. 6, Lucinda 4, George W. 2, Thomas J. 1/12 7-4-27

1880 CENSUS

J.T. Shelton 23, L. 18 (w), Mary DUNCAN 75 (m) 3-20-164

J.M. Shelton 57, M.J. 44 (w), W.H. 24 (s), M.J. 20 (d), S.E. 19 (d), A.J. 15 (s), L.S. 13 (d), G.W. 11 (s), Thomas 10, E.M. 7 (d) 3-20-165

1900 CENSUS

Erasmus A. Shelton 54 (May 1846-Va/Va/Va-M 32), Lydia 54 (Oct 1845-Va/Va/Va-M 32-4-4) 13-196B-128/130 [E.A. married Lydia Jane Umbarger on 20 Jan 1868 in Wythe Co., Va.]

George Shelton 31 (July 1868-M 2)(Brickmason), Minie 20 (Mar 1880-Indian Territory/Oh/Ky-M 2-1-1), Hester 1 (Nov 1898) 7-264B-276/281

James Shelton 53 (Unk 1847-M 33), Paralee 50 (July 1849-M 33-9-8), Rebecca 17 (Ap 1883), William 12 (May 1888), Kate 10 (Nov 1889), Savannah 8 (Aug 1891), Viola 6 (Mar 1894) 15-271B-69

James M. Shelton 43 (Mar 1857-M 21) (Brickmaker), Leahes C. 38 (June 1861-M 21-10-8), James H. 19 (July 1880)(Brickmaker), David W. 18 (Nov 1881) (Coal Miner), Cordia M. 16 (Oct 1883), William E. 12 (Aug 1888), Robert F. 9 (Sep 1890), Flora E. 7 (Nov 1892), Ina B. 5 (May 1895-Tex), Bessie R. 2 (Aug 1897) 10-324B-93/97

MARRIAGES

Agnes Shelton to Ben Hutcheson q.v.
Cora B. Shelton to Cal G. Hiley q.v.
Emma Shelton to S. H. Hickman q.v.
Emma Shelton to John Wheeler q.v.
George Shelton to Minnie Conley, 8 Jan 1898 (9 Jan), R.C. Knight JP, B.W.H. Lewis W 2-238
Lucinda Shelton to James S. Wilkey q.v.
Mary A. Shelton to John Elsa q.v.
Sarah C. Shelton to T. R. Wade q.v.
William H. Shelton to Catharine Kelly, 5 Oct 1877 (6 Oct), W.W. Low JP 1-#1515
W.W. Shelton to Tammie Gillespie, 26 Aug 1890 (same), L.M. Morris or Moores ?? 1-604

- - - - - - - - - - - - -

SHEPARD

1860 CENSUS

Sarah Shepard 80 (NC): see Anderson Edmons

- - - - - - - - - - - - -

SHERIDAN

MARRIAGE

Henry W. Sheridan to Annie M. Wilson, 16 Ap 1892, John K. Larkin, Priest 4-40

- - - - - - - - - - - - -

SHERLEY / SHERLY / SHIRLEY / SHERRLEY

1860 CENSUS

Rufus B. Sherly 32 (Merchant), Malinda 34, Rufus 2, Green B. KEYS 27 (Artist), Milo HOLLAWAY 13 (Clerk), Mary I. or J. SHARPSHIRE 28 4-37-319

1870 CENSUS

James C. Shirley 36, Sarah J. 33, James 14, Landon 12, John 10, Martha Jane 3, Nancy E. 8, Millie A. 1 8-11-78

Rufus B. Sherley 41 (Retail Merchant), Malinda 42, Rufus 12, William T. 9, Mollie SHRAPHIER 36, Elijah GREEN 15 4-8-49

1880 CENSUS

Isaac Sherly 33, M.E. 27 (w), J.C. 10 (s), S.J. 8 (d), Linda 3 (d), F.B. 4/12 (s) 8-15-129

S.J. Sherley 44, Jimmy 24 (s), Sandy 23 (s), John 22 [name & age marked through], Nancy 20, Jane 13, Millie 11, Betta 9, Joseph 7, Letta 4 8-15-131

1900 CENSUS

Kittie Shirley 22, Ethel 2: see Hettie Mills

Isaac N. Shirley 53 (Nov 1846-M 25), Mary E. 47 (Jan 1853-M 25-12-9), Joseph 17 (Sep 1882), Charles I. 15 (Mar 1885), Alice L. 12 (July 1887), Rosa A. 9 (Feb 1891), George H. 6 (Dec 1893), Maud E. 4 (Ap 1896), Emma K. CLINGAN 20 (Aug 1879)(Servant) 13-295A-103/105

Landy Shirley 22 (May 1877-M 0), Lea A. 28 (Ap 1872-M 0-1-1), Ida M. 5/12 (Dec 1899) 13-295B-104/106

Sarah J. Shirley 64 (Sep 1835-T/T/NC-Wd 9-7), James 44 (June 1855), Landy 43 (Nov 1856), Martha 33 (June 1866), Joseph 27 (June 1872) 13-296B-133/135

Thomas B. Shirley 21 (Jan 1879-M 0), Minnie 21 (Ap 1879-M 0-0) 3-295B-105/107

MARRIAGES

B.L. Sherly to Cassa Fills, 1 Sep 1870 (no return) 1-#1163
Blanch Sherrley to J. W. Adams q.v.
Kitty Shirley to Thomas Fitts q.v.
Landy Shirley to Lee Story, 12 Sep 1899 (same), N.D. Reed MG, G.W. Spivey W 3-32
Lettie Shirley to Augusta C. Davis q.v.
Margaret E. Shirley to G. A. Fraley q.v.
Mary J. Sherley to Robert Davis q.v.
Milley Sherley to John B. Swafford q.v.
Nancy Shirley to Dick Raulston q.v.
Sarah G. Sherley to William Fitts q.v.
Thomas Shirley to Minton Morgan, 30 Sep 1899 (7 Oct), Sherman Wilson MG, J. Martin W 3-44

- - - - - - - - - - - - -

SHERMAN / SHURMAN / SHEWMAN

1900 CENSUS

Robert M. Sherman 46 (Jan 1854-Oh/Oh/Oh-M 25)(Grocer), Rosa D. 42 (July 1857-Oh/Pa/Oh-M 25-5-5), Walter D. 18 (Mar 1882-Oh)(Grocery Salesman), Bessie A. 13 (Feb 1887), Harriet B. 9 (Mar 1891) 10-327A-146/154

MARRIAGES

C.E. Shewman to Laura B. Gollohen, 31 July 1895, R.A. Owens MG 4-90

Eli Shurman to Susie West, 25 Mar 1890, M.C. Bruner MG 4-19
Mrs. Sally Sherman or Shannon to J. B. Edwards q.v.
S. E. Shuman or Sherman to J. J. Jolley q.v.

- - - - - - - - - - - - -

SHERRILL / SHERILL / SHIRREL

MARRIAGES
H.C. Sherrill to Luretta Hollaway, 28 Feb 1887 (10 Mar), W.H. Munroe ?? 1-524
Lee Sherill to Clara Godsey, 21 July 1900, L.L. Barton JP 4-107
Martha Sherrill to Joseph Reed q.v.
Mary Sherrill to Robert Reed q.v.

- - - - - - - - - - - - -

SHERTZAHN

1900 CENSUS
Elbert Shertzahn 55 (Jan 1845-Oh/Oh/Oh-M 10), Elbe 30 (Feb 1870-Oh/Oh/Oh-M 10) 1-190A-213/225 (Spring City)

- - - - - - - - - - - - -

SHIDELER

1900 CENSUS
William L. Shideler 66 (Aug 1833-Oh/Pa/T-M 45)(Contractor), Rachel 65 (May 1835-Oh/Maine/Maine-M 45-3-0) 10-326B-134/140

- - - - - - - - - - - - -

SHIELDS

1900 CENSUS
Mich Shields 34 (July 1865-Germany/Do/Do-1868/32/Na-M 11)(Truck Farmer), Martha 32 (Feb 1868-M 11-4-3), Morgan10 (June 1889), John 8 (June 1891), Anny 1 (Dec 1898) 10-254B-88
Stephen Shields 42 (June 1857-M 14)(Furnaceman), Martha 31 (June 1868-T/Va/T-M 14-9-5), Edgar 12 (Dec 1887), Nellie 10 (Oct 1889), Robert 6 (Ap 1894), Jennie 2 (July 1897), Alether 7/12 (Oct 1899) 10-329A-19/204 (B)
William Shields 29 (Nov 1870-T/Ky/T-M 4), Anny B. 27 (June 1872-M 4-0) 10-255A-98/98

MARRIAGES
Stephen Shields to Martha Day, 15 Aug 1885 (17 Aug), Byrd Terry ?? 1-498
William Shields to Annie McDonald, 25 Dec 1895, J.A. Whitner MG 4-89

- - - - - - - - - - - - -

SHIFLET

1870 CENSUS
Jeremiah Shiflet 65 (NC)(House Carpenter), Ann C. 61 (NY) 1-3-18

- - - - - - - - - - - - -

SHILLITO / SHILLETON

1880 CENSUS
J.S. Shilleton 72, M.A. 64 (w), E. 30 (d), R. 27 (d), A. 25 (d), F.J. 23 (s), Ella 20 4-11-86 [James S. married Mary Ann Porter about 1847]
1900 CENSUS
Francis J. Shilleto 43 (Mar 1857-Pa/Pa/Pa), Emily 51 (si) (Feb 1849-Pa), Rachel 48 (si)(Dec 1851-Pa), Alice 45 (si)(Jan 1855-Pa) 14-221A-145/149
MARRIAGE
Ellen Shellito to H. C. Darwin q.v.

- - - - - - - - - - - - -

SHINN

MARRIAGE
Amanda A. Shinn to Joseph Simon q.v.

- - - - - - - - - - - - -

SHIPLEY

1860 CENSUS
Miron(?) Shipley 21: see Robert Pierce
1870 CENSUS
Orson A. Shipley 35, Delilah 30, Lenora A. GASS 10, Samuel E. 8, Nancy E. CAMPBELL 20 8-19-128
1880 CENSUS
Jessee Shipley 28, Aljarene 28, James 6, Melvin 3 2-38-314
W.O. Shipley 22, T.G. 20, A.S. 1 (d), L.J. HUTCHENS 40, Chasing 16 (d), Charles S. 13 (s), Isaac N. 7 (s), Thos LYONS 18 8-16-135
1900 CENSUS
Benjamin Shipley 50 (Mar 1850-Ky/Ky/Ky-M 19)(RR Section Foreman), Anna 41 (Aug 1858-M 19-9-7), Sidney 15 (Jan 1885)(Coal Miner), Mattie P. 13 (Mar 1887), Nancy M. 9 (Nov 1890), Grace E. 6 (June 1893), Callie M. 5 (May 1895), Emma L. 2 (May 1898) 3-306B-317/329
Gilbert Shipley 26 (May 1874-M 5), Harriet 25 (Oct 1874-T/Ga/Ga-M 5-3-2), Lee 1 (June 1898), Onest 1/12 (Ap 1900) 13-297A-135/137
Nathaniel Shipley 50 (Unk 1850-Wd), Joseph 20 (Oct 1879), Lottie 19 (Ap 1881), Richard 16 (Dec 1883), John 15 (Unk 1885), Susan 12 (July 1887), Sallie 10 (July 1889), George 6 (Sep 1893), King 3 (Sep 1896) 15-268B-15

MARRIAGES
Almeda Shipley to John Francis q.v.
Arlene Shipley to George Francisco q.v.
Calvin Shipley to Kittie Mills, 17 Mar 1895, J.W. Clouse JP 4-77
Delila Shipley to James Corvin q.v.
Effie Shipley to Florence Ottinger, 27 Oct 1898 (same), W.R. Grimsley MG, C.E. Aslinger & Elance Shipley W 2-339
Gilbert Shipley to Harriet Mills, 24 Mar 1894, J.W. Clouse JP 4-77
H. E. Shipley to N. M. Keith q.v.
J.B. Shipley to Esther Abel, 24 June 1897 (same), W.R. Grimsley MG, R. Keith W 2-156

James P. Shipley to Louisa Jane Howard, 7 Feb 1867 (10 Feb), P.G. Campbell JP 1-#935
Jessie P. Shipley to M.G. Dotson, 16 June 1885 (21 June), J.W. Peace ?? 1-496
Jim Shipley to Caroline Roe, 20 Dec 1893, J.W. Clouse JP 4-60
Laura Shipley to William Suggs q.v.
Lottie Shipley to Thomas Brooks q.v.
Louisa A. Shipley to John Aslinger q.v.
Mary Shipley to Orson Crawley q.v.
Mary E. Shipley to John J. Parker q.v.
Minnie Shipley to J. R. Cox q.v.
Mollie Shipley to Charley Strickland q.v.
Nehemiah Shipley to Emaline Scroggins, 1 Jan 1856 (3 Jan), L.W. Crouch ?? 1-#546
Owin A. Shipley to Delila R. Gass, 23 Feb 1867 (24 Feb), J.A. Kelly MG 1-#939
Thomas Shipley (23, Roane Co) to Mary Ann Milen (18, White Co), 9 July 1882, J.Q. Shaver MG, W.A. Howard & John Thomas W (of Hamilton Co) 4-8(77)
W.F. Shipley to Alice May, 15 Aug 1898 (same), W.L. Lillard JP, R.J. Killough W 2-310

\- - - - - - - - - - - - -

SHOCKLEY

1900 CENSUS
Alexander Shockley 26: see Katie Sims (B)

\- - - - - - - - - - - - -

SHOEMAKER

1900 CENSUS
Noah Shoemaker 60: see James H. Jackson
MARRIAGES
Elizabeth Shoemaker to W. D. Peeler q.v.
Ellen Shoemaker to James Crisp q.v.

\- - - - - - - - - - - - -

SHOOK / SHOCK

1870 CENSUS
Peter Shock 54, Martha M. 45, Mary E. 19, Hugh L. 15, Sarah V. 14, William FRANKLIN 9 3-20-145
MARRIAGE
Thomas Shook (26, Rhea Springs) to Rachel Clementine Harwood [license] or Howard [index] (24, White Co), 15 Oct 1881, W.W. Lowe JP, Ad McClendon & J. Holland W 4-5(47)

\- - - - - - - - - - - - -

SHOOP

1880 CENSUS
William Shoop 36, Louisa 28, Mary 8, Sarah 4, Thomas 1 1-13-109

\- - - - - - - - - - - - -

SHORT

1860 CENSUS
Francis M. Short 22, Jane 21 (Ky), John 1 9-98-667
Miller E. Short 21, Sarah J. 15 1-94-641
1870 CENSUS
Sally Short 25, Mary 8, Margarette 6: see James Johnson
1880 CENSUS
John Short 20, Artie 19 1-8-60
Mary Short 18, Margaret 16: see George Roddy
MARRIAGES
Francis M. Short to Blancha J. Rhea, 28 Jan 1857 (28 Jan), E. Brewer JP 1-#592
James Short to Ellenor Cox, 22 Ap 1859 (no return) 1-#681
John W. Short to Arlie Loy, 22 June 1878 (23 June), W.W. Low JP 1-#1563
Robert Short to Elvira Barnett, 8 Sep 1857 (same), R.T. Howard MG 1-#616
Sarah J. Short to George P. Roddy q.v.

\- - - - - - - - - - - - -

SHOUGHT

1900 CENSUS
Sam Shought 53 (Feb 1847-T/T/NC-M 19)(Stone Cutter), Aline 46 (Mar 1854-M 19-7-5), Lizzie 15 (June 1884), Sammie 12 (Mar 1887), Robin 7 (Mar 1893), Birtie 4 (June 1895) 7-266B-309/314

\- - - - - - - - - - - - -

SHUBERT

MARRIAGE
Jane Shubert to G. W. Milican q.v.

\- - - - - - - - - - - - -

SHUBYRD / SHEUBIRD

MARRIAGES
Anna Shubyrd to Crocket Beason q.v.
Looney Shuebird to Mencores(?) Grayham q.v.

\- - - - - - - - - - - - -

SHUFELT

1880 CENSUS
Jere Shufelt 75 (Carpenter & Joiner), Ann 72 12-3-25

\- - - - - - - - - - - - -

SILANCE

MARRIAGE
Mattie Silance to George Thomas Wright q.v.

\- - - - - - - - - - - - -

SILAS

1900 CENSUS
Henry Silas 35: see Milton Ragin (B)

\- - - - - - - - - - - - -

SILVERS

1900 CENSUS

George Silvers 32 (Jan 1868-Ky/Ky/Ky-M 7)(RR Section Foreman), Molly 25 (Nov 1874-M 7-5-2), Mandy M. 3 (Feb 1897), Saffall C. 1 (Ap 1899) 8-315B-104/108

- - - - - - - - - - - - -

SIMONS / SIMMONS / SIMMAMONS

MARRIAGES

Albert Simons to Hattie Day, 22 Mar 1899 (same), W.L. Lillard JP & W 2-395

Harry Simons to Annie Billingsley, 14 Jan 1890 (same), J.W. Williamson MG 1-587

Joseph Simon to Amanda A. Shinn, 25 May 1886 (16 May) [sic], M.C. Bruner MG 1-506

Lena Simons to Burket Marshall q.v.

Synda Simmons to Katie Walker, 22 Jan 1897 (same), J.W. Williamson MG, John McIntyrs(?) W 2-105

William Simmamons to Martha Romines, 23 Jan 1879 (28 Jan), J.F. Perry MG 1-#1601

- - - - - - - - - - - - -

SIMPSON / SAMPSON

1880 CENSUS

Madison Simpson 55 (Mill Clerk), Nancy 47, John 19, Rebecca 14, James 12, Dougan 9, Luke 7, Elizabeth 5 2-27-218

1900 CENSUS

Charles Sampson 51: see James D. Smith

Jack Simpson 42 (Nov 1855-M 23), Manervia 39 (Nov 1863-M 23-14-6), Charley 21 (May 1878), Harvy 20 (Ap 1879), Willie 14 (d)(July 1888-M 0-0), Jessee P. 7 (d)(Nov 1892), Walter C. 3 (Jan 1892), Jimmie M. 1 (Mar 1899), Leaser BRYANT 18 (boarder)(Mar 1882), Walter MILLS 22 (boarder)(Nov 1877) 10-252A-48 (B)

James B. Simpson 29 (Sep 1870-T/T/NC-M 9)(Shinglemaker), Mahala 27 (May 1873-M 9-4-3), Carl P. 6 (Oct 1893), Marjay 4 (Feb 1896) 14-215B-52/53

John W. Simpson 43 (Nov 1856-M 17), Mary L. 34 (Aug 1865-Ky/Ga/Ky-M 17-5-4), Maggie L. 18 (May 1884-Ky), Pearl 15 (May 1885-Ky), William E. 10 (Aug 1889), Nellie P. 4 (Sep 1895) 14-221A-152/156

Robert T. Simpson 50 (Jan 1849-M 32)(Teamster), Mary A. 54 (Ap 1846-Ky/Ky/Ky-M 32-5-4), Charles W. 26 (June 1874-Ky)(Teamster), John C. 24 (Dec 1875-Ky)(Farm Laborer), Lafayette KELLY 18 (nw)(Dec 1881-Ky/Ky/Ky) (at school), Minnie 15 (ne) (Dec 1885) (at school) 14-217B-94/96

Wiley Simpson 29 (Dec 1870-M 12), Emma 22 (Oct 1877-M 12-5-4), Alice M. 10 (May 1889), Daisey I. 7 (Sep 1892), Edward F. 4 (Nov 1895), Lucinda 3/12 (Feb 1900), Amos O'NEAL 19 (June 1880)(Servant) 2-194B-67/69

William F. Simpson 25 (Ap 1875-Ga/Canada/Ga-M 0)(Coal Miner), Belle 19 (Feb 1887-T/Va/T-M 0-0-0) 13-300A-191/196

MARRIAGES

Charlie Simpson to Jessie Monday, 10 Sep 1900, Wm White MG 4-109

F.A. Simpson to Julia H. King, 18 July 1874 (6 Aug), J.J. Ingle JP 1-#1344

J.C. Simpson to Myrtle Monday, 17 June 1900, W.M. White MG 4-108

J.W. Simpson to Eliza M. Ivey, 3 June 1886 (4 June), J.P. Thompson JP 1-538

James Simpson to Mahala F. Thompson, 9 Mar 1892, R.A. Dickson JP 4-43

Rebecca Simpson to Amos McEroy(?) q.v.

Sarah Simpson to William H. McCully q.v.

Simon Simpson to Ellen Thompson, 14 Sep 1889 (15 Sep), A. Reect(?) MG 1-581

Wyley L. Simpson to Emma Drake, 31 Aug 1888 (same), J.S. Roddy MG 1-549

- - - - - - - - - - - - -

SIMS / SIMMS

1900 CENSUS

Hattie Sims 38: see Ada Crockett

James B. Sims 53 (Jan 1847-M 12), Louisa C. 57 (Ap 1843-M 12-0), John BOLTON 6 (gs)(Nov 1892) 3-207A-121/132

John Sims 26 (Jan 1874-Ga/NC/Ga-M 0)(Laborer, Blast Furnace), Florence 22 (Dec 1877-M 0-0-0) 8-311A-3/3 (B)

Katie Sims 35 (Unk-Miss/Unk/Ga-M 2-2-1)(Boardinghouse Keeper): *Boarders:* George HOLSTON 17 (Nov 1882-Miss/Mo/Miss), Jeff HURD 23 (May 1877) (Furnaceman), Alexander SHOCKLEY 26 (Aug 1873), William FOUST 24 (Jan 1875-T/NC/Va), Moses HOWELL 13 (Unk-T/T/Mo) 10-338B-221/235 (B)

MARRIAGES

Albert Sims to George(?) Collins, 25 Nov 1891, S.W. Burnett MG 4-35

George Sims to Florence Williams, 20 May 1885 (same), P.P. Brooks ?? 1-494

John Simms to Florence Lay, 4 Oct 1899 (same), R.J. Smith ??, J.J. Jolly W 3-47

- - - - - - - - - - - - -

SINGLETON

1860 CENSUS

David Singleton 56 (NC), Viney 20, William 18, Eliza A. 16, Rebecca 14, Catharine 9, Faney 7, Joseph EATON 23 7-6-40

1870 CENSUS

David Singleton 68 (NC), Vina 28, Eliza A. 26, Mary C. 20, Fanny 18, Rens ANDERSON 20, Rebecca 24, Amanda 6/2 7-1-5

1880 CENSUS

David Singleton 76, Frankey 25, R.A. 5, James 7: see W.A. Kelley

1900 CENSUS

Franky Singleton 41: see Dack Jenno

MARRIAGES

Annie Singleton to Dock Gennoe q.v.

Catharine J. Singleton to S. L. Shaver q.v.

Eliza Ann Singleton to William A. Kelly q.v.

Elizabeth Singleton to John Allen q.v.
Nancy Singleton to George W. Milican q.v.
Nancy A. Singleton to Harris Ryan q.v.
Nancy J. Singleton to Joshua Eaton q.v.
Rebeca Singleton to E. A. Renow q.v.
Susan E. Singleton to William D. Smith q.v.

- - - - - - - - - - - - -

SISSON

MARRIAGE
J.R. Sisson to Ella Kirby, 9 Aug 1887 (same), Calvin Morgan JP 1-529

- - - - - - - - - - - - -

SITTON

MARRIAGE
James A. Sitton to Cordelia L. Bales, 23 Mar 1890 (same), W.S. Cagle M 1-597

- - - - - - - - - - - - -

SIVILS– see CIVILS

- - - - - - - - - - - - -

SKILLERN

1900 CENSUS
Frank W. Skillern 47 (July 1852-M 25)(Life Insurance Agent), Alice 43 (May 1857-M 25-2-2), Mattie J. 24 (Nov 1875)(Music Teacher), Kate 23 (Feb 1878-Tex) 8-313A-48/49
Rachel Skillern 40 (Unk 1860)(Washwoman) 15-271B-58/58 (B)

- - - - - - - - - - - - -

SKINER

1870 CENSUS
Seborn Skiner 28 (Ga), Adaline 35, Leasey 4, Samuel B. 2 8-21-146 (B)

- - - - - - - - - - - - -

SKUL

1900 CENSUS
Jane Skul 52 (May 1848-NY/NY/NY-S), Mary 50 (si)(July 1847-NY-Wd 0)(School Teacher) 2-179A-6/7

- - - - - - - - - - - - -

SKYLES

MARRIAGE
John Skyles to Dottie A. Hamlin, 7 June 1893, J.M. Benson JP 4-59

- - - - - - - - - - - - -

SLAGLE

MARRIAGE
G.H. Slagle to Nancy Ann Davis, 22 Sep 1858 (no return) 1-#657

- - - - - - - - - - - - -

SLATEN

1900 CENSUS
Archie H. Slaten 19 (July 1880-Ala/Ala/Ala)(Store Clerk) 13-302A-223/232

- - - - - - - - - - - - -

SLAUGHTER / SAUGHTER

1870 CENSUS
John Saughter 24, Mary Jane 20 6-15-109
MARRIAGE
John J. Slaughter to Mary Jane Waystuff, 2 Nov 1869 (same), T.N.L. Cunnyngham JP 1-#1121

- - - - - - - - - - - - -

SLAWSON

1900 CENSUS
Albert G. Slawson 41 (Oct 1858-Oh/NY/NY-M 1)(Tinner & Machinist), Cora 32 (Feb 1868-Ind/Ind/Ind-M 1-0), Wm H. 15 (July 1884-Oh/Oh/Oh)(Hardware Clerk), Ethel G. 12 (Sep 1887), Mervin L. 9 (Aug 1890), May M. 7 (May 1893), Jeannie TOLLE 27 (sil)(Mar 1873-Kan/Ky/Ky) 10-322B-57/60
MARRIAGE
A.G. Slawson to Cora D. Temple, 25 June 1898 (26 June), W.A. Howard MG, R.J. Killough W 2-315

- - - - - - - - - - - - -

SLUPE

MARRIAGE
W.K. Slupe or Sleepe to Ed [sic] E. Sanks, 17 May 1878 (no return) 1-#1558

- - - - - - - - - - - - -

SMALL / SMALLS

1900 CENSUS
Milar S. Small 47 (Sep 1852-NC/NC/NC-M 23), Mary 49 (May 1851-T/SC/T-M 23-5-3), Pearl 16 (Jan 1884), Isham A. (Sep 1887) 13-307A-326/338
Nancy A. Small 42 (Oct 1857-Wd 7-6), J. Edgar 22 (May 1878), Ola 20 (Feb 1880), Mollie 18 (Feb 1882), Chester H. 16 (Feb 1884), Flossie 11 (Aug 1888), Soonnie 5 (Aug 1894) 3-201A-24/25
Nora Small 15: see Jesse W. Iverster
Samuel H. Small 45 (Dec 1854-M 24)(Coal Miner), Millie A. 43 (Ap 1857-M 24-11-9), Walter S. 17 (Dec 1882)(Coal Miner), Henry C. 14 (May 1886), Emma 12 (July 1887), Ronnie 11 (May 1889), Josie C. 9 (Dec 1890), Maudie M. 8 (May 1892), Fred 5 (Oct 1894),

Sallie 4 (Nov 1895), Ella 2 (July 1897) 11-293B-89/90
William Small 40 (July 1859-M 13)(Coal Miner), Liza 30 (Dec 1869-M 13-4-1), Florence 12 (Mar 1888), Bridget MAHAN 17 (Feb 1883-Ky/T/T)(Servant) 8-280B-236/238

MARRIAGES

George W. Small to Elizabeth Parker, 22 Aug 1861 (4 Sep), no MG or JP 1-#759
Jimmie(?) Small to Martha Johnson, 17 Sep 1887 (18 Sep), M.C. Bruner MG 1-564
Reuben Small to Jane Britt(?), 1 Dec 1854 (2 Dec), Joseph Vanpelt MG 1-#472
Roda Small to John Henderson q.v.
William Smalls to Annie Coats(?), 12 July 1886 [on page with 1890 & 1891], M.C. Bruner MG 4-21

- - - - - - - - - - - - -

SMART

1900 CENSUS

George Smart 45: see Jackson Suddath (B)

- - - - - - - - - - - - -

SMEDLEY / SNEEDLEY

1870 CENSUS

George W. Smedley 29, Penelope C. 22, Mary E. 3, William A. 1 8-9-58

1880 CENSUS

G. W. Smedley 39, Penelope 38, Mary 14, William 11, Charles 8, George 4, John H. 8-16-136

1900 CENSUS

George W. Smedley 59 (June 1840-M 39), Penellipi C. 53 (Ap 1847-M 39-9-6), George 24 (Mar 1876), Henry 21 (Ap 1879), Alice 18 (May 1882), James 12 (Oct 1887), Hester 8 (Nov 1891) 15-269B-34
Mary Smedley 25, Walter 9: see Henry Banks
Willie Smedley 2: see Melvin Foust

MARRIAGES

Charley Sneedley to Mary L. Banks, 22 Sep 1891, James Corvin MG 4-46
M.E. or H.E. Smedley to J. H. Travis q.v.
Mary Sneedley to N. P. McNabb q.v.
William Smedley to Allice Banks, 17 May 1890 (18 May), W.S. Hale MG 1-601

- - - - - - - - - - - - -

SMITH

1860 CENSUS

Anthony Smith 17: see Richard Knight
Anthony Smith 57, Mary 55, Mary 27, Anthony L. 19, Thomas 16, Nancy C. 13, David B. 10, Ellen C. 6, Harriet M. 4, Nancy C. 9 7-7-45
Banister Smith 59 (Va), Eliza 55 (Va), James 31, Sarah 31, Eliza 9, Peggy 1, Polly E. 11/12 7-6-42
Benjamin D. Smith 16: see Jesse Harwood
Charles D. Smith 37, Hannah C. 26, Lewis E. 6, Malissa A. 4, Nancy E. 2 4-52-358
Coleman Smith 27, Margaret 23, Sarah A. 1 2-72-487
Daniel Smith 67 (Va), Patsey 67 (NC) 9-97-661
Edmond Smith 27, Isabella 23, William R. ?*, Marcus C. ?* 6-105-714 [*ink blob over ages]
Eliza A. Smith 57, Mary 26, William D. 16, Sevier 6, John 3, Anthony 21 7-7-49
Harris M. Smith 33, Martha 32, Nancy J. 14, Sarildabeth C. 11, Elzy M. 9, William A. 6, Charles T. 5, Martha E. 1 4-52-359
Henry S. Smith 24, Martha J. 22, James R. 1, Eliza A. 1 7-7-48
Jacob Smith 25, Jane 19, Mary F. 2 3-61-419
John M. Smith 23, Martha 15 (NC), William A. 11/12 (Ga), Stanten 21 (Ga), Eliza E. 16 7-7-47
Joseph D. Smith 25, Mary 22, Zyelpha 7, Wright 3 3-61-420
Margarita Smith 40, John T. 16, Susannah M. 14, Sarah L. 10 3-59-409
Moses Smith 65, Sarah 64, Phebe 25, George 22, Louisa 19, Eliza VARNER 32 4-53-361
Nancy Smith 63 (Va) 4-51-346
Nathaniel H. Smith 35 (Carpenter), Elizabeth 35, Eliza J. 13, John W. 11, Henry F. 9, Hariet 6, Adda 4, Betsy 6 6-111-761
William Smith [*] 18, Susan 25 7-3-18 [*could be Smitt]
William Smith 34, Nancy 41, Sarah E. 11, John W. 9, Jefferson 7, Darius W. 2, Mary 4/12 6-104-708
William S. Smith 26, Elizabeth 23, Mary C. 3, Nancy E. 2 4-48-324

1870 CENSUS

Andrew J. Smith 45, Mary E. 42, Isabella 11, Samuel A. 10, John H. 8, Benjamin 6, Sarah P. 5, William M. 2 3-9-67
Banister Smith 67 (Va), Nancy R. 33, Robert 14, Marcus C. 10, Alice P. 2 6-1-6
Benjamin D. Smith 26, Mary F. 22 (NC), Mary J. 2 3-16-117
Charles D. Smith 48 (Ala), Hannah C. 40, Lewis E. 16, Malissa A. 14, Nancy E. 12, Minerva T. 9, Charles N. 8, Horace 3 4-6-38
Coleman Smith 37, Margaret 25, Sarah A. 12, Frankey 10, John R. 6, Eliza 3, Mary 7/12 2-16-114
Elizabeth Smith 28: see William R. Champion
Harriette Smith 42, James 15, Madison 13, Letitia 11, Eliza E. 6 1-13-85 (B)
Horace Smith 44, Martha 43, Nancy J. 25, Surridabeth C. 22, William A. 16, Charles L. 14, Martha E. 11, Horace S. 7, Sarah A. 3 4-3-19
Jacob W. Smith 44 (House Carpenter), Zerena 31 (Ky), Mary F. 12, William C. 10, Turner T. 8, Melissa 7, Amanda T. 3 3-3-15
James Smith 42, Sarah 44, Margarette 13, Mary 10, Willis 9, Jane 5 6-2-8
James Smith 26, Tennessee 24, Peter 5 3-10-68
James R. Smith 11, Eliza A. 10, Mary E. 8: see Thomas J. Phelfrey
John Smith 45, Caroline 41, James 21, Thomas 16, Andrew 15, Louisa 13, William 13, John D. 7, Sarah E. 4, Bailey 1, Tennessee 1 6-17-120
John J. [or H.] Smith 31, Sarah 22, John T. 6/12, Nancy MATHES 17 7-5-34
John T. Smith 26, Mary A. 24, Margarette 3/12, Margarette A. SMITH 50 3-11-81
Martha Smith 71: see David Mitchell
Nancy Smith 73 (Va) 4-4-23

Nathaniel H. Smith 48 (Cabinet Workman), Sarah E. 43, John W. 21 (School Teacher), Henry 19, Henriette 16, Mary A. 14, Elizabeth 12, Nathaniel B. 10, Susan 8, Martha 5, Malinda R. 1 6-10-64

Samuel Smith 60, Thomas 16, Elizabeth 14 3-17-123 (B)

Samuel Smith 60, Letitia 23, Mariah 21, Thomas 15, Mariah 23, Mira 8, Thomas 6, Toba 4, Frona 2 3-17-125 (B)(Mu)

Sterling Smith 65 (B): see Jeremiah C. Wasson

William Smith 27, Susan E. 24, Elizabeth 4, Mary 3, Scrap 4/12 6-6-37

William J. Smith 59, Mariah 54, Eliza 15, James 13, William 8 7-4-32

William S. Smith 36, Julia A.E. 33, Mary C. 15, Nancy E. 12, Charles M. 9, William R. 8, John H. 5, Hester E. 1, John P. BANDY 28 4-4-21

1880 CENSUS

Banister C. Smith 79, Nancy E. 40 (w), Marcus C. 17, Allis P. 11, Banister C. 9 5-5-45

C. Smith 52, M.E. 50, A.E. 21 (d), S.E. 21 (s), B.F. 17 (d), S.L.O. 14 (d), N.M. 13 (s), M.S. 9 (d), R.E. McMURRAY 33 (boarder) 3-26-212

Charles Smith 17 (B): see Nile Broyles

Clabe Smith 30, Martha 28, Susan 15, R. 12 (s), J. 10 (s), S. 8 (s), J.C. 7 (s), T. 6 (s), A.C. 2 (s), Clabe 1/12 (s) 3-29-234 (B)

Coleman Smith 48, Margaret 39, Francis 18, John 14, Eliza 12, Mary 10, Rebecca 8, George 6, William 2 2-36-293

D. Smith 58, H.C. 48, N.E. 22 (d), M.L. 20 (d), C.N. 17 (s), H.J. 13 (s), Nancy 1 (gd) 3-19-153

E.M. Smith 29, E.L. 25, E.H. 14, S.M. 8, John 7, L.C. 6, Wm 3, Sam 3/12 4-34-281

G.M. Smith 31, Nancy E. 29, Mary A.J. 8 5-1-3

Henry Smith 34, F.A. 33, W.A. 4 (s), F.E. 3 (d), J.M. 9/12 (d) 4-36-297 (B)

Horace Smith 54, Martha 52, S.H. 18 (s), S.A. 14 (d), M.R. 10 (d) 4-34-278

Israel Smith 21, Hannah 23, Florence 6, John 3, Martin 1 2-32-261

J.T. Smith 36, M.A. 34, S.C. 8 (d), W.W. 6 (s), S.L. 4 (d), T.T. 8/12 (s) 3-19-147

James Smith 22: see G. B. Brady

James Smith 38, Tennessee 37, Peter 15, R.(?) 8 (s) 3-15-118

John Smith 47, J.F. 10 (s), Samey 8 (s), Allice 6, Eliza 4, Malicy 2 7-29-247

L.A. Smith 24, S.E. 19, S.F. 5 (d) 8-14-122

Lutitia Smith 25 (Washwoman), Dora 8, Nancy DETHERAGE 25 (Washwoman), Jane 5, Thomas 1, James B. HINCH 30 2-25-201 (B)(Mu)

Mirah Smith 21: see Cyrus Henry

Nathaniel H. Smith 56 (Cabinet Workman), Sarah E. 51, Adda 24, Millie E. 20, Nathaniel B. 18, Martha M. 14, Malinda R. 9 6-23-13 (Jefferson St., Washington)

Samuel Smith 77, M.S. 40 (d), Thom 24 (s) 3-29-235 (B)

Sarah Smith 53, Willis 19, Matilda G. 14, William T. 10 5-7-59

Sid Smith 16(?), William A. SMITH 25, Liza J. 25 (w), John H. 5, Sarah A. 2, Martha C. 4/12 5-2-17

Tate Smith 23, A.H. 22, A.L. 4, L.H. 1 4-34-280

Thom W. Smith 29, Lincy A. 27, Harriet A. 8, Willis O. 5, Andy W. 1 5-8-74

W.H. Smith 34, M.M. 36, W.E. 14 (s), M.E. 12 (d), R.B. 10 (s), L.G. 7 (d), T.C. 4 (s), B.E. 1 (s) 8-21-180

W.J. Smith 64, M. 65, J.W. 23 (s) 7-29-252

William Smith 16, P.M. 18: see M.E. Rhea

William Smith 38, Nancy 37, Bettie 13, James 12, George 10, William 6 1-11-88

William R. Smith 22, S.A. 20 (w) 7-29-248

1900 CENSUS

Ab Smith 21, Anna 16: see James K. Abel

Albert Smith 51 (Jan 1849-M 30), Mary 49 (July 1851-M 30-10-8), Jacphes 21 (June 1878), Anie 20 (Feb 1880), Gurty 12 (Jan 1888), Biddie 8 (Nov 1891), Minnie 6 (Ap 1894), Jessi 3 (Ap 1897) 1-188B-185/194

Amanda Smith 48 (Dec 1851-D 6-2)(Seamstress), Norman 19 (Nov 1880)(Day Laborer), Wayne 16 (May 1884) (Furnace Hand) 10-325A-102/106

Amos Smith 50 (Dec 1849-M 27)(Coal Miner), Nancy 45 (Nov 1854-M 27-9-9), Cora 16 (May 1884), Walter 13 (June 1886), Maud 11 (Aug 1888), Frank 9 (Feb 1891), Stella 6 (June 1893) 8-288A-395/397

Andy W. Smith 29 (Aug 1878-T/Ga/T-M 0), Roda 18 (Sep 1881-M 0-0) 5-233A-104

Aron T.(?) Smith 27 (Mar 1873-M 6), Ida E. 23 (Oct 1876-T/SC/T-M 6-2-2), Myrtle 5 (Ap 1895), Robert N. 1 (June 1898) 6-241B-29

Bailey B. Smith 32 (July 1867-M 12)(Coal Miner), Margaret C. 26 (Sep 1873-M 12-5-4), Henry C. 10 (Mar 1890), Maynard W. 6 (June 1893), Perry E. 3 (June 1896), Olia A. 8/12 (Sep 1899) 9-229A-30

Banister Smith 47: see John B. Brady

Benjamin Smith 27 (Feb 1873-Wd), Frank A. 1 (s)(Mar 1899) 3-205B-103/113

Charly Smith 24 (Nov 1875-M 6)(RR Hand), Nellie 23 (May 1877-M 6-3-1), Wash 11/12 (June 1899) 1-188B-186/195

Chas T. Smith 44 (Jan 1856-M 25), Delia S. 44 (Mar 1856-T/NC/T-M 25-8-8), Laura B. 18 (Mar 1882), Arvyzeny 15 (d)(Oct 1884), Martha L. 12 (Dec 1887), Bertha A. 9 (Nov 1890), Walter M. 6 (Jan 1894), Joel B. 4 (May 1896) 4-227A-262/266 (Rhea Springs & Washington Road)

Coleman Smith 67 (Jan 1833-T/T/Ireland-Wd), Mary D. 30 (Sep 1870), Rebecca P. 28 (Dec 1872), George W. 25 (Mar 1875)(Saw Mill Laborer), William N. 22 (Mar 1878), James C. 19 (Oct 1880) 2-191A-1/1

Dan Smith 54 (Dec 1845-M 15), Magie 40 (Mar 1860-Va/Va/Va-M 15-7-6), Mary 15 (Feb 1885), Bertha 14 (Mar 1886), James 20 (Nov 1879), Marty 9 (Jan 1891), Charley HANKS 19 (lodger)(Mar 1881) 7-263B-255/260 (B)

Edward Smith 45 (Oct 1854-Ga/Ga/Ga-M 2)(RR Section Hand), Sallie 28 (Dec 1880-M 2-2-1), Edward 10/12 (Aug 1899), Amanda 16 (d)(Dec 1883), Fred D. 17 (s) (Aug 1882) 5-233B-106 (B)

Elizabeth Smith 71 (Oct 1827-T/Va/Va-Wd 1-1), Lena 31 (Oct 1868)(Dressmaker) 8-312B-37/40

Elizabeth Smith 46 (Feb 1853-Wd 10-10), Larkin 20 (Feb 1880), Larnce 18 (Nov 1881), Mary 14 (May 1884), Sarah 11 (Nov 1888), Henderson 10 (Nov 1889) 1-186A-136/142

Estrell Smith 55 (Ap 1845-NY/NY/NY-M 25), Leah 44 (Ap 1856-Mich/NY/NY-M 25), Ila 20 (s)(Sep 1879-Mich),

Flada(?) 13 (Dec 1886-Mich), Dora 9 (May 1891-Mich), Alto 2 (d)(Sep 1897) 12-179B-27/29

George Smith 50: see Charles W. Ault

George Smith 18: see Clay Devault

George W. Smith 44 (June 1855-Ga/Ga/NC-M 12)(Miller), Elmira 38 (Ap 1862-T/Va/Va-M 12-4-4), Rindia B. 10 (Aug 1889), James T. 4 (Oct 1895), Charles A. 2 (Jan 1898), Maud E. 8/12 (Sep 1899), Harriet HOLLOWAY 80 (ml)(Jan 1820-Va/Va/Va-Wd 8-8), Nancy E. 44 (sil)(Sep 1855-T/Va/Va-S) 2-198A-128/133

Gus Smith 26, Laura 24: see Thomas Riddle

Henry Smith 35 (Aug 1864-M 5)(Coal Miner), Laura 24 (Sep 1875-M 5-2-2), Pearl M. 6 (Mar 1894), Earnest H. 1 (Feb 1899) 11-290B-17

Henry L. Smith 20 (Sep 1879-M 3), Adda 23 (July 1876-M 3-0) 4-227A-264/268

Henry R. Smith 16, Alice 14: see Joseph Campbell

Horace S. Smith 36 (Feb 1863-M 4), Emma 28 (Nov 1871-M 4-3-3), Elbert S. 7 (Aug 1892), Henry C. 2 (July 1897), John H. 1 (Jan 1898), unnamed 1/24 (May 1900) 3-203A-61/65

Humpry(?) Smith 49 (Mar 1851-Wd)(Painter), Ella 12 (Feb 1888-Ark/T/T), Alic 9 (d)(Aug 1890-Ark), Frances 7 (Aug 1892-Ark). George 5 (Sep 1894-Ark), Mack 3 (Oct 1898-Ark) 1-183B-92/95

Ida Smith 10: see Henry Pearman

Isaac N. Smith 58 (Ap 1842-T/SC/Unk-M 40), Martha R. 60 (May 1840-T/T/SC-M 40-4-4), Charley E. 19 (Feb 1881) 6-241A-28

Isbell Smith 66 (July 1834-Wd 8-1)(Washwoman), Alice 31 (d)(Aug 1869-D 0) 10-250A-7

James Smith 14: see Robert Ray

James D. Smith 32 (Mar 1868-M 4)(Hotel Keeper), Carrie 35 (Ap 1865-M 4-2-2), Pearl 1 (Nov 1868), Ruth MATHEWS 19 (June 1880)(Servant), Chas SAMPSON 51 (boarder)(July 1849-Pa/Eng/Ver)(RR Engineer), Thomas BURKHALTER 23 (boarder)(Oct 1876-Ala/T/Ala) 14-213A-12/12

James R. Smith 33 (July 1866-NC/NC/NC-M 0)(Teamster), Jennie 23 (June 1876-Ky/Ky/Ky-M 0-1-1), Fred L. 4/12 (Feb 1900), Jane SMITH 64 (m)(May 1836-NC/NC/NC-Wd 5-4) 2-197B-123/128

Jeff Smith 47 (May 1853-M 10), Elizabeth 30 (Jan 1870-M 10-6-3), Lucinda 9 (Aug 1890), Willie 7 (Ap 1893) 4-227B-280/284 (Back Valley Road)

Jefferson D. Smith 36 (Dec 1863-M 3)(Coal Miner), Alace M. 26 (Mar 1874-M 3-4-3), John J. 10 (Feb 1870), Earnest B. 3 (Nov 1896), Lenore M. 5/12 (Nov 1899) 9-229A-29

Joesas Smith 25 (May 1875-M 2), Matti 20 (Ap 1880-M 2-1-1), Eller 5/12 (Dec 1899) 1-185A-117/123

John F. Smith 30, Nancy A. 28, John A. 9, Samuel A. 6, Wm R. 2: see Alexander Ridley

John H. Smith 26 (Sep 1873-M 3), Martha T. 20 (July 1879-M 3-1-1), Willie H. 2 (Oct 1897) 3-203A-62/66

Josie Smith 33 (Jan 1867-M 19-7-5)(Boarding House Keeper), Beulah 15 (July 1884), Cornelia 14 (Nov 1885-Ga), Obelia 13 (Oct 1886), Essay 3 (Sep 1896); _Boarders:_ William SNELLING 16 (Aug 1883-Ga/Ga/Unk)(Coal Miner), James 50 (Unk-Ga/Ga/Ga)(Coal Miner) 10-330B-217/230 (B)

Lawrence Smith 18: see John F. Miller

Lee A. Smith 45 (Nov 1854-Ga/T/Ga-M 17)(Deputy Sheriff), Sue B. 35 (May 1865-T/Unk/Va-M 17-6-3), Lee E. 14 (Ap 1886), Laura B. 5 (July 1894), Liney REVIS 18 (d)(Dec 1881-M 0), William B. REVIS 32 (sl)(Nov 1869-M 0)(Engineer, Station Engine) 10-331A-228/243

Letitia Smith 47 (Jan 1853-S 1-1)(Washwoman), Cora 26 (d)(May 1874)(Washwoman) 14-215A-43/44 & 14-215B-54/54 (B)

Lizzie Smith 17, Maggie 12, Ida 10: see Sarah James

Louis E.(?) Smith 46 (Jan 1854-M 19), Lavina E. 34 (July 1865-M 19-4-4), Maud M. 17 (d)(Ap 1883), Anna G. 14 (Jan 1886), Ernest H. 11 (Sep 1888), Gertie G. 1 (Aug 1898) 3-201B-33/36

Margaret A. Smith 80 (Mar 1820-Wd 4-2) 3-205A-90/98

Martha Smith 46 (Mar 1854-Wd 2-2), Anie 20 (d)(Ap 1880), Marrie 10 (gd)(Feb 1890) 1-189B-210/221 (Spring City) (B)

Martha Smith 75 (Mar 1825-Wd 12-9), Amanda R. 30 (d)(Ap 1870), Oliver F. 5 (gs)(Mar 1895) 4-227A-263/267 (Rhea Springs & Washington Road)

Maud Smith 46 (Ap 1854-Wd 8-5), Walter 22 (Aug 1877), Chas 19 (Unk), Bob WRAY 19 (boarder)(Unk)(Coal Miner), Bessie 14 (boarder)(Sep 1885) 8-311A-9/9 (B)

Monroe Smith 46 (Ap 1854-Wd)(Coal Miner), Rudd 17 (Ap 1883)(Coal Miner), Dallas 8 (Mar 1892) 1-0-321B-32/33 (B)

Nancy H. Smith 41: see Charles W. Irwin

Nancy J. Smith 45 (Jan 1845-Wd 10-6), Reese E. 18 (Ap 1887)(Drayman), John M. 15 (Dec 1884)(Stable Laborer), John BLEVINS 21 (boarder)(Ap 1879)(RR Laborer) 14-219B-130/133

Oliver Smith 26 (Ap 1874-M 2), Rennie 21 (Jan 1879-M 2-0) 8-316A-115/119

Reuben H. Smith 22 (Mar 1878-M 1)(Coal Miner), Sally C. 18 (July 1881-M 1-1-1), Roy V. 2 (Dec 1897), Missouri K. TRAVIS 42 (ml)(Jan 1858-Wd 4-4), Perry SMITH 20 (b)(May 1880)(Coal Miner) 13-301B-213/221

Robert Smith 41 (Dec 1858-M 20)(House Carpenter), Polly A. 41 (May 1859-M 20-11-8), Howard 17 (Oct 1882), Samuel 14 (Mar 1886)(Livery Stable Hand), Callie 12 (Jan 1888), Mathew 9 (Dec 1890), Charles 6 (Mar 1894), Niner 4 (Jan 1896), Emma 2 (Dec 1898), Stella 3/12 (Feb 1900) 10-324B-101/105

Samuel A. Smith 37 (Nov 1862-M 14), Susan 32 (Aug 1867-M 14-3-3), George W. 12 (Jan 1888), Cora D. 10 (Ap 1890), Nora A. 5 (Ap 1895) 3-201B-37/40

Samuel W. Smith 27 (Sep 1872-M 0)(Coal Miner), Ollie M. 25 (May 1875-M 0-1-1), Ellen 1/12 (May 1900) 9-229A-27

Sarah M. Smith 64: see Laninia Brooks

Tennessee Smith 55 (Aug 1844-Wd 5-4), Petter 33 (Oct 1866), J. Wright 18 (June 1881), Thomas B. 11 (Ap 1889) 3-204A-77/83

Theodore T. Smith 20 (Aug 1879), Sue C. 28 (si)(Dec 1871), Lara 23 (si)(June 1886), Rositon(?) SMITH 18 (June 1881)(Servant) 3-207B-134/147

Thomas Smith 55 (Ap 1845-M 28), Lovel B. 44 (Feb 1856-M 28-11-7), Kissie J. 20 (July 1879), William P. 13 (Feb 1887), Mary M. 10 (July 1889), Alfred I. 8 (May 1892), Alexander 6 (Mar 1894), Martha A. 2 (June 1898) 6-245A-99/100

Thomas Smith 78 (Ap 1822-T/NC/Ky-M 52), Lorinda 77 (Mar 1823-M 52-5-5), Sarah M. 47 (d)(Oct 1852),

Elizabeth 37 (d)(Oct 1862) 8-280B-239/242

Thomas Smith 43 (June 1856-M 4)(Coal Miner), Estella 27 (Nov 1876-M 4-3-3), Wiley 18 (July 1881)(Coal Miner), Ila 13 (July 1886), Anna 9 (July 1891), Agnes 4 (May 1896), Carl 2 (Mar 1898), Irene 1/12 (Ap 1900) 8-280A-234/236

Thomas F. Smith 39 (Dec 1860-M 15)(Coal Miner), Kizzie 31 (Feb 1869-M 15-8-4), Allie N. 15 (Nov 1885), John A. 11 (Dec 1888), Jessie P. 3 (July 1896), Mandy M. 1 (May 1899) 13-308A-344/356

Thomas J. Smith 52 (May 1848-M 8)(RR Laborer), Edna 25 (Dec 1874-M 8-2-2), Nathan J. 5 (Aug 1874), Samuel L. 3 (Feb 1897), Bertha MARSH 13 (si)(May 1897) 14-218A-109/111 (B)

Thomas W. Smith 48 (Feb 1852-Ga/T/Ga-M 28), Lucy A. 46 (May 1854-M 28-10-8), James M. 19 (June 1881), Samuel W. 16 (May 1884), Martha W. 13 (Feb 1887), Nellie P. 10 (Feb 1890), Mary L. 6 (June 1893), Columbus C. 3 (Dec 1896) 5-230A-39

Tom Smith 17, Mate 15: see Lon Weathington (B)

Turner Smith 38 (Dec 1861-M 15), Mary 32 (Sep 1867-T/NC/T-M 15-6-6), Bertha 13 (Jan 1887), Philip 11 (Oct 1888), Anderson 8 (Oct 1891), Renie 7 (Dec 1892), Baily 6 (Mar 1894), Richard 2 (Jan 1898) 7-264B-278/283

William Smith 26 (Aug 1873-M 5)(Coal Miner), Anna 25 (Sep 1874-M 5-3-3), Walter 3 (July 1896), Carl 2 (Ap 1898), Myrtle 6/12 (Dec 1899) 15-273A-96

William Smith 26 (Unk 1874-M 6), Tuba A. 25 (Nov 1874-M 6), J. Chattman 6 (Mar 1895), John G. 4 (Sep 1895) 3-201A-29/31

William Smith 32 (Jan 1869-M 16), Lyda 32 (May 1869-Ga/Ga/Ga-M 16-9-6), Oston 11 (Mar 1889), Amanda 9 (Dec 1890), Cora 5 (May 1895), Florence 6/12 (Aug 1899) 5-237B-186

William Smith 40 (Mar 1860-NC/NC/NC-M 8), Lorena 33 (Feb 1867-M 8-0) 14-221A-153/157

William Smith 45 (Aug 1854), Jonah HENDERSON 15 (nw)(Ap 1885), Horace HENDERSON 13 (nw)(Nov 1886) 5-238B-207

William Smith 47 (Feb 1853-M 16), Louiza 30 (Ap 1870-M 16-11-4), Josephine 13 (May 1887), Lillie B. 9 (Mar 1891), William B. 6 (May 1894), Ida M. 4 (Mar 1896) 5-237A-176

William A. Smith 35 (Oct 1864-Ky/Ky/Ky-M 15)(Teamster), Roann 31 (Ap 1869-Ky/Ky/Ky-M 15-2-2), Annie B. 7 (Nov 1893-Ky), Esideth M. 3 (May 1897) 2-191B-19

William A. Smith 48 (Jan 1852-M 28), Eliza J. 46 (Dec 1853-M 28-9-8), Martha C. 20 (Jan 1880), Delia 15 (July 1884), Thos A. 14 (Dec 1885), Nula 10 (May 1890), Della J. 8 (Mar 1892), Minta 6 (May 1894) 3-202A-42/45

William B. Smith 71 (July 1829-T/NC/T-M 30)(Carpenter), Nancy A. 49 (June 1850-T/Va/Va-M 30-9-8), Laura B. 29 (May 1861), Nanny C. 25 (Mar 1875), Owney 15 (July 1884), Mattie 11 (July 1888), Clay 10 (Ap 1890), Maud HALL 20 (d)(Mar 1880-M 0-0), Gracy SMITH 5 (gs)(Mar 1894) 10-254A-78

Wilum D. Smith 37 (Nov 1892-M 7), Margett 30 (Oct 1893), Allice 3 (June 1896), Bryan 2 (Feb 1898), Richard 4/12 (Feb 1900) 1-184A-1-6/111

William R. Smith 28 (Oct 1871-M 6), Mary A. 20 (July 1879-M 6-2-2), John E. 4 (Sep 1895), James H. 1 (Nov 1898) 3-205A-85/92

William W. Smith 26 (Ap 1874-M 1), Mary I. 26 (Nov 1873-M 1-2-2), John E. 1 (Sep 1898), Dora A. 4/12 (Feb 1900), Thomas SUTTON 12 (Oct 1887)(Servant) 3-208A-143/156

MARRIAGES

A.L. Smith to Martha Rice, 10 July 1873 (same), W.R. Henry JP 1-#1287

Ab Smith to Annie Lively, 24 Feb 1900 (25 Feb), F.M. Cook MG, L.P. Smith W 3-128

Ada Smith to W. S. Hamilton q.v.

Addie Smith to Andy Sharp q.v.

Alice Smith to J. C. McClelland q.v.

Alice Smith to James Conners q.v.

Andy Smith (28, Murry Co) to L.V. Jenkins (22, Hawkins Co), 30 Ap 1883, I.W. Holt JP, M.G. Gibson & S.F. Gibson W 4-14(132)

Ann Smith to Hanibal Hurst q.v.

Annie Smith to Thompson I. Riddle q.v.

Arminda Smith to J. M. Riggs q.v.

Bailey Smith to Margaret Carter, 23 Nov 1887 (14 Nov), Calvin Morgan JP 1-542

Banister Smith to Elizabeth Travis, 29 Aug 1867 (same), R.T. Howard MG 1-#966

Banister C. Smith to Issabella C. Smith, 29 Nov 1867 (same), R.T. Howard MG 1-#982

Banister C. Smith to Sudia Barton, 27 Aug 1898 (same), D. Davis MG & W 2-318

Bessie L. Smith to Joseph R. Butler q.v.

Bettie Smith to Solomon Henry q.v.

C.D. Smith to H.C. Casey, 1 Jan 1853 (2 Jan), D. Broyles JP 1-#400

C.H. Smith to M.A. Crow, 1 Aug 1892, John Price MG 4-48

Charles T. Smith to Dealy S. Fisher, 11 Ap 1875 (12 Ap), A. Hann MG 1-#1410

Charley Smith to Nellie Long, 17 Dec 1893, J.M. Hinds MG 4-79

Clem Smith to Daniel Morgan q.v.

Coleman Smith to Margaret Dodson, 31 Dec 1857 (same), A.D. Paul JP 1-#626

Dartha Smith to P.P. Foust, 1 Sep 1856 (no return) 1-#569

E.C. Smith to M.S. Donahoe, 26 Mar 1887 (same), W.S. Hale MG 1-556

E.M. Smith to Margaret M. Denskin or Dunkin, 11 Aug 1869 (12 Aug), W.F. Buttram MG 1-#1099

E. J. Smith to Joel Dotson q.v.

Elijah Smith to E.B. Clifton, 7 Oct 1872 (6 Nov), J.P. Roddy MG 1-#1257

Eliza Smith to Charley King q.v.

Eliza Smith to William Neely q.v.

Eliza Smith to Howard Burdit q.v.

Eliza C. Smith to Samuel Henderson q.v.

Elizabeth Smith to Giles H. Ryan q.v.

Elizabeth Smith to John M. Brown q.v.

Elizabeth Jane Smith to P. Wyrick q.v.

F.C. Smith to Sarah Gaddis, 20 Aug 1898, no MG or JP, R.J. Killough W 2-311

F.F. Smith to Sarah Deatherage, 25 Oct 1884 (26 Oct), T.H. McPherson JP 1-469

Frances E. Smith to James A. Ivil q.v.

Franey Smith to James Schrimpshire q.v.

Frank Smith to Mattie Hampton, 30 Mar 1885 (same), W.A. Green JP 1-505

George Smith to Mariah McMillen, 18 Sep 1885 (19 Sep), J.P. Brown ?? 1-519
George Smith to Mary Ann Rhea, 22 Aug 1860 (23 Aug), T.H. McPherson JP 1-#723
George W. Smith to Susan McMullen, 27 Nov 1890, R.S. Mason JP 4-19
Gus Smith to Elvira Holloway, 23 Sep 1887 (25 Sep), B.F. Holloway JP 1-536
Gus L. Smith to Laura(?) L. Vandergriff, 2 June 1900 (3 June), A.P. Hayes JP, L.A. Smith W 3-160
H. A. Smith to S. A. Wilkey q.v.
H.F. Smith to S.M. Lankford, 2 July 1898, M.K. Fugate JP 4-94
H.S. Smith to Martha E. Fugate, 23 Dec 1887 (25 Dec), Taylor Russell JP 1-559
H.T. Smith to Tennie A. Krischban, 10 Mar 1900 (bond only), G.W. Johnson W 3-132
Harriet Smith to G. W. Atchley q.v.
Harris Smith to Amanda E. Marshall, 17 Mar 1888 (18 Mar), W.T. West M 1-542
Henry L. Smith to Addie Shelby, 18 Sep 1897, R.A. Dickson JP 4-98
Ida Smith to Jacob Henderson q.v.
Isabella Smith to Starling Smith q.v.
Issabella C. Smith to B. C. Smith q.v.
J.B. Smith to Ida M. Walker, 20 Oct 1897 (same), J.A. Whitner MG, R.L. Keith W 2-201
J.F. Smith to M.C. Owens, 6 Dec 1888 (9 Dec), D. Richardson MG 1-557
J.T. Smith to Byrney E. May, 24 Feb 1900 (same), W.L. Lillard JP, R.L. Keith W 3-124
Jackson Smith to Mary McMurry, 9 Jan 1858 (no return) 1-#627
Jackson A. Smith to Alfie Hicks, 23 Dec 1897 (same), G.W. Brewer MG, L.L. Woollen W 2-230
James Smith to Mattie Thompson, 27 Nov 1898, A.M. Broyles JP 4-96
James Smith to O.T. Ray, 31 Dec 1863 (same), no MG or JP 1-#816
James M. Smith to Nancy Porter, 1 Aug 1871 (same), A.J. Pritchett MG 1-#1202
James W. Smith to Margaret Burditt, 6 Oct 1876 (same), J. Waller MG 1-#1464
Jane Smith to William Brown q.v.
Jane Smith to Samuel Gravet q.v.
Jane Smith to V. L. Hurst q.v.
Jeff Smith to Alice McClendon, 18 July 1896 (same), H.B. Burdett MG, G.W. Smith W 2-46
John Smith to Henrietta Hill, 20 Sep 1888 (30 Aug), J.B. Phillips ?? 1-553
John Smith to L.A. Alexander, 5 Ap 1893, J.J. Krischbaum MG 4-53
John Smith to Martha Turner, 12 Sep 1896, L.E. Smith JP 4-96
John Smith to Mary Crawford, 12 July 1898 (16 July), W.R. Fugate JP, J.W. Varner(?) W 2-299 [bond crossed out]
John F. Smith to Nancy Ridley, 17 Aug 1889 (20 Aug), Eli Hays JP 1-586
John H. Smith to Sarah Jane Mathis, 19 Feb 1867 (same), A.P. Early MG 1-#937
John J. Smith to E. Beasly, 12 July 1872 (no return) 1-#1242
John J. Smith to Mary E. Grice, 22 Jan 1881 (same), J.A. Shaver MG 1-298
John P. Smith to Mariah Moore, 17 July 1861 (same), A.W. Frazier JP 1-#756
John T. Smith to Mary A. Foust, 20 July 1869 (same), James Carson MG 1-#1094
Jonas Smith to Jennie Atkenson, 3 Sep 1899, R.A. Dickson JP 4-101
L.A. Smith to Sarah Brewer, 20 Sep 1879 (same), J.M. Bramlett MG 1-#1676
L.A. Smith to Rhoda Walker, 23 Sep 1899 (bond only), no MG or JP 3-39
L.E. Smith (28) to Viney Mitchell (19), 20 Nov 1881, J.M. Bramlett MG, Joseph Dagley & Joseph Godbehere W 4-4(34)
L. J. Smith to T. N. L. Cunnyngham q.v.
L.S.H. Smith to Hannah Miller, 18 July 1873 (same), Allen L. King MG 1-#1288
Laeond Smith to Calvin Lenoir q.v.
Lezzie Smith to J. M. McCabe q.v.
Lennie Smith to W. S. Hamilton q.v.
Lilly Smith to Henry Bankston q.v.
Lizzie Smith to John Goins q.v.
Lona L. Smith to C. H. Humphreys q.v.
Louella Smith to J. W. Selvidge q.v.
Louisa Smith to William H. Rector q.v.
Lui Smith to William N. Smith q.v.
Luther Smith to Leander Gillespie, 11 Oct 1887 (13 Oct), C. Gillespie ?? 1-535
Luther Smith to Mollie Locke, 4 Sep 1892, R.A. Dickson JP 4-51
Lutitia Smith to Frank Young q.v.
Lyna A. Smith to Richard Revis q.v.
M.C. Smith (21) to Martha Ryan (16), 21 Dec 1881, A.J. Pritchett MG, B.C. Cofer & W. Smith W 4-6(56)
M.D. Smith to Minnie Gilbreth, 22 Jan 1889 (6 Feb), J.J. Robinett MG 1-565
M. G. Smith to J. F. Vandergriff q.v.
M. L. Smith to S. S. Harris q.v.
Malissa Smith to H. E. Rogers q.v.
Malissa E. Smith to A. J. Perry q.v.
Maggie Smith to James F. Dunlap q.v.
Maggie Smith to Charley B. Rudd q.v.
Malissa Smith to John W. Porter q.v.
Mandie or Maudie Smith to Dalt Hall q.v.
Mariah Smith to John T. Prater q.v.
Martha Smith to Joseph Campbell q.v.
Margaret A. Smith to M. L. Loftis q.v.
Marthy E. Smith to John E. Hurst q.v.
Mary Smith to James Yancy q.v.
Mary Smith to Robert T. Cooper q.v.
Mary Smith to Robert Flevopin q.v.
Mary Ann Smith to Vanburen Copeline q.v.
Mary C. Smith to James H. Mariott q.v.
Mary D. Smith to G. O. Cates q.v.
Mary E. Smith to R. M. Hartbarger q.v.
Mary E. Smith to J. C. Phillips q.v.
Mary E. Smith to Charley Gorden q.v.
Mary F. Smith to John E. White q.v.
Mary F. Smith to Walter Lyles q.v.
Mary L. Smith to Howard B. Birdett q.v.
Mary M. Smith to Canada Hurst q.v.
Mattie Bell Smith to William Jones q.v.
Mattie M. Smith to James Young q.v.
Maud Smith to M. E. D. Coffer q.v.

Minnie A. Smith to R. L. Armor q.v.
Miriah Smith to John Cranmore q.v.
Mollie Smith to Andrew Caloway q.v.
Mollie Smith to Thomas Smith q.v.
Munroe Smith to Hattie Jones, 9 Dec 1899 (10 Dec), G.T. Mussington MG, L.M. Brown W 3-83
N. J. Smith to James Massey q.v.
Nancy Jane Smith to Lewis Fugate q.v.
Olli Smith to Rena Doran, 12 Mar 1898 (13 Mar), W.S. Hale MG, L.A. Smith W 2-257
Onis Smith to James Phillips q.v.
Powell Smith to Sallie Turner, 26 Sep 1885 (same), W.S. Hale MG 1-500
Prescilla Smith to J. M. Hoss or Haze q.v.
Robert Smith to Susan Dawson, 6 Nov 1864 (9 Nov), W.W. Low JP 1-#1077
Rudy H. Smith to Sallie Mathis, 4 June 1898 (5 June), W.S. Hale MG, J.W. Smith W 2-289
S.H. Smith to Emma Beard, 1 Dec 1895, L.E. Smith JP 4-89
S. M. Smith to N. B. Foust q.v.
Samuel W. Smith to Ollie Baine, 24 June 1899 (25 June), A.P. Hayes JP, J.H. Burwick W 3-3
Sarah Smith to Sam Jones q.v.
Sarah Smith to C. G. Murphy q.v.
Sarah Smith to James Denton q.v.
Sarah A. Smith to Thomas J. Barger q.v.
Starling Smith to Issabella Smith, 12 May 1860 (15 May), A.W. Frazier JP 1-#711
Susan Smith to John H. Miller q.v.
Susan Smith to Robert Marshall q.v. (B)
T.H. Smith to Amanda Curtis, 20 July 1886 (22 July), J.Q. Shaver MG 1-502
Thomas Smith to Mollie Smith, 13 Nov 1900, R.A. Dickson JP 4-106
Thomas Smith to Lucy Hurst, 24 Oct 1871 (same), A.J. Pritchett MG 1-#1213
Thomas J. Smith to Edna Johnson, 25 Nov 1892, G.G. Swann MG 4-73
Turner Smith to Sarah Bennet, 18 Oct 1882 (20 Oct), J.W. Thompson MG 1-473
Turner P. Smith to Mary A. Scroggins, 16 Ap 1886 (17 Ap), T.H. McPherson JP 1-487
V. C. Smith to J. B. Brady q.v.
W.A. Smith to Lottie J. Minick, 26 May 1877 (27 May), J.M. Bramlett MG 1-#1500
W.J. Smith to Celia Mathis, 11 Mar 1880 (same), G.H. Ryan JP 1-#1722
W.J. Smith to Lena Walker, 5 Ap 1894, W.S. Hale MG 4-68
W.J. Smith to Lillie A. Stinett, 21 Sep 1900 (same), H.B. Burdett MG, W.N. Smith W 3-222
W.R. Smith to M.A. Hurst, 12 Mar 1894, J.M. Hill JP 4-64
W.T. Smith to Mary E. Davis, no date, probably June 1892, J.R. Clark MG 4-38
W.W. Smith to Bell Fugate, 23 Dec 1897 (same), W.K. Fugate JP 2-235
Will Smith to Lynda Lefew, 22 Mar 1892, W.M. Morgan JP 4-39
William Smith to Maggie Garrison, 25 Nov 1892, James Johnson MG 4-48
William Smith to Phebe Snyder, 17 Dec 1892, J.F. Hash MG 4-47
William Smith to Susan Woods, 18 May 1852 (same), G.A. Goins MG 1-#380
William Smith to Malissa A. Kelly, 28 Jan 1868 (same), John M. Kelly MG 1-#1000
William Smith to Lorina Blevins, 12 May 1892, M.S. Holloway JP 4-74
William Smith to Susanah Cates, 16 Jan 1860 (18 Jan), Thos Knight JP 1-#7-7
William Smith to Eveline Mathis, 20 Sep 1884 (same), C.T. Houts MG 1-480
William C. Smith to Nancy S. Lawhorn, 26 Feb 1889 (same), S.W. Tindell ?? 1-565 & 1-566
William D. Smith to Susan E. Singleton, 21 May 1865 (21 May 1864)[sic], J.L. Brown JP 1-#831
William H. Smith to Susan McAlpine, 16 Aug 1873 (17 Aug), J. Howard MG 1-#1296
William N. Smith to Lui Smith, 19 Jan 1878 (same), A.J. Pritchett MG 1-#1663
William R. Smith to Susan A. Grice, 6 Aug 1878 (7 Aug), J.A. Shane(?) JP 1-#1573
William S. Smith to Elizabeth Bandy, 14 Feb 1856 (same), R.T. Howard MG 1-#534
Willis Smith to Martha Webb, 26 Nov 1885 (same), A.J. Pritchett MG 1-514
Willis Smith to Susan Sneed, 16 Feb 1899 (17 Feb), J.M. Bramlett MG, R.J. Killough W 2-383

SMITHERS / SMUTHERS / SMOTHERS

1880 CENSUS
Charlie Smothers 28 (Mu): see Jere Wasson
MARRIAGES
Charley Smuthers (26) to Sallie Ryan (22), 8 Feb 1883, Thompson Ashburn MG, Oliver Lyon & Lawson Rhea W 4-15(141) (B)
Jack Smithers to Lizie Lewis, 23 Feb 1889 (23 Mar), S.W. Wych ?? 1-584

SMITTY

1860 CENSUS
James Smitty 18: see James Rhea

SNEED

1870 CENSUS
Robert Sneed 52 (Blacksmith), Adaline 22, Thomas 18, John 16, George 10, William S. 7, Andrea J. 6, Robert 3, Samuel H. 1 6-2-7
1880 CENSUS
Bob Sneed 27, S.A. 22 (w), C.A. 6 (d), H.D. 5 (d), M.E. 2 (d) 4-35-289
Robert Sneed 62 (Blacksmith), Eda A. 48 (w), Andrew J. 16, William S. 17, Robert D. 13, Samuel H. 11, Manda A. 10, James R. 8, Susanaker 5, Jerry D. 3, Rachel J.B. 2/12, George W. 19 5-6-46
Thomas Sneed 24, R. 20 (w), John 1 (s), Burl RUDD 46 (Hired Man) 3-15-116

Z.T. Sneed 34, Martha A. 37, Lettie C.V. 18, Sarah L. 16, John Anner J. 12 (d), James H. 10, Robert S.L. 9, Zachariah T. 6, Mat H. 5, Andrew A.M. 2 6-15-140/142; John RIGGLE 92 (f)("living with us"), Faribee 67 (w) 6-15-141/142

1900 CENSUS

Andy J. Sneed 35 (Nov 1864-M 8), Hannah J. 32 (Oct 1867-M 8-5-4), William H. 7 (Oct 1892), Lucy A. 5 (Sep 1894), Ernest E. 3 (Sep 1896), Wilson A. 1 (Dec 1898) 6-240A-7

Eda A. Sneed 54 (Feb 1846-T/SC/SC-Wd 12-12), Jeremiah M. 21 (Sep 1878), Nasha F. 15 (Dec 1884), Pink A. 13 (May 1887), Joseph B. 11 (May 1889) 5-235A-144

James B. Sneed 55 (July 1844-M 26), Susan R. 42 (July 1857-T/T/Ga-M 26-11-9), Hanna D. 24 (Nov 1875) (Flour Mill Hand), Emma G. 19 (Sep 1880), William J. 18 (Mar 1882)(Telegraph Message Boy), Daisey 14 (Oct 1885), Floyd T. 9 (Aug 1890), Lillie M. 7 (Feb 1893), Freddie G. 1 (Nov 1898) 10-324B-96/100

Richard Sneed 28 (Feb 1872-M 8), Martha A. 26 (Jan 1874-M 8-2-2), William N. 5 (May 1895), Robert J. 2 (Jan 1898), William S. 34 (b)(July 1865-Wd), George R. 8 (nw)(Aug 1891) 6-242A-48

Samuel H. Sneed 34 (Sep 1865-M 1), Callie 26 (Feb 1874-M 1-0) 6-244B-92

William S. Sneed 34, George R. 8: see Richard Sneed

MARRIAGES

A.J. Sneed to Annie Hicks, 28 Dec 1890, J.L. Brison(?) JP 4-22

Amanda Sneed to J. D. Pritchett q.v.

Annie Sneed to B. F. Moore q.v.

E. J. Sneed to S. D. Rudd q.v.

Ella Sneed to Oscar G. Lewis q.v.

J.R. Sneed to Susan Webb, 22 Mar 1873 (23 Mar), A.J. Pritchett MG 1-#1281

Jim Sneed to Nancy Housley(?), 8 Dec 1888 (9 Dec), Jesse P. Thompson JP 1-554

R.D. Sneed to Margaret J. Parker, 15 Sep 1888 (16 Sep), W.G. Curton MG 1-561

Richard Sneed to Mattie Curtain, 6 Mar 1892, J.R. Clark MG 4-42

Samuel H. Sneed to Caldonia Henderson, 30 Sep 1898 (2 Oct), J.M. Bramlett MG, W.F. Sneed W 2-328

Susan Sneed to Willis Smith q.v.

T.J. Sneed to Eliza J. Hensley, 9 Oct 1890, H. Burdett MG 4-81

Thomas Sneed to Rebecca M. Rudd, 5 June 1875 (6 June), J. Waller MG 1-#1400

W.S. Sneed to Callie Walker, 2 Nov 1890, W.G. Curton MG 4-22

- - - - - - - - - - - - -

SNELLING / SNELLINGS

1900 CENSUS

James Snellings 61: see Salie(?) Gillespie (B)

William Snelling 16, James 50: see Josie Smith (B)

- - - - - - - - - - - - -

SNELSON

1860 CENSUS

William Snelson 55, John R. MYNATT 25, Susannah 27, James B. 2, Preston MYNATT 21 2-70-480

1870 CENSUS– None

1880 CENSUS

William Snelson 84 1-15-125

- - - - - - - - - - - - -

SNODGRASS

1860 CENSUS

Elijah Snodgrass 25: see Osker Cook

MARRIAGE

M. M. Snodgrass to W. B. Goad q.v.

- - - - - - - - - - - - -

SNOW

1860 CENSUS

James Snow 25 (Blacksmith), Manerva 27, Albert 7, Martha 4 6-111-757

Plesant Snow 35, Nancy 32 (NC), Charlotte 11, Marion 10, Samuel 8, Margaret 6, Elizabeth 5, James 2, Sarah 1 8-24-164

1870 CENSUS

Pleasant H. Snow 45 (Wagonright), Nancy C. 42, Charlotte 21, Francis M. 20, Margarette E. 16, Elizabeth 14, James 12, Sarah J. 10, William R. 7, Mary A. 5, Pleasant H. Jr. 2, Rachel E. 2/12 8-1-3

1880 CENSUS

Pleasant Snow 50, Nancy 53, C. 32 (d), Marion 30 (s), Margaret 21, James 23, Sarah 21, W.L. 17 (s), M.A. 15 (d), P.H. 12 (s), R.E. 10 (d) 11-38-312

1900 CENSUS

Sarah J. Snow 40 (Dec 1859-NC)(Hotel Keeper), Rachel E. 29 (si)(Ap 1871-T/T/NC); *Boarders:* Earnest MEDLEY 19 (June 1880-T/NC/T)(Mine Laborer), Joseph A. MEDLEY 22 (Mar 1878-T/T/NC), John EVENS 28 (Sep 1871-SC/SC/SC) 11-292B-65

MARRIAGES

F.M. Snow to S.C. Bean, 14 July 1884 (20 July), S.F. Hale MG 1-491

James Snow to Bettie Mosley, 20 Oct 1886

Lizzy Snow to James J. Mathes q.v.

Maggie Snow to G. R. Locke q.v.

Mary Snow to George W. Morgan q.v.

Mrs. S. C. Snow [nee Bean] to W. A. Anderson q.v.

P. J. Snow or Senow to H. O. Oliver q.v.

William R.L. Snow to Mattie McCormick, 11 Jan 1891

- - - - - - - - - - - - -

SNOWDEN

1900 CENSUS

Jennie(?) Snowden 38 (June 1861-NC/NC/NC-Wd 4-4) (Washwoman), Ernest 16 (Jan 1884)(Station Boiler Fireman), Jesse 13 (June 1886), Dixon 11 (Mar 1889) 8-311A-6/6

John Snowden Unk (Unk-Wd)[written in pencil, very dim] 8-314A-73/76

MARRIAGE

Cora A. Snowden to Henry J. Price q.v.

- - - - - - - - - - - - -

SNYDER / SNIDER

1870 CENSUS

William M. Snider 18: see Nicholas G. Moore

1880 CENSUS– None

1900 CENSUS

Charles M.(?) Snyder 39 (May 1861-Ind/Ind/Ind-M 4)(Tel Lineman), Elizabeth 27 (Mar 1873-Ky/Ky/Ky-M 4-0) 10-322A-41/43

Jackson Snyder 23 (Dec 1876)(Coal Miner), Caroline L. 67 (m)(July 1832-Wd 3-2), Callie 19 (si)(Ap 1887) 13-304B-273/283

James M. Snyder 53 (Dec 1849-M 28), Mary E. 49 (Feb 1851-M 28-13-11), Tinnie 20 (Sep 1879), Mary M. 19 (June 1881), George W. 16 (July 1883), William H. 16 (Jan 1884), John A. 15 (Feb 1885), Celia D. 13 (Sep 1886), James S. 11 (June 1889), Luther M. 9 (Dec 1890) 3-205B-103/112
[James M. married Mary E. Martin]

Mattie Snyder 22: see Sarah M. Gaines

William M. Snyder 48 (Aug 1851-M 4)(Dentist), Olive F. 25 (July 1874-M 4-0), Garland 21 (Dec 1878)(RR Brakeman) 14-216B-73/74

MARRIAGES

Andrew Snyder to Lou Schill, 16 Aug 1892, R.S. Mason JP 4-41

I. B. Snyder to Mitchell Sorrells q.v.

Lizzie Snyder to Oddie Blink q.v.

Lucy Snyder or Sydneys to Holliday Russell q.v.

Phebe Snyder to William Smith q.v.

- - - - - - - - - - - - -

SOLOMON

1900 CENSUS

Thomas M. Solomon 49 (July 1850-M 18), Mary E. 46 (Sep 1853-M 18-5-3), Mary P. 16 (Aug 1883), Annie B. 13 (Aug 1886), Lora E. 12 (Dec 1887), Charles B. 9 (Oct 1890), Thomas O. 7 (Aug 1892) 11-291A-26

MARRIAGE

T.M. Solomon (31, Meigs Co) to Mary Elizabeth Morgan (28), 1 Sep 1881, J.A. Nicholson MG, John K. Brown (Meigs Co), A. Johnson, & James A. Rose (Bledsoe Co) W 4-2(12)

- - - - - - - - - - - - -

SORRELS / SORRELLS

1900 CENSUS

Andrew M. Sorrels 30 (Dec 1869-NC/NC/NC-M 5), Ibbie 24 (Dec 1875-M 5-2-2), James E. 5 (July 1894), William A. 1 (Jan 1899) 3-205A-94/102

MARRIAGE

Mary Sorrel to Harrison Winley q.v.

Mitchell Sorrells to I.B. Snyder, 18 Aug 1894, J.M. Hill JP 4-75

- - - - - - - - - - - - -

SOWARD / SOWERS

1900 CENSUS

John Sowers 27, Rena 16: see Chris Hood

John Soward 27: see Thomas F. Shaver

MARRIAGES

Elizabeth Soward(?) to James Yoder q.v.

John Soward to Renor Hughes, 13 June 1900 (same), J.T. Shaver MG, J.B. Corvin W 3-166

William Soward to Samantha A. Cranmore, 7 June 1894, W.S. Hale MG 4-66

William J. Soward(?) to Elizabeth Shadwick, 28 July 1886 (29 July), W.S. Hale MG 1-502

- - - - - - - - - - - - -

SPANGLER / SPANIER

1900 CENSUS

James L. Spangler 41 (June 1858-M 21), Nancy E. 40 (May 1860-M 21-12-10), Frankie A. 16 (Mar 1884), William H. 14 (Jan 1886), Emily J. 12 (Feb 1888), Lillie A. 9 (July 1890), Italy M. 8 (Ap 1892), Ader E. 6 (Ap 1894), Charles O. 4 (Jan 1896), Ella L. 2 (Feb 1898), infant 1/12 (Ap 1900), infant 1/12 (Ap 1900) 13-295A-99/101

MARRIAGE

W.H. Spanier [license] or Spurrin [index] to Alice M. Jones, 27 Dec 1886 (28 Dec), C. Morgan JP 1-514

- - - - - - - - - - - - -

SPARKS

1900 CENSUS

Allen Sparks 46 (Oct 1853-Ky/Ky/Ky-M 5), Sarah F. 26 (Mar 1874-M 5-2-2), Edith E. 14 (Sep 1885-Ky), Coleman S. 10 (June 1889), Judson C. 4 (Jan 1896), Walter T. 2 (Feb 1898), Elizabeth 62 (a)(Dec 1837-Ky/Ky/Ky-S) 11-291B-42

Charles A. Sparks 28 (Mar 1872-Ky/Ky/Oh-M 8), Margaret J. 27 (June 1872-M 8-4-4), Lora A. 7 (June 1892), Letha E. 6 (Ap 1894), Lucius I. 4 (Feb 1896), Loy O. 2 (Dec 1897) 13-307B-333/345

Everett C. Sparks 21 (Dec 1878-Ky/Ky/Oh-M 4)(Coal Miner), Hattie A. 18 (Mar 1881-M 4-2-2), Fred C. 3 (May 1897), Velma M. 11/12 (June 1899) 13-307A-331/343

MARRIAGES

A.S. Sparks to Sarah F. Edmondson, 3 Ap 1895, Jas M. Mannin MG 4-81

C.A. Sparks to M.J. Harwood, 26 Aug 1891, C.E. Mowrey JP 4-32

Everett Sparks to Hattie Owens, 23 May 1896 (24 May), F.M. Bandy MG, J.M. Kelley W 2-24

Hade or Haile Sparks to Letha Card, 28 Mar 1896 (29 Mar), W.R. Grimsley MG, John R. Brown W 2-8

- - - - - - - - - - - - -

SPEARS

1880 CENSUS

John Spears 59, Deseth 46, Samuel 21, Martha 19, Adline 2 8-16-133

MARRIAGE
Brown Spears to Adelia Gass, 27 Dec 1879 (28 Dec), F.J. Paine JP 1-#1696

- - - - - - - - - - - - -

SPENCE

1860 CENSUS
James Spence 39 (NC), Mahala 48, Mary A. 11, Albion 8 7-5-34
Stephen Spence 59 (NC), Martha 58 (NC), Benjamin F. 20, George M.D. 16 7-4-23
Stephen Spence 28: see John L. Ramsey
1870 CENSUS
James Spence 50 (NC), Mahala 60, Eliza WILSON 5, Albion SPENCE 18, Susan Woods SPENCE(?) 6 7-6-49
Stephen Spence 69 (NC), Mary A. 49, Albert DUNWOODY (B) 22, Easter CHATTIN (B) 16 7-3-23
1880 CENSUS
Albie Spence 28, Hattie 22, Locke 4/12 (d) 7-27-231
G.M.D. Spence 35, M.J. 39, J.S. 13 (s), G.F. 11 (s), Mollie 9, M.I. 6 (d), James 3, William 8/12 7-25-220
James Spence 61, Ma Kal 70 (w) 7-27-232
Stephen Spence 79, M.A. 60 (w) 7-26-221
1900 CENSUS
Albia Spence 48 (Aug 1851-M 22), Hattie 41 (May 1859-M 22-8-7), James L. 18 (Feb 1882), Wales 15 (Nov 1884), Marel 12 (Mar 1888), Emma 5 (Sep 1894) 7-267A-322/327
James Spence 21, Anna L. 22: see Charles W. Todd
Malinda Spence 81 (Ap 1809-Wd 1-1)(Landlady), Luckey 20 (gd)(Feb 1880), Addr R. 13 (gs)(Oct 1886), Kattie 8 (gd)(Nov 1891) 7-267A-323/328
MARRIAGES
Albert N. Spence to Adaline Abels, 24 Sep 1855 (same), W.C.(?) Hollins JP 1-#522
Albion Spence to Harriett A. Eldridge, 8 Oct 1877 (9 Oct), R.E. Smith MG 1-#1525
G.F. Spence to Nora Benson, 15 Jan 1895, J.A. Whitner MG 4-73
George M. Spence to Matty Foust, 15 Jan 1866 (17 Jan), John Whaley MG 1-#883
James R. Spence to Annie Lee Todd, 13 June 1897 (same), R.C. Knight JP & W 2-150
Jane Spence to Edward Roddy q.v.
Mary Ann Spence to Richard Knight q.v.
Mollie Spence to J. D. Hardin q.v.
Myra Ann Spence to James A. Cash q.v.
Oliver M. Spence to T.L. Kincannon, 30 Jan 1884 (3 Feb), J.H. Marrs ?? 1-484
Sarah Spence to William G. B. Purcer q.v.
Stephen Spence to Mary Ann Hankins or Hawkins, 15 June 1867 (23 June), T.N.L. Cunnyngham JP 1-#954

- - - - - - - - - - - - -

SPENCER

MARRIAGES
John S. Spencer to Isie(?) Grice, 3 Dec 1888 (4 Dec), Jas or Jno R. Walker MG 1-556
Julia Spencer to John Wilson q.v.

- - - - - - - - - - - - -

SPILLER

1900 CENSUS
Manie Spiller 25 (May 1875-T/Va/T-M 3), Aevy 22 (Aug 1877-M 3-2-2), Gertrude 4 (Jan 1896), Albertie 1 (Oct 1898) 10-256A-117/121 (B)
MARRIAGE
Munroe Spiller to Ivey Hughes, 6 Nov 1896 (same), J.B. Phillips MG, J.P.H. Davis W 2-81

- - - - - - - - - - - - -

SPISER

MARRIAGE
J.M. Spiser to Annie E. Hail, 31 Dec 1887, Jas Corvin MG 4-45

- - - - - - - - - - - - -

SPIVEY

1900 CENSUS
George W. Spivey 55 (Nov 1844-T/Va/T-M 6), Carrie E. 30 (Dec 1869-M 6-3-3), Claud E. 5 (Oct 1894), James C. 4 (Ap 1896), Warren 1 (May 1899) 13-298A-154/157
Holliday Spivey 28 (Sep 1871-M 7), Louella 24 (Sep 1875-M 7-4-4), John L. 6 (Nov 1893), Rosa Lee 5 (Mar 1895), Paul 3 (Oct 1896), Marie 1 (Aug 1898), Sally GOOD 16 (July 1883)(Servant) 13-298B-159/162 [G.H. Spivey married Luella Gamble on 12 Oct 1892 in Meigs County]
MARRIAGE
George W. Spivey to Carrie E. Story, 22 Jan 1894, A.C. Peters MG 4-71

- - - - - - - - - - - - -

SPRADLING

1870 CENSUS
Martin Spradling 19: see B. R. McDonald

- - - - - - - - - - - - -

SPRING / SPRINGS

1900 CENSUS
Abner Spring 45 (Unk 1853-M 20), Allie 50 (Unk 1850-M 20-10-10), Charles 20 (Unk 1880), Lettie 19 (1881), Ruthy 17 (1883)(Coal Miner), Bird 15 (1885)(Coal Miner), Margaret 12 (1888), Fred 9 (1891), Milden 5 (1895), Lucilley 1 (1899) 15-274A-114 (B)
Charles Springs 21: see Henry Angel (B)
Ethel Spring 12 (B): see Brown Swafford
Goldie Springs 35 (Unk 1865), Martha 60 (sil)(Feb 1840-T/Ga/T-Wd 5-3), Martha 34 (ne)(May 1866-M 15-6-5), Cave 12 (nw)(June 1887), Charles 8 (nw)(Oct 1891), Emma 6 (ne)(Jan 1894), Hallie 4 (ne)(Nov 1895), John L. 1 (nw)(Nov 1899) 13-299A-173/177 (B)
Ida Springs 3/12: see Roscoe Bennett (B)
Reace Springs 13, Mandie 11: see W. Mathew Hix (B)
Reese Springs 14 (Nov 1885), Maud 10 (si)(Feb 1890) 10-331B-249/264 (B)

MARRIAGE
William H. Spring to Anna Mary Byerley, 25 Dec 1893, Will Leroy Patton MG 4-61

- - - - - - - - - - - - -

SPYATT

1880 CENSUS
Eliza Spyatt(?) 54: see T. P. Cambron

- - - - - - - - - - - - -

STACHILD

1900 CENSUS
Floyd E. Stachild 37 (Aug 1862-Oh/NY/NY-M 11)(Saw Mill Sawyer), Annie M. 32 (Nov 1867-Ind/Oh/Ind-M 11-2-2), Minnie E. 10 (Nov 1889), Rosa S. 6 (July 1893) 2-191B-17/17

- - - - - - - - - - - - -

STALLINGS

1900 CENSUS
Margaret L. Stallings 48 (Aug 1851-T/NC/T-Wd 2-2), Mary 27 (Ap 1873-Ala/T/T) (Milliner), Joseph 20 (Mar 1880) 10-323B-76/80
MARRIAGE
James H. Stallings to Lucinda Shannon, 14 Sep 1886 (same), I.W. Holt JP 1-509

- - - - - - - - - - - - -

STANDIFER

1880 CENSUS
A.J. Standifer 52, Mary 48, S.A. 15 (d), E.D. 11 (d), G.W. 19 (s), Maggie 18 (dl), A.F. 1 (gs) 8-8-65
MARRIAGES
Frances Standifer to Thomas Long q.v.
G.W. Standifer to Margaret Harelston, 27 Dec 1877 (30 Dec), A.J. Mathis MG 1-#1538
Lucy Standifer to Taylor Jones q.v.
Mary Standifer to Berryman Mathis q.v.
Samuel Standifer to Annie Hughes, 5 Mar 1889 (6 Mar), L.M. Morris ?? 1-568

- - - - - - - - - - - - -

STANFIELD / STANDIELD

1860 CENSUS
George M. Stanfield 23, Evaline 17 1-87-597
Minerva Stanfield 8, Thursey E. 4: see Howard Montgomery
1870 CENSUS
Minerva Stanfield 18, Thursday E. 14: see Thomas H. Montgomery
1880 CENSUS– None
1900 CENSUS
Nancy L. Stanfield 58 (July 1841-T/Va/T-Wd 5-4) 8-314A-68/71
MARRIAGES
H.W. Stanfield to L.V. Hutchinson, 6 Jan 1886 (7 Jan), J.Q. Shaver MG 1-500
Susan Standfield to T. H. Montgomery q.v.
Susie Standfield or Cranfield to Lee Price q.v.
T. E. Stanfield to George Burchard q.v.

- - - - - - - - - - - - -

STANLY / STANLEY

1860 CENSUS
John Stanly 29, Nancy A. 20, Plesant 4 8-12-77
1870 and 1880 CENSUS– None
1900 CENSUS
Mary Stanley 56 (May 1844-Wd 4-3), John 21 (June 1878), Stanton 19 (Nov 1880), Susan 17 (Jan 1883), William C. FRALEY 39 (b)(May 1861) 15-269A-23
MARRIAGES
Elizabeth Stanley to Martin Ives q.v.
John Stanley to Edna Sexton, 18 Sep 1900 (21 Sep), W.W. Cranmore MG, J.Y. Spangler W 3-221
Molly Stanley to Charles Whitaker q.v.
Pleasant Stanley to Tennessee Corvin, 21 Aug 1878 (22 Aug), W.A. Green JP 1-#1577
Polly Ann Stanly to George Ives q.v.
W.R. Stanly to M.M. Harrel, 19 Feb 1888, James Howe MG 4-45

- - - - - - - - - - - - -

STANSBERRY / STANSBURY

1880 CENSUS
Luke Stansbury 46 (Brickmason), Margaret 35, Andrew 12 or 22, Reece 20 (Brickmason), James 10, Ida 8, William 6, Sarah 1, Darthula FINE 16 (Servant, Cook etc.) 2-39-323
1900 CENSUS
James Stansbury 40 (May 1860-M 24), Mary 39 (Oct 1860-SC/SC/SC-M 24-7-6), John 20 (Dec 1879-Ga)(Coal Miner), Earl 16 (Mar 1884-Ga)(Coal Miner), Fred 10 (Ap 1890-Ga), Robert 7 (Feb 1893-Ga), Jennie 3 (Dec 1896), Cane 23 (s)(Feb 1877-Ala-M 0)(Coal Miner), Yota 19 (dl)(Sep 1880-Ga/T/SC-M 0-0) 8-285A-328/330
John D. Stansberry 38 (Jan 1862-T/T/SC-M 10)(Quarry Foreman), Mattie 36 (May 1864-T/T/NC-M 10-7-6), Willie 10 (Nov 1889), Arva 8 (Jan 1892), James 7 (Ap 1893), Morgan 4 (Aug 1895), Clifford 2 (June 1897), Walter 1 (Dec 1898) 8-281A-246/248
MARRIAGE
J.D. Stansberry to Mattie Morgan, 30 Nov 1889 (same), W.M. Morgan JP 1-585

- - - - - - - - - - - - -

STANTON

1900 CENSUS
George W. Stanton 38 (Ap 1862-M 16)(Physician), Louisa E. 34 (Nov 1866-T/T/Ala-M 16-8-6), William G. 13 (Nov 1886), Nelley J. 8 (Sep 1891), John D. 7 (Jan 1893), Charles L. 5 (Feb 1895), Mary T. 3 (Aug 1896), Arther A. 6/12 (Dec 1899) 2-191A-2/2

- - - - - - - - - - - - -

STAPLES / STAPLEY

1900 CENSUS
Dean Staples 19: see Viola Leigh (B)
Harriet A. Stapley 70: see Jack Lee (B)
MARRIAGE
Tama or Tanna Staples to L. Lane q.v.

- - - - - - - - - - - - -

STARRING / STARING

1900 CENSUS
Lew Staring 27 (Aug 1872-NY/NY/NY-M 1), Lucindy 23 (Ap 1877-M 1-1-1), Ralph 3/12 (Mar 1900) 12-180B-43/46
MARRIAGE
Lewis M. Starring to Lucinda R. Stebbins, 6 Sep 1899, Thos J. Miles ?? 4-100

- - - - - - - - - - - - -

STEEDMAN

MARRIAGE
Nathan Steedman to Adelia E. Morgan, 31 Dec 1890, J.R. Walker MG 4-24

- - - - - - - - - - - - -

STEEL / STEELE / STEAL

1860 CENSUS
Nancy Steele 45, Nancy 24, James 21, Susan 18, Samuel 14, William 12, Isaac 9, Bird 3 8-10-66
1870 CENSUS
William A. Steele 53 (Va)(House Carpenter), Mary 49, William 21, John 17, Jane 13, Louvenia 11 8-14-96
1880 CENSUS
John N. Steele 25, Lucey A. 28, John H. 1/12 5-11-99
W.A. Steel 60, M.T 58, M.E. 19 (d) 8-20-170
1900 CENSUS
John Steel 18: see Sam Ellis
Polly Steele 79: see Joseph B. Corvin
MARRIAGES
Jane T. Steel to James M. Dobbs q.v.
John N. Steel to Loucy Ann Scott, 5 July 1879 (no return) 1-#1619
Lavinia Steel to George W. Walker q.v.
Martha Lavina Steel to Joseph B. Corvin q.v.
Mary F. Steel to Eli Corvin q.v.
Nancy E. Steele to Woodson A. Walker q.v.

- - - - - - - - - - - - -

STEGALL

1870 CENSUS
William Stegall 27 (Ala), Mary Jane 24, Allace 5, Minnie A. 3, John P.N. 5/12 2-7-49
MARRIAGES
Lula Stegall to D. B. Jackson q.v.
William A. Stegall to Mary J. McChristian, 8 Sep 1863 (no return) 1-#807

- - - - - - - - - - - - -

STENIS

1880 CENSUS
J.D. Stenis 36, E.O.(?) 38, W.F. 8 (s), N.P. 3 (d), J.A. 1 (s) 3-14-112

- - - - - - - - - - - - -

STENSON

1900 CENSUS
Foster Stenson 24: see Maggie Roddy

- - - - - - - - - - - - -

STEPHENS / STEVENS

1860 CENSUS
Isaac Stephens 52, Polly 30, William 8, Nancy J. 5, Josiah A. 2 8-25-172
Sarah Stephens 62: see Samuel Pearson
1870 CENSUS
Rebecca Stephens 25: see William G. Willson
1880 CENSUS
Caroline Stevens 42: see James Drake
1900 CENSUS
Fawn Stevens 6: see Will Payne (B)
Henry Stevens 38 (Jan 1862-M 16), Lydia 33 (Mar 1877-M 16-5-3), Bradford 15 (Dec 1884), Lillie M. 12 (Aug 1887), Arnold 4 (Aug 1896) 8-285A-330/332 (B)
John Stephens Unk (RR Laborer), Ina Unk 4-215B-54/55 (B)
John A. Stephens 29 (June 1870-M 0)(RR Laborer), Ida 23 (May 1877-M 0-0) 14-214B-25/26 (B)
Lawrence Stevens 28: see John Cates (B)
Margarett Stevens 66: see James B. Blevins
William Stephens 51 (Sep 1848-T/T/Va)(School Teacher), Sallie E. 44 (Mar 1856-M 27-6-3), Mark 18 (Nov 1881), Carrie 12 (Jan 1888), Thomas 10 (Sep 1889) 8-314A-65/68 [Wm E. married Sarah Elizabeth Swaford in 23 Dec 1873]
William Stephens 27 (May 1873-M 1), Partheni 22 (1878-M 1) 3-202B-56/59 (B)
William S. Stephens 51 (Feb 1849-M 22), Eller 47 (Dec 1853-M 22-5-5), Walter L. 20 (July 1879), Mark M. 19 (Mar 1881), Poselee 17 (Mar 1883), Dolal A. 15 (Nov 1884), Edcar A. 9 (Feb 1891) 10-255A-93
MARRIAGES
Addie L. Stephens to Albert H. Morgan q.v.
Adeline Stephens to Henry Wassom q.v.
Birdie Stephens to Herman Brown(?) q.v.
Calvin Stephens to Elizabeth Burkhart, 16 Dec 1856 (no return) 1-#585
Catharine Stephens to Lorenza Williams q.v.
Clearissa Stephens to Thomas Rhea q.v.
Isaac G. Stevens to Margarett L. Pierce, 25 Dec 1861 (same), A.P. Early MG 1-#766
J.B. Stephens to M.E. Kimbrough, 2 May 1882, J.P. Kefauver MG 4-9(83)
Jack Stephens to Martha Dagley, 7 Dec 1878 (no return) 1-#1591
Jacob A. Steven to Amanda S. Welch, 19 Dec 1894, H. Burditt MG 4-81
John A. Stephens to Ida Johnson, 28 Nov 1897, R.A. Dickson JP 4-99

Nancey Stephens to Edward Hill q.v.
Rebecca Stephens to A. D. Moore q.v.
Terza(?) Stevens to J. H. Burditt q.v.
Tishie Stephens to Taylor Clark q.v.
W.L. Stephens to Laura J. Bales, 22 Feb 1891, R.A. Bartlett MG 4-24

- - - - - - - - - - - - -

STEPHENSON

MARRIAGE

H. C. Stephenson to H. S. Giles q.v.

- - - - - - - - - - - - -

STEWART / STUART

1880 CENSUS

Moses Stewart 21 (Miner), Lousa 27, Ellen 4 2-30-238
William Stewart 54 (Ditcher), Julia 55, Julia 17, Thomas 13 2-24-195

1900 CENSUS

John R. Stewart 29 (Mar 1871-Iowa/Ind/Conn), Nellie E. STEWART 56 (m)(Sep 1843-Conn/Pa/Conn-Wd 4-4), Kate B. 27 (si)(Dec 1872-Iowa), Martha WILSON 79 (gm)(May 1821-Conn/Conn/Mass-Wd) 11-290A-10
Long S. Stewart 25 (Mar 1875-NC/Unk-M 0), Vinie 23 (Oct 1876-Ga/Ga/Ga-M 0-1-1), Annie 3 (Aug 1896-Ga/NC/Ga), William MOATS 50 (fl)(Unk 1850-Ga/Unk-Wd) 13-298A-151/154
Mattie Stewart 38 (May 1862-Wd 1-0)(Cook at Hotel), Winnie CLINE 68 (m)(June 1831-T/NC/NC-S 1-1), Joseph BUTLER 29 (boarder)(Ap 1871-Va/Va/Va-M 8)(Barber) 10-330B-218/231 (B)

MARRIAGES

Emma I. Stuart to John L. Varnell q.v.
I.M. Stewart to Edna Elson, 1 Mar 1893, J.Q. Shaver MG 4-52
Lin Stuart to Vina Motes, 10 Feb 1900 (same), Sherman Wilson MG 3-122
Loth Stuart to Calvin Tharp q.v.
Mary Stewart to W. B. Bolton q.v.
Mattie E. Stewart to C. B. Wolfe q.v.
Maynard Stewart to Candace Gentry, 12 Feb 1898 (13 Feb), W.A. Green JP, R.J. Killough W. 2-251
Nelie Stewart to Charley McDonald q.v.
Sarah Stewart to Anderson P. Swafford q.v.
Thomas Stewart to Mary S.A. Nelson, 2 Nov 1887 (3 Nov), R.H. Bartlett MG 1-540
Tinnie Stewart to John Sharp q.v.
Willis Stewart to Clara Ransom, 20 Jan 1890 (same), S.W. Wych ?? 1-596

- - - - - - - - - - - - -

STIBBINS / STEBBINS / STUBBIN

1880 CENSUS

Harbin Stebbins 41, Mary 32, Jonathan 10, Ada 8, Mary 5, Lucinda 3 12-3-24

1900 CENSUS

Charles Stubbin 61 (Sep 1838-NY/NY/NY-M 31), Mary 52 (May 1848-NY/NY/NY-M 31-6-5), Mary 25 (Dec 1874)(School Teacher), Leoner 13 (d)(Feb 1887) 12-180B-42/45

MARRIAGES

Lucinda R. Stebbins to Lewis M. Starring q.v.
Lucy A. Stibbins to Evan Moore q.v.

- - - - - - - - - - - - -

STINECIPHER / STINCIPHER / STONECIPHER / STOANSIPHER

1870 CENSUS

Jesse Stoansipher 50, Elizabeth 38, Asa 14, David J. 10, George W. 8, Nancy E. 5, Andrew J. 3, Mary C. 8/12 2-7-47

1880 CENSUS

Jack Stinecypher 19: see Rebecca Waterhouse (B)
Jessee Stinecipher 59, Asa 22, David 20, George 17, Andrew 12, Jessee 8 2-35-284

1900 CENSUS

Andrew J. Stinecipher 33 (July 1867-M 7), Amanda J. 23 (Mar 1877-M 7-1-1), George W. 6 (Jan 1894) 2-191A-7/7
Asa N. Stinecipher 43 (Aug 1856-M 13), Amanda 38 (May 1862-M 13-8-8), Doral S. 12 (Nov 1887), Florence 11 (Ap 1889), Mary E. 9 (Oct 1890), Sabra C. 8 (Mar 1892), Roda L. 6 (Jan 1894), Addie M. 4 (Sep 1895), Jesse F. 2 (Sep 1897), Carl J. 8/12 (Sep 1899) 1-192A-22/22
David J. Stinecipher 40 (Ap 1860-M 10), Ollie 29 (Jan 1871-M 10-0), Jesse STINECIPHER 79 (f)(June 1820-T/NC/Unk-Wd) 2-191A-8/8

MARRIAGES

A.J. Stonecipher to Amanda J. Treadway, 5 Jan 1893, Jas Johnson JP 4-52
Asa Stincipher to Amanda Ingle, 25 Oct 1886 (28 Oct), J.P. Roddy MG 1-511
D.J. Stincipher to Ollie Treadway, 21 Jan 1900 (28 Jan), W.R. Clack JP 1-600
Jesse Stonecipher to Elizabeth Newport, 19 Feb 1855 (22 Feb), Asa Newport MG 1-#484

- - - - - - - - - - - - -

STINETT / STINNET / STENETT

1900 CENSUS

George Stinett 40 (Sep 1859-M 19), Anna 38 (June 1861-M 19-6-5), Walter 14 (June 1885), George 12 (Jan 1888), Pearl 8 (Mar 1892), Clint 5 (Aug 1894) 2-194A-56/58
John Stenett 62 (Dec 1837-M 42), Martha J. 57 (May 1843-M 42-14-11), Lilly A. 15 (July 1884), Ludella 12 (Jan 1888) 6-242B-61
John R. Stinnett 29 (Sep 1870-M 8), Bettie J. 29 (Dec 1870-M 8-4-4), Mary E. 7 (Jan 1893), John A. 4 (Sep 1895), Rosana A. 2 (July 1897), Maud E. 10/12 (July 1899) 9-228A-9

MARRIAGES

Lillie A. Stinett to W. J. Smith q.v.
Rosie Stinnet to Samuel Neil q.v.

- - - - - - - - - - - - -

STINGER

MARRIAGE
Jack Stinger to Tennessee Armor, 12 Mar 1873 (13 Mar), Timothy P. Darr MG 1-#1280

- - - - - - - - - - - - -

STOCKEY / STOOKEY

1900 CENSUS
Lernu(?) Stockey 63 (Mar 1837-Mo/Va/Mo-M 26), Marri 55 (Ap 1845-Oh/Md/Va-M 26-5-3), Netti 10 (Dec 1890-Oh) 1-188B-184/193
MARRIAGE
Carl Stookey to Elie Holloway, 4 Jan 1899, L.M. Cartright MG 4-100

- - - - - - - - - - - - -

STOCKTON

MARRIAGE
Mary C. Stockton to Onslow G. Marsh q.v.

- - - - - - - - - - - - -

STOCKWELL

1870 CENSUS
Ephraigm Stockwell 37 (NY), Olive 27 (Ind) 2-9-57

- - - - - - - - - - - - -

STOFER

MARRIAGE
John Stofer to Polly Howard, 1 Mar 1888 (2 Mar), F.M. Bandy MG 1-546

- - - - - - - - - - - - -

STOKES

1900 CENSUS
Albert Stokes 40 (Unk 1860-Ga/Ga/Ga-M 10), Mollie 49 (June 1850-M 10-8-0), Earnest NORTHOP 10 (s) (Unk 1890), George COX 4 (s)(Feb 1896) 8-285A-331/333 (B)
MARRIAGE
Herbert Stokes to Mollie McDonald, 27 Aug 1886 (29 Aug), P.P. Brooks ?? 1-504

- - - - - - - - - - - - -

STONE

1860 CENSUS
Eliza Stone 18, Sarah 16, James W. 9, James M. 1: see Hampton Sales
1870 and 1880 CENSUS– None
1900 CENSUS
McDuffy Stone 27 (Unk 1873-Ala/Ala/Ala-M 4), Roxey 25 (Dec 1874-Ga/Ga/Ga-M 4-0) 3-275A-124 (B)
Rebecca Stone 59 (Aug 1840-T/NC/T-Wd 11-8), John 32 (Aug 1867)(Drug Salesman), George 19 (Mar 1881) 8-316B-130/134
MARRIAGES
Annie Stone to James Raulston q.v.
C.F. Stone to Loretta Ganaway, 4 Feb 1879 (same), E.L. Barnett MG 1-#1504
McDuffy Stone to Roxie Harden, 17 Aug 1896 (23 Aug), J.W. Williamson MG, W.M. Thompson [signed by X] W 2-57
Mary Stone to G. H. Sales q.v.
William Stone to Hattie King, 18 Dec 1888 (20 Dec), A.W. Frazier JP 1-566

- - - - - - - - - - - - -

STONER

1900 CENSUS
Harry A. Stoner 17: see Charles W. Irwin

- - - - - - - - - - - - -

STOOPS

1860 CENSUS
Mary Stoops 42 (Va), Lucinda 21, Mary 17, Matilda A. 7, Sarah J. 9/12 7-3-19
MARRIAGES
Lucinda Stoops to Christopher Romines q.v.
Mary Stoops to William Minnis q.v.

- - - - - - - - - - - - -

STORY / STOREY

1900 CENSUS
William T. Storey 28 (June 1871-Ga/Ga/Ga-M 9)(Coal Miner), Margaret L. 26 (Jan 1874-M 9-3-3), Charles W. 7 (Feb 1893), Ava V. 3 (Aug 1896), Maggie 1 (Ap 1899) 13-303A-242/252
MARRIAGES
Allice F. Story to William Bowlin q.v.
Carrie E. Story to George W. Spivey q.v.
Ida Belle Story to Samuel H. Flemmings q.v.
Lee Story to Kandy Shirley q.v.

- - - - - - - - - - - - -

STOUT

1880 CENSUS
Caswell Stout 31, Luretta 18, Lula D. 1/12 5-4-31
1900 CENSUS
Caswell T. Stout 51 (Aug 1848-T/T/Va-M 21), Loretta 38 (Oct 1861-M 21-6-6), Lullu D. 20 (Ap 1880), Seburn C. 17 (Sep 1882), Willie W. 15 (Sep 1884), Else J. 13 (Sep 1886), Fred W. 11 (June 1888), Anna L. 6 (July 1893) 5-230A-40
Elbert K. Stout 47 (July 1852-T/T/Va-M 19), Mary E. 40 (Aug 1859-Mo/T/T-M 19-7-6), William R. 18 (Feb 1882), Emmit B. 14 (Nov 1885), Thirza 11 (Dec 1888), Roy E. 8 (May 1892), John C. 5 (Mar 1895), Edith L. 2 (Mar 1898) 2-191B-11/11
MARRIAGES
B.B. Stout to Cordelia Whittenburg, 4 Jan 1881 (same), Z. Rose MG 1-298
C.T. [Caswell Taylor] Stout to Loretta Gannaway, 4 Feb 1879 (same) 1-#1604

Elbert K. Stout to Mary E. Underwood, 14 Jan 1881 (16 Jan), J.P. Roddy MG 1-298
Ella Stout to John V. Gray q.v.
John Stout to Louisa J. Whittenburg, 21 Jan 1862 (same), R.A. Giddion MG 1-#771
John W. Stout to Mary Jane Johnson, 20 Dec 1866 (same), W.L. Humphry JP 1-#923

- - - - - - - - - - - - -

STOVALL

1900 CENSUS
James Stovall 26 (Mar 1874-Ga/Ga/Ga-M 7), Sarah 27 (July 1872-M 7-1-0), William BLACKWALL 23 (bl)(Mar 1876-Ga/T/T) 6-248B-164/165
John Stovall 20: see Mattie Jones (B)
Robert Stovall 22: see Philip Henry (B)
MARRIAGE
W.J. Stovall to Nancy Johnson, 30 Dec 1885 (same), J.M. Bramlett MG 1-497

- - - - - - - - - - - - -

STOVER / STEVER

1900 CENSUS
Abraham I. Stever 59 (Jan 1840-Oh/Pa/Pa-M 11), Rachel 50 (Jan 1850-M 11-1-1), Adaline 18 (June 1882-Oh), James G. 7 (May 1893), Nancy DYER 55 (sil)(May 1845) 5-237A-175
MARRIAGE
Isiah Stover or Stever to Rachell Dyer, 20 Mar 1889 (24 Mar), Eli Hayes JP 1-571

- - - - - - - - - - - - -

STRADER

1900 CENSUS
Daniel Strader 51 (Dec 1848-M 25), Polley A. 42 (Feb 1858-M 25-9-4), Mary F. 25 (Dec 1874), William J. 20 (Mar 1880-Mo), Emily A. 13 (Aug 1886), Walter W. 7 (June 1892), Mary M. CURNUTT [CORNETT?] 75 (ml)(Aug 1824-Wd 5-2) 2-197A-104/109

- - - - - - - - - - - - -

STRATTON

1880 CENSUS
Eastland Stratton 68, Mary 50 12-1-6

- - - - - - - - - - - - -

STREBECK / STREBICK / SOREBECK

1860 CENSUS
George H. Sorebeck* 48 (Md)(Carpenter), Elenor C. 42, Haretta E. 18, Orren W. 16, Mary F. 13, Onslow B. 11 5-32-209
[* on 1850 Census name is spelled Strebeck]
MARRIAGE
Molly F. Strebick to William S. Kelly q.v.

- - - - - - - - - - - - -

STRICKLAND / STRICKLAN

1900 CENSUS
George W. Strickland 62 (Sep 1837-Ala/Ala/Ala-M 32) (Coal Miner), Mahala 49 (Sep 1850-T/Germany/Do-M 32-7-4), John A. 17 (Sep 1882-Ga)(Coal Miner), James E. 15 (Feb 1885)(Coal Miner) 13-302A-225/234
Olliver Strickland 40 (Mar 1860-Ark/Ark/Ga-M 12), Belle 34 (Oct 1865-M 12-4-3), Louisa 13 (July 1886), Orval 7 (Dec 1892), Jennie 21 (dl)(Aug 1878-M 5-1-0), James 35 (b)(Unk 1865-M 6), Horace PEAK 24 (boarder)(Unk 1876) 8-275B-136 (B)
MARRIAGES
Calvin Strickland to Maria Foster, 16 June 1893, Eli Price MG 4-54
Charley Strickland to Molley Shipley, 30 Mar 1897 (same), W.R. Grimsley MG, James Owens W 2-134
Oliver Stricklan to Bell Henderson, 15 Aug 1887 (same), Byrd Terry MG 1-530
Walter Strickland to Jennie Preston, 23 Jan 1895, G.M. Christman ?? 4-83

- - - - - - - - - - - - -

STRINGER

1900 CENSUS
Alic Stringer 17: see Manro Cravin
MARRIAGE
Mattie Stringer to George W. Ballew q.v.

- - - - - - - - - - - - -

STRONG

MARRIAGE
William M. Strong to Julia Louisa Baker, 25 Aug 1893, John T. Price MG 4-62

- - - - - - - - - - - - -

STUBBS

MARRIAGE
William M. Stubbs to Brunette Roberson, 6 Dec 1866 (no return) 1-#922

- - - - - - - - - - - - -

STULTZ / STULCE

MARRIAGES
S.A. Stulce to M.L.A. Bowen(?), 30 Aug 1891, J.J. Burnett MG 4-30
Thomas J. Stuters or Stulce to Nettie Emery or Emory, 16 Ap 1897 (same), D.V. Culver MG, J.R. Taylor W 2-138
William Stultz to Laura Hayes, 27 Mar 1889 (same), W.S. Hale MG, T.W. Morgan & Will Stultz W 2-397

- - - - - - - - - - - - -

STURDEVANT

1900 CENSUS

Melvin C. Sturdevant 35 (Ap 1865-Ill/Ind/Ind-M 13)(Missionary Adv), Maggie J. 38 (Feb 1862-Ill/Eng/Eng-M 13-2-1), Johnathan 11 (Oct 1888-Ill) 13-309A-368/382

- - - - - - - - - - - - -

STURGIS

MARRIAGE

C.L. Sturgis to Manda J. McCain, 30 Nov 1877 (2 Dec), ?.C. Cullom(?) MG 1-#1529

- - - - - - - - - - - - -

STUTTON

MARRIAGE

J.H. Stutton to Alice Christine, 13 Ap 1885 (16 Ap), W.A. Green JP 1-505

- - - - - - - - - - - - -

SUDDATH / SUDDETH / SUDDITH / SUTHERS

1870 CENSUS

George Suddath 57 (Va), Vina 53 (Va), Enoch F. 15 8-4-28 (B)

1880 CENSUS

Enoch F. Suddeth 23, Fanney 23 1-27-210/215 (B)

Jack Suddeth 33, Dinah 25, Susan 1/12, Lewis BILES 25 (boarder), Susan JONES 28 (boarder)(Milkmaid) 2-32-259 (B)(Mu)

1900 CENSUS

Enoch Suthers 53 (Oct 1846-M 3), Florence 26 (June 1873-M 3-3-3), William 19 (Mar 1881), Fritz WATKINS 9 (ss)(Oct 1890), Lillie 7 (sd)(Ap 1893), Ellen 1 (sd) (Mar 1899) 15-271A-54 (B)

Jackson Suddath 55 (Jan 1845-M 27), Eliza 43 (May 1857-T/Ga/Va-M 27), James E. 16 (May 1884), Thomas K. 12 (Dec 1887)(Water Carrier), Willie L. 10 (Ap 1890), Carrie M. POWELL 24 (d)(Oct 1875-M 9), George SMART 45 (boarder)(Unk) 8-317B-143/148 (B)

Sam Suddath 51 (Nov 1848)(Barber), William 26 (nw)(Dec 1873)(Hotel Porter) 8-311B-17/18 (B)

MARRIAGES

Enoch Suddeth to Fannie Hale, 2 May 1880 (6 May), W.S. Hale MG 1-#1728

Enoch Suddith to Sarah Andrews, 27 Dec 1890, L.M. Moore MG 4-20

Enoch Suddith to Florence Gillespie, 1 Jan 1897 (3 Jan), A. W. Randolph MG 2-99 (B)

Frank Suddath (22, Roane Co) to Nattie Suddath (19, Roane Co), 7 May 1881, T.N.L. Cunnyngham JP, Luns or Lewis Delaney & Lee Day W (both of Dayton) 4-3(25) (B)

- - - - - - - - - - - - -

SUGGS

1900 CENSUS

Mollie A. Suggs 57, Mamia 20: see Homer Halliburton

MARRIAGES

Jack Suggs to Oleptia Carroll, 1 Ap 1899 (2 Ap), J.P. Houston MG, W.M. Getty W 2-398

Jeff Suggs to Mattie Hickman, 6 July 1888 (same), W.R. Grimsley MG 1-552

Thomas Suggs to Louisa Gibson, 23 Sep 1894, J.W. Clouse JP 4-72

William Suggs to Laura Shipley, 30 Mar 1897 (same), W.R. Grimsley MG, James Colvin W 2-135

- - - - - - - - - - - - -

SUIAGROD

1900 CENSUS

John B. Suiagrod(?) 32 (Jan 1868-M 11)(RR Foreman), Bettie 26 (Feb 1874-M 11-3-1), Roy 8 (Nov 1891) 8-315B-105/109

- - - - - - - - - - - - -

SULLAS

1900 CENSUS

John Sullas 53 (Unk 1847-Wd), Charles 21 (Unk 1879), Samuel 16 (Unk 1884), Henry 15 (Unk 1885) 8-275B-143 (B)

- - - - - - - - - - - - -

SULLIVAN / SULIVAN

1880 CENSUS

John Sullivan 50, T.M. 46, R.W. 23 (s), J.D. 21 (s), T.J. 19 (s), F.V. 11 (s), C.E. 7 (s), S.E. 4 (d), S.A. SULLIVAN 53 (si) 11-37-300 [NOTE: The following entry also appeared on the 1880 Meigs County Census: John Sullivan 50, Temperance M. 46, William R. 23, Joseph D. 21, Thomas J. 19, Franklin V. 10, Celia E. 8, Sarah E. 5 2-42-382]

T.P. Sullivan 35, D.A. 42 (w), J.P. 20 (s), John 4 (s) 4-33-268

MARRIAGES

Cislia S. Sullivan to Robert Cox q.v.

Daniel Sullivan to Frances Randolph, 3 Oct 1891, C.J. Titus JP 4-31

J.A. Sullivan to Eliza Howard, 18 Nov 1897 (same), M.B. Hicks JP 2-209

J.D. Sullivan to Minny Alexander, 29 Dec 1887 (same), W.R. Grimsley JP 1-542

James Sullivan to Molly Clark, 17 Nov 1873 (same), W.R. Henry JP 1-#1309

John Sullivan to Hester Ferguson, 12 Sep 1898 (18 Sep), L.F. Smith ??, H.J. Sullivan W 2-322

Permenia E. Sullivan to David Oldham q.v.

Robert B. Sullivan to Sarah Trusley, 2 Ap 1852 (no return) 1-#370

T.P. Sullivan to Dycey Bradshaw, 21 Aug 1873 (22 Aug), W.M. Clark JP 1-#1297

W.F. Sullivan to Lizzie Carpenter, 26 Nov 1893, W.R. Grimsley MG 4-60

W.R. Sullivan to Ellen B. Kelley, 4 Sep 1886 (same), E.J.H. Pryor ?? 1-525

SULLY

MARRIAGE

J.F. Sully to Margaret Cushing, 29 Sep 1897 (same), Hugh Brady MG, T.N. Barton W 2-189

SUTTLES / SUTTLER

1870 CENSUS

Boswell Suttles 44 (NC), Rebecca 42, James 17 (Ga), Stephen 15 (Ga), Doctor 13 (Ga), Francis 8 (Ga), Joseph 1 5-3-17

Francis Suttles 62 (NC), Mary Ann 50 (SC), Burton J. 18, Wm R. 15 (Ga), Mary Ann 12, Thomas F. 7 5-8-60

John Suttles 19, Martha J. 22, Rebecca 5/12 5-3-18

1880 CENSUS

Martha J. Suttles 33 ("husband in penitentary"), Mary C. 7, Hester E. 5, Matilda E. 3 6-15-139/141

1900 CENSUS

Boz Suttles 74: see Joseph Suttles

Dock Suttles 23 (Feb 1877-M 7), Sally 22 (Mar 1888-M 7-4-3), Cally 6 (Jan 1894), Hary L. 3 (July 1896), Wyley 1 (July 1898) 10-257B-141/145

Fill Suttles 51 (Aug 1842-T/NC/Ga-M 7), Lizabeth 30 (May 1870-M 7-5-5), Matlin 15 (Oct 1884), Becky J. 14 (May 1886), Lilly 12 (Nov 1887), Franky 10 (June 1889), Henery B. 9 (May 1891), William 7 (May 1893), Colly 3 (Mar 1896), John 1 (Feb 1899), Cordail ELISON 15 (sd)(Oct 1884), Bob MASTON 11 (ss) (May 1889), Josey A. 8 (sd)(June 1891) 10-257A-139/143

Griffin Suttles 21: see Elic Molton

John W. Suttler 49 (Aug 1850-Ga/Ga/Ga-M 33)(Coal Miner), Martha J. 52 (July 1847-M 33-9-4), Josie Ina 10 (Dec 1889), John E. EATON 11 (gs)(Oct 1888), Chas R. 8 (gs)(July 1891) 13-302B-227/236

Joseph Suttles 32 (Jan 1868-M 10)(Coal Miner), Rhoda 24 (July 1875-Ala/Ga/Ga-M 10-6-5), Henry H. 8 (July 1891-Ala), Rosa B. 7 (Dec 1892-Ala), Boz 6 (Dec 1893-Ala), Florence 3 (Sep 1896-Ala), Clem 3/12 (Feb 1900-Ala), Boz SUTTLES 74 (f) (Jan 1826-Wd) (Blacksmith) 8-284A-306/308

Ruff Suttles 28, Lizzia 24, Corra 7: see Jessie Kieth (B)

MARRIAGES

B.F. Suttles to Frankie Ruth, 20 Sep 1888 (same), M.C. Bruner MG 1-563

Dock Suttles to Sarah E. Collins, 29 July 1893, J. L. Brown(?) JP 4-57

Hester Suttles to W. E. Phelfrey q.v.

M. C. Suttles to J. J. Eatons q.v.

Minnie Suttler to Joseph Martin q.v.

Philip Suttles to Lizzie Collins, 7 June 1894, J.B. Trotter MG 4-66

Rufus Suttles to Lizzie Keith, 11 Jan 1900 (same), R.C. Knight JP, J. Major(?) W 3-107

S.L. Suttles to A.E. Byerly, 6 Feb 1878 (same), Peter Roddy MG 1-#1545

Tilda or Tillie Suttles to James Millican q.v.

SUTTON

1900 CENSUS

Charles Sutton 22: see Elisha K. Giles

Jane Sutton 44 (Feb 1856-D 5-5), James R. 21 (Dec 1878), Mary A. 17 (Oct 1882), Susie A. 9 (Oct 1890) 3-202B-53/56

Thomas Sutton 12: see William W. Smith

SWABY / SWABEY

1900 CENSUS

Edson C. Swabey 33 (Feb 1867-Oh/England/Va-M 6)(Real Estate Agent), Clara B. 33 (Feb 1867-Oh/Mass/NY-M 6-2-2), Laura 4 (Jan 1896-Ind), Hellen 1/12 (Ap 1900), Addison M. BARTLETT 37 (bl)(June 1862-Oh/Mass/NY) 10-329A-189/202

MARRIAGE

Stanley W. Swaby to Myrtle Grace Curtis, 24 May 1893, Lee T. Fisher MG 4-55

SWAFFORD

1860 CENSUS

Jefferson J. Swafford 39 (Miss), Martha 29, Susan E. 10, Mary E. 6, Jackson 5, Nancy J. 3, Cynthia 1 8-16-105

1870 CENSUS

Jefferson J. Swafford 49 (Miss), Martha 40, Susan 19, Mary Elizabeth 17, Jackson A. 15, Nancy 12, Syntha 10, Larkin 8, Martha E. 6, John 1 8-6-36

Mary E. Swafford 17: see Bryan R. McDonald

Nancy A. Swafford 20, Aaron 11/12, Margarette 12: see John Pierce

1880 CENSUS

Charles Swafford 4 (Mu): see M. J. Darwin (B)

L.N. Swafford 28, Ambilia J. 19, Major M. 3, unnamed 2/12 (s) 5-2-14

Thomas Swafford 48, Rachel 35, Sarah N. 11, Susan M. 9 6-18-169/172

1900 CENSUS

Alexander Swafford 20: see Arabela J. Reel

Andrew Swafford 35 (May 1865-T/Miss/Miss)(Hotel Stewart) 10-331B-245/260 (B)

Brown Swafford 33 (June 1864-M 4)(Lawyer), Hannah G. 30 (Mar 1870-M 4-1-1), Samuel C.(?) 3 (Ap 1897), Ethel SPRINGS (B) 12 (Unk 1888)(Servant) 15-270B-52

Charles Swafford 30 (Nov 1869-M 10), Florra 29 (Ap 1871-M 10-2-2), Revis 9 (Dec 1890), Arrants 21 (Sep 1895) 6-247A-138/139

David Swafford 48 (Feb 1852-T/NC/Ga-M 8), Mary J. 46 (Ap 1854-M 8-2-2), William E. 20 (Mar 1880), John W. 18 (Mar 1882) 5-232A-83 (B)

Elizabeth Swaford 50 (Unk-Wd 5-4)(Washwoman) 8-318A-156/161 (B)

Harry Swafford 7: see Calumma Brown (B)

Henry Swafford 26 (May 1874-M 5), Mary 22 (May 1878-M 5-0), David HARMONY 30 (bl)(Unk 1870-M 15) 8-284B-317/319 (B)
Hester Swafford 19: see Sam Walters (B)
James Swafford 36 (June 1863-M 8)(Coal Miner), Anna 25 (Nov 1874-Ga/Ga/T-M 8-2-2), Ollie M. 7 (June 1892), William 4 (June 1895) 8-289B-426/429
John Swafford 27 (Mar 1873-M 6), China 25 (Unk-M 6-4-4), Reece 7 (Jan 1893), Maggie 4 (Dec 1895), Lillie 3 (Oct 1896), Ethel 1 (Aug 1898) 8-316A-125/129 (B)
John Swafford 30 (Ap 1870-M 6)(Coal Miner), Millie 29 (Aug 1870-M 6-2-1), Dewey 1 (Aug 1898), Ellen CLINGAN 19 (Ap 1881) 13-296B-130/132
John Swafford 31 (Nov 1868-M 3), Belle 22 (Feb 1878-M 3-2-2), Ida 4 (May 1896), Ruby 3 (May 1897) 11-291A-29
John Swafford 33 (Ap 1867-M 2), Dicie 20 (Unk 1880-M 2-1-2), Lela 5 (Mar 1895), Arlo M. 4 (Jan 1896), Danie L. 1 (Mar 1899) 15-271B-53 (B)
John R. Swafford 53 (June 1846-M 27), Matilda 45 (Dec 1854-M 27-7-5), Luiza 19 (Feb 1881), Elizabeth 16 (Nov 1883), George N. 11 (Oct 1888), William L. 8 (Aug 1890) 9-229A-21
Lewis Swafford 35 (Unk-M 2)(Coal Miner), Mary L. 25 (Dec 1874-M 2), Lizzie COCKRAN 45 (ml)(Sep 1854-Wd 7-3) 8-312B-36/38 (B)
Lizzie Swafford 16: see Joseph Ballard
Louis Swafford 18: see Enoch Ritchie
Major Swafford 24 (Mar 1876-M 4), Texas 25 (Oct 1874-M 4-3-3), Minerva 3 (Dec 1896), May 1 (June 1898), Pearl 1/12 (Ap 1900), Leslie GRAYHAM 16 (boarder)(Unk) 6-247B-143/144
Margaret Swafford 45 (Unk-Ga/Ga/Ga-D 2-2) (Cook at Hotel), Mary 22 (Aug 1877)(Washwoman), Bettie BLAIN 24 (d)(Nov 1875-M 6-2-2)(Washing & Ironing), Lillie 5 (gd)(Ap 1895), Charles 3 (gs)(Mar 1897) 10-330B-222/236 (B)
Minnie Swafford 17, Colonel 13: see Sallie Bettis (B)
Samuel Swafford 18: see John Killpatrick
Thomas Swafford 40 (Sep 1859-M 20)(Coal Miner), Miranda 35 (Mar 1865-M 20-5-4), Samuel 20 (s)(Aug 1879)(Coal Miner), Alonzo 17 (Oct 1882)(Coal Miner), Pearl 14 (Mar 1886), Thomas A. 9 (Aug 1890) 8-284B-321/323 (B)
Thomas Swafford 67 (Nov 1832-T/Miss/T-M 25)(crippled), Margarett A. 65 (Nov 1834-NC/NC/NC-M 25-3-1) 5-232A-80
William Swafford 28: see John W. Reynolds (B)
Willie Swafford 18: see William Young (B)

MARRIAGES

Anderson P. Swafford to Sarah Stewart, 16 Aug 1873 (17 Aug), Wm A. Clack JP 1-#1295
Anna Emaline Swafford to John Thurman q.v.
Bettie Swafford to Jack Meadows(?) q.v.
Booty John Swafford to Emma Walker, 9 Sep 1886 (10 Sep), C. Morgan JP 1-503 & 1-508
David Swafford to Emaline Worthington, 4 May 1890, F.M. Capps JP 4-16
Emeline Swafford to Gilbert Clark q.v.
Hass Swafford to Annie Jackson, 10 Aug 1896 (same), J.B. Phillips MG & W 2-55
Henry Swafford to Mary Cozart, 15 Mar 1894, J.B. Phillips MG 4-75
J.A. Swafford to Carrie E. Flinn, 9 Ap 1898 (bond only), I.N. Sherley [signed by X] W 2-267
J.M. Swafford to Cordelia Black, 15 Jan 1892, Wm Morgan JP 4-33
Jane Swafford to Luther Morgan q.v.
Jervin Swafford to S. H. Hall q.v.
Jesse B. Swafford to Hannah G. Darwin, 18 Dec 1895, J.A. Whitner JP 4-92
John B. Swafford to Milley Shirley, 14 Aug 1894, G.W. Curtain MG 4-70
Louis Swafford to Mary Hughes, 25 Oct 1897 (same), W.S. Hale MG, Marnie(?) Spicer(?) [signed by X] W 2-204
Lucretia Swafford to Albert Trewhitt(?) q.v.
M.M. Swafford to Texas Young, 7 Aug 1896 ("no license issued"), Wm Brown W 2-53
Maggie Swafford to John W. Rannel q.v.
Manervia Swafford to Thomas C. Morgan q.v.
Martha E. Swafford to J. P. Sexton q.v.
Mary Swafford to James F. Pickett q.v.
Mary Swafford to Richard Hughes q.v.
Mary E. Swafford to W. O. Hale q.v.
Mary J. Swafford to Samuel Keith q.v.
Mary Jane Swafford to John Casey q.v.
N. J. Swafford to S. P. Sexton q.v.
Sallie Swafford to William Webb q.v.
Sallie Swafford to Charles McDonald q.v.
Samuel Swafford to Hester Walters, 25 Mar 1889 (26 Mar), D.B. Jackson MG, Tom Swafford W 2-396
Sarah Swafford to Samuel Kirby q.v.
Susan Swafford to David Woody q.v.
Susan E. Swafford to J. A. Myerson q.v.
Susan M. Swafford to Levi Emory q.v.
T.W. Swafford to Margarit Blain, 1 Jan 1887 (same), J.B. Phillips MG 1-514
Thomas Swafford to Randia Hutcheson, 17 Feb 1888 (28 Feb), M.G. Bruner MG 1-564
Wesley Swafford to Sallie Cooper, 16 Mar 1895, S.W. Burnett MG 4-78

SWAIN / SWAN / SWIN

1900 CENSUS

George F. Swain 46 (Oct 1853-Oh/England/Do-M 24), Mary J. 42 (May 1858-Oh/Oh/Oh-M 24-7-6), Nora B. 17 (Nov 1883-Oh), Elsie M. 8 (Aug 1891-Oh), Letha 4 (Feb 1896-Oh), Willard G. 2/12 (Mar 1900) 9-228B-20
Henry Swain 23, Sherman 19: see Alvin Hayes
John Swan 26 (Nov 1873-Ga/Ga/Ga)(RR Laborer), Reuben JACKSON 37 (Jan 1863-Ga/Ga/Ga-M)(RR Laborer), Henry CROFFORD 20 (Mar 1880-Miss/Do/Do)(RR Laborer), Andrew BRADY 38 (May 1862-M)(RR Laborer) 14-215A-39/40 (B)
William Swin 53 (Feb 1850-NY/NY/Ga-M 6)(Carpenter), Martha 52 (Oct 1847-T/N/NC-M 6-5-2), Hattie GRAY 27 (sd)(Ap 1873-T/T/Ireland-M 3-1-1), Herbert 17 (sgs)(July 1882-Ark/T/Ark) 10-261A-214/219

MARRIAGES

Frances Swain to Andy Montgomery q.v.
Leina Swan to James Tucker q.v.
Willie Swan to Josie Sharp, 14 Mar 1888 (15 Mar), W.S. Hale MG 1-545

SWEARINGON

1900 CENSUS
Carrie B. Swearingon 36 (Mar 1864-Oh/Oh/Oh-D 2-2)(RR Depot Agent), Francis B. 7 (Mar 1893), Mary M. 5 (Aug 1894) 13-305A-285/295

- - - - - - - - - - - - -

SWEATMAN

MARRIAGE
William Sweatman to Nancy A. Mathis, 2 Oct 1854 (3 Oct), Elijah Brewer(?) JP 1-#461

- - - - - - - - - - - - -

SWEETON / SWEETEN

1870 CENSUS
John M. Sweeten 21: see Snelson Roberts
MARRIAGE
James [John] M. Sweeton to Louisa C. Locke, 1 Mar 1871 (same), Geo W. Renfro MG 1-#1192
[Louisa C., dau of Addison Locke]

- - - - - - - - - - - - -

SWICKER

1900 CENSUS
James E. Swicker 38 (Aug 1861-Va/Va/Va-M 8)(Minister), Lillie D. 28 (Aug 1871-Va/Va/Va-M 8-3-3), Olive M. 6 (Sep 1893-Va), Lucy V. 5 (Jan 1895-Va), James A. 2 (May 1898) 5-234A-125

- - - - - - - - - - - - -

SWIFT

1880 CENSUS
Gelilia Swift 41, Garet 2: see Jesse West
1900 CENSUS
Worthy Swift 36 (May 1864-England/Do/Do-1880/20/Na-M 6)(Coal Miner), Alice 35 (July 1864-M 6-1-1), Zella 1 (Mar 1899) 8-286A-346/348
MARRIAGE
Worthy Swift to Alice Chadwick, 12 Nov 1895, J.H. Seward MG 4-91

- - - - - - - - - - - - -

SYDNEYS - see SNYDER

- - - - - - - - - - - - -

SYKES / SIKES

1860 CENSUS
Dimpsy Sykes 69 (NC), Charlotte 57, Loddeck 18, Betsy PENS(?) 38 (NC) 8-24-162
Joseph Sykes 22, Mary C. 21, John 1, Dempsy 3/12, John W. ACRE 61 (NC) 8-24-163
Margaret Sykes 23 (School Teacher): see Joseph Parks
1870 CENSUS
Dempsey Sykes 80 (NC), Lodica 28, Nancy I. 23, Samuel 3/12 8-1-4
Joseph Sykes 32, Mary C. 30, John 11, Dempsy 10, Nancy C. 8, Lodica F. 6, Mary J. 3, William T. 11/12 8-1-5
1880 CENSUS
Loderick Sykes 49, N.I. 34 (w), John 9, B. 7 (s), A.D. 5 (d), E.D. 1 (s), John WHITE 40 (Hired) 11-38-311
1900 CENSUS
Bee F. Sykes 28 (Dec 1871-M 1), Mattie 27 (Aug 1872-T/Va/T-M 1) 11-292B-71
Lodic Sykes 58 (July 1842-T/NC/NC-M 31), Nancy 53 (Aug 1846-T/T/Ga-M 31-6-5), Delia L. 25 (Jan 1875), Edward 21 (Nov 1878), Nora E. 14 (May 1886) 11-293A-72
MARRIAGES
B.F. Sykes to Martha Esminger, 9 Sep 1898 (11 Sep), W.A. Howard MG, L.J. Sykes W 2-321
Joseph Sykes to Mary C. Acre, 21 Aug 1857 (same), Wm Morgan JP 1-#609
Lordick Sykes to Nancy White, 28 Dec 1868 (31 Dec), A.P. Early MG 1-#1038
Wm Sykes to Nancy Fountenberry, 21 Oct 1852 (25 Oct), C.A. Wollard MG 1-#389

- - - - - - - - - - - - -

SYKLES

MARRIAGES
Henry Sykles to Nancy Harden, 28 July 1894, J.W. Clouse JP 4-72
Jones Sykles to Massie Harden, 28 July 1894, J.W. Clouse JP 4-72

- - - - - - - - - - - - -

SYLER

MARRIAGE
Henry Syler to Dolla Bluff, 4 Dec 1885 (same), S.M. Burnett MG 1-501

- - - - - - - - - - - - -

TALLENT / TALENT / TALLANT / TOLLETT

1860 CENSUS
Michael Talent 31, Elizabeth J. 30, William L. 10, Susannah E. 4, Nancy J. 2 2-74-504
1870 CENSUS
Garet Talant 46, Nancy 39, Robert F. 17, Edward F. 15, Levi 13 (s), Martha 10, Henry 8, Mary 5, Babe 3 (s), Sarah 1, Elizabeth TALANT 68 (Va) 2-8-56
[Garrett married Nancy Hartbarger on 15 Aug 1850 in Roane County]
1880 CENSUS
Catharine Tallent 68: see J. F. Tallent
Edward Talent 25 (Carpenter), Syntha 22, Bertha 1 2-36-291
Garret Talent 54, Nancy 51, Lee 22, Martha 20, Henry 18, Mary 16, Jack 14, Puss 10 (d), Lydia 8. Tobe 6 (s) 2-36-290
J.F. Tallent 35, Bel 26 (w), Effa 7 (d), Jas S. 1 (s), Manda GROSS 48 (ml), Catharine TALLENT 68 (m), Bob GROSS 10 (ss) 8-12-98 [John Tallant married C.B. Gross on 10 Jan 1878 in Meigs County]

Johnath Tallent 42 (Blacksmith), S.J. 40, J.J. 17 (s), M.A. 13 (d), B.B. 1 (d) 8-1-7

Robert F. Tallant 27 (Blacksmith), Margaret 30, Noah J. 7, John F. 4, Peter 2, Floyd 2/12 10-29-227/234 [R.F. married Margaret Cox, 7 Ap 1872, Marshall Co., Ala.]

1900 CENSUS

Andrew J. Tallent 33 (Jan 1867-M 4), Eliza A. 25 (Jan 1875-M 4-3-3), Eunice C. 3 (Jan 1897), Reva 7/12 (Oct 1899), Eva 7/12 (Oct 1899), Harden CLARK 18 (bl)(Nov 1881) 2-192B-32/33
[Andrew Jackson Tallent married Eliza Ann Clark]

Bertha A. Tallent 21, Alma 17, Edward F. 14: see Mar--?-- O. Harrison

Floyd E. Tallent 20 (Mar 1880-T/T/Ga)(Liveryman) 8-312A-26/27

Garrett Tallent 74 (May 1826-T/Va/Va-Wd) (Landlord), Martha J. 40 (d)(Nov 1859)(School Teacher), Mary C. 34 (d)(Sep 1865), Maud 31 (d)(Mar 1869) 2-195A-75/78

Henry Tallent 40 (June 1860-M 1), Sarah 16 (Ap 1884-M 1), Luler 41 (si)(Jan 1833)(Cook) 1-188A-176/185

James Tallant 34 (July 1862-M 16), Nancy A. 35 (Jan 1865-M 16-7-7), Lester 15 (May 1885), May 13 (May 1887), Anna L. 11 (Dec 1888), James 10 (May 1890), Joseph A. 8 (Feb 1892), William A. 6 (Nov 1893), Kate T. 4 (Ap 1896) 15-270A-38

James F. Tollett 40 (May 1860-M 10), Florence T. 25 (July 1874-M 10-3-3), Thomas J. 7 (Mar 1893), Jessie 4 (May 1896), Dosie 2 (Sep 1898) 14-223A-185/189

John Tallent 24 (July 1875-Ga/T/Ga-M 2)(Fireman, Stat Engine), Alice 25 (Mar 1875-M 2-1-1), Lovenia 9/12 (Sep 1899) 8-316B-131/135

Johnathan Tallent 61 (Nov 1838-M 3)(Blacksmith), Nancy 34 (May 1866-M 3-0), Bertha B. 21 (Ap 1879), Cora C. 16 (Aug 1883) 13-305B-292/304

Louie G. Tallent 42 (June 1857-M 19), Henrietta 39 (June 1860-M 19-1-1), Clarence C. 18 (Sep 1881) 2-192A-25/25

Maggie Tallent 51 (Feb 1849-Ga/SC/SC-Wd 6-6), Pete C. 22 (Sep 1877)(Livery Stable Prop), Dolly 17 (Nov 1882), Willie R. 15 (Ap 1885) 8-314A-84/87

Noah J. Tallent 27 (Feb 1873-T/T/Ala-M 4)(Livery Stable Keeper), Maggie 22 (Dec 1877-M 4-2-2), Pansy M. 3 (Jan 1897), Frances M. 1 (Dec 1898) 10-321A-28/29

Quintion A. Tallent 26 (July 1873-M 0), Ethel 17 (June 1882-M 0-0) 2-191B-10/10

MARRIAGES

Bertha Tallent to I. A. Green q.v.

E.F. Talent to S.J. McChristian [McCuistion], 3 July 1878 (4 July), Sewell Phillips MG 1-#1565

Ida Tallent to Samuel Vinson q.v.

J.F. Tallent to Florence Rice, 16 July 1890 (17 July), J.L. McPherson JP 1-602

James J. Tallent to Nancy R. Travis, 30 July 1884 (3 Aug), I.W. Holt JP 1-545

John Tallent to Alice Corvin, 17 Nov 1898 (same), R.C. Knight JP & W, James Rodgers W 2-344

Johnathan Tallent to Nancy Elzy, 29 May 1897 (30 May), J.S. Best MG, E.A. Shelton W 2-146

L.G. Tallent to Henrietta Cash, 16 Nov 1880 (17 Nov), James Cash MG 1-293

Lidia L. Tallent to J. F. Gilliam q.v.

M. A. Tallent to J. H. Travis q.v.

Noah Tallant to Maggie Moore, 28 June 1896 (same), A.P. Hayes JP, E. Vane W 2-34

Q.A. Tallent to Ethel Phillips, 10 Dec 1899, A.M. Broyles JP 4-103

Sitha Tallent to W. F. Miller q.v.

W.H. Tallent to S.A. McLarrin [McClarrin], 8 Oct 1899, R. A. Hutsell MG 4-103

\- - - - - - - - - - - - -

TALLEY / TALLY
(see also TILLEY)

1880 CENSUS

James Talley 28: see J.L. McPherson

1900 CENSUS

Nathaniel Tally 6, Arnold 4: see Calumma Brown (B)

MARRIAGES

J. W. Talley to Jennie Wade, 23 Mar 1890 (same), J. R. Hoover MG 1-599

Ping(?) Talley to Addie Bridgeman, 8 Jan 1890 (same), J.W. Wright MG 1-592

William Talley to Sarah Lavender, 4 Nov 1891, W. A. Howard MG 4-30

\- - - - - - - - - - - - -

TALMADGE

1900 CENSUS

Edward M. Talmadge 61 (Feb 1839-NY/France/Scotland-M 38)(Carpenter), Sarah R. 52 (Aug 1847-Pa/Pa/Pa-M 38-4-2), Mary A. 11 (Dec 1888) 11-291B-35

\- - - - - - - - - - - - -

TANKERSLY / TANKSLEY

1900 CENSUS

John Tankersley 39 (June 1860-M 3), Daisy E. 23 (Unk 1877-NC/NC/NC-M 3-1-1), Roger 2 (Jan 1898) 3-209B-169/184

Thomas Tanksley 36 (Ap 1864-M 14), Sath 30 (May 1870-M 14-6-6), Bell 13 (Ap 1887)(Quiltmaker), Adies 11 (d)(Mar 1889), Samuel 9 (Feb 1891), Robbert 5 (May 1895), Thomis 3 (Feb 1897) 1-184B-114/120

MARRIAGES

John Tanksley to Samantha Harwood or Howard, 24 Jan 1891, J.W. Cowles(?) JP 4-21

John B. Tanksley to Daisey B. Rollins, 10 Feb 1897, A.M. Broyles JP 4-98

T.M. Tanksley to Sarah J. Wilson, 29 Dec 1886 (30 Dec), T.H. McPherson JP 1-516

\- - - - - - - - - - - - -

TANNSEL

1900 CENSUS

Ellen Tannsel(?) 31 (Mar 1869-Oh-S)(Farm Boss) 12-179B-24/26

Emma Tannsel(?) 65 (Feb 1835-Oh/Oh/Oh-Wd 2-2), Edith 34 (July 1865-Oh), Martha 33 (Jan 1867-Oh)(School Teacher) 12-179B-23/25

\- - - - - - - - - - - - -

TAP

1900 CENSUS
Frank Tap(?) 25 (May 1874-M 5), Suse(?) 24 (June 1875-M 5-1-1), Tomie 2 (May 1898) 1-183A-83/86

- - - - - - - - - - - - -

TARWATER

1880 CENSUS
James Tarwater 30 (Mineralogist) 2-29-231
William Tarwater 29 (General Carpenter), Sarah 21, Ida 6, Edward 4, Charles 1/12, Rebecca JOLLY 20 (Servant, Cook); *Boarders:* Isaac CLARK 16, William WHITLOCK 30 (Miner), Isaac HILL 34 (Miner) 2-29-229

- - - - - - - - - - - - -

TATE

1900 CENSUS
Emma Tate 28: see John Vance

- - - - - - - - - - - - -

TAUZER

1860 CENSUS
James P. Tauzer 15, Mary J. 12: see Susan Monday
MARRIAGE
Mary Jane Tauzer to Daniel O. Hartbarger q.v.

- - - - - - - - - - - - -

TAYLOR

1860 CENSUS
Doskey Taylor 50: see Lewis Morgan
1870 CENSUS
Albert H. Taylor 24, Mariah 23, Andrew 5/12, James F. YOKELY 59, John W. 11 2-15-109
Benjamin F. Taylor 38 (Ky)(Saddler) 3-16-118
1880 CENSUS
B.F. Taylor 52 (Saddler): see Calvin Jones
James Taylor(*) 30, L.A. 23 (w), W.A. 2 (s), C.C. 9/12 (d) 9-32-275 [* possibly Taylor James]
James O. Taylor 38, Julia O. 37, Walter G. 8, Theophilus M. 7, Luther P. 6, Mary E.J. 3, John B. 6/12 6-14-132/135 [James Taylor married Julia Findley on 2 Dec 1870 in Meigs County]
John Taylor 39, T.M. 32, J.N. 9 (s), W.O. 8 (s), N.J. 6 (d), J.W. 5 (s), H.A. 4 (d), C.K. 2 (d)[marked through, probably deceased], S.E. 2/12 7-26-227 [John married Tennessee Lillard on 12 Ap 1868 in Meigs Co]
1900 CENSUS
Arthur Taylor 8: see William Dill (B)
Asberry Taylor 21: see Susan Majors
Earl ?. Taylor 73 (Ap 1827-T/T/NC-M 50), Tempy 72 (Oct 1827-M 50-5-1), Mark 17 (gs)(June 1882) 12-181-56/59
Elmore R. Taylor 40 (July 1859-M 13)(Merchant), Louiza J. 38 (Mar 1862-M 13-2-2), Anna M. 19 (Oct 1890), Bulah 6 (July 1893), Theodore* 27 (July 1873-S) (Merchant. Partner) 5-234A-118 [* probably Theopolis, son of James O. and Julia Taylor] [E.R. married Louisa Jane Locke on 29 May 1887 in Meigs Co.]
George W. Taylor 24 (Feb 1876-M 3), Lula J. 17 (Dec 1882-M 3-2-2), Mattie 1 (Dec 1898), Oscar R. 3/12 (Mar 1900) 2-199A-155/160
Julia Taylor 56 (Dec 1843-Ga/Ga/Ga-Wd 6-6), Luther P. 25 (Oct 1874), Emma 23 (Oct 1876), John 20 (Oct 1879), William 16 (Feb 1884), Rosebud 3 (gd)(Sep 1896) 6-243A-69
Mary Taylor 33, Jessie 4: see Martha Gamble
Mahan(?) Taylor 52 (Ap 1842-NY/NY/Near East-M 29), Firena(?) 52 (Nov 1847-Conn/Conn/Conn-M 29-3-3) (School Teacher), Rodgers 24 (Oct 1875-Conn)(Store Clerk), Mary 22 (Aug 1877-Conn)(School Teacher) 12-179A-5/5
Milo Taylor (no dates)– non resident in District 12
Walter G. Taylor 28 (Dec 1871-T/T/Ga-M 1), Anna 31 (May 1869-M 1-1-1), Emma E. 8/12 (Oct 1899) 6-246B-128/129
Willis Taylor 58 (Ap 1842-SC/SC/SC-M 7), Lucy 40 (May 1860-M 7-3-1), Mattie ANTON 30 (sd)(Aug 1879), Willie FOUST 2/12 (sgs)(Ap 1900), Josie CASPER 23 (sil)(Ap 1872-T/Ky/T-M 5-1-0) 8-313B-58/61 (B)
Wilum G. Taylor 42 (Ap 1858-M 13), Lizzie 38 (Feb 1862-M 13-6-6), John 18 (Jan 1882), Isaac 16 (Aug 1883), Pegie 14 (Sep 1885), Robbert 12 (Mar 1888), Lillie 9 (Sep 1890), Bartlett(?) 6 (Sep 1893), James 6 (nw) (Oct 1893) 12-180B-53/56
MARRIAGES
Amanda Taylor to T. J. Bice q.v.
Ella Taylor to James Morgan q.v.
G.F. Taylor to Sarah J. Ferguson, 16 July 1888 (17 July), M.C. Bruner MG 1-561
G.W. Taylor to Lula Bohannon, 1 Dec 1897 (7 Dec), L.E. Smith JP, W.G. Taylor W 2-218
George G. Taylor to Lucinda Gallaher, 24 May 1898 (same), J.B. Phillips MG 2-285
John Taylor to Dolly Burns, 6 Aug 1898 (bond only), Jasper Hall W 2-110
John Taylor to Sally Burns, 6 Aug 1898 (7 Aug), J.A. Whitner MG, R.J. Killough W 2-316
Lynda F.M. Taylor to George A. Bader q.v.
Margarett Taylor to James Kelly q.v.
Maud Taylor to Alfred T. Brown q.v.
T.M. Taylor to Abbie Hall, 5 Sep 1900 (same), J.E. Smecker ??, E.R. Taylor W 3-210

- - - - - - - - - - - - -

TEAGUE / TEAGE / TEIGE / TIEGUE

1860 CENSUS
Adam Tague 30, Elizabeth 38, Hetty L. 18, John W. 16, Allen 5, William 25, Pleasant M. 13 8-15-103
Amanda Teague 19: see Andrew J. Bankston
MARRIAGES
Caroline Teage to A. J. Bankston q.v.
Elizabeth Teige to Harvy McCarrole q.v.
J.A. Tieague to Lucinda Roper, 22 May 1880 (23 May), S. Breeding JP 1-#1730
Joseph Teague to Edwir or Elmie Ray, 3 Sep 1888 (7 Sep), J.S. Roddy MG 1-555
Saphira Teague to Conrad Newman q.v.
W.C. Teague to Nancy Corwin or Caswin, 17 June 1863 (no return) 1-#800

- - - - - - - - - - - - -

TEASLEY / TINSLEY

1900 CENSUS

Elbert A. Teasley 45 (Oct 1854-T/Ga/Ga-M 19)(Coal Miner), Alace 40 (May 1860-Oh/Oh/Oh-M 19-6-5), Nellie M. 14 (Mar 1886), George W. 12 (Feb 1888), Thomas H. 9 (July 1890), John A. 7 (May 1893), James F. 1 (Aug 1898) 9-229B-33

Fred Teasely 22, Sallie 16: see Franklin McMillan

John Tinsley 56 (Mar 1844-T/Va/Va-M 25), Martha 43 (Ap 1857-T/NC/NC-M 25-4-2), Jeff WOODY 28 (Sep 1871-M 8)(Coal Miner) 10-254A-77

MARRIAGE

Fred Tinsley to Sudia McMillen, 22 Dec 1899 (25 Dec), A.P. Hayes JP, F. Teasey & T.J. Knight W 3-94

G.W. Tinsley to Margaret A. Travis, 20 Dec 1887 (25 Dec), J.H. Parrott MG 1-540

M. S. Tinsley to J. A. Brooks q.v.

- - - - - - - - - - - - -

TEDDER

MARRIAGE

Spince Tedder to Sallie Gillespie, 5 Mar 1883 (6 Mar), S. Phillips MG 1-480

- - - - - - - - - - - - -

TEETERS / TEETON

1900 CENSUS

Jacob Teeters 50 (Oct 1849-T/Unk/Va-M 19), Sarah 39 (May 1861-T/Unk/Ind-M 19-7-5), William 17 (May 1883), Noah 14 (Mar 1886), Jane 10 (Dec 1889), Alfred 8 (Dec 1891), Oscar 6 (May 1894) 13-295B-106/108

MARRIAGE

Nancy Teeters to William Dodson q.v.

- - - - - - - - - - - - -

TEFESTALER / TEPHTALLOW / TESSETELLER / TEFFENTELLER/ TEFTALEN [TEEFER– present spelling]

1880 CENSUS

J.G. Tefestaler 40, M.J. 38, W.L. 18 (s), M.J. 38 (si?) 3-23-185

S.D. Teftalen 28 (Blacksmith), M.E. 21, L.M. 1/12 (d) 3-23-184

1900 CENSUS

William S. Teffenteller 35 (Aug 1864-M 16), Malissa 30 (Oct 1869-M 16-8-7), Lillie M. 15 (Jan 1885), John C. 12 (Mar 1888), Bertha L. 10 (Oct 1889), James W. 8 (Jan 1892), Mary M. 7 (May 1893), Maud E. 4 (Mar 1896), Dasey E. 4/12 (Feb 1900) 5-233A-101

MARRIAGES

Joseph Henry Tephtallow (57, Blount Co) to Mrs. R.C. Broyles, nee Jane Mansell (36, Putnam Co), 4 Dec 1881, M.F. Moore(?) MG, B.T.(?) Rhea & T.J. Bramlett W 4-4(35)

S. A. Tesseteller or Teffeteller to G. W. West q.v.

William Tefferteller to Malica Neal, 18 Ap 1885 (19 Ap), Anthony Smith MG 1-488

- - - - - - - - - - - - -

TELLOW / TELLINS

1900 CENSUS

Flora Tellow 20 (Mar 1880)(Servant), Emma 18 (si)(Mar 1882), Adil CHATTIN 3/12 (ne)(Feb 1900) 10-251B-30 (B)

MARRIAGE

Flora Tellins to Evan Jones q.v.

- - - - - - - - - - - - -

TEMPLE

MARRIAGE

Cora D. Temple to A. G. Slawson q.v.

- - - - - - - - - - - - -

TEMPLETON

1860 CENSUS

Mary Templeton 42, Sarah E. 14, William A. 12, Mary J. 10, Emly A. 7, Catharine TEMPLETON 34, John C. 4 10-29-195

1870 CENSUS

William A. Templeton 23, Mary J. 20, Emily A. 18 10-1-8

1880 CENSUS

W.A. Templeton 33, Rebecca J. 26, Rebecca MOORE 72 (m), William D. 37, Mary J [*] 30, Adda E. [*] 27 10-29-221/226 [*probably TEMPLETON]

1900 CENSUS

Ashel Templeton 53 (Oct 1846-M 23), Rebecca J. 45 (May 1835-M 23-0), Marry 41 (si)(Feb 1848), Mancy BOGLE 17 (nw)(Ap 1883-NC/Va/T) 10-255A-100/101

MARRIAGES

Catharine Templeton to R. M. Martin q.v.

W.A. Templeton to R.J. Moore, 30 Nov 1876 (same), J.W. Williamson MG 1-#1473

- - - - - - - - - - - - -

TERRY

1870 CENSUS

Boyd Terry 26, Amanda 25, Barthula 6 8-13-90 (B)

1880 CENSUS

Amanda Terry 28: see John Chadrick

C.H. Terry 39, Z.J. 38, Wm 12, Teresa 10, Mary 8, Louella 5, Howard 3 4-5-40

John Terry 15: see A. Dixon

- - - - - - - - - - - - -

THATCHER

1900 CENSUS

Louis P. Thatcher 47 (Dec 1853-M 13), Edna 32 (Jan 1868-M 13-6-5), Burton C. 11 (Oct 1888), Samuel E. 9 (June 1890), Hugh L. 7 (July 1892), Elizabeth 6 (Mar 1894), Louis P. 4 (Ap 1896), Speich JONES 20 (Nov 1879-Germany/Do/Do)(Servant) 14-213B-21/22

- - - - - - - - - - - - -

THOMAS

1860 CENSUS

Fred G. Thomas 30: see P.T. Rawlings

James Thomas 35, Mary I. 23, Sarah J. 6, John 4, Franklin 2, Joshua GREENWOOD 45 (SC), Elizabeth GREENWOOD 44 (SC) 3-64-440

Wilson Thomas 40 (NC), Joseph D. 17, Manerva 15, Emly 5 1-95-649

1870 CENSUS

Biby Thomas 66 (NC), Nancy 35, Sarah 9 4-10-64

Charles Thomas 27, Amanda 26, William THOMAS 70 (Va), Margarette 67, Mary Ann 29, Sarah M. 7, Rebecca E. 5, John T. 1 4-10-65

1880 CENSUS

William Thomas 33 (Miner), Martha (B) 23 (w), Susan BROWN (B) 19 (sil) 2-31-250

1900 CENSUS

Annie P. Thomas 39 (Sep 1860-Wd), Katie 17 (July 1882), Howard 13 (Mar 1887), Robert 11 (Sep 1888), Mattie 9 (Sep 1890), Willie 7 (Nov 1892), Jacob 5 (Mar 1895), Gracie 2 (Mar 1898) 6-240B-21

Bird Thomas 45 (Aug 1854-T/T/Ga-M 25)(Coal Miner), Jennie 46 (Sep 1853-T/Ky/T-M 25-8-5), Ida B. 24 (Oct 1875), Edna S. 22 (Aug 1877), Cora A. 18 (Mar 1882), Gertrude E. 12 (Jan 1888), Eva M. 6 (Dec 1893) 13-304B-272/282

Carrie Thomas 8: see Valentine Rowen (B)

E.S.C. Thomas 17: see Aber Emery (B)

Fannie Thomas 28: see James J. Abel

George Thomas 19: see Elijah B. Ewing

James Thomas 37 (Ap 1863-M 7)(Coal Miner), Lucinda 36 (Mar 1864-T/Ky/Ky-M 7-3-3), Nellie 6 (Jan 1894), Joseph E. 4 (Feb 1896), Cornelia 1 (Mar 1899), Ada 13 (Feb 1887), Walter 11 (Mar 1889) 10-328A-174/184 (B)

Jesse D. Thomas 70 (Nov 1829-Oh/Va/NJ-Wd), Maud 33 (Dec 1866-Oh/Oh/Oh), Fred A.B. 32 (Mar 1868-Oh), Daisey A. 28 (June 1871-Oh), Mary 21 (Nov 1878-Oh), William H. RIDGLEY 72 (bl)(Sep 1827-WVa/Md/Md-S) 6-240A-3

John M. Thomas 33 (Sep 1866-M 10), Nettie 27 (Aug 1872-M 10-8-3), Cynthia A. 3 (Jan 1897), Vesta 1 (Dec 1898), infant 0 (May 1900) 13-296B-131/133

John T. Thomas 52 (Dec 1847-T/Va/Va-M 27), Sarah E. 45 (July 1854-M 27-13-11), James V. 15 (Dec 1884), Sarah Ida 14 (Jan 1886), Martha J. 12 (May 1888), John Lee 10 (Aug 1889), Robert Carl 7 (Aug 1892), David A. 6 (Mar 1894), Charles 4 (Ap 1896) 13-298A-152/155

Maggie Thomas 14: see Roscoe Bennett (B)

Mervin(?) Thomas 45 (Mar 1855-M 15), Nannie 49 (Ap 1851-M 15-1-1) 12-179A-14/16

Nettie Thomas 18: see Moses Porter (B)

Parthenia Thomas 49 (Aug 1850-Wd 5-2), Eugene P. BREEDLOVE 22 (s)(Mar 1878-Ky/SC/T)(Machinists Helper), Margaret A. BRANDON 18 (d)(Aug 1881-Ky-M 0-0), Taylor W. BRANDON 18 (sl)(July 1881-M 0)(Slate picker, Mines) 10-331A-232/247

Partise Thomas 39 (Jan 1861-Wd 1-1), William B. 14 (Dec 1885) 13-305A-287/298

Patrick Thomas 35 (Sep 1864-M 6)(Coal Miner), Julia E. 25 (June 1874-M 6-3-3), Carrie E. 5 (Feb 1895), Lizzie 3 (Dec 1896), Reese 1/12 (Ap 1900) 13-303B-252/262

Webster Thomas 75 (Dec 1824-Oh/NJ/Va-M 47)(House Carpenter), Susan E. 69 (Ap 1831-Oh/Va/Va-M 47-6-3), James H. 33 (s)(Oct 1866-M 6), Minnie S. 31 (d)(Ap 1869-Oh), Edna T. BLACK 21 (gd)(Jan 1879-Oh)(School Teacher), Edith B. 17 (gd)(Mar 1883-Ky), Joseph W. 15 (gs)(Aug 1884-Oh)(Compositor) 10-325B-119/123 [Webster married Susan Elmira Howell on 8 July 1852; information from headstone]

MARRIAGES

Alice Thomas to Jesse Iles q.v.

Andrew Thomas to Lizzie Aselinger, 1 Dec 1892, J.A. Shaver MG 4-46

Annie Thomas to A. E. Williams q.v.

Bird Thomas to Tilda Jane Frailey, 30 Dec 1874 (31 Dec), R.H. Jordan MG 1-#1382

C.G. Thomas to Katie Romans, 16 Mar 1894, W.G. Curton MG 4-73

Charley Thomas to Fannie Fleming, 5 Feb 1892, A.S. Munroe MG 4-33 (B)

D.L. Thomas to Parthena Breedlove, 25 June 1891, J.A. Darr MG 4-25

Ella Thomas to R. M. Bohannon q.v.

Esther Thomas to Will Baskett q.v.

George Thomas to Rosa Gravis, 22 Jan 1898 (23 Jan), W.M. Turner MG, J.M. Thomas W 2-244

J.H. Thomas to Annie P. Roddy, 11 June 1888 (12 June), S.Phillips MG 1-550

James Thomas to Darthula Purcell, 3 Feb 1886 (same), P.P. Brooks ?? 1-499

John Thomas to Nettie Francisco, 1 Feb 1890 (2 Feb), W.M. Turner MG 1-598

John A. Thomas to Vicy E. Howard, 26 Jan 1872 (no return) 1-#1224

Kate Thomas to J. A. Bryant q.v.

Katie C. Thomas to Rufus K. Brown q.v.

Louella Thomas to William M. Hale q.v.

Lula Thomas to J. F. Rutherford q.v.

Martha J. Thomas to Frank A. Greer q.v.

Mary Thomas to Write Perkins q.v.

Mary Thomas to J. E. Gibson q.v.

Mary Thomas to Thomas Davis q.v.

Mary Thomas to J. H. Angel q.v.

May Bell Thomas to Hugh Blevins q.v.

S. C. Thomas to J. F. Morton q.v.

Sharlett Thomas to John Argent(?) q.v.

Sallie Thomas to Enzzr Bettis q.v. (B)

T.D. Thomas to Ella Lillard, 14 Dec 1889 (15 Dec), no MG or JP 1-589 & 1-599

W. Thomas to Hannah Duggen, 15 Mar 1886 (14 Mar)[sic], P.P. Brooks ?? 1-486

W.G.M. Thomas to Mary L. McMillen, 18 May 1887 (20 May), R.C. Rankin MG 1-524

\- - - - - - - - - - - -

THOMASON / THOMISON / THOMSON / THOMISSON / TOMISON

1860 CENSUS

William P. Thomason 48 (Va), Nancy 44, John 21, Rhody T. 18, William P. 16, Zachary T. 13, Sarah V. 11, Harriet L. 9, James G. 7, Robert L. 5, Walter 7/12 6-102-698 [W.P. married Nancy Smith]

1870 CENSUS
Henry Thomison 20 (B): see Samuel J. Frazier
William P. Thomison 23: see William Allen
William P. Thomison 58 Va), Nancy 54 (Va), Rhoda 28, Virginia 22, Harriette L. 20, James 18, Robert 16, Walter F. 10, John INGLE 24 6-5-34
1880 CENSUS
James G. Thomisson 26: see Robert L. Allen
William P. Thomisson 36 (Retired Hotel Keeper), Cornelia A. 26 (w), Willie J. 2, Cora L. 9/12 5-9-86
W.P. Thomisson 67, Nancy 65, Sarah V. 29, Robert L. 24, Walter F. 20 6-20-184/188
1900 CENSUS
James G. Thomison 47 (Ot 1852-T/Va/Va-Wd)(Physician), Gebe 8 (d)(Aug 1891-T/T/Ky), Felix 6 (s)(Aug 1893), Ralph 4 (Ap 1896), Mary EVANS 14 (sd)(June 1886), Mary E. GRASTY 71 (ml)(Jan 1829-T/Va/Va-Wd 11-6) 8-313A-45/48
Robert Thomison 45 (Oct 1854-T/Va/Va-M 6), Ada 43 (June 1856-M 6-1-1), John 15 (Aug 1884), Mabel 6 (Jan 1894) 8-288A-400/402
Walter F. Thomison 40 (Oct 1859-M 10)(Physician), Ella 26 (June 1873-M 10-3-3), Maud 9 (Ap 1891), Clara 6 (Aug 1893), Agnew 1 (June 1898) 8-314A-72/75
William P. Thomison 56 (Jan 1844-T/Va/Va-M 24), Carmelie 46 (Oct 1853-M 24-9-8), William J. 22 (July 1877), Cora L. 20 (Sep 1879), Richard T. 17 (Aug 1890), Edward V. 7 (Aug 1892), James B. 2 (Mar 1898) 5-232B-92/92
MARRIAGES
Eliza Jane Thomson to Joseph Wright q.v.
Hallie [Harriet L.] Thomison to William Johnson q.v.
J.G. Thomison (27, Washington) to Della Darwin (18, Dardnell, Ark), 26 July 1882, T. Ashburn MG, Miss Flora Grier(?) & Richard Rodgers W 4-8(75)
J.G. Thomison to Lena R. Evans, 28 Oct 1890, Scott T. Cumming(?) MG 4-25
Mary E. Thomison to W. G. Allen q.v.
R.L. Thomison (28, Washington; Merchant) to C.L. Greer (18, Pikeville), 24 Ap 1883, T. Ashburn MG, Sue Johnson & Johnnie Allen W (both of Dayton) 4-14(138)
Rhoda T. Thomison to James H. Ford q.v.
W.F. Thomison to Ella Darwin, 31 Mar 1890 (1 June), J.R. Walker MG 1-601
William P. Thomison to Cornelia Peters, 1 June 1876 (same), A.P. Early MG 1-#1447

- - - - - - - - - - - - -

THOMPSON / TOMPSON

1860 CENSUS
Absalom Thompson 50, Malinda 49, Sarah C. 19, Margaret A. 17, Jesse A. 15, Thomas K. 13, Absalom L. 7, Elizabeth J. 5 2-75-514
Francis M. Thompson 26, Elizabeth R. 25, James P. 2, Louisa A. 5/12 1-83-566
Jackson Thompson 35 (NC)(Hammerman), Malinda 25, Bluford T. 9, Margaret M. 2, Columbus 5/12 4-44-296
James F. Thompson 30, Charity A. 30, Moses F. 4, William A. 2, John 1/12, Catharine THOMPSON 50, VanBuren THOMPSON 21 9-101-688
James M. Thompson 32, Eliza 34, James P. 8, Betsy A. 9/12 7-4-25
Jesse P. Thompson 42, Jane M. 38, William F. 6, Jesse C. 3, Mary McADOO 18 1-91-623
John L. Thompson 45, Nancy 30, Margaret J. 10, James 8, Addison 5, Elizabeth 2, Nancy 5/12 2-79-538
John W. Thompson 34 (Physician), Harriet 40, Catharine J. 8, Thomas H. 6, Samuel W. 4, John R. 1, Zachariah A. 1, Ruth McCULLA 27, Permelia 6 4-53-362
Joseph Thompson 50 (Conn), Julia A. 50, George 20, Ann E. 17 8-25-167
Mary Thompson 70: see Daniel Broyles
Moses C. R. Thompson 47, Lorena 38, William R. L. THOMPSON 35, Martha 29, James T. 7, William C. 2, Moses 10/12 1-92-625
Thomas K. Thompson 38, Margaret 40, Priscilla 35 2-79-536
1870 CENSUS
Absolem S. Thompson 60, Malinda 56, Margarett A. 27, Thomas K. 23, Absolem L. 17, Elizabeth J. 15, Nancy E. 8 1-9-60
Elbert Thompson 46, Mary 15, Hannah 13, Jack 11, Julia A. 8, Jane 6, John E. 4 (B): see John W. Thompson
George W. Thompson 30, Hettie S. 29 8-11-76
James A. Thompson 24, Jane 27, James M. 3, William G. 1 4-7-43
James F. Thompson 41, Charity 40 (NC), Moses F. 14, William A. 13, John L. 11, James E. 9, Joseph P. 7, Nancy J. 5, Doctor D.E. 3, Squire M. 1 1-19-125
James M. Thompson 43, Louisa 45, Elizabeth A. 10, William 4 7-6-47
James P. Thompson 19, Mariah E. 20 (Ill), Eliza Jane 1/12 7-6-48
Jesse A. Thompson 27, Mary D. 26, Sarah M. 1 2-17-122
Jesse P. Thompson 53, Jane 46, William F. 16, Henry C. 12, Perry 7, Mary 7, Vesta 2, Ellen KERSEY 15 1-6-40
John Thompson 56 (NC), Malinda 36, Bluford T. 16, Margarette 3, Noradem M. 10 (s), Andrew 8, Nancy A. 6, Tennessee 4, Kimble 2, Nancy COLLINS 66 (NC) 1-19-123
John Thompson 47, Frances 46, Mary A. 26, William A. 22, Leonidas G. 19, Eliza Jane 16, Malbera F. 13, Martha R. 9, Autany P. 6 4-1-8
John W. Thompson 47 (Physician), Harriette 51, Catharine Jane 18, Thomas H. 16, Samuel W. 15, John R. 12, Zachariah A. 12, James B. 8, Elbert THOMPSON (B) 46, Mary (B) 16, Hannah (B) 13, Jack (B) 11, Julia (B) 8, Jane (B) 6, John E. (B) 4 4-2-12
Joseph Thompson 58 (Mass), Julia Ann 58 (Conn), Ann E. 22 (Conn) 8-1-6
Martha Thompson 40, Caroline 14, Eliza 12, Manerva 10 6-14-102
Mary Thompson 10: see James O. Daniel
Mary Thompson 80: see Daniel Broyles
Moses C.R. Thompson 56, Sirena 47 1-7-41
Nancy Thompson 40 (NC), Margaret J. 20, James E. 18, Adisson 14, Elizabeth 12, Nancy 10, Thomas K. 8, John G. 6 2-3-18
Sarah Thompson 37, Eliza Jane 17, Margarette A. 15, Barbara E. 14, Mary L. 12, Malinda C. 10, Martha E. 9, Hester A.F. 8 4-16-105
Thomas K. Thompson 49, Margaret 51, Prissiller L. 47, Sarah HARRIS 12 2-3-16

Vanburen Thompson 35, Sarah 20, Kilsey B. THOMPSON62 (m) 1-7-42

William R.S. Thompson 45, Martha 36, James F. 17, William G. 13, Moses B. 11, General C. 9, Doctor B. 6, Thomas B. 3, Joseph H. 9/12 1-11-74

1880 CENSUS

A.J. Thompson 18, A. 13, Lettie 13: see A. J. Wyrick

E. Thompson 52, A.C. 26 (w), Jane 16, J.E. 14 (s), J.H. 7 (s), Parthena 3 4-32-263 (Mu)

Hannah Thompson 22 (B): see Virginia Leuty

Hester A. Thompson 17: see Elbert D. Pierce

J.A. Thompson 33, Jane 34, J.M. 13 (s), M.G. 11 (s), Alice 7 11-42-332

J.W. Thompson 56 (Doctor?), Mary 45 (w), Jack 21, T.H. 23 (s), Jas M. 18, Emma 20 (ne), Jane CLARK 47 (sil) 4-9-75

James Thompson 27: see Rebecca Hoyal

James Thompson 26, Elizabeth 21, Martha 1/12 1-17-143

James Thompson 50, Charity 50, William 22, John 20, James 19, Joseph 17, Nancy 15, Doctor 13, Squire 10, Lorinda 9, Mahala 7, May DUNLAP 8 (ne) 1-19-160

Jessee Thompson 62, Perry 17 (s), Mary 17 (d), Vesta 12 (d) 2-42-340

John Thompson 53, M.F. 57, M.A. 35 (d), Dora 21 (d), Tiney 18 (d), Belle 5 (gd), George MEE 17 (hired), W.H. HOLLOWAY 15 (Clerk) 11-43-340

Joseph Thompson 36 (Steamboat Pilot), Lydia 39, John 9, Alice 7, James 6, Susan 2, Sarah THOMPSON 62 (m), Sarah WROE 62 (c) 2-27-211

Justin Thompson 18 (Mu): see W. T. Gass

M.M. Thompson 38, Polly 35, Mary 11, James 9, John 7, Delthah 5, S.M. 3 (d), Sam 8/12, M. BRYANT 27 (boarder) 3-17-135 (B)

Mary Thompson 15: see J. M. McPherson

Minerva Thompson 18: see Stephen Breeding

Moses Thompson 24, Elvira 23, unnamed 1/12 (s) 1-10-78

N.M. Thompson 23: see Charles Reed

Nancy Thompson 49, Adison 24, Elizabeth 22, Thomas 18, John 15 2-41-337

Syrene Thompson 56, General 18 (nw), Katie 5 (adopted d) 1-8-63

Th--?--al Thompson 24, Clvin 5: see B.T. Waldo

Thomas Thompson 59, Margaret 61 (si), Priscilla 57 (si) (Cook), Margaret 8 (ne) 2-42-339

Vanburen Thompson 44, Sarah 34, Mary 8, Esquire 7, Thomas 5, Wright 3, Green 1 12-2-11

William Thompson 54, Matilda 45, Clarissa 16, William 18, Florence 12, James 11 12-6-52

William Thompson 55, Martha 49, William 22, Moses 20, Thomas 12, Doctor 17, Joseph 10, Lucy REECE 24 (Servant) 1-17-140

1900 CENSUS

Beng [D.B.?] Thompson 37 (Sep 1862-M 7), Ellie 29 (June 1870-M 7-2-2), Creed 6 (Mar 1894) Bessi 2 (Nov 1897), Banistae 38 (b)(Sep 1861) 1-187A-169/177

Claud Thompson 20: see James W.V. Scoville

Elbert Thompson 75 (Jan 1825-M 15), Joseph 25 (July 1874), Parthina ?? [Joseph & Parthina marked through] 3-204A-74/80 (B)

Emett Thompson 18: see Jacob E. Garrison

Frank Thompson 28 (Mar 1872-M 8)(RR Laborer), Margaret 28 (Mar 1872-M 8-3-2), Esepoine(?) 6 (s)(Dec 1893), Earnest 4 (Mar 1896) 14-216A-62/63

Gathers Thompson 30 (May 1870) 1-188A-180/189

James Thompson 47 (June 1853-M 20), Betsy 44 (Jan 1856-M 20-10-9), James 19 (Jan 1881), Moses 17 (Nov 1882), Cinda 15 (Dec 1884), Lara 13 (Oct 1886), Jacob 11 (Ap 1887), Willi 8 (Ap 1892), John 6 (Ap 1894), Clide 2 (June 1897) 1-188A-177/186

James A. Thompson 21: see James Evens

James A. Thompson 54 (Jan 1846-M 30), Jennie 58 (Ap 1842-M 30-5-3), James M. 28 (May 1872), William G. 26 (June 1874), Amanda A. 24 (Ap 1876) 14-221A-149/153

James F. Thompson 70 (Sep 1829-T/Va/Va-M 45)(Gardner), Charaity 70 (Sep 1829-N/NC/NC-M 45-11-6), Douglas D. 32 (May 1868)(Bartender), Joseph B. 14 (gs)(Feb 1886) 14-219A-125/128

Jeff Thompson 55 (Jan 1845-Ga/Ga/Ga-M 16)(Day Laborer), Elsa 40 (Mar 1860-M 16-0), Mathew M. MORRIS 45 (boarder)(Unk 1855-Ga/Ga/Ga-M ?) 14-216B-74/75 (B)

Joe Tompson 51 (B): see Huston Shaver

John(?) Thompson 39 (Feb 1861-M 16), Ellen 42 (Sep 1857-M 16-6-6), Clide 20 (Ap 1880)(Store Clerk), James 18 (Feb 1882)(Miller), Annie 14 (Dec 1885), Jerephes 13 (Feb 1887), Miram 6 (July 1893), Charles 5 (Dec 1894) 1-189B-206/215 (Spring City)

John R. Thompson 41 (Sep 1858-M 16), Cynthia A. 37 (Jan 1863-Ky/Ky/Ky-M 16-0), Albert WEST (B) 30 (Oct 1869-Ga/Ga/Ga)(Servant) 2-199A-148/153

Maria Thompson 29 (Ap 1871-T/T/Va-Wd 4-4)(Private Cook), Robert 10 (July 1889)(Servant), Mary 8 (Aug 1891), Author 5 (May 1895), Oscar 2 (Sep 1897), Leana MARIOTT 25 (si)(Nov 1895) 2-198A-127/132 (B)

Mary A. Thompson 57, Martha A. 40, Autensa P. 34: see James W. Wright

Milla Thompson 39 (Nov 1860-Wd 6-4), Walter K. 12 (Nov 1887), Carl T. 10 (Nov 1889), Homer B. 9 (June 1891), Earl C. 5 (July 1894) 14-217A-91/93

Thomas Thompson 33 (May 1867-M 10), Sallie 32 (Sep 1867-M 10-1-0) 1-188A-175/184

Tom Thompson 36 (Unk-M 19)(Hostler, Livery Stable), Fanny 39 (Ap 1861-M 19-7-5), Charley 18 (Jan 1882), Jeannetta 16 (July 1883), Cordelia 13 (May 1887), Willie 7 (June 1892), Mattie B. 5 (June 1894), Charlotte RUNYONS 70 (ml)(Unk-Wd 5-3) 10-329-192/205 (B)

William Thompson 18 (B): see John Holloway

William A. Thompson 42 (Nov 1857-M 5)(RR Carpenter), Myra E. 41 (May 1859-M 5) 14-223A-194/198

Wilum Thompson 75 (Jan 1825-T/Va/Va-Wd) 1-187A-169/178

MARRIAGES

Alma Thompson to Samuel Durham q.v.

Ann E. Thompson to James Gregory q.v.

Anney Thompson to J. R. Myres q.v.

Bell Thompson to James Wright q.v.

Bell Thompson to Henry Knox q.v.

Bettie Thompson to Rufus W. Morgan q.v.

Catharine Thompson to William Dodson q.v.

Catharine J. Thompson to John McFerson q.v.

D.B. Thompson to Ella Hanney, 5 Mar 1893, J.M. Hinds MG 4-73

E.H. Thompson to L.E. Clark, 11 Jan 1884 (same), John Howard MG 1-477

Ellen Thompson to Simon Simpson q.v.

Elvira Thompson to James E. Thompson q.v.
Emma Thompson to F. A. Parks q.v.
Evander Thompson to Emaline Watson, 13 Sep 1858 (25 Sep), A. Low JP 1-#656
F.M. Thompson to Rebecca Cash, 3 July 1855 (10 July), T.J. Gillespie JP 1-#506
Hannah Thompson to Samuel Waterhouse q.v.
J.E. Thompson to C. E. March, 5 Nov 1884 (same), B.F. Holloway JP 1-482
J.W. Thompson to Lydda Ann Roddy, 27 Ap 1868 (no return) 1-#1009
Jackson Thompson to Malinda Collins, 4 Ap 1859 (no return) 1-#679
James A. Thompson to Jeane Holloway, 12 Oct 1866 (14 Oct), B. Abernathy LMEC 1-#913
James E. Thompson to Elvira Thompson, 17 Oct 1891, C.J. Titus JP 4-31
James E. Thompson to Charity McClendon, 17 Dec 1854, Thos V. Atchley JP 1-#474
James F. Thompson to Elizabeth S. Dunlap, 21 Dec 1878 (22 Dec), Edward Pyott MG 1-#1593
James J. Thompson to Elizabeth Enos, 4 Sep 1869 (5 Sep), J. Howard MG 1-#1111
Jane Thompson to James Filyan(?) q.v.
Jeff Thompson to Alice Rhea, 17 May 1886 (18 May), J.P. Thompson JP 1-538
Jerry A. Thompson to Mary A. Breedin, 16 Dec 1867 (17 Dec), W.W. Low JP 1-#989
Jesse P. Thompson to Manervia J. Thompson, 15 Ap 1852 (same), J.I. Cash MG 1-#371
John Thompson to E.J. Martin, 15 May 1856 (same), L.W. Ferguson JP 1-#571
John Thompson to Mary A. Harris, no date [on page with 1877] 1-#1499
K.M. Thompson to Adaline Perkins, 13 Nov 1886 (same), E.S. Cox JP 1-509
Lorina E. Thompson to W. T. Gray q.v.
M. ?. Thompson to John R. Baldwin q.v.
M. M. Thompson to William W. Lowe q.v.
Mahala F. Thompson to J. Simpson q.v.
Manervia J. Thompson to Jesse P. Thompson q.v.
Margarett Thompson to Wesley Wyrick q.v.
Margarett J. Thompson to A. C. Miller q.v.
Margaret A. Thompson to J. W. Dovanite q.v.
Marion(?) Thompson to Annie Bailey, 8 May 1889 (same), J.B. Phillips MG 1-575
Martha Thompson to William W. Campbell q.v.
Mary Thompson to W. H. Prigmore q.v.
Mary L. Thompson to H. C. Holloway q.v.
Mattie Thompson to James Smith q.v.
Mattie Thompson to James Elder q.v.
Mitchell Thompson to Mary Archie, 15 Dec 1900 (20 Dec), R.C. Knight JP, Tom Ford [signed by X] W 3-257
Moses F. Thompson to Elvira A. Garrison, 22 Feb 1879 (no return) 1-#1607
Nancy A. Thompson to Jessie Turner q.v.
Nanie Thompson to Samuel A. Day q.v.
Nicy Thompson to Jacob Byerly q.v.
Peggy A. Thompson to Thomas Martin q.v.
Robert W. Thompson to Emma Ferguson, 26 Dec 1897, E.W. Mort ?? 4-99
Russell Thompson to Nicy Majors, 9 Sep 1852 (same), Wm Floyd JP 1-#388
S. A. Thompson to George Morris q.v.
S.F. Thompson to Maggie Harris, 4 Dec 1892, J.E. Waterhouse JP 4-48
Sallie Thompson to J. M. Price q.v.
Samuel G. Thompson to Louvena Hutchinson, 20 Nov 1858 (no return) 1-#673
Sarah Thompson to W. E. McCully q.v.
Sarah F. Thompson to Josiah Dawson q.v.
Sarah F. Thompson to J. Brightwell q.v.
Sary N. Thompson to N. T. Martin q.v.
Susan Thompson to Mack Willis q.v. (B)
T.H. Thompson to Mollie or Mettie Caldwell, 8 May 1886 (9 May), A.P. Early MG 1-515
T. M. A. Thompson to James Morrison q.v.
Thomas B. Thompson to Sallie Cox, 6 Nov 1888 (13 Jan 1889), D.L. Farris(?) JP 1-567
Thomas B. Thompson to Lizzie Burnett, 4 Mar 1897, E.P. Searle MG 4-98
Vanburen Thompson to Sarah Sales, 2 Jan 1870 (?? Feb), John Howard MG 1-#1134
Vesta J. Thompson to John Phillips q.v.
W.R.S. Thompson to Martha M. Dudley, 19 Jan 1852 (22 Jan), D. Broyles JP 1-#368
W.R.S. Thompson to E.J. Loy, 26 Aug 1894, Jas Johnson JP 4-72
William Thompson to Florence Wreen(?), 9 Oct 1899 (1 Nov), J.L. McPherson JP, W.C. Bailey W 3-49
William Thompson to Louisa Johnson, 24 May 1884 (26 May), C.M. Ingram MG 1-471
William Thompson to Sarah Lemmons, 16 Ap 1857 (same), E.E. Wasson JP 1-#597
William A. Thompson to Myra E.A. Loving(?), 21 Nov 1894, James Johnson JP 4-77

\- - - - - - - - - - - - -

THORP / THARP / THORPE

1860 CENSUS

Calvin Tharp 30, Sophy 25, Prescilla 12, Mary E. 8, James W. 3, William H. 1, Clara HIGHBARK 55 4-47-316
Jesse Thorpe 35, Betsy 40, Susan 2, Thomas 8, Francis 3 2-73-495
Sarah Tharp 45, Burrim(?) 16 4-47-317

1870 and 1880 CENSUS– None

1900 CENSUS

Joseph Thorp 24 (May 1876-M 5), Mary E. 21 (Nov 1878-M 5-2-2), George A. 2 (Dec 1897), William F. 2/12 (Oct 1899), Nancy C. PRICE 35 (ml)(July 1844-NC/NC/NC-Wd 1-1), Julia A. 17 (sil)(July 1882-T/T/NC) 5-235B-151 [Joseph married Mary Price on 20 Dec 1896 in Meigs County]

MARRIAGES

Bertie Tharp to Hugh Ray q.v.
Calvin Tharp to Loth Stuart, 15 June 1857 (same), L.W. Ferguson JP 1-#603
George Thorp to Lula Usur or Usom, 7 Feb 1896, A. P. Hayes JP 4-95
Hattie Tharp to Henry Majors q.v.
Jessee Tharp to N.E. Allison, 2 Aug 1853 (5 Aug), Daniel Broyles JP 1-#415

\- - - - - - - - - - - - -

THURMAN

1860 CENSUS
Jackson Thurman 28, Patsy A. 28, Sarah 9, Catharine E. 2 6-106-722
1870 CENSUS
Andrew Thurman 21, Rachel L. 21 4-13-86
Evander Thurman 34, Emaline 30, Cordelia 10, Nancy 8, Marion A. 6, Mary WATSON 35 1-8-51
Henry Thurman 48, Margarette 28, James R. 15, Jesse C. 13, John M. 11, Joseph 9, Granville T. 8, John C. 6 4-10-66
Hillard Thurman 55 (SC), Jane 45, Mary A. 11 8-3-19
Jackson Thurman 45 (SC), Martha M. 34, Catharine E. 12, Mary A. 9, Jefferson 8 6-16-112
1880 CENSUS
Charles Thurman 38, Amanda 38, S.M. 16 (d), R.E. 14 (d), J.T. 12 (s), J.C. 9 (s), S.S. 5 (d), E.M. 2 (s) 3-29-230
Evander Thurman 45, Emaline 45, A. 21 (d), Nancy 18, M.A. 15 (s) 4-9-74
Henry Thurman 52, M.E. 32, J.W. 25, J.M. 19, G.T. 19, J.C. 16, Mary 38 (si) 4-2-14
Jackson Thurman 58, Martha M. 47 6-17-156/160
Joseph Thurman 18: see James Brady
1900 CENSUS
Calvin Thurman 76 (Unk 1824-NC/NC/NC-M 45), Mary 66 (Unk 1834-NC/NC/NC-M 45-12-10), Texas 33 (d) (Sep 1866-Ga-Wd 1-1), Florida 13 (gd)(Mar 1887), Manuel 21 (s)(Unk 1879-Ga)(Coal Miner), Levi 23 (Unk 1877-Ga-M 1)(Coal Miner), Neal 19 (dl)(Unk 1881-M 1-0), Minnie GOTHARD 25 (d)(Nov 1874-M 9-1-0) 8-280A-234/236
Charles Thurman 26 (Unk-M 1), Martha 18 (Mar 1882-Ala/Ala/Ala-M 1-1-1), Bertha 1/12 (May 1900), Aron 16 (b)(Unk), Marion 4 (nw)(July 1895) 6-247A-134/135
Evander Thurman 64 (Oct 1835-T/Va/T-D) 14-222B-178/182
Will Thurman 24 (Dec 1875-M 6), Mary 21 (June 1878-M 6-4-4), Lulia 5 (Oct 1874), Ethel V. 3 (Nov 1896), Gracy A. 2 (Jan 1898), Will 0/12 (May 1900), Mona RANDOLPH 22 (sil)(Aug 1877) 10-256B-128/132 (B)
MARRIAGES
Elijah Thurman to Minnie Jeffreys, 16 Dec 1892, William Morgan JP 4-68
Elisha A. Thurman to Rachel L. Neil, 17 Mar 1870 (same), Bailey Minicks JP 1-#1146
Elizabeth Thurman to Joseph Dodd q.v.
Evander Thurman to Martha Worley, 2 Ap 1896, G.R. Baldwin JP 4-92
Henry Thurman to Mary Arthur, 12 Feb 1890 (14 Feb), R.S. Mason JP 1-598
J.C. Thurman to Lori Hall, 15 Mar 1884 (same), J.H. Weaver MG 1-471
Jane Thurman to James T. Henderson q.v.
Kansas Thurman to Body Author q.v.
John Thurman to Anna Emaline Swafford, 7 Dec 1858 (8 Dec), Wm Morgan JP 1-#674
Levi Thurman to Hattie Holden(?), 22 Aug 1895, W.L. Lillard JP 4-86
Levi B. Thurman to Cornelia Doran, 4 July 1899 (same), R.C. Knight JP, J.C. Black W 3-6
Lula Thurman to G. W. Webb q.v.
Lutitia Thurman to Georg Price q.v.
Mary Thurman to John Gothard q.v.
Mary Thurman to Thomas C. Wright q.v.
Mary Ann Thurman to James M. Cox q.v.
N. P. Thurman to E. G. Harris q.v.
Nancy Thurman to Thomas Allen q.v.
Nannie Thurman to Andy Majors q.v.
Polly Thurman to Marion Watson q.v.
Sallie Thurman to Jesse Ivester q.v.
Sarah Jane Thurman to J. I. Everett q.v.
Van Thurman to Tennie Neal, 23 Nov 1893, J.E. Waterhouse JP 4-62
William Thurman to Mary Randolph, 31 Dec 1892, H. Hinton MG 4-62

- - - - - - - - - - - - -

THYAW

1900 CENSUS
John Thyaw 30 (Mar 1870-NC/NC/NC-M 4)(Coal Miner), Lizzie 20 (May 1880-T/Ga/Ga-M 4-2-1), Stella 8/12 (Sep 1899), Bessie 11 (d)(July 1888), Lawrence 9 (s)(Ap 1891) 8-279B-219/221

- - - - - - - - - - - - -

TICHENER

MARRIAGE
O.L. Tichener to Mamie Kenedy, 17 Dec 1892, W.S. Neighbors MG 4-49

- - - - - - - - - - - - -

TIDWELL

MARRIAGE
John Tidwell to Adaline McNeal or McKeal, 16 Aug 1900 (same), G.W. --?-- MG, S.H. Ellis W 3-198

- - - - - - - - - - - - -

TIGNER

1900 CENSUS
Louis Tigner 41: see Alonzo Lane (B)

- - - - - - - - - - - - -

TILLEY / TILLY
(see also TALLEY)

1880 CENSUS
L. C. Tilley 40: see John Lee
Thomas D. Tilley 30 (Merchant), Sallie J. 30, Ann E. 5, John J. 3 6-22-7 (Madison Street, Washington)
1900 CENSUS
E. Lee Tilley 23 (Ap 1877-M 3), Vira 25 (Sep 1874-M 3-0), Wray TURNER 27 (sil)(Unk 1873) 3-209A-161/175
John A. Tilley 46 (Ap 1854-M 21), Mary J. 45 (Aug 1854-M 21-9-8), John B. 15 (Mar 1885), Robert T. 12 (Mar 1888), Caty J. 9 (Mar 1891), Walter H. 6 (Aug 1893), Bess 3 (Oct 1896), Maud P. 11/12 (June 1899) 4-225B-232/236

Newton A. Tilley 44 (Jan 1856-T/NC/T-M 24), Caroline 44 (July 1855-M 24-10-10), Nancy L. 14 (Jan 1886), Harriet 12 (July 1887), Earnest 10 (July 1889), Andrew 9 (Aug 1890), Evans 7 (Oct 1892), James T. 4 (Mar 1896), Elijah P. 20 (s)(Ap 1880), Lillie M. 16 (d)(Mar 1884), Eliza TILLEY 74 (m)(Ap 1826-Wd 6-3) 14-222A-165/169

MARRIAGES

Frances J. Tilley to Joseph Dunn q.v.
Lillie Tilly to John W. Pogue q.v.
Lizie Tilly or Tilley to John Martin Hartley q.v.

- - - - - - - - - - - - -

TINDELL

1880 CENSUS

S.W. Tindell 36 (Minister), Catharine 18 (w), Lilly 5 (d) 3-18-143

1900 CENSUS

Samuel W. Tindell 55 (Oct 1844-M 23)(School Teacher), Kattie C. 38 (Dec 1861-M 23-8-7), Pearl 19 (Nov 1880)(School Teacher), Susie 17 (Ap 1883)(School Teacher), Samuel W. 14 (Feb 1886), Hiram C. 12 (Dec 1887), Mary P. 5 (Oct 1894), Edith A. 4 (Oct 1895), Pauline A. 1 (Sep 1898) 3-205B-95/103

MARRIAGE

S.W. Tindell to Caty Chattin, 13 July 1878 (no return) 1-#1368

- - - - - - - - - - - - -

TINKER

1880 CENSUS

John Tinker 30, Mary 21, William 2 (s), Belle GREEN 10 (d) 2-29-236

- - - - - - - - - - - - -

TINSLEY– see TEASLEY

- - - - - - - - - - - - -

TIPTON

1900 CENSUS

Aliton Tipton 19: see Leauther Woods
Edgar P. Tipton 41 (Sep 1858-M 7)(Coal Miner), Nancy J. 38 (May 1862-M 7-3-3), Richard T. 5 (Sep 1894), Edgar P. Jr. 3 (Sep 1896), Louisa 1 (Feb 1899) 13-304A-270/280

MARRIAGES

Annie Tipton to Alex Cox q.v.
E.P. Tipton to Nancy J. Hawkins, 20 Sep 1893, Z. Bain MG 4-56

- - - - - - - - - - - - -

TODD

1880 CENSUS

Charles M. Todd 38, Angaliner 33, Lena R. 5, Amaline 2 10-29-223/228

1900 CENSUS

Charles M. Todd 59 (June 1840-SC/SC/SC-M 4), Mary 49 (Feb 1851-T/NC/T-M 4-0), Kate 18 (Mar 1882), Anna L. SPENCE 22 (d)(Feb 1878-T/SC/T-M 2-0), James SPENCE 21 (sl)(June 1878-M 2) 15-269B-32 [Chas married Mary Fuller on 12 June 1895 in Meigs Co]

MARRIAGES

Annie Lee Todd to James R. Spence q.v.
Nellie E. Todd to J. R. Miller q.v.
Charles M. Todd to Angeline Paine, 10 June 1874 (11 June), A.P. Early MG 1-#1339

- - - - - - - - - - - - -

TOLIVER

1900 CENSUS

Heart Toliver 49 (June 1851-M 16)(Coke Puller), Laura 45 (July 1854-M 16-6-6), Janie 15 (Sep 1885), Mary 14 (Dec 1885), Hugh 14 (Ap 1886), George 11 (Ap 1889), Robert 7 (Aug 1892), Sallie 4 (June 1898), Arthur SCOTT 18 (boarder)(Mar 1882)(Coke Puller) 10-257B-147/151 (B)

- - - - - - - - - - - - -

TOLLE / TOEL

1900 CENSUS

Jennie Tolle 27: see Albert G. Slawson
John J. Tolle 54 (June 1845-Ky-M 25), Josephine A. 51 (Dec 1848-Ind/NC/Ind-M 25-6-6), Philip S. 19 (Sep 1880-Kan)(Coal Miner), Mabel C. 21 (June 1878-Kan), John B. 15 (Dec 1884-Kan), Mary A. 9 (Oct 1890) 11-290A-3

MARRIAGE

Nellie Toel to John Ewers q.v.

- - - - - - - - - - - - -

TOLSTEN

MARRIAGE

William Tolsten to Abigal Myres, 2 Ap 1866 (3 Ap), William A. Green JP 1-#895

- - - - - - - - - - - - -

TORBETT / TORBET

1860 CENSUS

Sarah Torbett* 68 (Va), Susan J. 42 (Va), Mary E. 29 (Va), Sarah M. 31, Lucy J.** 28, Tennessee** 7 4-49-334 [*nee McCadden; widow of John][**widow & dau of Augustus Torbett]
Thomas F. Torbett 29, Mary E. 21, James A. 2 4-51-350

1870 CENSUS

Mary E. Torbett 32, James R. 12, Selah MARSH 72 (NC) 4-9-58
Sarah Torbet 78 (Va), Susan J. 52 (Va), Mary E. 40 (Va), Sarah M. 44 (Va), Lucy Jane 42 (Va), Tennessee 17 4-5-30

1880 CENSUS

E.M. Torbett 52 (m), James 22 (s), C.J. COOK 22 (ne) 4-35-287
M.E. Torbett 61, S.M. 48: see I.N. Whttenburg

1900 CENSUS

James A. Torbett 41 (June 1858-M 19), Mary A. 37 (Nov 1860-M 19-8-8), Thomas F. 17 (Sep 1882), John C. 16 (May 1884), James S. 13 (June 1886), Loet W. 12 (Jan 1888), Alfred H. 10 (Jan 1890), Oliver C. 7 (Aug 1892), Craty 4 (Jan 1896), Hugh L. 1 (July 1898), James H. TORBETT 76 (u)(June 1823-Va/Va/Va-Wd) 14-221B-160/164

MARRIAGES

James A. Torbet (25, Rhea Springs) to Mary A. Holland (24, Rhea Springs), 19 Dec 1882, J.M. Bramlett MG, Thos Holloway & John McClendon W 4-8(72)

R.B. [Rush B.] Torbett to N.E. [Nancy Emaline] Whittenburg, 2 Nov 1852 (4 Nov), J.W. Thompson MG 1-#391

Thomas F. Torbett to Mary E. Marsh, 10 July 1857 (same), Levi W. Ferguson JP 1-#606

Virginia Torbett to O. A. Marsh q.v.

- - - - - - - - - - - - -

TOWNSELL

MARRIAGE

Jessie Townsell to George Hayes q.v.

- - - - - - - - - - - - -

TOWNSEND

1900 CENSUS

Edward Townsend 68 (Oct 1831-Mass/Do/Do-M 35), Elizabeth 53 (Mar 1845-Ga/SC/SC-M 35-7-4), Lusander 24 (Ap 1876-Ga), Jessie HAYES 18 (d)(Jan 1882-Ga-Wd 1-1), George R. 2 (gs)(May 1898) 8-276A-149/149

John Townsend 21 (July 1878-Ga/Mass/Do-M 1), Sarah E. 20 (Oct 1879-M 1-1-1), Maggie E. 4/12 (Jan 1900) 8-275B-148

MARRIAGE

John Townsend to Sarah McMillen, 21 Dec 1898 (same), N.D. Reed MG, Pete Cahill W 2-360

- - - - - - - - - - - - -

TRAIN

1900 CENSUS

Charles Train 43 (June 1856-Mich/Mass/Conn-M 20), Celia G. 47 (May 1853-Mich/NY/NY-M 20-3-3), Florence 17 (Aug 1882-Mich)(Teacher), Beulah 13 (Ap 1887-Mich), Leroy 13 (Ap 1887-Mich) 14-213A-13/13

- - - - - - - - - - - - -

TRAMBLE / TRAMELL / TRAMWELL

1900 CENSUS

James C. Tramble 21: see Sarah Trusly

MARRIAGES

J.C. Tramble to Maggie McMahan, 8 Ap 1898 (10 Ap), F.M. Cook MG, Wm Woody [signed by X] W 2-266

J.C. Tramell or Tramwell to Alice Trusley, 12 Sep 1900 (same), W.L. Lillard JP, Bill Brandon(?) W 3-215

- - - - - - - - - - - - -

TRAMELT

MARRIAGE

Annie Tramelt to Henry Heaton q.v.

- - - - - - - - - - - - -

TRAVIS

1860 CENSUS

Joseph Travis 61 (Carpenter), Lovenia 58, Butler 39 [probably incorrect], Caroline 15, John H. 13, Joseph 10, Samuel 6, Thomas 3, Wesly WRIGHT 24, Elvira 17 6-103-700

Samuel Travis 27, Rebecca 19 3-54-368

1870 CENSUS

Benjamin B. Travis 37, Lucinda 27, Samuel 17, William 11, John 6, Margarette A. 1, Mary CARROLL 21 5-2-8

Joseph Travis 71, Louvenia 67, Rachel 32, Thomas 12, John 9, James 7 6-1-2

Thomas C. Travis 38 (House Carpenter), Nancy 36 (Ky), William H. 14, Sarah E. 10, Joseph H. 7, Nancy A. 5, Thomas L. 3, Margarette C. 1 8-21-142

1880 CENSUS

John H. Travis 32, Rachel J. 34, Mary A. 10, James H. 9, Benjamin F. 7, Charley G. 5, John R. 3, Martha E. 8/12 6-16-144/146

Samuel Travis 27, Ellen 23, James A. 4, Walter 9/12 6-19-179/183

T.C. Travis 49, Nancy 46, J.H. 18 (s), Ann 15, T.S. 14 (s), Maggie 11, J.V. 9 (s), Tip 7 (s), P.G. 3 (s) 8-17-144

William H. Travis 24, May 18, G.W. 2, J.E. 1 8-3-21

1900 CENSUS

Benjamin B. Travis 73 (July 1826-Wd), Lucinda 22 (Unk), Jacob F. 29 (s)(May 1871-M 2)(Brakeman), Miranda M. 16 (dl)(July 1883-M 2-1-1) 6-240A-5

George T. Travis 27 (Jan 1873-M 5)(Coal Miner), Sarah H. 26 (Oct 1873-M 5-3-2), Edith P. 2 (Oct 1897), Vesta P. 1 (Ap 1899) 13-306A-303/315

James Travis 28 (Jan 1872-M 11), Ida 28 (May 1872-M 11-5-2), Albert 10 (Mar 1890), Vesta 4 (Dec 1895) 6-246A-118/119

John Travis 37 (Jan 1863-M 8), Lula 27 (Mar 1873-M 8-3-2), Blanche 4 (June 1895), Garvie 2 (Nov 1897) 8-277A-172

Missouri K. Travis 42: see Reuben H. Smith

Peter H. Travis 22 (Nov 1877-M 1), Nannie 17 (Feb 1883-M 1-1-1), Luther 7/12 (Oct 1899) 15-269B-36

Thomas Travis 35 (Unk 1865-M 7), Nettie 30 (Feb 1870-M 7-3-3), Flossie 6 (Jan 1894), Grover 4 (May 1896), Ella 2 (Nov 1897), Eli HALL 19 (bl)(Feb 1881) 15-273A-97

Thomas C. Travis 40 (Mar 1860-M 13), Ellen 38 (Ap 1862-T/NC/NC-M 13-6-4), Floyd 8 (Dec 1891), Birid 6 (Feb 1894), Lester 3 (June 1896), Claud 1 (Nov 1899), Maggie WEST 16 (Feb 1884)(Servant) 7-261B-221/226

Thomas C. Travis 68 (June 1831-M 44), Nancy 65 (Nov 1834-T/NC/NC-M 44-11-9), Emma 14 (Mar 1886) 15-269B-35

MARRIAGES

B.B. Travis to Susan Chambers, 13 Mar 1862 (same), John Howard MG 1-#775

B.B. Travis to Loucinda Watts, 8 Aug 1867 (same), Wm F. Buttram MG 1-#963
Eliza C. Travis to S. D. Houston q.v.
Elizabeth Travis to Banister Smith q.v.
Ellen Travis to William Hale q.v.
Elvira Travis to W. T. Wright q.v.
G.T. Travis to Hattie Doran, 14 Ap 1895, W.S. Hale MG 4-79
J.F. Travis to Miranda Henderson, 2 Aug 1897 (3 Aug), W.A. Howard MG, W.P. Darwin W 2-165
J.H. Travis to M.E. or H.E. Smedley, 4 June 1885 (7 June), W.S. Hale MG 1-495
J.H. Travis to M.A. Tallent, 15 Aug 1891 [probably 1892], H.B. Burdett MG 4-42
J.H. Travis to Missouri Mathes, 26 Mar 1897 (27 Mar), W. S. Hale MG 2-132
James H. Travis to Ida Eaves, 16 Feb 1889 (17 Feb), J.L. Hemp or Hughes ?? 1-569
John Travis to Lula Martin, 20 Mar 1892, W.S. Hale MG 4-43
John H. Travis to E.J. Roddy, 11 Nov 1869 (same), W.F. Buttram MG 1-#1123
Lillie Travis to Oscar Runyan q.v.
M. C. Travis to R. C. Newman q.v.
Maney M. Travis to Georg M. Harrison q.v.
Margaret A. Travis to G. W. Tingsley q.v.
Mary Travis to H. H. Jackson q.v.
Nancy R. Travis to James J. Tallent q.v.
P.G. Travis to Mattie Hale, 23 Dec 1893 (same), W.S. Hale MG, T.C. Travis W 2-361
Rachel Travis to Joseph Wyott q.v.
Samuel Travis to Mary Ann Furgusson, 13 Ap 1853 (same), R.T. Howard MG 1-#409
Samuel Travis to Nancy Murphey, 1 Dec 1855 (2 Dec), John Howard JP 1-#533
Samuel Travis to Rebecca Jolly, 21 July 1859 (same), D. Homer MG 1-#686
Samuel Travis to Ellen M. Roddy, 3 Nov 1874 (5 Dec), W.W. Dodd MG 1-#1377
T.E. Travis to Nettie Hall, 20 Nov 1892, W.S. Hale MG 4-48
Thomas Travis to Ella Bolen, 14 Jan 1887 (16 Jan), J.A. Shaver MG 1-517
Thomas C. Travis to Nancy Buttram, 18 Aug 1855 (19 Aug), John Wyott JP 1-#514
Vird Wright, nee Travis, to Allen Hale q.v.
William Travis to Molly Amos, 5 June 1875 (same), Calvin Morgan JP 1-#1399

\- - - - - - - - - - - - -

TREADWAY / TREADAWAY / TREDWAY

1860 CENSUS
Daniel B. Treadway 26, Catharine 22, Eva 3, Landon C.H. 1 2-70-477
John Tredway 22, Malinda 19, William T. 1 2-80-543
1870 CENSUS
Levi Tredway 30, Mary Jane 24, Charles D. 3, Eddy 1, Barbara HARDBARGER 17, Phillip 20, Daniel 18 1-11-71
1880 CENSUS
Levi Treadaway 39 (Miller), Mary 35, Charlie 12, Edward 10, Oley 8, Thomas 4, Amanda 2, Mary 1 1-16-134
William Treadaway 21, Sarah 20, Lou Ella 1/12 1-13-106
1900 CENSUS
John W. Treadway 24 (Feb 1876-M 1), Bell 23 (Nov 1876-M 1-0), Bertha 18 (si)(June 1886) 15-273B-102
Levi Treadway 59 (Mar 1841-M 34), Mary 56 (Feb 1844-M 34-12-8), Edward 31 (Dec 1869), Thomas 25 (Dec 1874), Mary 21 (Nov 1879), Robert 19 (Jan 1881), George 12 (Ap 1887) 1-183B-93/96
Moses(?) Treadway 32 (Aug 1867-M 9), Cora 27 (May 1871-M 8-4-4), Manda 8 (Dec 1891), Bessie 7 (May 1892), Charles 5 (Nov 1894), Latice(?) 3 (s)(Nov 1897) 1-183B-94/97
Robert Treadway 19: see Zachariah T. Keedy
William Treadaway 30: see George Gray (B)
Wilum F. Treadway 41 (Dec 1858-M 21), Sarah 40 (Jan 1860-M 21-6-6), Luler(?) 20 (Nov 1879), Charles 17 (Aug 1882), Lanis 15 (Ap 1885), Erie 5 (d)(Feb 1895), Eddi 2 (d)(Oct 1877) 1-187A-165/173
MARRIAGES
Amanda J. Treadway to A. J. Stonecipher q.v.
E.F.M. Treadaway to Ellen Parker, 3 Dec 1860 (no return) 1-#734
John R. Treadaway to Malinda Hughes, 2 Jan 1858 (8 Jan), A.H. Long JP 1-#651
Levi Tredaway to Mary Fine, 16 July 1866 (18 July), W.W. Low JP 1-#1061
Ollie Treadway to D. J. Stincipher q.v.
Robert Treadway to Hester Keedy, 1 Sep 1900 (2 Sep), Wm A. Green JP 3-208
Sarah Treadaway to William Holloway q.v.
William Treadway to Sarah Holloway, 8 Jan 1879 (9 Jan), J.P. Roddy MG 1-291

\- - - - - - - - - - - - -

TRENTHAM

1860 CENSUS
James H. Trentham 40, Nancy J. 20, Sophea 18, William M. 16, Andrew J. 14, James M. 11, Charles A. 6, Robert 5 4-40-273
1870 CENSUS
John J. Trentham 23, Mary E. 23, Harriette A. 2, James M. 10/12 1-18-120
Nancy J. Trentham 30, William M. 26, Charles N. 16, Robert M. 14 4-4-26
1880 CENSUS
A.J. Trentham 35, M.E. 33 (w), H.A. 12 (d), J.M. 11 (d), J.W. 9 (s), E.W. 7 (d), A.D. 5 (d), E. 2 (d) 11-42-338
Robert Trentham 24, M.A. 22 (w), W.R. 2/12 (d), N.J. 40 (si) 3-30-244
1900 CENSUS
Andrew J. Trentham 55 (Oct 1844-M 35), Mary E. 53 (Dec 1846-T/T/Va-M 35-9-8), Harett A. 32 (June 1868), James N. 30 (Sep 1869), Chapman 19 (Jan 1881), Ida B. 17 (Ap 1883), Birtha L. 8 (July 1891) 3-211B-206/224
John Trentham 27 (Nov 1872-M 6), Ann 22 (Mar 1878-M 6-2-2), Rainy 5 (Jan 1895), Mary L. 9/12 (Oct 1899) 14-222A-170/174

Nancy Trentham 60: see William J. Mitchell
Robert M. Trentham 54 (Sep 1845-M 20), Mary A. 43 (Dec 1856-M 20-8-6), Nancy R. 20 (Mar 1880), Carrie B. 18 (Ap 1882), Mary E. 14 (July 1885), Sarah M. 12 (Feb 1888), Anna C. 8 (Jan 1892), Easther J. 6/12 (Nov 1899) 4-225B-237/241

MARRIAGES

A.J. Trentham to Mary Hollaway, 23 Feb 1867 (no return) 1-#940
Ada Trentham to James H. Allen q.v.
Ida Trentham to J. Charley B. Clack q.v.
John Trentham to Anney Alley, 21 Jan 1894, R.M. Trentham JP 4-65
R.M. Trentham to Mary Ann Walker, 13 Mar 1879 (12 Mar) [sic], D.V. Culver MG 1-#1609

- - - - - - - - - - - - -

TRENTWAN

1900 CENSUS

John Trentwan 30 (Nov 1869-M 10)(Coal Miner), Lula 29 (Ap 1871-M 10-5-3), William 9 (Nov 1890), Bertha 8 (May 1892), Carl 3 (Oct 1896) 8-276B-167/168

- - - - - - - - - - - - -

TREWHIT / TREWHITT

1900 CENSUS

Albert Trewhit 24 (Sep 1875-M 2), Rula 22 (Dec 1877-M 2-0) 8-275A-131 (B)

MARRIAGE

Albert Trewhitt to Lucretia Swafford, 12 Aug 1898 (same), J.B. Phillips MG, Allen Jones W 2-307

- - - - - - - - - - - - -

TREWIER

1870 CENSUS

Lucinda Trewier 28 (Ala), James 40 (Ala), James 11 (Ala), Casander 9 (Ala), William 7 (Ala), Elizabeth 5 (Ala), Andrew J. 2 10-1-2

- - - - - - - - - - - - -

TRIM

1860 CENSUS

Ander Trim 63, Eliza A. 45 (Pa), Cynthia L. 36, Sidney JOHNSON 27, Henegar 5, Delvora 1, James C. TRIM 49 6-109-749

MARRIAGES

Casandra Trim to Robert Killough q.v.
Catharine Trim to John Peterson q.v.
Elizabeth Trim to John Kirsey q.v.
Sidney Trim to John Johnson q.v.

- - - - - - - - - - - - -

TRIMMING

MARRIAGE

Obediah Trimming to Louisa J. Mitts, 15 Oct 1881, James Corvin M 4-44

- - - - - - - - - - - - -

TRIPLET

1900 CENSUS

Noah Triplett 30: see Jack Moore (B)

MARRIAGE

Callie Triplet to Berry Carter q.v.

- - - - - - - - - - - - -

TROTTER

1900 CENSUS

George Trotter 17: see William Murphy
John Trotter 44 (Oct 1855-T/SC/SC-M 26), Julia A. 42 (June 1857-M 26-16-11), Charley 21 (Dec 1878), Roby S. 15 (Feb 1885), Frank 13 (Feb 1887), James W. 11 (Dec 1888), Dara E. 9 (Oct 1890), Lucy 7 (Dec 1892), Carial 5 (Oct 1894), Pearl 3 (Dec 1896), Mynott 8/12 (Oct 1899) 7-262A-230/235

MARRIAGE

Tennessee C. Trotter to R. L. Montgomery q.v.

- - - - - - - - - - - - -

TROUT

1880 CENSUS

Matilda Trout 14, William 10, John 7, Jasmine 5: see Houston Maxwell

- - - - - - - - - - - - -

TROUTMAN

1900 CENSUS

John A. Troutman 39 (Sep 1860-NC/NC/NC-M 16), Edna 29 (May 1871-NC/Unk/NC-M 16-8-5), Sarah J. 15 (Mar 1885-NC), Daniel 13 (Aug 1886-NC), Charles P. 7 (Dec 1892), John M. 3 (July 1896), George F. 2/12 (Mar 1900) 13-295B-107/109

- - - - - - - - - - - - -

TRUE / TRIEU / TRUEX / TRUAX

1880 CENSUS

J.C. True 20, M.C. 20 3-21-173
William True 56, Susan 56 4-34-282

1900 CENSUS

J. William True 49 (Unk 1851-M 25), Mary C. 45 (Nov 1854-M 25-6-5), George E. 17 (Sep 1882), Judia A. 14 (Sep 1885), Henry W. 12 (Aug 1887), Mary E. 10 (Feb 1890), Nannie 6 (Nov 1893) 3-211B-204/222
William Truax 38 (Aug 1861-Oh/Oh/Oh-M 13)(Blacksmith), Lillie 28 (Aug 1871-M 13-4-3), Nellie 10 (Jan 1890), Orval 8 (Dec 1891), Willie 2 (Aug 1897) 8-288A-396/398

MARRIAGES

Mrs. E. I. Trieu to J. B. S. Hutson q.v.
W. J. Truex to Lillie Morgan, 20 Aug 1887 (21 Aug), A.E. Barnes ?? 1-527

- - - - - - - - - - - - -

TRUSLY / TRUSLEY / TRISLEY

1860 CENSUS
Delana Trusly 39, Elizabeth 44, William F. 9, Mary A. 5, Ezekiel T. 1 7-3-15
John Trusly 18: see Newton Edmonds
Nancy J. Trusley 31, William 2: see Cornelius Shaver
1870 CENSUS
Elizabeth Trusley 53 (SC), William F. 20, Mary A. 15, Ezekiel T. 11 7-1-2
1880 CENSUS
E.T. Trusely 21, Matilda A. 21 6-16-148/152
John Trusley 31, Martha N. 29, Jeff D. 11, Robert L. 12, Willie 8, Sidney D. RAWLINS 23 (Servant Girl) 10-26-201/207
W.F. Trusly 29, A.E. 26, J.S. 4 (s), Ann 10/12 8-17-149
1900 CENSUS
Henry Trusley 19 (Feb 1881-M 1)(Frayman, Flour Mill), Mary 20 (May 1880-T/Oh/T-M 1-0) 10-329A-184/197
Sarah Trusly 40 (Unk 1852-Va/Va/Va-S 5-5), Green 14 (July 1885)(Miner), Bessie 8 (Oct 1891), Alice JOHNSON 22 (d)(July 1877-M 3-0), Charles 32 (sl)(Sep 1867-Oh/Oh/Oh-M 3)(Machinist), James C. TRAMBLE 21 (boarder)(Unk 1871-Ga/Ga/Ga-Wd)(Coal Miner) 8-280B-243/245
MARRIAGES
Alice Trusley to C. H. Johnson q.v.
Alice Trisley(?) to J. C. Tramell or Tramwell q.v.
Ella Trusley to Robert Yoader q.v.
Henry Trusley to May Weatherby, 24 May 1899 (same), F.M. Cook MG & W 2-418
James Trusley to L.J. Hayney, 11 Feb 1898 (12 Feb), T.F. Shaver MG, J.A. Thomas W 2-249
John Trusly to Martha Woody, 23 Ap 1874 (same), A.J. Mathis MG 1-#1334
Mary A. Trusley to James Martin q.v.
Sarah Trusley to Robert B. Sulivan q.v.
Thomas Trusley to Matilda Howser, 10 Jan 1880 (11 Jan), W.S. Hale MG 1-#1760
W.R. Trusley to Mary Elder, 2 Sep 1886 (same), A.W. Curtis ?? 1-502
William Trusley to Gertie Brown, 26 Feb 1899, Z.T. Manis MG 4-103

TUCK

1880 CENSUS
Moses Tuck 56, N.A. 50 (w), M.E. 22 (d), Moses 18 (s), M.A. 16 (d), Joseph 13, John T. 12, I.B. 12 (d), Flora 10, N.W. 8 (s), S.C. 6 (d) 7-23-196

TUCKER

1870 CENSUS
George L. Tucker 39 (NC), Samuel HARRIS 21, Tennessee 17 7-3-21
1880 CENSUS
Isaac Tucker 16 (B): see Julia Kelley
MARRIAGES
G.L. Tucker to Manervia M. Frazier, 15 July 1863 (13 July) [sic], B. Frazier MG 1-#801
James Tucker to Liena Swan, 2 Mar 1887 (same), W.S. Hale MG 1-522
John Tucker to Emma Shaufner(?), 15 Aug 1891, D. J. Young ?? 4-32
Joseph Tucker to Elva Hunter, 9 Dec 1894, W.L. Lillard JP 4-75
Minerva Tucker to W. W. Cunnyngham q.v.
Minnie Tucker to Major Ricketts q.v.
Richard Tucker to Lucy Woods, 5 Dec 1888 (same), John Howard MG 1-556
Tiney or Liney Tucker to Bart Hale q.v.

TUDOR / TUTORS

1900 CENSUS
John J.(?) Tudor 45 (Dec 1854-M 25), Elizabeth 44 (Feb 1856-M 25-2-2), James B. 23 (June 1876-Ky-Wd), Vesta EDWARDS 17 (d)(Nov 1882-M 0-0), Wm M. EDWARDS 23 (sl)(July 1876-M 0), Eliza BROWN 9 (orphan)(Oct 1890) 4-226B-254/258
MARRIAGE
Ella Tutors to Ephraim Coston q.v.
N. V. Tudor to W. M. Edwards q.v.

TUICBELL

1900 CENSUS
Clyde S. Tuicbell 32: see James W. Duncan

TULALDO

1860 CENSUS
Bluford Tulaldo 9, Margaret 4: see Nancy Collins

TULLOM / TULLON

1900 CENSUS
Lillie Tullon 11: see John Martin (B)
MARRIAGE
Sallie Tullom to William Chattin q.v.

TULLAS / TULLISS / TULLOSS / TULLESS

1900 CENSUS
Frank Tulliss 27 (Jan 1873-M 5), Emma 25 (Ap 1875-M 5-0) 8-316B-128/132 (B)
George Tullas 20 (B): see Margaret Ault
Henry Tulless 51, Sadie 17: see Maria Henson (B)
James A. Tullas 91 (Ap 1809-Ga/Va/Va-Wd) 6-243B-80
MARRIAGES
Charles Tulloss(?) to Ora Washington, 22 Aug 1900 (bond only), John Tulloss(?) W 3-203
Frank Tullass to Emma Hughes, 23 Dec 1894, J.W. Clouse JP 4-79

Henry Tulliss(?) to Lizzie Rucker, 13 May 1893, J.W. Williamson MG 4-40

- - - - - - - - - - - - -

TUMLIN

1900 CENSUS

George Tumlin 45 (Dec 1854-Ga/Ga/Ga-M 3), Margaret J. 16 (June 1884-M 3-1-1), Ray 11/12 (June 1899), Mary Ann TUMLIN 65 (m)(May 1835-Ga/Ga/Ga-Wd 1-1) 10-256B-122/126

MARRIAGES

G.W. Tumlin to Sadie West, 1 Mar 1891, R.S. Mason JP 4-23

George W. Tumlin to Maggie Millican, 16 Aug 1897 (same), W.L. Lillard JP, N.M. Hirsh W 2-166

- - - - - - - - - - - - -

TURK

1900 CENSUS

Nancy Turk 40: see William Y. Denton

MARRIAGES

A.R. Turk to M.E. Gipson, 18 July 1873 (20 July), W.H. Selvidge MG 1-#1289

B.N. Turk to S.R. King, 21 Jan 1867 (30 Jan), S.W. Hyden MG 1-#932

Henry Turk to Phebe Ray, 17 Feb 1886 (same), Taylor Russell JP 1-512

Mary Turk to George W. Harris q.v.

- - - - - - - - - - - - -

TURLEY

1900 CENSUS

Calvin J. Turley 47 (Nov 1852-Oh/Va/Va-M 21), Althea B. 46 (Oct 1853-Oh/Oh/Oh-M 21-0), Thos T. CULVER 32 (boarder)(Mar 1868-Oh/NY/Ky) 11-291B-34

- - - - - - - - - - - - -

TURNER

1870 CENSUS

Moses Turner 24, Mary J. 20, Samuel 7/12: see Jas Corvin

1880 CENSUS

Robert Turner 52 Alise 46, E.S. 22 (s), L.A. 17 (d), S.J. 15 (d), E.P. 12 (d), M.E. 9 (d), Thussey 7 (d), J.H. 5 (s) 3-13-104

1900 CENSUS

Enoos H. Turner 44 (Feb 1856-M 23), Mary 40 (Unk 1860-M 23-10-10), Lucy 19 (Aug 1880), Ailsy 18 (May 1882), Della 14 (May 1886), Rheuben 11 (July 1888), Maggie 10 (Feb 1890), March 7 (July 1892), Jessie 6 (May 1891), Baillem 5 (s)(Mar 1895), Flora 3 (Jan 1897) 3-202B-50/53

Jackson Turner 23 (Unk 1877-Idaho/Unk-M 7/12), Cara A. 14 (Feb 1886-M 7/12) 3-208A-144/157

James Turner 67 (Unk-Ga/Ga/Ga) 8-319A-172/178

James F. Turner 23 (July 1876-M 3), Sarah B. 24 (Feb 1876-M 3-1-1), Erven B. 1 (June 1898) 14-221B-164/168

John A. Turner 29 (Feb 1871-M 11), Sidney C. 24 (Jan 1876-T/Va/T-M 11-5-5), James E. 10 (June 1890), Claud G. 7 (Dec 1892), Charles 5 (Jan 1895), Bige 3 (s)(June 1897), Clifford F. 6/12 (Jan 1900) 3-210A-178/193

Judge Turner 22, Josephine 23: see Creasia Hudson (B)

Mary Jane Turner 50 (Nov 1849-T/Va/T-Wd 11-6), James L. 27 (s)(Mar 1873-M 0), Phene 19 (dl)(Oct 1880-M 0-0), Marl 20 (Oct 1879), Frank 18 (Aug 1881), Sally 14 (Jan 1886), Edward 16 (Aug 1883), George W. CORVIN 33 (b)(Jan 1867-Wd), Ollie CORVIN 5 (ne) (Oct 1894) 13-297B-146/149

Reuben Turner 70 (June 1829-M 49), Alsa 67 (June 1832-M 49-8-8) 14-221B-163/167

Rheubin B. Turner 29 (Aug 1870-M 7), May S.J. 28 (Nov 1871-Ky/Ky/Ky-M 7) 3-211A-195/213

Samuel L. Turner 36 (Mar 1864-M 15), Carrie A. 37 (Feb 1863-M 15-8-7), Major L. 14 (Jan 1886), John D. 13 (Ap 1887), Ruben L. 11 (Ap 1889), Nettie B. 8 (Aug 1891), William M. 7 (May 1893), Hettie A. 4 (Sep 1895), Amos P. 7/12 (Oct 1899) 9-228B-12

Wray Turner 27: see E. Lee Tilley

MARRIAGES

Eliza P. Turner to J. B. Lavender q.v.

Enos Turner to Mary M. Rivas, no date [on page with 1878] 1-#1584

J.C. Turner to S.C. Fugate, 21 June 1889 (same), J.H. Hale JP 1-579

J.L. Turner to Phena Corvin, 18 Nov 1899 (19 Nov), W.G. Curton MG, J.D. Burkholder(?) W 3-23

Jack Turner to Carrie Phillips, 22 Oct 1899, M.F. McCuston MG 4-104

Jessie Turner (19, Campbell Co) to Nancy A. Thompson (18), 3 July 1881, J.A. Hixon MG, J.M. McPherson & C.J. McPherson W 4-3(28)

Judge Turner to Josie Hutcheson, 6 Dec 1899 (same), D.B. Jackson MG, J. Banks W 3-80

L.P. Turner to Tennie Ivuster, 27 Jan 1887 (17 Jan)[sic], I.W. Holt JP 1-522

Lewis Turner to Harriet Howard, 11 Feb 1899, no MG or JP, Mark Turner [signed by X] W 2-379

Lucy Turner to James Shelby q.v.

Margarett A. Turner to John Wassum q.v.

Martha Turner to Aaron Crawley q.v.

Martha Turner to John Smith q.v.

Sallie Turner to Powell Smith q.v.

William Turner to Palestine Howard, 24 July 1874 (26 July), Wm C. Wilson MG 1-#1346

- - - - - - - - - - - - -

TYLER

1900 CENSUS

Tom Tyler 25 (Ap 1875-M 0), Sallie 17 (June 1882-M 0-0) 7-262B-237/242 (B)

MARRIAGE

Thomas A. Tyler to Sallie Breeden, 30 Sep 1899 (1 Oct), D.B. Jackson MG, Will Thurman W 3-45

- - - - - - - - - - - - -

UHL

1900 CENSUS

William Uhl 40 (Ap 1860-Oh/Germany/Do-M 15)(RR Station Agent), Fannie F. 35 (Jan 1865-Ky/Ky/Ky-M 15-2-2), Wilence 12 (Nov 1887-Ky), Nellie 3 (Oct 1894) 8-315B-103/107

- - - - - - - - - - - - -

UMBARGER

1900 CENSUS

Samuel Umbarger 36 (Mar 1864-T/Germany/Do-M 8)(Coal Miner), Beatrice 22 (Oct 1879-M 8-2-2), Claud 3 (Mar 1897), Vivian 11/12 (June 1899), Arthur ROSE 20 (bl)(May 1880)(Coal Miner) 8-276B-165/167

MARRIAGE

Samuel Umbarger to Beatris L. Rose, 19 Oct 1892, J.D. Winchester MG 4-53

- - - - - - - - - - - - -

UNDERWOOD

1860 CENSUS

Eliza Underwood 40: see Nathan Whittenburg

1870 CENSUS

Clementine Underwood 10: see Asa Newport

Eliza Underwood 52: see Nathan Whittenburg

1880 CENSUS

Eliza Underwood 62: see N. Whittenburg

Mary Underwood 20: see Francis Majors

1900 CENSUS

Alice Underwood 17: see James W. Angel

Thomas Underwood 36 (Aug 1863-M 9), Amand E. 24 (May 1876-NC/NC/NC-M 9-5-5), Minnie M. 7 (July 1892), Parina E. 6 (Feb 1894), Rosa E. 5 (May 1895), Thomas L. 3 (May 1897), Ollie E. 5/12 (Dec 1899) 3-211B-203/221

MARRIAGES

P.M. Underwood to Mary J. Abel, 25 Oct 1877 (same), J.P. Roddy MG 1-#1520

Margarett Underwood to Frances M. Majors q.v.

Mary E. Underwood to Elbert K. Stout q.v.

Mattie Underwood to J. E. Morgan q.v.

- - - - - - - - - - - - -

UPTON

1880 CENSUS

Robert Upton 20 (B): see Samuel Gilespie

Thomas Upton 18 (B): see Nathan Yearwood

- - - - - - - - - - - - -

USOM

MARRIAGE

Jahu Usom to Barbria B. Walker, 9 July 1867 (same), S.H. Cate MG 1-#957

Lula Usom to George Thorp q.v.

- - - - - - - - - - - - -

USTER

MARRIAGE

Henry Uster to Lottie M. Johnson, 13 Feb 1888 (same), J.W. Holt JP 1-551

- - - - - - - - - - - - -

UTTER

MARRIAGE

J.G. Utter to Eliza J. Eaton, 13 Dec 1891, A.W. Frazier JP 4-35

- - - - - - - - - - - - -

VALENTINE

1880 CENSUS

Ronnie Valentine 35 (B): see J.H. Rogers

- - - - - - - - - - - - -

VANCE

1900 CENSUS

Edward Vance 23 (Dec 1876-Oh/Oh/Oh-M 0), Elizabeth 22 (Jan 1878-M 0-0) 8-277A-173

John Vance 48 (Mar 1852-Pa/Pa/Pa-M 27)(Superintendent, Coke Oven), Idella 43 (July 1856-Pa/Pa/Pa-M 27-1-1), Emma TATE 28 (Mar 1872-Kansas/Do/Do)(Servant) 8-277A-174/175

MARRIAGE

Edward Vance to Lizzie Whitford or Whitfield, 14 Dec 1899 (same), R.C. Knight JP, N.J. Tallent W 3-88

- - - - - - - - - - - - -

VANDERGRIFF

MARRIAGES

J.F. Vandergriff to M.G. Smith, 25 Ap 1896 (26 Ap), Wm A. Green JP, J. A.(?) Brown W 2-16

Laura(?) L. Vandergriff to Gus L. Smith q.v.

Lizaie Vandergriff to Nich A. McCabe q.v.

Martha Vandergriff to David Gothard q.v.

- - - - - - - - - - - - -

VANDVENTER

MARRIAGE

W.D. Vandventer to Nannie Reed, 13 Dec 1889 (same), R.S. Mason JP 1-590

- - - - - - - - - - - - -

VANN

MARRIAGE

Fannie Vann to Jonah Clark q.v.

- - - - - - - - - - - - -

VANORSDAL

1900 CENSUS
Clarence O. VanOrsdal 8, Oden L. 6: see Jacob Gass

- - - - - - - - - - - - -

VARNELL

MARRIAGES
John L. Varnell to Emma I. Stuart, 31 Oct 1893, W.L. Patton MG 4-55
W.H. Varnell to Virginia C. Morgan, 1 Sep 1875 (2 Sep), J.W. Williamson MG 1-#1407

- - - - - - - - - - - - -

VARNER

1860 CENSUS
David Varner 10: see Josiah Dawson
Eliza Varner 32: see Moses Smith
MARRIAGES
Elizabeth L. Varner to John Fox q.v.
P.M. Varner to Sarah Ann Hughes, Jan 15, 1852 (same), C.A. Holland MG 1-#359
William Varner to Elizabeth Jones, 10 May 1856 (no return) 1-#547

- - - - - - - - - - - - -

VARNEY

1900 CENSUS
Stephen H. Varney 67 (Feb 1833-Maine/Do/Do-M 40), Jane 69 (May 1831-Eng Canada/Ver/Scotland-M 40-0) 14-215A-38/39

- - - - - - - - - - - - -

VAUGHN

1860 CENSUS
Alfred Vaughn 16: see George Minick
Benjamin Vaughn 18: see James Carson
John Vaughn 35 (NC)(Trader), Fanny 34, Benjamin 18, Alfred 16, Joseph 14, James 12, William 10, Amos 8, Susan 6, Nancy 4, Eliza 2 6-104-706
1870 CENSUS
Charles Vaughn 13, James 11, Ernest 7, Mabel 4: see James Robinson
1880 CENSUS
B.F. Vaughn 38, N.A. 36, Wm A. 9, J.L. 7 (s), C.O. 2 (s) 4-32-258
Earnest Vaughn 17, Mabel 13, Idella 10: see Jas Robinson
John Vaughn 59, Fannie 62 4-2-16
1900 CENSUS
Ida Vaughn 12: see Caroline Pullum
James L. Vaughn 28 (Mar 1872-T/Ga/T-M 1/4), Eva May 22 (Feb 1878-M 1/4) 3-200A-10
John N. Vaughn 31 (Dec 1868-M 11)(Grist Miller), Ada 32 (Sep 1867-M 11-6-4), James F. 8 (Oct 1891), William R. 7 (May 1893), Bessie A. 3 (May 1897), Mintie 1 (Ap 1899), Charles 21 (b)(May 1879) 5-237B-191
Mable Vaughn 31: see Danil Robinson
Nancy Vaughn 57 (Sep 1843-Wd 5-4), William A. 21 (Nov 1869-T/Ga/T), Charles O. 21 (May 1879), Ollie COX 21 (Sep 1879)(Servant) 3-200A-9/9
MARRIAGES
A.J. Vaughn to M.A. Robinson, 18 Nov 1856 (no return) 1-#583
B.W. Vaughn to M.L. Gray, 11 June 1857 (no return) 1-#602
Elizabeth Vaughn to William Harrison q.v.
James Vaughn to Eva Beard(?), 12 Jan 1900 (14 Jan), L.E. Smith JP, J.E. Small W 3-108
Mabel Claire Vaughn to John Hously q.v.
Maggie Vaughn to Justin Rose q.v.
Nancy J. Vaughn to Charles B. Dyer q.v.

- - - - - - - - - - - - -

VEACH

1900 CENSUS
Harvey Veach 19: see George Brandon

- - - - - - - - - - - - -

VETITO / VITTITO / VEDETOE

1880 CENSUS
James Vedetoe 20: see James Hayes
MARRIAGES
Clark Vittito to Amanda McCulley, 27 Ap 1895, J.M. Hinds MG 4-85
Frances Viteto(?) to Thomas Waldon q.v.
Joseph Vetito to Elizabeth Haze, 6 Nov 1855 (8 Nov), E. Bower JP 1-#528
Polly Vetito to John Hudleston q.v.

- - - - - - - - - - - - -

VIALS / VILES [VYLES]

1900 CENSUS
Lucy B. Viles 44 (July 1855)(Tayloress), Charles H. 21 (May 1879)(Grocery Salesman), Mary E. 70 (m)(Jan 1830-Wd 9-4) 10-326B-138/145
[Lucy, widow of Samuel P. Vyles]
MARRIAGE
Sarah Vials to William Denton q.v.

- - - - - - - - - - - - -

VICTORY

1860 CENSUS
Edmond A. Victory 30, Manerva J. 21, John R. 3 2-77-521

- - - - - - - - - - - - -

VINCENT / VINCEN / VINSON

1900 CENSUS
Andy H. Vincent 42 (Ap 1858-M 20), Mandy E. 35 (Nov 1864-M 20-8-5), Savannah T. 18 (July 1881), James T. 12 (June 1888), Bettie J. 7 (June 1893), Charles 10 (May 1890), Samuel 1 (Mar 1899), James L. MILTON 26 (Jan 1874)(Servant) 3-204B-83/90

Charles Vincent 50 (Feb 1850-M 24), Ellen 51 (Sep 1848-M 24-7-7), Craton E. 22 (Dec 1877), Susie M. 18 (Nov 1881), Samuel 12 (Jan 1888), Ida 11 (Ap 1889), Belle 8 (Jan 1892), Nancy M. 7 (Feb 1893) 6-245A-102/103

Samuel Vincent 30 (Jan 1870-M 4), Ida A. 22 (Jan 1878-M 4-2-2), William F. 3 (Feb 1897), Martha D. 1 (Nov 1898), Wm BROWN 21 (July 1878)(Servant), Walter BROWN 11 (Ap 1889)(Servant) 3-204B-81/88

William J. Vincent 66 (July 1833-M 46), Evaline 61 (Sep 1838-M 46-11-6), Josie 22 (June 1868), William F. 21 (Oct 1878) 3-204B-81/87

MARRIAGES

Bettie J. Vincent to A. J. Hicks q.v.

Lula Vinson to W. H. Morgan q.v.

Mary Vincen to W. G. Hughes q.v.

Samuel Vinson to Ida Tallent, 8 Dec 1895, W.K. Fugate JP 4-89

Susie Vinson or Vinsen to E. J. Dodd q.v.

- - - - - - - - - - - - -

VINYARD / VINEYARD

1880 CENSUS

N.J. Vinyard 54, W.A. 55, Harrit 32, Mary 31, Roby 28, J. W. 23 (s), W.G. 21 (s), John McCOSLEN(?) 19 (Hired Man) 3-23-186

1900 CENSUS

Frank Vineyard 45: see Valentine Rowen (B)

MARRIAGES

J.W. Vineyard to A.A. Ewing, 31 Oct 1882 4-11

W.Y. or W.G. Vinyard to Adelia McPherson, 27 July 1889 (31 July), S.S. Hale MG 1-576

- - - - - - - - - - - - -

VITTILA

1900 CENSUS

Wilum Vittila(?) 25 (Jan 1875-M 3), Rosey 20 (Ap 1880-M 3-2-2), Morgan 2 (Ap 1898), Maud 3/12 (Feb 1900) 12-182A-69/72

- - - - - - - - - - - - -

VOILS

1880 CENSUS

James Voils 50, M.A. 40, William 18, E.J. 15, Mary 12, J.B. 9, J.M. 6, L.A. 2 3-30-243

- - - - - - - - - - - - -

VREELAND

1900 CENSUS

George S. Vreeland 44 (Feb 1856-Kan/Unk-M 16)(Bookkeeper), Jennie B. 42 (Mar 1858-Va/Va/Va-M 16-5-4), Rachael D. 15 (Mar 1885-Mo), Lula H. 13 (Aug 1886-Kan), Mary W. 11 (Aug 1888-Kan), Katie K. 7 (May 1893), Clarence 5/12 (Dec 1899) 13-300A-189/194

- - - - - - - - - - - - -

WADE

1860 CENSUS

Granville H. Wade 25, Nancy 30, Sarah L. 7, Perma(?) C. 3, James M. 1, Lewis J. DAVIS 35 6-66-458

1870 CENSUS

Granville H. Wade 37 (Blacksmith), Nancy 40, Lenea C. 12, James M. 12, Vina E. 8, Tennessee 6, Thomas R. 4, Susan C. 7/12 3-3-19

1880 CENSUS

Darthula Wade 22, Floyd 5/12 (Mu): see Mary J. Locke

G.H. Wade 45, Nancy 54 (w), J.M. 20 (s), V.E. 18 (d), M.S. 16 (d), F.R. 14 (s)

1900 CENSUS

Granville H. Wade 68 (Mar 1832-T/Va/Va-M 49), Nancy 73 (Sep 1826-T/Va/T-M 49-8-4), John L. 18 (July 1887), Nancy E. RUSSELL 15 (gd)(Oct 1884), Thomas RUSSELL 11 (gs)(Jan 1889) 3-211B-200/218

Henry Wade 45: see George Gray (B)

John H. Wade 59: see James S. Porter

Rosa Wade 50 (Unk-Ala/Ala/Ala-D 10-5), Samuel 13 (Oct 1886-T/Va/Ala), Alfred 11 (May 1889), Mary 8 (Jan 1892); _Boarders:_ Charles WHITE 25 (Unk 1875-M 3), Ollie RENFRO 22 (1888), Daniel 25 (1875-M 1), James MASON 25 (1875), John NEAL 19 (1881-Ga) 8-275A-130 (B)

Thomas R. Wade 34 (July 1866-T/Va/Va-M 11), Sarah E. 39 (Mar 1861-M 11-6-5), Granville H. 10 (Feb 1890), George N. 8 (Aug 1891), Lennie S. 6 (Sep 1893), John R. 4 (Oct 1895), James M. 1 (Ap 1898) 3-208B-156/169

MARRIAGES

James M. Wade (23, Meigs Co) to Mary E. Proffitt (17), 31 Sep 1882, Taylor Russell JP, J.W. & T.L. Russell W 4-12(115)

Jennie Wade to J. W. Talley q.v.

L. C. Wade to Thomas Russell q.v.

Pollard R. Wade to Alice M. Morgan, 12 Jan 1885 (14 Jan), I.W. Holt JP 1-462

Sarah L. Wade to Hesekiah Ginnow q.v.

Tennessee Wade to James W. Russell q.v.

Thomas R. Wade to Sarah C. Shelton, 11 Ap 1889 (14 Ap), S.S. Hale MG 1-574

Vinie Wade to Archer Lenem q.v.

W.L. Wade to Margaret Johnson, 11 Sep 1886 (12 Sep), Jas E. Rogers MG 1-504

Wesley Wade to Josie Ferguson, 2 Aug 1890, R.S. Mason JP 4-16

- - - - - - - - - - - - -

WALDO

1880 CENSUS

B.T. Waldo(?) 28, Adela 23, N.J. 9 (s), H.M. 6 (s), Wm O. 2 (s), Th--?--al THOMPSON 24, Calvin THOMPSON 5 (s) 4-2-12

1900 CENSUS

David(?) Waldo 26 (Ap 1874-M 6)(Teamster), Thursa C. 21 (Sep 1877-Y/NC/NC-M 6-2-2), Austin B. 4 (Oct 1895), Sarah G. 3/12 (Mar 1900) 4-224B-215/219 (Spring City & Dayton Road)

Mary Waldo 76 (Oct 1823-NJ/NJ/NJ-Wd 10-9), Edswaeste(?) 38 (s)(Dec 1861-Oh/Oh/NJ) 8-285B-338/340

MARRIAGE

Andy Waldo to Patsey Reed, 5 Oct 1892, L.L. Barton JP 4-49

WALDON / WALDEN

1900 CENSUS

Hugh or Henry Walden 30 (Oct 1869-Ga/Ga/Ga-M 11) (Miner), Mary 29 (June 1870-M 11-4-4), Mary 10 (Feb 1890), Juliette 8 (Ap 1892), Willie 5 (July 1894), Wilbern 2 (June 1897) 8-283B-197/299

John M. Walden 50 (May 1850-Ga/Ga/Ga-M 20)(Coal Miner), Elizabeth R. 65 (May 1835-SC/SC/SC-M 20-8-7), Mack C. 22 (July 1877-Ga)(Coal Miner) 13-303B-254/264

MARRIAGES

Mahala Waldon to Frank Jefferson q.v.

Rebecca F. Waldon to J. A. Webb q.v.

Thomas Waldon to Frances Viteto(?), 13 Nov 1885 (14 Nov), W.R. Clack JP 1-488

WALDRUP

1880 CENSUS

H. M. Waldrup 30: see W. M. Foust

WALKER

1860 CENSUS

David Walker 42, Nancy 42, Samuel 17, Eldridge 15, William 12, Braxton 9, Polly A. 2 4-48-325

John P. Walker 34, Sarah 31, Benjamin F. 9 8-11-73

1870 CENSUS

David Walker 51, Nancy 51, Braxton 19, Polly Ann 12, Sarah I. 8 4-3-18

George W. Walker 32 (Va), Hannah 29, George W. 9, James B. 7, Woods A. 4, Byrd T. 2 10-3-23

James B. Walker 30, Orlina 29, Mary T. 9, Sarah F. 6, Samuel M. 4, James W. 2 8-9-55

John A. Walker 23 (Va), Caroline 23, James A. 3, Nancy J. 2, John T. 10/12, Mary C. JOHNS 28 8-10-62

John P. Walker 43, Sarah 40, Benjamin F. 19, Sarah C. 11, William B. 4, George T. 4 8-8-48

Joseph M. Walker 20, Aminda C. 23, Margaretta J. 2/12 8-2-13

Samuel Walker 26, Sarena 25, Rebecca J. 2 4-5-27

Thomas N. Walker 63 (Va), Charity A.D. 53 (Va) 8-2-8

Thomas N. Walker Jr. 25, Martha A. 24, Louisa Jane 2, Alice J.P. 1, Margarette D.E. 16, Millard F. 13 8-2-9

Woodson A. Walker 33 (Va), Nancy E. 32, Ellen 6, Alexander 4, James W. 2 8-22-153

1880 CENSUS

B.F. Walker 29, Elaine 26, J.B. 9 (s), James B. 6 (s), C.B. 3/12 (d) 8-3-28

David Walker 62, Nancy 62, S.E. 18 (d), W.F. 12 (s) 4-34-276

Frankey Walker 18: see F. J. Paine

George Walker 42, Martha 30, Simpson 12, Thomas 1[illegible], Robert 10, Frank 9, Charles 6, Joseph 4, A.M. 2 (s), Martha 1 3-17-134 (B)

George W. Walker 40, Hannah 37, George 19, James 16, Woodson 13, Thomas 10, Mary F. 9, Nancy C. 6, Robert L. 4, Martha 7/12 10-29-224/229

H. M. Walker 21, M. 20, J.C. 1 (s) 7-22-192

J. B. Walker 28: see S. R. Rogers

J.P. Walker 54, Sarah 52, B.F. 34 (s), S.C. 21 (d), W.B. 14 (s), J.T. 14 (s), S.A. [probably Ida] 11 (d) 11-39-314

James B. Walker 40, Orlena 39, Mary A. 18, Sarah F. 16, James W. 11, Robert L. 9, Nancy J. 7, George L. 6, Leana B. 2, Josephine 6/12 6-15-136/138

Jane Walker 49, S.K. 24 (d) 8-8-66

Robert C. Walker 24, Nor--?--los 32, Sarah J. 7, William H. 4, Leora E. 3 6-14-130/131

Sam Walker 26, C. 19 (w), John McBIVINS(?) 40, Lyda 33, E. 11, Robert 7, John 3 3-15-117

Sam Walker 39, C.E. 35, J.A. 6 (d), Floyd 4, W.B. 4/12 (d) 4-33-273

W.A. Walker 43, N.E. 42, Ellen 16, James 12, Nuton 9 (s), J.A. 6 (s), M.J. 4 (d), Woods 2 (s) 8-12-97

William Walker 43, Alley 26 (w), William 16, M.A. 7 (d), J.J. 12 (s), T.C. 9 (s), M.J. 7 (d), J.F. 5 (s), R. 3 (s), J.M. 2 (s) 11-37-304

1900 CENSUS

Addison Walker 30 (Jan 1870-M 3)(Coal Miner), Elizbeth C. 35 (Jan 1865-M 3-6-3), Luvibia 10 (Sep 1889) 13-303A-239/249

Bird Walker 40 (Mar 1860-T/Va/T-M 20), Tennessee 37 (June 1862-T/Va/T-M 20-9-7), Mack 16 (Feb 1884), Sarah 12 (July 1887), Ella 10 (Aug 1889), Nora 9 (Aug 1890), Jessie 7 (Feb 1893), Morris 5 (May 1895) 13-297B-150/153

Bonnie Walker 21: see Samuel H. Allen

Bradford ?. Walker 56 (Oct 1843-NY/Mass/Mass-M 30) (Drayman), Delia 52 (July 1847-Conn/Do/Do-M 30-8-5), Mercelia A. 24 (July 1875-Minn)(Professional Nurse), Delia E. 22 (Aug 1877-Minn)(Professional Nurse), Blanche D. 20 (Nov 1879-Minn), Grace L. 18 (Mar 1882-Minn), Seth T. 26 (July 1873-Minn-M 0) (Minister), Edith 20 (dl)(Mar 1880-Mass-M 0-0)(Professional Nurse) 10-325B-115/119

Carrie Walker 43: see James W. Walker

Cyrus I. Walker 23 (Oct 1876-T/Va/T-M 0), Delia E. 19 (Dec 1880-T/T/Ind-M 0-0) 13-308A-342/354

Edd Walker 9/12, Iness 4, Andnon 6: see James Cook (B)

Filmore Walker 42 (Unk 1858-M 10)(Coal Miner), Emma 30 (Unk 1870-T/Va/Va-M 10-5-3), Thomas 12 (Mar 1887)(Coal Miner), Charles 8 (Sep 1891), Florence 2 (Ap 1898) 8-284A-309/311

Floyd Walker 23 (Jan 1877-M 2), Lillie 22 (Ap 1878-M 2-0) 4-226A-250/254

George W. Walker 62 (Feb 1838-Va/Va/Va-M 40), Hannah 58 (June 1842-M 40-10-8), Vesta 17 (June 1882), Nanna V. 11 (Jan 1889-Ky), Frank 9 (Mar 1891-Ky) 6-244A-89

Grant Walker 35 (Ap 1865-M 3), Lucinda 35 (July 1864-M 3-3-2), James McKEMP 12 (ss)(Unk) 10-330B-216/229 (B)

James Walker 31 (Aug 1868-M 12), Sarah 30 (June 1869-M 12-2-2), Clara 11 (Jan 1889), Nola 5 (Aug 1894), James HICKS 20 (bl)(Nov 1879) 8-277B-180/181

James A. Walker 34 (Sep 1865), John F. 23 (b)(Oct 1876), Maggie 18 (si)(May 1882), Caroline WALKER 60 (m) (Unk 1840-T/SC/Ga-Wd 11-8), Elizabeth RAINS 29 (si)(June 1870-M 5-2-2), Wright RAINS 31 (bl)(Ap

1869-M 5), Burnette 5 (nw)(Dec 1894), John W. 2 (nw)(Ap 1898) 13-304B-275/285

James F. Walker 25 (Oct 1874-M 8), Maggie A. 26 (Feb 1874-M 8-3-3) 11-290A-2

James F. Walker 43 (Oct 1856-M 19), Mary E. 41 (Jan 1859-Va/Va/Va-M 19-1-1), Birdie MARTIN 38 (sil) (Jan 1862-Va/Va/Va-Wd 0) 5-235B-154

James W. Walker 38 (Ap 1862-T/T/NC-M 18), Sarah 35 (July 1864-M 18-8-8), Carrie B. 17 (Mar 1883), Nancy E. 15 (Ap 1885), Jennie B. 11 (Sep 1888), Lula T. 10 (Jan 1890), John W. 6 (Ap 1894), Ella 4 (Jan 1896), Henry F. 1 (Nov 1898), William A. 1 (Nov 1898), Jennie BIGERSTAFF 69 (m)(Jan 1831-NC/NC/NC-Wd 1-1), Carrie WALKER 43 (si)(Feb 1857) 3-204A-72/77

John Walker 14: see Joseph Ballard

John Walker 14 (B): see Thomas G. Moss

John R. Walker 24 (Sep 1875-M 7), Jane 25 (June 1874-M 7-4-2), Thomas F. 4 (Jan 1896), Dicy E. 1 (Feb 1899) 4-225B-240/244 (Rhea Springs & Washington Road)

Lee Walker 36 (Oct 1863-M 14), Martha 33 (Nov 1866-M 14-6-5), Freeman 13 (Aug 1886), Jesse 6 (Mar 1894), Moulton(?) 5 (Ap 1895), Willie 3 (Jan 1897), George 1 (Feb 1899), Auther 0/12 (May 1900) 1-183A-87/90

Robert Walker 22 (Mar 1878-T/Va/T-M 4), Caroline 32 (June 1867-M 4-2-2), Samuel 2 (Mar 1898), Lens 4/12 (Jan 1900) 6-243B-74

Robert Walker 24: see Rees Gwillim

Robert Walker 35 (Unk 1865-M 12)(Coal Miner), Nannie 35 (Unk 1865-M 12-5-3), Roy 9 (Unk 1891), Bessie 3 (Unk 1897), Lillian 1 (May 1899) 8-283B-304/306

Samuel Walker 39 (Jan 1861-M 18), Martha E. 34 (Dec 1865-Ky/Ark/Ark-M 18-9-8), Thomas G. 15 (May 1885), Deborah 13 (Dec 1886), Earnest 11 (Dec 1888), Flossie A. 9 (Oct 1890), Martha P. 7 (Aug 1892), Esther 6 (May 1894), Guy 3 (June 1896), David H. 2 (Dec 1897) 13-309B-380/394

Samuel Walker 57 (Feb 1843-M 35), Serena C. 55 (Ap 1845-M 35-5-3), Ida 25 (Dec 1874), Bessie 12 (Sep 1887) 4-226A-249/253 (Rhea Springs & Washington Road)

Thomas Walker 32 (Jan 1868-M 10)(Coal Miner), Esta 27 (Dec 1872-Ga/Ga/Ga-M 10-5-5), Minnie 8 (Sep 1891), Johnie 6 (July 1893), Julia 5 (Feb 1894), Gather 3 (Nov 1896), Jack 1 (Nov 1898) 8-284A-310/312

Thomas Walker 35 (May 1865-T/Va/T-M 7), Susie 24 (Jan 1876-M 7-3-3), Fred 4 (Sep 1895), Artie E. 1 (June 1898), Woods A. 1/12 (Ap 1900) 6-242B-53 [Thomas married Susan Hughes on 2 Sep 1894 in Meigs County]

William Walker 35 (Dec 1864-M 10), Tina 30 (May 1870-M 10-1-1), John L. 3 (Aug 1896) 8-283B-300/302

William Walker 36 (Jan 1864-M 15)(Coal Miner), Lizzie 32 (Mar 1865-M 15-7-6), Myrtle 12 (Jan 1888), Daisy 10 (Sep 1889), Arthur 8 (July 1891), Della 7 (Mar 1893), Nora 2 (June 1897), Mattie 4/12 (Feb 1900) 8-284A-308/310

William H. Walker 28 (Ap 1872-M 3)(Coal Miner), Mamie 22 (May 1878-Ga/Ga/Ga-M 3-2-1), Grace I. 10/12 (July 1899), Grover C. NORRIS 11 (bl)(Sep 1888-T/Ga/Ga) 13-304A-259/269

William H. Walker 59 (Nov 1840-M 25)(School Teacher), Martha W. 44 (Oct 1855-M 25-4-2), Hila B. CORDELL 12 (ward)(June 1887-T/T/Ga), Pearl 11 (ward) (Jan 1889-Washington/T/Ga) 10-325B-118/122

William M. Walker 62 (Sep 1837-T/Va/Va-M 23), Elsie 47 (July 1852-M 23-11-8), Richard F. 23 (Feb 1877), Samuel N. 18 (Feb 1882), Minnie K. 16 (Jan 1884), Etta M. 12 (Feb 1888), Benjamin H. 10 (Feb 1890), Hattie P. 8 (Dec 1891), Lodenie L. 6 (Mar 1894), Fred A. 4 (Oct 1895) 11-293A-78

Woods Walker 34 (Mar 1866-T/Va/T-M 5), Lucinda 22 (July 1877-M 5-3-2), Robert T. 2 (Nov 1897), Hannah E. 5/12 (Dec 1899) 6-242A-52

MARRIAGES

A.W. Walker to Malia Johnson, 30 Ap 1898 (same), W.S. Hale MG, J. Boltmeter(?) W 2-274

B.T. Walker to S. J. Miller q.v.

Barbria B. Walker to John Usom q.v.

Bary [Braxton] Walker to E.A.J. Odom, 14 Ap 1879 (no return) 1-#1612

Bell Walker to John McMillian q.v.

Callie Walker to W. S. Sneed q.v.

Craty Walker to Wright Raines q.v.

Cyrus Walker to A.D. Marler, 23 Aug 1899 (same), W.R. Grimsley MG, S.I. Walker & Tom McMillin W 3-24

Elizabeth Walker to William Walker q.v.

Emma Walker to B. J. Swafford q.v.

Emma Walker to S. R. Dixon q.v.

Frank Walker to Viney McClendon, 2 Nov 1887 (same), T.H. McPherson JP 1-530

G.W. Walker to Cansada Woody, 25 Oct 1884 (same), A.J. Pritchett MG 1-469

George W. Walker to Lavinia Steele, 17 Oct 1874 (18 Oct), W.A. Green JP 1-#1363

Grant Walker to Synda Ransom, 17 Oct 1896 (18 Oct), C.A. Alexander MG, J.R. Darwin W 2-113

Ida Walker to W. D. Lillard q.v.

Ida M. Walker to J. B. Smith q.v.

J.B. Walker to S.E. Gardenhire, 20 Aug 1894, R.S. Mason JP 4-71

J.F. Walker to L.N. Ryan, 11 Dec 1898, W.M. White MG 4-109

J.W. Walker to Sallie E. Hayes, 17 Sep 1889 (8 Sep)[sic], W.S. Hale MG 1-582

James Walker to Sarah Hicks, 16 June 1888 (21 June), Calvin Morgan JP 1-570

James Walker to Maggie Bosley, 20 Sep 1891, R.S. Mason JP 4-31

James B. Walker to Ella Garland, 7 May 1887 (8 May), J.W. Williamson MG 1-523

James F. Walker to Mary E. Baldwin, 18 July 1880 (same), James H. Locke JP 1-295

Jannie Walker to S. H. Burwick q.v.

John A. Walker to Caroline Johns, 21 June 1865 (23 June), J.H. Keith MG 1-#834

John B. Walker to Priss(?) M. Bell(?) [ink blobs], 2 Sep 1844, D.V. Culver MG 4-70

John R. Walker to Jane L. Brady, 12 Sep 1893, A.L. Parker MG 4-84

Josie Walker to Walter J. Green q.v.

Katie Walker to Synda Simmons q.v.

Lee Walker to Martha J. Bowlis(?), 8 Mar 1891, W.R. Clack JP 4-22

Lena Walker to W. J. Smith q.v.
Liza Walker to D. W. Burwick q.v.
M. F. Walker to William Perry q.v.
Mabel Walker to Robert Keith q.v.
Maggie Walker to Sam Johnson q.v.
Malissa Walker to James Henry q.v.
Margaret D.E. Walker to James F. Pickett q.v.
Margaritt S.(?) Walker to Michall Enos q.v.
Martha E. Walker to Tate Frailey q.v.
Mary Walker to William Brooks q.v.
Mary Walker to Charles T. Rudd q.v.
Mary Ann Walker to R. M. Trentham q.v.
Mary M. Walker to John D. Whittenburg q.v.
Nancey Walker to Marion Green q.v.
Nancy Walker to John R. Green q.v.
Newton Walker to Margarett Wallace, 24 Dec 1863 (20 Dec)[sic], J. Howard MG 1-#814
R.W. Walker to Mary A. Jones, 4 Sep 1886 (5 Sep), I.W. Holt JP 1-511
Rhoda Walker to L. A. Smith q.v.
Robert Walker to Nannie Jacquish, 13 June 1890 (same), R.S. Mason JP 1-602
Robert Walker to Nancy C. Gibson, 1 Jan 1894 [probably 1896], P.G. Roddy MG 4-87
S.A.J. Walker to Permelia C. Holland, 6 Feb 1866 (same), J. Howard MG 1-#887
S.T. Walker to Edith Holbrook, 31 May 1900 (same), W. Woodford MG, E. Fisher W 3-150
Sallie Walker to Samuel Frazier q.v. (B)
Samuel Walker to Serena E. Wheeler, 3 Nov 1866 (4 Nov), J.W. Thompson MG 1-#916
Samuel Walker to M.C. Burton, 10 Nov 1879 (13 Nov), T.H. McPherson JP 1-#1686
Sarah C. Walker to William D. Rigsby q.v.
Sarah E. Walker to T. J. Nash q.v.
T.B. Walker to Martha J. Hughes, 7 July 1890, J.W. Williamson MG 4-16
T.H. Walker to L.A. Green, 11 May 1890 (same), E.F. Gwinn JP 1-602
Thomas Walker to Manervia Maddison, 1 Sep 1863 (no return) 1-#806
Thomas Walker to Mary E. Lemons, 24 Ap 1874 (?? Ap), Jas Johnson JP 1-#1335
W.R. Walker to Tinie Bean, 17 Dec 1889 (22 Dec), J.R. Walker MG 1-595
W.T. Walker to Margaret Dobbs, 22 July 1865 (23 July), J.M. Kelly MG 1-#839 & 1-#1260
W.W. Walker to Mamie Norris, 20 Mar 1897 (21 Mar), W. A. Green JP & W 2-129
Wallace Walker to Rosa James, 16 Aug 1884 (21 Aug), Jas Wallace MG 1-465
William Walker to Elizabeth Walker, 10 July 1874 (same), E.N. Ganaway JP 1-#1341
William Walker to Alsie Jane Johnson, 23 Sep 1875 (same), C. Morgan JP 1-#1414
William Walker to Elizabeth Olinger, 31 July 1886 (1 Aug), C. Morgan JP 1-503
William T. Walker to Sarah Land, 14 June 1854 (same), Wm C. Hollins JP 1-#451 & 1-#468 [name is Wm Thomas Walker in last entry]
Woodson A. Walker to Nancy E. Steele, 9 Jan 1863 (18 Jan), J.W. Foust JP 1-#793

\- - - - - - - - - - - - -

WALL / WALLS

1900 CENSUS
Andrew Wall 21, Jacob 22: see Henry Foster (B)
MARRIAGE
Andrew Walls to Girtie Preston, 28 June 1900 (same), W.L. Patton MG, Joe Tally W 3-173 (B)

\- - - - - - - - - - - - -

WALLACE / WALLIS

1860 CENSUS
George W. Wallace 53 (Ky), Elizabeth 49, Elvira J. NEIL 29, Eglantine 11, Mary Ann 8, Sterling 3, Wallace P. HILL 10 3-63-438
James Wallace 25 (Lawyer): see James W. Gillespie
1870 and 1880 CENSUS– None
1900 CENSUS
Ward Wallis 56 (Aug 1843-England/Do/Do-1880/20/Na-M 28), Lucy 56 (Ap 1844-Canada/England/Pa-1880-M 28-6-5), James L. 28 (Feb 1872-Can), Florence 22 (Jan 1878-Can)(Teacher), Lena L. 20 (July 1879-Can), Blanch 17 (Sep 1882-N Dak) 14-222A-173/177
MARRIAGES
Carrie Wallis to H. B. Heiskell q.v.
Margarett Wallace to Newton Walker q.v.

\- - - - - - - - - - - - -

WALLER / WELLER / WALLEN

1860 CENSUS
James F. Wallen 29, Elizabeth J. 28, Samuel J.D. 2, Matilda 1, Mary 1 8-25-169
1870 CENSUS– None
1880 CENSUS
W. Wallar 53, Malind 47, Amand 19, Floyd 14 7-22-193
1900 CENSUS
Addie B. Waller 14: see Thomas N.L. Cunnyngham
James Waller 37 (Unk-M 13), Evaline 37 (July 1862-M 13-6-5), Caleb 10 (July 1889), Edna E. 7 (Aug 1892), Rhoda 5 (Mar 1895), Rosa C. 2 (June 1897), Charlie L. 9/12 (May 1900) 6-247A-142/143 [James married Evaline Vincent on 22 Feb 1887 in Meigs County]
Leonard O. Waller 33 (Nov 1866-Oh/Oh/Oh-M 4), Lou E. 24 (Ap 1876-M 4-2-2), Hardie S. 4 (May 1896), Pearl S. 1/12 (Ap 1900) 11-290A-9
Malinda Waller 65: see Julia Barnett
Marshal Waller 19: see Marquis Morrison
Wiley N.(?) Waller 22 (Sep 1877-M 0), Millie 16 (June 1883-M 0-0) 5-231B-65
William Waller 30 (Nov 1869-M 8)(Printer), Kittie 26 (Aug 1873-Calif/Do/Do-M 8-4-4), Varney 7 (Nov 1892), Nealey 5 (Ap 1895), Violla 3 (May 1895), John Vehersond 1 (Feb 1899) 10-250A-6
MARRIAGES
Ada Weller to James Burwick q.v.
E. M. Waller to William Colville q.v.
George Waller to Susan Rogers, 26 Mar 1884 (same), A.J. Pritchett MG 1-518
Hattie Waller to James McMarty or McMurtry q.v.
J.F. Waller or Wallis to Martha Majors, 22 Nov 1890, A.W. Frazier JP 4-18

Martha Waller to J. J. Eaton q.v.
Matilda Waller to Fred Galimo q.v.
Mern or Mun Waller to Eva Mathis, 26 July 1889 (28 July), W.S. Hale MG 1-578
Samuel Waller to Clara Birchfield, 28 Jan 1894, Henegar Morgan JP 4-70
Susannah Waller to J. F. Essex q.v.
W. Waller to Mrs. Malinda Pritchett, 18 Sep 1879 (same), .J. Pritchett MG 1-#1675
Wyley Waller to Millie Gosset, 15 Nov 1899 (same), J.M. Bramlett MG, A.D. Gosset W 3-71

- - - - - - - - - - - - -

WALLINGFORD

1900 CENSUS
John G. Wallingford 46 (Jan 1854-Ky/Md/Ind-M 10)(Shoe Merchant), Minnie F. 31 (Dec 1868-Ind/Ind/Ind-M 10-0), Robert W. MARYMAN 62 (fl)(Oct 1837-Ind/Pa/ Ireland-Wd) 10-328A-167/177

- - - - - - - - - - - - -

WALTERS / WALTER

1900 CENSUS
Charles Walter14: see William M. Wiggins
Elsie Walters 22: see Floyd Rankins (B)
Kyle Walters 51: see Mary Conley
Sam Walters 51 (June 1848-M 22), Clara 38 (Unk-M 22-6-6), Alice 22 (May 1878), Bertha 14 (July 1885), Oliver 13 (Mar 1887), Carrie 8 (May 1892), William 1 (Feb 1849), Hester SWAFFORD 19 (d)(Ap 1881-M 1-1-1), Joseph Lans 3 (gs)(May 1897), Alberta PICKLE 8/12 (gd)(Oct 1899) 8-318A-154/159 (B)
MARRIAGES
Addie Walters to Floyd Rankins q.v.
Hester Walters to Samuel Swafford q.v.
William Walters to Louisa Horner, 8 Sep 1876 (9 Sep), James Johnson JP 1-#1460

- - - - - - - - - - - - -

WALTON

MARRIAGE
John Walton (21) to Jane Kirby (28), 27 Ap 1883, Anthony Smith MG, John Miller & Benjamin Kirby W 4-14(136)

- - - - - - - - - - - - -

WAMPLER / WAUPLY / WIMPLER

1880 CENSUS
Catharine Wimpler 48, Malind 19, William 10, James 10: see Rolen Denham
1900 CENSUS
William Wampler 32 (Sep 1867-M 8), Lineller 23 (Sep 1876-M 8-5-4), Fredy C. 6 (Jan 1892), Richard A. (June 1895), Andy M. 3 (Dec 1896), John W. 7/12 (Oct 1899) 7-262B-241/246
MARRIAGES
Allis Wampler to Gad Rogers q.v.
M. M. Wampler to J. R. Hooper q.v.
Molly Wauply to Jeff Woody q.v.
William Wampler to Eddie Brown(?), 13 Ap 1891, T.F. Shaver JP 4-22

- - - - - - - - - - - - -

WARD

1860 CENSUS
David Ward 21, William 18: see Alfred Hucheson
David F. Ward 44 (Ky), Jane 37, James 17, George W. 19, William 15, Ezekiel 13, Mary J. 11, David 9, Jackson 7, Newton 2 8-15-98
William Ward 20: see James Carson
1870 CENSUS
George W. Ward 53 (NC), Minerva 46 (NC), Emily J. 20 (NC), Alves G. 18 (NC), Clerinda 12 1-8-52
Henry Ward 28 (NC), Lydia 23, John H. 7, Sarah J. 4, George W. 3 3-3-16
Iverson Ward 23 (NC), Nancy 23, Mary T. 4. Susan E. 2 3-3-17
Margaret M. Ward 34, Ibba Jane 8, Mary E. 5, James W. 1 8-17-119
William Ward 35 (Va), Lucy A. 22 (Va), William N. 6, George P. 3, Byrd L. 6/12 2-19-141
William N. Ward 32, Louissa 33, Thomas J. 4 1-8-53
1880 CENSUS
A.G. Ward 28, Martha 27, M.E. 6 (d), E.L. 4 (d), J.W. 5/12 (s) 3-19-148
G.W. Ward 64, M.E. 55, E.J. 24 (d) 3-28-221
Henry Ward 40, Lydia 34, John 17, Sarah 14, George 13, Clarinda 4, Cora 2 3-28-220
I.S. Ward 30, M.H. 31, S.E. 11 (d), W.B. 8 (s), M.L. 5 (d), W.H. 2 (s) 3-28-222
William Ward 40, Louisiana 43, Thomas 14, William 10, Martha 6, Elias 1 1-19-159
1900 CENSUS
Absalom Ward 52 (Unk 1848-NC/NC/NC-M 31)(Shoe Repairer), Sarah 54 (Unk 1846-M 31-6-4), William 16 (May 1884), James B. 27 (Oct 1872-M 6), Alice 17 (dl)(Sep 1882-M 6-1-1), Paul 2 (gs)(Dec 1897) 8-287A-380/382
Edward Ward 35 (Oct 1864-Oh/Oh/Oh-M 3), Alta B. 21 (June 1878-M 3-2-2), Joanna 3 (Sep 1897), Lorinda J. 1 (Ap 1899) 5-236B-171
John H. Ward 59: see James S. Porter
William F. Ward 54 (Jan 1846-T/Ky/T-M 27), Catharine 44 (Nov 1855-Ala/Ala/Ala-M 27-8-6), Leonard F. 22 (Mar 1878-Fla), William W. 18 (Jan 1882-Fla), David C. 15 (June 1884-Fla), Rosa L. 12 (Oct 1887-Fla), Tomie C. 8 (Mar 1892-Fla), Minnie S. 2 (Aug 1897-Fla) 8-289A-419/422
MARRIAGES
Ada Ward or Wood to Charles Coleman q.v.
Alvin G. Ward to Martha Duncan, 13 Nov 1873 (14 Nov), H.B. Heiskell JP 1-#1311
Amanda Ward to J. K. P. Abel q.v.
B.P. Ward to Mary P. Wasson, 12 Jan 1884 (4 Feb), T.H. McPherson JP 1-482
Carry Ward to James I. Wilson q.v.
Cassi Ward or Wood to Thomas W. Prater q.v.

Clarenda Ward to Samuel Miller q.v.
Emma C. Ward to J. B. Zeigler q.v.
Francis M. Ward to Martha E. Woody or Wendy, 31 July 1890 (3 Aug), R.T. Howard MG 1-6-4
J.B. Ward to Alice Sexton, 8 Sep 1895, F.M. Cook MG 4-85
J.N. Ward to N.A. Horner, 6 Aug 1864 (8 Aug), Jas Carson MG 1-#1079
James H. Ward to Lyda Knox, 28 July 1860 (29 July), Jas Carson MG 1-#722
John Ward to Kate Mitchell, 31 Oct 1890, A.W. Frazier JP 4-18
Sallie Ward to Charley Davis q.v.
Sarah Ward to W. E. Crawford q.v.
W.E. Ward to Altie J. Burdett, 23 Dec 1896 (24 Dec), J.M. Bramlett MG, T.P. Houston W 2-94
William M. Ward to Louissanna Compton, 6 Dec 1869 (no return) 1-#1129

\- - - - - - - - - - - -

WARE / WARES

1880 CENSUS
Francis Ware 21: see Franklin Waterhouse
1900 CENSUS
Jeston Wares 71, Amanda 6, Dewit 3: see John B. Kirby

\- - - - - - - - - - - -

WARNACK

1880 CENSUS
William Warnack 23: see Stephen Cawood

\- - - - - - - - - - - -

WARNER

1900 CENSUS
John C. Warner 36 (Oct 1863-Oh/Germany/Oh-M 8)(RR Laborer), Emma R. 27 (May 1873-Ind/Pa/Oh-M 8-3-2), George W. 7 (Mar 1893-Ind), Earl A. 6 (Mar 1894-Ind) 13-309A-373/397
Louiza M. Warner 54 (Nov 1845-Oh/Ind/NY-Wd 7-5), Jennie 24 (Sep 1875-Oh/Eng/Oh), Mary E. 21 (Feb 1879-Oh), David W. 17 (Sep 1882-Oh)(Engins Pump S), David M. 14 (Dec 1885-Oh), Robert 13 (May 1887-Oh) 5-233B-114
Sarah Warner 65: see Mary T. Cofer
MARRIAGE
Emaline Warner to Alfred Watson q.v.

\- - - - - - - - - - - -

WARREN

MARRIAGES
Catharine Warren to Anthony Logan q.v.
Tennessee Warren to John Cofen or Cossen q.v.

\- - - - - - - - - - - -

WASHAM / WASHUM

1900 CENSUS
Dollie Washum 25, Nola 15: see Frank L. Crowder
MARRIAGE
Josie Washam to John Crowder q.v.

\- - - - - - - - - - - -

WASHBURN / WASHBORNE

1900 CENSUS
George W. Washborne 28 (Jan 1872-M 4)(Coal Miner), Mollie K. 24 (July 1875-M 4-0) 13-303A-243/253
James M. Washburn 63 (Aug 1836-Ga/Mass/Ga-M 38) (Shoemaker), Sarah A. 55 (Feb 1345-Ga/NC/Ga-M 38-10-7), John W. 21 (Mar 1879)(Coal Miner), Emma F. 18 (June 1881) 10-329A-187/200
William Washburn 35 (Unk 1865-M 13)(Coal Miner), Mollie 30 (Unk 1870-M 13-5-5), Jack 12 (Unk 1888), Anna 10 (1890), Blanche 8 (1892), Maud 6 (1894), Mellie 1 (1899) 8-289B-427/430 [Wm H. married Mollie Atchley on 31 July 1887 in Meigs County]
MARRIAGES
George Washburn to Mollie Knight, 30 June 1896 (1 July), G.W. Brewer MG, J.F. Johnson W 2-35
John Washburn or Washborne to Eliza Center, 8 Sep 1900 (12 Sep), Henneger Morgan JP, Nigle(?) Purser W 3-213

\- - - - - - - - - - - -

WASHING

1880 CENSUS
Wm Washing 2, Charlie 1/12, Cordelia 5: see Justin Kerby

\- - - - - - - - - - - -

WASHINGTON

1900 CENSUS
George Washington 35 (1865-Ga/Ga/Ga-Wd), Walter 20 (1880-Ga), Elvira 16 (1884-Ga), Maggie CONNELLY 20 (boarder)(1880-Ga/Ga/Ga) 8-275B-141 (B)
Sam Washington 73 (Jan 1827-Ga/Ga/Unk-M 0)(Shoemaker), Mary 50 (Dec 1849-SC/SC/SC-M 0-8-5) 7-262-232/237 (B)
MARRIAGES
Ora Washington to Charles Tulloss(?) q.v.
Samuel Washington to Mary Ravin, 22 July 1899 (23 June), G.S. Sanders MG, Muncie Corvin W 3-13

\- - - - - - - - - - - -

WASMAN

1900 CENSUS
Harley Wasman 40 (Mar 1860-T/Va/Va-M 12), Adah 35 (Ap 1865-M 12-6-5), Larry 10 (Feb 1890), Emma 8 (Jan 1892), Cathran 6 (Jan 1894), Anis 3 (June 1894), James 1 (June1898), Charles HOYAL 26 (boarder)(Ap 1875)(RR Hand) 1-186B-151/159 (B)
Rener(?) Wasman 27 (May 1871-Wd 2-2), Millie(?) 9 (d) (July 1890), Charles 2 (Ap 1898) 1-189B-206/216 (Spring City)

\- - - - - - - - - - - -

WASSON / WASSOM / WASSUM

1860 CENSUS

Andrew Wassom 38, Mary J. 21, Hetta M. 3, Jacob L. 1 4-42-286

Benjamin J. Wasson 37 or 57 (NC), Anna 45 (SC), William H. 20, Doctor 15, Jane 12 1-94-638

Henry Wassom 35 (Wagonmaker), Mary 36, John W. 16, George W. 14, Casey 12, William MOORE 19 3-57-393

Jacob L. Wassom 19, Mary A. 18, Victoria 4/12: see Hemp McFalls

Jeremiah Wasson 23, Martha M. 19, Luella 3, Chapman 1 1-86-596

Joab Wassom 34, Sarah J. 24, Eliza A. 4, John J. 2 3-58-394

John Wassom 42, Margaret 44, Caroline 16, Angaline 12, Eliza 10, James 3 6-105-710

John J. Wasson 21, Martha J. 18 4-47-315

Mira [Myrum] Wassum 45 (SC), Zachary T. 11, Texanah G. or L. 9, Hanah 6 4-43-293

Thomas Wasson 24, Mary 16 3-59-405

1870 CENSUS

Andrew Wassum 50, Mary J. 32, Hettie M. 13, Jacob L. 11, Andrew 9, Mary J. 7, Sarah B. 5, Eliza A. 2, Rebecca N. 5/12 3-6-36

Ellen Wasson 35, Franklin 14, John 12, Edward 10 6-6-35

George W. Wassom 24 (Blacksmith), Nancy 26, Thomas 5, Robert 3, Mary 8/12 2-6-39 [G.W. married Nancy Ann Robertson]

Jacob L. Wassom 28, Mary Ann 26, Victoria 10, John C. 8, James G. 7, Julia A. 4, Mira 2, Wright 3/12, Hannah 16 4-14-91

Jeremiah C. Wasson 33 (Merchant), Martha M. 28, Lueller 12, Jeremiah C. 11, John B. 9, Laura 9/12, James J. ABERNATHY 34 (Clerk in Store), N. LOW 69 (England)(Music Teacher), Francis LOW 24 (Eng), Joseph McLEER 27 (Merchant), Susan McLEER 20, A. McDERMET 30 (Merchant), Margaret P. McDERMIT 28, Jane McDERMET 3, Mary WASSON (B) 28 (Va), Samuel (B) 10, Virginia (B) 8, Henry (B) 6, James (B) 6/12, Lame WASSON (Mu) 15 (Miss) (Laborer), Sterling SMITH (B) 65 (Laborer), Edward OVERBY (B) 21 (Miss) 2-14-99

John W. Wasson 27, Susan 29, Allie 9 2-6-40

Zachariah T. Wassom 22, Samantha E. 23, Isabella Ann 3 4-17-110

1880 CENSUS

Amanda Wasson 16, Stephen 26 (Mu)(B): see Robert Robinson

Andrew Wassum 80: see Haly Wassum

Emaline Wasson 23 (B): see James Howel

George Wassom 35 (Carpenter & Joiner), Nancy 36, Thomas 14, Robert 12, Mary 10, Mabel 8, Betty 6, George 4, Charlie 3, Ella 1 2-25-202

Haly Wassum 59, M.S. 43 (w), J.L. 22 (s), Andrew 22, M.J. 17 (d), S.B. 15 (d), E.A. 12 (d), Rebecca 10, Annie 8, Amanda 6, Texas 2, Andrew 80 (f) 3-16-125

Hosea Wasson 70, Emilin 60, Margaret 36, Mary 23, Henry 28, John 18, William 16, Thomas 14, Birtie 12, Artie 10, James 6, Jacob 2 2-23-186 (B)

J.W. Wassom 36 (Blacksmith), S.A. 40 (w) 4-8-66

Jere Wasson 43 (Physician), Martha 41, Louella 22, Chapman 21 (Store Clerk), John 19 (Store Clerk), Lillie 10, Anna 8, Ada 6, Martha 4, Blanch 1/12, Daniel WILLIAMS 37 (Hotel Clerk), Thomas HARRISON (B) 50 (Servant, Cook), Alice (Mu) 31 (Cook), Emma (Mu) 18, Lula (B) 5, Susan (B) 2/12, William DANIEL (Mu) 20 (Servant, Barber), John COLES (B) 37 (Servant, Cook & Barber), Eliza JONES 42 (Servant, Milk Maid), Lulu 16 (Servant, Cook), George 12 (Servant), John BROWN (B) 22 (Servant, Waiter at Table), Fanny HINCH (B) 25 (Servant, Ironer), Lulu (B) 1/12, James GOOSEBY (B) 30 (Servant, Barber), Sarah (B) 17 (Servant, Cook), Charles SMUTHERS (Mu) 28 (Servant, Hostler), Scott RAMSEY 27 (boarder)(Merchant), L.L. Sampler 25 (boarder)(Deputy Marshall) 2-25-198

Mary Wassom 60: see Cyrus Henry

W. M. Wasson 54 (B): see James Real

1900 CENSUS

Bertie Wasson 29 (Feb 1871-T/Ky/T-Wd 6-4)(Washwoman), Lillie 15 (Feb 1885), Safronie 11 (May 1889), Joseph 9 (Mar 1891), Lawrence 8 (Feb 1892); *Boarders:* Charles LOCKE(?) 24 (July 1875), William KELLY 26 (Jan 1874)(Coal Miner), James JOHNSON 60 (Jan 1840-Va/Va/Va-M 7), Elmira 40 (Jan 1860-T/T/Ky-M 7-12-1), Charlie H. McCEAVER 10 (Dec 1889) 8-315A-96/100 (B)

Chapman Wasson 41 (Nov 1858-M 13)(General Merchant), Katherine 35 (July 1864-Ky/Ky/Ky-M 13-4-4), Gay 12 (Feb 1888), Owen 8 (Ap 1892), Blanche 5 (Jan 1894), Marthy 6/12 (Nov 1899) 2-197B-119/124

Hulda Wasson 56 (Unk 1844-Wd 12-6), Alice 27 (Mar 1873), George C. 25 (Aug 1874)(Hotel Waiter), Julia 22 (Oct 1877), Benjamin K. 20 (Dec 1879)(RR Laborer), James N. 15 (Jan 1886)(Servant), Henry 13 (Jan 1887)(Servant), William HICKEY 5 (gs)(Ap 1895), Robert LOCK 3 (gs)(Sep 1896), James C. LOCK 2 (gs)(Jan 1898) 2-198A-131/136 (B)

James or Jessy E. Wasson 22 (Feb 1878)(Grocery Salesman) 2-199A-149/154

Jeremiah C. Wasson 63 (Sep 1836-T/T/Ky-M 45)(Physician), Martha M. 61 (Jan 1839-T/NC/T-M 45-16-6), Adah P. 26 (Ap 1874)(Saleswoman), Mike C. DAVIS 18 (gs)(May 1882), Martha E. 16 (gd)(May 1884), Mamie L. 14 (gd)(Mar 1886), Frank M. GAGE 31 (boarder)(Ap 1869)(Physician), Well PHILLIPS (B) 59 (Aug 1840-M)(Servant) 2-197B-121/126

John W. Wassom 56 (Dec 1843-M 32)(Blacksmith), Susan E. 61 (May 1839-M 32-1-1), John H. SECREST 40 (sl)(July 1853-Ind/Oh/Oh-M 6)(Machinist), Alice L. 38 (d)(July 1851-M 6-5-1), Thomas B. LYLE 14 (June 1885) 14-219B-137/140

Lorinda Wassom 30, James C. 2: see Charles Reed

Robert W. Wassom 32 (Dec 1867-M 2), Mary B. 22 (Mar 1878-M 2-0), John W. GARRISON 34 (bl)(Dec 1865) 3-202-43/46 [Robert married Belle Garrison on 5 Jan 1898 in Meigs County]

Stephen Wasson 48 (Oct 1851-M 20), Amanda 38 (Sep 1861-M 20-10-7), Robert W. 19 (May 1881), Wilbert 16 (Dec 1883), John J. 11 (Aug 1888), Susan M. 9 (Ap 1891), Margaret 6 (Sep 1893), Alma 2 (July 1897), infant 1/12 (d)(Ap 1900) 14-221A-155/159 (B)

MARRIAGES

Alice Wasson to James Locke q.v.

Andrew Wasson to Mary J. Wassom, 25 Aug 1855 (26 Aug), L.W. Furguson JP 1-#523

Annie A. Wasson to P. T. Ferguson q.v.

Bell Wassom to A. L. Long q.v.

C. E. Wassom to Charles Reede q.v.

Cassa Wassum to ?. H. Henry q.v.

E.P. Wasson to Lorinda Gray, 8 Aug 1894, R.A. Dickson JP 4-72

Eliza Wasson to Jerry Billberry q.v.

Emaline Wasson to Melvin Phillips q.v.

Hannah Wasson to Jessee W. Cash q.v.

Henry Wassom to Adeline Stephens, 8 May 1889 (same), C.J. Titus JP 1-574

J. Wasson to Mary Davis, 20 Aug 1859 (same), Geo W. Wallace JP 1-#1657

Jacob L. Wassom to Samantha E. Furgusson, 19 Dec 1858 (no return) 1-#675

Jacob L. Wassum to Mary Ann McFalls, 19 Ap 1859 (21 Ap), E.E. Wasson JP 1-#680

John Wassum to Margarett A. Turner, 12 Sep 1858 (same), G.W. Wallace JP 1-#654

John Wassom to Susan Carpenter, 15 July 1868 (same), T.N.L. Cunnyngham JP 1-#1018 [Susan, widow of Thomas Carpenter; dau of Bennett C. & Lydia Tunnell Franklin]

John Wasson to Saline Outen, 26 May 1883 (27 May), B.F. Holloway JP 1-476

John B. Wasson to Annie Howe, 5 June 1889 (6 June), L.B. Caldwell ?? 1-574

Lillie M. Wasson to J. H. Gay q.v.

Martha Wasson to D. F. Hickey q.v.

Mary Wassom to Solomon Henry q.v.

Mary J. Wassom to Andrew Wasson q.v.

Mary F. Wassom to B. P. Ward q.v.

Naomia Wasson to Willis Drake q.v.

Rebecca Wasson to Arthur L. Miller q.v.

Stephen Wasson to Amanda Robinson, 12 Dec 1879 (8 Dec), Jacob Mann MG 1-#1719

Texanna Wasson to H. L. W. Ferguson q.v.

William J. Wasson to Barbary Ellen Ingle, 20 Dec 1854 ("in due time"), T.V. Atchley JP 1-#477

Zachariah T. Wassum to Samantha McFalls, 6 Mar 1866 (7 Mar), W.W. Low JP 1-#1074

- - - - - - - - - - - - -

WATERHOUSE

1860 CENSUS

Darius Waterhouse 45 (Physician), Harriet 32, Vesta E. 12, Elisha F. 11, Cyrus 8, Allice 4 6-109-743

Franklin Waterhouse 36, Lorenda R. 37, James E. 15, Elvira 10, Louisa A. 7, Richard G. 4, Harriet P. 1, Luke EDINGTON 30 1-88-602

1870 CENSUS

Alexander Waterhouse 31 (Ga), Sarah 29, Darthula 12, Albert 3, Mary J. 9/12 6-7-46 (B)

Darius Waterhouse 55 (Physician), Harriette C. 41, Vesta E. 21, Elisha F. 20, Cyrus 17, Alice 15, Darius 8, Harriette C. 6, Euclid 3, Caroline PAINE (B) 20, William PAINE (Mu) 2 6-6-40

Franklin Waterhouse 47, Lorinda R. 49, James E. 25, Elvira 20, Louisa 17, Richard G. 14, Harriette S. 11, Prudilla 9 1-8-48

Silva Waterhouse 40, Jordan 19, Albert 17, Jonathan 13, Rebecca 13, Thomas 10, Samuel 8 1-7-46 (B)

1880 CENSUS

Franklin Waterhouse 56, Lorinda 59, Elvira 30, Hariet 21, Lorinda FERGUSON 10 (gd), Francis WARE 21 (Servant) 1-20-165

Harriett Waterhouse 50, Vesta E. 31, E. Frank 30, Cyrus 27, Allis 22, Darus 18, Garrutt C. 15, E--?-- [Euclid] 12 6-21-186/190

James Waterhouse 35, Tennessee 28, Ada 8 1-20-164

John Waterhouse 26 (B): see Andrew Anderson

Martha Waterhouse 12 (B): see James W. Gillespie

Rebecca Waterhouse 24, William 9, Mary 3, Jack STINECYPHER 19 (boarder), Isaac BROWN 24 (boarder) 1-13-111 (B)

Thomas Waterhouse 25, Eliza A. 24, Samuel 5, John 3, Fanny N. 1 6-13-125/126 (Mu). [Thomas married Liza Tolliferro on 28 Dec 1871 in Meigs County]

1900 CENSUS

Cyrus Waterhouse 48: see Ebb S. Cox

Euclid Waterhouse 32 (Aug 1867-M 0), Birdie 30 (Nov 1869-T/NC/T-M 0-0) 13-298B-161/164

Frank Waterhouse 50 (Ap 1850-M 19), Tennie J. 39 [sic] (Dec 1850-M 19-5-5), Pauline 16 (Feb 1884), James 13 (Oct 1886), Harriet 11 (Jan 1889), Alice 7 (Nov 1892), Olivia 5 (Mar 1895) 6-247A-136/137

Harriet Waterhouse 73 (Feb 1827-Wd 9-6), Alice 43 (Aug 1856), Darius 39 (Feb 1861), Young COLVILLE 54 (nw)(Nov 1845), Hannah COXEY 25 (May 1875) (Servant) 6-244A-85

James(?) Waterhouse 55 (Ap 1845-M 23), Linnie 49 (Ap 1851-M 23-3-2), Vidia 19 (Oct 1880), Daysy 16 (Mar 1884) 1-189B-204/213 (Spring City)

Rena(?) Waterhouse 79 (m)(Jan 1821-Wd 4-4), Eller 50 (d) (Oct 1849), Carson EDMON 25 (border)(Jan 1875) (RR Hand) 1-189B-203/212 (Spring City)

Samuel Waterhouse 36 (Ap 1864-M 20)(Hustler), Hannah M. 36 (May 1864-M 20-4-2), James H. 12 (Mar 1888), Anna M. 5 (Aug 1894) 14-219A-124/127 (B)

MARRIAGES

Bell Waterhouse to William Cox q.v.

E.F. Waterhouse to Tennie D. James, 27 May 1881 (6 Ap), D. Munroe(?) MG 1-297

Eliz Waterhouse to W. C. Zigler q.v.

Harriet S. Waterhouse to D. C. Clendenin q.v.

James E. Waterhouse to Ann E. Day, 24 Nov 1870 (same), S. Phillips MG 1-#1178

Rebecca Waterhouse to Isaac Brown q.v.

Sallie Waterhouse to Lee Day q.v.

Samuel Waterhouse to Hannah Thompson, 23 June 1883 (same), T.H. McPherson JP 1-481

Samuel Waterhouse to Bell Douglass, 17 Aug 1892, D.E. Broyles JP 4-50

Vesta J. Waterhouse to Milo M. Furgusson q.v.

- - - - - - - - - - - - -

WATERMAN

MARRIAGE
Lucinda Waterman to James Woody q.v.

- - - - - - - - - - - - -

WATERS / WATTERS

1900 CENSUS
Albert Waters 39 (July 1860-Mich/Oh/Mich-M 16)(Carpenter), Sarah A. 36 (Dec 1863-Canada/Do/Oh-M 16-2-2)(Teacher), Leon D. 13 (Ap 1887-Mich), Glenn D. 11 (Ap 1889-Mich) 8-288B-404/406
Joseph H. Watters 60 (Jan 1840-Oh/Oh/Oh-M 29), Alma J. 49 (Sep 1850-Oh/Oh/Oh-M 29-2-0), Mary J. KERR 72 (ml)(Dec 1827-Oh/Pa/Va-Wd 6-4) 2-197B-114/119

- - - - - - - - - - - - -

WATHENS / WATHERN / WEATHERNS

MARRIAGES
Josephine Wathern(?) to Wylie D. Posey q.v.
Mariah Weatherns to Charley McDonald q.v.
Sallie Wathens or Mathers to William R. Holt q.v.

- - - - - - - - - - - - -

WATKINS / WADKINS

1900 CENSUS
Fritz Watkins 9, Lillie 7, Ellen 1: see Enoch Suthers (B)
James Wadkins 22: see Emma Gillespie (B)
Reese K. Watkins 51 (Mar 1849-M 25)(Physician), Jennie W. 47 (July 1852-M 25-7-5), Mary B. 22 (May 1878), Ethel T. 17 (Feb 1883), Mattie N. 14 (Jan 1886), Cleo 12 (Sep 1888), Leith N. 9 (Nov 1890) 14-220A-142/146
Sidney M. Watkins 47 (July 1852-Oh/Oh/Oh-M 25)(Banker), Sarah E. 47 (June 1853-Oh/Oh/Oh-M 25), Amy A. 19 (Sep 1880-Oh) 14-213B-20/21
William A. Watkins 40 (Dec 1869-Ga/Ga/Unk-M 11), Sarah G. 29 (Mar 1871-Ga/SC/Ga-M 11-3-2), James W. 10 (Sep 1889-Ga), Millard B. 4 (Jan 1896-Ga) 3-207A-125/136

MARRIAGE
Grace B. Watkins to N. R. Cartright q.v.

- - - - - - - - - - - - -

WATSON

1860 CENSUS
James Watson 51 (Va)(Blacksmith), Anna J. 35 2-79-539
Marion Watson 26, Susan E. 28, Manerva 30, William 8, Leander 3, Rebecca J. 1: see James Crisp
Orvey Watson 22: see William Gray

1870 CENSUS
John Watson 32, Sarah J. 31, Mary E. 14, Malinda 6, Vesta Ann 3, Rachel P. 1 3-5-33
Marion Watson 35 (Laborer), William C. 9, Mira 7, John W. 4, James M. 2 1-10-68
Mary Watson 35: see Evander Thurman
Nathan Watson 60, Sarah 52, James 27, Martha 20, Alfred 16, Rachel O. 12, Sarah E. 10 6-12-86
Nathan Watson 22, Rebecca 22 (Ga), James N. 3/12: see John H. Beasley

1880 CENSUS
Adam Watson 35, Hannah 33, M.A. 16, Joseph 12, Wm McDONALD 23 4-2-9
Lee Watson 25 (Miner), Mary 23, Nancy 1/12 2-31-253
Marion Watson 48, Sallie 42, Sarah 23, Lorinda 19, William 19, Elmirah 17, John 13, James 11, Samuel 8, Charles 2 12-3-28
Nathan Watson 34, Rebecca 33, James N. 10, Sarah M. 7, William 5, Rachel A. 2, Lulia 9/12 5-3-25
William Watson 75, Sarah 55 (w), Martha 25, R.O. 21 (d), S.E. 19 (d) 4-32-261

1900 CENSUS
Alfred Watson 50 (Unk 1850-M 20), Emma 36 (May 1864-M 20-9-4), Sarah J. 14 (Ap 1886), Nancy 11 (July 1888), Mettie 9 (June 1890), Nathan 6 (Oct 1893) 8-281A-253/255
James M. Watson 31 (Feb 1869-M 1), Lillie 19 (Oct 1880-M 1-1-1), Alvine 8/12 (Oct 1899), Amanda BROGLIN 24 (sil)(Aug 1875) 3-207A-127/138
Joseph Watson 31: see Sanders Dunlap
Perry Watson 25: see Franklin McMillan

MARRIAGES
Adam Watson to Mahala Jordan, 28 June 1836 (29 June), Asa Newport MG 1-#549
Alfred Watson to Emaline Warner, 28 Jan 1879 (29 Jan), A.J. Pritchett MG 1-#1603
Charlotte Watson to William Gray q.v.
Elizabeth Watson to John Beasly q.v.
Emaline Watson to Evander Thompson q.v.
James Watson to Ann Ledbetter, 1 Nov 1858 (2 Nov), S.H. Dickey JP 1-#664
James Watson to Lillie Mitchell, 22 Oct 1898 (23 Oct), H.B. Burditt MG, Nathan Watson W 2-337
Joseph Watson to Sarah Harwood, 31 Aug 1854 (no return) 1-#469
Manger Watson to I. L. Baker q.v.
Manerva Watson to Thomas Dodson q.v.
Manervia Watson to William Rector q.v.
Marion Watson to Emeline Crisp, 4 May 1860 (no return) 1-#709
Marion Watson to Polly Thurman, 4 Dec 1884 (same), D.V. Culver JP 1-492
Marion Watson to Sarah Cantrell, 2 Nov 1874 (3 Nov), G.W. Renfro MG 1-#1366
Martha A. Watson to James Mitchell q.v.
Mary Watson to Arthur Mize q.v.
Nathan Watson to Rebecca Beasly, 10 July 1869 (11 July), R.T. Howard MG 1-#1104
Nathan Watson to Mahala Norriss, 8 July 1884 (same), A.J. Pritchett MG 1-508
Rachel Watson to James Owens q.v.
T.M. Watson to C.C. Gorman, 27 Aug 1891, James Johnson JP 4-31
W.M. Watson to Manerva J. Cassady, 8 July 1856 (10 July), no MG or JP 1-#552
Wesley Watson to Nancy J. Pritchett, 29 Sep 1853 (same), R.T. Howard MG 1-#424
William M. Watson to Anney Lemmons, 25 Ap 1871 (27 Ap), H.B. Heiskell JP 1-#1194

- - - - - - - - - - - - -

WATTS

1870 CENSUS
William Watts 31, Mary 28, Mary E. 9, Pleasant H. 7, Sarah F. 5, Martha J. 3, Tennessee A. 1 6-105-718
1880 CENSUS
J. W. Watts 20: see John Morgan
MARRIAGE
Loucinda Watts to B. B. Travis q.v.

- - - - - - - - - - - - -

WAYSTUFF

MARRIAGE
Mary Jane Waystuff to J. J. Slaughter q.v.

- - - - - - - - - - - - -

WEATHERBY / WEATHERBEE / WEATHERLY

1900 CENSUS
William Weatherbee (Aug 1853-Mich/Do/Do-M 10)(Coal Miner), Martha E. 23 (June 1876-T/Ga/T-M 10-4-2), George H. 17 (Jan 1883)(Coal Miner), Hattie E. 15 (Sep 1884), Annie B. 4 (Sep 1895), William A. 2 (Aug 1897), Lizzie QUEEN 13 (July 1886-Ga/Ga/Ga) (Servant), John QUEEN 20 (boarder)(May 1880-Ga/Ga/Ga)(Coal Miner) 13-307A-330/342
MARRIAGES
May Weatherby to Henry Trusley q.v.
May Wetherly to Walter Hale q.v.
Will Weatherly to M. L. Renow, 10 Oct 1891, W. Morgan JP 4-36

- - - - - - - - - - - - -

WEATHERNS– see WATHENS

- - - - - - - - - - - - -

WEATHINGTON / WEATHERINGTON
(see also WORTHINGTON)

1900 CENSUS
Frank J. Weatherington 29 (Nov 1870-M 8)(Coal Miner), Mattie 30 (Feb 1870-M 8-4-4), William J. 6 (May 1894), Nellie 4 (Dec 1895), Nora F. 2 (Sep 1897), Clara 1 (Feb 1899) 10-254B-87
Lon Weathington 20 (Ap 1880)(Coke Puller), Charley HUGHES 21 (July 1878)(Coke Puller); *Boarders:* Hiram WEATHERINGTON 18 (Ap 1882)(Coke Puller), Isom HUGHES 34 (Oct 1865)(Coke Puller), Mose JOHNSON 20 (Mar 1880)(Coke Puller), Wright HUGHES 39 (Ap 1861-T/Va/T-Wd)(Coke Puller), Alford HUGHES 26 (Oct 1873)(Coke Puller), Alford ROWLINS 22 (June 1878-T/Ver/T)(Coke Puller), Tom SMITH 17 (Mar 1883)(Coke Puller), Mate SMITH 15 (Feb 1885)(Coke Puller) 10-258B-160/164 (B)
MARRIAGES
Foust Weathington to Alice Berry, 2 Ap 1897 (5 Ap), J.B. Trotter MG 2-136
Frank Weathington to Bettie Bird, 20 June 1892, S.S. Franklin JP 4-39

- - - - - - - - - - - - -

WEAVER

1900 CENSUS
David Weaver 70 (Mar 1830-Oh/Pa/Md-M 48), Mary A. 67 (July 1832-Oh/NC/Va-M 48-2-2), Harrison LEWIS 7 (Feb 1893)(Servant) 3-201A-27/28
John W. Weaver 68: see Emma Dorsett
Louis H. Weaver 38 (July 1862-Oh/Oh/Oh-M 13), Minnie O. 28 (June 1872-Oh/Oh/Oh-M 13-0) 3-201A-27/29
Martin C. Weaver 47 (Feb 1853-Ky/Ky/Ky-M 21)(RR Agent), Alace J. 45 (Sep 1854-Ky/Ky/Ky-M 21-3-3), Anna A. 16 (Aug 1883), Harry L. 14 (Mar 1885), Cela B. 10 (May 1889) 5-233B-113
MARRIAGE
A.E. Weaver to Sallie Middleton, 12 Jan 1888 (12 June) [sic], M.C. Bruner MG 1-564

- - - - - - - - - - - - -

WEBB

1860 CENSUS
Betsy Webb 60, Viny 40, Rue 26, Thomas J. 24 3-62-428
Hanibal Webb 22, Nelly A. 18, Susan A. 3, James A. 6/12 3-68-463
1870 CENSUS
Andrew Webb 56, Susanna 49, Sarah C. 20, Mahala R. 18, James L. 6 6-3-17
Ham D. Webb 34, Nelly A. 30 (Ga), Susan A. 13, James A. 11, William F. 8, Martha E. 4, Jasper N. 3 6-2-12
William Webb 29, Martha 29, Ida M.E. 5, William T. 3, Mille A. 1, Henry OGILL 20, Nancy A. 18 5-3-16
1880 CENSUS
F.J. Webb 39, E.J. 38, A.H.(?) 17 (s), J.A. 15 (d), L.N. 13 (s), Monta 12 (s), W.D. 14 (s), Minnie 6, Ellen 4, R. 2 (d), Mary RICHARDS(?) 26 (sil) 3-24-195
H.D. Webb 47, N. Ann 40, S.O. 22, James A. 20, William F. 18, Martha E. 15, Easter N. 12, Joseph M. 10, John B. 6, George W. 4 5-1-2
H.P. Webb 8: see John Gray
James L. Webb 15: see John W. Opal
M. Webb 45, M.M. 3: see A.J. Pritchett
Sallie Webb 43, Willie 2 6-25-191/195
William C. Webb 43, Martha J. 42, Ida T.E. 16, William T. 13, Millie A. 9, Martha V. 7, Homadothed D. 6 (s), Mary E. 3, Yancy F. 8/12 (s) 5-5-44
1900 CENSUS
Boss Webb 23 (Ap 1877-M 4), Anna 22 (Ap 1878-M 4-3-2), Martha 4 (May 1896), William F. 1 (June 1898) 5-231A-57
David Webb 25 (Feb 1875-M 6), Martha W. 24 (Aug 1875-M 6-3-2), Ada 4 (Aug 1895), Lee 3 (Feb 1897) 5-234A-122
Frank Webb 62 (Jan 1838-M 17), Maggie 47 (May 1853-M 17-7-6), Lizie 16 (Ap 1884), Susan J. 13 (Dec 1886), Lizzie 11 (July 1888), Alfred 10 (Dec 1889) 6-241B-39
George Webb 24 (Nov 1875-M 3), Lue 23 (Oct 1876-M 3-1-1), Burkett 2 (Feb 1898) 5-236B-164

Hamond D. Webb 66 (Dec 1833-T/NC/SC-M 2), Elizabeth 53 (Dec 1846-M 2-0), Joseph 30 (Oct 1869-M 2), Jane 17 (dl)(June 1882-M 2-1-0) 5-236B-163
Jack Webb 19: see Dollie Corvin
James Webb 32 (Jan 1868-M 12)(Stat Engine Fireman), Larvah 34 (Ap 1866-M 12-4-4), Luther 11 (Aug 1888), Clarence 9 (July 1890), Della 7 (Mar 1893), Belle 3 (Jan 1897) 10-327-145/153
James A. Webb 18 (Aug 1881-M 0), Anna 19 (Ap 1881-M 0-0) 6-241B-38
James A. Webb 40 (Nov 1859-M 6), Rebecca F. 23 (Nov 1876-M 6-0), Charles 15 (nw)(Ap 1885) 5-231B-62
Joseph Webb 30 (Feb 1870-M 7), Carrie M. 28 (Aug 1871-Pa/Pa/Pa-M 7-7-2), Susan I. 3 (June 1896), Ulicia 1 (May 1899) 5-236B-169
Lizzie Webb 55: see James Pelfrey
Nora Webb 6: see Charles Wilkey
Richard S. Webb 34 (Feb 1866-Ga/Ga/Ga-M 6), Isabella 24 (Oct 1875-Ind/Ind/Mo-M 6-0), Arazona 15 (Feb 1885-Ga/Ga/Ga), Arthur J. 12 (Dec 1887-Ga), Walter 10 (Sep 1889-Ga) 11-292B-70
William Webb 32 (Nov 1867-M 13), Nellie J. 30 (June 1869-M 13-5-5), John 12 (Ap 1888), James H. 7 (Sep 1892), William T. 5 (Sep 1894), Mary E. 2 (Feb 1896), Mattie L. 1 (Sep 1898) 5-235A-137
William C. Webb 63 (Oct 1836-T/NC/NC-M 46), Martha S. 63 (Sep 1836-T/NC/NC-M 46-11-7), Yancy F. 20 (Oct 1879), Alexander ROFF 22 (boarder)(Jan 1878) 5-236A-160

MARRIAGES

Andrew Webb to Nancy J. Etherton, 26 Feb 1876 (same), John Miller MG 1-#1439
Callie Webb to Charley Wilkey q.v.
Darth Webb to Martha Myers, 24 Feb 1893, H.B. Burdett MG 4-69
Ella Webb to Jacob Byerley q.v.
Franklin Webb (20) to Dolly Cahan (14), 19 Sep 1881, J.M. Bramlett MG, James Jones & Peter Minnick W 4-4(40)
G.W. Webb to Lula Thurman, 29 Mar 1897 (same), H.B. Burdett MG, F. Webb W 2-133
H.D. Webb to Lizza Beasley, 7 Ap 1898 (same), W.A. Howard MG 2-265
J.A. Webb to Rebecca F. Waldon, 10 Mar 1895, J.W. Gillespie JP 4-79
J.L. Webb to L.V. Wyatt, 15 Oct 1887 (same), E.S. Cox JP 1-533
Jacob Webb to Nancy H. Clour, 18 Jan 1875 (19 Jan), S. Phillips MG 1-#1388
James Webb to Emma Byerley, 24 Mar 1900 (bond only), J.M. Webb W 3-135
Jasper Webb to Cora Dixon, 25 Oct 1891, H.B. Burdett MG 4-41
Jennie Webb to Joe Adkins q.v.
John B. Webb to Tress Scrimpshire, 9 Mar 1894, J.W. Gillespie JP 4-76
Joseph Webb to Jane Burditt, 1 Feb 1898 (6 Feb), J.M. Bramlett MG, H.D. Sneed W 2-247
Mahala Webb to William Norris q.v.
Margaret Webb to W. C. Gossett q.v.
Martha Webb to Willis Smith q.v.
Mila W. or A. Webb to John Mize q.v.
Nancy Webb to Henry Ogle q.v.
Susan Webb to J. R. Sneed q.v.
Susan J. Webb to John Buchanan or Bushman q.v.
W.B. Webb to Nely J. Mize, 19 Dec 1885 (same), H.B. Burditt MG 1-497
William Webb to Sallie Swafford, 15 Ap 1886 (16 Ap), S.D. Burnett ?? 1-484
Yank Webb to Della Ogle, 24 Nov 1900 (same), W.G. Curton MG, Ben(?) Webb W 3-246

WEBSTER

1870 CENSUS

Caroline Webster 31: see William T. Gass

1880 CENSUS

Caroline Webster 35 1-19-158

1900 CENSUS

Caroline Webster 50 (Unk 1850-NC/NC/NC-Wd) 3-202B-52/55

WEEKS

1860 CENSUS

John Weeks 26: see William Key
Thomas Weeks 31, Esther A. 28, Betsy J. 7, George W. 5, Peter M. 3, Franklin P. 2 3-56-380

1870 and 1880 CENSUS– None

1900 CENSUS

Elisha M. Weeks 36 (Ga/Ga/Ga-M 16), Mary J. 34 (Dec 1865-Ga/T/T-M 16-10-8), William C. 14 (Aug 1885-Ga)(Coal Miner), Willis A. 13 (Oct 1886-Ga), Winslow 10 (Ap 1890-Ga), Reno C. 8 (June 1891-Ga), Florence M. 7 (May 1893), Burton J. 5 (July 1894-Ga), Webster A. 4 (Jan 1896-Ga), Pryor 11/12 (June 1899-Ga) 13-301B-212/220

MARRIAGES

Mary Ann Weeks to Daniel M. Bailes q.v.
Thomas A. Weeks to H.A. McCully, 7 Dec 1853 (8 Dec), John O. Torbett JP 1-#430

WEIGLE

1880 CENSUS

W.A. Weigle 37 (House Carpenter), Pallia 36, E.S. 12 (d), J.W. 10 (s), A.A. 8 (s), E. 5 (s), C.A. 2 (d) 8-1-9

WELCH / WELSH

1870 CENSUS

Preston Welch 36 (Shoemaker), Elendor 24, Mary A. 6, Rachel J. 3, Joseph L. 2, George W. 5/12, Rachel WHELER 58, Caroline WHELER 12 2-4-23

1880 CENSUS

Brox Welch(?) 28, E.L. 25, B.F. 5/12 (s) 4-34-283
Preston Welch 43 (Shoemaker), Ellen 33, Mary 14, Rachel 12, Joseph 11, George 10, Addie 9, Nellie 7, Anna 5, John 2 2-23-190

1900 CENSUS

John M. Welch 33 (Mar 1867-M 6)(Lumber Dealer), Minnie J. 27 (Oct 1872-M 6-1-1), Merle R. 3 (Dec 1896) 14-218A-114/116

MARRIAGES

Amanda S. Welch to Jacob A. Stevens q.v.

Alex Welsh to Mashie Allison, 19 Aug 1900 (same), W.G. Curton MG, J. Martin W 3-201

Hays Welsh to Mary Dobbs, 11 Aug 1900 (12 Aug), W.G. Curton MG, R.T. Sutton(?) W 3-197

Hugh E. Welch to A.T. Banks, 10 May 1899, no MG or JP, J.A. Denton W 2-410

J.M. Welch to Minne Allison, 26 June 1893, John T. Price MG 4-59

Mollie Welch to W. L. Brooks q.v.

Newt Welsh to Maggie McMillin, 27 Feb 1897 (28 Feb), W.G. Curton MG, Tim Martin W 2-119

Rachel Welch to R. S. Cox q.v.

- - - - - - - - - - - - -

WELLINGTON

1900 CENSUS

B. Forrest Wellington 27 (Ap 1873-M 3)(Coal Miner), Alice 23 (Jan 1877-M 3-2-2), John 2 (Dec 1897), Maggie 3/12 (Feb 1900) 13-298B-164/168

William Wellington 56 (Feb 1844-M 30), Margaret 53 (June 1846-M 30-11-8), Robert 23 (Oct 1876), James 21 (Feb 1879), Thomas 19 (Dec 1880), Edward 16 (July 1883), Houston 14 (Jan 1886), Martha J. 12 (Feb 1888) 13-298B-164/167

- - - - - - - - - - - - -

WEST

1860 CENSUS

Jeffrey West 39, Olinda 38, Leonna 14, Warren 12, Napolen 10, Mary 7, Isaac P. 4, Album T. 2, Martha PREWET 18 5-38-254

Mary West 71 (Va), Manerva 16 4-49-331

1870 CENSUS

Edward West 52 (NC), Sidda 47 (NC), Eli 21 (NC), Charity L. 19 (NC), Jesse 17 (NC), Rebecca 14 (Ga), Jonathan 11 (Ga), George W. 8 (Ga), Martin 4/12 2-16-112

Mary West 50 (Va), Paula I. McCULLY 17 4-1-2

Orlinda West 49, Warren 24, Napoleon 20, Mary 17, Isaac P. 15, Allion 11, Thomas C. 9 5-9-69

William West 24, Mary A. 24, Sarah E. 3, James L. 2, John L. 1 2-12-83

1880 CENSUS

Edmond West 55, Matilda 21, Jonathan 20, George 18, Martin 9, Ida 4 12-5-46

James West 26: see Aaron Ray

Jesse West 31, Julia 27, Bette 7, Vashtar 6, Zack 5, Nebunezer(?) 3, Gelilia SWIFT 41 (sil)(Nurse), Garnet SWIFT 2 (ne) 2-29-237

John West 59, Sephia A. 30 (w), Jane N. 13, Mary A. 12, James 11, Susan 6, William F. 2 6-13-122 (B)

Leander West 29, Sarah L. 21, William S. 8, Charles T. 3, Rolly F. 1, Mary B. 3/12 5-4-34

Thomas West 38, Margaret 33, Calvin 10, Susanna 8, Mary 6, Lottie 5, George 2 1-8-59

1900 CENSUS

George West 30 (Feb 1870)(Attorney) 10-326B-136/143

Georgia A. West 24, William 5, Richard A. 0/12: see Mary Pryor

Jacob West 16: see Lewatz(?) Bowman

James H. West 72 (Aug 1827-Md/Md/Md-M 40), Sophia 47 (Unk-M 40-11-7), John H. 19 (June 1880), Charles 13 (Feb 1887), Henry J. 11 (Feb 1889), Louisa A. 9 (May 1891), Lula B. 5 (Nov 1894) 6-243A-64 (B)

John West 21: see John C. Malone

Johnson West 41 (Feb 1859-M 18), Haret 40 (Nov 1859-M 18-10-6), Eddi 15 (June 1884), Charly 10 (Mar 1891), Tarnis(?) 8 (May 1892), Lucy 5 (July 1894), Dallas 3 (Sep 1896), Rack 11/12 (June 1899), Emma GILLUM 64 (ml)(Sep 1835-Wd 7-7) 12-181B-62/65

Leander J. West 56 (Dec 1843-NC/NC/NC-M 27), Sarah 42 (May 1858-M 27-14-9), Raleigh L. 21 (Sep 1878)(RR Laborer), Minnie 16 (Mar 1884), Kittie 11 (Jan 1889), Grace 9 (Sep 1890), John 6 (Dec 1893), Ida M. 4 (May 1896) 5-238B-204

Maggie West 16: see Thomas C. Travis

MARRIAGES

Calvin G. West to Florence Cox, 23 July 1891, J.P. Roddy MG 4-29

Cinda(?) West to Wm R. Bowles q.v.

Della West to J. T. Marshall q.v.

E. West to Tilda Shelvy, 14 Ap 1879 (no return) 1-#1613

Enoch West to Netyie(?) Reynolds, 22 Dec 1899, J.H. Keylon JP 4-103

G.W. West (21) to S.A. Tesseteller or Teffeteller, 1 Jan 1882, S. Breeding JP, A. Morriss & Y. Rose W 4-7(69)

James West to Sopha Buttler, 28 Nov 1872 (30 Nov), G.W. Renfro MG 1-#1230

John West to George Ann Pryor, 24 Dec 1891, W. Morgan JP 4-36

Jonathan G. West (22, Polk Co) to Harriett Gilliam (22), 23 May 1882, A. Selser MG, John Short & John Lawson W 4-9(88)

Sadie West to G. W. Tumlin(?) q.v.

Samantha West to Green Pryor q.v.

Susie West to Eli Shurman q.v.

William T. West to Margarett Monday, 15 Aug 1867 (18 Aug), Wm R.S. Thompson JP 1-#964

- - - - - - - - - - - - -

WESTER / WISTER

1880 CENSUS

Pink Wester 50, Amelia 26 (d)(Washwoman), Alice 12 (gd), Sophronia 6 (gd), Martha 1 (gd) 2-38-309 (B(Mu)

1900 CENSUS

John W. Wester 69 (Sep 1830-T/NC/Va-M 40), Hanna J. 71 (Mar 1829-M 40-6-4) 2-193A-40/41 (B)

MARRIAGE

Ellen Wester to James Rodgers q.v.

- - - - - - - - - - - - -

WESTFIELD

MARRIAGE
John Westfield to Amanda Wilkey, 19 Ap 1893, J.D. Gaither MG 4-53

- - - - - - - - - - - - -

WETMORE

1900 CENSUS
Edwin F. Wetmore 47 (Sep 1852-Oh/Oh/Oh-M 18)(Fruit Grower), Ada M. 41 (Ap 1859-Oh/Denmark/Do-M 18-4-4), Myrtlie E. 16 (June 1883-Oh), Mildred M. 10 (Jan 1890), Alton J. 6 (Dec 1893), Carrie P. 4 (Feb 1896), Daly C. BEAN 24 (boarder)(Aug 1875-T/Va/T) 11-292B-62

- - - - - - - - - - - - -

WHALEY / WHALY / WALEY

1860 CENSUS
John S. Whaley 28, Elizabeth J. 28, Mary A. 3, Thomas M. 1, Catharine C. 1/12, John A. 21 7-1-3
John Whaly 59 (Ky)(Methodist Preacher), Polly 56, Theodore 20, James C. 15, Wilder F. 12, Adaline 22, Anderson 20 10-28-189
Thomas H. Whaley 30, Mary A. 30, John T. 10, Mary E. 8, Rachel F. 6, Laura M. 3, Ema A. 1 7-1-2
1870 CENSUS
Elizabeth Whaley 38, Mary A. 13, Thomas M. 11, Sallie C. 10 10-3-21
Sarah Whaley 24: see J. W. Williamson
1880 CENSUS
Jery Whaly 22, E.J. 20, Eliza CATES 50 (ml), E.A. 40 (d), Joseph L. 13 (gs), Johny 11 (gs), J.R. 6 (gs) 7-26-225
Pat Whaley(?) 45, Catharine 40, John 16, Charley 11, Annie 9, Willie 6, Adila 6, Kitie 4, Sarah 10/12 8-14-124
1900 CENSUS
Thomas Whaley 41 (Sep 1858-M 2)(Bookkeeper), Ann 48 (Dec 1852-M 2-0), Claud 12 (s)(Nov 1887), Edcar 11 (s)(Ap 1889), Taylor 8 (s)(Aug 1891) 10-250B-20

MARRIAGES
Elizabeth Whaley to Joseph Dodd q.v.
J.D. Whaley to Lucinda Cates, 9 Dec 1876 (11 Dec), J.R. Crawford JP 1-#1474
James O. Whaley to Mary Keith, 9 Nov 1865 (no return) 1-#854 & 1-#872
Mary A. Whaley to W. B. Fisher q.v.
S. W. Whaley to G. W. Callahan q.v.
Sallie Whaley to Barwick Brady q.v.
T.M. Whaley to Low Hicks, 20 Dec 1886 (21 Dec), J.H. Keith MG 1-514
T.M. Whaley to Mrs. Ann Purser, 22 Dec 1897 (23 Dec), G.W. Jackson MG 2-228
Tennessee C. Whaley to A. C. P. Igou q.v.
Thomas F. Whaley to Rachel J. Howell, no date (29 Oct 1870), J.H. Keith MG 1-#1171
Wilbert F. Whaley to Mary Davis, 26 Dec 1865 (21 Dec) [sic], J.H. Keith MG 1-#859

- - - - - - - - - - - - -

WHEELER / WHELER

1860 CENSUS
John Wheeler 61 (Va), John M. 23, Charles N. 20, Serena E. 15, Joshua10 4-50-339
1870 CENSUS
John Wheeler 73 (Va) 4-3-15
John Wheeler 27 (Physician): see Addison Locke
Rachel Wheler 58, Caroline 12: see Preston J. Welch
1880 CENSUS
J.D. Wheeler 30, E.J. 29, J.F. 5 (s), Richard 3, J.S. 1 (s), B.F. 3/12 (s) 4-33-272
John Wheeler 26 (Shoemaker), Fanny 31, Charlie 7 2-24-191
Samuel Wheeler 46 (Physician), Sarah 32, James 2, Dora 1 1-9-71
1900 CENSUS
Caswell Wheeler 54, Adra 15: see Conrad Evans
John H. Wheeler 25 (May 1875-M 5), Anna 27 (Unk 1873-M 5-2-1), Ollie 2 (Dec 1897), Ollie A. WHEELER 15 (si)(May 1885) 3-208B-155/168
Robert Wheeler 40 (Dec 1859-Ga/NC/NC-M 8)(Saloon Keeper), Laura E. 29 (Aug 1870-T/T/Ga-M 8-3-2), Nannie E. 7 (July 1892), Joseph A. 4 (Jan 1896) 10-325A-103/107
Samuel J. Wheeler 67 (Mar 1833-Wd)(Physician), James 22 (July 1878), Dara 19 (Jan 1881), Samuel 15 (Sep 1884), Pharis PAUL 45 (Jan 1853-Wd 1-1)(Servant) 1-186A-142/150
MARRIAGES
Callie Wheeler to Jesse Hale q.v.
George K.M. Wheeler to Elizabeth A. Peoples, 28 Oct 1857 (no return) 1-#618
J.D. Wheeler to E.S. Holland, 9 Aug 1873 (13 Aug), John Howard MG 1-#1293
John Wheeler to Emma Shelton, 23 Dec 1894, A.M. Broyles JP 4-74
S.J. Wheeler to C.C. Johnson, 26 May 1868 (same), Wm H. Bell MG 1-#1011
Serena E. Wheeler to Samuel Walker q.v.
William M. Wheeler to M.M. Fisher, 13 Nov 1858 (14 Nov), S.H. Dickey JP 1-#669

- - - - - - - - - - - - -

WHEELOCK

1900 CENSUS
Noah W. Wheelock 60 (Mar 1840-M 36)(Tinsmith), Mary C. 55 (Nov 1844-M 36-4-2) 14-214B-32/33
MARRIAGE
W.E. Wheelock to Amanda B. Neal, 3 Mar 1891, H.C. Neal MG 4-21

- - - - - - - - - - - - -

WHITAKER / WHITACRE

MARRIAGES
Charles Whitaker to Molly Stanly, 5 May 1886 (6 May), J. W. Simpson ?? 1-510
Elizabeth Whitacre (21, Putnam Co) to Stephen Wilhoit q.v.
Thomas Whitacer to Sarah Brown(?), 21 Aug 1892, Jas Corvin MG 4-46

- - - - - - - - - - - - -

WHITE

1860 CENSUS
James White 40, Jane 45, John 17, James P. 18, Nancy 13, Manerva 12, William 11, Carson 7, Penelope 4 3-64-443
James F. White 36, July E. 32, Jacob 11 4-49-333
John White 36, Mary 45, James R. 17, John T. 15, William H. 12, Lewis R. 4, Rebecca M. PORTER(?) 15 3-64-444
Martin White 26 (Ala)(Lawyer), Mary 28, Alexander 1 6-112-767
Mary White 68, Nancy LOUVEL(?) 10 8-17-112
1870 CENSUS
Alfred White 9 (B): see Sarah Howerton
Jacob B. White 22, James F. 48, Julia 43, Madison BURSON(?) 14, Susan A. MITCHELL 32, Booney V. 23, Nancy WOODARD 50 3-4-28
James White 53, Visa L. 46 (NC), Virginia C. 9, Henry 5 3-11-78
James P. White 27, Eliza 28, Franklin 2, Penelope 15 3-19-138
John White 50, Mary 53, Lewis 16 3-8-130
1880 CENSUS
John White 40: see Deadrick Sykes
Miles White 19: see L. P. Essex
Peyton White 39, E. 42, Frank 13, William 11, Thomas 7, M.J. 4 (d), R. GOSSETT 19 (boarder) 3-22-179

1900 CENSUS
Andrew White 40: see Emma Buckhanon (B)
Charles White 25: see Rosa Wade (B)
Edward White 41 (Mar 1859-NC/Unk-Wd)(RR Section Hand) 10-328A-165/175 (B)
Georgia White 5: see Lee A. Kelly (B)
Hattie White 30 (Dec 1869-M 10-4-4), Myrtle 9 (Dec 1890), Ethel 7 (Jan 1893), Ruth 3 (July 1895), Willie 2 (Aug 1897), Jake GILL 35 (boarder)(Unk) 8-311B-18/19 (B)
Jacob White 32: see Jack Moore (B)
James White 59 (Feb 1841-M 35), Eliza 59 (Unk 1841-T/Va/Va-M 35-7-4), Martha 22 (Dec 1877), Jay F. 18 (Unk 1882) 3-207B-132/145
John White 60: see Milton McDonald
Julius White 35 (Mar 1865-M 10)(RR Section Foreman), Jennie 32 (Sep 1867-M 10-3-2), William G. 9 (Mar 1892), Leona 7 (Jan 1893) 14-214B-28/29
Rene White 17: see Harvey Creaseman
William White 55 (Dec 1844-England/Do/Do-1866/34/Na-M 30)(Iron Foundryman), Sarah 53 (Mar 1847-Ireland/Do/Do-1862/38/?-M 30-8-6), William E. 27 (July 1872-Pa)(Machinist), Josie 26 (May 1874-Pa), Charles A. 23 (Nov 1876-Pa)(Foundryman), Maud 22 (May 1878-Pa), Henry 20 (July 1880-Pa)(Foundryman), John 18 (Jan 1882-Pa)(Foundryman) 10-322B-54/57
William White 57 (June 1842-T/WVa/NC-M 36)(Clergyman), Rebekah 54 (May 1845-M 36-11-9), Rutha E. 19 (Ap 1881), Benjamin F. 17 (Jan 1883), Samuel R. 11 (Mar 1889) 2-197A-109/114
William White 65 (Ap 1835-T/Va/Va-M 24), Malinda J. 58 (Ap 1842-M 24-5-4), Berry L. 32 (Sep 1867)(Coal Miner) 8-278B-203/205

MARRIAGES
Ben White to Hettie Henderson, 30 Oct 1889 (same), L.M. Moore ?? 1-592
Della A. White to Samuel M. Keathley q.v.
Eliza J. White to John A. Porter q.v.
Enoch White to Matilda E. Hughes, 5 Mar 1877 (8 Mar), L.W. Pence MG 1-#1489
Enoch White to Nettie Hayes, 8 Oct 1893, A.D. Hubbard MG 4-61
Fannie White to W. S. Bridgeman q.v.
Houston White to Nancy McCully, 8 Oct 1867 (same), D. Broyles JP 1-#975
James White to Jane Fike, 23 Feb 1861 (no return) 1-#746
James White to Dellie Kelly, 9 Nov 1899, W.K. Fugate JP 4-104
James W. White to Vicey Horner, 2 Mar 1867 (same), T. N.L. Cunnyngham JP 1-#1004 [on page with 1868, but according to divorce papers, James and Louisa V., widow of Rev. David Horner, were married on 15 Sept 1864]
John E. White to Mary F. Smith, 9 Aug 1873 (10 Aug), W.M. Dodd MG 1-#1292
Lewis White to M.J. Mitchell, 27 June 1874 (28 June), N. Whittenburg MG 1-#1340
Lillie M. White to John R. Davis q.v.
Louis B. White to Sallie Moore, 6 May 1885 (8 May), Jas R. Crawford JP 1-494
Lyda E. White to R. M. Green q.v.
Malinda White to John Jordan q.v.
Manervia F. White to H. B. Fry q.v.
Nancy White to Lodrick Sykes q.v.
Penelopy White to Jesse McCollend q.v.
Sallie L. White to John P. Roddy q.v.
W.H. White to L.J. Miller, 14 Sep 1883 (16 Sep), I.W. Holt JP 1-481
Wiley White to Eliza Williams, 17 Nov 1892, D.H. Hindman(?) JP 4-51
William White to Laura Jones, 7 Mar 1890 (same), L.M. Moore ?? 1-593

WHITEHEAD

1880 CENSUS
Asa Whitehead 37 (Boot & Shoemaker), Hannah 30, Minnie 9 12-1-4
John Whitehead 30, Margaret 24, James 5, Sarah 3, William 2 2-32-260

WHITEHOUSE

1900 CENSUS
Ada Whitehouse 5, Cornelia 2: see James L. Brown (B)

WHITFIELD / WHITEFIELD

1880 CENSUS
George W. Whitfield 36, E.J. 30, Billy 12, James 11, John 9, Elige 7, Eliza 4 8-17-143

1900 CENSUS

John Whitfield 28 (Jan 1872-T/Ga/T-M 8)(Locamotive Engineer), Carrie 27 (Jan 1873-M 8-3-3), Edith 7 (Sep 1892), Meta 5 (Aug 1894), Claud 2 (Jan 1898) 8-276A-156/157

Ligh(?) Whitefield 22 (Dec 1878-T/Ga/T-M 3)(RR Engineer), Ginthy 23 (May 1877-M 3-3-3), Ray 2 (Dec 1897), Paul 1 (Jan 1899), Haggie 1/12 (Ap 1900) 10-259B-181/185

May Whitfield 7: see Annie Scott

William Whitfield 32 (Jan 1868-T/Ga/Ga-M 4)(Locamotive Engineer), Heaster 19 (July 1880-M 4-1-1), Nellie 2 (Ap 1898) 10-323A-67/71

MARRIAGES

Elijah Whitfield to Syntha Williams, 26 Aug 1897 (same), W.L. Lillard JP, Wm Wilkey W 2-168

Ida Whitfield to John Gillespie q.v.

James P. Whitfield or Whitford to Carrie Ford, 23 Dec 1891, R.A. Bartlett MG 4-37

L. Whitfield to Tennie Erwin, 10 Dec 1893, W.S. Hale MG 4-59

Lizzie Whitfield or Whitford to Edward Vance q.v.

William Whitfield to Hester Cooley, 26 Sep 1896 (27 Sep), W.L. Lillard JP, T.J. Bruner W 2-69

- - - - - - - - - - - - -

WHITLOCK

1880 CENSUS

William Whtlock 30: see William Tarwater

- - - - - - - - - - - - -

WHITLOW

1900 CENSUS

Samuel Whitlow 22 (Unk 1888), Hugh KEITH 26 (boarder)(1874-M 0), Sanford CARTER 22 (boarder)(1878), Sally SEA 20 (boarder)(1880) 8-275A-126 (B)

- - - - - - - - - - - - -

WHITMORE

MARRIGE

Fannie Whitmore or Whitemer to Tom Davis q.v.

- - - - - - - - - - - - -

WHITNER

1900 CENSUS

John A. Whitner 40 (Dec 1859-Ga/NC/NC-M 15)(Minister), Mina 38 (June 1861-Ill/Canada/England-M 15-5-5), Carl V. 13 (Sep 1886), Irene D. 11 (Dec 1888), Ollie M. 9 (Ap 1891), George A. 4/12 (Aug 1899), Myron PARKER 8 (ss)(Sep 1881-T/Pa/Ill)(Grocery Salesman), Elizabeth WHITNER 76 (m)(Feb 1824-NC/NC/NC-Wd 6-5) 8-314B-88/91

- - - - - - - - - - - - -

WHITTENBURG

1860 CENSUS

Christopher Whittenburg 55, Mary 54, Eliza J. 21, Mary A. 20, Manerva T. 18 4-50-342

Eglantine A. Whittenburg 32, Sarah A. 5, James W. 3 4-50-337

Henry Whittenburg 41, Eliza B. 38, Jesse M. 20, William E. 18, Ira N. 14, Prudence 12, Mary E. 8, Margaret J. 3 4-48-326

Ira M. Whittenburg 33, Mary B. 24, Anjaletta 5, Adelia C. 2 4-48-327

Nathan Whittenburg 39 (School Teacher), Sarah J. 37, Eliza C. 2, Amanda E. 10/12, Eliza UNDERWOOD 40 3-69-470

Newton H. Whittenburg 37, Sarah A. 54 (Va) 4-53-363

S.T. Whittenburg 46 (Trader), Charlotte J. 33, Margaret E. 16, Sarah J. 14, James 12 1-93-632

Samuel Whittenburg 46, Sarah H. 36, William A. 14, Timothy N. 10, Edmond G. 7, Henry H. 5, Marthy J. 2 4-49-336

William Whittenburg 63, Mary A. 51, Sarah F. 17, John A. 15, Stephen P. 13, Amos F. 11 4-54-365 [William married Mary A. Stout]

1870 CENSUS

Christopher Whittenburg 66, Mary 65, Mary Ann C. 29, Marena T. 25 4-5-28

Ira M. Whittenburg 43, Mary B. 34, Angaletta J. 15, Adela C. 12, Mary I. 6, Mary P. 1, David FARNER 14 4-4-25

Mary A. Whittenburg 58, Sarah F. 26, Stephen P. 23, Amos F. 21 4-2-11

Nathan Whittenburg 52, Sarah J. 46, Eliza C. 12, Amanda E. 10, Jefferson D. 9, Margarette J. 7, Eliza UNDERWOOD 52 3-2-8

William Whittenburg 10, Sarah E. 7: see Peter McCullough

1880 CENSUS

A.M. Whittenburg 31, M.C. or M.E. 26, M.(?)B. 5 (d), A.C. 3 (d) 4-32-264

Delia Whittenburg 22: see Rebecca Hoyal

I.N. Whittenburg 53, M.B. 44, D.C. 22 (d), M.J. 16 (d), M.P. 12 (d), E.J. 9 (d), W.R. 1 (s), M.E. TORBETT 61 (boarder), S.M. TORBETT 48 (boarder) 4-33-275

Mary Whittenburg 40: see Thomas Godbehere

Nathan Whittenburg 62, Sarah 55 (w), Amanda 20, Jefferson 18, Margaret 17, Eliza UNDERWOOD 62 (sil) 1-15-130

1900 CENSUS

Ira M. Whittenburg 73 (Nov 1826-T/Pa/T-Wd), Robarson W. 21 (s)(Aug 1877) 3-201B-32/35

Sarah Whittenburg 77 (May 1823-T/SC/SC-Wd 3-2), Eliza UNDERWOOD 83 (si)(Jan 1817-Wd 0-0)(Quiltmaker), Jeff WHITTENBURG 40 (s)(Jan 1860) 1-183A-86/89 [Sarah, widow of Nathan]

MARRIAGES

Amanda Whittenburg to W. G. Roddy q.v.

Augusta Whittenburg to Peter McCully q.v.

Austillie J. Whittenburg to A. T. Marsh q.v.

Cordelia Whittenburg to B. B. Stout q.v.

Eliza J. Whittenburg to J. R. Campbell q.v.

H.N. Whittenburg to Sarah A.L. Barksdale, 12 May 1852 (same), J.B. Lawson ?? 1-#373

Ira M. Whittenburg to Mary B. Ganaway, 31 Oct 1853 (5 Nov), J.W. Thompson MG 1-#426
John D. Whittenburg to Mary M. Walker, 5 May 1853 (6 May), J.W. Thompson MG 1-#429
John W. Whittenburg to E.A. Broyles, 23 July 1851, Wm Ganaway MG 1-#345
Louisa J. Whittenburg to J. Stout q.v.
M. E. Whittenburg to James L. Roddy q.v.
M. T. Whittenburg to W. L. Godbyhere q.v.
N. E. Whittenburg to R. B. Torbett q.v.
Samuel Whittenburg to Rhoda R. Ganaway, 19 Nov 1860, J.W. Thompson MG 1-#732
Sarah Jane Whittenburg to J. E. Montgomery q.v.

- - - - - - - - - - - - -

WHITTLE

MARRIAGE
James Whittle to Virginia Peterson, 17 July 1886 (18 July), James R. Crawford JP 1-507

- - - - - - - - - - - - -

WIBEL

1900 CENSUS
Samuel Wibel 42: see Chrstopher Neal

- - - - - - - - - - - - -

WIDST

1860 CENSUS
Catharne Widst(?) 60 (Pa), Susan 18 8-17-111

- - - - - - - - - - - - -

WIGGINS

1900 CENSUS
Elija Wiggins 21 (Dec 1878-M 2), Cora 16 (June 1883-M 2-1-1), William E. 9/12 (May 1900), Martha WIGGINS 17 (si)(Mar 1883) 3-208B-149/162
Lila Wiggins 19: see John C. Willson
William M. Wiggins 57 (Nov 1842-T/NC/NC-M 32), Catharine 46 (Unk 1854-M 32-12-9), Sarah 14 (Sep 1885), Nancy 11 (Dec 1888), William J. 8 (Nov 1891), James R. 6 (Mar 1894), John DRAKE 24 (1876)(Servant), Chas WALTER 14 (1886)(Servant) 3-208B-152/165
MARRIAGES
Cinda J. Wiggins to John C. Wilson q.v.
Elijah Wiggins to Cora Presswood, 6 Feb 1898, E.W. Mort ?? 4-99
Lillie Wiggins to Tim Couch q.v.
Susanah Wiggins to James W. Mitchell q.v.

- - - - - - - - - - - - -

WILBANKS

1900 CENSUS
Barry(?) Wilbanks 30 (Oct 1869-T/Ga/Ala-M 5), Maggie 20 (Ap 1880-Ala/Unk-M 5-2-2), Samie 5 (Oct 1894-Ga), Mollie 3 (Feb 1897-Ala) 10-255A-96
Joe Wilbanks 27 (Sep 1872-T/Ga/Ala-M 2), Anny 23 (July 1876-M 2-1-1), Johney 2 (Feb 1898) 10-255A-97

- - - - - - - - - - - - -

WILBUR

1900 CENSUS
Charles Wilbur 52 (July 1847-Ga/T/France-M 20)(Grocer), Sarah 43 (Aug 1856-Ind/Ga/Ind-M 20-3-3), Charles 17 (July 1882-Ind)(Grocery Salesman), Veni 13 (May 1887-Ind), Myrtle 7 (Aug 1892) 10-320B-7/7

- - - - - - - - - - - - -

WILCOXSON

MARRIAGE
David Wilcoxson to Margaret Keener, 16 Nov 1891, A.W. Frazier JP 4-38

- - - - - - - - - - - - -

WILEY

1860 CENSUS
Ellen Wiley 13: see Jason I. Panner

- - - - - - - - - - - - -

WILHOIT / WILLHOIT

MARRIAGES
Fosie Wilhoit to Ras Elder q.v.
G.W. Willhoit to W.G.Z. Jordan, 20 July 1878 (no return) 1-#1570
Stephen Wilhoit (22, Putnam Co) to Elizabeth Whitacre (21, Putnam Co), 10 Ap 1883 (Washington), T.N.L. Cunnyngham JP, C.W. Johnson & J.L. Locke W 4-14(133)

- - - - - - - - - - - - -

WILIBY

MARRIAGE
William Wiliby to Sarah M. Crisp, 3 Sep 1864 (same), W.W. Low JP 1-#1086

- - - - - - - - - - - - -

WILKENS / WALKINS

1860 CENSUS
Isaac Wilkens 44, Caroline 31, David 14, James 12, Sarah 9, Jane 7, Mary 5, John 2 1-87-599
MARRIAGE
Lena Walkins to Reuben Jefferson q.v.

- - - - - - - - - - - - -

WILKERSON / WILKARSON

1870 CENSUS
George Wilkerson 34, Martha 24 (Ga), Smionolia 5 (Ga), Thomas 3, Robert 1 3-20-142 (B)(Mu)
1880 CENSUS– None
1900 CENSUS
Charles H. Wilkerson 26 (Mar 1874-T/Ky/Ga), Robert F. 30 (b)(Oct 1869), Addie 19 (si)(May 1881), Essie 16 (si) (1884), Hester 14 (Mar 1886), Steelie 15 (b)(Aug 1884), Harrison 2 (b)(July 1897) 3-204A-74/79 (B)

Frank Wilkarson 25: see Richard Hickey (B)

George W. Wilkerson 59 (July 1840-T/T/Ga-M 1), Hattie 40 (June 1860-Ga/Ga/Ga-M 1-0), Mary E. 9 (gd)(Nov 1890), Syntha 6 (gd)(June 1894), Doshia M. 4 (gd) (July 1896) 3-205B-102/111 (B)

Huell Wilkerson 18 (B): see Charles Day

James Wilkerson 31: see Cate Guirver(?) (B)

Thomas Wilkerson 32 (Unk 1868-M 10), Mary E. 27 (Oct 1872-M 10-6-6), Caroline 10 (Feb 1890), Lilly M. 8 (July 1891), Martha J. 6 (July 1893), Cora P. 4 (Sep 1895), Laura A. 2 (Aug 1897), John I. 1 (Ap 1899) 3-206A-109/119 (B)

MARRIAGE

George Wilkerson to Hattie Williams, 26 Nov 1898 (27 Nov), D.B. Jackson MG, R.J. Killough W 2-38

\- - - - - - - - - - - - -

WILKES / WILKS

1900 CENSUS

Dolly Wilkes 28: see William Eberhart (B)

William M. Wilks 34: see Mattie Jones (B)

MARRIAGE

Eugene Wilkes to Dollie Fuller, 21 Mar 1900 (same), R.C. Knight JP, Charley Phillips [signed by X] W 3-234

\- - - - - - - - - - - - -

WILKEY / WILKIE / WILKY

1860 CENSUS

Columbus Wilkey 18, Rosannah 18 6-108-734

Samuel Wilkey 45, Cynthia 37, Rhoda A. 16, Sylvester 14, Kissier 12, Abby J. 10, Hugh E. 8, Celia 5, Alexander 3, Patrick H. 1, John SHAVER 85 6-107-733

1870 CENSUS

Samuel Wilkie 50, Synthia 47, Adda J. 19, Sela 15, Alexander 12, Patrick 10, Martin 7 6-5-30

Silvester Wilkey 23, Rebecca 30, Versa J. AULT 9, George M. 8, Hugh L. WILKEY 3/12 3-20-147

1880 CENSUS

Calm [Campbell] Wilkey 30, Emily 20 (w), James 15, Martha 9, Mary 7, Wenni 5, Catharine 3, Belle 3, Andrew 1/12 2-38-307

Christopher Wilkey 38, Ellen T. 30 (w), Abner D. 20, Robert C. 13, William D. 12, Samuel 8, James C. 7, Charles A.(?) 4 6-16-141/143

Richard Wilkey 27, Mary 20, Mary 12, Campbell 10, William 6, Eliza 5, John 4, Smith 2, Hottner(?) 11/12 4-6-47

S.L. Wilkey 33, R. 36, Mary 7, Cynthia 5, Rob 4, Susan 3, J.S. 1/12 (s) 3-26-211

Syntha Wilkey 56, Patrick 18, Martin 16 6-12-117

William Wilkie 33, Lorena 25, Martin 12, Cresa 11, Viney 7, Alexander 4, Charlie 2, Nathan 1/12 4-6-48

1900 CENSUS

Abner D. Wilkey ?? (-?- M 17), Eliza A. 39 (Mar 1861-M 17), James H. 16 (Dec 1883), Columbus C. 12 (Aug 1887), Alta B. 5 (Aug 1894), Sarah J. DODD 63 (ml) (Mar 1837-Wd 2-1) 3-200B-17/18

Albert Wilkey 20 (May 1880-M 2)(Well Digger), Josie 18 (Aug 1881-M 2-0), Lucinda WILKEY 47 (m)(Unk-Wd 1-1) 10-325B-113/117

Bill Wilkey 25 (Mar 1875-M 4), Harett 22 (Feb 1877-M 4-5-3), Bessie(?) DOLEN(?) 7 (sd)(Dec 1892), Myrtle 5 (sd)(Sep 1895), George WILKEY 7/12 (s)(Oct 1899) 7-265A-280/285

Cane Wilkey 27 (Sep 1872-M 7), Ada 22 (Jan 1878-M 7-3-3), Virgil H. 5 (July 1894), Clemmie E. 3 (Feb 1897), Mintie 1 (Oct 1898) 6-247A-137/138

Charley Wilkey 23 (Ap 1877-M 1), Callie 21 (Sep 1878-M 1-1-1), Nora WEBB 6 (sd)(Aug 1893) 7-265A-279/284

Columbus C. Wilkey 49 (Oct 1851-M 30), Ellen 50 (Aug 1850-M 30) 3-200B-18/19

Elzie Wilkey 24 (Mar 1876-M 3), Jennie 20 (Dec 1879-M 3-2-1), Jessie L. 7/12 (Oct 1899), Samuel HARTLEY 20 (boarder)(Jan 1880) 6-247A-141/142

Emily Wilkey 40 (Unk 1860-Va/Va/Va-Wd 3-3), Andy 20 (Oct 1879), Ike 17 (Mar 1883), Manda 16 (May 1884) 10-260B-206/211

James Wilkey 36 (Aug 1863-T/T/Va-M 13), Sindy 34 (Feb 1866-M 13-6-4), Pearlie A. 10 (Oct 1889), Emma 5 (July 1894), Bell 3 (Nov 1896), James A. 1 (Nov 1898), Patrick 15 (c)(Oct 1884-T/Eng/T) 10-260B-212/217

James C. Wilkey 28 (Nov 1871-M 8), Sallie M. 25 (Oct 1874-M 8-3-2), Nellie M. 6 (Sep 1893), Pearl 1 (Nov 1899) 3-200B-20/21

John Wilkey 22 (Mar 1879-M 1), Anna 21 (Jan 1879-M 1-0) 6-241A-31

Martin Wilkie 34 (Oct 1865-M 10)(Coal Miner), Easter E. 36 (Sep 1863-M 10-7-4), Luveny 7 (Aug 1892), Ethel 5 (Oct 1894), Floyd 2 (July 1897), Earnest 0/12 (May 1900) 10-324A-85/89

Martin Wilkey 36 (Sep 1863)(Grocery Dealer), Thomas 21 (nw)(Nov 1877), Vira 20 (ne)(Mar 1880), Eveline McMURRY 50 (boarder)(Mar 1850)(Seamstress) 6-243A-68

Martin Wilkey 66 (May 1834-T/T/NC-M 40), Nancy 66 (July 1833-NC/NC/NC-M 40-0), Rebecca 42 (si)(May 1858) 10-260B-205/210

Mary Wilkie 27 (Sep 1870)(Washwoman), Katy 23 (si) (May 1877-Wd 0), Andy 19 (b)(Oct 1880) 8-311A-11/12

Patrick Wilkey 15: see James Wilkey

Patrick Wilkey 40 (Jan 1860-M 11), Mary 30 (June 1869-M 11-2-2), Earl 10 (Feb 1890), Roy 8 (nw)(Mar 1892) 6-243-67

Richard Wilkey 50 (Unk-M 24), Martha 49 (Unk-M 24-12-9), Author 20 (Unk), Ella 17 (Oct 1883), Daniel 15 (Ap 1884), Asey 8 (Oct 1891), Isaac 18 (nw)(Mar 1882), Luther 2 (May 1898) 6-246B-124/125

Samuel A. Wilkey 30 (Mar 1870-M 8), Harriet A. 28 (Oct 1871-T/Ga/T-M 8), Euclid T. 7 (July 1892), Malinda J. 5 (Ap 1895), Roscoe L. 1 (June 1898), Thomas W. McDOWELL 23 (Mar 1877)(Servant) 3-200B-19/20

Sill Wilkey 53 (Oct 1846-M 30)(Merchant), Rebecca 60 (Nov 1839-M 30-3-3), Robert L. 24 (Feb 1876)(Store Clerk), Susan E. 22 (Mar 1878), John L. 20 (May 1880) 5-233B-108

William Wilkey 54 sic (Feb 1856 sic-M 35), Lovina 48 (Mar 1852-M 35-13-8), Nathan 18 (May 1882), Sallie 17 (Oct 1883), Mary 10 (Aug 1889), Luller 7 (May 1893), Annie 18 (ne)(Dec 1881) 7-265A-286/291

William D. Wilkey Unk (Unk-M 1), Nancy L. 21 (Feb 1879-M 1-1-1), Esteline E. 3/12 (Feb 1900), Lula M. McDOWELL Unk (sil)(Unk) 3-301-23/24

MARRIAGES

A.L. Wilkey to Amanda J. Harrison, 15 Dec 1877 (16 Dec), John Howard MG 1-#1531
Abba J. Wilkey to William Minick q.v.
Abner D. Wilkey (20) to Eliza Dodd (21), 16 July 1882, T.H. McPherson JP, J.C. Garrison & Jane Garrison W 4-10(91)
Albert Wilkey to Josie Gossit, 27 Aug 1898 (28 Aug), J.W. Williamson MG, Martin Wilkey W 2-317
Amanda Wilkey to John Westfield q.v.
Amanda Wilkey to Joseph Martin q.v.
C.C. Wilkey to Rosanna Jolly, 4 Aug 1859 (no return) 1-#694
Cain Wilkey to Ada Reed, 4 June 1893, S.S. Franklin JP 4-58
Celia Wilkey to Edward L. Collins q.v.
Charley Wilkey to Callie Webb, 8 Jan 1898 (bond), 7 Jan (license & return), J.W. Purcer or Renoir JP, Martin Wilkey W 2-370
Cyntha Wilkey to H. B. Williams q.v.
Elza or Elijah Wilkey to Jennie Dunning, 7 May 1897 (9 May), W.L. Lillard JP, Francis Howard W 2-144
Frances Wilkey to Samuel A. Bollis q.v.
James Wilkey to Martha Roberts, 8 Jan 1868 (9 Jan), W.W. Lowe JP 1-#996
James Wilkey to Sallie Garrison, 27 Sep 1891, W.A. Howard MG 4-32
James W. Wilkey to Lucinda Shelton, 22 Dec 1886 (30 Dec), Taylor Russell JP 1-512
John Wilkey to Ann King, 24 Feb 1899 (25 Feb), W.R. Henry JP 2-387
Katie Wilkey to W. L. Hughes q.v.
Kissiah Wilkey to A. J. Hunter q.v.
Louisa Wilkey to George Bishop q.v.
Lulla Wilkey to Samuel McMillan q.v.
Mart Wilkey to Liza Scroggins, 22 July 1889 (23 July), L.F. Shane(?) JP 1-581
Martha Wilkey to Barton Cox q.v.
Mary Wilkey to W. C. Paine q.v.
Minnie Wilkey to David McJunkins q.v.
Patrick Wilkey to Mary Burnett, 3 Mar 1889 (same), J.M. Bramlett MG 1-573
Rhoda Ann Wilkey to R. C. Montgomery q.v.
S.A. Wilkey to H.A. Smith, 19 Sep 1891, J.M. Bramlett MG 4-37
S.L. Wilkey to Rebecca A. Ault, 8 Aug 1869 (same), W.F. Buttram MG 1-#1096
Samuel Wilkey to Rosa Lourey, 8 Dec 1896 (same), F.F. Shaver MG, W. Wilkey W 2-86
Syntha Wilkey to Stephen Gentry q.v.
Trussie Wilkey to F. A. Harwood q.v.
Vina Wilkey to Cornelius Shaver q.v.
W.D. Wilkey to Dalla Perry, 12 Nov 1893, D.E. Broyles JP 4-61
William Wilkey to Vader or Varder McDowell, 4 Aug 1898 (7 Aug), J.M. Bramlett MG 2-306

- - - - - - - - - - - - -

WILL / WILLS

1860 CENSUS
Rudiz or Reedz Will 13: see William Dyke
MARRIAGE
William Wills to Lucy Johnson, 9 Mar 1885 (4 Ap), S.W. Barnett MG 1-459

- - - - - - - - - - - - -

WILLARD

MARRIAGE
Issabella M. Willard to William A. Witt q.v.

- - - - - - - - - - - - -

WILLETT

1900 CENSUS
John W. Willett 41 (Oct 1858-Ala/T/T-M 18), Susan 41 (May 1859-M 18-1-1), Joseph 15 (Mar 1885) 5-236A-145 [John W. married Susan Maples on 25 June 1882 in Meigs County]

- - - - - - - - - - - - -

WILLIAMS

1860 CENSUS
E. S. Williams 47 (Conn), Sarah 37 (Conn), Lusey 13 (Conn), Charles 11 (Conn), Mary F. 7 (Conn), Lura C. 5, Orehy 3, Harret F. 6/12 8-24-166
1870 CENSUS– None
1880 CENSUS
Daniel Williams 37: see Jere Wasson
Perry Williams 27, J. 23, Homer 3, J.T. 1 (s) 4-11-90
1900 CENSUS
James Williams 26: see James M. Nelson
John Williams 51: see Lee A. Kelly (B)
Lizzia Williams 20, Edward 6, Carl 2, Paul 6/12: see Jake Hickey (B)
Richard H. Williams 39 (Nov 1860-M 14), Sallie A. 32 (Jan 1868-M 14-6-2), Anna M. 13 (Oct 1886-Ky), Albert W. 10 (Nov 1889) 3-203A-59/63
Thomas M. Williams 57 (Oct 1846-Wales/Do/Do-1872/ 28/ Na-Wd)(Capitalist) 10-323A-70/74
William E. Williams 47 (Nov 1852-T/NC/NC-M 17), Hattie E. 35 (Feb 1865-M 17-7-5), James A. 13 (Sep 1886), Miler U. 11 (Feb 1889), Elizabeth E. 6 (Sep 1893), William P. 4 (Nov 1896), Neatia M. 2 (May 1898) 2-195B-84/87
MARRIAGES
A.E. Williams to Annie Thomas, 19 Oct 1889 (20 Oct), Jas J. Robinett MG 1-593
Alice Williams to Silas Blancet q.v.
David Williams to Mary J. Abel, 19 June 1890, F.M. Capps JP 4-16
Eliza Williams to Wiley White q.v.
Florence Williams to George Sims q.v.
George Williams to Lucy Hailes, 14 Dec 1886 (17 Dec), J. Phillips MG 1-541

H.B. Williams to Cyntha Wilkey, 9 Nov 1895, A.P. Hayes JP 4-89
Hattie Williams to George Wilkerson q.v.
James Williams to Lizzie Hickey, 28 Jan 1894, J.W. Cowles JP 4-65
Lorenza Williams to Catharine Stephens, 1 June 1886 (3 June), J.P. Brown ?? 1-487
Malinda J. Williams to Samuel O'Neal q.v.
Mary Williams to John Powers q.v.
Mary A. Williams to William Evans q.v.
Matty Williams to Jack Bryant q.v.
Moses Williams to Jane Capps, 20 Feb 1886 (same), P.P. Brooks ?? 1-499
Nancy Ann Williams to M. A. Edmonds q.v.
Rafe Williams to Martha Jackson, 19 Dec 1887 (same), E.S. Cox JP 1-536
Reese G. Williams to Flora or Florence Fine, 18 May 1898 (3 July), W.A. Howard MG, N.D. Reed W 2-277
Syntha Williams to Elijah Whitfield q.v.
T.C. Williams to Mrs. Lorinda Gray, 23 June 1892, James Johnson JP 4-38
Will Williams to Ginger Logan, 16 Nov 1890, L.M. Morris MG 4-23
William Williams to H.E. McChristian, 13 June 1883 (16 Jan), Jas Johnson JP 1-518
William Williams to Hanny Cool, 27 Dec 1900 (same), L. Haworth MG 1-591

- - - - - - - - - - - - -

WILLIAMSON

1870 CENSUS
John W. Williamson 39 (SC), Evaline 34, Alice L. 9, Albert H. 7, Minnie A. 4, Orville V. 2, Sarah WHALEY 24 10-4-26

1880 CENSUS
John W. Williamson 47 (Minister), Evaline 48, Allis L. 19, Albert H. 18, Minnie A. 14, Orville V. 12, John W. 8, Sarah E. 6, Marvin E. 3, Mary F. 3/12 10-26-204/210

1900 CENSUS
John W. Williamson 69 (Mar 1831-SC/SC/SC-M 42), Eva 63 (July 1836-M 42-9-7), Minnie 33 (Aug 1866)(Stenographer), Edwin M. 22 (Feb 1878)(Teamster), Mary S. 20 (Mar 1880) 8-314B-80/83

MARRIAGES
Eliza Williamson to Taylor Clack q.v.
John W. Williamson to Evaline Paine, 18 Nov 1858 (no return) 1-#670
R.A. Williamson to Bettie Wycuff, 19 Feb 1887 (20 Feb), Calvin Morgan JP 1-531

- - - - - - - - - - - - -

WILLIS

1870 CENSUS
James Willis 18, Larinda 20, Scup 1/12 4-9-60
John M. Willis 23 (School Teacher), Maggie J. 19 2-5-29
William V. Willis 53, Lucinda 51, Mary L. 21 4-17-113

MARRIAGES
J. Newton Willis to Lucinda Hollaway, 6 July 1869 (7 July), G.W. Renfro MG 1-#1102
John W. Willis to Margaret Howard, 21 June 1868 (same), R.T. Howard MG 1-#999
Mark Willis (40; occupation, Stonemason) to Susan Thompson (38), 28 Jan 1883, D.V. Culver MG, Bob Robinson & Amanda Wasson W 4-13(122)

- - - - - - - - - - - - -

WILSON / WILLSON

1860 CENSUS
John A. Wilson 26, Matilda J. 20, William P. 1 4-52-357
Samuel Wilson 20 (Itenerant): see Richard Bailey
Sarah Wilson 51 (NC), William M. 28 (Dentist), Jane 21, Isabella 18, Woods C. 16, Sarah E. 14, Elizabeth 11, Robert T. 6, Harrison LOYED 14 (bound) 3-57-389 [Sarah's husband, James C. Wilson, evidently was erroneously omitted from the census since he was not deceased]
William D. Wilson 43 (NC), Elizabeth 34, John 16, Mary 14, Emely 12, Jane 10, William 8, Joseph 6 7-2-11

1870 CENSUS
Eliza Wilson 5: see James Spence
Elizabeth Wilson 76: see William H. Dodd
James Wilson 42, Mary C. 39 (SC), Mission 9, William C. 8, Charlotte 3 7-6-40
James C. Wilson 65 (Wheelwright), Sarah B. 57, Sarah E. 19, Elizabeth 17, Robert 16, Ann M. 13 3-5-31
John Wilson 27, Martha 26, David 6, Sallie 4, William 2 3-18-132
Ruth Wilson 25 (Ala): see Samuel J. Frazier
Samuel Wilson 27, Malinda J. 22, Robert C. 4, Abner D. 7, William D. 2, Samuel 5/12 6-6-39
William D. Wilson 52 (NC), Elizabeth 44 (NC), Martha J. 17, William 15, Joseph 13 3-16-120
William G. Willson 44, Susan C. 43 (SC), William A. 10, Rebecca STEPHENS 25, Mary Jane BROWN 14 8-12-85
William M. Wilson 38 (Physician): see Phillip T. Rawlings

1880 CENSUS
J.C.(?) Wilson 45, A. 41, M. 15, Sarah 12, Amy 5, H.B. 4, J.M. 2, Thomas 2/12 3-16-126 (B)
James Wilson 75 (Wheelwright), S.B. 70, Sarah 27, Josephine 17 (adopted d) 3-16-129
John Wilson 37, M.C. 34, David 15, S.J. 13 (d), William 11, J.C. 9 (s), J.I. 7 (s), M.A. 5 (d), R.G. 3 (s), G.W. 6/12 (s) 3-26-207
William Wilson 49 (Physician), Amanda 31, Sarah 6, John 4, William 1, Helen HARDBARGER 45 (Servant, Cook) 2-27-215 [Wm M. married Amanda Melvina Brown on 26 Oct 1871 in Roane County]
William Wilson 25 (B): see E. S. Fugate

1900 CENSUS
Alice Wilson 11: see Elijah Norris
Charles R. Wilson 56 (Unk 1843-T/NC/NC-M 35)(Coal Miner), Elvira 50 (June 1849-M 35-9-6), Ulus S. 17 (Aug 1882), Eugene 15 (Mar 1885), Walter 10 (July 1889) 8-281B-263/265
Clem Wilson 32, Emily 14: see Maggie Roddy
James I. Wilson 27 (Feb 1873-M 7), Anthy C. 22 (Jan 1878-M 7-3-3), Charles F. 6 (Feb 1894), Gurtie 3 (Jan 1896), Annie 2 (Jan 1897) 3-206A-108/118

James R. Wilson 33 (Feb 1867-M 13), Mary J. 37 (Feb 1863-M 13-6-5), Martha E. 10 (June 1889), William D. 9 (Dec 1890), Samuel H. 7 (Dec 1892), Rosa E. 4 (Jan 1896), George J. 4/12 (Jan 1880) 8-285B-340/342

Jean B. Wilson 10, Hazen A. 6, Hattie M. 4: see Addie R. Neal

Jefferson Wilson 38, William 19: see Hiram Moore (B)

John Wilson 23 (Mar 1877-M 2), Clara W. 18 (Oct 1881-M 2-1-1), Helen 10/12 (July 1899) 8-282A-264/266

John C. Wilson 30 (Ap 1870-M 8)(Ferryman), Loucinda J. 27 (Dec 1872-M 8-0), James McINTYRE 21 (Aug 1878)(Servant), Lila WIGGINS 19 (sil)(Ap 1881) 3-208B-151/164

John F. Wilson 78 (July 1821-Oh/Va/Ky-M 24)(Retired Physician), Minerva A. 52 (Sep 1847-Ind/NC/Ky-M 24), Lena 14 (Jan 1886-Ind), Polly 10 (Aug 1889-Ind) 3-308B-353/366

John H. Wilson 56 (Oct 1843-NC/NC/NC-M 36), Martha 55 (Nov 1844-M 36-12-10), Rufus 21 (Nov 1878), Granville W. 20 (Feb 1880), Hattie E. 18 (Feb 1882), Theodore 13 (Nov 1886), Annie 10 (Feb 1890) 3-206B-117/118

John H. Wilson 47 (July 1852-Ind/Ky/Ky-M 15)(Drayman), Annie 41 (Aug 1858-Ky/Ky/Ky-M 15-3-2), Albert C. 11 (Nov 1888), William W. 9 (May 1893) 10-326A-128/132

Julia A. Wilson 59: see Aaron A. Reed

Martha Wilson 79: see John R. Stewart

Mary Wilson 69: see Samuel Gill

Rena Wilson 19: see Jack Moore (B)

Samuel A. Wilson 28 (Nov 1871-M 4)(Coal Miner), Sarah S. 37 (Jan 1863-T/Germany/Do-M 4-0), Jennie J. 8 (si)(Nov 1891) 13-304B-271/281

Sherman Wilson 33 (Ap 1867-M 11)(Fisherman), Mattie 24 (Unk 1876-M 11-5-5), Edgar 9 (Ap 1891), Bertha 7 (Mar 1893), Lena 5 (Feb 1895), Carl 4 (Mar 1896), Clide 1 (Ap 1899) 15-271B-64

Thomas Wilson 30: see Columbus McMillan

William Wilson 31 (Feb 1869-M 8), Arabella 22 (Ap 1878-M 8-2-2), Claude 6 (Oct 1893), Walter H. 7/12 (Oct 1899) 14-221A-151/155 [W.B. Wilson married Arabela Peak on 17 Aug 1892 in Meigs County]

William Wilson 58 (Unk 1844-M 4), Mary L. 43 (Oct 1856-NY/Germany/Do-M 4-5-4), Charles 23 (Sep 1876) (Coal Miner), William I. 20 (July 1879), Napoleon 16 (June 1883)(Mail Carrier), Nathan 13 (July 1886), Jessie J. 8 (Nov 1891), Nelson RIGSBY 11 (ss)(Nov 1888), Effie M. 9 (sd)(Mar 1891), Ina 5 (sd)(Aug 1894), Iva 5 (sd)(Aug 1894) 8-281B-260/262

William M. Wilson 68 (Oct 1831-M 28)(Landlord), Amanda M. 52 (Ap 1848-M 28-7-5), Sarah C. 26 (Ap 1874), William M. 21 (Sep 1878), James R. 18 (Aug 1881), Mary R. 14 (Oct 1885), George T. 12 (Nov 1887) 2-199A-156/161

MARRIAGES

Amanda A. Wilson to David Kyle q.v.

Ann E. Wilson to J. S. Chumley q.v.

Annie Wilson to John Arwine q.v.

Annie M. Wilson to Henry W. Sheridan q.v.

Beckey Wilson to James Griffin q.v.

C.H. Wilson to Maggie Monnsey, 13 Dec 1894, C.E. Muncey JP 4-75

Dealtha J. Wilson to Spencer G. Clack q.v.

Denira Wilson to A. J. Ayheart q.v.

Emily Wilson to Samuel H. Brady q.v.

G.W. Wilson to Nancy Johns, 15 Feb 1859 (same), G.W. Wallace JP 1-#1655

Ida Wilson to Samuel Gill q.v.

J.F. Wilson to Della M. Freily, 17 July 1897 (18 July), C.E. Mowrey JP, Pete Schell W 2-161

J.H. Wilson to Sarah A. Dodd, 30 Mar 1864 (no return) 1-#825

J.H. Wilson to Rachel Mathews, 26 Jan 1870 (same), T.N.L. Cunnyngham JP 1-#1140

J.H. Wilson to Ida Neal, 2 Jan 1895, J.A. Torbett JP 4-82

James I. Wilson to Carry Ward, 16 Sep 1893, J.M. Hill JP 4-56

James R. Wilson to Mary J. Oldham, 6 Aug 1888 (7 Aug), C. Morgan JP 1-570

Jane Wilson to John Harwood q.v.

John Wilson to Lula Gardner, 18 May 1885 (19 May), W.S. Hale MG 1-495

John Wilson to Julia Spencer, 17 Aug 1886 (28 Aug), S. Phillips MG 1-502

John C. Wilson to Cinda J. Wiggens, 10 July 1892, J.W. Cowles JP 4-52

Johnson Wilson to Clara M. Woods, 23 Ap 1898 (bond only), John Wilson & Wm L. Wilson [signed by X] W 2-271

L. C. Wilson to H. W. James q.v.

Leonora Wilson to D. H. Lee q.v.

Lynda Wilson to Rufus Hartbarger q.v.

Margaret A. Wilson to Alfred Medows q.v.

Margaret I. Wilson to John S. Clack q.v.

Mary Wilson to Joseph Gillespie q.v.

Minnie Wilson to Cyrus Ellison q.v.

Nancy Jane Wilson to William Cranfield q.v.

R.J. Wilson to Doris McCall, 26 Aug 1900, R.M. Trentham JP 4-106

Ruth Wilson to H. B. Haywood q.v.

Sallie Wilson to David McDonald q.v.

Sallie Wilson to C. W. McMillian q.v.

Sallie A. Wilson to James Anderson q.v.

Samuel Wilson to Sarah Bower, 7 Feb 1896, W.A. Green JP 4-94

Sarah J. Wilson to T. M. Tanksley q.v.

Sherman Wilson to Mattie Ellison, 15 June 1890, W.M. Morgan JP 4-23

Tillie Wilson to John Brackett q.v.

Vesta Wilson to Asberry Goines q.v.

W.T. Wilson to Laura Ellis, 9 Dec 1886 (same), J.P. Brown ?? 1-512

William L. Wilson to M.L. Rigsby, 31 Aug 1896 (same), A. Brunsy(?) MG, John Morgan W 2-62

\- - - - - - - - - - - - -

WINFIELD

1900 CENSUS

Frank R. Winfield 41 (July 1858-Oh/NJ/Oh-M 18)(House Carpenter), Myra 59 (Nov 1840-Oh/Oh/Oh-M 18-6-5), Frank 15 (Aug 1884-Oh), Clarence 13 (Oct 1886), Dean 10 (Dec 1889), Wallis 8 (Nov 1891), Harrold 3 (Feb 1897) 10-325A-104/108

\- - - - - - - - - - - - -

WINFREY / WINEFREY / WINPHREY WINPEY

1860 CENSUS
John Winphrey 34, Phebe 28 (Va), Eliza J. 11, George L. 9, Rachel C. 6, Lucinda 3 4-40-269
1870 CENSUS
Phebe Winfrey 40, Eliza Jane 20, Rachel C. 16, Lucinda 14, America 8, Amanda M. 7, Laura 3/12 4-12-79
1880 CENSUS
Phebe Wimpey 45, A.M. 17 (d), Laura 8 (d) 4-4-27
MARRIAGES
America Winefrey to John Roberts q.v.
Eliz J. Winfrey to William A. Brown q.v.
John Wimpey to L. J. Hoyle, 5 May 1888, Jas Corvin MG 4-44
John Winfrey(?) to Lisa(?) Hale, 25 Nov 1890, J.W. Williamson MG 4-19
M. Lucinda Winfrey to Maddison Love q.v.
Manda Winfrey to Andrew Carrol q.v.
Rachel C. Winfrey to William G. Kennedy q.v.

- - - - - - - - - - - - -

WINLEY / WINTEY

MARRIAGE
Harrison Winley or Wintey to Mary Sorrel(?), 13 Jan 1888 (same), J.L. Henry JP 1-541 [last name was spelled Wimberly in index]

- - - - - - - - - - - - -

WINNE / WINNIS

1900 CENSUS
Amma C. Winne 75 (Aug 1824-NY/NY/NY-Wd 8-2)(Pensioner) 14-215B-51/52
John M. Winne 49 (Jan 1851-NY/NY/NY-M 28), Elizabeth 45 (May 1855-T/T/NC-M 28-9-8), Harry 19 (July 1880-Iowa), Samuel 15 (June 1884), John 13 (Jan 1887), Martha J. 11 (Mar 1889), Lewis 8 (Ap 1892) 6-244A-82
Mary Winnis 45: see Henry Jackson (B)

- - - - - - - - - - - - -

WINSETT

1870 CENSUS
Nancy E. Winset 27: see Thomas B. Coulter
1880 CENSUS– None
1900 CENSUS
James Winsett 20: see Henry Mowry or Moulry
MARRIAGES
James C. Winsett to Lizzie Bean, 29 June 1900 (1 July), J.M. Manning MG, Asa C.(?) Wooden W 3-176

- - - - - - - - - - - - -

WINSEY

1860 CENSUS
William R. Winsey 16: see Leonard Edens

- - - - - - - - - - - - -

WINTERS

MARRIAGE
James Winters to E.L. Morgan, 12 June 1894, Wm Morgan JP 4-72

- - - - - - - - - - - - -

WINTON

1880 CENSUS
Timothy Winton 28, Stena 64, Robert 4, Eglentine 2, Wash FRANKLIN 25 (Miner), George CATE 22 (Miner) 2-30-240 (B)

- - - - - - - - - - - - -

WISEMAN

MARRIAGES
A. B. or A. R. Wiseman to B. A. Frazier q.v.
Nancy Wiseman to David Morgan q.v.

- - - - - - - - - - - - -

WISEMER / WISSMER / WAISMER

1860 CENSUS
Leonard Waisner 25: see Manerva Brunet
MARRIAGES
Cornelius Wissmer to Narcissa C. Paul, 8 Nov 1855 (16 Nov), J.I. Cash MG 1-#500
Sarah J. Wisemer to W. A. Murphy q.v.

- - - - - - - - - - - - -

WITHSHAN

MARRIAGE
John Withshan to Nancy Kerby, 31 Aug 1876 (same), John Waller or Miller MG 1-#1457

- - - - - - - - - - - - -

WITT

1900 CENSUS
May Witt 20: see George Elliott
Martha Witt 21, Harriet 17: see Thomas Conner
William Witt 23 (Sep 1876-M 6), Maggie 24 (May 1876-M 6-2-2), Jasper F.S. 4 (Dec 1895), Henry V. 2 (Ap 1898) 3-203A-66/71
MARRIAGES
C. S. Witt to W. P. Kyles q.v.
Eliza Witt to John H. Jacquess q.v.
William A. Witt to Issabella N. Willard, 25 Nov 1855, W.H. Bell MG 1-#529

- - - - - - - - - - - - -

WOLF / WOLFE

1870 CENSUS
Sampson Wolf 41 (Pa), Mary 33 (Pa), Charles 12 (Iowa), William 10 (Iowa), Elmer 8 (Iowa), Chem 4 (Pa), Grant 2 1-21-141

1880 CENSUS

Sampson Wolf 52, Mary 45, Charles 22, William 20, Elmer 18, Katie 14, Grant 12, Franklin 9, Anna 5 12-5-39

1900 CENSUS

Rezin Wolfe 75 (Jan 1825-Oh/Oh/Ky-Wd), Harry B. 23 (June 1876-Oh-M 1), Vesta 23 (dl)(July 1876-M 1-0) 11-292A-49

Sam Wolf 71 (Nov 1828-Pa/Pa/Pa-Wd)(Physician), Annie 26 (d)(Jan 1874) 12-180B-49/52

MARRIAGES

C.B. Wolfe to Mattie E. Stewart, 27 Nov 1897 (28 Nov), C.E. Mowrey JP 2-214

Harry Wolfe to Vesta Richey, 15 Oct 1898 (16 Oct), W.A. Howard MG, J.O. Hickman W 2-333

W.H. Wolf to S.C. Burchard or Burchart, 17 Mar 1889 (same), R.S. Mason JP 1-568

- - - - - - - - - - - - -

WOLFORD / WOFARD / WOFFORD

1900 CENSUS

George Wolford 20 (June 1879-M 1), Hattie 19 (Aug 1880-T/NC/T-M 1-1-1) 10-258B-165/169 (B)

MARRIAGE

George Wofard or Wofford to Hattie Avery, 2 June 1889 (same), D.B. Jackson MG, James Colyer W 2-421

- - - - - - - - - - - - -

WOMACK / WOMAC / WOMICK / WAMMOCK

1870 CENSUS

George Womick 9 (B): see Newton Brown

Richard Womack 24, Jane 28, Nelson 11, Alice 5 7-8-58 (B)

1880 CENSUS

Jane Wammock 42, Mary A. 14, Detha A.C. 8, William H. 6 6-24-26 (B)

Nelson Womack 19 (B): see W. S. Gillespie

1900 CENSUS

Ida Womack 19: see Isaac K. Brown

Jesse Womac 28: see Mary Norris (B)

MARRIAGES

Anna Womack to Thomas Cook q.v.

J.H. Womack to Ida Darwin, 21 Jan 1886 (same), A.P. Early MG 1-515

Jacob Womack to Mary Ann Mitchell, 24 Dec 1860 (same), John Howard MG 1-#739

Jesse Womack to Anna Brown, 5 May 1887 (same), John Howard MG 1-523

- - - - - - - - - - - - -

WOOD / WOODS

1880 CENSUS

William Woods 15 (B): see Jessee Roddy

1900 CENSUS

Lauther Woods 24 (May 1876-M 1)(Carpenter), Bessie 24 (Mar 1876-T/Ala/T-M 1-0), Aliton TIPTON 19 (bl) (Aug 1880-T/Ala/T) 10-259A-170/174

MARRIAGES

Ada Wood or Ward to Charles Coleman q.v.

Cassy Wood or Ward to Thomas W. Prater q.v.

Clara Woods to Johnson Wilson q.v.

Dinah Woods to Foster Ross q.v.

James K. Woods to Permelia Buckner, 17 Dec 1864 (same), R.J. Gains JP 1-#1071

Joseph B. Wood to Elizabeth Campbell, 12 Ap 1866 (13 Ap), W.W. Low JP 1-#1091

Lucy Woods to Richard Tucker q.v.

M.A. Woods to A.F. Hutcheson, 22 Sep 1851 (24 Sep), H. Douglas MG 1-#350

Riley Wood to Lucy Osborn, 24 July 1886 (same), A.W. Frazier JP 1-5-1

Robert Wood to Martha Fitchgearl, 9 Mar 1878 (10 Mar), James Johnson JP 1-#1549

S. A. Woods to W. H. Porter q.v.

Susan Woods to William Smith q.v.

Thomas H. Woods to Emely Jaquish, 8 Aug 1868 (9 Aug), J.L. Brown JP 1-#1022

- - - - - - - - - - - - -

WOODALL

1900 CENSUS

Blennie Woodall 19: see Samuel W. Litchfield

- - - - - - - - - - - - -

WOODBY

MARRIAGE

Nancy Woodby to William Hodge q.v.

- - - - - - - - - - - - -

WOODEN

MARRIAGE

W.A. Wooden to Mary McCallen, 18 Ap 1885 (19 Ap), P.P. Brooks ?? 1-460

- - - - - - - - - - - - -

WOODFORD

1900 CENSUS

William Woodford 38 (Ap 1862-England/Do/Do-M 2) (Clergyman), Lillie B. 27 (Ap 1863-Ill/Ind/Ill-M 2-0), Winnie R. 14 (June 1885-Oh), Nellie E. 13 (Feb 1887-Oh), Fred H. 11 (May 1889-Oh), Ethel M. 8 (May 1892-Oh) 13-309B-376/390

MARRIAGE

William Woodford to Lillie May Bland, 20 May 1898 (22 May), N.W. Allen MG, W.L. Lillard W 2-281

- - - - - - - - - - - - -

WOODSON

1880 CENSUS

Carington Woodson 40, Jane 25 (w), Elizabeth 11 (d) 1-12-88 (B)

- - - - - - - - - - - - -

WOODWARD / WOODARD

1860 CENSUS
Nancy Woodward 50, Betsy 65: see Robert Michel
Margaret Woodard 36: see Joseph W. Cook
1870 CENSUS
Nancy Woodard 50: see Jacob B. White
MARRIAGE
Darthula Woodward to Elisha Ellison q.v.

- - - - - - - - - - - - -

WOODY / WOODEY / WOODAY

1860 CENSUS
David Woody 21, Permelia J. 26, Martha E. 2 6-103-699
Elizabeth Woodey 20: see Joshua Dawson
Jane Woody 34, Martha A. 17, Hughe 13, Canezada J. 6 5-32-212
Nicholas Woody 73, Martha 52, Catharine 24, Emaline 23, John 21, Amanda 19, Belzena 3 6-113-774
1870 CENSUS
David Woody 32 (NC), Pamelia J. 35, Martha E. 12, Nancy E. 8, Mary C. 4, William 1 5-1-2
Jane Woody 42, Martha A. 21, Canzada 15, Hugh 21 5-2-10
Martha Woody 74 (SC), Catharine 35, Emaline 33, John 24, Amanda 22 5-2-9
1880 CENSUS
Jane Woody 58, Canzada J. 22 6-19-170/173
Martha Woodye 83 (blind), Catharine 49 (d), John 33 (s) 6-17-163/167
1900 CENSUS
Clarles(?) E. Woody 17, Darius C. 11, Lillie B. 7: see Belle J. Martin
David Woodey 79 (July 1820-T/SC/SC-M 10), Susan 25 (July 1879-M 10-3-3), David 8 (Dec 1891), Thomas 4 (Feb 1896), Bryant 6/12 (Oct 1899), Mary McCLELLAND 89 (si)(May 1811) 5-232B-91
Eler Woody 25 (Ap 1875-Wd 2-2), Myrtle 4 (July 1895), Lee 2 (Sep 1897), James BOWEN 19 (b)(Ap 1882) 10-254A-76
Hugh Woodey 52 (May 1848-Wd), John 23 (Ap 1877), Squire 17 (July 1882) 5-232A-82
Jeff Woody 28: see John Tinsley
John Woody 28 (Jan 1872-M 10), Kittie 28 (Jan 1871-M 10-6-6), Minnie 12 (Ap 1888), Birtha 9 (Jan 1891), William 7 (Feb 1893), Ramal 5 (Dec 1894), Cora 3 (Oct 1896), Lula 1 (Feb 1899) 3-205A-92/100
William Woody 30 (Aug 1869-M 10), Susan R. 31 (Ap 1869-M 10-3-3), Nellie J. 7 (Mar 1893), William H. 4 (Jan 1896), Esutla 1 (Feb 1899), Jasper DOSS 50 (Sep 1849-T/T/Ga) 8-317B-144/149
MARRIAGES
Annie Woody to Casper Cunnyngham q.v.
Bell Woody to John Martin q.v.
Cansada Woody to G. W. Walker q.v.
Jennoe Wooday to Tom McMillen q.v.
David Woody to Permelia Parker, 26 Aug 1857 (no return) 1-#611
David Woody to Susan Swafford, 3 July 1889 (same), W.G. Curtin ?? 1-576
James Woody to Lucinda Waterman, 23 Aug 1853 (25 Aug), T.P. Jack JP 1-#419
Jeff Woody (19) to Molly Wauply (19, Greene Co), 1 Jan 1882, J.Q. Shaver MG, John Trusley & J.A. Shaver W 4-10(92)
John Woody to Kittie Harfeston, 28 Nov 1891, J.W. Pearce MG 4-35
John Woody to Mollie Collins or Colier, 15 Sep 1900 (16 Sep), W.A. Howard MG, Casper Cunningham W 3-216
M. A. R. Woody to William C. Myres q.v.
Martha Woody to John Trusly q.v.
Martha E. Woody to Francis M. Ward q.v.
Nancy Woodey to Miles Harris q.v.
Vesta Woodey to J. D. Morgan q.v.
William Woody to Ellen Bowen, 11 Sep 1894, W.L. Lillard JP 4-72

- - - - - - - - - - - - -

WOOLFOLK

1900 CENSUS
Mitchell C. Woolfolk 35 (Dec 1864-Ga/Ga/Ga-M 8)(RR Section Hand), Annie 31 (June 1868-Ala/Va/Va-M 8-1-0), James BOYTIN 16 (nw)(Jan 1884-Ala/Ala/Ala) 10-330A-210/223 (B)

- - - - - - - - - - - - -

WOOLLEN

1900 CENSUS
George W. Woollen 54 (Ap 1846-Ky/Unk-M 32)(Deputy Sheriff), Sallie 53 (Dec 1846-Ky/Ky/Ky-M 32-11-9), May 26 (Dec 1873-Ky)(Dressmaker), Daisey 24 (Dec 1875-Ky)(Dressmaker), George K. 18 (Dec 1881-Ky) (Telegraph Operator), Orah L. 16 (Dec 1883-Ky) (Clerk, Provision Store), Imogene 13 (July 1886), Ernest E. 11 (Ap 1889) 10-321B-31/32
[G.W. married Sarah E. Goodman about 1867]
MARRIGE
Lillian T. Woollen to A. J. England q.v.

- - - - - - - - - - - - -

WORLEY

1900 CENSUS
William Worley 33: see Joseph E. Raines
MARRIAGES
Lula Worley to Will Lavender q.v.
Martha Worley to Evander Thurman q.v.

- - - - - - - - - - - - -

WORTHINGTON
(see also WEATHINGTON)

1900 CENSUS
John T. Worthington 6: see Caroline Pullum
MARRIAGES
Alice Worthington to Ed Hill q.v.
Emaline Worthington to David Swafford q.v.
Ida Worthington to Monroe Hickman q.v.
Louis Worthington to Mary Pullman, 29 Ap 1893, D.H. Hindman JP 5-54

- - - - - - - - - - - - -

WRAY

1900 CENSUS
Bob Wray 19, Bessie 14: see Maud Smith (B)

- - - - - - - - - - - - -

WREN / WREEN

1870 CENSUS
Mary Wren 74: see Joseph S. Evans
1880 CENSUS
Mary Wren 84: see Joseph S. Evans
MARRIAGE
Florence Wreen(?) to William Thompson q.v.

- - - - - - - - - - - - -

WRIGHT

1860 CENSUS
Calvin Wright 33 (NC), Louisa 26, William 12, Joseph 8, Wesley 6, Florence 1/12 6-102-692
Elizabeth Wright 61: see J. C. Ferguson
Madison Wright 18: see John W. Foust
Marcus L. Wright 22 (NC), Jane 20 (Ky), Louisa E. 3/12 6-105-717
Pleasant M. Wright 47, Sarah 45, Amanda 17, John 12, Obediah 10/12 8-19-125
Sampson Wright 34, Susan 29, Mary F. 14, Nancy E. 9, Joseph T. 7, Josephine 7, Malissa A. 5, Rachel H. 7/12 6-108-736 [Sampson married Susan Hitchcock]
Wesly Wright 24, Elvira 17: see Joseph Travis
1870 CENSUS
Damarcus L. Wright 34 (NC), Jane 27 (Ky), Elizabeth 10, Eliza J. 8, James A. 5, Margarette 3 3-9-63
John Wright 23, Nancy R. 19 8-10-63
Pinkney Wright 21 (Ala), Louisa 20, Lodenia 1, Nancy 18 (Ala) 6-17-124
Sampson Wright 49 (NC), Susan 44 (NC), Nancy 19 (NC), Joseph 17 (NC), Josephine 17 (NC), Melissa A. 12, Rachel H. 10, James S. 7, Florence 4, Jacob F. 2 3-10-73
Wesley Wright 37 (NC), Elvira 23, Sarah Jane 7, Lewis 5, Elizabeth 3, James P. 1 5-3-21
William Wright 26, Sarah E. 23, Mary A. 2, Sarah O. 1 6-5-27
1880 CENSUS
Florence Wright 20: see Henry Devault
J. A. Wright 14: see Thomas McPherson
John Wright 32, Aarabelle 28 (w), Mary 10, Thomas 7, Rufus 6, Peter 3 4-3-20
Joseph Wright 27, E. 25, William 2, Strother 1, M.A. 12 (c) 3-16-124
L.C. Wright 33, W.E. 11 (d), J.S. 9 (s), M.J. 7 (d), J.B.(?) 4 (s), L.H. 1 (d) 11-38-309
Sampson Wright 59, S.A. 54, Nancy 29, Nettie 21, Samuel 17, Jacob 12, William 10, H.J. 3 (gd) 3-13-107
Stephen Wright 30, M.J. 32, J.D. 11 (s), T.J. 8 (s), J.W. 7 (s), R.C.L. 4 (s) 4-6-43
Viney E. Wright 36, Lewis D. 16, Elizabeth O. 14, James P. 11, Viney E. 10, Elmore L. 6, John W. 4, John F. 4/30 10-195/200
William Wright 24: see A. Hodge

1900 CENSUS
Andrew Wright 24 (B): see Merrol L. Fugate
Charles E. Wright 3: see James W. Boles
Elmore Wright 34, Virginia E. 34: see Joseph Brown
George T. Wright 30 (July 1869-Ga/Ga/Ga-M 0), Mattie 24 (Mar 1876-T/NC/NC-M 0-0) 8-313A-49/52 (B)
Henry Wright 21: see Valentine Rowen (B)
Henry J. Wright 42 (Ap 1858-Mich/NY/NY-M 19), Hattie M. 40 (May 1860-Mich/NY/NY-M 19-3-3), Edith M. 18 (Jan 1882-Mich), Maud E. 13 (Mar 1887), Bertha A. 6 (June 1893) 11-291B-45
James W. Wright 30 (Sep 1869-Oh/Oh/Oh-M 7), Cora B. 28 (Ap 1872-M 7-2-2), Myrtie E. 5 (Jan 1895), Iva L. 2 (Jan 1898), Mary A. THOMPSON 57 (m)(Sep 1842-Wd 3-3), Martha R. 40 (si)(Ap 1860), Autensa P. 34 (si)(Aug 1865) 14-221A-144/148
John Wright 52 (May 1848-NC/NC/NC-M 17)(Carpenter), Elizabeth 50 (Jan 1831-M 17-5-3), Johny 12 (Jan 1888-Ala), Marthy 10 (Feb 1890-Ala), Miny 8 (May 1892) 10-253B-70
Joseph E. Wright 50 (May 1850-Ga/Ga/Ga-Wd), Levada M. 20 (Nov 1879), Myrtle E. 18 (Sep 1881), Claude K. 16 (Nov 1883), Vester 15 (Feb 1885), Jordan 13 (Mar 1887), Pearl G. 8 (Dec 1891), Floy C. 6 (Feb 1894), Currie E. 4 (Mar 1896) 13-306B-314/326
Joseph T. Wright 53 (Feb 1847-NC/NC/NC-M 23), Eliza J. 44 (July 1855-M 23-9-8), Strother M. 21 (May 1879), John I. 18 (Feb 1882), Sampson G. 17 (May 1883), Anthony J. 15 (Ap 1883), James S. 13 (Feb 1887), Samuel C. 9 (June 1890), Eva D. 5 (Dec 1894) 3-203B-68/73
Louisa Wright 51 (Unk-T/Ireland/T-Wd 5-3), Annie [N-ER(?) [ink blob] 21 (d)(Unk-M ?), Clay 27 (sl)(Unk-M ?) 11-291B-40
Martha E. Wright 26: see Sams J. Henderson
Nancy Wright 63 (Jan 1837-T/Va/T-Wd 6-5), John 32 (Mar 1868)(Locamotive Fireman), James 27 (May 1873) (Day Laborer) 10-323A-65/69
Thomas Wright 28 (Ap 1871-M 10)(Coal Miner), Maggie 27 (Ap 1873-T/Ga/Ga-M 10-2-1), Hershell E. 3 (Nov 1896) 11-291B-39
William D. Wright 22 (Nov 1877-M 4), Cordie 20 (Feb 1880-M 4-2-2), Cora J. 4 (Jan 1896), Ella G. 1 (Oct 1898), Hugh McCHOLISTER 36 (Unk 1864)(Servant) 3-206A-106/116

MARRIAGES
Alice Wright to A. J. Bowman q.v.
Amanda Wright to Raymon Ottinger q.v.
Ann Wright to William McMurry q.v.
C.W. Wright to Maggie Cole, 27 Dec 1884 (28 Dec), L.H. McPherson JP 1-462
Calvin Wright to Elizabeth Roddy, 1 Oct 1860 (same), John Howard MG 1-#728
D.L. Wright to Laura Brady, 20 Aug 1887 (21 Aug), J.Q. Shaver MG 1-532
Elizabeth Wright to James Peterson q.v.
Elmore Wright to Mrs. Virginia E. Bunn, 12 Feb 1898 (12 Feb), G.W. Brewer MG, E.B. Madaris W 2-250
F.C. Wright to Catharine Ballard, 5 Nov 1855 (8 Nov), A. Campbell JP 1-540
Fannie Wright to John Buchannon q.v.
Florence Wright to E. A. Cagle q.v.
Florence Wright to Samuel Hood q.v.

George Thomas Wright to Mattie Silance, 19 May 1900 (same), J.W. Williamson MG 3-155 (B)
Ida Wright to John Crosby q.v.
J.F. Wright to Minnie Pool, 4 July 1900 (same), T.D. Shelton MG, R.H. Aslinger W 3-181
J.M. Wright to Lizzie Robberts, 9 Aug 1892, J.W. Cowles JP 4-48
J.T. Wright to M.M. Hicks, 11 May 1890 (same), E.F. Gwinn JP 1-602
J.W. Wright to Vera McClelland, 14 Dec 1895, G.W. Brewer MG 4-90
James Wright to Bell Thompson, 24 Dec 1892, Will L. Patton MG 4-84
Jefferson Wright to Emma Johnson, 7 May 1898 (same), H. Hallmark MG, Jack Wright & Charles Galloway [signed by X] W 2-276
John Wright to N.R.B. Land, 12 July 1869 (same), Wm L. Humphrey JP 1-#1105
Joseph Wright to Eliza Jane Thomson, 13 Jan 1877 (14 Jan), W.W. Low JP 1-#1483
Lezzil Wright to Charley Brady q.v.
Louisa Wright to John W. Hughes q.v.
Maggie Wright to James Millard q.v.
Marcus Wright to Jane Majors, 2 May 1859 (2 Mar)[sic], John Wyatt JP 1-#683
Mary Wright to Robert McBroom q.v.
Mary Wright to James Kennedy q.v.
Mary A. Wright to S. M. Ganaway q.v.
Mason Wright to Sarah E. Davis, 9 Nov 1865 (same), John Howard MG 1-#853
Mrs. Louisa Wright to Abraham Payne q.v.
Ollie Wright to J. F. Hall q.v.
Rhoda Wright to Walter Dodd q.v.
Sallie Wright to M. V. Ides or Iles q.v.
Sallie Wright to Albert Hutcheson q.v.
Sarah D. Wright to P. K. Barton q.v.
Sarah J. Wright to James Dodd q.v.
Sary Wright to John M. Lincoln q.v.
Thomas C. Wright to Mary Thurman, 6 Nov 1858 (same), Wm Morgan JP 1-#666
Vird Wright, nee Travis, to Allen Hale q.v.
W.T. Wright to Elvira Travis, 22 July 1860 (same), John Howard MG 1-#719
William T. Wright to Cordia(?) Cagle, 10 Feb 1896, J.H. Keylon JP 4-93
W.T.G. Wright to Sarah J. Mitchell, 12 Ap 1852 (18 Ap), W. Ganaway MG 1-#364

\- - - - - - - - - - - -

WROE

1880 CENSUS
Sarah Wroe 62: see Joseph Thompson

\- - - - - - - - - - - -

WRYDENHOUR

MARRIAGE
Sarah Wrydenhour to William Lea q.v.

\- - - - - - - - - - - -

WUMBLE

1900 CENSUS
Lorinda G. Wumble(?) 68: see John King

\- - - - - - - - - - - -

WYATT / WYOTT

1860 CENSUS
John Wyatt 52 (Carpenter), Milly 52, Henry JAMES 16 (bound) 6-110-751
Joseph Wyott 35 (Va), Rachel 23, Benjamin 1 6-103-702
Thomas C. Wyatt 36, Prudence 36, Elizabeth J. 12, William A. 10, Margaret M. 5 6-102-696
1870 CENSUS
John Wyatt 62, Margarette 35, Samuel 11, Mary A. HARDEN 45 6-11-73
1880 CENSUS
?.N. Wyott 37, M.J. 38, P.J. 13, N.A. 11, T.M. 6, R.H. 4, M.J. 1: see J. E. McMury
Darthula Wyatt 28, Monna E. 6, Ulsie 4 (B): see Henry A. Crawford
James Wyatt 16: see Henry A. Crawford
Margaret J. Wyatt 7: see Thomas Peterson
Martha J. Wyott 37, Larne Vir 13, John H. 4, Eliza J. 2 6-23-14
1900 CENSUS
Jacob D. Wyatt 36 (Dec 1863-M 13)(Carpenter), Mattie M. 30 (Nov 1869-Maine/Do/Do-M 13-5-4), Walter E. 12 (Dec 1887), Frank B. 9 (Sep 1890), Herbert 7 (Ap 1893), Willard L. 2 (Ap 1898), Millie A. 9 (ne)(Jan 1891) 11-291B-46
John Wyatt 28 (Aug 1875)(Blacksmith), Martha J. 60 (m) (Mar 1840-T/T/SC-Wd 1-1), Eliza 23 (si)(Feb 1877), Pearl 3 (ne)(Dec 1896) 10-326B-140/148
John Wyatt 42 (Nov 1857-M 26)(Coal Miner), Nancy 39 (Mar 1861-M 26-6-5), Laura 19 (Dec 1881), Nettie 17 (May 1883), Pearl 14 (Oct 1885) 8-282A-266/268
John R. Wyatt 39 (Feb 1861-T/Va/T-M 19)(RR Carpenter), Mary E. 38 (Nov 1862-M 19-8-7), Alace L. 15 (Dec 1884), Ellen F. 12 (July 1887), Rachel E. 9 (May 1891), Raye C. 6 (Dec 1893), Thomas L. 6 (Dec 1893), James C. 3 (Feb 1897), Andrew J. ENGLISH 56 (boarder)(Feb 1844-Ga/Ga/Ga-Wd) 5-235B-152
MARRIAGES
Amanda E. Wyott to John W. Barger q.v.
Dora Wyatt to Roe Callahan q.v.
Flora Wyatt to R. J. Hoge q.v.
John Wyott to Margarett Gingery, 22 May 1864 (same), John Howard MG 1-#830
John Wyott to Nancy M. Peterson, 1 July 1871 (2 July), A.P. Early MG 1-#1200
John R. Wyatt to Ellen Mize, 19 Aug 1880 (same), A.J. Pritchett MG 1-295
Joseph Wyott to Rachel Travis, 27 Jan 1857 (28 Jan*), Elijah Brewer* JP 1-#591
[*date of solemnization & JP marked through]
L. V. Wyatt to J. L. Webb q.,v.
Laura Wyatt to Jack Jones q.v.
Maggie Wyott to Frank Blevins q.v.
Milley Wyott to Robert Ford q.v.

\- - - - - - - - - - - -

WYBEL

1900 CENSUS
Mina Wybel 2: see Homer Halliburon

WYCUFF

1900 CENSUS
Charles Wycuff 29 (Unk-M 4), Eliza 28 (Ap 1872-Ga/NC/NC-M 4-2-1), Higey T. HURLEY 12 (ss)(Feb 1888-T/Ga/Ga) 8-314A-70/73
Jim P. Wycuff 55 (Oct 1844-T/NC/NC-M 30)(Lime Burner), Carlines 60 (Mar 1840-T/NC/NC-M 30-5-3), Nancy 26 (Nov 1873-Wd 2-2), John 22 (Aug 1877), Roy MORGUN 8 (gs)(Aug 1891), Maggie W. 6 (gd) (May 1894), Jeff J. BREIDER 41 (nw)(Mar 1859) (Bartender) 10-253A-61
MARRIAGES
Annie Wycuff to Lee Marcum q.v.
Bettie Wycuff to R. A. Williamson q.v.
Charley Wycuff to Eliza A. Hurley, 12 Nov 1895, J.W. Williamson MG 4-95
Flora Wycuff to Joseph Pogue q.v.
S. L. Wycuff to J. J. Aley q.v.

WYLER

MARRIAGE
Thomas H. Wyler to Nora L. Holloway, 26 Ap 1897, R.A. Dickson JP 4-98

WYRICK / WEIRICK

1860 CENSUS
Adam S. Wyrick 19 (Va), Bathia 19, Edettia(?) A. 8/12 4-45-306
Andrew Wyrick 70 (Va), Catharine 72 (Pa), John A. 24 (Va) 4-40-270
Andrew J. Wyrick 37 (Va)(Carpenter), Margaret E. 25, Lena A. 3, Manford L. 1 4-45-305
Martin Wyrick 46 (Va), Sophia 40 (Va), Mary 24, Margaret 19, Anderson 16, Martin 9, William 7, Catharine 5, Audley 3 4-45-304
Solomon Wyrick 30 (Va), Mary A. 29, Andrew 8, Peney 6, Thomas 5, William G. 2, George W. 5/12 4-40-271
William Wyrick 34 (Va)(Mason), Ann 24, Wiley W. 21, Mary 20, Sarah M. 11 4-45-303
1870 CENSUS
Adam S. Wyrick 38 (Va), Bethiah 30, Edatha R. 10, Martha A. 8, William B. 6, Phebe Jane 4, James A. 1 4-17-116
Andrew J. Wyrick 48 (Va)(House Carpenter), Elizabeth 34, Mumford L. 11, Carry A. 13, Everett B. 9, Lydia B. 7, Savannah J. 5, Parzada 2 4-12-77
Phillip Wyrick 22, Eliza Jane 22 6-10-66
Samuel Wyrick 66, Momerad(?) 41, White M. 13, Elizabeth 8, Maras 5 4-13-87
Solomon Wyrick 40 (Va), Elizabeth 35, Andrew J. 18, Parlena 17, Thomas 10, William 7, George 6, Sally A. 4, John 2 4-12-80
William Wyrick 45 (Va)(Brickmason), Annie 35, Samuel L. 14, Alfred 35 (Va), Pollie 32, Adam 6, William S. 5, Margaret L. 2 2-17-121
William S. Wyrick 58 (Blacksmith), Nancy 60 (Ky), Pheby E. 31, Margaret E. 26 2-17-120
1880 CENSUS
A.J. Wyrick 58, M.E. 43 (w), S.A. 24 (d), E.B. 19 (s) (Merchant), L.B. 17 (d), S.J. 13 (d), E.P. 11 (d), J.B. 8 (s), R.N. 5 (d), A.J. THOMPSON 18 (nw), A. 13 (nw), Lettie 13 (ne) 4-5-34
Alfred Wyrick 50, Polly 42, A.L. 16 (s), M.S. 14 (s),
Margaret 11, A.B. 8 (d), S.D. 1 (s) 4-4-26
James Wyrick 24, M.E. 24, D.A. 3 (d), Tom(?) 1 (s) 4-34-284
Locke Wyrick 21, M.E. 21, R.C. 1 (d) 4-5-33
Simon Wyrick 70 (Blacksmith), Sarah C. 52, Lentitia CUMBO 27 ("parted this --?-- long ago"), Robert L. 4/12 (s)("with mother"), David L. 12 (gs), Margaret ROBERDS 28 ("one of the family") 6-21-187/191
William Wyrick 54 (Bricklayer), Anna 45, M. 14 (c), John NASH 14 (nw), Samuel 12 (nw), Lean(?) WYRICK 5 (ne) 4-3-24
William Wyrick 67 (Blacksmith), Pelista 49 (w), Phebe 42 (d), Ellenor 8 (gd), Elizabeth FINE 17 (gd) 2-26-205
1900 CENSUS
Andrew J. Wyrick 78 (Jan 1822-Va/Va/Pa-Wd), Cena 43 (d)(Nov 1856), Lida B. 37 (Jan 1863), Nora R. 25 (June 1874), Rachel S. 16 (gd)(Sep 1883), Leslie D.A. 13 (gs)(June 1886), Emma F. FERGUSON 31 (d)(Nov 1868-D), Carrie B. FERGUSON 6 (gd)(Aug 1893) 4-225A-229/233 (Creek Road)
Etta F. Wyrick 28: see William Collins
James Weirick 69 (May 1831-M 24)(Book Agent), Kate 37 (Oct 1862-M 24-7-6), Mabel 23 (Oct 1876), Frederick 21 (Sep 1878), Minnie 19 (Nov 1880), Kate 17 (Nov 1882), Adella 15 (Nov 1884), Ozora 11 (Ap 1891) 14-213A-11/11
Lee A. Wyrick 55 (Oct 1844-Va/Va/Va-M 30), Rebecca 45 (May 1855-M 30-10-9), Nannie 19 (May 1881), Lillie 16 (Jan 1884), Luther 12 (Mar 1888), Jesse 10 (Nov 1889), Pearl 8 (May 1892), Graddy 5 (June 1894) 6-224A-83
Mumford L. Wyrick 41 (Sep 1858-T/Va/T-M 9)(Coal Miner), Louisa J. 25 (Ap 1875-Ark/NC/T-M 9-3-3), Iris 19 (May 1881), Rufus B. 7 (Oct 1892), Beatrice 4 (Oct 1895), Willie W. 0/12 (May 1900) 8-279A-217/219
MARRIAGES
Adam Wyrick to Bethia Furgusson, 29 July 1858 (same), J.O. Torbett JP 1-#645
Andrew Wyrick to Elizabeth Collins, 1 Mar 1855 (same), J.O. Torbett JP 1-#487
Anna Wyrick to William H. Wyrick q.v.
Bell Wyrick to Henry Matherly q.v.
Bell Wyrick to John Collins q.v.
Clyde Wyrick to Nettie Long, 20 July 1898 ("license returned not executed, no marriage"), George C. Miller W 2-301
Clyde Wyrick to Maggie Melton, 10 Oct 1900 (same), W.S. Hale MG, E. Fisher W 3-233
E. J. Wyrick to James Owings q.v.
Emma Wyrick to P. W. Ferguson q.v.

G.W. Wyrick to Margarit C. Ponder, 13 Ap 1885 (14 Ap), W.R. Clack JP 1-486
James L. Wyrick to Nancy E. Poston or Ponder, 13 July 1874 (10 July), A.L. King MG 1-#1342
James L. Wyrick to Marthy C. Godby, 12 Feb 1876 (17 Feb), W.W. Low JP 1-#1433
John A. Wyrick to Polly Wyrick, 19 Jan 1861 (no return) 1-#742
Josie Wyrick to John Barry q.v.
Lean Wyrick to John Devault q.v.
Locke Wyrick to Mariah E. Davis, 4 May 1878 (16 May), Robert E. Smith MG 1-#1557
Luncy Wyrick to John T. Collins q.v.
Malinda Wyrick to Robert H. Barger q.v.
Margarett E. Wyrick to H. W. Ponder q.v.
Margaret M. Wyrick to Robert Perkins q.v.
Mary J. Wyrick to Elbert Huffman q.v.
Orris Wyrick to David Scroggins q.v.
Phillip Wyrick to Elizabeth Jane Smith, 21 Oct 1869 (same), A.P. Early MG 1-#1118
Polly Wyrick to John A. Wyrick q.v.
Samuel Wyrick to Fanny J. Neal, 22 Sep 1871 (no return) 1-#1209
Sarah Wyrick to Franklin Houpt q.v.
Sarahan Wyrick to W. S. Alley q.v.
Solomon Wyrick to Mary Elizabeth Martin, 24 May 1851 (25 May), J.O. Torbett JP 1-#338
Syntha Wyrick to B. B. Blye q.v.
Wesley Wyrick to Margarett Thompson, 2 June 1877 (same), B.F. Holloway JP 1-#1503
William H. Wyrick to Anna Wyrick, 2 Ap 1857 (same), E.E. Wasson JP 1-#593
William S. Wyrick to Calista E. Fine, 23 Nov 1874 (6 Dec), W.W. Low JP 1-#1374

- - - - - - - - - - - - -

YANCY

MARRIAGES

James Yancy to Amanda Miller, 9 Sep 1875 (10 Sep), Allen L. King MG 1-#1409
James Yancy to Mary Smith, 6 Nov 1877 (7 Dec)[sic], Jas Johnson JP 1-#1524

- - - - - - - - - - - - -

YARBER / YARBOUGH

1880 CENSUS

W.A. Yarber 24, V.E. 24 (w), H. 3 (s) 8-11-95

1900 CENSUS

Lucinda Yarber 69 (Jan 1831-T/SC/NC-Wd 4-4), Daniel S. 29 (July 1870-T/NC/T) 5-230B-49

MARRIAGES

J.N. Yarber to Menny Fortner, 13 Mar 1886 (14 Mar), W.A. Green JP 1-498
W.A. Yarbough to E.A. Green, 16 Aug 1876 (17 Aug), J.W. Pence MG 1-#1456

- - - - - - - - - - - - -

YARNELL

1900 CENSUS

Mark Yarnell 26 (Unk 1874-M 5), Lina 21 (Mar 1879-M 5-2-2), Ethel 4 (Ap 1896), Maurie 1 (d)(Nov 1898) 8-282B-283/285

MARRIAGES

Cornelia Yarnell to Joseph Brown q.v.
Lizza Yarnell to John Johnson q.v.

- - - - - - - - - - - - -

YATES

1900 CENSUS

James N. Yates 47 (June 1852-M 16), Mintie 38 (Sep 1861-M 16-9-8), John W. 15 (Aug 1884), Robert 13 (Aug 1886), Bertha 12 (Nov 1887), James C. 9 (Jan 1891), Jennie M. 9 (Jan 1891), Harvey L. 6 (Oct 1893), Flossie M. 2 (June 1897), Rhodolphus 7/12 (Oct 1899) 6-242A-50
Marley Y. Yates 46 (Feb 1854-M 0), Sary J. 42 (Ap 1858-M 0-1-1), James 17 (Oct 1882), Annie 14 (July 1885), Walter 10 (Aug 1884), Henry 4 (Ap 1896) 6-245B-106/107
Martin E. Yates 45 (Oct 1854-M 10), Josephine 29 (Oct 1870-M 10-4-4), Fred J. 11 (Sep 1888), Rhoda A. 5 (July 1894), Rilda E. 2 (Ap 1898), Matilda L. 2 (Ap 1898) 6-246A-113/114

MARRIAGES

Irvin Yates to Josephine Aiken, 13 Oct 1888 (14 Oct), R.S. Mason JP 1-557
Marley Yates to Sarah Byerley, 6 Dec 1894, H.A. Crawford JP 4-74
Marley Yates to Sarah J. Byerley, 26 Dec 1899 (27 Dec), H. A. Crawford JP & W 3-100
Minerva Yates to John Cantrell q.v.
Norman Yates to Mintiey Callahan, 6 Oct 1883 (7 Oct), W. S. Hale MG 1-477

- - - - - - - - - - - - -

YEARWOOD

1880 CENSUS

Nathan Yearwood 57, Elizabeth 35 (w), Thomas UPTON 18 (Servant), James RUCKER 11 (Servant), John HENDERSON 20 (boarder)(Miner), Harvey GLASS 20 (boarder)(Miner) 2-28-227 (B)(Mu)
Scruggs Yearwood 31, Mary 26, Zia 1, Mark HODGE 24 (Servant), Hans HATFIELD 46 (Servant), James SCRUGGS 22 (boarder) 2-32-257

MARRIAGE

Sarah E. Yearwood to William Gravett q.v.

- - - - - - - - - - - - -

YODER / YOADER

1900 CENSUS

James Yoder 24 (Oct 1875-M 7), Elizabeth 22 (Nov 1877-M 7-3-3), John 6 (Sep 1893), Walter 3 (Ap 1897), Matilda 2/12 (Mar 1900) 15-269B-30

William Yoder 28 (May 1872-M 6)(Coal Miner), Mary E. 26 (July 1873-Ga/Ga/Ga-M 2-2-2), Louis 11 (Feb 1889), James 9 (Feb 1891), Sim B. (Feb 1892), Willie 6 (Ap 1894), Ida 1 (June 1898) 8-280A-231/233

William D. Yoder 62 (Jan 1838-Ga/Ga/Ga-M 32), Martha S. 48 (Unk 1852-M 32-12-7), Lula A. 18 (Unk 1882), Louis J. 16 (Dec 1883), Dora 12 (June 1887), Rosa E. 10 (Jan 1890), Robert 21 (s)(July 1878-M 2), Ella 17 (dl)(Unk 1883-T/Ga/T-M 2-0-0) 15-272A-76

MARRIAGES

James Yoder to Elizabeth Seward(?), 7 Sep 1893, F.M. Cook MG 4-68

Joe A. Yoder to J. T. Shadwick q.v.

Robert Yoder to Ella Trusley, 21 Nov 1898 (same), F.M. Cook MG, Chas Johnson W 2-346

- - - - - - - - - - - - -

YOKLEY

1870 CENSUS

James B. Yokley 13: see Andrew McCamey

James F. Yokley 59, John W. 11: see Albert H. Taylor

- - - - - - - - - - - - -

YOUNG

1860 CENSUS

Henry Young 45 (Oh)(Miller), Emaline 22 (Oh) 3-58-400

John R. Young 14: see Newton M. Brown

1870 CENSUS

Henry Young 59 (Oh)(Wood Carver), Elvina S. 29, Joseph E.J. 3, Henry B. 9/12 3-7-48

1880 CENSUS

Amanda Young 18, Easter 4, Mira 2/12 (B): see Joe McKinney

Henry Young 69, E.V. 35 (w), J.E. 13 (s), H.B. 10 (s) 3-26-208

James Young 22, Sarah 21, Edward 1 2-28-224

James L. Young 20 ("living with brother") [between James West, #6-13-122, and Joseph A. Killough, #6-13-123]

John W. Young 25, Margaret S. 28 6-21-190/193

Lucy Young 84 (Mu): see Sam Bell

1900 CENSUS

Jeffrey Young 38 (Feb 1862-M 15)(Coal Miner), Rosa 30 (June 1869-T/NY/Ga-M 15-7-5), Frank 13 (Oct 1886), Lulie 11 (Aug 1888), Florence 9 (Sep 1890), Annie 7 (Nov 1892), James 5 (Feb 1895) 15-274A-110

John Young(?) 65 (Jan 1835-M 15), Manda 29 (Jan 1871-M 15-4-4)(Washwoman), Edward 12 (Ap 1888), Fred 10 (Ap 1870), Henry 2 (May 1898), Dall 2/12 (Jan 1900) 1-184A-104/108 (B)

John S. Young 27 (Sep 1872-M 4)(School Teacher), Annie M. 26 (Ap 1874-T/Ga/Ga-M 4-1-0) 2-197B-120/125

John W. Young 47 (Ap 1853-T/Va/T-M 26)(Coal Bunker Foreman), Margaret S. 52 (Mar 1848-Ga/SC/T-M 26-2-1), James T. 18 (June 1881)(Coal Miner) 10-329A-188/201

William Young 40 (Unk 1860-M 7), Maggie 27 (Unk 1873-M 7-2-2), Josie RANKINS 9 (sd)(Nov 1890), Willie SWAFFORD 18 (ss)(Ap 1882), Isaiah YOUNG 21 (b) (Unk 1879) 15-274A-112 (B)

MARRIAGES

Amanda Young to Henry McCaleb q.v.

Frank Young to Lutitia Smith, 13 Jan 1900 (same), G.W. Brewer MG 3-111

Harriet Young to Frank Cody q.v.

Henry Young to Elveny Barnett, 18 Sep 1865 (same), John Howard MG 1-#848

Henry Young to Annie Perry, 5 Aug 1891, M.F. Moore MG 4-37

I.B. Young(?) to Tennie Cox, 25 Jan 1894, J.L. McPherson JP 4-71

James Young to Mattie M. Smith, 22 May 1886 (same), John Howard MG 1-487

James Young to Lew(?) Richards, 1 Ap 1899, L.E. Smith JP 4-100

Joseph Young to Mary M. Robinson, 23 Dec 1887 (25 Dec), H.B. Burdett MG 1-546

T.A. Young to Rachel E. Rice, 17 Aug 1872 (18 Aug), A.J. Pritchett M 1-#1245

Texas Young to M. M. Swafford q.v.

W.J. Young to Ida Manning, 20 Mar 1892, W.M. Morgan JP 4-39

William Young to Maggie Rankins, 6 July 1895, A.P. Hayes JP 4-87

- - - - - - - - - - - - -

YOUNT / YAUNT

1900 CENSUS

Samuel Yount 63 (Dec 1836-Oh/NC/Pa-M 34), Nancy A. 63 (Oct 1836-Oh/Oh/Oh-M 34-6-4), Linus F. 30 (Oct 1869-Oh), Sarah L. 24 (Jan 1876-Oh) 14-221A-146/150

MARRIAGE

Lilley Yount to J. L. Rector q.v.

Lucy Yaunt to Charles L. Mealer q.v.

- - - - - - - - - - - - -

ZEBE

1900 CENSUS

Clift Zebe 25 (Jan 1875) 8-314A-77/80 (B)

- - - - - - - - - - - - -

ZIGLER / ZEIGLER / ZIGGLER

1860 CENSUS

George W. Ziggler 11, Margaret 7, Nancy A. 4, Amanda 10/12: see Samuel Dodson

1870 CENSUS

Benjamin F. Zigler 55 (Va), Susanna 48, Benjamin T. 22, Susan 19, Sarah 16, Rachel R.J. 14, Robert M. 9, Laura A. 6 5-1-5

Joseph A. Zigler 51 (Va), Mary Ann 48, William C. 23, Joseph B. or R. 19, Thomas B. 17, Joseph C. 8, Mary E. 6, Ambus L. HAWKINS 28 5-1-7

William Q. Zigler 29, Louisa C. 37 (NC), William O. 2, James M.G. 1, John 22 5-1-1

1880 CENSUS

Benjamin T. Zigler 64 (Justice of the Peace), Laura 16 (d) 6-25-192/196

Joseph Zeigler 60 (Blacksmith), Mary 58, Joseph 18, Lizzie 16 2-21-170

W.Q. Zigler 39, L.C. 45 (w), W.O. 13 (s), M.J. 11 (s), A.B. 6/12 (s) 8-2-15

MARRIAGES

J.B. Zeigler to Emma C. Ward, 17 May 1895, G.T. Francisco ?? 4-81

J.B. Zeigler to Jennie Pearce, 7 July 1900 (same), R. Walker ??, E. Fisher W 3-183

Lizzie Ziegler to J. H. Burnett q.v.

R. J. Zeigler to J. H. Brown q.v.

Sarah Zegler to William B. Brown q.v.

Sarah Ziegler to Frank Arnold q.v.

W.C. Zigler to Eliza Waterhouse, 1 Jan 1872 (3 Jan), G.W. Renfro MG 1-#1221

- - - - - - - - - - - - -

ZIMERLE

MARRIAGE

Olly Zimerle to James W. Prestly q.v.

- - - - - - - - - - - - -

ZIMMERMAN

MARRIAGE

Catharine Zimmerman to R. Gibson q.v.

- - - - - - - - - - - - -

ZINNAMON

MARRIAGE

Mary Zinnamon to John Brewer q.v.

- - - - - - - - - - - - -

ZOLLANDER

MARRIAGE

Ode Zollander to Julia Baker, 13 May 1899 (same), R.C. Knight JP, Mitchell Woolford W 2-414

- - - - - - - - - - - - -

ZUNISTIAN

MARRIAGE

John Zunistian to Ina Everett, 22 Jan 1898 (bond only), John Zunstine & R.J. Killough W 2-243

- - - - - - - - - - - - -

APPENDIX A– HEADS OF HUSEHOLD

The following list of household heads is arranged in the order they appear in the census. When persons with other last names were included in the household, they appear in parenthesis. The page number (A), dwelling house number (B), and family number (when different)(C) are also shown in the order taken.

1860 CENSUS

DISTRICT 7 (WASHINGTON P.O.)

(A)	(B)	
1	1	John Crawford (Griffett)
	2	Thomas H. Whaley
	3	John S. Whaley
	4	Benjamin O'Kelley
	5	John Howell
2	6	John W. Hughes
	7	Cornelius Shaver (Key, Trusley)
	8	John Q. Shaver
	9	H. M. Cunningham
	10	Margaret Jones
	11	William D. Wilson
3	12	Harris Ryan
	13	William Kelley
	14	James E. Foust
	15	Delana Trusly
	16	James T. Bolen (Trusly)
	17	Margaret Beddo
	18	William Smith
	19	Mary Stoops
	20	Newton Edmonds (Trusly)
4	21	Benjamin O'Kelly
	22	Thomas M. Bolen
	23	Stephen Spence
	24	William Purser
	25	James M. Thompson
	26	Pleasant M. Purser (Renfrow)
	27	Valentine Allen
5	28	James Perser
	29	Anonamons Fondren
	30	Henry Fisher (Gourd)
	31	Martha Renfrow
	32	William Coval (Renfrow)
	33	Lucinda Cates
	34	James Spence
	35	John L. Ramsey (Spence)
	36	Richard Knight (Smith)
6	37	James A. Cash
	38	Benjamin F. Land
	39	Barbary Frazier
	40	David Singleton (Eaton)
	41	Willis Coffer
	42	Banister Smith
	43	William Key (Weeks)
7	44	Thomas Knight
	45	Anthony Smith
	46	Harvy Roddy
	47	John M. Smith
	48	Henry S. Smith
	49	Eliza A. Smith
8	50	Thomas C. McDowell
	51	Elisha Moore

DISTRICT 8 (SMITHS CROSS ROADS P.O.)

(A)	(B)	
9	52	Sanders D. Broyles
	53	Charles Reivley (Lauderdale)
	54	Washington Morgan (Dunwoody)
	55	James Sexton
	56	John W. Foust (Wright, Bell)
	57	Tollover Sexton
	58	Elizabeth Sexton
	59	Halley Sexton
10	60	Jack Bell (Gothard)
	61	William Clingan
	62	William Hickman
	63	David Moore
	64	Robert Moore
	65	Lewis McDonald
	66	Nancy Steele
	67	David Fox
11	68	George Milligan
	69	Newton M. Brown (Young)
	70	Joseph Newell (Canns?)
	71	Alfred Hucheson (Ward)
	72	James Colville
	73	John P. Walker
12	74	Henry M. Haley
	75	Solomon Coate
	76	Emalin Gothard
	77	John Stanly
	78	William Harrison
	79	Andrew J. Bankston (Teague)
	80	Abraham Bryson
	81	George W. Jackson
	82	Margaret Peirce
13	83	Robert Peirce (Shipley)
	84	John R. Hickamon
	85	Elias Hickamon
	86	Henry Hickamon
	87	Isaac Huchison
	88	John Cates
	89	John Gray
	90	William L. Johnson
	91	James W. Johnson
14	92	Christian Montgomery
	93	Hester Bandy
	94	Charles D. Bean
	95	Jacob Newman
	96	Andrew J. Nelson
	97	Abgail Duncan
	98	David F. Ward
15	99	Samuel Hogue
	100	Andrew J. Nichols
	101	Nicholas Marler
	102	Adam Tague
	103	Sterling Holloway
	104	A. Nicholas
16	105	Jefferson H. Swafford
	106	Robert B. Bargen
	107	William A. Green
	108	James A. McPherson Green)
	109	James Nash
	110	William Myers
17	111	Catharine Widst(?)
	112	Mary White (Louvel)
	113	John Everet
	114	John C. Rodgers
	115	George Gothard
	116	Russel Duncan
	117	Cassian Picket
	118	William Shadrick
18	119	Martin Morgan
	120	Lesly Myers
	121	James McDonald
	122	Howard A. Montgomery
	123	Polly Burwick
	124	Sarah Morgan
19	125	Plesant M. Wright
	126	James M. Cuningham
	127	Stephen Gray
	128	Catharine Martin (Gray)
	129	Wilrey Myers
	130	John W. Hulse (Holes)
20	131	Francis M. Bandy
	132	Josiah C. Green
	133	C. W. Abel (Foust)
	134	George W. Everet
	135	Margaret Abel
	136	John W. Bean
	137	John R. Abel
	138	Robert F. Abel
	139	James W. McGuyer
21	140	James Kelly
	141	Sarah Land
	142	John H. Bryant
	143	John Foust
	144	Philip T. Foust
22	145	Larkin Gothard
	146	Azariah Barton
	147	James R. Abel
	148	Ira G. Gothard
	149	Mary A. Johnson (Moss)
22	150	Elijah Grueswell
	151	Joseph A. Howell
	152	Philip Foust (Acre)
23	153	Joshua Riddle (Benson)
	154	Elizabeth Foust
	155	John Barwick
	156	P. M. Picket
	157	Cornelius Broyles
	158	John C. Gothard
	159	Lewis Morgan
24	160	John Chatten
	161	Hamilton Burchwood

24 162 Dimpsy Sykes (Pens?)
163 Joseph Sykes (Acre)
164 Plesant Snow
165 Leonard Edens (Winset)
166 E. S. Williams
25 167 Joseph Thompson
168 Charles Morgan
169 James F. Wallen
170 Cyrus Jordan
171 Washington Morgan
172 Isaac Stephens
173 Mary Johnson
26 174 William L. Humpreys
175 Robert W. Bice
176 William Morgan (Green)
177 Richard Gregory

DISTRICT 10
(SMITHS CROSS ROADS P.O.)

27 178 Francis M. Morgan
179 Calvin Morgan
180 William B. Flemings
181 John McDonald
182 Daniel Hodges
183 Roland F. McDonald (Richards)
184 John H. Keith (Lowery)
185 Nicholas Keith (Michell)
28 186 W.B. Johnson (Bean, McFarland)
187 John Jewell
188 Lewis Morgan (Taylor)
189 John Whaley
190 Nancy McDonald
191 William B. Everitt
29 192 Bryant R. McDonald
193 Alexander Patten
194 J. N. Ragsdale (Bruce, Dalrymple)
195 Mary Templeton
196 Elias Morgan
197 Rufus Morgan (Bice)
30 198 David Morgan (Green)
199 John Atchly
200 Mike R. Barley
201 Henry Hampton
202 Ambos Arthur (David)

DISTRICT 5
(WASHINGTON P.O.)

31 203 John Newman
204 William Chumly
205 Jacob Barily
206 James F. Ladd (Rogers)
207 Joseph Evans
208 John E. Fraley
209 George H. Soreheck(?)
32 210 George W. Hostler
211 Jasper Barely
212 Jane Woody
213 Martin Loftiss
214 George Loftss
215 William Enus
216 John Day (Grimsley)
33 217 Thomas Hanes
218 Henry C. Collins
219 Joseph Broyles
220 Jeremiah Denton
221 Micajah Howerton
222 William Mitchell
223 Andrew J. Pritchet
224 James Mathews
225 Cobb Gravet
34 226 James Pierce (Loftiss)
227 Elbert Pierce
228 Joseph Hicks
229 David M. Landrith
230 Scott Hale (McFarland)
231 James A. Darwin
35 232 James P. Collins
233 Darus Loftiss (Denton)
234 James C. Phillips
235 Jacob Hamilton (Rector)
236 Jesse Rector
237 James Rector
238 Edward W. Ganawy
239 Wm Ganaway (Hampton)
36 240 Thomas C. Ganaway
241 Wm K. Ganaway (Broyles)
242 William A. Graham (Nash)
243 Franklin Milligan (McCulla)
244 Dorcus F. Fisher (Eaton)
245 George W. Fisher
246 Samuel W. Gibson
37 247 Samuel Shelvy
248 James McKahan
249 Henry Eaton (Chatten)
250 Baily Minick
251 William Cumpton
252 James Barnet
253 Joseph Garrison (Hase)
38 254 Jeffrey West (Prewet)
255 Robert Michel (Woodward)
256 Orville Paine (Brown)
257 Thomas T. Barnet
258 Berreman G. Mathews
259 Anderson Edmons (Shepard)
39 260 Greenberry McDaniel
261 John R. Henderson
262 Joshua Gentry
263 Obediah H. Brown
264 James Detherage (Carroll)
265 Jossiah Rice
40 266 Merrel McUen
267 Ruthe Mason

DISTRICT 4
(WASHINGTON P.O.)

40 268 Elisha Brown
269 John Winphrey
270 Andrew Wyrick
271 Solomon Wyrick
272 Nancy Martin (Harris)
273 James H. Trentham
41 274 Henry Miller (Essex)
275 Margaret Mitchell
276 Manerva Martin
277 Louisa Essex
278 Nancy Collins (Tulaldo)
279 James C. Fergason
280 William Collins
42 281 Polly Bird
282 Robert Ferguson (Neele)
283 Samuel B. Fergason
284 Levi Fergason
285 John Miller (Brabson)
286 Andrew Wasson
287 Peter W. Miller
43 288 Peter McCully (Graham)
289 Calvin Neil
290 William T. Gass
291 Mary Essex
292 John Duckworth
293 Miram Wassum
294 Hamp McFalls (Wasson)
44 295 Lewis C. Fergason (Brown)
296 Jackson Thompson
297 Jesse S. Brown
298 Edward Harris
299 David Keziah
300 Robert McFalls
301 Farly Brady
45 302 Thomas K. Green (Goard)
303 William Wyrick
304 Martin Wyrick
305 Andrew J. Wyrick
306 Adam S. Wyrick
307 William Gray (Watson)
308 William Fullington
46 309 Andrew Collins
310 Henry Davis (Kiziah)
311 Thomas Darwin
312 Jonathan Caldwell
313 Audley Caldwell
314 Miles Atchley

DISTRICT 4
(SULPHUR SPRINS P.O.)

47 315 John J. Wasson
316 Calvin Tharp (Highbark)
317 Sarah Tharp
318 Burton Leuty
319 Rufus B. Sherly (Keys, Holloway, Sharpshire)
320 Harvey Roberson
321 John Fellyow (Quillen, Coxey)
322 Thomas L. Franklin
323 James S. McPherson
48 324 William S. Smith
325 David Walker
326 Henry Whittenburg
327 Ira M. Whittenburg
328 Henderson Fisher
49 329 Aggy McCulla (McCarrol)
330 Charles W. Ault
331 Mary West
332 Alfred Collins
333 James F. White
334 Sarah Torbet
335 Malakiah Campbell
336 Samuel Whittenburg
50 337 Eglantine A. Whittenburg
338 Joseph Eaton
339 John Wheeler
340 William H. Bradley
341 William Porter
342 Christopher Whittenburg
343 Jacob Foust
51 344 Thomas Godbehere
345 William C. Hodge
346 Nancy Smith
347 Passafy T. Frazier
348 Thomas R. Holland
349 Alfred March (Cook)
350 Thomas T. Torbett
351 Thomas March
52 352 Joseph Cantrel
353 Daniel Broyles (Thompson)

52 354 Evan Breeden (Owens)
355 William M. Owens
356 William Jolly
357 John A. Wilson
358 Charles D. Smith
359 Harris M. Smith
53 360 Margaret Rose
361 Moses Smith (Varner)
362 John W. Thompson(McCulla)
363 Newton H. Whittenburg
364 Adam Booker
365 William Whittenburg

DISTRICT 3
(WASHINGTON P.O.)

54 366 John Jolly
367 Doctor W. Horner
368 Samuel Travis
369 William McMurry
370 John Edmonds
371 Francis A. Cash
55 372 James Carson (Ward,Vaughn)
373 George Minick (Vaughn)
374 John D. Chattin
375 William Brotherton
376 William R. Ridener
377 Ruben W. Porter
378 Calvin Henry
379 Samuel Porter
56 380 Thomas Weeks
381 Joseph W. Sellers
382 George W. Ahart
383 Elizabeth Knox
384 James Knox
385 Benjamin Knox
386 Thomas Pearson
387 John Garrison
57 388 Josiah Dawson (Varner,Woody)
389 Sarah Wilson (Loyed)
390 Thomas McPherson (James, Gengery, Redener?)
391 Samuel Pearson (Stephens?)
392 James L. Hanson
393 Henry Wasson (Moore)
58 394 Joab Wasson
395 John D. or G. Fisher
396 Hiram Henry
397 James Campbell
398 Joseph Peterson
399 James M. Cox
400 Henry Young
401 Joseph W. Cook (Woolard)
59 402 William Daughtery
403 William Graham (Nash)
404 Elizabeth Barton
405 Thomas Wasson
406 James H. Pass
407 Henry Arnold
408 Elizabeth Hubbard
409 Margarita Smith
60 410 Thomas N. Cunningham
411 William Collins (Moore)
412 Pinkney Collins
413 Ruth Howard
414 Martha Fewget(?) (Sales)
415 Pleasant Rhea
416 Garlington Bramlet (Edmonds)
61 417 Drury A. Bacon (Bird)
418 Elbert S. Cox (Bean)
419 Jacob Smith
420 Joseph Smith
421 Columbus Major (Coleman)
422 Elizabeth Gear (Dotson)
423 John Kennedy (McMurry)
62 424 Daniel Kennedy
425 Malinda Roberson (Carrol)
426 Sarah McMurry
427 Solomon Henry
428 Betsy Webb
429 George Henry
430 Cyrus Henry
431 George W. Ault (Hartly, James)
432 Wyley H. Cunningham
63 433 Marcus L. Gamble
434 Thomas Houston
435 Peter Minick
436 William Clack
437 Catharine Rush (McClaran)
438 George W. Wallace (Neil, Hill)
439 Rufus M. Harwood
64 440 James Thomas (Greenwood)
441 Andrew Johns (Witson)
442 George W. Lowry
443 James White
444 John White (Porter)
65 445 John A. Porter
446 Stanton W. Leuty
447 Robert N. Clack (Chatten)
448 William P. Foust
449 Jesse Harwood (Blythe)
450 George Hale
66 451 James W. Jolly
452 William Fewget
453 Nicholas Fine (Jones)
454 James H. Hawkins
455 Samuel Duckworth
456 David Davis
457 Isaac Davis
458 Granville H. Ward (Davis)
67 459 James Rhea (Smitty)
460 Hampton Sales (Stone)
461 Andrew J. Jolly
462 James Powers
68 463 Hanibal Webb
464 Gilbert Reed
465 David S. Brunnet (Fine)
466 Francis Roberson
467 John McAlpine
468 John Coxey (James)
469 Sally Marshel
69 470 Nathan Whittenburg (Underwood)
471 John Rector
472 Andrew Lowe (McAdoo)

DISTRICT 2
(SULPHUR SPRINGS P.O.)

70 473 Landon Rector
474 John C. Abernathy (Bennett)
475 Smith Brady
476 Hugh Roberts
477 Daniel B. Tredway
478 John P. Moulton
479 John Godsey
480 William Snelson (Mynatt)
71 481 Philip L. Carter
482 John Davis
483 James E. Bohanan
484 John T. Clack (Donaldson)
485 Samuel Allen
72 486 Abraham Emory
487 Coleman Smith
488 Andrew Marney
489 Allen Bacon
490 Thomas Miller
491 William Miller
492 Enoch Floyd
493 Archibald McCaleb
494 George W. Kirklan
73 495 Jesse Thorp
496 Lucinda Gillespie
497 Micajah Clack
498 Charles Brady
499 Prudence Parker
500 Thomas Clark
74 501 Thomas Keziah
502 Manerva Brunet (Waisner)
503 Leonard Long
504 Michael Talent
505 John H. Fine
506 Isaac Fine
507 Archibald D. Paul (Clark)
508 Samuel Dotson (Zigglar)
75 509 John Johnson
510 David McCulla
511 Nile M. Broyles
512 Stephen Breeden
513 Thomas Breeden (Reese)
514 Absalom Thompson
76 515 William Capps
516 Harriet Adams
517 John Hosse
77 518 Addison C Day (Lauderdale)
519 Samuel H. Dickey (Reevely)
520 Margaret Fine (Dickey)
521 Edmond A. Victory
522 Smith Harris
523 Dicey Ervin
524 William Rector
78 525 George W. Renfro
526 John C. Gillespie
527 Andrew J. Bryson
528 Agnes Peters
529 David E. Gillespie
530 Sarah A. Roberson
531 John Monroe (Lemons)
532 William Giles
79 533 William T. Guin
534 James Kincannon (Lauderdale)
535 Edward Pyott
536 Thomas K. Thompson
537 Wyly A. Ault (Howard)
538 John L. Thompson
539 James Watson
80 540 William M. Foust
541 James I. Cash
542 Ruben Lemons
543 John Tredway
544 Joel Dotson
545 Lilburn Boughman (Bell)
546 Henry T. Rogers
547 Zachariah Key (Dodson)
81 548 James Gillam
549 John House
550 Susan Monday (Fawger)
551 Martin McCully (Harris)
552 Dawson Harris
553 Willis Burchfield

DISTRICT 1
(PRESTONVILLE P.O.)

82 554 Major C. Gillam
555 James P. Hollaway
556 Nathaniel M. Gillam
557 Wiley Kersey
558 Thomas J. Casney(?)
559 Steven(?) Monday
560 James M. Majors
561 James H. Pyott
562 Calvin G. Dudley
563 Hiram Mahaffy
83 564 Richard L. Garrison
565 Preston G. Campbell
566 Francis M. Thompson
567 John L. Marsh
568 Jacob Green
569 Elias Crisp
570 Carey Bargen
84 571 John H. Ferguson (Wright)
572 Nicholas H. Long
573 Benjamin Reese
574 Osker Cook (Snodgrass)
85 575 Onslow Marsh
576 Samuel Robinson
577 Hugh Rhea
578 William Dyer
579 Charles Dyer
580 Richard Bailey (Wilson)
581 William G. Clark
582 Wesley Casey
583 Calvin Garrison
86 584 Paskill K. Busum
585 John Lemons
586 Jeremiah Wasson
587 John Dyer
588 Pryor Barton
589 Aron Gray
590 Isaac Hollaway
87 591 Pleasant Hollaway
592 Nancy Adams
593 Elijah Barton
594 James Hollaway
595 Thomas J. Barton
596 Jacob Garrison
597 George M. Stanfield
598 John R. Crisp
599 Isaac Wilkens
88 600 Joseph P. Hollaway
601 Miller M. Fergason
602 Franklin Waterhouse (Edington)
603 John Roberson (Collins)
604 John Gist
605 Mat Cox
89 606 James Roberson
607 Robert Patterson
608 Lenville Mynott
609 Stephen S. Keywood
610 Edward Ferguson
611 Joel Dotson
612 William Hughes
613 Nancy Munday (Reese)
90 614 Abner Dotson
615 James Crisp (Watson)
616 William T. Holoway
617 Robert D. Hines
618 Major Holoway (Majors)
91 619 Richard W. Holoway
620 Jacob Gibson
621 James Johnson
622 Allen Hughes
623 Jesse P. Thompson (McAdoo)
624 William W. Cash
92 625 Moses C.R. Thompson
626 William Hill
627 Larkin Majors (Huddleston)
628 Silas Pearson
629 Edmond Jenkins
630 Elias Majors
631 Jesse P. Roddy (Bell)
93 632 S. T. Whittenburg
633 Wm G. Roddy (Preston)
634 Susan Roddy
635 Rozannat(?) Hood
636 Jacob Boles
94 637 Alexander Jolly
638 Benjamin J. Wasson
639 Edmund Johnson
640 Asa Newport
641 Miller E. Short
642 Daniel Roberson
643 John W. Kerrick
644 Mary Bean
95 645 Eldridge Clifton
646 John Kersey
647 Susan Delana
648 John Kelly
649 Wilson Thomas
650 Davd M. Roddy
651 Addison Locke (Knight)
96 652 Yancy Loy
653 David Majors

DISTRICT 9
(PRESTONVILLE P.O.)

97 654 Thomas Condiff
655 Henry Rhea
656 Elijah Brewer
657 David Hanks
658 James H. Hase
659 John Hase
660 Pleasant Munday
661 Daniel Smith
662 John Michell
98 663 James W. Grisham
664 Stewart H. Pugh
665 Thomas Lemons (Brady)
666 Aaron Rhea
667 Francis M. Short
668 Warren Rhea
669 John Rhea
670 Daniel W. Knox (Bell, Lea)
671 James Hase
99 672 Willis McClendon
673 Sanders McClendon
674 James Brady
675 Merril Brady (McClendon)
676 Dennis McClendon (Brady)
677 Jason I. Panner (Donald, Wiley)
678 Isaac Morris
100 679 William Lea
680 Thomas Lea
681 Elizabeth Dunlap
682 John Dunlap
683 Jacob L. Dunlap
684 Daniel McFalls
685 Francis McFalls
686 Sarah Danny
101 687 William Lemmons
688 James F. Thompson
689 Austin J. Evans (Edington)
690 John Dotson

DISTRICT 6
(WASHINGTON P.O.)

102 691 William Dyke (Witt)
692 Calvin Wright
693 Samuel B. Murphy
694 Sallie Ryan (Clements)
695 Samuel Melis
696 Thomas C. Wyatt
697 Robert Peterson
698 William P. Thomason
103 699 David Woody
700 Joseph Travis (Wright)
701 Joseph Brown
702 Joseph Wyott
703 William Ives
704 Calvin Myers
705 Ely Campbell
104 706 John Vaughn
707 Robert T. Howard
708 William Smith
709 Polly Prewit
105 710 John Wassom
711 John W. Pritchett (James)
712 John Peterson
713 Michael Birely
714 Edmond Smith
715 William M. Birely
716 Samuel McAdoo (Falkner)
717 Marcus L. Wright
718 William Watts
106 719 Thomas Peterson
720 William C. Edmonds
721 Allen Holland
722 Jackson Thurman
723 Elijah Buttram
724 Elzy Buttram
725 James H. Locke
107 726 William Campbell
727 William Bennet
728 Ruben Owens
729 Leodice Bell (Richards)
730 Newton Locke (Henry,Humphrey)
731 Franklin Locke
732 Rutha L.E. Frazier
733 Samuel Wilkey (Shaver)
108 734 Columbus Wilkey
735 R.C. Montgomery (Barnett,Henry)
736 Sampson Wright
737 Rebecca Cox
738 Kezziah Moore
739 Alfred Burton
740 Pinkney Burton
741 Jordan Moore
742 Spencer Boltin
109 743 Darius Waterhouse
744 Robert N. Gillespie (Crawford)
745 Joseph Parks (Love, Sykes, Paine, Bean)
746 John Kersey
747 P.T. Rawlings (Thomas)
748 Jacob Kelly (Darwin)
749 Ander Trim (Johnson)
110 750 John W. Chambers
751 John Wyott (James)
752 William Guin

110 753 Elijah Rudd
754 James T. Nanny (Hacker)
755 Pulaski Killough
756 John Harwood (Presley)
111 757 James Snow
758 George W. Cobb
759 John M. Huston (Colston)
760 Robert Kellough
761 Nathaniel H. Smith
762 John James
763 Wm B. Killough (Brown)
764 William Allen
112 765 John S. Evans (Moore)
766 John B. Murphy (Peterson, Blevins)
767 Martin White
768 R. F. Monzy
769 George W. Ball
770 John Hoyal
771 Albert P. Early (Frazier)
113 772 Warner E. Colville
773 Adam Rawlings
774 Nicholas Woody
775 William N. Merriott
776 Jas W. Gillespie (Wallace)
777 DeWitt C. Ragsdale
778 Samuel R. Hackett

1870 CENSUS

DISTRICT 1
(SULPHUR SPRINGS P.O.)

1 1 James Holloway (Garrison)
2 Caroline J. Barton (Knight)
3 John Jones
4 Thomas Jones
5 Addison Locke (Wheeler)
6 Lucy Evans
7 John W. Gray
2 8 George W. Renfro
9 William H. Harris (Lee, Mathews)
10 Andrew J. Bryson (Burnett)
11 Samuel H. Holloway (Haws, Cunningham)
12 John Edwards
13 Caroline Locke
14 Malinda Loy
3 15 Jacob Garrison
16 Charles F. Ederton
17 Lynus Batchelder
18 Jeremiah Shiflet
19 John Radcrisp
20 Albert Morris
21 William Lemmon
22 Abner Dekey
23 Francis A. Cash
4 24 William F. Ball
25 John H. Devaney
26 Samuel C. Dunkin(?)
27 Lucy Parks
28 Luther M. Heiskell
5 29 John Robinson
30 James Robinson (Vaughn)
31 Sarah Roper (Russel)
32 David Feicher
33 Rufus Hardbarger
34 Columbus Gibson
6 35 Major Holloway
36 Isaac W. Holloway
37 Austin Evans
38 Robert D. Hanes
39 William Cash (Reed)
40 Jesse P. Thompson (Kersey)
7 41 Moses C.R. Thompson
42 Vanburen Thompson
43 Stephen Cawood (Reed, Craig)
44 John M. Lemons
45 Luke T. Edington
46 Silva Waterhouse
8 47 William Gardenhire
48 Franklin Waterhouse
49 James M. Moss
50 Milan M. Ferguson
51 Evander Thurman (Watson)
52 George W. Ward
53 William N. Ward
54 Franklin Dagley
55 Snelson Roberts (Sweeten, Davis, Reese)
9 56 Onslo G. Marsh
57 Sarah Cantrell (Lemmons)
58 Leandia Mariott
59 Sanders McClendon
60 Absolem S. Thompson
61 John Parker
62 George Parker
10 63 Wiley G. Clark
64 Hugh B. Heiskell (Marney)
65 Benjamin Reese
66 Nicholas H. Long
67 Susanna Ray
68 Marion Watson
11 69 William Gray
70 Nancy Monday
71 Levi Tredway (Hardbarger)
72 Joel Dodson
73 Elizabeth Parten
74 William R.S. Thompson
12 75 James Lemmons (Clark)
76 Richard L. Garrison
77 Allen H. McFalls
78 Richard Holloway
79 Major C. Gilliam
80 James S. Holloway
81 Sally S. Gilliam
13 82 Malinda Gillespie (Roddy)
83 Chesley D. Corbin
84 Thomas J. Harvey (Hull)
85 Harriette Smith
86 Alexander Hanes/Haimes
87 Elizabeth Bratcher
88 David M. Roddy
14 89 James P. Lawyer (Munday)
90 Peter Bell (Loden)
91 Sarah Clark
92 William G. Roddy (Preston, Cawood)
93 Thomas Preston
15 94 Elizabeth Roddy
95 Henry Roddy
96 James L. Roddy
97 Susan Roddy
98 Joseph Brown
99 James Johnson (Short, Bell)
100 Edmond Johnson
16 101 John Hayes
102 John Henry (Russell)
103 Amanda Bean
104 David Majors
105 Alderago Clifton (Moore)
17 106 Thomas Cogens
107 Adam Kirkland
108 James F. Newport
109 Asa Newport (Underwood)
110 William H.H. McCulley
111 William F. Majors
112 William E. Lonas
113 Jacob Boals
114 Hughey Ray
18 115 William Cox
116 Robert Robinson
117 Pleasant Johnson
118 Joseph Hood
119 Pleasant M. Holloway
120 John J. Tratham
121 Wm R. Edington (McAdoo)
19 122 Polly A. Dunlap
123 John Thompson (Collins)
124 James O. Daniel (Thompson)
125 James F. Thompson
126 Mary Scarberry
127 James I. Garrison
128 William Dunlap
20 129 Elizabeth Dunlap
130 Sarah A. Gibbs
131 John McClondal
132 Elbert S. Martin
133 Ann Morris
134 Aaron Morris
135 Claborn Fugat
21 136 James Brady
137 Willis McClondal
138 Erastus Coal
139 Richard Lemmons
140 Valentine Roberts
141 Sampson Wolf
22 142 William Lemmons
143 Yancy Loy
144 Aaron Ray
145 Aaron Ray Jr.
146 Henry Ray
147 Angeline Brady
148 James T. Monroe
149 Elijah Brewer
150 Pleasant Munday
23 151 James Hayse
152 William O. Chadwick
153 Jennetta Anderson

DISTRICT 2
(SULPHUR SPRINGS P.O.)

1 1 Rufus Hood
2 John Boals
3 Semeour Palmour (Brwer)
4 Shelby Monda
5 Martin McCullough
6 George Boals
2 7 Daniel Boals
8 James D. Gilliam
9 Henry L. Rogers
10 Calvin Dudley
11 Jesse Ingle
3 12 Thomas H. Ingle
13 William Dodson
14 James I. Cash
15 William M. Foust
16 Thomas K. Thompson
17 Henry Homey
18 Nancy Thompson
4 19 James H. Pass
20 Edward Pyott
21 Thomas K. Monsey
22 John E. Pyott
23 Preston J. Welch (Wheeler)
5 24 George W. Foust
25 James H. Pearson
26 Henry Robinson
27 James H. Monday
28 John W. Foust
29 John M. Wills
30 John Drake
31 William C. Carson
32 Hannah P. Day (Lauderdale)
33 Joseph B. Peters
34 Milo S. Holoway
6 35 William F. Rous
36 Willim W. Neal
37 Robert B. Bohannon
38 Agnes Peters
39 George W. Wassom
40 John W. Wasson
41 Willis Drake
42 William R. Clack
43 Micajah Clack
44 Spencer Clack
7 45 Huston Hurst
46 Samuel Baker
47 Jesse Stoansipher
48 David McCuiston
49 William Stegall
50 Miles H. McCuiston
8 51 James B. McCaleb
52 Jacob Green (Reas)
53 Martin Hurst (Gray, King)
54 Allen L. King
55 George Farmer
56 Garet Talant
9 57 Ephraigm Stockwell
58 Nancy A. Jolly
59 William Brown
60 Sarah Manney(?)
61 Andrew Manney
62 John Patten
63 Elbert Brown
64 Thomas J. Brown
65 William R. Miller
10 66 John Donalson
67 Arch McCaleb
68 Peter McCaleb
69 James L. Coke
70 Albert McCaleb
71 Joseph Roberts
72 Arcada Lee
11 73 Thomas Miller
74 Moses Miller
75 Lucinda Gillespie (Jolley, Robenson)
76 Nancy Gillespie
77 Jefferson Gillespie
78 Auston Gillespie
79 Ralph Gillespie
12 80 Philip Gillespie
81 Sidney Gillespie
82 Shepherd Donalson
83 William West
84 Wilbern Clark
85 John Brown
86 Newton Brown (Womick)
87 Ben C. Franklin
88 Hiram Robeson
89 James H. Gilbreth
90 William R. Ponder
13 91 David Clark
92 Preston Campbell
93 Stephen Breeding (Brown)
94 Thomas Breeding (Reece)
95 John Howard
96 Olaver Lyon
97 Barry Abernathy
98 John C. Abernathy
14 99 Jeremiah C. Wasson (Low, Abernathy, McLeer, McDermet, Smith, Overbey)
100 Samuel Craighead
101 Nile M. Broyles
102 Samuel H. Dickey (Bean, Curley)
103 Richard Johnson
15 104 Thomas B. McElwee
105 Joseph Reynolds
106 Noah Robinson
107 Elizabeth Haselbarger (Brown)
108 Andrew McCamey (Yokely)
109 Albert H. Taylor (Yokely)
16 110 Charles Brady (Gipson)
111 Pleasant Majors
112 Edward West
113 Sebastion S. King
114 Coalman Smith
115 Lenard Long
116 William J. Oasis
17 117 Rebecca Poll [Paul]
118 James Bohanan
119 Francis McCabe
120 William S. Wyrick
121 William Wyrick
122 Jesse A. Thompson
123 William M. Oans [Owens]

DISTRICT 3
(SULPHUR SPRINGS P.O.)

1 1 John K. Franklin
2 William W. Lowe
3 Calista E. Fine
4 George W. Duckworth
5 John Duckworth
6 John Felyaw (Quillen)
7 James Kincannon
2 8 Nathan Whittenburg (Underwood)
9 Temperance McCarpen
10 Adaline Shadwick
11 Jeston Kirby
12 Jane Hair
13 Isaac Byrd
14 Aaron C. Owens (Keelon)
3 15 Jacob W. Smith
16 Henry Ward
17 Iverson Ward
18 Wm J. McLerrin (Hamer)
19 Granville H. Wade
20 George W. Lemmons
21 John A. Porter
4 22 George Minnick
23 Josiah Dawson
24 John F. Dawson (McNew)
25 Jesse Harwood
26 Thos H. McPherson (Jones)
27 James Garrison
28 Jacob B. White (Burson?)
5 29 William C. Hodge
30 John P. Marshall
31 James C. Wilson
32 Marion Horn
33 John Watson
34 James M. Cox
6 35 Ruth Howard
36 Andrew Wassum
37 Abraham Hodge (Boofer)
38 Keziah Lefew (McDuffy)
39 James R. Barnett
40 Calvin Neal
41 Carter Rolan
42 Benjamin F. Rhea

DISTRICT 3
(WASHINGTON P.O.)

7 43 Peter McCullough
44 Nancy C. Cofer
45 Calvin Reynolds
46 Peter Minnick (McMurry,Mariot)
47 James McCullough
48 Henry Young
49 Mary Bramlet
50 Andrew J. Matthews
51 Isaac Barnett
8 52 William Graham
53 Joseph Graham
54 Calvin Millican
55 Elizabeth McCullough
56 Franklin Milican
57 Pinkney Collins
58 Calvin Henry
59 Solomon Henry
60 Thomas L. Franklin
9 61 Bennet J. Franklin
62 Julia A. Carmicall
63 Damarcus L. Wright
64 James Henry
65 Daniel Kennedy
66 Joseph W. Sellers
67 Andrew J. Smith
10 68 James Smith
69 Marion Ray
70 Eldridge Merrell
71 James Kennedy
72 John C. Carson

10 73 Sampson Wright
11 74 Amedia Rice
75 John Low
76 John Marshall
77 William Marshall (Lewis)
78 James White
79 William Broyles
80 Martha Johnson
81 John T. Smith
82 Thomas N.L. Cunnyngham
12 83 William Giles
84 Peter Dooley
85 Marion Dooley
86 Robert F. Cook (Gaines)
87 Hesakiah Genow
13 88 John Ball
89 William McMurry
90 James G. Ewing
91 Joab Foust
92 John Foust
93 Napoleon Foust
94 Samuel O. Foust
95 Susan Robinson
96 William Doughty
97 Richard Riggins
14 98 George W. Kelley

DISTRICT 3
(SULPHUR SPRINGS P.O.)

14 99 Thomas Brotherton
100 George H. Hail
101 Hugh B. Fry
102 John A. Scott
103 Robert N. Clack
104 Catharine Rush
105 Sebra Fry
106 James J. Bell
15 107 Willie M. Moyers
108 Joel Merrill
109 Letitia W. Foust
110 Julia A. Harwood
111 William Fuget (Buttram)
112 John R. Cock
16 113 Martha Fugat (Sails)
114 Marion Clark
115 David Davis (Duckworth)
116 James Ray
117 Benjamin D. Smith
118 Benjamin F. Taylor
119 Rufus Davis
120 William D. Willson
17 121 Samuel Ray
122 Lawson Ray
123 Samuel Smith
124 Henry Ray
125 Samuel Smith
18 126 James Genow
127 William R. Genow
128 David Genow
129 Hugh Collins
130 John White
131 Joshua Greenwood
132 John Willson
133 Spencer Clack
134 Micajah Clack (Harris)
19 135 George Hail
136 James Hail
137 Samuel Brady
138 James P. White
139 William M. Clack
140 Susan Chattin
141 William Ward
20 142 George Wilkerson
143 James Carson
144 John S. Clack (McNew)
145 Peter Shock (Franklin)
146 Charles Brady
147 Silvester Wilkey
21 148 William Coval
149 Uria Henry
150 Elvira Cunningham
151 Jane Cunningham

DISTRICT 4
(SULPHUR SPRINGS P.O.)

1 1 Reubin Porter
2 Mary West (Macully)
3 William P. Collins
4 William McCully (Oans)
5 Charles W. Ault
6 Robert A. Phillips
7 Gilbert Reed
8 John Thompson
2 9 Jane M. Gannaway (Hinch, Rogers)
10 William Cunningham
11 Mary A. Whittenburg
12 John W. Thompson
3 13 William Pritchett
14 Thomas J. Barton
15 John Wheeler
16 William F. Guinn
17 Wm K. Ganaway (Broyles)
18 David Walker
19 Horace Smith
4 20 M. Elzy
21 William S. Smith (Bandy)
22 Pacify T. Frazier
23 Nancy Smith
24 Thomas Godbyhere
25 Ira M. Whittenburg (Farmer)
26 Nancy J. Trentham
5 27 Samuel Walker
28 Christopher Whittenburg
29 James Mitchel
30 Sarah Torbet
31 Margarette Rose
32 Henderson Fisher
33 Louisa J. Crow
6 34 William Jolly
35 William McGill
36 Evan Breeding (Oans)
37 Oliver O. Henry
38 Charles D. Smith
39 Thos R. Holland (McNew)
40 John Mitchell
7 41 James M. Grasham
42 Daniel Broyles (Thompson)
43 James A. Thompson
44 George W. Harsler
45 James M. Dorton
46 Lott Johnson (McDonald)
8 47 Jas F. Ladd (Gillespie, Garrison)
48 Joel L. McPherson
49 R. B. Sherley (Green, Shraphier)
50 Burton Leuty
51 Zachariah Rose (McNabb)
52 James Reed
9 53 William H. Rector
54 Thomas Grant (Henderson)
55 Starling H. Holloway
56 James D. McPherson
57 Thomas J. Marsh (Kelly)
58 Mary E. Torbett (Marsh)
59 John T. Powers
60 James Willis
10 61 H. H. Miller (Duismoor, Pierce)
62 Christopher C. Carrol
63 Samuel Shelby
64 Biby Thomas
65 Charles Thomas
66 Henry Thurman
67 Malaki Campbell
11 68 Jasper N. Cook
69 Wm T. Gass (Webster, Darwin)
70 Mary Essick
71 Jane Hicks
72 Jonas Boofer
73 Newton C. Hicks
74 Orinda Marsh
75 Levi W. Ferguson
12 76 William C. Mitchel
77 Andrew J. Wyrick
78 Mary A. Collins
79 Phebe Winfrey
80 Solomon Wyrick
13 81 John T. Ferguson
82 Hugh L.W. Ferguson (Essex)
83 Mitchell Neal
84 James Neal
85 George W. Marshall
86 Anderson Thurman
87 Samuel Wyrick
88 Vesta Ferguson
89 Obediah Brown
14 90 Samuel B. Ferguson
91 Jacob L. Wassom
92 Samuel Caldwell
93 Delilah Kelly
94 Francis M. Hill
95 Robert McFalls
96 David Mitchell (Smith)
15 97 Andrew J. Jolly
98 Jonathan Caldwell
99 Moneaa(?) Gass
100 Merril Brady
101 Henry C. Rogers
102 Thos C. Darwin (Brady, Gourd)
16 103 David Casey
104 Emily Matthews
105 Sarah Thompson
106 James H. Beard (Brown)
107 John T. Miller
108 Wright S. Miller
17 109 Rebecca Miller
110 Zachariah T. Wassom
111 John N. Miller (Darwin)
112 Joseph Garrison (McDonald)
113 William V. Willis
114 Farley Brady
115 John Essex
116 Adam S. Wyrick
18 117 Edly P. Caldwell
118 Joseph Holloway

DISTRICT 5
(WASHINGTON P.O.)

1 1 William Zigler
2 David Woody
3 Robert N. Crow
4 Alfred A. Day
5 Benjamin F. Zigler
6 Rachel Day (Armor)
7 Joseph A. Zigler (Hawkins)
2 8 Benjamin B Travis (Carroll)
9 Martha Woody
10 John Woody
11 David Kyle
12 Alfred Day (Rankins, McDonald)
13 Jasper Byrely
3 14 Henry H. Gamble (Norman, Fitz-gerald)
15 Flavius J. Paine
16 William Webb (Ogill)
17 Roswell Suttles
18 John Suttles
19 Joseph S. Evans (Wren)
20 Jane Locke
21 Wesley Wright
4 22 Edward Denton
23 Jeremiah Denton
24 James J. Denton
25 James Coval
26 Baily Minnix
27 Roland Gass (Duismore)
5 28 James B. Blevins
29 James P. Collins
30 James Phillips
31 Elbert D. Pierce
32 Andrew J. Pritchett
33 John Beshears
34 Martin Loftis
35 Martin L. Loftis
36 Joseph A. Bell
37 Martha J. Darwin
6 38 Micajah Howerton (Collins)
39 Sarah Howerton (White)
40 James M. Beasly
41 James E. Beasly
42 Caleb Gravet
43 James A. Darwin (Blevins)
44 Charles Darwin
45 Ruth Mason
46 Elvira Paine
7 47 Francis M. Loftis
48 Green McDonald
49 Thomas H. McDaniel
50 Giles H. Ryan
51 Berryman G. Matthews
52 John H. King
53 William Henderson
54 Albert Lane
8 55 George W. Gideon (Reno)
56 Elisha Brown
57 James Detherage (Gidion, Jolly)
58 William R. Carroll
59 William C. Harris
60 Francis Suttles
61 Thomas Ganaway
62 Joseph A. Broyles
9 63 Henry C. Darwin
64 William P. Darwin (Blevins)
65 Lewis C. Ferguson
66 Nancy J. Fisher
67 Watson Roberts
68 Churchwell A. Brown
69 Orlinda West
10 70 Mary McClendal
71 William W. Partn(?)
72 William A. Compton
73 James G. Broyles
74 Edmond Ganaway
75 William Ganaway
76 Jacob M. Hamilton (Rector)

DISTRICT 6
(WASHINGTON P.O.)

1 1 Squire Blevins
2 Joseph Travis
3 John Brown
4 Leroy Britterson
5 Joseph Brown
6 Banister Smith
2 7 Robert Sneed
8 James Smith
9 Jeremiah Moore
10 William Buttram
11 Thomas J. Phelfrey (Smith)
12 Ham D. Webb
3 13 Isaiah Rice
14 Adam McCullough
15 James McCullough
16 James Phelfrey
17 Andrew Webb
18 Joseph Eaton
19 Henry Eaton
4 20 Elbert S. Cox
21 Mary Hairce
22 Moses F. Moore
23 Thompson Hurce
24 Rebecca Cox (Pritchett, Jones)
25 Julia Kelley (Collins)
26 Thomas A. Houston
5 27 William Wright
28 Robert Montgomery (McMurry)
29 Gustavus Murphy
30 Samuel Wilkie
31 David Ryan
32 Newton J. Brown
33 James Rice (McErvin)
34 Wm P. Thompson (Ingle)
6 35 Ellen Wasson
36 Samuel Ingle
37 William Smith
38 Harvey Roddy (Peterson)
39 Samuel Wilkie
40 Darius Waterhouse (Paine)
7 41 Samuel J. Frazier (Wilson, Thom-ison)
42 Charles Crocket
43 Uria Rawlings (Garrison)
44 John M. Houston
45 Allen Gillespie
46 Alexander Waterhouse
8 47 Philip T. Rawlings (Wilson)
48 David Rawlings
49 Pulaski Killough
50 Robert Killough
51 James T. Nanny
52 Robert Peterson
53 John Peterson
9 54 Henry Fisher
55 Robert N. Gillespie
56 John James
57 Joseph J. Hoge
58 Henry A. Crawford
59 Mary Gillespie (Ramsey)
60 Albert P. Early (Collins)
61 Anonymus Fondren
10 62 David Davis
63 William Chumly
64 Nathaniel H. Smith
65 William R. Henry (Brewer, Locke)
66 Phillip Wyrick
67 Sarah J. Parks (Howard)
11 68 Frances Chambers
69 William Allen (Thompson)
70 Samuel Fondren
71 James M. Gillespie
72 William Greene(?)
73 John Wyatt (Harden)
74 Richard W. Colville
75 Robert T. Howard
76 Jacob Dilmon
77 Thomas Peterson
12 78 Thomas Frazier
79 Ana Frazier
80 John Hoyal (Johnson)
81 Warner E. Colville
82 Rachel Myers
83 Franklin L. Bean
84 Frankln Locke (Kellon)
85 Alfred Locke
86 Nathan Watson
13 87 Caswell Litner
88 [skipped]
89 Anderson Locke
90 James H. Locke
91 Houston Mansel
92 Mary Robinson
93 William Campbell
94 Thomas Campbell
14 95 James Campbell
96 Scott Hail
97 Nancy Mariott
98 John A. Matthews
99 James K. Hail
100 James P. Brandin(?)
100? Thomas C. Potter
101 James Harris
15 102 Martha Thompson
103 Cyrus Henry (Locke)
104 George W. Henry
105 Mary Richey
106 Robert Parker
107 John Parker
108 Alfred Etherley
109 John Slaughter
110 Abraham Dyer
111 Allen Holland (Dilemon)
16 112 Jackson Thurman
113 James J. Everett
114 Elijah L. Rudd
115 Hannah Gillespie (Nichols)
116 John Gillespie
117 James Ryan
118 Smith Moore
119 Alexander Frazier
17 120 John Smith
121 William D. Byrely
122 Harris Ryan
123 Thomas A. Allen
124 Pinkney Wright
125 Sarah Ryan
126 Louisa Ryan

DISTRICT 7
(SMITHS CROSS ROADS P.O.)

1 1 Jesse A. Shaver
2 Elizabeth Trusley
3 William Kelley
4 John W. Hughes
5 David Singleton (Anderson)
6 Delpha Knight
7 Neeley Keith
8 Lawson Cameron
9 John G. Shaver
2 10 James F. Bowling
11 Henry Gillespie
12 James Prater (Paduse)
13 Richard Knight
14 Asberry F. Fisher
15 William Morgan
16 Thomas M. Bowling
17 Michael Byrely (Romines)
18 Jacob Byrely (Chumley)
3 19 Parham Boling
20 Elizabeth Howel
21 George L. Tucker (Harris)
22 James N. Grice
23 Stephen Spence (Chattin, Dunwoody)
24 Richard C. Knight (Rawlings)
25 Pinkney Burton
26 Franklin Matherly (Byrely)
4 27 James M. Shelton
28 McHenry Hughes
29 David Moore
30 John H. Beasley (Watson)
31 Samuel D. Housely
32 William J. Smith
5 33 John W. Porter
34 John J. Smith (Mathes?)
35 Alfred Burton
36 Eliza A. Garrison
37 William L. Irvin (Early)
38 Elizabeth Burton (Collins, Hubbert)
39 Bartley C. Craig
6 40 James Wilson
41 William H. Dodd (Wilson)
42 Thomas H. Cash
43 James A. Cash
44 Nicholas Frazier (Christian)
45 William Evans
46 Thomas B. Scrogins
47 James M. Thompson
48 James P. Thompson
49 James Spence (Wilson)
7 50 Lucinda Cates
51 Vallentine Allen
52 Albert D. Moore
53 Pleasant M. Purser
54 William Purser
55 Franklin Broyles
56 Richard L. Manzy
57 James R. Craword (Griffith)
8 58 Richard Womack
59 Abner W. Frazier
60 Joseph B. Dodd
61 Ambers Arther
62 Calvin Hughes
63 Cornelius Shaver

DISTRICT 8
(SMITHS CROSS ROADS P.O.)

1 1 John Freiley
2 Francis M. Capes
3 Pleasant H. Snow
4 Dempsey Sykes
5 Joseph Sykes
6 Joseph Thompson
7 Thomas B. Hughes
2 8 Thomas N. Walker
9 Thomas N. Walker Jr.
10 Charles Morgan
11 Franklin B. Morgan
12 Washington Morgan
13 Joseph M. Walker
14 James H. Morgan
15 Mary E. Ennis
16 Jackson Keith
3 17 Eli Campbell
18 William K. Gray
19 Hillard Thurman
20 Jas Carvin (Turner, Fox, Coulter)
21 Joel W. Hoge
4 22 Christina Montgomery
23 Nichodemus Marler
24 Arvazine Nichols
25 Lewis McDonald
26 John A. Foust
27 Hamilton Burchard
28 George Suddath
29 John Hodges (Edwards, Green)
5 30 Martin Morgan
31 Samuel McDonald
32 Thos H. Montgomery (Stanfield)
33 William D. Averett (Morgan)
34 Mary Burwick
6 35 James A. McPherson
36 Jefferson J. Swafford
37 John O. Johnson (Rogers)
38 Joseph Brown
39 James L. Dungan (Pierce?)
40 Abigail Dungan (Gothard)
7 41 Charles L. Dungan
42 Miles A. Dungan
43 Edmond Couch
44 Marvel Couch
45 Sarah J. Morgan
46 John W. Bean
8 47 James M. Fann
48 John P. Walker
49 Stephen Gray (Alexander)
50 Isaac A. Martin (Gray)
51 Henry Hickman
52 Eijah Boman (Holt)
53 Sarah A. Morgan
54 James J. Kelley
9 55 James B. Walker
56 Mary A. Abel
57 John R. Abel
58 George W. Smedley
59 Susan Rogers
60 Abraham Bryson
61 Andrew Cowen
10 62 John A. Walker (Johns)
63 John Wright
64 Cain W. Abel (Foust)
65 James H. Cox
66 Abner A. Carter
67 William F. Morgan
68 Larkin Gothard
11 69 John McDonald
70 Jesse Pierce
71 James A. Foster (Brown)
72 Phillip T. Foust
73 James B. Green
74 Milo S. Riddle
75 John L Riddle
76 George W. Thompson
77 Mary R. Abel
78 James C. Shirley
12 79 James Peirce (Johnson)
80 Thomas Howard
81 Caroline Dean
82 Samuel Latmir
83 Darius C. Hutcheson
84 Murphey Orlander
85 Wm G. Wilson (Brown,Stephens)
13 86 Mordica Ford
87 Vilena(?) Hutchison (Norman)
88 Alfred Hutchison (Crain,Goodson)
89 Samuel W. Hutcheson
90 Byrd Terry
91 Lewis F. McDonald
92 Richard H. Jordan (Chadwick)
14 93 William A. Jordan (Buice)
94 Charles P. Howard
95 David Fox
96 William A. Steele
97 Pleasant M. Carvin
98 James C. Buttram
99 Andrew J. Bankston (Cowen)
100 Sanders D. Broyles
15 101 James J. Abel (Fleming)
102 Nicholas G Moore (Elder, Snider)
103 John H. Keith
104 James M. Benson
105 Asabel Johnson
106 Phillip Foust
107 William P. McGill
108 Mary A. Johnson
16 109 Lewis Morgan
110 John Jewel (Lea)
111 Thomas J. Coulter
112 Thos B. Coulter (Fuller, Winset)
113 Francis Bower
114 Leander Neal
17 115 Alexander Hickman
116 Daniel Raulston
117 William R. Johns
118 Eliza A. Holt
119 Margaret M. Ward
120 Wm R. Champion (Smith)
18 121 William Hickman (Buice)
122 William S. Kelley (Cahana)
123 William A. Green
124 — F. Richards (Cranmore)
125 John M. Burwick
126 Henry M. Housely
19 127 John Pierce (Swafford)
128 Orson A Shipley (Gass, Campbell)
129 Dolly Foust
130 William B. Benson
131 Henry Davis
132 Thomas K. Green
133 Calvin A. Morgan
134 Abraham O'Neal
20 135 George Gothard
136 William L. Humphrey
137 William Morgan
138 Richard Grigory

20 139 Lesley Myers
140 Willie Fleming
141 Nicholas Keith
21 142 Thomas C. Travis
143 Jeremiah Browder
144 Mary Bell
145 John H. Coalman (Everet)
146 Sebern Skiner
147 Holly Sexton
148 Elizabeth Sexton
149 Samuel Bell
22 150 Charles M. Hutcheson
151 Jefferson Hutcheson
152 Robert Kyle
153 Woodson A. Walker
154 Polly A. Edwards
155 John Couch (Moyers)
156 George McDonald
157 David W. Oldham (Buttren)
158 Decalb C. Melton

NOTE: There was no District 9 in 1870.

DISTRICT 10
(SMITHS CROSS ROADS P.O.)

1 1 Gideon T. Morgan
2 Lucinda Trewier
3 Nat Nichols
4 Eliza Picket
5 Henry Logan
6 Elis H. Morgan
7 Martha Macahan
8 William A. Templeton
2 9 Bryan R. McDonald (Spradling, Swafford)
10 Edley A. Jewel
11 Nancy McDonald
12 Calvin Morgan
13 Robert F Alexander (Everet)
14 Daniel Hodges
15 William B. Fleming
3 16 Margarette Jones
17 John O. David
18 Green A. McDonald
19 Aubern McDonald
20 Rebecca Moore
21 Elizabeth Whaley
22 James Jewell (McDonald)
23 George W. Walker
4 24 Martha G. Johnson
25 James G. Butram
26 John W. Williamson (Whaley)
27 Lucinda Morris
28 Rowlen F. McDonald
29 James Rogers (Byrely)

I hereby certify that the whole number of pages in the foregoing Return made by me on Schedule I is 143 [written on left margin "125 pages"] and that this Return has been well and truly made according to the tenor of my oath of office. John P. Walker, Assist Marshal
Dated October 7th 1870
Sub 24, East Tenn

1880 CENSUS

Supervisor's District No. 2, Enumeration District No. 108 Inhabitants in Civil District No. 12 [also in Districts 1 and 2] in the County of Rhea, State of Tennessee, enumerated by me on the 1st day of June, 1880. S. A. Pyott

NOTE A– The Census year begins June 1, 1879 and ends May 31, 1880

NOTE B– All persons will be included in the Enumeration who were living on the 1st day of June, 1880. No others will. Children born since June 1, 1880, will be omitted. Members of Families who have died since June 1, 1880 will be included.

NOTE C– Questions Nos 13, 14, and 23 are not to be asked in respect to persons under 10 years of age.

[The following instructions included the questions to be asked or columns to be filled in]

1 Dwelling houses numbered in order of visitation
2 Families numbered in order of visitation
3 The names of each person whose place of abode on 1st day of June 1880 was in this family
4 Color: White= W, Black=B, Mulatto=M, Chinese=C, Indian=I
5 Sex: Male=M, Female=F
6 Age at last birthday prior to June 1, 1880; If under 1 year, give months in fractions
7 If born within the census year, give month
8 Relationship of each person to the head of this family; whether wife, son, daughter, servant, boarder, or other
9 Single /
10 Married /
11 Widowed / Divorced=D
12 Married during Census year /
13 Profession, occupation or trade of each person, male or female
14 Number of months this person has been unemployed during the Census year
15 Is the person (on the day of the Enumerator's visit) sick or temporarily disabled, so as to be unable to attend to ordinary business or duties? If so, what is the sickness or disability?
16 Blind
17 Deaf & Dumb
18 Idiots
19 Insane
20 Maimed, Crippled, Bedridden, or otherwise disabled
21 Attended School within the Census year /
22 Cannot read
23 Cannot write
24 Place of Birth of this person, naming State or territory of US, or the Country, if of foreign birth
25 Place of Birth of the Father of this person, naming the State or territory, etc [same as above]
26 Place of Birth of the Mother of this person, etc. [same as above]

DISTRICT 12

1 1 Andrew J. Jolly (Foster)
2 Riley Edington
3 Wilson Churchill
4 Asa Whitehead
5 Francis Edgerton
6 Eastland Stratton
7 Samuel Lockerby
8 Chester Foster
9 Franklin Dagley
2 10 Martin Abbot
11 Vanburen Thompson
12 John Edwards
13 Elizabeth Dunlap
14 Obediah Brown
15 Henry Fortner
16 Isaac Morris
17 James Carney
18 Mary Coles (Dye)
19 Charles Jewett (Powel, Andrews)
3 20 Ebinezer Gooding
21 Hiram Huntington
22 Joachin Diare
23 Nelson Parmalee
24 Harbin Stebbing
25 Jere Shufelt [Shiflet]
26 Adison Lemons
27 David Dye
28 Marion Watson
4 29 James Brady
30 Jessee May (Fresby)
31 Richard Lemons
32 John Lemons
33 William Brown
34 William Revis
35 James McNeal
36 James Daniel
37 James Lemons
38 Samuel Lemons
5 39 Sampson Wolf
40 Eliza Loy
41 William Danill
42 Henry Ray
43 William Cox
44 Angeline Brady
45 Randolph Gibson
46 Edmond West
6 47 Samuel Baker
48 Robert Miller
49 Robert Clifton
50 Pleasant Monday
51 James Hayes (Brewer, Videtoe)
52 William Thompson
53 Peter Clifton
54 Amos Clifton
7 55 Duncan Grassham
56 Henry Roddy
57 David Fortner
58 Amos Gillespie

DISTRICT 1

8 59 Thomas West
60 John Short
61 Joe McKinney (Young)
62 Jasper McClarin
63 Syrene Thompson
64 Austin Evans
65 James Robinson (Vaughn)
66 Dilsie Robinson
67 Luke Heiskell
9 68 James Filyoe (Martin)
69 Burrell Pope
70 Bazelia Buinn
71 Samuel Wheeler
72 Mary Marsh
73 Alfred Marsh (Cook)
74 William Castleman (Darwin)
75 Jane Barton (Northrap)
76 Redman Crisp
10 77 Elvira Holloway
78 Moses Thompson
79 Luke Edington
80 William Filyoe
81 George Shaw
82 Samuel Holloway (Haws)
83 William Shelby
84 Nancy Scarbrough (Dunlap)
85 Houston Maxwell (Trout?)
11 86 Andrew Cawood (Scott)
87 Abner Dickey
88 William Smith
89 Benjmin Shelow (Sleep, Fletcher, Krichbaym)
90 John Duncan
91 William Dean
92 Sarah Evans (Locke)
93 John Robinson (Perkins, River)
12 94 Isaac Heiskell
95 Stephen Cawood (Craig, Moore, Warnack)
96 Sarah Waller
97 Malinda Queen
98 Archibald Mullens
99 Carington Woodson
100 Henry Cole
101 Pleasant Holloway
102 Aaron Marrs
13 103 Robert Hinds
104 Isaac Holloway
105 Major Holloway
106 William Treadaway
107 James Holloway
108 Columbus Gibson
109 William Shoop
110 David Roddy
111 Rebecca Waterhouse (Stinecipher, Brown)
112 Jessee Roddy (Marney, Woods)
14 113 William Roddy (Johnson)
114 Polk Brown (Shull)
115 Margaret Carter
116 Aaron Ray (West)
117 Jacob Roos (Clark)
118 Susan Roddy (Gillespie)
119 Gracie Roddy (Gillespie)
120 James Roddy
121 John Justice
15 122 George Roddy (Short, McCaleb)
123 James Johnson
124 Nettie Roddy (Day, Eskridge)
125 William Snelson
126 George Brown (Miller)
127 John Majors
128 Francis Majors (Underwood)
129 Amanda Bean
130 Nathan Whittenburg (Underwood)
131 Jacob Krichbaum (Harry)
16 132 Nancy Galion
133 Adam Kirklin (Selvage)
134 Levi Treadaway
135 Richard Garrison
136 Moses Miller
137 Wilburn Clark
17 138 Joel Dotson (Gilliam)
139 Hugh Ray
140 William Thompson (Reece)
141 Martin Ingle
142 Wade McFalls (Holloway, Reece)
143 James Thompson
144 Samuel Duncan
145 Major Gilliam
18 146 Benjamin Reece
147 David Pierce (Phillips)
148 John Hunt
149 Margaret Long
150 Zacharia Long
151 Hugh Heiskell (Gillespie)
152 Rebecca Hoyal (Evans, Whittenburg, Thompson)
153 Jacob Green
154 Asbury Cash
19 155 Samuel Knox
156 Sarah Lemons
157 Mary Dunlap
158 Carolin Webster
159 William Ward
160 James Thompson (Dunlap)
161 Malinda McClendon
162 Wesley Case (Shelby)
163 Caroline Locke (Broiles, Peters)
20 164 James Waterhouse
165 Franklin Waterhouse (Ferguson, Ware)

DISTRICT 2

21 167 George Foust
168 John Foust
169 John Gaunce
170 Joseph Zeigler
171 Jacob Dyer (Houston)
172 Susan Neal (Cox, Abernathy)
173 Robert Robinson (Gillespie, Gooseby, Wasson, Phillips)
22 174 James Monday
175 Nancy Peters
176 Andrew Bryson
177 John Bryson
178 Charles Mills
179 Joseph Peters
180 John Chadrick (Terry)
181 John Abernathy (Day, Cleag)
182 Eliza Abernathy (Brookman)
183 Andrew Anderson (Brown, Manis, Galbraith, McWhirter, Obien, Paris, Waterhouse)
23 184 Joel Crosby
185 Dwight Culver
186 Hosea Wasson
187 William Payne
188 Alexander Dye
189 James Howe (Wasson)
190 Preston Welch
24 191 John Wheeler
192 David Oansby
193 John Neal (Adkins, Darwin)
194 Franklin Duckworth
195 William Stewart
196 Thomas Robinson (Henegar)

24 197 Martha Marsh
198 Jere Wasson (Williams, Harrison, Daniel, Coles, Jones, Brown,Hinch, Gooseby, Smuthers, Ramsey, Sampler)
25 199 John Pyott (McClendon)
200 Samuel Dickey (Kelly)
201 Lutitia Smith (Detherage, Hinch)
202 George Wassom
26 203 John Brown (Rose)
204 Nile Broyles (Eastland,Ray,Smith)
205 William Wyrick (Fine)
206 James Mitchell
207 William Crabtree
208 Smith Brady (Sellers)
209 George Pinion (Kirby)
27 210 Green McDaniel
211 Joseph Thompson (Wroe)
212 Thomas Green
213 Miles Prestwood
214 William Godsey
215 Wm Wilson (Hardbarger)
216 John Roberts
217 Samuel Miller
218 Madison Simpson
219 George Minic (Fraley)
28 220 Peter Dooley (Gilespie)
221 Isaac Fine (Pass)
222 Henry Giles
223 Lucinda Gilespie (Andrews, Donaldson)
224 Samuel Gilespie (Upton,McCaleb, Jolley)
224? James Yancy
225 Calvin Gilespie (Henderson, Donaldson, Capps)
226 Nancy Gilespie (Hampton)
227 Nathan Yearwood (Upton, Rucker, Henderson, Glass)
29 228 William McCarrol (Burnet)
229 William Tarwater (Clark, Whitlock, Jolley, Hill)
230 Jeff Gillespie
231 James Tarwater
232 Edward Billings
233 John Donaldson
234 Joseph Jones
235 Marion Dooley
236 John Tinker (Green)
237 Jessee West (Swift)
30 238 Moses Stewart
239 Lee Calvin (Green)
240 Timothy Winton (Franklin, Cate)
241 James Drake (Stevens)
242 William Gray
243 Elizabeth Dotson
244 Angeline Jolly
245 James Honeycut (Derrick)
31 246 John Lasson
247 James Roberts
248 Robert McGowen
249 John Jones
250 William Thomas (Brown)
251 Andrew Moore (Brown)
252 Martin Necling
253 Lee Watson
254 Sarah Aiken
255 Robert Bell
32 256 Thomas McLemore
257 Scruggs Yearwood (Hodge, Hatfield, Scruggs)

258 Benjamin Jemesom
259 Jack Suddeth (Biles, Jones)
260 John Whitehead
261 Israel Smith
262 Thomas Miller (Long)
263 Arch McCaleb (Gillespie)
264 Charles Hughes
265 Albert Peak
33 266 Eli Gillespie
267 Albert McCaleb
268 John Boles (Hembree)
269 William Boles (Firzgerald)
270 Daniel Boles
271 Jeff Gillespie
272 Phillip Gillespie
34 273 Wash Donaldson (Gillespie)
274 Hiram Donaldson
275 Sarah Gillespie
276 George Farmer
277 James Hood
278 Rufus Hood
35 279 Joseph Hood
280 Robert Hood
281 Micajah Clack (Baker)
282 Samuel Baker
283 Spencer Clack
284 Jessee Stinecipher
285 Leonard Long
286 Miles McCristian
287 Granville Hurst (Long)
288 Fanny Gray
36 289 Andrew Gibson
290 Garret Talent
291 Edward Talent
292 George Eldridge
293 Coleman Smith
294 Henry Jolly
295 Wesley Bell
296 James Casire
37 297 Rebecca Paul (Osborne, Rucker)
298 Leander Clark
299 Russel Miller
300 William Owens
301 Albert Morris
302 Thomas Miller
303 Emiline Garrison
304 William Dotson
38 305 Stephen Breeding (Thompson)
306 James Owens
307 Calm Wilkey
308 John Hurst
309 Pink Wester
310 Elijah Dyer
311 William Hashbarger
312 John Baldwin
313 Betsy Hashbarger
314 Jessee Shipley
315 James Brady (Thurman)
39 316 Hamilton Ponder
317 Shep Donaldson
318 Martin McCullough
319 Jessee Boles
320 Daniel Farmer (Caroll)
321 John Boles
322 Luke Stansbury (Fine)
40 323 James Gilliam
324 Franklin McCabe (Long)
325 Jessee Ingle
326 Thomas Ingle (Browning)
327 John Bracher (Monday)
328 Thomas Cash

41 329 James Cash
330 Henry DeVault (Cash, Wright)
331 Margaret Foust
332 John McCarrol
333 Margaret Breeding (Reece)
334 Justin Kerby (Washing)
335 Samuel Craighead
336 Joseph Bryant
337 Nancy Thompson
338 James Pass
42 339 Thomas Thompson
340 Jessee Thompson
341 William Martin
342 William Bell
343 Margaret Pyott (Durham)
344 Milo Holloway

"I certify that I have thus completed the enumeration of the Districts assigned me, and that the returns have been duly and truthfully made in accordance with law and my oath of office." S.A. Pyott, Enumerator
Rhea Springs, Rhea Co., Tenn.
June 22, 1880

DISTRICT 4

"Surveyor's Dist. No. 2, Enumeration Dist. No. 109, June 1, 1880." B.F. Holloway

1 1 J.W. Caldwell (Marney,Elliott, Cates)
2 B.F. Roberson (Aiken)
3 John Franklin
4 J.M. Caldwell
5 Manerva Caldwell
6 Bennet Franklin
7 James Monroe
8 R.W. Holloway (Hays)
2 9 Adam Watson (McDonald)
10 Henry McDonald
11 R.C. Lyons
12 B.T. Waldo(?) (Thompson)
13 M.L. Mee(?)
14 Henry Thurman
15 William T. Mee(?)
16 John Vaughn
17 William Harrison(?)
3 18 L.W. Ferguson
19 James Monday
20 John Wright
21 William Mitchell
22 S.B. Ferguson
23 L.P. Essex (White)
24 William Wyrick (White)
25 J.T. Ferguson
26 William McCullough
4 26 Alfred Wyrick
27 Phebe Wimpey
28 John Roberts
29 John Essex
30 H.H. Miller
31 J.T. Miller
32 H.(?) Drury(?)
5 33 Liche(?) Wyrick
34 A.J. Wyrick (Thompson)
35 Henry Beard (Reese)
36 Noah Duncan
37 Farley Brady (Martin)
38 W.W. Barton

5 39 Nath Harrison (Neal)
40 C.H. Terry
41 Pryor Dyer
6 42 Jane Hicks
43 Stephen Knight
44 Isaac Runyon
45 B.M. Collins (Dyer)
46 Newton Hicks
47 Richard Wilkey
48 William Wilkie
7 49 Gilbert Reed (Fugate, Sharp)
50 John Reed
51 John Jones
52 W.B. Schoolfield
53 P.G. Mitchel
54 David Mitchell
55 David Mitchell
56 T.C. Darwin
57 H.S. Amos (Filyan)
58 R.C.M. Cunnyngham (Blevins)
8 59 Samuel Blevins
60 A. Griffith (Rhea)
61 William Cates
62 J.W. Duncan
63 L.J. Hainira or Haines
64 Jessee Dickey (Hays, Renfro, Prigmore)
65 Daniel Odem (Gass)
66 J.W. Wassom
67 James Pearson
9 68 Calvin Janow (Taylor)
69 G.R. Baldwin
70 D.M. Copenhan (Edwards)
71 S.T. Blevins (Holloway, Mills, Eidson, Essex, Marritt)
72 Jack Davis
73 J.H. Gross
74 Evander Thurman
75 J.W. Thompson (Clark)
10 76 John Lee (Feniran, Tillery)
77 A. or H. Essex
78 G.W. Duckworth
79 Oliver Lyons (Maples)
80 James Real (Wasson)
81 Alfred Shelby
82 C.C. Hite
83 Virginia Leuth (Thompson, Reynolds, Alexander)
11 84 J.W. Casta(?) (Reed)
85 Harvey Johnson
86 J.I. Shilleton
87 G.W. Marshall
88 David Meyer
89 Charles Reed (Thompson)
90 Perry Williams
91 W. F. Rose
12 92 J.(?) C. Casey
93 I.L. Philpot
94 Julia Kelley (Cox, Castelberry, Kelley, Tucker)
95 E. Cunnyngham (Files, Day, Gillespie, Eaves)
96 H.L. Gillespie
97 W.M. Gillespie
98 T.(?) Rudd
99 Thomas McCuiston
100 C.A. Brown (Garrison)

DISTRICT 3

13 101 A. McClendon
102 Calvin Henry
103 Posey Marshall
104 Robert Turner
105 E. Marl (Canada)
106 Charles Brady
107 Thompson(?) Wright
14 108 A. Hodges (Wright)
109 Thomas Foust
110 Pinkney Barton
111 Gus Murphey
112 J.D. Stenis
113 H.R. Porter (Harshaw)
114 S.H. Coal or Cole (Browder)
15 115 J.F. Mee
116 Thomas Sneed (Rudd)
117 Sam Walker (McBivins?)
118 James Smith
119 Elija McMurry
120 William Hodges (Milligan)
121 N.B. Foust
122 L. Crawford
123 N.E. Rhea (Smith)
16 124 Joseph Wright
125 Haly Wassum
126 J.C.(?) Wilson
127 S.A. Johnson
128 James Majors
129 James Wilson
17 130 A.G. Bryant
131 John Clack
132 Robert G. Cook
133 S.M. Cook (Rayburn)
134 George Walker
135 M.M. Thompson (Bryant)
136 A. Brewye(?) (Kelly)
18 137 Amos Peak
138 H. Janow
139 J.T. Lankford
140 J.W. Lankford
141 Luke Murat (Huston)
142 Susan Chattin
143 S.W. Tindell
144 William Clack
145 Levi Rudd
146 L.M. Foust
19 147 J.T. Smith
148 A.G. Ward
149 Susan Hale
150 Jeff Marshall
151 William Hawrd [Howard]
152 A.H. Miller
153 D. Smith
154 Nancy Mitchell
155 James Janow
20 156 J.? Kincanon (Lauderdale)
157 G.W. Wade
158 John L. Ramsey (Henry)
159 Lossen Cole
160 S.S. Ramsey
161 William Lowe
162 N.J. Collins
163 S.M. Patton
164 J.T. Shelton (Duncan)
165 J.M. Sheton [Shelton]
21 166 D.M. Hutsell
167 E. Kembrough (Breeding)
168 W.H. Long
169 Henry Rhea
170 Lawson Rhea
171 J.H. Erwin
172 Edmunds Aiken
173 J.C. True
22 174 David Davis
175 H. Baldwin
176 John Jarvis
177 F.C. Fugate
178 J.A. Scroggins
179 Peyton White
180 James Ewing
181 M.M. Cagle
23 182 W. Cagle
183 S. Saphels
184 S.D. Teftalen
185 J.C. Tefestaler
186 N.J. Vinyard (McCoslen?)
187 E.D. Hart (Breeding)
188 Henry Feulks
24 189 J.E. Cleage
190 L.M. Johnson
191 James Kelly
192 Susan Hitt
193 George W. Johnson (Leuty)
194 —utin Heck(?)
195 F.J. Webb (Richards?)
196 G.W. Fielding
197 John Grey (Webb)
25 198 James Saphels
199 Robert Phillips
200 Clebe Fugate
201 E.S. Fugate (Wilson)
202 James Perry
203 J.H. Harwood
204 W.M. Fugate
26 205 Robert Perkins
206 F. Russell
207 John Wilson
208 Henry Young
209 Frank Milican
210 William Giles
211 S.S. Wilkey
212 C. Smith (McMurray)
27 213 S.O. Foust (James)
214 Thomas Doud (Nelson)
215 Thomas McPherson (Wright)
216 James Garrison
217 Ruth Harwood
218 J.F. Dosson
28 219 B.F. Dosson
220 Henry Ward
221 G.W. Ward
222 I.S. Ward
223 Sam Miller
224 H. Kisler
225 G.M. Kisler
226 Mae Campbell
227 L.M. Parks
228 J. I.(?) Dagley
229 Peter(?) Blink(?)
29 230 Charles Thurman
231 E.L. Melbia
232 Willis Drake
233 E. Janow
234 Clabe Smith
235 Samuel Smith
236 Thomas Rhea

29 237 A.C. O'Neal (Janow)
238 Mary Harwood (Blythe)
30 239 Nat Jones(?)
240 Lewis Rhea
241 R.M. Davis
242 James Hale or Cole
243 James Voils
244 Robert Trentham
245 D. Broyles
246 I.N. Broyles

DISTRICT 4

31 247 C. Holloway
248 S.E. Holland
249 Caroline Brady
250 W.(?) R.(?) Renden(?)
251 Thomas Godbehere (Whittenburg)
252 Thomas Godbehere
253 Calvin Neal
254 F. McCullough
255 W.M. McCullough
256 Calvin McCoy
257 James Barnett (Cox)
32 258 B. ? Vaughn
259 W.H. Long(?)
260 John Cox (Perry)
261 William Watson
262 James Eseal
263 E. Thompson
264 A.M. Whittenburg
265 Seth Alley
33 266 S. Holloway
267 Mary Caldwell
268 T.P. Sullivan
269 S.H. Miller
270 H.M. Miller
271 Sam Litel
272 J.D. Wheeler
273 Sam Walker
274 Tom Holloway
275 I.N. Whittenburg (Torbett)
34 276 David Walker
277 M. Rose
278 Horace Smith
279 William Rector
280 Tate Smith
281 E.M. Smith
282 William True
283 Brox Welch(?)
284 James Wyrick
35 285 W. McClendon
286 John McClendon (Brown, Ivings)
287 E.M. Torbett (Cook)
288 John Philyan (Quillon)
289 Bob Sneed
290 J.L. McPherson (Long, Talley)
291 Frances Carter
292 Joseph McPherson
36 293 B.F. Holloway
294 Jeff Brooks (Gardenhire)
295 P.W. Brooks
296 J.P. Holloway
297 Henry Smith
298 L(?) J. Henderson
299 W.T. Gass (Thompson)

DISTRICT 11

37 300 John Sullivan
301 David Oldham
302 W. Morgan (Gothard, Gates?)
303 J.B. Evart
304 William Walker
305 F.R. Morgan
306 J.M. Hall
38 307 Charles Morgan
308 G.W. Campbell
309 Burton Peirce (Gothard)
309[sic] L.C. Wright
310 A.L. Cunnyngham
311 Deadrick Sykes (White)
312 Pleasant Snow
39 313 F.B. Hughes
314 J.P. Walker
315 F.M. Cass
316 H.D. Chambers
317 John Bridgemon
318 M.D. Duanyng
319 L.C. Gothard
320 Thomas Edmundson
40 321 J.B. Evart
322 James Burwick
323 E.L. Campbell (Evert)
324 Martha Campbell
325 L.G. Rogers
326 W.F. Morgan
327 Houston Morgan
328 Wm McPherson (Burwick)

41 329 J.M. Burwick
330 Walker Hughes (McCaroy?)
42 331 Thomas Barton
332 J.A. Thompson
333 H.L.W. Ferguson
334 E.A. Foster
335 Millis Owens
336 Riley Dagley
337 James Ivins
338 A.J. Trentham
340 J.M. McPherson (Thompson)
43 341 John Thompson (Mee,Holloway)

"I certify that the foregoing is a correct list of the persons residing in the 109 Enumeration Dist of the 2nd Super-visors Dist of Tennessee, comprising the 3rd, 4th, and 11th Civil Districts of Rhea County on the 1st day of June 1880 made by me in compliance with the sixth section of the Act of Congress appointed Ap 20, 1880."

B.F. Holloway, Enumerator

DISTRICT 5

1 1 A.J. Pritchett (Meanalley, Webb)
2 H.D. Webb
3 G. M. Smith
4 J.C. Phillips
5 E. Denton
6 T.J. Pelfrey
7 Mary Hurst
8 G.W. Busby(?)
9 W.H. Eaton
2 10 J.M. Houston (Linn)
11 P. Collins
12 Sirena J. Gentry
13 Moses F. Moore (Brown?)
14 L.M. Swafford
15 J.W. Barnett
16 Bailey Minix (Gambell)
17 Sid Smith
18 Moses Hughes
3 18[sic] James Jackson
19 John H. Busby
20 Thomas W. Busby
21 John Busby
22 Elbert D. Pierce (Thompson)
23 David Reed
24 James B. Blevins (Piercce)
25 Nathan Watson
26 L.C. Ferguson
4 27 Thomas J. Bramlett
28 George W. Edmonds
29 Jones Boofer
30 John P. Fritts
31 Caswell Stout
32 James Jones
33 James P. Collins
34 Leander West
35 James W. Landreth
36 Jacob M. Hamilton
5 37 John H. Hamilton
38 James G. Broyles
39 John W. Green
40 Rufus M. Sharp
41 Ed M. Ganaway
42 William Compton
43 Darus Broyles
44 William C. Webb
45 Banister C. Smith
6 46 Robert Sneed
47 J.S. Evans
48 Izzabel Cordial
49 Daniel Gllespie
50 Robert Evens
51 Robert C. Broyles
52 Taylor Jones
53 C.R. Robinson
54 Ann R. Dodson
7 55 Sherard Gay
56 R.W. Gambell
57 Samuel J. Brown
58 Jacob F. Shelley
59 Sarah Smith
60 Banister Coffer
61 Jesse C. Abercrombie
62 Martin L. Loftis
63 Harris James
64 Edward L. Gregg
65 Charles Darwin
66 Edward Ody
67 Jerry Denton
68 Sarah A. Caldwell
8 69 James Caldwell
70 Elvira Beevers (Mason)
71 George Howerton
72 Sarah Howerton
73 M.J. Darwin (Swafford)
74 Thomas W. Smith
75 John M. Bramlett
76 James Coss
77 Aaron Evans
78 Alexander Coffer
79 Joseph Hoge

9 79[sic] John Brewer (Garrison)
80 Mary Enous(?)
81 Rufus Calahan
82 W.G. Allen (McCroy)
83 R. McDonald
84 White Morgan
85 Andrew Brown
86 William P. Thomisson
87 Samuel Doran
88 H.H. Gambill (Norman, Reed, Cahan)
10 89 Cela J. Revis
90 Nathan W. Rice
91 Elvira Paine (Colville)
92 J.W. Porter
93 F.J. Paine (Walker)
94 Robert W. Crow
95 David Kyle
96 David Hodge
97 Houston A. Hodge
11 98 James H. Scott
99 John N. Steel
100 William M. Gravett
101 Harris R. Phillips
102 Joseph M. Fry
103 Charley Gebts(?)
104 Hugh Cruz(?)
105 William Carson
106 William T. Darwin (Cox, Collins)
107 James Denton
108 Alfred Dyer

DISTRICT 6

[NOTE: Households and family numbers were a mess in this district. B.J.B.]

12 109/109 Henry H. Ryan
110/110 Thos A. Houston (Lawson)
111/111 Leander Pierce
112/112 James C. Kenedy
113/113 Samuel Day
114/114 Andy Kelley
115/115 Andus Johnson
116/116 Henry A. Pearman
116 Mary Rudd
117/117 Syntha Wilkey
118/118 Edward T. Collins
119/119 John A. Porter
13 120/120 Samuel L. Coval
121 Elizabeth Harrison
121/121 William R. Henry
122/122 James West
? James L. Young
123 Joseph A. Killough
123/124 David Davis
124/125 Muck Medain
125/126 Thomas Waterhouse
126/127 Sarah J. Day
127/128 David Byrd
14 128/129 James H. Locke
129/130 Mary Robinson
130/131 Robert C. Walker
130/130[130/132] Elder Kibble
131/133 Isaach Brown
131/134 Jinnie Campbell
132/135 Frank Foust
? / ? James O. Taylor
133/135 Jack Johnson (Day)
134/136 David C. Rose
15 135/137 Samuel Frazier
136/138 James B. Walker
137/139 Mary Richie
138/140 Cyrus Henry (Wassom, Smith, Gass, Hackney)
139/141 Martha J. Suttles
140/142 Z.L Sneed (Riggle)
16 141/143 Christopher Wilkey
142/144 Robert W. Lillard
143/145 Margarett Guin
144/145 John H. Travis
145/147 Harvey Roddye
146/149 John Achinson
147/150 Isom Keith
148/151 James M. Martin
149/152 E.T. Trusley
150/153 Joel L. Henry
151/154 Anderson Parker
152/155 John Coxey
17 153/156 Samuel Parker
154/157 Newton L. Henry
155/158 Asbury Locke
156/159 Joseph B. Dodd
156/160 Jackson Thurman
157/161 Elijah A. Riggle
158/162 Peter G. Roddye
159/163 James D. Roddye
160/164 Mary J. Locke (Wade)
161/165 Lewis Delonis (Davis)
162/166 James Campbell
163/167 Martha Roddye
164/168 John Mise
18 165/169 Joseph Brown Sr.
166/170 James H. Brown
167/170 William B. Brown
168/171 Ben B. Davis
169/172 Thomas Swafford
170/173 Jane Woddy
171/174 James W. Hill
172/175 Elbert L Cox (Burwick)
19 172/176 Arter M. Potter
173/177 William Murphey
174/178 Caleb Gravett
175/179 Wyatt A. Day
175/180 Thos Peterson (Wyatt)
176/181 George P. Parker
177/182 William Harris
178/182 Jack Gillespie
179/183 Samuel Travis
20 180/184 James W. Rice (Harden)
181/185 Samuel H. Fraley
181/186 Squire B. Fraley
182/186 James A. Fraley
183/187 Henry A. Crawford (Wyatt, Gillespie)
184/188 W.P. Thomsson
185/189 James W. Dodd
21 185/189 John T. Roddye (Colville)
186/190 Harriet Waterhouse
187/191 John T. Collins
187/191 Simon Wyrick (Cumbo, Robards)
188/191 Jas W. Gillespie (Rawlings, Johnson, Waterhouse, Mariott)
189/192 Elijah L. Rudd
190/193 John W. Young
191/194 Richard W. Colville (Paine)

TOWN OF WASHINGTON

Madison Street
22 1 N.Q. Allen
2 Albert D. Earley
3 John James
4 T.N.L. Cunnyngham
5 Robert L. Allen (Tomisson, Darwin, Sanford)
6 Valentine Allen
7 Thomas D. Tilley
8 Francis Cambers [Chambers]
9 John Howard (Bean, Mason)
10 Sarah J. Parks
11 John Peterson (Load, Frazur)
23 12 W.S. Gillespie (Chadick, Freeman, Womack)

Jefferson Street
13 Nathaniel H. Smith
14 Martha J. Wyatt
15 Pulaski Killough

High Street
16 William Campbell
17 William H. Campbell
18 Orlena Nanney (Henry)

Rural Street
19 John A. Blevins
20 Isac Bird (Clark)
21 John Price
24 22 Jas A. Howard (McDonald)
23 Jacob Dillman
24 Robert J. Killough
25 Eliza Frazier
26 Jane Wammock
27 C.S. Killough

Jail House
John W. Opal, Jailor (Webb–nw)
Lewis Moore, prisoner

[END OF TOWN OF WASHINGTON]

DISTRICT 6 (CONTINUED)

25 186/190 Louisa J. Laurey (Crow, Rogers)
187/191 Barley Craig
188/192 James M. Carney (Johnson)
189/193 John M. Howard
190/194 Alfred Locke
191/195 Sallie Webb
192/196 Benjamin T. Zigler
193/197 Robert A. Gillespie (Frazier)
194/198 Samuel J.A. Frazier
195/199 James Frazier

DISTRICT 10

26 195/200 Viney E. Wright
196/201 Daniel N. Powell
197/202 Johnathan Mulky
198/203 James Rogers
198/204 Sarah A. Blye
199/205 Peter Howerton
200/206 Alfred Etherly (Cowan)
201/207 John Trusley (Rawlins)
202/208 James Costalo
203/209 Elaigon(?) McClendon
204/210 John W. Williamson
27 205/211 Levena Buttram (Green)
206/212 Martha G. Johnson (Wheeler)

27 207/213 George D. Moore
208/214 James M. Benson (Harris)
209/214 John Brewer
210/215 Enoch F. Suddeth
? ? Joe A. Shannon
28 211/216 Willi M. Shannen
212/217 Sam McDonald
213/218 Jeff Campbell
214/219 Nancy McDonald (Sawyers)
215/220 Isaac Dyer
216/221 Benjamin Dyer
217/222 Calvin Morgan
218/223 Ostear Barton
219/224 John D. Morgan
220/225 Elias H. Morgan
29 221/226 W.A. Templeton (Moore)
222/227 R.F. McDonald
223/228 Charles M. Todd
224/229 George W. Walker
225/230 H.O. Leuty
226/231 Lewis McDonald
226/232 Samuel Bergans
226/233 Harris Copeland
227/234 Robert F. Tallant
30 227/234 William N. Morgan
227/235 William S. Hail
227/236 Martha J. Hail
228/237 Margaret James
228/238 Mary A. Gothard
229/239 Margaret F. Allen
230/239 John O. David
231/240 Louisa Ryon (Randolph)
232/241 Sarah A. Mariott (Kelley)
233/242 William B. Benson
234/243 Rolen Denhasn (Wimpler)
31 234/244 Joseph Broyles
235/245 William Broyles

"I certify that I have this day completed the enumeration of the district assigned me and that the returns have been duly and faithfully made in accordance with law and my oath of office the 7th day of July 1880."
John Howard, Enumerator

DISTRICT 8
(DAYTON P.O.)

1 1 T.A. Allen (Riddle, Day)
2 J.J. Abel
3 Mary Ann Abel
4 W.T. Broyles (Flemming)
5 George Johnson
6 S.D. Bridgeman
7 Johnath Talbert
8 F.A. Fisher
9 W.A. Weigle
10 M.S. Morrison (Abel)
2 11 H.C. Rose
12 I.N. Hope
13 William Morgan
14 Lihu Baker
15 W.Q. Zigler
16 S.D. Broyles
17 Daniel Hodge
18 A. Johnson (Fleming?)
19 Larkin Gothard
20 W.N. Ault (Pope)
3 21 William H. Travis
22 J.S. Crannion(?) (Patton)
23 N.D. Reed
24 J.E. Ingle
25 S.W. Hutchenson
26 B.W.H. Louis
27 J.H. Jewell
28 B.F. Walker
29 R.F. Alexander
4 29 Joel Rogers
30 J.S. Dungen
31 W.A. Johnson (Flemings)
32 John A. Foust
33 Louis Morgan
34 F.J. Miller
35 Pryor Barton
36 F.M. Morrison
5 36 W.D. Pealer
37 Joseph Foster
38 M.S. Riddle
39 M.H. Hughes
40 J.H. Cox (Abel)
41 J.K.P. Abel
42 J.R. Abel
43 W.G. Renon
6 44 A.S. Abel
45 R.F. Land (Montgomery, Gaerett)
46 J.M. Kelley
47 I.A. Martin
48 N. Marler
49 T.J. Kelley (Alexander)
50 C.T. Bean (Gray)
51 J.W. Canse
52 S.(?)R. Rogers (Walker)
7 53 Francis Bower
54 John Coregan
55 J.A. Kelly
56 R.O. Jordon
57 J.H. Bankston
58 C.W. Abel (Hinch)
59 Mary R. Abel
60 C.C. Myres
61 J.J. Kelley
8 62 J.H. Hickman
63 Robert Edwards
64 J.W. Green
65 A.J. Standifer
66 Jane Walker
67 Tom Phillips
68 Cash Dysen (Roberson)
69 John Hickman
70 W.R. Johns
71 A. Hickman
9 72 T.B. Coulter
73 T.J. Coulter
74 Rufus Cauley (Lamb)
75 W.A. Green
76 F.M. Capps Jr.
77 S.I. Rogers (Bean)
78 Wesly Rains
79 W.H. Morgan
10 80 R.T. Coulter (Chambers, Dyland)
81 W.B. Nicholds
82 A.N. Denigan
83 A.S. Alexander
84 R.T. Martin (Hoge)
85 C.S. Dungan
86 W.J. Banks (Lautermilk, Cates)
87 J.J. Merill
11 88 C.A. Morgan
89 Sam McDonald
90 B.F. Rigsby
91 M.J. Morgan
92 H.F. Morgan
93 M.G. Gipson
94 G.H. Debord (Gates, Shannon)
95 W.A. Yarber
96 H.H. Chadwick
12 97 W.A. Walker
98 J.F. Tallent (Grass, Tallent)
99 W.B. Gothard
100 W.M. Foust (Waldrup)
101 Mary Morgan
102 A.T. Nicholds
103 W.D. Avrett (Morgan)
104 G.H. Burchard
105 H. Burchard
106 T.H. Montgomery
13 107 C.T. Montgomery
108 J.A. Morgan
109 John Chadwick
110 J.W. Morgan
111 A.S. Morgan
112 Katharine Foust
113 James Moore
114 Y.P. Oldham
115 J.F. Perry
116 T.R. Green
14 117 H.C. Rogers
118 John Jewell
119 Sallie Flemmings
120 Jane Rankin
121 W.J. Cofer
122 L.A. Smith
123 J.H. Rogers (Lock,Bell,Valentine, Nathan(?), Gillespie)
124 Pat Waley(?)
15 125 Hanah Bryson
126 M. Mayers (Gregory)
127 J.O. Johnson (Corvin,Gass,Hoge)
128 J.T. Corvin
129 Isaac Sherly
130 William R. Moyer
131 S.A. Sherley
132 Dan Royston
16 133 John Spears
134 Eliza McGuire
135 W.O. Shipley (Hutchens, Lyons)
136 G.W. Smedley
137 Charly Keith (McDonald)
138 F.A. Harris (Martin)
139 A. Dixon (Terry)
140 Jeff Hutchenson
17 141 Munro Hughes
142 S.F. McDonald
143 George W. Whitfield
144 T.C. Travis
145 J.C. Butram (Morgan)
146 Joseph Bell
147 H.C. Collins
148 Mary Bell
149 W.F. Trusly
18 150 M.A. Sexton
151 Sam Bell (Young)
152 William Elleson
153 J.P. Sexton
154 W.D. Byrly (Suttels)
155 Elizabeth Sexton
156 James Crommin(?)
157 William Henderson
158 R. Kyle
19 159 William Hail
160 Jock Keith
161 A.J. Bankston

19 162 Milo Sexton
163 M. McClendon
164 P.M. Corvin
165 J.L. Kiser
20 166 Thomas Dobbs (Corvin)
167 J.M. Dobbs
168 John Corvin (J.A. Gothard ?)
169 E. Gothard
170 W.A. Steal
171 W.H. Hickman
172 Joseph Rose
173 H.M. Hensly
174 A.C. Morgan
175 P.T. Foust
176 H.D. Riddle (Green)
21 177 J.L. Nicholds
178 Godfre Noie(?) or Nase(?)
179 Isaac Nase(?)
180 W.H. Smith
181 Laidy Darwin
182 J.M. Jewell
183 T.M. Bolen
184 R.H. Jewell (Balew)
185 G.B. Brady (Lindsey, Smith)

DISTRICT 7

22 186 John Robertson
187 John F. Bolen
188 H.M. Perser (Manard, Lauson)
189 R.N. Dyre
190 W.A. Brayde
191 M.R. Romines (Barly)
192 H.M. Walker
193 W. Wallar
194 Smith Moore
23 195 Martha McCoy
196 Moses Tuck
197 Martha Dixon
198 S.J. Shaver
199 T.F. Shaver
200 Jasper Byrly
201 J.O. Shaver (McAllen)
24 202 A. Auther
203 A. Frazier
204 Joe Dodd
205 B.J. Franklin
206 H.F. Matherly
207 Joe Morgan (Byrely, Watts)
208 T.S. Franklin (Huskins)
209 John Hausly
210 W. Dryemon (Hubbard)
211 A. Rawlings
25 212 J. Prater (Bramlett)
213 T.J. Knight (Clemmens, Majors)
214 Sam Byrely
215 Jacob Byerley
216 S.R. Hausly
217 J.E. Hausly
218 M. Chumly
219 Sam Hensly (Bajed)
220 G.M.D. Spence
26 221 Stephen Spence
222 A.A. Morgan
223 F.M.C. Broyles
224 David Moore
225 Jery Whaly
226 J.A. Early (Erwin, Rogers)
227 John Taylor
228 James Day
27 229 T.M. Jewell (Crawford)
230 J.A. Bajed
231 Albie Spence
232 James Spence
233 J.R. Crawford (Garrison, Dixon, Griffen)
234 R. Knight
235 R.O. Purser
236 P.M. Purser
237 Wily Logan
28 238 Elys Mackadow
239 W.B. Purser
240 James Prator
241 N.G. Moore
242 A.W. Powell
243 T.P. Cambon (Spyatt?, Ives)
244 Rolly McDonald
29 245 M.S. Gambell (Reuess?)
246 W.A. Kelley (Singleton)
247 John Smith
248 William R. Smith
249 S.L. Shaver
250 Nancy Grice
251 G.H. Ryon
252 W.J. Smith

DISTRICT 9

30 253 S.L. Henderson
254 T.H. McDonald
255 T.J. Mathis
256 C.F. Henderson
257 William Henderson
258 Calvin Sharp
259 A. Jordan
260 Isaac Jolley (Burdett)
261 Gid Sharp (McMillin)
31 262 James Dathrage (Giddon)
263 D. Kennedy
264 J.E. McMury (Wyott)
265 Rector Ganaway
266 M.A. Ganaway
267 Peter Minnik
268 E.E. Gittkens
269 C.L. Cobb
270 W.H. Miller
271 John Coxey (Marshall)
32 272 W.T. Purser
273 Mary Dyril
274 H.R. Rains (Castelbery)
275 James Taylor / Taylor James
276 Tom Good
277 T.J. Kiker
278 H. Arther
279 W.B. Fisher
280 A.C. Chatin

[NOTE: No summay statement appeared at end of District 9. H.B. Benson was the enumerator]

1900 CENSUS

DISTRICT 12
(GRANDVIEW P.O.)
Nathaniel L. Brown, Enumerator

179A 1 1 Robert Reed
2 2 Thomas Cary
3 3 David Billingsly (Robinson)
4 4 Bidgan(?) Hubbard
5 5 Mahan(?) Taylor
6 John F. Feree
6 7 Jane Skul
7 8 Nelson Higby
8 9 Nelson Highby Jr.
9 10 Mary N. Juett [Jewtt]
10 11 Charles Hawk (Quick)
11 12 Moulton Cammaris
13 Elbert Goadder
12 14 Anna Huntington(?)
13 15 Thomas Meariet
14 16 Mervin(?) Thomas
179B 15 17 Wilm Clark (Dana)
16 18 Almy Childs
17 19 Martar Abbit
18 20 Hairny(?) Hoyl(?)
19 21 Martan Pattan
20 22 Ben(-?-) Bengerman (Hart)
21 23 Thomas Pope
22 24 Laran Sawyer (Diper)
23 25 Emma Tannsel(?)
24 26 Ellen Tannsel(?)
25 27 Julli Kirkler
26 28 Charles Califf
27 29 Estrell Smith
180A 28 30 Lafayette L. Barton
29 31 Frank Sawers
30 32 Danie Allender
31 33 George Mars
34 George Mars Jr.
32 35 Isaac Mars (Parmer)
33 36 Wash McFaniles(?)
34 37 Dan Edward
35 38 Susan Edward
36 39 Shuman(?) Edward
37 40 Sam Jolly
38 41 Anderson Jolly Jr.
39 42 Leander Forster(?)
180B 40 43 Blanch Franklin
41 44 Jestas Forstar (Daniel,Allen)
42 45 Charles Stubbin
43 46 Len Staring
44 47 Cilia Parmerlee (Philip)
45 48 Mary Cash
46 49 Larance Sandrans
47 50 Nannie Robberts
48 51 Henry Hileary
49 52 Sam Wolf
50 53 Robert L.(?) Gentry

180B 51 54 Rilley Danals
52 55 Wilum Furguson
53 56 Wilum G. Taylor
181A 54 57 Sarah Brock
55 58 Lafayette Burnett
56 59 Earl ? Taylor
57 60 Mary Brady
58 61 arlow Reed
59 62 John Crens(?)
60 63 Plas Brady
181B 61 64 John D. Allen (Lay, Burnett)
62 65 Johnson West (Gillin)
63 66 John Henry(?) Gass (Clife?)
64 67 John Dunlap
65 68 Wilum M. Bauldin
66 69 Wilum J. Jolley
182A 67 70 Wilum Darnals(?)
68 71 Charles Mandy
69 72 Wilum Vittila(?)
70 73 Vigia(?) Lodan(?)
71 74 James Loden
72 75 Sarah Evens
73 76 Plas(?) Monday
182B 74 77 Randolph Gibson
75 78 Samuel Ray
76 79 James Ray
77 80 Henry Ray
78 81 Henry Coolmill(?)
79 82 Samuel Lemmon (Dannels)
80 83 Adison Lemans
81 84 James Hays

Non-residens in District 12
(no household numbers)

Milo Taylor
Charles Abbitt
Charles Gentry
Jem Jansan
Blanchy Lockwood
Jessie Cash
James Craft

DISTRICT 1
Nathaniel L. Brown, Enumerator

183A 82 85 Macey Miller
83 86 Frank Tap(?)
84 87 John Bean
85 88 Amos(?) Clifton
86 89 Sarah Whitenburg
87 90 Lee Waulker
88 91 James Pryor(?)
89 92 John Hips
183B 90 93 Robert B. (?) Linsey
91 94 Tenn Crisburn(?)
92 95 Humpry(?) Smith
93 96 Levi Treadway
94 97 Moses(?) Treadway
95 98 Add Kirklen
99 Joseph McDonald (Guillin?)
96 100 Julli(?) Garrison
97 101 George W. Farner
98 102 Joab Ross
184A 99 103 Wilum Roddy
100 104 Miller Cooper
101 105 Elmor Cooper
102 106 John Roddy
103 107 Henry Collop(?)
104 108 John Young
109 James Buttlar
105 110 James Roddy
106 111 Wilum D. Smith
107 112 Francis M. Majors
108 113 Aaron Cooper
109 114 Frank M. Sharp
184B 110 115 Wilum Bristoe
111 116 Hugh Ray
117 Samuel Peters
112 118 Samuel Rose
113 119 Purcy Alley
114 120 Thomas Tanksley
115 121 Bryant B. Roddy
116 122 James W. Hamton
185A 117 123 Joesas Smith
118 124 Robbrt Bails
119 123 Andrew Cramer (Clarke?)
120 126 Charles Ross
121 127 James Miller
122 128 Hanna(?) Moses
123 129 Lewis Cawood
124 130 George Laveinder
125 131 John Dunken
126 132 John M. Cassey
127 133 Wilum N. Shelby
128 134 Hiram Miller
129 135 Frank Edington (Halaway)
185B 130 136 Luty(?) Holloway(?)
131 137 Luke(?) Edington
132 138 Sam Hartbarger
133 139 Sam McClendon (Hill, Chinp?)
134 140 John J. Criss(?)
135 141 Aryle Marsh
186A 136 142 Elizabeth Smith
137 143 James Chrisp
138 144 David Rhea (Bollen)
139 145 James Hoyal
146 Henry Hart
140 147 Witcher Barton
141 148 Burt--s Regester
149 Jessie C. Reed
142 150 Saml J. Wheeler (Paul)
143 151 Shaw P. Medod(?)
144 152 Pery Rusel
186B 145 153 Luther Haskel
146 154 Thomas McGee
147 155 Bre--t Robbinson
148 156 Elin Dunn(?)
149 157 James Bell
150 158 Dannial Haskel (Hunt)
151 159 Harley Wasman (Hoyal)
152 160 Dick Gillum
153 161 Columbis Gibson
154 162 Paul McAlley
187A 155 163 Wilum McCully
156 164 Danil Robinson (Vaughn)
157 165 James Preston
158 166 Anderson Cawood
159 167 Jane Murphy
160 168 John Brown
161 169 Charlie Brown
162 170 Aron Maise
163 171 Robbert D. Hupans(?)
164 172 Frank Holoway
165 173 Wilum F. Treadway
187B 166 174 James Haynes
167 175 Wilum Halliet (Gibson)
168 176 James Gibson
169 177 Beng Thompson
178 Wilum Thompson
170 179 Jessi Pryor
171 180 James Evens (Thompson)
172 181 Squir Evans
173 182 Aaron Danty
188A 174 183 Sterlin Finley
175 184 Thomas Thompson
176 185 Henry Tallent
177 186 James Thompson
178 187 Martin Bishop
179 188 James Cunningham
180 189 Gathers Thompson
181 190 Niles C. Hides (Mize)
182 191 Thomas Roddy
183 192 Major D. Hinds (Angle)
188B 184 193 Lemu(?) Stockey
185 194 Albert Smith
186 195 Charly Smith
187 196 Oster J. Evens
188 197 Zac Long
189 198 Humpry Haskel
190 199 Marlar Garret
191 200 Stephen Nitito(?)
192 201 George Filyan

SPRING CITY

189A 193 202 Herbert Payne (Leuty)
194 203 James Dululch(?) (Edington)
195 204 Nath(?) McCulley
196 205 Polley Dunlap
197 206 John Dunlap
198 207 Nuton Casey (Kelley, Calwell)
199 208 John Chilcoat(?)
200 209 Darysy Bell
201 210 James Getgood
202 211 David J. Mency
189B 203 212 Rena Waterhouse (Edmon)
204 213 James(?) Watterhouse
205 214 Andrew Mency
206 215 John(?) Thompson
216 Rener(?) Wasman
207 217 John Earley
208 218 Tom Mare
209 219 James Radger
220 J.A. Radger
210 221 Martha Smith
222 James Ricker
211 223 John Herrich
190A 212 224 Jeff Jeno
213 225 Elbert Shertzahn

DISTRICT 2
RHEA SPRINGS
Andrew J. Tallent, Enumerator

191A 1 1 Coleman Smith
2 2 George W. Stanton
3 3 James F. Byrd
4 4 Isaac A. Grasham
5 5 Miles H. McCuiston (Carden)
6 6 Saml D. McCuiston (Price)
7 7 Andrew J. Stinecipher
8 8 David J. Stinecipher
9 9 Crane D. Reed
191B 10 10 Quinton A. Tallent
11 11 Elbert K. Stout
12 12 Wm R Clack (Johnson)
13 13 David McCullough (Gilliam)
14 14 Daniel Bowler(?)
15 15 Sidney H. Gillium

191B 16 16 William V. Gillium
17 17 Floyd E. Stachild
18 18 George McCuiston
19 19 William A. Smith
192A 20 20 Mike McNetis
21 21 William H. McCain
22 22 Asa N. Stinecipher
23 23 Thomas H. Ingle
24 24 Addison McCullough
25 25 Louie G. Tallent
192B 26 26 James M. Foust
27 27 William Bell
28 William E. Jolley
28 29 Margiat Bell
29 30 James H. Pearson
30 31 Franklin Martin
31 32 John B. Breeding
32 33 Andrew J. Tallent (Clark)
33 34 Thomas J. Gillespie
34 35 Haram Donaldson
193A 35 36 John Sharp
36 37 Philip Gillespie
37 38 Elic Gillespie
38 39 Thomas J. Gillespie
39 40 James Martin (Gillespie)
40 41 John W. Wester
41 42 John L. Miller
42 43 George R. Henry (Hembry)
43 44 Philip Bohannon
193B 44 45 Chitten Miller
45 46 William W. Drake
46 47 Elexander Keylon
47 48 William H. Boles
49 William W. Boles
48 50 Charles F. Roberson (Landford)
49 51 Albert Hornsby (Johnson)
50 52 Polk Donaldson
51 53 Josey McCaleb (Blair)
194A 52 54 Wm Blair (McCaleb)
53 55 Taylor M. Childs (Prater)
54 56 Jacob B. Ewing (Frazier)
55 57 Arthur C. Ewing
56 58 George Stinett
57 59 Samuel McCaleb
58 60 James Canellar(?)
59 61 George W. Dodson
60 62 Thomas J. Manis
61 63 Elbert M. Patterson
62 64 Wm R. Miller (Dodson)
194B 63 65 John Pickel (Holloman)
64 66 James W. Boles (McMurry, Wright)
65 67 Elbert R. Brown
66 68 James N. Long
67 69 Wiley Simpson (O'Neal)
68 70 Charles Hicks
69 71 James L. Benson
70 72 Henry R. Jolley
71 73 Robert L. Jolley
72 74 James H. Keylon (Ellis)
195A 73 75 James Henderson
76 Harriet Gilleand
74 77 John W. Long
75 78 Garrett Tallent
76 79 Kelley Moore
77 80 George W. Donaldson
78 81 James Cunningham (Jones, Clark)
79 82 Charles Hughes (Scott)
195B 80 83 Thomas Hughs
81 84 Wm T. Hicks (Kirby)
82 85 John B. Kirby (Wares)
83 86 John M. Ewing
84 87 William E. Williams
85 88 Jacob E. Garrison (Thompson)
86 89 Samuel S. Brady (Gillespie)
87 90 John W. Dolan
196A 88 91 John Cunningham
89 92 Henry J. Bell (Pinion)
90 93 Charles L. McElwee
91 94 Wm G. Cook
92 95 John N. Moore
93 96 George W. Gibson
94 97 William Kirby
95 98 James H. Monday
96 99 James P. Brady
196B 97 100 Robert M. Phillips
98 101 Enoch C. Broyles
99 102 Balam Lavender
100 103 James A. Drake
101 104 Jesse L. Baler
102 105 James Reese (Cox)
106 Dock B. Reese (Graham)
103 107 James L. Garrison
197A 104 109 Daniel Stroder (Curnutt)
105 110 James Gregory (Prestwood)
106 111 Beriah Craighead
107 112 William Kelly (Sharpe)
108 113 Jas H. Jackson (Shoemaker)
109 114 William White
110 115 George Ensley
111 116 John C. Ensley
112 117 William N. Angel
197B 113 118 Luke L. Coulter (Pass)
114 119 Joseph H. Watters (Kerr)
115 120 John I. Hawland
116 121 George W. Foust
117 122 David C. Kemmer
118 123 Elie T. Sawyers
119 124 Chapman Wasson
120 125 John S. Young
121 126 Jeremiah C. Wasson (Davis, Gage, Phillips)
122 127 Andrew Anderson
123 128 James R. Smith
198A 124 129 Frank Marsh
125 130 Perry McWillis (Harbison)
126 131 Robert Robinson
127 132 Maria Thompson (Mariot)
128 133 Geo W. Smith (Holhoway)
129 134 Andrew Brady
130 135 Francis A. McCabe
131 136 Hulda Wasson (Lock,Hikey)
132 137 Henry Rhea
198B 133 138 Evan Moore
134 139 James W. Russell
135 140 Elizabeth A. Fuller (Berger)
136 141 Greely G. Foust
137 142 Frank DeLuce
138 143 William H. Perkins
139 144 Stephen Gartner
140 145 Ely Adkins
141 146 Ellen S. Gance
142 147 John McCabe
143 148 Jake Hickey (Williams)
199A 144 149 Benjamin Bracher (Green, Chaplin)
145 150 Thomas J. Monday
146 151 Addison M. Broyles
147 152 James H. Galbraith
148 153 John R. Thompson (West)
149 154 Jas or Jesse E. Wasson
150 155 Patrick T. Ferguson
151 156 Jacob B. Crofts
152 157 Rebecca A. Rush
153 158 Andrew J. Ensley
154 159 Thomas J. Green
155 160 George W. Taylor
156 161 William M. Wilson
199B Blank

DISTRICT 3

Thomas D. Gannaway, Enumerator

200A 1 1 John R. Neal
2 2 Franklin Millican
3 3 G. Calvin Neal
4 4 W. Calvin Neal
5 5 W. Mathew Hix (Springs)
6 6 John D. Chambers
7 7 James A. Chambers
8 8 William M. Russell
9 9 Nancy Vaughn (Cox)
10 10 James L. Vaughn
200B 11 11 Julia Barnett
12 12 Arch Berry
13 13 Joe(?) McMillan
14 William Harwood
14 15 George W. Pritchet
15 16 Thomas H. Burditt
16 17 John Berry
17 18 Abner D. Wilkey (Dodd)
18 19 Columbus C. Wilkey
19 20 Saml A Wilkey (McDowell)
20 21 James C. Wilkey
201A 21 22 Nancy Rose
22 23 William G. Housley
23 24 Wm D. Wilkey (McDowell)
24 25 Nancy A. Small
25 26 Willie J. Cox (Marshel)
26 27 John Phillips
27 28 David Weaver (Lews)
29 Louis H. Weaver
28 30 M. Therlow Reed
29 31 William Smith
30 32 James L. Pritchet
31 33 William Pritchet
201B 32 34 Wilard S.(?) Knight
35 Ira N. Whittenburg
33 36 Louis E.(?) Smith
34 37 John Hurst
35 38 George W. Fisher (Lowery)
36 39 John W. Dagley
37 40 Samuel A. Smith
38 41 W. Owen Fisher
39 42 John H. Fisher
40 43 Mary Northrup
202A 41 44 Thomas J. Barger
42 45 William A. Smith
43 46 Robt W Wassom (Garrison)
44 47 C. Columbus Jones
45 48 John A. Porter Sr.
46 49 John W. Hill (Rectar)
47 50 Elisha K. Giles (Sutton)
48 51 John Cunningham
202B 49 52 John H. Crow
50 53 Enoos H. Turner
51 54 Samuel Durham
52 55 Caroline Webster

202B 53 56 Jane Sutton
54 57 John B. Coulter
55 58 William J. Blevins
56 59 William Stephens
57 60 John Holloway (Thompson)
203A 58 61 Gillan S. Price
62 H. Adlanne Boyd
59 63 Richard H. Williams
60 64 Wm H. Rector (McCabe)
61 65 Horace S. Smith
62 66 John H. Smith
63 67 Mauda Guess
64 68 James Leuty
65 69 William H. Long
70 Tara McIntyre
66 71 William Witt
203B 67 72 John W. Harwood
68 73 Joseph L. Wright
69 74 Newton Cagle (Drake)
70 75 Samuel F. Day
71 76 Enoch Ritchie (Swafford)
204A 72 77 Jas W. Walker (Bigerstaff)
73 78 Charles Day (Wilkerson)
74 79 Charles H. Wilkerson
80 Elbert Thompson
75 81 Wm Day (Gaut, Ray, True)
76 82 Eliza A. McMaury
77 83 Tennessee Smith
204B 78 84 Anthony N. Arnwine
79 85 James G. Howard
80 86 John H. Pugh
81 87 William J. Vincent
88 Samuel Vincent (Brown)
82 89 Andrew J. Perry (Smith)
83 90 Andy H. Vincent (Milton)
205A 84 91 Mary S. Foust
85 92 William R. Smith
86 93 James G. Ray
87 94 James Gibson
95 Sarah Neal
88 96 Robert Pointer
89 97 Robert Ray (Buck, Smith)
90 98 Margaret A. Smith
91 99 F. Merion Marler
92 100 John Woody
93 101 William J. Cowan
94 102 Andrew M. Sorrels
205B 95 103 Samuel W. Tindell
96 104 Jas L. McCuiston (Johns)
97 105 Thomas Atkerson
98 106 James H. Martin
99 107 Jerry Bilberry
100 108 Amanda McPherson
109 James W. McPherson
101 110 John S.(?) Long
102 111 George W. Wilkerson
103 112 James M. Snyder
113 Benjamin Smith
206A 104 114 James A. Garrison
105 115 Morgan Hackler
106 116 Wm D Wright (McColister)
107 117 Fred W. Chattin (Brown)
108 118 James L Willson
109 119 Thomas Wilkerson
110 120 Susan Chattin
111 121 Henry M. Bogart
112 122 Sarah M. Gaines (Snyder)
206B 113 123 John Cates
114 124 Lafayette Gott
115 125 John M. McClure

116 126 Pleas Cranfield
117 127 David Kile
128 John H. Willson
118 129 John W. Cochrum
119 130 Milton G McDonald (White)
207A 120 131 James Kelly
121 132 James B. Sims (Bolton)
122 133 John T. Kelly
123 134 Sol Harwood (Coach)
124 135 Joseph A. Davis
125 136 William A. Watkins
126 137 James Leuty
127 138 James M. Watson (Broglin)
128 139 Elizabeth Ewing
129 140 Henry T. Roddy
130 141 Roda Hill
142 James A. Hill
207B 130 143 Bart Ewing
131 144 James Mitchell
132 145 James White
133 146 James B. Bogart
134 147 Theodore T. Smith
135 148 William M. Clack
136 149 Wm A Hashbarger (Rucker)
137 150 Merril L. Fugate (Genow, Wright)
138 151 Jas M. Owens (Barnett)
208A 139 152 Wm A. Armstrong (Parker)
140 153 James S. Porter (Ward)
141 154 James Shell
142 155 Rheuban F. Porter
143 156 Wm W. Smith (Sutton)
144 157 Jackson Turner
145 158 Elbert S. Fugate
146 159 Claburn Fugate Jr.
147 160 Claburn Fugate Sr.
208B 148 161 William L. Hill
149 162 Eliza Wiggins
150 163 Mattie Rider
151 164 John C. Willson (McIntyre, Wiggins)
152 165 William M. Wiggins (Drake, Walter)
153 166 Richard Ray
154 167 Robert B. Kimbrough
155 168 John H. Wheeler
156 169 Thomas L. Wade
157 170 Richard Hickey (Wilkerson)
209A 157 171 Thos G. Moss (Walker)
158 172 Calvin C. Brown
159 173 John Collins
160 174 Barry Crestwood
161 175 E. Lee Tilley (Turner)
162 176 George I. Hale
163 177 Andrew Hickey
164 178 Daniel F. Hickey (Phillips)
209B 165 179 William Sedman
166 180 Mary J. Hale
167 181 Newton Robbins
182 Margarett E. Parker
168 183 William J. Pendergrass (Harwood, Hamilton)
169 184 John Tankersley
170 185 Frank W. Long
171 186 Robert W. Melton
172 187 David Jenow
173 188 William Mincy
174,189 Charles C. Lowe
210A 175 190 Timothy McNutt
176 191 Ephraim H. Manus
177 192 Mattie E. Hill

178 193 John A. Turner
179 194 William K. Fugate Sr.
180 195 John E. Fugate
196 James Fugate
210B 181 197 Mary McPhail
198 Zac Fugate
182 199 Louis Fugate
183 200 James Genow
184 201 Louis Fugate
185 202 William Fugate
186 203 Andrew J. Bankston
204 Samuel W. Bankston
187 205 Wm O. Bankston (Rector)
188 206 William M. Fugate
211A 189 207 David M. Mitchell
190 208 Charles Mitchel
191 209 William J. Porter
192 210 Winfield S McGann (Brady)
193 211 George M. Marshel
194 212 James F. Kincannon
195 213 Rheubin B. Turner
196 214 James A. Johnson
197 215 Samuel H. Miller
211B 198 216 James M. Kincannon
199 217 John A. Riggs
200 218 Granville H. Wade (Russell)
201 219 Asa C. or E. Graham
202 220 Dock Graham
203 221 Thomas Underwood
204 222 J. William True
205 223 Thomas W. Kincannon
206 224 Andrew J. Trentham
212A 207 225 Thomas A. Parks
208 226 Henry H. Parks
209 227 Ruthy Harwood
210 228 William B. Hawkins (Perry)
212B Blank

DISTRICT 14
SPRING CITY

Charles G. Miller, Enumerator

WARD 1

Rhea Avenue

213A 1 1 William Hook
2 2 D. Estaing Githens
3 3 James F. Rider
4 4 Nathan R. Cartwright
5 5 Jeff Cash
6 6 Lattimore B. McNabb
7 7 Rebecca Bryson
8 8 Curt Caldwell
9 9 Rufus Baker
10 10 George Elliott (Hicks, Witt, Kennedy)
11 11 James Weirick
12 12 James D. Smith (Sampson, Mathews, Burkhalter)
13 13 Charles Train

East 2nd Street

213B 14 14 Charles G. Mller

Piccadilly Avenue

15 15 James McKeehen
16 16 Samuel P.C. Robinson
17 17 Joseph McPherson
18 Smith Moulton

213B 18 19 Lemuel M. Cartright (Burkman)
19 20 Edwin D. Osborn
20 21 Sidney M. Walkins
21 22 Louis P. Thatcher (Jones)

East 1st Street
214A 22 23 Mart F. Reid
23 24 James McCabe

Picadilly Avenue
24 25 Newton F. Moulton
25 26 John A. Stephens

WARD 2

East 2nd Street
26 27 William Cate
27 28 Thomas W. Crisp
28 29 Julius White
29 30 George W. Oakes
30 31 Eph Meadows
31 32 James Meadows (Eldridge)

Rhea Avenue
214B 32 33 Noah W. Wheelock
33 34 Mariel K. Rhea (Hison)
34 35 George Proctor

Jackson Avenue
35 36 Mattie Blevins

Rhea Avenue
35 37 William H. Russell
215A 37 38 Phena Lambert

Jackson Avenue
38 39 Stephen H. Varney
39 40 John Swan (Jackson, Brady, Crofford)
40 41 Jas W. Duncan (Stuichell)
41 42 James W.V. Scoville (Thompson)
42 43 Elijah B. Ewing (Lowe, Thomas)
43 44 Letitia Smith
44 45 Hillary Nestor
45 46 Addison Long
46 47 Thomas Early
47 48 Emma Holloway
215B 48 49 James M. Griffin
49 50 Isaac Murrey (Bridgman)
50 51 Leonard Harmon (Pattison)
51 52 Anna C. Winne
52 53 James B. Simpson

Rhea Avenue
53 54 Letitia Smith
54 55 John Stephens
55 56 James Reed (McCaleb)
56 57 George W. Jones
57 58 Dallas Baker (Robinson)

WARD 3

West 1st Street
216A 58 59 Milton Galloway (Quinn)
59 60 James Garrison
60 61 Ambrose Griffith (Felty)
61 62 Edmond Angel
62 63 Frank Thompson
63 64 William Gibson
64 65 Floyd Gallahon
65 66 John C. Locke
66 67 Thomas B. Holloway

Harrison Street
67 68 Jefferson Brooks
68 69 John Robbens
69 70 Frank Rhea
70 71 Thomas Rhea
71 72 John A. Gamble

Jackson Avenue
72 73 Joseph E. Phillips
216B 73 74 William M. Snyder
74 75 Jeff Thompson (Morris)
75 76 James M. Cox (Phipps)
76 77 Milo M. Holloway
77 78 Alfred Gross
78 79 Thomas J. Eaves
79 80 Charles Beuois
80 81 Lou A. Blair
81 82 Jesse C.(?) McGee
82 83 Robert C. Cunnyngham
83 84 Rufus M. Robinson
217A 84 85 John A.(?) Gamble
85 86 John Hinch
86 87 Noah L. Cate (Miller)
88 William McDonald
87 89 John Patton
88 90 Elmore Holloway (Essex)
89 91 Calonis(?) Russell (Henderson)
90 92 Henry C. Collins
91 93 Milla Thompson
92 94 Calvin D. Lavender
93 95 Robert A. Dickson
217B 94 96 Robert T. Simpson (Kelly)
95 97 Francis M. Breeden
96 98 Thomas F. Shelby
97 99 Samuel Shelby (Burdett)
98 100 Sarah J. Lavender
99 101 William S. Lavender
100 102 Eugene Allender
101 103 John C.(?) Dodson (Riggs)
102 104 Ellis Riggs
103 105 John Lyons
104 106 Richard C. Lyons
105 107 Jackson Peak

Street in Gap
218A 106 108 George R. Baldwin
107 109 John B. Jester
108 110 James Knight
109 111 Thos J. Smith (Marsh)

West 2nd Street
110 112 Zeno Fisischer
111 113 James H. Rogers
112 114 Victoria Caldwell (Darwin)
113 115 Wm F.P. Brown (Robinson)
114 116 John M. Welch
115 117 John H. Allison
116 118 Robert C. Cox
119 Naoima Gollahon
117 120 James H. Hodge

West 1st Street
218B 118 121 Byron Runyan

WARD 4

Rhea Avenue
219A 119 122 Mart Reid
120 123 Thos B. Reid (Edington)
121 124 Jesse B. Regester
122 125 Samuel E. Paul
123 126 James W. Angel (Underwood, Gollahar)

West 3rd Street
124 127 Samuel Waterhouse
125 128 James F. Thompson
126 129 Smith B. Richards (Reed)

West 2nd Street
127 130 Robert Johnson
128 131 Laura A. Gillespie
129 132 Olivia J. Richards
219B 130 133 Nancy J. Smith (Blevins)
131 134 Joseph D. Hardin
132 135 John S. Hardin (Neal)
133 136 Frank Beatis
134 137 Amos A. Lemons

West 1st Street
135 138 Addie R. Neal (Wilson)
136 139 James Regester
137 140 John W. Wassom (Lyle, Learest?)
138 141 John W. Angel (Haley, Bradley)
139 142 Andrew Calloway
220A 143 John Rector

Price Hill
140 144 Brainard Perkins
141 145 Henry T. Price
142 146 Reese H. Watkins
143 147 Thomas G. Gillespie (Millican, Loftin)
(END, SPRING CITY ENUMERATION)

Spring City and Rhea Springs Road
221A 144 148 Jas W. Wright (Thompson)
145 149 Francis J. Shilleto
146 150 Samuel Yount
147 151 Viola Griffith
148 152 Nanna Hutcheson (Renfro)
149 153 James A. Thompson
150 154 George L. Crosby
151 155 William Wilson
152 156 John W. Simpson
153 157 William Smith
154 158 Hardin Hope
155 159 Stephen Wasson

Rhea Springs and Washington Road
221B 156 160 William C. Payne (Hoyal)
157 161 William D.(?) Fillers
158 162 Conrad Evans (Wheeler)
159 163 Andrew J. Garrison (Fugate, McClendon)
160 164 James A. Torbett
161 165 Willis McClendon
162 166 Benjamin S. McClendon
163 167 Reuben Turner
164 168 James F. Turner

Ridge Road 2 and 3 miles southeast of Spring City
222A 165 169 Newton R. Tilley
166 170 John F.(?) Holland
167 171 Elijah H. Holland
168 172 William P. Broyles
169 173 Henry C. Darwin
170 174 John Trentham
171 175 Isaac N. Broyles
172 176 John F. Broyles
173 177 Ward Wallis

Location not indicated
222B 174 178 Elizabeth G. Robinson

On Mountain Path
175 179 Henry McDonald

Spring City and Dayton Road
176 180 Sellers Brady
177 191 David Moyer
178 182 Evander Thurman
179 183 William R. Gregory
180 184 Titus Shearer
181 185 Chas Reed (Wassum, Gray)
182 186 Hugh L. Ferguson
183 187 Oscar L. Barton
184 188 Jessie Cash

Back Valley Road
223A 185 189 James F. Tollett [Tallent]
186 190 Thomas J. Henderson
187 191 Tullock Neal
188 192 Fred A. Gregory (Aylworth)
189 193 Sanders Dunlap (Watson, Hayes)
190 194 James T. Monroe (Rice)
191 195 Richard Holloway (McFalls)

Shutin Gap Road
192 196 John C. Duncan
193 197 James F. Pope
194 198 William A. Thompson
195 199 Monroe Pope

Shutin Gap & Bledsoe County Road
223B 196 200 Elisha A. Neuby
197 201 Fayete C. Neuby
198 202 Robinson Neuby
199 203 Reiley N. Neuby
200 204 James F. Neuby

DISTRICT 4

Charles G. Miller, Enumerator

Spring City and Dayton Road
224A 201 205 William L. Burnett
202 206 James M. Alley
203 207 Byron S. Denton
204 208 John F. Miller (Smith)
205 209 Joseph Mitchell
206 210 James H. Beard
207 211 John H. DeVaney
208 212 Joseph R. McFalls
209 213 Peter L. Eberly
210 214 Jacob Gass (Palmer, VanOrsdal)
211 215 Jas L.(?) Pelfrey (Gass)
224B 212 216 Thomas J. Hall
213 217 Davis ?. Parker
214 218 George W. Shelby
215 219 Daniel Waldo
216 220 John Burditt
217 221 Perry Pierce
218 222 Edward McMillan
219 223 Richard D. Davis

Back Valley Road
220 224 John T. Ferguson
221 225 Richard T. Ferguson (Holloway)
222 226 James F. Henderson
225A 223 227 Louis P. Essex
224 228 Low M. Neal
225 229 John F. McCulloch (McCoy)

Clear Creek Road
226 230 George E. Finney
227 231 Lottie F. Brown
228 232 Scott W. Alley
229 233 Andrew J Wyrick (Ferguson)
230 234 Alfred McPheters

Ridge Road East of Spring City and Dayton Road
225B 231 235 William L. Godbehere
232 236 John A. Tilley
233 237 Edward Jannow
234 238 Thos H. Robinson (Bryson)
235 239 William R. Dagley
236 240 George P. Ensor
237 241 Robert M. Trentham
238 242 Wm J. Mitchell (Trentham)

Rhea Springs and Washington Road
239 243 Patrick O. Sullivan
240 244 John R. Walker
226A 241 245 Frank Brogdon
242 246 Robert Bell
243 247 John Rosenbaulm
244 248 John M. McPherson (Henry)
245 249 Anna Crosby (Clark)
246 250 Allen Godbehere
247 251 Jasper W. McClarin (Godbehere)
248 252 Mary Scarbrough (McClendon)
249 253 Samuel Walker
250 254 Floyd Walker
251 255 William Shelby
252 256 Andrew T. Holloway
226B 253 257 John M.(?) Rose
254 258 John J.(?) Tudor (Edwards, Brown)
255 259 Ansel G. McClendon (Madgett)
256 260 David Shelby
257 261 Adison L. Fisher
258 262 Dorcus P. Fisher
259 263 Joseph Hurst
260 264 Robert F. Porter
261 265 John A. Porter
227A 262 266 Charles L. Smith
263 267 Martha Smith
264 268 Henry L. Smith
265 269 Wyley A.(?) Barger
266 270 John T. Phillips

Spring City and Washington Road
267 271 John W. Beasley
268 272 James S. Harrison
269 273 Seth Alley
270 274 William D. Schoolfield

Road on Line of 3rd and 4th Districts
227B 271 275 John M. Campbell
272 276 John Houston (McMilen)
273 277 James Dyer
274 278 Cornelius H. Knight
275 279 Villers(?) E. Knight
276 280 Walter B. Knight
277 281 Christopher Neal (Wibel)

Clear Creek Road
278 282 William H. Porter
279 283 William P. Runyan

Back Valley Rod
280 284 Jeff Smith

DISTRICT 9

C. C. Hayes, Enumerator

228A 1 1 Alfred J. Collins
2 2 James W. Pelfry (Lemons)
3 3 Philip W. Allen
4 4 Frank Lemons
5 5 John W. Kennedy
6 6 Daniel Kennedy
7 7 Alfred W. Graves
8 8 Lavadia A. Sharp
9 9 John R. Stinnett
10 10 Alexander Ridley (Reece, Smith)
11 11 William G. Brown
228B 12 12 Samuel L. Turner
13 13 Sams J. Henderson (Wright)
14 14 Andrew Dunahoo
15 15 John H. King (Russell)
16 16 Hariet Henderson (Pearce)
17 17 John W. Conley
18 18 Alvin Henderson
19 19 William M. Dunn
20 20 George F. Swain
229A 21 21 John R. Swafford
22 22 James F. McDonald
23 23 Charles Harrison
24 24 William L. Rowe
25 25 William R. Henry
26 26 Charles M. Bain (Holland)
27 27 Samuel W. Smith
28 28 Green H. Pryor
29 29 Jefferson D. Smith
30 30 Bailey D. Smith
31 31 Lewis Farmer
32 32 Joseph N. King
229B 33 33 Elbert A. Teasley
34 34 George A. Hughes
35 35 Charles C. Hayes

DISTRICT 5

C. C. Hayes, Enumerator

230A 36 36 John A. Davis
37 37 York Davis
38 38 Martha Shadden
39 39 Thomas W. Smith
40 40 Caswell T. Stout
41 41 Malinda Morgan (Bartram)

230A 42 42 Darius E. Broyles
43 43 Thomas C Collins (Comton)
230B 44 44 James B. Blevins (Pease, Stevens)
45 45 William E.M. Denton
46 46 George A. Eakins (Pelfry)
47 47 Garrett M. Besley
48 48 Thomas W. Beasley
49 49 Lucinda Yarber
50 50 James Cox
51 51 John L. Howardon
231A 52 52 George Howardon
53 53 James Howardon
54 54 Andrew Gass
55 55 Mary R. Darwin
56 56 James Denton
57 57 Boss Webb
58 58 Hugh A. Locke
59 59 Alfred Paine (Ezell)
60 60 Samuel Montgomery
61 61 Eliza Campbell
62 62 James A. Webb
63 63 Joseph W. Furrey
64 64 James Ezill
65 65 Wiley N.(?) Waller
66 66 James J. Ezell
67 67 George M. Ezell
68 68 Mary J. Hickey
231B 69 69 Martha Gamble (Taylor, Reuise, McBrune)
70 70 James Castolo
71 71 Rubern L.(?) Hanby
72 72 James C. Moore (Phillips)
232A 73 73 Clinton Norman
74 74 Ellen Kyle
75 75 Sharlott E. Rice
76 76 Rufus R. Callahan
77 77 James A. Hill
78 78 Samuel H. Frailey
79 79 Willim M. Myers
80 80 Thomas Swafford
81 81 Samuel Burgin (McDonal, Coplan)
82 82 Hugh Woodey
83 83 David Swafford
84 84 John Mikels
232B 85 85 Joseph Eakens
86 86 Alexander Cofer (Seals)
87 87 Norman A. Haynes
88 88 William Howard
89 89 William P. Ferguson (Sharp)
90 90 Thomas Gravett
91 91 David Woodey (McClelland)
92 92 William P. Thomison
93 93 James B. Campbel
94 94 James Newell
233A 95 95 Thomas Conner (Witt)
96 96 Henry Porter
97 97 John Porter
98 98 Theodore J. Marshall
99 99 Beuford McCollins
100 100 Isaac Runyon
101 101 William S. Teffenteller
102 102 Harison Lewis
103 103 Robert F. Runyan
104 104 Andy W. Smith
105 105 Arther C. Ferguson
233B 106 106 Edward Smith
107 107 William L. Able (McKinsey)
108 108 Sill Wilkey
109 109 Wiley H. Cunningham (Miller, Darwin)
110 110 Elijah L. Rudd
111 111 Pleasant E. Hunter
112 112 Thomas H. Evans
113 113 Martin C. Weaver
114 114 Louiza M. Warner
115 115 Bird Clay (Murry, Hughes)
234A 116 116 John L. Mahoney
117 117 Onslo G. Gannaway (Love)
118 118 Elmore R. Taylor
119 119 William M. Cox
120 120 William T. Gass (Broyles)
121 121 Frances E. Love
122 122 David Webb
123 123 Alfred B. Darwin
124 124 William E. Rodgers
125 125 James E. Swicker
126 126 Joseph E. Evans
127 127 Maggie F. Evans (Ford)
128 128 James R. Sharp
129 129 Jacob M. Hamilton
234B 130 130 Joseph Miller (Denton)
131 131 Willam P. Darwin (Coxey, Paine)
132 132 Robert McBroom
133 133 Henry Hare
134 134 George ?. Genow
135 135 Guy M. Denton
136 136 George W. Metzgar
235A 137 137 William Webb
138 138 Sarah L. Ogle
139 139 William C. Paine
140 140 James T. Darwin
141 141 William M. Beaver
142 142 Thomas D. Kelley
143 143 Andrew H. Brewer
144 144 Eda A. Sneed
145 145 Alvira Beaver (Mason)
146 146 John W. Willett
147 147 Noris Richardson
235B 148 148 William Gravett
149 149 Samuel Boyer
150 150 Jefferson N. Marshall
151 151 Joseph Thorp (Price)
152 152 John R Wyatt (English)
153 153 Jacob Beirly
154 154 James F. Walker (Martin)
236A 155 155 John J. McHone
156 156 John H. Hamilton
157 157 James H. Locke
158 158 John Atkinson
159 159 John L. Eddington (Hines, Grice)
160 160 William C Webb (Roff)
161 161 Cyrus C. Bramlet
162 162 Samuel Brown
236B 163 163 Hamond D. Webb
164 164 George Webb
165 165 Roley Jones
166 166 John Avery
167 167 Wm P. McCullough
168 168 Sarah Duckworth (McAntire)
169 169 Joseph Webb
170 170 John Beasley
171 171 Edward Ward
172 172 Howard Burdett
237A 173 173 Mary Dyer
174 174 Wesley B. Millerd
175 175 Abraham I. Stever (Dyer)
176 176 William N. Smith
177 177 Isaac L Commons (Herbeck)
178 178 James Harrison
179 179 Jacob S. Miller
180 180 Albert Dye
181 181 Lee Landreth
237B 182 182 John Bramlet
183 183 John M Houston (Newman)
184 184 James Jones
185 185 Robert W. Collins
186 186 William Smith
187 187 Canada Hurst
188 188 Thomas Houston
189 189 Byron Pelfrey
190 190 Hanable Hurst
191 191 John N. Vaughn
192 192 Robert N. Beard
238A 193 193 John Killpatrick (Swafford)
194 194 William Dyre (Prater)
195 195 Frank R. Jourdain
196 196 Isaac W. Barnett (Cline)
197 197 William E. Collins
198 198 Robert M. Boofer
199 199 Lutitia McDowel (Johnson)
200 200 James T. Boofer
201 201 Baily Minick
238B 202 202 Joseph C. McDowell
203 203 Thomas J. Barton
204 204 Leander J. West
205 205 Arabela J. Reel (Swfford, Hail)
206 206 John L. Collins
207 207 William Smith (Henderson)
208 208 William Gannaway
209 209 Rhoda N. Pearce
239A 210 210 Thomas Gannaway
211 211 James Landreth
212 212 James C. Broyles

DISTRICT 6

F. E. Porter, Enumerator

240A 1 1 Joseph Haas
2 2 Anna Henderson
3 3 Jesse D. Thomas (Ridgley)
4 4 Douglas Morgan
5 5 Benjamin B. Travis
6 6 Tate Frailey
7 7 Andy J. Sneed
8 8 Charles Medaris (Perkins)
9 9 William B. Brown
10 10 Bert L. Marshall
11 11 Joseph Brown (Wright)
12 12 Jim H. Brown
240B 13 13 Nathaniel C. Brown
14 14 Lewis Morgan
15 15 James S. Gravett
16 16 John Mize
17 17 John Mize Jr.
18 18 Nancy Bankston
19 19 William D. Ogle
20 20 Richard S. Gaston
21 21 Aron P. Thomas
22 22 John Porter
241A 23 23 James R. Byrd
24 24 Charles Rudd
25 25 Rheuben A. Hill
26 26 Charles M. Pelfry
27 27 Casper Cunnyngham
28 28 Isaac N. Smith

241A 29 29 Aron T.(?) Smith
30 30 Lot Cagle
31 31 John Wilkey
32 32 James T. King
241B 33 33 Elizabeth Campbell (Moles)
34 34 Albert O. McClelland
35 35 Charles J. Copinger
36 36 J. Tolbert Cooley
37 37 George S. Cooley
38 38 James A. Webb
39 39 Frank Webb
40 40 Bart Craig
41 41 Isaac Byrd
242A 42 42 Joseph Campbell
43 43 Jerry L. Denton
44 44 Joseph L. Goodwin
45 45 Wm Collins (Wyrick)
46 46 John Price
47 47 Santuelli(?) Franklin
48 48 Richard Sneed
49 49 James Dovers
50 50 James M. Yates
51 51 Jim Campbell
52 52 Woods Walker
242B 53 53 Thomas Walker
54 54 Joel T. Henry
55 55 Mary Buchanon (Jenkins)
56 56 Belle J. Martin (Woody)
57 57 William R. Clark
58 58 John Buchanon
59 59 Susan Hall
60 60 William McDonald
61 61 John Stenett
62 62 Giles H. Ryan (Drake)
243A 63 63 William Ryan (Hinkle)
64 64 James H. West
65 65 Joseph Ballard (Swafford, Walker)
66 66 Edward L. Collins
67 67 Patrick Wilkey
68 68 Martin Wilkey (McMurry)
69 69 Julia Taylor
70 70 James L. Brown
71 71 Robert Moles
72 72 Alfred Locke
243B 73 73 James Gravett
74 74 Robert Walker
75 75 William Rockholt
76 76 Catherine Morris
77 77 Wm Y. Denton (Howard, Bradshaw, Highfield, Turk, Housley, McClendon)
78 78 Jane Locke
79 79 John M. Reed
80 80 James A. Tullas
81 81 Oscar Franklin
244A 82 82 John M. Winne
83 83 Lee A. Wyrick
84 84 Barton K. Mynatt
85 85 Harriet Waterhouse (Colville, Coxey)
86 86 Frank M. Rockholt (Byrd)
87 87 William B. Kelley
88 88 Susan Hale
89 89 George W. Walker
90 90 Philip H. Harsh
244B 91 91 Henry A. Crawford (Gillespie, Roberts)
92 92 Samuel H. Sneed
93 93 Andrew Aiken (Hicks)
94 94 George N. Dodd
95 95 Thomas H. Dodd (Minnick)
96 James N. Dodd
96 97 Luther Marlow
97 98 George N. Marlow
98 99 Lorenza Roberts
245A 99 100 Thomas Smith
100 101 William Morgan
101 102 Fred Morgan
102 103 Charles Vincent
103 104 William R. Crow (Hale)
104 105 John Bishop
245B 105 106 Henry Morgan
106 107 Marley Y. Yates
107 108 Archey Bowles
108 109 Benjamin Harris
109 110 Asberry Locke (Booker)
110 111 John T. Roddy
111 112 Thomas Hale (Locke)
112 113 William C. Harris
113 114 Martin E. Yates
246A 114 115 George W. Kerley
115 116 James Berry (Hickmot)
116 117 Matthew Allen
117 118 Jesse Kerley
118 119 James Travis
119 120 William Smith
120 121 James Filyow
121 122 Casey Henry
122 123 William Harris
123 124 Daniel L. Kerley
246B 124 125 Richard Wilkey
125 126 William L. Locke
126 127 George Dunn
127 128 James M. Beyrley
128 129 Walter G. Taylor
129 130 James A. Houston (Kimbro, Robinson)
130 131 Bert Revis (McCullough)
131 132 John P. Cory
132 133 Richard R. Brown (Kimbro)
247A 133 134 John H. Morgan
134 135 Charles Thurman
135 136 Jud Sharp
136 137 Frank Waterhouse
137 138 Cane Wilkey
138 139 Charles Swafford
139 140 James M. Ballard
140 141 James A. Clark
141 142 Elzie Wilkey (Hartley)
142 143 James Walker
247B 143 144 Major Swafford (Grayhan)
144 145 James Kennedy (McMurry)
145 146 James D. Collins
146 147 James N. Pelfrey (Webb)
147 148 William E. Pelfrey
148 149 Vincent Hurst
149 150 James Crane (Cox)
150 151 John Lewis
151 152 James Cartright
152 153 Joseph Gibbs
248A 153 154 Jesse F. Collins
154 155 Casper Howard
155 156 John M. Hartley
156 157 Luke M. King (Price)
157 158 James Carney
158 159 David Ryne
159 160 Isaac K. Brown (Womack, Martin, Lawson)
160 161 Roy Harris
248B 161 162 Samuel Frazier
162 163 John Couch
163 164 Meridith M. Paul (Harwood)
164 165 James Stovall (Blackwall)
165 166 John McMahan (Cox)
166 167 Wm Lockmiller (Campbell)
167 168 William Couch
168 169 Elizabeth Roddy
169 170 Oscar H. Hill (Johnson)
170 171 William Harwood
249A 171 172 James M. Cagle (Hawkins)
172 173 Peter Roddy
173 174 John Pogue (Parker, Bunn)
174 175 Marlone(?) Lockmiller
175 176 Thomas Coppinger
176 177 Geo M Harrison (Chambers)
177 178 Samuel Colbughar
178 179 Julius A. Kennedy
179 180 Jack Ryan (Henry)

DISTRICT 10

James W. Romines, Enumerator

250A 1 1 Albert Pursur
2 2 Elizabeth Pursur (Fisher)
3 3 Thomas F. Shaver (Soward)
4 4 Thomas Henderson
5 5 James Pursur (Dickson, Chaten)
6 6 William Waller
7 7 Isabell Smith
8 8 Dan Elders
9 9 Floyd Mayriott
10 10 William Nippur
11 11 William Curr
250B 12 12 Robert Pursur
13 13 Anderson Hendrick (Fuller, Bolen)
14 14 Newton Henry
15 15 Andy Kelly
16 16 Edd W. Parker
17 17 Abbey Dodd
18 18 Andy Ervin
19 19 Asariah Fisher (Knight)
20 20 Thomas Whaley
21 21 Joseph Killough
251A 22 22 Mameray J. Pursur
23 23 Bird Lowery (Carter, Lawson, Montgomery)
24 24 Elmer Randolph
25 25 Johh Pursur
26 26 Tom McDonald
27 27 Birrel C. Hinch (Carlile?)
28 28 Will Hickson
251B 29 29 Jordan Davis (Hutchins)
30 30 Flora Tellow (Chattin)
31 31 Ascar Lewis
32 32 Will Rains (Donhoo)
33 33 William Randolph (Goodall. Robertson)
34 34 John Morgan (Brown)
35 35 Ras Elder
36 36 Amos McDonald
37 37 Dave Galiger
252A 38 38 Sam Galiger
39 39 John Housely
40 40 Souisen Barton
41 41 William McDonald
42 42 Matilda Doss
43 43 Rachel Dooley (Rucker)
44 44 Jessie Keith (Suttles)

252A 45 45 Nancy Keith
46 46 James Knight
47 47 Isom Chatten
48 48 Jack Simpson (Mills,Bryant)
252B 49 49 Aber Emery (Frild, Thomas, Malone)
50 50 Frank Henry
51 51 Joseph B. Dodd
52 52 Earnest D.(?) Keith
53 53 Earnest Ganiway
54 54 Mack McLane
55 55 Robert J. Kilouge (Kertain, Ivester)
56 56 Sody E. Jewell
253A 57 57 Ben B. Blye
58 58 Bailes W.J. Lewis (Hedge-coth)
59 59 Henry Matherly
60 60 Thomas Matherley
61 61 Jim P. Wycuff (Breider, Morgun)
62 62 George Johnson
63 63 Lewis L. Powell
64 64 Albert Broyls (Roberts)
65 65 Jim Coaplin (Broyles, Cliff)
66 66 Acar Galiger
253B 67 67 Philip Henry (Crawford, Reed, Stovall, Johnson)
68 68 Ben McDonald (Day, Harris, Keith)
69 69 Richard Kelley
70 70 John Wright
71 71 Eligah Newton (Baton)
72 72 Jim Anderson (Conley, Grifin)
73 73 Tom McClelland
74 74 Elbert Hamilton
254A 75 75 Sam Doren(?) (Coffer)
76 76 Eler Woody (Boran)
77 77 John Tinsley (Woody)
78 78 William B. Smith (Hall)
79 79 Joseph Jackson
80 80 Brahat Coaller Jr (Holeman)
81 81 William B. Clonius
82 82 John A.B. Boyd
254B 83 83 Charley Melton
84 84 William M. Crege(?)
85 85 Thomas L. Rodgers
86 86 Frank Barton
87 87 Frank J. Weatherington
88 88 Mich Shields
89 89 George Griffen
90 90 Ben Dyer (Cowin, Henery)
91 91 Elijah B. Hudson
255A 92 92 Henry J. Brady
93 93 William S. Stephens
94 94 Andrew A. Morgan
95 95 Robert Howard
96 96 Barry(?) Wilbanks
97 97 Joe Wilbanks
98 98 William Shieds
99 Homer Halliburton (Wybel, McDonald, Suggs)
99 100 Elmer Conly
100 101 Ashel Templeton (Bogle)
101 102 Askinean Arthur (Harris)
102 103 West Hawkins
255B 104 Sam Harris
103 105 William Buetenner(?)
106 John Pressneal
104 107 William Presnell
105 108 Hinery Hansby
106 109 Mathew(?) Black
107 110 Humbusby(?) Hillard
108 111 Mary Pryer (West)
109 112 Barton Cox
110 113 Ralie Hansby
256A 114 Samuel Housely
111 115 James Cook (Walkes)
112 116 James Clards
113 117 Will Pryer
114 118 Will Hale
115 119 James Jackson (Mays)
116 120 Isac Hale
117 121 Manie Spiller
118 122 George Brook
119 123 Jeffe Pritchett
120 124 James Cox
256B 121 125 John Henderson
122 126 George Tumlin(?)
123 127 Wm Johnson (Russell)
124 128 Carter Phillips (Pryor)
125 129 William Phillips
126 130 Ali Mayatt
127 131 James Randolph
128 132 Will Thurman (Randolph)
129 133 Jerry Robertson
257A 130 134 Louis Martin
131 135 Alford Etherley (Griffie)
132 136 John Blevins
133 137 Robert McDonald
134 138 Wyatt Day
135 139 William Collins
136 140 George Collins
137 141 Horras Dillard
138 142 Jasper Dillard
139 143 Fill Suttles (Elison,Maston)
257B 140 144 Sam Ellis (Steel)
141 145 Dock Suttles
142 146 Richard T. Greer
143 147 Tom Hensley
144 148 Lue Allen
145 149 Lewis Chatten
146 150 Willis Hunt
147 151 Heart Toliver (Scott)
258A 148 152 Smith McNab
149 153 Emma Buckhanon (White)
150 154 John Sharp
151 155 Mary Lightfoot (Robertson, Phillips)
152 156 William Scarbrough
153 157 William Bess
154 158 Edd L. Crege
155 159 Carey Gipson
156 160 Charley Avery
157 161 Henery Knight
158 162 Will Brown
258B 159 163 John Condru
160 164 Lon Weathington (Hughes, Johnson, Rowlins, Smith)
161 165 John Henderson
162 166 Bernelia Clack
163 167 Perry Miligan
164 168 James Miligan (Eaton)
165 169 George Wolford
166 170 Robert Corn (Brigman)
167 171 Henry Flore(?) (Parker)
168 172 William H. Leadford
169 173 Isaac Dodd
259A 170 174 Lauther Woods (Tipton)
171 175 James R. Denton
172 176 Will C. Denton
173 177 John Hughes (Shaw, Mathews)
174 178 Charley Maler
175 179 James Dodd
176 180 Frank Gooden
177 181 Scott Gooden (Scott)
178 182 James Porter
179 183 Charly Gooden
180 184 Balu(?) McJunkins
259B 181 185 Ligh(?) Whitefield
182 186 Henry Hawkins
183 187 Silas Potter
184 188 John Potter (Posey)
185 189 William Roberts
186 190 Roe Calihan
187 191 Allie Huskins (Coleman)
188 192 Oscar Hawkins
189 193 John Hughes (Lowery)
190 194 Lon Gossett (Ledford)
191 195 John Lowery
192 196 Thomas C. Hays
260A 193 197 Nancy Crawford (Barns)
198 Sam T. Scott
194 199 Pafee(?) Hale
195 200 Bob Mason
196 201 Mack Killough
197 202 George Hughys
198 203 Wm Sawyeur (Bishop)
199 204 Zach Benison
200 205 John T. Howard (Bean, Fraley)
201 206 John T. Mathew
202 207 Peter Robertson
260B 203 208 Ike Dyer
204 209 Wm Murphy (Trotter)
205 210 Martin Wilky
206 211 Emery Wilkey
207 212 Wm H. Jones (Hensley)
208 213 Eli McDonal (Lutty)
209 214 Dock Jenno (Singleton)
210 215 David Mayatt
211 216 Tilman Mace (Hamilton)
212 217 James Wilkey
261A 213 218 John Mitchel
214 219 William Swin (Gray)
215 220 James Jewell

DISTRICT 7

James W. Romines, Enumerator

261B 216 221 Jesse Coleman
217 222 Frank S. Knight
218 223 William D. Pursur (Byerley)
219 224 James Pursur
220 225 Miller Pursur
221 226 Thos C. Travis (West)
222 227 Nancy Bishop
223 228 James Burnett
224 229 Emma Hall
225 230 John M. Bolin
226 231 Ray Pursur (Knight)
262A 227 232 Thomas Gallenday(?)
228 233 Haray Blye
229 234 John H. Jewell
230 235 John Trotter
231 236 Charley Carr (Bingam)
232 237 Sam Washington
233 238 James Melton
234 239 John Morgan (Hamilton)
235 240 James Morgan

262A 236 241 Jeffe Patten
262B 237 242 Tom Tyler
238 243 Patrick Daniel
239 244 John Shavin
240 245 Jessee Shavin
241 246 William Wampler
242 247 Lafayett Shaver
243 248 Nealy(?) Shaver
244 249 John B. Brady (Smith)
245 250 Sam Arnold
263A 246 251 Huston Shaver (Thompson)
247 252 John M. Shaver
248 253 Marion Coleman
249 254 John Boyd
250 255 Jerry Burnett
251 256 Rudd Boyd
252 257 James Robertson
263B 253 258 Charley Hood
254 259 Hiram Patten
255 260 Dan Smith (Hanks)
256 261 William Fisher
257 262 Thomas Knight (Elders, Elers)
258 263 Ruffus Hood
259 264 Sam Hood (McCullough)
260 265 Albert Fitzgerald
264A 261 266 Ben McCullough
262 267 James Gillespie
263 268 Lucy Matherley (Byerley)
264 269 Phill Harris
265 270 Thos Bowles (Keith)
266 271 Kirk Loydd (Hamilton)
267 272 William Coleman
268 273 Freeling T. Shaver
264B 269 274 Mary Conley (Roberts, Walters)
270 275 John ?. Horten (Conley)
271 276 Thos Jeffertson (Bridgman, Day)
272 277 Jeff Price
273 278 James Scott
274 279 John Powers
275 280 Elic Hill
276 281 George Shelton
277 282 Joseph Leadford
278 283 Turner(?) Smith
265A 279 284 Charley Wilkey (Webb)
280 285 Bill Wilkey (Dolen?)
281 286 James Lawry
282 287 Henry Rice
283 288 Call Scroggins
284 289 William Kelley
285 290 Jeff Drue
286 291 William Wilkey
287 292 Henry(?) Burchard
288 293 Frank Harwood
265B 289 294 Michel Douglas
290 295 Stuvor Lawrence (Sanders)
291 296 Green Holms
292 297 Abe Chattin
293 298 Guss Cambel
294 299 Charly Raybin
295 300 Manro Cravin (Powers, Stringer)
296 301 Frank Byreley (Ollin,Knight)
297 302 Nancy Hously
298 303 Elic Molton (Suttles)
299 304 Charley Jewell
300 305 John S. Hicks
266A 301 306 John Cochran
302 307 Jeff Moses
303 308 Sam Byerly
304 309 Clay Devault (Smith)
305 310 Newt Henry (Bowins)
306 311 Elizah Huff
307 312 James Earley
266B 308 313 Charley Knight
309 314 Sam Shought
310 315 Jack Byerly
311 316 William Milton
312 317 James Prater (Call)
313 318 John Mayott (Brown)
314 319 Frank Dixon (Coffer,Kelley)
315 320 Kattie Muloy(?)
316 321 Tom Combow(?) (Loyd)
267A 317 322 David Brown
318 323 James W. Romines
319 324 Richard Knight
320 325 Robert Hood
321 326 William Byrley
322 327 Albia Spence
323 328 Malinda Spence
324 329 Miral A. DeVault
325 330 James Chumly
267B 326 331 John Purcur (Burnell, Crawford)
327 332 Ann Parker
328 333 Jim Shaver (Davis)
329 334 Henry Reynolds (Billburry)

DISTRICT 15
Henry King Banks, Enumerator

268A 1 1 Louis F. McDonald (Brooks, Helton)
2 2 Jehu N. McClure
3 3 Stanton McDonald (Bennett)
4 4 Thos J Mathews (Fairbanks)
5 5 Andrew Fairbanks
6 6 John Corvin (Gothard)
268B 7 7 Hariet Corvin (Abel)
8 8 Anna(?) Brooks
9 9 James Corvin (Dennis)
10 10 Mandy Harvison
11 11 John Brooks
12 12 Richard Jordan
13 13 Dollie Calvin (Webb)
14 14 Sarah Emmet
15 15 Nathaniel Shipley
16 16 John C. Decker
269A 17 17 James C.(?) Cranmore
18 18 Robert L. Duckworth
19 19 William Davis
20 20 Henry Banks (Smedley)
21 21 Wolford Hayle
22 22 John Chote
23 23 Mary Stanley (Fraley)
24 24 Calvin Morgan
25 25 Pleasant Corvin
26 26 James Goddard
27 27 Francis M. Cook
269B 28 28 Jonah Scott
29 29 Elijah Norris (Wilson, Land, Hartbarger)
30 30 James Yoder
31 31 Frank Helton (Franklin, Rains)
32 32 Charles W. Todd (Spence)
33 33 Nancy Martin
34 34 George W. Smedley
35 35 Thomas R. Travis
36 36 Peter G. Travis
37 37 George W. Romines
270A 38 38 James Tallent
39 39 Benjamin Pugh
40 40 Moses Bottomlee
41 41 Samuel B. Arnold (Bell)
42 42 William Arnold
43 43 Ebb S. Cox (Waterhouse)
270B 44 44 Arch Goins
45 45 William Gholston
46 46 George W. Johnson
47 47 John Goins (Gaddis)
48 48 James P. Sexton
49 49 Arch C. Broyles
50 50 Cornelius D. Broyles
51 51 Valentine Allen
52 52 Brown Swafford (Spring)
271A 53 53 John Swafford
54 54 Enoch Suthers (Watkins)
55 55 Samuel Day
56 56 William W. Cunnyngham (Burnett)
57 57 Mary E. Hale (Bankston)
58 58 Rachel Skillern
59 59 Floyd Rankins (Walters)
60 60 William Gillespie
61 61 Joseph Gillespie
62 62 John Gill
63 63 George Goins
271B 64 64 Sherman Wilson
65 65 Peter Ellison
66 66 John Collier
67 67 Samuel Gill (Wilson)
68 68 Charles Nelson (Furbanks)
69 69 James Shelton
70 70 Jessie B. Jordan
71 71 John Dyer
72 72 George R. Kyle
272A 73 73 Robert Kyle
74 74 Caroline McDonald (Kyle)
75 75 James Eakins
76 76 William D. Yoder
77 77 John Shadrick
78 78 Ferrel Hall
79 79 Jack Moore (Triplett, White, Cates, Wilson, Breedlove)
80 80 Nancy Rankin (Norton, Cunningham)
81 81 Jessie A. Lovelace
272B 82 82 Jeff D. Gaither (Kyle)
83 83 George Cunningham
84 84 Jefferson Claig
85 85 John W Reynolds (Swafford)
86 86 Humphrey Hackett (Lotharage)
87 87 John Birch
88 88 John Good
89 89 Anderson Dodd (Henderson)
90 90 John C. Malone (West)
273A 91 91 Robert L. Allen
92 92 James Crawford (Kelly)
93 93 Charles Robertson
94 94 Joseph Ellis (Rogers)
95 95 Franklin H. Abel (Coulter)
96 96 William Smith
97 97 Thomas Travis (Hall)
98 98 John Hall
273B 99 99 George Azz

273B 100 100 Valentine Rowen (Thomas, Vineyard, Wright)
101 101 Patrick Maley
102 102 John W. Treadway
103 103 Richard L. Ellis
104 104 William Kyle
105 105 Rachel(?) Shankle
106 106 John R. Abel
107 107 Henry Jackson (Winnis)
108 108 James A. Kelly
109 109 Thos Painter (Rowden)
274A 110 110 Jeffrey Young
111 111 James J. Bohannon
112 112 Wm Young (Rankins, Swafford)
113 113 Solomon Henry
114 114 Abner Spring
115 115 Joseph Kelly
116 116 William Lockmiller
274B 117 117 John Rush (Presley)
118 118 John Gill
119 119 Louis F.(?) Elder
120 120 John F. Ivy

DISTRICT 8

Henry K. Banks, Enumerator

275A 121 121 Milton N. Johns (Mitchell)
122 122 Wesley Mathis
123 123 Joe Mitchell
124 124 McDuffy Stone
125 125 Bup Matlock (Kelly)
126 126 Samuel Whitlow (Keith, Carter, Sea)
127 127 John Pearson
128 128 Florence Ray (Mayfield)
129 129 Alice Hart
130 130 Rosa Wade (White, Renfro, Mason, Neal)
131 131 Albert Trewhit
132 132 Nancy Mitchell (Mayfield)
133 133 Matilda Johns
134 134 Rice Hodge (Knott)
275B 135 135 Ella Love (McDuffy)
136 136 Olliver Strickland (Peak)
137 137 Dock Bridgman
138 138 Jack Meadows
139 139 Henry Foster (Wall)
140 140 Bonnie Brown
141 141 George Washington (Connelly)
142 142 Lee A. Kelly (Medlock, Jink, White, Williams, Sharp)
143 143 John Sullas
144 144 David Lane (Bennett)
145 145 Milton Ragin (Silas, Archy)
146 146 Charles Callaway (Baker)
147 147 Thomas Ford (Melton)
148 148 John Townsend
276A 149 Edward Townsend (Hayes)
149 150 Wm Lindsey (Herring, Buffington)
150 151 Geo M. Neuman (Kilgore)
151 152 Samuel McJunkin
152 153 Richard Gallahar (Roberts)
153 154 Samuel H.(?) Hickman (Sabin)
154 155 Eli H. Jones
155 156 William A. Rogers
156 157 John Whitfield
276B 157 158 Frank L Crowder (Washum)
158 159 Martin Lyons
159 160 Joseph Gallaher
160 161 William McWells (Cunningham)
161 162 William Bird
162 163 William J. Norman
163 164 Joseph Gibson (Campbell)
164 165 John Sharp
165 166 George McMillan
166 167 Samuel Umbarger (Rose)
167 168 John Trentwan
277A 168 169 James Morgan
169 170 Franklin McMillan (Watson, Teasely, Pritchet)
170 171 William F. Head
171 172 John Travis
172 173 Edward Vance
173 174 William Holden
174 175 John Vance (Tate)
175 176 Samuel Henderson
176 177 William Majors
177 178 David Bess
178 179 Wesley Britt (Bain, Ferguson)
277B 179 180 Alvin Hayes (Swain)
180 181 James Walker (Hicks)
181 182 Calvin Morgan (Abel)
182 183 Arza Adams
184 Arva Morgan (Green, Houser)
183 185 Kate Gothard
184 186 Ed T. Morgan (Romines)
185 187 Martha J. Morgan
186 188 Lucien Hale (Armor)
187 189 David Gwillim
278A 188 190 Rees Gwillim (Walker)
189 191 William A. Brand
190 192 Henry C. Morgan
191 193 William D. Center
192 194 James McJunkin
193 195 Newton Johnson
194 196 John W. Buttram
195 197 James Majors
196 198 Thomas Hale
197 199 Samuel H. Nixon (Kiker)
278B 198 200 George Nixon
199 201 William Rose
200 202 Alvin P.(?) Morgan (Green)
201 203 Mary West
202 204 Calvin Green
203 205 William White
204 206 William Bridgman
205 207 Sarah Green
206 208 James Head
207 209 Joseph Hogue
279A 208 210 Frank Rigsby (Merrel)
209 211 David Bell
210 212 Frank Lynch
211 213 Susan Dunaho
212 214 Ulusor Boyd (Payne)
213 215 Henry Morgan
214 216 John Holmes (Carter)
215 217 Lafayette Gambill
216 218 Charles Sharp (Moonyhan)
217 219 Mumford L. Wyrick
218 220 John W. Nash
279B 219 221 John Thyaw
220 222 Harvey Franklin (Lampkin, Lively)
221 223 Joseph Harris (Lane)
222 224 Robert Jakes (Maness)
223 225 Louis Hawkins
224 228 Isaac Dunaho
225 227 Susan Majors (Eaton, Taylor)
226 228 Lorenza Poole
280A 227 229 Mollie Hibbs (Marler)
228 230 James K. Abel (Smith)
229 231 Louis Sharp (Brown, Jenkins)
230 232 James(?) Ottinger
231 233 William Yoder
232 234 Thomas Nash (Gardenhire)
233 235 Calvin Thurman (Gothard)
234 236 Thomas Smith
280B 235 237 Samuel Caldwell
236 238 Wm Small (Mahan)
237 239 Hurman Johnson
238 240 George Lemons
239 241 Thomas Smith
240 242 Jasper Miller
241 243 Melvin Burrell
242 244 Caroline Lane
243 245 Sarah Trusly (Johnson, Tramble)
244 246 Robert Hogue
245 247 William Ayers
281A 246 248 John D. Stansberry
247 249 John L. Bridgmon
248 250 Edward Blackford
249 251 Albert Evans
250 252 Edward Jones (Insley)
251 253 Elitt Jones
252 254 Samuel McDonald
253 255 Alfred Watson
281B 254 256 Milton Henry
255 257 Elizabeth Shadrick (Elliott)
256 258 David C. King
257 259 William Nelson
258 260 Columbus McMillan (Wilson)
259 261 Jennie Blackburn
260 261 Wm Wilson (Rigsby)
261 263 Charles W. Ault (Smith)
262 264 George Kiker
263 265 Charles R. Wilson
282A 264 266 John Wilson
265 267 John Neal (Ivester)
266 268 John Wyatt
267 269 Joseph Giles (Bently,Jordan)
268 270 Henry Mowry (Winsett)
269 271 Andy Holden
270 272 Thomas Alexander
271 273 Robert Armor
272 274 Theodore Morgan
273 275 John D. Morgan
282B 274 276 Gideon B. Morgan (Barton)
275 277 Robert Green
276 278 Fred Green
277 279 William A. Pass
278 280 Calvin Morgan
279 281 Hattie E. Greer
280 282 William Hicks
281 283 John Johnson (Love)
282 284 Mattie Rector (Pass)
283 285 Mack Yarnell
284 186 Wm J. Caldwell (Pryor)
285 287 Henry F. Morgan
283A 286 288 John A. Rose
287 289 Polly Mahan

283A 288 290 George W. Presly
289 291 George Fields (Baker)
290 292 Hannibal Green
291 293 James Bottomlee
292 294 Mary J. Rogers (Horney)
293 295 Jeneral F. Collier (Green)
283B 294 296 Joseph Green
295 297 Lark Hunter (Raiden)
296 298 Andy Carter (Johnson)
297 299 Hugh or Henry Walden
298 300 John Hughes (Baddirvans, Holden)
299 301 Jack Arndale
300 302 William Walker
301 303 George Alley
302 304 Wm Rogers (Denton)
303 305 Lee Clouse
304 306 Robert Walker
284A 305 307 Richard Atkins (Sharp)
306 308 Joseph Suttles
307 309 Whit Dillard
308 310 William Walker
309 311 Filmore Walker
310 312 Thomas Walker
311 313 Mandy Burk
312 314 Green Dillard
284B 313 315 Bud Carter
314 316 Steve Kelly
315 317 Ella Cradle
316 318 Wairick K. J–?—
317 319 Henry Swaford (Harmony)
318 320 John Crawford
319 321 Isaac Bogger (Foster)
320 322 Jas Campbell (Avy, Bogges)
321 323 Thomas Swafford
322 324 Thomas Herring
323 325 George Dickson
324 326 Chas Bird (Bigby, Harbin)
285A 325 327 Elia Brown
326 328 Jefferson Hutchison
327 329 Emily E. Harper
328 330 James Stansbury
329 331 Jack Lee (Stapley, Hankins)
330 332 Henry Stevens
331 333 Albert Stokes (Northop,Cox)
332 334 William Shadrick
333 335 Walter Arden
334 336 Walter Gannaway
335 337 Edmond Gannaway
285B 336 338 King Benson
337 339 James Benson
338 340 Mary Waldo
339 341 Thomas Riddle (Smith)
340 342 James R. Wilson
341 343 Milton Howser
342 344 Serena Morgan
343 345 Charles James
344 346 James G. Rudd
345 347 Adolphus Morgan
286A 346 348 Worthy Swift
347 349 Emily Oldham
348 350 Margaret Harverson
349 351 James F. Minton
350 352 James Oldham
351 353 Sarah Riley
352 354 Creed Shadrick (Davis)
353 355 Prudence Shadrick
354 356 Samuel T. Shadrick
355 357 William Dyer
356 358 Rufus Dyer
357 359 Chas Denning or Dunning
358 360 Alonzo Denning or Dunning
359 361 Riley Minton
286B 360 362 Hard Shadrick
361 363 Elijah Pool
362 364 Munroe Morgan
363 365 Aruogia(?) Gothard
364 366 Julia A. Morgan (Burwick)
365 367 Wiley A. Ault
366 368 James England
367 369 John Acuff (Gardenhire, Cunningham)
368 370 James M. McMillan
369 371 Margaret James
370 372 Malinda Crockett
287A 371 373 Jonas Coleman
372 374 Sarah Cooper (Condar)
373 375 William Jones
374 376 James Everitt
375 377 William Arrants (Sexton)
376 378 Walter Green
377 379 Hiram Riddle
378 380 George Foust (McPherson)
379 381 Lemul Bowman (West)
380 382 Absalom Ward
381 383 Melvin Foust (Green, Smedley)
382 384 Samuel James
287B 383 385 Spencer Burrel
384 386 Jesse Green
385 387 Daniel Curtis
386 388 Julian Bird
387 389 Chris Hood (Hughes, Sowers)
388 390 Thomas Sanford (Cox)
389 391 James Griffin (Cook)
390 392 Rufus Hughes
391 393 Matthew Maury (Anderson)
392 394 John R. Abel
393 395 Henry M. Hensley (Rothjeb)
394 396 Margaret A. Ault (Tullas)
288A 395 397 Amos Smith
396 398 William Truax
397 399 Thos Prater (Keener)
398 400 Mathew R. Gibson
399 401 John Clingan
400 402 Robert Thomison
401 403 Tipton Broyles
402 404 Elijah Atkinson (Cunningham)
288B 403 405 William Burchard
404 406 Albert Waters
405 407 Henry Burchard
406 408 James Nicholds
407 409 Charles Hickman
408 410 James Pickle
409 411 William Morgan
410 412 Houston Morgan
411 413 George Burchard
289A 412 414 James Hickmont
415 William Montgomery
413 416 White Morgan
414 417 Richard Henderson
415 418 Jacob Montgomery
416 419 Raulston Montgomery
417 420 Howard Montgomery
418 421 Thomas Nichols
419 422 William F. Ward
420 423 William Henderson
421 424 Nash Bottomlee
289B 422 425 Hamilton Burchard
423 426 John McMillan
424 427 John Bottomlee
425 428 James A. Black
426 429 James Swafford
427 430 William Washburn
428 431 Thomas Earhart
429 432 Charity Earhart
430 433 John A. Patterson (Hayes)

DISTRICT 11

Roy R. Reynolds, Enumerator

290A 1 1 Morris Humphrey
2 2 James F. Walker
3 3 John J. Tolle
4 4 Frank W. Birchfield
5 5 John T. Ewers
6 6 William R. Burdett
7 7 William F. Morgan
8 8 John C Reno (Blalock)
9 9 Leonard O. Weller
10 10 John R. Stewart (Wilson)
11 11 James F. Pickett
290B 12 12 James T. Pickett
13 13 Mar— F. Rigsby
14 14 Henry Keeney
15 15 William D. Rigsby
16 16 Wigfall Lillard
17 17 Henry Smith
18 18 George W. Morgan (Locke)
19 19 Noah H. Euvrand
20 20 James M. Clark
21 21 Rufus W. Morgan
291A 22 22 Charles Morgan
23 23 Elisha M. Kimbrough
24 24 Josephus Morgan
25 25 Brownlow Morgan
26 26 Thomas M. Solomon
27 27 James E. Eaton
28 28 Adelbert Eaton
29 29 John Swafford
30 30 Frank R.(?) Morgan
31 31 Luther R. Morgan
32 32 Robert J. Rigsby
33 33 Samuel J. Rigsby
291B 34 34 Calvin J. Turley (Culver)
35 35 Edward M. Talmadge
36 36 William Elder
37 37 Newton J. Edmundson
38 38 John B. Headlee
39 39 Thomas Wright
40 40 Louise Wright
41 41 Walker B. Headlee
42 42 Allen Sparks
43 43 John Olinger
44 44 Charles E. Mowry
45 45 Henry H. Wright
46 46 Jacob D. Wyatt
292A 47 47 Judson B. Hill
48 48 Joseph E. Euvrard
49 49 Rezin Wolfe
50 50 Joseph R. Acuff
51 51 Jacob N. Bean
52 52 William J. Acuff
53 53 Robert T. Ritchie
54 54 Reuben B. Lee
55 55 Josephine Lee
56 56 David Ritchie
57 57 Malauchton Miller
58 58 Nancy A. Freiley
59 59 Edward P. Hutchins

292B 60 60 Sarah M. Hutchins
61 61 Bryant H. Melendy
62 62 Edwin F. Wetmore (Bean)
63 63 Duarie Lee
64 64 David Dickerson
65 65 Sarah J. Snow (Medley, Evens)
66 66 Aaron A Reed (Wilson)
67 67 Clinton Medley
68 68 John T. Ensminger
69 69 Albert E. Lee
70 70 Richard S. Webb
71 71 Bee F. Sykes
293A 72 72 Lodic Sykes
73 73 James D. Blankenship
74 74 Noah Myers
75 75 John D. Olinger
76 76 Frank J. Grice (Johnson)
77 77 William B. Lowry
78 78 William M. Walker
79 79 Abraham Payne
80 80 James D. Gothard
81 81 Frank Pickard
82 82 Matilda L. Pickard
83 83 Lewis G. Rogers
293B 84 84 John M. Burwick (Fisher)
85 85 John H. Burwick
86 David H. Burwick
86 87 Howard Keely
87 88 Samuel Burwick
88 89 James O.(?) Rogers
89 90 Samuel H. Small
90 91 David Oldham
91 92 Robert Rogers
92 93 John W. Morgan
93 94 Robert L. Reed
94 95 David W. Reed (Barnes)
95 96 William R. Reed
96 97 Watson Reed

DISTRICT 13
Roy R. Reynolds, Enumerator

295A 97 98 George W. Everett
99 Rufus H. Everett
98 100 John W. Barger
99 101 James L. Spangler
100 102 Vesta Gannaway
101 103 Joseph Martin
102 104 William C. Line (Raulston)
103 105 Isaac N. Shirley (Clingan)
295B 104 106 Land Shirley
105 107 Thomas B. Shirley
106 108 Jacob Teeters
107 109 John A. Troutman
108 110 Hugh Barger (Hatfield)
109 111 James F. Gad
110 112 Zachariah T. Keedy (Treadaway)
111 113 Rufus Goin
112 114 Nancy Queen
296A 113 115 Arch N. Lewis
114 116 William M. Russell
115 117 Charles D. Bean
116 118 Marcus Russell
117 119 Neely M. Keith
118 120 Charles L. Coulter
119 121 George B. Alexander
120 122 Daly A. Green (Boling)
121 123 James M. Alexander
122 124 Bradford Goin
296B 123 125 Charles Cook (England)
124 126 Aaron Crawley (Marshall)
125 127 John Morrison
126 128 Cue B. Alley (Crawley)
127 129 Thomas Brooks
128 130 Earnest A. Shelton
129 131 Frank Lander
130 132 John Swafford (Clingan)
131 133 John M. Thomas
132 134 Hattie Mills (Shirley)
133 135 Sarah J. Shirley
297A 134 138 Gilbert Martin (Lee)
135 137 Gilbert Shipley
136 138 Charles McAfee
137 139 John B. Doss
138 140 Charles Howard
139 141 Hugh Doss
140 142 Gus Doss
141 143 John Doss
144 Jane Kilgore
142 145 Deck Raulston
297B 143 146 Joseph B. Corvin (Steele)
144 147 William M. Brooks
Thomas Corvin
146 149 Mary Jane Turner (Corvin)
147 150 Jane S. Dobbs
148 151 James Myers (Powers)
149 152 William R. Myers (Cantrell)
150 153 Bird Walker
298A 151 154 Long S. Stewart (Moats)
152 155 John T. Thomas
153 156 Solomon Harden
154 157 George W. Spivey
155 158 J. Crockett Corvin
156 159 Thomas A. Corvin
157 160 William Lyons
298B 158 161 Harvey Creaseman (White)
159 162 Holliday Spivey (Good)
160 163 Rachael Colston
161 164 Euclid Waterhouse
162 165 John Fine
163 166 Robert Brannon
164 167 William Wellington
168 B. Forrest Wellington
165 169 Jeptha Randolph
299A 166 170 James Fox
167 171 John McKinney
168 172 George Moats (McKinney)
169 173 Newton Moats
170 174 James A. Crawley
171 175 Elijah Boles
172 176 James T. James
173 177 Goldie Springs
299B 174 178 Charles M. Davis
175 179 Louis A. Blake (Prady, Julian, Myers, Martin)
176 180 John A. Anderson
181 Charles E. Johnson
177 182 David Davis
178 183 James M. Nelson (Coulter, Williams)
179 184 William Grimsley (Houston)
180 185 George L. Schatzel (Fiscus)
300A 181 186 George D. Clemons
182 187 W. Edward McDonald
183 188 William C. Myers
184 189 William L. Lacewell
185 190 William K. Gray
187 191 Henry T. Fox
187 192 William Fox
188 193 George McDonald (Fox)
189 194 George S. Vreeland
190 195 William M. Lawson
191 196 William F. Simpson
197 Alonzo S. Price
300B 192 198 George W. Owens
193 199 William H. Morgan
194 200 Martin L. Loftis
195 201 William A. Green
202 Albert S. Green
196 203 Frank M. Bower
197 204 James Miller
198 205 Wm W. Edwards (Gill)
199 206 Columbia H Myers (Brown)
301A 200 207 Joel A Lasham or Lawhorn
201 208 Miller Goin (Creaseman, May)
202 209 James H. Hickman
203 210 Thomas H. Holmes
211 George W. Holmes
204 212 Robert B. Barger (Howard)
205 213 Francis Bower
206 214 John H. Brackett
207 215 Meredith A. Neal
301B 208 216 Thomas E. May
209 217 Theodore Flora
210 218 Peter B. Clouse
211 219 William F. Corvin
212 220 Elisha M. Weeks
213 221 Reuben H Smith (Travis)
214 222 Andy J. Hawkins
215 223 Jacob H. Cross (Helton)
302A 216 224 Asbury Goins
217 225 Edward J. Abel
218 226 Jas D. Rigsby (Morris)
219 227 William T Barger (Best, Johnson)
220 228 William S. Hale
221 229 William L. Jones
222 230 Thomas H. Johnson
223 231 Alfred C. Houston
232 Archie H. Slaten
224 233 John C. Connelley
225 234 George W. Strickland
302B 226 235 John Doss
227 236 John W. Suttler (Eaton)
237 John Green
228 238 Jesse W. Ivester (Small)
229 239 Andy Majors (Pluning)
230 240 Charles Jones
231 241 Edwin B. Osborn
232 242 Joseph O. Bilbrey
233 243 Colum–ru Ervin
234 244 George W. Davis
235 245 John Best (Pryor)
236 246 Morgan Dalton
303A 237 247 Jasper S. Fain
238 248 John M. Colwell
239 249 Addison Walker
240 250 Columbus(?) Colwell
241 251 Andy Miles
242 252 William T. Storey
243 253 George W. Washburne
244 254 Ollie Corvin
245 255 Newton J. Bowman
246 256 Jas M. Rogers (Brumlow)
247 257 Emily Rogers
248 258 Thomas B. Coulter
249 259 John B. Rogers
303B 250 260 Samuel B. Hoge
251 261 Thomas I. Helton

303B 252 262 Patrick Thomas
253 263 Edward L. Jenkins
254 264 John M. Walden
255 265 Rachael Formens(Brown)
256 266 David A. Holt
257 267 Jasper J. Alley
258 268 Wm H. Hensley (Hamby)
304A 259 269 William H. Walker (Norris)
260 270 Robert F. Axmaker
261 271 Emanuel Hensley
262 272 George E. Furman
263 273 William A. Anderson
264 274 Henry A. Davis
265 275 William T. Green
266 276 Andrew Gillespie
267 277 Robert Edwards (Houston)
268 278 William McEwen (Gregory)
269 279 Henry Clouse
270 280 Edgar P. Tipton
304B 271 281 Samuel A. Wilson
272 282 Bird Thomas
273 283 Jackson Snyder
274 284 Daniel Mitchell
275 285 James A. Walker (Rains)
276 286 Joseph Rose (Griffin)
277 287 Jas A. Hoback (Dixon)
278 288 Jack E. Calhoun
279 289 James Brown
280 290 Jas C. Denson (Corvin)
305A 281 291 James J. Green
282 292 Robinson Nail
283 293 Sylvester Bird
284 294 Charles C. Nail
285 295 Carrie B. Swearingon
286 296 Francis W. Bacon (Daniels, Rogers)
287 297 Joseph Iseminger
298 Partise Thomas
288 299 Job W. Carlock (Furlong)
289 300 Henry H. Buguo
290 301 Sidney Brownbeage
305B 291 302 Frank McDonald
292 303 Arvell Leech
304 Johnathan Tallent
293 305 Robert McGill
294 306 Marion Helton
295 307 Robert McDonald (Scott)
296 308 William F. Alley
297 309 Wm A. Jordan (Johnson)
298 310 William Griffith
299 311 Levi Hoback
300 312 James M. Grimsley
301 313 James W. Rose
302 314 John B. Roach (Rose)
306A 303 315 George T. Travis
304 316 Samuel Dungan
305 317 William Beard
306 318 Samuel S. Blevins
307 319 Tate Martin (Hughes)
308 320 Lucinda E. Dungan
309 321 John Bolin (Jordan, Evans)
310 322 Benjamin Goin
311 323 John R. Brown
312 324 George W. Foster (Brown)
313 325 Ozias Jordan
314 326 Joseph E. Wright
306B 315 327 Jacob C. Bean
316 328 John W. Clouse
317 329 Benjamin Shipley
318 330 Joseph E. Rains (Worley, Pearsley)
319 331 Laurence J. Card
320 332 John A. Reed
321 333 Edward J. Farmer
322 334 Monroe R. Miller (Hall)
307A 323 335 Nancy Bolin
324 336 James R. Barger
325 337 Sarah J. Card
326 338 Milar S. Small
327 339 William R. Rogers
328 340 William M. Bean
329 341 Samuel W. Litchfield (Pine, Manous, Woodall)
330 342 Wm Weatherbee (Queen)
331 343 Everett C. Sparks
307B 332 344 William Sharp
333 345 Charles A. Sparks
334 346 Alfred T. Marler
335 347 Nichodemus Marler
336 348 Francis M. Marler
337 349 James Rolston
338 350 Ruth Martin
339 351 Joseph P. Martin
340 352 John D. Gad
341 353 Calvin H. McMillan
308A 342 354 Cyrus I. Walker
343 355 John R. Green
344 356 Thomas F. Smith
345 357 John F. Henderson
346 358 Robert O. Jordan
347 359 Charles H. Cantrell
348 360 Oscar J. Green
361 William P. Johns
349 362 James J. Davis
350 363 Printos S. Messer
308B 351 364 Andrew C. Bird
352 365 Clara ?. Phillips (Conklin Phillipot)
353 366 John F. Wilson
354 367 Hugh T. Blevins
355 368 Cyria M. Gannaway
356 369 James Jordan
357 370 Joseph B. Everett
358 371 Robert T. Carter
359 372 Patrick D. Myers
309A 360 373 James L. McKinzie
361 374 William T. Drummond
362 375 John M. Hall (Henegar)
363 376 Mary C. Morrison (Sharp)
364 377 Rinnie T. Letson
365 378 Joseph W. Franklin
366 379 James B. Morton
367 380 Erwin P. Giles
381 Noah W. Allee
368 382 Melvin C. Sturdevant
369 383 Winnie E. Bell
370 384 Robt M. Kilgore (Eldredge)
309B 371 385 William M. Sexton
372 386 Olie Hayward (Buntin)
373 387 John C. Werner
374 388 Allen F. Harrison (Rose)
375 389 Andrew B. Caravile (Gregg)
376 390 William Woodford
377 391 Edwin R Gillett (Davenport)
378 392 John F. Jeffers
379 393 Henry B. Landis
380 394 Samuel Walker
310A 381 395 John Dennis
382 386 William R. Grimsley
383 397 Norris P. Lawrence (Hughes)
384 398 Wilford Lawrence
385 399 Charles W. Irwin (Foster, Finch, Fulton, Morey, Davis, Martin, Rogers, Dortch, Rikard, Hanson, Pavey, Greenwood, Smith, Stoner, Paul, Baugh, Mitchell, Archer)
386 400 Etta M. Cobban
310B 387 401 John Bean
388 402 Charles F. Bean
389 403 James Letner
390 404 John Jones

DISTRICT 8

M. B. Hicks, Enumerator

CITY OF DAYTON

(that part south of Big Richland Creek)

311A 1 1 Robert L. Lyons
2 2 Henry Logan (Fleming, Haskell)
3 3 John Sims
4 4 Matildas Bridgman
5 5 Isam Eskridge (Deloin)
6 6 Jennie(?) Snowden
7 7 Perry Johnson
8 8 Elizabeth Potter (Broyles)
9 9 Maud Smith (Wray)
10 Waldo Jackson
10 11 Ellen Hyde
11 12 Mary Wilkie
12 13 Roscoe Bennett (Gibson, Springs, Thomas)
311B 13 14 Phoebe Rhea (Brown,Cates)
14 15 Joseph B. Hale
15 16 George L. Morgan
16 17 Elizabeth Morgan
17 18 Sam Suddath
18 19 Hettie White (Gill)
19 20 Jas Holland (Arnold)
20 21 Wayne(?) Cranmore
21 22 Louis Gormany
22 23 Eli Gossett (Ellis)
23 24 Samuel H. Ellis
312A 24 25 Joseph Decker
25 26 Camill Bowler
26 27 Floyd E. Tallent
27 28 James Rudd (Goins)
29 Sarah James (Smith)
28 30 Moses Grier (Essex, Harrison, Owens, King, Jenkins, Kennedy, Boring, Curtis)
29 31 Robert P. Abel (Cook)
30 32 Myra J. Hodges (Cunningham)
31 33 William F. Blevins
32 34 William B. Benson Jr. (Miller)
33 35 John King (Wumble?)
312B 34 36 Charles Nelson
35 37 James W. Acuff
36 38 Lewis Swafford (Cockran)
39 James S. Day
37 40 Elizabeth Smith
38 41 Joseph Daniels
39 42 Aquilla M. Hale
40 43 Vaughn Crow (Mullenix)
41 44 Danie May (Senter)

312B 42 45 Henry C. Rose
313A 43 46 William B. Benson
44 47 Emmett P. Johnson
45 48 James G. Thomison (Evans, Grasty)
46 49 Frank W. Skillern
47 50 John McKinley (Newman)
48 51 George C. McKenzie
49 52 George T. Wright
50 53 Melvin Hight (Dyer)
51 54 Maria Henson (Tolless)
313B 52 55 Walter C. Gossett
53 56 Hart P.(?) Arthur
54 57 W-?-ain Brunnagin (Brooks)
55 58 Nimrod Pickle
56 59 Joe Banks (McDonald, Boggess)
57 60 Bell Kimball (Bogel)
58 61 Willis Taylor (Anton, Foust, Casper)
59 62 Malinda H. Chamber
60 63 Reuben Brun
61 64 Samson Bridgman Jr.
62 65 George Bunn
314A 63 66 John Cates (Stevens)
64 67 Joseph Price
65 68 William Stephens
66 69 Henry C. Benson
67 70 William Dill (Taylor)
68 71 Nancy L. Stanfield
69 72 William G. Purser
70 73 Charles Wycuff (Hurley)
71 74 James M. Robeson
72 75 Walter F. Thomison
73 76 John Snowden
74 77 Allen Hale
75 78 William McDonald (Edwards)
76 79 Thomas Bridgeman
77 80 Clift Zebe
314B 78 81 John B. Beugler (Chase)
79 82 Mary B. Minton
80 83 John W. Williamson
81 84 Will L. Patten (Rose)
82 85 William Brown
83 86 John Abel
84 87 Maggie Tallent
85 88 William G. Allen
86 89 Matthew Gibson
87 90 Sarysan D. Tridgman (Lillard)
88 91 John A. Whitner (Parker)
315A 89 92 Fannie Jones (Hughes)
90 93 Sallie Bettis (Ninn, Swafford)
91 94 Mary H. Bunn (Eskridge)
92 95 Elisha S. Gibson
93 96 Wm McConnell (Gerton)
94 97 Mary Bradford (Hunt,Mack)
98 Ada Gormany
95 99 James McDonald
96 100 Bertie Wasson (Locke?, Kelly, Johnson, McCeaver)
315B 97 101 William Castleman
98 102 Betsy J. Miller
99 103 John S. Evans (Maddison)
100 104 Fannie Miller
101 105 Marshall Johnson
102 106 A. F. Nye
103 107 William Uhl
104 108 George Silvers
316A 105 109 John B. Suiagood
106 110 Francis M. Morrison
107 111 William Donaldson
108 112 Mar–? O. Harrison (Tallent)
109 113 Thomas K. Green
110 114 Thomas Banks
111 115 Mary J. Ervin (Brooks)
112 116 James E. Abel (Rowan)
113 117 James J. Abel (Jewell, Thomas)
114 118 Mary T. Cofer (Warner)
115 119 Oliver Smith
116 120 Robert Pullan
117 121 Mettie Jones (Powell,Carter, Buckner,Stovall, Wilks, Peassall)
118 122 William A. Johnson
119 123 Frederick R. Rogers
120 124 Nathan D. Reed (Gilbreath)
121 125 Frank Reed
122 126 Patrick Haughey (Gallager)
316B 123 127 Edward H. Ivey
124 128 Will Payne (Stevens)
125 129 John Swafford
126 130 William C. Gunter
127 131 Andy Lowry
128 132 Frank Tulliss
129 133 Samuel Fleming
130 134 Rebecca Stone
131 135 John Tallent
136 Henry Dodson
132 137 Roe Ridley
133 138 John Gordon
134 139 John Rue (Larson,Toury?)
317A 135 140 Thomas S. Blackburn
136 141 William H. Alexander
137 142 John H. Best (Queen)
138 143 George Franklin
139 144 Arne Johnson
140 145 Thos Edwards (Dew)
141 146 Ellen Peak (Jolly)
142 147 James Gains
317B 143 148 Jackson Suddath (Powell, Smart)
144 149 William Woody (Doss)
145 150 Henry Bankston
146 151 Nathan B. Moore
147 152 Ben(?) B. McAndrens
148 153 Thomas P. Collins
149 154 Wm J. Buchanan (Piesall)
150 155 James M. Newell
151 156 Asahel Johnson
152 157 Joseph Roberts
318A 153 158 Joseph Morgan
154 159 Sam Walters (Swafford, Pickle)
155 160 Cate Guirver(?) (Jones, Wilkerson, Carmack, Hill)
156 161 Elizabeth Swafford
157 162 Salie(?) Gillespie (Carter, Snellings)
158 163 David Coulter
159 164 Martha Lincoln
160 165 Hattie Henderson (Johnson, Jackson)
166 Jennie Dickson (Barney, Alexander)
318B 161 167 Alex Ridley (Maley)
162 168 Charles Harper (Gordon)
163 169 Calumma Brown (Tally, O'Rankins, Swafford)
164 170 George Miller (Perkins)
165 171 Columbus Gillespie (Boyd)
166 172 Alonzo Lane (Tigner)
167 173 William H. Rogers (Dixon, Hutchinson)
168 174 James Riley
169 175 James Jackson (Bryant, McDermit)
170 176 John Martin (Tullon)
171 177 Solomon Rose or Rise
319A 172 178 James Turner
173 179 Miranda Bennett
174 180 Mary Collins

DISTRICT 10

Webster Thomas, Enumerator

CITY OF DAYTON

(that part north of Big Richland Creek)

Railroad Street

320A 1 1 Benjamin F. Mealer (Hicks, Gillespie, Gwillim, Deakins, Gann, Ayers, Holloway, Gray, Early, Saillie, S?agrange, Dane, Douglas, Billingsly)

Main Street

320A 2 2 George W. Goodrich (Miller, Minton, Hoover, Gardenhire, Frazier, Moody, Heiney, Schoolfield, Ayers)
3 3 Marquis Morrison (Jones, Holloman, McCabe, Waller, Kent, Lokey)
320B 4 4 John E. Ewers
5 5 John C. Cunnyngham
6 6 Thomas ?. Barton
7 7 Charles Wilbur
8 8 James L. Dean
9 9 Albert Dodson
10 10 Mary J. Baker
11 11 James Howard
12 12 Sallie E. Dickey
13 13 William Maryman
14 14 Andrew P. Haggard
15 15 John A. Denton
321A 16 16 James Brandon
17 17 Charles Keylon
18 18 Otto Greunitz
19 19 Sarah L. Benson
20 William Robeson
20 21 Joseph Hicks
21 22 Ambrose A. Pierce
22 23 John M. Howard (Hayes)
23 24 W[illegible]e B.(?) Miller
24 25 Lizzie Crawford
25 26 Joseph Brooks
26 27 George Henderson
27 28 James H. Hood
28 29 Noah J. Tallent
29 30 John W. Francis (Daniels)
30 31 Emma Dorsett (Weaver)
321B 31 32 George W. Woolen

321B 32 33 Monroe Smith
33 34 Scruggs Lockmiller
34 35 Lihu Baker
35 36 Andrew Dick
37 Edward O. Rankin
36 38 Hoyt C. Bridgman

First Avenue

37 39 William L. Barnes
38 40 Maggie A. Rose
39 41 Perry M. England
322A 40 42 Alvin C. Gibson (Sells)
41 43 Charles M.(?) Snyder
42 44 Addie Hutsell
43 45 Rufus L.(?) Doran (Monneyhan)
44 46 Emma Gillespie (Jolly, Wadkins, Hembrick, Allen, Gilbert)
45 47 Nicholas G. Moore
46 48 Andrew J. England
47 49 Alexander Dickson
48 50 Bennet J. Franklin (Detar)
49 51 Melinda Hodge
322B 52 Nancy J. Hillyard
50 53 Alfred Carney
51 54 James Franklin
52 55 Benjamin F. Moore
53 56 Thomas J. Campbell
54 57 William White
55 58 Henry Gonia
56 59 Maggie Roddy (Wilson, Stenson, Carter, Pearson)
57 60 Albert G. Slawson (Tolle)
323A 58 61 Charles Middleton
59 62 Charles Brady
60 63 August Schill
61 64 Rhoda Hamilton (Pickle)
65 John McEntire (Cummings, Fleming)
62 66 Mary Holmes (Jones)
63 67 Annie Scott (Whitfield)
323A 64 68 Ada Crockett (Sims)
65 69 Nancy Wright
66 70 James Jones
67 71 William Whitfield
68 72 Franklin Martin
69 73 Wm Bomires (Blevins)
70 74 Thomas M. Williams
71 75 John K. Merton

Second Avenue

323B 72 76 Harry D. Martin (Brown)
73 77 Thomas Pelfrey (Rudd)
74 78 Perry Pelfrey
75 79 Dwight Culver (Arnold)
76 80 Margaret L. Stallings
77 81 Hezekiah Elder
78 82 Richard C. Knight
79 83 Jas F.(?) Henninger (Kiker)
80 84 Callie Howard (James)
81 85 William L. Givens
324A 82 86 John C. Dodd
83 87 Caroline Pullum (Glen, Vaughn, Worthington)
84 88 Earl G. Nye
85 89 Martin Wilkie
86 90 Alexander Bennett
87 91 James Harris
88 92 Benjamin G McKenzie
89 93 William Doyle
90 94 George Brandon (Rogers, Veach)
91 95 Abraham Pryor
92 96 Anderson Parker
324B 93 97 James L.(?) Shelton
94 98 Green B. Brady (Lindsey)
95 99 Benjamin F. Barcus
96 100 James B. Sneed
97 101 Major McDowell
98 102 John Cox
99 103 Jerry Hawkins
100 104 Julia Deblieux
101 105 Robert Smith

Third Avenue

325A 102 106 Amanda Smith
103 107 Robert Wheeler
104 108 Frank R. Winfield
105 109 Napoleon M. Hensley
106 110 James C. Abel
107 111 Nathaniel B. Brady
108 112 John F. Dawson (Aikens)
109 113 Milo Barton
110 114 Lizzie Baily
111 115 Iseael Kesler
112 116 Geo W. Millican (Cooper)
325B 113 117 Albert Wilkie
114 118 John Bryant
115 119 Bradford ?. Walker
116 120 Thos N.L. Cunnyngham (Waller)
117 121 James F. Johnson (Eldridge)
118 122 William H. Walker (Cordell)
119 123 Webster Thomas (Black)
120 124 Bertie Brandon

Fourth Avenue

121 125 Alexander Johnson
122 126 Susan McPherson
326A 123 127 David A. Elrod (Jones)
124 128 German See (Douglas)
125 129 George Mussington
126 130 George W. Gray
127 131 John ?. Nelson
128 132 John H. Wilson
129 133 Elizabeth J.(?) Atchley
134 George D. Dickey
130 135 Henry Pearman (Smith)
131 136 William L. Lillard
132 137 Nathaniel R. Roberts (Dyer)
138 Charles H. Powell
326B 133 139 Samuel T. Roberson (Bell)
134 140 William L. Shideler
135 141 Joseph Martin
136 142 William Bailey
143 George West
137 144 Lavinia Brooks (Smith)
138 145 Lucy B. Viles
139 146 James H. Johnson
147 William T.B. Poole
140 148 John Wyatt
141 149 John W. Hudson (Henderson)
142 150 Rebecca Donaldson
143 151 John B. Reedy
144 152 Hany Schaefer (Hindman)
327A 145 153 James Webb
146 154 Robert M. Sherman
147 155 Benjamin F. Patton
148 156 John C. Abernathy
149 157 George W. Brewer
150 158 Armitt P.(?) Jones
151 159 Peter J. Clift
152 160 Marshal L. Eskridge
153 161 Andrew McC. Cate
327B 154 162 John Perry

Market Street

155 163 Marion/Martin Shalliday
156 164 Jeferson D. Burkhalter (Loualen)
157 165 John F.(?) Humphrey (McBee, Campbell)
158 166 Philip T. Foust
167 Samuel H. Pearcy
159 168 Samuel Harris
160 169 Theodore Moench
161 170 William Eberhart (Wilkes, Bruner)
162 171 Elbert Henson
163 172 Benjamin Cathbert
173 Willie Helton
164 174 William Caraway
328A 165 175 Edward White
166 176 Joseph Phillips (Osborn Alsoop)
167 177 John G. Wallingford (Maryman)
168 178 Robert Keith

Washington Street

169 179 Henry C.(?) Hawkins
170 180 George V.(?) Harris
171 181 Isaac W. Angel
172 182 Matthew Jones
173 183 Hiram Moore (Ooten, Wilson, Melton, McClendon, Burrel)
174 184 James Thomas
328B 175 185 Archie Rollings
176 186 James Fair
187 Mary Cornett (Powell)
177 188 Amos Clifton (McCullus)
189 David McDonald
178 190 Marion Dooley (Magsby)
179 191 James McClearin (McDermit)
192 William J. Lowry
180 193 Alfred C. Blevins
181 194 Samuel H. Allen (Walker)
182 195 Parrin Gitgood
329A 183 196 Albert Rollings
184 197 Henry Trusley
185 198 Catharine B. Gallagher
186 199 Alexander Clingan
187 200 James M. Washburn
188 201 John W. Young
189 202 Edson C. Swebey (Bartlett)
190 203 James H. Crisp
191 204 Stephen Shields
192 205 Tom Thompson (Runyons)
193 206 Mary Houston
329B 194 207 Samuel Bacon (Roddy)
195 208 Moses Howell
196 209 Moses Porter (Thomas)
197 210 Mary Morris (Womac, Harmon)
198 211 Viola Leigh (Staples)
199 212 Lovie McNabb
200 213 Jennie Coleman

Spring Street

329B 201 214 Frances C. Baskett
202 215 Orlena Cathey
203 216 James H. Crawford
204 217 Frederick Doll (Barnett)
205 218 George Gray (Jones, Treadaway, Readdy, Sawyers, Wade)
206 219 Jennie Benson (Keith)
207 220 Lucion M. Brown
330A 208 221 Isaac H. Gains

Fox Street

209 222 Peter T. Morris
210 223 Mitchell C. Woolfork (Boytin)
211 224 Henry Angel (Springs)
212 225 James McDonald
213 226 Joseph Brown
214 227 James Love
215 228 Guy Holman
330B 216 229 Grant Walker (Kemp)
217 230 Josie Smith (Snellings)
218 231 Mattie Stewart (Cline,Butler)
232 Clint Freeman
219 233 Irene Copeland (Huff)

Front Street

220 234 Christopher Jones (Rider)
221 235 Katie Sims (Holston, Hurd Shockley, Howell)
222 236 Margaret Swafford (Blair)
223 237 William Fifer (Knox, Campbell)
331A 238 Thomas Horton
224 239 Belle Hawkins

Railroad Street

225 240 Creasis(?) Hudson (Turner, Howard)
226 241 William Branam (Moore, Russell)
331A 227 242 John Hicks
228 243 Lee A. Smith (Revis)
229 244 Jasper N. Cooley

Cedar and Walnut Streets

230 245 Thomas K. Knight
231 246 John M. Hill
232 247 Parthenia Thomas (Brandon, Breedlove)
331B 233 248 Angeline M. Gilmore

Railroad Street and "Pick Ups"

234 249 Joseph C. Jones (Bright, Montgomery)
235 250 Thomas J. Brewer
236 251 James R. Gillespie
237 252 James T. Crawford
238 253 Homer L. Meyers
239 254 John M. Hayes
240 255 Benjamin F. Pleasant
241 256 Roy V. Myers
242 257 James R. Hoover
243 258 James J. Lawrence
244 259 John C. Brown
345 260 Andrew Swafford
246 261 Louisa McMillan
247 262 Thomas A. Gross
248 263 Wm M. Brown (Goins)
249 264 Reese Springs

www.ingramcontent.com/pod-product-compliance
Lightning Source LLC
Chambersburg PA
CBHW080243030426
42334CB00023BA/2679

* 9 7 8 0 7 8 8 4 7 6 0 2 0 *